DISCOVER NEW YORK

New York

Are we meeting your travel needs?

Send written comments to:

AAA Member Comments
1000 AAA Drive, Box 61
Heathrow, FL 32746-5063

Published by:
AAA Publishing
1000 AAA Drive
Heathrow, FL 32746-5063
Copyright AAA 2004

**Advertising Rate and Circulation
Information**
Call: (407) 444-8280

Printed in the USA by
Quebecor World, Buffalo, NY

Photo Credit: (Cover & Title Page)
Adirondack Park
© David Muench / Corbis

 Printed on recyclable paper.
Please recycle whenever possible.

Stock #4618

New York

TourBook Navigator

Follow our simple guide to make the most of this member benefit 9-25

Comprehensive City Index

Alphabetical list for the entire book 627

■ New York

Featured Information

4

Hilton™

hilton.com

DOUBLETREE®

doubletree.com

E

EMBASSY SUITES
HOTELS®

embassysuites.com

That card in your wallet is a license to save.

Just check in. Choose from over 800 AAA approved locations in the Hilton family. Across the US, you can count on special **Stay and Save**™ AAA rates that'll help stretch your travel budget. From luxurious resort getaways, to value-priced accommodations with all the amenities you'd expect from the Hilton family, Show Your Card & Save® at any

participating hotel. For special rates, call our dedicated AAA number at **1-877-655-5694**.

Hilton
Garden Inn®

hiltongardeninn.com

HOMEWOOD
SUITES

Hilton

homewoodsuites.com

Hilton HHonors™
Points & Miles®

New York's Route 97
Scenic Byway:

It's all
the Buzz!

And it's right here in Sullivan County. The Route 97 Scenic Byway is a beautiful corridor that parallels the Delaware River along the border between New York and neighboring New Jersey and Pennsylvania. Explore dramatic cliffs and sweeping vistas. Watch bald eagles soar through a winter sky. Hunt for antiques and treasures in our quaint communities. Fish or canoe the river wild. Talk about a picture at an exhibition.

Only 90 minutes from New York City. And we know how to make you feel welcome.

For more information visit www.scva.net or call 1-800-882-CATS

antiques

eagle watching

fall foliage

winter sports

SULLIVAN COUNTY
THE CATSKILLS   I ♥ NY

When planning your next trip, check out the many time saving tools and member saving benefits on www.aaa.com to make your travels fun, easy and affordable. Highlights include:

Internet TripTik®/Traveler. Ranked #1 by the *Wall Street Journal*, ITT provides sightseeing and dining recommendations, online hotel reservations at great rates and, of course, AAA's famous maps, driving directions and custom routes!

Online TourBook®. Reserve rooms at great rates PLUS get AAA Diamond ratings for lodgings and restaurants and insider tips on attractions and local events!

AAA Drive Trips. Over 50 driving tours nationwide with precise directions and candid area overviews*

Vacation Getaways. Take to the skies, hit the high seas or select a tour and receive exclusive benefits from AAA's Preferred Travel Partners.

Travel Accessories. Order luggage, car games for the kids, accessories, and more to make travel easy.

Travel Guides. Get a 5% discount on AAA's famed travel guides and learn your destination inside out.

Disney® Vacations. Get exclusive benefits and savings on AAA Vacations® Disney vacation packages.

Hertz Rental. Up to 20 % discount from AAA's Exclusive Car Rental Partner.

Show Your Card & Save. Search for savings on lodging, travel, entertainment, retail, and e-Merchants in the database.

AAA Travel Money. Get no-fee travelers cheques, foreign currency and prepaid cards.

AAA Map Gallery*. Know the best way to go wherever you travel.

Cash Back. Get a 5% rebate every time you use your AAA credit card to gas up.

AAA Approved Auto Repair. Enter your zip code to get your car road-trip ready at the nearest AAR shop.

Click on www.aaa.com for numerous products and services that will make your next trip easy to plan, more enjoyable and full of value. **Travel to www.aaa.com TODAY for all your vacation planning needs!**

www.aaa.com

Travel With Someone You Trust®

Products and Services available through participating AAA and CAA Clubs.

8

WITH SO MANY RAMADA LOCATIONS, THE DISTANCE BETWEEN THEM ISN'T MUCH. (GOOD THING)

SAVE
15%

Visit one of our participating properties in New York and enjoy a clean, comfortable room at a great rate. Also, take advantage of one of the world's largest hotel reward programs, "Trip Rewards℠". Visit ramada.com for details.

RAMADA®
A very good place to be.™

For reservations or more information, visit us online or call today.
RAMADA.COM/VALUES or 1.800.4.RAMADA
en español 1.888.709.4021
Ask for Great Value Rates (promo code LPGV)

Trust

the AAA TourBook® guide for objective travel information. Follow the pages of the TourBook Navigator to thoroughly understand this unique member benefit.

Making Your Way Through the AAA Listings

Attractions, lodgings and restaurants are listed on the basis of merit alone after careful evaluation, approval and rating by one of our full-time, professionally trained Tourism Editors. Annual evaluations are unannounced to ensure that our Tourism Editors see an establishment just as our members would see it.

Those lodgings and restaurants listed with an (fyi) icon have not gone through the same evaluation process as other rated properties. Individual listings will typically denote the reason why this icon appears. Bulleted recreational activity listings are not inspected but are included for member information.

An establishment's decision to advertise in the TourBook guide has no bearing on its evaluation or rating. Advertising for services or products does not imply AAA endorsement.

How the TourBook is

Organized

Geographic listing is used for accuracy and consistency. This means attractions, lodgings and restaurants are listed under the city in which they physically are located—or in some cases under the nearest recognized city. The Comprehensive City Index located in the back of the book contains an A-to-Z list of cities. Most listings are alphabetically organized by state, province, region or island; city; and establishment name. A color is assigned to each state or province so that you can match the color bars at the top of the page to switch from ❶ Points of Interest to ❷ Lodgings and Restaurants.

Destination Cities and Destination Areas

The TourBook guide also groups information by destination city and destination area. If a city is grouped in a destination vicinity section, the city name will appear at its alphabetical location in the book, and a handy cross reference will give the exact page on which listings for that city begin. Maps are placed at the beginning of these sections to orient you to the destinations.

❸ Destination cities, established based on government models and local expertise, are comprised of metropolitan areas plus nearby vicinity cities.

Destination areas are regions with broad tourist appeal. Several cities will comprise the area.

All information in this TourBook guide was reviewed for accuracy before publication. However, since changes inevitably occur between annual editions, we suggest you contact establishments directly to confirm prices and schedules.

Points of Interest Section

Orientation maps
near the start of each Attractions section show only those places we call points of interest. Coordinates included with the city listings depict the locations of those cities on the map. A GEM symbol (♥) accents towns with "must see" points of interest which offer a *Great Experience for Members®*. And the black ovals with white numerals (**22** for example) locate items listed in the nearby Recreation Areas chart.

Destination area maps
illustrate key travel areas defined by local travel experts. Communities shown have listings for AAA approved attractions.

National park maps
represent the area in and around the park. Some campground sites and lodges spotted on the maps do not meet AAA/CAA criteria, but are shown for members who nevertheless wish to stay close to the park area.

Walking or self-guiding tour maps
correspond to specific routes described in TourBook guide text.

City maps
show areas where numerous points of interest are concentrated and indicate their location in relation to major roads, parks, airports and other landmarks.

Lodgings & Restaurants Section

Destination area maps
illustrate key travel areas defined by local travel experts. Communities shown have listings for AAA-RATED® lodgings and/or restaurants.

Spotting maps
show the location of lodgings and restaurants. Lodgings are spotted with a black background (**22** for example); restaurants are spotted with a white background (**23** for example). Spotting map indexes have been placed immediately after each map to provide the user with a convenient method to identify what an area has to offer at a glance. The index references the map page number where the property is spotted, indicates if a property is an Official Appointment and contains an advertising reference if applicable. It also lists the property's diamond rating, high season rate range and listing page number.

Downtown/city spotting maps
are provided when spotted facilities are very concentrated. GEM points of interest also appear on these maps.

Vicinity spotting maps
spot those properties that are outside the downtown or city area. Major roads, landmarks, airports and GEM points of interest are shown on vicinity spotting maps as well. The names of suburban communities that have AAA-RATED® accommodations are shown in magenta type.

Featured Information Section

Driving distance maps
are intended to be used only for trip-distance and driving-time planning.

Sample Attraction Listing

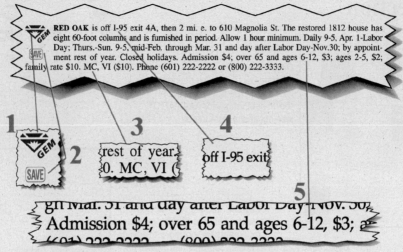

RED OAK is off I-95 exit 4A, then 2 mi. e. to 610 Magnolia St. The restored 1812 house has eight 60-foot columns and is furnished in period. Allow 1 hour minimum. Daily 9-5. Apr. 1-Labor Day; Thurs.-Sun. 9-5, mid-Feb. through Mar. 31 and day after Labor Day-Nov.30; by appointment rest of year. Closed holidays. Admission $4; over 65 and ages 6-12, $3; ages 2-5, $2; family rate $10. MC, VI ($10). Phone (601) 222-2222 or (800) 222-3333.

1

2

3 rest of year. 0. MC, VI (

4 off I-95 exit

5

gh Mar. 31 and day after Labor Day-Nov. 30;
Admission $4; over 65 and ages 6-12, $3; a
(601) 222-2222   (800) 222-3333

1 This attraction is of exceptional interest and quality and therefore has been designated a AAA GEM—offering a *Great Experience for Members* ®.

2 [SAVE] Participating attractions offer AAA/CAA, AAA MasterCard or AAA Visa cardholders a discount off the attraction's standard admission; members should inquire in advance concerning the validity of the discount for special rates. Present your card at the admission desk. A list of participating points of interest appears in the Indexes section of the book. The SAVE discount may not be used in conjunction with other discounts. Attractions that already provide a reduced senior or child rate may not honor the SAVE discount for those age groups. All offers are subject to change and may not apply during special events, particular days or seasons or for the entire validity period of the TourBook. Shopping establishments preceded by a SAVE icon also provide discounts and/or gift with purchase to AAA/CAA members; present your card at the mall's customer service center to receive your benefit.

3

AX=American Express	DS=Discover	MC=MasterCard
CB=Carte Blanche	JC=Japan Credit Bureau	VI=VISA
DC=Diners Club		

Minimum amounts that may be charged appear in parentheses when applicable.

4 Unless otherwise specified, directions are given from the center of town, using the following highway designations: I (interstate highway), US (federal highway), Hwy. (Canadian or Caribbean highway), SR (state route), CR (county road), FM (farm to market road), FR (forest road), MM (mile marker), Mex. (Mexican highway).

5 Admission prices are quoted without sales tax. Children under the lowest age specified are admitted free when accompanied by an adult. Days, months and age groups written with a hyphen are inclusive. Prices pertaining to points of interest in the United States are quoted in U.S. dollars; prices for Canadian province and territory points of interest are quoted in Canadian dollars; prices for points of interest in Mexico and the Caribbean are quoted as an approximate U.S. dollar equivalent.

Bulleted Listings: Casino gambling establishments are visited by AAA personnel to ensure safety; casinos within hotels are presented for member information regardless of whether the lodging is AAA approved. Recreational activities of a participatory nature (requiring physical exertion or special skills) are not inspected. Wineries are inspected by AAA Tourism Editors to ensure they meet listing requirements and offer tours. All are presented in a bulleted format for informational purposes.

AAA. Every Day.

These Show Your Card & Save® partners provide the listed member benefits. Admission tickets that offer greater discounts may be available for purchase at the local AAA/CAA club. A maximum of six tickets is available at the discount price.

Attraction Partners

SeaWorld/Busch Gardens

SAVE Save $4 at SeaWorld and Busch Gardens

SAVE Save $3 at Sesame Place, Water Country USA and Adventure Island

SAVE Save 10% on select up-close dining. Reservations are required; visit Guest Relations for details

Six Flags Theme Parks

SAVE Save $4 on general admission at the gate

SAVE Save $12 on general admission at the gate each Wednesday

SAVE Save 10% on selected souvenirs and dining (check at main gate for details)

Universal Orlando (www.aaa.com/Universal)

SAVE Save $4 on a 2-day/2-park pass or $5 on a 3-day/2-park pass at Universal Orlando's theme parks (savings apply to tickets purchased at the gate)

SAVE Save 10% on select dining and souvenirs at both Universal Orlando theme parks and at select Universal CityWalk Orlando restaurants (except Emeril's)

Universal Studios Hollywood

SAVE Save $3 on a 1-day Universal Hollywood pass (savings applies to tickets purchased at the gate)

SAVE Save 10% on select dining and souvenirs at Universal Studios Hollywood and Universal CityWalk

Gray Line

SAVE Save 10% on sightseeing tours of 1 day or less

Restaurant Partners

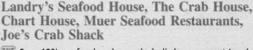

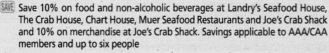

Landry's Seafood House, The Crab House, Chart House, Muer Seafood Restaurants, Joe's Crab Shack

SAVE Save 10% on food and non-alcoholic beverages at Landry's Seafood House, The Crab House, Chart House, Muer Seafood Restaurants and Joe's Crab Shack and 10% on merchandise at Joe's Crab Shack. Savings applicable to AAA/CAA members and up to six people

Hard Rock Cafe

SAVE Save 10% on food, beverage, and merchandise at all U.S., Canada, and select international locations. Members also save 10% at The Hard Rock Vault.

Mexican Partners

Ahorra con AMA

SAVE An alliance between AAA/CAA and AMA (Mexican Automobile Association) provides members visting Mexico savings from Mexicana Airlines, Tony Roma restaurants and Six Flags of Mexico

---

Visit aaa.com to discover all the great Show Your Card & Save® discounts in your area.

Sample Lodging Listing

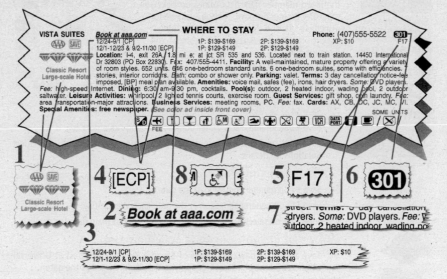

1 **AAA** or **CAA** indicates our Official Appointment (OA) lodgings. The OA program permits properties to display and advertise the **AAA** or **CAA** emblem. We highlight these properties with red diamonds and classification. Some OA listings include special amenities such as free continental breakfast; expanded continental breakfast or full breakfast; early check-in/late check-out; free room upgrade or preferred room, such as ocean view or poolside (subject to availability); free local phone calls; and free daily newspaper. This does not imply that only these properties offer these amenities. The **AAA** or **CAA** sign helps traveling members find accommodations that want member business.

◆◆◆ ◆◆ or ◆◆◆ ◆◆◆ The number of diamonds—not the color—informs you of the overall level of quality in a lodging's amenities and service. More diamond details appear on page 16.

Classic Resort Large-scale Hotel or Classic Resort Large-scale Hotel: All diamond rated lodgings are classified using three key elements: style of operation, overall concept and service level. See pages 22-23 for details about our Lodging Classifications and Subclassifications.

Member Values

SAVE Official Appointment properties guarantee members a minimum 10% discount off the standard room rates published in TourBook guides or the lowest public rate available at the time of booking for the dates of stay, for standard rooms.

S$D Establishments offer a minimum senior discount of 10% off the listed rates. This discount is available to members 60 or older.

ASK Many properties offer discounts to members even though the lodgings do not participate in a formal discount program. The **ASK** is another reminder to inquire about available discounts when making your reservations or at check-in.

Discounts normally offered at some lodgings may not apply during special events or holiday periods. Special rates and discounts may not apply to all room types. Some Member Values may not apply in Mexico or the Caribbean.

To obtain published rates or discounts, you must identify yourself as a AAA or CAA member, request AAA rates when making reservations and have written confirmation sent to you. The SAVE or senior discount may not be used in conjunction with other discounts. At registration, show your membership card and verify the room rate.

Discounts normally offered at some lodgings may not apply during special events or holiday periods. Special rates and discounts may not apply to all room types. Some Member Values may not apply in Mexico or the Caribbean.

The rates listed for approved properties are provided to AAA by each lodging and represent the regular (rack) rate for a standard room. Printed rates, based on rack rates and last room availability, are rounded to the nearest dollar. Rates do not include taxes and discounts. U.S., Mexican and Caribbean rates are in U.S. dollars; rates for Canadian lodgings are in Canadian dollars.

2 Book at aaa.com - Internet Reservations
Indicates AAA/CAA members can conveniently check room availability and make reservations in a secure online environment at aaa.com.

3 Rate Lines
Shown from left to right: dates the rates are effective; meal plan provided with rates (see Meal Plan Indicators-if no plan noted, rate includes room only); rates for 1 person or 2 persons; extra person charge (XP); and any applicable family plan indicator.

Rates Guaranteed
AAA/CAA members are guaranteed that they will not be charged more than the maximum regular rate printed in each rate range for a standard room. Rates may vary within the range depending on season and room type. Listed rates are based on last standard room availability. Rates for properties operating as concessionaires for the U.S. National Park Service are not guaranteed due to governing regulations. Rates in the Mexico TourBook are not guaranteed and may fluctuate based on the exchange rate of the peso.

Exceptions
Lodgings may temporarily increase room rates, not recognize discounts or modify pricing policies during special events. Examples of special events range from Mardi Gras and Kentucky Derby (including pre-Derby events) to college football games, holidays, holiday periods and state fairs. Although some special events are listed in AAA/CAA TourBook guides, it is always wise to check, in advance, with AAA travel professionals for specific dates.

Discounts
Member discounts will apply to rates quoted, within the rate range, applicable at the time of booking. Special rates used in advertising, and special short-term, promotional rates lower than the lowest listed rate in the range, are not subject to additional member discounts.

4 Meal Plan Indicators
The following types of meal plans may be available in the listed room rate:
AP = American Plan of three meals daily
BP = Breakfast Plan of full hot breakfast
CP = Continental Plan of pastry, juice and another beverage
ECP = Expanded Continental Plan, which offers a wider variety of breakfast items
MAP = Modified American Plan of two meals daily
See individual listing "Terms" section for additional meal plans that are not included in the room rate.

> Check-in times are shown in the listing only if they are after 3 p.m.; check-out times are shown only if they are before 10 a.m.

5 Family Plan Indicators
F = Children stay free
D = Discounts for children
F17 = Children 17 and under stay free (age displayed will reflect property's policy)
D17 = Discount for children 17 and under

6 Lodging Locators
Black ovals with white numbers are used to locate, or "spot," lodgings on maps we provide for larger cities.

7 Unit Types
Unit types, amenities and room features preceded by the word "Some" indicate the item is available on a limited basis, potentially within only one unit.

8 Lodging Icons
A row of icons is included with each lodging listing. These icons represent the member values, member services, and facilities offered by that lodging. See page 19 for an explanation of each icon.

The Lodging Diamond Ratings

AAA Tourism Editors evaluate and rate each lodging based on the overall quality, the range of facilities and the level of services offered by a property. The size, age and overall appeal of an establishment are considered as well as regional architectural style and design.

While guest services are an important part of all diamond ratings, they are particularly critical at the four and five diamond levels. A property must provide a high level of service, on a consistent basis, to obtain and support the four and five diamond rating.

These establishments typically appeal to the budget-minded traveler. They provide essential, no-frills accommodations. They meet the basic requirements pertaining to comfort, cleanliness, and hospitality.

These establishments appeal to the traveler seeking more than the basic accommodations. There are modest enhancements to the overall physical attributes, design elements, and amenities of the facility typically at a modest price.

These establishments appeal to the traveler with comprehensive needs. Properties are multifaceted with a distinguished style, including marked upgrades in the quality of physical attributes, amenities and level of comfort provided.

These establishments are upscale in all areas. Accommodations are progressively more refined and stylish. The physical attributes reflect an obvious enhanced level of quality throughout. The fundamental hallmarks at this level include an extensive array of amenities combined with a high degree of hospitality, service, and attention to detail.

These establishments reflect the characteristics of the ultimate in luxury and sophistication. Accommodations are first-class. The physical attributes are extraordinary in every manner. The fundamental hallmarks at this level are to meticulously serve and exceed all guest expectations while maintaining an impeccable standard of excellence. Many personalized services and amenities enhance an unmatched level of comfort.

The lodging listings with **fyi** in place of diamonds are included as an "information only" service for members. The icon indicates that a property has not been rated for one or more of the following reasons: too new to rate; under construction; under major renovation; not evaluated; or may not meet all AAA requirements. Those properties not meeting all AAA requirements are included for either their member value or because it may be the only accommodation available in the area. Listing prose will give insight as to why the **fyi** designation was assigned.

Guest Safety

Room Security

In order to be approved for listing in AAA/CAA TourBook guides for the United States and Canada, all lodgings must comply with AAA's guest room security requirements.

In response to AAA/CAA members' concern about their safety at properties, AAA-RATED® accommodations must have dead-bolt locks on all guest room entry doors and connecting room doors.

If the area outside the guest room door is not visible from inside the room through a window or door panel, viewports must be installed on all guest room entry doors. Bed and breakfast properties and country inns are not required to have viewports. Ground floor and easily accessible sliding doors must be equipped with some other type of secondary security locks.

Tourism Editors view a percentage of rooms at each property since it is not feasible to evaluate every room in every lodging establishment. Therefore, AAA cannot guarantee that there are working locks on all doors and windows in all guest rooms.

Fire Safety

Because of the highly specialized skills needed to conduct professional fire safety inspections, AAA/CAA Tourism Editors cannot assess fire safety.

Properties must meet all federal, state and local fire codes. Each guest unit in all U.S. and Canadian lodging properties must be equipped with an operational, single-station smoke detector. A AAA/CAA Tourism Editor has evaluated a sampling of the rooms to verify this equipment is in place.

> **For additional fire safety information, read the page posted on the back of your guest room door, or write:**
>
> **National Fire Protection Association**
> **1 Batterymarch Park**
> **P.O. Box 9101**
> **Quincy, MA 02269-9101**

Requirements for some features, such as door locks and smoke detectors/sprinkler systems, differ in Mexico and the Caribbean. If a property met AAA's security requirements at the time of the evaluation, the phrase "Meets AAA guest room security requirements" appears in the listing.

Access for Mature Travelers and Travelers with Disabilities

Qualified properties listed in this guide are shown with symbols indicating they meet the needs of the hearing-impaired or offer some accessible features for mature travelers or travelers with disabilities.

Hearing Impaired

Indicates a property has the following equipment available for hearing-impaired travelers: TDD at front desk or switchboard; visual notification of fire alarm, incoming telephone calls, door knock or bell; closed caption decoder; text telephone or TDD for guest room use; telephone amplification device, with shelf or electric outlet next to guest room telephone.

Accessible Features

Indicates a property has some accessible features meeting the needs of mature travelers and travelers with disabilities. Lodging establishments will provide at least one guest room meeting the designated criteria as well as accessible restrooms and parking facilities. Restaurants provide accessible parking, dining rooms and restrooms.

AAA/CAA strongly urges members to call the property directly to fully understand the property's exact accessibility features. Some properties do not fully comply with AAA/CAA's exacting accessibility standards but may offer some design standards that meet the needs of some guests with disabilities.

AAA/CAA does not evaluate recreational facilities, banquet rooms, or convention or meeting facilities for accessibility.

Service Animals

No fees or deposits, even those normally charged for pets, may be charged for service animals. Service animals fulfill a critical need for their owners—they are *not* pets.

The Americans With Disabilities Act (ADA) prohibits U.S. businesses that serve the public from discriminating against persons with disabilities. Some businesses have mistakenly denied access to persons who use service animals. ADA, a federal mandate, has priority over all state and local laws, as well as a business owner's standard of business, which might bar animals from the premises. Businesses must permit entry to guests and their service animals, as well as allow service animals to accompany guests to all public areas of a property. A property is permitted to ask whether the animal is a service animal or a pet, and whether the guest has a disability. The property may not, however, ask questions about the nature of the disability, the service provided by the animal or require proof of a disability or certification that the animal is a service animal.

Note: These regulations may not apply in Canada, Mexico or the Caribbean.

What The Lodging Icons Mean

Member Values
(see p. 14)

AAA or **CAA** Official Appointment

SAVE Offers minimum 10% discount or lowest public rate *(see p. 14)*

ASK May offer discount

SD Offers senior discount

fyi Informational listing only

Member Services

✈ Airport transportation

🐕 Pets allowed

🍴 Restaurant on premises

🍴+ Restaurant off premises (walking distance)

24🍴 24-hour room service

🍸 Cocktail lounge

👶 Child care

Accessibility Feature
(see p. 18)

&M Accessible features

♿ Roll-in showers

👂 Hearing impaired

Safety Features
(Mexico and Caribbean only)

S Sprinklers

D Smoke detectors

Leisure Activities

🎲 Full service casino

🏊 Pool

🏋 Health club on premises

🏋+ Health club off premises

🏹 Recreational activities

In-Room Amenities

⊠ Designated non-smoking rooms

AC No air conditioning

TV No TV

CTV No cable TV

VCR VCR

🎬 Movies

DATA PORT Data port/modem line

✆ No telephones

🧊 Refrigerator

🍱 Microwave

☕ Coffee maker

Availability and Additional Fees

If an in-room amenity is available only on a limited basis (in one or more rooms), the term "SOME UNITS" will appear above those icons. Fees may be charged for some of the services represented by the icons listed here. The word "FEE" will appear below each icon when an extra charge applies.

SOME UNITS

&M 👂 **VCR** 🎬 ☕ / ⊠ **DATA PORT** 🧊 /
        FEE FEE   FEE

Preferred Lodging Partners

SAVINGS. SELECTION. SATISFACTION. — When contacting one of the partners listed, you will be given AAA's best rates for your dates of stay. Your valid membership card must be presented at check-in.

SATISFACTION GUARANTEE — If you are not satisfied with any part of your stay, you must provide the property the opportunity to correct the situation during your stay. If the matter cannot be resolved, you will be entitled to recompense for a portion of, or your entire, stay. Satisfaction guarantee varies by chain.

Select the chain you want and have your membership card available when making a reservation and checking in.

Making Reservations

When making reservations, you must identify yourself as a AAA or CAA member. Give all pertinent information about your planned stay. Ask about the lodging's pet policy, or the availability of any other special feature that is important to your stay. Request written confirmation to guarantee: type of room, rate, dates of stay, and cancellation and refund policies. At registration, show your membership card. Note: Age restrictions may apply.

Confirm Deposit, Refund and Cancellation Policies

Most establishments give full deposit refunds if they have been notified at least 48 hours before the normal check-in time. Listing prose will note if more than 48 hours notice is required for cancellation. However, when making reservations, confirm the property's deposit, cancellation and refund policies. Some properties may charge a cancellation or handling fee.

When this applies, "cancellation fee imposed" will appear in the listing. If you cancel too late, you have little recourse if a refund is denied.

When an establishment requires a full or partial payment in advance, and your trip is cut short, a refund may not be given.

When canceling reservations, phone the lodging immediately. Make a note of the date and time you called, the cancellation number if there is one, and the name of the person who handled the cancellation. If your AAA/CAA club made your reservation, allow them to make the cancellation for you as well so you will have proof of cancellation.

Review Charges for Appropriate Rates

When you are charged more than the maximum rate listed in the TourBook guide for a standard room, question the additional charge. If management refuses to adhere to the published rate, pay for the room and submit your receipt and membership number to AAA/CAA within 30 days. Include all pertinent information: dates of stay, rate paid, itemized paid receipts, number of persons in your party, the room number you occupied, and list any extra room equipment used. A refund of the amount paid in excess of the stated maximum will be made if our investigation indicates that unjustified charging has occurred.

Get the Room You Reserved

When you find your room is not as specified, and you have written confirmation of reservations for a certain type of accommodation, you should be given the option of choosing a different room or finding one elsewhere. Should you choose to go elsewhere and a refund is refused or resisted, submit the matter to AAA/CAA within 30 days along with complete documentation, including your reasons for refusing the room and copies of your written confirmation and any receipts or canceled checks associated with this problem.

How to Get the Best Room Rates

You'll find the best room rate if you book your reservation in advance with the help of a travel professional or agent at your local AAA/CAA office.

If you're not yet ready to make firm vacation plans or if you prefer a more spontaneous trip, take advantage of the partnerships that preferred hotel chains have arranged with AAA. Phone the toll-free number 866-AAA-SAVE that has been set up exclusively for members for the purpose of reserving with these Show Your Card & Save® chain partners.

Even if you were unable to make a reservation, be sure to show your membership card at the desk and ask if you're being offered the lowest rate available for that time. Many lodgings offer reduced rates to members.

Lodging Classifications

To ensure that your lodging needs/preferences are met, we recommend that you consider an establishment's classification when making your travel choices.

While the quality and comfort at properties with the same diamond rating should be consistent (regardless of the classification), there are differences in typical décor/theme elements, range of facilities and service levels. Please see the descriptions below.

Hotel Royal Plaza, Lake Buena Vista, FL

Large-scale Hotel
A multistory establishment with interior room entrances. A variety of guest unit styles is offered. Public areas are spacious and include a variety of facilities such as a restaurant, shops, fitness center, spa, business center, or meeting rooms.

Small-scale Hotel
A multistory establishment typically with interior room entrances. A variety of guest unit styles is offered. Public areas are limited in size and/or the variety of facilities available.

Baymont Inn, Dallas/Ft. Worth-Airport North, TX

Best Western Deltona Inn, Deltona, FL

Motel
A one- to three-story establishment typically with exterior room entrances facilitating convenient access to parking. The standard guest units have one bedroom with a bathroom and are typically similar in décor and design throughout. Public areas are limited in size and/or the variety of facilities available.

Country Inn
Similar in definition to a bed and breakfast, but usually larger in scale with spacious public areas and offers a dining facility that serves at least breakfast and dinner.

Greenville Inn, Greenville, ME

1884 Paxton House Inn, Thomasville, GA

Bed & Breakfast
Small-scale properties emphasizing a high degree of personal touches that provide guests an "at home" feeling. Guest units tend to be individually decorated. Rooms may not include some modern amenities such as televisions and telephones, and may have a shared bathroom. Usually owner-operated with a common room or parlor separate from the innkeeper's living quarters, where guests and operators can interact during evening and breakfast hours. Evening office closures are normal. A continental or full, hot breakfast is served and is included in the room rate.

Condominium
Vacation-oriented or extended-stay, apartment-style accommodations that are routinely available for rent through a management company. Units vary in design and décor and often contain one or more bedrooms, living room, full kitchen, and an eating area. Studio-type models combine the sleeping and living areas into one room. Typically, basic cleaning supplies, kitchen utensils and complete bed and bath linens are supplied. The guest registration area may be located off-site.

Sands of Kahana, Kahana, Maui, HI

Desert Rose Inn, Bluff, UT

Cabin/Cottage
Vacation-oriented, small-scale, freestanding houses or cabins. Units vary in design and décor and often contain one or more bedrooms, living room, kitchen, dining area, and bathroom. Studio-type models combine the sleeping and living areas into one room. Typically, basic cleaning supplies, kitchen utensils, and complete bed and bath linens are supplied. The guest registration area may be located off-site.

C Lazy U Ranch, Granby, CO

Ranch
Typically a working ranch with an obvious rustic, Western theme. In general, equestrian-related activities are featured, but ranches may include other animals and activities as well. A variety of guest unit styles is offered in a family-oriented atmosphere.

Vacation Home
Vacation-oriented or extended-stay, large-scale, freestanding houses that are routinely available for rent through a management company. Houses vary in design and décor and often contain two or more bedrooms, living room, full kitchen, dining room, and multiple bathrooms. Typically, basic cleaning supplies, kitchen utensils, and complete bed and bath linens are supplied. The guest registration area may be located off-site.

ResortQuest, Hilton Head Island, SC

Lodging Subclassifications

The following are subclassifications that may appear along with the classifications listed above to provide a more specific description of the lodging.

Casino
Extensive gambling facilities are available such as blackjack, craps, keno, and slot machines. **Note:** This subclassification will not appear beneath its diamond rating in the listing. It will be indicated by a dice icon and will be included in the row of icons immediately below the lodging listing.

Classic
Renowned and landmark properties, older than 50 years, well-known for their unique style and ambience.

Historic
These properties are typically over 75 years of age and exhibit many features of a historic nature with respect to architecture, design, furnishings, public record, or acclaim. Properties must meet one of the following criteria:
- Maintained the integrity of the historical nature
- Listed on the U.S. National Register of Historic Places
- Designated a U.S. National Historic Landmark
- Located in a U.S. National Register Historic District

Separate criteria designate historic properties in Canada, Mexico and the Caribbean.

Resort
Recreation-oriented, geared to vacation travelers seeking a specific destination experience. Travel packages, meal plans, theme entertainment, and social and recreational programs are typically available. Recreational facilities are extensive and may include spa treatments, golf, tennis, skiing, fishing, or water sports, etc. Larger resorts may offer a variety of guest accommodations.

Sample Restaurant Listing

WHERE TO DINE

KINGSTON'S RESTAURANT Classic   **Dinner:** $16-$35   **Phone:** 555/987-1600   (18)
Location: I-459, exit 13 (US 31); adjacent to Riverchase Galleria; in The Wynfrey Hotel. 1000 Riverchase Galleria 35244. **Hours:** 5 pm-10 pm. Closed major holidays; also Sun. **Reservations:** suggested. **Features:** Boasting an upscale atmosphere and excellent American cuisine, the fine dining establishment is the ideal setting for a special, intimate dinner. Its newly renovated dining rooms offer an elegant setting for a truly memorable meal. Dressy casual; cocktails. **Parking:** on-site. **Cards:** AX, DC, DS, MC, VI.

American

5 Classic

3 **Cards:** AX, DC, DS, MC, VI.

6 (18)

1 American

2 **Dinner:** $16-$35

4

1   or   indicates our Official Appointment (OA) restaurants. The OA program permits properties to display and advertise the   or   emblem. We highlight these properties with red diamonds and cuisine type. The   or   sign helps traveling members find restaurants that want member business.

  or   The number of diamonds—not the color—informs you of the overall level of quality for food and presentation, service and ambience. Menus for red Diamond restaurants can be viewed on <u>aaa.com.</u>

A cuisine type is assigned for each restaurant listing. AAA currently recognizes more than 90 different cuisine types.

2 Prices represent the minimum and maximum entree cost per person. Exceptions may include one-of-a-kind or special market priced items.

3 AX = American Express
CB = Carte Blanche   DS = Discover   MC = MasterCard
DC = Diners Club   JC = Japan Credit Bureau   VI = VISA

4 These three icons are used in restaurant listings. When present, they indicate: the presence of a cocktail lounge, the lack of air conditioning, and/or that the restaurant has a designated non-smoking section or is entirely smoke-free.

5 If applicable, restaurants may be further defined as:

Classic—renowned and landmark restaurant operations in business longer than 25 years, known for unique style and ambience.

Historic—properties must meet one of the following criteria:
- Listed on the U.S. National Register of Historic Places
- Designated a U.S. National Historic Landmark
- Located in a U.S. National Register Historic District

Separate criteria designate historic properties in Canada, Mexico and the Caribbean.

6 These white ovals with black numbers serve as restaurant locators and are used to locate, or "spot," restaurants on maps we provide for larger cities.

The Restaurant Diamond Ratings

AAA Tourism Editors are responsible for determining a restaurant's diamond rating based on established criteria.

These criteria were established with input from AAA trained professionals, members, and restaurant industry experts. They are purposely broad to capture what is typically seen throughout the restaurant industry at each diamond rating level.

These establishments appeal to a diner seeking good, wholesome, no-nonsense eating at an affordable price. They typically provide simple, familiar, and unadorned foods served in a sensible, casual or self-service style. Often quick service and family oriented.

Examples include coffee shops, diners, cafeterias, short order, and modest full service eateries.

These establishments provide for dining needs that are increasingly complex, but still reasonably priced. They typically exhibit noticeable efforts in rising above the ordinary in many aspects of food, service and decor. Service is typically functional yet ambitious, periodically combining informal style with limited self-service elements. Often well-suited to traditional, special occasion, and family dining.

Examples include a varied range of specific concept (theme) and multi-purpose establishments.

These establishments impart an increasingly refined and upscale, adult-oriented experience. This is the entry level into fine dining. Creative and complex menus offer a blend of traditional and trendy foods. The service level is typically semi-formal with knowledgeable and proficient staff. Routinely these restaurants appeal to the diner in search of an experience rather than just a meal.

Examples include high-caliber, chic, boutique, and conventional restaurants.

These establishments impart a luxurious and socially refined experience. This is consistent fine dining. Menus typically reflect a high degree of creativity and complexity, featuring elaborate presentations of market-driven or traditional dishes. A cultured, professional, and highly proficient staff consistently demonstrates a profound desire to meet or exceed guest expectations. Restaurants of this caliber are geared to individuals with an appetite for an elite, fine-dining experience.

Examples include dining rooms associated with luxury lodgings, or exclusive independent restaurants often found in metropolitan areas.

Often renowned, these establishments impart a world-class and opulent, adult-oriented experience. This is "haute cuisine" at its best. Menus are often cutting edge, with an obvious dedication to use of only the finest ingredients available. Even the classic dishes become extraordinary under the masterful direction of highly acclaimed chefs. Presentations are spectacular, reflecting impeccable artistry and awareness. An expert, formalized staff continuously anticipates and exceeds guest expectations. Staff members' unfailing attention to detail appears effortless, well-rehearsed and unobtrusive. Undoubtedly, these restaurants appeal to those in search of the ultimate dining experience.

Examples include renowned dining rooms associated with luxury lodgings, or exclusive independent restaurants often found in metropolitan areas.

The restaurants with **fyi** in place of diamonds are included as an "information only" service for members. These listings provide additional dining choices but have not yet been evaluated.

YOU'RE READY...

NOW YOU'RE READY FOR ANYTHING.

Travelers Cheques
Available in US Dollars, Canadian Dollars, Euros, and Pounds Sterling; AAA VISA® Travelers Cheques are accepted worldwide.

Cash Passport Card
With AAA Cash Passport you can withdraw cash in the local currency from any VISA® ATM in the world.

Credit Card
The AAA VISA® Credit Card is accepted in over 24 million locations around the world.

Foreign Currency
We supply over 100 different currencies and can advise which is the best for your destination.

AAA TRAVEL MONEY
Know Before You Go.

Visit Participating AAA offices **Click** aaa.com and go to Travel Money **Call** 866-339-3378

Savings for all Seasons

Hertz rents Fords and other fine cars. ® REG. U.S. PAT. OFF. © HERTZ SYSTEM INC., 1999/2606-99.

No matter the season, Hertz offers AAA members exclusive discounts and benefits.

Operating in 150 countries at over 7,000 locations, Hertz makes traveling more convenient and efficient wherever and whenever you go. Hertz offers AAA members discounts up to 20% on car rentals worldwide.

To receive your exclusive AAA member discounts and benefits, mention your AAA membership card at time of reservation and present it at time of rental. **In addition**, to receive a free one car class upgrade, in the United States mention PC# 929714, in Canada mention PC# 929725 and in Puerto Rico mention PC# 929736 at the time of reservation. Offer available through 12/31/04.

For reservations and program details, call your AAA Travel office or the Hertz/AAA Desk at **1-800-654-3080**.

Show Your Card & Save
AAA. Every Day.

Hertz ®
exactly.

ALL I WANT IS...

New York

The Big Apple
Skyscrapers, theater, museums, shopping, bustling crowds— New York City

Take a Sip
New York state's wines compare with the world's finest

Niagara Falls
The power of Mother Nature is awesome

Historic Canals
When the Great Lakes met the Hudson River, commerce flowed

Explore the Outdoors
Raft, hike, boat, fish, bike, canoe, ski—you can do it all in New York

Cape Vincent
© Tom Algire
SuperStock

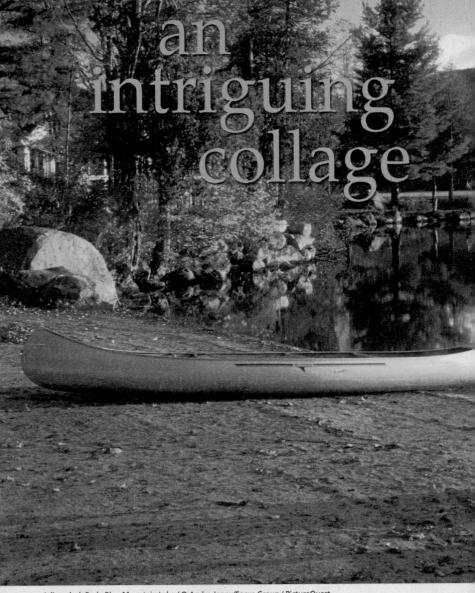

an intriguing collage

Adirondack Park, Blue Mountain Lake / © Andre Jenny/Focus Group / PictureQuest

Take an escalator to an observation floor in Manhattan's towering Empire State Building, and you'll view a busy panorama of asphalt and skyscrapers.

As spectacular as that sight may be, it's a one-dimensional snapshot of the state of New York. The broader picture encompasses much more.

A rich maritime and farming heritage characterizes Long Island, a resort playground with pristine beaches, breathtaking mansions and quaint lighthouses.

The Catskills and the Adirondacks give you adventure—by water, by land and by air.

The past is the draw in the Hudson Valley, in which Franklin D. Roosevelt's ancestral home is counted among the many historic sites.

Albany, the state capital, is noted for its art and architecture, while vineyards are the trademark in the fertile Finger Lakes region.

You'll find romance at Niagara Falls and in the Thousand Islands, an area with scenic trails and warm beaches.

History and sports are the focus in the Leatherstocking region where the Erie Canal system and baseball and soccer legends are celebrated.

And varied cultures—American Indian and Amish—in Chautauqua-Allegheny grant you the opportunity to expand your horizons.

Its many images and varied attractions make New York an intriguing collage.

Brazilian. Chinese. German. Irish. Italian. Korean. Mexican. Polish. Russian. South African. Vietnamese.

These nationalities represent a mere handful of the full shelf of ethnic spices that add zest to the New York City melting pot. The city's cultural stew is an epicurean *piéce de résistance*.

Similarly, the tantalizing attractions of the state as a whole combine in a recipe equally appetizing.

Among the most savory ingredients is history, and you'll find it in several flavors.

One traces the turmoil and strife of the Revolutionary War. Nearly a third of the war's battles were fought on New York soil—at such places as Johnstown, Saratoga, Schuylerville and White Plains. Weapons, uniforms, paintings and documents relating to the struggle for independence fill a museum at Fort Ticonderoga.

The story of the Underground Railroad is another. Many slaves found freedom taking cover in the safe houses along the route. Among those preserved sites are the Harriet Tubman Home in Auburn; the H. Lee White Marine Museum in Oswego; and the John Brown Farm State Historic Site in Lake Placid. Displays in Fenton History Center in Jamestown provide a wealth of information about the abolitionist network.

Yet a third recounts America's love of sports. In addition to being the home of numerous professional teams, the Empire State boasts halls of fame for several sports, including boxing, horse racing and soccer. Most notable, though, is Cooperstown's National Baseball Hall of Fame and Museum, which pays homage to the national pastime.

Architectural Smorgasbord

Add to this historical stock samples of diverse styles of architecture.

Albany's Capitol, one of few such buildings without a dome, bears intricate carvings that give it a decidedly French feel. The Beaux-Arts style characterizes the Vanderbilt Mansion National Historic Site in Hyde Park. A Greek Revival flair marks the Rose Hill Mansion in Geneva.

Fold in a rich dollop of art. Renowned museums in Albany, Buffalo and New York show off the talents of such artists as Willem de Kooning, Pablo Picasso, Auguste Rodin

Giovanni da Verrazano, representing the King of France, is the first European to set foot on New York soil; Henry Hudson claims the region for the Dutch in 1609.

1524

President William McKinley is assassinated while attending the Pan-American Exposition in Buffalo.

1901

New York enters the Union as the 11th state.

1788

1626
Peter Minuit buys Manhattan Island from American Indians for 60 guilders (about $24), and New Amsterdam is established.

New York Historical Timeline

1825
The completion of the Erie Canal links the Great Lakes and the Hudson River.

and Andy Warhol. Exquisite glass is the centerpiece at Corning Glass Center.

The Statue of Liberty, equal parts architecture and art, rises up from Liberty Island as a 151-foot-tall symbol of freedom on a 154-foot-high pedestal.

Sprinkle in a pinch of nature's architectural treasures. Brick walkways weave through the stalactites and stalagmites in Howe Caverns in Howes Cave. Huge outcroppings comprise the Panama Rocks in Panama.

Top it all off with a heaping spoonful of something home-grown—presidential homesteads. Millard Fillmore, Franklin D. Roosevelt, Theodore Roosevelt and Martin Van Buren all were New York natives.

Liquid Assets

Pour in plenty of water. Hugging varied borders are the Atlantic Ocean, Long Island Sound, lakes Champlain, Erie and Ontario, and the Delaware and St. Lawrence rivers. The aptly named Finger Lakes, 11 glacial lakes, gash vertical blue streaks in the landscape south of the stretch of I-90 linking Rochester and Syracuse.

Breathtaking waterfalls—including 215-foot Taughannock Falls in Ithaca, Rainbow Falls in Watkins Glen and the honeymooner's paradise of Niagara Falls—cascade and plummet all over the state.

Tour Goat Island, which separates the Niagara River to form Horseshoe and American falls, then venture onto nearby Three Sisters Islands to view the thundering rapids up close and personal.

Constructed to link major waterways and thereby open trade west of the Appalachians, the famed Cayuga-Seneca, Champlain, Erie and Oswego canals occupy their own niche in New York lore.

Accompany each course with a glass of premium wine from one of six major viticultural regions: Cayuga Lake, the Finger Lakes, Hudson River, Lake Erie, the Long Island Hamptons and the Long Island North Fork. More than 100 vineyards produce upwards of 20 million gallons of such varieties as chardonnay, pinot noir and cabernet sauvignon each year.

Bon appetit!

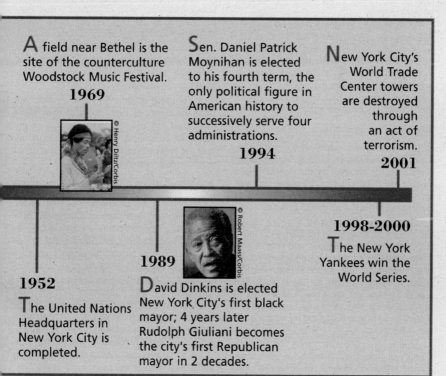

A field near Bethel is the site of the counterculture Woodstock Music Festival.
1969

© Henry Diltz/Corbis

Sen. Daniel Patrick Moynihan is elected to his fourth term, the only political figure in American history to successively serve four administrations.
1994

New York City's World Trade Center towers are destroyed through an act of terrorism.
2001

1998-2000
The New York Yankees win the World Series.

© Robert Maass/Corbis

1989
David Dinkins is elected New York City's first black mayor; 4 years later Rudolph Giuliani becomes the city's first Republican mayor in 2 decades.

1952
The United Nations Headquarters in New York City is completed.

Recreation

Forests. Mountains. Valleys. Waterways. If you're looking for fun in the great outdoors, New York has it all.

From the heights of the rugged Adirondacks to the pine barrens of Long Island, New York entices explorers of all stripes with miles upon miles of **hiking** trails. Notable among them are the Appalachian, Erie Canal, Finger Lakes and Northville-Lake Placid trails; the Long Island Greenbelt; and the Long Path, which links New York City with the Adirondacks. In winter many of these routes are popular for cross-country skiing.

Get a different perspective while **spelunking** alongside the subterranean river in Howe Caverns, in Howes Cave.

Steady yourself on two wheels and go **bicycling** along the 35-mile Mohawk-Hudson Bikeway, near Albany; through the 32 miles of trails in Old Erie Canal State Park, east of Syracuse; and on the 60-mile Barge Canal Recreationway, which traverses Monroe and Orleans counties.

If **horseback riding** is your thing, visit Allegany State Park, Connetquot State Park Preserve or Rockefeller State Park Preserve. Nearly 100 miles of trails are divided between the three.

Looking to go **canoeing** or **kayaking**? The Adirondacks are a good place to start. The range boasts 2,800 lakes and ponds in addition to thousands of miles of rivers. Explore the scenic wilderness in the Saint Regis canoe area—57 lakes and ponds near Saranac Lake—or head for Old Forge and navigate the Adirondack Canoe Route.

Running on the River

If you're new to **white-water rafting**, try a run on the Delaware, Genesee or Sacandaga rivers. Thrills abound on the feistier Black, Moose and Salmon rivers. Combine spectacular scenery and turbulent waters and you get the Hudson River, a perennial favorite.

There are plenty of other ways to play in the water. More than 4,000 lakes—including two of the Great Lakes and the Finger Lakes—add up to scores of options for **boating, swimming** and **water skiing**. The 524 miles of waterways in the New York State Canal System link the Great Lakes with the Hudson River and other northeastern inland waters to form another prime locale for pleasure boating.

Shipwrecks off the coast of Oswego County in Lake Ontario make for great **scuba diving**. Also of interest to divers is Lake George, where the well-preserved *Land Tortoise* sank; Lake Champlain, home of a legendary beast akin to the Loch Ness Monster; Long Island Sound; and the crystal-clear waters of the Thousand Islands-Seaway region.

Cast a line in one of New York's bodies of water, and you're in for a **fishing** adventure. Fresh waters yield bass, trout, perch, muskie, salmon and panfish. Bluefish, fluke, striper and weakfish swim in the surf. Long Island is noted for its cod, blackfish and flounder.

Three outstanding fishing streams—Beaver Kill, Neversink and Willowemoc—are within Catskill Forest Preserve in Catskill.

Playing on the Edge

For a rush of adrenaline, try **rock climbing** in the Adirondack, Catskill, Shawangunk or Taconic mountains; **parasailing** over Lake George; or **hang gliding** over the Rondout River near Ellenville. You'll also feel that excitement while **surfing** in the ocean off Long Island, **windsurfing** on the Finger Lakes or **snowmobiling** through Finger Lakes National Forest.

Exhilaration also is the name of the game at such **downhill skiing** hot spots as Belleayre Mountain, near Highmount; Big Tupper Ski Area in Big Tupper Lake; Gore Mountain in North Creek; Holiday Valley, near Ellicottville; Hunter Mountain in Hunter; Lake Placid/Whiteface in Wilmington; Windham Mountain in Windham; and Titus Mountain in Malone.

A **camping** excursion is sure to free you from the rigors of everyday life. The state's more than 500 campgrounds are all over the place: in backwoods spots reached only by boat or foot, along the shores of lakes and rivers, on the beautiful Atlantic coast.

Recreational Activities

Throughout the TourBook, you may notice a Recreational Activities heading with bulleted listings of recreation-oriented establishments listed underneath. Similar operations also may be mentioned in Destination City recreation sections. Since normal AAA inspection criteria cannot be applied, these establishments are presented only for information. Age, height and weight restrictions may apply. Reservations often are recommended and sometimes are required. Addresses and/or phone numbers are provided so visitors can contact the attraction for additional information.

Fast Facts

POPULATION: 18,976,457.

AREA: 49,576 square miles; ranks 30th.

CAPITAL: Albany.

HIGHEST POINT: 5,344 ft., Mount Marcy.

LOWEST POINT: Sea level, Atlantic Ocean.

TIME ZONE(S): Eastern. DST.

MINIMUM AGE FOR DRIVERS: Minimum driving age is 16 with restrictions, 18 without. In New York City no one under 17 may drive.

MINIMUM AGE FOR GAMBLING: 18.

SEAT BELT/CHILD RESTRAINT LAWS: Seat belts required for driver, front-seat passengers and back-seat passengers ages 4-16. Child restraints required for under 4.

HELMETS FOR MOTORCYCLISTS: Required.

RADAR DETECTORS: Permitted.

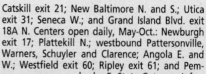

FIREARMS LAWS: Vary by state and/or county. Contact the New York State Police Headquarters, Building 22, State Campus, Albany, NY 12226; phone (518) 457-6811.

HOLIDAYS: Jan. 1; Martin Luther King Jr. Day, Jan. (3rd Mon.); Lincoln's Birthday, Feb. (1st Mon.); Washington's Birthday, Feb. (3rd Mon.); Memorial Day, May (last Mon.); July 4; Labor Day, Sept. (1st Mon.); Columbus Day, Oct. (2nd Mon.); Election Day, Nov.; Veterans Day, Nov. 11; Thanksgiving; Dec. 25.

TAXES: New York's statewide sales tax is 4 percent, with local options for additional increments of up to 4.5 percent. Localities may impose taxes on lodgings, admissions or restaurant meals. New York City imposes a 13.25 percent plus $2 room tax as well as additional sums depending on the room rate.

STATE INFORMATION CENTERS: Centers on/near the New York State Thruway (I-87) open daily year-round: Sloatsburg N.; Harriman exit 16; Catskill exit 21; New Baltimore N. and S.; Utica exit 31; Seneca W.; and Grand Island Blvd. exit 18A N. Centers open daily, May-Oct.: Newburgh exit 17; Plattekill N.; westbound Pattersonville, Warners, Schuyler and Clarence; Angola E. and W.; Westfield exit 60; Ripley exit 61; and Pembroke E. State Gateway Information Centers open daily year-round: Binghamton rest area (I-81) N.; Thousand Island International Bridge S. and Beekmantown rest area (Adirondack Northway) S.

FURTHER INFORMATION FOR VISITORS:

Department of Economic Development
Division of Tourism
One Commerce Plaza
Albany, NY 12245
(518) 474-4116
(800) 225-5697 (50 states and possessions)

New York Convention and Visitors Bureau
810 Seventh Ave.
New York, NY 10019
(212) 484-1200
(800) 692-8474

RECREATION INFORMATION:

New York State Office of Parks, Recreation and Historic Preservation
Agency Building #1
Empire State Plaza
Albany, NY 12238
(518) 474-0456
(800) 456-2267 (reservations)

FISHING AND HUNTING REGULATIONS:

Division of Fish and Wildlife
State Environmental Conservation Department
50 Wolf Rd.
Albany, NY 12233
(518) 457-3521

NATIONAL FOREST INFORMATION:

Forest Supervisor
Finger Lakes National Forest
5218 State Route 414
Hector, NY 14841
(607) 546-4470
(877) 444-6777 (reservations)

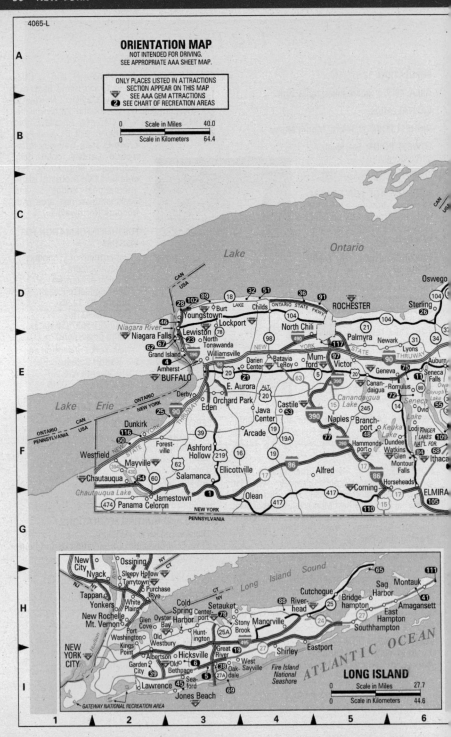

4065-L

ORIENTATION MAP
NOT INTENDED FOR DRIVING.
SEE APPROPRIATE AAA SHEET MAP.

ONLY PLACES LISTED IN ATTRACTIONS
SECTION APPEAR ON THIS MAP
▽ SEE AAA GEM ATTRACTIONS
❷ SEE CHART OF RECREATION AREAS

0   Scale in Miles   40.0
0   Scale in Kilometers   64.4

LONG ISLAND

0   Scale in Miles   27.7
0   Scale in Kilometers   44.6

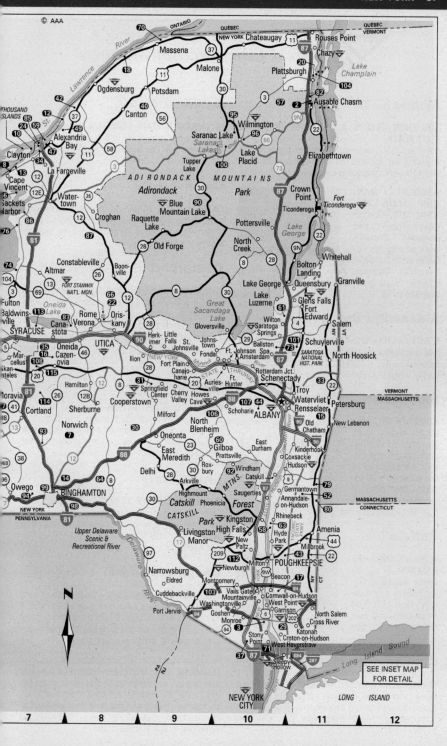

Points of Interest Offering A
Great Experience for Members®

Albany (F-10)

GOVERNOR NELSON A. ROCKEFELLER EMPIRE STATE PLAZA—In the heart of New York's capital, the plaza is a government complex consisting of the state capitol and the state museum in addition to a performing arts center. See p. 59.

SCHUYLER MAN-SION STATE HIS-TORIC SITE—George Washington and Benjamin Franklin were among the no-tables entertained in this 1761 Georgian home; its owner Phillip Schuyler was a general during the Revolutionary War. See p. 59.

Alexandria Bay (B-8))

BOLDT CASTLE—Hotel magnate George C. Boldt had this replica of a Rhineland castle built for his beloved wife; construction was immediately halted when she died in 1904. See p. 60.

Blue Mountain Lake (C-9)

ADIRONDACK MU-SEUM—Nearly two centuries of Adiron-dack culture and his-tory are explored in this museum's 20 in-door and outdoor exhibits overlooking Blue Mountain Lake. See p. 64.

Buffalo (E-3)

ALBRIGHT-KNOX ART GALLERY—A stately Greek Revival build-ing houses a particu-larly fine collection of modern and con-temporary art. See p. 71.

Canandaigua (E-5)

SONNENBERG GARDENS—Elegant gardens and a Queen Anne-style mansion reflect the summer-time lakeside lifestyle experienced by an affluent Victorian-era couple from New York City. See p. 75.

Castile (E-4)

LETCHWORTH STATE PARK—The Genesee River Gorge, three waterfalls and scenic roads, trails and views are the highlights of this state park. See p. 76.

Catskill (F-10)

CATSKILL GAME FARM—Animals and birds from around the world coexist in this zoological park; a petting zoo lets children and young animals meet each other. See p. 76.

Centerport (H-3)

VANDERBILT MUSEUM—William K. Vanderbilt II, great-grandson of Cornelius Vanderbilt, began work on his estate in the early 1900s; the 43 acres contain landscaped grounds, a planetarium, Vanderbilt's home and a marine museum reflect-ing his interest in the sea and marine life. See p. 77.

Chautauqua (F-2)

CHAUTAUQUA INSTITUTION—Begun in 1874 as a center for Sunday-school teachers, the institution has evolved into a summer arts and education center known for its lectures and entertainment offerings. See p. 77.

Chazy (A-11)

THE ALICE T. MINER MUSEUM—This gray stone Colonial Revival house museum contains glass, porcelain, prints, paintings, carpets, furniture and textiles, primarily from the 18th and 19th centu-ries. See p. 78.

Cooperstown (F-8)

THE FARMERS' MUSEUM—Nineteenth-century rural life in upstate New York is depicted here in a restored 1845 village, a farmstead and a stone dairy barn now used to house exhibits; craftspeo-ple in period attire practice their trades. See p. 79.

FENIMORE ART MUSEUM—Collections of folk and fine art are exhibited in this museum on Ot-sego Lake, as is memorabilia associated with au-thor James Fenimore Cooper, who was raised in Cooperstown; a separate wing is devoted to American Indian art. See p. 80.

NATIONAL BASEBALL HALL OF FAME AND MUSEUM— You won't strike out by visiting this museum where baseball legends are enshrined; the museum traces the history of the nation's pastime from its 19th-century beginnings to the present. See p. 80.

Corning (G-5)

CORNING MUSEUM OF GLASS— The artistry and history of glass, its uses and its manufacturing process are explained through museum exhibits and glassblowing demonstrations. See p. 81.

ROCKWELL MUSEUM OF WESTERN ART— Western and Native American art is the focus here, pardner. See p. 81.

Darien Center (E-4)

SIX FLAGS DARIEN LAKE— You will definitely be entertained at this complex where roller coasters, water parks, stage shows and thrill rides are all part of the fun. See p. 83.

Fort Stanwix National Monument (D-8)

FORT STANWIX NATIONAL MONUMENT— Built in 1758, the original fort protected the Mohawk Valley during the French and Indian and Revolutionary wars; its reconstruction contains archeological exhibits and living-history demonstrations. See p. 87.

Fort Ticonderoga (C-11)

FORT TICONDEROGA— The fort's strategic position on Lake Champlain led to its constant changes in ownership—from the French to the British to the Americans and back to the British; now restored, it has a museum with period artifacts. See p. 88.

Garrison (H-10)

BOSCOBEL— Saved from destruction in the mid-1900s, this restored 1804 Federal-style mansion is on a bluff overlooking the Hudson River. See p. 150.

Geneva (E-6)

ROSE HILL MANSION— The 1839 Greek Revival mansion overlooking Seneca Lake has 21 rooms furnished in period that can be seen on guided tours. See p. 89.

Glens Falls (D-11)

THE HYDE COLLECTION ART MUSEUM— An Italian Renaissance-style villa is the setting for an extensive collection of 15th- to 20th-century art which includes European antiques and works by European old masters and American artists. See p. 90.

Hammondsport (F-5)

GLENN H. CURTISS MUSEUM— The achievements of a speed enthusiast and aviation entrepreneur who held the first pilot's license issued in the United States are chronicled. See p. 91.

PLEASANT VALLEY WINE CO.— The cellars carved into the hillside and the wooden and stone structures of this winery date to its 1860 founding, adding to its Old World feeling; the Great Western Winery Visitor Center features tours, tastings and exhibits. See p. 91.

Howes Cave (E-9)

HOWE CAVERNS— Tours of the prehistoric cave proceed through chambers of stalagmites and stalactites and end with a quarter-mile boat ride on underground Lake of Venus. See p. 92.

Hudson (F-11)

AMERICAN MUSEUM OF FIREFIGHTING—The history of firefighting in America is examined from its early 18th-century origins to the present. See p. 93.

OLANA STATE HISTORIC SITE—Landscape painter Frederic Church's attention to the design details of his Moorish villa and landscaped grounds 1870-91 resulted in a singular work of art. See p. 93.

Hyde Park (G-10)

FRANKLIN D. ROOSEVELT MUSEUM AND LIBRARY—Home of the first presidential library, the museum includes family possessions as well as photographs, speeches and gifts from heads of state; a section is devoted to FDR's wife Eleanor. See p. 94.

HOME OF FRANKLIN D. ROOSEVELT NATIONAL HISTORIC SITE—FDR's home has been maintained as it was when he died in 1945; the graves of the president and his wife are in a rose garden. See p. 94.

STAATSBURGH STATE HISTORIC SITE—A 65-room mansion, built in 1832 and enlarged in 1895, sits on a 900-acre site; elaborately decorated, the house has marble fireplaces, ornate furniture and artifacts from around the world. See p. 94.

VANDERBILT MANSION NATIONAL HISTORIC SITE—Frederic Vanderbilt's elegant mansion, built during the "Gilded Age" of the late 19th-century, contains original furnishings; the grounds afford scenic views of the Hudson River and the Catskill Mountains. See p. 94.

Ithaca (F-6)

TAUGHANNOCK FALLS STATE PARK—The waterfall for which the park is named cascades 215 feet between 400-foot-tall rocky cliffs; trails offer a choice of views from either above or below the falls. See p. 95.

Jones Beach (I-3)

JONES BEACH STATE PARK—The attraction here is swimming—at ocean-front beaches, a bay beach or in two pools; a 2-mile-long boardwalk follows part of the shoreline. See p. 96.

Kingston (G-10)

SENATE HOUSE STATE HISTORIC SITE—This stone house belonging to Abraham Van Gaasbeek was where the governmental system of New York state was adopted in 1777; a museum contains works by area artists. See p. 97.

Lewiston (E-3)

EARL W. BRYDGES ARTPARK—A hybrid, this 200-acre state park along the Niagara River gorge is both a performing arts complex and a recreational facility; visitors flock here for dance, opera and music concerts as well as for hiking and exploring nature trails. See p. 166.

Lockport (D-3)

LOCKPORT LOCKS AND ERIE CANAL CRUISES—Passengers experience "locking up" and "locking down" as the boat makes its way through double working locks during a narrated tour of the historic Erie Canal. See p. 167.

Mayville (F-2)

CHAUTAUQUA BELLE——This replica of an old-fashioned stern-wheeler transports guests on tours of Chautauqua Lake. See p. 102.

Mumford (E-5)

GENESEE COUNTRY VILLAGE & MUSEUM—Craftspeople and guides in period costume portray life in a typical 19th-century country village; nature trails and a gallery of sporting and wildlife art complete the complex. See p. 104.

Newburgh (H-10)

WASHINGTON'S HEADQUARTERS STATE HISTORIC SITE—The general had his headquarters in this house 1782-83 as he directed troops during the Revolutionary War; a museum contains exhibits about the Continental Army. See p. 105.

New Paltz (G-10)

HUGUENOT HISTORICAL SOCIETY TOURS—Houses built by the original settlers still stand in the historic district. See p. 105.

New York (I-10)

AMERICAN MUSEUM OF NATURAL HISTORY—A freestanding dinosaur greets visitors in the rotunda; his relatives and other fossil displays are the highlights of this natural history museum. See p. 121.

BRONX ZOO—The animals in this 265-acre park, a landmark since 1899, reside in natural habitats. See p. 133.

BROOKLYN BOTANIC GARDEN—A 52-acre garden grows in Brooklyn; formal and informal gardens include a fragrance garden for the blind, a Japanese garden, a conservatory and a bonsai museum. See p. 134.

CENTRAL PARK—An 840-acre oasis in the middle of bustling Manhattan, the park contains lakes, skating rinks, an Egyptian obelisk, a wildlife conservation center, gardens and a theater; see it all by buggy ride, horse-drawn hansom cab or a walking tour conducted by a park ranger. See p. 125.

CHINATOWN—This little bit of China in New York City's Lower East Side is an exotic ethnic neighborhood of Asian restaurants, street vendors and shops stocked with everything Oriental. See p. 116.

THE CLOISTERS—A branch of the Metropolitan Museum of Art, The Cloisters is known for medieval art; five French cloisters, gardens, 15th-century tapestries and illuminated manuscripts carry out the theme. See p. 132.

DAHESH MUSEUM OF ART—Works by artists trained in European academies embody classical ideals. See p. 125.

ELLIS ISLAND—Audiotapes guide visitors around the processing station where millions of hopeful immigrants entered the country to begin a new life. See p. 121.

EMPIRE STATE BUILDING—This 1931 art deco building has long symbolized New York City; its two observatories afford panoramic views, one from the 86th floor, the other from the 102nd. See p. 125.

FEDERAL HALL NATIONAL MEMORIAL—This historic site was where our fledgling nation protested "taxation without representation," where the first Congress met and where George Washington was inaugurated; a museum contains exhibits pertaining to these events. See p. 116.

FRICK COLLECTION—Philanthropist Henry Clay Frick's collections of paintings, Oriental rugs, Limoges enamels and other art treasures are displayed. See p. 125.

LINCOLN CENTER FOR THE PERFORMING ARTS—This 14-acre complex encompasses the halls and theater where the New York Philharmonic, the Metropolitan Opera, the New York Ballet and the New York City Opera perform. See p. 126.

METROPOLITAN MUSEUM OF ART—One of the world's great museums, the Metropolitan's collections span 500 years of art history. See p. 128.

MUSEUM OF JEWISH HERITAGE—A LIVING MEMORIAL TO THE HOLOCAUST—Personal narratives, photographs and artifacts guide visitors through the 20th-century Jewish experience. See p. 119.

THE MUSEUM OF MODERN ART—More than 100,000 pieces of modern art, including paintings, sculptures, drawings, prints and photographs, comprise MoMA's comprehensive collection of 20th-century works. See p. 128.

NEW YORK BOTANICAL GARDEN—Stop and smell the roses here, and also visit a glass palacelike conservatory and specialty gardens featuring mountain flowers, plants native to the eastern United States, day lilies, perennials and herbs. See p. 133.

RIVERSIDE CHURCH—The 74 bronze bells of its carillon ring out three times each Sunday at this interdenominational church. See p. 133.

ROCKEFELLER CENTER—A city within a city, Rockefeller Center is well-known as the home of Radio City Music Hall and the "Today" show. See p. 129.

ROSE CENTER FOR EARTH AND SPACE—The secrets of the cosmos are revealed through multifaceted exhibits, interactive stations, high-definition images and the Hayden Planetarium's spectacular space show. See p. 121.

ST. PATRICK'S CATHEDRAL—Surrounded by skyscrapers, the twin spires of St. Patrick's have been a Manhattan landmark since 1879. See p. 129.

SOLOMON R. GUGGEN-HEIM MUSEUM—Frank Lloyd Wright's circular design for the museum is a perfect complement for the modern art collection hung along its sloping walkway. See p. 133.

STATUE OF LIBERTY NATIONAL MONUMENT AND ELLIS ISLAND—Lady Liberty, a gift from France in 1884, has welcomed millions of immigrants to America's shores; nearby Ellis Island was the entry point. The statue has an immigration museum in its base. See p. 120.

UNITED NATIONS HEADQUARTERS—Flags of all member nations mark this complex of buildings where the countries of the world meet to discuss global problems. See p. 130.

Niagara Falls, New York (D-3)

CAVE OF THE WINDS TRIP—Get a topsy-turvy view of the American Falls from wooden walkways at its base. See p. 161.

GOAT ISLAND—Skirt the edges of both the Canadian and American falls from mid-stream. See p. 161.

MAID OF THE MIST—Rides on these boats take visitors directly in front of the powerful falls. See p. 161.

NIAGARA AEROSPACE MUSEUM—Find out about western New York's contributions to aviation history. See p. 163.

NIAGARA FALLS—Visit Niagara Falls State Park to get splendid views. See p. 163.

POWER VISTA—The electrifying story of the harnessing of the falls' power is explained at the Niagara Power Project's visitor center. See p. 163.

Niagara Falls, Ontario (D-3)

JOURNEY BEHIND THE FALLS—Get a behind and bottom-up view of Horseshoe Falls from this unusual vantage point. See p. 169.

MAID OF THE MIST—You'll be grateful for the waterproof clothing provided on this boat trip in front of the falls. See p. 170.

MARINELAND—After you've seen the spectacular shows, make a spectacle of yourself on the roller coaster. See p. 170.

NIAGARA FALLS—A favorite of honeymooners, daredevils and millions of tourists, the majestic falls are a true natural wonder. See p. 172.

QUEEN VICTORIA PARK—If the falls have dampened your spirit, let these fine floral displays perk you up. See p. 176.

RIPLEY'S BELIEVE IT OR NOT! MUSEUM—Explore the outer limits of reality at this museum of the unusual. See p. 176.

WHIRLPOOL AERO CAR—Get a bird's-eye view of the Niagara Gorge and the whirlpool from this cable car. See p. 177.

WHITE WATER WALK—You'll be swept away by this close-up view of the rolling Niagara River rapids. See p. 177.

Ogdensburg (A-8)

FREDERIC REMINGTON ART MUSEUM— Paintings, bronzes, watercolors and drawings by the great artist of the American West are exhibited in this museum near his birthplace. See p. 179.

Old Bethpage (I-3)

OLD BETHPAGE VILLAGE RESTORATION—Long Island's pre-Civil War history is documented through a collection of buildings moved here from various locations. See p. 179.

Oyster Bay (H-3)

PLANTING FIELDS ARBORETUM STATE HISTORIC PARK—In addition to 409 acres of greenhouses, gardens and natural habitats, the historic site's grounds are graced with a 65-room Tudor Revival mansion with 16th- and 17th-century furnishings. See p. 182.

Queensbury (D-11)

THE GREAT ESCAPE AND SPLASHWATER KINGDOM—One of New York's largest theme parks keeps visitors active with thrill rides, live shows, a water park, roller coasters and attractions just for children. See p. 185.

Riverhead (H-4)

ATLANTIS MARINE WORLD—The Lost City of Atlantis holds the secrets of deep blue sealife, from eels to octopi and stingrays to sharks. See p. 186.

Rochester (D-5)

GEORGE EASTMAN HOUSE—The estate of the founder of Eastman Kodak Co., restored to its early 20th-century appearance, contains gardens and the International Museum of Photography and Film. See p. 187.

MEMORIAL ART GALLERY—A diverse 11,000-piece collection includes artifacts from ancient Greece, two ornate Egyptian coffins and contemporary art glass. See p. 188.

ROCHESTER MUSEUM & SCIENCE CENTER—This museum, which specializes in science, technology and the environment, also presents star and laser sound-and-light shows in its planetarium. See p. 188.

THE STRONG MUSEUM—The story of everyday life in America is related through collections of items dating from 1820—toys, house-wares and home furnishings, clothing and advertising materials. See p. 188.

Saratoga Springs (D-10)

LAKE GEORGE OPERA FESTIVAL—Operas are presented by a regional repertory company in June and July; the company strives to develop young American artists and provide a combination of new and traditional works. See p. 192.

Sleepy Hollow (H-2)

KYKUIT, THE ROCKEFELLER ESTATE—Four generations of Rockefellers have occupied the Hudson River estate built for Standard Oil mogul John D. Rockefeller. See p. 153.

Springfield Center (E-9)

GLIMMERGLASS OPERA—Opera is performed in repertory on the shores of Otsego Lake in a theater whose walls open to reveal views of the countryside. See p. 196.

Tarrytown (H-2)

WASHINGTON IRVING'S SUNNYSIDE—On the banks of the Hudson River, Washington Irving's estate includes a charming stone mansion that still has the wisteria he planted at its entranceway; interpreters in period costume conduct tours. See p. 154.

Utica (E-8)

MUNSON-WILLIAMS-PROCTOR ARTS INSTITUTE—The institute, which consists of an art museum, a performing arts program and an art school, has fine collections of American and European art. See p. 200.

Watkins Glen (F-6)

WATKINS GLEN STATE PARK—Scenic gorges sculpted by nature, waterfalls, rocky cliffs and a bridge over the chasm are high points at this popular state park. See p. 201.

West Point (H-10)

UNITED STATES MILITARY ACADEMY—Many of America's military heroes were trained at this venerable academy overlooking the Hudson River. See p. 202.

WEST POINT MUSEUM—This museum at the military academy contains exhibits about military and academy history and extensive collections of artifacts from Revolutionary War days to the present. See p. 203.

Wilmington (B-10)

WHITEFACE MOUNTAIN VETERANS' MEMORIAL HIGHWAY—Constructed 1929-35 as a tribute to New Yorkers killed in World War I, the 6-mile road provides numerous scenic mountain and lake viewpoints. See p. 204.

Youngstown (D-3)

OLD FORT NIAGARA—On the grounds of Fort Niagara State Park, the fort was constructed by the French and has served under the flags of three nations. See p. 167.

RECREATION AREAS

	MAP LOCATION	CAMPING	PICNICKING	HIKING TRAILS	BOATING	BOAT RAMP	BOAT RENTAL	FISHING	SWIMMING	PETS ON LEASH	BICYCLE TRAILS	WINTER SPORTS	VISITOR CENTER	LODGE/CABINS	FOOD SERVICE
NATIONAL FORESTS *(See place listings)*															
Finger Lakes (F-6) 16,000 acres in north-central New York on a ridge between Seneca and Cayuga lakes, via I-90, I-81, I-86 and SR 17.		●	●	●				●		●		●			
NATIONAL RECREATION AREAS *(See place listings)*															
Gateway															
Breezy Point District (I-2)			●					●	●	●			●		●
Jamaica Bay District (I-2) Horse rental.			●	●	●			●		●	●		●		●
Staten Island Unit (I-2)			●	●	●			●	●	●	●		●		●
NATIONAL SEASHORES *(See place listings)*															
Fire Island (I-4) 6,220 acres on Fire Island, off the s. shore of Long Island.		●	●	●				●	●	●			●		●
STATE															
Allan H. Treman Marine (F-6) 1 mi. n. of Ithaca on SR 89.	109		●		●	●		●	●						
Allegany (G-3) 60,398 acres (two areas) s. of Salamanca on State Park Rd. 1. Cross-country skiing; horse rental.	1	●	●	●	●	●	●	●	●	●	●	●	●	●	●
Ausable Point (B-11) 500 acres 12 mi. s. of Plattsburgh on US 9.	2	●	●		●	●		●	●						●
Bear Mountain (H-10) 5,067 acres 5 mi. s. of West Point off US 9W. Museum, nature trails, zoo. *(See West Point p. 202)*	3	●	●	●	●	●	●	●	●	●	●	●	●	●	●
Beaver Island (E-3) 1,081 acres 8 mi. w. of Buffalo on southern tip of Grand Island. Snowmobiling.	4		●	●	●			●	●	●		●			●
Belmont Lake (I-3) 459 acres 4 mi. n. of Babylon off Southern State Pkwy. exit 38. Bridle paths.	5		●	●	●		●	●	●	●	●				
Bethpage (I-3) 1,475 acres 1 mi. n. of Farmingdale. Cross-country skiing, golf, tennis, tobogganing; bridle paths.	6		●	●						●	●	●			●
Bowman Lake (F-8) 653 acres 8 mi. n.w. of Oxford off SR 220. Nature trails.	7	●	●	●				●	●	●	●	●			●
Burnham Point (B-7) 12 acres 3 mi. e. of Cape Vincent on SR 12E.	8	●	●		●	●		●		●					
Buttermilk Falls (F-6) 751 acres s. of Ithaca on SR 13. Cross-country skiing.	9	●	●	●				●	●	●		●		●	
Canoe-Picnic Point (B-7) 70 acres on southern tip of Grindstone Island; access is by boat only.	10	●	●		●			●		●			●		
Cayuga Lake (E-6) 141 acres 3 mi. e. of Seneca Falls on SR 89. Sledding; recreation building.	11	●	●		●	●		●	●	●			●		
Cedar Island (B-7) 10 acres on Cedar Island w. of Chippewa Bay; access is by boat only.	12	●	●		●			●		●					
Cedar Point (B-7) 48 acres 6 mi. w. of Clayton on SR 12E.	13	●	●		●	●	●	●	●	●					
Chenango Valley (C-7) 1,071 acres 13 mi. n.e. of Binghamton on SR 369. Nature trails.	14	●	●	●	●		●	●	●	●		●	●		●
Cherry Plain (F-11) 175 acres 2 mi. n. of Stephentown on Miller Rd.	15		●	●	●			●	●	●					
Chittenango Falls (E-7) 192 acres 4 mi. n. of Cazenovia on SR 13.	16	●	●	●				●		●					
Clarence Fahnestock Memorial (H-11) 6,800 acres 11 mi. w. of Carmel on SR 301. Cross-country skiing.	17	●	●	●	●		●	●	●	●		●	●		●
Clark Reservation (E-7) 310 acres 3 mi. s.e. of Syracuse on SR 173. Playground.	108		●	●				●	●	●					
Coles Creek (A-8) 1,800 acres 5 mi. e. of Waddington on SR 37.	18	●	●		●	●		●	●	●					
Connetquot Preserve (I-3) 3,473 acres near Oakdale/Bohemia on SR 27. Historic. Cross-country skiing; bridle paths.	19		●					●					●		
Cumberland Bay (A-11) 350 acres 1 mi. n. of Plattsburgh off US 9.	20	●	●					●	●	●	●				
Darien Lake (E-4) 1,845 acres 2 mi. w. of Darien Center on US 20. Cross-country skiing, snowmobiling.	21	●	●	●	●			●	●			●		●	

RECREATION AREAS

	MAP LOCATION	CAMPING	PICNICKING	HIKING TRAILS	BOATING	BOAT RAMP	BOAT RENTAL	FISHING	SWIMMING	PETS ON LEASH	BICYCLE TRAILS	WINTER SPORTS	VISITOR CENTER	LODGE/CABINS	FOOD SERVICE
Delta Lake (D-8) 400 acres 6 mi. n.e. of Rome on SR 46. Snowmobiling.	22	•	•	•	•	•		•	•	•	•	•			•
Devil's Hole (E-3) 42 acres 4.5 mi. n. of Niagara Falls. Scenic. Nature trails.	23		•	•				•	•						
DeWolf Point (B-7) 13 acres on Wellesley Island in the St. Lawrence River.	24	•			•	•		•	•					•	
Evangola (F-2) 733 acres 5 mi. s.w. of Angola on SR 5.	25	•	•	•	•			•	•	•		•			•
Fair Haven Beach (D-6) 865 acres 1 mi. n. of Fair Haven off SR 104A. Cross-country skiing, snowmobiling; nature trails.	26	•	•	•	•	•	•	•	•	•		•	•	•	•
Fillmore Glen (F-7) 939 acres 1 mi. s. of Moravia on SR 38.	27	•	•	•					•	•		•			•
Fort Niagara (D-3) 504 acres at the mouth of the Niagara River off SR 18F. Snowmobiling, tobogganing. *(See Youngstown p. 167)*	28		•	•	•	•	•	•	•	•		•	•		•
Four Mile Creek (D-3) 248 acres 4 mi. e. of Youngstown on SR 18.	102	•		•				•	•						
Franklin Delano Roosevelt (H-10) 952 acres w. of Yorktown Heights off the Taconic State Pkwy. Snowmobiling.	29		•	•	•			•	•	•	•	•			•
Gilbert Lake (F-8) 1,569 acres 12 mi. n.w. of Oneonta off SR 205. Cross-country skiing.	30	•	•	•	•	•	•	•	•	•		•		•	•
Glimmerglass (E-9) 593 acres 4 mi. s. of East Springfield. Snowmobiling.	31	•	•	•	•	•		•	•	•		•			•
Golden Hill (D-4) 510 acres 5 mi. n.e. of Barker off SR 148. Snowmobiling.	32	•	•		•	•		•		•		•			
Grafton Lakes (E-11) 2,357 acres .5 mi. s. of Grafton off SR 2. Cross-country skiing; nature trails.	33		•	•	•		•	•	•	•		•			•
Grass Point (B-7) 66 acres 5 mi. s. of Alexandria Bay off SR 12.	34	•	•		•	•		•	•						
Green Lakes (E-7) 1,700 acres 4 mi. n.e. of Fayetteville on SR 290. Cross-country skiing.	35	•	•	•	•		•	•	•	•	•	•		•	•
Hamlin Beach (D-4) 1,243 acres 5 mi. n. of Hamlin on Lake Ontario. Cross-country skiing; nature trails.	36	•	•	•	•	•		•	•	•		•	•		•
Harriman (I-10) 46,613 acres 5 mi. w. of Stony Point on SR 210. Cross-country skiing; nature trails.	37	•	•	•	•	•	•	•	•	•		•			•
Heckscher (I-3) 1,657 acres 1 mi. s. of East Islip off Southern State Pkwy. Cross-country skiing; bridle paths.	38	•	•	•	•			•	•	•	•				•
Hempstead Lake (I-2) 775 acres 2 mi. s. of Hempstead. Tennis; bridle paths, nature trails.	39							•	•		•				
Higley Flow (B-9) 1,200 acres 2 mi. w. of South Colton off SR 56. Cross-country skiing; nature trails.	40	•	•	•	•			•	•	•		•			•
Hither Hills (H-6) 1,755 acres 8 mi. w. of Montauk on SR 27.	41	•	•	•				•	•						•
Jacques Cartier (B-7) 461 acres 2 mi. w. of Morristown off SR 12. Cross-country skiing.	42	•	•		•	•		•	•			•			
James Baird (G-11) 590 acres 11 mi. e. of Poughkeepsie on Taconic State Pkwy. Cross-country skiing, golf.	43		•	•				•	•			•			•
John Boyd Thacher (E-10) 2,000 acres 4 mi. n. of New Salem on SR 157. Nature trails.	44		•	•				•		•		•			
Jones Beach (I-3) 2,413 acres on the ocean shore of Long Island off Meadowbrook or Wantagh Pkwy. Golf. *(See Jones Beach p. 96)*	45		•					•	•		•		•		•
Joseph Davis (D-3) 388 acres 2.5 mi. s. of Youngstown off Robert Moses Pkwy.	46		•	•				•	•	•		•			
Keewaydin (B-7) 180 acres 1 mi. w. of Alexandria Bay on SR 12.	47	•			•	•		•	•						
Keuka Lake (F-5) 621 acres 6 mi. s.w. of Penn Yan off SR 54A. Snowmobiling.	48	•	•	•	•	•		•	•	•		•			
Kring Point (B-8) 51 acres 10 mi. n.e. of Alexandria Bay.	49	•	•		•	•		•	•					•	
Lake Erie (F-2) 355 acres 2 mi. n. of Brocton on SR 380. Snowmobiling, tobogganing.	50	•	•	•				•	•	•		•			•
Lakeside Beach (D-4) 734 acres 1.5 mi. e. of Kuckville on SR 18. Cross-country skiing.	51	•	•					•	•	•		•			•

RECREATION AREAS

	MAP LOCATION	CAMPING	PICNICKING	HIKING TRAILS	BOATING	BOAT RAMP	BOAT RENTAL	FISHING	SWIMMING	PETS ON LEASH	BICYCLE TRAILS	WINTER SPORTS	VISITOR CENTER	LODGE/CABINS	FOOD SERVICE
Lake Taghkanic (G-11) 1,568 acres 12 mi. s.e. of Hudson on SR 82. Cross-country skiing, snowmobiling.	52	•	•	•	•	•	•	•	•			•		•	•
Letchworth (F-4) 14,336 acres 2 mi. n. on SR 19A to Denton's Corners, then 2 mi. e. Scenic. Cross-country skiing; nature trails. *(See Castile p. 76)*	53	•	•	•				•	•	•	•	•		•	•
Long Point (E-6) 108 acres 4 mi. s. of Aurora off SR 90 to Lake Rd.	55		•		•	•		•							
Long Point (C-7) 23 acres 11 mi. s.w. of Three Mile Bay off SR 12E.	56	•	•		•	•		•							
Long Point on Lake Chautauqua (F-2) 360 acres 1 mi. s. of Maple Springs off I-86/SR 17. Snowmobiling.	54		•	•	•	•	•	•				•			•
Macomb Reservation (B-10) 600 acres 3 mi. w. of Schuyler Falls off SR 22B. Cross-country skiing.	57	•	•	•				•	•			•			
Margaret Lewis Norrie (G-10) 329 acres 3 mi. n. of Hyde Park on US 9.	58	•	•	•	•	•		•				•	•		•
Mary Island (B-7) 13 acres at n.e. end of Wellesley Island; access is by boat only.	59	•	•	•				•							
Max V. Shaul (F-9) 15 acres 5 mi. s. of Middleburgh on SR 30.	106	•	•	•				•	•	•					
Mine Kill (F-10) 15 mi. s. of Middleburgh via SR 30.	60		•	•	•	•		•	•			•	•		
Minnewaska State Park (G-10) 10 mi. w. of New Paltz via US 44/SR 55. Cross-country skiing.	112		•	•				•	•	•	•	•	•		
Montauk Point (H-6) 724 acres 4 mi. e. of Montauk on SR 27. Nature Trails.	111		•	•				•							•
Moreau Lake (D-10) 645 acres 4 mi. s. of Glens Falls off US 9. Cross-country skiing; nature trails.	61	•	•	•	•	•		•	•	•		•	•		•
Newton Battlefield Reservation (G-6) 330 acres 5 mi. e. of Elmira via SR 7.	105		•	•									•	•	
Niagara Falls (E-2) 433 acres at foot of Falls St. in Niagara Falls. Scenic. Nature trails, recreation programs. *(See Niagara Falls p. 163)*	62		•	•						•	•		•		•
Ogden and Ruth Livingston Mills Memorial (G-10) 575 acres 5 mi. n. on US 9 to Old Post Rd. Cross-country skiing, golf.	63		•	•				•				•	•		•
Oquaga Creek (F-8) 1,482 acres 9 mi. s. of Sidney off SR 206.	64	•	•	•	•			•	•	•		•	•		•
Orient Beach (H-5) 357 acres 3.5 mi. e. of Orient off SR 25.	65		•	•				•	•						•
Pinnacle (G-5) 2 mi. s. of Addison off Ackerson Rd. Golf.	110		•	•									•		•
Pixley Falls (D-8) 375 acres 6 mi. s. of Boonville off SR 46.	66	•	•	•				•		•			•		•
Point Au Roche (A-11) 850 acres 4 mi. n. of Plattsburgh e. of SR 9. Cross-country skiing; nature center.	104		•	•				•	•	•	•	•	•		•
Reservoir (E-3) 132 acres 2 mi. n. of Niagara Falls at jct. SRs 265 and 31.	67		•	•						•	•				
Robert H. Treman (F-6) 1,025 acres 5 mi. s.w. of Ithaca off SR 327.	68	•	•	•				•	•	•				•	
Robert Moses (I-3) 1,000 acres on the w. end of Fire Island on the Atlantic Ocean, accessible via the Robert Moses Causeway from Captree State Park. *(See Fire Island National Seashore p. 86)*	69		•		•			•	•						•
Robert Moses (A-8) 4,122 acres 2 mi. n.e. of SR 37 on Barnhart Island. Scenic. Downhill skiing; nature trails. *(See Massena p. 102)*	70	•	•	•	•	•		•	•	•	•	•	•		•
Rockland Lake (I-10) 1,079 acres 3 mi. n. of Nyack on US 9W. Cross-country skiing; nature trails.	71		•	•	•	•		•	•	•	•	•	•		•
Sampson (E-6) 1,853 acres 5 mi. n. of Ovid on SR 96A. Recreation building.	72	•	•	•	•	•		•	•	•		•			•
Saratoga Spa (E-11) 2,002 acres n. of I-87 exit 13N in Saratoga Springs. Cross-country skiing, snowmobiling. *(See Saratoga Springs p. 192)*	73		•	•				•	•			•	•		•
Selkirk Shores (D-7) 980 acres 5 mi. w. of Pulaski on SR 3. Snowmobiling.	74	•	•	•	•	•		•	•	•		•		•	•

RECREATION AREAS

RECREATION AREAS	MAP LOCATION	CAMPING	PICNICKING	HIKING TRAILS	BOATING	BOAT RAMP	BOAT RENTAL	FISHING	SWIMMING	PETS ON LEASH	BICYCLE TRAILS	WINTER SPORTS	VISITOR CENTER	LODGE/CABINS	FOOD SERVICE
Seneca Lake (E-6) 141 acres 1 mi. e. of Geneva off US 20. *(See Geneva p. 89)*	75		•		•	•		•	•	•					•
Southwick Beach (C-7) 313 acres 32 mi. s.w. of Watertown off SR 3. Nature trails.	76	•	•	•				•	•	•			•		•
Stony Brook (F-5) 577 acres 3 mi. s. of Dansville on SR 36. Snowmobiling.	77	•	•	•				•	•				•		•
Sunken Meadow/Governor Alfred E. Smith (H-3) 1,266 acres 1 mi. n. of Kings Park. Cross-country skiing, golf, sledding; bridle paths.	78		•	•				•	•			•	•		•
Taconic-Copake Falls (F-11) 4,647 acres 1 mi. e. of Copake Falls on SR 344. Nature trail.	79	•	•	•				•	•					•	
Taconic-Rudd Pond (G-11) 210 acres 3 mi. n. of Millerton.	80	•	•	•	•	•	•	•	•	•					•
Taughannock Falls (F-6) 783 acres 8 mi. n. of Ithaca on SR 89. *(See Ithaca p. 95)*	81	•	•	•				•	•	•			•		• •
Thompson's Lake (E-10) 50 acres 3 mi. s.w. of East Berne on SR 157A.	107	•	•	•				•	•	•					
Valcour Landing (B-11) 4 mi. s. of Plattsburgh off US 9.	82	•	•		•			•							
Verona Beach (D-8) 1,735 acres 1 mi. s. of Sylvan Beach off SR 13. Cross-country skiing, snowmobiling.	83	•	•	•				•	•	•			•		•
Watkins Glen (F-6) 1,000 acres adjoining Watkins Glen at the s. end of Seneca Lake. Recreation building. *(See Watkins Glen p. 201)*	84	•	•	•				•	•				•	•	•
Wellesley Island (B-7) 2,636 acres 2 mi. n. of Alexandria Bay via the Thousand Islands Bridge.	85	•	•	•	•	•	•	•	•	•			•		•
Westcott Beach (C-7) 319 acres 4 mi. s.w. of Sackets Harbor off SR 3.	86	•	•	•				•	•	•					•
Whetstone Gulf (C-8) 1,902 acres 3 mi. s. of Martinsburg off SR 26. Nature trails.	87	•	•	•				•	•	•			•		•
Wildwood (H-4) 769 acres 3 mi. e. of Wading River off SR 25A. Cross-country skiing.	88	•	•					•	•			•	•		
Wilson-Tuscarora (D-3) 390 acres 1 mi. w. of Wilson on SR 18.	89		•	•				•	•	•					
OTHER															
Adirondack Park (C-9) 6,000,000 acres in upstate New York. Horse rental. *(See place listing p. 57)*	90	•	•	•	•	•	•	•	•	•	•	•	•	•	•
Braddock Bay (D-5) 2,295 acres 10 mi. w. of Rochester on Lake Ontario. Nature trails.	91		•	•	•	•	•	•				•	•		•
Catskill Forest Preserve (F-10) 287,989 acres in the Catskill Mountains. *(See Catskill p. 76)*	92	•	•	•	•			•	•			•			
Dorchester Park (F-7) 1,242 acres 2 mi. n. of Whitney Point on SR 26.	93	•	•	•	•	•	•	•	•	•					
Genesee Valley Park (D-5) 2.5 mi. s.w. of Rochester on Elmwood Ave. Golf (18-hole), ice skating, tennis.	117		•	•					•						
Greenwood Park (G-7) 440 acres 13 mi. n. of Endicott on SR 26.	94	•	•	•	•			•	•	•		•	•		•
Highland Forest (E-7) 2,700 acres 4 mi. e. of Fabius on SR 80.	114		•	•						•	•	•	•		
Jamesville Beach Park (E-7) 250 acres off SR 173 on Apulia Rd. in Jamesville.	115		•	•				•	•	•					•
Lake Colby (B-10) 1 mi. n. of Saranac Lake Village on SR 86.	95		•		•	•		•	•				•		
Lake Flower (B-10) in Saranac Lake Village on SR 86. Canoeing, tennis.	96		•		•	•	•	•	•					•	•
Mendon Ponds (E-5) 2,462 acres 12 mi. s.e. of Rochester on SR 65. Nature trails.	97	•	•	•				•	•			•	•	•	
Nathaniel Cole (G-8) 370 acres 5 mi. e. of Kirkwood on Colesville Rd.	98	•	•	•	•	•		•	•						•
Oneida Shores Park (D-7) 390 acres on Bartell Rd. off I-81 exit 31 in Brewerton.	113	•	•		•	•		•	•	•					•
Otsiningo (G-7) 84 acres 1 mi. n. of Binghamton on US 11.	99		•	•				•			•	•	•		

RECREATION AREAS

	MAP LOCATION	CAMPING	PICNICKING	HIKING TRAILS	BOATING	BOAT RAMP	BOAT RENTAL	FISHING	SWIMMING	PETS ON LEASH	BICYCLE TRAILS	WINTER SPORTS	VISITOR CENTER	LODGE/CABINS	FOOD SERVICE
Point Gratiot (F-2) 75 acres on Lake Shore Dr. W. in Dunkirk.	116	•						•	•	•	•				
Saranac Lakes (B-10) Three lakes.	100														
Lower Saranac Lake .5 mi. w. of Saranac Lake off SR 3W. Horse rental.		•	•	•	•	•	•	•	•				•		•
Middle Saranac Lake 3 mi. w. of Saranac Lake off SR 3W.		•	•	•	•			•	•				•		
Upper Saranac Lake 11 mi. w. of Saranac Lake off SR 3W. Horse rental.		•	•	•	•	•	•	•	•				•	•	
Saratoga Lake (E-11) 3 mi. e. of Saratoga Springs via SR 9P.	101	•	•		•	•	•	•	•				•		•	•
Thomas Bull Memorial Park (H-9) 652 acres s.w. of Montgomery on SR 416. Golf, tennis.	103		•			•		•	•		•		•		•

New York Temperature Averages
Maximum / Minimum
From the records of the National Weather Service

	JAN	FEB	MAR	APR	MAY	JUNE	JULY	AUG	SEPT	OCT	NOV	DEC
Albany	31/14	33/15	42/24	57/36	70/46	79/56	84/61	81/59	73/50	62/40	48/31	35/19
Bear Mountain	33/19	33/19	43/28	55/38	67/48	75/56	79/63	78/61	71/54	60/44	47/33	36/22
Binghamton	30/15	31/15	39/23	53/34	65/45	74/55	79/60	77/58	70/50	59/40	45/30	33/19
Buffalo	30/17	30/16	38/23	52/34	65/44	75/55	80/59	79/58	72/51	60/44	46/32	33/21
New York	40/28	40/27	48/34	59/43	71/53	80/63	85/69	83/68	76/61	66/51	54/41	42/30
Oswego	32/18	32/18	40/26	51/36	62/45	72/55	79/62	76/61	70/54	59/44	47/34	35/22
Rochester	33/18	33/17	40/24	55/36	67/46	78/56	83/61	80/59	73/52	62/42	48/33	36/22
Syracuse	32/17	32/17	40/25	55/37	68/47	78/57	82/62	81/60	72/52	61/42	47/33	35/21

Exploring New York

For descriptions of places in bold type, see individual listings.

Adirondack Mountains

Stretching over 6 million acres and consisting of 46 peaks more than 4,000 feet tall, the Adirondack Mountains encompass thousands of miles of rivers and streams and more than 2,000 lakes and ponds. Low winter temperatures and heavy snowfall create excellent conditions for winter sports.

Lakes Champlain and George form the region's eastern border, while the Mohawk and St. Lawrence river valleys define its southern and northern limits.

Providing access to the region's mountainous interior are SRs 9N/86 and 73 from I-87; and SRs 30 and 12/28 from I-90.

A popular spot for hot-air balloonists between the Hudson River and Lake George, **Glens Falls** features the Hyde Collection of fine arts in a Florentine-style mansion. Cruise boats depart from the village of **Lake George** to explore the 365 islands of 32-mile-long Lake George.

The village also serves as a base for exploring lakeshore recreational facilities and historical sites. Scenic Lake Shore Drive links the village to **Fort Ticonderoga,** which controlled the narrow isthmus between lakes Champlain and George during Colonial times.

Extending southward 120 miles from Canada, Lake Champlain varies in width from one-quarter of a mile to 12 miles.

From **Plattsburgh,** Port Kent and Essex, ferries reach Vermont.

Off I-87, **Ausable Chasm** has a series of waterfalls and rapids. Plattsburgh, near the Canadian border, played a strategic role in the War of 1812.

SRs 9N/86 and 73 wind through about 50 miles of small farms, resort communities and rugged mountains before joining near **Lake Placid.** East of town is **Wilmington,** where 4,867-foot Whiteface Mountain ranks as the highest skiing peak in the East.

© Adirondack Scenic Railroad

Escape to the Empire State

West of Lake Placid is the town of **Saranac Lake,** where author Robert Louis Stevenson sought relief from tuberculosis and wrote extensively.

Blue Mountain Lake, at the junction of SRs 30 and 28, features the Adirondack Museum, which provides a thorough background on the region. Along Raquette Lake near the town of **Tupper Lake** lie the extravagant "Great Camps" of the Victorian-era industrialists.

Catskill Mountains

American Indians called this heavily forested section of the Appalachian escarpment *Onteora,* or "land in the sky." With its trout-filled streams and established resorts, the Catskill region is popular among artists and entertainers.

Four routes reach the Catskills from the Hudson River Valley. From the town of **Catskill,** scenic SRs 23 and 23A climb the steep 1,000-foot wall of the Catskills' eastern edge. SR 23 reaches the ski resort of **Windham** and continues on to **Oneonta.**

Before joining SR 23 at **Prattsville,** SR 23A winds upward through scenic Kaaterskill Clove to the mountain ski resort of Hunter. From **Kingston,** SR 28 passes Ashokan Reservoir and heads into the heart of the 278,000-acre Catskill Forest Preserve. From there, SR 28 crosses one of the least developed sections of the Catskills.

SR 17 between Harriman State Park/I-87 and **Binghamton** allows access to resort towns. Monticello serves as a base for exploring the headwaters of the Delaware River.

Winter recreational opportunities in the Catskills include hiking and snowshoeing. For ski enthusiasts, the Catskills offer snowmaking capacity for more than 1,100 acres, a combined vertical drop in excess of 8,890 feet and more than 200 trails. Cross-country skiing is available in state parks, the Catskill Forest Preserve and at area ski centers.

Mohawk Valley

The Mohawk Valley Heritage Corridor is a mosaic of picturesque landscapes and legendary places where great events shaped the history of America. Homeland to the Iroquois Confederacy, the region stretches 130 miles from the Hudson River to Oneida Lake and includes Albany, Fulton, Herkimer, Montgomery, Oneida, Saratoga, Schenectady and Schoharie counties as well as the Oneida Indian Nation.

Heroic battles fought and won in the area became the turning point in the Revolutionary War. Once one of the busiest thoroughfares from the Atlantic seaboard, waves of settlers traversed the area heading westward through the Adirondack and Appalachian mountains. Many settled along the Erie Canal, creating a vibrant 19th century center of industrial innovation and commerce.

The primary east-west route is the I-90/NYS Thruway toll road from **Albany** to **Utica.** Albany was the site of the first general congress of all the Colonies in 1754. Northwest of Albany, **Schenectady** displays its Dutch heritage in the restored Stockade District. With the opening of the Erie Canal in 1825, **Amsterdam,** just west of Schenectady, became an important industrial town.

Nearby **Johnstown** remains a glove-making center and contains the site of one of the last battles of the Revolution. Utica, 60 miles west, developed with the canal. **Rome,** a portage station that connected the Hudson River to the Great Lakes before the Erie Canal, grew up around the site of **Fort Stanwix,** which played an important role in the Revolutionary War.

Central

Pivotal in the growth of water-powered industry and the opening of the West via the Erie Canal, central New York consists of rolling hills, dense forests and ample rivers. The region is demarcated by the Hudson River to the east; the Adirondacks, Mohawk River and Oneida Lake to the north; the Finger Lakes to the west; and the Catskills to the south.

© Richard A. Cooke / Corbis

James Fenimore Cooper's novels chronicled the area's pioneer days and gave the region its nickname, Leatherstocking Country. As the Erie Canal system became obsolete, many of the towns declined; except for scattered dairy farms, much of the countryside has reverted to its natural state.

From Schenectady, I-88 heads southwest across rolling farmland to Binghamton. Two scenic routes offer access to the southern portion of the region: SR 12 runs from Binghamton to Utica, and SR 28 runs from Oneonta to **Cooperstown.**

Beginning with the collection of salt from Onondaga Lake, **Syracuse** blossomed into a leading industrial and university city. Chittanango Falls State Park to the southeast contains one of the state's most beautiful waterfalls.

Binghamton developed after the opening of the Chenango Canal, which created a direct route between Pennsylvania coal fields and the Erie Canal. At the turn of the 20th century Eastern European immigrants sought work in shoe factories, leaving their mark in golden, onion-domed churches.

From Oneonta, home of the National Soccer Hall of Fame, SR 28 heads to Cooperstown, the home of the National Baseball Hall of Fame and the setting for James Fenimore Cooper's novels. Near the town of **Howes Cave** are caverns that contain a river, a lake and the floor of an ancient ocean.

Finger Lakes

Glaciers carved 11 deep, narrow, finger-shaped lakes and the distinctive drumlin ridges and left a landscape bearing names reminiscent of the Iroquois Indian civilization. Artistic retreats, wineries and parkland are a few of the region's attractions. The **Finger Lakes** lie south of I-90 between Syracuse and **Rochester,** northeast of SR 17/I-86/I-390 between Binghamton and Rochester, and west of I-81 between Syracuse and Binghamton.

The following routes allow access to the shorelines of the principal lakes: SR 13 between **Cortland, Ithaca** and **Elmira;** scenic SR 89 along Cayuga Lake between Ithaca and the Montezuma National Wildlife Refuge; and SR 14 along Seneca Lake from **Geneva** via **Watkins Glen** to Elmira. The region's most popular wineries line SRs 89, 14 and 54 at Keuka Lake.

At the northern end of Owasco Lake, **Auburn** is an agricultural center with fine Victorian houses. **Seneca Falls,** at the head of Cayuga Lake, was the birthplace of the women's rights movement. At the southern end of the lake, Ithaca boasts Cornell University. Nearby Taughannock Falls plunges 215 feet.

In Geneva, at the northern tip of Seneca Lake, is the Greek Revival-style Rose Hill estate. Watkins Glen, at the southern end of the lake, is known for auto racing and a state park where a stream has cut unusual patterns in the rocks as it drops 700 feet in a series of 18 waterfalls.

South of Seneca and Keuka lakes is Elmira, where Mark Twain spent his summers. **Corning,** synonymous with glass manufacturing, displays its products at the Corning Museum of Glass. Northwest of Corning via SR 54 is **Hammondsport,** associated with the state's grape and wine industry. **Canandaigua,** at the north end of Canandaigua Lake, serves as a performing arts and grape-growing center.

Home of the Eastman Kodak Co., Rochester is known for its parks, gardens and estates. South off I-390, Mount Morris provides access to Letchworth State Park's "Grand Canyon of the East."

The Hamptons

When city streets begin to bake in the summer sun—an event that occurs with increasing regularity after Memorial Day—thousands of New Yorkers head for the cooler retreats of Long Island Sound and the Atlantic Ocean. Poshness seems to increase as one travels eastward on **Long Island.**

Generally speaking, the working class heads for such closer spots as Coney Island and **Jones Beach.** Free spirits trek to the **Fire Island National Seashore.** Young professionals splurging on group house rentals migrate to Westhampton. The truly rich and famous, however, congregate in multimillion-dollar beach houses in an area of summer colonies known as the Hamptons.

SR 27 winds through this area of vineyards, marinas, farmlands and sandy beaches. Luxurious resort communities dot the landscape. At the junction of SRs

council had voted to ban cars more than 3 years old and to reserve parking for vehicles worth more than $30,000 were reputedly accepted at face value by some Southamptonites. Twelve-foot hedges acting as green sentries shield the huge mansions on Gin Lane from the roadway.

Huguenot church, New Paltz / © Lee Snider / Corbis

114 and 27 are the magnificent estates of **East Hampton.**

In **Montauk,** Montauk Lighthouse—commissioned by President George Washington in 1796—stands at the easternmost tip of Long Island. From Montauk a ferry departs for Block Island, R.I., during the summer. The season also is enlivened by numerous fishing tournaments.

Perhaps the best-known and most exclusive Hampton is **Southampton,** east on SR 80 from SR 27. Settled in 1640 and named after the aristocratic Earl of Southampton, the town's social distinctions and conservative politics are firmly rooted.

According to one story, satires printed in a neighboring village's newspaper stating that the town

Culture manages to maintain a foothold in Southampton even amid the rusticity of sand and salt spray. In the summer there is some sort of festival—wine, antique, art, theater—held almost every week.

Contrary to popular belief, the Hamptons region is not all high society glitter. Tucked among the fashionable enclaves is **Sag Harbor,** once one of the world's largest whaling centers. Other communities on Long Island Sound's south fork include **Amagansett, Bridgehampton** and Quogue.

Hudson River Valley

The size of the Hudson River estuary led explorer Henry Hudson to believe he had discovered a passage to the Orient. Because of its navigability, the river developed into a strategic waterway that attracted invading armies, facilitated exploration and trade westward, sustained the Industrial Revolution and guaranteed the growth of New York City as an international port.

Montauk Point Lighthouse Museum / © Peter Finger / Corbis

Breathtaking bridges span 400-foot cliffs; farms and estates line the valley; and recreational possibilities abound in the Catskills and Taconic mountains to the west and east.

Primary routes paralleling the Hudson from **New York City** include the spectacular Palisades Interstate Parkway and US 9W on the west bank via the George Washington toll bridge; the faster New York Thruway toll road (I-87), via the Tappan Zee toll bridge; the scenic Henry Hudson Parkway/US 9/SR 9D/SR 9G route on the east bank; and the faster Saw Mill River Parkway/Taconic State Parkway road farther east.

Just north of New York City on the east bank off SR 9A is **Yonkers,** a major industrial town containing the Georgian-style Philipse Manor Hall. **Tarrytown** occupies a cove under the Tappan Zee Bridge on SR 9. Washington Irving's "Legend of Sleepy Hollow" described the town; Sunnyside was the author's home.

Sleepy Hollow, formerly North Tarrytown, contains the 18th-century Dutch-style Philipsburg Manor as well as John D. Rockefeller's Kykuit and the Union Church of Pocantico Hills. **Ossining's** claim to fame is the infamous maximum-security prison Sing Sing. Nearby **Croton-on-Hudson** contains Van Cortlandt Manor, the estate of a Colonial Dutch patroon.

At the Bear Mountain Bridge north of Peekskill, scenic SR 9D follows the Hudson River, which narrows at the rugged cliffs of the Hudson Highlands. In the shadow of 1,000-foot Storm King Mountain, **Garrison** features the Boscobel mansion, an example of Federal architecture. **Poughkeepsie** is built on rocky terraces rising 250 feet above the Hudson and is home to Vassar College.

Just north, **Hyde Park** has the Home of Franklin D. Roosevelt National Historic Site, Eleanor Roosevelt's Val-Kill retreat and the FDR Library. Nearby **Rhinebeck** contains Beekman Arms, said to be the oldest hotel in the United States, and the Old Rhinebeck Aerodrome, known for vintage aircraft and summer air shows.

Finally, the former whaling town of **Hudson,** the northernmost point of interest along the river's east bank, features unusual Olana, a blend of castle and mosque designed by painter Frederick Church.

On the Hudson's west bank about 41 miles north of New York City is Bear Mountain State Park, where the river begins slicing through the Appalachian mountain chain. An observation deck provides views of four states—New York, New Jersey, Connecticut and Massachusetts. Guarding this narrow stretch is **West Point,** home of the vast United States Military Academy. **Newburgh** served as Gen. George Washington's headquarters during the Revolutionary War from April 1792 until August 1783.

New Paltz, established by French Huguenots in the 17th century, boasts some of the oldest neighborhoods in America. **Kingston,** a Dutch trading post, lies at the mouth of the Delaware and Hudson Canal, which transported Pennsylvania coal and the Catskill Mountain bluestone that was destined to be the curbing and sidewalks of Manhattan.

Rip Van Winkle's legendary nap took place in the town of **Catskill,** which also is the beginning of scenic SR 23 northwest over East Windham Mountain.

As home to the United States' second largest state government, Albany provides diverse architecture ranging from the original Dutch settlement of Quackenbush and the Schuyler Mansion State Historic Site to the sleek high-rises of the Empire State Plaza complex of government buildings.

At the nearby confluence of the Mohawk and Hudson rivers lies industrial **Troy.** Along with neighboring communities, Troy forms the Hudson-Mohawk Urban Cultural Park, which commemorates the area's crucial role in 19th-century commerce and industry.

The northern end of the Hudson Valley is celebrated for horse racing and the health-giving properties of its springs. **Saratoga Springs** developed into a premier Victorian horse racing resort. It also is the summer home of the New York City Ballet and the Philadelphia Orchestra. Although summer activities center on Thoroughbred races and the arts, the town also is becoming a year-round sports and convention center.

Southeast via SR 29 and US 4 is **Saratoga National Historical Park,** which commemorates the Battles of Saratoga, fought on Sept. 19 and Oct. 7, 1777, and considered the turning point of the American Revolution.

Long Island

A bedroom community of Manhattan, the westernmost portion of Long Island is truly an extension of New York City, since it contains Brooklyn and Queens, two of the city's boroughs.

As Long Island extends eastward about 125 miles, the most densely populated areas give way to farms, vineyards, posh resorts and old whaling ports.

Glaciers scraped this low-lying extension of the New England coastal plain to produce the low bluffs of the North Shore along Long Island Sound and the moraines in the center of the island. The Atlantic Ocean continues to shape the dune-covered barrier islands of the South Shore.

Most of Long Island is less than a 2-hour drive from Midtown Manhattan. The Long Island Expressway, I-495, runs east-west through the center of the island, allowing convenient access to most points of interest. Highlights of the island include 20th-century mansions and 17th-century saltbox houses.

SR 25A offers a more leisurely, scenic route along the North Shore, while the Southern State Parkway and Sunrise Highway, SR 27, provide access to the South Shore.

As an alternative to driving, the Long Island Railroad links Manhattan to most major towns on Long Island.

The elegant estates that inspired F. Scott Fitzgerald's novel "The Great Gatsby" line the western half of the North Shore, also called the Gold Coast. Old Westbury Gardens, in the town of **Old Westbury,** once served as the estate of industrialist John S. Phipps.

Sagamore Hill National Historic Site, near **Oyster Bay,** was Theodore Roosevelt's summer White House. The 1885 house displays his family memorabilia. From this point SR 25A leads to **Centerport,** where the Vanderbilt mansion stands overlooking Northport Harbor. The Spanish

Oyster Bay / © Gibson Stock Photography

Revival home is furnished with period pieces.

The eastern terminus of I-495 is at **Riverhead,** where Long Island separates into two peninsulas, the North and South Forks. SR 25 skirts the farms of the North Fork to Orient Point, where the Cross Sound Ferry sails to New London, Conn. From Riverhead, SR 24 merges with scenic SR 27 to follow the South Fork to its eastern terminus, also called The Hamptons.

Along the South Shore of Long Island heading west, SR 27 parallels undeveloped Fire Island National Seashore and the more commercialized Jones Beach, both popular recreation spots for New York City residents.

New York City

New York City is indebted to the tough bedrock that anchors the lofty skyscrapers of **Manhattan,** heart of the culturally rich, energetic "Big Apple."

With one of the highest traffic densities in the nation, as well as scarce and expensive parking, Manhattan poses problems for the motorist. For those driving between Upper, Midtown and Lower Manhattan, take the route consisting of controlled-access sections of FDR Drive, East River Drive, Harlem River Drive, I-95, the West Side Elevated Highway and the Henry Hudson Parkway (SR 9A).

The outlying boroughs of New York City also have much to offer. From Upper Manhattan, the Cross-Bronx Expressway (I-95) and the Major Deegan Expressway (I-87) reach **The Bronx.** Highlights here include the New York Botanical Garden, covering some 250 acres and featuring 28 specialty gardens, and the Bronx Zoo, one of the country's largest urban zoos.

From Midtown Manhattan the Long Island Expressway (I-495) via the Queens Midtown toll tunnel reaches **Queens,** which has Flushing Meadows-Corona Park, site of the 1939-40 and 1964-65 New York World's Fairs.

From Lower Manhattan, **Brooklyn** is reached via the Brooklyn Battery toll tunnel and the Prospect Expressway; the Brooklyn and Manhattan bridges also link Manhattan to the borough. Brooklyn contains the Brooklyn Botanic Garden, Brighton Beach and the vintage Coney Island Boardwalk.

Staten Island, reached from Brooklyn via the Verrazano-Narrows toll bridge or by the Staten Island Ferry, is home to Historic Richmond Town, a restored 100-acre village recreating 3 centuries of local history.

Thousand Islands-St. Lawrence River

Called the "jewels in the crown of the Empire State," the **Thousand Islands** range in size from 2 square feet to 20 square miles and are a paradise for anglers, boaters and swimmers. Although the region was the scene of some of the bloodiest battles of the War of 1812, Canada and the United States now cooperate along their "Fourth Seacoast" in operating the **Great Lakes-St. Lawrence Seaway System** and in generating electricity.

A principal route through the region is I-81, between Syracuse

and the Thousand Islands International Bridge. A scenic combination of SRs 12E and 12 then follows the St. Lawrence southwest to Lake Ontario. In the opposite direction SRs 12 and 37 lead to **Massena.**

Along I-81 in wooded, gently rolling farmland is **Watertown,** the birthplace of the Woolworth five-and-dime store chain. **Sackets Harbor,** a nearby lakeside

© Empire State Building

resort, saw a U.S. victory against British warships during the War of 1812. From Fishers Landing the Thousand Islands International Bridge to Ontario offers a perspective of some of the rocky, pine-covered islands.

Boat tours from **Alexandria Bay** or **Clayton** offer a closer perspective of Boldt Castle on Heart Island, a 1900 turreted stone castle.

SR 12/37 crosses semiwooded farmland to **Ogdensburg,** the oldest settlement in upstate New York and the boyhood home of artist Frederic Remington. A museum displays some of his American West-themed paintings.

Farther northeast, an 80-foot drop in the river marks the location of Massena, the U.S. end of the Moses-Saunders Power Dam, which generates 2 million kilowatts for Ontario and New York state. The town lies on the St. Lawrence Seaway, a series of connecting locks, lakes and rivers that compensate for rapids and the 602-foot change in altitude from the mouth of the St. Lawrence to the Great Lakes.

Western

Thundering Niagara Falls and the Allegheny Mountains draw visitors to New York's western region, which is bordered by the Niagara River and Lake Erie to the west, the Pennsylvania border to the south, Lake Ontario to the north and the Finger Lakes to the east.

The principal routes include I-90 between Rochester via **Buffalo** and the Pennsylvania border and I-290/190 around Buffalo to **Niagara Falls** and Lake Ontario. From its junction with I-390, I-86/SR 17 traverses the Allegheny Mountains and crosses Chautauqua Lake.

New York's second largest city, Buffalo serves as a major international port and manufacturing center. It also has strong ethnic neighborhoods and such architectural treasures as the Albright-Knox Art Gallery and the Guaranty Building sky-scraper. The Peace toll bridge provides access to Canada. Just east off US 20 amid rolling farm country is **Darien Center,** where there is a Six Flags amusement park.

From Buffalo I-190 leads to Niagara Falls via **Grand Island,** a residential community in the middle of the Niagara River.

For a spray-catching close-up of the falls themselves—which consist of the massive American Falls, tiny Bridal Veil Falls and the magnificent Canadian Horseshoe Falls—ride the *Maid of the Mist* around the base of the falls, or hike near the Cave of the Winds on Goat Island, where walkways bring you to within 25 feet of the American Falls.

© Gibson Stock Photography

The falls power one of North America's largest hydroelectric projects, which is the focus of Power Vista, the Niagara Power Project's visitor center. An observation building affords wonderful views of the falls, while working models and displays explain how the generators operate. The Rainbow and Whirlpool Rapids toll bridges lead into Canada.

Lockport, 17 miles east of Niagara Falls on SR 31, preserves the history of the Erie Canal. Visitors can see the original locks, no longer active, and ride a boat through working locks.

From Niagara Falls, follow the Robert Moses Parkway or SR 18F north along the Niagara River, which churns through the breathtaking Niagara Escarpment. Fort Niagara, outside of **Youngstown,** guards the strategic mouth of the Niagara River on Lake Ontario. Built by the French in 1726, the fort played an important role during Colonial times.

Between Buffalo and the Pennsylvania border, southbound I-90 parallels a section of the old Underground Railroad through rolling vineyards and fruit orchards within sight of Lake Erie. **Chautauqua,** a Victorian-style summer resort and center of a wine-producing region on the shores of Chautauqua Lake off SR 394, offers a variety of arts-and education-related activities.

Near the southeastern end of the lake is **Jamestown,** known for its furniture and wood products. From Jamestown, I-86/SR 17 heads eastward through forested mountains to 60,398-acre Allegany State Park, New York's largest state park.

Farther east, **Salamanca** is the home of the Seneca-Iroquois National Museum. The collection portrays the life and culture of the Iroquois.

Rock City Park in nearby **Olean** allows hikers to examine 500-million-year-old quartz boulders that project from the edge of the Allegheny Mountains.

Stay.

Visit New York and save with Choice Hotels.®

AAA members always save with Choice Hotels. Call today and ask for our AAA Rate* and save at more than 25 participating hotels in upstate New York. Or call your local AAA travel agent.

Albany	Ithaca
Amherst	Lake George
Batavia	Latham
Binghamton	Lockport
Buffalo	Newark
Catskill	Niagara Falls
Cheektowaga	North Syracuse
Clifton Park	Ogdensburg
Cooperstown	Plattsburgh
Corning	Queensbury
Cortland	Rochester
Dunkirk	Rome
East Greenbush	Saugerties
Glenmont	Schenectady
Hamburg	Syracuse
Henrietta	Williamsville
Hornell	

866.446.6900

We'll see you there.

CHOICE HOTELS INTERNATIONAL®

Points of Interest

ADIRONDACK PARK (C-9)

Encompassing about two-thirds of upstate New York, Adirondack Park embraces some 6 million acres of both private and state land. Nearly half of it is wilderness. Physical features range from rugged mountains and sheer cliffs to low rolling uplands, beaver meadows, swamps and a grassy plain.

Among the 42 mountains that exceed 4,000 feet in elevation is 5,344-foot Mount Marcy, the highest in the state. Some 2,800 lakes and ponds, 1,200 miles of rivers and more than 30,000 miles of brooks and streams cover the landscape, allowing a mere 1,100 miles of highway and 120 miles of railroad to squeeze between the park's southwest border at Remsen and the northeast border at Lake Placid.

The park's geologic base reveals the contrasts of eons of change. Part of the main mountain chain is an outcropping of the Laurentian, or Canadian, Shield, a rare surfacing of some of the oldest and hardest known rock forged in the Earth's interior. Other areas contain fossil-rich strata formed millions of years later at the bottom of prehistoric seas.

Ecosystems, which range from alpine and subalpine to boreal and lowland lake to wetland, present an overlapping of northern and southern forest types with an occasional stand of virgin timber. With the exception of small areas near lakes George and Champlain, the park harbors no poisonous snakes.

The area was named after the Algonquin Indians. The Iroquois Indians called Algonquin *Ha-De-Ron-Dah* or "bark eaters" because they ate certain kinds of tree bark. The domain of hunters and loggers during the 18th and early 19th centuries, the Adirondacks were not "discovered" until after the Civil War. They evolved into a woodland retreat for the wealthy, who built luxurious resorts, private camps *(see Raquette Lake p. 185)* and summer homes on the lakes.

The wild and peaceful setting is being preserved for recreation. There are scenic views at every turn, some still bearing the vestiges of logging activity and the stubborn scars left by the forest fires of 1899, 1903 and 1908, and the hurricane of 1950.

Recreational possibilities span the seasons; boating, bird-watching, camping, canoeing, fishing, horseback riding, downhill and cross-country skiing, snowmobiling and snowshoeing are available. Areas with major development include Blue Mountain Lake, Lake George and Lake Placid *(see place listings pp. 64, 98 and 99).*

Two interpretive visitor centers provide indoor and outdoor exhibits and programming about the park. Both centers offer a surfaced trail system with interpretive signage.

The visitor center at Paul Smiths, 1 mile north of SR 86 on SR 30, provides information about the history, people and ecology of the Adirondack Park region. Features of the Newcomb Center, 14 miles east of Long Lake on SR 28N, include an exhibit about the birth and development of the conservation and preservation movements and the 20-minute multi-image presentation "Adirondack Passages." Comprehensive information about the park and its outdoor recreation opportunities can be obtained by contacting the Department of Environmental Conservation, P.O. Box 296, SR 86, Ray Brook, NY 12977; phone (518) 897-1200.

The visitor centers are open daily 9-5; closed Thanksgiving and Dec. 25. Free. Phone (518) 327-3000. *See Recreation Chart the AAA Northeastern CampBook.*

ALBANY (F-10) pop. 95,658, elev. 30′

See map page 58.

Albany is the state capital. The city's modern governmental complex, construction of which began in 1962, contrasts with its pastoral surroundings along the Hudson River.

Although French trappers were in the area in the mid-1500s, it was not until 1609 that Dutch fur traders arrived and established a trading center and fort. The first permanent settlement was founded in 1624 by 18 Walloon families, French Protestants who left the Spanish Netherlands seeking religious freedom. The settlement was called Beverwyck until it was transferred to England and renamed in honor of the Duke of York and Albany.

Albany was chartered in 1686 with Pieter Schuyler as the first mayor. By 1750 it had become an important trading center. Robert Fulton's *North River Steamboat* made the first successful steamboat run from New York to Albany in 1807. The opening of the Erie Canal between Buffalo and Albany in 1825 and the city's growth as a major railroad terminus greatly increased its importance.

Albany's notable citizens have included U.S. presidents Martin Van Buren, Millard Fillmore and Theodore and Franklin Roosevelt as well as authors Herman Melville and Henry James.

Albany is an expanding cultural center with museums, theaters and historic buildings. Governor Nelson A. Rockefeller Empire State Plaza *(see attraction listing)*, a 98.5-acre, 11-building complex that comprises state government offices and cultural and convention facilities, commands downtown Albany.

Other cultural showcases include the Palace Theatre, home of the Albany Symphony Orchestra, and Park Playhouse, one of the larger outdoor theaters on the East Coast. The Capital Repertory Theatre, the area's resident professional equity theater, presents a variety of plays year-round.

The Albany Heritage Area Visitor Center, at the intersection of Broadway and Clinton avenues at 25

Quackenbush Sq., has hands-on exhibits tracing the history of Albany; phone (518) 434-0405. The Henry Hudson Planetarium within the visitor center presents shows Saturdays.

Nestled along the Hudson River waterfront in downtown Albany is the Corning Preserve, a narrow strip of land several miles long that has nature trails popular for jogging, walking, bicycling and inline skating. The site also beckons picnickers and is frequently used for concerts and festivals.

Albany County Convention and Visitors Bureau: 25 Quackenbush Sq., Albany, NY 12207; phone (518) 434-1217 or (800) 258-3582.

Self-guiding tours: The Albany Heritage Area Visitor Center has self-guiding walking tour information.

Shopping areas: Colonie Center, Wolf Road and Central Avenue, has Macy's and Sears as its anchor stores, while Crossgates Mall, on Crossgates Mall Road, counts Filene's, JCPenney, Lord & Taylor and Macy's among its more than 230 stores.

[SAVE] **ALBANY INSTITUTE OF HISTORY AND ART,** 125 Washington Ave., presents permanent and changing exhibits about the art, culture and history of Albany and the Hudson Valley region. Collections include Hudson River School landscapes, early Dutch limner portraits, Albany silver, and 18th- and 19th-century New York furniture, sculpture, pewter, ceramics and decorative

arts. The museum also houses an Egyptian collection and a library.

Allow 1 hour minimum. Wed.-Sat. 10-5, Sun. noon-5; closed holidays. Admission $7; senior citizens and students with ID $5; ages 6-12, $3. Phone (518) 463-4478.

CATHEDRAL OF ALL SAINTS is at 62 S. Swan St. This 1884 Gothic Revival Episcopal church has stained glass, mosaics, stone carvings, 17th-century choir stalls carved in Belgium, and historic and artistic objects. Allow 30 minutes minimum. Daily 9-3. Donations. Phone (518) 465-1342.

CATHEDRAL OF THE IMMACULATE CONCEPTION is at 125 Eagle St. This 1852 neo-Gothic Revival Catholic cathedral has a carved pulpit, stained glass and historic and artistic objects. Open Mon.-Fri. 7-5:30, Sat.-Sun. 8-6. Guided tours are given Tues. and Thurs. at 1, May-Sept. Free. Phone (518) 463-4447.

COURT OF APPEALS BUILDING, 20 Eagle St. at Pine St., opposite Academy Park, dates from 1842. This Greek Revival structure houses New York's highest court and features a courtroom designed by Henry Hobson Richardson. Mon.-Fri. 10-noon and 2-4, or by appointment. Free. Phone (518) 455-7711.

DUTCH APPLE CRUISES, 141 Broadway at Madison Ave., offers 2-hour narrated sightseeing cruises

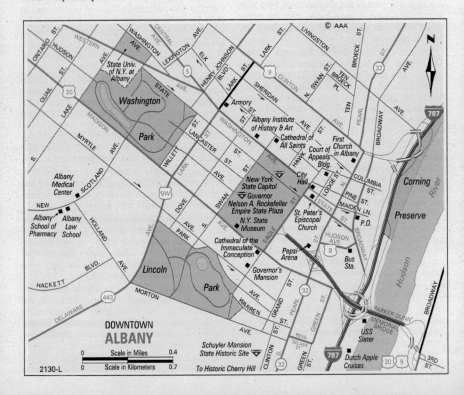

on the Hudson River. Cruises with meals are available. Departures daily at 11 and 2, May-Oct. Schedule may vary; phone ahead. Fare $10; ages 5-12, $6. Departures require a minimum of 20 persons. MC, VI. Phone (518) 463-0220.

FIRST CHURCH IN ALBANY (Reformed), 110 N. Pearl St., was founded in 1642. Its pulpit and weather vane both date from 1656. Mon.-Fri. 8:30-3. Donations. Phone (518) 463-4449.

GOVERNOR NELSON A. ROCKEFELLER EMPIRE STATE PLAZA, downtown between Madison Ave. and State St., houses a governmental center, a performing arts center, a meeting center, the New York State Museum and a collection of modern American art. A free tour of the art collection is available by reservation. The 42-story Corning Tower Building features an observation deck. Allow 1 hour minimum. Observation deck daily 10-2:30; closed Jan. 1, Easter, Thanksgiving and Dec. 25. Free. Phone (518) 474-2418 for general information or (518) 473-7521 to arrange a tour of the art collection.

New York State Capitol, bounded by Washington Ave. and Swan, State and Eagle sts., was built in the late 1800s and houses the governor's office and the New York State Senate and Assembly. Carvings on the Million Dollar Staircase depict famous people in American history as well as friends and relatives of the sculptors. Guided 1-hour tours daily at 10, noon, 2 and 3; closed Jan. 1, Easter, Thanksgiving and Dec. 25. Free. Phone (518) 474-2418.

New York State Museum is in the Empire State Plaza. Multimedia exhibits focus on the Adirondack wilderness, the New York City metropolis and American Indians of the state. The latter exhibit includes a full-size replica of an Iroquois longhouse. Participatory programs about art, history, science and technology are offered. Carousel rides are available. Allow 1 hour, 30 minutes minimum. Daily 9:30-5; closed Jan. 1, Thanksgiving and Dec. 25. Donations. Phone (518) 474-5877.

SAVE **HISTORIC CHERRY HILL** is between First and McCarty aves. at 523½ S. Pearl St. The 1787 Georgian-style house, once the center of a Colonial farm, contains furniture, silver, china, glass, letters and clothing from five generations. Allow 1 hour minimum. Guided tours on the hour Tues.-Sat. 10-3, Sun. 1-3, July-Sept.; Tues.-Fri. noon-3, Sat. 10-3, Sun. 1-3, Apr.-June and Oct.-Dec. Closed major holidays. Fee $4; over 62, $3; college students with ID $2; ages 6-17, $1. Phone (518) 434-4791.

ST. PETER'S EPISCOPAL CHURCH is 1 blk. e. of the Capitol at State and Lodge sts. The 1859 French Gothic church contains stained-glass windows, elaborate floor mosaics, a replica of the Queen Anne silver presented in 1712 and a British general's grave beneath the vestibule. Open Mon.-Fri. 8-4. Organ recitals are given Fri. at 12:30, Sept.-June. Donations. Phone (518) 434-3502.

SCHUYLER MANSION STATE HISTORIC SITE, 32 Catherine St., was the residence of Philip Schuyler, a noted Revolutionary War general and U.S. senator from New York. His daughter Betsy married Alexander Hamilton in the house. Guided tours on the hour Wed.-Sun. 10-5, Apr.-Oct.; by appointment rest of year. Closed Columbus Day. Fee $4; senior citizens and students with ID $3; ages 5-12, $1. Phone (518) 434-0834.

SHAKER HERITAGE SOCIETY, off I-87 exit 4, then 1.5 mi. w. on Albany-Shaker Rd. (CR 151), is on the site of what is said to be the country's first Shaker settlement, established in 1776. The complex includes the 1848 Shaker Meeting House, with displays of furniture, tools and handicrafts; the cemetery where sect founder Mother Ann Lee is buried; and a nature preserve with trails. Picnicking is permitted. Allow 1 hour minimum. Tues.-Sat. 9:30-4; closed first 2 weeks in Jan. Guided tours are given Sat. at 11:30 and 1:30, June-Oct. Donations. Tour fee $3, under 13 free. Phone (518) 456-7890.

SAVE **USS SLATER** is off I-787N exit 2, then n. on Broadway to the Snow Dock, or e. off I-787S exit 3B. This restored World War II destroyer escort offers a look at the floating environment for 216 men. Highlights include the crew's quarters, officers' country, radio room, galley and bridge with combat information center. Guided tours are available. Some steep stair climbing is required. Allow 30 minutes minimum. Wed.-Sun. 10-4, Apr.-Nov. Admission $6; ages 6-14, $5. Phone (518) 431-1943.

ALBERTSON (I-2) pop. 5,200, elev. 140'

CLARK BOTANIC GARDEN, 193 I.U. Willetts Rd., is reached from the Northern State Pkwy. and Long Island Expwy. via Willis Ave. S. exits. Rose, wildflower, vegetable and herb gardens as well as woodlands are available. Allow 1 hour minimum. Daily 9-4; closed Jan. 1, Thanksgiving and Dec. 25. Free. Phone (516) 484-8600.

DID YOU KNOW

European settlers
introduced the apple
to New York
in the 1600s.

ALEXANDRIA BAY (B-8)
pop. 1,088, elev. 274'

[SAVE] **1000 ISLANDS SKYDECK,** a 400-foot observation tower between the spans of the Thousand Islands International Bridge, offers excellent views of the Thousand Islands. On a clear day visibility is more than 40 miles. Daily 9-dusk, mid-Apr. to late Oct. (weather permitting). Admission $7.95; ages 6-12, $4.45. Bridge toll $3 per private vehicle. AX, MC, VI. Phone (613) 659-2335.

AQUA ZOO is off I-81 exit 50 n. to 43681 SR 12. The aquarium offers more than 50 exhibits of marine life, fossils and shells along with a wide variety of coral samples from around the world. Allow 30 minutes minimum. Daily 10-7, Memorial Day-Labor Day. Admission $5; ages 3-13, $4.50. DS, MC, VI. Phone (315) 482-5771.

[GEM] **BOLDT CASTLE,** on Heart Island, is accessible by ferry service or boat tours *(see attraction listings)*. The turreted, stone, 120-room, six-story castle was begun in 1900 by George C. Boldt, the proprietor of New York's Waldorf-Astoria hotel and Philadelphia's Bellevue-Stratford. Intended as a summer home for his wife, it was abandoned when he died in 1904, never to be furnished or occupied.

For more than 70 years the estate deteriorated to a state of almost complete disrepair. Restoration of the castle, yacht house, towers, service buildings and gardens has been ongoing since 1977. Exhibits depict the lives of the Boldts and the development of the 1000 Islands.

Picnicking is permitted. Food is available. Allow 1 hour, 30 minutes minimum. Daily 10-7:30, July-Aug.; 10-6:30, early May-June 30 and Sept. 1-second Mon. in Oct. Admission $4.75; ages 6-12, $3. Ferry or tour fares are not included in castle admission. Phone (800) 847-5263.

Boldt Yacht House, reached via ferry from the castle, is on Wellesley Island. The restored yacht house features a collection of antique wooden boats. Allow 30 minutes minimum. Ferry departs every 30 minutes from the castle. Yacht house open daily 10-6:30, late May-late Sept. Fare $3; ages 6-12, $2.

[SAVE] **EMPIRE BOAT LINES** departs from 4 Church St. (Upper Harbor). A narrated 3-hour sightseeing tour of the St. Lawrence River's Thousand Island region features scenic and historic points of interest as well as views of magnificent homes and stops at castlelike mansions. Dinner cruises also are available.

Allow 1 hour, 30 minutes minimum. Tours depart daily at 11:30 and 4, July-Aug.; Sat.-Sun. at 11:30 and 4, mid-May through June 30 and Sept.-Oct. Fare $15; ages 7-14, $10. Fare does not include admission to Boldt Castle. Reservations are recommended. Schedules and fares may vary; phone ahead. AX, MC, VI. Phone (315) 482-8687.

MINNA ANTHONY COMMON NATURE CENTER, off I-81 exit 51 in Wellesley Island State Park *(see Recreation Chart and the AAA Northeastern CampBook),* is a 600-acre wildlife sanctuary with 8 miles of trails. The visitor center has nature exhibits. Trails are available for cross-country skiing.

Allow 30 minutes minimum. Center open Mon.-Sat. 8 a.m.-8:30 p.m., Sun. 8:30-5, July-Aug.; Mon.-Sat. 8:30-4:30, Sun. 10-4:30, rest of. year (weather permitting). Trails open daily dawn-dusk. Admission $7 per private vehicle, July-Aug.; free rest of year. Phone (315) 482-2479.

[SAVE] *UNCLE SAM* BOAT TOURS, I-81 exit 50N to foot of James St., offers 2.25-hour sightseeing cruises of the 1000 Islands region aboard double- and triple-deck paddle wheelers; the trip includes a stop at Boldt Castle *(see attraction listing)* in season. A ferry to Boldt Castle also is available. Lunch and dinner cruises are available in summer.

Sightseeing cruise departs daily every hour 10-4:30, May-Sept.; schedule varies in Apr. and Oct. Ferry departs daily every 30 minutes 10-6, July-Aug.; every hour 10-5, mid-May through June 30 and Sept. 1 to mid-Oct. One-hour evening cruise departs daily at 7, mid-June through Labor Day. Three-hour Seaway Island Cruise departs daily late June-Labor Day. Sightseeing cruise $14; over 65, $13; ages 4-12, $6.75. Ferry $7; ages 4-12, $4.25.

One-hour evening cruise $9; ages 4-12, $4.50. Seaway Cruise $15; ages 4-12, $8. Fares do not include admission to Boldt Castle. DS, MC, VI. Phone (315) 482-2611 or (800) 253-9229. *See color ad p. 60.*

ALFRED (F-5) pop. 3,954, elev. 1,671′

THE SCHEIN-JOSEPH INTERNATIONAL MUSEUM OF CERAMIC ART AT ALFRED, in Binns-Merrill Hall on Main St. at Alfred University, houses contemporary American ceramics and ceramic technology, pottery of the ancient Americas, and ceramics from Africa, Asia and Europe. The Fosdick-Nelson Gallery, located in Harder Hall, presents changing exhibits.

Allow 30 minutes minimum. Museum open Tues.-Sun. 10-5 and by appointment; closed holidays. Gallery open Mon.-Fri. 11-4, Sat. noon-5, Sept.-May; by appointment rest of year. Free. Phone (607) 871-2421 for the museum or (607) 871-2442 for the Fosdick-Nelson Gallery.

ALTMAR (D-7) pop. 351

SALMON RIVER FISH HATCHERY, 7 mi. e. of Pulaski off SR 13 following signs, has fish tanks and videotape monitors that explain hatchery operations. Allow 30 minutes minimum. Daily 9-4, Apr.-Nov. Free. Phone (315) 298-5051.

AMAGANSETT (H-6) pop. 1,067, elev. 64′

Despite its lack of a natural harbor, Amagansett has been a fishing village since it was settled in 1690. In the 18th and early 19th centuries the whaling industry was one of the town's most important sources of commerce and employment as well as the basis for an enduring folklore immortalizing old salts and the big ones that got away. *Also see Long Island p. 101.*

EAST HAMPTON TOWN MARINE MUSEUM is .5 mi. s. of jct. SR 27 and Atlantic Ave. on Bluff Rd. Dioramas and exhibits depict early whaling and modern fishing industries. A gunning shanty display with bird decoys, a children's discovery room and a garden also are on the grounds. Allow 1 hour minimum. Daily 10-5, July-Aug.; Sat.-Sun. 10-5 in June and Sept. 1-Columbus Day. Admission $4, over 64 and children $2. Phone (631) 267-6544 or (631) 324-6850.

AMENIA (G-11) pop. 1,115

WINERIES

• **Cascade Mountain Winery**, 3 mi. n. on SR 22, then 3.5 mi. w. on Webutuck School Rd., following signs. Thurs.-Mon. 11-5; closed Thanksgiving and Dec. 25. Phone (845) 373-9021.

AMHERST—*see Buffalo p. 73.*

AMSTERDAM (E-10) pop. 18,355, elev. 275′

Amsterdam, settled in 1783, became an important industrial center with the opening of the Erie Canal in 1825. After the Utica & Schenectady Railroad came through 11 years later, the town entered its commercial heyday with more than 100 industrial plants manufacturing such goods as carpets, brooms, buttons, clothing and linseed oil.

Montgomery County Chamber of Commerce: 366 W. Main St., P.O. Box 309, Amsterdam, NY 12010; phone (518) 842-8200 or (800) 743-7337.

FORT JOHNSON—*see place listing p. 87.*

NOTEWORTHY INDIAN MUSEUM, 100 Church St., houses American Indian artifacts and exhibits that trace Mohawk habitation in central New York. Displays include beadwork, baskets, pottery and a scaled-down replica of a Mohawk longhouse. Guided tours are available. Allow 1 hour minimum. Tues.-Fri. 11-5, Sat. 11-4, July-Aug.; by appointment rest of year. Free. Phone (518) 843-4761.

WALTER ELWOOD MUSEUM AND ART GALLERY is reached via I-90 exit 27, w. on SR 5, 3 blks. n. on Evelyn St., then w. to 300 Guy Park Ave. Permanent displays include a blacksmith shop, a nature room, a cabin dating from the time the first European settlers arrived in America, Victorian furnishings and exhibits about Eskimos, the Iroquois Indians and the Mohawk Valley. Allow 1 hour minimum. Mon.-Fri. 10-3; closed holidays. Donations. Phone (518) 843-5151.

ANNANDALE-ON-HUDSON (G-11)

SAVE **MONTGOMERY PLACE** is .2 mi. off SR 9G. Built in 1805 by the widow of Revolutionary War general Richard Montgomery, the Federal mansion was later transformed to the Classical Revival style by noted architect Alexander Jackson Davis. Gardens reflect the influence of 19th-century horticulturist Andrew Jackson Downing. The 434-acre Hudson River estate includes a coach house, chalet-style cottage, greenhouse and nature trails.

Picnicking is permitted. Wed.-Mon. 10-5, Apr.-Oct.; Sat.-Sun. 10-5 in Nov.; Sat.-Sun. noon-5, early to mid-Dec. Last tour begins 1 hour before closing. Guided tour $7; over 60, $6; ages 5-17, $4. Grounds only $4. AX, MC, VI. Phone (845) 758-5461.

ARCADE (F-4) pop. 2,026, elev. 1,455′

ARCADE AND ATTICA RAILROAD, on SR 39 at 278 Main St., offers a historical and educational 15-mile steam locomotive train ride. Various themed excursions are held throughout the year, including a trip to Beaver Meadow sanctuary in March, a Civil War trip the third weekend in August and Santa runs in December.

Allow 3 hours minimum. Departures Wed. and Sat.-Sun. at 12:30 and 3, Fri. at 1, July-Aug.; Fri. at 1, Sat.-Sun. at noon, 2 and 4, first 3 weekends in Oct.; Sat.-Sun. at 12:30 and 3, in June, Sept. and the last weekend in Oct.; Sat.-Sun. at noon and 2, first 3 weekends in Dec. Fare $10; senior citizens $9; ages 3-11, $7; under 3 on lap free. Reservations are recommended for themed tours. MC, VI. Phone (585) 496-9877 or (585) 492-3100.

ARKVILLE (F-9) elev. 1,373'

[SAVE] **DELAWARE AND ULSTER RAIL RIDE,** 43510 SR 28, offers 1- and 1.75-hour round-trip train rides through the scenic Catskill Mountains. The depot displays railroad memorabilia. Twilight and train robbery rides also are offered. Departures Wed.-Fri. at 11 and 2, Sat.-Sun. at 11, 1, 2:30 and 3:45, July-Aug.; Sat.-Sun. and holidays at 10, 12:30, 2 and 3:15, Memorial Day weekend-June 30 and Sept.-Oct. Fare $7-$10; over 63, $6-$8; ages 3-12, $5-$6. MC, VI. To verify schedule and fares phone (845) 586-3877, or (800) 225-4132 in New York.

ASHFORD HOLLOW (F-3)

GRIFFIS SCULPTURE PARK, off SR 219 on Ahrens Rd., displays 200 steel, aluminum and bronze sculptures in meadows overlooking the rolling countryside. The park, which is in a 400-acre nature preserve, offers 10 miles of hiking trails. Picnicking is permitted. Daily 9-dusk, May-Oct.; by appointment rest of year. Donations. Phone (716) 667-2808.

AUBURN (E-6) pop. 28,574, elev. 694'

In 1793 Auburn's location at the northern tip of Owasco Lake attracted its first settler, surveyor and Revolutionary War hero Col. John Hardenbergh. He built a cabin and a mill on the site. In 1805 the town was named for a locale in Oliver Goldsmith's poem "Deserted Village." Five years later the community boasted 90 dwellings and 17 mills.

The opening in 1817 of the state prison, built on land donated by citizens, and the establishment in 1829 of a theological seminary, which is affiliated with Union Theological Seminary, stimulated additional growth. Prison labor was cheap and, until 1882, legal. By the early 1920s the town was firmly entrenched as an industrial center and market for the region's agricultural products.

Fort Hill Cemetery, 19 Fort St., contains part of a hill thought to have been erected by Moundbuilders as well as the graves of William Seward, secretary of state under Presidents Lincoln and Andrew Johnson; former slave and Underground Railroad champion Harriet Tubman; and Logan, a Mingo Indian orator who led a war party in 1774 in retaliation for the murder of his family. *Also see Finger Lakes p. 86.*

Cayuga County Office of Tourism: 131 Genesee St., Auburn, NY 13021; phone (315) 255-1658 or (800) 499-9615.

CAYUGA MUSEUM/CASE RESEARCH LAB MUSEUM, 203 Genesee St., has changing and permanent Cayuga County history displays and 19th-century furnishings. The Case Research Laboratory, site of the invention of early sound motion pictures, is on the grounds. Tues.-Fri. 10-5, Sat.-Sun. noon-5; closed Easter, Thanksgiving and Dec. 25. Donations. Phone (315) 253-8051.

EMERSON PARK, 2.5 mi. s. via SR 38A on Owasco Lake, covers 133 acres and contains the Cayuga County Agricultural Museum. Boating, fishing, picnicking and swimming are permitted. Food is available. Museum open Wed.-Sun. 11-4, Memorial Day weekend-Labor Day. Park open daily 6 a.m.-dusk, mid-May through Labor Day. Park admission $2 per private vehicle. Museum admission by donation. Phone (315) 253-5611.

HARRIETT TUBMAN HOME, 1.5 mi. s. on SR 34 at 180 South St., features a 25-minute videotape about the life of the former slave who delivered more than 300 slaves from the South on the Underground Railroad. During the Civil War Tubman rendered invaluable service to the Union Army as a nurse, scout and spy. A guided tour includes her simple house and the home for the aged built and run in her honor.

Allow 1 hour minimum. Tours are given on the hour Tues.-Fri. 10-3, Sat. 10-2, Feb.-Oct.; by appointment rest of year. Admission $5; over 60 and college students with ID $3; ages 5-17, $2. Phone (315) 252-2081.

HOOPES MEMORIAL PARK, 1.2 mi. e. on US 20 at E. Genesee St., contains a miniature lake and rose gardens. Daily 7 a.m.-9 p.m. Free. Phone (315) 252-9300.

SCHWEINFURTH MEMORIAL ART CENTER, 205 Genesee St., houses changing exhibitions featuring works by area children, senior citizens and contemporary New York artists as well as an annual quilt exhibit. Tours, lectures, art classes, workshops and videotapes supplement the exhibits. Allow 1 hour minimum. Mon.-Sat. 10-5, Sun. 1-5, Nov.-Dec.; Tues.-Sat. 10-5, Sun. 1-5, rest of year. Closed major holidays. Admission $3, under 10 free. An additional fee may be charged during special exhibits. Phone (315) 255-1553.

WARD W. O'HARA AGRICULTURAL MUSEUM, 2.5 mi. s. on SR 38A, across from Emerson Park, contains farm and household implements recalling rural life 1800-1930. Settings include a general store, creamery, blacksmith shop, veterinarian's office and kitchen. A large collection of farming equipment features locally manufactured tractors, wagons and agricultural machinery. Picnicking is permitted. Allow 1 hour minimum. Daily 11-4, July 1-Labor Day; Sat.-Sun. 11-4, Memorial Day-June 30. Free. Parking $2. Phone (315) 253-5611.

[SAVE] **WILLARD MEMORIAL CHAPEL,** 2 blks. e. of SR 34 at 17 Nelson St., is an example of the interior design work of Louis Comfort Tiffany and the Tiffany Decorating and Glass Co. The 1892 Romanesque Revival chapel has carved wooden pews, stained-glass windows, leaded-glass chandeliers, mosaic floors, and oak wainscoting and furnishings. Guided tours are available. Allow 1 hour minimum. Tues.-Fri. 10-4 and by appointment; closed holidays. Admission $3. Phone (315) 252-0339.

SAVE **WILLIAM H. SEWARD HOUSE,** 33 South St., was the home of the secretary of state under Presidents Abraham Lincoln and Andrew Johnson. It contains original family furnishings, clothing, antique toys and mementos of Seward's career. A painting by Emanuel Leutze depicts Seward's negotiations for the purchase of Alaska. Allow 1 hour minimum. Tues.-Sat. 10-4, Sun. 1-4, July 1 to mid-Oct.; Tues.-Sat. 1-4, mid-Oct. through Dec. 31 and Feb.-June. Closed major holidays. Admission $5; over 59, $4; students with ID, $2; under 12 free. Phone (315) 252-1283.

AURIESVILLE (E-9) elev. 304'

NATIONAL SHRINE OF NORTH AMERICAN MARTYRS, off I-90 exits 27 or 28, on SR 5S, marks the site of the Mohawk village of Ossernenon, where Father Isaac Jogues and his companions were killed in the 1640s. They were later canonized as martyrs. It also is the birthplace of the Blessed Kateri Tekakwitha, a Mohawk Indian who is a candidate for canonization.

The site includes an American Indian museum and the Big Round Church, which seats 6,500. Picnicking is permitted. Food is available. Allow 2 hours minimum. Shrine daily dawn-dusk. Information center daily 10-4, May-Oct. Donations. Phone (518) 853-3033.

AUSABLE CHASM (B-11)

SAVE **AUSABLE CHASM** is reached via I-87 exit 34. The 1.5-mile-long gorge has waterfalls and rapids formed by the Ausable River; in places the rocky walls rise perpendicularly 200 feet above the river. The tour combines a participatory raft ride with a .75-mile self-guiding nature-trail walk that involves climbing many stairs; a return-trip bus ride is available. Wear comfortable shoes.

Picnicking is permitted. Allow 2 hours minimum. Daily 9:30-5, July 1-Labor Day; 9:30-4, Memorial Day-June 30 and day after Labor Day-Columbus Day. Fare (includes nature trail) $24; over 55, military with ID and ages 12-17, $21.95; ages 5-11, $19.95. Nature trail $15.95; over 55, military with ID and ages 12-17, $13.95; ages 5-11, $11.95. AX, DS, MC, VI. Phone (518) 834-7454.

RECREATIONAL ACTIVITIES
White-water Rafting

• **Hudson River Rafting Co.,** off I-87 exit 34 to SR 9. Write P.O. Box 468, North Creek, NY 12853. Trips depart daily mid-May to mid-Oct. Phone (800) 537-1211.

BALDWINSVILLE (D-7)
pop. 7,053, elev. 389'

BEAVER LAKE NATURE CENTER, 8477 E. Mud Lake Rd., covers 675 acres, including 238-acre Beaver Glacier Lake. Up to 10,000 geese stop in the area during spring migration, and many return in the fall. Eight trails traverse forest, meadows, lakeshore and wetlands. Trail highlights include boardwalks, an observation tower, interpretive signs, telescopes and a bog with orchids and insect-eating plants. Guided canoe trips are offered in summer. Daily 7:30-dusk; closed Dec. 25. Admission $1 per private vehicle. Phone (315) 638-2519.

BALLSTON SPA (E-10) pop. 5,556, elev. 288'

NATIONAL BOTTLE MUSEUM, 76 Milton Ave., promotes the study, appreciation and preservation of the American mouth-blown bottle industry. Exhibits include permanent and changing displays of bottles, containers and glass-blowing tools. A videotape describes glassblowing and mold blowing techniques. The museum also has a research library. Allow 30 minutes minimum. Daily 10-4, June-Sept.; Mon.-Fri. 10-4, rest of year. Donations. Phone (518) 885-7589.

BATAVIA (E-4) pop. 16,256, elev. 956'

Batavia was only a junction of the old Genesee Road and Tonawanda Creek Indian trails when Robert Morris bought more than 3 million acres in western New York from Massachusetts in 1797. Having obtained the Indian title to the land by the Big Tree Treaty, Morris sold most of his holdings to the Dutch Holland Land Co. The town is named for the Netherlands republic from which the owners originated.

Genesee County Chamber of Commerce: 210 E. Main St., Batavia, NY 14020; phone (585) 343-7440 or (800) 622-2686.

HOLLAND LAND OFFICE MUSEUM, 131 W. Main St., is in the original 1815 Holland Land Co. office. Exhibits deal with the early history of Genesee County, with emphasis on the Holland Purchase. Allow 30 minutes minimum. Mon.-Sat. 10-4, Memorial Day-Labor Day; Tues.-Sat. 10-4, rest of year. Closed county holidays. Donations. Phone (585) 343-4727.

DID YOU KNOW

The nickname Empire State is derived from a comment about the seat of empire made by George Washington in 1784.

BEACON (H-10) pop. 13,808, elev. 150'

In 1663 Francis Rombout bought all the land he could see from the top of Mount Beacon from the native inhabitants. Catharyna Brett inherited the property and managed the holdings until her death in 1764. During the Revolutionary War fires burning on the summit of Mount Beacon to warn Gen. George Washington of British movements up the Hudson River gave the mountain and the city their names.

Madame Brett's Homestead, 50 Van Nydeck Ave., has been the residence of seven generations of the family and is said to be the oldest house in Dutchess County. The 1709 building is open the first Sunday of each month May through December; phone (845) 831-6533.

BINGHAMTON (G-8) pop. 47,380, elev. 866'

The site of Binghamton was bought by Philadelphia merchant William Bingham in 1786 and settled by Joseph Leonard and other pioneers the following year. Originally called Chenango for the river it bordered, the settlement was renamed Binghamton in honor of the man whose donations of land allowed it to grow into a village and later into a full-fledged town.

Railroads, photography equipment and cigar making were the town's major industries before 1900, but shoe manufacturing became the dominant enterprise in the early 20th century. Such high-tech corporations as Universal Instruments and Link Flight Simulation, which manufactures aerospace equipment, later came to the forefront. IBM established its first plant in nearby Endicott.

Gold- and onion-domed churches of various Eastern European cultures are found throughout Broome County. Binghamton also includes among its cultural assets a branch of the State University of New York. The Anderson Center for the Performing Arts at Binghamton University presents performing artists of national and international acclaim. The Forum on Washington Street hosts cultural productions.

The Binghamton area has six antique woodcarved carousels that visitors can ride from Memorial Day through Labor Day (weather permitting). George F. Johnson, who donated the carousels to local parks, stipulated that the municipalities never charge a fee for a ride. The carousels are at C. Fred Johnson Park in Johnson City; George W. Johnson Park in Endicott; Highland Park in Endwell; Recreation Park in Binghamton; Ross Park Zoo in Binghamton (*see attraction listing*); and West Endicott Park in Endicott.

Greater Binghamton Chamber of Commerce: Metro Center, 49 Court St., P.O. Box 995, Binghamton, NY 13902; phone (607) 772-8860 or (800) 836-6740.

Self-guiding tours: Brochures outlining walking tours of scenic and historic attractions in the Triple Cities—Binghamton, Endicott and Johnson City— are available at the chamber of commerce.

Shopping areas: Oakdale Mall, 3 miles west on Reynolds Road (SR 17 exit 70N), has JCPenney, Kaufman's and Sears among its 126 stores. Kohl's anchors Parkway Plaza, on SR 434 at SR 17 exit 70S. Clinton Street's Antique Row, off SR 17 exit 72, attracts antique enthusiasts.

ROBERSON MUSEUM AND SCIENCE CENTER, 30 Front St., is a regional museum of 19th- and 20th-century art, history, folk life, science and natural history. It is composed of the historic 1907 Roberson Mansion and a museum, planetarium and science gallery. Also on site is the Binghamton Visitor Center, which features permanent and changing heritage displays and a slide presentation.

Allow 2 hours minimum. Tues.-Sat. 10:30-4:30 (also Thurs. 4:30-8); closed major holidays. Planetarium shows are offered Thurs. and Sat.; phone for schedule. Admission $6, over 61 and students with ID $4, family rate $20. Phone (607) 772-0660.

ROSS PARK ZOO, 60 Morgan Rd., is a 25-acre facility. Animals include lions, tigers, spectacled bears, endangered red wolves, otters, blackfooted penguins and golden lion tamarins. Signs explain each animal's habitat, diet and social structure. A 1919 carousel operates daily Memorial Day through Labor Day. Picnicking is permitted. Allow 1 hour, 30 minutes minimum. Daily 10-5, Apr.-Oct. Admission $5; senior citizens and ages 3-12, $3.50. Carousel free. Phone (607) 724-5461.

Discovery Center of the Southern Tier is at 60 Morgan Rd., entered through Ross Park Zoo. Hands-on activity stations invite children to fly a jet plane, ride a fire engine, shop in a grocery store or present the news on television. Allow 1 hour minimum. Tues.-Fri. 10-4, Sat. 10-5, Sun. noon-5; closed Jan. 1, Easter, Memorial Day, Labor Day and Dec. 25. Admission $5; over 18, $4; under 2 free. Phone (607) 773-8661.

BLUE MOUNTAIN LAKE (C-9) elev. 1,789'

To the north of Blue Mountain Lake, Blue Mountain rises 3,759 feet. Splendid views of the region are available from the summit, reached by a 3-mile trail. *Also see Adirondack Park p. 57.*

Blue Mountain Lake Association: Main Street, Blue Mountain Lake, NY 12812; phone (518) 352-7659.

ADIRONDACK MUSEUM, on SR 30, explores the culture, environment and history of the Adirondack region from the early 1800s to the present. The museum, on 32 acres overlooking Blue Mountain Lake, has 22 indoor and outdoor exhibits about logging, boating, recreation and mining. Visitors also can enjoy an elegant private railroad car, a collection of freshwater boats, a schoolhouse and a cottage with rustic furniture.

The crowd-pleasing Photobelt exhibit features selections from an extensive collection of historic Adirondacks photographs. Special displays are introduced each season.

Food is available. Allow 3 hours minimum. Daily 10-5, Memorial Day weekend to mid-Oct. Admission $14; over 62, $13; ages 7-17, $7. AX, DS, MC, VI. Phone (518) 352-7311.

BOLTON LANDING (D-11)

A resort area on the west shore of Lake George, Bolton Landing originated as an American Indian encampment on a wilderness trail. It later became the Bolton Landing stage stop on the Great Road. Wealthy families made the area their summer home. Scenic SR 9N runs north and south and is part of a lake shore route through the Adirondack Mountains.

Bolton Chamber of Commerce: P.O. Box 368, Bolton Landing, NY 12814; phone (518) 644-3831.

MARCELLA SEMBRICH OPERA MUSEUM, .5 mi. s. on SR 9N to 4800 Lakeshore Dr., contains mementos of the early 20th-century opera star's career. Lakeside walking paths on the grounds lead to vistas. Allow 30 minutes minimum. Daily 10-12:30 and 2-5:30, June 15-Sept. 15. Admission $2, under 12 free. Phone (518) 644-9839 or (518) 644-2492.

BOONVILLE (D-8) pop. 2,138, elev. 1,135′

Boonville was named for Garret Boon, an agent of the Holland Land Co., which owned property in the region at the end of the 18th century. The Black River Canal and the Black River Railroad brought prosperity to the town in the mid-1800s. Many of the grand houses of that period are on Schuyler Street. Hulbert House, a Georgian coach inn, was built in 1812.

Boonville Area Chamber of Commerce: P.O. Box 163, 122 Main St., Boonville, NY 13309; phone (315) 942-5112.

BRANCHPORT (F-5) elev. 736′

WINERIES

- **Hunt Country Vineyards,** off SR 54A at 4021 Italy Hill Rd. Mon.-Sat. 10-6, Sun. noon-6, July-Oct.; Mon.-Sat. 10-5, Sun. noon-5, rest of year. Phone (315) 595-2812 or (800) 946-3289.

BRIDGEHAMPTON (H-5)
pop. 1,381, elev. 50′

BRIDGEHAMPTON HISTORICAL MUSEUM is at 2368 Montauk Hwy. The early 19th-century Greek Revival Corwith House displays local artifacts and is furnished in various periods dating from the late 18th century. Working antique engines and farm machines can be found in the Hildreth-Simons Machine Shop; the George W. Strong Wheelwright Shop displays tools used in wagon repair. Guided tours Tues.-Sat. 11-4, June 1-Sept. 15; Mon.-Fri. 11-4, Mar.-May and Sept. 16-Dec. 31. Donations. Phone (631) 537-1088.

Buffalo

How Buffalo was named remains a mystery, although the site has never been called anything else. Ironically there have never been buffalo in Buffalo; even the shaggy beasts at the Buffalo Zoological Gardens are technically North American bison. One theory blames the misnomer on a mispronunciation of the French *beau fleuve*, or "beautiful river." The river in question is the Niagara.

The French explorer Robert La Salle paddled his canoe down the Niagara in 1628. A small French settlement was established in 1758. It was burned by the British the following year, but the settlers held fast. Joseph Ellicott informed them in 1800 that the Holland Land Co. had bought the land. Ellicott mapped out plans for a town to be called New Amsterdam and patterned after Washington, D.C.

The town was built, but residents insisted on calling it Buffalo. Put to the torch again by the British during the War of 1812, the town was quickly reconstructed. In 1818 the first Great Lakes steamboat, *Walk-on-the-Water*, was built, the first of two major events that turned a small village into a major city in only 16 years.

The second event was the opening of the Erie Canal in 1825. By connecting numerous trade and transportation routes, the canal made Buffalo the nucleus of the shipping trade between the Great Lakes region, Canada and the eastern United States. Ten years later the addition of railroads to Buffalo's transportation network boosted the city's growth potential even higher.

Buffalo's major industries include glass, rubber, plastics, electronics and airplane and automobile manufacturing. High-technology has emerged as a viable successor to the city's imperiled heavy industries. Agriculture also plays an important economic role, particularly the growing of fruits and vegetables. Grain distribution and flour and feed production have been part of the local economy since the 1950s. The city also is the home of the only player piano roll manufacturer in the world.

Buffalo has produced important people as well. Two of its residents, Millard Fillmore and Grover Cleveland, became president. Fillmore is buried in Forest Lawn Cemetery. Theodore Roosevelt was sworn in at the Wilcox Mansion on Delaware Avenue after President William McKinley's assassination at the city's Pan-American Exposition in 1901.

Other former Buffalo residents include William G. Fargo of the Wells Fargo stagecoach line, as well as the inventors of the windshield wiper, the pacemaker and the electric chair. Ellsworth Statler opened the first Hotel Statler on Delaware Avenue in 1908 with the slogan "A room with a bath for a dollar and a half."

Buffalo Museum of Science / © Gibson Stock Photography

Erie Basin Marina / © Gibson Stock Photography

Samuel Clemens, a resident in the 1870s, was editor of the *Buffalo Express*. Author Taylor Caldwell also called Buffalo home. Such musical classics as "When Irish Eyes Are Smiling," "My Wild Irish Rose" and "Over the Rainbow" were penned by Buffalo composers. Edwin P. (Ned) Christy launched the Christy Minstrels show in Buffalo.

Frank Lloyd Wright left his mark on Buffalo with the Darwin D. Martin House, on Jewett Parkway. Some say it is one of his best examples of prairie architecture. Wright also designed Martin's summer retreat, Graycliff Estate *(see attraction listing p. 73)*, in nearby Derby.

Buffalo can aptly be called a college town; its 18 higher educational facilities range in curriculum from liberal arts to business to vocational training. The State University of New York at Buffalo is the largest university in the state; D'Youville College on Porter Avenue is noted for its nursing program.

The Albright-Knox Art Gallery *(see attraction listing p. 71)*, Kleinhans Music Hall and other cultural centers balance industrial practicality with aesthetic appreciation. At the stadiums and arenas cheering the local teams is almost a prerequisite for citizenship in a town known for its high attendance at sporting events.

Approaches

By Car

From Rochester and other points east I-90 approaches Buffalo's northeast corner. It then joins I-190 and travels south, paralleling the city's eastern boundary before continuing west along the Lake Erie shoreline. The segment of I-290 that connects I-90 from the east and I-290 going north to Niagara Falls is called the Youngmann Expressway.

I-190 approaches the city from the northwest, passing through the west side before cutting across town and joining I-90 to the east. Toll barriers along I-190 are inbound only and are found between the Scajaquada Expressway (SR 198) and the Peace Bridge and between I-90 and Ogden Street. Travelers using I-90 from the west can either go northwest through the city via I-190 or northeast via I-90. Both I-90 and I-190 are part of the New York State Thruway.

Entering the area from the south are US 219 (Southern Expressway) from Springville and SR 400 (Aurora Expressway) from South Wales. Both join I-90 headed northeast. SR 5 from Dunkirk joins I-190 just below Seneca Street; SR 5 then becomes Main Street, cutting northeast. US 62 (Bailey Avenue), going north and south, bisects Buffalo.

The Kensington Expressway (SR 33) comes in from the east; the Scajaquada Expressway (SR 198) enters from the west off I-190. At the intersection of these two expressways, the Scajaquada ends; the

(continued on p. 70)

The Informed Traveler

City Population: 292,648

Elevation: 680 ft.

Sales Tax: The sales tax in Buffalo is 8 percent. There also is a 7 percent tax levied on lodgings and a 5 percent tax on rental cars.

WHOM TO CALL

Emergency: 911

Police (non-emergency): (716) 853-2222

Time: (716) 844-1717

Weather: (716) 844-4444

Hospitals: Buffalo General, (716) 859-5600; Mercy Hospital, (716) 826-7000; Sisters of Charity Hospital, (716) 862-1000.

WHERE TO LOOK

Newspapers

The *Buffalo News* is the local daily newspaper. Also available are more than 40 weekly and special-interest publications.

Radio

Buffalo radio station WEBR (970 AM) is an all-news/weather station; WBFO (88.7 FM) is a member of National Public Radio.

Visitor Information

Information is available from the Greater Buffalo Convention and Visitors Bureau, 617 Main St., Buffalo, NY 14203; phone (716) 852-0511 or (800) 283-3256. For parks information phone (716) 851-5806.

TRANSPORTATION

Air Travel

Airport Taxi Service provides limousine transportation to the airport from major hotels and the Ellicott Street Bus Terminal daily 6 a.m.-11 p.m.; phone (716) 633-8294. The Niagara Shuttle runs to major hotels in Niagara Falls daily; phone (800) 551-9369.

Rental Cars

Hertz, (716) 632-4772 or (800) 654-3080, offers discounts to AAA members. For listings of other agencies check the telephone directory.

Rail Service

Amtrak has two connecting stations: one at Exchange Street near the junction of Main and Seneca streets and another on Dick Road, in the Cheektowaga area.

Buses

Greyhound Lines Inc. operates out of the Ellicott Street Bus Terminal downtown; phone (800) 231-2222. For Empire Trailways information phone (800) 295-5555.

Taxis

Cab companies include Airport Taxi Service, (716) 633-8294; Broadway, (716) 896-4600; and City Service, (716) 852-4000. The rate is $1.80 per mile. For a complete list of taxi services check the telephone directory.

Public Transport

The major Metro bus routes operate daily 5 a.m. to midnight. Service varies by route, but buses generally run every 20 minutes on weekdays. The base fare is $1.25; exact fare is required. Zone charges apply in the suburbs; transfers are 25c. Tokens can be purchased at Metro offices and local banks.

A light rail rapid transit system runs from Memorial Auditorium at the base of Main Street through Buffalo Place and the theater district, ending at the State University of New York at Buffalo campus. Rail fares are the same as bus fares, with free transfers available between the two systems. Route maps are available at the Transportation Center at 181 Ellicott St.; phone (716) 855-7211.

Destination Buffalo

*T*he "Queen City" has something for everyone. Travel back in time to the days of the dinosaurs at the Buffalo Museum of Science or watch history come alive at the Naval and Military Park.

*C*heer on football's Bills or watch hockey's Sabres slice the ice. For a taste of Buffalo, sample its spicy chicken wings or visit the Buffalo and Erie County Historical Society, where more than 700 Buffalo-made products include Cheerios.

Theodore Roosevelt Inaugural National Historic Site, Buffalo.
The nation's 26th president was sworn in here just hours after the assassination of President William McKinley. (See listing page 71)

Buffalo and Erie County Historical Society.
Keepers of the past, both the society and the building constructed for the 1901 Pan-American Exposition have lots of stories to tell. (See listing page 71)

Buffalo Niagara CVB and Angel Art Ltd.

North Tonawanda

190

290

Grand Island

ON NY

Amherst
Williamsville

Buffalo

90

20

CANADA USA

20

U.S. 20

See Vicinity map p. 70

400

Derby

Orchard Park

East Aurora

90

219

Eden

Pedaling History Bicycle Museum, Orchard Park.
Boneshakers and folding paratroopers are just some of the cycling curiosities to behold. (See listing page 74)

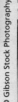

© Gibson Stock Photography

*P*laces included in this AAA Destination City:

Albright-Knox Art Gallery, Buffalo.
Although its collections span centuries, the city's premier art museum is renowned for its modern art. (See listing page 71)

Kensington Expressway continues south to downtown and east to Buffalo-Niagara Falls International Airport on Genesee Street.

Getting Around

Street System

Buffalo's major streets branch off from its central business district in a radial pattern. Because Lake Erie borders the city's southwest side, most roads begin downtown and branch out to the north and east. Niagara Square is the primary downtown intersection. From the square Delaware Avenue runs north and south; Niagara Street goes diagonally northwest to the Black Rock Canal and then heads north. Genesee Street extends northeast from Niagara Square to the airport.

Main Street, 2 blocks east of Delaware Avenue, runs north and south downtown but branches off to the northeast at Ferry Street. Main Street downtown and to the northeast is SR 5; however, to the south SR 5 is known as Fuhrmann Boulevard and then

Hamburg Turnpike as it goes farther south down the Lake Erie shoreline.

Because of the creation of Buffalo Place, a pedestrian mall downtown, Main Street has been permanently closed to traffic from the theater district to the foot of Main Street. To maintain traffic flow, two sets of one-way streets are on either side of the mall. To the east, Elm Street runs north and Oak Street runs south; to the west, Franklin Street runs north and Pearl Street runs south. Buffalo's metro rail line also traverses this area.

Seneca Street and Abbott Road are two main east-west routes connecting downtown and the southeast suburbs. Clinton Street begins 4 blocks east of Niagara Square at Lafayette Square and heads alternately south and east, detouring the two-block section from Michigan Avenue to Pine Street.

The downtown speed limit is 30 mph. Unless otherwise posted, right turns at red lights are permitted after a complete stop; left turns at red lights from a one-way street to another one-way street are permitted after a complete stop. Rush hours, 7-9 a.m. and 4-6 p.m., should be avoided.

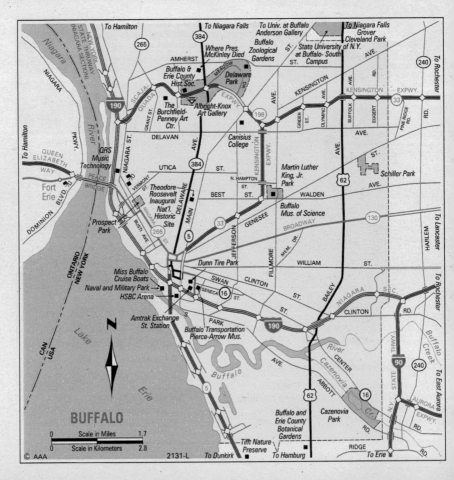

Parking

Metered parking is available downtown, but spaces fill quickly. With patience, unmetered spaces also can be found. Many parking garages are available at $4-$5 per day. Underground parking is offered at Main Place, One M&T Plaza and One Marine Midland Center.

What To See

ALBRIGHT-KNOX ART GALLERY, just s. of jct. SR 198 on Elmwood Ave., is a Greek Revival building housing paintings and sculptures dating from 3000 B.C. to the present. The contemporary collection of American and European art is especially notable and includes works by Willem de Kooning, Henri Matisse, Pablo Picasso and Jackson Pollock.

Food is available. Allow 2 hours minimum. Tues.-Sat. 11-5, Sun. noon-5; closed Jan. 1, July 4, Thanksgiving and Dec. 25. Admission $6, over 62 and students with ID $5, under 12 free, family rate (two adults and two children) $12. Phone (716) 882-8700.

BUFFALO AND ERIE COUNTY BOTANICAL GARDENS is at 2655 South Park Ave. (US 62). The gardens are in South Park, which was designed by Frederick Law Olmsted in the late 1890s. A restored, triple-domed glass conservatory patterned after England's Crystal Palace houses tropical and subtropical plants grouped by region, in the Victorian style. Other features include an arboretum, an evergreen collection, flowering annuals, a bog garden, a lake, dinosaur topiaries and an extensive ivy collection. Allow 1 hour minimum. Mon.-Fri. 9-4 (also Wed. 4-6), Sat.-Sun. 9-5. Donations. Phone (716) 827-1584.

BUFFALO MUSEUM OF SCIENCE, 1020 Humboldt Pkwy. at Northampton St. (Best St. exit from SR 33), has exhibits about Egyptians, dinosaurs, insects, space and endangered species as well as a children's discovery room. The Kellogg Observatory offers sun shows in the summer.

Allow 2 hours minimum. Tues.-Sat. 10-5, Sun. noon-5; closed Jan. 1, July 4, Thanksgiving and Dec. 25. Admission $6; over 61, college students with ID and ages 3-17, $4. AX, MC, VI. Phone (716) 896-5200.

BUFFALO TRANSPORTATION PIERCE-ARROW MUSEUM is at 263 Michigan Ave. at Seneca St. The development of transportation in the Buffalo area is chronicled through exhibits of automobiles, motorcycles, bicycles and such related motoring memorabilia as signs, parts and accessories. Of particular interest is a collection of Pierce-Arrow automobiles and hood ornaments. Muscle cars also are displayed. Allow 1 hour minimum. Wed.-Sun. noon-5, Apr.-Sept.; Fri.-Sun. noon-5, rest of year. Admission $7; over 60, $6; ages 6-17, $3. MC, VI. Phone (716) 853-0084.

THE BURCHFIELD-PENNEY ART CENTER, in Rockwell Hall on Elmwood Ave. on the Buffalo State College campus, has a variety of changing exhibits and presentations. Featured is a collection of watercolor paintings by Charles E. Burchfield. Permanent exhibits include a re-creation of Burchfield's studio and Roycroft furniture and decorative objects. Allow 30 minutes minimum. Tues.-Sat. 10-5, Sun. 1-5. Admission $5; over 64, $4; ages 6-18, $3. Phone (716) 878-6011.

DELAWARE PARK, 2 mi. n. on Elmwood Ave., then e. on Iroquois Dr., offers tennis, bicycling and golf.

Buffalo and Erie County Historical Society, 25 Nottingham Ct., is housed in the only remaining building from the 1901 Pan-American Exposition. Exhibits highlight the commercial and industrial development of the Buffalo area. An archive library is available.

Allow 1 hour minimum. Exhibits Mon.-Sat. 10-5, Sun. noon-5. Library Wed.-Fri. 1-5, Sat. noon-5. Closed Jan. 1, Thanksgiving and Dec. 25. Admission $4; over 60, $3; students with ID $2.50; ages 7-12, $1.50; family rate (two adults and two children) $7.50. Library $4. MC, VI. Phone (716) 873-9644.

SAVE Buffalo Zoological Gardens, 2 mi. n. on Elmwood Ave., then e. on Iroquois Dr. to Delaware Park, has indoor and outdoor displays of more than 1,000 animals and birds on 23.5 acres. A highlight is the greater one-horned rhinoceros. Special exhibits include a wildlife building, lion and tiger outdoor habitat, gorilla rain forest and children's zoo. Carousel and train rides are available in season.

Food is available. Allow 1 hour, 30 minutes minimum. Gates open daily 10-5, June 1-Labor Day; daily 10-4, rest of year. Admission $7; ages 2-14, $3.50; over 62, $3. Parking $3. DS, MC, VI. Phone (716) 837-3900.

NAVAL AND MILITARY PARK, on Lake Erie at the foot of Pearl and Main sts. at 1 Naval Park Cove, is one of the few inland naval parks in the country. Visitors can board fighting ships, the guided-missile cruiser USS *Little Rock*, the destroyer USS *The Sullivans* and the World War II submarine USS *Croaker*. Displays include aircraft, scale models of ships and airplanes, and a videotape about the park's features and history. Daily 10-5, Apr.-Oct.; Sat.-Sun. 10-4, in Nov. Admission $6; over 61 and ages 6-16, $3.50. Phone (716) 847-1773.

THEODORE ROOSEVELT INAUGURAL NATIONAL HISTORIC SITE (Wilcox Mansion), 641 Delaware Ave., is an 1838 Greek Revival structure. Theodore Roosevelt was sworn in as the 26th president in the library. Displays include items relating to President William McKinley's assassination and President Roosevelt's inauguration, a slide presentation and changing art exhibits.

Allow 1 hour minimum. Mon.-Fri. 9-5, Sat.-Sun. noon-5; closed Jan. 1, Easter, Memorial Day, July 4, Labor Day, Thanksgiving and Dec. 24-25 and 31.

Admission $3; over 62, $2; ages 6-14, $1. Phone (716) 884-0095.

TIFFT NATURE PRESERVE is w. on SR 5 to 1200 Fuhrmann Blvd. The park encompasses 264 acres with nature trails, a wildflower garden and a 75-acre cattail marsh. The visitor center contains mounted specimens of local wildlife and displays detailing the preserve's development. Guided walks are offered Sundays at 2. Picnicking, fishing, cross-country skiing and snowshoeing are permitted.

Park open daily dawn-dusk. Visitor center open Tues.-Fri. 9-2, Sat. 9-4, Sun. noon-4; closed Jan. 1, Thanksgiving and Dec. 24-25. Donations. Phone (716) 825-6397.

UNIVERSITY AT BUFFALO ANDERSON GALLERY, SR 33W (Main St. exit), then n. on Englewood Ave. to Martha Jackson Pl., offers changing exhibits of post-World War II art, many with a regional theme. Display media range from paintings and photographs to sculpture. Wed.-Sat. 11-5, Sun. 1-5. Free. Phone (716) 829-3754.

What To Do

Sightseeing

Those unfamiliar with Buffalo may wish to begin their sightseeing with an aerial view of the city from the observation deck on the 28th floor of City Hall at Niagara Square downtown; phone (716) 851-4200. The deck is open Mon.-Fri. 9-3; closed holidays.

Many of Buffalo's historic structures have been renovated or restored; Allentown, a historic preservation district just south of North Street between Elmwood Avenue and Main Street, has Victorian buildings, ethnic restaurants, art galleries and boutiques. Information about tours of Allentown is available from the Allentown Association, 414 Virginia St., Buffalo, NY 14201; phone (716) 881-1024.

Boat Tours

MISS BUFFALO **CRUISE BOATS** depart from the Erie Basin Marina at Marine Dr. and Erie St. Offered is a variety of 2-hour, narrated sightseeing tours of the Buffalo River and area waterways. Meal cruises with entertainment also are available. Sightseeing cruises depart Tues.-Sun., June-Sept.; departure days and times vary according to type of cruise. Fare $12; ages 3-9, $8. AX, DS, MC, VI. Phone (716) 856-6696.

Bus Tours

Bus tours of Buffalo are offered by AFT Tours Inc., phone (716) 646-4682; Apex Transportation Services, phone (716) 632-4666; Bedore Tours Inc., (716) 285-7550; SAVE Gray Line of Buffalo & Niagara Falls, (716) 694-3600, (716) 695-1603 or (800) 695-1603; and Motherland Connextions Inc., (716) 282-1028.

Industrial Tours

QRS MUSIC TECHNOLOGY, .5 mi. n. of the Peace Bridge at 1026 Niagara St., offers guided tours of the world's only manufacturer of player piano rolls. Tours are limited to 15 persons and are not recommended for small children. Mon.-Fri. at 10 and 2; closed Jan. 1, Good Friday, Memorial Day, July 4, Labor Day, Thanksgiving and Dec. 24-25 and 31. Fee $2; under 12, $1. Phone (716) 885-4600.

Walking Tours

Guided 30-minute to 2-hour walking tours of Allentown, Main and N. Pearl streets or Delaware Avenue depart from the Wilcox Mansion, 641 Delaware Ave. Parking is available in the rear of the building. A tour of the downtown area departs near the library. Guided tours run April through October; a minimum of six persons is required. Fee $5; ages 5-12, $2.50. Phone (716) 884-0095 for tour schedule; reservations must be made 2 weeks in advance.

Forest Lawn Cemetery, 1411 Delaware Ave., offers bird-watching and sculpture on 269 acres. A brochure outlining a self-guiding tour is available at the cemetery office inside the Delaware Avenue entrance Mon.-Fri. 8:30-4:30, Sat. 8:30-4; phone (716) 885-1600.

For information about other self-guiding tours contact the Greater Buffalo Convention and Visitors Bureau *(see The Informed Traveler)*.

Sports and Recreation

Buffalo has an extensive municipal park system where sports enthusiasts can find ample playing space. More than 100 **baseball** and **softball** diamonds are available, as are 84 **tennis** courts and three **soccer** fields. Sports such as **lawn bowling** and **cricket** also are offered. **Swimming** can be enjoyed at local pools and beaches.

Running tracks are available for walkers, joggers and runners. **Basketball** courts and **football** fields are scattered throughout town; six indoor ice rinks offer year-round **ice skating**.

Skiing is very popular in the region. Nine major areas with chair lifts, T-bars and other facilities are within close driving distance of the city; Kissing Bridge and Holiday Valley are less than an hour away. Other winter sports such as **tobogganing, sledding** and **snowmobiling** are permitted in public parks.

Those who consider spectating a sport in its own right will find plenty of company in Buffalo, where stadiums and arenas are filled with professional fans. Football lovers can see the Buffalo Bills at Ralph Wilson Stadium; phone (716) 649-0015. The Buffalo Bisons play baseball at Dunn Tire Park; phone (716) 843-4373. Slicing the ice in the HSBC Arena every winter is the Buffalo Sabres **hockey** team; phone (716) 855-4100. Buffalo's numerous colleges and universities also offer a wide variety of sporting events.

Four-legged athletes offer their share of excitement to **horse racing** buffs as well. **Harness racing** is held at the Buffalo Raceway in Hamburg; phone (716) 649-1280 for schedule.

Note: Policies concerning admittance of children to pari-mutuel betting facilities vary. Phone for information.

Shopping

The variety of stores offering fashions, fads and foods for every taste and budget make shopping in Buffalo an adventure. The downtown shopping area extends from Main and Church streets north to Main and Chippewa streets, and west along Elmwood and Delaware avenues. Buffalo Place offers a wide variety of shops. Main Place Mall stretches along Main Street from Swan to Goodell streets. Boutiques line Delaware Avenue as well.

The Bon-Ton and Kaufmann's are two major department stores. Antique and specialty gift shops are found in the Allentown area, Buffalo's version of Greenwich Village. Bargain hunters will appreciate the Ammex Tax & Duty Free Shop at The Peace Bridge.

Broadway Market at Broadway and Fillmore streets is an indoor marketplace in an Old World setting offering fresh produce, baked goods, crafts and specialty items. The Hertel, North Main Street and Riverside commercial areas also offer a wide range of shops.

Walden Galleria, at I-90 and Walden Avenue, offers more than 200 stores including The Bon-Ton, JCPenney, Kaufmann's, Lord & Taylor and Sears.

Theater and Concerts

Shea's Performing Arts Center, an ornate 1926 theater at 646 Main St., presents performances year-round. For information about schedules and tickets phone (716) 847-0850. The Theatre of Youth (TOY) Company performs children's shows in the Allendale Theatre; phone (716) 884-4400.

The rejuvenated theater district also includes The New Phoenix Theatre at 95 Johnson Pkwy., phone (716) 855-2225; Studio Arena Theater at 710 Main St., phone (716) 856-5650; and Ujima Theatre at 545 Elmwood Ave., phone (716) 883-0380. Plays and musicals are presented September through early June. Shakespeare in Delaware Park gives free outdoor performances June through August; phone (716) 856-4533.

The Alleyway Theatre, One Curtain Up Alley, is a professional theater company dedicated to performing new plays in off-Broadway style; phone (716) 852-2600. The Irish Classical Theatre Co. performs international classics and plays from Irish literature at 625 Main St.; phone (716) 853-4282. Just outside of downtown at 320 Porter Ave. is the Kavinoky Theatre-D'Youville College; phone (716) 881-7668.

Special Events

In May the city is enlivened by the Hellenic Festival, offering cultural displays, folk dancing and Greek food. During the second weekend in June the Allentown Art Festival in the historic Allentown district displays the works of local artisans.

July 1-4, Buffalo and Fort Erie, Ontario, celebrate brotherhood during the Friendship Festival. Festivities include arts and crafts exhibits, a cultural parade, equestrian jumping, concerts and fireworks. Buffalo's best restaurants prepare epicurean delights from chicken wings to cheesecakes for the second weekend of July's Taste of Buffalo festival.

At the Erie County Fairgrounds, 12 miles south off I-90 exit 56 in Hamburg, one of the nation's oldest and largest county fairs takes place in mid-August. The second week in August brings the Lake Erie Can Am Challenge Walleye Tournament, in which anglers from Canada and the United States vie to catch the largest total weight of walleye perch. Buffalo's Winterfest, celebrated from December to January, is highlighted by ice skating, snow sculpture competitions and other activities.

The Buffalo Vicinity

AMHERST (E-3) pop. 116,510, elev. 260′

Amherst borders Buffalo-Niagara Falls International Airport, which is the focus of major air service to the Buffalo-Niagara Falls area. In the center of town is one of two campuses belonging to the State University of New York at Buffalo.

Amherst Chamber of Commerce: 325 Essjay Rd., Suite 200, Amherst, NY 14221; phone (716) 632-6905.

[SAVE] **AMHERST MUSEUM** is reached from I-990 to SR 263, then n. on New Rd. to 3755 Tonawanda Creek Rd. Featured are 12 restored 19th-century buildings. Highlighting local history are a costume collection, a children's discovery room and a hands-on Erie Canal exhibit.

Allow 2 hours minimum. Museum open Tues.-Fri. 9:30-4:30, Sat.-Sun. 12:30-4:30, Apr.-Oct.; Tues.-Fri. 9:30-4:30, rest of year. Buildings open May 15-Oct. 15. Closed holidays. Admission $5; ages 5-12, $1.50; family rate $12. DS, MC, VI. Phone (716) 689-1440.

DERBY (E-3) pop. 1,200, elev. 707′

[SAVE] **GRAYCLIFF ESTATE** is at 6472 Old Lake Shore Dr. Frank Lloyd Wright designed this summer estate in 1927 for Darwin and Isabelle Martin. The manor house on a cliff overlooking Lake Erie incorporates Wright's vision of "organic architecture," blending with the natural landscape. Allow 1 hour minimum. Guided tours depart Tues.-Thurs. at 11 and 2, Fri. at 3 and 7, Sat. at 11, noon, 1, 2, 3 and 7, Sun. at 1, 2, 3 and 4. Closed Easter, Thanksgiving and Dec. 25. Reservations are required. Admission $10, students with ID $5, under 10 free. MC, VI. Phone (716) 947-9217.

EAST AURORA (E-4) pop. 6,673

East Aurora is home to Roycroft Campus, an art community founded in 1895 by Elbert Hubbard, a former salesman and marketing genius turned artist, writer, publisher and craftsman. Hubbard, a leader in the American Arts and Crafts movement, went on to design a simple, straight-line style of furniture that remains popular. The Elbert Hubbard Museum, 363 Oakwood Ave., features a collection of Roycraft arts and crafts.

A restored 1826 cottage built by Millard Fillmore before he became president is on Shearer Ave. and includes some of Fillmore's furnishings and presidential memorabilia.

Explore and More, 300 Gleed Ave., has interactive learning and play stations for children up to age 10; phone (716) 655-5131.

Greater East Aurora Chamber of Commerce: 431 Main St., East Aurora, NY 14052; phone (716) 652-8444.

Self-guiding tours: A brochure about 14 historic buildings, including the Roycroft Inn, on Roycroft Campus is available from the chamber.

TOY TOWN MUSEUM, 1.1 mi. e. of SR 16/78 to 636 Girard Ave., is dedicated to preserving the heritage of toys from the early 1900s to the present. Toy Works, designed for children over 7, is the museum's interactive learning lab. Allow 30 minutes minimum. Mon.-Sat. 10-4. Free. Phone (716) 687-5151.

EDEN (E-3) pop. 3,579, elev. 797′

THE ORIGINAL AMERICAN KAZOO CO., 8703 S. Main St., is a factory that produces metal kazoos. The factory floor is closed to visitors, but there is a special area for viewing the production process. Exhibits depict the musical toy's West African origins as well as modern production methods. Guided tours are available by reservation. Allow 30 minutes minimum. Tues.-Sat. 10-5, Sun. noon-5; closed holidays. Free. Phone (716) 992-3960.

GRAND ISLAND (E-2) pop. 18,621

MARTIN'S FANTASY ISLAND, off I-190 exit 19N, is a theme park with rides, shows and attractions. A water park, miniature golf course and canoes are available. Picnicking is permitted. Allow 4 hours minimum. Daily 11:30-8:30, mid-June through Labor Day; Sat.-Sun. 11:30-8:30, mid-May to mid-June. Admission $18.95; under 48 inches tall $14.95; over age 65, $9.95; under age 2 free. AX, DS, MC, VI. Phone (716) 773-7591.

NORTH TONAWANDA (E-3) pop. 33,262

The Erie Canal spurred the development of North Tonawanda and its neighbor Tonawanda with a flourishing lumber industry. Today, the canal provides numerous recreational opportunities, including walking and biking along the Canalway Trail.

Chamber of Commerce of the Tonawandas: 15 Webster St., North Tonawanda, NY 14120; phone (716) 692-5120.

THE HERSCHELL CARROUSEL FACTORY MUSEUM, 180 Thompson St., preserves one of several local factories that produced carousels and band organs. Exhibits detail the process of hand-carving the various carousel animals and other objects. Of special note is a restored and working 1916 carousel. A children's carousel also is available. Daily 11-5, July-Aug.; Wed.-Sun. 1-5, Apr.-June and Sept.-Dec. Admission $4; over 60, $3; ages 2-12, $2. Phone (716) 693-1885.

ORCHARD PARK (E-3) pop. 3,294, elev. 886′

Founded by Quakers in the early 1800s, Orchard Park now is home to the NFL's Buffalo Bills, who play in Ralph Wilson Stadium. An outdoor lovers dream, the area offers 1,500-acre Chestnut Ridge Park, complete with hiking trails and picnicking areas. Winter brings snow to the hills, perfect for tobogganing and sledding.

Orchard Park Chamber of Commerce: 4211 N. Buffalo Rd., Suite 14, Orchard Park, NY 14127; phone (716) 662-3366.

(SAVE) **PEDALING HISTORY BICYCLE MUSEUM** is at 3943 N. Buffalo Rd. With more than 300 antique and reproduction bicycles, this museum is said to be the country's largest of its kind. Displays include a collection of children's wheeled vehicles dating from the 1890s; boneshakers, built during the 1860s and so named because of the jarring riders experienced; wooden highwheels; and folding paratrooper bicycles used during World War II. Allow 1 hour minimum. Mon.-Sat. 11-5, Sun. 1:30-5, Apr. 2-Jan. 14; Fri.-Sat. and Mon. 11-5, Sun. 1:30-5, rest of year. Closed Jan. 1, Thanksgiving and Dec. 25. Admission $6; over 62, $5.40; ages 7-15, $3.75; family rate $17.50. MC, VI. Phone (716) 662-3853.

WILLIAMSVILLE (E-3) pop. 5,573

In 1804, Jonas Williams built a mill along Ellicott Creek and expanded his businesses, which included several grist mills, a sawmill, a tannery, a distillery and power-generating dams and raceways. He owned and operated so much of the area that it became know as Williams Mills, and later Williamsville. Present-day Williamsville Water Mills continues the operation begun in 1811.

Surrounded on all sides by the larger town of Amherst, the Village of Williamsville maintains geographic and political independence.

Amherst Chamber of Commerce: 325 Essjay Rd., Suite 200, Williamsville, NY 14221; phone (716) 632-6905.

WILLIAMSVILLE WATER MILLS, 56 Spring St., is a restored 1811 water-powered mill with historical exhibits. Cider is made early September through March 31. Mon.-Sat. 10-6, Sun. 11-6. Free. Phone (716) 632-1162.

The previous listings were for the Buffalo Vicinity. This page resumes the alphabetical listings of cities in New York.

BURT— *see Niagara Falls p. 166*

CANAJOHARIE (E-9) pop. 2,257, elev. 317'

In an area settled by Dutch and Germans in the early 1700s, Canajoharie gets its name from an American Indian expression meaning "the washed pot." The pot is a large pothole in the nearby Canajoharie Creek Gorge. A 45-foot waterfall can be seen at the gorge from Wintergreen Park.

The village is part of the historic Mohawk Valley Heritage Corridor, home of the Iroquois Confederacy *(see Exploring New York p. 50)*; phone (518) 673-1045 for information.

Canajoharie-Palatine Chamber of Commerce: P.O. Box 38, Canajoharie, NY 13317.

CANAJOHARIE LIBRARY AND ART GALLERY, s.w. off New York Thruway exit 29 at Church St. and Erie Blvd., contains watercolors and oils by such American painters as John Singleton Copley, Winslow Homer, George Inness, Albert Pinkham Ryder, John Singer Sargent and Gilbert Stuart. Other displays feature local history; industry, including the Beech-Nut and Life Savers companies; and genealogy.

Guided tours are available by appointment. Allow 30 minutes minimum. Mon.-Thurs. 10-7:30, Fri. 10-4:30, Sat. 10-1:30; closed holidays. Free. Phone (518) 673-2314.

CANANDAIGUA (E-5) pop. 11,264, elev. 685'

Canandaigua stands on the shore of the lake that shares its name. The town is on the site of the Seneca Indian village *Kan-an-dar-gue*, destroyed by Gen. John Sullivan in 1779. Considered to be one of the most beautiful of the Finger Lakes, Canandaigua Lake is 17 miles long and averages about a mile wide. It harbors bass, pickerel, pike and trout. Around the lake are thousands of acres of vineyards. *Also see Finger Lakes p. 86.*

Thoroughbred horse racing takes place Friday through Tuesday, early April through late November, at Finger Lakes Race Track, 8 miles north on SR 96 just east of its junction with SR 332; for information phone (585) 924-3232.

Note: Policies concerning admittance of children to pari-mutuel betting facilities vary. Phone for information.

Canandaigua Chamber of Commerce: 113 S. Main St., Canandaigua, NY 14424; phone (585) 394-4400.

CAPTAIN GRAY'S BOAT TOURS, 770 S. Main St., offers 1-, 2- and 3-hour narrated cruises on Canandaigua Lake. One-hour cruises depart daily at 11, 1, 3, 5 and 7, June 1-Labor Day. Fare for 1-hour cruise $8.50; under 12, $4. Phone (585) 394-5270.

[SAVE] **GRANGER HOMESTEAD AND CARRIAGE MUSEUM** is at 295 N. Main St. This restored 1816 Federal-style homestead was built by Gideon Granger, U.S. postmaster general under Presidents Thomas Jefferson and James Madison. The Carriage Museum has more than 44 horse-drawn vehicles made or used in the region 1810-1920.

Guided tours of the house and museum are given on the hour Tues.-Sun. 1-4, June-Aug.; Tues.-Fri. 1-4, mid-May through May 31 and Sept. 1 to mid-Oct. Admission $5; over 61, $4; ages 7-16, $1. Phone (585) 394-1472.

[SAVE] **ONTARIO COUNTY HISTORICAL SOCIETY MUSEUM,** 55 N. Main St., features exhibits about local and regional history. Archives and a genealogy research room also are available. Allow 1 hour minimum. Tues.-Sat. 10-4:30 (also Wed. 4:30-9); closed holidays. Museum admission $2. Research room $5. Phone (585) 394-4975.

ROSELAND WATERPARK is at 250 Eastern Blvd. (US 20). The park includes a giant wave pool, body flume, raft ride, tube slide and children's splash pool. Kayaks and paddleboats are available to rent. Water shows are performed on a 38-acre lake. Allow 1 hour minimum. Daily 10:30-8, late June to mid-Aug.; 11-7, mid- to late June and mid-Aug. to early Sept. Admission $19.99; ages 4-10, $16.99; over 60 and under 4, $4.99. Additional fee for lockers, paddleboats and kayaks. Parking $3. MC, VI. Phone (585) 396-2000.

[GEM] [SAVE] **SONNENBERG GARDENS** is n. off SR 21 (Gibson St.) at 151 Charlotte St., near New York State Thruway (US 90) exits 43 and 44. The 1887 Queen Anne-style mansion served as the summer retreat of Frederick Ferris, founder of the First National Bank of the City of New York, and his wife Mary Thompson, the daughter of a former New York governor. A variety of colors and textures accent the mansion's rustic facade. The interior reflects the Victorian-era penchant for mixing architectural styles, as seen in the English Tudor entry hall, medieval great hall, Colonial dining room, and Arts and Crafts trophy room.

Sonnenberg is a German word meaning "sunny hill." The 50-acre estate overlooking Canandaigua Lake consists of more than a dozen elegant, manicured theme gardens with fountains, streams, ponds, statues and greenhouses. Tram rides are available.

Food is available. Allow 2 hours minimum. Daily 9:30-5:30, Memorial Day-Labor Day; 9:30-4, early May-day before Memorial Day and day after Labor Day to mid-Oct. Admission $8.50; over 59, $7.50; ages 5-14, $3.50. Admission prices may vary during special events. MC, VI. Phone (585) 394-4922.

CANASTOTA (D-7) pop. 4,425, elev. 436'

CANASTOTA CANAL TOWN MUSEUM, 122 Canal St., is in an 1874 house. Displayed are antiques, Erie Canal historical items and local memorabilia including photographs, maps, dolls, a water pump at an old-fashioned kitchen sink and examples of the handmade crystal for which Canastota was well-known in the early 1900s. Allow 30 minutes minimum. Tues.-Sat. 10-4, July-Aug.; 1-4, May-June and Sept.-Oct. Closed holidays. Admission $2, under 16 free. Phone (315) 697-3451.

INTERNATIONAL BOXING HALL OF FAME, off New York State Thruway (I-90) exit 34 at 1 Hall of Fame Dr., offers videotapes and displays of such boxing memorabilia as robes, gloves and ticket stubs. Allow 30 minutes minimum. Mon.-Fri. 9-5, Sat.-Sun. 10-4; closed Easter, Thanksgiving and Dec. 25. Admission $7; over 65, $6.50; ages 7-15, $5.50. AX, DS, MC, VI. Phone (315) 697-7095.

CANTON (B-8) pop. 5,882, elev. 375'

Canton was settled by Vermonters in the early 1800s. The names for this town and nine others in the county were chosen from the world atlas in the hope that familiar names would help the land sell more easily. In 1861 Frederic Remington, sculptor and painter of the American West, was born in Canton, where his father was editor of the newspaper. Canton is home to St. Lawrence University, a liberal arts institution of about 2,000 students, which was founded in 1856.

Canton Chamber of Commerce: P.O. Box 369, Canton, NY 13617; phone (315) 386-8255.

ST. LAWRENCE COUNTY MUSEUM, 3 E. Main St., was the home of U.S. senator and New York governor Silas Wright. The exterior and first-floor interior have been restored to the 1830-50 period. Permanent and changing exhibits relate to St. Lawrence County history; a research library is available. Allow 1 hour minimum. Museum and library open Tues.-Sat. noon-4 (also Fri. 4-8); closed holidays. Museum free. A research fee is charged. Phone (315) 386-8133.

CAPE VINCENT (C-7) pop. 760, elev. 253'

CAPE VINCENT HISTORICAL MUSEUM, next to Horns Ferry Dock on lower James St., features area history displays. A genealogy room is available by appointment. Allow 30 minutes minimum. Daily 10-4, July-Aug.; by appointment rest of year. Donations. Phone (315) 654-4400.

CASTILE (E-4) pop. 1,051, elev. 1,397'

LETCHWORTH STATE PARK, 2 mi. n. on SR 19A to Denton's Corners, then 2 mi. e., is noted for the three waterfalls of the Genesee River Gorge. Middle Falls, a 107-foot cascade, is lighted nightly until 11. The walls of the 17-mile gorge reach heights up to 600 feet, offering views of the river and surrounding area. Scenic roads and trails pass through the park.

Food is available. Allow 4 hours minimum. Daily 6 a.m.-11 p.m. Admission $6 per private vehicle daily, Apr.-Oct. and Sat.-Sun. and holidays Dec.-Feb.; free rest of year. Phone (585) 493-3600. *See Recreation Chart.*

William Pryor Letchworth Pioneer and Indian Museum, in Letchworth State Park, has a varied display of artifacts. Allow 3 hours minimum. Daily 10-5, mid-May to mid-Oct. Free. Phone (585) 493-2760.

CATSKILL (F-10) pop. 4,392, elev. 67'

Near Catskill is the scene of Rip Van Winkle's legendary nap. The area affords a number of scenic drives, such as the section of SR 23 northwest over East Windham Mountain and SR 23B over Hunter Mountain.

Greene County Promotional Department: P.O. Box 527, Catskill, NY 12414; phone (518) 943-3223 or (800) 355-2287.

CATSKILL FOREST PRESERVE, comprising 287,989 acres in the Catskill Mountains, is particularly beautiful in June when the laurel blooms and in October when the leaves turn. Slide Mountain, with a height of 4,180 feet, is the highest point in the preserve. The preserve also is the location of Beaver Kill, Neversink and Willowemoc, three of the best fishing streams in the state. Daily 24 hours. Free. Phone (845) 256-3000. *See Recreation Chart.*

CATSKILL GAME FARM is off I-87 exit 21, w. 6.5 mi. on SR 23, then 5.5 mi. s. on SR 32. This farm has animals and birds from around the world, including rare or threatened species. Also included are amusement rides, recreation facilities and a petting zoo. Animal shows are presented daily, Memorial Day weekend-Labor Day. Food is available. Allow 2 hours minimum. Daily 9-5, May-Oct. Admission $16.75; ages 4-11, $12.95. MC, VI. Phone (518) 678-9595.

CAZENOVIA (E-7) pop. 2,614, elev. 1,205'

Cazenovia embraces the end of Cazenovia Lake, originally called *Ho-wah-ge-neh* (lake where the yellow perch swim) by American Indians. In 1793 John Lincklaen, a land agent for the Holland Land Co., settled in this area and renamed the site for Theophile Cazenove, the general agent for the company. The village first prospered as the economic crossroads of the region.

The invention of the modern game of football is credited to Cazenovia native Gerrit Smith Miller, who adapted it from a form of rugby around 1860.

Greater Cazenovia Area Chamber of Commerce: 59 Albany St., Cazenovia, NY 13035; phone (315) 655-9243 or (888) 218-6305.

LORENZO STATE HISTORIC SITE is off SR 13, .2 mi. s. of US 20 at 17 Rippleton Rd. The 1807 mansion overlooking Cazenovia Lake contains original furnishings. The grounds include a formal garden and a carriage collection. Allow 1 hour minimum. Wed.-Sun. 10-4:30. Guided tours are available May-Oct. Admission $5; over 61 and students with ID, $4; ages 5-11, $1. Phone (315) 655-3200.

CELORON (G-2) pop. 1,295

SUMMER WIND CHAUTAUQUA LAKE CRUISES depart from the dock in Lucille Ball Memorial Park, 1 mi. n. of SR 394. Two-hour sightseeing cruises on Chautauqua Lake are given. Cruises with meals also are offered. Sightseeing cruises depart Mon.-Fri. at 12:30 and 3, Sat. at noon, Sun. at 10 and 1, July-Aug.; departure times vary May-June and Sept.-Oct. Fare $13.95; ages 4-12, $8.95. Reservations are recommended. AX, DS, MC, VI. Phone (716) 763-7447.

CENTERPORT (H-3) pop. 5,446, elev. 50′

VANDERBILT MUSEUM is 1.5 mi. n. of SR 25A to 180 Little Neck Rd. Overlooking Northport Harbor, the 43-acre estate of William K. Vanderbilt II contains a Spanish Revival-style mansion, boathouse, seaplane hangar, marine and natural history museum, planetarium and gardens with water and architectural features. The house is filled with original furnishings, family memorabilia, decorative arts, firearms, ethnic objects and natural history specimens. A highlight is a 3,000-year-old mummy purchased in 1931.

The marine museum has one of the largest privately owned collections of marine specimens in the world. Also on the grounds is the Dino-Stars exhibition, with life-size dinosaur replicas and interactive touch screens.

Guided tours are available. Mansion open Tues.-Sat. 10-5, Sun. and holidays noon-5, late June-Labor Day; Tues.-Fri. noon-5, Sat.-Sun. and holidays 11:30-5, May 1-late June and day after Labor Day-Oct. 31; Tues.-Fri. noon-4, Sat. noon-5, Sun. and holidays 11:30-5, rest of year. Closed Jan. 1, Easter, Thanksgiving and Dec. 24-25 and 31. Last admission 1 hour before closing. Grounds $5; senior citizens and students with ID $3; under 12, $2. Mansion tour $3. Dino-Stars $2. Phone (631) 854-5555 or (631) 854-5579.

Planetarium, on Little Neck Rd., contains astronomy and science exhibits, telescopes, an observatory and a sky theater with a 60-foot-diameter dome. The Goto projector creates special effects with multiple projections of stars, the moon, and planets. Children's programs and a magic show also are offered. Sky shows Fri. at 8, Sat. at 11, noon, 1, 2 and 3, Sun. at 11, noon, 1 and 2:30. Magic show Sunday at 3. Admission $2. Magic show $12. Phone (631) 854-5555 or (631) 854-5579.

CHATEAUGAY (A-10) pop. 798, elev. 1,010′

HIGH FALLS PARK, 1 mi. w. on SR 11 to Cemetery Rd., following signs, features a 120-foot waterfall, which is reached by nature trails through a wooded area. Signs identify trees and plants; picnic facilities adjoin a playground. Daily 9-9, May 15-Sept. 30; 3-8, Oct. 1-15. Admission $2; over 64, students with ID and ages 6-11, $1. Phone (518) 497-3156.

CHAUTAUQUA (F-2) pop. 4,666, elev. 1,427′

A summer arts and education center bordering Chautauqua Lake, Chautauqua Institution is a secluded community whose population reaches as high as 7,500 during the summer. Victorian cottages line narrow wooded streets that slope down to the water. Boating, fishing and swimming are among the activities available at the lake.

Chautauqua County Visitors Bureau: P.O.Box 1441, Chautauqua, NY 14722; phone (800) 242-4569.

CHAUTAUQUA INSTITUTION is on SR 394. Founded in 1874 as an educational center for Sunday-school teachers, the institution has become known for its concept of presenting lectures and entertainment to large groups. Chautauqua Institution offers activities for all ages in the arts, education, religion and recreation, including symphony, opera, theater and dance. For further information contact Chautauqua Institution, Box 28, Chautauqua, NY 14722.

Lectures and popular entertainment are presented in the amphitheater June 26-Aug. 29. Daily gate ticket prices range between $11 and $36. AX, MC, VI. Phone (800) 836-2787.

CHAZY (A-11) pop. 4,181, elev. 151′

Chazy was founded in 1763 by Jean Fromboise. During the Revolution the British forces of Gen. John Burgoyne overran the area, and Fromboise was forced to flee. After the war Fromboise returned to Chazy, where he planted the region's first apple orchard. The McIntosh orchards in Chazy are some of the largest in the world.

DID YOU KNOW

Kingston, Poughkeepsie and New York City all served as the state's capital before the honor went to Albany in 1797.

Another notable area resident was William H. Miner, an 1800s railroad industrialist and philanthropist. One of his gifts to the town is the Miner Institute, an agricultural and environmental science center.

THE ALICE T. MINER MUSEUM is reached via I-87 exit 41, 1 mi. e. on US 191, then .5 mi. s. on US 9 to 9618 Main St. The Colonial Revival gray stone house museum contains collections primarily from the 18th and 19th centuries. Included are prints, paintings, porcelain, glass, carpets, furniture and textiles. Allow 1 hour, 30 minutes minimum. Guided tours are given Tues.-Sat. at 10, 11:30, 1 and 2:30, Feb. 1-Dec. 22. Fee $3; over 61, $2; students with ID $1; under 5 free. Phone (518) 846-7336.

CHERRY VALLEY (E-9)

pop. 592, elev. 1,326′

Settled in 1740, Cherry Valley was an important stagecoach stop on the Cherry Valley Turnpike, now US 20. A large stone monument in the village cemetery commemorates the victims of the Massacre of 1778, when 700 American Indians and Tories killed or captured most of the residents.

[SAVE] **CHERRY VALLEY MUSEUM,** 49 Main St., exhibits household articles, Civil War and Revolutionary War memorabilia, books and documents, pumpers, clothing and farm implements. Allow 1 hour minimum. Daily 10-5, Memorial Day weekend-Oct. 15; by appointment rest of year. Admission $3; over 59, $2.50; under 11 free with an adult. Phone (607) 264-3303 or (607) 264-3098.

CHILDS (D-4)

COBBLESTONE SOCIETY MUSEUM is at jct. SRs 104 and 98 at 14393 Ridge Rd. This collection of seven historic buildings includes three cobblestone structures: an 1834 church, an 1840 parsonage once owned by Horace Greeley and a one-room schoolhouse built in 1849. Four frame buildings house blacksmith, harness and print shops as well as 19th- and 20th-century farming tools and implements.

Guided tours are available. Allow 1 hour, 30 minutes minimum. Tues.-Sat. 11-5, Sun. 1-5, June 23-Labor Day; Sun. 1-5, day after Labor Day-Oct. 31. Admission $3.50; over 54, $3; ages 5-17, $2. Phone (585) 589-9013.

CLAYTON (B-7) pop. 1,821, elev. 276′

The Thousand Islands extend more than 10 miles above and below the village of Clayton on the St. Lawrence River. The Handweaving and Arts Center offers workshops in folk arts and crafts.

Clayton Area Chamber of Commerce: 510 Riverside Dr., Clayton, NY 13624; phone (315) 686-3771 or (800) 252-9806.

[SAVE] **ANTIQUE BOAT MUSEUM** is 6 mi. s.w. of 1000 Islands Bridge (I-81) on SR 12N at 750 Mary St. This collection of freshwater wooden boats includes American Indian dugout and birch bark canoes, St. Lawrence skiffs and early 20th-century speedboats, launches and pleasure craft. Featured are the *Dixie II,* the *Miss Canada III* and other Gold Cup boats along with the personal boats of Presidents Ulysses S. Grant and James Garfield. Boat rides are available.

Allow 1 hour, 30 minutes minimum. Daily 9-5, early May-early Oct.; hours vary rest of year. Admission $8; over 54 and military with ID $7; students with ID $6; ages 6-17, $4. MC, VI. Phone (315) 686-4104.

[SAVE] **THE THOUSAND ISLANDS MUSEUM** is at 312 James St. Life along the St. Lawrence River is depicted through historical artifacts, antiques and exhibits about hunting, fishing and commerce. Among the displays are record muskies and award-winning decoys. Daily 10-4, mid-May to mid-Oct. Admission $2, students with ID $1, under 6 free. Phone (315) 686-5794.

[SAVE] *UNCLE SAM* BOAT TOURS depart from the Riverside Dr. dock. Three-hour narrated Seaway Island tours aboard double- and triple-deck boats are offered. Cruises include an optional stop at Boldt Castle *(see Alexandria Bay p. 60).* Tours depart daily at 9:30, 12:30 and 3:30, July-Aug. Fare $16; ages 4-12, $8. Fare does not include admission to Boldt Castle. DS, MC, VI. Phone (315) 686-3511 or (800) 253-9229 for departure times.

COLD SPRING HARBOR (H-3)

pop. 4,975, elev. 100′

COLD SPRING HARBOR WHALING MUSEUM, on Main St. (SR 25A), offers self-guiding tours and audio cassette tapes that tell the story of the whaling industry and its impact on the area. Displays include a fully equipped whaleboat, whaling implements, marine paintings, ship models and a diorama depicting 1850 Cold Spring Harbor. Changing exhibits and a family activity room also are offered. Daily 11-5, Memorial Day-Labor Day; Tues.-Sun. 11-5, rest of year. Admission $3; over 64, $2; ages 5-18, $1.50. Phone (631) 367-3418.

CONSTABLEVILLE (D-8) pop. 305

CONSTABLE HALL, .5 mi. e. of SR 26, is an 1819 Georgian mansion. The house contains original furnishings, artifacts and a library. The grounds include a garden. Allow 1 hour minimum. Guided tours Tues.-Sat. and Mon. holidays 10-4, Sun. 1-4, June 1-Oct. 15. Admission $3; ages 6-13, $1.50. Phone (315) 397-2323.

Everything you need to travel. Including this handy bookmark.

Book in advance and as a AAA/CAA member you'll always save at Choice hotels.* Plus, it's easy to earn nights or flights with our reward programs at any of our over 3,000 locations across the U.S. Just visit your local AAA/CAA office or call 800.228.1AAA to book your next stay.

CHOICE HOTELS
INTERNATIONAL ®

**choicehotels.com
800.228.1AAA**

The Power of Being There. **Go** ®
CHOICE HOTELS INTERNATIONAL

Call us at 800.228.1AAA or visit us on the Web at choicehotels.com for more information and reservations.
©2003 Choice Hotels International, Inc. All rights reserved.

Lodging Listing Symbols

Member Values
(see pg. 14)

- (AAA) Official Appointment
- [SAVE] Offers minimum 10% discount
- [SAVE] SYC&S chain partners
- [ASK] May offer discount
- [S$] Offers senior discount
- [fyi] Informational listing only

Member Services

- Airport transportation
- Pets allowed
- Restaurant on premises
- Restaurant off premises (walking distance)
- 24-hour room service
- Cocktail lounge
- Child care

Accessibility Features
(see pg. 18)

- Accessibility features
- Roll-in showers
- Hearing impaired

Leisure Activities

- Full Service Casino
- Pool
- Health Club on premises
- Health Club off premises
- Recreational activities

In-Room Amenities

- Non-smoking rooms
- No air conditioning
- No TV
- No Cable TV
- VCR
- Movies
- Data port/modem line
- No telephones
- Refrigerator
- Microwave
- Coffee maker

Call property for detailed information about fees & restrictions relating to the lodging listing symbols.

CHOICE HOTELS
INTERNATIONAL®

Your trip across America starts here.

CHOICE HOTELS
INTERNATIONAL®

choicehotels.com
800.228.1AAA

COOPERSTOWN (F-8)
pop. 2,032, elev. 1,270′

Cooperstown was founded in 1786 by Judge William Cooper, father of James Fenimore Cooper, who wrote "The Last of the Mohicans" and other tales. Nine-mile-long Otsego Lake, set among hills and forests, is the "Glimmerglass" of Cooper's stories. The original appearances of many of the town's picturesque buildings and houses have been carefully maintained.

Another renowned Cooperstown resident was Gen. Abner Doubleday, who, by official decree of the National Baseball Commission in 1908, was credited with founding the game of baseball in 1839 while a student at a military academy. However, more recent research indicates that credit also is due to the man who devised the playing field and many of the rules, New York City resident Alexander Joy Cartwright.

Cooperstown Chamber of Commerce: 31 Chestnut St., Cooperstown, NY 13326; phone (607) 547-9983.

BREWERY OMMEGANG is at 656 CR 33. In the 19th century, 80 percent of all hops grown in America came from Otsego County. Tours of this farmstead brewery cover the history of hops and the process of making traditional Belgian beers, from recipes to fermentation to cellaring. Tastings are offered. Allow 1 hour minimum. Mon.-Fri. noon-7, Sat.-Sun. 11-7, late May-early Sept.; daily noon-5, rest of year. Closed Jan. 1, Thanksgiving and Dec. 25. Admission $4. MC, VI. Phone (607) 544-1800 or (800) 544-1809.

THE FARMERS' MUSEUM, 1 mi. n. on Lake Rd. (SR 80), is a living-history museum on land owned and farmed by James Fenimore Cooper 1813-29. Craftspersons demonstrate commercial trades and domestic skills in the restored buildings of an 1845 village, which includes a general store, blacksmith shop, pharmacy, tavern and wallpaper manufactory. Formal, kitchen and medicinal herb gardens accent the grounds.

Of particular interest is a working farmstead with oxen and heritage breeds of chickens and cows. Structures include a farmhouse, animal sheds, a smokehouse and a 1918 dairy barn that features changing exhibits with rural life themes. Interpreters at the Iroquois log house, a restored dwelling from the Seneca Tonawanda Reservation, demonstrate American Indian life, culture and history.

Food is available. Allow 2 hours minimum. Daily 10-5, May 18-Oct. 11; Tues.-Sun. 10-4, Oct. 12-31; Tues.-Sat. 10-4, Apr. 1-May 17. Admission $9; over 64, $8; ages 7-12, $4. Combination tickets with Fenimore Art Museum and/or National Baseball Hall of Fame and Museum are available. AX, DS, MC, VI. Phone (607) 547-1450, or (607) 547-1500 for recorded information, or (888) 547-1450. *See color ad p. 270.*

Combination Tickets

Individual admission and combination tickets are available for The Farmers' Museum, Fenimore Art Museum and the National Baseball Hall of Fame and Museum *(see attraction listings).*

Combination admission for all attractions $22; ages 7-12, $9.50. National Baseball Hall of Fame and Museum and either The Farmers' Museum or Fenimore Art Museum $15; ages 7-12, $6.50. Fenimore Art Museum and The Farmers' Museum $14.50; ages 7-12, $6.50. Phone (607) 547-1400.

Digital Archives

DID YOU KNOW

The American symbol "Uncle Sam" comes from the label "U.S." stamped on barrels of beef being shipped to troops by a Troy, N.Y., meat packer during the War of 1812.

FENIMORE ART MUSEUM is 1 mi. n. on Lake Rd. (SR 80). This museum features fine collections of American art in a neo-Georgian structure with terraced gardens overlooking Otsego Lake. James Fenimore Cooper memorabilia, 19th-century American paintings, folk art, decorative art, historic photographs and changing exhibitions are presented.

Of particular interest are the Thaw Collection of North American Indian Art in the American Indian wing and the Mohawk Bark House, a reproduction of a late 18th-century Iroquois hunting and fishing camp. Special exhibits in 2004 cover such topics as the works of Winslow Homer, Victorian clothing, railroad photographs by O. Winston, the Girl Scouts centennial and the story of Geronimo.

Food is available. Daily 10-5, May 18-Oct. 11; Tues.-Sun. 10-4, Apr. 1-May 17 and Oct. 12-Dec. 31. Closed Thanksgiving and Dec. 25. Admission $9; over 64, $8; ages 7-12, $4. Combination tickets with The Farmers' Museum and/or National Baseball Hall of Fame and Museum are available. AX, DS, MC, VI. Phone (607) 547-1400, or (607) 547-1500 for recorded information, or (888) 547-1450. *See color ad p. 270.*

NATIONAL BASEBALL HALL OF FAME AND MUSEUM, 25 Main St., chronicles the history of baseball through photographs, artifacts, player memorabilia, sports ephemera and interactive terminals. Exhibits cover such topics as women in baseball and the World Series. The museum's centerpiece is a gallery with plaques representing Hall of Fame inductees.

Daily 9-9, Memorial Day weekend-Labor Day; 9-5, rest of year. Closed Jan. 1, Thanksgiving and Dec. 25. Admission $9.50; over 65, $8; ages 7-12, $4; military with ID free. A combination ticket with The Farmers' Museum and Fenimore Art Museum is available. AX, MC, VI. Phone (607) 547-7200 or (888) 425-5633. *See color ad p. 270.*

CORNING (G-5) pop. 10,842, elev. 938′

Corning, on a plateau divided by the Chemung River, traces its economic origins to the manufacture of glass. After the completion of the Chemung Canal in 1833, Erastus Corning of Albany bought real estate in the area and built a railroad from Pennsylvania to the canal. In 1868 the Flint Glass Co. of Brooklyn relocated to Corning and reorganized, selling two-fifths of the company to local residents. Home to the Corning Museum of Glass *(see attraction listing),* Corning is recognized as one of the world's glass centers.

Historic Market Street, the main commercial district, has been restored to its late 19th-century appearance and features tree-lined brick sidewalks, shops and restaurants. Visitors can watch glass making in progress at several galleries along Market Street. A shuttle bus provides transportation between Market

Street and the Corning Museum of Glass every 20 minutes. *Also see Finger Lakes p. 86.*

The Spence Crest Nature Center, off Denison Pkwy. on Powderhouse Rd., is situated on 200 acres of rolling wooded grounds and includes 7 miles of nature trails and interpretative displays. Opportunities for hiking, fishing, picnicking, cross-country skiing and snowshoeing are available; phone (607) 962-2169.

Greater Corning Area Chamber of Commerce: 1 W. Market St., Suite 302, Corning, NY 14830; phone (607) 936-4686.

CORNING MUSEUM OF GLASS, off I-86 exit 46 following signs to 1 Museum Way, is home to one of the world's most comprehensive glass collections, which spans 35 centuries of glassmaking. Galleries showcase pieces from around the world, while interactive exhibits tell of glass inventions and technology.

The Hot Glass Show, in a theater-style setting in the working glass factory, presents narrated glassblowing demonstrations by master glassblowers. Visitors can also watch artisans create miniature glass animals. Hands-on glass working sessions are offered for a fee.

Food is available. Allow 3 hours minimum. Daily 9-8, July 1-Labor Day; 9-5, rest of year. Closed Jan. 1, Thanksgiving and Dec. 24-25. Admission $12, under 18 free. AX, DS, MC, VI. Phone (800) 732-6845. *See color ad.*

THE CORNING-PAINTED POST HISTORICAL SOCIETY MUSEUM COMPLEX, 59 W. Pulteney St., is home to various restored building representing the area's history. The Benjamin Patterson Inn is a restored 1796 inn containing 19th-century furniture and crafts. The Browntown Schoolhouse retains the flavor of the late 19th century, and the 1860s Starr Barn contains an agricultural exhibit. The complex also features a blacksmith shop and a 1784 log cabin. Allow 1 hour minimum. Mon.-Fri. 10-4, mid-Mar. to mid-Dec.; closed major holidays. Admission $3.50; over 59, $3; ages 6-17, $1.50; family rate $10. Phone (607) 937-5281.

ROCKWELL MUSEUM OF WESTERN ART is at 111 Cedar St. in the Market Street Historic District. The museum displays a comprehensive collection of traditional and contemporary Western and Native American paintings and sculpture. Also included is a children's art trail. Until the 1970s, the Romanesque revival-style brick building served as Corning's city hall, fire station and jail.

Guided tours are available. Allow 1 hour minimum. Mon.-Sat. 9-8, Sun. 11-8, July 1-Labor Day; Mon.-Sat. 9-5, Sun. 11-5, rest of year. Closed Jan. 1, Thanksgiving and Dec. 24-25. Admission $6.50; over 59, $5.50; ages 6-17, $4.50; family rate $20. AX, DC, DS, MC, VI. Phone (607) 937-5386 to verify hours and prices.

WEST END GALLERY, 12 W. Market St., showcases original oils and watercolors by regional artists. Exhibits change every 6 to 8 weeks. Allow 30 minutes minimum. Mon.-Fri. 10-5:30 (also Thurs.-Fri. 5:30-8), Sat. 10-4, Sun. noon-5. Free. Phone (607) 936-2011.

CORNWALL-ON-HUDSON (H-10)
pop. 3,058, elev. 12'

MUSEUM OF THE HUDSON HIGHLANDS, .7 mi. s.w. off SR 218 on The Boulevard, is devoted to the natural and cultural history of the Hudson Valley. The natural history wing has live native animals; the Ogden Gallery presents changing art exhibits, films and lectures; and the central wing has changing exhibits. Nature trails traverse the 75-acre grounds. Thurs.-Sat. 10-4, Sun. noon-5; closed Jan. 1, Easter, July 4, Thanksgiving and Dec. 24-25 and 31. Admission $2. MC, VI. Phone (845) 534-5506.

CORTLAND (F-7) pop. 18,740, elev. 1,130'

Established in 1808, Cortland was named for Gen. Pierre Van Cortlandt, New York's first lieutenant governor. The Cortland Repertory Theatre presents five main-stage productions mid-June through August in the turn-of-the-20th-century Pavilion Theatre. The theater is in Dwyer Memorial Park on Little York Lake, 8 miles north on SR 281. Further information is available from the Cortland Repertory Theatre Business Office, 37 Franklin St., Cortland, NY 13045; phone (607) 756-2627.

Cortland County Convention and Visitors Bureau: 34 Tompkins St., Cortland, NY 13045; phone (607) 753-8463 or (800) 859-2227.

SAVE **THE 1890 HOUSE MUSEUM,** 1 blk. s.w. on SR 13 at 37 Tompkins St., is a Victorian mansion with period furnishings, cherry and oak woodwork, elaborate wall stenciling and stained glass. Tues.-Sun. 1-4; closed major holidays. Admission $4, senior citizens and students with ID $3, under 12 free. Phone (607) 756-7551.

COXSACKIE (F-11) pop. 2,895, elev. 139'

Named for an American Indian word meaning "hoot of an owl," Coxsackie was an exclusively Dutch settlement from the late 1600s until 1790, when other settlers arrived. In 1775, 225 of the villagers wrote and signed a declaration of independence protesting "arbitrary and oppressive acts of the British Parliament"—a year before their counterparts farther south drafted their own declaration.

The village, situated along the banks of the Hudson River, features Colonial and Victorian houses. Riverside Park offers a panorama of the Hudson River and the Berkshire Mountains.

SAVE **BRONCK MUSEUM** is off US 9W to Pieter Bronck Rd. Dutch Hudson Valley history is reflected in the main houses of stone and brick, the oldest dating from 1663. Buildings include a New World Dutch barn and a 13-sided barn. Allow 1

hour minimum. Wed.-Fri. noon-4, Sat. and Mon. holidays 10-4, Sun. 1-4, Memorial Day-Oct. 15. Last admission is at 3:30. Admission $4; ages 12-15, $2; ages 5-11, $1.50. Phone (518) 731-6490.

CROGHAN (C-8) pop. 665, elev. 847'

SAVE **AMERICAN MAPLE MUSEUM,** on Main St. (SR 812), illustrates the history of maple production through displays of lumbering and syrupmaking equipment. The museum also contains the Maple Industry Hall of Fame. Mon.-Sat. 11-4, July 1-Labor Day; Fri.-Sat. and Mon. 11-4, mid-May through June 30 and day after Labor Day-early Oct. Phone to verify schedule. Admission $4; ages 5-14, $1; family rate $10. Phone (315) 346-1107.

CROSS RIVER—see New York p. 150.

CROTON-ON-HUDSON—
see New York p. 150.

CROWN POINT (C-11) pop. 2,119, elev. 126'

CHAMPLAIN MEMORIAL LIGHTHOUSE is 7.5 mi. n.e. following SR 9N/22, then e. on CR 903 to the New York end of the Lake Champlain Bridge. The original light station was constructed in 1858. A new light and memorial were erected by Vermont and New York in 1912 to honor Samuel de Champlain, who discovered the lake in 1609. The bas-relief "La Belle France" by Auguste Rodin was a gift from France.

Picnicking and camping are permitted. Allow 30 minutes minimum. Mon.-Fri. 10-4, Memorial Day-Labor Day (weather permitting). Admission $4. Phone (518) 597-3603.

CROWN POINT STATE HISTORIC SITE is 7.5 mi. n.e. at the New York end of the Lake Champlain Bridge. The site contains the preserved ruins of fortifications occupied during the French and Indian and Revolutionary wars. A museum has history and archeology exhibits that focus on the 1734 French Fort St. Frederic and the 1759 British Fort Crown Point. An orientation film is offered.

Allow 2 hours minimum. Grounds open daily dawn-dusk, May-Oct. Museum open Wed.-Mon. 9-5. Grounds admission Sat.-Sun. and holidays $5. Museum admission $3; senior citizens and students with ID, $2; ages 6-12, $1. Phone (518) 597-3666.

PENFIELD HOMESTEAD MUSEUM, off I-87 exit 28, 12 mi. e. on SR 74, then 3 mi. n. on Corduroy Rd. (CR 2), is a complex of 19th-century buildings in the Ironville Historic District. Structures include the 1827 home of Allen Penfield and ruins of the Crown Point Iron Co. works, reputedly the first industrial operation to use electricity. The house museum has displays about iron mining, the Civil War and 19th-century residents. Allow 2 hours minimum. Thurs.-Sun. 10-4, July-Aug.; Thurs.-Sat. 10-4, May 15-June 30 and Sept. 1-Oct. 15. Admission $4; under 6, $2. Phone (518) 597-3804.

CUDDEBACKVILLE (H-9)

SAVE **NEVERSINK VALLEY AREA MUSEUM** is at 26 Hoag Rd. in the D&H Canal Park. Within a 300-acre historical park that includes a 1-mile portion of the D&H Canal, the museum contains exhibits and photographs as well as miniature replicas and artifacts pertaining to area history and the canal's importance to community development. A self-guiding canal walking tour is available. Allow 1 hour, 30 minutes minimum. Wed.-Sun. noon-4, Apr.-Nov. Admission $3; ages 6-17, $1.50. Phone (845) 754-8870.

CUTCHOGUE (H-5) pop. 2,849, elev. 40'

The Corchaug Indian word Cutchogue means "it splits off land." The Old House, built in 1649, was moved to Cutchogue's Village Green in 1661 from nearby Southold. Exposed sections inside show construction features. Also on the Village Green are the 1700 Wickham Farmhouse and the 1840 Old Schoolhouse. *Also see Long Island p. 101.*

Cutchogue-New Suffolk Chamber of Commerce: P.O. Box 610, Cutchogue, NY 11935; phone (631) 734-2335.

WINERIES

• **Castello di Borghese/Hargrave Vineyard**, on North Country Rd. (CR 48) at Alwah's Ln. Sun.-Thurs. 11-5, Fri.-Sat. 11-6. Phone (631) 734-5111 or (800) 734-5158.

DARIEN CENTER (E-4) elev. 931'

GEM SAVE **SIX FLAGS DARIEN LAKE** is 6 mi. s. of I-90 exit 48A on SR 77 at 9993 Allegheny Rd. This entertainment complex features more than 100 rides, live shows and attractions with five roller coasters, including Superman-Ride of Steel, one of the Northeast's tallest coasters. Highlights also include Looney Tunes Seaport kids area, Batman Thrill Spectacular stunt show, and Hook's Lagoon water park. National recording artists appear throughout the season at the 20,000-seat Darien Lake Performing Arts Center. Also on the grounds are camping facilities.

Food is available. Park opens at 10:30, May-Oct. Days of operation and closing times vary; phone ahead. Admission $31.99, under 49 inches tall $19.99, senior citizens $18.99, under age 3 free. Admission $18.99 after 5 p.m. (all ages). Parking $7. AAA members save 10 percent on select in-park dining and merchandise. Check at the park's Guest Relations window for details. AX, DS, MC, VI. Phone (585) 599-4641.

DELHI (F-9) pop. 2,583, elev. 1,360'

SAVE **DELAWARE COUNTY HISTORICAL ASSOCIATION**, 2.5 mi. n.e. on SR 10, features seven historic buildings. Included are the 1797 Frisbee House and a barn, schoolhouse, blacksmith shop, 19th-century gun shop and turnpike tollhouse as well as the Christian Church at Fitch's Bridge.

Changing art and history exhibits are shown in two galleries. The complex also houses a research library. A half-mile nature trail is available.

Picnicking is permitted. Allow 1 hour minimum. Galleries open Tues.-Sun. 11-4, Memorial Day-Oct. 15; Mon.-Fri. 11-4, rest of year. Museum open Tues.-Sun. 11-4, Memorial Day-Oct. 15. Admission $3; under 12, $1.50. Phone (607) 746-3849.

DERBY — *see Buffalo p. 73*

DUNDEE (F-5) pop. 1,690, elev. 994'

WINERIES

• **Glenora Wine Cellars**, on SR 14. Daily 10-8, July-Aug.; daily 10-6, May-June and Sept.-Oct.; Mon.-Sat. 10-5, Sun. noon-5, rest of year. Closed Jan. 1, Easter, Thanksgiving and Dec. 25. Phone (800) 243-5513.

DUNKIRK (F-2) pop. 13,131, elev. 613'

Founded as Chadwick's Bay in 1805, Dunkirk was renamed in 1817 because its harbor was said to resemble that of Dunkerque, France. On Thanksgiving 1946 the citizens of Dunkirk aided their war-impoverished namesake with a shipment of more than $100,000 worth of emergency supplies.

Dunkirk's harbor, which has been a key factor in the town's commercial growth, offers numerous recreational opportunities, including fishing, boating, swimming and water skiing. Lake Erie State Park is 7 miles west *(see Recreation Chart)*. The Lily Dale Assembly, 8 miles south of US 90 exit 59, offers a diversified summer program of lectures and workshops about spiritualism.

Northern Chautauqua Chamber of Commerce: 212 Lake Shore Dr. W., Dunkirk, NY 14048; phone (716) 366-6200.

DUNKIRK HISTORICAL LIGHTHOUSE AND VETERANS PARK MUSEUM is n. on Lighthouse Point Dr. off SR 5. The lighthouse was built in 1875 on the site of the first Point Gratiot lighthouse, established in 1826. The museum, housed in the keeper's quarters, displays armed services and war memorabilia as well as exhibits related to the lighthouse and its keepers. Also on the grounds is a Coast Guard and submarine exhibit room.

Allow 1 hour minimum. Mon.-Tues. and Thurs.-Sat. 10-4, July-Aug.; Mon.-Tues. and Thurs.-Sat. 10-2, late Apr.-June 30 and Sept.-Oct. Museum and grounds $5; ages 4-12, $2. Grounds $1. Phone (716) 366-5050.

DUNKIRK HISTORICAL MUSEUM, .5 mi. s. of SR 5 at 513 Washington Ave., contains permanent and changing exhibits about local businesses, schools and veterans as well as paintings by local artists. In addition to the displays, the museum offers a small library and information about local attractions. Allow 30 minutes minimum. Mon.-Fri.

noon-4 and by appointment; closed holidays. Donations. Phone (716) 366-3797.

WINERIES

- **Woodbury Vineyards Winery**, .5 mi. s. off I-90 exit 59, 1 mi. e. on US 20, then 1 mi. s. on Roberts Rd. Daily 9-7, late June-Labor Day; Mon.-Sat. 9-5, Sun. noon-5, rest of year. Closed major holidays. Phone (716) 679-9463.

EAST AURORA—*see Buffalo p. 74.*

EAST DURHAM (F-10)

[SAVE] **IRISH AMERICAN HERITAGE MUSEUM**, on SR 145, has changing exhibits about Irish-American culture and history. A 7-minute film providing background information about the museum and an audiovisual reading library for research purposes also are available. Allow 1 hour minimum. Wed.-Sun. noon-4, Memorial Day-Labor Day. Admission $3.50; over 64, students with ID and under 12, $2; family rate $9. Phone (518) 634-7497 June-Sept. or (518) 432-6598 rest of year.

EAST HAMPTON (H-6) pop. 1,334, elev. 55′

This section of Long Island's south shore has many fashionable summer colonies and estates. The Clinton Academy, the first chartered academy in the state, has changing local history exhibits; phone (631) 324-1850. *Also see Long Island p. 101.*

East Hampton Chamber of Commerce: 79A Main St., East Hampton, NY 11937; phone (631) 324-0362.

EAST HAMPTON TOWN MARINE MUSEUM— *see Amagansett p. 61.*

GUILD HALL OF EAST HAMPTON, 158 Main St., is a cultural center with changing art exhibits, theater presentations and educational programs. Mon.-Sat. 11-5, Sun. noon-5, Memorial Day-Labor Day; Wed.-Sat. 11-5, Sun. noon-5, rest of year. Admission $5, senior citizens $4. Phone (631) 324-0806.

"HOME SWEET HOME" is across the village green from SR 27 at 14 James Ln. Dedicated to the memory of playwright, actor and diplomat John Howard Payne, who wrote the song "Home Sweet Home," the house contains 17th- and 18th-century furniture and a collection of English ceramics and lusterware. An herb garden and the 1804 Pantigo Windmill also are on the grounds. A garden with period plantings surrounds the house. Allow 30 minutes minimum. Mon.-Sat. 10-4, Sun. 2-4, Apr. 15-Sept. 30; Fri.-Sat. 10-4, Sun. 2-4, Oct.-Nov. Closed Thanksgiving. Admission $4; ages 2-12, $2. Phone (631) 324-0713.

THE MULFORD FARMHOUSE, across the village green from SR 27 at 10 James Ln., is a 4-acre site that preserves the original 17th-century settlement of Maidstone. Highlights include decorative arts exhibits, information about East Hampton's architectural styles and tours by costumed interpreters.

Daily 10-5, June-Aug. Admission $4, senior citizens $2. Phone (631) 324-6869.

EAST MEREDITH (F-9) elev. 1,353′

[SAVE] **HANFORD MILLS MUSEUM**, on CRs 10 and 12, is a restored 19th-century water- and steam-powered milling and industrial complex. Exhibits and demonstrations are featured at the sawmill and gristmill. Other buildings include a feed mill, barn, hardware store, wagon and lumber shed and restored farmhouse. Guided tours are available. Allow 1 hour minimum. Daily 10-5, May-Oct. Admission $6; ages 6-12, $3. MC, VI. Phone (607) 278-5744 or (800) 295-4992.

EASTPORT (I-5) pop. 1,454, elev. 25′

SHRINE OF OUR LADY OF THE ISLAND is midway between Long Island Expwy. (I-495) exit 70 and Sunrise Hwy. (SR 27) exit 61 on Eastport Manor Rd. The 70-acre site includes wooded walkways, the stations of the cross, gardens, statues and chapels. Picnicking is permitted. Grounds open daily 24 hours. Chapels open daily 9:30-4. Free. Phone (631) 325-0661.

EDEN—*see Buffalo p. 74.*

ELDRED (H-9) elev. 1,000′

On the edge of the Catskills, Eldred is home to the Eldred WWII Museum at 201 Main St. Dedicated to preserving the history of the war, the museum contains various displays and offers a videotape presentation. For additional information phone (814) 225-2220.

ELIZABETHTOWN (B-11) pop. 1,315, elev. 550′

One of the most picturesque drives in northern New York is US 9, which extends south through the Boquet River Valley.

[SAVE] **ADIRONDACK HISTORY CENTER**, 7590 Court St., offers displays covering such topics as pioneer settlement, wilderness exploration, transportation and the local community. The center also has a forest fire observation tower and a formal garden. Allow 1 hour minimum. Mon.-Sat. 9-5, Sun. 1-5, Memorial Day weekend-Columbus Day. Admission $3.50; over 59, $2.50; ages 6-18, $1.50. Phone (518) 873-6466.

ELLICOTTVILLE (F-3) pop. 472, elev. 1,549′

In winter Ellicottville's snow-festooned evergreens lure skiing enthusiasts. The 60,398 acres of nearby Allegany State Park *(see Recreation Chart and the AAA Northeastern CampBook)* provide cold-weather devotees with opportunities for cross-country skiing, snowmobiling and ice fishing, while those who prefer the summer sunshine can hike, bike, fish, swim, camp and ride horseback.

For an unusual site, view a herd of buffaloes on the hill adjacent to the ski slopes at the B&B Buffalo Ranch on Horn Hill Road.

Ellicottville Chamber of Commerce: P.O. Box 456, Ellicottville, NY 14731; phone (716) 699-5046 or (800) 349-9099.

Shopping areas: Washington Street is home to various antiques and specialty shops.

RECREATIONAL ACTIVITIES

Skiing

• **Holiday Valley Resort,** s. on US 219. Write Holiday Valley Rd., Ellicottville, NY 14731. Other activities are available. Mon.-Thurs. 9 a.m.-10 p.m., Fri.-Sun. 8:30 a.m.-10:30 p.m., late Nov.-Easter (weather permitting). Phone (716) 699-2345.

ELMIRA (G-6) pop. 30,940, elev. 854′

Nine years after the decisive 1779 battle of New-town, the first permanent settlers built their cabins on the site that is now Elmira. According to local tradition, the city was named after a neighborhood child who wandered into an 1808 meeting where local politicians were trying to decide on a town name.

Samuel Clemens, better known as Mark Twain, married Elmira native Olivia Langdon in 1870; thereafter the Clemens family spent its summers at Olivia's sister's farm. It was in Elmira that Twain wrote "The Adventures of Huckleberry Finn" and other classic works.

Woodlawn National Cemetery contains more than 3,000 graves of Confederate soldiers who died in the local prisoner of war camp. Year-round entertainment is available at the Clemens Performing Arts Center at Clemens Center Parkway and Gray Street.

From early July through late August the Trolley Into Mark Twain Country travels past historic and architectural points of interest; phone the chamber of commerce for more information. Sailplane rides are available from Schweizer Soaring School at the Elmira-Corning Regional Airport and from Harris Hill Soaring Corporation *(see attraction listing).* Also see Finger Lakes p. 86.

Chemung County Chamber of Commerce: 400 E. Church St., Elmira, NY 14901; phone (607) 734-5137 or (800) 627-5892.

Self-guiding tours: Maps and brochures outlining a self-guiding tour of the Near Westside historic neighborhood are available from the chamber of commerce; phone (607) 733-4924.

Shopping areas: Arnot Mall, exit 51 off SR 17 between Elmira and Corning, has 117 stores, including The Bon-Ton, JCPenney, Kaufmans and Sears.

[SAVE] **ARNOT ART MUSEUM** is at 235 Lake St. Housed in an 1833 Greek Revival mansion, the museum's collections include 17th-, 18- and 19th-century Dutch, Flemish, French and German paintings as well as 19th- and 20th-century American art and sculpture. Noteworthy is the museum's collection of contemporary realism. Allow 30 minutes minimum. Tues.-Sat. 10-5, Sun. 1-5; closed major holidays. Admission $5; over 60 and students with ID $4.50; ages 6-12, $2.50; family rate $12.50; free to all Sat.-Sun. Phone (607) 734-3697.

[SAVE] **CHEMUNG VALLEY HISTORY MUSEUM,** 415 E. Water St., contains regional historical artifacts and information about Mark Twain and the Elmira Prison Camp. A research library is available. Allow 1 hour minimum. Museum Tues.-Sat. 10-5, Sun. 1-5. Library Mon.-Fri. noon-5. Closed holidays. Admission $2; senior citizens and ages 5-12, $1. Phone (607) 734-4167.

GRAVE OF MARK TWAIN, facing East Hill in Woodlawn Cemetery at the n. end of Walnut St., is identified by a monument that is 12 feet high or "mark twain." The expression, which Samuel Clemens adopted as his byline, refers to the 2-fathom (12-foot) water depth necessary for riverboats to pass through a river.

Clemens' son-in-law, the distinguished musician Ossip Gabrilowitsch, is buried at his request at Clemens' feet. Grave markers bear quotes from the author's works. Daily dawn-dusk. Free.

HARRIS HILL SOARING CORPORATION, I-86/SR 17 exit 51S, then w. on CR 64 in Harris Hill Park, features flights in modern high-performance sailplanes above the scenic Chemung Valley. Allow 1 hour minimum. Daily 10-6, June 15-Labor Day weekend; Sat.-Sun. 10-6, Apr. 1-June 14 and day after Labor Day-Oct. 31. Fare $65. MC, VI. Phone (607) 734-0641.

MARK TWAIN STUDY, on the Elmira College campus, is an octagonal study built in the form of a Mississippi riverboat pilothouse. A gift from Clemens' sister-in-law, the study once overlooked the city from atop East Hill and still contains some of its original furniture. Guided tours of the study and Hamilton Hall's Mark Twain exhibit are available. Mon.-Sat. 9-5, mid-June through Aug. 31; by appointment rest of year. Free. Phone (607) 735-1941.

[SAVE] **NATIONAL SOARING MUSEUM** is off I-86/SR 17 exit 51 following signs to Harris Hill Park. Featured is a collection of gliders and sailplanes. Interactive exhibits include a computerized flight simulator lab and a full-size glider simulator. Allow 1 hour minimum. Daily 10-5; closed Jan. 1, Thanksgiving and Dec. 24-25. Admission $6; over 60, $5; college students with ID and ages 6-17, $4. AX, DS, MC, VI. Phone (607) 734-3128.

SULLIVAN'S MONUMENT AT NEWTOWN BATTLEFIELD, 3 mi. e. on I-86/SR 17, was the site of a Revolutionary War campaign staged by Gen. John Sullivan and Brig. Gen. James Clinton. Occasional battle re-enactments are presented throughout the year. Hiking and biking trails are available as well as campsites, cabins, playgrounds and picnic areas. Allow 30 minutes minimum. Daily 10-dusk, Fri. before Memorial Day-Columbus Day. Free. Phone (607) 732-6067.

FINGER LAKES

American Indian folklore holds that the Finger Lakes were formed when God placed his handprint on some of the most beautiful land ever created. There are actually 11 finger-shaped lakes beginning just east of I-390 and extending east almost to I-81 south of Syracuse; the northern boundary straddles I-90, with I-86 and SR 17 defining the southern edge.

The lakes are named for the tribes of the Six Nations of the Iroquois: the Cayugas, Mohawks, Onondagas, Oneidas, Senecas and Tuscaroras. SRs 14 and 89, which parallel the western shores of Seneca and Cayuga lakes, respectively, are major north-south routes cutting through the center of the region. Seneca and Cayuga are the largest lakes. Boating, fishing and swimming are popular area recreational pastimes.

Information about regional attractions can be found in place listings for Auburn, Branchport, Canandaigua, Corning, Elmira, Geneva, Hammondsport, Horseheads, Ithaca, Lodi, Montour Falls, Moravia, Naples, Palmyra, Seneca Falls, Skaneateles and Watkins Glen.

FINGER LAKES NATIONAL FOREST (F-6)

Elevations in the forest range from 1,400 ft. at the southeast corner near Reynoldsville to 1,860 ft. at Hector Backbone. Refer to AAA maps for additional elevation information.

Finger Lakes National Forest lies on a ridge between Seneca and Cayuga lakes, via I-90, I-81 and SR 17. New York's only national forest was officially designated as such in October 1985. The forest comprises just 16,000 acres and is one of the country's smallest national forests.

More than one-third of the land provides pasture for beef and dairy cattle. The remaining area is used for camping, hiking on the 33-mile trail system, horseback riding, fishing and hunting. Midsummer draws blueberry pickers, and winter attracts cross-country skiers and snowmobilers to the gently rolling hillsides. The Forest Service office is about 9 miles north of Watkins Glen on SR 414; the office is open weekdays 8-4:30. Free.

For further information contact the District Ranger, Finger Lakes National Forest, 5218 SR 414, Hector, NY 14841. Phone (607) 546-4470. *See Recreation Chart.*

FIRE ISLAND NATIONAL SEASHORE (I-4)

Fire Island National Seashore encompasses most of the lands between Robert Moses State Park *(see attraction listing)* and Smith Point County Park off the south shore of Long Island. Low shrubs and beach grass along the Atlantic shore protect sand from erosion; in sheltered portions, high thickets and groves of pitch pine are common.

Wildlife is abundant along the seashore. Anglers can find bass, blowfish, bluefish, fluke, mackerel, weakfish and winter flounder. Waterfowl are numerous October through March; white-tailed deer, red foxes and rabbits also can be seen.

The seashore is accessible by car near its eastern end at Smith Point County Park, via the Robert Moses Causeway from the west or by mainland ferry service that leaves Bay Shore, Sayville and Patchogue in summer. A visitor center at Smith Point West next to Smith Point County Park has exhibits and visitor information; a ranger is on duty year-round. A national wilderness area extends west for 7 miles.

The lightkeeper's quarters of the mid-19th-century Fire Island Lighthouse is a visitor center with exhibits about the history of the site. To reach the lighthouse, park at the east end of Robert Moses State Park and walk about a quarter-mile over a dirt trail. Physically impaired persons can park at the lighthouse; phone (631) 289-4810.

Sailors Haven, 1 mile west of the private community of Cherry Grove, offers a marina, beach and picnic areas. A self-guiding nature trail leads through the Sunken Forest. Access to Sailors Haven is by boat or walk-on ferry from Sayville; phone (631) 589-0810. Round-trip fare is $9; ages 2-11, $5. Visitor services are offered during the summer.

The William Floyd Estate is at 245 Park Dr. in Mastic Beach. The preserved house of one of the signers of the Declaration of Independence reflects the changes in styles during the 250 years of Floyd family ownership. Guided house tours and self-guiding grounds tours are available; phone (631) 399-2030.

For further information contact the Superintendent, Fire Island National Seashore, 120 Laurel St., Patchogue, Long Island, NY 11772. Phone (631) 289-4810. *See Recreation Chart and the AAA Northeastern CampBook. Also see Long Island p. 101.*

ROBERT MOSES STATE PARK is on the w. end of Fire Island on the Atlantic Ocean, accessible via the Robert Moses Cswy. from the Long Island Expwy. or the Southern State Pkwy. Recreational facilities include a pitch-and-putt golf course, boat anchorages, a fishing pier and bathhouses. Picnicking is permitted. Daily dawn-dusk, Memorial Day-Labor Day; Sat.-Sun. dawn-dusk, day after Labor Day-Oct. 31; 7-5:30, rest of year. Free. Parking $8, Memorial Day-Labor Day; $5, rest of year. Phone (631) 669-0449. *See Recreation Chart.*

FONDA (E-9) pop. 810, elev. 291'

THE NATIONAL SHRINE OF BLESSED KATERI TEKAKWITHA AND NATIVE AMERICAN EXHIBIT is .5 mi. w. on SR 5. The shrine honors the place where this American Indian girl was baptized and lived almost half her life. Also included is the 1663 Caughnawaga Indian village, an excavated and staked-out Iroquois village, and American Indian artifacts exhibits. Picnicking is permitted. Allow 2 hours minimum. Daily 9-7, May 1-Nov. 1. Donations. Phone (518) 853-3646.

FORESTVILLE (F-3) pop. 770, elev. 928'

WINERIES

• **Merritt Estate Winery**, 2264 King Rd. Mon.-Sat. 10-5, Sun. 1-5. Phone (888) 965-4800.

FORT EDWARD (D-11) pop. 3,141, elev. 144'

On the portage trail between the Hudson River and Lake Champlain, Fort Edward was fortified throughout the French and Indian and Revolutionary wars. During the Revolutionary War, local citizen Jane McCrea was murdered on the way to see her fiancé in the British Army. Her grave can be seen at Union Cemetery on Broadway.

Fort Edward Chamber of Commerce: P.O. Box 267, Fort Edward, NY 12828; phone (518) 747-3000.

[SAVE] **OLD FORT HOUSE MUSEUM**, .5 mi. s. on US 4 to 22-29 Lower Broadway, was built in 1772. A tavern and courthouse under British rule, it was the Revolutionary War headquarters for Gens. Philip Schuyler, John Burgoyne and John Stark. On the grounds are a 19th-century tollhouse and schoolhouse, the 1870 Washington County Fair building, a turn-of-the-20th-century water works building, a law office and a research center.

Allow 1 hour, 30 minutes minimum. Daily 1-4, June 1-Labor Day and the first Sat. in Dec.-Dec. 22; Sat.-Sun. 1-5, day after Labor Day to mid-Oct. Closed July 4. Admission $4, under 18 free. Phone (518) 747-9600.

FORT HUNTER (E-10)

Alongside the Erie Canal in Fort Hunter is Schoharie Crossing, a 3-mile nature trail with interpretive signage and picnic facilities.

Vestiges of the original Erie Canal locks, as well as structures from two other phases of canal construction, can be seen at Schoharie Crossing State Historic Site on Schoharie Street. The site preserves the six remaining arches from the Schoharie Aqueduct, built in the late 1830s to carry the Erie Canal over Schoharie Creek, as well as a restored 1850 canal store. A visitor center is open Wednesday through Sunday, the first Wednesday in May through the last weekend in October. The site also offers nature and bike trails; phone (518) 829-7516.

FORT JOHNSON (E-10) pop. 491

FORT JOHNSON is on SR 5 w. of SR 67. Sir William Johnson's 1749 fieldstone house was fortified during the French and Indian War and remains virtually unchanged. It contains original family furnishings, a rare 18th-century privy and artifacts reflecting Mohawk Valley history. Wed.-Sun. 1-5, May 15-Oct. 15. Admission $2, under 12 free. Phone (518) 843-0300.

FORT PLAIN (E-9) pop. 2,288, elev. 317'

FORT PLAIN MUSEUM, from jct. SRs 80 and 5S, w. on SR 5S to 389 Upper Canal St., is the site of a Revolutionary War fort that was the headquarters for the western defense. Exhibits include an extensive collection of American Indian artifacts, an Erie Canal room and information about area agriculture. Guided tours are available. Allow 1 hour minimum. Wed.-Sun. 1-4, mid-May through Labor Day; by appointment rest of year. Donations. Phone (518) 993-3419 for fort information or (518) 993-2527 for the museum.

[GEM] FORT STANWIX NATIONAL MONUMENT (D-8)

Off SR 26 in Rome, Fort Stanwix was built during the French and Indian War. In 1776, at the outbreak of the Revolution, the fort was repaired and restored by American rebels. Attacked by a force of British, Tories and American Indians in 1777, it successfully withstood a 3-week siege. The fort contains exhibits. Costumed interpreters re-enact 18th-century life in a military outpost. Open daily 9-5, Apr.-Dec.; closed Thanksgiving and Dec. 25. Free. Phone (315) 336-2090.

FORT TICONDEROGA (C-11)

SAVE Approximately 1 mile east of Ticonderoga on SR 74, Fort Ticonderoga was built in 1755 by the French, who named it Fort Carillon. Bordering Lake Champlain, the fort controlled the connecting waterway between Canada and the American Colonies. In 1758 the French successfully defended Fort Carillon against the British, but in 1759 British general Jeffery Amherst captured, rebuilt and renamed the fort.

Ethan Allen and his Green Mountain Boys, along with Benedict Arnold, took the fort in a bloodless surprise attack in 1775; the next year Arnold assembled the first American fleet and fought the Battle of Valcour Island on Lake Champlain. In 1777 Gen. John Burgoyne captured the fort for the British. It remained under British control for the remainder of the American Revolution.

Fort Ticonderoga has been restored on the original foundations according to the French plans. The museum contains collections of weapons, utensils, paintings and papers dealing with the Colonial and Revolutionary periods. A well-marked battleground surrounding the fort was the site of the British and Colonial defeat in 1758 by the French under the Marquis de Montcalm. Costumed interpreters give historical narratives.

Fort open daily 9-5, early May-late Oct. Cannon firings and fife-and-drum corps performances are offered July-Aug. Admission $12; over 60, $10.80; ages 7-12, $6. AX, MC, VI. Phone (518) 585-2821.

MOUNT DEFIANCE is 1 mi. s.e. off SR 22/74 via a blacktop road. British cannon mounted at this point forced Gen. Arthur St. Clair to surrender American-held Fort Ticonderoga in 1777. At an elevation of 853 feet, the overlook provides a panorama of Lake Champlain, the valley and the Green Mountains. Daily 9-5, early May to mid-Oct. Free. Phone (518) 585-2821.

FULTON (D-7) pop. 11,855, elev. 393′

Fulton lies along the Oswego River about 11 miles south of Lake Ontario. The town was founded in the late 18th century by Dutch settlers from the Hudson and Mohawk valleys.

In the 1820s the Oswego Canal opened, linking the Erie Canal and Lake Ontario and boosting Fulton's economy. Locks enabled boats to negotiate the falls of the Oswego River, which drop 14 feet, and a series of rapids to the north, which drop another 30 feet. An observation area in Canal Park overlooks the lower locks. Recreation Park, on Lake Neahtahwanta at the west end of town, offers sports facilities.

Exhibits related to Fulton's history can be seen at the Pratt House, 177 S. First St.; phone (315) 598-4616.

Greater Fulton Chamber of Commerce: 41 S. 2nd St., P.O. Box 148, Fulton, NY 13069; phone (315) 598-4231.

GARDEN CITY (I-2) pop. 21,672, elev. 88′

Near Garden City is Roosevelt Field, where Charles A. Lindbergh began his historic transatlantic flight in 1927. *Also see Long Island p. 101.*

Garden City Chamber of Commerce: 230 7th St., Garden City, NY 11530; phone (516) 746-7724.

Shopping areas: Roosevelt Field Shopping Center, off Meadowbrook Parkway exit M2W, is near Garden City. Among its 185 stores are JCPenney and Macy's.

CATHEDRAL OF THE INCARNATION (Episcopal), Cathedral Ave. at 6th St., is of 13th-century Gothic style. The 1885 church is noted for its hand-carved mahogany woodwork and rare marble. Mon.-Fri. 9:30-4, Sat.-Sun. 8-noon. Hours may vary; phone ahead. Free. Phone (516) 746-2955.

SAVE **CRADLE OF AVIATION MUSEUM,** 1 Davis Ave., features exhibits and more than 70 aircraft chronicling Long Island's role in civilian and military aviation history, from the first official air mail flight in 1911 to the Grumman plant's production of Apollo lunar modules in the 1960s. Charles Lindbergh flew from Roosevelt Field to Paris in 1927. IMAX films feature aviation themes. Allow 1 hour, 30 minutes minimum. Daily 10-5; closed Thanksgiving and Dec. 25. Admission $7; ages 2-14, $6. AX, MC, VI. Phone (516) 572-4111.

LONG ISLAND CHILDREN'S MUSEUM is at 11 Davis Ave. Through multimedia exhibits children are challenged to be creative while learning about a variety of topics including communications, music and the environment. Allow 2 hours minimum. Tues.-Sun. 10-5, July-Aug.; Wed.-Sun. and Mon. holidays 10-5, rest of year. Closed Jan. 1, Easter, Memorial Day, July 4, Labor Day, Thanksgiving and Dec. 24-25. Admission $8; over 65, $7. MC, VI. Phone (516) 224-5800.

GARRISON—see New York p. 150.

GATEWAY NATIONAL RECREATION AREA (I-2)

Comprising the Sandy Hook Unit in New Jersey and three units in New York City, Gateway National Recreation Area offers urban residents and visitors a chance to enjoy nature and the sea.

The Breezy Point Unit, on Rockaway Peninsula, includes Jacob Riis Beach, historic Fort Tilden and the westernmost point of the peninsula. The Jamaica Bay Unit includes Jamaica Bay Wildlife Refuge in Queens (*see New York p. 135*), Canarsie Pier, Plumb Beach and Floyd Bennett Field in Brooklyn. The Staten Island Unit consists of Great Kills Park and Miller Field. The Sandy Hook Unit in Highlands, N.J., includes a beach, a lighthouse and Fort Hancock.

Historical, educational, cultural and recreational events are presented throughout the year. The beaches are open daily, Memorial Day weekend-Labor Day. For further information contact the Public Affairs Office, Gateway National Recreation Area, Headquarters, Bldg. 69, Floyd Bennett Field, Brooklyn, NY 11234. Phone (718) 354-4606. *See Recreation Chart.*

GENEVA (E-6) pop. 13,617, elev. 671′

On Seneca Lake, largest of the Finger Lakes, Geneva is the center of a rich agricultural and nursery region. Nearby Seneca Lake State Park *(see Recreation Chart)* offers numerous types of aquatic recreation.

A local wine research and development center explores new ways of growing grapes and making wine. Numerous vineyards can be found in the area via a wine trail off I-90 exit 42.

The Geneva Historical Society Museum, 543 S. Main St. (SR 14) in the Prouty-Chew House, has permanent and changing exhibits about local history; phone (315) 789-5151. *Also see Finger Lakes p. 86.*

Geneva Area Chamber of Commerce: 35 Lakefront Dr., P.O. Box 587, Geneva, NY 14456; phone (315) 789-1776.

Self-guiding tours: A brochure outlining a self-guiding walking tour of Geneva's historic S. Main Street is available from the Geneva Historical Society.

Self-guiding walking tours of the Hobart and William Smith College campus are detailed in a brochure available at the Alumni House, 615 S. Main St.; phone (315) 781-3700.

THE MIKE WEAVER DRAIN TILE MUSEUM is on SR 96A at East Lake Rd., 1.5 mi. s. of jct. SR 5 and US 20; visitors should go to nearby Rose Hill Mansion for an escort to the museum. The museum displays 350 styles of drain tile dating from 100 B.C. to the present. Mon.-Sat. 10-3, Sun. 1-4, May-Oct. Admission $1. Phone (315) 789-3848 or (315) 789-5151.

ROSE HILL MANSION is 3 mi. e. on SR 96A, 1 mi. s. of jct. US 20/SR 5. This beautifully restored 1839 mansion on 30 acres of land overlooks Seneca Lake. Furnished in the Empire style of the period, the house is one of America's finest examples of Greek Revival architecture. Many furnishings are original to the Swan family, who occupied the mansion 1850-90. Twenty-one rooms are open to the public.

Guides provide detailed explanations of furnishings and demonstrations of how items of that period were used in daily life. Paint colors, wallpaper and textiles in the house are typical of the period, as is the extensive use of wall-to-wall carpeting. Allow 1 hour, 30 minutes minimum. Mon.-Sat. 10-4, Sun. 1-5, May-Oct. Admission $3; over 62 and ages 10-18, $2. Phone (315) 789-3848.

GERMANTOWN (G-11) pop. 862, elev. 11′

CLERMONT STATE HISTORIC SITE, 4 mi. s. on SR 9G, then 1 mi. w. on CR 6 following signs., comprises the 500-acre Hudson River estate of Chancellor Robert R. Livingston, delegate to the second Continental Congress and member of the committee to draft the Declaration of Independence. The original circa 1730 mansion was burned by the British in 1777 and rebuilt 1779-82. The grounds contain historical nature trails and restored formal gardens.

Grounds open daily 8:30-dusk. Visitor center open Tues.-Sun. and Mon. holidays 10:30-5, Apr.-Oct.; Sat.-Sun. 11-4, rest of year. Guided mansion tours are given every 30 minutes Tues.-Sun. and Mon. holidays 11-5, Apr.-Oct.; Sat.-Sun. 11-4, rest of year. Last tour begins 30 minutes before closing. Grounds admission (includes mansion tour) Sat.-Sun. and Mon. holidays $5, Mon.-Fri. free, Apr.-Oct.; free, rest of year. Mansion tour $5; senior citizens and students with ID $4; ages 5-12, $1. Phone (518) 537-4240.

GILBOA (F-10) pop. 1,215, elev. 960′

Off SR 342 just west of the Schoharie Creek bridge is a group of fossil tree stumps that represent the oldest known species of trees on Earth. Known as *eospermatopteris,* they were seed-bearing tree ferns that grew in the shore muds of an ancient Devonian sea west of the present Catskill Mountains. The fossils are identified by a historical marker.

GLEN COVE (H-2) pop. 26,622, elev. 115′

GARVIES POINT MUSEUM AND PRESERVE is n. on Glen Cove Rd. to the fire station, then following signs to 50 Barry Dr. This 62-acre preserve overlooking Hempstead Harbor has 5 miles of nature trails and a museum with regional archeology and geology exhibits as well as changing displays. Tues.-Sun. 10-4; closed Jan. 1 and Dec. 25. Admission $2; ages 4-14, $1. Phone (516) 571-8010.

GLENS FALLS (D-11) pop. 14,354, elev. 376′

Part of a land grant settled in 1759, Glens Falls grew up around the power-producing 60-foot falls on the Hudson River—a site known to the indigenous population as *Chepontuo,* "a difficult place to get around." The village was destroyed by the British in 1780 and resettled in 1788 by Col. John Glen. His mills established the town as an industrial center.

Adirondack Regional Chamber of Commerce: 5 Warren St., P.O. Box 158, Glens Falls, NY 12801; phone (518) 798-1761.

Shopping Areas: Aviation Mall, a quarter-mile east of I-87 exit 19, is a major local shopping center. Among its 80 stores are JCPenney and Sears. A series of factory outlet stores are located off I-87 exit 20.

CHAPMAN HISTORICAL MUSEUM, 348 Glen St., is in the restored, Victorian-era DeLong House.

Two exhibition galleries contain changing area history exhibits and Seneca Ray Stoddard's photographs of the Adirondacks. Tues.-Sat. 10-5; closed major holidays. Guided tours are given Tues.-Fri. 1-4, Sat. 10-4. Admission $2, senior citizens and students with ID $1, under 12 free. Phone (518) 793-2826.

THE HYDE COLLECTION ART MUSEUM is at 161 Warren St. The museum encompasses a furnished Florentine-style villa and three additional galleries. Exhibits include works of art by European and American masters from the 4th century B.C. to the 20th century.

Allow 1 hour, 30 minutes minimum. Tues.-Sat. 10-5 (also Thurs. 5-7), Sun. noon-5; closed national holidays. Guided tours are offered Tues.-Sun. 1-4. **Note:** The house will be closed for renovations until late spring. Galleries will remain open during this time. Free. Phone (518) 792-1761.

RECREATIONAL ACTIVITIES

Hot Air Ballooning

- SAVE **Adirondack Balloon Flights** depart near I-87 (Adirondack Northway) exit 19. Write P.O. Box 65, Glens Falls, NY 12801. Departures daily Apr.-Nov. Reservations are required. Phone (518) 793-6342.

GLOVERSVILLE (D-9) pop. 15,413, elev. 796'

FULTON COUNTY MUSEUM, 2.5 mi. w. of SR 30A at 237 Kingsboro Ave., offers historical displays with emphasis on the manufacture of leather and gloves, for which the city was named. Also exhibited are Victorian clothing, regional 19th-century folk art and memorabilia of the Sacandaga Amusement Park, which was flooded when the dam that created Great Sacandaga Lake was built. Allow 1 hour minimum. Tues.-Sat. 10-4, July-Aug.; Tues.-Sat. noon-4, May-June and in Sept. Donations. Phone (518) 725-2203.

DID YOU KNOW

Approximately one-third of all battles fought during the Revolutionary War were fought on New York soil.

GOSHEN (H-10) pop. 5,676, elev. 431'

The Goshen Public Library, (845) 294-6606, contains the signatures of Alexander Hamilton and Benedict Arnold among its historical artifacts. The collection and a genealogical library are available by appointment only.

The Historic Goshen Track is one of the oldest harness racetracks in the United States and the sporting world's first national historic landmark. Self-guiding walking tours of the barn and blacksmith shop are offered; phone (845) 294-5357.

Note: Policies concerning admittance of children to pari-mutuel betting facilities vary. Phone for information.

Chamber of Commerce of Orange County: 40 Matthews St., Suite 103, Goshen, NY 10924; phone (845) 294-8080.

HARNESS RACING MUSEUM & HALL OF FAME, 240 Main St., honors the sport of harness racing. The Tudor-style building, originally a stable, houses a collection of Currier & Ives trotting prints, a timeline tracing the sport's history, and trotting memorabilia and interactive exhibits. A 3-D simulator takes visitor for a ride. The Hall of Fame showcases the people and horses that have contributed to the sport. Allow 1 hour minimum. Daily 10-6; closed Jan. 1, Thanksgiving and Dec. 25. Admission $7.50; over 61, $6.50; ages 6-15, $3.50. AX, DS, MC, VI. Phone (845) 294-6330.

GRAND ISLAND—see Buffalo p. 74.

GRANVILLE (D-11) pop. 2,644, elev. 403'

SAVE **THE PEMBER MUSEUM OF NATURAL HISTORY,** 33 W. Main St., is a Victorian-period museum housing specimens of birds and mammals, rocks and minerals, shells, eggs and other objects related to natural history. Hiking trails are open year-round at the Pember Nature Preserve; trail maps are available at the museum. Programs and guided nature hikes are available by appointment. Allow 1 hour minimum. Tues.-Fri. 1-5, Sat. 10-3. Admission $2.50; senior citizens and under 18, $1. Phone (518) 642-1515.

GREAT LAKES-ST. LAWRENCE SEAWAY SYSTEM

Extending from the Atlantic Ocean to the headwaters of the Great Lakes, the Great Lakes-St. Lawrence Seaway System is a 2,342-mile marine highway. It was completed in 1959 as a joint venture between the United States and Canada. The United States dredged the Thousand Islands section and constructed the Wiley-Dondero Ship Channel and two locks with auxiliary facilities near Massena.

Canada built canals and four locks in territorial waters between Cornwall, Ontario, and Montréal, Québec; built a canal and lock at Iroquois, Ontario; and deepened channels of the Welland Canal. *For information about points of interest in the St. Lawrence Seaway area, see Alexandria Bay, Clayton, Massena, Ogdensburg and Thousand Islands pp. 60, 78, 102, 179 and 198.*

GREAT RIVER (I-3) pop. 1,546, elev. 21′

BAYARD CUTTING ARBORETUM, on SR 27A (Montauk Hwy.), covers 697 acres, more than 140 acres of which are open to the public. Plantings include azaleas, evergreens, hollies, rhododendrons and wildflowers. A 68-room Tudor-style house, the former Cutting residence, features lavish woodwork, stained-glass windows and large fireplaces as well as a natural history museum with a collection of mounted birds and American Indian artifacts.

Food is available mid-April through Labor Day. Allow 2 hours, 30 minutes minimum. Arboretum open Tues.-Sun. 10-dusk. Cutting House and museum Tues.-Sun. 10-5, Apr.-Oct.; 10-4:30, rest of year. Admission $6 per private vehicle Tues.-Sun., early Apr.-Labor Day, and Sat.-Sun., day after Labor Day-Oct. 31; free rest of year. Phone (631) 581-1002.

HAMILTON (E-8) pop. 3,509, elev. 1,109′

Colgate University is on SR 12B. The Case Library houses exhibits and rare books; Alumni Hall displays archeological and ethnological materials; and the Dana Arts Center contains the Picker Art Gallery and the University Theater. Free guided campus tours can be arranged through the admissions office; phone (315) 228-7401.

HAMMONDSPORT (F-5) pop. 731, elev. 740′

The Keuka Lake community of Hammondsport is the center of the state's grape and wine industry as well as the home of aviation pioneer Glenn H. Curtiss. *Also see Finger Lakes p. 86.*

GLENN H. CURTISS MUSEUM, .5 mi. s. on SR 54, displays early motorcycles, engines and aircraft, many of which were developed for military use by Glenn H. Curtiss in his Hammondsport manufacturing plant.

A skilled mechanic, speed enthusiast and aviation pioneer, Curtiss won the title "fastest man in the world" for a motorcycle speed record set in 1907; the next year he piloted the first documented public flight in the United States. With the U.S. Navy's purchase of its first airplane—a Curtiss design—in 1911, Curtiss became known as the Father of Naval Aviation.

In addition to a tribute to the first female aviators, galleries feature Curtiss family art objects, early automobiles and turn-of-the-20th-century furnishings and memorabilia.

Allow 1 hour, 30 minutes minimum. Mon.-Sat. 9-5, Sun. 11-5, May-Oct.; Mon.-Sat. 10-4, Sun. noon-5, Nov.-Dec. and in Apr.; Thurs.-Sat. 10-4, Sun. noon-5, rest of year. Closed Jan. 1, Easter, Thanksgiving and Dec. 24-25. Admission $6; over 65, $4.50; ages 7-18, $3.50; family rate $17. AX, DS, MC, VI. Phone (607) 569-2160.

KEUKA MAID DINNER BOAT departs from the Hammondsport town dock on SR 54, .2 mi. n. of SR 54A. The ship is a 500-passenger, three-deck vessel that operates on Keuka Lake. Allow 2 hours, 30 minutes minimum. Trips depart Tues.-Sat. at 12:30 and 6:30, Sun. at noon and 6:30, May-Oct. Boarding begins 30 minutes before departure. Fare (without meals) $15. Reservations are required 1 day in advance. AX, DS, MC, VI. Phone (607) 569-2628 or (888) 372-2628.

THE WINE AND GRAPE MUSEUM OF GREYTON H. TAYLOR is off SR 54A, 1 mi. n. on Greyton H. Taylor Memorial Dr., next to Bully Hill Vineyards. Displays trace the process of wine production. The wood and stone building dates from the late 19th century and houses antique equipment used for tending the vineyards and producing wines and brandy; coopers' tools and local historical memorabilia also are displayed. Mon.-Sat. 9-5, Sun. noon-5, May-Oct. Donations. Phone (607) 868-4814.

WINERIES

• **Bully Hill Vineyards,** off SR 54A, then 2 mi. to 8843 Greyton H. Taylor Memorial Dr. Tours are offered on the hour Mon.-Sat.10-4, Sun. noon-4. Phone (607) 868-3610 or (607) 868-3210.

• **Pleasant Valley Wine Co.,** off SR 54 and CR 88 following signs. Daily 10-5, Apr.-Dec.; Tues.-Sat. 10-4, rest of year. Closed Jan. 1, Easter, Thanksgiving and Dec. 25. Phone (607) 569-6111.

HERKIMER (E-9) pop. 7,498, elev. 398′

Settled in 1725 by German Palatines, Herkimer began as a dairying center, then became a focus of state politics and conventions during the early 1800s. In 1865 Warner Miller perfected the process of making paper from wood pulp, which cut the cost of newsprint and caused a huge increase in newspaper, magazine and book publishing.

A trial at the Herkimer County Courthouse inspired Theodore Dreiser's novel "An American Tragedy." More recent local activities include digging for "Herkimer Diamonds," which are actually rare, exceptionally clear, double-terminated quartz crystals. An open-pit mine and museum can be found on SR 28; phone (315) 891-7355.

Herkimer County Chamber of Commerce: 28 W. Main St., Mohawk, NY 13407; phone (315) 866-7820 or (877) 984-4636.

HERKIMER COUNTY HISTORICAL SOCIETY, 400 N. Main St., provides an overview of agriculture, industry and domestic life in Herkimer County from the 1700s to the 1990s. A guided tour of the old county jail and a dollhouse collection are available. Allow 1 hour minimum. Mon.-Fri. 10-4, Sat. 10-3, July-Aug.; Mon.-Fri. 10-4, rest of year. Closed holidays. Museum free. Jail or dollhouse tour $1, family rate $2.50. Phone (315) 866-6413.

HICKSVILLE (I-3) pop. 41,260, elev. 149'

SAVE **HICKSVILLE GREGORY MUSEUM,** at Heitz Pl. and Bay Ave., is in the 1895 Heitz Place Courthouse. The museum's mineral collection features specimens from throughout the world. A butterfly and moth collection emphasizes species native to Long Island. Visitors can see the 1915 jail, where inmates were supervised by a constable who resided in quarters above the courtroom. Audiovisual programs and changing exhibits also are offered.

Allow 1 hour minimum. Tues.-Fri. 9:30-4:30, Sat.-Sun. 1-5; closed major holidays. Admission $5; over 59 and ages 4-14, $3; family rate $15. Phone (516) 822-7505.

LONG ISLAND REPTILE MUSEUM, 70 Broadway, contains some 3,000 live reptiles and amphibians from around the world. Animal shows and a petting zoo are featured. Allow 1 hour minimum. Daily 10-6; closed Thanksgiving and Dec. 25. Admission $9.95; over 61 and ages 2-12, $7.95. DS, MC, VI. Phone (516) 931-1500.

HIGH FALLS (G-10) pop. 627, elev. 256'

SAVE **DELAWARE & HUDSON CANAL MUSEUM,** .5 mi. s. of SR 213 on Mohonk Rd., is devoted to the history of a 108-mile canal that linked the company's coal fields to the Hudson River at Kingston 1828-98. Exhibits depict 19th-century canal life and canal boat activities. Also included are photographs, artifacts, dioramas and working models of a lock and a gravity railroad car. A self-guiding tour of the nearby "Five Locks" also is available. Allow 1 hour minimum. Thurs.-Sat. and Mon. 11-5, Sun. 1-5, Memorial Day-Oct. 25. Admission $3; under 12, $1. Phone (845) 687-9311.

HIGHMOUNT (G-9) elev. 795'

A winter sports center, Highmount is near Belleayre Mountain, said to have the highest base elevation in the Northeast. Downhill and cross-country skiing are popular.

HORSEHEADS (F-6) pop. 6,452, elev. 915'

Horseheads is named for the remains of the pack horses Gen. John Sullivan used to transport his men from Pennsylvania to western New York to fight the Six Nations of the Iroquois. On the return trip the horses collapsed, and Sullivan destroyed an estimated 300 of them at this site. Their sun-bleached skulls were all that remained when the first European settlers arrived in 1789. The Horseheads Historical Society Museum houses local historical artifacts in addition to works by early 20th-century political cartoonist Eugene "Zim" Zimmerman. *Also see Finger Lakes p. 86.*

SAVE **NATIONAL WARPLANE MUSEUM** is off SR 17 exit 51 following signs to Elmira-Corning Regional Airport. Exhibits include military aircraft and artifacts from 1919 through the Desert Storm conflict. Among the rare aircraft are a flying-condition B-17 and the only known flyable PBY in

original military configuration. A restoration hangar shows work in progress.

Allow 1 hour minimum. Mon.-Fri. 10-4, Sat. 9-5, Sun. 11-5; closed Jan. 1, Thanksgiving and Dec. 25. Hours may vary; phone ahead. Admission $7; over 62, $5.50; ages 6-17, $4; family rate (two adults and three children) $18. AX, DS, MC, VI. Phone (607) 739-8200.

HOWES CAVE (E-9) elev. 795'

GEM **HOWE CAVERNS** is off I-88 exit 22, 1.7 mi. e. on SR 7, then 1.5 mi. n. following signs. The 80-minute guided tour begins as elevators descend into the prehistoric caverns, 160 to 200 feet underground. Brick walkways follow the subterranean river through chambers with stalactites and stalagmites to the departure point for a boat ride on the underground Lake of Venus. The caverns have a constant temperature of 52 degrees Fahrenheit (12 C).

Geode cutting and gemstone mining are available all year. Pony rides are offered (weather permitting) at an animal farm July 1-Labor Day.

Food is available. Allow 2 hours minimum. Tours daily 8-8, July-Aug.; 9-6, rest of year. Closed Thanksgiving and Dec. 25. Fee $16; over 65 and ages 12-15, $14; ages 5-11, $8. AX, DS, MC, VI. Phone (518) 296-8900. *See color ad p. 271.*

SAVE **IROQUOIS INDIAN MUSEUM,** off I-88 exit 22, 1.7 mi. e. on SR 7, then 1 mi. n. on Caverns Rd., is devoted to the Iroquois people, their culture and the preservation of their heritage. The museum houses a collection of contemporary Iroquois artwork as well as archeological and historical exhibits. A children's museum contains hands-on exhibits. Nature trails through a 45-acre park are available.

Allow 1 hour minimum. Tues.-Sat. 10-5, Sun. noon-5, Apr.-Dec.; closed Easter, Thanksgiving and Dec. 24-25. Admission $7; senior citizens and ages 13-17, $5.50; ages 5-12, $4. MC, VI. Phone (518) 296-8949.

HUDSON (F-11) pop. 7,524, elev. 67'

Named after Henry Hudson, who landed at this site in 1609, Hudson was chartered in 1785 and missed being the state capital by just one vote. This once booming whaling port and port of entry has one of the country's largest assortments of 19th-century architecture.

The 1811 Robert Jenkins House and Museum contains Hudson River School paintings, local artifacts, whaling lore and a genealogical library. Several antique shops line Warren Street in the business district. Promenade Hill overlooks the Hudson River and the Catskills.

Columbia County Tourism Department: 401 State St., Hudson, NY 12534; phone (518) 828-3375 or (800) 724-1846.

AMERICAN MUSEUM OF FIREFIGHT-ING, at the Fireman's Home at 117 Harry Howard Ave., was founded in 1925. One of the country's oldest museums of its type, it contains more than 86 firefighting machines, one of which dates from 1725. An extensive collection of firefighting equipment and memorabilia depicts the evolution of firefighting. Allow 30 minutes minimum. Daily 9-4:30; closed major holidays. Free. Phone (518) 828-7695.

OLANA STATE HISTORIC SITE is off New York State Thruway (I-87) exit 21 to SR 23E, then 1 mi. s. to 5720 SR 9G. The Victorian estate was the home of Frederic Edwin Church, landscape painter of the Hudson River School. The mansion, built 1870-76 in the Persian style, commands a view of the Hudson River Valley and the Catskills. The visitor center offers a film and exhibit about Church. Recreational opportunities include hiking and cross-country skiing.

Picnicking is permitted. Allow 2 hours minimum. Grounds daily 8-dusk. Visitor center Tues.-Sun. 10-5, early Apr.-late Nov. Last tour begins 1 hour before closing. Tour $7; over 62, $5; ages 5-12, $2. Tours are limited to 12 persons; reservations are recommended. Phone (518) 828-0135.

HUNTINGTON (H-3) pop. 18,403, elev. 205'

Huntington is the birthplace of poet Walt Whitman and the place where patriot Nathan Hale was arrested. Situated on Long Island's North Shore, Huntington is characterized by rolling hills, bluffs and picturesque harbors. The John Lloyd Manor House, built 1766-67, is a restored local historic site. The Lloyd Neck Black Oak, north from SR 25A on West Neck Road, measures 19 feet, 7 inches in circumference and is the largest known black oak in the United States.

Huntington Township Chamber of Commerce: 164 Main St., Huntington, NY 11743; phone (631) 423-6100.

Shopping areas: Walt Whitman Mall, 2 miles north of I-495 exit 49N on the east side of SR 110, serves the Huntington area. Macy's is among its 100 stores.

HECKSCHER MUSEUM, in Heckscher Park at 2 Prime Ave., contains a permanent collection of nearly 1,900 pieces of European and American art ranging from works by Renaissance masters to contemporary local artists. Also offered are changing exhibits, educational programs and lectures. Allow 30 minutes minimum. Tues.-Fri. 10-5 (also first Fri. of the month 5-8:30), Sat.-Sun. 1-5; closed Thanksgiving and Dec. 25. Admission $5; over 64 and students with ID $3; ages 6-12, $1. Phone (631) 351-3250.

HUNTINGTON HISTORICAL SOCIETY HOUSE MUSEUMS are at 2 High St. and 434 Park Ave. The David Conklin Farm House, on High

Street, was built in 1750 and contains period furnishings, including a chair used by George Washington on a 1790 visit to Long Island. The Dr. Daniel W. Kissam House, built in 1795, reflects the lifestyle of an affluent local physician and is restored to its 1840s appearance. Allow 30 minutes minimum. Conklin House open Tues.-Fri. and Sun. 1-4. Hours may vary; phone ahead. Kissam House open by appointment. Admission (each house) $2.50, children $1. Phone (631) 427-7045.

NATHAN HALE MEMORIAL MONUMENT, 1 mi. n. of SR 25A on SR 110 and Mill Dam Rd., marks the spot where the patriot spy was captured. Daily 24 hours. Free.

WALT WHITMAN BIRTHPLACE STATE HISTORIC SITE is off SR 110 at 246 Old Walt Whitman Rd. The 1819 farmhouse is where Walt Whitman spent his early childhood years. Visitors can delve into Whitman's life and poetry through a series of exhibits that trace the poet's development from his boyhood on Long Island to his international prominence as one of the country's visionaries. Available are more than 130 portraits of Whitman as well as original letters, manuscripts and artifacts.

Picnicking is permitted. Allow 30 minutes minimum. Mon.-Fri. 11-4, Sat.-Sun. noon-5, last week in June-Labor Day; Wed.-Fri. 1-4, Sat.-Sun. 11-4, rest of year. Closed major holidays. Admission $3; over 62 and students with ID $2; ages 7-12, $1. Phone (631) 427-5240.

HYDE PARK (G-10) pop. 20,851, elev. 8'

Hyde Park is the home of the Culinary Institute of America, a vocational training school for aspiring chefs. The school was founded in 1946 with 16 students; its most recent enrollment is about 1,800. The institute occupies a former Jesuit seminary on US 9 overlooking the Hudson River. The institute's four restaurants are open to the public by reservation.

Hyde Park Chamber of Commerce: 4389 Albany Post Rd., P.O. Box 17, Hyde Park, NY 12538; phone (845) 229-8612.

ELEANOR ROOSEVELT NATIONAL HISTORIC SITE is off SR 9G, .5 mi. n. of St. Andrews Rd. to 4077 Albany Post Rd. Val-Kill, the main cottage, was Mrs. Roosevelt's weekend and holiday retreat during her husband's presidency. After President Franklin D. Roosevelt died in 1945, she lived in the cottage until her death in 1962. The grounds include gardens, outbuildings, woodland trails and a pond. The site's access road is unpaved and narrow; check locally for road conditions.

Guided tours are available. Allow 1 hour minimum. Daily 9-5, May-Oct.; Sat.-Sun. 9-5, rest of year. Closed Jan. 1, Thanksgiving and Dec. 25. Admission $8, under 17 free. Combination ticket $22 (includes the Franklin D. Roosevelt Museum and Library, Home of Franklin D. Roosevelt National

Historic Site, and Vanderbilt Mansion National Historic Site). DS, MC, VI. Phone (845) 229-9115, or (845) 229-2501 Sat.-Sun.

FRANKLIN D. ROOSEVELT MUSEUM AND LIBRARY, next to the Home of Franklin D. Roosevelt National Historic Site, was the first presidential library. The museum's displays of photographs, artworks, official documents and speeches, gifts from admirers and heads of state, and family possessions and letters chronicle the lives and careers of President and Mrs. Roosevelt.

Allow 1 hour, 30 minutes minimum. Daily 9-6; closed Jan. 1, Thanksgiving and Dec. 25. Admission $14, under 17 free. Combination ticket $22 (includes the Eleanor Roosevelt National Historic Site, Home of Franklin D. Roosevelt National Historic Site, and Vanderbilt Mansion National Historic Site). DS, MC, VI. Phone (845) 229-8114.

HOME OF FRANKLIN D. ROOSEVELT NATIONAL HISTORIC SITE, 2 mi. s. on US 9, consists of more than 200 acres and includes the home and graves of President and Mrs. Roosevelt. The 1826 house remains almost exactly as it was at the time of the president's death in 1945. The estate includes stables, icehouses, a walking trail and a tourist information center. The graves, marked by a plain white marble monument, are in the Rose Garden, northeast of the house.

Allow 1 hour, 30 minutes minimum. Daily 9-5; closed Jan. 1, Thanksgiving and Dec. 25. Admission $14, under 17 free. Combination ticket $22 (includes the Eleanor Roosevelt National Historic Site, Franklin D. Roosevelt Museum and Library, and Vanderbilt Mansion National Historic Site). DS, MC, VI. Phone (845) 229-9115, or (845) 229-2501 Sat.-Sun.

STAATSBURGH STATE HISTORIC SITE is 5 mi. n. on US 9 to Old Post Rd. The 65-room mansion was built in 1832 and remodeled and enlarged in 1895 by architect Stanford White for Ogden and Ruth Livingston Mills. It contains marble fireplaces, wood paneling, gilded plaster work, ornate furniture and art objects from around the world. The Ogden and Ruth Livingston Mills Memorial Park has recreational facilities (see Recreation Chart).

Allow 1 hour minimum for tour. Mansion open Wed.-Sat. 10-5, Sun. noon-5, Apr. 1-Labor Day; Wed.-Sun. noon-5, day after Labor Day-last Sun. in Oct. Guided house tours are conducted every half-hour. Last tour begins 30 minutes before closing. Grounds open daily 8-dusk. Admission $5; over 62, $5; students with ID $4; ages 5-12, $1. Phone (845) 889-8851.

VANDERBILT MANSION NATIONAL HISTORIC SITE is 2 mi. n. on US 9. This 1898 mansion exemplifies the Beaux-Arts architecture of the late 19th-century "Gilded Age." The French and Italian furnishings are original

pieces. Also exhibited are Flemish and French tapestries and Oriental rugs. The grounds afford views of the Hudson River.

Allow 1 hour minimum. Daily 9-5; closed Jan. 1, Thanksgiving and Dec. 25. Admission $8, under 17 free. Combination ticket $22 (includes Eleanor Roosevelt National Historic Site, Franklin D. Roosevelt Museum and Library, and Home of Franklin D. Roosevelt National Historic Site). DS, MC, VI. Phone (845) 229-9115.

ILION (E-8) pop. 8,610, elev. 392′

REMINGTON ARMS CO. PLANT TOUR departs from the museum entrance on Catherine St. Visitors walk 1.5 miles through the plant to view the gun-making process. No cameras, backpacks or strollers are allowed on the tour. Allow 1 hour minimum. Tours depart Mon.-Fri. at 10 and 1, Memorial Day-Labor Day. Free. Phone (315) 895-3200.

Remington Museum, on Catherine St., offers a display of firearms ranging from flintlock rifles to rare pistols and revolvers. Other Remington products from the past include a 19th-century typewriter and a 1900s bicycle. A videotape presentation is offered. Allow 30 minutes minimum. Mon.-Fri. 8-5, Sat. 10-4; closed holidays. Phone (315) 895-3200.

ITHACA (F-6) pop. 29,287, elev. 836′

Ithaca is at the southern tip of Cayuga Lake. Buttermilk Falls (see Recreation Chart), Taughannock Falls (see attraction listing) and Robert H. Treman (see Recreation Chart) state parks offer recreational opportunities. The Cayuga Wine Trail begins at this point and continues north on scenic SR 89, passing several wineries along the western shore of the lake.

Founded in 1892 as a conservatory of music, Ithaca College, atop South Hill off SR 96B, offers drama and music presentations and a public art gallery. Campus tours are available through the admissions office; phone (800) 429-4274. Also see Finger Lakes p. 86.

Ithaca/Tompkins County Convention and Visitors Bureau: 904 E. Shore Dr., Ithaca, NY 14850; phone (607) 272-1313 or (800) 284-8422.

CORNELL UNIVERSITY is on the n.e. side of town. The Herbert F. Johnson Museum of Art is open Tues.-Sun. 10-5. Chimes at the University Clock Tower are played regularly when school is in session. Other places of interest on the campus include Triphammer Bridge, with its view of Fall Creek Gorge, Triphammer Falls and Beebe Lake; the Olin Library; Anabel Taylor Hall; and the Lua A. Minns Memorial Gardens.

Central campus tours depart from the main lobby of Day Hall Mon.-Fri. at 9, 11, 1 and 3, Sat. at 9, 10:30 and 1, Sun. at 1, Apr.-Nov.; daily at 1, rest of year. Closed Jan. 1 and Dec. 24-25. Phone (607) 254-4636.

Cornell Plantations, 2.5 mi. n. on SRs 79 and 366 at One Plantation Rd., lie along the Cascadilla and

Fall Creek gorges. The plantations contain trails, botanical gardens, ponds, streams, woodlands, swamps, a lake and an arboretum. Picnicking is permitted. Allow 1 hour minimum. Daily dawn-dusk. Free. Phone (607) 255-3020.

Sapsucker Woods, 3 mi. n.e. of the main campus at 159 Sapsucker Woods Rd., is the home of the Cornell Laboratory of Ornithology research center. Four miles of sanctuary trails wind through woodlands and swamps filled with nesting and migrating birds. The Lyman K. Stuart Observatory overlooks a bird-feeding garden and a 10-acre pond. Displayed is a collection of paintings by ornithological painter Louis Agassiz Fuertes.

Allow 1 hour minimum. Observatory open Mon.-Thurs. 8-5, Fri. 8-4, Sat. 10-4; closed Jan. 1 and Dec. 25. Trails open daily 24 hours. Donations. Phone (607) 254-2473.

[SAVE] **SCIENCENTER** is at 601 First St. This interactive science museum features numerous hands-on displays that allow visitors to explore scientific principles while having fun. Exhibits include "whisper dishes,"or long-range voice projectors, and a hydraulic raceway, two-story ball machine and giant walk-in camera.

Allow 2 hours minimum. Mon.-Sat. 10-5, Sun. noon-5, July-Aug.; Tues.-Sat. 10-5, Sun. noon-5, rest of year. Admission $6; over 64, $5; ages 3-17, $4. Phone (607) 272-0600.

STEWART PARK, on Cayuga Lake .5 mi. n. on Meadow St., has a carousel, a goldfish pond and a rose garden. Adjoining the park are the Fuertes Wild Fowl Preserve and the Renwick Bird Sanctuary. Picnicking is permitted. Allow 30 minutes minimum. Daily 8 a.m.-10 p.m. Free.

TAUGHANNOCK FALLS STATE PARK is 8 mi. n. on SR 89. The 215-foot Taughannock Falls is in a .75-mile-long glen with sides rising from 350 to 400 feet. Trails follow the edge of the gorge. The park offers a weekly schedule of guided tours and nature programs. Camping and swimming are permitted in season.

Park open daily 8 a.m.-dusk. Trails open mid-May to mid-Oct. Admission $7 per private vehicle, June 1-Labor Day; $5, day after Labor Day-Columbus Day; free rest of year. Phone (607) 387-6739. *See Recreation Chart and the AAA Northeastern CampBook.*

TOMPKINS COUNTY MUSEUM AND DEWITT HISTORICAL SOCIETY, 401 E. State St., presents seasonal exhibits focusing on local industries, arts and ethnic groups. A reference room is available Tuesdays, Thursdays and Saturdays. Museum open Tues.-Sat. 11-5; closed Jan. 1, July 4, Thanksgiving and Dec. 25. Donations. Phone (607) 273-8284.

JAMESTOWN (G-2) pop. 31,730, elev. 1,323'

Jamestown's founder, James Prendergast, built the town's first dam and sawmill in 1811, taking advantage of the vast white pine forests on the hills overlooking the southeast tip of Chautauqua Lake. By the mid-1800s Jamestown was one of the state's leading producers of furniture and wood products. Locally produced "pearl ash" was used to make glass, and the town was nicknamed Pearl City.

Old-fashioned family fun can be found at Midway Park, on SR 430 in nearby Maple Springs. Highlights include picnic areas, a roller skating rink and several amusement rides, including bumper boats and go-carts; phone (716) 386-3165.

Jamestown Area Chamber of Commerce: 101 W. 5th St., Jamestown, NY 14701; phone (716) 484-1101.

Self-guiding tours: Jamestown is the site of many 19th-century commercial and industrial buildings, churches and private houses. Brochures detailing self-guiding walking tours are available from the Fenton History Center Museum & Library *(see attraction listing).*

Shopping areas: Chautauqua Mall, 3 miles west on SR 394, includes The Bon-Ton, JCPenney and Sears among its 60 stores.

ART GALLERY, in the James Prendergast Library at 509 Cherry St., contains 19th- and 20th-century French, German and American paintings as well as changing exhibits. Allow 30 minutes minimum. Mon.-Fri. 9-8:30, Sat. 9-5, Sun. 1-3:30, Nov.-Apr.; Mon.-Fri. 9-8:30, Sat. 9-4:30, rest of year. Free. Phone (716) 484-7135.

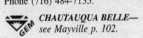 *CHAUTAUQUA BELLE—* see Mayville p. 102.

SAVE **FENTON HISTORY CENTER MUSEUM & LIBRARY** is at 67 Washington St. (SR 60), just s. of Washington St. bridge. The 1863 Italian villa-style mansion of New York Gov. Reuben E. Fenton features a restored Renaissance Revival drawing room, other period rooms, changing topical exhibits and a reference/genealogy library. An annual holiday exhibit highlights historic and ethnic observances and celebrations.

Guided tours are available by appointment. Allow 1 hour minimum. Mon.-Sat. 10-4 (Library also open Mon. 4-9), Sun. 1-4, Thanksgiving-Jan. 6; Mon.-Sat. 10-4 (Library also open Mon. 4-9), rest of year. Admission $5; ages 4-12, $4; family rate $20. Phone (716) 664-6256.

JAMESTOWN AUDUBON NATURE CENTER, 2 mi. s. on SR 60, 3 mi. s. on US 62, then .5 mi. e. to 1600 Riverside Rd., is a 600-acre wildlife sanctuary with 5 miles of nature trails through wetlands, fields and pine forests. Also featured are an arboretum, a bald eagle enclosure, an herb and butterfly garden, and towers and overlooks for viewing wildlife habitats. An interpretive center has hands-on exhibits, more than 200 mounted bird specimens and prints by Jamestown native and noted wildlife artist Roger Tory Peterson.

Allow 1 hour minimum. Sanctuary daily dawn-dusk. Interpretive building Mon.-Sat. 10-4:30, Sun. 1-4:30; closed holidays. Donations. Phone (716) 569-2345.

SAVE **LUCY-DESI MUSEUM,** 212 Pine St., celebrates the lives and entertainment careers of Jamestown-native Lucille Ball and her co-star husband Desi Arnaz through interactive displays, personal belongings and video screenings. **Note:** The museum is scheduled to move to W. Third Street in 2004. Phone ahead to verify hours and prices. Mon.-Sat. 10-5:30, Sun. 1-5, May-Oct.; Sat. 10-5:30, Sun. 1-5, rest of year. Closed Jan. 1 and Dec. 25. Admission $5; over 55 and ages 6-18, $3.50. AX, DS, MC, VI. Phone (716) 484-0800.

ROGER TORY PETERSON INSTITUTE OF NATURAL HISTORY, 311 Curtis St., is a national center for nature education named for the award-winning naturalist and author of a popular series of natural history field guides. Featured are wildlife art and nature photography exhibits. Trails and a butterfly garden are on the 27 wooded acres. Tues.-Sat. 10-4, Sun. 1-5. Admission $4, students with ID $2, family rate $12. Phone (716) 665-2473.

JAVA CENTER (F-4)

BEAVER MEADOW NATURE CENTER, 1610 Welch Rd., features several nature trails, including one that passes near a couple of old farmsteads and others that follow the edge of Beaver Pond. A visitor center contains exhibits. Allow 1 hour minimum. Tues.-Sat. 10-5, Sun. 1-5; closed Jan. 1, July 4, Thanksgiving and Dec. 25. Donations. Phone (585) 457-3228.

JOHNSTOWN (E-9) pop. 8,511, elev. 650′

Johnstown was founded by and named for Sir William Johnson, a British general and Superintendent of Indian Affairs during the mid-1700s. Johnstown has been a center of the glove-making industry since its earliest days, as has the adjoining city of Gloversville *(see place listing p. 90).* Elizabeth Cady Stanton, a pioneer of women's rights, was born in Johnstown in 1815.

Johnstown Battlefield preserves the site of what was probably the Revolutionary War's last battle, fought Oct. 25, 1781, 6 days after Gen. Charles Cornwallis surrendered at Yorktown.

The Fulton County Court House, on W. Main Street between N. William and N. Melcher streets, was erected in 1772 and is the only Colonial courthouse standing in the state. The courthouse and five other historic sites are highlighted on a free guided walking tour departing from the corner of Main and Market streets. For a tour schedule and to make reservations contact Historic Johnstown Walking Tour; phone (518) 762-8309.

JOHNSON HALL STATE HISTORIC SITE, .2 mi. w. off SR 29 on Hall Ave., is a 1763 Georgian mansion. The house was a center for American Indian trade and negotiations prior to the Revolution. Diorama and period exhibits are in the original stone house flanking the main house. Picnicking is permitted. Allow 1 hour minimum. Guided tours Wed.-Sat. and Mon. 10-5, Sun. 1-5, May 1-Labor Day; Wed.-Sun. 10-5, day after Labor Day-Oct. 31. Fee $4; over 65, $3; ages 6-12, $1. Phone (518) 762-8712.

JONES BEACH (I-3)

JONES BEACH STATE PARK, covering 2,413 acres on the ocean shore of Long Island off Meadowbrook or Wantagh Pkwy., offers supervised swimming in Zach's Bay, oceanfront beaches and two pools. Bathhouses are available; a boardwalk follows part of the shoreline.

Facilities at Field 4 include a pitch-and-putt golf course and court games. Free events include softball games and outdoor dancing. Planned programs are presented weekends.

Park open daily dawn-midnight, second weekend in June-Labor Day; dawn-dusk, rest of year. Parking daily $8, mid-May to mid-Sept; Sat.-Sun. and holidays $6, early Apr. to mid-May and mid-Sept. to early Dec.; free, rest of year. Phone (516) 785-1600. *See Recreation Chart.*

KATONAH—*see New York p. 150.*

KINDERHOOK (F-11) pop. 1,275, elev. 288'

COLUMBIA COUNTY MUSEUM, 5 Albany Ave., has a genealogical library, a regional art gallery and changing exhibits of historical artifacts. Allow 30 minutes minimum. Mon.-Fri. 10-4, Memorial Day-Labor Day; Mon., Wed. and Fri. 10-4, rest of year. Closed holidays. Donations. Phone (518) 758-9265.

JAMES VANDERPOEL HOUSE, 16 Broad St., is an 1820 Federal-style house containing period furniture and decorative arts. Guided tours are available. Allow 1 hour minimum. Thurs.-Sat. 11-5, Sun. 1-5, Memorial Day weekend-Labor Day weekend; closed federal holidays. Admission $3; over 55, college students with ID and ages 12-18, $2. Combination admission with the Luykas Van Alen House $5; over 54 and ages 12-18, $3. Phone (518) 758-9265.

LUYKAS VAN ALEN HOUSE AND ICHABOD CRANE SCHOOLHOUSE are 1 mi. s. on SR 9H. The 1737 farmhouse is furnished with period furniture and 18th-century decorative arts. The 1850 one-room schoolhouse has been restored to its 1920s appearance and displays Columbia County school artifacts. Allow 1 hour minimum. Guided tours Thurs.-Sat. 11-5, Sun. 1-5, Memorial Day weekend-Labor Day weekend; closed federal holidays. Admission $3; over 55, college students with ID and ages 12-18, $2. Combination admission with the James Vanderpoel House $5; over 54 and ages 12-18, $3. Phone (518) 758-9265.

MARTIN VAN BUREN NATIONAL HISTORIC SITE, 2 mi. s. on SR 9H to 1013 Old Post Rd., is the estate of the eighth U.S. president. The 1797 mansion was remodeled in the Italianate style. Guided tours are available. Allow 1 hour, 30 minutes minimum. Daily 9-4, mid-May to late Oct.; Sat.-Sun. 9-4, rest of year. Admission $3, under 17 free. Phone (518) 758-9689.

KINGS POINT (H-2) pop. 5,076

U.S. MERCHANT MARINE ACADEMY, on Steamboat Rd. facing Long Island Sound, trains and educates officers for the Merchant Marine and Naval Reserve. The grounds include the estate of automobile manufacturer Walter Chrysler, the American Merchant Marine Museum and the U.S. Merchant Marine Memorial Chapel. Allow 1 hour minimum. Campus open daily 9-5. Museum open Tues.-Fri.

10-3, Sat.-Sun. 1-4:30. Closed federal holidays. A photo ID is required for admission. Hours may vary; phone ahead. Campus free. Museum admission by donations. Phone (516) 773-5000.

KINGSTON (G-10) pop. 23,456, elev. 295'

Established as a Dutch trading post in 1614, Kingston became a permanent settlement in 1652. The first state constitution was drafted and adopted in Kingston in 1777, when the city became the first capital. Several Colonial houses are in the Kingston area; one of the most notable is the Bevier House, which serves as the Ulster County Historical Society Headquarters and Museum.

Chamber of Commerce of Ulster County: 1 Albany Ave., #G3, Kingston, NY 12401; phone (845) 338-5100.

Self-guiding tours: Brochures outlining a walking tour of the historic Uptown Stockade area, Midtown and Rondout Creek corridor are available at the Heritage Area Visitor Center, 20 Broadway; phone (845) 331-7517 or (800) 331-1518. Brochures also are available May through October from the visitor center at 308 Clinton Ave., and at city hall, 420 Broadway; phone (845) 331-9506 or (845) 331-0080, respectively.

ASHOKAN RESERVOIR is w. off SRs 28 and 28A, in the Catskills. The reservoir provides New York City with more than 500 million gallons of water daily when full. A scenic 40-mile route encircles the impoundment. Phone (845) 657-2304.

SAVE **HUDSON RIVER CRUISES** depart from Rondout Landing on Broadway in the Historic Rondout Waterfront District aboard the MV *Rip Van Winkle.* The 2-hour narrated cruise passes several lighthouses and magnificent Hudson River mansions. A music cruise also is available. Allow 2 hours minimum. Two-hour cruise departs Tues.-Sun. at 11 and 2, July-Aug.; at 2, May-June and Sept.-Oct. Fare $15; over 60, $14; ages 4-11, $6. DS, MC, VI. Phone (845) 340-4700 or (800) 843-7472 for schedule information.

OLD DUTCH CHURCH AND CEMETERY is on Main St. between Wall and Fair sts. The church was established in 1659; the cemetery dates from 1661 and contains the grave of George Clinton, first governor of the state. Mon.-Fri. 10-4 and by appointment. Free. Phone (845) 338-6759.

GEM **SENATE HOUSE STATE HISTORIC SITE,** 312 Fair St., was the meeting site of the first New York State Senate. A museum features Hudson Valley furnishings and art exhibits relating to John Vanderlyn and other Hudson Valley artists. Rooms in the Senate House are furnished as they would have appeared in 1777 when the New York State Senate met in the home of Abraham Van Gaasbeek.

Allow 30 minutes minimum. Guided tours Wed.-Sat. and Mon. 10-5, Sun. 11-5, mid-Apr. to Oct. 31.

Fee $4; over 62, $3; ages 5-12, $1. Phone (845) 338-2786.

VOLUNTEER FIREMEN'S HALL AND MUSEUM OF KINGSTON, 265 Fair St., houses a parade carriage, a display of 1800s fire convention badges and a collection of souvenir mugs. The museum has a functioning fire alarm system and a fire company parlor, complete with a working player piano and ornately carved furniture with the fire company's initials on each piece. Wed.-Fri. 11-3, Sat. 10-4, June-Aug.; Fri. 11-3, Sat. 10-4, Apr.-May and Sept.-Oct. Donations. Phone (845) 331-0866 or (845) 331-1247.

LA FARGEVILLE (C-7) pop. 588, elev. 375'

[SAVE] **AGRICULTURAL MUSEUM,** 6 mi. s. on SR 180, illustrates the development of agriculture in the region. The complex includes a one-room schoolhouse, a church/meetinghouse and a cheese factory. Guided tours daily 9-4, June-Sept.; by appointment only in May. Admission $5. Phone (315) 658-2353.

LAKE CHAMPLAIN (A-11)

Extending from Canada southward for 120 miles, Lake Champlain varies from a quarter-mile to 12 miles wide. Two-thirds of its cubic area lies in Vermont; the rest, except for a small Canadian portion, is in New York. Lake Champlain accommodates large vessels and, with its Hudson River connector, the Champlain Canal, makes navigation possible from New York City to Montréal and the Great Lakes.

Legends of Lake Champlain's own version of the Loch Ness Monster have persisted since Samuel de Champlain sighted what he described as a serpentine creature 20 feet long, as thick as a barrel and with a head like a horse. Occasional sightings of the elusive creature, affectionately named "Champ," still occur, but whether or not a distant cousin of the Scottish sea serpent really resides in the lake remains a matter of speculation.

[SAVE] **LAKE CHAMPLAIN FERRIES** offer scenic links between New York and Vermont via three separate crossings: Plattsburgh to Grand Isle, Vt.; Essex to Charlotte, Vt.; and Port Kent to Burlington, Vt. Plattsburgh ferry (crossing time 12 minutes) operates daily 24-hours year-round. Essex ferry (crossing time 20 minutes) operates year-round, ice conditions permitting. Port Kent ferry (crossing time 1 hour) runs mid-May to mid-Oct. AAA clubs have complete schedules and fare information. Phone (802) 864-9804.

LAKE GEORGE (VILLAGE) (D-10)
pop. 985, elev. 325'

The village of Lake George is at the southern end of the 32-mile-long lake. Of the 365 islands dotting the lake, 92 have been developed for camping *(see Adirondack Park p. 57 and the AAA Northeastern CampBook)*. On the southern shore along Beach Road are a public beach, departure points for steamboat and cruise boat rides and areas where speedboats, parasails and horse-drawn carriages may be rented.

Million Dollar Beach, east of US 9 on Beach Road, is a popular swimming beach with a bathhouse, lifeguard, lockers, picnic facilities and volleyball courts. It is open Memorial Day through Labor Day; phone (518) 668-3352 to verify hours and prices. Scenic Lake Shore Drive (SR 9N) follows the west shore between the towns of Lake George and Ticonderoga *(see place listing p. 198).*

Lake George Chamber of Commerce: P.O. Box 272, Lake George, NY 12845; phone (518) 668-5755 or (800) 705-0059.

Shopping areas: Several factory outlet centers including Adirondack Factory, French Mountain Commons, Lake George Plaza and Log Jam are located along "Million-Dollar-Half-A-Mile" on SR 9 off I-87 exit 20.

FORT WILLIAM HENRY MUSEUM is on US 9 (Canada St.) in the center of town. This 1755-57 British fort was the subject of James Fenimore Cooper's "The Last of the Mohicans." The replica contains barracks, stockades, dungeons and fort artifacts. Living-history demonstrations include canon and musket firing, a bomb toss and musket ball molding. The Archeological Hall contains an exhibit about the 1997 archeological dig.

Allow 2 hours minimum. Daily 9 a.m.-8 p.m., July-Aug.; 10-5, May-June and Sept.-Oct. Tour $9.30; over 60, $8.40; ages 3-11, $6.78. AX, DS, MC, VI. Phone (518) 668-5471.

 THE GREAT ESCAPE AND SPLASHWATER KINGDOM—*see Queensbury p. 185.*

LAKE GEORGE BATTLEFIELD PARK, .5 mi. s. off US 9, contains the ruins of Fort George, an American Indian monument and a memorial to Jesuit missionary Father Jogues. Picnicking is permitted. Daily 10-6, late June-Labor Day; Sat.-Sun. 9-8, early May-late June. Park free. Parking $6. Phone (518) 668-3352. *See the AAA Northeastern CampBook.*

 LAKE GEORGE OPERA FESTIVAL— *see Saratoga Springs p. 192.*

LAKE GEORGE STEAMBOAT CO., with cruises departing from Steel Pier, offers a narrated 4.5-hour Discovery Tour and 2.25-hour Paradise Bay cruises aboard the *Mohican.* One-hour paddle wheeler cruises are available aboard the *Minne-ha-ha.* Two-hour excursions aboard the *Lac du Saint Sacrement* are available with or without a meal. Two-hour moonlight cruises also are offered.

Discovery Tour departs daily at 9, June 21-Labor Day. Paradise Bay cruise departs daily at 2:30, Memorial Day weekend-Columbus Day. Paddle wheeler cruise departs daily 10-7:30, June 21-Columbus Day. Cruises on the *Lac du Saint Sacrement* depart daily at noon, May -Oct. Round-trip Discovery Tour $18.50; ages 3-11, $8.75. Paradise Bay cruise $14.75; ages 3-11, $7.50. Paddle wheeler cruise $9.50; ages 3-11, $5.75. *Lac du Saint Sacrement* cruise (excludes meal) $14.75; ages 3-11, $6.75. Reservations are recommended for lunch and dinner cruises. AX, DS, MC, VI. Phone (518) 668-5777 or (800) 553-2628.

PROSPECT MOUNTAIN VETERANS MEMORIAL HIGHWAY, I-87 exit 21, then 1 mi. n. on US 9, provides a scenic 5.5-mile drive to a crest overlooking Lake George. The summit is reached via bus or a hiking trail. Picnicking is permitted. Allow 1 hour minimum. Daily 9-5, Memorial Day-Oct. 21. Admission $6 per private vehicle. Phone (518) 668-5198 Memorial Day-Oct. 21 or (518) 668-3352 rest of year.

SHORELINE CRUISES OF LAKE GEORGE leave from the lakefront at 2 Kurosaka Ln. Narrated tours explain the scenic and historic sites along the shore. Sunset, moonlight and entertainment cruises also are available One-hour sightseeing cruises depart daily every 30 minutes, May-Oct. Two-and-a-half-hour Paradise Bay cruises depart daily at 1. One-hour cruise $8.50; ages 3-11, $4.50. Paradise Bay cruise $12; ages 3-11, $6. MC, VI. Phone (518) 668-4644 or (800) 894-2427.

LAKE LUZERNE (D-10)
pop. 2,240, elev. 624'

RECREATIONAL ACTIVITIES
White-water Rafting
- **Hudson River Rafting Co.** off I-87 exit 21, 11 mi. s. on SR 9N to Mill St., then w. to Main St. Write P.O. Box 47, North Creek, NY 12853. Trips daily July-Aug.; Sat.-Sun., mid-May to late June and Sept.-Oct. Reservations are recommended. Phone (518) 696-2964 or (800) 888-7238.

LAKE PLACID (B-10) pop. 2,638, elev. 1,864'

The village of Lake Placid lies on the shores of Mirror Lake and Lake Placid; the former provides a backdrop for the Main Street commercial district. Host of the 1932 and 1980 Winter Olympics, the area boasts downhill skiing at Whiteface Mountain, 8 miles north, as well as other competitive and recreational sports activities at both state-operated and private facilities.

Summer recreational facilities include foot and bicycle paths, private and public beaches, tennis courts, six golf courses, hiking trails and the indoor Olympic Arena for summer ice skating. Boats can be rented at either lake. Whiteface Mountain provides gondola rides over grassy ski slopes, and the Whiteface Mountain Veterans' Memorial Highway *(see Wilmington p. 204)* runs almost to the summit.

The United States Olympic Training Center, 421 Old Military Rd., offers self-guiding tours of its facilities; phone (518) 523-2600. The Uihlein-Cornell

Sugar House on Bear Cub Road contains maple sugar exhibits and demonstrations.

Lake Placid/Essex County Visitors Bureau: Olympic Center, 216 Main St., Lake Placid, NY 12946; phone (518) 523-2445 or (800) 447-5224.

HIGH FALLS GORGE—*see Wilmington p. 203.*

JOHN BROWN FARM STATE HISTORIC SITE is 2 mi. s. on SR 73, then .7 mi. s. on John Brown Rd. A monument and restored farmhouse mark the burial spot of abolitionist John Brown. A self-guiding trail passes through the grounds, which are accessible year-round. Cross-country skiing is permitted in winter. Guided farmhouse tours are available. Allow 30 minutes minimum. House open Mon. and Wed.-Sat. 10-5, Sun. 1-5, May 1-late Oct. Admission $2. Phone (518) 523-3900.

LAKE PLACID BOAT RIDES, 1 mi. n. on Mirror Lake Dr. at Lake Placid Marina, offers narrated 1-hour cruises. Departures daily at 10:30; 1, 2:30 and 4, June 22-Labor Day; Mon.-Fri. at 10:30 and 2:30, Sat.-Sun. at 10:30, 2:30 and 4, May 18-June 21; daily at 10:30, 1:30 and 3, day after Labor Day-Oct. 20. Fare $7.25; over 62, $6.25; ages 3-12, $5.25. MC, VI. Phone (518) 523-9704 to verify schedule and fares.

LAKE PLACID/NORTH ELBA HISTORICAL SOCIETY MUSEUM, 2 blks. from SRs 73 and 86 at 89 Averyville Rd., chronicles Lake Placid's history over the last 200 years. The waiting room and the baggage room of this former train station now house displays of primitive farm implements, musical instruments, period photographs and memorabilia, and 1932 and 1980 Olympic material. A train engine also is featured. Allow 30 minutes minimum. Thurs.-Sun. 9-4, Tues.-Wed. noon-4, June-Sept. Donations. Phone (518) 523-1608.

OLYMPIC CENTER, 218 Main St. off SR 86, is a multipurpose facility hosting numerous world- and national-class sports events. Originally built for the ice events of the 1932 Winter Olympic Games, the center received an additional wing to host the 1980 Winter Olympic Games—providing a total of four indoor ice rinks. Other sites include the Whiteface Mountain facilities, MacKenzie-Intervale Ski Jumping Complex and Verizon Sports Complex.

Allow 4 hours minimum. Center open daily 9-5. Summer Olympic Site Passport (includes admission to all venues) offered daily 9-5, mid-June to mid-Oct. Winter Passport available late Dec. to mid-Mar. Passport $19. Phone (518) 523-1655.

1932 & 1980 Lake Placid Winter Olympic Museum, within the Olympic Center at 218 Main St., explores the legacy of the 1932 and 1980 Olympic Games. Video booths feature athletes' uniforms and equipment as well as changing exhibits. Allow 30 minutes minimum. Daily 10-5; closed Jan. 1, Easter, Thanksgiving and Dec. 25. Admission $5; over 62, $4; ages 7-12, $3. Phone (518) 523-1655.

MacKenzie-Intervale Ski Jumping Complex, 2 mi. s.e. of the village on SR 73, is a year-round training and event facility. The Kodak Sports Park is a freestyle skiing training center. In the winter the site is home to international competition and training; in summer plastic matting is used to simulate snow. Featured is a 26-story tower with a glass-enclosed elevator and a view of Mount Marcy and surrounding peaks.

Daily 9-4. Admission $8; with chairlift pass and elevator to top of ski jump; over 61 and ages 5-12, $5. Phone (518) 523-1655 or (518) 523-2202.

Verizon Sports Complex, 7 mi. s.e. on SR 73, offers more than 50 miles of groomed cross-country ski trails and a combined bobsled/luge/skeleton track. Bobsled rides are offered year-round.

Open daily 9-4. Bobsled ride Wed.-Sun. 10-4 (weather permitting). Day-use fees (special events excluded) $5. Cross-country ski area $14; senior citizens and under 12, $12. Bobsled rides $30-$40. Phone (518) 523-4436 or (800) 462-6236.

SANTA'S WORKSHOP—*see Wilmington p. 203.*

LAWRENCE (I-2) pop. 6,522, elev. 30'

ROCK HALL MUSEUM, 199 Broadway, is a restored 1767 Georgian Colonial mansion furnished in the style of the late 18th century. A garden and picnic area are on the grounds. Wed.-Sat. 10-4, Sun. noon-4; closed holidays. Free. Phone (516) 239-1157.

LE ROY (E-5) pop. 4,462, elev. 863'

SAVE LE ROY HOUSE MUSEUM AND JELL-O GALLERY, I-90 exit 47, then s. on SR 19 to 23 E. Main St., was built in the early 19th century. Seven rooms are furnished in period, including a basement kitchen and a children's playroom. An exhibit about Jell-O, the dessert food invented in Le Roy in 1897, is presented in another building on the property. Allow 30 minutes minimum. Jell-O Gallery Mon.-Sat. 10-4, Sun. 1-4, May-Oct.; Mon.-Fri. 10-4, rest of year. Le Roy House Mon.-Fri. 10-4, Sun. 1-4, May-Oct.; Closed Jan. 1, Easter, Thanksgiving and Dec. 25. Admission $3; ages 6-11, $1.50. MC, VI. Phone (585) 768-7433.

LEWISTON—*see Niagara Falls p. 166.*

LITTLE FALLS (E-9) pop. 5,188, elev. 370'

Water has always been a factor in the development of the city of Little Falls. Although in the city's earliest days the falls may have created a navigational problem, they soon became a natural blessing; their presence spurred the onset of settlement in the gorge and became a source of water power. Lock #17, with a drop of 40 feet, is the largest lock on the Barge Canal. As transportation improved, trade increased, and Little Falls soon became a stopping point between New York City and the western part of the state.

Historic Canal Place is a revitalized industrial area that includes two refurbished 19th-century stone mill buildings set amidst two parks along the Mohawk River. The area includes antique and art galleries as well as other shops and restaurants and a visual and performing arts center. An underground walkway connects Historic Canal Place with Main Street.

Of interest is the Little Falls Historical Society Museum at 319 S. Ann St. Exhibits housed in the restored 1833 bank building include local memorabilia, genealogical files, a bank vault and Victorian clothing; phone (315) 823-0643.

Self-guiding tours: Brochures detailing self-guiding tours of the city's landmarks, historic areas and natural wonders are available at the Little Falls Historical Society Museum or at the Urban Renewal Office, 46 Main St.; phone (315) 823-3560.

Shopping areas: Little Falls Antique Center, 25 W. Mill St. in Historic Canal Place, offers two floors of antiques and decorative arts displayed in an 1855 stone mill building. Several art galleries also call this area home.

HERKIMER HOME STATE HISTORIC SITE, 3 mi. e. on SR 169 at interchange 29A, was the home of American Revolutionary War general Nicholas Herkimer. The 1764 house contains historic furnishings, artifacts and memorabilia. The site includes a Colonial herb and vegetable garden. A visitor center presents an audiovisual program about Palatine German settlers and late 18th-century Colonial life.

Allow 1 hour minimum. Guided tours begin on the half-hour Tues.-Sat. 10-5, Sun. 11-5, mid-May through Oct. 31. Tour $4; over 62, $3; ages 5-11, $1. Phone (315) 823-0398.

LIVINGSTON MANOR (G-9)
pop. 1,355, elev. 1,400'

Livingston Manor is at the southern edge of Catskill Forest Preserve in the Catskill Mountains. Camping, hiking and fly fishing in the Willowemoc and Beaver Kill trout streams are popular recreational pursuits.

Sullivan County Visitor's Association: 100 North St., P.O. Box 5012, Monticello, NY 12701; phone (845) 794-3000.

CATSKILL FLY FISHING CENTER AND MUSEUM is off SR 17 exit 96, then 2 mi. w. to 1031 Old SR 17. Exhibits interpret the history, science and art of fly fishing. The center's 35 acres feature nature trails and trout streams. Picnicking is permitted. Allow 30 minutes minimum. Daily 10-4, Apr.-Oct.; Tues.-Fri. 10-1, Sat. 10-4, rest of year. Admission $3; under 12, $1. MC, VI. Phone (845) 439-4810.

LOCKPORT—*see Niagara Falls p. 166*

LODI (F-6) pop. 338

WINERIES

- **Wagner Vineyards and Micro Brewery**, just s. of SR 96A on SR 414. Daily 10-5. Brewery open Mon.-Sat. 10-5, Sun. noon-5. Closed Jan. 1, Thanksgiving and Dec. 25. Phone (607) 582-6450.

LONG ISLAND

Ask both a New Yorker and a geography student to define Long Island, and you will get two different answers. Geographically speaking, the island encompasses 1,723 square miles within its boundaries, which extend 125 miles to the east of Manhattan.

A New Yorker pictures the island a bit differently, however. Because two counties—Queens and Kings (Brooklyn)—of the island's four are boroughs of New York City, only the remaining Nassau and Suffolk counties form Long Island in the minds of many city dwellers. Queens and Brooklyn account for the majority of the island's total population.

The northern side of Nassau county forms the island's Gold Coast, whose beautiful gardens and elegant estates were the aspirations of Jay Gatsby in F. Scott Fitzgerald's novel "The Great Gatsby." Some of New York's most well-known beaches extend from western Nassau County along the southern shore through Suffolk County. These include Jones Beach State Park *(see Jones Beach p. 96)* and Fire Island National Seashore *(see place listing p. 86).*

At the eastern end of Suffolk County are the North and South Forks, site of some of New York's most productive farmland. The more urban South Fork also is known as the Hamptons. The populations of these quiet towns swell each summer with the wealthy, the famous and others who wish to escape the hectic and humid city.

From such 20th-century mansions as Old Westbury House in Nassau County to the 17th-century saltboxes of Sag Harbor in Suffolk County, carefully preserved buildings and houses dot Long Island.

Places and towns on Long Island with individual place listings are (clockwise around the island from the northwest) King's Point, Glen Cove, Oyster Bay, Cold Spring Harbor, Centerport, Stony Brook, Setauket, Riverhead, Cutchogue, Bridgehampton, Sag Harbor, Montauk, Amagansett, East Hampton, Southampton, Eastport, Manorville, Shirley, Fire Island National Seashore, West Sayville, Oakdale, Great River, Jones Beach, Old Bethpage, Old Westbury, Albertson, Lawrence and Garden City.

Long Island Convention and Visitors Bureau: 330 Motor Pkwy., Hauppauge, NY 11788. The Suffolk County branch office is on the Long Island Expressway between exits 51 and 52 eastbound, and the Nassau County branch office is off the Southern State Parkway between exits 12 and 13 eastbound; phone (631) 951-3440 or (877) 386-6654.

LYONS (E-6) pop. 5,831, elev. 406'

WAYNE COUNTY HISTORICAL SOCIETY MUSEUM, 2 blks. w. of the County Court House at Butternut and Church sts., is housed in a brick mansion and an attached stone jail built in 1854. Displays include antiques, farm implements, ship artifacts and exhibits depicting the area's early judicial system. The restored horse barn contains transportation artifacts and agricultural and domestic equipment.

Guided tours are available by appointment. Allow 1 hour minimum. Mon.-Fri. 10-4, Sat.-Sun. by appointment, July 4-Labor Day; Tues.-Fri. 10-4, Sat.-Sun. by appointment, rest of year. Closed holidays. Donations. Phone (315) 946-4943.

MALONE (A-10) pop. 6,075, elev. 756'

FRANKLIN COUNTY HOUSE OF HISTORY, 51 Milwaukee St., features guided tours of an 1850s home complete with period furniture, photographs and household items. There also are displays about weaving, spinning and broommaking. A genealogical library is available. Allow 30 minutes minimum. Tues.-Sat. 1-4, June 1-Sept. 4; Sat. 1-4 and by appointment, rest of year. Closed holidays. Donations. Phone (518) 483-2750.

WILDER FARM—BOYHOOD HOME OF AL-MANZO WILDER is 2.5 mi. e. of SR 30 on US 11, 1 mi. s. on CR 23, then 1 mi. s. on Donahue and Stacy rds., following signs. The boyhood home of Laura Ingalls Wilder's husband Almanzo was the setting for her novel "Farmer Boy." It is furnished in period. A visitor center museum displays family photographs and a model of the farm as described in the book. On the grounds are three barns copied from drawings of barns built by James Wilder.

Picnicking is permitted. Guided tours are given Tues.-Sat. 11-4, Sun. 1-4, and by appointment, Memorial Day weekend-Labor Day. Last tour begins 1 hour before closing. Admission $5; ages 5-16, $2.50. Phone (518) 483-1207 or (518) 483-4516 to verify prices.

MANORVILLE (H-4) pop. 11,131

THE ANIMAL FARM, .2 mi. n. off SR 27 exit 59 or 3 mi. s. of I-495 (Long Island Expwy.) exit 69 to 296 Wading River Rd., is a refuge for neglected and unwanted animals. The petting zoo is designed so children may touch, feed and have close contact with farm and exotic animals. Pony rides are available. Picnicking is permitted. Food is available. Mon.-Fri. 10-5, Sat.-Sun. 10-6, Apr.-Oct. Admission $12; over 65 and ages 2-16, $10. AX, MC, VI. Phone (631) 878-1785.

SAVE **LONG ISLAND GAME FARM WILDLIFE PARK,** off I-495 (Long Island Expwy.) exit 70, then 2.2 mi. s. on Chapman Blvd. following signs, has a wildlife collection, a petting zoo and performing animal shows. Themed nature trails and several rides also are available.

Picnicking is permitted. Allow 2 hours, 30 minutes minimum. Daily 10-6, Memorial Day-Labor Day; 10-5, mid-Apr. through day before Memorial Day and day after Labor Day to mid-Oct. Admission Memorial Day-Labor Day $15.95; ages 2-11 and over 60, $13.95. Admission prices vary rest of season; phone ahead. DS, MC, VI. Phone (631) 878-6644.

MARCELLUS (E-7) pop. 1,826, elev. 492′

CENTERS FOR NATURE EDUCATION/BALTIMORE WOODS is off SR 175, then .4 mi. n. on Bishop Hill Rd. Seven trails wind around a recreated pioneer homestead, herb garden, open fields, two spring-fed streams and undisturbed hillside forests of mixed hardwood and old-growth timber. Interpreted programs about the ecology of the area are offered. Allow 2 hours minimum. Daily dawn-dusk. Free. Phone (315) 673-1350.

MASSENA (A-9) pop. 11,209, elev. 24′

An 80-foot drop in the St. Lawrence River along the Great Lakes-St. Lawrence Seaway System *(see place listing p. 90)* has been a two-fold boon to Massena. Two locks, the Bertrand Snell and Dwight D. Eisenhower, were built to overcome the descent, while the Moses-Saunders Power Dam was constructed to take advantage of it. Approximately 3,000 ships from international ports carry passengers and cargo through the locks each year.

Viewing decks and parking are available at the Dwight D. Eisenhower Visitor Center off SR 37, open Memorial Day through Labor Day. Recorded information about upbound and downbound shipping traffic is available; phone (315) 769-2422.

Greater Massena Chamber of Commerce: 50 Main St., P.O. Box 387, Massena, NY 13662; phone (315) 769-3525 or (315) 769-5000.

Shopping areas: St. Lawrence Centre Mall on SR 37 features more than 100 stores, including JCPenney and Sears, as well as specialty shops. An Ammex Tax & Duty Free Shop is at the American Bridge Plaza in Rooseveltown, northeast off SR 37.

MASSENA MUSEUM, 200 E. Orvis, contains items of local interest, including an 1882 hotel book signed by President Chester A. Arthur, a carved Victorian hearse adapted for winter with sled runners, Victorian furnishings and an exhibit of aluminum artifacts from area manufacturers. A town historian is available mornings. Allow 30 minutes minimum. Mon.-Fri. 10-4; closed major holidays. Free. Phone (315) 769-8571.

ROBERT MOSES STATE PARK is 2 mi. n.e. of SR 37 on Barnhart Island. This 4,122-acre park overlooks lock operations. An information center offers seaway brochures and a marina provides a boat ramp and boat rentals. Park open daily dawn-dusk, mid-May through Columbus Day. Information center open daily 8-10, Memorial Day-Labor Day; daily 9-5, day after Labor Day-Columbus Day. Beach open daily June 1-Labor Day. Park free. Beach $7, reduced admission after 4. Phone (315) 769-8663. *See Recreation Chart and the AAA Northeastern CampBook.*

MAYVILLE (F-2) pop. 1,756, elev. 1,303′

Located on the northwest shore of Chautauqua Lake, Mayville began as a portage point between Lake Erie and the Allegheny and Ohio rivers. Boating, hiking, bicycling, fishing, snowmobiling and cross-country skiing are among the recreational opportunities available nearby.

Mayville/Chautauqua Chamber of Commerce: P.O. Box 22, Mayville, NY 14757; phone (716) 753-3113.

GEM *CHAUTAUQUA BELLE,* on SR 394 on the Chautauqua Lake waterfront, is a replica of an old-fashioned, steam-powered sternwheeler offering 1 hour, 30 minute cruises. Cruises depart daily at 11, 1:15 and 3, Memorial Day-Labor Day. Fare $14; ages 13-18, $8.50; ages 6-12, $5. AX, DS, MC, VI. Phone (716) 753-2403 to verify schedules and fares.

MILFORD (F-9) pop. 511

SAVE **COOPERSTOWN & CHARLOTTE VALLEY RAILROAD**, .3 mi. e. on SR 166 to Milford Depot at 136 E. Main St., offers scenic 8-mile sightseeing trips to Cooperstown in 1928 passenger coaches. A museum is in the restored 1869 depot. Departures Sat.-Thurs., mid-June through Labor Day, Sat.-Sun., Memorial Day to mid-June and Sat. after Labor Day to mid-Oct. Evening and holiday excursions also are offered. Departure days and times may vary; phone for schedule. Fare $8; over 62, $7; ages 4-12, $5. AX, MC, VI. Phone (607) 432-2429.

MILLBROOK (G-11) pop. 1,429, elev. 567′

WINERIES

- **Millbrook Vineyards & Winery**, 3.5 mi. n. on SR 82 to Shunpike Rd. (CR 57), then 3 mi. e. following signs to 26 Wing Rd. Daily noon-7, Memorial Day-Labor Day; noon-5, rest of year. Closed major holidays. Phone (845) 677-8383 or (800) 662-9463.

MILTON (G-10) pop. 1,251

WINERIES

- **Royal Kedem Winery**, 1519 SR 9W (Dock Rd.). Sun.-Thurs. 10:30-4:30; closed Jewish holidays. Phone (845) 236-4281.

MONROE (H-10) pop. 7,780, elev. 607′

MUSEUM VILLAGE is 1.2 mi. w. on SR 17M or off SR 17 exit 129. This 17-acre outdoor museum has exhibit buildings with collections of 19th-century Americana. Included are a drugstore, schoolhouse and natural history museum. Demonstrations of 19th-century crafts, family workshops and farm animals also are featured. Food is available. Open Mon.-Fri. 10-2, Sat.-Sun. 11-5, June-Nov.; Mon.-Fri. 10-2, Apr.-May. Admission $8; over 59, $6; ages 4-15, $5. MC, VI. Phone (845) 782-8247.

MONTAUK (H-6) pop. 3,851, elev. 9′

Once inhabited by the Montaukett Indians, Montauk is a resort on a peninsula along the south shore of extreme eastern Long Island. The "cod ledge" off the banks of Montauk is one of the most renowned fishing areas in the world.

Hither Hills State Park *(see Recreation Chart and the AAA Northeastern CampBook)* and Montauk Point State Park *(see Recreation Chart)* has various recreational facilities. Montauk County Park also offers recreational facilities as well as the 1799 Third House Museum. *Also see Long Island p. 101.*

A ferry to Block Island, R.I., departs from Viking Landing daily at 9, late May-Columbus Day; Fri.-Sun. at 9, mid- to late May. The ferry returns at 4:30; phone (631) 668-5700.

MONTAUK POINT LIGHTHOUSE MUSEUM, on Montauk Point 6 mi. e. on SR 27, is in one of the oldest active lighthouses in the country. The 1796 lighthouse was commissioned by George Washington in 1792. Visitors may climb the 137 steps to the top of the tower. Exhibits about maritime history and a videotape are available.

Allow 1 hour minimum. Open daily at 10:30, Memorial Day-Columbus Day; closing times vary. Phone for winter schedule. Admission $6; senior citizens $5; under 13, $3. Parking $5. Under 41 inches tall are not permitted in the tower. Phone (631) 668-2544 or (888) 685-7646.

SECOND HOUSE MUSEUM is .5 mi. w. at e. jct. of Old Montauk Hwy. and SR 27. This late 18th-century house contains period artifacts and a one-room school. Allow 1 hour minimum. Thurs.-Tues. 10-5, Memorial Day-Columbus Day. Admission $2; ages 6-12, $1. Phone (631) 668-5340.

MONTGOMERY (H-10) pop. 3,636, elev. 388′

HILL-HOLD MUSEUM, n.e. on SR 416, re-creates life on an 1830s Hudson Valley farm. The grounds contain an herb garden, a one-room schoolhouse and barnyards with livestock. Original furnishings include pieces that were crafted on the farm. Allow 1 hour minimum. Wed.-Sun. 10-4:30, early May-Oct. 31; phone for December holiday schedule. Admission $3; under 16, $2; family rate $7. Phone (845) 291-2404 or (845) 457-4905.

MONTOUR FALLS (F-6)
pop. 1,797, elev. 456′

Montour Falls occupies the site of Catharines Town, a village ruled by and named for Queen Catharine Montour of the Iroquois Nation. A score of waterfalls flow through the seven glens that surround the town.

Havana Glen has hiking trails past numerous waterfalls, pools and cascades as well as camping facilities. Picnicking is permitted. Chequa-gua Falls, 156 feet high, is at the head of Main Street; the falls are illuminated at night. Seneca Lake is immediately north of the village; a marina is open daily from mid-April to mid-October. Recreational opportunities include boating, camping and fishing. Picnicking is permitted.

Nearby Catharine Creek is known for its rainbow and brown trout fishing, which is at its best April through December. *Also see Finger Lakes p. 86.*

SCHUYLER COUNTY HISTORICAL SOCIETY MUSEUM, 108 N. Catharine St., is housed in the 1830 Old Brick Tavern, the county's oldest brick building. The Georgian-style building displays period artifacts that characterize 19th-century life in rural upstate New York. Among the exhibits are antique farm implements and tools of various trades, American Indian relics, ladies' fashions, antique toys and medical memorabilia. The bedrooms are furnished in period.

Allow 1 hour minimum. Mon.-Thurs. 10-4, Sat. noon-4, Mar.-Nov.; Mon.-Thurs. 10-4, rest of year.

Closed major holidays. Donations. Phone (607) 535-9741.

MORAVIA (E-7) pop. 4,040, elev. 802′

MILLARD FILLMORE CABIN is 1 mi. s. on SR 38 in Fillmore Glen State Park. The cabin is a replica of the one in which the 13th president was born. The Fillmore birthplace, designated by markers within Fillmore Glen State Park *(see Recreation Chart and the AAA Northeastern CampBook)*, is 4 miles east via Skinner Hill Road. Park open daily dawn-dusk. Cabin open daily 8 a.m.-dusk, early May-early Oct. Admission $6 per private vehicle, late June-Labor Day; $7 per private vehicle, rest of year. Phone (315) 497-0130.

MOUNTAINVILLE (H-10)

STORM KING ART CENTER, off SR 32 on Old Pleasant Hill Rd., is a 500-acre outdoor sculpture park and museum with more than 120 sculptures. The permanent collection contains pieces by Magdalena Abakanowicz, Siah Armajani, Alexander Calder, Mark di Suvero, Louise Nevelson, Isamu Noguchi and David Smith; exhibitions change annually. Allow 2 hours minimum. Daily 11-5:30, Apr. 1-late Oct.; 11-5, late Oct. to mid-Nov. Admission $9, senior citizens $7, students with ID $5, under 5 free. Free to all Sat. 5-8, July-Aug. Phone (845) 534-3115.

MOUNT VERNON—*see New York p. 151.*

MUMFORD (E-5) elev. 617′

GENESEE COUNTRY VILLAGE & MUSEUM, 1.2 mi. w. of SR 36 on Flint Hill Rd. (George St.), has more than 57 19th-century structures that have been moved from their original sites, restored and authentically furnished. Costumed villagers portray 19th-century daily life, while craftspeople demonstrate spinning, weaving, cooking and other skills and crafts. An art gallery displays some 700 works by nationally-acclaimed artists. A nature center features more than 5 miles of interpretive trails.

Picnicking is permitted. Food is available. Allow 4 hours minimum. Tues.-Sun. and holidays 10-5, July-Aug.; Tues.-Fri. 10-4, Sat.-Sun. and holidays 10-5, mid-May through June and Sept. 1 to mid-Oct. Last admission 1 hour before closing. A trolley runs daily July-Aug. Combined admission to village, museum, nature center and art gallery $12.50; over 61 and college students with ID $9.50; ages 4-16, $7. Gallery of Sporting Art admission $5; over 61 and college students with ID $4; ages 4-16, $3. Nature center admission $3; over 61 and college students with ID $2.50; ages 4-16, $2. AX, MC, VI. Phone (585) 538-6822.

NAPLES (F-5) pop. 1,072, elev. 818′

Near the southern end of Canandaigua Lake, Naples is in the vicinity of three scenic glens—Parrish, Tannery and Grimes—with many waterfalls.

Rainbow trout fishing is popular. *Also see Finger Lakes p. 86.*

CUMMING NATURE CENTER is 1.2 mi. w. on Clark St., then 7 mi. n. on Gulick Rd. to 6472 Gulick Rd. Part of the Rochester Museum & Science Center *(see Rochester p. 188)*, this 900-acre environmental center in Bristol Hills has 6 miles of themed trails for nature walks and cross-country skiing and snowshoeing; equipment rentals are available. Featured are natural history programs, exhibits and seasonal events. Trails open Mon.-Fri. 9-4, Sat.-Sun. 9-5. Visitor center open Sat.-Sun. 9-5. Closed for seasonal maintenance mid-Nov. to late Dec. Admission $3. Phone (585) 374-6160.

WINERIES

- **Widmer's Wine Cellars Inc.**, 1 Lake Niagara Ln. Mon.-Sat. 10-5, Sun. noon-5, May-Oct.; daily 1-4, rest of year. Closed Jan. 1, Easter, Thanksgiving and Dec. 25. Phone (800) 836-5253.

NARROWSBURG (H-9) pop. 414, elev. 716′

Narrowsburg is sandwiched between Sullivan County's lake region and the Upper Delaware Scenic and Recreational River *(see place listing p. 199)*, which forms a meandering boundary between New York and Pennsylvania. A public boat launch is nearby. Visitors can obtain information about river recreation at an information center on Main Street.

Sullivan County Visitor's Association: 100 North St., P.O. Box 5012, Monticello, NY 12701; phone (845) 794-3000.

SAVE **FORT DELAWARE MUSEUM OF COLONIAL HISTORY**, .7 mi. n. on SR 97, is an 18th-century stockade with blockhouses, three log cabins, a gun platform, storehouses, a blacksmith shop, an armory, an animal yard and an herb garden. The fort is patterned after the mid-1700s Cushetunk settlement. Guides in period dress present lectures, demonstrations and slide and videotape shows about Colonial arts and crafts.

Allow 1 hour minimum. Wed.-Sun. 10-5:30, June 30-Labor Day; Sat.-Sun. and holidays 10-5:30, Memorial Day weekend-June 27. Admission $4; over 54, $3.25; ages 6-16, $2.25. Phone (845) 252-6660.

NEWARK (E-5) pop. 9,682, elev. 457′

HOFFMAN CLOCK MUSEUM, 2 blks. s. of SR 31 in the Newark Public Library at 121 High St., displays antique clocks. Allow 1 hour minimum. Tues.-Fri. 9:30-9, Sat. 10-3, Mon. noon-9. Free. Phone (315) 331-4370.

NEWBURGH (H-10) pop. 28,259, elev. 164′

The site of George Washington's headquarters for more than a year during the Revolutionary War, Newburgh later based its economy on a thriving whaling industry. With the demise of whaling the town successfully turned its ships to other trade in the late 1800s; its seafaring tradition is still evident. Downtown Newburgh's 455-acre historic district contains 18th- and 19th-century structures.

The Chamber of Commerce, Inc.: 11 Racquet Rd., Newburgh, NY 12550; phone (845) 567-6229.

Self-guiding tours: Brochures for self-guiding tours of the historic district are available from the Newburgh Historical Society, 189 Montgomery St.; phone (845) 561-2585.

WASHINGTON'S HEADQUARTERS STATE HISTORIC SITE, Liberty and Washington sts., was Gen. George Washington's headquarters from April 1782 until August 1783 and the place from which Washington ordered the end of the Revolutionary War. The 1750 Hasbrouck House is furnished as a military headquarters. A museum contains exhibits relating to the Continental Army and a 6-acre park includes the 1887 Tower of Victory monument. Wed.-Sat. and Mon. 10-5, Sun. 11-5, mid-Apr. to late Oct. Admission $4; over 61, $3; ages 5-11, $1. Phone (845) 562-1195.

NEW CITY—*see New York p. 151.*

NEW LEBANON (F-11) pop. 2,454

MOUNT LEBANON SHAKER VILLAGE, s. of US 20 on Shaker Rd., was the home of the Shakers 1785-1947. Known for their celibate lifestyle and community living, the Shakers designated this village the "Center of Union," a site of spiritual importance equivalent to that of the Vatican for Catholics or Mecca for Muslims. Visitors can learn about the traditions, architecture and handmade furniture unique to the sect. The village has 26 buildings.

Guided tours are available by appointment. Allow 1 hour, 30 minutes minimum. Fri. 10-4, Sat.-Sun. 10-5, June-Oct.; by appointment rest of year. Admission $5; over 59, $4.50; under 16, $3; under 5 free; family rate (two adults and two children) $12. MC, VI. Phone (518) 794-9500.

NEW PALTZ (G-10) pop. 6,034, elev. 252′

New Paltz was established by French Huguenots on land purchased from the Esopus Indians. Stone houses built 1692-1894 stand on Huguenot Street as reminders of the original settlement.

New Paltz Chamber of Commerce: 124 Main St., New Paltz, NY 12561; phone (845) 255-0243.

HUGUENOT HISTORICAL SOCIETY TOURS, beginning at DuBois Fort on Huguenot St., visits a selection of buildings in a 300-year-old Huguenot village comprising six houses, the fort and a reconstructed 18th-century stone church. Established in 1677, New Paltz was home to 12 French Huguenot refugee families whose descendents lived in the houses well into the 20th century. Many of the houses contain family furnishings reflecting various periods of ownership. Architectural styles range from Colonial to Victorian.

Tours depart Tues.-Sun. 10-4, May-Oct. Fee $10; over 62, $9; college students with ID and ages 6-17, $5. Children must be with an adult. MC, VI. Phone (845) 255-1660 or (845) 255-1889.

NEW ROCHELLE—*see New York p. 151.*

New York

City Population: 8,008,278 Elevation: 54 ft.

Popular Spots

Central Park .... *(see p. 125)*

Empire State Building............. *(see p. 125)*

Metropolitan Museum of Art ... *(see p. 128)*

Brooklyn Bridge / © Alan Schein Photography / Corbis

New York is a city of such extremes that any visitor would be hard pressed to describe it without resorting to superlatives. Words like biggest and best come to mind when referring to America's most populated city. The superlatives are not always positive though. The enormous number of people, pace of life and stark urban landscape contribute to an often grim and sometimes frustrating experience when walking along its streets. Despite problems common to any major city, New York attracts 34 million visitors each year to its man-made canyons.

A true archipelago, the 314 square miles that make up New York City are a series of islands that embrace five boroughs, or administrative districts: Manhattan, Brooklyn, Queens, Staten Island and the Bronx. More than 8 million people live in the city's metropolitan area, which includes Long Island and parts of southern New York State, northeastern New Jersey and southwestern Connecticut.

The city's early history laid the foundation for that "New York state of mind"—a powerfully independent, rambunctious outlook on life. Both the Dutch and English spent years quarreling over the rights to Manhattan after its official discovery in 1609 by Englishman Henry Hudson (the Hudson River's namesake), who navigated the area's waterways.

Fifteen years later it was the Dutch who claimed the area by forming a settlement called New Amsterdam, a principal colony of New Netherland. Two years later Peter Minuit, sailing with the Dutch West India Company, finagled the purchase of Manhattan from the local Indians for trinkets worth about 60 guilders, or $24.

The English returned in 1664 and, angered by their trade rivalries with the Dutch in Europe, seized New Amsterdam. A more autocratic form of government was instituted, and the area was renamed New York after King Charles II's brother,

the Duke of York. Just 9 years later the Netherlands launched a surprise attack on New York, reclaiming the area and christening it New Orange. In 1674 New York changed hands for the last time, the result of the Treaty of Westminster between England and the Netherlands. In 1686 New York became the first city in the colonies to be granted a royal charter.

The 1825 opening of the Erie Canal furthered development by connecting the city with Buffalo, the Great Lakes and parts of the West. Overseas trade burgeoned. The increase in international stature had another important effect: Those in other parts of the world, victims of failed revolutions or poverty or motivated by an adventurous spirit, bid farewell to their homelands and set sail for a haven promising greater opportunities.

From the mid-19th to the mid-20th centuries New York was the official port of entry for millions of immigrants. From 1855 to 1890 newcomers first landed at Castle Garden in Lower Manhattan, near what is now Battery Park. As the numbers swelled, the federal government was forced to find a larger facility, and an island in the New York Bay seemed the logical choice. Ellis Island, southwest of the tip of Lower Manhattan, was first used as a dump site for ships' ballast and later as a fort. Named after its

Getting There — starting on p. 112

Getting Around — starting on p. 114

What To See — starting on p. 116

What To Do — starting on p. 137

Where To Stay — starting on p. 376

Where To Dine — starting on p. 380

© Tom Holton / SuperStock

owner, Samuel Ellis, the 27.5-acre island was transformed into a processing station.

Waves of immigrants swept onto the shores of Ellis Island. German, Irish, Scandinavian and central European families clutched sacks filled with personal items. Frightened, anxious and weary from their arduous passage, Italians, Poles, Czechs and Russians waited for entrance into the United States.

The red-brick buildings were cramped and drafty, containing scowling immigration inspectors standing between a fresh start or heartbreaking deportation. Many of those permitted to stay began new lives not far from where they had disembarked. It was these immigrants, mostly skilled laborers and those willing to work cheaply, who built the city's bridges, tunnels, roads and elevated transportation systems—infrastructure that helped New York make the leap from city to metropolis.

With this sudden surge in population came a boom in economic enterprises, from manufacturing to entertainment. New citizens worked furiously not only to improve their island home but to make New York one of the most influential cities in the world.

Increasing interdependence of the five boroughs roused city leaders to discuss merging. Although Brooklyn initially resisted, Manhattan, the Bronx, Queens, Staten Island and Brooklyn consolidated to form Greater New York on Jan. 1, 1898.

This proverbial melting pot fostered a strong sense of ethnic pride within neighborhoods, and newcomers' craftsmanship lent a striking beauty to the city streetscape. Embellishments on many of New York's older buildings stand as a testament to painstaking Old World artistry.

Considered the city's first skyscraper, the 285-foot-tall brick and limestone Flatiron Building was built in 1902 on the south side of Madison Square. This impressive Italian Renaissance structure was shaped like a wedge of pie to fit into the triangular area between Broadway and Fifth Avenue. Two years later the IRT, the city's first subway line, began operations, running from City Hall to 145th Street. Today subways in New York City are much more extensive: They move 1.2 billion people a year over 656 miles of track.

In 1931 the Empire State Building became a distinctive Art Deco-style landmark in the city's skyline. Rising some 1,454 feet above Manhattan, construction of the 102-story office building sped along at almost a floor a day. Forty years later this impressive architectural feat was topped by the World Trade Center, each of its two towers 110 stories tall. The buildings were destroyed by terrorists in 2001.

(continued on p. 110)

Destination New York City

*F*rom classic opera at Lincoln Center to a walk on the wild side at the Bronx Zoo, the Big Apple has something for everyone.

*Y*ou say you like museums? Well, there are some 150 with exhibits ranging from dinosaurs to Degas. Do you have the theater bug? Stop on Broadway to catch a show. Got your head in the clouds? Check out the diverse architecture of the city's skyscrapers. And if things are moving too swiftly, hop in a buggy for a quiet ride through the city's backyard— Central Park.

© NYC & Company, Inc.

Museum of the City of New York, Upper Manhattan.
A treasure trove of documents and photographs, costumes and textiles, and paintings, prints and toys illuminates the city's colorful past. (See listing page 133)

© American Museum of Natural History

American Museum of Natural History, Midtown Manhattan.
T-rex welcomes visitors to the museum's fourth-floor fossil and dinosaur exhibit halls. (See listing page 121)

*P*laces included in this AAA Destination City:

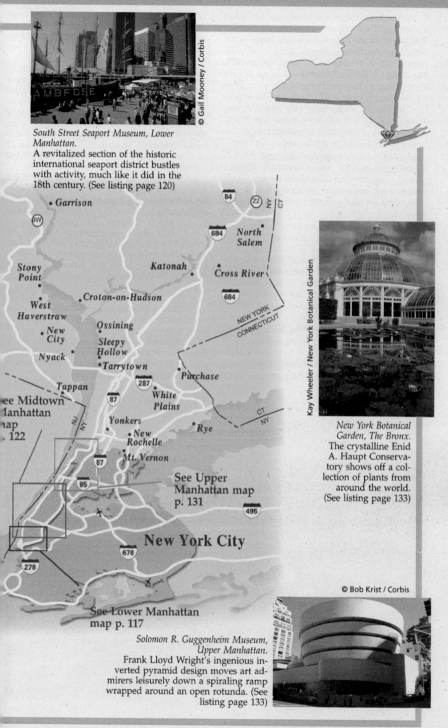

South Street Seaport Museum, Lower Manhattan.
A revitalized section of the historic international seaport district bustles with activity, much like it did in the 18th century. (See listing page 120)

© Gail Mooney / Corbis

Kay Wheeler / New York Botanical Garden

New York Botanical Garden, The Bronx.
The crystalline Enid A. Haupt Conservatory shows off a collection of plants from around the world. (See listing page 133)

© Bob Krist / Corbis

Solomon R. Guggenheim Museum, Upper Manhattan.
Frank Lloyd Wright's ingenious inverted pyramid design moves art admirers leisurely down a spiraling ramp wrapped around an open rotunda. (See listing page 133)

In New York bridges and tunnels are themselves attractions. They include the Verrazano-Narrows Bridge, the second longest single span bridge in the world, and the Holland Tunnel, a marvel of engineering skill at the time of its completion in 1927. The Brooklyn Battery Tunnel is one of the world's longest, and the Bayonne Bridge is one of the longest steel arch bridges in the world. But The Brooklyn Bridge is undoubtedly the world's best known—and most purchased—bridge. The ability to sell the Brooklyn Bridge to gullible visitors was long a standard of a con man's worth.

In 1948 what is now the 4,930-acre John F. Kennedy International Airport opened in Queens. Kennedy and La Guardia, also in Queens, along with Newark International, in nearby New Jersey, combine to service some 86.5 million passengers annually.

New York's population explosion fueled a building boom and job growth and generated worldwide recognition. Unfortunately its ethnic diversity gave rise to racial tensions. Harlem, in Upper Manhattan, was considered the most notable African-American community in the United States in the 1920s—a haven for intellectuals, artists and writers. But as overcrowding and racial discrimination began to eat away at the city, several destructive blows were dealt.

In 1963, Dr. Martin Luther King Jr. delivered his stirring "I Have a Dream" speech during the March on Washington; racial tensions in New York continued to escalate. And activist Malcolm X was killed in 1965 at a Harlem rally. In 1966 a race riot broke out in East Brooklyn; the following year more violence erupted in East Harlem. African-Americans and other minority groups gathered together for a cause—social and economic justice and improvements to their neighborhoods.

If the '60s were socially volatile, the '70s were financially bereft. In 1978, after more than 10 years of spending and borrowing, the city narrowly avoided bankruptcy. New Yorkers blamed their failing economy on spendthrift politicians and sought a mayor who could reverse the city's downward fiscal slide; they chose Democrat Edward Koch, the son of Polish Jewish immigrants. Mayor Koch, who reigned for 12 years, was revered for his brazen outspokenness and his dedication to the middle class.

As New York finally emerged from its financial doldrums, its beloved 151-foot-tall Lady of the Harbor re-emerged from a cocoon of scaffolding after a much-needed makeover. During an $85 million restoration project, American and French workers replaced worn sheets of copper to enhance the statue's blue-green patina. Elevators and stairs leading to the crown also were replaced. The torch, having long since fallen into disrepair because of the strain of visitors seeking an unobstructed view of the city, was restored as well.

In 1986 the centennial of the Statue of Liberty was observed after completion of the restoration. Americans celebrated the beauty of Lady Liberty in grand style with fireworks, marching bands and tall ships on parade in the harbor. The festivity was a fitting tribute to the lady who offered solace to those millions following the light from her torch in search of refuge from poverty and strife.

Central Park / © Bruce Burkhardt / Corbis

The Informed Traveler

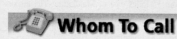

Whom To Call

Emergency: 911

Police (non-emergency): Use local precinct phone number.

Time: (212) 976-1616 or (718) 976-1616

Temperature: (212) 976-1212

Hospitals: Beth Israel, (212) 420-2000; Cabrini, (212) 995-6000; Elmhurst, (718) 334-4000; New York University Downtown Hospital, (212) 312-5000; New York University Medical Center, (212) 263-7300.

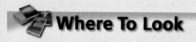

Where To Look

Newspapers

New York City has numerous English and foreign language newspapers. The most popular English language papers are *Newsday*, *New York Daily News*, *New York Post*, *New York Times* and *The Wall Street Journal*.

Radio

New York radio stations WCBS (880 AM) and WINS (1010 AM) are all news/weather stations; WNYC (93.9 FM or 820 AM) is a member of National Public Radio.

Visitor Information

The New York Convention and Visitors Bureau operates an information center at 810 Seventh Ave. Maps in six languages and visitor guides are available for free. Phone (212) 484-1200. For visitors literature phone (212) 397-8222 or (800) 692-8474.

What To Pack

The best times to visit New York are spring and fall. Not only is the weather more comfortable than in summer and winter, but the scenery is downright breathtaking. May and October daytime high temperatures are generally in the mid- to upper 60s. Dress moderately—slacks, jacket and comfortable footwear are appropriate—and bring a slightly heavier sweater or coat for cooler evening temperatures.

Summer in New York City can be stifling unless you are near the coast, where cool sea breezes temper the heat. For summer sightseeing bring lightweight clothing, sunglasses, and comfortable sneakers or thick-soled sandals (the pavement can get very hot).

© Rose Hartman / Corbis

New York winters can be trying. Daytime temperatures average in the upper 30s or low 40s; at night temperatures can drop into the 20s. Although most of your sightseeing will be indoors, winter gear should be layered in order to acclimate to warm restaurants and crowded theaters. *For additional information see temperature chart on p. 48.*

Sales Tax: The sales tax in New York City is 8.25 percent. The tax on hotel rooms is 13.62 percent plus 2 percent occupancy fee. Car rental tax is 13.62 percent.

Getting There

By Car

Entering the city from the north, the New York Thruway (I-87) connects with the Major Deegan Expressway, following the east side of the Harlem River through the Bronx and connecting with the Bruckner Expressway (I-278) at the Triborough Bridge. This route bypasses Manhattan and allows easy access to Brooklyn, Queens and other points on Long Island.

Also from the north, the New England Thruway (I-95) leads through the eastern part of the Bronx to either the Bronx-Whitestone Bridge or to the Throgs Neck Bridge, again bypassing Manhattan and allowing easy access to Long Island. Both routes also connect with various points in Manhattan, including the Cross Bronx Expressway (I-95), heading east-west, which leads to the Henry Hudson Parkway (SR 9A), running north-south along the Hudson River.

I-80 from the west in New Jersey runs congruently with I-95 as it approaches the George Washington Bridge. Once across the bridge it continues east to connect with roads leading to Long Island or swings south on Henry Hudson Parkway or Harlem River Drive to Franklin D. Roosevelt Drive (East River Drive) and downtown Manhattan.

The New Jersey Turnpike (I-95) is the major southern access road to the city. Motorists traveling to Brooklyn and points east should take New Jersey exit 10 to SR 440E (the West Shore Expressway on Staten Island) to I-278E, which crosses Staten Island. Then use the Verrazano-Narrows Bridge to Brooklyn and Long Island.

Lower Manhattan is best approached from the New Jersey Turnpike via the Holland Tunnel. Motorists heading for mid-Manhattan should continue on the turnpike to exit 16E and the Lincoln Tunnel approach.

Air Travel

The New York City area has three airports. John F. Kennedy and La Guardia, two of the world's busiest airports, are in Queens; Newark Airport is in New Jersey.

John F. Kennedy Airport, the area's largest, is located in Queens off the Van Wyck Expressway (I-678) about 15 miles east of Manhattan. The airport is undergoing renovation work to improve its terminals, roadways and arrivals buildings. Work is scheduled to be completed by 2006.

From JFK to Manhattan, take the Van Wyck Expressway to Grand Central Parkway, then head west on the Long Island Expressway. To reach Lower Manhattan, take the Brooklyn Queens Expressway and access either the Brooklyn, Manhattan or Williamsburg bridges leading into the city. To reach Midtown Manhattan, stay on the Long Island Expressway, which feeds directly into the Queens Midtown Tunnel. Drive time is about 1 hour.

Or take the subway: Take the A train directly from the Howard Beach JFK Airport station. The Q10 bus also connects JFK airport to Union Turnpike (E or F train), 121st Street (J or Z train) and Lefferts Boulevard (A train) stations; phone (718) 995-4700 for schedules.

AirTran, the Port Authority of New York and New Jersey's airport rail system, ushers airline passengers from the airport to the Howard Beach terminal for subway connections to Manhattan or to Jamaica Station to catch a subway or the Long Island Rail Road. For AirTran schedules and information about connections and transfers, phone (718) 244-4444.

Just 8 miles east of Midtown in northwest Queens, La Guardia Airport handles many domestic flights. The airport was named after the city's former mayor, Fiorello La Guardia (1934-45), who is credited with helping develop the metropolitan area's accessibility for the aviation age.

Upon leaving La Guardia Airport, take Grand Central Parkway west to the Triborough Bridge, then to Franklin D. Roosevelt Drive. Going north on FDR Drive takes you into Harlem; traveling south on FDR Drive takes you to Midtown Manhattan. Drive time is about 40 minutes.

New York Airport Service provides bus service from La Guardia and JFK airports to Manhattan and to the Jamaica, Queens, Long Island Rail Road

station. The bus stops in Manhattan at the Port Authority bus terminal, 41st Street and Park Avenue, Grand Central Terminal and most midtown hotels. Fares are: from La Guardia to Manhattan $10; from JFK to Manhattan $13; from either airport to Jamaica $5; between La Guardia and JFK $11; from La Guardia to hotels $12; and from JFK to hotels $15. Buses run frequently; for schedules and other information phone New York Airport Service at (718) 875-8200.

SuperShuttle departs from all La Guardia terminals and drops off passengers at Manhattan hotels. Fares range $13-$22 and the schedule varies according to passenger demand; phone (212) 315-3006. SuperShuttle also offers shuttle service from all three airports in vans designed to handle wheelchairs; reservations are required. Fares are $19 from Kennedy, La Guardia or Newark.

The Q48 bus provides service from La Guardia to the 111th Street or Main Street stations (both via the 7 train). On the subway, take the Q33 bus from La Guardia to Roosevelt Avenue station (via the E, F, G or R train) or the 74th Street/Broadway station (via the 7 train). For additional information, phone MTA, (718) 330-1234.

New Jersey's Newark International Airport handles domestic and transatlantic flights. Located on Newark Bay about 16 miles southwest of Manhattan, Newark is an ideal fly-in point for those proceeding to Lower Manhattan or points along the borough's western side. Take the New Jersey Turnpike to the Holland Tunnel for access to Lower Manhattan, and follow the signs to the Lincoln Tunnel if you are headed for Midtown Manhattan. It will take you about 40 minutes to reach the city.

Express buses from Newark International stop at the Port Authority Bus Terminal at W. 42nd Street and Eighth Avenue in Midtown Manhattan; Olympia Trails Bus Service buses depart every 20 minutes from 5 a.m. to midnight. One-way fare is $12; phone (908) 354-3330.

New Jersey Transit bus #62 runs between Newark International and selected points in Newark, including Newark's Penn Station, where PATH subways depart for Broadway at 33rd Street. Buses leave Mon.-Fri. and Sun. every 20-30 minutes from

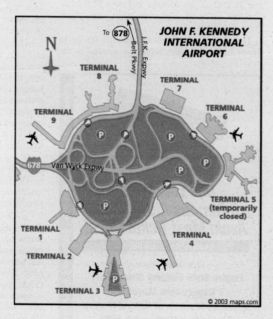

6 a.m. to 2 a.m., and Sat. every 30 minutes from 6:30 a.m. to 2 a.m. The fare is $1.10.

AirTrain's rail system links Newark International Airport with Newark International Airport Station, where passengers can transfer to Amtrak or New Jersey Transit trains to continue on to New York City; phone (888) 397-4636.

Taxis are plentiful at all airports; a taxi ride from Kennedy, La Guardia or Newark to Midtown Manhattan costs $35 plus tolls and tip.

Hertz, 310 E. 48th St., offers discounts to AAA members; phone (800) 654-3080. All major car rental agencies have offices in New York City and at each airport.

Rail Service

If you enter the city by rail, you will arrive at either Grand Central Terminal or Pennsylvania Station, both in the heart of Manhattan. Built in 1913, Grand Central, at Park Avenue and E. 42nd to 44th streets, is an architectural delight. It supports Metro-North commuter trains, including the New Haven, Harlem and Hudson lines traveling to the northern suburbs and suburban Connecticut. This commuter railroad serves Westchester, Putnam, Rockland and Dutchess counties in New York as well as Fairfield and New Haven counties in Connecticut. For information phone (212) 532-4900 or (800) 638-7646.

Amtrak runs out of New York's Pennsylvania Station, Seventh Avenue and 31st Street. Penn Station also supports Long Island Railroad trains and New Jersey Transit trains. For schedules, fares and reservations phone (800) 872-7245.

PATH trains, also originating from Penn Station, run 24 hours a day to stops in Lower Manhattan. The fare is $1.50. For more information phone (800) 234-7284.

The Staten Island Railway limits its service to Staten Island, from the St. George terminal to the Tottenville terminal. The fare is $1.50. Phone (718) 966-7478 for information or schedules.

Buses

The Port Authority Bus Terminal, Eighth to Ninth avenues between W. 40th and 42nd streets, is the main terminal for the city; phone (212) 564-8484.

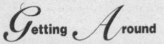

Getting Around

Street System

Manhattan streets were laid out in an easy-to-follow grid pattern back in the early 1800s. Unfortunately, maneuvering within the city is not as simple nowadays. For those unfamiliar with Manhattan traffic, the best driving advice is: DON'T. If you absolutely must drive, timing doesn't really mean much. Although rush hours are 7-9:30 a.m. and 4:30-6:30 p.m., city streets are always busy.

Be alert at all times. The traffic density of streets in Manhattan is probably the highest in the country. A good street map is helpful. When driving in the other boroughs a street index and map are necessities. **Note:** Drivers should keep car doors locked at all times.

In Manhattan consecutively numbered streets run east/west, and avenues cross north/south. Fifth Avenue is the dividing line between east and west streets. Most avenues are one-way and are alternately northbound and southbound. In general, even-numbered streets are eastbound and odd-numbered streets are westbound. Most downtown streets are one-way. Exceptions are Canal, Houston, 14th, 23rd, 34th, 42nd, 57th and 125th streets, which run both east and west.

As you make your way into Lower Manhattan, the city's efficient grid pattern system falls apart in the Greenwich Village and SoHo areas. From Houston Street south, both the numbered streets and Fifth Avenue come to an abrupt end.

Crosstown traffic usually moves faster on 14th, 23rd, 34th, 42nd and 57th streets, because these streets are wide. Northbound and southbound traffic moves faster, at least during non-rush hours, on one-way avenues: These northbound avenues are First, Third, Madison, Avenue of the Americas (Sixth Avenue) and Eighth, while the southbound avenues include Second, Lexington, Fifth, Seventh and Ninth. Gridlock is a particular hazard of driving in the city; it is illegal to stand or stop in the middle of an intersection or to make left turns, except where otherwise indicated.

For those who do not wish to use surface streets to travel, East River Drive and West Side Highway provide elevated, controlled-access roads around the city. **Note:** Avoid the parkways and expressways during rush hours.

The speed limit on downtown streets is 30 mph, or as posted. **No one under 17 is allowed to drive**

in **New York City,** even with a valid driver's license from another state.

Parking

Finding a parking space may be the most difficult aspect of your visit to New York City. Parking is prohibited on most downtown Manhattan streets and is next to impossible in entertainment districts. If you do find a space, read the curbside signs to avoid having the car towed and paying a $185 towing fee plus a fine and storage fee.

Very few accommodations have free parking, and Midtown Manhattan parking lots and garages average about $13 an hour. Guests staying at a hotel with parking facilities often find it is easiest to leave the car in the lot or garage and use public transportation or taxis.

The best strategy available for those wishing to avoid the heavy traffic and exorbitant parking fees in Manhattan is to "park and ride" with the daily commuters. From Queens, parking is available near the #7 Flushing line at Shea Stadium, 126th Street and Roosevelt Avenue, from 5-5: fee before 11, $5; after 11 and after 5 p.m. for Mets games $8.

Another garage is located at Queens Plaza and Jackson Avenue above the Queens Plaza IND subway line and one block from the Queensboro Plaza IRT subway line. Fee $1.50 per half-hour; $8 maximum per 12 hours.

Commuters and visitors from New Jersey have the option to park at NY Waterway's Weehawken, Hoboken and Jersey City terminals and ride a ferry to Lower or Midtown Manhattan. Connecting bus transportation from the Manhattan ferry terminals into the city is available. For schedules, fares and parking fees phone (800) 533-3779.

Taxis

With more than 12,000 licensed yellow medallion cabs roaming the streets, the taxi is one of the most frequently used modes of transportation by visitors. Yellow medallion taxis are the only vehicles authorized to pick up street hails. To avoid being "taken for a ride" and paying more than you should, always give the driver the intersection nearest to your destination as well as the full street address.

Once the meter starts, it continues running. Even at a standstill in traffic, you pay. Taxi fares begin at $2, then increase 30c each additional fifth of a mile, or 30 cents for each 90 seconds waiting in traffic. A 10 to 20 percent tip is customary. A 50c per fare surcharge applies between 8 p.m. and 6 a.m., plus any bridge and tunnel tolls. One fare generally covers all passengers—taxis can carry four people maximum (three in the back seat, and one in the front).

Complaints or lost articles can be reported to the Taxi and Limousine Commission; phone (212) 692-8294. When calling, passengers must provide the taxicab identification number.

Public Transportation

Compared to some cities, public transportation in New York is a good bargain. A $2 fare buys you an unlimited-mileage ride as long as you do not get off. In Manhattan subways traverse the length of Avenue of the Americas (Sixth Avenue), Broadway,

Manhattan / © Photorush / Corbis

Seventh and Eighth avenues and several portions of both Lexington and Park avenues.

Crosstown subways operate on 14th, 42nd, 53rd and 60th streets. In addition there is a shuttle train from Grand Central Terminal to Times Square (intersection of Seventh Avenue and Broadway from 42nd to 43rd streets) where passengers can transfer free of charge to other lines.

Subways also are fast. The New York City subway system accommodates some 1.2 billion riders annually because it is fast, efficient and one of the cheapest ways of getting around. Although New York City subways can be intimidating, directional signs and maps are posted at each station.

Using them is a snap if you heed these four pearls of wisdom: Avoid using the system during weekday rush hours (usually 8-9:30 a.m. and 5-6:30 p.m.) and late at night; ride in the conductor's car if possible (located in the middle of the train); try to avoid using the subway restrooms; and avoid the express and take the local trains (although not as fast as the express, the local trains stop at each station, so missing the correct stop is less likely).

MetroCard, a thin plastic fare card, replaced the familiar tokens for subway admission. You can purchase individual cards at subway station vending machines, neighborhood merchants and tourist information centers. The Pay-Per-Ride MetroCard is good for 11 rides and costs $15. Unlimited ride cards for 1, 7 or 30 days range $7-$70. The card can be used on all New York City buses and at all subway stations.

Maps for both subway and bus routes are available at the Grand Central, Pennsylvania and Columbus Circle stations and the New York Convention and Visitors Bureau.

Note: In the *What To See* section attraction listings will often include the nearest subway (S) station or stations. Consult a subway map to determine which train line is nearest and most direct; not every train runs from each station.

Riding the aboveground rails is another option. The Metro North Railroad serves Westchester, Putnam and Dutchess counties. For schedules phone (212) 532-4900 in New York City, or (800) 638-7646 elsewhere in New York. The Long Island Rail Road serves Nassau and Suffolk counties; for schedule information phone (516) 822-5477.

From New Jersey, the NJ Transit stops every hour at Harmon Meadow Boulevard; phone (973) 762-5100.

More than 200 bus routes serve New York City. Buses run uptown on Tenth, Eighth, Sixth, Madison, Third and First avenues and downtown on Ninth, Seventh, Fifth and Second avenues. Some of the major east-west crosstown bus routes are 14th, 23rd, 34th, 42nd, 57th, 65th and 79th streets. Upon boarding, ask the bus driver for a free transfer from an uptown or downtown bus to a crosstown bus, or vice versa.

Most bus stops have Guide-A-Ride signs, showing bus stops and transfer points along that route. Fare on the Manhattan and Bronx lines is $2; exact change (no bills) is required. For information concerning the subway and city-operated buses phone the New York Transit Authority at (718) 330-1234.

LOWER MANHATTAN

AMERICAN NUMISMATIC SOCIETY, 140 William St. at Fulton St., has more than 600,000 coins and medals; a selection is displayed. A research library also is available. Tues.-Fri. 9-4:30; closed holidays. **Note:** The museum is scheduled to open in early 2004. Phone ahead to verify hours, admission and exhibition details. Interim exhibits are offered at the Federal Reserve Bank. Free. Phone (212) 234-3130.

BATTERY PARK, at the s. tip of Manhattan Island (S: South Ferry), was the site of a fort established by the first Dutch settlers in 1624. The park affords views of New York Harbor and the Statue of Liberty. The East Coast War Memorial is inscribed

with the names of American servicemen who died on the seas during World War II. "The Sphere," a sculpture representing world peace, was salvaged from the World Trade Center after Sept. 11, 2001. Daily 24 hours. Free.

Castle Clinton National Monument (S: South Ferry, Bowling Green) commemorates the 1811 West Battery Fort built to defend New York Harbor. The fort was U.S. Army headquarters during the War of 1812. Tickets to the Statue of Liberty *(see attraction listing p. 120)* are available. Daily 8:30-5. Closed Dec. 25. Free. Phone (212) 344-7220.

THE BOWERY, extending from Chatham Sq. n. to E. 4th St., was once the city's liveliest district and later the habitat of the homeless.

 CHINATOWN, near Chatham Sq., w. of the Bowery (S: Canal St.), includes Mott, Pell and Doyers streets. Chinese restaurants and shops line these streets and vendors crowd the busy sidewalks.

CITY HALL faces City Hall Park at Chambers St. and Broadway (S: City Hall). Near this spot, in the presence of Gen. George Washington, the Declaration of Independence was read to the Army on July 9, 1776. Mon.-Fri. 10-3:30. Free. Phone (212) 788-3000.

COOPER UNION FOUNDATION BUILDING is at E. 7th St. and Third Ave. When constructed in 1859 to house industrialist and inventor Peter Cooper's free college, this Italianate brownstone was the tallest building in New York City. The Great Hall served as a public forum and a platform for speeches by Abraham Lincoln, Frederick Douglass, Sioux Chief Red Cloud, Mark Twain, P.T. Barnum and Theodore Roosevelt. Allow 30 minutes minimum. Mon.-Sat. noon-5. Free. Phone (212) 353-4195.

ELLIS ISLAND—
see Statue of Liberty National Monument and Ellis Island p. 121.

FEDERAL HALL NATIONAL MEMORIAL, Wall and Nassau sts. (S: Wall St., Rector St.), was built in 1842 and is on the site of the first U.S. Capitol. The museum contains material pertaining to George Washington's inauguration, the Bill of Rights and old Federal Hall. Special events and programs also are available. Mon.-Fri. 9-5; closed major holidays. Free. Phone (212) 825-6888.

FEDERAL RESERVE BANK, 33 Liberty St. (S: Fulton St., Wall St.), offers tours by appointment that include a brief explanation of the Federal Reserve System. The history and significance of money is chronicled through the American Numismatic Society's exhibit of more than 800 coins, medals and currency used worldwide. Allow 1 hour

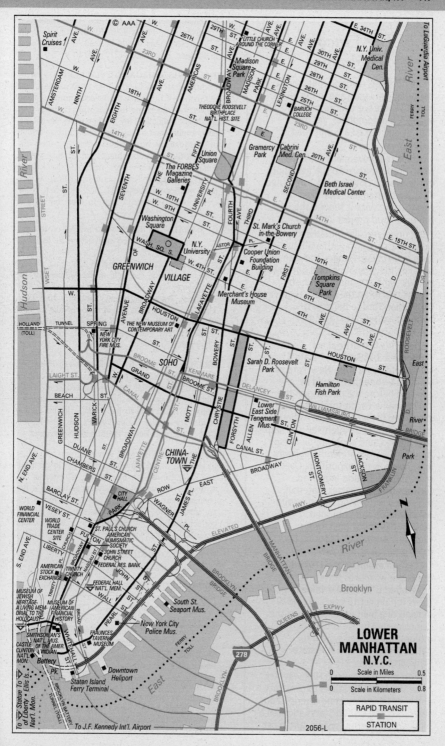

© AAA

Spirit Cruises

Hudson River

East River

To LaGuardia Airport
FERRY   TOLL

LITTLE CHURCH AROUND THE CORNER

Madison Square Park

N.Y. Univ. Medical Cen.

THEODORE ROOSEVELT BIRTHPLACE NAT'L. HIST. SITE

BARUCH COLLEGE

Union Square

Gramercy Park

Cabrini Med. Cen.

The FORBES Magazine Galleries

Beth Israel Medical Center

Washington Square

N.Y. University

St. Mark's Church in-the-Bowery

GREENWICH   VILLAGE

Cooper Union Foundation Building

Tompkins Square Park

Merchant's House Museum

HOLLAND (TOLL)   TUNNEL   SPRING

THE NEW MUSEUM OF CONTEMPORARY ART

NEW YORK CITY FIRE MUS.

SOHO

Sarah D. Roosevelt Park

HOUSTON

LAIGHT ST.

KENMARE

Hamilton Fish Park

BEACH

GRAND

BROOME ST.

CANAL

DELANCEY

Lower East Side Tenement Mus.

WILLIAMSBURG BRIDGE

East River Park

CHINA-TOWN

CANAL ST.

BROADWAY

WORLD FINANCIAL CENTER

CITY HALL

ELEVATED

MANHATTAN BRIDGE

WORLD TRADE CENTER SITE

ST. PAUL'S CHURCH AMERICAN NUMISMATIC SOCIETY

JOHN STREET CHURCH

FEDERAL RES. BANK

Brooklyn

AMERICAN STOCK EXCHANGE

TRINITY CHURCH

FEDERAL HALL NAT'L. MEM.

MUSEUM OF JEWISH HERITAGE. A LIVING MEMORIAL TO THE HOLOCAUST

MUSEUM OF AMERICAN FINANCIAL HISTORY

South St. Seaport Mus.

QUEENS EXPWY.

SMITHSONIAN'S NAT'L MUS. OF THE AMER. INDIAN

FRAUNCES TAVERN MUSEUM

New York City Police Mus.

CASTLE CLINTON NAT'L. MON.   Battery

278

BROOKLYN BATTERY TUNNEL (TOLL)

LOWER MANHATTAN N.Y.C.

Downtown Heliport

East River

Staten Island Ferry Terminal

To Statue To of Liberty • Ellis Is. Nat'l. Mon.

To J.F. Kennedy Int'l. Airport

2056-L

Scale in Miles   0   0.5

Scale in Kilometers   0   0.8

RAPID TRANSIT

STATION

The Lincoln Highway

The horseless carriage rolled onto the American landscape in the 1890s. By 1910 there were more than 450,000 registered automobiles, yet the country still lacked a public road system.

Organized movements for better roads brought issues to the attention of the federal government, which had not participated in major road construction since it funded the National Road project in 1806.

But one particular initiative captured the public's support with a unique idea. In 1913 Carl Fisher—the man who built the Indianapolis Motor Speedway in 1909—and automobile industry leaders chartered the Lincoln Highway Association for the purpose of defining a direct coast-to-coast automobile route.

The LHA's first official act was to delineate a 3,389-mile, 12-state continuous route from New York to California—one that would be passable before the opening of the 1915 Panama-Pacific International Exposition in San Francisco. Although not perfect, the throughway was ready as promised, and a motion picture of America's transcontinental highway was shown at the exposition. Over time, the association improved surfaces by using better materials, shortened the driving distance with realignments and published guidebooks about the Lincoln Highway. Automobile touring had never been so good.

Through example, the LHA educated the public as well as state and federal governments about the value of good roads for almost 15 years. The 1919 moving of a military convoy over the "Lincolnway" foretold the utility of an integrated highway system for national defense and interstate commerce.

With the 1921 Federal Highway Act came the funds for states to construct and maintain connecting arteries. Four years later the United States adopted a highway numbering system, and most

minimum. Exhibit open Mon.-Fri. 10-4. Bank tours are given Mon.-Fri. at 9:30, 10:30, 11:30, 1:30 and 2:30. Reservations should be made at least 1 week in advance. Free. Phone (212) 720-6130.

THE FORBES MAGAZINE GALLERIES is at 62 Fifth Ave. at 12th St. (S: 14th St./Broadway, 14th St./Sixth Ave.). Among the eclectic array of items collected by magazine founder Malcolm Forbes are toy boats, miniature toy soldiers, presidential papers, trophies and loving cups, and various versions of the Monopoly board game. A fine art gallery displays 19th-century paintings, and another gallery contains 12 Faberge eggs designed for Russian czars. Photography is not permitted. Allow 30 minutes minimum. Tues.-Wed. and Fri.-Sat. 10-4; closed holidays. Free. Under 16 must be with an adult. Phone (212) 206-5548.

[SAVE] **FRAUNCES TAVERN MUSEUM,** on the second and third floors of 54 Pearl St. at Broad (S: Whitehall St./South Ferry), was built in 1719 and became a tavern in 1762. In 1783 Gen. George Washington bade farewell to the officers of the Continental Army at the site. It housed the first American War Department. Tues.-Fri. 10-5 (also Thurs. 5-7), Sat. 11-5; closed major holidays except Washington's Birthday and July 4. Admission $3; senior citizens and ages 6-18, $2. Phone (212) 425-1778.

GRAMERCY PARK, E. 20th St. between Third Ave. and Park Ave. S., is a private park surrounded by a high iron fence. The gates are locked at all times. Since 1831 only persons living in the immediate vicinity have had keys to the grounds. In this section of the city are the National Arts Club, The Players Club, a statue of Edwin Booth and a synagogue.

GREENWICH VILLAGE extends from 14th St. s. to Houston St. and Washington Sq. w. to the Hudson River (S: W. 4th St., 8th St., Christopher St., Astor Pl.). Known for many years as the city's Bohemian center, "the Village" is famed for its restaurants, curio shops, bookstores, art shows, coffeehouses and nightclubs. *For a walking tour description, see What To Do, Sightseeing p. 137.*

HARBOR EXCURSIONS—
see What to Do, Sightseeing p. 137.

JOHN STREET CHURCH (United Methodist), 44 John St. (S: Fulton St., Broadway-Nassau St.), was dedicated as Wesley Chapel in 1768 and is said to be the oldest Methodist society in the United States. The church was torn down and rebuilt in 1817 and 1841. It contains many Methodist relics. Mon., Wed. and Fri. 11-4 and by appointment. Free. Phone (212) 269-0014.

LOWER EAST SIDE TENEMENT MUSEUM, 90 Orchard St. at Broome St. (S: Essex St., Delancey St.), recognizes the nation's urban, working class immigrants through exhibits based on the lives of tenement residents. Some 7,000 people from 20 countries occupied apartments in the 97 Orchard St. building 1863-1935.

Guided tours depart from the visitor center. Neighborhood walking tours also are offered. Allow 1 hour minimum. Visitor center daily 11-5:30. Guided tours are given every 40 minutes Tues.-Fri. 1-4:30, every 15 minutes Sat.-Sun. 11-4:30; closed Jan. 1, Thanksgiving and Dec. 25. Admission $10, over 65 and students with ID $8, under 5 free. AX, MC, VI. Phone (212) 431-0233.

MERCHANT'S HOUSE MUSEUM is at 29 E. 4th St., between Lafayette St. and The Bowery (S: 8th St, Astor Pl., Broadway/Lafayette St.). This elegant 1832 Greek Revival town house was occupied continuously by hardware merchant Seabury Tredwell's family 1835-1933. Marble mantelpieces, mahogany pocket doors, furniture by local cabinetmakers, decorative accessories and intact personal possessions such as clothing, needlework and photographs present a composite of a prosperous 19th-century lifestyle. Allow 1 hour minimum. Thurs.-Mon. 1-5; closed holidays. Tours are given Sat.-Sun. on the half-hour. Admission $6, over 65 and students with ID $4, under 13 free. AX, DC, MC, VI. Phone (212) 777-1089.

MUSEUM OF AMERICAN FINANCIAL HISTORY, 28 Broadway (S: Whitehall, Bowling Green) in the heart of the financial district, chronicles the history of American capital and finance including the stock market, business and industry, and finance in politics. Allow 30 minutes minimum. Tues.-Sat. 10-4; closed major holidays. Admission $2. Phone (212) 908-4110.

MUSEUM OF JEWISH HERITAGE—A LIVING MEMORIAL TO THE HOLOCAUST, 18 First Pl. in Battery Park City (S: Bowling Green, South Ferry, Whitehall), chronicles the 20th-century Jewish experience through artifacts, photographs and videotaped personal narratives in three exhibits: Jewish Life a Century Ago introduces the Jewish culture; the Holocaust is remembered by survivors in The War Against the Jews; and Jewish Renewal highlights the post-World War II achievements of the Jewish people. A Torah recovered from the Nazis is displayed in a hexagon-shaped room.

The six-sided building, itself a monument to Jewish heritage, symbolizes the points of the Star of David and the 6 million Jews who died in the Holocaust. An audiotape tour narrated by actress Meryl Streep and violinist Itzhak Perlman highlights the museum's artifacts.

Allow 2 hours minimum. Sun.-Thurs. 10-5:45 (also Thurs. 5:45-8), Fri. and eve of Jewish holidays 10-5, May 1-late Oct.; Sun.-Fri. 10-5:45 (also Thurs. 5:45-8), Fri. and eve of Jewish holidays 10-3, rest of year. Closed Thanksgiving and Jewish holidays. Last admission is 1 hour before closing. Admission $10; senior citizens, $7; students with ID $5; under 12 free. Audiotape tour $5. Advance purchase tickets are available. MC, VI. Phone (212) 509-6130.

The Lincoln Highway
(continued)

of the Lincoln route became US 30, 40 and 50. The association disbanded in 1928, but not before it engaged Boy Scout troops across the country to place some 3,000 concrete Lincoln Highway markers along the route in all 12 states: New York, New Jersey, Pennsylvania, Ohio, Indiana, Illinois, Iowa, Nebraska, Wyoming, Utah, Nevada and California. Many of these markers still exist.

Times Square in **New York City** was the official eastern terminus of the Lincoln Highway, which consisted of only 1 mile of road in New York state. From Broadway, motorists departed what Lincoln Highway guidebooks called "one of the most congested thoroughfare points in the world" and drove west on 42nd Street to the Hudson River, then caught a ferry to Weehawken, N.J. The Holland Tunnel, from Canal Street in Lower Manhattan to Jersey City, N.J., was completed about 1927; however, the Weehawken ferry served motorists crossing from Midtown Manhattan until the Lincoln Tunnel was built at 39th Street in the late 1930s. **Look for these New York Lincoln Highway landmark towns in this TourBook guide.**

For more information about the old Lincoln Highway, contact the new Lincoln Highway Association, P.O. Box 308, Franklin Grove, IL 61031; phone (815) 456-3030.

NEW YORK

New York City

Digital Archives

THE NEW MUSEUM OF CONTEMPORARY ART, 583 Broadway (S: Prince St., Houston St.), displays works focusing on experimental ideas as well as exhibits portraying the development of emerging artists. Tues.-Sun. noon-6 (also Thurs. 6-8 p.m.); closed holidays. Admission $6, senior citizens and students with ID $3, under 18 free. Admission Thurs. after 6, $3. Phone (212) 219-1222.

NEW YORK CITY FIRE MUSEUM, 1 blk. n. of the Holland Tunnel at 278 Spring St. (S: Spring St.), displays the combined collection of fire memorabilia from the New York City Fire Department and The Home Insurance Co. The 1904 Beaux Arts-style firehouse has firefighting vehicles and tools from Colonial days to the present as well as displays about infamous fires, the firefighter and the history of fire insurance. A memorial exhibit honors firefighters who died Sept. 11, 2001.

Allow 1 hour minimum. Tues.-Sat. 10-5, Sun. 10-4; closed major holidays. Admission $5; senior citizens and students with ID $2; under 12, $1. Phone (212) 691-1303.

NEW YORK CITY POLICE MUSEUM, 100 Old Slip between Water and South sts. (S: South Ferry, Wall St.), houses police vehicles, weapons, uniforms, shields and memorabilia. A forensics exhibit details the process of identifying evidence, artifacts and personal items removed from the World Trade Center site. Interactive exhibits allow visitors to explore a crime scene or experience a day in the life of emergency service personnel. Allow 1 hour minimum. Tues.-Sat. 10-5; closed major holidays. Donations. Phone (212) 480-3100.

NEW YORK UNIVERSITY is at 50 W. 4th St., dominating the e. and s. sides of Washington Sq. (S: W. 4th St., 8th St., Christopher St., Astor Pl.). Samuel F.B. Morse developed the electric telegraph and John W. Draper took the first photographic portrait at this spot. Guided tours are given Mon.-Fri. at 10:30 and 3:30. Free. Phone (212) 998-4500.

ST. MARK'S CHURCH IN-THE-BOWERY (Episcopal), Second Ave. at 10th St. (S: Astor Place, Broadway, 8th St.), was built in 1795. Peter Stuyvesant, the last Dutch governor of New Netherland, is buried in the church. Mon.-Fri. 10-4. Donations. Phone (212) 674-6377.

ST. PAUL'S CHAPEL (Episcopal), Trinity Parish, is at Broadway and Fulton St. (S: Fulton St., Chambers St.). Dedicated in 1766, the church is purported to be the oldest public building in continuous use now standing in Manhattan. George Washington and Gov. George Clinton had designated pews. Mon.-Sat. 10-6, Sun. 10-4; closed holidays. Donations. Phone (212) 602-0874.

SMITHSONIAN'S NATIONAL MUSEUM OF THE AMERICAN INDIAN is next to Battery Park in the Alexander Hamilton U.S. Custom House at One Bowling Green (S: South Ferry). Artifacts depict the art, culture and lifestyles of North, Central and South American Indians since prehistoric times. Collections include tools, weapons, ornaments, clothing, utensils, containers, toys and means of transport. The Beaux Arts-style building was constructed at the turn of the 20th century and features exterior sculpture and a large rotunda with elaborate murals. Allow 1 hour minimum. Daily 10-5 (also Thurs. 5-8); closed Dec. 25. Free. Phone (212) 514-3700.

SOHO, an acronym for "south of Houston Street," is 3 blks. s. of Washington Square Park. Avantgarde galleries, shops and eateries line the streets between West Broadway, Houston, Lafayette and Canal streets. SoHo's trademark cast-iron buildings appealed to poor artists, who transformed the area into one of the city's hot spots.

SAVE **SOUTH STREET SEAPORT MUSEUM** is bounded by South, John, Pearl and Dover sts. (S: Broadway-Nassau St., Fulton St.). This 12-block historic district was a flourishing 17th- and 18th-century port. The museum is comprised of landmark buildings, refurbished warehouses and the "Street of Ships." Of interest are art galleries, a print shop with antique presses, a 1923 tugboat pilothouse and a lighthouse memorial to the victims of the 1912 *Titanic* disaster.

Food is available. Allow 2 hours minimum. Daily 10-6, Apr.-Sept.; Wed.-Mon. 10-5, rest of year. Admission $5, under 12 free. AX, MC, VI. Phone (212) 748-8600.

Museum Ships are docked at Pier 16 in the East River. Vessels along the "Street of Ships" include the *Pioneer*, an 1885 schooner; the 1908 *Ambrose*, a floating lighthouse used to guide ships through lower New York Bay; and the *Peking*, a restored, four-masted German merchant vessel launched in 1911. Guided tours are available.

STATUE OF LIBERTY NATIONAL MONUMENT AND ELLIS ISLAND is in Upper New York Bay on Liberty Island. The statue was presented to the United States by France in 1884 in commemoration of the two countries' alliance during the American Revolution. Measuring 151 feet high on a 154-foot-high pedestal, it is the tallest statue of modern times.

The American Museum of Immigration in the base traces the history of immigration into the United States; also presented is an exhibit about the history of the statue. Nearby Ellis Island (*see attraction listing*) was the main point of entry into the United States for immigrants 1892-1954.

Liberty Island is only accessible by ferry service, available daily from Battery Park in Lower Manhattan and from Liberty State Park in Jersey City, N.J. A round-trip ticket includes stops at both Liberty Island and Ellis Island.

Food is available. Allow 2 hours minimum. Boats depart from Battery Park and Liberty State Park daily 9:30-3:30 (weather permitting); closed Dec. 25. Hours may vary; phone ahead. **Note:** Due to security concerns, the statue and museum have been closed indefinitely; only the grounds are open to the public. Ferry $10; over 61, $8; ages 4-12, $4. Phone (212) 363-3200 for the monument, (201) 915-3401 for Liberty State Park, (212) 269-5755 for ferry departures from New York, or (201) 435-9499 for ferry departures from New Jersey.

Ellis Island, in New York Harbor near the Statue of Liberty (S: South Ferry), was the nation's main point of entry for millions of immigrants 1892-1954. Exhibits chronicle the history of the processing station and the island. The site also includes the Immigration Library and an oral history studio. The American Immigrant Wall of Honor is a series of stainless steel panels engraved with the names of nearly 400,000 immigrants.

Ellis Island is only accessible by ferry service, available daily from Battery Park in Lower Manhattan and from Liberty State Park in Jersey City, N.J. A round-trip ticket includes stops at both Liberty Island, the site of the Statue of Liberty National Monument, and Ellis Island.

Audiotapes that relate the history of the island, explain the exhibits and outline a walking tour are available. Arrive early to avoid crowds. Allow 4 hours minimum. Museum open daily 9-5. Boats depart from Battery Park and Liberty State Park daily 9:30-3:30 (weather permitting); closed Dec. 25. Hours may vary; phone ahead. Museum free. Ferry $10; over 61, $8; ages 4-12, $4. Phone (212) 269-5755 for general information or New York ferry departures, (201) 435-9499 for New Jersey ferry departures, or (212) 363-3200 for the museum.

THEODORE ROOSEVELT BIRTHPLACE NATIONAL HISTORIC SITE, 28 E. 20th St. between Park Ave. S. and Broadway (S: 23rd St., Park Ave. S.), is the reconstructed boyhood home of the only United States president born in New York City. It was his home 1858-72. Galleries and 1865-period rooms relate the story of young Teddy. The four floors contain items pertaining to Roosevelt's youth, ranch life, presidency and exploring days. Guided tours on the hour Tues.-Sat. 9-5; closed federal holidays. Last tour begins 1 hour before closing. Admission $3, under 17 free. Phone (212) 260-1616.

TRINITY CHURCH (Episcopal), Broadway at Wall St. (S: Rector St., Wall St.), was originally built 1696-97. In 1754 it was the first site of King's College (now Columbia University). The present edifice was completed in 1846. Alexander Hamilton and Robert Fulton are buried in the church. Church museum open Mon.-Fri. 9-11:45 and 1-3:45, Sat. 10-3:45, Sun. 1-3:45. Guided tours Mon.-Sat. at 2, Sun. at 11:15 and 2. Free. Phone (212) 602-0800.

WALL STREET (S: Wall St.), the financial keystone of the country, takes its name from the wooden wall erected by the Dutch burghers in 1653 to protect the colony from attack. The New York Stock Exchange is at 11 Wall St.

WASHINGTON SQUARE, foot of Fifth Ave., is the scene of art shows in the spring and fall. Washington Arch, designed by Stanford White, stands at the head of the square.

MIDTOWN MANHATTAN

AMERICAN CRAFT MUSEUM, 40 W. 53rd St. (S: 5th Ave., 53rd St.), exhibits artistic handicrafts in fabrics, ceramics, metals, wood and architecture. Allow 1 hour, 30 minutes minimum. Daily 10-6 (also Thurs. 6-8 p.m.); closed Jan. 1, July 4, Thanksgiving and Dec. 25. Admission $8, over 64 and students with ID $5, under 12 free. Phone (212) 956-3535.

[SAVE] **AMERICAN FOLK ART MUSEUM**, 45 W. 53rd St. (S: Fifth Ave./53rd St.), celebrates American creativity through exhibits of folk art dating from the 18th century to the present day. Allow 1 hour, 30 minutes minimum. Tues.-Sun. 10:30-5:30 (also Fri. 5:30-7:30); closed Jan. 1, July 4, Thanksgiving and Dec. 25. Admission $9, over 61 and students with ID $7, under 12 free; free to all Fri. 6-8 p.m. AX, MC, VI. Phone (212) 265-1040.

AMERICAN MUSEUM OF NATURAL HISTORY, Central Park West at 79th St. (S: 79th St./Broadway, 81st St./Central Park W.), explores American Indian, Asian, Pacific Island, South American, Aztec and Mayan cultures through changing and permanent exhibits.

Six fossil halls with more than 600 specimens trace the development of vertebrates and feature interactive exhibits. In the Hall of Biodiversity visitors can experience the sounds and smells of a rain forest and learn how the world's species and ecosystems are being preserved.

The Hall of Human Biology and Evolution educates visitors on the marvels of the human body through the use of models, dioramas, animation and holograms. An IMAX theater shows films about natural, scientific and anthropological subjects.

Guided tours and food are available. Allow 3 hours minimum. Daily 10-5:45; closed Thanksgiving and Dec. 25. IMAX films are shown daily; phone ahead for schedule. Admission (includes Rose Center) $12; over 59 and students with ID $9; ages 2-12, $7. Combination ticket for museum, Rose Center and Hayden Planetarium space show $22; over 59 and students with ID $16.50; ages 2-12, $13. Theater or special exhibition $7; over 59 and students with ID $5; ages 2-12, $4. AX, CB, DC, DS, JC, MC, VI. Phone (212) 769-5100. *See ad p. 114.*

Rose Center for Earth and Space is on 81st St. at Central Park West or entered through the American Museum of Natural History (S: 81st St./Central Park W., 79th St./Broadway). Exhibits explore Earth's origins, geology, climate, habitats and relationship to the universe.

Visitors will find answers to frequently asked questions about the cosmos in the Hall of the Universe, which features images taken from satellites and through telescopes. Rocks and minerals are displayed in the Hall of Planet Earth.

The 360-foot-long Cosmic Pathway traces 13 billion years of cosmic evolution, equating each human step on the walkway to 75 million years of celestial development. In the Scales of the Universe

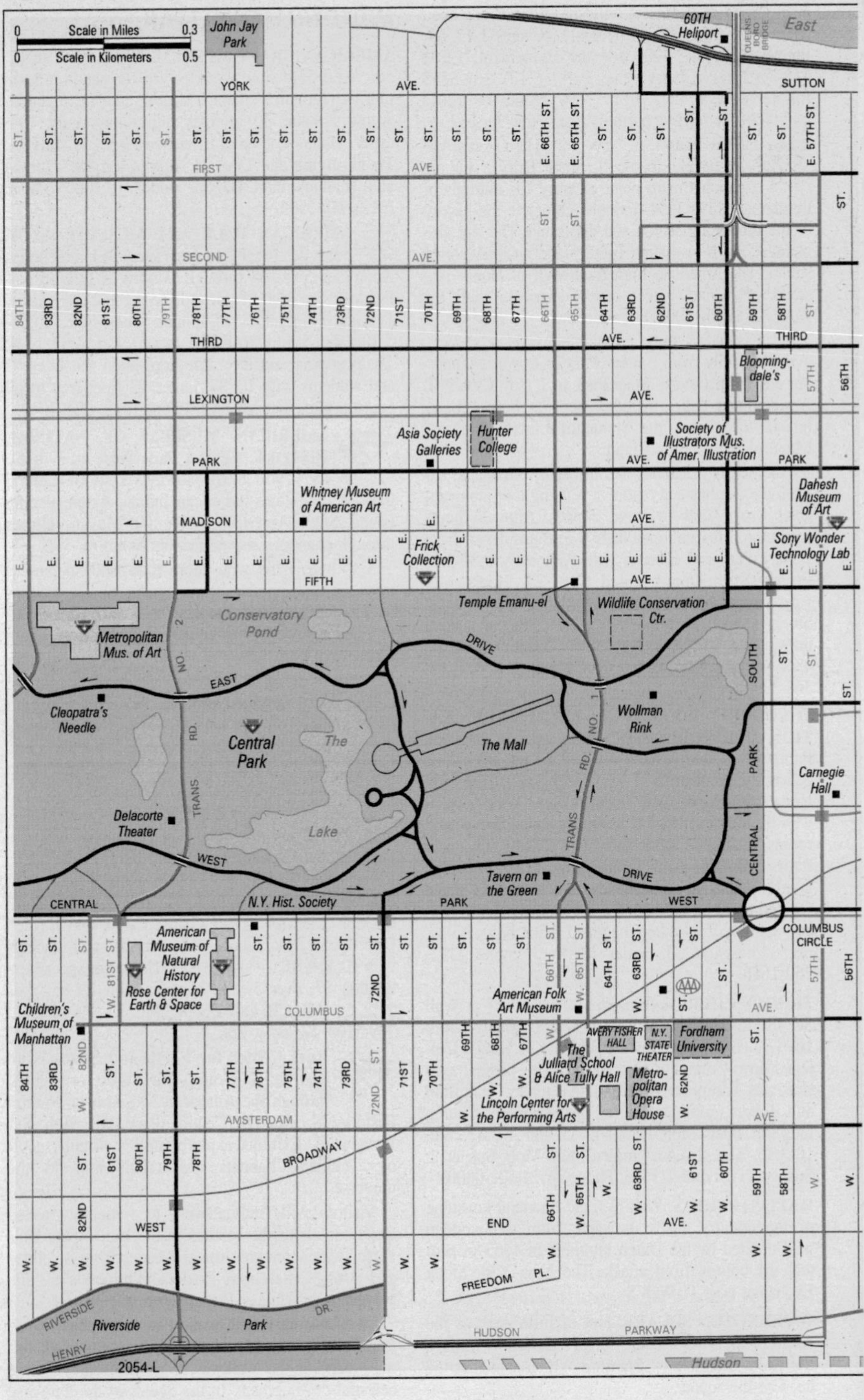

East

60TH Heliport

John Jay Park

Scale in Miles 0.3
Scale in Kilometers 0.5

YORK AVE.

SUTTON

E. 57TH ST.
E. 66TH ST.
E. 65TH ST.

ST.

FIRST AVE.

SECOND AVE.

84TH
83RD
82ND
81ST
80TH
79TH
78TH
77TH
76TH
75TH
74TH
73RD
72ND
71ST
70TH
69TH
68TH
67TH
66TH
65TH
64TH
63RD
62ND
61ST
60TH
59TH
58TH

THIRD AVE.

THIRD

57TH
56TH

LEXINGTON AVE.

Bloomingdale's

Asia Society Galleries

Hunter College

Society of Illustrators Mus. of Amer. Illustration

PARK AVE.

PARK

Dahesh Museum of Art

Whitney Museum of American Art

MADISON AVE.

Sony Wonder Technology Lab

Frick Collection

FIFTH AVE.

Temple Emanu-el

Wildlife Conservation Ctr.

Conservatory Pond

DRIVE

Metropolitan Mus. of Art

EAST

RD. NO. 2

Cleopatra's Needle

Central Park

The Mall

RD. NO. 1

Wollman Rink

SOUTH ST.

The

Lake

TRANS RD.

Delacorte Theater

CENTRAL PARK

Carnegie Hall

WEST

TRANS DRIVE

Tavern on the Green

CENTRAL

N.Y. Hist. Society

PARK

WEST

COLUMBUS CIRCLE

American Museum of Natural History

Rose Center for Earth & Space

W. 81ST ST.

72ND

60TH
63RD
64TH
65TH

57TH
56TH

American Folk Art Museum

Children's Museum of Manhattan

COLUMBUS

84TH
83RD
82ND
81ST
80TH
79TH
78TH
77TH
76TH
75TH
74TH
73RD
72ND
71ST
70TH
69TH
68TH
67TH

The Julliard School & Alice Tully Hall

AVERY FISHER HALL

N.Y. STATE THEATER

Fordham University

Metropolitan Opera House

62ND

AMSTERDAM

Lincoln Center for the Performing Arts

66TH
65TH

63RD
61ST
60TH
59TH
58TH

BROADWAY

WEST

END

AVE.

W.

FREEDOM PL.

RIVERSIDE

Riverside Park

DR.

HUDSON PARKWAY

HENRY

2054-L

Hudson

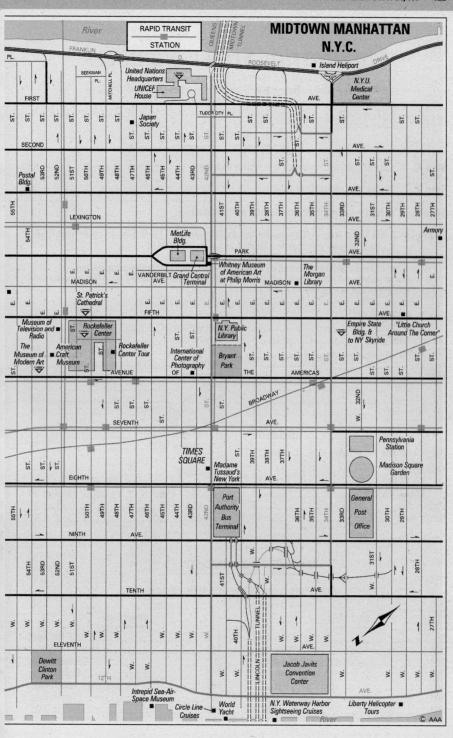

MIDTOWN MANHATTAN
N.Y.C.

Key to
Manhattan Street Numbers

Correct use of this formula will locate the cross-street of virtually
any address in Manhattan.

NORTH-SOUTH AVENUES

Step A: Cancel the last figure of the house number.

Step B: Divide the remainder by 2.

Step C: Add the key number, or deduct as indicated.

Example: 1165 Third Ave. A: Cancel the last figure—result 116. B: Divide by 2—result 58.
C: Add 10 (key number for Third Ave.)—result 68th St.

*On streets or address numbers preceded by an asterisk, omit Step B from the computation.
**On streets or address numbers preceded by two asterisks, omit Steps A and B from the computation
  and divide the house number by 10.

Ave. A, B, C, D	3	Tenth Ave.	13
First Ave.	3	Eleventh Ave.	15
Second Ave.	3	Amsterdam	59
Third Ave.	10	Columbus	59
Fourth Ave.	8	Lexington	22
Fifth Ave.:		Madison	27
1—200	13	Park	34
201—400	16	West End	59
401—600	18	Central Park West**	60
601—775	20	Riverside Dr.**:	
776—1286*	Deduct 18	1—567*	73
Avenue of the Americas	Deduct 12	Above 567*	78
Seventh Ave.:		Broadway:	
1—1800	12	1—754 are below 8th St.	
Above 1800	20	754—858	Deduct 29
Eighth Ave.	9	858—958	Deduct 25
Ninth Ave.	13	Above 1000	Deduct 31

EAST-WEST NUMBERED STREETS

Addresses begin at the streets listed below.

East Side		West Side	
1	Fifth Ave.	1	Fifth Ave.
101	Park Ave.	101	Avenue of the Americas
201	Third Ave.	201	Seventh Ave.
301	Second Ave.	301	Eighth Ave.
401	First Ave.	401	Ninth Ave.
501	York or Ave. A	501	Tenth Ave.
601	Ave. B	601	Eleventh Ave.

exhibit, models of human and cosmic objects are juxtaposed to show their relative size.

The Hayden Planetarium's space show "Passport to the Universe" takes viewers on a virtual trip through the Milky Way to the edge of the universe. Allow 2 hours minimum. Daily 10-5:45 (also Fri.-Sat. 5:45-8:45); closed Thanksgiving and Dec. 25. Space show daily 10:30-4:30 (also Fri.-Sat. 4:30-7:30). Admission (includes museum) $12; over 59 and students with ID, $9; ages 2-12, $7. Combination ticket for center, museum and space show $22; over 59 and students with ID, $16.50; ages 2-12, $13. Reservations are recommended for space shows. AX, CB, DC, DS, JC, MC, VI. Phone (212) 769-5100.

ASIA SOCIETY GALLERIES, 725 Park Ave. at 70th St. (S: 68th St.-Hunter College), presents Asian cultural programs and changing exhibits of Asian art. Tues.-Sun. 11-6 (also Fri. 6-9 p.m.); closed major holidays. Admission $7, over 64 and students with ID $5. Phone (212) 288-6400.

CARNEGIE HALL is at 57th St. and Seventh Ave. The 1891 Italian Renaissance-style structure is renowned for its perfect acoustics and exquisite architecture and decor. The center plays host to prominent orchestras and international performers. The Rose Museum offers a historical perspective. Museum open Thurs.-Tues. 11-4:30. Tours are conducted Mon.-Fri. at 11:30, 2 and 3, mid-Sept. through June 30. Performance schedule varies; phone ahead. Fee for tour $6; over 61 and students with ID $5; under 12, $3. Phone (212) 247-7800.

CENTRAL PARK, extending from 59th to 110th sts. and from Fifth Ave. to Central Park W., was designed as a refuge for New York City residents by architects Frederick Law Olmsted and Calvert Vaux. The park contains 843 acres of wooded and landscaped grounds with gardens, lakes, ice-skating rinks, a swimming pool and a carousel.

The Central Park Zoo and Wildlife Conservation Center, 64th Street and Fifth Avenue, displays wildlife in naturalistic surroundings. The formal, 6-acre Conservatory Garden, 105th Street and Fifth Avenue, contains English, French and Italian landscape styles. The Conservatory Water, near 74th Street and Fifth Avenue, is a model boat pond.

Belvedere Castle, a Victorian folly constructed in 1872, now houses the Henry Luce Nature Observatory, which features exhibits about the park's ecosystems and wildlife. A park visitor center at 65th Street is in a restored dairy building that served as a 19th-century refreshment center.

Picnicking is permitted. Food is available. Visitor center Tues.-Sun. 9-5, mid-Apr. through Oct. 15; 11-5, rest of year. Zoo and wildlife conservation center Mon.-Fri. 10-5, Sat.-Sun. 10-5:30. Guided park walking tours are given Wed. and Fri.-Sun. **Note:** Visit the park during daylight hours only. Park free. Zoo and wildlife conservation center $6; over 64, $1.25; ages 3-12, $1. Phone (212)

360-3456, or (212) 861-6030 for the zoo, (212) 794-6564 for the visitor center, or (212) 360-3444 for event information.

CHILDREN'S MUSEUM OF MANHATTAN, in the Tisch Building at 212 W. 83rd St. between Broadway and Amsterdam Ave. (S: 86th St./Broadway), presents permanent and changing exhibits that teach children about the creative processes using art, science and nature participatory exhibits and activity stations. Allow 1 hour minimum. Tues.-Sun. 10-5, July 1-Labor Day; Wed.-Sun. and school holidays 10-5, rest of year; closed Jan. 1, Thanksgiving and Dec. 25. Admission $6; over 64, $3; under 1 free. AX, MC, VI. Phone (212) 721-1223.

DAHESH MUSEUM OF ART, 580 Madison Ave. between 56th and 57th sts., is named for a Lebanese writer and philosopher with a penchant for 19th- and 20th-century European academic art. Art schools, particularly the French Academy, prescribed rigorous training for students while expecting them to possess a high level of technical skill and familiarity with lofty Western subjects. The goal was to prevent the perception that painting was a mere craft.

The collection includes paintings, drawings, watercolors, sculptures and prints representing the main academic categories: history paintings, landscapes, portraiture, still lifes, genre scenes, animal depictions and orientalism. Tues.-Sun. 11-6; closed holidays. Admission $9; over 61 and students with ID $4, under 12 free. Phone (212) 759-0606.

EMPIRE STATE BUILDING, 350 Fifth Ave. at 34th St. (S: 33rd St., 34th St. Herald Sq.), is one of the world's tallest office buildings. The Art Deco building, soaring 1,454 feet, has 2 million square feet of office space. Elevators run to the observatory on the 86th floor (1,050 feet), where visitors can see approximately 50 miles. Another elevator rises to the circular glass-enclosed observation tower on the 102nd floor (1,250 feet).

Completed in 1931, the building is made of Indiana limestone and granite trimmed with sparkling stainless steel. The lobby features marble imported from Belgium, France, Germany and Italy as well as eight original art works depicting the Seven Wonders of the Ancient World and the Eighth Wonder of the Modern World—the Empire State Building. The top 30 floors of the building are lit year-round from dusk to midnight with changing colors throughout the year.

Observation tower open daily 9:30 a.m.-midnight. Last ticket sold 45 minutes before closing. **Note:** Visitors may encounter long lines. Tower admission $11; over 61 and ages 12-17, $10; military with ID, $9; ages 6-11, $6. Multilingual audiotape $5. Lobby exhibits free. Phone (212) 736-3100. *See ad p. 114.*

FRICK COLLECTION is at 1 E. 70th St. between Fifth and Madison aves. (S: 68th St.-Hunter College). Housed in the Henry Clay Frick mansion erected 1913-14, the collection features the paintings, antiques, decorative art and furnishings owned by the industrialist and philanthropist. Paintings include works by Thomas Gainsborough, Frans Hals, Claude Monet, Johannes Vermeer and James McNeill Whistler. Also displayed are Limoges enamels, Oriental rugs, porcelains and sculpture.

Allow 1 hour minimum. Tues.-Sat. 10-6 (also Fri. 6-9 p.m.), Sun. 1-6; closed Jan. 1, July 4, Thanksgiving and Dec. 24-25. Admission $12; over 62, $8; students with ID $5. Under 10 are not admitted; ages 11-15 must be with an adult. Phone (212) 288-0700.

GARMENT DISTRICT, bounded by Sixth and Eighth aves. and 34th and 40th sts., accounts for one-third of the clothes manufactured in this country. During working hours this is one of the busiest areas of the city, with workers pushing racks of clothes down the street and transporting bolts of cloth between factories.

GRAND CENTRAL TERMINAL, 42nd St. between Lexington and Vanderbilt aves. (S: Grand Central), is the city entrance through which half a million commuters pass every day. The 1913 Beaux Arts terminal serves the MTA Metro-North Railroad and has a subway stop connecting the station to city destinations. Shops and restaurants are on the premises. Be sure to gaze up at the constellation mural on the 120-foot-high ceiling of the main concourse. Tours are given Wed. and Fri. at 12:30. Free. Phone (212) 697-1245.

MetLife Building, next to the Grand Central Terminal, rises 59 stories and is one of the world's largest office buildings.

INTERNATIONAL CENTER OF PHOTOGRAPHY is at 1133 Avenue of the Americas at 43rd St. (S: 42nd St.). Established in 1974, the gallery is devoted to the exhibition, preservation and study of all aspects of photography—from master photographers to newly emerging talent, from photo journalism to the avant-garde, and from photograph aesthetics to technique. Exhibits change every 3 months. Allow 30 minutes minimum. Tues.-Thurs. 10-5, Fri. 10-8, Sat.-Sun. 10-6; closed Jan. 1, July 4, Thanksgiving and Dec. 25. Gallery tours are offered Tues. at 2. Admission $10, over 64 and students with ID $7, under 12 free. AX, DS, MC, VI. Phone (212) 857-0000.

SAVE **INTREPID SEA-AIR-SPACE MUSEUM** is docked at Pier 86 on W. 46th St. at 12th Ave. (S: 42nd St., then M42 bus; 49th St., 50th St. or 51st St., then M50 bus). The decommissioned *Intrepid,* an aircraft carrier used in World War II and Vietnam, also was a space program recovery ship before being converted into a museum. The hangar deck houses the U.S. Navy Hall, *Intrepid* Hall, Pioneers Hall and Technologies Hall; the flight deck has historic aircraft. Multimedia presentations are offered.

Mon.-Fri. 10-5, Sat.-Sun. and holidays 10-6, May-Sept.; Tues.-Sun. 10-5, rest of year. Closed Thanksgiving and Dec. 25. Last ticket sold 1 hour before closing. Admission $14; over 64 and ages 12-17, $10; ages 6-11, $7; ages 2-5, $2. AX, MC, VI. Phone (212) 245-0072. *See ad p. 114.*

JAPAN SOCIETY, 333 E. 47th St. between First and Second aves. (S: Grand Central Station/42nd St.), presents exhibits of traditional and contemporary Japanese art. Films, performing arts and topical lectures are offered. Mon.-Fri. 11-6, Sat.-Sun. 11-5, during exhibits. Hours may vary; phone ahead. Admission $5, over 64 and students with ID $3. Ticket prices may vary with each event. Phone (212) 752-0824 for current exhibits.

GEM **LINCOLN CENTER FOR THE PERFORMING ARTS,** 62nd to 66th sts. between Columbus and Amsterdam aves. (S: 66th St./Broadway), is a 14-acre complex of educational and artistic institutions. The buildings were designed by some of the nation's finest architects.

Tours leave the center concourse daily at 10:30, 12:30, 2:30 and 4:30; closed Jan. 1, July 4, Thanksgiving and Dec. 25. Tour fee $12.50; over 64 and students with ID $9; ages 6-12, $6. Guided 1-hour tours are limited to 19 persons per tour. Reservations are required. Phone (212) 875-5350.

Alice Tully Hall is the home of the Chamber Music Society of Lincoln Center.

Avery Fisher Hall, Broadway at 65th St., is the home of the New York Philharmonic Orchestra.

The Juilliard School contains four auditoriums and classrooms for music students.

Metropolitan Opera House is the home of the renowned Metropolitan Opera.

New York Public Library for the Performing Arts (Library and Museum of the Performing Arts) has extensive archives covering music, theater and dance. The Bruno Walter Auditorium presents chamber concerts, dance recitals, poetry readings and other events. Exhibition areas are devoted to displays about the performing arts. Library open Tues.-Sat. noon-6 (also Thurs. 6-8 p.m.); closed holidays. Phone (212) 870-1630.

New York State Theater, Columbus Ave. and 63rd St., houses the New York City Ballet and the New York City Opera.

"LITTLE CHURCH AROUND THE CORNER" is at 1 E. 29th St. near Fifth Ave. (S: 28th St.). It is also known as the Church of the Transfiguration (Episcopal). Daily 8-6. A guided tour is offered Sun. at 1. Donations. Phone (212) 684-6770 or (212) 684-6771.

SAVE **MADAME TUSSAUD'S NEW YORK** is at 234 W. 42nd St. between Seventh and Eighth aves. (S: 42nd St./Times Square). Realistic wax figures representing icons of popular culture, entertainment, sports, politics and New York history are staged in interactive vignettes.

AAA MEMBERS SAVE **15%**

COME EXPRESS YOURSELF FREELY.

THE AMAZINGLY LIFE-LIKE WAX FIGURES OF THE BEST-KNOWN PERSONALITIES FROM NEW YORK AND AROUND THE WORLD ARE NOW INTERACTIVE. THIS MAY INCLUDE PUTTING YOURSELF IN THEIR PLACE - IT'S ABOUT TIME.

SAVE 15%

AAA MEMBERS RECEIVE A 15% DISCOUNT ON ADMISSION AND ON ALL PURCHASES WHEN VISITING MADAME TUSSAUDS NEW YORK

LOCATED AT 234 WEST 42ND STREET (BETWEEN 7TH & 8TH AVENUES). 1.800.246.8872. OPEN 365 DAYS A YEAR FROM 10:00AM UNTIL 10:00PM. LAST TICKET SOLD AT 8:00PM. WWW.NYCWAX.COM.

PRESENT YOUR AAA MEMBERSHIP CARD AT THE BOX OFFICE AND RECEIVE 15% OFF. CANNOT BE COMBINED WITH ANY OTHER OFFER. OFFER EXPIRES 4/1/05. CELEBRITIES APPEAR IN WAX. ON OCCASION MADAME TUSSAUDS NEW YORK MAY CLOSE EARLY FOR SPECIAL EVENTS. CALL FOR UPDATES.

MADAME TUSSAUDS NEW YORK

* C 2 1 0 0 0 4 *

Show Your Card & Save

AAA. Every Day.®

The Opening Night Party exhibit depicts a glitzy, after-theater gathering of such luminaries as Woody Allen, Bette Midler and Donald Trump. Likenesses of John F. Kennedy, the Dalai Lama and Diana, Princess of Wales are featured in The Gallery, an exhibit centered on notables of the world.

Hope, an exhibit about Sept. 11, 2001, portrays scenes of bravery and patriotism. Other exhibits follow Madame Tussaud's triumph during the French Revolution and offer a behind-the-scenes look at creating wax portraiture.

Allow 1 hour, 30 minutes minimum. Daily. 10-8. Hours may vary; phone ahead. Admission $25; over 59, $22; ages 4-12, $ 19. AX, DS, MC, VI. Phone (212) 512-9600 or (800) 246-8872. *See color ad p. 127 & ad p. 407.*

SAVE MADISON SQUARE GARDEN is at 4 Penn Plaza, between Seventh and Eighth aves. and 31st and 33rd sts. (S: 34th St.). The Garden has facilities for simultaneous major events and is the home of the city's basketball and hockey teams. Behind-the-scenes guided tours visit the 20,000-seat main arena, the theater, restaurants, a luxury suite and locker rooms. Allow 1 hour minimum. Tours are given daily 10-3 except during performances and games; phone ahead. Fee $16; under 12, $12. Phone (212) 465-5800.

GEM METROPOLITAN MUSEUM OF ART, 1000 Fifth Ave. at 82nd St. (S: 86th St./ Lexington Ave.), is one of the great museums of the world. Among the collections are Egyptian, Greek and Roman art; Near Eastern art and antiquities; European and Oriental paintings and sculpture; arms and armor; musical instruments; arts from Africa, Oceania and the Americas; modern art; ancient glass; and European and American decorative arts.

The Iris and B. Gerald Cantor Roof Garden provides a vantage point overlooking Central Park and features many modern sculptures including "The Burghers of Calais" by Auguste Rodin.

Allow 3 hours minimum. Tues.-Sat. 9:30-5:30 (also Fri.-Sat. 5:30-9), Sun. 9-5; closed Jan. 1, Thanksgiving and Dec. 25. Admission $12, over 64 and students with ID $7, under 12 free. Admission includes The Cloisters in Upper Manhattan *(see attraction listing p. 132).* Phone (212) 535-7710.

THE MORGAN LIBRARY, 29 E. 36th St. at Madison Ave. (S: 34th St.), a palazzo-style building of Renaissance architecture, was the private library of J. Pierpont Morgan. Rare editions and illuminated manuscripts are featured as well as art objects, paintings, sculpture and a glass-enclosed garden court. Changing art and literature exhibits also are presented.

Food is available. Tues.-Thurs. 10:30-5, Fri. 10:30-8, Sat. 10:30-6, Sun. noon-6; closed holidays. Admission $8, over 64 and students with ID $6, under 12 free. Phone (212) 685-0008.

GEM THE MUSEUM OF MODERN ART, 11 W. 53rd St. (S: Fifth Ave./53rd St.), offers a survey of 20th-century paintings, sculptures, drawings, prints, photographs, architectural models and plans, design objects, films and videotapes. Classic, artistic or documentary movies are shown Thursday through Tuesday.

Food is available. Allow 2 hours, 30 minutes minimum. Thurs.-Tues. 10:30-5:45 (also Fri. 5:45-8:15); closed Thanksgiving and Dec. 25. **Note:** The museum is closed for renovations until early 2005. During this time exhibits can be seen at MoMA QNS, 33rd Street and Queens Boulevard in Queens; phone ahead to verify hours. Admission $12, over 65 and students with ID $8.50, under 16 free with an adult, donations Fri. 4-7:45. Phone (212) 708-9480. *See ad p. 114.*

MUSEUM OF TELEVISION AND RADIO, 25 W. 52nd St. (S: 5th Ave.), maintains a collection of some 50,000 radio and television program tapes. Visitors can select material from the museum's library, then watch or listen to it at one of 96 radio and television consoles. Tues.-Sun. noon-6 (also Thurs. 6-8 p.m. and Fri. 6-9 p.m.); closed Jan. 1, July 4, Thanksgiving and Dec. 25. Admission $10; over 64 and students with ID $8; under 13, $5. Phone (212) 621-6600.

NEW YORK HISTORICAL SOCIETY, 2 W. 77th St. at Central Park W. (S: 79th St./Broadway, 81st St./Central Park W.), houses a museum, print room and reference library. Allow 1 hour, 30 minutes minimum. Tues.-Sun. 10-6; closed Jan. 1, Thanksgiving and Dec. 25. Admission $8; over 64 and students with ID $5; under 12 free. Phone (212) 873-3400.

NEW YORK PUBLIC LIBRARY, 42nd St. and Fifth Ave. (S: 42nd St./Ave. of Americas, Fifth Ave.), houses a research library that contains more than 5 million volumes, including 21 specialized collections of American history, art, periodicals and Slavic, Jewish and Oriental literature. Main room open Tues.-Wed. 11-7:30, Thurs.-Sat. and Mon. 10-6; closed federal holidays. Free. Phone (212) 930-0800.

SAVE NY SKYRIDE is on the 2nd floor of the Empire State Building, Fifth Ave. and 34th St. (S: 33rd St., 34th St. Herald Sq.). Two 40-seat, big-screen, flight-simulator theaters feature a ride over various city landmarks, including the Statue of Liberty and Times Square. Motion simulators synchronized to the film's action move and tilt the seats, giving passengers the feel of soaring over Manhattan, gliding through Wall St., and riding Coney Island's Cyclone roller coaster. The experience includes two pre-shows.

Allow 30 minutes minimum. Daily 10-10. Admission $14.50; over 65 and ages 6-18, $13.50; ages 5-11, $12.50. AX, MC, VI. Phone (212) 279-9777.

PARK AVENUE, between 46th and 60th sts., is the site of major office buildings which incorporate innovative architectural features. Among the most impressive structures are the Seagram Building, 375 Park Ave.; the Lever House, 390 Park Ave.; and the corporate headquarters of Manufacturer's Hanover Bank, 270 Park Ave.

ROCKEFELLER CENTER, Fifth Ave. to Avenue of the Americas (Sixth Ave.) and 48th to 51st sts. (S: 47th St./50th St., 49th St., 50th St., 51st St.), is a model of urban planning and design, housing 24 acres of underground shops and restaurants. A self-guiding tour brochure is available at the information desk. Phone (212) 698-2950, or (212) 632-3975 for information.

NBC Studio Tours, departing from the NBC Experience Store at 30 Rockefeller Plaza, gives 70-minute behind-the-scenes tours of the production areas of several television shows. Tours depart every 15 minutes Mon.-Sat. 8:30-5:30, Sun. 9:30-4:30. Ticket sales begin at 8. Tours $17.75; senior citizens and ages 6-16, $15. Under 6 are not permitted. MC, VI. Phone (212) 664-3700 or (212) 664-7174.

Radio City Music Hall is on Avenue of the Americas (Sixth Ave.) between W. 50th and W. 51st sts. This 1932 Art Deco theater presents musical stage spectaculars with the Rockettes as well as theatrical productions and live concerts. Guided 1-hour tours departing from the lobby are available. Mon.-Fri. 11-3, Sun. noon-3. Tour $17; under 12, $10. AX, MC, VI. Phone (212) 247-4777.

SAVE **Rockefeller Center Tour** departs from the NBC Experience Store at 30 Rockefeller Plaza. Guided outdoor walking tours explore the art, architecture and history of the "city within a city." Highlights include more than 100 works of art, the Channel Gardens, the ice skating rink and the spot where "Today" show onlookers hang out. Allow 1 hour minimum. Tours are given daily on the hour 10-4; closed Thanksgiving and Dec. 25. Fee $10; senior citizens and ages 6-16, $8. Reservations are recommended. AX, DS, MC, VI. Phone (212) 664-3700.

ST. PATRICK'S CATHEDRAL (Roman Catholic), Fifth Ave. at 50th St. (S: 47th St./50th St., 49th St., 50th St., 51st St.), is one of the largest churches in the United States, with a seating capacity of 2,400. The rose window is 26 feet across, and the pipe organ has more than 7,380 pipes. Twin spires 330 feet high grace the 14th-century Gothic-style structure.

The foundations of the church were laid before the Civil War, but the church was not open until 14 years after the war ended. Guided tours are available by appointment. Daily 6:30 a.m.-8:45 p.m. Phone (212) 753-2261.

SOCIETY OF ILLUSTRATORS MUSEUM OF AMERICAN ILLUSTRATION, 128 E. 63rd St. (S: 59th St./Lexington Ave.), displays changing exhibits

CityPass

CityPass offers savings to those who plan visits to many New York City attractions. The pass covers the price of admission to six sites: American Museum of Natural History, Empire State Building Observatory, NY SKYRIDE, Solomon R. Guggenheim Museum, *Intrepid* Sea-Air-Space Museum and Museum of Modern Art. The pass also includes a 2-hour Circle Line Harbor Cruise.

CityPass ticket booklets can be purchased at visitor information centers and at any of the participating attractions. The tickets, valid for 9 days from the first date of use, are $48; ages 6-17, $34. *See ad p. 114.*

Digital Archives

New York Pass

SAVE New York Pass can be used at 40 New York City attractions, including the Empire State Building, Solomon R. Guggenheim Museum and Circle Line Harbor Cruises. The purchase price includes a 125-page guidebook, admission to selected attractions without waiting in line and discounts or special offers at 25 restaurants, shops, theaters and helicopter rides.

Passes for 1, 2, 3 or 7 days range $49-$135, children $39-$95. New York Pass is available at Madame Tussaud's New York, NY SKYRIDE, Planet Hollywood, and the Port Authority of New York, at Eighth Avenue and 42nd St.; phone (877) 714-1999. *(See color ad p. 408).*

Central Park Zoo / © Kevin Schafer / Corbis

by noted illustrators of the past and present. Lectures and special demonstrations also are held. Allow 1 hour minimum. Tues.-Fri. 10-5 (also Tues. 5-8), Sat. noon-4. Free. Phone (212) 838-2560.

SONY WONDER TECHNOLOGY LAB, between 55th and 56th sts. at 550 Madison Ave. (S: 53rd St./ 5th Ave.), is an interactive science and technology museum that emphasizes hands-on state-of-the-art communications technology. Allow 1 hour minimum. Tues.-Sat. 10-6 (also Thurs. 6-8 p.m.), Sun. noon-6. Free. Phone (212) 833-8100.

TEMPLE EMANU-EL, Fifth Ave. and 65th St. (S: 68th St.), was founded in 1845 and is one of the world's largest reformed synagogues. Completed in 1929, the building features striking architecture, mosaics and stained-glass windows. Visitors are welcome to the festivals and a community service offered on high holy days. Sun.-Thurs. 10-4:30, Fri. 10-3; closed to visitors prior to Jewish festivals and on high holy days. Free. Phone (212) 744-1400.

UNICEF HOUSE, 3 United Nations Plaza at 44th St. between 1st and 2nd Ave. (S: 42nd St.), offers multimedia presentations about world peace, global development and the future of the world. Allow 1 hour minimum. Mon.-Fri. 9-5. Donations. Phone (212) 326-7000.

UNITED NATIONS HEADQUARTERS, on First Ave. between 42nd and 48th sts. (S: Grand Central/42nd St.), is along the East River. The visitors entrance is at First Ave. and 46th St. The complex consists of the majestic Secretariat Building, the domed General Assembly Building, the Conference Building and the Hammarskjold Library. Each building was designed and decorated by celebrated architects and artisans.

Tours lasting 1 hour depart from the public lobby daily 9:30-4:45; closed major holidays and the last week in Dec. Tour $10.50; over 61, $8; students with ID $7; grades 1-8, $6. Under 5 are not permitted on tour. Phone (212) 963-8687 for tour information.

WHITNEY MUSEUM OF AMERICAN ART, 945 Madison Ave. at 75th St. (S: 77th St.), presents modern sculptures, paintings, photographs, drawings, films and videotapes. An inverted pyramid construction allows 30,000 square feet of exhibition space in a building only 97 feet tall.

Allow 1 hour, 30 minutes minimum. Wed.-Thurs. and Sat.-Sun. 11-6, Fri. 1-9; closed Jan. 1, Thanksgiving and Dec. 25. Admission $12, over 61 and college students with ID $9.50, under 12 free with an adult; free to all Fri. 6-9 p.m. Phone (212) 570-3676.

WHITNEY MUSEUM OF AMERICAN ART AT PHILIP MORRIS, 120 Park Ave. at 42nd St. (S: 42nd St./Grand Central Station), presents changing exhibits on the ground floor and in the sculpture court. Museum talks are held Wednesday at 1. Gallery open Mon.-Fri. 11-6 (also Thurs. 6-7:30 p.m.); closed holidays. Sculpture court open Mon.-Sat. 7:30 a.m.-9:30 p.m., Sun. 11-7. Free. Phone (917) 663-2453.

UPPER MANHATTAN

AUDUBON TERRACE MUSEUM GROUP, Broadway at 155th St. (S: 157th St./Broadway), houses several museums with varying displays and exhibits. The Children's Museum of the Native American is open only to school groups.

American Academy of Arts and Letters, 633 W. 155th St., with gallery entrance on Audubon Terr., offers two exhibits a year. Thurs.-Sun. 1-4, in Mar. and mid-May to mid-June; closed major holidays. Free. Phone (212) 368-5900.

Hispanic Society of America, Broadway at 155th St., exhibits Spanish and Portuguese sculpture, paintings and decorative arts. Tues.-Sat. 10-4:30, Sun. 1-4; closed holidays. Free. Phone (212) 926-2234.

CATHEDRAL OF ST. JOHN THE DIVINE (Episcopal), 112th and Amsterdam Ave. at 1047 Amsterdam Ave. (S: 110th St. Cathedral Pkwy.), was begun in 1892. Built entirely of stone, including Maine granite and Indiana limestone, St. John's is two football fields long and 17 stories high. The Biblical Garden contains more than 100 plants mentioned in Scripture; the Peace Fountain is by Greg Wyatt.

Allow 1 hour minimum. Daily 7-6. Guided tours Tues.-Sat. at 11, Sun. at 1. Guided tour $5, senior citizens and students with ID $4. Phone (212) 316-7490.

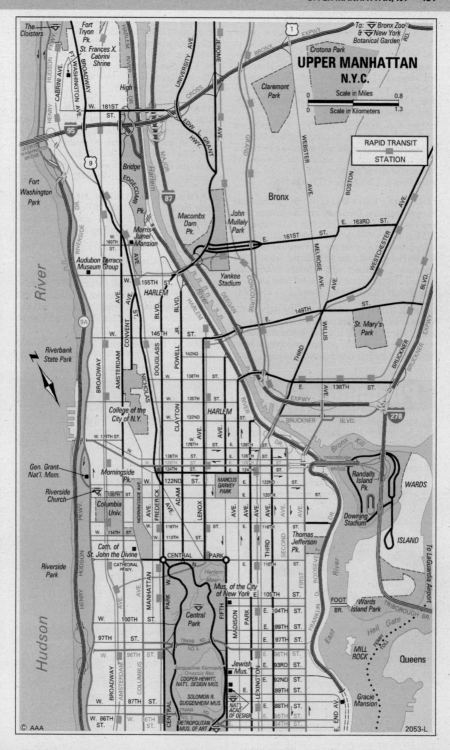

The Cloisters
Fort Tryon Pk.
St. Frances X. Cabrini Shrine
High
W. 181ST ST.
95
9
Bridge
EDGECOMB
Pk.
87
Morris Jumel Mansion
W. 160TH ST.
Audubon Terrace Museum Group
W. 155TH ST.
HARLEM
9A
Riverbank State Park
College of the City of N.Y.
W. 145TH ST.
142ND
POWELL
W. 138TH ST.
W. 135TH ST.
W. 132ND
HARLEM
CLAYTON
W. 129TH ST.
126TH ST.
Gen. Grant Nat'l. Mem.
Morningside Pk.
124TH ST.
122ND ST.
Riverside Church
120TH ST.
Columbia Univ.
W. 114TH ST.
116TH ST.
W. 113TH ST.
Cath. of St. John the Divine
CATHEDRAL PKWY.
Riverside Park
CENTRAL PARK
Harlem Meer
Mus. of the City of New York
105TH ST.
Central Park
W. 100TH ST.
W. 97TH ST.
TRANS RD. NO. 4
96TH ST.
Jacqueline Kennedy Onassis Res.
COOPER-HEWITT NAT'L DESIGN MUS.
Jewish Mus.
93RD
92ND
89TH
SOLOMON R. GUGGENHEIM MUS.
NAT'L ACAD. OF DESIGN
W. 87TH ST.
W. 86TH ST.
86TH
TRANS RD. NO. 3
METROPOLITAN MUS. OF ART
E. 88TH
E. 84TH
© AAA

1
EXPWY
To: Bronx Zoo & New York Botanical Garden
Crotona Park

UPPER MANHATTAN N.Y.C.

Scale in Miles
0   0.8
Scale in Kilometers
0   1.3

RAPID TRANSIT
STATION

Claremont Park
Bronx
Macombs Dam Pk.
John Mullaly Park
E. 163RD ST.
E. 161ST ST.
Yankee Stadium
CONCOURSE
E. 149TH
St. Mary's Park
E. 138TH ST.
BRUCKNER BLVD.
278
Bronx Kill
TRIBOROUGH BRIDGE
Randalls Island Pk.
WARDS
Downing Stadium
ISLAND
E. 128TH ST.
E. 126TH ST.
E. 124TH ST.
MARCUS GARVEY PARK
E. 122ND ST.
E. 120TH
LENOX
THIRD
SECOND
E. 116TH ST.
Thomas Jefferson Pk.
E. 110TH ST.
FRANKLIN D. ROOSEVELT DR.
East River
To LaGuardia Airport
TRIBOROUGH BR.
FOOT BR.
Wards Island Park
Hell Gate
MILL ROCK
Queens
FERRY TOLL
Gracie Mansion
E. 104TH ST.
E. 99TH ST.
E. 97TH ST.
E. 96TH ST.
MADISON
LEXINGTON
E. END AV.

Fort Washington Park
Hudson River
2053-L

Bronx
WEBSTER AVE.
BOSTON
WESTCHESTER AVE.
MELROSE AVE.
WILLIS
Bruckner EXPWY
BRUCKNER BLVD.
DR.
2053-L

THE CLOISTERS is in Fort Tryon Park, first exit n. of George Washington Bridge off Henry Hudson Pkwy. (S: 190th St. or M4 bus "Cloisters" on Madison Ave. to end). Devoted to medieval art, this branch of the Metropolitan Museum of Art includes parts of five French cloisters, a Romanesque chapel and extensive gardens. Collections include statues, paintings, stained-glass windows and tapestries.

Tues.-Sun. 9:30-5:15, Mar.-Oct.; 9:30-4:45, rest of year. Closed Jan. 1, Thanksgiving and Dec. 25. Admission $12, over 64 and students with ID $7, under 12 free. Admission includes the Metropolitan Museum of Art in Midtown Manhattan *(see attraction listing p. 128)*. Phone (212) 923-3700.

COLUMBIA UNIVERSITY is in Morningside Heights, between Broadway and Amsterdam Ave. and 114th and 120th sts. (S: 116th St.). Founded in 1754 as King's College, it includes Columbia College, School of Engineering and Applied Sciences, and several graduate and professional schools. The university is affiliated with Teachers College and Barnard College for women. Guided tours are given Mon.-Fri. at 11 and 2. Free. Phone (212) 854-4900.

COOPER-HEWITT, NATIONAL DESIGN MUSEUM is in the landmark Andrew Carnegie Mansion at 2 E. 91st St. (S: 86th St.). This Smithsonian Institution affiliate features historic and contemporary drawings, prints, textiles, ceramics, wall coverings, glass, metalwork and woodwork that present perspectives on the impact of design on daily life. The 250,000-piece collection representing cultures from around the world spans some 3,000 years. Tues.-Thurs. 10-5, Fri. 10-9, Sat. 10-6, Sun. noon-6; closed holidays. Admission $10, senior citizens and students with ID $8, under 12 free. Phone (212) 849-8400.

DYCKMAN HOUSE, 204th St. and Broadway (S: 207th St.), dates from 1784 and is the only Dutch farmhouse remaining on Manhattan Island. It is furnished in the style typical of wealthy colonists. Tues.-Sun. 10-4; closed Jan. 1, July 4, Thanksgiving and Dec. 25. Hours may vary; phone ahead. Admission $1. Phone (212) 304-9422.

GENERAL GRANT NATIONAL MEMORIAL, Riverside Dr. and 122nd St. (S: 116th St.), is the tomb of President Ulysses S. Grant and his wife. Daily 9-5; closed Jan. 1, Thanksgiving and Dec. 25. Free. Phone (212) 666-1640.

JEWISH MUSEUM, 1109 Fifth Ave. at 92nd St. (S: 86th St.) is said to be the largest Jewish museum in the world outside of Israel. Culture and Continuity: The Jewish Journey is a permanent exhibition that traverses 4,000 years of Jewish art, history and culture. Also available are changing art exhibits and a family interactive exhibit.

Allow 1 hour minimum. Sun.-Thurs. 11-5:45 (also Thurs. 5:45-8), Fri. 11-3; closed major and

Jewish holidays. Admission $10, over 64 and students with ID $7.50, under 12 free, by donation Thurs. 5-8. Phone (212) 423-3200.

[SAVE] **MORRIS-JUMEL MANSION,** 65 Jumel Terr. between 160th and 162nd sts., .5 blk. e. of St. Nicholas Ave. (S: 163rd St.), served as British and American army headquarters during the Revolutionary War. Built around 1765, the mansion is one of Manhattan's oldest surviving residential structures; it houses Colonial, Revolutionary, Federal and American Empire furniture. Wed.-Sun. 10-4, Mon.-Tues. by appointment; closed major holidays. Admission $3, over 64 and students with ID $2, under 12 free with an adult. Phone (212) 923-8008.

MUSEUM OF THE CITY OF NEW YORK, Fifth Ave. and 103rd to 104th sts. (S: 103rd St./Lexington Ave.), is devoted to the life and history of the city. Weekend educational and entertainment programs are held in the auditorium. The museum also offers seasonal walking tours of various parts of the city *(see What To Do, Sightseeing p. 141)*. Wed.-Sun. 10-5; closed holidays. Admission $7, over 64 and students with ID $4, family rate $12. Phone (212) 534-1672.

NATIONAL ACADEMY OF DESIGN, 1083 Fifth Ave. at 89th St. (S: 86th St.), displays a permanent collection of artworks as well as changing drawing, painting, sculpture and architectural exhibits. Allow 30 minutes minimum. Fri.-Sun. 11-6, Wed.-Thurs. noon-5; closed major holidays. Admission $8; over 64, students with ID and under 16, $4.50. AX, MC, VI. Phone (212) 369-4880.

RIVERSIDE CHURCH, 490 Riverside Dr. between 120th and 122nd sts. (S: 116th St.), houses a 74-bell carillon that is played Sunday at 10:30, 12:30 and 3. The carillon is the heaviest and the second largest in the world. Bell tower open Tues. and Sun. 11-4. Admission $2; college students with ID and ages 11-18, $1. Under 6 are not permitted in the bell tower. **Note:** The bell tower is temporarily closed for renovations. Phone (212) 870-6700.

ST. FRANCES X. CABRINI SHRINE, 701 Fort Washington Ave. (S:190th St. or M4 bus to 190th St.), is dedicated to the first American saint, who is the patron saint of immigrants. Displayed are objects and clothes that belonged to her. Allow 30 minutes minimum. Daily 9-5; closed Memorial Day, July 4, Labor Day and Thanksgiving. Free. Phone (212) 923-3536.

SOLOMON R. GUGGENHEIM MUSEUM, 1071 Fifth Ave. at 89th St. (S: 86th St./Lexington Ave.), was designed by Frank Lloyd Wright. The domed circular section of the building creates an interesting visual effect; paintings are hung along the spiraled walkway. In addition to the permanent collection, the museum exhibits late 19th- and early 20th-century and contemporary paintings and sculpture.

Food is available. Allow 2 hours minimum. Sat.-Wed. 10-5:45, Fri. 10-8; closed Thanksgiving and Dec. 25. Admission $15, over 64 and students with ID $10, under 12 free with an adult. AX, MC, VI. Phone (212) 423-3500. *See ad p. 114.*

THE BRONX pop. 1,332,650

BARTOW-PELL MANSION MUSEUM, e. of the Orchard Beach exit of the Hutchinson River Pkwy., then .5 mi. n. to 895 Shore Rd. (S: Pelham Bay Park), occupies a site bought from the Siwanoy Indians in 1654. The first house was destroyed during the Revolutionary War; the existing mansion was built 1836-42. Furnished in period, it is the only home of its era in this region. Gardens adorn the grounds.

Gardens open daily 8:30-dusk. Mansion open Wed. and Sat.-Sun. noon-4, Thurs.-Fri. and Tues. by appointment; closed Jan. 1, Easter, July 4, Thanksgiving weekend and Dec. 25. Mansion admission $2.50, senior citizens and students with ID $1.25, under 12 free. Phone (718) 885-1461.

BRONX COMMUNITY COLLEGE is in University Heights on University Ave. and W. 181st St. (S: 183rd St.). On campus is the Hall of Fame for Great Americans, open daily 10-5. Free. Phone (718) 289-5100.

BRONX ZOO, off the Bronx River Pkwy. at exit 6/Fordham Rd. (S: Pelham Pkwy., E. Tremont Ave.), displays more than 4,000 animals in naturalistic indoor and outdoor habitats on 265 wooded acres. Congo Gorilla Forest, a 6.5-acre simulated African rain forest, is home to one of the largest gorilla troops in a North American zoo plus such endangered or threatened species as Wolf's monkeys, mandrills, okapis and hornbills.

At Tiger Mountain visitors can learn about Siberian tigers through demonstrations given by animal keepers. JungleWorld is an indoor tropical Asian setting with gibbons, langurs, bats and other wildlife.

Food is available. Mon.-Fri. 10-5, Sat.-Sun. and holidays 10-5:30, Apr.-Oct.; daily 10-4:30, rest of year. Admission Apr.-Oct. $11; over 64 and ages 2-12, $8. Admission rest of year $10; over 64 and ages 2-12, $7. All-inclusive admission (includes gate, ride and exhibit fees) May-Oct. $20; over 64 and ages 2-12, $16. Parking $7. Phone (718) 367-1010.

FORDHAM UNIVERSITY, Third Ave. at E. Fordham Rd., near n.w. Bronx Park (S: Fordham Rd.), was founded in 1841 as an independent Jesuit university. Fordham's 10 schools have three campuses: Rose Hill, Lincoln Center and Tarrytown. Guided tours of Rose Hill and Lincoln Center are available. Rose Hill tours are given Mon.-Fri. at 10, noon and 2, Sat.-Sun. by appointment. Lincoln Center tours are given at Mon.-Fri. at noon. Tour schedules may vary; phone ahead. Free. Phone (718) 817-1000.

NEW YORK BOTANICAL GARDEN, 200th St. and Kazimiroff Blvd. (S: Bedford Park Blvd.), was founded in 1891 and is one of the world's largest botanical gardens, covering 250 acres. The grounds have 28 specialty gardens and plant collections. The palacelike, glass-enclosed Enid A. Haupt Conservatory contains plants displayed in settings similar to their tropical, subtropical and desert habitats.

Outdoor gardens include the Peggy Rockefeller Rose Garden, the Rock Garden, the Native Plant Garden and the Jane Watson Irwin Perennial Garden as well as 50 acres of original forest that once covered the city. The 12-acre, indoor/outdoor Everett Children's Adventure Garden has 40 hands-on activities for discovering plants and nature, plus mazes and topiaries. Other features include narrated tram rides, children's activities and guided walking tours.

Brooklyn / © James Marshall / Corbis

Picnicking is permitted. Food is available. Grounds open Tues.-Sun. 10-6, Apr.-Oct.; 10-5, rest of year. Hours vary for conservatory and children's, rock and native plant gardens; phone ahead. Closed Thanksgiving and Dec. 25.

Grounds $6; over 64, $3; students with ID $2; ages 2-12, $1; free to all Wed. and Sat. 10-noon, Apr.-Oct. Conservatory $5; over 64 and students with ID $4; ages 2-12, $3. Children's garden $3; over 64 and students with ID $2; ages 2-12, $1. Rock and native plant gardens $1; over 64, students with ID and ages 2-12, 50c. Combination ticket $10; over 64, $7.50; ages 2-12, $4. Tram $2, ages 2-12, $1. Parking $5. Phone (718) 817-8700.

VAN CORTLANDT HOUSE MUSEUM is at Broadway and 246th St. in Van Cortlandt Park. This 1748 mansion features 17th- and 18th-century Dutch, English and American furnishings. Tues.-Fri. 10-3, Sat.-Sun. 11-4; closed holidays. Admission $5, over 59 and students with ID $1.50; under 12 free. Phone (718) 543-3344.

WAVE HILL, off the Henry Hudson Pkwy. at W. 249 St. and Independence Ave., was built in 1843 and features a 28-acre garden and cultural center overlooking the Hudson River. The Glyndor House presents changing horticultural exhibits. Guided walks among the herb, wildflower and aquatic gardens are held Sunday at 2:15; special events are held periodically.

Allow 1 hour minimum. Tues.-Sun. 9-5:30, mid-Apr. to mid-Oct.; Tues.-Sun. 9-4:30, rest of year. Closed Jan. 1, Martin Luther King Jr. Day, Presidents Day, Thanksgiving and Dec. 25. Admission $4, senior citizens and students with ID $2, under 6 free; free to all Tues. all day and Sat. 9-noon. Free rest of year. Phone (718) 549-3200.

WOODLAWN CEMETERY, Webster Ave. at E. 233rd St. (S: Jerome Ave.), was established in 1863 and contains more than 250,000 graves, including those of Duke Ellington, Herman Melville, Joseph Pulitzer and Elizabeth Cady Stanton. Sculpture adorns the landscaped grounds. Musical programs, tours and special events are held regularly. Open daily 8:30-5 (weather permitting). Free. Phone (718) 920-0500.

BROOKLYN pop. 2,465,326

NEW YORK AQUARIUM, on the Coney Island Boardwalk (S: West 8th St. N.Y. Aquarium, Coney Island Stillwell Ave.), exhibits marine life in outdoor pools and indoor tanks. The Oceanic tank features a Beluga whale. Local species are featured in the Hudson River exhibit. The Gulf Stream Habitat examines the various fish that are swept up the river by the stream during the summer. The Sea Cliffs exhibit is a replica of the rocky Pacific coast and features walruses, sea otters, seals and penguins. Daily 10-5. Admission $11; over 65 and ages 2-12, $7. Parking $7. Phone (718) 265-3474.

BROOKLYN BOTANIC GARDEN has entrances at Flatbush Ave. and Empire Blvd. and at Washington Ave. and Eastern Pkwy. (S: Eastern Pkwy., Prospect Park). Its 52 acres include the Garden of Fragrance for the visually impaired; the Japanese Hill-and-Pond Garden; and the Conservatory, housing tropical plants and a bonsai museum under three glass pavilions.

Allow 1 hour minimum. Garden open Tues.-Fri. 8-6, Sat.-Sun. and holidays 10-6, Apr.-Sept.; Tues.-Fri. 8-4:30, Sat.-Sun. and holidays 10-4:30, rest of year. Conservatory open Tues.-Sun. and holidays 10-5:30, Apr.-Sept.; Tues.-Sun. 10-4, rest of year. Admission $5, over 64 and students with ID $3, under 16 free, free to all Tues. all day and Sat. 10-noon, free to over age 64 Fri. Phone (718) 623-7200.

BROOKLYN CHILDREN'S MUSEUM, 145 Brooklyn Ave. (S: St. Mark), contains more than 77,000 artifacts. Children learn through touching, entering or interacting with exhibits. Arrive early on weekends to avoid crowds. Wed.-Fri. 1-6, Sat.-Sun. and holidays 11-6; closed Jan. 1, Thanksgiving and Dec. 25. Admission $4. Phone (718) 735-4400.

BROOKLYN HISTORICAL SOCIETY MUSEUM,
128 Pierrepont St. at Clinton St. (S: Borough Hall/ Court St./Jay St.), is in the restored 1881 Queen Anne-style building designed by George B. Post, architect of the New York Stock Exchange building. The museum's central exhibit chronicles the life of Brooklyn's working class over 400 years through re-created living and working environments, displays of locally manufactured products and recorded stories. Allow 1 hour minimum. Wed.-Sat. 10-5 (also Fri. 5-8); Sun. noon-5. Admission $6, over 64 and students with ID $4, under 12 free. Phone (718) 222-4111.

[SAVE] **BROOKLYN MUSEUM OF ART,** Eastern Pkwy. and Washington Ave. at Prospect Park (S: Eastern Pkwy./Brooklyn Museum), houses collections of Egyptian, African, Asian, Oceanic, classical, New World and ancient Middle Eastern art as well as American paintings, 29 Colonial period rooms representing the 17th through 20th centuries, and an outdoor sculpture garden.

Wed.-Fri. 10-5, Sat.-Sun. 9-6 (also first Sat. of each month 6-11 p.m.); closed Jan. 1, Thanksgiving and Dec. 25. Admission $6; students with ID $3; over 62, $3; under 12 free with an adult. Parking $6. Phone (718) 638-5000.

CYPRESS HILLS NATIONAL CEMETERY is on Jamaica and Hale aves. (S: Cypress Hills). The original 3,170 graves are casualties received from Civil War hospitals in the New York City vicinity. Daily 9-4:30. Free.

FORT GREENE PARK, at Myrtle and DeKalb aves., and St. Edwards and Cumberland sts. (S: Fulton St./Lafayette Ave.), contains Martyrs' Monument, designed by Stanford White and dedicated to the Continental soldiers who died on British prison ships in Wallabout Bay. Daily dawn-dusk. Free.

NEW YORK TRANSIT MUSEUM, jct. of Boerum Pl. and Schermerhorn St. under the Board of Education building (S: Borough Hall, Court St., Jay St.), has photographs, equipment, artifacts and memorabilia that trace the development of the city's bus and subway systems. Numerous trains and vehicles are displayed, some of which can be entered. Tues.-Fri. 10-4, Sat.-Sun. noon-5; closed major holidays. Admission $5; over 61 and ages 3-17, $3. Phone (718) 694-5100.

PROSPECT PARK, between Prospect Park W. and Prospect Park S.W. and Flatbush and Parkside aves. (S: 7th Ave./Grand Army Plaza), contains a Quaker graveyard, gardens, woodlands, waterfalls, trails, a zoo, boating facilities, pools, and Lefferts Historic House, an 18th-century homestead museum containing furnishings and relics. Grand Army Plaza, at the north entrance at Flatbush Avenue and Eastern Parkway, has an arch commemorating Civil War heroes and a memorial to John F. Kennedy.

Park open daily dawn-dusk. Lefferts Historic House open Fri.-Sun. 1-4, Apr.-Nov. Free. Phone (718) 965-8951, (718) 965-8999 for recorded information, or (718) 789-2822 for Lefferts Historic House.

ST. JOHN'S EPISCOPAL CHURCH, 9818 Fort Hamilton Pkwy. (S: 95th St.), was founded in 1834. Generals Robert E. Lee and Thomas "Stonewall" Jackson were members of the congregation while at Fort Hamilton. Mon.-Fri. 9-1. Free. Phone (718) 745-2377.

QUEENS pop. 2,229,379

AMERICAN MUSEUM OF THE MOVING IMAGE, 35th Ave. and 36th St. in Astoria (S: Steinway St.), chronicles the art, history, technique and technology of motion pictures, television, video and digital media. The museum occupies a renovated building on the site of the former Astoria Studio, a 1920s facility used by Paramount Pictures. Interpretive programs, changing exhibitions and screenings are offered. Strollers are not permitted. Wed.-Thurs. 11-5, Fri. 11-7, Sat.-Sun. 11-6. Admission $10; over 65 and students with ID $7.50; ages 5-18, $5. Phone (718) 784-0077 or (718) 784-4777.

FLUSHING MEADOWS CORONA PARK is bounded by Roosevelt Ave., Van Wyck Expwy., Union Tpke. and 111th St. (S: Willets Point/Shea Stadium). Site of New York's World Fairs 1939-40 and 1964-65, the park has bicycle paths, the Queens Wildlife Conservation Center, a carousel, freshwater fishing, pitch-and-putt golf, an indoor ice-skating rink and a marina. Baseball, cricket, football and softball fields are available, as are boccie courts. Picnicking is permitted. Daily 9-dusk. Free. Phone (718) 760-6565.

THE ISAMU NOGUCHI GARDEN MUSEUM, 32-37 Vernon Blvd. (S: Broadway), displays sculpture in 12 galleries and an outdoor garden. Allow 2 hours minimum. Thurs.-Fri. and Mon. 10-5, Sat.-Sun. 11-6. Guided tours are given at 2:30. Admission $5, senior citizens and students with ID $2.50. Phone (718) 204-7088.

JAMAICA BAY WILDLIFE REFUGE is 3 mi. s. on Crossbay Blvd. off Belt Pkwy. exit 17. The 9,155-acre refuge contains varied habitats, including freshwater ponds, marshes, bays, fields, wooded areas and islands. It is a major stopover for migrating birds; some 329 species have been recorded since the mid-1950s. A 1.75-mile walking trail allows visitors to see the early stages of forest development. Allow 2 hours minimum. Refuge daily 8:30-dusk. Visitor center daily 8:30-5. Free. Phone (718) 318-4340.

NEW YORK HALL OF SCIENCE, 111th St. and 46th Ave. in Flushing Meadows Corona Park (S: 111 St.), is a hands-on science and technology center. Many of the exhibits are geared toward making scientific processes understandable for children. The center also has a multimedia library.

Allow 2 hours minimum. Tues.-Fri. 9:30-5, Sat.-Sun. 10:30-6, Mon. 9:30-2, July-Aug.; Tues.-Thurs. 9:30-2, Fri. 9:30-5, Sat.-Sun. noon-5, rest of year.

Closed Jan. 1, Labor Day, Thanksgiving and Dec. 25. Admission $9; over 61 and ages 5-17, $6; free to all Fri. 2-5, Sept.-June. Parking $7. MC, VI. Phone (718) 699-0005.

QUEENS BOTANICAL GARDEN is at 43-50 Main St.; take I-495 (Long Island Expwy.) exit 23 to Main St., then 1 mi. n. to Dahlia Ave. (S: Main St.). Trails and paths wind through rose, rock and formal gardens, and a live beehive is the focal point in a wildflower meadow. Special programs, educational tours and projects are offered throughout the year. Tues.-Fri. 8-6, Sat.-Sun. 8-7, Memorial Day-Sept. 30; daily 8-4:30, rest of year. Donations. Phone (718) 886-3800.

QUEENS COUNTY FARM MUSEUM is off Cross Island Pkwy. exit 27, .4 mi. e. on Jericho Tpk., then 1.7 mi. n. on Little Neck Pkwy. This 7-acre historical farm is said to be the largest remaining plot of agricultural land within the New York City limits. The complex includes a shingled 1772 farmhouse restored to its 1856 appearance; a wagon shed, two barns and three greenhouses built after 1927; animal pens with cows, goats, pigs and sheep; and productive fruit orchards and vegetable gardens. Allow 1 hour minimum. Grounds daily 9-5. House tours are given Sat.-Sun. 10-5; closed Jan. 1, Easter, Memorial Day, July 4, Thanksgiving and Dec. 25. Free. Admission is charged during special events. Phone (718) 347-3276.

QUEENS MUSEUM OF ART, in the New York City Building at Flushing Meadows Corona Park (S: Willets Point/Shea Stadium) *(see attraction listing),* offers changing art exhibitions. Allow 1 hour minimum. Tues.-Fri. 10-5, Sat.-Sun. noon-5; closed Jan. 1, Thanksgiving and Dec. 25. Admission $5, senior citizens and students with ID $2.50, under 5 free. Phone (718) 592-9700.

STATEN ISLAND pop. 443,728

ALICE AUSTEN HOUSE is off I-278 Bay St. Exit, n. 1 mi. to Hylan Blvd. then e. to 2 Hylan Blvd. This Victorian house, carefully restored to its 1890s appearance, displays photographs taken from the late 1800s through the first half of the 20th century by Alice Austen, who lived here 1866-1929. Allow 1 hour minimum. Thurs.-Sun. noon-5. Admission $2, under 12 free. Phone (718) 816-4506.

HISTORIC RICHMOND TOWN is s. of I-278 via Richmond Rd./Clove Rd. exit. This living history village and museum complex interprets 3 centuries of daily life and culture on Staten Island. Restored houses, shops and public buildings from the 1690s to the 1900s feature furnished interiors and exhibits. Guides in period dress lead tours and conduct participatory programs.

Allow 2 hours minimum. Wed.-Sat. 10-5, Sun. 1-5, July-Aug.; Wed.-Sun. 1-5, Feb.-June and Sept.-Dec. Closed Easter, Thanksgiving and Dec. 25. Tours are given Sat.-Sun. at 2. Admission $5; over 61 and college students with ID $4; ages 5-17, $3.50. Phone (718) 351-1611.

JACQUES MARCHAIS MUSEUM OF TIBETAN ART is at 338 Lighthouse Ave.; take I-278W to Richmond Rd., then 5 mi. s. to Lighthouse Ave. Designed like a small Tibetan mountain temple, the museum collects, preserves and displays Tibetan, Tibeto-Chinese, Nepalese and Mongolian art objects and paintings. Terraced sculpture gardens, a lily and fish pond and a view of the Lower Bay provide a serene atmosphere. Lectures, demonstrations and performances are offered on selected Sunday afternoons.

Allow 1 hour minimum. Wed.-Sun. 1-5, Apr.-Nov.; by appointment Wed.-Sun. 1-5, rest of year. Closed Thanksgiving, day after Thanksgiving and Dec. 25. Admission $3; over 64, $2.50; ages 1-12, $1; Sun. programs $3 additional. Phone (718) 987-3500.

SNUG HARBOR CULTURAL CENTER, Clove Rd. exit off I-278, then 3 mi. n. to 1000 Richmond Terr., was founded in 1801 as the nation's first maritime hospital and home for retired sailors. Restored buildings include Main Hall, with its Newhouse Center for Contemporary Art, and Veterans Hall, a concert venue.

The 83-acre Staten Island Botanical Garden includes formal displays of annuals, a variety of themed gardens, a Chinese garden, sculpture and fountains. Newhouse Center Sun.-Fri. 11-5, Sat. 11-7. Garden Tues.-Sun. dawn-dusk. Center $2. Chinese garden $5, senior citizens and students with ID $4. Grounds free. Phone (718) 273-8200 or (718) 448-2500.

Staten Island Children's Museum, in the Snug Harbor Cultural Center, contains exhibits about art, science and humanities. Hands-on workshops, performances and special events designed for preschool through eighth grade children are presented throughout the year. Allow 1 hour, 30 minutes minimum. Tues.-Sun. noon-5; closed Jan. 1, July 4, Thanksgiving and Dec. 25. Admission $5, under 1 free. Phone (718) 273-2060.

SAVE **STATEN ISLAND INSTITUTE OF ARTS AND SCIENCES,** 75 Stuyvesant Pl. (5-minute walk from the ferry terminal in St. George), displays art, natural science and history collections as well as exhibits about Staten Island and its people. The archives and library have documents dating from the early 1700s. Allow 1 hour minimum. Tues.-Sat. 9-5, Sun. 1-5; closed major holidays. Admission $2.50; students with ID $1.25; over 64, $1. Phone (718) 727-1135.

SAVE **STATEN ISLAND ZOO,** in Barrett Park, West New Brighton at 614 Broadway, is an educational zoo with mammals, birds, reptiles and tropical fish. Exhibits include a representation of a tropical rain forest, an aquarium, a serpentarium and a children's center emphasizing domestic animals that help man. Allow 1 hour minimum. Daily 10-4:45; closed Jan. 1, Thanksgiving and Dec. 25. Admission $5; over 59, $4; ages 3-14, $3; free to all Wed. after 2. Phone (718) 442-3100.

What To Do

Sightseeing

Boat Tours

Boat tours can make sightseeing even more exciting. One of the best sightseeing bargains in the city is a ride on the Staten Island Ferry. Leaving South Ferry in Battery Park every day at least once an hour, the free ride provides views of the Lower Manhattan skyline and the Statue of Liberty. Avoid the ferry during peak commuter hours, Mon.-Fri. 8-10 and 4-6; phone (718) 390-5253.

The 1885 schooner *Pioneer* offers 2-hour excursions of New York Harbor Tues.-Sun., June-Sept.; Sat.-Sun., Apr.-May. Tickets are sold at the Pier 16 ticket booth; phone (212) 748-8786.

CIRCLE LINE CRUISES departs from Pier 83, W. 42nd St. at the Hudson River. Two-hour narrated sightseeing trips of Lower Manhattan afford views of the Statue of Liberty and the Manhattan skyline. Highlights of a 3-hour cruise around the island include three rivers, docks, seven bridges and more than 25 landmarks. Trips of varying lengths as well as evening cruises and combination trips also are available. Cruises daily Apr.-Nov; Wed.-Mon., in Mar. and Dec.; Thurs.-Mon., rest of year. Departure times vary. Closed Dec. 25. Fare for 2-hour cruise $21; over 64, $17; under 13, $10.50. Fare for 3-hour cruise $26; over 64, $20; under 13, $13. AX, DC, DS, MC, VI. Phone (212) 563-3200. *See ad p. 114.*

[SAVE] NY WATERWAY HARBOR SIGHTSEEING CRUISES departs from Pier 78 at W. 38th St. and 12th Ave. Offered are a 2-hour sightseeing cruise around the island of Manhattan, a 90-minute tour of New York Harbor and a 1-hour Lower Harbor cruise. Twilight, entertainment, dinner and holiday cruises also are available. Bus transportation is available from local hotels.

Manhattan and harbor cruises depart daily, mid-May to early Nov.; schedule varies rest of year. One-hour harbor cruises depart daily, late May-late Oct. Departure times vary according to type of cruise; phone for schedule. Manhattan cruise $24, senior citizens $19, children $12. Harbor cruise $19, senior citizens $16, children $9. Lower harbor cruise $12, senior citizens $11, children $7. AX, CB, DC, DS, MC, VI. Phone (201) 902-8711 or (800) 533-3779.

SPIRIT CRUISES departs from Pier 61, Chelsea Piers, off W. 23rd St., and from Weehawken, NJ. Offered are narrated 2-hour lunch cruises on the East and Hudson rivers. Music and entertainment are provided. Dinner cruises are available but are not narrated.

Lunch cruises are available daily; phone for departure times. Lunch cruises $28-$46. Reservations

are recommended. Inquire about refund policies. AX, DC, DS, MC, VI. Phone (212) 727-2789.

WORLD YACHT, Pier 81 and W. 41st St. on the Hudson River, offers brunch and dinner cruises of New York harbor. Passengers can experience marvelous views of the Statue of Liberty and the city's skyline. Live entertainment is provided. Allow 3 hours minimum. Dinner cruises depart daily at 7, brunch cruises Sun. at 12:30; closed Jan. 1 and Dec. 25. Boarding is 1 hour prior to departure.

Dinner cruise (jacket required) Sun.-Thurs., $69.95, Fri.-Sat. $79. Brunch cruise $43.90. Parking $20. Reservations are required. AX, MC, VI. Phone (212) 630-8100.

Bus Tours

To see the most in the least amount of time, take a bus tour. There are numerous bus tours that cover all parts of the city; information is available either from your local AAA club or by phoning the bus lines directly.

[SAVE] Gray Line New York offers a variety of sightseeing tours in double-deck buses. The All Loops Tour includes the Uptown, Downtown and Night Loop/Holiday Lights Tour. A motor coach tour of Manhattan includes lunch. Tickets can be purchased at the Gray Line Visitors Center, 777 Eighth Ave. (between 47th and 48th streets); phone (212) 445-0848 or (800) 669-0051. *See color ad p. 112.*

Helicopter Tours

[SAVE] LIBERTY HELICOPTER TOURS departs from the VIP Heliport at W. 30th St. at 12th Ave. A helicopter sightseeing tour of the Big Apple includes views of the Statue of Liberty, the Manhattan skyline, Central Park and the George Washington Bridge. Photo identification is required. Allow 1 hour minimum. Daily 9:30-8:30. Fee for 5-7 min. tour $56; 10-12 min. $101; 15-17 min. $162. AX, MC, VI. Phone (212) 967-6464.

Walking Tours

[AAA] **Walking Tour: Greenwich Village**

See map following. The tour takes 3-5 hours, depending on your pace and the number of listed sites you visit along the way. Those that appear in bold type have detailed listings in the What to See section. Even if you decide not to visit a listed site, reading the listing when you reach that point should make the tour more interesting.

Although just a short subway ride from the scurrying throngs and imposing skyscrapers of Midtown, Greenwich Village seems a world apart. Characterized by quiet side streets, secluded courtyards, tree-shaded parks and brick townhouses, the Village is about as pedestrian-friendly a place as you are likely to find in a huge city like New York. A stroll along its relatively peaceful sidewalks offers a break from the frenetic bustle that characterizes much of Manhattan. Walking also happens to be the best way to experience the funky ambience of this famously unconventional neighborhood.

Not only do Village residents have a long history of defying convention, the streets themselves defy the ordered grid that makes navigation so easy in other areas of Manhattan. Fortunately there are plenty of street signs, and contrary to popular stereotype, New Yorkers are often very willing to assist with directions.

The walking tour begins and ends in Greenwich Village's leafy heart: **Washington Square,** at the southern end of Fifth Avenue. To get there, take the A, C, E, F or S train to the West 4th Street Subway Station; the park is a block east. You might be disappointed to learn that New York City's subway tokens have gone the way of the pterodactyl, but the fare cards (called MetroCards) that have replaced those distinctive little coins are easy to use, easy to obtain and much lighter in your pocket. The base MetroCard fare is $1.50 per ride. A Fun Pass, which is good for unlimited rides for 1 day on city subway trains and buses, is available for $4 at MetroCard vending machines.

Originally a marsh, the area that is now Washington Square Park was used as a cemetery in the late 1700s. Excavations a century later uncovered numerous skeletons and headstones, much to the dismay of the well-heeled residents who lived along the park's borders at the time. Today you would have a hard time envisioning Washington Square's funeral past, particularly on summer weekends when the park fills with children, chess players, joggers, skaters, couples with baby strollers, people walking their dogs, food vendors, street entertainers, musicians rehearsing and tourists sitting on benches and resting their weary feet. Adding a youthful air to this already vibrant environment are the students of **New York University.** One of America's largest private universities, N.Y.U. owns many of the buildings surrounding the park, making Washington Square a de facto part of the school campus.

Presiding over this crazy quilt of humanity is the square's majestic ❶ Washington Memorial Arch. Dedicated in 1895, the 77-foot-high, white-marble monument at the end of Fifth Avenue was designed by Stamford White to commemorate the centennial of George Washington's inauguration. It replaced an earlier wooden arch temporarily constructed less than a block north on Fifth Avenue. "Washington in War," a statue of the first president wearing military attire, was added to one side of the arch in 1916 and a second, called appropriately enough "Washington in Peace," was installed in 1918. Other park monuments include a statue of Giuseppe Garibaldi, known as the Father of Modern Italy, and a bust of Alexander Lyman Holley, who perfected the Bessemer process of manufacturing steel, giving rise to the U.S. steel industry.

Walk over to the park's central fountain and proceed from there to Washington Square South. The bell tower to your right is part of Italian Renaissance-style ❷ Judson Memorial Church, built in 1896. The church was noted for its stained-glass windows, which were designed at the turn of the 20th century by eminent artist John La Farge.

Turn left and head over to Washington Square East. The massive red stone building to your right with fluted walls is N.Y.U.'s ❸ Elmer Bobst Library. Set on a pedestal adjacent to the library is a piece of ornate stonework from the university's original Gothic building, which was demolished in the late 1800s. Founded in 1831, N.Y.U. occupies buildings throughout the Village. You'll recognize them by the large violet banners emblazoned with the school's symbol: a flaming torch.

Turn left again and follow Washington Square East to Washington Square North. The building at the corner of Washington Square East and Waverly Place is the university's ❹ Main Building, which stands on the site of the original Gothic structure mentioned earlier. Famous occupants of that first building include painter Winslow Homer, poet Walt Whitman, author Henry James and electric telegraph developer Samuel Morse, who, interestingly enough, taught painting and sculpture and is credited with establishing America's first academic fine arts department. Within the current Main Building is the Grey Art Gallery, where you can see an array of visual arts on display.

Now walk west along Washington Square North. The ❺ Greek Revival townhouses here were built in 1833 for wealthy New Yorkers, but most now belong to the university. Henry James grew up around the corner, and his grandmother lived in a townhouse on this very block. James drew heavily on his aristocratic upbringing in Greenwich Village when he wrote his novel, "Washington Square."

Proceed north on Fifth Avenue to ❻ Washington Mews, a peaceful pedestrian-only alley on your right. You'll notice a towering Art Deco

© AAA   2112-L

building, built in 1926, on the other side of the mews. Stables once lined this narrow brick-paved street, but they were replaced by desirable apartments long ago. As you exit onto University Place, the buildings on your right and left are the French and German departments of N.Y.U.

Walk 4 blocks north on University Place to East 11th Street and turn left. Half way down the block on the north side is a small 19th-century building tucked in between two larger buildings and hidden behind trees. This is the **7** Conservative Synagogue of Fifth Avenue, which, like the residences along Washington Mews, was originally used as a stable. Across the street, a plaque to the left of the door at 20 East 11th St. indicates that Eleanor Roosevelt, one of the Village's many famous residents, kept an apartment here in the 1930s and '40s.

Continue west and turn right at Fifth Avenue to the broad stairway of the **8** Salmagundi Club, an artist's organization founded in 1871 as the New York Sketch Club. Members have included Childe Hassam, Louis Comfort Tiffany and N.C. Wyeth. The club took its current name from "The Salmagundi Papers," Washington Irving's satirical take on social life in early 19th-century New York. Incidentally, it is within "The Salmagundi Papers" that Irving first referred to New York as Gotham, which has been a nickname for the city ever since. The club has occupied the 1853 Italianate mansion—the last of its kind remaining on this stretch of Fifth Avenue—since 1917.

Across Fifth Avenue from the club is the Gothic Revival-style **9** First Presbyterian Church. Completed in 1846, the church was modeled after the Church of St. Saviour in Bath, England. Just a bit farther south on Fifth Avenue, at the corner of 10th Street, looms another example of Gothic Revival architecture: the 1841 Church of the Ascension.

North of the First Presbyterian Church, between 12th and 13th, you'll find the **FORBES Magazine Galleries.** Inside, countless toy soldiers of every description are displayed marching or engaged in battle. Toy boats, historical documents, collectible trophies, Monopoly board games and Faberge Easter eggs round out this eclectic hodgepodge amassed by the late Malcolm Forbes.

Return to 11th Street and head west. A wall and wrought iron fence on the south side of 11th near Sixth Avenue protects a small corner of a once-larger cemetery. **10** The Second Cemetery of the Spanish and Portuguese Synagogue dates back to 1805. Take a peek through the bars into the dim, well-tended space beyond, which is filled with tombstones of various shapes and sizes beneath sheltering evergreen trees.

Continue to Sixth Avenue, turn right and turn right again on West 10th Street. On the south side of 10th is a row of **11** Anglo-Italianate town-houses connected by a single shallow terrace with an ornate iron railing. These residences

Henry Clay Frick Mansion
© The Frick Collection, New York

were built in the 1850s and designed by James Renwick, Jr., who also designed historic Grace Church at 802 Broadway; St. Patrick's Cathedral on Fifth Avenue between 50th and 51st streets; and the Smithsonian Castle in Washington, D.C.

Retrace your steps back to Sixth Avenue and cross the street. The building with the pyramid-topped clock tower to your left is **12** Jefferson Market Courthouse, completed in 1887. In the hearts of Villagers this Victorian Gothic landmark ranks second only to the Washington Memorial Arch, although in the early 1960s "Old Jeff" came perilously close to demolition. Angered Villagers came to the rescue, and after a 1967 restoration, it reopened as a branch of the New York Public Library. Behind the courthouse, where a women's prison once stood, is a volunteer-maintained viewing garden.

Across West 10th Street from the courthouse you'll find **13** Patchin Place, a quiet, dead-end street lined with three-story residences. These were built in 1848 as boardinghouses for waiters at a nearby hotel, but in the 20th century Patchin Place counted several renowned writers among its residents, including poets e.e. cummings and John Masefield, authors Theodore Dreiser and John Reed and playwright Eugene O'Neill. Just around the corner on Sixth Avenue is Milligan Place, another picturesque courtyard lined with former boardinghouses, these built in 1852.

Proceed west on 10th Street to Seventh Avenue and turn left. The intersection ahead where seven streets come together is **14** Sheridan Square, roughly the geographical center of Greenwich

Village. With so many streets meeting in one spot, the square has earned a reputation for disorienting visitors. Just try to remember your position relative to Seventh Avenue, the main thoroughfare.

A statue of Civil War general Philip Henry Sheridan, for whom the square was named, stands in Christopher Park, which is the triangular park to your left created by the intersection of Seventh Avenue and Christopher and Grove streets. For such a small area, Christopher Park seems crowded with statues. Opposite the general is a grouping of four whitewashed bronze figures known as the Gay Liberation Monument, evidence of the Village's tolerant live-and-let-live ethos. Nearby, a second triangular park created by the intersection of Washington Place, 4th Street and Barrow Street features a viewing garden.

Go back to Seventh Avenue and continue south to where Seventh intersects with Bleeker and Barrow streets. Turn right on Barrow and follow it for one block to Bedford. Another right will bring you to 86 Bedford St., better known as ⑮ Chumley's, a restaurant opened in 1922 that served as a speakeasy during Prohibition. A veritable Who's Who list of literary greats have frequented Chumley's over the years, including James Agee, e.e. cummings, Theodore Dreiser, F. Scott Fitzgerald, Lillian Hellman, Edna St. Vincent Millay, John Dos Passos, Upton Sinclair and John Steinbeck.

Return to Bedford and Barrow, turn right and then make a left on Commerce Street. Where the street curves to the left stands the ⑯ Cherry Lane Theater, founded by Edna St. Vincent Millay in 1924. One of the city's first off-Broadway venues, the theater has showcased challenging, experimental plays by the likes of Eugene Ionesco, David Mamet, Harold Pinter and Sam Shepard for more than 75 years.

Follow the bend in Commerce Street until you're back on Bedford, then make a right, after which you will immediately be confronted by two Greenwich Village superlatives. On the corner at 77 Bedford St. is the ⑰ Isaacs-Hendricks House, which was built in 1799 and is recognized as the oldest in the Village. By comparison, the house next door at 75½ Bedford, built in 1873, is a relative newcomer. With just one glance, however, you can guess what it's claim to fame is. At under 10 feet wide, 75½ Bedford has earned the reputation as the narrowest house in the Village. Edna St. Vincent Millay lived there briefly during the 1920s.

Walk south on Bedford to Seventh Avenue and turn right. Turn right again on Leroy Street, which for a short stretch is known as ⑱ St. Luke's Place. The impressive row of Italianate townhouses along the street's north side was constructed in the 1850s for New York's mercantile elite. Ornate facades, grand entryways, tall windows, shade trees and a park across the street

make these some of the most sought after addresses in the Village. Number 6 was the home of Jimmy Walker, mayor of the city 1926-32. Two lamps, which traditionally identify the mayor's house in New York, still frame the entrance.

Retrace your steps back to Seventh Avenue and cross it, following Leroy Street east to Bleeker. Make a right onto Bleeker in front of ⑲ Our Lady of Pompeii, a large Roman Catholic Church built in 1928 for the Italian immigrant community. Continue on Bleeker, but when you reach Sixth Avenue be careful: Four streets intersect here making it somewhat tricky to find where Bleeker resumes again. Follow Bleeker to MacDougal Street and stop. If your energy levels are beginning to dip, you're in luck. With a café at every turn, this intersection is known as café corner, a perfect spot to sit, relax and enjoy a cup of coffee.

After you've revived, proceed east on Bleeker to La Guardia Place. This area of the Village is thick with second-hand clothing and record stores, cafés and intimate nightspots offering live jazz and rock music. The Bitter End at the corner of Bleeker and La Guardia features live entertainment and even sports a plaque honoring the establishment for its "contribution to the artistic life of New York."

Turn left on La Guardia. Halfway up the block on the east side of the street you'll spy a bronze ⑳ statue of Fiorello La Guardia, New York City mayor 1934-45. The statue shows the diminutive 5'2" La Guardia, known as "the little flower," stepping forward, mouth open and hands poised as if clapping. While far from the dignified posture one might expect of an honored statesman, the statue captures the enthusiasm and energy of one of the city's most popular mayors, who served three consecutive terms during a difficult period in the city's history and is remembered for his sweeping reforms and efforts to curb corruption.

Continue north on La Guardia to West 3rd Street and turn left. On your left will be a bright red Victorian building housing the ㉑ Number 2 Fire Engine Co. Notice the painted carving of a woman's face over the arched main door. From 3rd Street turn right onto MacDougal, which is one block after Sullivan. The historic ㉒ Provincetown Playhouse, which opened in 1916, is on the left side of the street. The theater has played a pivotal role in fostering the early careers of many playwrights including Edna St. Vincent Millay and Eugene O'Neill as well as numerous actors, directors and set designers, and it continues to produce innovative plays to this day.

Just a few steps north and you're back at Washington Square Park. Before you finish your tour, however, walk farther north, crossing West 4th Street and Washington Place. The building at the corner of Waverly Place with the elaborate marquee was the ㉓ home of Eleanor Roosevelt 1942-49. A plaque to the left of the entrance pays tribute to the first lady. To return to the West 4th Street

Subway Station, backtrack to West 4th Street and turn right. The station is one block ahead of you.

Guided Walking Tours

Various guided walking tours are offered daily by the Municipal Art Society, based in the Urban Center at 457 Madison Ave. and 51st Street. Of interest is an in-depth look at Grand Central Terminal *(see attraction listing p. 126)*; phone (212) 935-3960.

The Museum of the City of New York *(see attraction listing p. 133)* conducts guided walking tours of Manhattan, Brooklyn, the Bronx, Queens and Staten Island April through October. Fees vary according to tour and reservations are required. For a brochure describing the various tours contact the Education Department, Museum of the City of New York, 1220 Fifth Ave., New York, NY 10029; phone (212) 534-1672, ext. 206.

Theme tours of Harlem, including jazz, soul food and art galleries, are available from Harlem, Your Way! Tours; phone (800) 382-9363. New York City Cultural Walking Tours, (212) 979-2388, offers guided tours that emphasize Manhattan's architecture and history. The 92nd Street YMCA provides walking tours that center on the art, history and architecture of various neighborhoods; phone (212) 996-1100. Adventure on a Shoestring specializes in community walking tours; phone (212) 265-2663.

Weaving history and architecture with insight into people and events that shaped the heart of Lower Manhattan, the Downtown Alliance's free guided Wall Street Walking Tour departs from the steps of the Smithsonian's National Museum of the American Indian *(see attraction listing p. 120)* every Thursday and Saturday at noon; phone (212) 606-4064.

The Times Square Business Improvement District offers tours highlighting landmarks, hotels and famous theaters. Tours depart from the Times Square Visitor Center Fridays at noon; phone (212) 768-1560.

Self-Guiding Walking Tours

An inexpensive way to see the city is by self-guiding walking tours. Various ethnic neighborhoods offer intriguing shops, restaurants and sidewalk fairs best sampled on foot.

Some of the best known communities include Little Italy, centering on Mulberry Street; the Jewish sector, on Essex and Orchard streets; the Middle Eastern enclave, along Atlantic Avenue; and the East Indian neighborhood, on Lexington Avenue. Check with a local AAA club for more information about what other areas would lend themselves to walking tours.

Talk-A-Walk offers audiotape tours of various Lower Manhattan attractions and the Brooklyn Bridge. The audiotapes can be obtained through the mail for $9.95 each (plus $2.90 for postage and shipping for up to six cassettes) by writing Talk-A-Walk, 30 Waterside Plaza, 10D, New York, NY 10010; phone (212) 686-0356.

Spectator Sports

No one takes sports quite as seriously as New Yorkers. Seven professional sports teams dominate the sports scene, including two football, baseball and ice hockey teams. Being a fan here involves

Central Park / © Mike Zens / Corbis

unfeigned loyalty: Just ask Yankees and Mets fans what happens when they share a baseball stadium, or how Dodgers fans felt when their team moved to Los Angeles.

Baseball

New Yorkers are especially passionate about the national pastime. The **New York Yankees**, who produced such legendary "Bronx Bombers" as Joe DiMaggio, Lou Gehrig, Mickey Mantle and Babe Ruth, play at **Yankee Stadium** in the Bronx. This American League club won the World Series in 1996, 1998, 1999 and 2000. The season runs from April to October; phone (718) 293-4300.

The **Mets**, New York City's National League team, stole the World Series from the Boston Red Sox in 1986. They play at **Shea Stadium** in Queens. The season runs from April to October; phone (718) 507-6387 or (718) 507-8499.

The majors have several Minor League baseball counterparts. The **Staten Island Yankees** kick off the season in June at **Richmond County Bank Ballpark at St. George**. For ticket information phone (718) 720-9265. The Mets-affiliated **Brooklyn Cyclones** play at **Keyspan Stadium** on Surf Avenue in Coney Island; phone (718) 449-8497. **EAB Park** in Central Islip is where the Atlantic League's **Long Island Ducks** swing into action; phone (888) 332-5600.

Basketball

When the **New York Knicks** hit the court at **Madison Square Garden** *(see attraction listing p. 128)*, fans are assured of an exciting game. The season runs from November to June; phone (212) 465-5867 for Knicks information, or (212) 465-6741 for the Garden.

New York loves its college hoopsters, too. The beloved **St. John's University Red Storm** occasionally play at Madison Square Garden; phone (718) 990-6211 for ticket information. The **Long Island University Blackbirds** and **St. Francis College Terriers** both hoop it up in Brooklyn; phone (718) 488-1030 for the Blackbirds and (718) 489-5489 for the Terriers. The **Fordham University Rams**, (718) 817-4307, play in the Bronx, while the **Wagner College Seahawks** take to the court at **Frederik Sutter Gymnasium** in Staten Island; phone (718) 390-3489.

Football

From September to December, Super Bowl III winners the **New York Jets** and two-time NFL champions the **New York Giants** scramble on the gridiron in **Giants Stadium** in East Rutherford, N.J., at the **Meadowlands** complex; phone (201) 935-8222 (Giants) or (516) 560-8200 (Jets). Tickets are scarce, so unless you know someone with a season pass, your plans may be sidelined.

Hockey

After a 54-year dry spell the **New York Rangers** brought home the coveted Stanley Cup in 1994 to the cheers of die-hard fans at Madison Square Garden; phone (212) 465-6741. The **New York Islanders**, Stanley Cup winners 1980-83, play out of **Nassau Coliseum** on Long Island. The season runs from November to April; phone (516) 794-4100.

Horse Racing

If you enjoy the ponies, try **Aqueduct Race Track** in Queens, (718) 641-4700; **Belmont Park Race Track** on Long Island, (718) 641-4700 or (516) 488-6000; and the Meadowlands in East Rutherford, N.J., (201) 935-3900. Harness racing can be seen at **Yonkers Raceway** in Yonkers; phone (914) 968-4200.

Note: Policies on admitting children to pari-mutuel facilities vary. Phone for specific information.

Recreation

When the hustle and bustle of the city streets is too much to handle, shift into a slower gear. New York's parks and beaches offer peaceful respite. The lush lawns, trees, shrubs and meadows as well as lakes, fountains, sculptures and bridges make **Central Park** *(see attraction listing p. 125)* a favorite spot with visitors and New Yorkers alike.

Bicycling

Roadways in Central Park are closed to motorized traffic year-round from Fri. 7 p.m.-Mon. 6 a.m. (also Mon.-Thurs. 10 a.m.-3 p.m. and 7-10 p.m.,

Fri. 10 a.m.-3 p.m., Apr.-Oct.). However, the transverse roads are always open to traffic. Access to three bicycle routes—6.1 miles, 5.2 miles or 1.7 miles in length—is possible by following the park drives, which encircle the park. Another option is to enter at 72nd Street and Central Park West Drive and pedal south to 59th Street, east to East Drive, then north on East Drive to 72nd Street. Exit at Fifth Avenue, or continue north along East Drive until your legs are tired.

For a scenic ride along the Hudson River, pedal around **Riverside Park**, off Riverside Drive on the Upper West Side.

Golf

Obviously you will not find a golf course in Manhattan, but the Department of Parks does operate 12 18-hole public courses in the other boroughs. On weekends golfers might have to wait as long as 8 hours before they are able to tee off; to learn of the waiting times, try the weekend news broadcasts over WNYC (93.9 FM or 820 AM).

Most fees are Mon.-Fri. $26, $23.50 after 1, $16.25 for twilight golf; Sat.-Sun. and holidays $29, $26 after 1, $17.25 for twilight golf. Cart fees are $26, and those under 18 must have a golf permit.

The first course listed under each borough is open all year; other courses are open the first weekend in April through the last weekend in November. Phone the individual courses or (718) 225-4653 for citywide reservations. The following courses accept reservations, but not for same-day playing: Clearview, Dyker Beach, La Tourette, Silver Lake, South Shore and Split Rock.

The Bronx: Pelham and Split Rock courses, 870 Shore Rd., Pelham Bay Park, (718) 885-1258; and Van Cortlandt, Van Cortlandt Park South and Bailey Avenue, (718) 543-4595.

Brooklyn: Dyker Beach, Seventh Avenue and 86th Street, (718) 836-9722; and Marine Park, Flatbush Avenue between Avenue U and the Belt Parkway, (718) 338-7113.

Queens: Clearview, 23rd Avenue and Willets Point Boulevard, (718) 229-2570; Douglaston Park, Commonwealth Boulevard and Marathon Parkway, (718) 224-6566; Forest Park, Forest Park Drive and Jackie Robinson, (718) 296-0999; and Kissena, 164-15 Booth Memorial Rd., (718) 939-4594.

Staten Island: La Tourette, 1001 Richmond Hill Rd., (718) 351-1889; Silver Lake, 915 Victory Blvd., (718) 447-5686; and South Shore, Hugenot Avenue and Arthur Kill Road, (718) 984-0101.

Horseback Riding

Equestrian activity in Manhattan is confined to trails in Central Park. The **Claremont Riding Academy**, 175 W. 89th St. between Amsterdam and Columbus avenues, rents horses for $45 an hour and also offers lessons; phone (212) 724-5100. Riders must be experienced in English riding, and reservations are required.

Jogging and Walking

These are the sports of necessity in New York City, particularly if you want to get from here to there in reasonable time. For those with only the sport in mind, the hottest spot is in Central Park on the 2-mile path surrounding the Reservoir. There also are designated jogger's lanes throughout the park.

Picturesque Riverside Park, between the Hudson River and Riverside Drive, also is a popular spot. Other patches of greenery include **Battery Park**, at the tip of Lower Manhattan *(see attraction listing p. 116)*; **Gramercy Park**, between E. 20th and 21st streets at Lexington Avenue *(see attraction listing p. 118)*; and **Washington Square Park**, in Greenwich Village.

Tennis

Eight Manhattan locations have courts: Central Park, 93rd Street and West Drive; **East River Park**, at Broome Street; **Fort Washington Park**, at 172nd Street; **Fred Johnson Park**, at W. 151st Street east of Seventh Avenue; **Inwood Hill Park**, 207th Street and Seaman Avenue; Riverside Park (two sections), at 96th and at 119th streets; and **Sunken Meadow Randalls Island**. The Department of Parks issues permits; phone (212) 360-8131.

Several courts are open to the public at the site of the U.S. Open, the **U.S.T.A. National Tennis Center** in Flushing Meadows, Queens. Your best bet is to phone (718) 760-6200 2 days in advance to make a reservation; the center is busy on weekends.

Water Sports

Since New York City is surrounded by water, a great way to escape the summertime heat is to visit one of its many beaches. **Jones Beach State Park** *(see Jones Beach p. 96)* is your best bet: With 6 miles of beaches, a boardwalk and a theater playing host to outdoor concerts, you'll forget all about hot blacktop. Beaches listed below can be reached by either bus or subway.

Head to **Coney Island Beach and Boardwalk** in Brooklyn to ride the wooden roller coaster or Ferris wheel; don't pass up a famous Nathan's hotdog for lunch. **Manhattan Beach**, Oriental Boulevard from Ocean Avenue to Mackenzie Street, also is in Brooklyn.

Pelham Bay Park and **Orchard Beach** are in the Bronx. **Jacob Riis Park** and **Jamaica Bay**, Beach 149th to Beach 169th streets, and **Rockaway Beach and Boardwalk**, Beach 9th to Beach 149th streets, are in Queens.

The following beaches are in Richmond (Staten Island): **Great Kills Park**, Hylan Boulevard, Great Kills; **South Beach and Boardwalk**, Fort Wadsworth

to Miller Field, Midland Beach; and **Wolfe's Pond Park**, Holten and Cornelia avenues, Prince's Bay.

Few people would believe you if you claimed to have gone boating in the middle of Manhattan, but it is possible. Rowboats are for rent in Central Park at **Loeb Boathouse**, 72nd Street and Fifth Avenue, for $10 an hour and a $30 deposit; phone (212) 517-2233, ext. 3. As for swimming, only a few municipal pools are still open: **Lasker Pool** on the north end of Central Park is one. Phone the New York City Parks and Recreation Swimming Information hotline at (718) 699-4219 for the latest on pool locations and openings.

© Paul Barton / Corbis

Looking for one-stop recreation? Visit **Chelsea Piers**, a 30-acre sports village along the Hudson River between 17th and 23rd streets. Highlights of the four renovated shipping piers include heated hitting stalls for golfers, a 25-yard swimming pool, an indoor running track, a hockey rink open to ice skaters and an outdoor roller rink. Sailing, kayaking and speedboat tours of the harbor also are offered. Various shops and eateries call the historic piers home; phone (212) 336-6666.

Winter Sports

When there is a chill in the air, New Yorkers head to the nearest ice skating rink to participate in a living portrait by Currier and Ives. The rink at **Rockefeller Center** *(see attraction listing p. 129)* has more glitz, especially when the giant Christmas tree is lit in December. Every year nearly 100,000 skaters are enticed to take a turn on the ice beneath a fabulous golden sculpture of Prometheus.

In 1986 real-estate tycoon Donald Trump paid to have **Wollman Memorial Rink** in Central Park refurbished, to the delight of fellow New Yorkers. Skating is from October to March. There also is a smaller venue on the north end of Central Park, **Lasker Rink**, and the **World's Fair Ice Skating Rink** in **Flushing Meadows Corona Park** is open all year and has rentals *(see attraction listing p. 135)*.

Shopping

New York is a shopping mecca for whatever your heart desires. You will have no trouble hunting down the basics or the extravagances in the stores lining block after enticing block.

While Peter Minuit got the best trade in the city's history—in 1626 he paid $24 for Manhattan Island, currently worth more than $50 billion—Manhattan is still a borough of bargains. The saying "I can get it for you wholesale" is nowhere more applicable.

Antiques

There are plenty of places in the city for antique lovers to indulge their whims. Good hunting grounds for antiques are along Madison Avenue; on Second and Third avenues from the upper 40s to the 80s; on E. 55th Street; and on 57th Street.

Manhattan Art and Antiques Center, 1050 Second Ave. between 55th and 56th streets in Midtown Manhattan, has nearly 100 shops with furniture, glassware, jewelry, pottery and other period pieces sold by a number of independent vendors.

For those looking for something a bit more down to earth, flea markets set up almost every weekend. Try the **Outdoors Annex Antiques Fair and Flea Market**, Sixth Avenue between W. 24th and 27th

Chinatown / © Gibson Stock Photography

streets, or the **SoHo Antiques Fair, Collectibles and Crafts**, Broadway and Grand streets.

Malls

Typical American malls do not exist in New York City. Such a compact urban area lacks the luxury of unlimited space and miles of parking; expect something a little different and quite a bit more extravagant here.

Stern's department store anchors the **Manhattan Mall**, W. 33rd Street at Sixth Avenue in Midtown

Manhattan, and its collage of 60 shops. The eight-floor mall boasts four glass elevators, marble flooring and free entertainment.

Large malls are mostly found outside Manhattan. **Kings Plaza Shopping Center** is an enclosed mall 1 mile north of Belt Parkway exit 11N in Brooklyn. Elmhurst, in Queens County, has **Queens Center**, 2 blocks west of the Long Island Expressway (I-495) on Queens Boulevard. **Staten Island Mall**, 2 miles south of I-278 on Richmond Avenue, has 170 stores, including Macy's and Sears.

The Market at Citicorp Center, on Lexington at 54th Street, is a seven-story building housing international restaurants and shops. The atrium contains an indoor garden cafe with skylights; free entertainment is offered daily.

From designer originals to sweet treats, one of the 200 stores at **Rockefeller Center** *(see attraction listing p. 129)* is bound to carry what you crave. **Trump Tower**, 725 Fifth Ave. at E. 56th Street, has an elegant collection of fashion, food and gift shops within its glass, marble and bronze atrium. The building, reputedly the tallest concrete structure in New York, includes walkways, hanging gardens and an 80-foot waterfall.

Shoppers make a day of it at the **South Street Seaport Museum** *(see attraction listing p. 120)* complex on the East River. Here, **Fulton Market** sells a variety of goods at what was once a fish market. Fresh produce is still available, and there are trendy retailers like **Ann Taylor** and **Abercrombie & Fitch**.

While one-stop shopping in suburbia means the mall, in Midtown Manhattan it means the department store. Among New York's leading department stores are **Bloomingdale's**, 1000 Third Ave. at 59th Street; **Lord and Taylor**, Fifth Avenue at 38th Street; and **Saks Fifth Avenue**, 611 Fifth Ave. at 50th Street. And let's not forget **Macy's**, known as the world's largest store, 151 W. 34th St. at Herald Square.

Takashimaya, 693 Fifth Ave. near 54th Street, is a popular Japanese store, and **Alfred Dunhill Ltd.**, 450 Park Ave. at 57th Street, is a haven for gifts.

Women's clothing is the specialty of **Bergdorf Goodman**, Fifth Avenue at 57th Street; and **Wallach's**, 4123 13th Ave. in Brooklyn. **Bolton's**, with several locations including 57th Street between Fifth and Sixth avenues, and **Loehmann's**, on Seventh Avenue at W. 16th Street, are renowned for their discounted women's apparel.

For men's clothing, try **A. Sulka & Co.**, Park Avenue at 56th Street; **Barney's**, 660 Madison Ave. at 61st Street; **British American House**, 488 Madison Ave.; **Brooks Brothers**, Madison Avenue at

44th Street; and **Paul Stuart**, Madison Avenue at 45th Street.

In Midtown Manhattan at 1540 Broadway in Times Square is **Planet Hollywood**, where the fascination with all that is Hollywood is captured in souvenirs ranging from designer T-shirts to key chains to leather jackets.

Outlets

Despite the emphasis on high-priced merchandise, New York also has plenty of bargains. The city prides itself on its discount clothing houses. Buying from exporters and wholesalers on **Seventh Avenue** can be rewarding, but there are some restrictions: usually cash-only transactions and no returns.

Clothing outlets are found all along Madison and Fifth avenues and along side streets between the Garment District (see attraction listing p. 126) and 85th Street.

Burlington Coat Factory, 707 6th Ave., is said to be the largest coat retailer in the country. It sells designer merchandise at a hefty discount. Go to **Syms**, 42 Trinity Pl. in the financial district, to buy bargain-priced men's and women's apparel. Do not expect doting salesclerks, and be ready to pay in cash.

In addition, you may find discounts of up to 80 percent on shoes, handbags and clothing at **Daffy's**, 111 Fifth Ave. at E. 18th Street in Lower Manhattan.

Specialty Districts

Often many shops of the same specialty are found within a radius of several blocks. These informal groupings are a boon for shoppers, who reap the benefits of convenience and competitive prices.

Art galleries are grouped between Fifth and Madison avenues from 45th to 85th streets; bookstores cluster between Madison and Fifth avenues, 46th to 57th streets, and 57th Street between Seventh and Third avenues. Flower markets adorn the 28th Street and Sixth Avenue area. And rumor has it that the **Diamond District**, W. 47th Street between Fifth and Sixth avenues near Rockefeller Center, is where most of the big deals on big rocks are made.

Macy's anchors the **34th Street Shopping District**, Midtowns Manhattan's 31-block retail, dining and entertainment hub bounded by Park and Tenth avenues and 31st and 36th streets.

Rows and rows of small retail shops sell shoes, suits, linens and more are at the **Historic Orchard Street Shopping District** on the Lower East Side.

Let it be known: **Fifth Avenue** is to shoppers what Baskin Robbins is to most ice cream lovers. For a seemingly limitless selection of goods visit the area from 54th to 59th streets, give or take a block in either direction. Here you can find **Tiffany & Co.** and **F.A.O. Schwarz**. Simply window shopping is quite a treat. Scoot down 57th Street, east or west, for more browsing at **Rizzoli Bookstore**, **Ann Taylor** and **Hermes**.

Shops that rival those on Fifth Avenue can be found on Manhattan's Upper East and West sides. Lots of glitter and plenty of funky threads can be found along **Columbus Avenue** (West Side) between 70th and 83rd streets. **Madison Avenue** (East Side) from 59th to 79th streets is another shoppers' playground, with dozens of retailers and restaurants galore. The **Crystal District** features the luxury boutiques of Daum, Baccarat, Lalique, Steuben and Swarovski on Madison Avenue between 58th and 63rd street.

For gourmet and specialty food items, follow your nose to Lower Manhattan's **Chelsea Market**, occupying a full block on Ninth Avenue between 15th and 16th streets. Built by Nabisco in 1890, this former commercial building is where the first Oreo cookie was baked.

Jewelry and handicraft items can be found in stores at **Greenwich Village** (see attraction listing p. 118). If you do not see what you want, describe it to the shopkeeper—who often also is the artisan—and he or she will either be able to make it for you or tell you where to obtain it.

Performing Arts

The soul of New York City—its unique vibrance and urban beat—bears witness to a love of the arts and a willingness to share this fascination with everyone. The choices are endless—theater, music, opera, dance, film; traditional or experimental; indoors or outdoors; free or ticketed. There is no escaping the delightful barrage of offerings.

Most types of performances take place at **Lincoln Center for the Performing Arts** (see attraction listing p. 126) at Broadway and 65th Street. Its plaza includes **Alice Tully Hall**, (212) 875-5050, the only public concert hall of orchestral size to be constructed in the city since 1891; **Avery Fisher Hall**, (212) 875-5030; **Juilliard School of Music**, (212) 769-7406; **Metropolitan Opera House**, (212) 362-6000; the **New York State Theater**, (212) 870-5570; **Vivian Beaumont and Mitzi E. Newhouse theaters**, (212) 239-6200; and the **Walter Reade Theater**, (212) 875-5600.

Dance

As the nation's cultural mecca, New York City invests a great deal of time and money into its expressive nature, including dance. The greats have all danced here, and Mikhail Baryshnikov, Gregory Hines and Rudolf Nureyev even embraced the city as their home turf.

In a class by itself, the **New York City Ballet** garners rave reviews for its performances of contemporary works under the guidance of well-respected, inventive choreographers. The troupe performs November through February at the New York State Theater at Lincoln Center. The **American Ballet Theatre** presents the classics and some newer ballets to a global audience at the nearby Metropolitan Opera House from April through June.

Modern dance enthusiasts flock to several distinguished venues, such as the **Joyce Theater** in

Rockefeller Center / © Gibson Stock Photography

Lower Manhattan. This dance emporium caters to all forms, from its ballet company in residence, the **Ballet Tech** to more contemporary, avant-garde works; phone (212) 242-0800.

In seasons past, Midtown Manhattan's **City Center,** the city's largest concert hall, has played host to such great modern troupes as the **Alvin Ailey Dance Company,** the **Dance Theater of Harlem,** the **Joffrey Ballet** and the **Paul Taylor Dance Company.** The venue is on 55th Street between Sixth and Seventh avenues; phone (212) 581-1212.

Film

Moviegoing is an event in New York City. You can see the latest blockbusters, an oldie but goodie and everything in between. Foreign and domestic art films are abundant, with both small and large houses catering to those in the mood for an offbeat documentary or underground film.

The Walter Reade Theater at the Lincoln Center schedules repertory showings, sometimes by genre or director. It's an ideal setting for studying film. The **Florence Gould Hall,** 55 E. 59th St., Midtown Manhattan, also shows films; phone (212) 355-6160.

Several museums and art societies hold their own film revivals. In Queens, head to the **American Museum of the Moving Image** for an American film series. In Midtown Manhattan **Asia Society Galleries, The Museum of Modern Art** (rare classics) and **Museum of Television and Radio** have showings. *See attraction listings under What To See.*

Foreign and independent films are shown throughout the city. Try the **Film Forum,** 209 W.

Houston St.,(212) 627-2035; **The Joseph Papp Public Theater,** 425 Lafayette St., (212) 260-2400; or **Millennium,** 66 E. Fourth St., (212) 673-0090.

Music

Musical director Kurt Masur conducts the illustrious **New York Philharmonic Orchestra,** the oldest symphony in the United States, in Avery Fisher Hall at the Lincoln Center for Performing Arts September through June. In July and August the Philharmonic performs free concerts under the stars in various city parks. The innovative **American Symphony Orchestra** also performs in Avery Fisher Hall.

The **Chamber Music Society** of Lincoln Center performs in Alice Tully Hall at the Lincoln Center from September through May, often in conjunction with visiting ensembles and famous soloists. Don't forget to check out the **Brooklyn Academy of Music (BAM)**, 30 Lafayette Ave., which boasts an active opera performance schedule as well as its orchestra in residence, the **Brooklyn Philharmonic.** Phone (718) 636-4100.

The famed **Carnegie Hall**, 57th Street and Seventh Avenue, plays host to celebrated orchestras, noted conductors and a variety of performers *(see attraction listing p. 125).* **Town Hall,** noted for its fine acoustics and excellent seating layout, is between Sixth and Seventh avenues on 43rd Street; phone (212) 840-2824.

There are dozens of classical music locales throughout the city and plenty of performances to choose from, even concerts for children put on by the **Little Orchestra Society;** phone (212) 971-9500 for current offerings. The group normally appears at Florence Gould Hall, 55 E. 59th St., the **Sylvia and Danny Kaye Playhouse,** 695 Park Ave., and Lincoln Center.

For complete, current information about outdoor concerts, phone the City Parks Events Hotline at (212) 360-3456.

Opera

Tenor Luciano Pavarotti brings the house down every time he performs with the **Metropolitan Opera Company** in the elegant surroundings of the Metropolitan Opera House at Lincoln Center. The Met's season runs from September to April and normally includes crowd pleasers like "La Boheme," "Rigoletto" and "Figaro." Founded in the late 1880s, the Met continues to captivate audiences.

The **New York City Opera,** which performs September to April, assembles at the Lincoln Center's New York State Theater. This younger company also is known for fine performances, including "Carmen" and "Madame Butterfly." The **Amato Opera Theatre** offers a classic repertoire at its Lower Manhattan location; phone(212) 228-8200 for performance dates and times.

Theater

New York is the theater capital of the world. Whether on Broadway, off-Broadway or off-off-Broadway, the glitzy bright lights of New York's theater district beckon showgoers from around the world. Simply put, theater *flourishes* in New York City.

Centered on the Times Square area between 41st and 53rd streets from Eighth to Sixth avenues are the theaters that have perpetuated the magic of Broadway—only two of these theaters are actually on Broadway. Glittering marquees announce the latest productions.

The categories of Broadway and off-Broadway indicate the size of the theater—all off-Broadway houses have fewer than 465 seats. This size distinction allows apparent contradictions in that some of the theaters in the Times Square area are classified as off-Broadway; other houses almost next door are described as Broadway theaters.

While the Broadway shows stick to the formula of name stars, writers and directors, the off-Broadway productions are noted for their experimental presentations and revivals. These sometimes equal or surpass the artistry of Broadway and are usually the offerings of young hopefuls, although it is not uncommon for a Broadway "name" to appear in them.

Some Broadway theaters have become as well-known as the mainstream blockbuster plays they have supported, like "*Les Miserables*" at the **Imperial** and "The Phantom of the Opera" at the **Majestic**. This is Andrew Lloyd Webber country. **The Ford Center for the Performing Arts** on 42nd Street is home to the revival production of one of Broadway's longest running musicals, SAVE "42nd Street" *(see color ad starting on p. 394).*

Off-Broadway has its share of fine productions and performers, many along W. 42nd Street in places like the **Playwright's Horizons.**

One celebrated off-Broadway theater is the **Provincetown Playhouse**, 133 MacDougal St. in Greenwich Village. In this theater the early works of Eugene O'Neill, e.e. cummings, Edna St. Vincent Millay and other literary notables were produced. **Cherry Lane Theatre**, 38 Commerce in Greenwich Village, is where many young actors got their start. Also in the Village is the **Sullivan Street Playhouse**, 181 Sullivan, where "The Fantasticks'" enjoyed the distinction of being the longest running show.

Queens Theatre in the Park, in the New York State Pavilion at Flushing Meadows Corona Park, presents a year-round schedule of plays, children's theater and dance; phone (718) 760-0064.

Off-off-Broadway is a free-for-all of experimental performances, usually by unknowns with something to say. Performances are staged at smaller venues and in out-of-the-way cafes.

Current theater listings appear in *New York* and *The New Yorker* magazines, in the newspapers and in *Variety*, a weekly newspaper devoted to the entertainment world, including off-Broadway theaters in Greenwich Village.

Tickets to Broadway shows are hard to come by but not impossible. Advance planning is the key to obtaining the best tickets for the best prices. Seats to Broadway shows are on sale anywhere from 3 months to 1 year in advance. Otherwise, TKTS booths at Times Square in Midtown Manhattan or near the South Street Seaport in Lower Manhattan

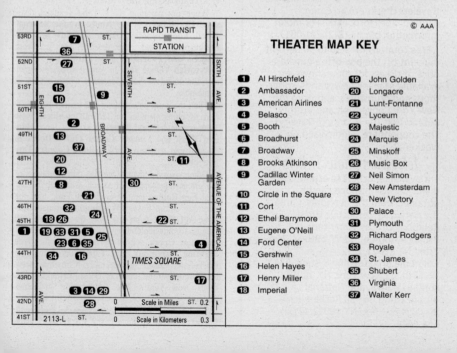

© AAA

THEATER MAP KEY

1 Al Hirschfeld	**19** John Golden
2 Ambassador	**20** Longacre
3 American Airlines	**21** Lunt-Fontanne
4 Belasco	**22** Lyceum
5 Booth	**23** Majestic
6 Broadhurst	**24** Marquis
7 Broadway	**25** Minskoff
8 Brooks Atkinson	**26** Music Box
9 Cadillac Winter Garden	**27** Neil Simon
10 Circle in the Square	**28** New Amsterdam
11 Cort	**29** New Victory
12 Ethel Barrymore	**30** Palace
13 Eugene O'Neill	**31** Plymouth
14 Ford Center	**32** Richard Rodgers
15 Gershwin	**33** Royale
16 Helen Hayes	**34** St. James
17 Henry Miller	**35** Shubert
18 Imperial	**36** Virginia
	37 Walter Kerr

Theater Ticket Bargains

Theater tickets for Broadway and off-Broadway shows are sold at a discount on performance day at two TKTS booths. The Times Square booth, in Midtown Manhattan, is at Broadway and 47th Street. Ticket purchase hours are 3-8 for Mon.-Sat. evening tickets; 10-2 for Wed. and Sat. matinee tickets. For Sun. matinee and evening tickets purchase hours begin at 11.

In Lower Manhattan tickets can be purchased at the South Street Seaport booth, on Front Street, Mon.-Sat. 11-6 for evening performances and 11-3:30 for Sun.

© R. Kord / Robertstock

evening shows. Matinee tickets must be purchased a day in advance.

A $3 surcharge is added to the ticket price. Only cash or travelers checks are accepted. Caution: lines form early. For more information phone (212) 221-0013.

Free coupons for a 30 to 50 percent discount off the box-office purchase price of tickets for some shows are available at many newsstands, coffee shops and drugstores, and from the New York Convention and Visitors Bureau (see The Informed Traveler). The coupons are seldom valid on weekends.

Television Show Tickets

If available, tickets to attend the major television shows can be obtained from the networks. Contact the networks' respective Guest Relations Offices: American Broadcasting Co., 38 W. 66th St., New York, NY 10023, (212) 456-3537; Columbia Broadcasting System, 524 W. 57th St., New York, NY 10019, (212) 975-2476; and National Broadcasting Co., 30 Rockefeller Plaza, New York, NY 10012, (212) 664-4444.

sell discounted tickets on the day of the performance (see Theater Ticket Bargains). Seating varies and there is a service charge, but the effort may be well worth your while. In addition, tickets generally are available at theater box offices a few hours before show time (usually 8 p.m.).

Or contact a ticket agency. Agencies charge a fee in addition to the price printed on the ticket; they also may charge a service fee for delivery of tickets to the hotel or box office.

Special Events

Most ethnic groups in New York City observe at least some of their native holidays with parades, festivals or celebrations. When dates vary for events listed below, only the month in which the event occurs is given. For a comprehensive listing of special events, contact the New York Convention and Visitors Bureau (see The Informed Traveler).

It is said that everyone loves a parade, and New Yorkers may love them more than most. Spring parades include **St. Patrick's Day** and **Greek Independence Day** in March; **Easter** in March or April; **American Ethnic** in April; **Solidarity Day**, **Armed Forces Day**, **Norwegian Constitution Day** and **Memorial Day** in May; and **Israeli Day**, held in the spring (the month varies).

Parades spanning the rest of the year include **Puerto Rican Day** in June; **Labor Day**, **Steuben Day**, **African-American Day** and **West Indian-American Day**, in September; **Pulaski Day**, **Desfile de la Hispanidad: Columbus Day** and **Columbus Day** in October; **Greenwich Village Halloween** on Oct. 31; and **Veterans Day** and **Macy's Thanksgiving Day Parade** in November.

When not parading, New Yorkers attend festivals: **Ukrainian** and the **Ninth Avenue International Food** in May; **Saint Anthony** in June; **Shakespeare**, held June through August; **Festa Italiana** and **Fourth of July Fireworks** in July; **Greenwich Village Jazz** in August and September; and **the Feast of San Gennaro**, which occurs in September.

Then there are celebrations that cannot be classified as either parades or festivals: **Chinese New Year** in late January; **Museum Mile** in June; **Harlem Week** and **Lincoln Center Out-of-Doors** in August; and the **New York is Book Country Day** in September.

Other seasonal events include the beginning of the circus engagement in March or April; the annual **Egg Rolling** contest in Central Park, held the Saturday before Easter; **Washington Square Outdoor Art Show** from late May through June and August to mid-September; the opening of the **Metropolitan Opera season** in September; the **Tree Lighting Ceremony and Christmas Carols** at Rockefeller Center in December; Christmas services throughout the month of December; and the famous **New Year's Eve Celebration** in Times Square.

Take note of such musical events as **Juilliard's Focus! Festival** in January; the **Rockettes' Easter**

Show at Radio City Music Hall; and the **Mostly Mozart Festival** at Lincoln Center in July or August. The **New York Film Festival** presents an international menu of movies from late September to mid-October.

Sporting events include the **U.S. Open Tennis Championships**; since 1978 such greats as Andre Agassi, Steffi Graf and Pete Sampras have played at the **Arthur Ashe Stadium** in Flushing. The tournament takes place annually in late August and early September. Following in November are the **Chase Championships of the Janex Women's Tennis Association Tour** and the **New York City Marathon**, which begins in Staten Island and ends in Central Park.

Nightlife

Come-and-go clubs are the norm in any large city, so always check *The New York Times'* "Weekend" section, *New York* magazine's *Cue* section or the *Village Voice* before planning an evening on the town. What may have been a rock club yesterday may be something else today. It also is worth noting that some of the more trendy places may require funky attire in order to get inside.

Cabaret

The Rainbow Room, on the 65th floor of 30 Rockefeller Plaza, may the most romantic spot in all of New York City. Diners have a spectacular view of the city, and chances are good that the entertainment will be by someone the caliber of Tony Bennett.

Looking for something a little less pricey and a bit more flashy? **The Duplex Cabaret and Piano Bar**, 61 Christopher St., invites audience participation in its downstairs piano bar and houses one of the longest-running cabaret acts in the city. Even the wait staff gets into the act. **Don't Tell Mama**, 343 W. 46th St., serves up something for everyone, from female impersonators to gospel vocalists.

The Oak Room at the Algonquin Hotel, 59 W. 44th St., is an old favorite that attract the likes of classy jazz stylists. Woody Allen sometimes entertains audiences at **Cafe Carlyle**, 35 E. 76th St.

Comedy Clubs

You're in for a real treat at **Stand-Up New York**, 236 W. 78th St., if you happen to be there when Robin Williams stops by for a few minutes on stage. Even on an off night, plenty of popular jokesters turn up to needle patrons at this Upper West Side club.

Cutting-edge comedians and some old favorites play at **Caroline's Comedy Club**, 1626 Broadway off Times Square. Rodney Dangerfield still may not have gotten any respect, but his comedy club **Dangerfield's**, 1118 First Ave., has become one of the oldest laugh factories in the city.

Manhattan / © Alan Schein Photography / Corbis

Dance Clubs

The city that never sleeps offers much in the way of dance clubs—from retro disco to swing dancing to a seductive waltz. Long lines are common at many establishments, and bouncers at the door sometimes handpick those lucky enough to enter the trendier places.

If the surroundings don't get you in the mood, surely the crowd will at the **Roxy**, 515 W. 18th St. It has one of the largest dance floors in town. Make a note: You can roller skate to disco here on Wednesday nights.

After more than 90 years, the **Copacabana**, 617 W. 57th St., is still moving to a Latin beat, and all that garish clothing of the 1970s makes a return for weekend disco dancing.

Crowds pack a former church at 660 Sixth Ave. Yes, there's dancing in the sanctuary at the **Limelight** and lots of people-watching going on in the choir loft. Deejays play Top 40 ditties and crowd favorites. Although some will argue that the Limelight is a bit passé, few can resist partying in church.

Jazz & Blues

Jazz and blues in New York are deeply woven into the city's musical fabric from the Swing Street days, when Dizzy Gillespie and Billie Holiday wowed crowds. These soulful musical strains thrive at clubs in the Greenwich Village area. The granddaddy of them all is **Village Vanguard**, 178

Seventh Ave., known around the world as a jazz showcase. Wynton and Branford Marsalis are just two of the many luminaries who have played here.

The following clubs pay tribute exclusively to jazz and blues: **Blue Note**, 131 W. Third St.; **Iridium Jazz Club**, 1650 Broadway at 51st St.; **Knickerbocker**, 33 University Pl.; **Metropolitan Cafe**, 31 Union Square W.; and **Tavern on the Green**, Central Park at W. 67th Street.

Rock

Places like **Madison Square Garden, Meadowlands** (in East Rutherford, N.J.) and **Radio City Music Hall** present current superstars.

On a smaller scale, **CBGB**, 315 Bowery, specializes in punk rock; **Knitting Factory**, 74 Leonard St., plays everything from John Prine to Yoko Ono; and **Wetlands**, 161 Hudson St., presents rap and funk.

The New York City Vicinity

CROSS RIVER (H-11)

WARD POUND RIDGE RESERVATION, jct. SRs 35 and 121, is a 4,700-acre park and wildlife sanctuary. Camping shelters and picnic areas are available, as are hiking and skiing trails and a wildflower garden. Plant, animal and American Indian artifacts displays are in the Delaware Indian Resource Center in the Trailside Nature Museum. Park open daily 8-dusk. Museum open Tues.-Sun. 9-4; closed Jan. 1, Thanksgiving and Dec. 25. Admission $8 per private vehicle. Phone (914) 864-7317.

CROTON-ON-HUDSON (H-11)
pop. 7,606, elev. 8′

Croton-on-Hudson, once part of the estate of Van Cortlandt Manor *(see attraction listing)*, was founded by Irish and Italian laborers working on the Croton Reservoir dam in the 1840s. During the 1920s the town became a fashionable haven for intellectuals, including poet Edna St. Vincent Millay, feminist Doris Stevens, journalist John Reed and economist Stuart Chase.

Croton Point Park is a retreat for recreation seekers. Surrounded on three sides by the Hudson River, the 504-acre park offers swimming, fishing, camping, cross-country skiing and hiking; a nature center also is available. At the southern tip of the peninsula is Teller's Point, where a small group of Revolutionary War patriots repelled HMS *Vulture* while British Maj. John Andre met onshore with Benedict Arnold to secretly plot the takeover of West Point. Unable to return to his ship, Andre fled and was captured near Tarrytown; the conspiracy was exposed.

SAVE **VAN CORTLANDT MANOR**, off US 9 at 525 S. Riverside Ave., is a restored 18th-century Dutch-English manor house on 20 acres of what was originally an 86,000-acre estate. The restored Ferry House and Ferry House Kitchen at the east end supplied food and lodging to travelers on the Albany Post Road. Family portraits, furniture, silver and porcelains are exhibited. Costumed interpreters demonstrate 18th-century craft skills.

Guided tours are available. Allow 1 hour minimum. Wed.-Mon. 10-5, Apr.-Oct.; Sat.-Sun. 10-4,

Nov.-Dec. Closed Thanksgiving and Dec. 25. Last tour begins 1 hour before closing. Admission $9 over 61, $8; ages 5-17, $5. AX, DS, MC, VI. Phone (914) 631-8200 or (914) 271-8981.

GARRISON (H-10)

BOSCOBEL is 8 mi. n. of Bear Mountain Bridge on SR 9D above the Hudson River Valley. The facade of the restored 1804 New York Federal-style mansion has three unusual draperies of carved wood. Other features include *trompe l'oeil* wallpaper, period furniture, china and silver. The grounds offer a panorama of the Hudson Valley and contain a gatehouse, an orangery, a springhouse and an herb garden.

Grounds Wed.-Mon. 9:30-5, Apr.-Oct.; Wed.-Mon. 9:30-4, Nov.-Dec. Guided tours are given 10-4:15, Apr.-Oct.; 10-3:15, Nov.-Dec. Closed Thanksgiving and Dec. 25. Grounds $7; ages 6-14, $5. Tour $10; over 62, $9; ages 6-14, $7. MC, DS, VI. Phone (845) 265-3638.

GRAYMOOR SPIRITUAL LIFE CENTER, US 9 just s. of SR 403, is on a mountaintop overlooking the Hudson River Valley. Home of the Franciscan Friars of the Atonement, the center contains many shrines and chapels. Picnicking is permitted. Grounds open daily dawn-dusk. Free. Phone (845) 424-3671.

KATONAH (H-11) elev. 226′

CARAMOOR HOUSE MUSEUM is off I-684 exit 6, just e. on SR 35, then 1.8 mi. s. on SR 22 to 149 Girdle Ridge Rd. This house museum is one of only five in the country whose original owners collected entire rooms, usually from European estates, to create their homes. Walter and Lucile Rosen built the Mediterranean-style house 1929-39 and filled it with Eastern, Medieval and Renaissance art and artifacts. The home sits on 100 acres with elaborate gardens. Allow 1 hour minimum. Wed.-Sun. 1-4, May-Oct; Tues.-Fri. by appointment, rest of year. Admission $8, under 16 free. Phone (914) 232-8076.

JOHN JAY HOMESTEAD STATE HISTORIC SITE, 400 Jay St. (SR 22), was the retirement home of the first chief justice of the United States and second governor of New York. The house has restored period rooms with family memorabilia and portraits by American artists. The grounds include landscape plantings and 19th- and 20th-century farm outbuildings.

Guided tours are available. Allow 1 hour minimum. Tues.-Sat. 10-4, Sun. 11-4, Apr.-Oct.; hours vary rest of year. Guided tours are given on the hour. Admission $7; over 62 and ages 5-12, $5. Phone (914) 232-5651.

KATONAH MUSEUM OF ART, SR 22 and Jay St., presents changing exhibits from major museums, artists and private collectors. Allow 30 minutes minimum. Tues.-Sat. 10-5, Sun. noon-5; closed major holidays and during the installation of new exhibits. Guided tours are offered Tues.-Sun. at 2:30. Admission $3, under 12 free. Phone (914) 232-9555.

MOUNT VERNON (H-2)
pop. 68,381, elev. 100′

In 1850, a merchant tailor named John Stevens founded the Industrial Home Association with the goal of helping working-class New Yorkers buy their own homes. More than 1,000 people joined, and the association collected enough dues to purchase 369 acres of farmland. In a vote to select the town name, Monticello was the original winner. With that name already taken, Mount Vernon won in the second round.

ST. PAUL'S CHURCH NATIONAL HISTORIC SITE is at 897 S. Columbus Ave. (SR 22). The 5-acre site includes a museum, a historic church and cemetery, and the remnants of a town village green. The church was used as a hospital during the Revolutionary War Battle of Pell's Point; Aaron Burr argued law in the church's makeshift courtroom after the war. Guided tours are available. Daily 9-5. Donations. Phone (914) 667-4116.

NEW CITY (G-1) pop. 34,038, elev. 163′

Several farms and orchards in the New City area allow visitors to pick their own strawberries and apples during harvest time.

New City Chamber of Commerce: P.O. Box 2222, New City, NY 10956; phone (845) 638-1395.

HISTORICAL SOCIETY OF ROCKLAND COUNTY is off Palisades Pkwy. exit 11, e. onto New Hempstead Rd., then n. at Main St. to 20 Zukor Rd. The museum presents changing exhibits, including a doll house and furnishings display in December. Guided tours of an 1832 restored Dutch farmhouse are offered some Sundays; phone for dates. Allow 30 minutes minimum. Tues.-Sun. 1-5; closed federal holidays and briefly between exhibits. Admission $5; ages 6-12, $3. Phone (845) 634-9629.

NEW ROCHELLE (H-2) pop. 72,182, elev. 72′

The New Rochelle area was settled in 1688 by Huguenot refugees who named their community after their old home, La Rochelle, in France. New Rochelle grew quickly due to its healthy shipbuilding industry, its location as a key port of trade with New York City and other nearby harbors and its position on the strategic Boston Post Road, the major route to cities farther north.

In the 1890s the town became a popular retreat for noted actors, artists and authors, including Eddie Foy, Agnes Booth and Frederic Remington. The town still is known as a wealthy suburb of commuters who work in New York City.

The Thomas Paine Cottage, 20 Sicard Ave., was the home of the American political theorist and writer. A museum 100 yards north houses Thomas Paine artifacts. Both are open to the public. Phone (914) 633-1776 for Friday through Sunday hours and fees.

New Rochelle Chamber of Commerce: 459 Main St., New Rochelle, NY 10801; phone (914) 632-5700.

NORTH SALEM (H-11) pop. 5,137

[SAVE] **HAMMOND MUSEUM AND JAPANESE STROLL GARDEN** is off I-684 exit 7, 4.3 mi. e. on SR 116, then n. on SR 124 to Deveau Rd., following signs. Decorative arts, Oriental art and nearly 500 photographs by Carl Van Vechten are displayed in the museum. The grounds feature fruit trees, waterfalls, ponds, a reflection pool, a bamboo grove and paths meandering to such thematic areas as the Zen Garden, Tea Garden and Mountain Walk. Wed.-Sat. noon-4, Apr.-Oct. Admission $5; over 61, $4; under 12 free. Phone (914) 669-5033.

NYACK (H-2) pop. 6,737, elev. 100′

Nyack's way of life has always been tied to the Hudson River: The Nyack Indians gathered oysters on its banks, European settlers established a prosperous river landing and today pleasure craft abound. Artist Edward Hopper was born in Nyack in 1882; his boyhood home is now a public art gallery.

The Nyacks Chamber of Commerce: P.O. Box 677, Nyack, NY 10960; phone (845) 353-2221.

Self-guiding tours: Brochures outlining several walking tours through historic and scenic areas in Nyack are available for a nominal fee from Friends of the Nyacks, P.O. Box 120, Nyack, NY 10960. Phone (845) 358-4973.

OSSINING (G-2) pop. 24,010, elev. 8′

TEATOWN LAKE RESERVATION, off Taconic Pkwy. onto SR 134 w., then 1 mi. n. to 1600 Spring Valley Rd., is an environmental education center and wildlife sanctuary with 12 miles of nature trails. Changing exhibits relating to mammals, birds, plants and geology are presented in a museum; native birds of prey unable to live in the wild also are displayed.

Guided tours of Wildflower Island, including a display of rare orchids, are available by appointment May 1 through Sept. 15. Nature center open

Tues.-Sat. 9-5, Sun. 1-5; closed major holidays. Grounds open daily dawn-dusk. Donations. Phone (914) 762-2912.

PURCHASE (H-2) elev. 355'

DONALD KENDALL SCULPTURE GARDENS, off Anderson Hill Rd. at PepsiCo, is a 114-acre garden with modern sculpture. Highlights include exotic trees and shrubs, a water lily pool and works by such artists as Henry Moore, Claes Oldenburg and Auguste Rodin. A self-guiding tour brochure is available. Daily dawn-dusk. Free. Phone (914) 253-2000.

[SAVE] **NEUBERGER MUSEUM OF ART** is at 735 Anderson Hill Rd. on the campus of Purchase College, State University of New York (SUNY), off I-287 exit 8E, off the Hutchinson River Pkwy. exit 28 or off I-684 exit 2 following signs. The museum presents a permanent collection and changing exhibits focusing on 20th-century American and European art as well as African art.

Allow 1 hour minimum. Tues.-Fri. 10-4, Sat.-Sun. 11-5; closed major holidays. Guided gallery talks are conducted Tues.-Fri. at 1, Sun. at 2 and 3, mid-Sept. through June 30. Admission $5, over 61 and students with ID $3, under 12 free, free to all first Sat. of the month. Phone (914) 251-6100.

RYE (H-2) pop. 14,955, elev. 49'

PLAYLAND, off I-95 exit 19 following signs to Playland Pkwy., is a recreational complex offering rides, a beach and boardwalk, a saltwater lake, riverboat excursions, an 18-hole miniature golf and a children's park. Playland was among the earliest totally planned amusement parks in the country. Features include original Art Deco buildings, a long grass mall, the Dragon Coaster and a vintage carousel. Free entertainment is provided daily.

Allow 3 hours, 30 minutes minimum. Tues.-Thurs. and Sun. noon-11, Fri.-Sat. and Mon. holidays noon-midnight, late June-Labor Day; Tues.-Thurs. 10-4, Fri.-Sat. and Mon. holidays noon-midnight, Sun. noon-11, mid-May to late June; Sat.-Sun. noon-midnight, day after Labor Day-Sept. 30. Hours may vary; phone ahead. Twenty-four ticket book $21; 16 tickets $16; 8 tickets $9. Individual ride tickets $1.25. Additional admission is charged for the beach, pool and miniature golf course. Parking Sat.-Sun. $7, Tues.-Fri. $5, holidays $10. MC, VI. Phone (914) 813-7000.

SLEEPY HOLLOW (H-2) pop. 9,212

Sleepy Hollow, North Tarrytown until 1996 when the residents voted to change the town's name, is on the east bank of the Hudson, where the river widens to form the Tappan Zee. In 1680, near where the Pocantico River flows into the Hudson, Frederick Philipse built a stone house, a church and other buildings. The church was popularized by Washington Irving in "The Legend of Sleepy Hollow."

HEADLESS HORSEMAN BRIDGE carries US 9 across the Pocantico River where the old bridge once stood from which, in Irving's story, the headless horseman hurled his pumpkin head at Ichabod Crane.

KYKUIT, THE ROCKEFELLER ESTATE is off SR 119; tours depart from Philipsburg Manor on US 9 *(see attraction listing)*. Home to four generations of the Rockefeller family, Kykuit, meaning lookout, is on a hilltop overlooking the Hudson River. Built in 1913 under the supervision of John D. Rockefeller's son Junior, the stone mansion is appointed with antiques, fine art and family memorabilia.

Fountains and a collection of 20th-century sculpture assembled by Nelson A. Rockefeller accent the terraced and formal gardens. The coach barn contains vintage automobiles and carriages.

Food is available. Allow 2 hours, 30 minutes minimum. Tours depart every 30 minutes Wed.-Mon. 10-3, late Apr.-early Nov. Garden and sculpture tours are given Wed.-Fri. and Mon. at 3. **Note:** Tours are not recommended for under age 10. Fee $22; over 61, $20; under 18, $18. AX, DC, DS, MC, VI. Phone (914) 631-9491.

PHILIPSBURG MANOR, on US 9, consists of an early 18th-century Dutch-American manor house, an operating gristmill, an oak-timbered dam and a barn. The stone manor house is furnished with period artifacts. Costumed guides lead tours, and a reception center offers exhibits and a film about the development and restoration of the manor.

Food is available. Allow 2 hours minimum. Wed.-Mon. 10-5, Apr.-Oct.; Wed.-Mon. 10-4, Nov.-Dec.; Sat.-Sun. 10-4, in Mar. Closed Thanksgiving and Dec. 25. Last tour begins 1 hour before closing. Admission $9; over 61, $8; ages 5-17, $5. AX, DS, MC, VI. Phone (914) 631-8200.

SLEEPY HOLLOW CEMETERY, on US 9, includes the graves of Washington Irving, Andrew Carnegie, William Rockefeller and Whitelaw Reid. Daily 8:30-4:30. Free. Phone (914) 631-0081.

UNION CHURCH OF POCANTICO HILLS is at 555 Bedford Rd. John D. Rockefeller, Jr. donated the land and funds for the construction of the nondenominational Protestant church in 1921. It contains stained glass windows by Henry Matisse and Marc Chagall. Allow 30 minutes minimum. Wed.-Fri. and Mon. 11-5, Sat. 10-5, Sun. 2-5, Apr.-Dec. Admission $4, under 6 free. Phone (914) 332-6659.

STONY POINT (H-10) pop. 11,744, elev. 32′

STONY POINT BATTLEFIELD STATE HISTORIC SITE is 8 mi. s. of the Bear Mountain bridge off US 9W on Park Rd. This was the location of a successful midnight assault by the American Corps of Light Infantry, commanded by Brig. Gen. Anthony Wayne, against a British garrison in July 1779. A museum presents exhibits and a slide show. Interpreters in period dress offer demonstrations with muskets and artillery; cooking and the usual tasks

of camp life also are portrayed. Guided grounds and lighthouse tours are available.

Picnicking is permitted. Allow 1 hour minimum. Grounds open Wed.-Sat. and Memorial Day, July 4 and Labor Day 10-5, Sun. 1-5, mid-Apr. through Oct. 31. Admission $5 per private vehicle. Increased admission may be charged during special events. Phone (845) 786-2521.

TAPPAN (H-2) pop. 6,757, elev. 50′

Historically, Tappan is best noted for being the setting for the prologue and denouement of the Benedict Arnold-Maj. John Andre conspiracy. At his DeWint House headquarters, Gen. George Washington gave the command of West Point to Arnold, who arranged to betray the garrison to the British.

However, Arnold's contact, Andre, was captured, and the plans were uncovered. Andre was jailed in the old Seventy-Six House and executed by hanging on what is known as Andre Hill. His body was later traded for that of Gen. Richard Montgomery, who was killed in the Siege of Quebec in 1775. Andre was interred in Westminster Abbey in 1821.

GEORGE WASHINGTON'S HEADQUARTERS AT TAPPAN (The DeWint House), 20 Livingston St. at Oak Tree Rd., was built in 1700 and was used on occasion by Gen. George Washington as an army headquarters during the Revolutionary War. This restored house features furnished period rooms. The Carriage House Museum contains Washington artifacts and various memorabilia. Daily 10-4; closed Jan. 1, Thanksgiving and Dec. 25. Donations. Phone (845) 359-1359.

TARRYTOWN (H-2) pop. 11,090, elev. 14′

"In the bosom of one of those spacious coves which indent the eastern shore of the Hudson, at that broad expansion of the river denominated by

DID YOU KNOW

Colin Powell, the nation's first African-American secretary of state, hails from the South Bronx.

the Tappan Zee there lies a small market town or rural port, which by some is called Greenburgh, but which is more generally and properly known as Tarry Town."

So Washington Irving described the town nearest the bucolic little glen that figures in "The Legend of Sleepy Hollow." Tarrytown is joined on the south by Irvington and on the north by Sleepy Hollow, formerly North Tarrytown. These three communities form the well-known Sleepy Hollow country.

According to Irving the name of Tarrytown was given by housewives "from the inveterate propensity of their husbands to linger about the village tavern on market days."

Near the boundary of Sleepy Hollow and Tarrytown British spy Maj. John Andre was captured, exposing Benedict Arnold's treachery.

Sleepy Hollow Chamber of Commerce: 54 Main St., Tarrytown, NY 10591; phone (914) 631-1705.

SAVE **LYNDHURST,** .2 mi. e. of jct. US 9 and I-287 at 635 S. Broadway (US 9) overlooking the Hudson River, is an example of an American Hudson River Gothic Revival mansion. The house is furnished in Gothic, Beaux Arts and French 19th-century styles. The interior has ribbed and vaulted ceilings, figured bosses, stained-glass windows and panels, and walls painted to resemble dressed stone. Landscaped grounds surround the mansion.

Allow 1 hour minimum. Tues.-Sun. and Mon. holidays 10-5, Apr. 15-Oct. 31; Sat.-Sun. 10-4, rest of year. Closed Jan. 1, Thanksgiving and Dec. 25. Last tour begins 45 minutes before closing. Admission $10; over 61, $9; ages 12-17, $4. Phone (914) 631-4481.

PATRIOTS' PARK, on US 9, contains Andre Brook, the dividing line between the Tarrytowns. Captors' Monument is topped by a bronze figure of John Paulding, one of the captors of British spy Maj. John Andre. Daily dawn-dusk. Free. Phone (914) 631-1705.

WASHINGTON IRVING MEMORIAL, W. Sunnyside Ln. at Broadway (US 9), is by Daniel Chester French, sculptor of the seated figure in the Lincoln Memorial in Washington, D.C. The memorial consists of a bust of the author with figures of characters from his stories. Daily 24 hours. Free. Phone (914) 631-1705.

GEM SAVE **WASHINGTON IRVING'S SUNNYSIDE,** .5 mi. s. of Tappan Zee Bridge on US 9 to W. Sunnyside Ln., was the home of Washington Irving 1835-59. Set at the bottom of a hill next to the Hudson River, this is the home the romantic Irving called his "little snuggery." The house was built in the late 17th century as a tenant farmer's cottage and was occupied in the 18th century by a branch of the Van Tassel family that figures in "The Legend of Sleepy Hollow."

Irving modified the house, planned the grounds and planted wisteria and ivy vines. The interior has features that were far advanced for their day, such as a bathtub with running water and a hot water tank in the kitchen fed by pipes from the pond that Irving called the "Little Mediterranean." Costumed guides explain the house and its furnishings, which include the author's library.

Picnicking is permitted. Allow 1 hour minimum. Wed.-Mon. 10-5, Apr.-Oct.; Wed.-Mon. 10-4, Nov.-Dec.; Sat.-Sun. 10-4 in Mar. Closed Thanksgiving and Dec. 25. Last tour begins 1 hour before closing. Admission $9; over 61, $8; ages 5-17, $5. AX, DS, MC, VI. Phone (914) 631-8200.

WEST HAVERSTRAW (I-11)
pop. 10,295, elev. 100′

The village of West Haverstraw is in the area 17th-century Dutch landholders called Haverstraw, meaning oat straw. Merchant trade out of Haverstraw Bay shored the community in the early years, giving way to textile milling and a lucrative brickmaking industry that grew to include 42 plants by 1885. Helen Hayes Hospital, founded in 1900 and later named in honor of the First Lady of the American Theater for her 49 years of service on its visitors' board, is one of the village's major employers.

The Ramapo Mountains, to the west, and Lake Sebago, off Seven Lakes Parkway, offer year-round recreational opportunities.

From its home port at Haverstraw Marina, Hudson Highlands Cruises offers narrated Hudson River sightseeing excursions between West Haverstraw and West Point aboard the MV *Commander*, a 1917 ferry boat commissioned by the U.S. Navy during World War I; phone (845) 534-7245.

MARIAN SHRINE, 2 mi. e. of Palisades Pkwy. exit 14 off Filors Ln., includes among its 200 acres an Italian marble rosary way, a replica of the St. John Bosco birthplace and a 48-foot bronze statue of the Rosary Madonna. Daily 9-5. Donations. Phone (845) 947-2200.

WHITE PLAINS (H-2) pop. 53,077, elev. 201′

Seat of Westchester County, White Plains was the birthplace of the state; the first Provincial Congress met at this site on July 10, 1776. Gen. George Washington headquartered here during the last phase of the Battle of White Plains.

County Chamber of Commerce: 235 Mamaroneck Ave., White Plains, NY 10605; phone (914) 948-2110.

Shopping areas: Galleria Mall is 2 blocks east of Bronx River Parkway exit 21 at 100 Main St. Among its 149 stores are JCPenney and Sterns.

WHITE PLAINS NATIONAL BATTLEFIELD SITE consists of three monuments, one at Chatterton Hill and two on Battle Avenue. The monuments mark Washington's position during the Battle of White Plains, fought Oct. 28, 1776. Daily 24 hours. Free.

YONKERS (H-2) pop. 196,086, elev. 300'

Once a village of the Manhattes Indians, the site of Yonkers was part of a parcel of land granted to Adriaen Cornelissen van der Donck by the Dutch West India Co. in 1646. His title, De Jonkheer, became the city's name.

Today the city is a major industrial center, supported by more than 100 different industries. Despite its nearness to New York City, the city is not a bedroom community—most of its breadwinners are employed in Yonkers.

Yonkers Chamber of Commerce: 20 S. Broadway, Suite 1207, Yonkers, NY 10701; phone (914) 963-0332.

Shopping areas: Cross County Shopping Center, south of Cross County Parkway exit 5, has 108 stores, including Sterns and Wanamakers.

THE HUDSON RIVER MUSEUM OF WESTCHESTER, 511 Warburton Ave. overlooking the Hudson River, includes changing exhibitions of 19th- and 20th-century American art from its permanent collection. The elements of art, history and science are combined in a given subject. Within the museum complex are the 19th-century Glenview Mansion and the Andrus Planetarium. Programs for senior citizens and children are offered regularly.

Food is available. Allow 1 hour, 30 minutes minimum. Museum open Wed.-Sun. noon-5 (also Fri. 5-8), May-Sept.; Wed.-Sun. noon-5, rest of year. Closed major holidays. Planetarium shows Fri. at 7, Sat.-Sun. at 1:30, 2:30 and 3:30. Museum $5; over 61 and under 13, $3. Planetarium $5; over 61 and under 13, $3; Fri. show free to all. Phone (914) 963-4550.

PHILIPSE MANOR HALL STATE HISTORIC SITE is at 29 Warburton Ave. This 17th-century residence of wealthy gristmill owner Frederick Philipse was the nucleus of a vast estate that eventually became the town of Yonkers. At one time it served as the city hall; today it is a museum of history, art and architecture. Guided tours are available. Allow 1 hour minimum. Wed.-Sat. noon-5, Sun. 1-4, Apr.-Oct.; by appointment rest of year. Closed holidays. Free. Phone (914) 965-4027.

Statue of Liberty / © Lester Lefkowitz / Corbis

**This ends listings for the New York City Vicinity.
The following page resumes the alphabetical listings of cities in New York.**

Niagara Falls

(including Niagara Falls, Ontario)

Young in geologic time, Niagara Falls were created by the recession and melting of a mammoth ice sheet. As the ice retreated some 50,000 years ago the land rose behind it, forming such ridges as the Niagara Escarpment. The melting ice formed a vast lake in what is now Lake Erie and its surrounding lowlands; the lake overflowed about 12,000 years ago, creating Niagara Falls.

The falls originally formed 7 miles north in what is now Lewiston. Due to erosion they are currently about midway between lakes Erie and Ontario on the Niagara River, a 37-mile-long strait that is bisected by the international boundary. The cities of Niagara Falls, N.Y., and Niagara Falls, Ontario, are connected by bridges across the river.

The Canadian, or Horseshoe, Falls are 176 feet high with a deeply curving crest of about 2,200 feet. The American Falls, higher at 184 feet, have a shorter, fairly straight crest of about 1,075 feet. The third and smallest of Niagara's falls, Bridal Veil, is separated from the other falls by Luna and Goat islands.

Untouched, the combined flow of the water over the falls would be about 1.5 million gallons per second; however, one-half to three-quarters of the river is diverted for the generation of electricity before it reaches the falls. Most of the siphoning is done at night. The water flow is reduced to about 700,000 gallons per second during the tourist season and to less at other times.

The first people to gaze upon this natural spectacle were ancestors of the Seneca Indians. They were the area's first inhabitants some 2,000 years ago. One of the earliest Europeans to view the falls was French priest Father Louis Hennepin in 1678. History recounts that upon seeing the spectacle Hennepin fell to his knees in prayer, saying of the falls that "the universe does not afford its parallel."

In the next few years the French built and rebuilt several forts at the mouth of the river. Old Fort Niagara *(see Youngstown p. 167)* was to play key roles in the major wars of the next 90 years. In 1759, during the French and Indian War, the British captured the fort. They held it until 1796 when they withdrew to Fort George in Canada.

Power Vista / Niagara Tourism & Convention Corporation

American Falls / © Andre Jenny/Focus Group / PictureQuest

The War of 1812 was the most devastating to hit Niagara Falls. Many small settlements on both sides of the river were looted and burned. Niagara Falls witnessed the Battle of Lundy's Lane, the war's bloodiest, on July 25, 1814. Neither side could claim victory in that fierce conflict. Five months later the Treaty of Ghent ended 2.5 years of fighting and reinstated the boundary line.

After the war Niagara Falls entered a new era of peace and prosperity. Settlement began in earnest, and by 1892 Niagara Falls was incorporated as a city. With the arrival of steamships in 1820, the Erie Canal in 1825 and the railroad in 1840, the town became accessible to tourists. An old saw predicts that "the love of those who honeymoon here will last as long as the falls themselves."

A different type of romance lured daredevils to the falls in the 1800s and early 1900s. The first stuntster was Sam Patch. He survived two dives into the waters below the falls. The first person to go over the falls in a barrel was Annie Taylor in 1901. William Fitzgerald took the plunge in 1961. He was arrested as soon as he surfaced, because stunts on the river and falls had by then been outlawed.

In 1895 the world's first commercial hydroelectric plant was built at the falls. The Niagara Power Project opened in 1961 with 13 generators and a total installed power of 2,190,000 kilowatts, one of the largest hydroelectric facilities in the world. But the power won't last forever; the falls are eroding about an inch per year. For the next 2,500 years, however, the falls will look much the same as they have since Father Hennepin's visit.

Approaches

By Car

Traffic arriving from the south can connect with a part of the New York State Thruway (I-90), which interchanges with both I-290 and I-190. I-190, an expressway spur, leads across Grand Island to Niagara Falls, connecting with the major arteries to downtown. For the most direct and scenic route to the falls from I-190 take the Robert Moses Parkway and follow the signs to Niagara Falls State Park (*see attraction listing p. 163*).

From points east, access is primarily via I-90, which collects traffic from across the state. From the Rochester area, however, SRs 31 and 104 each offer an alternate route to the city.

Approaches from the west are via any of several highways in Canada, with three bridges funneling traffic stateside: the Rainbow Bridge in the southwest part of the city near Prospect Park; the Whirlpool Rapids Bridge in the northwest just below Whirlpool State Park (*see attraction listing p. 164*); and the Lewiston-Queenston Bridge in Lewiston, which

(continued on p. 161)

The Informed Traveler

City Population: 55,593

Elevation: 571 ft.

Sales Tax: The sales tax in Niagara Falls is 7 percent. An additional 11 percent is levied for hotel/motel rooms, and 12 percent is added for rental cars.

WHOM TO CALL

Emergency: 911

Police (non-emergency): (716) 286-4711

Time and Temperature: (716) 844-1717

Hospitals: Mount St. Mary's, in Lewiston, (716) 297-4800.

WHERE TO LOOK

Newspapers

Niagara Falls has one daily paper, the morning *Niagara Gazette.* The *Buffalo News,* as well as such metropolitan dailies as the *New York Times* and the *New York Daily News* also are available.

Radio

Radio station WEBR (970 AM) is an all-news/weather station; WBFO (88.7 FM) is a member of National Public Radio.

Visitor Information

Information is available from the Niagara Falls Tourism and Convention Corp., 345 Third St., Suite 605, Niagara Falls, NY 14303, (716) 282-8992 or (800) 338-7890. For parks information contact the New York State Parks Commission in Prospect Park at (716) 278-1770.

TRANSPORTATION

Air Travel

The nearest airport offering major domestic and international flight service is the Buffalo-Niagara Falls International Airport at Genesee Street and Cayuga Road. Shuttle buses run between the airport and major hotels; phone (800) 551-9369. Taxi service is available with fares averaging $35. Short- and long-term parking is available at SunPark at 4099 Genesee St.; phone (716) 633-6040.

The Niagara Falls International Airport on Porter Road serves charter and private flights.

Rental Cars

Hertz, (716) 632-4772 or (800) 654-3080, offers discounts to AAA members. For listings of other agencies check the telephone directory.

Rail Service

Passenger rail service is available at the Amtrak station at Hyde Park Boulevard and Lockport Road; phone (716) 285-4224.

Buses

Connections by bus may be made at Rainbow Boulevard N. and Old Falls Street; phone (716) 285-9319.

Taxis

Cab companies include LaSalle Cab Co., (716) 284-8833, and United Cab Co., (716) 285-9331. Rates are $1.50 for the first half-mile, then 75c for each additional sixth of a mile. For a complete list of taxi services check the telephone directory.

Public Transport

The Niagara Frontier Transportation Authority (Metro) offers bus service within the city and outlying areas, including connections to Lockport and Buffalo. Service is generally from 5 a.m. to 10:30 p.m. Fares are $1.50 plus 25c for each additional zone; over 64, ages 5-11 and the physically impaired 65c plus 10c for each additional zone; phone (716) 285-9319.

Destination Niagara Falls

While the falls are Niagara's primary diversion, the area offers more than meets the eye.

See how the river's power is harnessed at Power Vista, the Niagara Power Project's visitor center. Cross a footbridge and hike wooded Goat Island. Say hello to a colony of Peruvian penguins at the Aquarium of Niagara. Or view some contemporary art at the Castellani Art Museum.

© James Nazz Corbis

Prospect Point Observation Tower, Niagara Falls. Elevators inside this 250-foot tower whisk visitors up to the observation deck or down to the *Maid of the Mist* boarding dock. (See listing page 163)

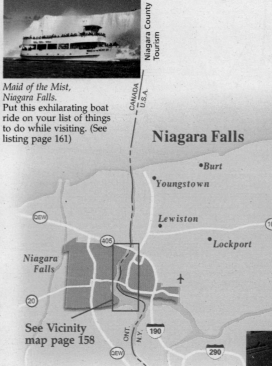

Niagara County Tourism

Maid of the Mist, Niagara Falls. Put this exhilarating boat ride on your list of things to do while visiting. (See listing page 161)

CANADA U.S.A.

Niagara Falls

•Burt

•Youngstown

Lewiston
•

Lockport

QEW

405

104

Niagara Falls

20

Power Vista, Niagara Falls. Interactive exhibits reveal how the Niagara Power Project transforms the power of the falls into electricity. (See listing page 163)

See Vicinity map page 158

ONT. N.Y.

190

QEW

290

Niagara County Tourism

Places included in this AAA Destination City:

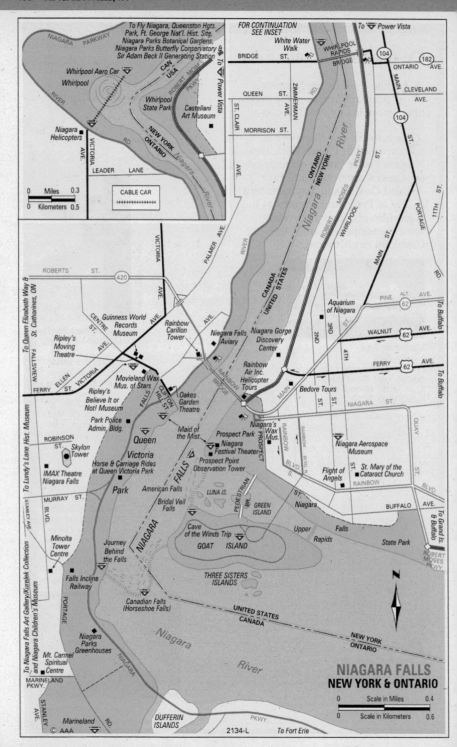

NIAGARA PARKWAY

To Fly Niagara, Queenston Hgts.
Park, Ft. George Nat'l. Hist. Site,
Niagara Parks Botanical Gardens,
Niagara Parks Butterfly Conservatory &
Sir Adam Beck II Generating Station

To Power Vista

FOR CONTINUATION
SEE INSET

White Water
Walk

WHIRLPOOL
RAPIDS

104
182

Whirlpool Aero Car
Whirlpool

BRIDGE

WHIRLPOOL
BRIDGE

ST.

ONTARIO

AVE.

MAIN

ST.

CLEVELAND
AVE.

Niagara
Helicopters

Whirlpool
State Park

Castellani
Art Museum

QUEEN ST.

ZIMMERMAN AVE.

ST. CLAIR

RD.

MORRISON ST.

104

AVE.

ST.

11TH

NEW YORK
ONTARIO

NIAGARA RIVER

LEADER LANE

ROBERT MOSES PKWY

ONTARIO
NEW YORK

WHIRLPOOL

ROBERT MOSES PKWY

MAIN ST.

ST.

PORTAGE

RD.

Miles 0.3
Kilometers 0.5

CABLE CAR

CABLE CAR

To Queen Elizabeth Way &
St. Catharines, ON

To Lundy's Lane Hist. Museum

VICTORIA AVE.

PALMER AVE.

RIVER

CANADA
UNITED STATES

Niagara River

ROBERTS ST.

420

CENTRE ST.

AVE.

AVE.

PINE ALT. AVE.

62

To Buffalo

Guinness World
Records Museum

Rainbow
Carillon
Tower

Niagara Falls
Aviary

Niagara Gorge
Discovery
Center

Aquarium
of Niagara

2ND

3RD

WALNUT

62

AVE.

Ripley's
Moving
Theatre

FALLSVIEW

ELLEN ST.

AVE.

VICTORIA

RAINBOW BRIDGE

Rainbow
Air Inc.
Helicopter
Tours

4TH

FERRY

62

AVE.

Movieland Wax
Mus. of Stars

CLIFTON HILL ST.

Oakes
Garden
Theatre

Bedore Tours

FERRY

To Buffalo

NIAGARA ST.

Ripley's
Believe It or
Not! Museum

FALLS ST.

Maid of
the Mist

Niagara's
Wax Mus.

QUAY ST.

Park Police
Admin. Bldg.

Queen

Prospect Park

PROSPECT ST.

Niagara Aerospace
Museum

ROBINSON ST.

Skylon
Tower

Victoria

Niagara
Festival Theater

RAINBOW BLVD. N.

Flight of
Angels

St. Mary of the
Cataract Church

IMAX Theatre
Niagara Falls

Horse & Carriage Rides
at Queen Victoria Park

Prospect Point
Observation Tower

RAINBOW

MURRAY ST.

Park

American Falls

LUNA IS.

PEDESTRIAN BR.

ST.

Niagara

BUFFALO AVE.

BLVD.

Minolta
Tower
Centre

Bridal Veil
Falls

NIAGARA FALLS

GREEN
ISLAND

Falls

To Grand Is.
& Buffalo

To Niagara Falls Art Gallery/Kurelek Collection
and Niagara Children's Museum

Journey
Behind
the Falls

Cave
of the Winds Trip

GOAT ISLAND

Upper
Rapids

State Park

ROBERT MOSES PKWY

Falls Incline
Railway

THREE SISTERS
ISLANDS

PORTAGE RD.

Canadian Falls
(Horseshoe Falls)

UNITED STATES
CANADA

NEW YORK
ONTARIO

Niagara

Niagara
Parks
Greenhouses

Mt. Carmel
Spiritual
Centre

NIAGARA RIVER

River

MARINELAND
PKWY.

STANLEY AVE.

Marineland

DUFFERIN
ISLANDS

PKWY.

To Fort Erie

2134-L

NIAGARA FALLS
NEW YORK & ONTARIO

Scale in Miles 0.4

Scale in Kilometers 0.6

© AAA

connects the northern end of I-190 with Canada's Hwy. 405.

Getting Around

Street System

In Niagara Falls the streets are laid out in the traditional grid pattern. Numbered streets run north to south, from First Street on the western edge of the city to 102nd Street on the eastern boundary. Named streets generally run east to west. Avenues run east to west, and roads and boulevards run north to south or diagonally.

The Robert Moses Parkway parallels the river as it runs along the extreme western and southern edges of Niagara Falls, while the Niagara Expressway (I-190) bypasses downtown traffic as it hugs the eastern edge before crossing into Canada.

Parking

Parking is plentiful on the U.S. side of the river and ranges from on-street parking to free or pay lots. State-owned lots are in Prospect Park and on the east and west ends of Goat Island. Pay lots average a minimum of $3 per day.

What To See

[SAVE] **AQUARIUM OF NIAGARA,** 701 Whirlpool St. at Pine Ave. (US 62), displays more than 1,500 aquatic animals ranging from the Great Lakes to the coral reefs and is home to the state's largest collection of Great Lakes fish. Visitors can see California sea lions, sharks, piranhas and more. Highlights include a colony of endangered Peruvian penguins and an outdoor harbor seal pool. The aquarium is the site of the 81st "Whaling Wall" by marinelife artist Wyland.

Open daily at 9. Closing hours vary; phone ahead. Closed Thanksgiving and Dec. 25. Penguins are fed daily at 9:30 and 2:30; seals are fed daily at 11 and 3:45; and sharks are fed on alternate days at 11:30. Admission $6.95; over 59 and ages 4-12, $4.95. AX, DS, MC, VI. Phone (716) 285-3575 or (800) 500-4609.

BEDORE TOURS, departs from the Howard Johnson at the Falls at 454 Main St., near the Rainbow Bridge and from area hotels. The U.S./Canadian Boat and Van Tour; the All-American Boat and Van Tour; and an evening tour, the Canadian Illumination Tour are among the excursions offered. Each tour visits the American, Horseshoe and Bridal Veil falls as well as other area attractions. The day tours also include sightseeing directly in front of the falls aboard the *Maid of the Mist* tour boats *(see attraction listing).*

Departures daily Apr. 1-Nov. 15. During peak season there are three tours daily. Fare for All-American and Canadian Illumination tours $54.95; ages 5-11, $29; under 5 on lap free. U.S./Canadian tour $59.95; ages 5-11, $32. Combination day and evening tours $99.90. Reservations are required.

AX, DS, MC, VI. Phone (716) 285-7550 or (800) 538-8433.

CAVE OF THE WINDS TRIP, on Goat Island *(see attraction listing),* follows wooden walkways to within 25 feet of the base of the falls. An elevator takes visitors 175 feet through the Niagara rock escarpment into the Niagara Gorge to view the falls from the bottom. After donning a raincoat and special footwear, visitors are guided to the Hurricane Deck, just 20 feet from the roaring Bridal Veil Falls, where a good dousing can be expected. Rainbows are generally visible day and night.

From October 30 through January 2 a gorge walk is available that takes visitors down to the first wooden structure at the base of the falls; phone for information.

Allow 1 hour minimum. Sun.-Thurs. 9 a.m.-10 p.m., Fri.-Sat. 9 a.m.-11 p.m., mid-May through Labor Day; daily 9-8, day after Labor Day-Oct. 1. Schedule may vary; phone ahead. Admission $8; ages 6-12, $7. Under age 6 must be at least 42 inches tall. AX, DC, DS, MC, VI. Phone (716) 278-1730. *See color ad p. 162.*

FLIGHT OF ANGELS is at 310 Rainbow Blvd. S. A tethered helium balloon rises 400 feet above the falls. Allow 30 minutes minimum. Daily 9 a.m.-midnight, June-Sept.; 10-10, Apr.-May and in Oct. Fare $18; under 13, $9; family rate $55-$60 (two adults and two or three children). MC, VI. Phone (716) 278-0824.

GOAT ISLAND, in the Niagara River, separates the Canadian and American falls. Easily accessible by foot or vehicular bridge, this wooded island has paved drives and walks that offer spectacular views from the edges of both falls.

The Three Sisters Islands, which lie in the rapids, are accessible by footbridge, as is Luna Island, which lies between the American and Bridal Veil falls.

MAID OF THE MIST boats depart from the dock at Prospect Point Observation Tower on the American side and is also listed in Niagara Falls, Ontario, where this information is included. The boats pass directly in front of the falls and enter the Horseshoe Basin.

Trips depart daily beginning at 9:15, Memorial Day weekend and mid-June through Labor Day; at 10, mid-Apr. through day before Memorial Day weekend (depending on ice conditions in the river), June 1 to mid-June and day after Labor Day-Oct. 24 (weather permitting). Closing times vary; phone ahead. **Note:** These hours reflect the American side; the Canadian side runs 15 minutes earlier. Fare (waterproof clothing included) $11.50; ages 6-12, $6.75. Elevator cost included. MC, VI. To confirm daily schedules phone (716) 284-8897 in N.Y. or (905) 358-5781 in Ontario. *See color ad p. 171.*

NIAGARA AEROSPACE MUSEUM is at 345 Third St. Exhibits trace the development of aviation from its beginnings to recent space exploration programs, with emphasis on achievements in western New York. A hall of fame highlights contributing scientists, inventors, entrepreneurs and aviators.

Among the full-size aircraft displayed are a replica of a 1910 Curtiss bamboo and wire airframe biplane; a GA-36 experimental airplane and a Piper Cub, both built in the 1930s; a Schweitser Sailplane flown during World War II; and a rare 1947 Bell 47B-3 helicopter. Other exhibits feature engines, flight simulators, model airplanes, photographs and aviation paraphernalia. Films of historical moments in aviation are shown in three small theaters.

Allow 1 hour, 30 minutes minimum. Daily 10-6, Memorial Day to mid-Sept.; hours vary rest of year. Admission $7; senior citizens and college students with ID $6; ages 5-18, $4. MC, VI. Phone (716) 278-0060.

NIAGARA FALLS is in the Niagara River between New York and Ontario. The falls are divided into three cataracts separated by islands. Horseshoe Falls, on the Canadian side, is the widest. Bridal Veil, the middle and smallest falls, surges between Goat and Luna islands. And the 184-foot American Falls is the highest.

While there are many opportunities to gaze at this spectacle, it was not always so. Mills and plants once blocked public access, and by the late 1860s most of the land around the falls was privately owned by entrepreneurs. In 1885 the falls were reclaimed for public enjoyment through the creation of the Niagara Reservation, the nation's first state park.

Excellent views of the river and falls are available from several vantage points within Niagara Falls State Park (see attraction listing). Each night the falls are illuminated for 2.5 to 3.5 hours after dusk. A variety of guided sightseeing tours also is available (see What to Do/Sightseeing).

NIAGARA FALLS STATE PARK, at Prospect Point, covers more than 400 acres. New York's oldest state park, it opened in 1885. The visitor center has information about area attractions. Park open daily dawn-dusk. Visitor center open daily at 8; closing time varies. Free. Phone (716) 278-1796. See Recreation Chart.

Niagara Festival Theater, in the visitor center at Niagara Falls State Park, presents a 23-minute film "Niagara: A History of the Falls." The movie recounts the events that made the falls famous. Shows every 60 minutes daily 10-8, May 16-Sept. 3; 10-6, Sept. 4-Oct. 1; 9-5, Apr. 1-May 15 and Oct. 2-Dec. 31. Admission $2; ages 6-12, $1. Phone (716) 278-1796.

NIAGARA GORGE DISCOVERY CENTER, .5 mi. n. of the Rainbow Bridge, is accessible from Robert Moses Pkwy. following signs. This museum offers interactive displays and a multiscreen theater presentation about the natural history of the Niagara Gorge and the falls. A geological garden, scenic overlook, climbing wall and gorge trailhead are on the grounds. Guided hikes are available for a fee. Daily 9-7, Memorial Day-Labor Day; 9-5, Apr. 1-day before Memorial Day and day after Memorial Day-Oct. 31. Admission $5; ages 6-12, $3. Phone (716) 278-1070.

NIAGARA'S WAX MUSEUM, 303 Prospect St., exhibits figures in scenes depicting the history of the area. Topographic maps and collections of memorabilia from the Niagara frontier also are displayed. Daily 9:30 a.m.-10:30 p.m., May-Sept.; 11-9 in Apr. and Oct.-Dec.; 11-5, rest of year. Admission $4.95; over 64, $4.45; ages 13-17, $3.95; ages 6-12, $2.95. AX, MC, VI. Phone (716) 285-1271.

OVER THE FALLS TOURS, offers pick-up service at area accommodations. A variety of sightseeing tours cover highlights of Niagara Falls, N.Y., and Niagara Falls, Ontario, including opportunities to visit Journey Behind the Falls, Cave of the Winds, Goat Island, the Minolta Tower Centre, Skylon Tower and ride the Maid of the Mist.

Allow 4 hours, 30 minutes minimum. Tours depart daily 8-7. Hours may vary; phone ahead. Fare $59.95; ages 5-12, $36.95; under 5 on lap free. Reservations are required. AX, DS, MC, VI. Phone (716) 283-8900 or (877) 783-8900.

POWER VISTA is 4.5 mi. n. of the falls on US 104, or reached from Robert Moses Pkwy., following signs. The Niagara Power Project's visitor center features more than 50 interactive exhibits explaining the development of hydroelectricity in the Niagara area. The Electric Lab features an operating model of a hydropower turbine. Modern energy efficiency is demonstrated in a Victorian house setting.

A large-scale terrain map provides a geographic overview of the Niagara Project, the source of one-seventh of the state's power. Just steps away, an outdoor observation deck 350 feet above the water affords views of the river, gorge and power plants.

Other exhibits highlight solar power, electric vehicles and local history. A mural by Thomas Hart Benton depicts Father Louis Hennepin viewing the falls for the first time. Daily 9-5; closed Jan. 1, Thanksgiving and Dec. 24-25 and 31. Free. Phone (716) 286-6661 or (866) 697-2386.

PROSPECT POINT OBSERVATION TOWER, next to the American Falls in Prospect Park, is a 260-foot structure that rises above the cliffs. Stairs lead from the tower to the Crow's Nest, an observation area beside the falls. Four elevators descend into the gorge, permitting access to the base of the falls and Maid of the Mist boats (see attraction listing), which board near the landing. Open daily at 9:30, early Apr.-late Oct.; closing time varies. Admission $1, under 6 free. Phone (716) 284-8897.

SAVE **RAINBOW TOURS OF NIAGARA** offers pick-up service at local lodgings. The 4- to 5-hour bus tours visit either the Canadian or American sides of the falls and include a ride on the *Maid of the Mist* boat. The American tour goes to Cave of the Winds, the Whirlpool, and Goat, Luna and Three Sisters islands. Canadian tour highlights include Dufferin Island, Minolta Tower Centre, Niagara Parks Geenhouses and the Floral Clock. Other tours are available. Daily 10-4. Hours may vary; phone ahead. Fare $62.95; senior citizens $57.95; ages 5-12, $34.95; under 5 on lap free. AX, DC, DS, MC, VI. Phone (716) 773-7087.

ST. MARY OF THE CATARACT CHURCH, 259 Fourth St., was built in 1847. Highlights include stonework, stained glass windows, a statue of St. John Neumann and the tallest steeple in Niagara Falls. Open daily 8-5. Free. Phone (716) 282-0059.

WHIRLPOOL STATE PARK, on the Robert Moses Pkwy. n. of the Whirlpool Bridge, is on a bluff overlooking the whirlpool that results from the Niagara River's 90-degree turn. Gorge and rim trails are available. Ramps and steps wind along the gorge. Daily dawn-dusk. Free. Phone (716) 278-1770 or (716) 285-3892.

CASINOS
• **Seneca Niagara Casino** is at 310 Fourth St. Daily 24 hours. Phone (716) 299-1100.

What To Do
Sightseeing
Sightseeing is what Niagara Falls is all about, and there is an amazing array of ways to view the falls. Many of the attractions listed in the What To See section are basically different forms of sightseeing.

Information about guide services and sightseeing companies is available from your local AAA club or from the Niagara Tourism and Convention Corp. *(see The Informed Traveler).* The New York State Parks Commission, (716) 278-1770, also has area sightseeing information.

Bus and Van Tours
Major tour bus companies include Coach USA, (716) 372-5500; Gavin Travel Service Inc., (716) 282-3715; Grand Island Transit, (716) 433-6777; SAVE Gray Line of Niagara Falls, (716) 695-1603; and SAVE Niagara Majestic Tours, (716) 285-2113.

NIAGARA SCENIC TROLLEY can be boarded at several locations on Goat Island and near Prospect Point Observation Tower *(see attraction listings).* Thirty-minute tours follow a 3-mile route and take visitors close to the falls and other points of interest as guides provide historical narration. Stopovers are made at six sites, and passengers have the option of getting on and off the trolley as they choose.

Sun.-Thurs. 9 a.m.-11:30 p.m., Fri.-Sat. 9 a.m.-12:30 a.m., July 1-Labor Day; Sun.-Thurs. 9 a.m.-10:30 p.m., Fri.-Sat. 9 a.m.-12:30 a.m., mid-May

through June 30; daily 9 a.m.-9:30 p.m., in Sept.; daily 9-9, Apr. 1 to mid-May; daily 9-6:30, Oct.-Dec.; daily 9-5, rest of year. Fare $5; ages 6-12, $3. Phone (716) 278-1730.

Helicopter Tours

RAINBOW AIR INC. HELICOPTER TOURS, departing from 454 Main St., offer views of both the American and Canadian falls. Allow 1 hour minimum. Daily 9-dusk. Fare for 10-minute tour $60. MC, VI. Phone (716) 284-2800.

Sports and Recreation
Niagara Falls has several city and state parks that offer recreational opportunities, as do nearby lakes Erie and Ontario. Most parks offer picnicking, scenic views and **nature trails;** several have **fishing, swimming, tennis** courts, **bike trails** and playgrounds. **Boating** and fishing are available at many sites on lakes Erie and Ontario, which also have sandy beaches for swimming.

In the southeast are Griffon, Hennepin, Jayne and LaSalle parks; in the southwest, Niagara Falls State Park *(see attraction listing p. 163 and Recreation Chart)* comprises Prospect Park, Upper Rapids Park and Goat Island. In the northwest are Devil's Hole and Whirlpool state parks and Centre Court and Unity city parks.

In the center of Niagara Falls at Hyde Park Boulevard and Pine Avenue is Hyde Park, the largest of the city parks. Hyde Park has two nine-hole public **golf** courses and a swimming pool.

During winter several of the nature trails in the area's parks convert to **cross-country skiing** and **snowmobile** trails. **Downhill skiing** is available within an hour's drive at Kissing Bridge, the Alpine Recreation Area or Tamarack Ridge, all southeast on SR 240.

For further information about recreational facilities phone the state parks commission at (716) 278-1770, or the city parks service at (716) 286-4943.

Shopping
Souvenirs of the falls can be found downtown on Main Street, just a few minutes from the Rainbow Bridge. Three Sisters Trading Post offers gifts, souvenirs and American Indian crafts. Nearby Artisans Alley at 10 Rainbow Blvd. is a shop and gallery featuring the works of more than 600 artisans. A 1-mile strip of Pine Avenue/Niagara Falls Boulevard known as Little Italy is lined with unique shops, Italian eateries and an open-air market. Summit Park Mall, on Williams Road between SR 384 and US 62, is anchored by Bon-Ton and Sears.

For those on a budget or just looking for a good deal, SAVE Prime Outlets at 1900 Military Rd. offers savings on such items as clothing, glassware, jewelry, shoes, accessories and toys; stores include Bass, Liz Claiborne, Ralph Lauren and Mikasa.

Visitors to the Canadian side can shop for discounted merchandise at the Niagara Duty Free Shop. *See color ad p. 175.*

Note: Visitors to Niagara Falls, Ontario, should be aware that currency exchange rates vary by merchant and are sometimes lower than the official rate offered by banks. U.S. Customs regulations limit or prohibit the importation of certain goods (such as sealskin products) from Canada; further information is available at customs offices or in the Border Regulations section of the Canadian TourBooks.

Theater and Concerts

Theatrical and musical performances can be found in nearby Buffalo and at Earl W. Brydges ArtPark, 7 miles north on the Robert Moses Parkway in Lewiston *(see place listing p. 166).*

Special Events

Re-enactors from the United States and Canada create a 1759 historical battle during the **French and Indian War Encampment** held at Old Fort Niagara in early July. **Winterfest Niagara** lights up the city throughout the holiday season, late November through December, with a parade, musical performances and a fair.

The Niagara Falls Vicinity

BURT (D-3) pop. 400

SAVE **MURPHY ORCHARDS** is off Wilson-Burt Rd. at 2402 McClew Rd. Offered is a variety of narrated 30- and 90-minute theme tours of a working farm. Agricultural, wildlife or historical tours may include a tractor-drawn wagon ride through orchards, planting and cider pressing demonstrations, a visit to a petting zoo or information about the farm's role as a stop on the Underground Railroad. Visitors may also take a self-guiding tour and pick fruit. Picnicking is permitted. Food is available. Daily 8:30-5, May 1-Dec. 24. Guided tours require a minimum of 10 persons for departure. Grounds free. Thirty-minute tour fee $1.95. Ninety-minute tour fee $3.50. Reservations are required. AX, DS, MC, VI. Phone (716) 778-7926.

LEWISTON (E-3) pop. 2,781, elev. 363′

The site of Niagara Falls some 12,000 years ago, the Lewiston area later was home to various tribes, including the Attawandaronk, Hopewell and Seneca, who landed their canoes here to portage around the deadly rapids and falls of the Niagara River. Though also the site of portages by explorers in the late 1600s, the area was not settled until 1796, when the British surrendered nearby Fort Niagara.

Named for Gov. Morgan Lewis, Lewiston quickly grew into a center of trade and transportation; a tramway built by the British is said to have become America's first railroad. Another of Lewiston's innovations is the cocktail, which was invented by a local tavern proprietress who mixed some gin and herb wine in a tankard and stirred the drink with the tail feather of a stuffed cock pheasant.

CASTELLANI ART MUSEUM is on Senior Dr. on the Niagara University campus. The museum's permanent collection emphasizes 20th-century and contemporary art and includes works by Charles Burchfield, Louise Nevelson, Pablo Picasso and Andy Warhol. In addition there are collections of paintings, drawings, photographs and prints. Changing exhibits also are presented. Tues.-Sat. 11-5, Sun. 1-5; closed major holidays. Free. Phone (716) 286-8200.

GEM **EARL W. BRYDGES ARTPARK** is on S. 4th St. along the Niagara River gorge. This state park blends visual and performing arts with recreation and nature. The main theater presents Broadway musicals, big-band concerts and celebrity performances. A variety of family-oriented festivals and events is offered in an outdoor amphitheater.

Sculpture installations, working artists-in-residence and hands-on art activities round out the cultural offerings. Historic and geological sites and such recreational facilities as nature areas, fishing docks, and hiking and cross-country skiing trails make up the 150-acre complex.

Picnicking is permitted. Park open daily dawn-dusk. Theater performances are presented July-Sept.; phone for schedule and ticket information. Parking $5, July-Aug. Phone (716) 754-9000 or (800) 659-7275.

NATIONAL SHRINE BASILICA OF OUR LADY OF FATIMA, 1.5 mi. e. on US 104, 2 mi. n. on SR 18, then .5 mi. e. on Swan Rd., is an outdoor cathedral with more than 100 life-size statues, a giant rosary and a translucent domed chapel that has an observation deck on top. Picnicking is permitted. Food is available. Daily 9-5, early Jan. to mid-Nov.; 9-9, rest of year. Closed Thanksgiving and Dec. 25. Free. Phone (716) 754-7489.

WHIRLPOOL JET BOAT TOURS, departing from 115 S. Water St., offers 45-minute trips on the lower Niagara River on 48- to 54-seat jet boats. The river can be experienced on either "wet jet" trips, where a good soaking can be expected, or a "dry" version of the trip in a domed jet boat. Features of the tours, which are half historic/scenic and half white-water adventure, include historic forts, the Niagara Gorge, white-water rapids and the whirlpool. A complete rain suit and wet boots are provided for the "wet" trip.

Allow 2 hours minimum for preparation, tour and clothing changes. **Note:** A change of clothes is recommended for the "wet jet" trip. Participants should be in good health; a signed release is required. Trips are not recommended for those with heart, back or neck problems, and pregnant women may not take the tours. Trips depart daily 10-7, May-Oct. Schedule may vary; phone ahead. Arrive 30 minutes early to prepare for the trip. "Wet jet" fare $43; ages 6-13, $37. Jet dome fare $34; ages 6-13, $27. Under 6 are not permitted. Reservations are recommended. Inquire about refund policy. MC, VI. Phone (905) 468-4800 or (888) 438-4444.

LOCKPORT (D-3) pop. 22,279, elev. 544′

Lockport derived its name from the Erie Canal locks that overcome the difference in elevation along the Niagara Escarpment. The historic five flights of locks, built in 1825, can be seen from Pine Street Bridge or from the boats that offer narrated cruises along the canal and through working locks.

The town also boasts one of the widest bridges in the world, located downtown within walking distance from the locks, and an upside-down railroad bridge, built with its supporting structures facing downward to hinder competing canal shipping. Part of the original canal towpath is used today for hiking and walking.

The Towpath Trolley offers narrated sightseeing tours of the area July 4 through Labor Day; phone (716) 628-6095. *See color ad p. 162.*

Niagara Tourism and Convention Corp.: 345 Third St., Suite 605, Niagara Falls, NY 14303; phone (716) 282-8992 or (800) 338-7890.

Self-guiding tours: Brochures for a walking tour of the canal district are available at the municipal building on Main Street.

Shopping areas: Lockport Mall, 5737 S. Transit Rd., includes The Bon-Ton.

KENAN CENTER, 433 Locust St., is a regional cultural, educational and recreational complex on 25 acres. Kenan House, the 1800s Victorian mansion of William R. Keenan Jr., features a ladies' parlor and an art gallery. Taylor Theater is in a restored carriage house. The campus also includes formal gardens, a sports arena and playgrounds. Allow 1 hour minimum. Art gallery Mon.-Fri. noon-5, Sat.-Sun. 2-5, day after Labor Day-Memorial Day; Mon.-Fri. noon-5, Sun. 2-5, rest of year. Closed holidays. Free. Admission may be charged during special events. Phone (716) 433-2617.

[SAVE] **LOCKPORT CAVE AND UNDERGROUND BOAT RIDE** departs from the ticket office at 2 Pine St. near Main St. Tour activities include viewing the Erie Canal locks and industrial age ruins, walking through a 1,600-foot tunnel blasted out of solid rock in the mid-1800s and riding a boat on an underground waterway. Allow 1 hour, 30 minutes minimum. Tours depart Sun.-Fri. on the hour 11-5, Sat. and holidays 10-5, June 19-Labor Day; Sat.-Sun. on the hour noon-4, May 29-June 18 and Sept. 11-Oct. 11. Fare $8.25; ages 4-12, $5.50. AX, MC, VI. Phone (716) 438-0174.

[GEM] **LOCKPORT LOCKS AND ERIE CANAL CRUISES** depart from a restored 1840s stone warehouse at 210 Market St. off SR 31. Two- [SAVE] hour narrated Erie Canal cruises take passengers past the original 1800s locks, under an inverted trestle bridge and lift bridges, alongside the original towpath and through a rock cut. The boat passes through working locks, where it is locked up (raised) 50 feet to overcome the difference in elevation of the Niagara Escarpment; locking down is experienced on the return trip. The Erie Canal Heritage Museum has exhibits, photographs and artifacts.

Food is available. Picnicking is permitted. Trips depart daily at 10, 12:30, 3 and 5:30, June 21-Sept. 6; Sun.-Fri. at 12:30 and 3, Sat. at 10, 12:30 and 3, May 10-June 20 and Sept. 7-Oct. 17. Fare $12.50; over 64, $11.50; ages 4-10, $8. DS, MC, VI. Phone (716) 433-6155 or (800) 378-0352. *See color ad p. 162.*

NIAGARA COUNTY HISTORICAL SOCIETY, 215 Niagara St., is a complex devoted to county history. Exhibits include business and medical memorabilia, farm tools, Civil War items and Indian artifacts. Also displayed are the one-of-a-kind 1923 Junior R, a locally produced aluminum automobile, and a 1954

Pontiac, reputedly the first General Motors car with air conditioning. Allow 1 hour, 30 minutes minimum. Mon.-Sat. 10-5, Sun. 1-5, June-Aug.; Thurs.-Sun. 1-5, Sept.-Dec.; Wed.-Sat. 1-5, rest of year. Closed holidays. Admission $1. Phone (716) 434-7433.

Col. William M. Bond House, 143 Ontario St., is an 1824 brick house featuring 12 period rooms used as backdrops for changing exhibits. Allow 1 hour minimum. Sat.-Sun. and Thurs. 1-5, May-Dec. Donations. Phone (716) 434-7433.

YOUNGSTOWN (D-3) pop. 1,957, elev. 301'

FORT NIAGARA STATE PARK is at the mouth of the Niagara River off SR 18F, following signs to Robert Moses Pkwy. Tennis, basketball, boating, fishing and swimming facilities are available Memorial Day through Labor Day at this 504-acre park. Daily dawn-dusk. Free. Parking $5 daily, July 1-Labor Day and Sat.-Sun., Memorial Day weekend-June 30; free, rest of year. Swimming $3; ages 6-12, $1.50. Boat launch $5. Phone (716) 745-7273. *See Recreation Chart.*

[GEM] **Old Fort Niagara,** adjacent to the state park grounds, was begun by the French in 1726. [SAVE] Active under three flags, the fort contains many mounted cannons, a hot shot furnace, a drawbridge and pre-revolution buildings. The site includes the only fortified French castle in the United States; it has been restored and furnished to re-create its stark 18th-century atmosphere. Drills and ceremonies are presented daily July through Labor Day. Re-enactments are held throughout the year.

Allow 1 hour minimum. Daily 9-7:30, July-Aug.; Mon.-Fri. 9-6:30, Sat.-Sun. 9-7:30, in June; daily 9-5:30, Apr.-May and Sept.-Oct.; daily 9-4:30, rest of year. Closed Jan. 1, Thanksgiving and Dec. 25. Admission $8; over 64, $7; ages 6-12, $5. AX, DS, MC, VI. Phone (716) 745-7611.

DID YOU KNOW

Forty million gallons of water spill over Niagara Falls every minute.

Nearby Ontario

NIAGARA FALLS pop. 78,815

FALLS INCLINE RAILWAY, next to the Table Rock Point, operates twin cable-rail cars between the Fallsview tourist area and Table Rock Point areas. The historic railway transports visitors up and down the Niagara Escarpment. Rail cars operate daily, late Mar.-late Oct. (weather permitting). Phone ahead to confirm schedule. One-way fare $2.50. Phone (905) 357-9340. *See color ad p. 171.*

[SAVE] **GUINNESS WORLD RECORDS MUSEUM,** 4943 Clifton Hill, displays exhibits demonstrating world records in sports, science and nature. Videotapes depict accomplishments in outer space and high-speed travel. Daily 9 a.m.-2 a.m., June-Sept.; daily 10-10, Oct.-Mar.; otherwise varies rest of year. Admission $9.99; over 59 and students with ID $7.99; ages 6-12, $5.99. AX, MC, VI. Phone (905) 356-2299.

IMAX THEATRE NIAGARA FALLS, next to the Skylon Tower at 6170 Fallsview Blvd., presents "Niagara: Miracles, Myths & Magic," an exciting view of the falls on a screen six stories tall. The movie re-creates some of the historical events that have taken place in the Niagara Falls area, including a re-enactment of Annie Taylor's 1901 tumble over the falls in a barrel. Artifacts from those daredevils who have challenged the falls and rapids in the past are displayed. Other IMAX films also are shown.

Food is available. Films shown daily on the hour 9-9, Apr.-Aug.; 9-8, Sept.-Oct.; 10-4 (extended hours Fri.-Sat.), rest of year. Admission $12; over 64, $8.50; ages 4-12, $6.50. MC, VI. Phone (905) 358-3611 or (905) 374-4629. *See color ad p. 170.*

[GEM] **JOURNEY BEHIND THE FALLS,** 1.6 km (1 mi.) s. of Rainbow Bridge on the Niagara Pkwy. in Table Rock Point, contains elevators that descend to the base of the Horseshoe Falls. Three tunnels lead from the elevators and provide excellent vantage points for close-up views of the thundering falls and the Niagara River. The observation plaza is about 38 metres (125 ft.) below the gorge embankment and 8 metres (26 ft.) above the river's edge. Disposable raincoats are provided.

Saturdays and Sundays in July and August a Royal Canadian Mounted Police officer in ceremonial uniform is posted near the brink of the falls to pose with visitors for photographs. Complex opens daily at 9; closing times vary. Tunnels close 30 minutes before complex closing; phone ahead for closing times. Closed Dec. 25. Tunnel $10; ages 6-12, $6. AX, DC, JC, MC, VI. Phone (905) 354-1551.

LUNDY'S LANE HISTORICAL MUSEUM, 1.6 km (1 mi.) from the falls off Hwy. 420 at 5810 Ferry St., is on the site of one of the fiercest battles of the War of 1812, the Battle of Lundy's Lane, which was fought here July 25, 1814. The 1874 building contains military displays of that conflict and the Fenian Raids as well as Indian artifacts, a collection of Niagara Falls art and souvenir china and items that portray the life of the region's early settlers.

Allow 30 minutes minimum. Daily 10-5, May-Oct.; daily noon-4, Jan.-Apr.; Wed.-Sun. noon-4, rest of year. Admission $3; over 64 and students

with ID $2.50; ages 6-12, $2. Phone (905) 358-5082.

MAID OF THE MIST boats depart from the dock at Clifton Hill and River Rd. on the Canadian side. Since 1846 visitors have experienced the majesty and power of the falls from a series of boats, all named *Maid of the Mist*. Today's steel, double-deck, diesel-powered vessels enter the Horseshoe Basin, fight the mighty current and pass directly in front of the American and Horseshoe falls. Raincoat-clad passengers on the tossing, heaving ship are guaranteed a generous soaking from the spray of the cataract.

Trips depart daily beginning at 9, Memorial Day weekend and mid- June through Labour Day; at 9:45, mid-Apr. through day before Memorial Day weekend (depending on ice conditions in the river), June 1 to mid-June and day after Labour Day-Oct. 24 (weather permitting). Closing times vary; phone ahead. **Note:** These hours reflect the Canadian side; the American side runs 15 minutes later. Fare (waterproof clothing included) $13; ages 6-12, $8. Elevator cost included. MC, VI. To confirm daily schedules phone (905) 358-5781 in Ontario or (716) 284-8897 in N.Y.

MARINELAND, 7657 Portage Rd., is known for its marine shows, which feature killer whales, dolphins, walruses and sea lions. There also are a freshwater aquarium and wildlife displays with bears, elk and buffaloes and a deer petting park. At the interactive Friendship Cove visitors can touch a whale. Several rides are available, including Dragon Mountain, a large steel roller coaster. A few children's rides also are available. Show times vary according to the season.

Food is available. Daily 9-6, late June-Labour Day; 10-5, mid-May to late June and day after Labour Day-Oct. 31. Amusement rides open Victoria Day weekend-early Oct. Admission mid-May to mid-Oct. $32.95; over 59 and ages 5-9, $27.95. Reduced admission when rides are closed for the season. Parents should ask about height restrictions before paying admission. Phone to verify schedule and prices. AX, MC, VI. Phone (905) 356-9565.

MINOLTA TOWER CENTRE, overlooking the falls at 6732 Fallsview Blvd., rises 99 metres (325 ft.) above the ground and 203 metres (665 ft.) above the base of the falls, providing a magnificent view of the surrounding area. An indoor observation deck is at the top of the center.

Allow 1 hour minimum. Daily 7 a.m.-10 p.m., with extended hours during the summer. Admission $6.95, over 64 and students with ID $4.95, under 6 free with an adult. AX, DS, MC, VI. Phone (905) 356-1501 or (800) 461-2492.

MOUNT CARMEL SPIRITUAL CENTRE, n. of McLeod Rd. at 7021 Stanley Ave., just above the

The Authentic Falls Experience.

BUTTERFLY CONSERVATORY - Let your spirit soar.

NIAGARA FALLS
GREAT GORGE
ADVENTURE PASS

NIAGARA FALLS, CANADA

MAID OF THE MIST - Ride into the mist.

WHITE WATER WALK - Discover raging white water.

JOURNEY BEHIND THE FALLS - Feel the thunder.

ADULT PASS	YOUTH PASS
$34.95†† CDN	$21.95†† CDN

KIDS 5 & UNDER FREE!

Niagara Falls & Great Gorge Adventure Pass!

The Adventure Pass includes tickets to Maid of the Mist, White Water Walk, Journey Behind the Falls and the Butterfly Conservatory. You also get Priority Access at Journey Behind the Falls and the Butterfly Conservatory along with all day transportation on the People Mover and Incline Railway. **PLUS**! Receive valuable coupons, including a discount for the Whirlpool Aero Car. Buy your Pass on-line at **www.niagaraparks.com**, at participating Niagara Falls hotels or at the brink of the Falls.

Niagara
Parks

An agency of the Government of
Ontario since 1885

††Plus tax. Pass will be valid during the time the Maid of the Mist is sailing (approximately May to October 2004).

Niagara Parks Commission Passes

The Niagara Parks Commission offers discount passes that provide savings for guests interested in visiting several Niagara Falls attractions.

The *Niagara Falls and Great Gorge Adventure Pass* includes admission to four attractions—*Maid of the Mist,* Journey Behind the Falls, the Niagara Parks Butterfly Conservatory and White Water Walk— as well as an all-day transportation pass for the People Mover and Falls Incline Railway. The pass also includes coupons, including a discount for the Whirlpool Aero Car. The passport is available May through October. Fee $34.95; ages 6-12, $21.95.

The pass can be purchased at most major Niagara Parks Commission attractions and information centers and many hotels.

DID YOU KNOW

New York was the first state to establish a state park— Niagara Reservation, now known as Niagara Falls State Park.

---

falls, was founded in 1894; it is now used for religious retreats. The main altar has woodcarvings and paneling in American white oak. The center contains Our Lady of Peace Church, built in 1827. Daily 9-4. Free. Phone (905) 356-4113.

SAVE **MOVIELAND WAX MUSEUM OF STARS,** 4950 Clifton Hill, displays figures of film and television personalities in scenes that made them famous. Visitors can make replicas of their own hand in the Wax Hands Emporium. Daily 9 a.m.-1 a.m., May-Sept.; 10-10, rest of year. Admission $8.99; ages 4-12, $5.99. AX, MC, VI. Phone (905) 358-3061.

GEM **NIAGARA FALLS** is in the Niagara River on the international border between Canada and the United States. The thundering falls, consisting of the Horseshoe Falls on the Canadian side and American and Bridal Veil falls in the U.S., were formed by a retreating glacier 12,000 years ago. The Canadian falls, 54 metres (177 ft.) high and 675 metres (2,215 ft.) wide, derive their name from their crescent shape.

Often heard before they can be seen, the falls have long been a favorite of honeymooners, making the city of Niagara Falls a favorite of newlyweds. In addition to scenic overlooks in Queen Victoria Park, the grandeur of the falls also can be appreciated by boat, helicopter, observation towers and bridges. The falls are illuminated at night year-round.

NIAGARA FALLS ART GALLERY/KURELEK COLLECTION AND NIAGARA CHILDREN'S MUSEUM, 1.5 km (.9 mi.) s.e. of QEW exit 27 (Mc Leod Rd.) at 8058 Oakwood Dr., has an outstanding collection of works by Canadian artist William Kurelek, including the series known as "The Passion of Christ."

Also noteworthy are two sculptures: "Pierre Rock," a 10-metric-ton (11-ton) dolomite slab carved with symbols of pioneer achievement and dedicated to Canadian prime minister Pierre Trudeau, and "Stepova Baba" (Grandmother of the Steppes), a work at least 2,500 years old. The gallery also houses the Niagara Children's Museum. Mon-Fri. 11-5, Sat.-Sun. 1-5, June-Sept.; daily 1-5, rest of year. Donations. Phone (905) 356-1514.

NIAGARA FALLS AVIARY, next to the Rainbow Bridge at 5651 River Rd., is a journey through a mythical kingdom filled with colorful birds and other animals, tropical foliage, trees and waterfalls. The conservatory, with a lost kingdom theme, allows visitors to see tropical birds in an enclosed aviary and also interact with them in a free-flight environment. A nocturnal jungle amidst ancient ruins features bats, poison arrow dart frogs, owls and snakes.

Food is available. Allow 30 minutes minimum. Daily 9-9, May-Sept.; 9-5, rest of year. Closed Dec. 25. Admission $14.95; over 65, $13.95; ages 5-12,

$9.95. AX, DS, MC, VI. Phone (905) 356-8888 or (866) 994-0090. *See color ad p. 173.*

NIAGARA GLEN RIM TOUR departs from the Niagara Glen Nature Area, 7 km (4 mi.) n. on the Niagara Pkwy. This leisurely paced, 20-minute nature walk conducted by Niagara Parks Commission naturalists, takes visitors along the top of the Niagara Escarpment where native flora and fauna and a view of the gorge can be seen. The guides provide a history of the area and explain how it has changed over time. Tours are given daily every half hour 10-4, mid-May to mid-Sept. Fee $4, children $2. MC, VI. Phone (905) 358-8633.

(SAVE) NIAGARA HELICOPTERS, 3731 Victoria Ave., near the Whirlpool Rapids on the Niagara Pkwy., provides an aerial perspective of the falls and river during 9-minute flights. Headsets provide a taped narration. Daily 9-dusk (weather permitting); closed Dec. 25. Fare $100; ages 2-11, $55; couples $190; a family rate is available. AX, DC, MC, VI. For reservations phone (905) 357-5672. *See color ad.*

THE NIAGARA PARKS BOTANICAL GARDENS, 8 km (5 mi.) n. of the falls on Niagara Pkwy., is the home of The Niagara Parks School of Horticulture, said to be the only residential school in Canada for apprentice gardeners. Floral displays and both formal and informal gardens, including 2,300 varieties of roses, are on the 40-hectare (99-acre) site. Other sections include rock, herb, annual, perennial and vegetable gardens. The best viewing time is April through October, when the blooms are at their peak. Daily dawn-dusk. Guided 30-minute tours are available. Free. Phone (905) 356-8554.

Horse & Carriage Rides at The Niagara Parks Botanical Gardens depart from the gardens; timed tickets can be purchased at the Niagara Parks Butterfly Conservatory ticket booth. Forty-minute narrated tours conducted in covered, horse-drawn carriages provide an overview of the botanical gardens and a chance to see the horticulture students at work. Departures every 15 minutes daily 10-4, May-Oct. Hours may vary; phone ahead. Fare $15, children on lap free. MC, VI. Phone (905) 358-0025.

Niagara Parks Butterfly Conservatory, 2565 Niagara Pkwy. on the grounds of the Botanical Gardens, is home to some 2,000 free-flying butterflies. Waterfalls and various tropical flora line the pathways throughout the glass-enclosed conservatory. More than 40 butterfly species can be observed in a native butterfly garden outside the conservatory.

Allow 1 hour minimum. Daily 9-5 (closing times are extended Mar. 1-second Mon. in Oct.); closed Dec. 25. Timed-tickets are available. Admission $10; ages 6-12, $6. MC, VI. Phone (905) 358-0025. *See color ad p. 171.*

NIAGARA PARKS GREENHOUSES, .5 km (.2 mi.) s. of the Canadian Horseshoe Falls, have seasonal displays of local flowers and foliage, palm trees, more than 75 tropical birds and other tropical plants and aquatic life, all set in the midst of waterfalls and pools. There is also an outdoor fragrance garden for the visually impaired. Daily 9-5 (closing hours are extended mid-June through Labour Day); closed Dec. 25. Free. Phone (905) 354-1721 or (877) 642-7275.

OAKES GARDEN THEATRE, 1 km (.6 mi.) n. of the falls on the Niagara Pkwy. at the foot of Clifton Hill, is a Greco-Roman style amphitheater in a setting of rock gardens, lily ponds, terraces and promenades overlooking the American Falls. Daily dawn-dusk. Free. Phone (905) 354-5141.

SUPERB DINING ABOVE THE FALLS!

With two levels of fine dining to choose from, both overlooking the Falls.

Revolving Dining Room. At the height of dining excellence... featuring award-winning continental cuisine. One rotation hourly. Early dinner special at 4:30 & 5:00 PM.

Summit Suite Dining Room. The ultimate in buffet-style dining... breakfast, lunch and dinner. Family affordable. Sunday Brunch.

Observation Deck. Spectacular indoor/outdoor viewing.

5200 Robinson Street, Niagara Falls, Canada L2G 2A3
For Reservations Call: 905- 356-2651
Toll-Free: 1-888-686-1791 www.skylon.com

Skylon Tower

OH CANADA EH? DINNER SHOW is at 8585 Lundy's Ln. A taste of Canada's culture and traditions can be experienced at this production staged in a rustic log cabin decorated with Canadiana. A family-style Canadian meal is served during the show by such Canadians as Anne of Green Gables, singing Mounties, lumberjacks, a hockey player and other performing characters. Allow 2 hours, 30 minutes minimum. Shows are presented daily at 6:30 p.m., May-Oct.; schedule varies rest of year. Admission $49; ages 13-16, $39; under 13, $24.50. MC, VI. Phone (905) 374-1995 or (800) 467-2071. *See color ad.*

 QUEEN VICTORIA PARK, on the Niagara Pkwy. at the falls, originated in 1887. It is a 62-hectare (154-acre) landscaped park offering fine views of the falls and beautiful seasonal floral displays. The park is illuminated at night and is the site of many special events. Daily dawn-dusk. Free.

Horse & Carriage Rides at Queen Victoria Park depart from the Victoria Park Gift Shop on Niagara Pkwy. at the falls; timed tickets can be purchased at the gift shop. Fifteen-, 45- and 80-minute narrated tours in a horse-drawn carriage provide scenic views of the cataract as well as commentary about the falls and the Niagara area.

Departures daily 4-11, mid-May through Labour Day (weather permitting). Hours may vary; phone ahead. Fare $40 per carriage for 15-minute tour; $100 per carriage for 45-minute tour; $170 per carriage for 80-minute tour. MC, VI. Phone (905) 358-5935.

RAINBOW CARILLON TOWER, at the terminus of the Rainbow Bridge, presents concerts on its 55 tuned bells. Concerts are given Fri.-Sun. at 4 and 7 and before the Friday fireworks display, early June-Labour Day. Free.

RIPLEY'S BELIEVE IT OR NOT! MUSEUM, 4960 Clifton Hill, displays world-traveler Robert Ripley's collection of strange, odd and unusual items. Hundreds of exhibits feature curiosities and illusions such as interactive puzzles, an eight-legged buffalo and a shrunken human head. Daily 9 a.m.-2 a.m., mid-June to mid-Sept.; 10-10, mid-Mar. to mid-June and mid-Sept. through Dec. 31; 11-7, rest of year. Admission $10.95; over 55, $8; ages 6-12, $5.49. A combination ticket with Ripley's Moving Theatre is available. AX, MC, VI. Phone (905) 356-2238.

Ripley's Moving Theatre, 4983 Clifton Hill, offers two adventure rides in a motion simulator complete with wind, mist and snow effects. **Note:** The rides are not recommended for persons with back or neck problems. Daily 9 a.m.-2 a.m., mid-June to mid-Sept.; 10-10, mid-Mar. to mid-June and mid-Sept. through Dec. 31; 11-7, rest of year. Admission $12.95; over 55, $10.95; under 12, $7.69. Under 43 inches tall are not permitted. A combination ticket with Ripley's Believe It or Not! Museum is available. AX, MC, VI. Phone (905) 356-2261.

SKYLON TOWER, overlooking the falls at 5200 Robinson St., rises 160 meters (525 ft.) above the ground and 244 meters (800 ft.) above the base of the falls, providing a magnificent view of the surrounding area. Three levels at the top include a revolving dining room, a summit suite buffet and an indoor/outdoor observation deck; an entertainment center is at the base. Daily 8 a.m.-midnight, May 1 to mid-Oct.; otherwise varies. Observation deck $9.50; over 64, $8.50; ages 6-12, $5.50; family rate (two adults and two children under 12) $27. AX, DC, DS, JC, MC, VI. Phone

(905) 356-2651 to verify prices or (888) 673-7343. *See color ad p. 175.*

 **WHIRLPOOL AERO CAR,** on the Niagara Pkwy. 3.25 km (2 mi.) n. of Horseshoe Falls, is a cable car carrying passengers 76.2 metres (250 ft.) above the Niagara Gorge and back on a 529-metre-long (1,800-ft.) cableway, affording views of the rapids and nearby hydroelectric plants. Below the suspended aero car the churning river backs up into the 24-hectare (60-acre) Whirlpool Basin.

Allow 30 minutes minimum. Car operates daily 9-5, mid-Mar. to mid-Nov. (weather permitting); closed periodically for maintenance. Closing hours are extended mid-June through Labour Day. Last car departs 30 minutes before closing. Phone ahead to confirm schedule. Timed tickets are available. Round trip $10; ages 6-12, $6. AX, JC, MC, VI. Phone (905) 354-5711.

WHITE WATER WALK is n. of the Whirlpool Rapids Bridge on the Niagara Pkwy.

After taking an elevator to the river level, visitors can stroll along a boardwalk beside the rapids of the lower Niagara River. The scenic 305-metre (1,000 ft.) pathway along the edge of the river provides a close-up view of the rapids as they rush from the falls.

Daily 9-5 (closing times are extended Sat.-Sun.), mid-Mar. to mid-Nov. Last admission 30 minutes before closing. Phone ahead to confirm hours. Admission $7.50; ages 6-12, $4.50. AX, DC, MC, VI. Phone (905) 374-1221. *See color ad p. 171.*

CASINOS

• **Casino Niagara,** 5705 Falls Ave. Daily 24 hours. Phone (905) 374-3598 or (888) 946-3255.

This ends listings for the Niagara Falls Vicinity. The following page resumes the alphabetical listings of cities in New York.

NORTH BLENHEIM (F-9) elev. 791'

BLENHEIM-GILBOA PUMPED STORAGE POWER PROJECT, 3 mi. s. on SR 30, has two reservoirs. During the day water is released from the upper reservoir to create electricity, and at night electricity is used to pump water from the lower to the upper reservoir to repeat the process the next day. A 19th-century dairy barn houses the New York Power Authority's visitor center, which features interactive energy displays. Daily 10-5; closed Jan. 1, Thanksgiving and Dec. 25. Free. Phone (518) 827-6121 or (800) 724-0309.

Historic Lansing Manor Museum adjoins the power project's visitor center. The 1819 house was part of an 840-acre estate owned by John T. Lansing Jr., an aide to Revolutionary War general Philip Schuyler. The restored manor is furnished in period. Wed.-Mon. 10-5, Memorial Day weekend-Columbus Day. Free. Phone (518) 827-6121 or (800) 724-0309.

OLD BLENHEIM BRIDGE, on SR 30 across Schoharie Creek, was built in 1854 and is said to be the world's longest single-span wooden covered bridge. It is 232 feet long, 26 feet wide and has two driveways. The bridge is open only to pedestrians. Free. Phone (518) 827-6344.

NORTH CHILI (D-4) elev. 582'

VICTORIAN DOLL MUSEUM AND CHILI DOLL HOSPITAL, 4332 Buffalo Rd. (SR 33), 4.5 mi. w. on SR 33 exit 7B off I-490, has more than 2,000 identified dolls made of bisque, china, wax, tin and vinyl. Also displayed are toys, Victorian memorabilia, a puppet theater, a circus and a Noah's Ark. A doll hospital also is featured. Allow 1 hour minimum. Tues.-Sat. 10-4:30, Feb.-Dec.; closed holidays. Admission $2.50; under 12, $1.50. Phone (585) 247-0130.

NORTH CREEK (C-10) elev. 1,013'

North Creek is a popular access point for recreation in the surrounding Adirondack Park. Downhill and cross-country skiing are available 5 miles northwest off SR 28 at Gore Mountain, (518) 251-2411, and at Garnet Hill, (518) 251-2821. White-water rafting expeditions depart from downtown.

Gore Mountain Region Chamber of Commerce: 228 Main Street, North Creek, NY 12853; phone (518) 251-2612.

BARTON MINES GARNET MINE TOUR is 4.5 mi. n. on SR 28, then w. 5 mi. on Barton Mines Rd. One of the largest garnet mines in the world, it was begun in 1878. In 1983, the main mining operation moved to nearby Ruby Mountain. One-hour guided tours feature the original site and include a walk through an open-pit mine 800 feet below the summit of Gore Mountain.

Tours depart on the hour Mon.-Sat. 10-4, Sun. 11-4, late June-Labor Day; Sat. on the hour 10-4,

Sun. 11-4, day after Labor Day-Columbus Day. Admission (season pass) $9.50; ages 60-90, $8; ages 7-14, $6. Rocks collected cost $1 per pound. Phone (518) 251-2706 to verify schedule and prices.

RECREATIONAL ACTIVITIES

White-water Rafting

- **Hudson River Rafting Co.** is e. off I-87 exit 23, then n. on SR 9 to SR 28; trips depart from Cunningham's Ski Barn. Write P.O. Box 47, North Creek, NY 12853. Daily, Apr. 2 to mid-June; Tues., Thurs. and Sat.-Sun., mid-June through Labor Day; Sat.-Sun., day after Labor Day-Columbus Day. Reservations are recommended. Phone (518) 251-3215 or (800) 888-7238.

- **Mountains Unlimited Adventures**, departs from Main St., off I-87 exit 23. Write 336 Lakewood Rd., Waterbury, CT 06704. Departures daily at 9, Apr. 1-Columbus Day. Phone (888) 240-6976.

NORTH HOOSICK (E-11)

BENNINGTON BATTLEFIELD STATE HISTORIC SITE, 3 mi. e. on SR 67, is the site of one of the earliest decisive Colonial victories of the Revolutionary War. In 1777 Gen. John Stark and his New Hampshire, Vermont and Massachusetts militia captured a British expeditionary force. An interpretive sign explains the course of the battle. A hilltop picnic area overlooks the battlefield.

Allow 1 hour minimum. Daily 10-7, Memorial Day weekend-Labor Day; Sat.-Sun. 10-7, May 1-day before Memorial Day weekend and day after labor Day-Columbus Day (weather permitting). Free. Phone (518) 279-1155.

NORTH SALEM — *see New York p. 151.*

NORTH TONAWANDA — *see Buffalo p. 74.*

NORWICH (F-8) pop. 7,355, elev. 1,015'

NORTHEAST CLASSIC CAR MUSEUM, 24 Rexford St. (SR 23), has more than 100 restored automobiles dating from the turn of the 20th century to the 1960s. Included are Auburns, Cords, Duesenbergs, Packards and models by Chalmers Detroit, Holmes, Stutz and Pierce Arrow. An extensive collection of Franklin luxury cars also is featured. Mannequins in period clothing are displayed next to cars of the day.

Allow 1 hour minimum. Daily 10-5; closed Jan. 1, Thanksgiving and Dec. 25. Admission $8; over 65, $7; students with ID $4; under 6 free. AX, DS, MC, VI. Phone (607) 334-2886. *See color ad p. 70.*

NYACK — *see New York p. 151.*

OAKDALE (I-3) pop. 8,075, elev. 17'

CONNETQUOT RIVER STATE PARK PRESERVE, entered off SR 27, is a 3,400-acre refuge supporting many species of animals and plants. Guided nature walks and interpretive tours are conducted Wednesday through Sunday; reservations are required. Fishing is permitted with a New York license; equestrian permits are available by phoning the preserve. Tues.-Sun. 7-dusk, Apr.-Sept.; Tues.-Sun. 8-4, rest of year. Parking S6. Phone (631) 581-1005.

OGDENSBURG (A-8) pop. 12,364, elev. 276'

Situated on the banks of the St. Lawrence River, Ogdensburg was founded as the French Fort La Presentation in 1749 by the Sulpician missionary Abbé François Picquet. The fort, which also served as a mission, trading post and school, was damaged by the French before the British could capture it in 1760. On the ruins of La Presentation the British built Fort Oswegatchie, which was an important military stronghold during the Revolution.

In 1796 Oswegatchie was turned over to Col. Samuel Ogden, and in 1817 it was incorporated as the village of Ogdensburgh. The village dropped its "h" when incorporated as a city in 1868.

The Custom House, 127 Water St., designated the oldest federal government building in the United States, was built 1809-10. The building offered protection to both American and British soldiers during a battle on Feb. 23, 1813. Battle scars are visible near the roof peak on the north side of the building. It has served as the customhouse since 1928.

The New York State Armory, a massive castellated-style edifice, 225 Elizabeth St., was constructed 1897-98 by architect Isaac Perry. Built for the Fortieth Separate Co., the building has been historically significant due to its association with American military history.

Twin-towered St. Mary's Cathedral, at Hamilton and Greene streets, features a series of stained glass windows depicting prominent religious figures.

Greater Ogdensburg Chamber of Commerce: 1020 Park St., Ogdensburg, NY 13669; phone (315) 393-3620.

Shopping areas: An Ammex Tax & Duty Free Shop is at Bridge Plaza off SR 37. Gateway Centre also is off SR 37, and Seaway Shopping Center is on Canton Street.

FREDERIC REMINGTON ART MUSEUM, 303 Washington St., displays bronzes, oil paintings, watercolors and pen-and-ink illustrations by Frederic Remington, known for his depictions of the American West. The artist's tools, library, personal notes and furnishings from his home are on display. In addition the museum presents traveling exhibitions that relate to the artist's style, theme and time period.

Allow 1 hour minimum. Mon.-Sat. 10-5, Sun. 1-5, May-Oct.; Wed.-Sat. 11-5, Sun. 1-5, rest of year. Closed Jan. 1, Easter, Thanksgiving and Dec. 25. Admission $6; over 65 and students age 6-22, $5. Phone (315) 393-2425.

OLD BETHPAGE (I-3) pop. 5,400

OLD BETHPAGE VILLAGE RESTORATION, 1 mi. s. of Long Island Expwy. exit 48S on Round Swamp Rd., is a reconstructed pre-Civil War Long Island working farm village on 209 acres. Buildings moved from locations throughout the island reflect architectural styles dating from the early 1700s. Included are blacksmith shops, a church, homes, a store and an inn.

The 165-acre Powell farmstead, with the original family house and carriage shed, includes an English-style barn, a smokehouse and live animals. The Schenck farmhouse is one of the area's oldest Dutch structures. The Layton Store doubled as a family home in the 1860s and today contains period merchandise. Costumed guides explain each building and the activities of its former inhabitants.

Picnicking is permitted. Allow 2 hours minimum. Wed.-Sun. 10-5, May-Oct.; 10-4, Mar.-Apr. and Nov.-Dec. Closed Nov. 4 and 11, Thanksgiving and Dec. 25. Last admission is 1 hour before closing. Admission $7; over 59 and ages 5-12, $5. Phone (516) 572-8400.

OLD CHATHAM (F-11) elev. 551'

THE SHAKER MUSEUM AND LIBRARY is off Taconic Pkwy. (exit 295) and the N.Y. State Thruway Berkshire Spur exit (exit B-2) to CR 13, following signs to 88 Shaker Museum Rd. Twenty-six exhibit areas include painted shaker furniture, baskets, poplarware, domestic items and pre-1900 tools. Displays span more than 200 years of Shaker history. Wed.-Mon. 10-5, Apr. 29-Oct. 31. Admission $8; over 61, $6; ages 8-17, $4; family rate (two adults and two children). $18. Phone (518) 794-9100, ext. 100.

OLD FORGE (C-9) elev. 1,706'

Originating in Old Forge is a canoe trip through the eight lakes of the Fulton Chain as well as Raquette, Forked, Long and Saranac lakes. McCauley Mountain offers summer and winter recreation.

Central Adirondack Association: P.O. Box 68, Old Forge, NY 13420; phone (315) 369-6983.

ADIRONDACK SCENIC RAILROAD departs 1 mi. s. on SR 28 at Old Forge/Thendara Station. A 20-mile round-trip excursion to Otter Lake provides views of the Moose River region. Other excursions are available. Moose River 75-minute trip departs Wed.-Sun., Labor Day and Columbus Day at 12:30 and 2:45, June 25-Sept. 1 and Sept. 17-Oct. 12; Sat.-Sun. at 12:30 and 2:45, May 24-26, May 31-June 22, Sept. 6-14 and Oct. 18-19. Fare $12; over 62, $11; ages 3-12, $5. MC, VI. Phone (315) 369-6290 or (877) 508-6728.

ARTS CENTER/OLD FORGE, .3 mi. n. at 3260 SR 28, exhibits paintings, pottery, photography and other media as well as works from the permanent collection. Special month-long exhibitions are offered year-round. Workshops and performances also are offered. Allow 30 minutes minimum. Mon.-Sat.

10-4, Sun. noon-4; closed major holidays. Donations. Admission is charged during special exhibits. Phone (315) 369-6411.

ENCHANTED FOREST/WATER SAFARI, on SR 28, is a 60-acre family-oriented water theme park with 44 rides, including 31 heated water rides and attractions. Featured are five themed areas and The Shadow, a double-flume slide. Circus shows are offered twice daily. Food is available. Daily 9:30-7, June 26-Aug. 15; schedule varies June 10-25 and Aug. 16-Labor Day. Admission $21.95; ages 3-11, $18.95. DS, MC, VI. Phone (315) 369-6145.

SAVE **OLD FORGE LAKE CRUISES** depart from the SR 28 dock on Old Forge Pond. Narrated cruises on the scenic Fulton Chain of Lakes include a 2-hour sightseeing excursion, a 1.5-hour children's cruise and a 3-hour mailboat ride. Dinner and fireworks cruises also are available.

Sightseeing cruise departs daily June 26-Oct. 11; departure times vary. Cruises also are available May 22-June 25; phone for schedule. Children's cruise departs daily at 6:30, June 26-Sept. 4. Mailboat cruise departs Mon.-Sat. at 9:45, June 1-Sept. 15. Sightseeing cruise $11.50; ages 3-12, $8.50. Children's cruise $10; ages 3-12, $6. Mailboat cruise $14.50; ages 3-12, $10.50. MC, VI. Phone (315) 369-6473.

OLD WESTBURY (H-2) pop. 4,228

SAVE **OLD WESTBURY GARDENS** is at 71 Old Westbury Rd. between Long Island Expwy. (SR 495) and Jericho Tpke. (SR 25). The 1906 Westbury House is furnished with antique furniture and art, including paintings by Henry Raeburn, Sir Joshua Reynolds, John Singer Sargent and Richard Wilson. The grounds feature landscaping and formal gardens patterned after the English "great parks" of the 18th century.

Picnicking is permitted. Food is available. Allow 2 hours minimum. Guided tours are given Wed.-Mon. 10-5, late Apr.-Oct. 31. Holiday tour schedule varies Nov.-Dec. Admission $10; over 62, $8; ages 6-12, $5. Holiday tour fees may vary; phone ahead. Phone (516) 333-0048.

OLEAN (G-4) pop. 15,347, elev. 1,435′

Olean was founded at the headwaters of the Allegheny River in 1804 by Revolutionary War hero Maj. Adam Hoops. The settlement flourished as a supply depot and departure point for pioneers heading west on makeshift rafts and flatboats. With the completion of the Buffalo and Washington Railroad in the 1870s and a subsequent oil boom, Olean emerged as a major petroleum shipping center at the turn of the 20th century. The name Hoops gave his land 100 years earlier is derived from the Latin word *oleum*, meaning oil.

Olean Point Museum, 302 Laurens St., contains town memorabilia; phone (716) 376-5642. The restored Fannie E. Bartlett Historical House on Laurens Street is furnished in the Victorian style, recalling Olean's heyday; phone (716) 376-5642.

Greater Olean Area Chamber of Commerce: 120 N. Union St., Olean, NY 14760; phone (716) 372-4433.

ROCK CITY PARK, 5 mi. s. on SR 16, has paths and stairways that wind through 320-million-year-old quartz boulders projecting from the edge of the Allegheny Mountains. The site reputedly has the world's largest exposure of quartz conglomerate, also known as pudding stone. One stairway is believed to have been built by the Seneca Indians, who used the area as a fortress.

Picnicking is permitted. Food is available. Allow 1 hour minimum. Daily 9-6, May-Oct. (weather permitting). Admission $4.50; over 62, $3.75; ages 6-12, $2.50. Phone (716) 372-7790.

ONEIDA (E-7) pop. 10,987, elev. 427′

The Oneida Community was founded nearby in 1848 by John Noyes. A religious and social commune who called themselves Perfectionists, they shared all property and looked for ways of improving their self. The communal way of life was abandoned in 1881. However a joint stock corporation was formed to carry on the manufacturing activities. The present corporation has retained some cooperative features; Oneida Ltd. has factories and home offices in the area as well as in Sherrill, where silverware is made.

Of interest is the Oneida Community Mansion House at 170 Kenwood Ave. Begun in 1860, the home contains some 300 rooms that reflect the needs of the society that lived as one family. Guided tours present family portraits, Empire and Victorian furniture, costumes and historical photographs; phone (315) 363-0745.

Greater Oneida Chamber of Commerce: 136 Lenox Ave., Oneida, NY 13421-1745; phone (315) 363-4300.

MADISON COUNTY HISTORICAL SOCIETY HEADQUARTERS, 435 Main St., occupies the Gothic Revival mansion Cottage Lawn. The house offers changing exhibits about local history, a genealogical library and seven period rooms. The carriage barn has an agricultural museum which features a display about hops. Guided tours are given Mon.-Sat. 9-4, June-Sept.; Mon.-Fri. 9-4, rest of year. Closed major holidays. Tour $2; under 12, $1. Phone (315) 363-4136.

ONEONTA (F-8) pop. 13,292, elev. 1,083′

Oneonta is the Oneida Indian word for "cliffs abound" or "exposed rock in side of hills." The town is on the western edge of the Catskills, surrounded by hills.

Oneonta became the site of a major railroad car-building shop for the Albany & Susquehanna line in 1863. Twenty years later a handful of train yard workers formed the Brotherhood of Railroad Brakemen, the embryo of today's Brotherhood of Railroad Trainmen. When first built, the Delaware and

Hudson roundhouse was one of the largest turntables in the world.

Otsego County Chamber of Commerce: 12 Carbon St., Oneonta, NY 13820; phone (607) 432-4500.

NATIONAL SOCCER HALL OF FAME, I-88 exit 13 to 18 Stadium Cir., tells the story of soccer in America through interactive exhibits, videotape footage and artifacts, including the world's oldest soccer ball and the Women's World Cup trophy. Soccer buffs can test their skills in the Kick's Game Zone with 11 different games.

Allow 1 hour minimum. Daily 9-7, Memorial Day-Labor Day; 10-5, rest of year. Closed Jan. 1, Thanksgiving and Dec. 25. Phone ahead to verify schedule. Admission $8; ages 6-12, $6.50; over 54, $5.50. AX, DC, MC, VI. Phone (607) 432-3351.

SCIENCE DISCOVERY CENTER OF ONEONTA is in the Physical Science Building at State University College on Ravine Pkwy. This center promotes the enjoyment and understanding of science by children and adults through direct, hands-on experiences and educational fun. Allow 1 hour minimum. Mon.-Sat. noon-4, July-Aug.; Thurs.-Sat. noon-4, rest of year. Closed Good Friday, July 4, Thanksgiving and Dec. 25. Free. Phone (607) 436-2011.

YAGER MUSEUM, on the Hartwick College campus, includes holdings of Upper Susquehanna American Indian, South American pre-Columbian and Mesoamerican artifacts along with Southwestern pottery, baskets and rugs and a small collection of objects from Micronesia. Works in the fine arts collection range from European Renaissance through contemporary American paintings, sculpture and prints. Open Tues.-Sun. noon-4:30, Sept.-May; Wed.-Sun. noon-4:30, rest of year. Closed holidays. Free. Phone (607) 431-4480.

ORCHARD PARK—see *Buffalo p. 74.*

ORISKANY (D-8) pop. 1,459, elev. 423'

ORISKANY MUSEUM, 420 Utica St., exhibits items commemorating the Battle of Oriskany, fought during the Revolutionary War, as well as other military contributions from the area. An airplane and an anchor from the aircraft carrier USS *Oriskany,* which served during the Korean and Vietnam wars, also are displayed. Guided tours are available. Allow 30 minutes minimum. Tues. and Thurs.-Fri. 1-5, Sat. 4-8, May-Sept.; Tues. and Thurs.-Sat. 1-5, rest of year. Closed Dec. 25. Free. Phone (315) 736-7529.

OSSINING—see *New York p. 151.*

OSWEGO (D-6) pop. 17,954, elev. 298'

On Lake Ontario at the mouth of the Oswego River, Oswego was fought over by the French, English and Americans during most of the 1700s because of its strategic position at the end of the inland water route. By 1796 Oswego was firmly in

U.S. hands, and the town soon became a booming port. Oswego is the largest U.S. port on Lake Ontario and the home of the State University of New York at Oswego.

Greater Oswego Chamber of Commerce: 156 W. 2nd St., Oswego, NY 13126; phone (315) 343-7681.

FORT ONTARIO STATE HISTORIC SITE, 5 blks. n. of SR 104 on E. Fourth St., overlooks Oswego Harbor and Lake Ontario. The site was first fortified during the French and Indian War and remained in use through World War II, when it was the only American site to house Jewish refugees. Barracks, guard houses, a powder magazine, two officers' quarters, underground stone casements and the grounds have been restored to the 1868-72 time period. Costumed interpreters portray fort residents.

Picnicking is permitted. Allow 1 hour minimum. Tues.-Sun. 10-5, mid-May through Oct. 31. Admission $4; over 62 and students with ID, $3; ages 5-12, $1. Phone (315) 343-4711.

[SAVE] **H. LEE WHITE MARINE MUSEUM,** SR 104 to W. 1st St. then .5 mi. n. to end of pier, houses exhibits covering 300 years of Oswego and Great Lakes history. Included are displays about local American Indians, early settlement, navigation on Lake Ontario and the activities of the Underground Railroad in the area. A World War II tugboat and an Erie Canal barge can be toured. Allow 1 hour minimum. Daily 10-5, July-Aug.; daily 1-5, May-June and Sept.-Dec.; Mon.-Sat. 1-5, rest of year. Admission $3; ages 5-11, $1.50. AX, MC, VI. Phone (315) 342-0480.

RICHARDSON-BATES HOUSE MUSEUM, 135 E. 3rd St., contains period rooms dating from around 1890 with original Victorian pieces, an exhibit about county history and changing exhibits. Allow 1 hour minimum. Tues.-Fri. 10-5, Sat. 1-5, Apr.-Dec. Closed holidays. Admission $4, over 64 and students (to age 25) with ID $2, under 5 free; family rate $10. Phone (315) 343-1342.

OVID (F-6) pop. 612, elev. 816'

WINERIES

• **Cayuga Ridge Estate Winery** is 4 mi. e. via SR 96A and CR 138, then .5 mi. n. on SR 89. Daily 11-5, mid-May to mid-Nov.; Sat.-Sun. noon-4, rest of year. Guided tours are offered daily at 2:30, mid-May to mid-Nov. Phone (607) 869-5158.

OWEGO (G-7) pop. 20,365

THE TIOGA COUNTY HISTORICAL SOCIETY MUSEUM, 110 Front St., offers permanent and changing interpretive exhibits about local and regional history. Displays include American Indian artifacts, folk art portraiture and 19th-century tools, toys, fashions and transportation artifacts. Area genealogical information dating from 1800 also is available. Allow 30 minutes minimum. Museum open Tues.-Sat. 10-4. Research library open Tues.-Fri. 1-4, Sat. 10-4. Closed holidays. Museum free. Library $5. Phone (607) 687-2460.

OYSTER BAY (H-3) pop. 6,826, elev. 8'

Oyster Bay, discovered in 1653 by settlers from Massachusetts, found itself in the middle of a tug of war: The Dutch Government in New Amsterdam and the English Colonial government in Hartford were unable to agree on who had jurisdiction over Oyster Bay. The settlers made appeals to both governments for protection.

During the Revolutionary War the village was headquarters for British lieutenant colonel John Graves Simcoe, a close friend of Maj. John Andre, adjutant general of the British Army in North America. As Benedict Arnold's British contact, Andre played an instrumental role in the ensuing scandal and was executed as a British spy in 1780. From 1901 to 1909 Oyster Bay was the site of President Theodore Roosevelt's summer White House. *Also see Long Island p. 101.*

Oyster Bay Chamber of Commerce: P.O. Box 21, Oyster Bay, NY 11771; phone (516) 922-6464.

Self-guiding tours: Brochures detailing self-guiding tours of Oyster Bay are available from the chamber of commerce.

EARLE-WIGHTMAN HOUSE MUSEUM, 20 Summit St., was built in 1720 as a one-room home, with additional rooms added over the following 150 years by successive owners. One room has been renovated to reflect the 18th century, and a second room depicts a 19th-century parlor. Other rooms feature changing exhibits. An 18th-century garden is on the grounds.

Allow 30 minutes minimum. Tues.-Fri. 10-2, Sat. 9-1, Sun. 1-4; closed Jan. 1, July 4, Thanksgiving and Dec. 25. Donations. Phone (516) 922-5032.

PLANTING FIELDS ARBORETUM STATE HISTORIC PARK, w. via Mill River and Oyster Bay rds., covers 409 landscaped acres of greenhouses, gardens and natural habitat. Collections include rhododendrons, azaleas, camellias, orchids, ferns and bromeliads. The Synoptic Garden's ornamental shrubs and small trees are arranged alphabetically and are identified by botanical and common name and by family and country of origin.

Allow 1 hour, 30 minutes minimum. Arboretum daily 9-5; closed Dec. 25. Greenhouses daily 10-4:30. Camellia house daily 10-4. Admission free. Parking $4 daily, May-Sept. and Sat.-Sun. and holidays, rest of year. Phone (516) 922-9200.

Coe Hall, on the arboretum grounds, is a 65-room Tudor Revival mansion furnished with 16th- and 17th-century pieces. Carpets, paintings and tapestries were imported from Europe. Examples of stained glass from the 13th through 19th centuries are found throughout the house. The Buffalo Room

contains murals of buffalo and American Indians set against a Western landscape. Allow 30 minutes minimum. Daily noon-3:30, Apr.-Sept.; closed holidays. Admission $5; over 61, $3.50; ages 7-12, $1; under 7 free. Parking $5. Phone (516) 922-9210.

[SAVE] **RAYNHAM HALL MUSEUM,** 20 W. Main St., British headquarters during the Revolutionary War, was the home of Samuel Townsend, who was partially responsible for the capture of Maj. John Andre and the exposure of Benedict Arnold's plan to betray West Point. Allow 30 minutes minimum. Tues.-Sun. noon-5, July 1-Labor Day; Tues.-Sun. 1-5, rest of year. Closed holidays. Admission $4; over 65 and ages 6-18, $3. Phone (516) 922-6808.

ROOSEVELT BIRD SANCTUARY AND TRAILSIDE MUSEUM is 2 mi. e. on E. Main St. to 134 Cove Rd. Features include a memorial to President Theodore Roosevelt and a museum with examples of Long Island plant and animal life. Films and nature programs are presented on occasional weekends. Young Memorial Cemetery, next to the sanctuary, contains President Roosevelt's grave. Allow 30 minutes minimum. Mon.-Fri. 8:30-4:30, Sat.-Sun. 9-5; closed Jan. 1, Thanksgiving and Dec. 25. Donations. Phone (516) 922-3200.

SAGAMORE HILL NATIONAL HISTORIC SITE, 3 mi. e. via E. Main St. and Cove Neck Rd. to 20 Sagamore Hill Rd., was the home of President Theodore Roosevelt until his death in 1919. The house served as the "summer White House" during his administration. The 1885 house displays trophies, furniture and other memorabilia. The nearby Old Orchard Museum offers audiovisual programs and exhibits relating to the political career and family life of President Roosevelt.

Guided tours of the house are given daily on the hour 10-4, Memorial Day-day before Labor Day; Wed.-Sun. 9-5, rest of year. Closed holidays. Grounds open daily 9:30-dusk. Admission $5, under 16 free. Tour tickets go on sale at 9:30. AX, DS, MC, VI. Phone (516) 922-4447 or (516) 922-4788.

PALMYRA (E-5) pop. 3,490, elev. 442'

Palmyra was the birthplace of Mormonism and the early home of Joseph Smith. The Church of Jesus Christ of Latter-day Saints was organized and the "Book of Mormon" was published nearby in 1830. A visitor center on the Peter Whitmer Farm, where the church was founded, is 5 miles south of Waterloo on SR 96. *Also see Finger Lakes p. 86.*

ALLING COVERLET MUSEUM, 122 William St., has changing 19th-century coverlet and quilt displays. Daily 1-4, June 1-Sept. 15. Free. Phone (315) 597-6737.

BOOK OF MORMON HISTORIC PUBLICATION SITE, 217 E. Main St., is the site where the first 5,000 copies of the "Book of Mormon" were printed by E.B. Grandin. The restored site includes a bindery and the print shop. Allow 1 hour minimum. Forty-minute guided tours are given Mon.-Sat. 9-7, Sun. 11-7. Free. Phone (315) 597-5982.

HILL CUMORAH, 2 mi. n. of I-90 exit 43, is where Joseph Smith is said to have received from the angel Moroni the golden plates inscribed with the history of ancient Americans, from which he translated the "Book of Mormon." A 40-foot monument crowns the hill. The visitor center has an audiovisual tour centering on the life of Jesus Christ. Twenty-five minute guided tours are given Mon.-Sat. 9-9, Sun. 11-9, June-Aug.; Mon.-Sat. 9-6, Sun. noon-6, Apr.-May and Sept.-Oct.; hours vary rest of year. Free. Phone (315) 597-5851.

JOSEPH SMITH HOME, 4 mi. s. on SR 21 to Stafford Rd. (a few miles from Hill Cumorah), includes the Smith frame home, a reconstructed log home and the Sacred Grove. Guided tours of the homes are given Mon.-Sat. 9-9, Sun. 11-9, June-Aug.; Mon.-Sat. 9-6, Sun. 11-6, Apr.-May and Sept.-Oct.; hours vary rest of year. Free. Phone (315) 597-5851.

PANAMA (G-2) pop. 491, elev. 1,548′

PANAMA ROCKS, .2 mi. w. of jct. SR 474 and CR 33, then w. on CR 10, is an outcrop of Paleozoic sea islands compressed into quartz-conglomerate rock fractured by earthquakes and unearthed by glaciers. The huge rocks, some more than 60 feet high, extend along a half-mile ridge. Geologic features include cavernous dens, small caves, passageways and crevices. A 1-mile hiking trail is available. Visitors can also enjoy off-trail exploration and rock climbing.

Pets are not permitted. Picnicking is permitted. Daily 10-5, May 1 to mid-Oct. Admission $6; over 55 and ages 13-17, $4; ages 6-12, $3. Under 18 must be with an adult. Phone (716) 782-2845.

PETERSBURG (E-11) pop. 1,563, elev. 684′

BERKSHIRE BIRD PARADISE SANCTUARY, 2 mi. n. on CR 87 from jct. SR 2 and CR 87, then 1 mi. e. to 43 Red Pond Rd., is dedicated to the conservation of wild birds. The site is home to more than 1,000 birds, including raptors, tropical birds and birds of prey. Allow 1 hour minimum. Daily 9-5, mid-May through Oct. 31 Admission $8; under 12, $5. Phone (518) 279-3801.

PHOENICIA (G-9) pop. 381, elev. 795′

RECREATIONAL ACTIVITIES
Tubing

- [SAVE] **The Town Tinker Tube Rental**, 10 Bridge St., P.O. Box 404, Phoenicia, NY 12464. Daily 9-3:30, May 15-Sept. 30. Phone (845) 688-5553.

PLATTSBURGH (A-10)
pop. 18,816, elev. 109′

On Lake Champlain, Plattsburgh was the site of the Battle of Plattsburgh on Sept. 11, 1814. While Gen. Alexander Macomb restrained a superior British land force, the Americans, under Cmdr. Thomas Macdonough, scored a decisive naval victory in Plattsburgh Bay.

Plattsburgh North Country Chamber of Commerce: 7061 SR 9, P.O. Box 310, Plattsburgh, NY 12901; phone (518) 563-1000.

Shopping areas: Two major malls serve the Plattsburgh area. Champlain Centers Mall, a quarter-mile east on SR 3 from exit 37, and Consumer Square, farther east on SR 3, include Ames, JCPenney and Sears.

CLINTON COUNTY HISTORICAL MUSEUM, 48 Court St., contains a diorama of the 1814 Battle of Plattsburgh and the 1776 Battle of Valcour. Also displayed are domestic and historical artifacts and memorabilia, including a collection of Redford glass. Tues.-Fri. noon-4. Admission $4; over 64, $3; students with ID $2. Phone (518) 561-0340.

KENT-DELORD HOUSE MUSEUM, 17 Cumberland Ave., overlooks Lake Champlain at the mouth of the Saranac River. The Federal-style structure was commandeered by the British in 1814. They left behind an oak tea chest when they fled. American decorative arts and period furniture also are displayed. Exhibits interpret daily life 1800-1913, with emphasis on the War of 1812, the Civil War and women's issues of the late 19th century.

Tues.-Sat. noon-4, Mar.-Dec.; closed major holidays. Admission $5; students with ID $3; under 12, $2; ages 5-11, $1. Phone (518) 561-1035.

LAKE CHAMPLAIN FERRIES—
see Lake Champlain p. 98.

DID YOU KNOW

The Stars and Stripes
was flown in battle
for the first time
at Fort Stanwix
in Rome.

PLATTSBURGH STATE ART MUSEUM is at 101 Broad St., on the campus of the State University of New York at Plattsburgh. Displays include a collection of paintings, drawings and books by illustrator Rockwell Kent. The gallery also houses photographs by Ansel Adams, German expressionist prints and prints by Paul Cézanne, Albrecht Dürer and Peter Paul Rubens. Changing historical and contemporary exhibitions of mixed media and an outdoor sculpture garden also are available. Allow 30 minutes minimum. Daily noon-4; closed holidays. Donations. Phone (518) 564-2813 or (518) 564-2474.

PORT JERVIS (H-9) pop. 8,860, elev. 442'

An important 19th-century railroad and river transportation hub, Port Jervis was named for John B. Jervis, chief engineer of the Delaware and Hudson Canal. One of two railroad turntables built around the turn of the 20th century is still in operation.

Stephen Crane reputedly drew inspiration for "The Red Badge of Courage" while interviewing veterans of New York's 124th Regiment at the 1886 dedication of a Civil War monument in Veteran's Memorial Park.

GILLINDER GLASS FACTORY, corner Erie and Liberty sts., uses century-old techniques to produce commercial and decorative glass. Visitors to the factory floor can watch the pouring, pressing and cooling of molten glass. A museum chronicles the history of local glass making. Allow 1 hour minimum. Guided tours Mon.-Fri. at 10:15, 12:30 and 1:30. Tours $4; over 55 and under 16, $3.50. MC, VI. Phone (845) 856-5375.

PORT WASHINGTON (H-2)
pop. 15,215, elev. 140'

Port Washington Chamber of Commerce: 329 Main St., P.O. Box 121, Port Washington, NY 11050; phone (516) 883-6566.

SANDS POINT PRESERVE, 6 mi. n. of I-495 exit 36 on Searingtown Rd./Port Washington Blvd. at 95 Middleneck Rd., contains a 209-acre forest and shoreline preserve. Restored Guggenheim family homes display artifacts and antiques. Nature and science exhibits are on the grounds. Allow 2 hours, 30 minutes minimum. Grounds open Tues.-Sun. 10-5. Admission $6; over 59 and ages 3-12, $4. Special events incur an additional charge. Phone (516) 571-7900.

Castlegould, in Sands Point Preserve, is a huge 1902 stone castle that once served as a stable. It houses a visitor reception center and a main exhibit hall. Allow 1 hour minimum. Tues.-Sun. 10-5, Feb.-Oct. Visitor center free. Main exhibit hall $6; over 59, $4; ages 3-12, $3.

Falaise, in Sands Point Preserve, was built by Capt. Harry F. Guggenheim in 1923. The elegant Normandy-style manor house contains original furnishings and historic memorabilia relating to Guggenheim's support of aeronautical technology. Allow 1 hour minimum. Guided tours Wed.-Fri. noon-3, Sat.-Sun. noon-3:30, May-Oct. Last tour begins 1 hour before closing. Tour $6; over 59, $4. Under 10 are not permitted.

Hempstead House, in Sands Point Preserve, was the main residence. The design of the 1912 house includes features of an English Tudor castle. Tours of the main rooms and viewings of the Wedgwood china collection are offered Sat.-Sun. noon-4, May-Sept. Fee $2.

POTSDAM (A-9) pop. 9,425, elev. 397'

Potsdam was settled in 1803 by land agent Benjamin Raymond. Five years later a post office opened to serve a thriving community of more than 900. The Clarkson family ran a farm and a variety of businesses, built Trinity Church and founded the Thomas Clarkson Memorial College of Technology, now known as Clarkson University. Raymond built a schoolhouse, which became part of the state university system in 1949. Sandstone quarried in the area has been used for structures in Ottawa, Syracuse, and New York City.

Potsdam Chamber of Commerce: Potsdam Civic Center Box 717, Potsdam, NY 13676; phone (315) 265-5440.

GIBSON GALLERY, on SR 56 in Brainerd Hall at the State University of New York, College of Potsdam, presents changing exhibitions featuring student and regional, national and international artists throughout the year and houses a permanent collection and a sculpture park. Allow 1 hour minimum. Mon.-Fri. noon-5 (also Tues.-Thurs. 7-9 p.m.), Sat.-Sun. noon-4 and by appointment; closed during school breaks. Free. Phone (315) 267-2245 or (315) 267-2481.

POTSDAM PUBLIC MUSEUM, on SR 11 in the Civic Center, houses the Burnap Collection of English pottery, dating 1700-1870. The collection includes Delft chargers, Wedgwood, lusterware, transfer prints and relief wares. Also displayed are American decorative glassware, furniture and changing exhibits pertaining to local history. Tues.-Sat. noon-4, Sept.-May; Tues.-Fri. noon-4, rest of year. Closed holidays. Free. Phone (315) 265-6910.

POTTERSVILLE (C-10)

[SAVE] **NATURAL STONE BRIDGE AND CAVES** is 1 mi. n. of I-87 exit 26 on US 9, then 2.5 mi. w. following signs. A well-marked path leads through a series of caves, rock formations and underground waterways. Natural paths cover some uneven terrain. Rental shoes are available.

Picnicking is permitted. Allow 1 hour minimum. Daily 9-7, Memorial Day weekend-Labor Day; 10-6, day after Labor Day-Columbus Day. Admission $10; ages 5-12, $5. AX, DC, MC, VI. Phone (518) 494-2283.

POUGHKEEPSIE (G-11)
pop. 29,871, elev. 168′

Originally settled by the Dutch, Poughkeepsie became the state capital in 1777. Eleven years later the state ratified the U.S. Constitution. The city is built on the rocky terraces rising 250 feet above the Hudson River and the level plateau above. The Home of Franklin D. Roosevelt and the Vanderbilt Mansion national historic sites are nearby *(see Hyde Park p. 93)*.

Poughkeepsie Area Chamber of Commerce: 110 Main St., Poughkeepsie, NY 12601; phone (845) 454-1700.

THE FRANCES LEHMAN LOEB ART CENTER, on the campus of Vassar College at 124 Raymond Ave., contains more than 12,500 art objects. Exhibits include works from the permanent collection displayed chronologically in the Main Gallery and selections from the college's significant holdings in Asian art. Among the displays are works by Pieter Brueghel the Younger, Alexander Calder, Paul Cézanne, Georgia O'Keeffe and Jackson Pollock. Allow 1 hour minimum. Tues.-Sat. 10-5, Sun. 1-5; closed major holidays. Free. Phone (845) 437-5632.

[SAVE] **LOCUST GROVE, THE SAMUEL MORSE HISTORIC SITE,** 2 mi. s. of Mid-Hudson Bridge at 2683 South Rd. (US 9), was the home of artist, educator and telegraph inventor Samuel F.B. Morse 1847-72. Designed by A.J. Davis, the house contains period furnishings, china, art, original telegraph equipment and other Hudson Valley memorabilia. The 150-acre site includes hiking trails and historic formal gardens, carriage and ice houses, a picnic grove and a visitor center.

Allow 1 hour, 30 minutes minimum. Grounds daily 8 a.m.-dusk. House daily 10-3, May-Nov.; by appointment otherwise. Closed Thanksgiving. Fee $7; over 59, $6; ages 6-18, $3. MC, VI. Phone (845) 454-4500.

PRATTSVILLE (F-10) pop. 2,064, elev. 1,165′

ZADOCK PRATT MUSEUM, on SR 23 (Main St.), was the home of Prattsville's founder and U.S. representative Zadock Pratt. The 1828 house contains original and period furnishings; exhibits pertain to Pratt's lively and varied occupations, as well as to town and regional history. Thurs.-Mon. 1-4, Memorial Day-Columbus Day. Tours lasting 45 minutes are given on the hour. Last tour begins 1 hour before closing. Admission $2; under 13, $1. Phone (518) 299-3395 to verify schedule.

PURCHASE—*see New York p. 152.*

QUEENSBURY (D-11) pop. 25,441, elev. 293′

[GEM] **THE GREAT ESCAPE AND SPLASHWATER KINGDOM** is 3.7 mi. n. on US 9, just e. of I-87 Northway via exits 19 or 20. [SAVE] With 140 acres, this is one of the state's largest theme parks. More than 125 rides, live shows and attractions include the classic wooden coaster The Comet, and Canyon Blaster, a steel coaster almost 2,000 feet long that simulates a ride on a runaway mine train. In addition to six roller coasters, features include a full water park, Storytown USA and a variety of shows for children.

Allow 6 hours minimum. Park opens daily at 10, mid-May through Oct. 31; closing times vary. Admission $33.99, over age 54 and under 49 inches tall $19.99, under age 3 free. AX, DS, MC, VI. Phone (518) 792-3500.

 LAKE GEORGE OPERA FESTIVAL— *see Saratoga Springs p. 192.*

RAQUETTE LAKE (C-9) elev. 1,810′

[SAVE] **GREAT CAMP SAGAMORE,** 4 mi. s. from SR 28 following signs via a dirt road, was a rustic summer retreat built in 1897 and expanded in 1901. Exemplifying the 19th century's Great Camps, the lake-side main lodge features log and bark siding. Other buildings include the caretakers' quarters, a bowling alley and a dining hall.

A 2-hour guided tour is offered daily at 10 and 1:30, late June-Labor Day; Mon.-Fri. at 1, Sat.-Sun. at 10:30 and 1, day after Labor Day-Columbus Day. Sat. at 1:30, Memorial Day-late June. Admission $10, senior citizens and college students with ID $9, children $3. Reservations are recommended. MC, VI. Phone (315) 354-5311.

RENSSELAER (F-11) pop. 7,761, elev. 21′

Across the Hudson from Albany, Rensselaer was founded in 1631 by Dutch settlers sent by wealthy patron Killean Van Rensselaer. Fort Crailo was built in 1704 for protection against the indigenous inhabitants. It is said that "Yankee Doodle" was composed in Rensselaer in 1758 as a satire of the Provincial troops.

CRAILO STATE HISTORIC SITE is 1.5 blks. s. of jct. US 9 and US 20 at 9 ½ Riverside Ave. The museum houses exhibits that explain the history, development, culture and influence of Dutch settlements in the Upper Hudson Valley area. Allow 1 hour minimum. Guided tours are given every half-hour. Wed.-Sun. 10-5, early Apr.-Oct. 31; closed Easter. Last tour begins at 4. Grounds open dawn-dusk. Tour $3; senior citizens and ages 5-12, $1. Phone (518) 463-8738.

RHINEBECK (G-10) pop. 3,077, elev. 203′

[SAVE] **OLD RHINEBECK AERODROME,** .5 mi. n. on US 9 off SR 9G, then 1.5 mi. e. to 42 Stone Church Rd., presents antique airplanes from 1908-37. Fifteen-minute barnstorming rides in a 1929 open cockpit airplane are available a few weekends before and after air shows. Daily 10-5, May 15-Oct. 31. Air shows Sat.-Sun. at 2, mid-June to mid-Oct. Museum $6; senior citizens $5; ages 6-10, $2. Air shows $12; senior citizens $10; ages 6-10, $5. Plane rides $40. Phone (845) 752-3200.

RIVERHEAD (H-4) pop. 10,513, elev. 25′

ATLANTIS MARINE WORLD is at 431 E. Main St. Indoor and outdoor areas simulating the ruins of the Lost City of Atlantis feature eel, piranha, shark, octopus and tortoise exhibits along with one of the largest live coral reefs in North America. A stingray touch tank and an interactive salt marsh provide hands-on experiences.

Sea lion shows, shark feedings and educational programs are presented daily. Naturalist-led environmental boat tours of the Peconic River and Flanders Bay also are offered.

Guided behind-the-scenes tours are available. Allow 1 hour, 30 minutes minimum. Daily 10-5; closed Dec. 25. Boat trips daily at 11:30 and 2, May-Oct. (weather permitting). Admission $13.50; over 61, $12.50; ages 3-11, $10. Guided tours $5. Boat trip $17; over 61 and under 12, $15. AX, DS, MC, VI. Phone (631) 208-9200.

SPLISH SPLASH WATER PARK is .5 mi. w. of jct. I-495 and SR 25 at 2549 Splish Splash Dr. The 40-acre park contains such water rides as Splash Landing, Lazy River and Giant Twisters. Children's areas and tropical bird and sea lion shows also are featured.

Food is available. Allow a full day. Daily 9:30-7, mid-June through Aug. 19; Sat.-Sun. 9:30-5, Memorial Day to mid-June. Over 48 inches tall $27.99, over age 62 and children under 48 inches tall $20.99, under age 3 free. Parking $6. Prices may vary; phone ahead. AX, DS, MC, VI. Phone (631) 727-3600.

SUFFOLK COUNTY HISTORICAL SOCIETY, on SR 25 at 300 W. Main St., has permanent and changing exhibits about the history of Suffolk County, including early crafts, textiles, china, whaling and American Indian artifacts and a research library. Allow 1 hour minimum. Tues.-Sat. 12:30-4:30; closed holidays. Library open Wed.-Thurs. and Sat. 12:30-4:30. Donations. Library $2. Phone (631) 727-2881.

ROCHESTER (D-5) pop. 219,773, elev. 660′

Originally called the "Flour City" because of its milling industries, Rochester also became known as the "Flower City" because of its nurseries, parks and fruit and garden areas. Rochester leads in the manufacture of optical, surgical, dental, check-protecting and gear-cutting goods.

Some of the local parks preserve historical sites; others were created especially for recreation. Cobb's Hill Park between Highland Avenue and Culver Road contains Lake Riley, the old Erie Canal turning basin; phone (585) 428-6909. The city can be viewed from the hilltop. Upper Falls Park, on the Genesee River off St. Paul Street, has a 100-foot waterfall; phone (585) 325-2030. Originally used to power the city's flour mills, the falls continue to generate electricity.

Manhattan Square Park at Chestnut and Broad streets has a 100-foot observation tower; phone (585) 428-7541. Monroe County Park at Clover Street and Pond Road is a 2,500-acre park with a natural preserve and self-guiding trails; phone (585) 256-4950.

City Hall at Church and Fitzhugh streets presents exhibits in its Link Gallery; phone (585) 428-6690. Another landmark is Mount Hope Cemetery on Mount Hope Avenue. One of the oldest Victorian-era cemeteries in the nation, it contains the graves of Susan B. Anthony and Frederick Douglass; phone (585) 428-7999.

Rochester's contribution to education and technology is evident at the University of Rochester's Laboratory of Laser Energetics, where nuclear fusion research takes place. The Rochester Institute of Technology has the School for American Craftsmen and the National Technical Institute for the Deaf.

The Rochester Philharmonic Orchestra performs at the Eastman Theater; phone (585) 222-5000. The GEVA Theatre, 75 Woodbury Blvd., offers performances throughout the year; phone (585) 232-4382. Local theater and musical companies and touring Broadway troupes also offer productions. The Eastman School of Music is said to produce more professional musicians than any other conservatory in the country.

One of the most popular recreational pursuits is fishing. Lake Ontario and its tributaries offer ice fishing in winter and warm-water angling in summer. Abundant species include coho and giant chinook salmon, smelt, bass, pike and steelhead, rainbow and brown trout. Hiking and biking are popular along the Erie Canal Trail.

Greater Rochester Visitors Association, Inc.: 45 East Ave., Rochester, NY 14604; phone (585) 546-3070 or (800) 677-7282.

Self-guiding tours: Brochures detailing self-guiding walking tours of the downtown historic district and other areas are available from the visitors association.

Shopping areas: Several major enclosed malls serve the Rochester area. Near Greece in Rochester's northwest suburbs is The Mall at Greece Ridge Center, with 100 stores 1 mile west of I-390 at West Ridge Road; anchor stores are JCPenney, Kaufmann's and Sears.

Eastview Mall, on SR 96 near I-490 in Victor, counts Kaufmann's and Sears among its 106 stores. Northeast on SR 104 is the Irondequoit Mall, with JCPenney and Sears. Marketplace Mall, at W. Henrietta and Jefferson roads in Henrietta, has a Kaufmann's and 147 other stores.

Discounted merchandise can be found at the 70 stores of the Southtown Plaza, 3333 W. Henrietta Rd. at Jefferson Road, and the 27 stores at the Panorama Mall and Plaza, 3 miles east of I-490 on Penfield Road in Penfield.

Antiques and crafts are the specialty at Craft Company No. 6, 785 University Ave., and Village Gate Square, housed in a renovated 1800s printing factory at 274 N. Goodman St.

THE CENTER AT HIGH FALLS is at 60 Browns Race along the Genesee River. In a neighborhood that was once a flour milling center, this complex features exhibits tracing Rochester's development, artwork by local artists and an observation deck. Food is available. Allow 1 hour, 30 minutes minimum. Tues.-Fri. 10-4, Sat. noon-5; closed major holidays. Hours may vary; phone ahead. Free. Phone (585) 325-2030.

DURAND-EASTMAN PARK, 7 mi. n. off I-590, has a 2-mile frontage on Lake Ontario. Part of the Monroe County Arboretum, the park contains an 18-hole golf course and a large collection of flowering wild crab apples. Daily 10 a.m.-11 p.m. Free. Phone (585) 266-1372.

 GENESEE COUNTRY VILLAGE & MUSEUM—*see Mumford p. 104.*

GEORGE EASTMAN HOUSE is at 900 East Ave. This 50-room mansion, once occupied by George Eastman, founder of Eastman Kodak Co., has been restored to its early 1900s appearance. Formal gardens grace the 12.5-acre estate. The International Museum of Photography and Film houses changing displays of photography, film, technology and related literature.

The Dryden Theater presents evening film programs Wednesday through Sunday. Guided garden tours are offered May through September. A research library is available.

Allow 2 hours minimum. Mon.-Sat. 10-5 (also Thurs. 5-8), Sun. 1-5; closed Jan. 1, Thanksgiving and Dec. 25. Museum tours are given Tues.-Sat. 10-5, Sun. 1-5. Admission $8; over 59 and students with ID $6; ages 5-12, $3. Film programs $5.50. AX, MC, VI. Phone (585) 271-3361, or TTY (585) 271-3362.

HIGHLAND PARK, off I-490 exit 12 or 14 following signs to entrance, contains botanic gardens, a

conservatory and a collection of more than 1,200 lilac bushes. Allow 1 hour, 30 minutes minimum. Park open daily 10 a.m.-11 p.m. Conservatory open daily 10-4. Admission $1. Phone (585) 256-5878.

LANDMARK SOCIETY OF WESTERN NEW YORK is at 133 S. Fitzhugh St. The historical society's exhibit gallery and research library are in the 1840 Hoyt-Potter House. Guided tours of two historic house museums are offered. Campbell-Whittlesey House, 123 S. Fitzhugh St., is a restored Greek Revival house furnished to illustrate the lifestyle of a 19th-century flour miller. Stone-Tolan House, 2370 East Ave., was an early 19th-century rural tavern and farmhouse.

Allow 2 hours minimum. Mon.-Fri. 9-4, Mar.-Dec. Tours of Campbell-Whittlesey House are given Thurs.-Fri. noon-3. Tours of Stone-Tolan House are given Fri.-Sat. noon-3. Fee (one house) $3; ages 8-18, $1. Two houses $5; ages 8-18, $1.50. Phone (585) 546-7029.

MAPLEWOOD PARK, Lake Ave., contains one of the nation's largest municipal rose gardens. Allow 1 hour minimum. Daily 8-dusk. Free. Phone (585) 428-6444.

MEMORIAL ART GALLERY, 500 University Ave., features a collection of 11,000 art works spanning 50 centuries. Notable artists whose works are displayed include Mary Cassatt, Paul Cézanne, Winslow Homer, Henri Matisse and Claude Monet.

The museum's collection of antiquities includes a 16th-century Flemish painting and a pair of 4th-century Egyptian coffins. Contemporary glass sculpture by Dale Chihuly and works by American craft masters also are displayed.

Guided tours and food are available. Allow 2 hours, 30 minutes minimum. Wed.-Fri. 10-4 (also Thurs. 4-9), Sat. 10-5, Sun. noon-5, Tues. noon-4; closed major holidays. Admission $7; over 61 and college students with ID $5; ages 6-18, $2; $2 to all Thurs. after 5. DS, MC, VI. Phone (585) 473-7720, or TTY (585) 473-6152.

ROCHESTER HISTORICAL SOCIETY MUSEUM is at 485 East Ave. The museum is housed in Woodside, an 1840 Greek Revival mansion. A distinctive feature is the house's round, glazed cupola set on a square pedestal surrounded by balustrades. Rooms display portraits, period furnishings and costumes. An enclosed perennial garden laid out in parterres is beyond the rear veranda. The collections include a reference library, archives and genealogical information.

Allow 1 hour minimum. Mon.-Fri. noon-4, Memorial Day-Labor Day; Sun.-Thurs. noon-4, rest of year. Closed holidays. Admission $3; over 60 and college students with ID $2; ages 6-18, $1. Phone (585) 271-2705.

ROCHESTER MUSEUM & SCIENCE CENTER, 657 East Ave., provides visitors the opportunity to explore science and technology, the natural environment and the cultural heritage of the region. The museum has family-oriented activities and permanent and changing exhibits. Highlights include a collection of Haudenosaunee (Iroquois) artifacts. The museum also operates the Cumming Nature Center in Naples (see Naples p. 104).

Food is available. Allow 2 hours, 30 minutes minimum. Mon.-Sat. 9-5, Sun. noon-5; closed Thanksgiving and Dec. 25. Admission $7; senior citizens and college students with ID $6; ages 3-18, $5. DS, MC, VI. Phone (585) 271-1880.

Strasenburgh Planetarium, 657 East Ave., presents large-format science/nature films in the Star Theater. Current events star shows and laser sound-light shows also are presented. "I See the Sky" is designed for children ages 3-5 and is offered Saturdays at 10. The observatory is open May-Oct.; phone for schedule. Shows are presented daily; phone for times. Closed Thanksgiving and Dec. 25. Admission $6; college students with ID $5; over 59 and under 18, $4. Prices vary with type of show. Under 5 are not admitted to evening shows. DS, MC, VI. Phone (585) 271-1880 or (585) 271-4552.

SEABREEZE PARK/RAGING RIVERS WATER PARK, off I-590 and SR 104 at Culver Rd., is an amusement and water park with roller coasters, water slides, children's rides, a classic wooden carousel and a log flume. Live shows are presented.

Allow 4 hours minimum. Daily noon-10 (also Fri.-Sat. 10-11 p.m.), mid-June through Labor Day; Sat.-Sun. noon-10, May 1 to mid-June. Ride and slide pass $17.95, under 48 inches tall $13.95. Admission after 5 p.m. $10.95. Admission Plus Pass includes two ride tickets $7.50, under age 2 free. DS, MC, VI. Phone (585) 323-1900.

SENECA PARK ZOO, 2222 St. Paul St., along the Genesee River Gorge, features a Rocky Coasts Exhibit that offers underwater viewing of polar bears, sea lions and penguins. The zoo also houses African elephants and Bornean orangutans. Allow 1 hour minimum. Mon.-Fri. 10-5, Sat.-Sun. 10-5, Memorial Day-Labor Day; daily 10-5, rest of year. The grounds are open 1 hour later. Admission $5; over 63, $4; ages 3-11, $2. Phone (585) 467-9453.

THE STRONG MUSEUM, One Manhattan Sq., features a variety of interactive learning environments, including a "Sesame Street" exhibit where visitors can appear on a television screen with characters from the show. Children can scan groceries in a child-size supermarket, produce their own TV show, or visit an old-fashioned ice-cream fountain. Collections include dolls, dollhouses, miniatures and home furnishings as well as a toy hall of fame. A glass atrium features a historic street scene, vintage operating diner and 1918 carousel.

Allow 3 hours minimum. Mon.-Sat. 10-5 (also Fri. 5-8), Sun. noon-5; closed Jan. 1, Thanksgiving and Dec. 25. Admission $7; over 62, $6; college students with ID and ages 2-17, $5. DS, MC, VI. Phone (585) 263-2702, or TTY (716) 712-2702.

THE SUSAN B. ANTHONY HOUSE, 17 Madison St., was the home of the well-known civil rights leader during the most politically active period of her life. It also was the site of her famous arrest for voting in 1872. Guided tours of the red brick Victorian house feature personal items and a collection of suffrage material. A visitor center provides additional exhibits. Tues.-Sun. 11-5, Memorial Day-Labor Day; Wed.-Sun. 11-4, rest of year. Admission $6; over 62, $5; students with ID and under 13, $3. DS, MC, VI. Phone (585) 235-6124.

VICTORIAN DOLL MUSEUM AND CHILI DOLL HOSPITAL—*see North Chili p. 178.*

ROME (D-8) pop. 34,950, elev. 435'

Long before the Europeans discovered Rome, it was called *De-O-Wain-Sta,* an American Indian term meaning "the carrying place." In the city's center is a portage on the only practical water route south of the St. Lawrence River, which connected the Great Lakes with the Hudson River.

Francis Bellamy, author of the "Pledge of Allegiance to the Flag," is buried in the Rome cemetery. The Tomb of the Unknown Soldiers of the American Revolution is next to the city hall at 207 N. James St. It was designed by Lirimer Rich, who also planned the Tomb of the Unknown Soldier in Arlington National Cemetery in Virginia.

The Tug Hill plateau north of Rome receives up to 200 inches of snow a year. This region is renowned for its skiing, snowmobiling and year-round hunting and fishing.

Rome Chamber of Commerce: 139 W. Dominick St., Rome, NY 13440; phone (315) 337-1700.

ERIE CANAL VILLAGE, 3 mi. w. on SR 49 at 5789 Rome-New London Rd., is a re-creation of an 1840 community with museums and restored buildings. Demonstrations, audiovisual programs and farm, canal and Americana exhibits are featured. A 30-minute horse-drawn packet boat ride along a restored part of the canal and a 4.5-mile train ride also are offered.

Allow 1 hour, 30 minutes minimum. Wed.-Sat. 10-5, Sun., noon-5, Memorial Day weekend-Labor Day; Sat. 10-5, Sun. noon-5, day after Labor Day-Sept. 30. Admission $4; over 62, $3; ages 5-17, $2. Boat or train ride $5. AX, MC, VI. Phone (315) 337-3999.

FORT RICKEY CHILDREN'S DISCOVERY ZOO is 3 mi. w. on SRs 46 and 49. Hands-on presentations and two petting areas allow children to interact with animals. Displayed are such animals as bobcats, spider monkeys, llamas, bison and owls. Children also can enjoy pony rides, pedal boats, a

playground, a wet play fountain, a "ball crawl" and a catfish feeding area.

Picnicking is permitted. Food is available. Allow 1 hour, 30 minutes minimum. Daily 10-5:30, mid-June through Labor Day; Mon.-Fri. 10-4, Sat.-Sun. 10-5, early to mid-June; Mon.-Fri. 10-2, Sat.-Sun. 10-5, mid-May to early June. Admission $8; over 64 and ages 2-15, $6. MC, VI. Phone (315) 336-1930.

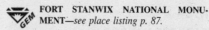 **FORT STANWIX NATIONAL MONUMENT**—*see place listing p. 87.*

ORISKANY BATTLEFIELD, 6 mi. e. on SR 69, is marked by a granite shaft. On Aug. 6, 1777, in the "bloodiest battle of the Revolution," Mohawk Valley militiamen en route to relieve Fort Stanwix were ambushed by a large force of Tories and Indians. The Colonists and Oneida Indian allies led by Gen. Nicholas Herkimer were victorious, though badly mauled, in the 6-hour battle. Guided tours are available. Allow 30 minutes minimum. Wed.-Sat. and Mon. holidays 9-5, Sun. 1-5, mid-May to mid-Oct. Free. Phone (315) 768-7224.

ROME-BOONVILLE GORGE, traversed by SR 46, is a narrow valley from Rome to North Western and a gorge from North Western to Boonville. Portions of the Black River Canal can be seen along the drive.

ROMULUS (E-6) pop. 2,036, elev. 717'

WINERIES

• **Swedish Hill Vineyard and Winery** is .5 mi. s. of jct. SR 336 at 4565 SR 414. Tours are given Mon.-Fri. at 1 and 3, Sat.-Sun. at noon, 2 and 4, May-Oct. Phone (315) 549-8326.

ROTTERDAM JUNCTION (E-10)

MABEE FARM HISTORIC SITE is at 1080 Main St. (SR 5S). The 9-acre preserved farmstead contains a 300-year-old Dutch Colonial house; a brick building that served as a trading post, slave quarters and auxiliary housing; an old inn; two barns; and the Mabee family cemetery. Farming methods, domestic chores, social habits and daily life of a typical Mohawk Valley farming family are interpreted. Allow 1 hour minimum. Tues.-Sat. 10-4, mid-May to late Sept. Admission $3. Phone (518) 887-5073.

ROUSES POINT (A-11) pop. 2,277, elev. 117'

Rouses Point is less than a mile south of the Canadian border; a U.S. Customs and Immigration Service office is in the village. At nearby Island Point are the ruins of Fort Montgomery, which replaced Fort Blunder. The construction of Fort Blunder was abandoned in 1818 when it was learned that the land belonged to Canada. Vermont can be reached via the Korean Veterans Memorial Bridge.

Northern Tier Chamber of Commerce: P.O. Box 44, Rouses Point, NY 12979; phone (518) 297-3040.

Shopping areas: An Ammex Tax & Duty Free Shop is on Five Lake Street and SR 9B.

ROXBURY (F-9) pop. 2,509, elev. 1,495′

RECREATIONAL ACTIVITIES

Skiing

- **Ski Plattekill**, Plattekill Mountain Rd., P.O. Box 187, Roxbury, NY 12474. Other activities are available. Daily Dec.-Apr. Phone (607) 326-3500 or (800) 633-3275.

RYE—*see New York p. 152.*

SACKETS HARBOR (C-7)
pop. 1,386, elev. 255′

A resort on eastern Lake Ontario, Sackets Harbor saw one of the first battles in the War of 1812, when five British battleships were repelled by one U.S. ship and a group of farmers on shore with a single cannon. The only British shot to land near the farmers was loaded into the cannon and returned; it took down the mast of the British flagship.

The Old Military Cemetery on Dodge Avenue has graves of soldiers from the War of 1812, including that of Gen. Zebulon Pike, discoverer of Pikes Peak.

[SAVE] Seaway Trail Discovery Center, in an 1871 limestone building at Ray and W. Main sts., serves as an orientation center for the scenic 500-mile Seaway Trail, which stretches from New York to Pennsylvania along Lake Erie, the Niagara River, Lake Ontario and the St. Lawrence River. The center has exhibits, a mural and driving maps; the trail is marked with interpretive signs.

Sackets Harbor Visitor Center: 301 W. Main St., Sackets Harbor, NY 13685; phone (315) 646-2321.

Self-guiding tours: A pamphlet describing a combination walking and driving tour past the historic buildings and sites of Sackets Harbor is available for a fee at the visitors center in the Sacket Mansion on W. Main Street.

SACKETS HARBOR BATTLEFIELD STATE HISTORIC SITE, at the village, was the site of two battles in the War of 1812, during which Sackets Harbor served as headquarters for the Army of the Northern Frontier and the Navy of the Great Lakes. The restored commandant's house dates from 1850. Behind the house the 1812 Navy Exhibit depicts a sailor's life aboard the *Jefferson* during the war.

Guided tours are available. Allow 1 hour minimum. Battlefield open daily 8-dusk. Museums open Tues.-Sat. 10-5, Sun. 11-5, mid-May through Labor Day; Fri.-Sat. 10-5, Sun. 11-5, day after Labor Day-Columbus Day. Last tour begins 1 hour before closing. Admission $3; senior citizens and students with ID $2; ages 6-12, $1. Phone (315) 646-3634.

SAG HARBOR (H-5) pop. 2,313, elev. 10′

Sag Harbor's sheltered position between the North and South Forks of Long Island made it important from its earliest days. As early as 1707 it

had assumed such stature as a port that the British Crown appointed an officer to stop the "running of illicit cargos into Sagg Harbour, the principal port of Long Island." The town was one of the first two ports of entry created by Congress in 1789.

The whaling industry was of primary importance to Sag Harbor's development. During this period the town was the source of many real and imagined heroes, including those of the sea stories of James Fenimore Cooper, who began his first novel in this area in 1824. Sag Harbor ranked as one of the largest whaling ports in the world before the industry died in 1871.

Antique hunters have long since replaced whale hunters. The streets of the town's historic district contain interesting buildings ranging from simple weathered saltbox cottages to the more ornate houses of its wealthy past. *Also see Long Island p. 101.*

Sag Harbor Chamber of Commerce: 459 Main St., P.O. Box 116, Sag Harbor, NY 11963; phone (631) 725-0011.

CUSTOM HOUSE, Main and Garden sts., is the restored home of a customs officer and postmaster of Sag Harbor in the late 1700s and early 1800s. Original and restored furnishings and artifacts are displayed. Allow 30 minutes minimum. Tues.-Sun. 10-5, July-Aug.; Sat.-Sun. 10-5, May-June and Sept.-Oct. Admission $3; senior citizens and ages 7-14, $1.50. Phone (631) 692-4664.

SAG HARBOR WHALING MUSEUM is on Main St. opposite the library. Exhibits include whaling equipment, scrimshaw, oil paintings, ships models, fishing gear, logbooks and other objects connected with Colonial eastern Long Island. Allow 30 minutes minimum. Mon.-Sat. 10-5, Sun. 1-5, May 15-Sept. 30. Admission $3; over 64, $2; ages 6-13, $1. Phone (631) 725-0770.

ST. JOHNSVILLE (E-9) pop. 1,685

Situated in the Mohawk Valley, St. Johnsville was first home to the Dutch in the mid-1600s, followed by the Palatine who were driven from their home along the Rhine River in Germany. They called the area "the Promised Land" because it resembled their homeland.

Hunting for "Herkimer Diamonds"—extremely clear, double-terminated quartz crystals found only in central New York—is a favorite pastime at Crystal Grove Diamond Mine, 5 miles north on CR 114; phone (518) 568-2914 or (800) 579-3426.

FORT KLOCK HISTORIC RESTORATION, 2 mi. e. on SR 5, is a fortified 1750 farmhouse built for trading and defense purposes. Partially furnished with antiques, the main house contains exhibits relating to rural 18th-century life. A schoolhouse, Dutch barn and blacksmith shop are next to the house. Picnicking is permitted. Allow 1 hour minimum. Tues.-Sun. 9-5, Memorial Day to mid-Oct.

Admission $2; ages 10-15, $1. Phone (518) 568-7779.

MARGARET REANEY MEMORIAL LIBRARY AND MUSEUM, 3 blks. e. of Main St. at 19 Kingsbury Ave., was built in 1909. Among the many historical displays are Civil War items, period rooms and farm and trade tools. The library contains approximately 25,000 volumes. Allow 1 hour minimum. Mon. and Fri. 9:30-5 and 6:30-8:30, Tues.-Wed. 9:30-5, Thurs. 1-5, Sat. 9:30-noon. Free. Phone (518) 568-7822.

SALAMANCA (F-3) pop. 6,097, elev. 1,389'

Salamanca's Iroquois heritage is evident in the abundance of local artisans who create traditional arts and crafts.

Salamanca Area Chamber of Commerce: 26 Main St., Salamanca, NY 14779; phone (716) 945-2034.

SALAMANCA RAIL MUSEUM, 170 Main St., is a restored 1912 Buffalo, Rochester and Pittsburgh Railway passenger depot. Artifacts, photographs and videotapes depict the role railroads played in area history. Mon.-Sat. 10-5, Sun. noon-5, May-Sept.; Tues.-Sat. 10-5, Sun. noon-5, in Apr. and Oct.-Dec. Closed Thanksgiving and Dec. 25. Donations. Phone (716) 945-3133.

SENECA-IROQUOIS NATIONAL MUSEUM is off US 17 exit 20 on the Allegany Indian Reservation, Broad St. extension. The museum's collection portrays the life and culture of the Iroquois Indians, with emphasis on the Seneca Nation. Guided tours are available by reservation 2 weeks in advance.

Allow 30 minutes minimum. Mon.-Tues., Thurs.-Sat. 9-5, Sun. noon-5, Apr. 1 to mid-Oct.; Mon.-Fri. 9-5, rest of year; closed major holidays. Admission $4; senior citizens and students with ID $3; ages 7-13, $2. Phone (716) 945-1738 or (716) 945-1760.

SALEM (D-11) pop. 964, elev. 490'

THE BATTEN KILL RAMBLER SCENIC TRAIN departs from Salem Station at 223 Main St./SR 22 and the Cambridge Station at 6 Broad St. The train takes passengers on 2- to 3-hour excursions through the scenic countryside along the Batten Kill River. The train also can be boarded at Cambridge. A fall foliage trip and other special events tours also are available.

Allow 2 hours, 30 minutes minimum. Train departs Thurs. at 10:30 and 1:30, Sat. at 11:30 and 2:30, Sun. at 1, July 1-Sept. 5; Sat. at 11:30, Sun. at 1, May 29-June 30. Fare $10; senior citizens $9; ages 3-12, $6. Phone (518) 692-2191.

SARANAC LAKE (B-9)
pop. 5,041, elev. 1,535'

First settled in 1819, Saranac Lake was a major tuberculosis treatment center during the late 1800s and early 1900s. The area's mountains and lakes make it a popular vacation site. Many cottages, inns and treatment centers from the late 1800s and early 1900s still stand along Saranac Lake's winding streets.

Saranac Lake Area Chamber of Commerce: 39 Main St., Saranac Lake, NY 12983; phone (518) 891-1990 or (800) 347-1992.

CHARLES DICKERT WILDLIFE MUSEUM, in the library on Main St., exhibits mounted specimens of species native to the Adirondacks. Mon.-Sat. 10-5:30 (also Thurs. 5:30-8), Sept.-June; Mon.-Fri. 10-5:30, Sat. 10-1, rest of year. Free. Phone (518) 891-4190.

ROBERT LOUIS STEVENSON COTTAGE, off jct. SRs 3 and 86 on Stevenson Ln. via Church and Main sts., was the author's home during the winter of 1887-88. The cottage and original furniture have been preserved. The museum reputedly holds the world's largest collection of Stevenson memorabilia. Tues.-Sun. 9:30-noon and 1-4:30, July 1 to mid-Sept.; by appointment rest of year. Admission $5, under 12 free. Phone (518) 891-1462.

SARATOGA NATIONAL HISTORICAL PARK (E-11)

Eight miles south of Schuylerville on US 4, the Battlefield of Saratoga National Historical Park embraces partially wooded country along the west side of the Hudson River. In addition to the 3,200-acre battlefield, the park is made up of two other areas: the Schuyler House in Schuylerville and the Saratoga Monument in Victory. The park commemorates the Battles of Saratoga, fought on Sept. 19 and Oct. 7, 1777, in which Gen. Horatio Gates' American forces defeated Gen. John Burgoyne's British forces.

On Oct. 17, 1777, Burgoyne surrendered to the Americans near Schuylerville (Old Saratoga), thus preventing British control of the Hudson and the east-west split of the Colonies that would have ensued. Some historians consider this victory to be the turning point of the Revolution. Eight miles from the battlefield stands the Saratoga Monument commemorating Burgoyne's surrender *(see Schuylerville p. 194)*. A 155-foot stone obelisk marks the approximate location where part of the British army was encamped the week before their surrender.

Ironically, the strategic planning and bravery of Benedict Arnold helped to secure an American victory at Saratoga. Just 3 years later he would attempt to turn West Point over to the British; but at the Breymann Redoubt he valiantly galloped through cross fire and received his second bullet wound in the same leg for the rebel cause. A marble boot, epaulets and an inscription document Arnold's heroics, but tactfully neglect to mention his name.

A visitor center on Fraser Hill, the highest point in the park, affords a view of the battlefield and surrounding area. Theater programs are available daily. Costumed interpreters present living-history programs.

A 9.5-mile scenic driving tour has 10 stops in the park. Costumed guides are available July through August at the Nielson House. There is a $5 per private vehicle fee for the tour. Bicycles are permitted on the driving tour roads for $3 per person. Hiking trails also are available for $3 per person; trails are free with the driving tour. Tour and trail charges are good for 7 days. An annual pass is available for $10. The tour road is closed from mid-November through early April due to the harsh weather conditions. Picnicking is permitted. Allow a full day. Daily 9-5; closed Jan. 1, Thanksgiving and Dec. 25. Park admission and visitor center free. Phone (518) 664-9821, ext. 224.

THE PHILIP SCHUYLER HOUSE, 8 mi. n. of the visitor center on US 4 in Schuylerville, is the restored summer house of Revolutionary War general Philip Schuyler. The two-story wooden house is furnished in period. Guided tours are available. Allow 1 hour minimum. Wed.-Sun. 10-4:30, mid-June through Labor Day. Free. Phone (518) 664-9821, ext. 224.

SARATOGA SPRINGS (D-10)
pop. 26,186, elev. 312'

Saratoga Springs is renowned for the beauty of its setting, the reputed health-giving properties of its waters and the gaiety of its summer life. The city boasts more than 1,000 examples of Victorian architecture in its eight historic districts.

The resort also is gaining popularity as a year-round sports and convention center. Equestrian events are popular year-round. Harness races are held from mid-February to mid-November and polo is played during the summer at Saratoga Equine Sports Center off Nelson Avenue; phone (518) 584-2110. In August spectators can watch the Thoroughbred races at Saratoga Race Course on Union Avenue, said to be the oldest course in the country; phone (518) 584-6200.

Note: Policies concerning admittance of children to pari-mutuel betting facilities vary. Phone for information.

Winter events focus on Saratoga Springs' many alpine and cross-country skiing facilities and ice skating and snowshoeing areas. The Saratoga Springs Heritage Area and Visitor Center, across from Congress Park, shows an orientation videotape and is open all year; phone (518) 587-3241.

Saratoga County Chamber of Commerce: 28 Clinton St., Saratoga Springs, NY 12866; phone (518) 584-3255.

Self-guiding tours: Brochures with maps detailing the points of interest downtown and in the surrounding area are available from the chamber of commerce and the visitor center.

Shopping areas: On SR 50 is the Wilton Mall, which includes JCPenney and Sears. Downtown Saratoga's Broadway Street features specialty stores with fine art, decorative crafts and antique books.

SAVE **CONGRESS PARK AND CANFIELD CASINO,** off Broadway (US 9), contains Italian sculpture gardens and works by Daniel Chester French, who created the seated Lincoln in the Washington, D.C., memorial. An 1870 casino houses the Historical Society of Saratoga Springs Museum, which traces Saratoga Springs' growth from a rural village to a flamboyant resort, and the Walworth Memorial Museum, which chronicles the saga of a prominent local family.

Allow 30 minutes minimum. Mon.-Sat. 10-4, Sun. 1-4, June-Sept.; Wed.-Sat. 10-4, Sun. 1-4, rest of year. Admission $4, over 59 and students with ID $3, under 12 free. Phone (518) 584-6920.

GEM **LAKE GEORGE OPERA FESTIVAL** presents performances at the Spa Little Theatre in Saratoga Spa State Park. This regional professional repertory company presents two to four main stage performances each season. The company is committed to the development of young American performers through an apprentice artist program.

The mainstage season runs June-July. Admission $32-$64, with reduced rates for senior citizens and students. Reservations are recommended. MC, VI. Phone (518) 584-6018 for general information or (518) 587-3330 for mainstage tickets.

SAVE **NATIONAL MUSEUM OF DANCE & HALL OF FAME,** 1 mi. s. at 99 S. Broadway (US 9), presents changing exhibits about professional dance. The museum also includes the Dance Hall of Fame. Dance classes can be observed in the Lewis A. Sawyer Studio. Allow 1 hour minimum. Tues.-Sun. 10-5. Admission $6.50; senior citizens and students with ID $5; under 12, $3. Phone (518) 584-2225.

NATIONAL MUSEUM OF RACING AND HALL OF FAME, 191 Union Ave. at Ludlow St., contains exhibits about the past, present and future of Thoroughbred racing in America. Displays include paintings and sculptures. The Hall of Fame honors horses, jockeys and trainers. Photographs, videotapes and a skeleton illustrate selective breeding and anatomy. In a simulated racetrack, videotapes of well-known trainers and jockeys explain training and racing techniques.

Allow 1 hour minimum. Daily 9-5, late July-Labor Day; Mon.-Sat. 10-4:30, Sun. noon-4:30, rest of year. Closed Jan. 1, Easter, Thanksgiving and Dec. 25. Admission $7, senior citizens and students with ID $5. Phone (518) 584-0400.

SARATOGA SPA STATE PARK, n. of I-87 exit 13N, features bathhouses, mineral springs and geyserlike spouters, four swimming pools, walking and hiking trails, two outdoor ice skating rinks, golf courses and picnic pavilions on 2,200 acres. The park also includes the Saratoga Performing Arts Center and the Spa Little Theatre. Allow 4 hours minimum. Daily 8 a.m.-dusk. Free. Parking daily $6, Memorial Day-Labor Day, Sat.-Sun. in May and day after Labor Day-Columbus Day; free, rest of year. Phone (518) 584-2535, or (518) 587-3330 for program and ticket information. *See Recreation Chart.*

YADDO, just w. of I-87 Northway exit 14 on Union Ave., is a private estate made available as a working community for visual artists, writers, filmmakers, choreographers and composers. Although the estate is private, the rose gardens are open to visitors daily 8-dusk. Free. Phone (518) 584-0746.

SAUGERTIES (G-10) pop. 4,955, elev. 159′

Saugerties has changed little since the days when riverboats stopped at its port on the Hudson. Victorian houses and small shops help to maintain the town's rural atmosphere.

OPUS 40 AND QUARRYMAN'S MUSEUM is 6 mi. w. on SR 212 from I-87 exit 20 to Glasco Tpke. following signs. Opus 40 consists of curvilinear pathways, pools and fountains of bluestone fitted to the contour of the land and surrounding a 9-ton monolith. The Quarryman's Museum houses 19th-century tools and household furnishings of the quarryman and other tradesmen.

Allow 1 hour minimum. Fri., Sun., most Sats. and Mon. holidays noon-5, Memorial Day-Columbus Day. Admission $6, over 61 and students with ID $5, under 5 free. Phone (845) 246-3400.

SCHENECTADY (E-10)
pop. 61,821, elev. 246′

On the Mohawk River at the eastern side of the scenic Mohawk Valley, Schenectady was founded in 1661 by Dutch settlers under the leadership of Arendt Van Curler. The Dutch influence is visible in much of the architecture of the historic Stockade District; this Front and Union streets area includes more than 66 homes and buildings built 1700-1850.

The G.E. Realty Plot historic district, bounded by Lenox Road, Nott Street, West Alley and Union Avenue, has some 130 homes dating from the early 1900s, when the neighborhood was created as an exclusive residential community for corporate executives of the General Electric Co. Among the earliest residents was GE engineer and television pioneer Ernest Alexanderson.

Schenectady's downtown renaissance is apparent in such urban revitalization projects as Jay Street Pedestrian Walkway, with shops and outdoor cafes. The Arts and Entertainment District incorporates Center City, an indoor soccer field, and Proctor's Theatre, a restored 1926 vaudeville house presenting touring Broadway shows, music events and classic films; phone (518) 382-3884.

Scenic attractions include the rose garden and nature trails in Central Park; an outdoor theater offers free performances. Jackson's Garden, 8 acres of formal gardens and woodland, is on the Union College campus; phone (518) 388-6000. Opened in 1795, the college purportedly was the first architecturally-designed campus in the country. The Stockade's Mohawk-Hudson Valley Bike-Hike Trail provides views of the Mohawk River.

The Chamber of Schenectady County: 306 State St., Schenectady, NY 12305; phone (800) 962-8007.

Self-guiding tours: Brochures detailing self-guiding tours of the city's historic areas are available at the Schenectady Heritage Area Visitors Center in the Schenectady Museum *(see attraction listing).*

Shopping areas: Rotterdam Square, off I-890 exit 2A on Campbell Road, has Filene's and Sears. Specialty stores can be found along Upper Union Street and the Jay Street Pedestrian Walkway.

SCHENECTADY COUNTY HISTORICAL SOCIETY MUSEUM, 32 Washington Ave., is housed in the 1895 Dora Jackson house. The museum contains 18th- and 19th-century furnishings, artifacts of Dutch heritage, an 1834 dollhouse and a genealogy library. Allow 1 hour minimum. Museum Mon.-Fri. 1-5. Library Mon.-Fri. 1-5, Sat. 9-noon; closed holidays. Admission $3, under 14 with adult $2, family rate $5. Library $5. Phone (518) 374-0263.

SCHENECTADY MUSEUM & PLANETARIUM AND SCHENECTADY HERITAGE AREA VISITORS CENTER, on Nott Terrace Heights between SR 5 and Union St., features a planetarium, a theater, a children's discovery area and exhibits about art, regional history and the history of the electrical industry.

Allow 2 hours minimum. Tues.-Fri. 10-4:30, Sat.-Sun. noon-4:30; closed major holidays. Planetarium show schedule varies; phone ahead. Museum $5; senior citizens $4; ages 4-12, $3. Museum and planetarium $6.50; senior citizens $5.50; ages 4-12, $4.50. Phone (518) 382-7890.

SCHOHARIE (F-10) pop. 1,030, elev. 611′

Schoharie, one of the oldest villages in upstate New York, was called Brunnen Dorf when it was settled in 1712. Many of the town's original buildings remain, including the 1770 George Mann House, the 1772 Swartz Tavern, the 1795 Lasell Hall and the Old Stone Fort *(see attraction listing).* One of the oldest buildings in Schoharie County, the restored 1743 Palatine House on Spring Street is known as the Old Lutheran Parsonage; the house serves as a museum.

The old Middleburgh-Schoharie Railroad Complex on Depot Lane has been restored and is a historic cultural center open weekends. It has original buildings and an 1890 passenger/baggage train car that houses a small museum.

Schoharie County Chamber of Commerce: P.O. Box 400, Schoharie, NY 12157; phone (518) 295-7033.

SAVE **OLD STONE FORT MUSEUM COMPLEX,** 1 mi. n. on N. Main St. to 145 Fort Rd., is a 1772 Dutch Reformed church, stockaded as a fort during the American Revolution. Other buildings include a 1760 Palatine house, an 18th-century Dutch barn, an 1830 law office, an 1890 schoolhouse and a historical and genealogy library. Furnishings, weaponry, automobiles, tools and farm implements are displayed.

Mon.-Sat. 10-5, Sun. noon-5, July-Aug.; Tues.-Sat. 10-5, Sun. noon-5, May-June and Sept.-Oct. Admission $5; over 62, $4.50; students with ID $1.50. MC, VI. Phone (518) 295-7192.

SCHUYLERVILLE (E-11)
pop. 1,197, elev. 146′

Schuylerville, originally a Native American camping ground, was settled by French refugees in 1688 and named Saratoga. In 1831 it was renamed Schuylerville after Revolutionary War general Philip Schuyler.

The turning point of the Revolutionary War took place in Schuylerville in 1777; the British army was trapped after retreating from the Battle of Saratoga *(see Saratoga National Historical Park p. 191).* The field of grounded arms is in the area. The Saratoga Monument commemorates British general John Burgoyne's surrender.

SEAFORD (I-3) pop. 15,791, elev. 9′

TACKAPAUSHA MUSEUM AND PRESERVE, off Seaford-Oyster Bay Expwy. exit 2E, .5 mi. e. on Sunrise Hwy., then .5 mi. s. on Washington Ave., occupies an 80-acre glacial outwash plain. Museum exhibits focus on the habitats and the life cycles of Long Island animals and plants. Changing videotapes and programs cover a variety of natural history topics. Nature trails traverse the wildlife sanctuary. Tues.-Sat. 10-4, Sun. 1-4; closed major holidays. Admission $2; ages 4-14, $1; under 4 free with an adult. Phone (516) 571-7443.

SENECA FALLS (E-6) pop. 6,861, elev. 473′

Seneca Falls is known as the birthplace of the women's rights movement. Notable former residents include Amelia Bloomer, who popularized the undergarments that bore her name, and Elizabeth Cady Stanton, organizer of the first Women's Rights Convention and an early feminist leader. The nation's first women's rights convention was held in Seneca Falls in 1848.

Several wineries lie within a 20-mile area of scenic SR 89, known as the Cayuga Wine Trail, which skirts the western shore of Cayuga Lake. As its name suggests, the Cayuga-Seneca Canal connects Cayuga and Seneca lakes and passes through diverse landscapes. The double locks at Seneca Falls create a 49-foot change in elevation. Houseboat rentals by the week are available locally; contact the chamber of commerce. *Also see Finger Lakes p. 86.*

Seneca County Chamber of Commerce: P.O. Box 70, Seneca Falls, NY 13148; phone (315) 568-2906.

MONTEZUMA NATIONAL WILDLIFE REFUGE, with its headquarters 5 mi. e. on US 20/SR 5, covers more than 7,000 acres. A link in the Atlantic flyway, the refuge is a nesting and resting spot for migratory waterfowl and other birds including geese, ducks and shorebirds. The refuge also has a resident population of bald eagles. Facilities include a visitor center, nature trail, boat launch, public fishing site and two observation towers. A self-guiding automobile tour is available. Bicycling is not permitted. Daily dawn-dusk. Visitor center open daily 10-3, Memorial Day-Labor Day. Free. Phone (315) 568-5987.

NATIONAL WOMEN'S HALL OF FAME, 76 Fall St., honors and celebrates the achievements of distinguished American women who have made contributions to the arts, athletics, business, government, philanthropy, humanities, science and education. Among the women enshrined in the hall are Susan B. Anthony, Amelia Earhart, Sandra Day O'Connor, Georgia O'Keeffe, Rosa Parks and Eleanor Roosevelt.

Allow 30 minutes minimum. Mon.-Sat. 10-4, Sun. noon-4, May-Oct.; Wed.-Sat. 11-4, Feb.-Apr. and Nov.-Dec. Closed major holidays. Admission $3, senior citizens and students with ID $1.50, family rate $7. Phone (315) 568-8060.

SENECA FALLS HISTORICAL SOCIETY, 55 Cayuga St., was founded in 1896 and occupies an imposing 1880 Queen Anne style mansion. It features Victorian period rooms, exhibits of local history and an extensive research library. The society also owns a collection of glass plate negatives relating to the Women's Rights Movement, which many historians consider to have begun in the town.

Guided tours are available. Allow 1 hour minimum. Tours are given on the hour Mon.-Fri. 9-4, (also Sat.-Sun. 1-4, July-Aug.); closed major holidays. Admission $3, students with ID $1.50, under 5 free, family rate $7.50. Phone (315) 568-8412.

WOMEN'S RIGHTS NATIONAL HISTORICAL PARK, 136 Fall St., chronicles the development of the women's rights movement. Highlights include changing exhibits, films and summer interpretive talks. Guided tours of the restored 1846 Elizabeth Cady Stanton Home at 32 Washington St. are offered on a varying schedule. Walking tours of Seneca Falls also are available.

Allow 1 hour minimum. Park and visitor center open daily 9-5; closed Jan. 1, Martin Luther King Jr. Day, Presidents Day, Thanksgiving and Dec. 25. Admission $3, under 17 free. House tour $1. Phone (315) 568-0024.

This is Woman's Hour is at 118 Fall St. A multimedia exhibit highlights the accomplishments of Mary Baker Eddy, pioneering thinker, author, and church and college founder. Mon.-Sat. 9-5, Sun.

noon-5, June-Aug; Mon.-Sat. 9-5, Sun. 2-5, in May and Sept.; Wed.-Sat. 9-5, rest of year. Closed major holidays. Free. Phone (315) 568-6488.

SETAUKET (H-3) elev. 189′

Setauket is part of a region called The Three Villages, which encompasses Setauket, Stony Brook and Old Field. Revolutionary War spies used the town as a headquarters; the town later became known for shipbuilding. William Sidney Mount captured the area's post-Revolutionary lifestyle on canvas in the mid-1800s from his mobile art studio.

The 1729 Caroline Church of Brookhaven is open on request; phone (631) 941-4245. Open by appointment, the Sherwood-Jayne House contains a varied furniture collection and hand-painted wall frescoes; phone (631) 692-4664. *Also see Long Island p. 101.*

Self-guiding tours: A brochure outlining a walking and driving tour of Setauket and the surrounding area is available from The Three Village Historical Society office at 93 North Country Rd., P.O. Box 76, East Setauket, NY 11733; phone (631) 751-3730.

THOMPSON HOUSE, 1 mi. n.e. of Stony Brook Station to 91 N. Country Rd., is a typical 17th-century saltbox house with period furnishings. Guided tours are available. Allow 30 minutes minimum. Fri.-Sun. 1-5, July-Aug.; Sat.-Sun. 1-5, Memorial Day-June 30 and Sept. 1-Columbus Day. Last tour begins 30 minutes before closing. Admission $3; over 64 and ages 7-14, $1.50. Phone (631) 692-4664.

SHERBURNE (E-8) pop. 1,455, elev. 1,048′

ROGERS ENVIRONMENTAL EDUCATION CENTER, 1 mi. w. on SR 80 off SR 12, provides 600 acres of habitat for plants and animals in a variety of aquatic, woodland and field environments. Short nature trails begin at the visitor center. Mounted North American birds are displayed. Six miles of trails are open year-round for hiking, cross-country skiing and snowshoeing. Educational programs are offered on Saturday.

Picnicking is permitted. Allow 1 hour minimum. Visitor center open Mon.-Fri. 8:30-4:45, Sat.-Sun. 1-4:45, June-Aug.; Mon.-Fri. 8:30-4:45, Sat. 1-4:45, rest of year. Grounds and trails open daily dawn-dusk. Free. Phone (607) 674-4017.

SHIRLEY (I-4) pop. 25,395

LONG ISLAND NATIONAL WILDLIFE REFUGE COMPLEX, .5 mi. s. on Smith St. off Montauk Hwy., has its headquarters in Wertheim National Wildlife Refuge. Wertheim offers boating, crabbing, fishing and a nature trail.

Morton National Wildlife Refuge is on Noyack Road *(see Southampton p. 195).* Target Rock National Wildlife Refuge, 4.5 miles north on W. Neck Road off SR 25A in Huntington village, then 3 miles east on Lloyd Harbor Road, has walking trails.

Refuges open Mon.-Fri. 8-4:30. Admission to Target Rock and Morton refuges $4 per private vehicle, $2 each for persons on bicycles or on foot, over 61 free. Admission to Wertheim free. Phone (631) 286-0485.

MANOR OF ST. GEORGE is off SR 27 (Sunrise Hwy.), 3.2 mi. s. on William Floyd Pkwy. On a 127-acre site overlooking Great South Bay, the three-story manor house displays furnishings from the early 1800s and paintings and documents concerning the estate, which was granted to Col. William Tangier Smith by the British Crown in 1693. Allow 30 minutes minimum. Wed.-Sun. 10-4, May-Oct. Free. Phone (631) 281-5034.

SKANEATELES (E-7) pop. 2,616, elev. 903′

MID-LAKES NAVIGATION CO., 1 blk. w. of jct. SRs 321 and 20 at 11 Jordan St., offers 1-hour sightseeing and 3.5-hour mailboat cruises. Dinner and lunch cruises also are available. Sightseeing cruises depart daily, July-Aug; departure times vary. Mailboat cruise leaves Mon.-Sat. at 10 a.m., July 1-Sept. 5. One-hour cruise $8; under 13, $5; family rate $25. Mailboat cruise $17; under 13, $11. AX, DS, MC, VI. Phone (315) 685-8500 or (800) 545-4318 for sightseeing schedule.

SLEEPY HOLLOW—*see New York p. 152.*

SOUTHAMPTON (H-5) pop. 3,965, elev. 45′

Settled in 1640 by English colonists from Massachusetts, Southampton is one of the oldest English settlements in New York. In the mid-19th century the proximity of its scenery and beaches to New York City began to draw summer visitors, who boarded with farmers and fishermen. The coming of the railroad to Southampton in 1870 brought thousands more persons, who began to buy land and build estates.

Soon the "Hamptons" gained the reputation as one of the East Coast's principal resorts for the wealthy and famous. The residents of the luxurious beachfront homes along Gin and Meadow lanes rub elbows with tourists and young professionals from the city as they shop at the boutiques and local branches of New York City stores along Job's Lane and Main Street.

In spite of the modern lines of some of the luxurious beach "cottages," Southampton Village has managed to retain much of its past. Roads with names like Ox Pasture and Meeting House Lane are lined with pleasant houses ranging in style from Colonial cedar shake to Victorian gingerbread.

The descendants of the Shinnecock Indians, who welcomed the first settlers, have a reservation next to the town off SR 27A. *Also see Long Island p. 101.*

Southampton Chamber of Commerce: 76 Main St., Southampton, NY 11968; phone (631) 283-0402.

Self-guiding tours: Information about self-guiding tours of Southampton by car, bicycle or foot is available from the chamber of commerce. Information also is available from the Southampton Historical Museum *(see attraction listing).*

MORTON NATIONAL WILDLIFE REFUGE, e. on SR 27 to exit 9, 2.5 mi. n. on N. Sea Rd. (SR 38), then 5 mi. e. on Noyack Rd., is a feeding, resting and nesting area for migratory birds on the Atlantic flyway, particularly for endangered piping plovers, least terns and ospreys. The refuge offers birdwatching, fishing, hiking and a visitor center. A nature trail traverses a forest and field, past wetlands and onto a bay beach.

Daily 30 minutes before dawn-30 minutes after dusk; public access is sometimes restricted. Admission $4 per private vehicle, $2 each for persons on bicycles or on foot, over 61 free. Phone (631) 286-0485. *See also Long Island National Wildlife Refuge Complex attraction listing in Shirley p. 195.*

PARRISH ART MUSEUM AND ARBORETUM, 25 Job's Ln., displays 19th- and 20th-century American art, including a collection of William Merritt Chase and Fairfield Porter. The grounds include an arboretum and statuary. Allow 1 hour minimum. Mon.-Sat. 11-5, Sun. 1-5, mid-June to mid-Sept.; Thurs.-Sat. and Mon. 11-5, Sun. 1-5, rest of year. Admission $5, senior citizens $1, students with ID and under 12 free. Phone (631) 283-2118.

SAVE **SOUTHAMPTON HISTORICAL MUSEUM,** off Main St. at 17 Meeting House Ln., consists of an 1843 whaling captain's home and 11 other buildings, including blacksmith, carpentry, cobbler and harness shops, a drugstore, a carriage house and a country store housed in a pre-Revolutionary barn. A whaling exhibit, a one-room schoolhouse and two original outhouses also are displayed.

Allow 1 hour minimum. Tues.-Sat. 11-5, Sun. 1-5, June 12-Dec. 31. Admission $4; over 64, $3; under 12, $2. Phone (631) 283-2494, (631) 283-0605 or (631) 283-1612.

SAVE **THE THOMAS HALSEY HOUSE,** .5 mi. s. on S. Main St., is a restored two-story 1648 house that is deemed the oldest frame house in the state. Built by one of the original settlers, Thomas Halsey, it contains 17th- and 18th-century furnishings. Behind the house is a Colonial herb garden. Allow 30 minutes minimum. Fri.-Sat. noon-5, Sun. 1-5, mid-June to mid-Oct. Admission $3; over 64, $2; under 12, $1. Phone (631) 283-2494.

SPRINGFIELD CENTER (E-9)

GEM **GLIMMERGLASS OPERA,** on Otsego Lake, 2 mi. s.w. on SR 80, features four operas performed in repertory at the Alice Busch Opera Theater. The theater has side walls that open to the landscape. Guided backstage tours are available. Opera previews are given 1 hour before performances.

Allow 1 hour minimum for tour; 2 hours, 30 minutes to 3 hours for performances. Performances July-Aug. Guided tours are given Sat. at 11 in Aug.; by appointment rest of year. Tickets $28-$104; previews and tours are free. AX, DS, MC, VI. Phone (607) 547-2255.

STERLING (D-6) pop. 3,432, elev. 320'

STERLING RENAISSANCE FESTIVAL is held off SR 104A at 15385 Farden Rd., following festival signs. The festival presents costumed minstrels and players, jousting, street theater, plays, games, madrigals, food and puppet shows, and crafts reminiscent of Renaissance England. Allow 3 hours minimum. Sat.-Sun. 10-7, July 5-Aug. 17. Admission $19.99; ages 6-12, $6.99. AX, MC, VI. Phone (315) 947-5783.

STONY BROOK (H-4) pop. 13,727

Settled by New Englanders in 1665, Stony Brook developed into a prosperous farming community whose economy was supplemented in the early 1800s by shipping and shipbuilding.

In 1940 Ward Melville sponsored the rehabilitation of Stony Brook's Main Street. The crescent-shaped shopping center was designed around a Republican-style post office overlooking a 2-acre village green on Stony Brook Harbor. Atop the building a mechanical, carved wooden eagle flaps its wings on the hour. *Also see Long Island p. 101.*

Self-guiding tours: Free brochures outlining a walking tour of Stony Brook's historic district are available in the shops at the Stony Brook Village Center on Main Street or by contacting the Ward Melville Heritage Organization, Box 572, Stony Brook, NY 11790; phone (631) 751-2244.

SAVE **DISCOVERY WETLANDS CRUISE,** departing from the waterfront dock on Shore Rd., offers a 90-minute pontoon boat cruise through the wetlands off the historic village of Stony Brook. Highlights include views of area cottages and estates, birds and waterfowl in addition to insights into the area's history, geology and ecology. Trips depart daily at high tide, May-Oct. Fare $18; under 12, $10. AX, MC, VI. Phone (631) 751-2244.

SAVE **THE LONG ISLAND MUSEUM OF AMERICAN ART, HISTORY AND CARRIAGES,** Main St. and SR 25A, is a 9-acre complex with exhibits of 19th- and 20th-century American art and history. In addition to museums and historic buildings, the complex also encompasses gardens and a family burial ground dating from 1796.

Allow 2 hours, 30 minutes minimum. Tues.-Sat. and Mon. holidays 10-5, Sun. noon-5. Closed Jan. 1, Thanksgiving and Dec. 24-25. Admission $5; over 60, $4; students with ID and ages 6-17, $3; free to college students with ID Wed. Admission Mon. holidays $1. Phone (631) 751-0066.

Art Museum presents changing exhibits of works by 19th- and 20th-century American artists.

Carriage Museum has eight galleries displaying approximately 90 horse-drawn wagons and sleighs, including European royal coaches, firefighting equipment and gypsy wagons.

History Museum, in a renovated lumber mill, has the Antique Decoy and Miniature Room galleries, and changing exhibits about American history.

Historic Buildings include the blacksmith shop, one-room schoolhouse, a 1794 barn and an 1867 carriage shed.

STONY BROOK GRIST MILL, on Harbor Rd. off Main St., is a working 1751 grist mill. A rare example of Dutch framing, the site is run by a miller as it was in the 18th and 19th centuries. Allow 30 minutes minimum. Wed.-Sun. noon-4:30; June-Aug.; Sat.-Sun. noon-4:30, Apr.-May and Sept.-Dec. Admission $2; under 12, $1. Phone (631) 751-2244.

STONY POINT—see New York p. 153.

SYRACUSE (E-7) pop. 147,306, elev. 522′

The growth of Syracuse as a prominent city is due to its geographic location and geologic wealth. In 1570 the Onondagas Indian chief Hiawatha chose the site as the location of the capital of the Iroquois Confederacy. The Jesuits founded a mission and fort called Fort Ste. Marie de Gannentaha in the area in 1656. Indian hostility caused the fort to be abandoned after 2 years.

Salt first brought the Indians and the French to the shores of Onondaga Lake; the first Anglo-American settlers came to boil the brine in 1788. The city of Syracuse was founded in 1805 and for many years supplied the bulk of the salt used in America.

Syracuse's American Indian population is concentrated south of the city in Nedrow at the Onondaga Indian Reservation, which is the seat of the Iroquois Confederacy.

Syracuse University, founded in 1870, occupies a 640-acre campus; its most outstanding feature is the Carrier Dome.

Greater Syracuse Chamber of Commerce: 572 S. Salina St., Syracuse, NY 13202; phone (315) 470-1800.

Self-guiding tours: Brochures detailing a walking tour of the downtown area are available from the Syracuse Heritage Area Visitor Center at the Erie Canal Museum *(see attraction listing).* Interpretive signs are located throughout the downtown area, describing the history of the city and the people who built it.

Shopping areas: Downtown Syracuse offers the historic Armory Square District with quaint shops and restaurants. Carousel Center, off I-81 exit 23, features more than 170 stores and shops including JCPenney, Kaufmann's and Lord & Taylor as well as cinemas and restaurants.

Three major shopping malls serve Syracuse's outlying suburbs. Fayetteville Mall, at the intersection of SR 5, E. Genesee and N. Burdick streets in Fayetteville, features Royal Discount Books, The Avenue Plus and T.J. Maxx as well as a merry-go-round and a food court. Great Northern Mall, at the intersection of SRs 481 and 31, has The Bon-Ton, Dick's Clothing and Sporting Goods, Kaufmann's, Sears, specialty shops, cinemas and a food court. Shoppingtown Mall, on E. Erie Boulevard in De Witt, has more than 100 stores including The Bon-Ton, JC Penney, Kaufmann's and Sears.

ERIE CANAL MUSEUM, 318 Erie Blvd. E., is in the 1850 Syracuse Weighlock Building. Designed to weigh 100-foot-long canal boats, this is reputedly the only surviving structure of its kind in the country. The museum features a full-size canal boat replica, exhibits detailing canal construction and early canal life, a penny-postcard arcade, changing exhibits and the Syracuse Heritage Area Visitor Center *(see Self-guiding tours).* Flash photography is not permitted. Allow 1 hour minimum. Tues.-Sat. 10-5, Sun. 10-3; closed major holidays. Donations. Phone (315) 471-0593.

EVERSON MUSEUM OF ART, 401 Harrison St., displays American paintings and sculpture from Colonial times to the present, and a large ceramics collection. The museum also displays changing exhibits. Food is available. Tues.-Fri. and Sun. noon-5, Sat. 10-5. Donations. Phone (315) 474-6064.

MID-LAKES NAVIGATION CO. LTD. cruises depart from Dutchman's Landing, 3 mi. w. of Liverpool; take I-90 to exit 38 (SR 57N) to John Glen Blvd., w. to SR 370, then w. on River Road to Hillside Rd. All-day Erie Canal cruises aboard the *City of Syracuse* offer good views of the city along the tree-lined Onondaga Lake portion of the canal. Jazz, brunch, lunch, dinner and sightseeing cruises are available.

Dinner cruises depart daily at 6. All-day cruise $38. Two-hour cruise $13. One-hour cruise $8. Reservations are required. AX, MC, VI. Phone (315) 685-8500 or (800) 545-4318.

MILTON J. RUBENSTEIN MUSEUM OF SCIENCE AND TECHNOLOGY, Franklin St. at W. Jefferson St., is a hands-on science museum with exhibits that explain scientific and technological phenomena. Displays address topics such as animals, chemistry, color, computers, gravity, light, sound and the stars. Demonstrations are offered. The Bristol Omnitheater offers showings on a six-story IMAX domed screen.

Museum open Tues.-Sun. 11-5. The Silverman Planetarium offers sky shows Mon.-Fri. at 2:15 and 4:15, Sat.-Sun. at 2:15. Shows for under age 5 are held Sat.-Sun. at 12:15. Phone for Omnitheater schedule. Museum admission $5; over 61 and ages 2-11, $4. Planetarium shows $1. Museum and Omnitheater $9.75; over 61 and under 12, $7.75. DS, MC, VI. Phone (315) 425-9068.

ONONDAGA HISTORICAL ASSOCIATION MUSEUM, 321 Montgomery St., features a permanent collection of items, paintings, photographs and memorabilia documenting 300 years of Onondaga history. The museum also has changing exhibits. Allow 1 hour minimum. Wed.-Sun. noon-4; closed holidays. Donations. Phone (315) 428-1864.

ONONDAGA LAKE PARK, off I-81 Liverpool exit 24, then 1.5 mi. w. on SR 370W to Ononadaga Pkwy., extends 6 mi. along the eastern shore. The park has a marina, a boat launch and athletic fields as well as the original Salt Spring and the Jesuit Well. Tram rides and inline skate and bicycle rentals are available mid-May through Columbus Day. The park's Salt Museum contains a replica of a 19th-century salt boiling block and other artifacts.

Picnicking is permitted. Food is available. Park open daily dawn-dusk. Museum open daily 11-4, May 1-Columbus Day. Free. Phone (315) 453-6712 or (315) 451-7275.

SAVE **ROSAMOND GIFFORD ZOO AT BURNET PARK** is off I-90 exit 36, then take I-81 s. to exit 22; from the e. take I-690 exit 10, following signs; from the w., take I-690 exit 8, following signs. The zoo displays domestic and exotic animals in simulated natural settings. Elephants are exhibited daily (weather permitting) and there is a Siberian tiger exhibit. The veterinary clinic and kitchen can be viewed through windows.

Allow 2 hours minimum. Daily 10-4:30; closed Jan. 1, Thanksgiving and Dec. 25. Admission $6; over 62 and students with ID, $4; ages 3-15, $3.50. Phone (315) 435-8511.

TAPPAN—*see New York p. 153.*

TARRYTOWN—*see New York p. 153.*

THOUSAND ISLANDS (B-7)

A French explorer called this region "Thousand Islands," although the islands number more than 1,700. Some of these islands in the St. Lawrence River are mere points of rocks and others are village size, but most can accommodate only a home or summer camp. Numerous stone castles and summer homes dot the islands, and many historical markers commemorate the arrival of the Loyalists to British North America.

The best way to see the islands is to take a boat tour offered by the boat lines described under Alexandria Bay and Clayton *(see place listings pp. 60 and 78)*. Between the spans of the Thousand Islands Bridge is the 1000 Islands Skydeck *(see Alexandria Bay p. 60)*.

The Thousand Islands embrace the St. Lawrence Islands National Park, which consists of 21 widely scattered units in the St. Lawrence River between Kingston and Brockville, Ontario, and a 96-acre (39-hectare) area at Mallorytown Landing on the mainland. Mallorytown Landing contains the park headquarters, picnic areas, a children's play area and a beach. A visitor center has displays about the

natural and cultural history and settlement of the Thousand Islands region.

Access to the park by private vehicle is available only at the Mallorytown Landing entrance. Day use facilities are open Victoria Day weekend through the second Monday in October. For additional information write the Superintendent's Office, St. Lawrence Islands National Park, 2 CR 5, RR 3, Mallorytown, ON, Canada K0E 1R0; phone (613) 923-5261

TICONDEROGA (C-11) pop. 5,167, elev. 277′

 **FORT TICONDEROGA**— *see place listing p. 88.*

TICONDEROGA HISTORICAL SOCIETY LIBRARY AND MUSEUM, 6 Moses Cir. at Montcalm St., is in a reproduction of John Hancock's Boston home. Displays include original and reproduction American furniture, Redford glass and historic town memorabilia. Facing the house is the bronze Liberty Monument by Charles Keck. Wed.-Sat. 10-4. Donations. Phone (518) 585-7868.

TROY (E-11) pop. 49,170, elev. 35′

Troy, an industrial city at the head of Hudson River navigation, was home to the man who inspired the national symbol of Uncle Sam. In the early 1800s meatpacker Sam Wilson's "U.S. Beef" meat stamp was jokingly interpreted as "Uncle Sam's Beef." Life became legend, and the character of Uncle Sam was born.

Troy's Rensselaer Polytechnic Institute is one of the nation's foremost technological institutions of higher learning and one of the oldest engineering schools in the English-speaking world. The school owns and operates Rensselaer Technology Park, the site of a growing number of Troy's high-tech companies.

Troy and neighboring communities form the Hudson-Mohawk Urban Cultural Park, which preserves the historical features at the confluence of the Hudson and Mohawk rivers. Included in the park are waterfalls, 19th-century mill districts and workers' houses, river fronts, canals, warehouses, music halls, churches and merchants' mansions. A 26-mile heritage trail links the park's various features, and 2nd Street offers many fine examples of 19th-century architecture.

An audiovisual program, exhibits and computerized area information kiosks are available Tuesday through Saturday at the RiverSpark Visitor Center, 251 River St., Troy, NY 12180; phone (518) 270-8667.

Rensselaer County Regional Chamber of Commerce: 31 2nd St., Troy, NY 12180; phone (518) 274-7020.

Self-guiding tours: A brochure detailing a self-guiding tour of the Hudson-Mohawk Urban Cultural Park and a brochure detailing a self-guiding walking tour through downtown historic districts and neighborhoods can be obtained at the River-Spark Visitor Center.

SAVE **HART-CLUETT MANSION,** 57 Second St., was built in 1827. The Federal-style mansion contains original and period furnishings, many of which were made locally. The adjoining Carr Building houses changing exhibits and a research library with historical information about Rensselaer County. A restored carriage house features transportation exhibits.

Guided tours are available. Allow 1 hour minimum. Carr Building Tues.-Sat. noon-5 (also Thurs. 5-8), Feb.-Dec. Mansion tours are given Thurs.-Sat. at 11. Research library Tues.-Fri. noon-5. Closed holidays and Christmas week. Admission $4; senior citizens and ages 12-18, $3. Mansion tour $2. Phone (518) 272-7232.

JUNIOR MUSEUM is at 105 Eighth St. This hands-on children's museum has exhibits relating to science, history and the arts. Planetarium and animal shows are offered daily. Allow 1 hour minimum. Wed.-Sun. 10-4, June-Aug.; Fri-Sun. 10-4, Wed.-Thurs. 10-2, rest of year. Closed major holidays. Admission $5, under 3 free. Phone (518) 235-2120, ext. 207, to verify prices.

UNCLE SAM TABLET, in Oakwood Cemetery, marks the grave of Samuel Wilson, the original "Uncle Sam." He was an Army beef contractor in the War of 1812; his trademark and caricature eventually became a national symbol. Daily 9-4:30. Free. Phone (518) 272-7520.

TUPPER LAKE (B-9) pop. 3,935, elev. 1,556'

Tupper Lake, which began as a lumber and sawmill village in the 1890s, is a resort in the Adirondacks. As the logging industry diminished, the town shifted its commercial interests to its other natural resources.

Fishing, swimming and boating opportunities abound at Tupper Lake, Lake Simond, Raquette River and Raquette Pond, easily reached from Tupper Lake.

The resort also boasts a municipal park with a beach, campground, tennis courts, 18-hole golf course and boat-launching sites. The nearby mountains are suited to skiing, climbing and hiking. Other recreation areas can be found in Adirondack Park (see Recreation Chart and the AAA Northeastern CampBook).

Tupper Lake Chamber of Commerce: 60 Park St., Tupper Lake, NY 12986; phone (518) 359-3328 or (888) 887-5253.

UPPER DELAWARE SCENIC AND RECREATIONAL RIVER

The Upper Delaware Scenic and Recreational River comprises 73 miles of the Upper Delaware River from just north of Port Jervis, Pa., to Hancock. Along this stretch the river changes from long, placid eddies to swift water and challenging rapids. It is paralleled on the New York side by SR 97, which has several scenic overlooks.

Almost all land along the river is privately owned; public river access areas are located on both the Pennsylvania and New York shores. Private campgrounds and canoe liveries are available near the river.

The Upper Delaware was an important transportation route for American Indians and early settlers. In 1828 the Delaware and Hudson Canal opened, bringing coal-laden boats from the Pennsylvania interior to the port of New York. However, problems soon developed at the point where the canal crossed the river: Slow-moving boats being towed across the river were constantly colliding with the huge log and timber rafts that were coursing down the river to sawmills and shipyards in Trenton, N.J., and Philadelphia. To solve the problem the canal company approved a plan to "build the canal above the water."

John Roebling, who later designed the Brooklyn Bridge, built the Delaware Aqueduct. The aqueduct is considered to be the oldest wire suspension bridge in America. The adjacent tollhouse contains exhibits interpreting the history of the Delaware and Hudson Canal, John Roebling and the Delaware Aqueduct. It is open Saturdays and Sundays, Memorial Day to mid-October.

Area wildlife includes bears, white-tail deer, beavers, otters, muskrats, minks, squirrels and rabbits. Birds include bald eagles, ospreys, great egrets, great blue herons, turkey vultures, Canada geese and several varieties of hawks and ducks.

Recreational opportunities include rafting, canoeing, boating and fishing. National Park Service programs are offered in the summer. Included are cultural and natural history walks, canoeing demonstrations and guided canoe tours

Information stations are located at the public boating access sites in Ten Mile River and at Skinner's Falls, as well as in Lackawaxen, Pa. An information center on Main Street in Narrowsburg (see place listing p. 104) generally is open Sat.-Sun. 9:30-4:30, Memorial Day weekend to mid-Oct. Phone (845) 252-3947 or (570) 729-7134.

UTICA (E-8) pop. 60,651, elev. 452'

Built on land granted to William Crosby in 1734, Utica was the site of Old Fort Schuyler, erected in 1758. Sparsely settled for many years, Utica did not begin to develop until after the Revolution; its real growth as a commercial and industrial center dates from the completion of the Erie Canal in 1825.

Mohawk Valley Chamber of Commerce: 520 Seneca St., Utica, NY 13502; phone (315) 724-3151.

SAVE **THE CHILDREN'S MUSEUM** is at 311 Main St. Interactive exhibits inspire children to learn about varied topics, including space exploration, local history, archaeology, weather, transportation and technology. Allow 1 hour minimum. Tues.-Sat. 10-4:30, Sun. noon-4:30; closed Jan. 1, Easter,

Thanksgiving and Dec. 25. Admission $4, under 1 free. MC, VI. Phone (315) 724-6129.

SAVE **THE MATT BREWING CO.**, Court and Varick sts., demonstrates the process of beer manufacturing and offers trolley rides June through August to the 1888 Tavern, where samples are served. Allow 1 hour minimum. Guided tours are given on the hour Mon.-Sat. 1-4, June-Aug.; Fri.-Sat. at 1 and 3, rest of year. Closed major holidays. Tour $3; ages 6-12, $1. Reservations are recommended Sept.-May. Phone (315) 624-2434 or (800) 765-6288.

GEM **MUNSON-WILLIAMS-PROCTOR ARTS INSTITUTE**, 310 Genesee St., is a fine arts center with programs in the visual and performing arts and an art museum. The museum's collections include American art from the Colonial period to the present, with an emphasis on 19th- and 20th-century paintings and sculpture. Works by European artists are displayed, as are examples of graphic and decorative arts. Fountain Elms Museum, an 1850 Victorian house, adjoins the center. Allow 1 hour, 30 minutes minimum. Tues.-Sat. 10-5, Sun. 1-5. Free. Phone (315) 797-0000.

ONEIDA COUNTY HISTORICAL SOCIETY, 1608 Genesee St., has exhibits about Utica, Oneida County and Mohawk Valley history. A reference library also is available. Allow 1 hour minimum. Tues.-Fri. 10-4:30, Sat. 11-3. Exhibits free. Library $5 per day. Phone (315) 735-3642.

SAVE **UTICA ZOO**, 99 Steele Hill Rd., has more than 200 animals from around the world. Included are North American grizzly bears, Asian tigers, Australian emus and wallabies, and California sea lions. Sea lion demonstrations are held Wed.-Mon. at noon and 3. Food is available. Allow 1 hour, 30 minutes minimum. Daily 10-5; closed Jan. 1, Thanksgiving and Dec. 25. Admission $4.50; over 65, $4; ages 4-12, $2.75; free to all Nov.-Mar. Phone (315) 738-0472.

VAILS GATE (H-10) pop. 3,319

KNOX'S HEADQUARTERS STATE HISTORIC SITE is at jct. SR 94 and Forge Hill Rd. The Georgian-style home of prominent businessman John Ellison served as Maj. Gen. Henry Knox's military headquarters during the Revolutionary War and housed Maj. Gen. Horatio Gates during the last months of the war. The site includes the house, mill ruins, a garden and hiking trails. Exhibits explore Hudson Valley life during the 18th and 19th centuries. Allow 1 hour minimum. Mon.-Sat. 10-5, Sun. 1-5, Memorial Day-Labor Day. Admission $3; over 65, $2; ages 5-12, $1. Phone (845) 561-5498.

NEW WINDSOR CANTONMENT STATE HISTORIC SITE, 1 mi. s. of I-84 on Temple Hill Rd. (SR 300), is the site of the last winter encampment of Gen. George Washington's Continental Army. Costumed interpreters demonstrate 18th-century military life, including musket and artillery drills, woodworking and blacksmithing. A visitor center

has exhibits about the Revolutionary War in the Hudson Highlands and on the cantonment. Picnicking is permitted. Wed.-Sat. and Mon. 10-5, Sun. 11-5, Apr. 15-Oct. 31. Admission $4; over 61, $3; ages 5-12, $1. Phone (845) 561-1765.

VERONA (E-8) pop. 6,425

CASINOS

• **Turning Stone Casino** is .5 mi s. on I-90 exit 33 at 5218 Patrick Rd. Daily 24 hours. Phone (315) 361-7711.

VICTOR (E-5) pop. 2,433

GANONDAGAN STATE HISTORIC SITE is w. on CR 41 (Boughton Hill Rd.) to SR 444. On the site of a 17th-century Seneca village are interpretive trails, a bark longhouse and a visitor center with displays and a half-hour videotape. An exhibit by Seneca artist Carson Waterman focuses on the Iroquois clan system. Allow 1 hour minimum. Trails open daily 8 a.m.-dusk (weather permitting). Visitor center open Tues.-Sun. 9-5, May 15-Oct. 31. Longhouse open Tues.-Sun. 10-4. Admission $2, senior citizens and students with ID $1. Phone (585) 924-5848.

WASHINGTONVILLE (H-10)
pop. 5,851, elev. 310'

WINERIES

• **Brotherhood Winery** (America's Oldest Winery), 2 blks. e. on SR 94 to 100 Brotherhood Plaza Dr. Daily 11-5, May-Dec.; Sat.-Sun. 11-5, rest of year. Closed Jan. 1, Thanksgiving and Dec. 25. Hours may vary; phone ahead to verify schedule. Phone (845) 496-3661.

WATERTOWN (C-7) pop. 26,705, elev. 454'

During an 1878 county fair F.W. Woolworth tested the idea of selling a fixed-price line of merchandise in a department store. The result of his experiment was the Woolworth store chain. Watertown also is noted as the home of Fort Drum.

Greater Watertown North Country Chamber of Commerce: 230 Franklin St., Watertown, NY 13601; phone (315) 788-4400.

JEFFERSON COUNTY HISTORICAL SOCIETY, 228 Washington St. in the 1878 Paddock Mansion, contains high-Victorian furnishings and decorative art, American Indian artifacts from Jefferson County, historic water turbines, Civil War memorabilia, coverlets and special exhibits. A re-created Victorian garden and a carriage barn with antique automobiles and farm implements also are on the premises. Guided tours area available by appointment. Allow 30 minutes minimum. Tues.-Fri. 10-5, Sat. noon-5, May-Nov.; Tues.-Fri. noon-5, rest of year. Closed major holidays. Donations. Phone (315) 782-3491.

THE SCI-TECH CENTER OF NORTHERN NEW YORK, 154 Stone St., is a hands-on science museum. Exhibits focus on light, sound and electricity. Guided tours are available by appointment. Allow 1 hour minimum. Tues.-Sat. 10-4; closed Jan. 1, July 4, Thanksgiving and Dec. 25. Admission $3; ages 3-18, $2; over 54, $1.50; family rate $10. Phone (315) 788-1340.

THOMPSON PARK, just e. off SR 12, has playground, swimming and tennis facilities. A 35-acre zoo featuring North American species also is featured. Picnicking is permitted. Daily 10-5; closed Thanksgiving and Dec. 25. Park free. Zoo $5; senior citizens, students with ID and ages 4-12, $3. MC, VI. Phone (315) 785-7775.

RECREATIONAL ACTIVITIES

White-water Rafting

- SAVE **ARO Adventures**, departing from various locations. Write P.O. Box 649, Old Forge, NY 13420. Trips depart Wed.-Mon. in Aug. and Wed.-Sun. in July; weekend trips are available May-June and Sept.-Oct. Phone (315) 369-3536 for reservations or (800) 525-7238 for information.

- **Hudson River Rafting Co.**, e. off I-81 exit 46, 1.5 mi. e. to Whitewater Way. Write P.O. Box 47, Watertown, NY 13801. Trips depart Mon.-Fri. at 11, Sat.-Sun. at 10 and 1, in Aug.; Tues.-Fri. at 11, Sat.-Sun. at 10 and 1, in July; Fri.-Sun. at 11, in June; Fri. and Sun. at 11, Sat. at 10 and 1, Sept. 7-Oct. 13. Phone (315) 782-7881 or (800) 888-7238.

WATERVLIET (E-11) pop. 10,207, elev. 50′

WATERVLIET ARSENAL MUSEUM, off I-787 exit 8, then 1 mi. s. on Broadway (SR 32), is the nation's oldest continuously active arsenal. Built in 1813, the arsenal is owned by the government and continues to produce large-caliber weapons. Housed in the 1859 cast-iron storehouse, the museum chronicles the history of big guns and displays cannon and other military equipment from the 16th century through the present. A restored 1900s machine shop demonstrates early artillery production. Sun.-Thurs. 10-3; closed holidays. A photo ID is required for admittance. Donations. Phone (518) 266-5805

WATKINS GLEN (F-6)
pop. 2,149, elev. 1,008′

At the southern tip of Seneca Lake, Watkins Glen is renowned for its summer auto racing at Watkins Glen International. Long before the roar of cars, this small town's most notable features were the nearby salt wells, which made this region one of the state's major salt producers. *Also see Finger Lakes p. 86.*

Several wineries can be found on either side of Seneca Lake, off SRs 14 and 414.

Schuyler County Chamber of Commerce: 100 N. Franklin St., Watkins Glen, NY 14891; phone (607) 535-4300.

CAPTAIN BILL'S SENECA LAKE CRUISES depart from the foot of Franklin St. Scenic 10-mile trips are offered; lunch, dinner and other cruises also are available. Sightseeing departures daily on the hour 10-8, July 1-early Sept.; daily on the hour 11-4, early Sept.-Oct. 15; Mon.-Fri. on the hour 11-4, Sat.-Sun. and holidays on the hour 10-8, May 15-June 30. Sightseeing fare $8.50; under 13, $4. AX, DS, MC, VI. Phone (607) 535-4541 or (607) 535-4680.

FARM SANCTUARY is at 3100 Aikens Rd.; take CR 409W (4th St.) 1.5 mi. to SR 23, then w. 8 mi. to Aikens Rd., following signs. This 175-acre working farm is home to hundreds of cows, pigs, turkeys and goats rescued from slaughterhouses and stockyards and nursed back to health. One-hour guided tours encourage visitors to pet the animals. Videotapes and photographs promote responsibility towards animals.

Tours on the hour Wed.-Sun. 11-3, June-Aug.; Sat-Sun. 11-3, in May and Sept.-Oct. Tour $2; ages 4-12, $1. Phone (607) 583-2225.

INTERNATIONAL MOTOR RACING RESEARCH CENTER AND MUSEUM is at 610 S. Decatur St. Films, photographs, memorabilia and ephemera document the history of motorsports. The collection includes fine art and rare posters depicting racing topics. A research library and archives are available. Allow 1 hour minimum. Mon.-Sat. 9-5; closed Jan. 1, Thanksgiving and Dec. 25. Free. Phone (607) 535-9044.

GEM **WATKINS GLEN STATE PARK** adjoins the village at the s. end of Seneca Lake. The scenic glen, which drops about 400 feet in 2 miles, is highlighted by rock formations and 19 waterfalls; Rainbow Falls is especially lovely. Cliffs rise 300 feet above the stream; a bridge 165 feet above the water spans the glen.

Buses to the head of the glen run every 15 minutes for those who wish to avoid climbing the 832 steps. The park offers a weekly schedule of guided tours and nature programs.

Allow 1 hour, 30 minutes minimum. Park open daily 8 a.m.-dusk. Gorge trail open daily 8 a.m.-dusk, mid-May through Nov. 10. Buses depart daily 9-6, late June-Labor Day; Sat.-Sun. 9-5, day after Labor Day-Columbus Day. Park admission free. Parking $7, mid-June through Labor Day; $6, rest of season. Bus fare $2.50. Phone (607) 535-4511. *See Recreation Chart and the AAA Northeastern CampBook.*

WINERIES

- **Chateau Lafayette Reneau**, 7 mi. n. on SR 414. Mon.-Sat. 10-6, Sun. 11-6, Apr.-Oct.; Mon.-Sat. 10-5, Sun. 11-5, rest of year. Phone (607) 546-2062.

WESTFIELD (F-2) pop. 3,481, elev. 728′

Those who like to walk will find plenty of room in which to travel in Westfield. The Chautauqua

Gorge extends 7 miles along a 100-foot-deep gorge between Westfield and Mayville. Barcelona Harbor offers fishing and a boat launch. It is the site of a historical lighthouse. Westfield is part of Chautauqua wine country, and several small wineries west of the city off US 20 offer wine tastings and guided tours in season.

Shopping areas: The Westfield streets are lined with various antiques shops, including Landmark Acres and Priscilla Nixon Antiques on W. Main Rd.; Militello Antiques at 31 Jefferson St.; and Antique Marketplace, Eley Place, Monroe's Mini Mall, Saraf's Emporium and W.B. Mollard Antiques, all on E. Main St.

THE McCLURG MANSION, jct. US 20 and US 394, was built in 1820 and contains period furniture, a pioneer kitchen, Colonial farm implements, American Indian artifacts and a military exhibit. Tues.-Sat. 10-4; closed most holidays. Hours may vary; phone ahead. Admission $1.50; over 59 and students with ID $1; under 12, 50c. Phone (716) 326-2977.

WINERIES

- **Johnson Estate Winery** is 2 mi. w. on US 20 (E. Main Rd.) Guided tours daily on the half-hour 10-5, July-Aug. Phone (716) 326-2191 or (800) 374-6569.
- **Vetter Vineyards** is 3 mi. e. to Prospect Rd., then right .5 mi. to US 20 (E. Main Rd.). Tastings daily 11-5. Phone (716) 326-3100.

WEST HAVERSTRAW—*see New York p. 154.*

WEST POINT (H-10) pop. 7,138, elev. 10′

BEAR MOUNTAIN STATE PARK is 5 mi. s. off US 9W. The George W. Perkins Memorial Drive winds to the 1,305-foot summit of Bear Mountain, where a tower and observation deck provide views of four states and the Hudson River Valley. Picnicking is permitted. Food is available. Park open daily dawn-dusk. Drive open daily 8-dusk (weather permitting), Apr.-Nov. Tower daily 9-4. Park admission free. Parking $5 Sat.-Sun. in winter. Phone (845) 786-2701. *See Recreation Chart.*

Trailside Museum and Zoo is s. on US 9W near the park entrance. A nature trail leads to animal enclosures, museums, trail-side exhibits, the outer breastworks of Fort Clinton and a statue of Walt Whitman. The museums feature animal habitat displays as well as geological, historical and natural exhibits. Allow 3 hours minimum. Daily 9-5:30, Memorial Day-Labor Day; 9-4:30, rest of year (weather permitting). Admission daily May 1-Labor Day, Sat.-Sun. and holidays rest of year, $1, children 50c; otherwise free.

UNITED STATES MILITARY ACADEMY is on the w. bank of the Hudson River off scenic Old Storm King Hwy. (SR 218); the academy also can be reached from US 9W. A visitor center just outside Thayer Gate (South Post) offers orientation films, exhibits, a replica of a cadet

barracks room, and maps and brochures while serving as the departure point for narrated, 1-hour bus tours of the campus. The academy grounds and buildings are not open to the public.

Tour highlights include Cadet Chapel, which features stained-glass windows and one of the largest church organs in the world, and Trophy Point, a repository of war relics dating from the American Revolution.

Visitor center daily 9-4:45; closed Jan. 1, Thanksgiving and Dec. 25. One-hour bus tours depart Mon.-Sat. 10-3:30, Sun. 11:15-3:30, Apr.-Oct.; daily at 11:15 and 1:15, rest of year. Extended tours are available daily May-Oct. No tours are given on home football Saturdays and during graduation week. Visitor center free. One-hour bus tour $7; under 12, $4. Reservations are recommended and a photo ID is required for tours. Phone (845) 938-2638 for the visitor center or (845) 446-4724 for bus tour information. *See color ad p. 202.*

West Point Museum is in Olmsted Hall at Pershing Center. West Point was declared the permanent depository of war trophies by Executive Order after the 1846-48 Mexican War. Exhibits chronicle the garrisoning of West Point and the subsequent establishment of the United States Military Academy in 1802. Military warfare from antiquity to modern times is surveyed through displays of hand-held weapons, heavy artillery and battle dioramas. Allow 1 hour minimum. Daily 10:30-4:15; closed Jan. 1, Thanksgiving and Dec. 25. Free. Phone (845) 938-2203.

WEST SAYVILLE (I-4) pop. 5,003, elev. 28'

LONG ISLAND MARITIME MUSEUM, e. on Montauk Hwy. on the grounds of the West Sayville Golf Course at 86 West Ave., displays ships models, paintings and artifacts. Allow 1 hour minimum. Mon.-Sat. 10-4, Sun. noon-4; closed Jan. 1, Easter, Election Day, Thanksgiving and Dec. 25. Donations. Phone (631) 854-4974.

WHITEHALL (D-11) pop. 2,667, elev. 123'

Settled by Capt. Philip Skene and about 30 other British families in 1759, Whitehall was originally named Skenesborough in the captain's honor. After the Revolutionary War, during which Skene supported the British, the town changed its name.

Whitehall Chamber of Commerce: 259 Broadway, Whitehall, NY 12887; phone (518) 499-2292.

Self-guiding tours: Historic buildings dating from 1824 are in a downtown area bounded by Broadway, Williams, Saunders and Clinton streets. A brochure detailing self-guiding walking and driving tours of Whitehall's historic areas is available at the Skenesborough Museum.

CARILLON CRUISES, departing from the dock at Skenesborough Museum, just n. of US 4 on SR 22, provides trips through Champlain Canal Lock 12 to Lake Champlain. A historical narrative about the Revolutionary War and the War of 1812 complements the tour. Sights include Fiddlers Elbow, Putts Rock, Galick Farm and South Bay. Allow 1 hour, 30 minutes minimum. Cruises depart Sun.-Tues. at 1, July-Aug. Additional cruises are available with a minimum of 15 passengers. Fare $9; senior citizens $8.50; ages 3-12, $4.50. Phone (802) 897-5331.

SKENESBOROUGH MUSEUM, just n. of US 4 on SR 22 in the center of town, includes a Navy room with models of 1776 and 1812 shipyards and ships models, a doll room, a military room and local historical artifacts. Mon.-Sat. 10-4, Sun. noon-4, mid-June through Labor Day; Sat. 10-3, Sun. noon-3, day after Labor Day to mid-Oct. Admission $2, senior citizens $1, students with ID 50c, family rate $5. Phone (518) 499-0716.

WHITE PLAINS—*see New York p. 154.*

WILLIAMSVILLE—*see Buffalo p. 74.*

WILMINGTON (B-10) pop. 1,131, elev. 1,019'

With the Ausable River and Whiteface Mountain nearby, the village of Wilmington offers scenic diversions as well as many opportunities for summer and winter recreation.

Whiteface Mountain Regional Visitors Bureau: P.O. Box 277, Wilmington, NY 12997; phone (518) 946-2255 or (888) 944-8332.

HIGH FALLS GORGE, 4.5 mi. s.w. on SR 86, is a deep ravine cut into the base of Whiteface Mountain by the Ausable River. A colorful variety of strata, rapids, falls and potholes can be seen from a network of well-constructed bridges and paths. The center of the gorge can be reached without climbing stairs. The main building features mineral displays.

Picnicking is permitted. Food is available. Allow 1 hour minimum. Daily 9-5:30, July-Aug.; 9-5, May-June and Sept.-Oct. Hours vary Nov.-Mar. Last admission is 30 minutes before closing. Downhill ski, snowboard and snowshoe rentals are available in winter; phone ahead for trail hours and rates. Admission $9.95; ages 4-12, $5.95. DS, MC, VI. Phone (518) 946-2278 to verify schedule and prices.

SANTA'S WORKSHOP, 1.5 mi. w. on SR 431 at North Pole, has Santa Claus, live reindeer, craft shops, live entertainment, children's rides and storybook characters. Rides are available late June through August and on fall weekends.

Allow 3 hours, 30 minutes minimum. Sat.-Wed. 9:30-4:30, June 1-Labor Day; Sat.-Sun. and Columbus Day 9:30-4, day after Labor Day to mid-Oct.; Sat.-Sun. 10-3:30, late Nov.-late Dec. Admission $15.95; ages 2-16, $12.95. DS, MC, VI. Phone (518) 946-2211 or (518) 946-2212 to verify schedule and prices.

WHITEFACE MOUNTAIN VETERANS' MEMORIAL HIGHWAY, 3.5 mi. w. via SR 431, is a 6-mile macadam road leading to a parking area near the summit of Whiteface Mountain. The 4,867-foot summit is reached by a .2-mile hiking trail or by an unusual electric elevator set in the cone of the peak. Wear proper footwear and warm clothing. On a clear day the summit house affords a view across more than 100 miles, including the St. Lawrence River and lakes Champlain and Placid.`

Allow 1 hour minimum. Daily 9-6, late June-Labor Day; 9-4, mid-May to late June and day after Labor Day to mid-Oct. (weather permitting). Admission per private vehicle (including driver) $8, each passenger $4; motorcycle (including driver) $5, passenger $4. Maximum private vehicle rate $25. Phone (518) 523-1655 or (518) 946-2223, ext. 319.

RECREATIONAL ACTIVITIES
Skiing
- **Whiteface Mountain Ski Center**, 3 mi. s. on SR 86. Write P.O. Box 1980, Wilmington, NY 12997. Other activities are offered. Lifts operate daily 8:30-4, mid-Nov. to mid-Apr. (weather permitting). Phone (518) 946-2223.

WILTON (D-10) pop. 12,511

GRANT COTTAGE STATE HISTORIC SITE is on the grounds of the Mount McGregor Correctional Facility; take exit 16 off I-87 and follow signs. This summer cottage is where Gen. Ulysses S. Grant spent his last days and completed his memoirs in 1885. The cottage has been left largely as it was the day he died. Wed.-Sun. 10-4, Memorial Day-Labor Day; Sat.-Sun. 10-4, day after Labor Day-second weekend in Oct. Admission $2.50; over 59, $2; ages 5-16, $1. Phone (518) 587-8277.

WINDHAM (F-10) pop. 359

RECREATIONAL ACTIVITIES
Skiing
- **Windham Mountain**, off SR 23W following signs. Write P.O. Box 459, Windham, NY 12496. Other activities are offered. Mon.-Fri. 9-4 (also Thurs.-Fri. 4-10 p.m.), Sat. 8-10, Sun. 8-4, Nov.-Mar. Phone (518) 734-4300.

YONKERS—*see New York p. 155.*

YOUNGSTOWN—*see Niagara Falls p. 167.*

AMERICA ON THE MOVE

A NEW EXHIBITION ON TRANSPORTATION IN AMERICAN HISTORY

1903 Winton, First Car to Cross the Country

National Museum of American History
14th and Constitution Ave. NW ◆ Washington, D.C.

Open Daily: 10 a.m. - 5:30 p.m. (Except December 25)

americanhistory.si.edu/onthemove

Free Admission

 Smithsonian
National Museum of American History
Behring Center

 AMERICA
ON THE MOVE

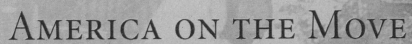

AMERICA ON THE MOVE
A NEW EXHIBITION ON TRANSPORTATION IN AMERICAN HISTORY

Smithsonian
National Museum of American History
Behring Center

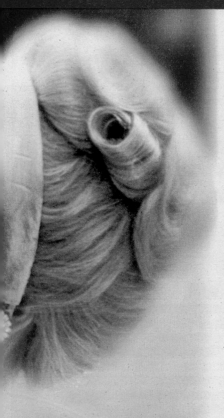

Because it's an enchanting time for a fairytale vacation.

Trust AAA Travel to take you there.

Storybook lands. Magical worlds. Fantastic voyages to paradise. Whatever your dream, there's a Disney vacation for you. And when you book select vacation packages through AAA Travel, you can enjoy exclusive AAA benefits and great values. Your fairytale is just a phone call away. Call or visit your AAA Travel office today.

Walt Disney World®

Disneyland®
RESORT
IN CALIFORNIA

Disney CRUISE LINE®

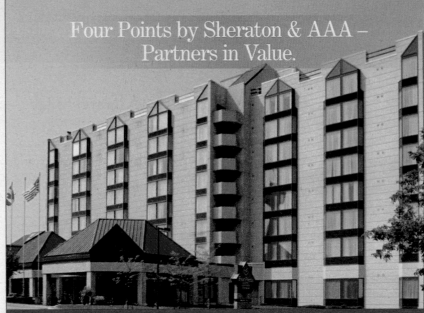

New York

New York Orientation
Map to destinations

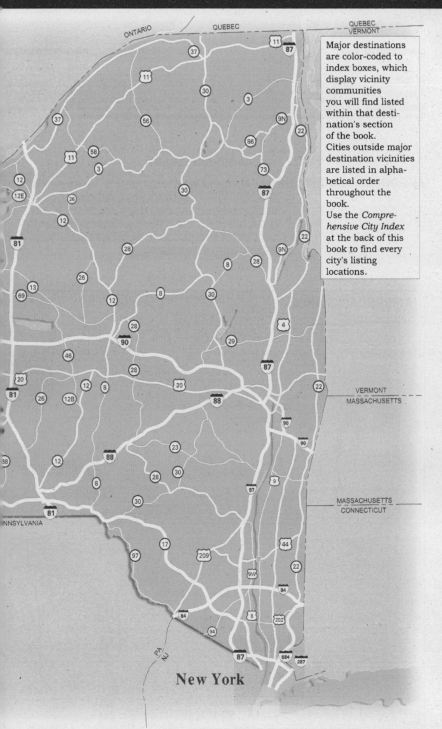

Major destinations are color-coded to index boxes, which display vicinity communities you will find listed within that destination's section of the book.
Cities outside major destination vicinities are listed in alphabetical order throughout the book.
Use the *Comprehensive City Index* at the back of this book to find every city's listing locations.

New York

ACRA

—— WHERE TO STAY ——

LANGE'S GROVE SIDE

(AAA) (SAVE)

Small-scale Hotel

11/16-4/30	1P: $60-$95	2P: $65-$95	XP: $20
6/27-9/1	1P: $50-$82	2P: $70-$82	XP: $10
5/1-6/26 & 9/2-11/15	1P: $40-$62	2P: $60-$82	XP: $10

Phone: (518)622-3393

Location: Jct SR 145, 3.3 mi w. 6047 SR 23 12405. Fax: 518/622-3393. **Facility:** 23 one-bedroom standard units. 1 story, exterior corridors. **Parking:** on-site. **Terms:** 2-3 night minimum stay - weekends, 3 day cancellation notice. **Dining:** 8:30 am-10 & 5:30-7 pm; closed 9/3-6/28, cocktails. **Pool(s):** heated outdoor. **Leisure Activities:** whirlpool, tennis court, recreation programs, ping pong, playground, shuffleboard. **Business Services:** fax (fee). **Cards:** AX, DC, MC, VI. **Special Amenities:** free continental breakfast and free local telephone calls.

Adirondacks Area

ADIRONDACK MOUNTAINS —See BOLTON LANDING, CHESTERTOWN, DIAMOND POINT, ELIZABETHTOWN, GLENS FALLS, INLET, KEESEVILLE, LAKE GEORGE, LAKE LUZERNE, LAKE PLACID, LONG LAKE, NORTH CREEK, OLD FORGE, QUEENSBURY, SARANAC LAKE, SCHROON LAKE, SPECULATOR, TICONDEROGA, TUPPER LAKE, WARRENSBURG & WILMINGTON.

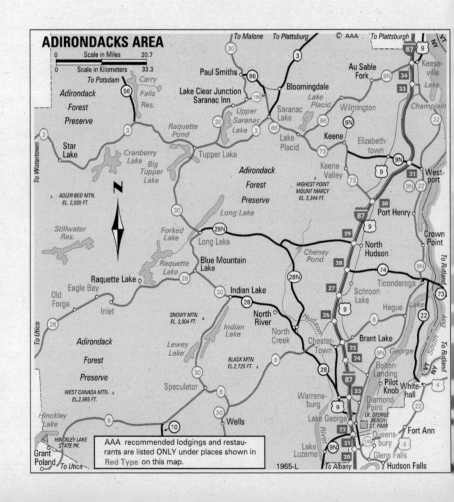

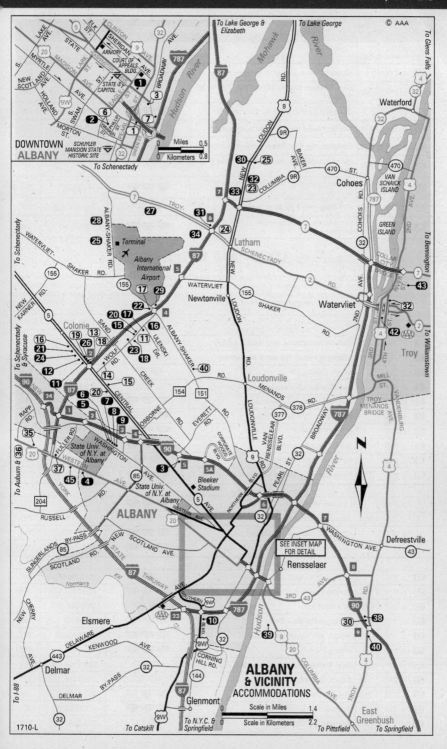

© AAA

DOWNTOWN ALBANY

To Lake George & Elizabeth

To Lake George

To Glens Falls

To Schenectady

To Schenectady

To Watervliet-

To Schenectady & Syracuse

To Auburn & 36

To I-88

To Catskill

To N.Y.C. & Springfield

To Pittsfield

To Springfield

To Williamstown

To Bennington

ALBANY & VICINITY ACCOMMODATIONS

Scale in Miles

Scale in Kilometers

1710-L

✈ Airport Accommodations

Spotter/Map Page Number	OA	ALBANY	Diamond Rating	Rate Range High Season	Listing Page
18 / p. 215		Albany Marriott, 2 mi se of terminal	♦♦♦	$184	266
20 / p. 215	AAA	**Best Western Albany Airport Inn, 2 mi se of terminal**	♦♦	$89-$159 SAVE	266
23 / p. 215		Courtyard by Marriott, 2 mi se of terminal	♦♦♦	$69-$239	266
22 / p. 215	AAA	**The Desmond Hotel, 1.5 mi e of terminal**	♦♦♦	$99-$169 SAVE	266
16 / p. 215	AAA	**Hampton Inn Wolf Road, 2 mi se of airport**	♦♦♦	$139-$169 SAVE	267
25 / p. 215	AAA	**Hilton Garden Inn-Albany Airport, just w of terminal**	♦♦♦	$99-$189 SAVE	267
17 / p. 215		Holiday Inn Turf on Wolf Road, 2 mi se of terminal	♦♦♦	$169-$209	267
15 / p. 215	AAA	**Red Roof Inn, 2 mi se of terminal**	♦♦	$88-$92 SAVE	267
28 / p. 215		Comfort Inn At Albany Airport, 0.5 mi w of terminal	♦♦♦	$99-$109	336

Albany and Vicinity

This index helps you "spot" where approved accommodations and restaurants are located on the corresponding detailed maps. Lodging rate ranges are for comparison only and show the property's high season; rates are per night, unless only weekly (W) rates are available. Restaurant rate range is for dinner, unless only lunch (L) is served. Turn to the listing page for more detailed rate information and consult display ads for special promotions.

Spotter/Map Page Number	OA	ALBANY - Lodgings	Diamond Rating	Rate Range High Season	Listing Page
1 / p. 215	AAA	**Crowne Plaza Hotel and Resort Albany**	♦♦♦	$99-$189 SAVE	220
2 / p. 215	AAA	**Albany Mansion Hill Inn & Restaurant**	♦♦♦	$145-$175 SAVE	219
3 / p. 215		Albany Quality Inn	♦♦	$79-$119	219
4 / p. 215	AAA	**Best Western Sovereign Hotel Albany**	♦♦♦	$89-$149 SAVE	219
5 / p. 215		The Albany Thruway Courtyard	♦♦♦	$114-$154	219
6 / p. 215		Fairfield Inn by Marriott-Albany	♦♦♦	$140-$180	220
7 / p. 215		CrestHill Suites	♦♦♦	$139-$289	219
8 / p. 215		TownePlace Suites-Albany	♦♦♦	$140-$180	220
9 / p. 215		Extended Stay America	♦♦	$369-$470	220
10 / p. 215	AAA	**Regency Inn & Suites** - see color ad p 218	♦♦♦	$79-$129 SAVE	220
		ALBANY - Restaurants			
1 / p. 215		La Serre Restaurant	♦♦♦	$14-$24	221
3 / p. 215	AAA	**Jack's Oyster House**	♦♦♦	$12-$20	221
6 / p. 215		Albany Mansion Hill Inn Restaurant	♦♦♦	$15-$24	221
7 / p. 215		Nicole's Bistro At Quackenbush House	♦♦♦	$17-$22	221
		COLONIE - Lodgings			
11 / p. 215		Ambassador Motor Inn	♦	Failed to provide	266
12 / p. 215	AAA	**Comfort Inn & Suites**	♦♦♦	$69-$350 SAVE	266
15 / p. 215	AAA	**Red Roof Inn**	♦♦	$88-$92 SAVE	267
16 / p. 215	AAA	**Hampton Inn Wolf Road**	♦♦♦	$139-$169 SAVE	267
17 / p. 215		Holiday Inn Turf on Wolf Road	♦♦♦	$169-$209	267
18 / p. 215		Albany Marriott	♦♦♦	$184	266
20 / p. 215	AAA	**Best Western Albany Airport Inn**	♦♦	$89-$159 SAVE	266
21 / p. 215	AAA	**Quality Inn-Albany Airport**	♦♦	$69-$199 SAVE	267
22 / p. 215	AAA	**The Desmond Hotel**	♦♦♦	$99-$169 SAVE	266
23 / p. 215		Courtyard by Marriott	♦♦♦	$69-$239	266
24 / p. 215	AAA	**Ramada Limited**	♦♦	$89-$140 SAVE	267

Spotter/Map Page Number	OA	COLONIE - Lodgings (continued)	Diamond Rating	Rate Range High Season	Listing Page
25 / p. 215	AAA	Hilton Garden Inn-Albany Airport - see color ad p 220	◆◆◆	$99-$189 SAVE	267
26 / p. 215		Albany Super 8 Motel	◆◆	$72-$85	266
		COLONIE - Restaurants			
11 / p. 215		Real Seafood Co	◆◆◆	$14-$28	268
13 / p. 215		Smokey Bones Barbecue & Grill Restaurant	◆◆	$8-$17	268
14 / p. 215		Bangkok Thai Restaurant	◆◆	$10-$17	267
15 / p. 215	AAA	Grandma's Country Restaurant	◆◆	$8-$15	268
16 / p. 215		Butcher Block Steak & Seafood Restaurant	◆◆	$13-$19	268
17 / p. 215		Scrimshaw	◆◆◆	$18-$30	268
18 / p. 215		Delmonico's Italian Steakhouse	◆◆	$18	268
19 / p. 215		Garcia's Mexican Restaurant	◆◆	$7-$14	268
20 / p. 215		Ralph's Tavern	◆	$5-$13	268
		LATHAM - Lodgings			
27 / p. 215		Residence Inn by Marriott Albany Airport	◆◆◆	$189-$209	337
28 / p. 215		Comfort Inn At Albany Airport	◆◆◆	$99-$109	336
29 / p. 215		Wingate Inn	◆◆◆	$150-$175	337
30 / p. 215	AAA	Century House Restaurant & Hotel	◆◆◆	$129-$225 SAVE	336
31 / p. 215		Clarion Inn & Suites	◆◆	$109-$239	336
32 / p. 215		Hampton Inn-Latham	◆◆◆	$134-$164	337
33 / p. 215	AAA	Holiday Inn Express-Airport	◆◆◆	$70-$130 SAVE	337
34 / p. 215	AAA	Microtel Inn	◆◆	$52-$119 SAVE	337
		LATHAM - Restaurants			
23 / p. 215		Kirker's Steak & Seafood	◆◆	$12-$22	337
24 / p. 215	AAA	Dakota	◆◆	$9-$18	337
25 / p. 215	AAA	Century House	◆◆	$16-$27	337
		EAST GREENBUSH - Lodgings			
38 / p. 215	AAA	Holiday Inn Express Hotel & Suites	◆◆◆	$116-$125 SAVE	280
39 / p. 215	AAA	Econo Lodge	◆◆	$59-$149 SAVE	280
40 / p. 215	AAA	Fairfield Inn by Marriott-Albany/East Greenbush	◆◆◆	$79-$139 SAVE	280
		EAST GREENBUSH - Restaurant			
30 / p. 215		Bennigan's Grill & Tavern	◆◆	$6-$17	280
		TROY - Lodgings			
42 / p. 215		Franklin Square Inn & Suites	fyi	$106-$269	584
43 / p. 215	AAA	Best Western-Rensselaer Inn	◆◆	$89-$119 SAVE	584
		TROY - Restaurant			
32 / p. 215		Holmes & Watson, Ltd	◆	$11-$15	584
		GUILDERLAND - Lodgings			
45 / p. 215	AAA	Holiday Inn Express Turf on Western Ave	◆◆◆	$99-$159 SAVE	300
		GUILDERLAND - Restaurants			
35 / p. 215		Metro 20 Diner	◆	$9-$16	300
36 / p. 215		Bavarian Chalet	◆◆	$10-$17	300
37 / p. 215		Londonderry Cafe	◆◆	$8-$17	300
		LOUDONVILLE - Restaurant			
40 / p. 215		Pearl of the Orient	◆◆	$7-$17	345

ALBANY pop. 95,658 (See map and index starting on p. 215)

──── **WHERE TO STAY** ────

ALBANY MANSION HILL INN & RESTAURANT   *Book at aaa.com*   Phone: 518/465-2038   **2**
AAA SAVE   All Year [CP]   1P: $145   2P: $175   XP: $20   F17
▼▼▼   **Location:** I-787, exit 3B (Madison Ave/US 20 W) to Philip St, 0.4 mi s. 115 Philip St at Park Ave 12202 (45 Park Ave).
Historic Bed   Fax: 518/434-2313. **Facility:** In an older neighborhood, the property features a rustic courtyard and is reno-
& Breakfast   vated with modern amenities; original buildings date to 1860 and 1913. 8 one-bedroom standard units. 2 stories (no elevator), interior/exterior corridors. **Parking:** on-site and street. **Terms:** office hours 9 am-5 pm,
check-in 4 pm, 5 day cancellation notice-fee imposed. **Amenities:** dual phone lines, voice mail, irons, hair
dryers. **Dining:** restaurant, see separate listing. **Guest Services:** valet laundry, area transportation-bus &
train station. **Business Services:** meeting rooms. **Cards:** AX, CB, DC, DS, MC, VI. **Special Amenities:** free continental breakfast and free newspaper.

SOME UNITS

ALBANY QUALITY INN   *Book at aaa.com*   Phone: (518)438-8431   **3**
▼▼▼▼   All Year [BP]   1P: $79-$119   2P: $79-$119   XP: $5   F18
Location: I-90, exit 5 (Everett Rd), just s, then e. 3 Watervliet Ave 12206. Fax: 518/438-8356. **Facility:** 215 units.
Small-scale Hotel   214 one-bedroom standard units, some with efficiencies. 1 one-bedroom suite. 2-9 stories, interior corridors.
Parking: on-site. **Terms:** cancellation fee imposed. **Amenities:** irons, hair dryers. **Pool(s):** small outdoor,
small heated indoor. **Leisure Activities:** exercise room. *Fee:* game room. **Guest Services:** valet and coin laundry, area transportation. **Business Services:** conference facilities. **Cards:** AX, CB, DC, DS, JC, MC, VI.

SOME UNITS

THE ALBANY THRUWAY COURTYARD   *Book at aaa.com*   Phone: 518/435-1600   **5**
▼▼▼▼   5/1-10/31   1P: $114-$154   2P: $114-$154
11/1-4/30   1P: $94-$154   2P: $94-$154
Small-scale Hotel   **Location:** I-90, exit 2 westbound, just s on Fuller Rd, then just e; eastbound, just e. 1455 Washington Ave 12206.
Fax: 518/435-1616. **Facility:** 78 units. 70 one-bedroom standard units. 8 one-bedroom suites. 3 stories, interior corridors. *Bath:* combo or shower only. **Parking:** on-site. **Terms:** cancellation fee imposed, [BP] meal plan available.
Amenities: video games, dual phone lines, voice mail, irons, hair dryers. **Pool(s):** small heated indoor. **Leisure Activi-
ties:** whirlpool, exercise room. **Guest Services:** valet and coin laundry. **Business Services:** meeting rooms, fax. **Cards:** AX,
DC, DS, JC, MC, VI.

SOME UNITS

BEST WESTERN SOVEREIGN HOTEL ALBANY   *Book at aaa.com*   Phone: (518)489-2981   **4**
AAA SAVE   All Year [BP]   1P: $89-$149   2P: $89-$149   XP: $10   F16
▼▼▼   **Location:** I-90, exit 2, 0.7 mi s, follow signs to US 20 (Western Ave). Located across from the state university. 1228
Small-scale Hotel   Western Ave 12203. Fax: 518/489-8967. **Facility:** 195 units. 193 one-bedroom standard units. 2 one-bedroom
suites. 5 stories, interior corridors. *Bath:* combo or shower only. **Parking:** on-site. **Terms:** small pets only
($10 extra charge). **Amenities:** video games, voice mail, irons, hair dryers. **Dining:** 6:30 am-11 pm. **Pool(s):**
small heated indoor. **Leisure Activities:** saunas, exercise room. **Guest Services:** valet laundry, area
transportation-bus & train station. **Business Services:** conference facilities, business center. **Cards:** AX, CB, DC, DS, MC, VI.
Special Amenities: free full breakfast and free local telephone calls.

SOME UNITS

CRESTHILL SUITES   *Book at aaa.com*   Phone: (518)454-0007   **7**
▼▼▼▼   7/22-8/31 [ECP]   1P: $139-$289   2P: $139-$289
5/1-7/21 & 9/1-10/31 [ECP]   1P: $129-$269   2P: $129-$269
Small-scale Hotel   11/1-4/30 [ECP]   1P: $119-$229   2P: $119-$229
Location: I-90, exit 2 westbound, just s on Fuller Rd, then just e; eastbound, just e. 1415 Washington Ave 12206.
Fax: 518/454-0003. **Facility:** 95 units. 42 one-bedroom standard units with kitchens. 33 one- and 20 two-bedroom suites with
kitchens. 3 stories, interior corridors. **Parking:** on-site. **Terms:** package plans - weekends, pets ($150 deposit). **Amenities:** video
library, high-speed Internet, dual phone lines, voice mail, irons, hair dryers. **Pool(s):** heated outdoor. **Leisure Activities:** exercise room. **Guest Services:** sundries, area transportation. **Business Services:** meeting rooms, business center. **Cards:** AX, CB,
DC, DS, MC, VI.

SOME UNITS

(See map and index starting on p. 215)

CROWNE PLAZA HOTEL AND RESORT ALBANY   *Book at aaa.com*   Phone: (518)462-6611   **1**

All Year   1P: $99-$189   2P: $99-$189

Location: At Lodge and State St; downtown. Located at Ten Eyck Plaza. 89 State St 12207. Fax: 518/462-2901. **Facility:** 384 units. 380 one-bedroom standard units. 4 one-bedroom suites ($249-$299). 15 stories, interior corridors. *Bath:* combo or shower only. **Parking:** on-site (fee) and valet. **Terms:** check-in 4 pm.

Large-scale Hotel   **Amenities:** CD players, dual phone lines, voice mail, irons, hair dryers. **Dining:** 6:30 am-10 pm, cocktails. **Pool(s):** small heated indoor. **Leisure Activities:** whirlpool. **Guest Services:** gift shop, valet laundry, area transportation-train station. **Business Services:** conference facilities, business center. **Cards:** AX, DC, DS, JC, MC, VI.

SOME UNITS

EXTENDED STAY AMERICA   *Book at aaa.com*   Phone: 518/446-0680   **9**

All Year Wkly   1P: $369-$450   2P: $389-$470   XP: $20   F3

Location: I-90, exit 2 westbound, just s on Fuller Rd, 0.5 mi e; eastbound, then just e. 1395 Washington Ave 12206. Fax: 518/446-0779. **Facility:** 134 one-bedroom standard units with efficiencies. 2 stories, interior corridors.

Small-scale Hotel   *Bath:* combo or shower only. **Parking:** on-site. **Amenities:** voice mail. **Guest Services:** coin laundry. **Cards:** AX, CB, DC, DS, MC, VI.

SOME UNITS

FAIRFIELD INN BY MARRIOTT-ALBANY   *Book at aaa.com*   Phone: 518/435-1800   **6**

7/8-8/31 [ECP]   1P: $140-$180
5/1-7/7 [ECP]   1P: $100-$120
9/1-4/30 [ECP]   1P: $90-$120

Small-scale Hotel   **Location:** I-90, exit 2 westbound, just s on Fuller Rd, then 0.6 mi e; eastbound, just e. 1383 Washington Ave 12206. Fax: 518/435-1800. **Facility:** 99 one-bedroom standard units. 3 stories, interior corridors. *Bath:* combo or shower only. **Parking:** on-site. **Terms:** cancellation fee imposed. **Amenities:** voice mail, irons, hair dryers. **Pool(s):** small heated indoor. **Leisure Activities:** whirlpool. **Guest Services:** valet laundry. **Business Services:** fax. **Cards:** AX, DC, DS, MC, VI.

SOME UNITS

REGENCY INN & SUITES   *Book at aaa.com*   Phone: (518)462-6555   **10**

8/1-9/5 [ECP]   1P: $79-$129   2P: $79-$129   XP: $10   F12
9/6-4/30 [ECP]   1P: $75-$119   2P: $75-$119   XP: $10   F12
5/1-7/31 [ECP]   1P: $70-$119   2P: $70-$119   XP: $10   F12

Location: On SR 9W; I-87, exit 23. 416 Southern Blvd 12209 (215 West 34th St, NEW YORK, 10002). **Small-scale Hotel**   Fax: 518/462-2547. **Facility:** 132 one-bedroom standard units. 1-2 stories (no elevator), interior/exterior corridors. *Bath:* combo or shower only. **Parking:** on-site. **Terms:** small pets only ($20 fee, $25 deposit). **Amenities:** voice mail, irons, hair dryers. **Leisure Activities:** Fee: 7 indoor tennis courts. **Guest Services:** valet and coin laundry. **Business Services:** conference facilities. **Cards:** AX, CB, DC, DS, JC, MC, VI. **Special Amenities:** free expanded continental breakfast and free local telephone calls. *(See color ad p 218)*

SOME UNITS

TOWNEPLACE SUITES-ALBANY   *Book at aaa.com*   Phone: 518/435-1900   **8**

7/8-8/31 [CP]   1P: $140-$180
9/1-12/31 [CP]   1P: $110-$140
5/1-7/7 [CP]   1P: $110-$130
1/1-4/30 [CP]   1P: $100-$120

Small-scale Hotel

Location: I-90, exit 2 westbound, just s on Fuller Rd, then 0.6 mi e; eastbound, just e. 1379 Washington Ave 12206. Fax: 518/446-8170. **Facility:** 101 units. 74 one-bedroom standard units with kitchens. 4 one- and 23 two-bedroom suites with kitchens. 3 stories, interior corridors. *Bath:* combo or shower only. **Parking:** on-site. **Terms:** cancellation fee imposed, pets ($75 fee). **Amenities:** voice mail, irons, hair dryers. **Pool(s):** small heated outdoor. **Leisure Activities:** exercise room. **Guest Services:** valet and coin laundry. **Cards:** AX, DC, DS, MC, VI.

SOME UNITS

(See map and index starting on p. 215)

——— WHERE TO DINE ———

ALBANY MANSION HILL INN RESTAURANT   **Dinner:** $15-$24   **Phone:** 518/465-2038   6
▼▼▼   **Location:** I-787, exit 3B (Madison Ave/US 20 W) to Philip St. 0.4 mi s; in Albany Mansion Hill Inn & Restaurant. 115
American   Philip St at Park Ave 12202. **Hours:** 5 pm-9 pm; hours may vary in summer. Closed major holidays; also Sun.
Reservations: suggested. **Features:** In a small, intimate setting, the restaurant is decorated in classic
American style. The succulent swordfish has a crusted mustard texture and taste, while the blueberry
creme brulee has a different, but very good flavor. Service is professional. Casual dress; cocktails. **Parking:** on-site.
Cards: AX, CB, DC, DS, MC, VI.
✕

JACK'S OYSTER HOUSE   **Lunch:** $5-$9   **Dinner:** $12-$20   **Phone:** 518/465-8854   3
AAA   **Location:** Just s of City Hall; downtown. 42 State St 12207. **Hours:** 11:30 am-10 pm. **Reservations:** suggested.
▼▼▼   **Features:** In the heart of the downtown business district, the lively, energetic restaurant is a favorite for
Seafood   fine dining. A lovely mural brightens the wall behind a reproduction of a Florentine bar. The menu centers
on seafood, such as oven-roasted sea bass with leek and mushroom compote and vintage port wine
sauce, expertly prepared by certified master chef Dale Miller. Save room for a homemade dessert, such as
exquisite Key lime brulee. Casual dress; cocktails. **Parking:** on-site. **Cards:** AX, CB, DC, DS, MC, VI.
⛾ ✕

LA SERRE RESTAURANT   **Lunch:** $7-$13   **Dinner:** $14-$24   **Phone:** 518/463-6056   1
▼▼▼   **Location:** Just s of State St; 3 blks e of state capitol building. 14 Green St 12207. **Hours:** 11:30 am-2:30 & 5-9
Continental   pm, Sat 5:30 pm-9:30 pm. Closed major holidays. **Reservations:** accepted. **Features:** Chilean sea bass,
rack of lamb and lobster ravioli are among specialties on the restaurant's inventive menu. The renovated
1829 white-gabled building resides in the heart of downtown. The atmosphere in the elegant dining room is
upscale and intimate. Dressy casual; cocktails. **Parking:** street. **Cards:** AX, CB, DC, MC, VI.
⛾ ✕

**NICOLE'S BISTRO AT
QUACKENBUSH HOUSE** Historic   **Lunch:** $6-$12   **Dinner:** $17-$22   **Phone:** 518/465-1111   7
▼▼▼   **Location:** Just off Clinton Ave exit; downtown. 25 Quackenbush Sq 12207. **Hours:** 11:30 am-2:30 & 5-10 pm. Sat
Nouvelle American   from 5 pm. Closed major holidays; also Sun. **Reservations:** suggested. **Features:** The converted
17th-century home is decorated in soft tones and charcoal sketches. Flavorful dishes, such as steak au
poivre and onion soup gratinee, are prepared with obvious thought to color and texture. The light, sweet
chocolate mousse is exquisite. Dressy casual; cocktails. **Parking:** on-site. **Cards:** AX, CB, DC, DS, MC, VI.
⛾ ✕

ALBION pop. 7,438

——— WHERE TO STAY ———

LAMONT'S ORCHARD VIEW BED & BREAKFAST   **Phone:** 585/589-7702
▼▼▼   1/1-4/30 [BP]   1P: $85-$100   2P: $85-$100   XP: $10
5/1-12/31 [BP]   1P: $85-$95   2P: $85-$95   XP: $10
Bed & Breakfast   **Location:** Jct SR 104, 1.4 mi s. 3027 Densmore Rd 14411. Fax: 585/589-7023. **Facility:** Smoke free premises. 4
one-bedroom standard units, some with whirlpools. 2 stories (no elevator), interior corridors. **Bath:** some
shared or private, combo or shower only. **Parking:** on-site. **Terms:** age restrictions may apply, 14 day cancellation notice-fee imposed. **Amenities:** hair dryers. **Cards:** AX, DC, MC, VI.
SOME UNITS
✕ ☎ / 📺 VCR /

ALEXANDRIA BAY pop. 1,088

——— WHERE TO STAY ———

OTTER CREEK INN   **Phone:** (315)482-5248
AAA SAVE   6/30-9/6   1P: $68-$99   2P: $68-$99   XP: $10   F5
▼▼▼   5/1-6/29 & 9/7-9/30   1P: $55-$68   2P: $55-$68   XP: $10   F5
Motel   **Location:** Jct Crossmon and Church sts, follow signs. 2 Crossmon St Extension 13607. Fax: 315/482-3672.
Facility: 32 one-bedroom standard units. 2 stories (no elevator), interior/exterior corridors. **Parking:** on-site.
Terms: open 5/1-9/30, 2 night minimum stay - weekends 7/1-8/31, 3 day cancellation notice, package plans.
Leisure Activities: boat dock, fishing, picnic tables. Fee: charter fishing. **Cards:** DS, MC, VI.
SOME UNITS
⊠ / ✕ 🍴 /

RIVEREDGE RESORT-HOTEL

Phone: (315)482-9917

6/25-9/5	1P: $179-$338	2P: $179-$338	XP: $20 F11
5/1-6/24 & 9/6-10/28	1P: $126-$288	2P: $126-$288	XP: $20 F11
10/29-4/30	1P: $99-$198	2P: $99-$198	XP: $20 F11

Resort
Small-scale Hotel

Location: I-81, exit 50N, 4.9 mi n on SR 12, 0.6 mi e on Walton, then just ne. 17 Holland St 13607. Fax: 315/482-5010. **Facility:** The resort offers comfortable rooms, each with a balcony overlooking the St. Lawrence River; shops and attractions are within walking distance. 129 units. 101 one-bedroom standard units. 28 one-bedroom suites, some with whirlpools. 4 stories, interior corridors. **Parking:** on-site and valet. **Terms:** check-in 4 pm, 1-2 night minimum stay - weekends, 15 day cancellation notice-fee imposed, [AP] & [MAP] meal plans available, package plans, pets ($20 extra charge). **Amenities:** video games, voice mail, irons, hair dryers. **Dining:** 2 restaurants, 7 am-10 pm; hours may vary in winter, cocktails, also, Jacques Cartier Dining Room, see separate listing, entertainment. **Pool(s):** outdoor, heated indoor/outdoor. **Leisure Activities:** sauna, whirlpools, fishing, exercise room. *Fee:* marina, massage. **Guest Services:** gift shop, coin laundry, area transportation-into village. **Business Services:** conference facilities. **Cards:** AX, DC, DS, MC, VI.

(See color ad p 221)

SOME UNITS

──── WHERE TO DINE ────

CAPT'S LANDING

American

Lunch: $5-$10 **Dinner:** $11-$21 **Phone:** 315/482-7777

Location: On Bayfront; center. 49 James St 13607. **Hours:** Open 5/18-10/14; 7 am-9 pm. **Reservations:** suggested. **Features:** Guests that step aboard the "barge made into a restaurant" at dockside actually are floating on Alexandria Bay. The friendly, casual staff serves seafood, pasta, beef and chicken as diners enjoy the view across the bay toward Boldt Castle. The barge does move on waves from passing boats. Casual dress; cocktails. **Parking:** on-site. **Cards:** AX, DS, MC, VI.

JACQUES CARTIER DINING ROOM
🔺 AAA
▽▽▽ ▽▽▽
Continental

Dinner: $24-$32   Phone: 315/482-9917
Location: I-81, exit 50N, 4.9 mi n on SR 12, 0.6 mi e on Walton, then just ne; in Riveredge Resort-Hotel. 17 Holland St 13607. **Hours:** Open 5/12-10/8; 6 pm-10 pm; 5 pm-9 pm off season. **Reservations:** suggested. **Features:** The dining room affords wonderful views of the St. Lawrence River and historic Boldt Castle. A harpist adds to the decidedly romantic atmosphere. Such dishes as Chilean sea bass and rack of lamb are carefully prepared and flavorful. Service is attentive, accomplished and unpretentious. Dressy casual; cocktails; entertainment. **Parking:** on-site and valet. **Cards:** AX, CB, DC, DS, MC, VI.

[&M] [X]

ALFRED pop. 3,954

——— WHERE TO STAY ———

SAXON INN
▽▽ ▽▽
Small-scale Hotel

Phone: 607/871-2600
5/1-12/20 & 1/5-4/30   1P: $93-$120   2P: $103-$120   XP: $10   F12
Location: On Alfred University campus. 1 Park St 14802 (Saxon Dr). Fax: 607/871-2650. **Facility:** 26 one-bedroom standard units. 2 stories, interior corridors. **Parking:** on-site, winter plug-ins. **Terms:** open 5/1-12/20 & 1/5-4/30. **Amenities:** voice mail, hair dryers. *Some:* irons. **Guest Services:** valet laundry. **Business Services:** meeting rooms, fax (fee). **Cards:** AX, DC, DS, MC, VI.

SOME UNITS
[ASK] [S⊙] [♿] [&M] [DATA PORT] / [X] [🛏] [▣] /

ALLEGANY pop. 1,883

——— WHERE TO STAY ———

COUNTRY INN & SUITES, OLEAN
▽▽▽ ▽▽
Small-scale Hotel

Book at aaa.com
1/1-4/30   1P: $89-$149   2P: $89-$149   XP: $10   F18
5/1-12/31   1P: $89-$129   2P: $89-$129   XP: $10   F18
Location: I-86, exit 25 westbound; exit 24 eastbound, 2 mi e. Located across from St. Bonaventure University. 3270 NYS Rt 417 W 14760. Fax: 716/372-7525. **Facility:** 77 units. 53 one-bedroom standard units, some with whirlpools. 24 one-bedroom suites. 3 stories, interior corridors. **Bath:** combo or shower only. **Parking:** on-site. **Terms:** cancellation fee imposed, [ECP] meal plan available. **Amenities:** dual phone lines, voice mail, irons, hair dryers. **Pool(s):** heated indoor. **Leisure Activities:** whirlpool, exercise room. **Guest Services:** valet and coin laundry. **Business Services:** meeting rooms, fax (fee). **Cards:** AX, DC, DS, MC, VI. *(See color ad p 554)*

SOME UNITS
[ASK] [S⊙] [♿] [🐕] [⊘] [🏊] [✦] [DATA PORT] [▣] / [X] [🛏] [▣] /

——— *The following lodging was either not evaluated or did not meet AAA rating requirements but is listed for your information only.* ———

MICROTEL INN & SUITES-OLEAN/ALLEGANY
[fyi]

Phone: 585/248-2440
All Year [CP]   1P: $39-$59   2P: $39-$59   XP: $5   F16
Too new to rate, opening scheduled for May 2004. **Location:** I-86. exit 24 (Allegany/St. Bonaventure). Located across from St. Bonaventure University. 3234 W State Rd 14706. Fax: 585/248-3271. **Amenities:** 50 units, pets, coffeemakers, microwaves, refrigerators. **Terms:** 14 day cancellation notice. **Cards:** AX, CB, DC, DS, MC, VI.

AMAGANSETT pop. 1,067

——— WHERE TO DINE ———

LOBSTER ROLL
▽▽▽
Seafood

Lunch: $8-$13   Dinner: $6-$18   Phone: 631/267-3740
Location: 4 mi e on SR 27. **Hours:** Open 5/1-10/15; 11:30 am-9:30 pm, Fri-Sun to 10 pm. **Features:** A seasonal institution, the local favorite is lovingly called "lunch" by those in the know. It may not look like much more than an old roadside seafood stand, but it's charming. Sit in the plastic-enclosed porch with flower baskets, hanging plants and red and white checkered tablecloths. The lobster roll is good, as are the fried oyster, clam roll, fish and chips, blue-claw crab cakes, marinated charbroiled fish and the puffers, tempura blow fish, fins and all. The pie is worth the splurge. Casual dress; beer & wine only. **Parking:** on-site. **Cards:** MC, VI.

[X]

AMHERST —See Buffalo p. 246.

AMITYVILLE pop. 9,441

——— WHERE TO DINE ———

ROSE COTTAGE
▽▽▽ ▽▽
Continental

Lunch: $9-$12   Dinner: $18-$30   Phone: 631/691-6881
Location: SR 27A, 0.5 mi e of SR 110. 348 Merrick Rd 11701. **Hours:** noon-3 & 5-9 pm, Fri & Sat-10 pm, Sun noon-8 pm. Closed: 1/1, 7/4, 12/25; also Mon. **Reservations:** suggested, weekends. **Features:** Enhancing the restaurant's French dialect decor are knotty pine walls, beamed ceilings, dried-flower wreaths and intimate lighting. An extensive wine list complements a menu that centers on steak and pasta. Casual dress; cocktails. **Parking:** on-site. **Cards:** AX, DC, DS, MC, VI.

[Y] [X]

AMSTERDAM pop. 18,355

——— WHERE TO STAY ———

SUPER 8 MOTEL
▽▽▽ ▽▽
Small-scale Hotel

Book at aaa.com
5/1-10/20 [CP]   1P: $60-$115   2P: $60-$115   XP: $4   F17
10/21-4/30 [CP]   1P: $50-$105   2P: $50-$105   XP: $4   F17
Location: I-90, exit 27 (SR 30 S). Rt 30 S 12010. Fax: 518/843-5888. **Facility:** 67 one-bedroom standard units. 2 stories (no elevator), interior corridors. **Parking:** on-site, winter plug-ins. **Amenities:** video library (fee). **Business Services:** fax (fee). **Cards:** AX, CB, DC, DS, MC, VI.

Phone: 518/843-5888

SOME UNITS
[ASK] [S⊙] / [X] [VCR] [DATA PORT] /
FEE

ANGELICA pop. 903

——— WHERE TO STAY ———

ANGELICA INN B&B
Phone: 585/466-3063

▼▼ ▼▼
All Year   2P: $75-$125   XP: $20

Historic Bed & Breakfast
Location: SR 17, exit 31, 0.5 mi w. 64 W Main St 14709 (PO Box 686). Fax: 585/466-3063. **Facility:** Individually furnished rooms create a pleasant atmosphere at this restored Victorian mansion. Smoke free premises. 6 units. 3 one-bedroom standard units, some with whirlpools. 2 two- and 1 three-bedroom suites ($100-$125), some with kitchens. 3 stories (no elevator), interior/exterior corridors. *Bath:* combo or shower only. **Parking:** on-site. **Terms:** 2 night minimum stay - seasonal weekends, 14 day cancellation notice-fee imposed, weekly rates available, [BP] meal plan available, small pets only (in designated units, owner's dogs on premises). **Amenities:** video library, hair dryers. **Guest Services:** gift shop. **Business Services:** meeting rooms. **Cards:** AX, DS, MC, VI.

SOME UNITS

🐾 ⊠ 🕿 / 🈹 🎦 VCR 🖭 🖾 🖵 /

APALACHIN pop. 1,126

——— WHERE TO STAY ———

THE DOLPHIN INN
Phone: (607)625-4441

▼▼ ▼▼
All Year [CP]   1P: $50-$62   2P: $55-$70

Small-scale Hotel
Location: SR 17, exit 66, just e. 7666 SR 434 13732. Fax: 607/625-4631. **Facility:** 50 one-bedroom standard units. 2 stories, interior corridors. *Bath:* combo or shower only. **Parking:** on-site. **Terms:** cancellation fee imposed, weekly rates available, package plans, pets ($10 deposit). **Leisure Activities:** exercise room. *Fee:* game room. **Business Services:** meeting rooms, fax (fee). **Cards:** AX, DS, MC, VI.

SOME UNITS

ASK SD 🐾 🍴 🐾 🎦 / ⊠ VCR DATA PORT 🖭 /
      FEE   FEE

——— WHERE TO DINE ———

DOLPHIN DINER   **Lunch:** $4-$7   **Dinner:** $6-$14   **Phone:** 607/625-5029

▼
American
Location: SR 17, exit 66, just e. 7670 SR 434 13732. **Hours:** 7 am-9 pm. Closed: 12/25. **Reservations:** accepted. **Features:** Easy on/off the highway for a delicious quick bite at this old-fashioned diner, offering traditional American fare served by friendly staff. Casual dress; cocktails. **Parking:** on-site. **Cards:** DS, MC, VI.

⊠

ARMONK —See New York p. 449.

AUBURN pop. 28,574—See also FINGER LAKES.

——— WHERE TO STAY ———

AUBURN MICROTEL INN & SUITES   *Book at aaa.com*
Phone: (315)253-5000

Ⓐ Ⓐ Ⓐ SAVE
10/31-4/30 [CP]   1P: $70-$110   2P: $75-$120   XP: $6   F18
5/1-10/30 [CP]   1P: $60-$100   2P: $70-$120   XP: $6   F18

▼▼ ▼▼
Small-scale Hotel
Location: Jct SR 34/38, just e on US 20/SR 5; center. 12 Seminary Ave 13021. Fax: 315/253-9090. **Facility:** 79 one-bedroom standard units. 3 stories, interior corridors. *Bath:* combo or shower only. **Parking:** on-site, winter plug-ins. **Terms:** small pets only ($15 fee). **Amenities:** dual phone lines, voice mail. *Some:* irons, hair dryers. **Leisure Activities:** exercise room. **Guest Services:** valet and coin laundry. **Business Services:** fax (fee). **Cards:** AX, CB, DC, DS, MC, VI. **Special Amenities:** free continental breakfast.

SOME UNITS

🐾 🍴 🛎 ⓜ 🐾 🎦 DATA PORT / ⊠ 🖭 🖾 🖵 /
      FEE

HOLIDAY INN-AUBURN/FINGER LAKES   *Book at aaa.com*
Phone: (315)253-4531

Ⓐ Ⓐ Ⓐ SAVE
7/1-8/31   1P: $84-$102   2P: $84-$102
5/1-6/30 & 9/1-10/15   1P: $78-$94   2P: $78-$94
10/16-4/30   1P: $67-$77   2P: $67-$77

▼▼ ▼▼ ▼▼
Small-scale Hotel
Location: SR 34, just n of US 20/SR 5. 75 North St 13021. Fax: 315/252-5843. **Facility:** 165 one-bedroom standard units, some with whirlpools. 5 stories, interior corridors. **Parking:** on-site, winter plug-ins. **Terms:** cancellation fee imposed, small pets only ($10 extra charge). **Amenities:** dual phone lines, voice mail, irons, hair dryers. **Dining:** 6:30 am-10 pm; hours vary in winter, cocktails. **Pool(s):** heated indoor. **Leisure Activities:** exercise room. **Guest Services:** valet and coin laundry, beauty salon. **Business Services:** meeting rooms. **Cards:** AX, CB, DC, DS, MC, VI. **Special Amenities:** free local telephone calls and free room upgrade (subject to availability with advanced reservations). *(See color ad p 289)*

SOME UNITS

SD 🐾 🍴 🍸 ⓜ 🏊 🐾 DATA PORT 🖭 / ⊠ VCR 🖭 🖾 /
   FEE   FEE FEE FEE

SLEEPY HOLLOW MOTEL
Phone: 315/704-0343

▼▼ ▼
5/1-9/15   1P: $59-$109   2P: $59-$109   XP: $10   F9
9/16-4/30   1P: $49-$99   2P: $49-$99   XP: $10   F9

Motel
Location: US 20, 1 mi e. 3401 E Genesee St 13021 (PO Box 461, SKANEATELES, 13152-0461). **Facility:** 15 one-bedroom standard units. 1 story, exterior corridors. **Parking:** on-site, winter plug-ins. **Terms:** 10 day cancellation notice-fee imposed, weekly rates available, pets ($15 fee). **Cards:** MC, VI.

SOME UNITS

🐾 DATA PORT / ⊠ 🖭 🖾 🖵 /
   FEE

SPRINGSIDE INN

Historic
Country Inn

All Year [CP] 1P: $100-$200 2P: $100-$200 XP: $20 F7
Phone: (315)252-7247
Location: On SR 38, 3.3 mi s. Located across from Owasco Lake. 6141 W Lake Rd 13021 (PO Box 327).
Fax: 315/252-8096. **Facility:** Well-landscaped lawn with gazebo and duck pond. Closed 12/25. 7 one-bedroom standard units, some with whirlpools. 3 stories (no elevator), interior corridors. *Bath:* combo or shower only. **Parking:** on-site. **Terms:** office hours 7 am-10 pm, 10 day cancellation notice-fee imposed.
Amenities: video library, voice mail. **Dining:** dining room, see separate listing. **Business Services:** meeting rooms. **Cards:** AX, MC, VI.

SOME UNITS

(ASK) (SD) (♦) (X) / (W) (⊟) (⊡) /

──────── WHERE TO DINE ────────

PARKER'S GRILLE & TAP HOUSE

American

Lunch: $5-$7 **Dinner:** $5-$7 **Phone:** 315/252-6884
Location: Center. 129 Genesee St 13021. **Hours:** 11 am-midnight, Sun from noon. Closed major holidays.
Features: Guests can partake of a casual meal amid brick walls, stained-glass lights and bright beer brand lights that feature the 20 draft and 50 bottled beer choices. New York state wines are featured. Grilled mesquite chicken, French onion soup and hot and cold sandwiches are representative of items served by the friendly staff. Casual dress; cocktails. **Parking:** street. **Cards:** AX, MC, VI.

(Y) (X)

SPRINGSIDE INN Historic

American

Dinner: $16-$25 **Phone:** 315/252-7247
Location: SR 38 S, 3.3 mi s; in Springside Inn. 6141 W Lake Rd 13021. **Hours:** 5 pm-9 pm, Sun 10:30 am-1 pm; seasonal hours may vary. Closed major holidays; also Mon, Tues 1/1-3/29. **Reservations:** suggested.
Features: Diners can sit on the porch overlooking Owasco Lake in summer or by the large fireplace in cooler weather. Friendly service in the restored 1850s inn ensures a pleasant meal any time of the year. Hot popovers, served immediately, are a treat. Dishes such as veal sauteed in wine sauce with portobello mushroom will satisfy the heartiest appetite. Dessert is displayed on a tempting tray; consider the "house sundae," served with three homemade sauces. Casual dress; cocktails. **Parking:** on-site. **Cards:** AX, MC, VI.

(Y) (X)

AVERILL PARK pop. 1,517

──────── WHERE TO STAY ────────

LA PERLA AT THE GREGORY HOUSE COUNTRY INN & RESTAURANT

Historic
Country Inn

5/1-12/31 [ECP] 1P: $100-$125 2P: $110-$135 XP: $15
1/1-4/30 [ECP] 1P: $75-$95 2P: $90-$110 XP: $15
Phone: (518)674-3774
Location: Center. 3016 SR 43 12018 (PO Box 401). Fax: 518/674-8916. **Facility:** This 1830s inn offers modern conveniences in a country-style, homey atmosphere; some guest rooms have balconies and all have coordinated decor themes. Smoke free premises. 12 one-bedroom standard units. 2 stories (no elevator), interior corridors. **Parking:** on-site. **Terms:** age restrictions may apply, 7 day cancellation notice, weekly rates available, small pets only.
Pool(s): small outdoor. **Cards:** AX, DC, MC, VI.

(ASK) (SD) (♦) (♦) (Y) (≈) (X) (DATA PORT)

AVOCA pop. 1,008—See FINGER LAKES.

AVON pop. 2,977

──────── WHERE TO DINE ────────

TOM WAHL'S

American

Lunch: $4-$7 **Dinner:** $4-$7 **Phone:** 585/226-2420
Location: On US 20/SR 5; center. 283 E Main St 14414. **Hours:** 10:30 am-10 pm. Closed major holidays.
Features: Good comfort food is ordered at the counter and prepared quickly. Among choices are roast beef on kimmelwick, barbecue beef and pulled pork sandwiches, and children's fun meals. Casual dress. **Parking:** on-site. **Cards:** AX, MC, VI.

(⅃M) (X)

BABYLON pop. 12,615

──────── WHERE TO DINE ────────

DON RICARDO'S MEXICAN RESTAURANT

Mexican

Lunch: $7-$13 **Dinner:** $10-$17 **Phone:** 631/587-0122
Location: Between Deer Park Ave and SR 231. 94 E Main St 11702. **Hours:** noon-10 pm, Fri-11 pm, Sat & Sun 1 pm-11 pm. Closed: 7/4, 11/25, 12/25. **Reservations:** suggested. **Features:** The first two dining rooms have the feel of a Mexican tavern, while the back room, made up of a brick courtyard with skylights and a stone fountain, exudes a friendly warmth. Menu offerings center on hearty and tasty Mexican and Spanish fare. Casual dress; cocktails. **Parking:** street. **Cards:** AX, MC, VI.

(X)

BAINBRIDGE pop. 1,365

──────── WHERE TO DINE ────────

OLDE JERICHO TAVERN

American

Cards: AX, MC, VI.

Lunch: $5-$8 **Dinner:** $12-$16 **Phone:** 607/967-5893
Location: Center. 4 N Main St 13733. **Hours:** 11:30 am-2 & 5-8 pm, Fri & Sat-9 pm, Sun noon-7 pm. Closed: Mon & Tues. **Features:** In business since 1793, the stately, Colonial tavern has a storied history, which is brought to life in pictures and postcards. Such tempting choices as ribs, peel-and-eat shrimp and black bean soup line the buffet. Fresh blueberry muffins are delicious. Casual dress; cocktails. **Parking:** on-site.

(Y) (X)

BALDWINSVILLE pop. 7,053

—— WHERE TO STAY ——

MICROTEL INN & SUITES   *Book at aaa.com*   **Phone:** (315)635-9556

AAA **SAVE**   All Year [ECP]   1P: $45-$100   2P: $50-$100   XP: $5   F18

Location: SR 690, exit SR 31 W, 0.6 mi e. 131 Downer St 13027. Fax: 315/635-1972. **Facility:** 61 one-bedroom standard units. 2 stories, interior corridors. *Bath:* combo or shower only. **Parking:** on-site. **Terms:** weekly rates available, small pets only ($5 fee). **Cards:** AX, DS, MC, VI. **Special Amenities:** free expanded con-

Small-scale Hotel   tinental breakfast.

SOME UNITS

⟨S D / FEE⟩ ⟨dog⟩ ⟨TV⟩ ⟨M⟩ ⟨&⟩ ⟨film⟩ ⟨DATA PORT⟩ / ⟨X⟩ ⟨refrig⟩ ⟨microwave⟩ ⟨coffee⟩ /

—— WHERE TO DINE ——

BLUEWATER GRILL   **Dinner:** $6-$22   **Phone:** 315/638-3342

Location: Downtown; on Seneca River waterfront. 2 Oswego St 13027. **Hours:** 4:30 pm-9:30 pm, Fri & Sat-10:30 pm; hours vary in summer. **Closed:** 1/1, 3/27, 12/25. **Reservations:** accepted. **Features:** On the riverside, the contemporary setting is fitting for casual, upbeat dining. On the menu are fresh seafood, entree salads,

American   wraps, nachos, steaks, pasta and even Yankee pot roast. Casual dress; cocktails. **Parking:** on-site.

Cards: AX, MC, VI.   ⟨Y⟩ ⟨X⟩

TASSONE'S WINE GARDEN   **Lunch:** $6-$10   **Dinner:** $10-$14   **Phone:** 315/635-5133

Location: Jct SR 370, 31 and Dexter St. Rt 370 13027. **Hours:** 11 am-9 pm, Fri-10 pm, Sat 11:30 am-10 pm, Sun noon-9 pm; hours vary in summer. Closed major holidays. **Reservations:** accepted. **Features:** Daily

Italian   specials include the popular 1.5-pound Cornish game hen stuffed with mushroom dressing and all-you-can-eat crab legs. Friendly hometown service can be expected in the casual wine-garden

atmosphere. Casual dress; cocktails. **Parking:** on-site. **Cards:** AX, MC, VI.   ⟨Y⟩ ⟨X⟩

BALLSTON LAKE

—— WHERE TO DINE ——

CARNEY'S TAVERN   **Lunch:** $4-$7   **Dinner:** $13-$18   **Phone:** 518/399-9926

Location: Center. 17 Main St 12019. **Hours:** 11 am-9 pm, Tues-Sat to 10 pm, Sun from noon. Closed: 3/27, 11/25, 12/25. **Features:** The original tin ceiling and bar back add to the authentic feel of the

American   mid-19th-century Colonial tavern. Traditional Irish pub fare, including the specialty Celtic steak, is at the heart of the menu. Homemade bread pudding is a mouthwatering treat. Casual dress; cocktails. **Parking:**

on-site. **Cards:** AX, DS, MC, VI.

BALLSTON SPA pop. 5,556

—— WHERE TO DINE ——

ECOBELLI'S RESTAURANT   **Lunch:** $5-$7   **Dinner:** $10-$18   **Phone:** 518/885-5900

Location: I-87, exit 12, 3.4 mi w on SR 67, then just s on SR 50. 1475 Schenectady-Saratoga Rd 12020. **Hours:** 11:30 am-2 & 4-9 pm, Fri & Sat 5 pm-10 pm, Sun 1 pm-9 pm. Closed: Mon off season.

Italian   **Features:** Classic-style Italian food is served in hearty portions and pleasant service in this restaurant conveniently located between Saratoga Springs, Albany and Schenectady. Casual dress; cocktails.

Parking: on-site. **Cards:** DS, MC, VI.   ⟨Y⟩ ⟨X⟩

GREAT BAY CLAM CO   **Lunch:** $5-$9   **Dinner:** $10-$20   **Phone:** 518/885-0583

Location: SR 50, 1.5 mi n of jct SR 50 (Doubleday Ave) and SR 67. 2149 Doubleday Ave 12020. **Hours:** 11:30 am-9 pm, Sat from 4 pm, Sun 12:30 pm-8:30 pm. Closed: 3/27, 11/25, 12/25; also Mon & Tues.

Seafood   **Reservations:** accepted. **Features:** Family-owned for 28 years, the popular restaurant prepares the freshest seafood available. Casual dress; cocktails. **Parking:** on-site. **Cards:** AX, DC, DS, MC, VI.   ⟨Y⟩ ⟨X⟩

SPA BRAUHAUS   **Dinner:** $10-$20   **Phone:** 518/885-4311

Location: I-87, exit 12, 1.5 mi w on SR 67 to E Line Rd, 2 mi n, then 0.3 mi e. 200 E High St 12020. **Hours:** 4 pm-10 pm, Sun noon-9 pm. Closed: 12/24, 12/25; also Mon (except 8/1-8/31) & Tues in winter.

German   **Reservations:** suggested. **Features:** A cozy atmosphere, warmed by a lighted fireplace on chilly evenings, welcomes families and diners. The traditional tureen of homemade soup brought to the table by a friendly

waiter starts off a hearty dining experience. Among choices are three ways of serving crispy Wiener schnitzel, which comes with red cabbage and spaetzle noodles. Dessert is made in-house. Casual dress; cocktails. **Parking:** on-site. **Cards:** CB, DC, MC, VI.   ⟨Y⟩ ⟨X⟩

BANGALL

—— WHERE TO STAY ——

The following lodging was either not evaluated or did not meet AAA rating requirements but is listed for your information only.

BULLIS HALL   **Phone:** 845/868-1665

⟨fyi⟩   Not evaluated. **Location:** Center. 88 Hunns Lake Rd 12506 (PO Box 630). Facilities, services, and decor characterize an upscale property.

BARNEVELD pop. 332

─── WHERE TO STAY ───

SUGARBUSH BED AND BREAKFAST   *Book at aaa.com*   **Phone:** (315)896-6860
▼▼ ▼▼   All Year   1P: $60-$80   2P: $85-$95   XP: $10
         Location: Jct SR 12, 0.3 mi se. 8451 Old Poland Rd 13304. Fax: 315/896-8828. **Facility:** Smoke free premises.
Bed & Breakfast   5 units. 4 one-bedroom standard units. 1 one-bedroom suite ($140-$150). 2 stories (no elevator), interior
corridors. *Bath:* combo or shower only. **Parking:** on-site. **Terms:** 8 day cancellation notice-fee imposed. [BP]
meal plan available. **Amenities:** hair dryers. **Leisure Activities:** cross country skiing, playground, volleyball. **Business Services:** fax. **Cards:** AX, DS, MC, VI.

SOME UNITS
(ASK) (S/D) (X) (X) (Z) / (K) (W) /

BATAVIA pop. 16,256

─── WHERE TO STAY ───

COMFORT INN   *Book at aaa.com*   **Phone:** (585)344-9999
(AAA) (SAVE)   7/1-9/8   1P: $89-$189   2P: $89-$189   XP: $10   F18
              5/1-6/30   1P: $79-$159   2P: $79-$159   XP: $10   F18
▼▼ ▼▼   9/9-4/30   1P: $69-$149   2P: $69-$149   XP: $10   F18
         Location: I-90, exit 48, just n on SR 98. Located in a quiet area. 4371 Federal Dr 14020. Fax: 585/345-7400.
Small-scale Hotel   **Facility:** 60 one-bedroom standard units, some with whirlpools. 2 stories (no elevator), interior corridors. *Bath:* combo or shower only. **Parking:** on-site. **Terms:** [ECP] meal plan available, pets ($10 fee).
Amenities: safes, irons. *Some:* hair dryers. **Pool(s):** outdoor. **Leisure Activities:** exercise room. **Guest Services:** valet laundry. **Business Services:** meeting rooms. **Cards:** AX, DC, DS, MC, VI. **Special Amenities:** free expanded continental breakfast and free local telephone calls.

SOME UNITS
(S/D) (hair) (bed) (&M) (access) (pets) (TV) (DATA PORT) / (X) (fridge) (suitcase) (microwave) /
FEE

DAYS INN   *Book at aaa.com*   **Phone:** (585)343-6000
(AAA) (SAVE)   5/1-9/7   1P: $59-$109   2P: $59-$109   XP: $10   -   F12
              9/8-12/31   1P: $55-$69   2P: $55-$69   XP: $10   F12
▼▼ ▼▼   1/1-4/30   1P: $49-$69   2P: $49-$69
         Location: I-90, exit 48, just s. 200 Oak St 14020. Fax: 585/343-5322. **Facility:** 119 one-bedroom standard units.
Small-scale Hotel   2 stories (no elevator), interior/exterior corridors. **Parking:** on-site. **Terms:** [AP] & [BP] meal plans available, pets ($10 extra charge). **Amenities:** hair dryers. **Dining:** 6:30-11 am, 11:30-3 & 4-9:30 pm, cocktails.
Pool(s): outdoor. **Leisure Activities:** lifeguard on duty. **Guest Services:** coin laundry. **Business Services:** meeting rooms, PC. **Cards:** AX, DC, DS, MC, VI. **Special Amenities:** free local telephone calls.

SOME UNITS
(S/D) (bed) (restaurant) (cocktail) (pets) (TV) / (X) (fridge) (microwave) /
FEE

HOLIDAY INN-DARIEN LAKE   *Book at aaa.com*   **Phone:** (585)344-2100
(AAA) (SAVE)   6/25-9/5   1P: $75-$129   2P: $75-$129   XP: $10   F18
              5/1-6/24   1P: $65-$99   2P: $65-$99   XP: $10   F18
▼▼ ▼▼   9/6-10/31   1P: $65-$89   2P: $65-$89   XP: $10   F18
              11/1-4/30   1P: $59-$89   2P: $59-$89   XP: $10   F18
Small-scale Hotel   **Location:** I-90, exit 48, just w. 8250 Park Rd 14020. Fax: 585/344-0238. **Facility:** 195 units. 147 one-bedroom
standard units. 48 one-bedroom suites ($89-$169). 5 stories, interior corridors. **Parking:** on-site. **Terms:** cancellation fee imposed, [AP], [BP], [CP] & [ECP] meal plans available, package plans, small pets only. **Amenities:** voice mail, irons, hair dryers. **Dining:** 6:30 am-2 & 5-10 pm; hours vary in winter, cocktails. **Pool(s):** outdoor, heated indoor. **Leisure Activities:** saunas, steamrooms, exercise room. *Fee:* game room. **Guest Services:** valet and coin laundry. **Business Services:** meeting rooms. **Cards:** AX, CB, DC, DS, JC, MC, VI. **Special Amenities:** free local telephone calls and free newspaper.

SOME UNITS
(S/D) (bed) (restaurant) (cocktail) (pets) (X) (TV) (DATA PORT) (microwave) / (X) (fridge) /

MICROTEL INN & SUITES   *Book at aaa.com*   **Phone:** (585)344-8882
(AAA) (SAVE)   6/25-9/2 [ECP]   1P: $99-$119   2P: $105-$125   XP: $6
              5/18-6/24 [ECP]   1P: $75-$95   2P: $81-$101   XP: $6
▼▼ ▼▼   5/1-5/17 & 9/3-4/30 [ECP]   1P: $69-$89   2P: $75-$95   XP: $6
         Location: I-90, exit 48, just w. 8210 Park Rd 14020. Fax: 585/344-7187. **Facility:** 52 one-bedroom standard units.
Small-scale Hotel   2 stories, interior corridors. *Bath:* combo or shower only. **Parking:** on-site. **Amenities:** video library (fee), high-speed Internet, voice mail, safes, irons, hair dryers. **Pool(s):** small heated indoor. **Leisure Activities:** whirlpool, exercise room. **Guest Services:** valet laundry. **Cards:** AX, DC, DS, MC, VI. **Special Amenities:** free expanded continental breakfast and preferred room (subject to availability with advanced reservations).

SOME UNITS
(S/D) (restaurant) (access) (pets) (TV) (DATA PORT) (microwave) / (X) (VCR) (fridge) (suitcase) /
FEE

PARK OAK INN   **Phone:** (585)343-7921
(AAA) (SAVE)   6/24-9/7   1P: $70-$89   2P: $75-$110   XP: $6   F10
              5/17-6/23   1P: $55-$80   2P: $60-$90.   XP: $6   F10
▼▼   9/8-4/30   1P: $40-$60   2P: $45-$70   XP: $6   F10
Motel   5/1-5/16   1P: $40-$60   2P: $45-$65   XP: $6   F10
         Location: I-90, exit 48, just n. 301 Oak St 14020. Fax: 585/343-6701. **Facility:** 20 one-bedroom standard units.
2 stories (no elevator), interior corridors. **Parking:** on-site. **Terms:** [ECP] meal plan available, small pets only
($4 fee). **Guest Services:** valet laundry. **Business Services:** fax (fee). **Cards:** AX, DS, MC, VI. **Special Amenities:** free expanded continental breakfast and free local telephone calls.

SOME UNITS
(S/D) (bed) (restaurant) / (X) (fridge) (suitcase) /
FEE

RAMADA LIMITED *Book at aaa.com*
Phone: (585)343-1000

(AAA) [SAVE]

◆◆◆◆ ◆◆◆◆

Small-scale Hotel

5/1-9/15	1P: $69-$119	2P: $69-$119	XP: $10 F
9/16-4/30	1P: $49-$89	2P: $49-$89	

Location: I-90, exit 48, just w. 8204 Park Rd 14020. Fax: 585/343-8608. **Facility:** 74 one-bedroom standard units. 2 stories, interior corridors. **Parking:** on-site. **Terms:** [CP] meal plan available, pets (must be attended). **Amenities:** irons, hair dryers. **Dining:** 6:30-11 am, 11:30-1:30 & 5-9 pm, Sat from 7 am, Sun 7:30 am-2 & 5-8:30 pm, cocktails. **Pool(s):** heated outdoor. **Guest Services:** valet laundry. **Business Services:** meeting rooms. **Cards:** AX, CB, DC, DS, MC, VI. **Special Amenities:** free expanded continental breakfast and free local telephone calls.

SOME UNITS

[icons]

RED CARPET *Book at aaa.com*
Phone: (585)343-2311

◆◆◆◆ ◆◆◆◆

Motel

6/22-9/9	1P: $65-$120	2P: $70-$120	XP: $6
5/18-6/21	1P: $55-$90	2P: $60-$95	XP: $6
9/10-4/30	1P: $42-$75	2P: $42-$85	XP: $6
5/1-5/17	1P: $50-$75	2P: $50-$80	XP: $6

Location: I-90, exit 48, just w. 8212 Park Rd 14020. Fax: 585/343-2053. **Facility:** 20 one-bedroom standard units. 2 stories (no elevator), interior/exterior corridors. **Parking:** on-site. **Terms:** cancellation fee imposed, [ECP] meal plan available, pets ($6 extra charge). **Guest Services:** valet laundry. **Business Services:** fax (fee). **Cards:** AX, DC, DS, MC, VI.

SOME UNITS

[ASK] [icons] FEE

SUPER 8
Phone: (585)345-0800

(AAA) [SAVE]

◆◆◆◆ ◆◆◆◆

Small-scale Hotel

5/1-9/7	1P: $59-$109	2P: $59-$109	XP: $7 F12
9/8-12/31	1P: $55-$69	2P: $55-$69	XP: $7 F12
1/1-4/30	1P: $49-$69	2P: $49-$69	XP: $7 F12

Location: I-90, exit 48, just s. 200A Oak St 14020. **Facility:** 54 one-bedroom standard units. 2 stories (no elevator), interior corridors. **Parking:** on-site. **Terms:** [AP] & [BP] meal plans available. **Cards:** AX, DC, DS, MC, VI. **Special Amenities:** free local telephone calls.

SOME UNITS

[icons]

─────── *The following lodging was either not evaluated or did not* ───────
meet AAA rating requirements but is listed for your information only.

HAMPTON INN
Phone: 585/815-0475

[fyi]

Small-scale Hotel

5/1-9/30 [ECP]	1P: $64-$139	2P: $64-$139	XP: $10 F18
10/1-4/30 [ECP]	1P: $54-$99	2P: $54-$99	XP: $10 F18

Too new to rate, opening scheduled for February 2004. Location: I-90, exit 48, just n. 4360 Commerce Dr 14020. **Amenities:** 100 units. **Terms:** 7 day cancellation notice. **Cards:** AX, DC, DS, MC, VI.

─────── **WHERE TO DINE** ───────

ALEX'S PLACE
Lunch: $4-$19   Dinner: $4-$19   Phone: 585/344-2999

◆◆◆◆

American

Location: I-90, exit 48, just w. 8322 Park Rd 14020. **Hours:** 11 am-11 pm, Fri & Sat-midnight, Sun noon-9 pm. Closed: 1/1, 11/25, 12/25. **Features:** Family-owned for more than 15 years, the cozy restaurant serves popular American fare, with a focus on steaks and seafood. Next to Batavia horse racetrack, this place is convenient for pre- or post-racing dining. Casual dress; cocktails. **Parking:** on-site. **Cards:** AX, MC, VI.

[icons]

MISS BATAVIA FAMILY RESTAURANT
Lunch: $3-$5   Dinner: $6-$8   Phone: 585/343-9786

(AAA)

◆◆◆◆

American

Location: 2 mi e on SR 5 E (Main St); center. 566 E Main St 14020. **Hours:** 6 am-9 pm. Closed: 1/1, 12/25; also closes early 11/22, 12/24 & 12/31. **Features:** Friendly hometown waitresses serve affordable, home-cooked meals. Built in 1933, the newly renovated diner offers pleasant surroundings. Casual dress. **Parking:** on-site. **Cards:** AX, DC, DS, MC, VI.

[icon]

PONTILLO'S PIZZA & PASTA
Lunch: $4-$7   Dinner: $4-$7   Phone: 585/343-3303

◆◆◆◆

Italian

Location: Just e on SR 5 (Main St); downtown. 500 E Main St 14020. **Hours:** 11 am-midnight, Fri & Sat-1 am, Sun noon-midnight; hours may vary in winter. Closed: 3/27, 11/25, 12/25. **Features:** Established in 1947, the casual family restaurant delivers traditional Italian and American dishes, such as chicken wings, homemade pasta and tasty pizza baked in stone-hearth ovens. Diners can watch food being prepared in the open kitchen. Outdoor patio seating is available. Casual dress; beer & wine only. **Parking:** on-site. **Cards:** AX, CB, DC, DS, MC, VI.

[icon]

BATH pop. 5,641—*See also FINGER LAKES.*

─────── **WHERE TO STAY** ───────

BATH SUPER 8 *Book at aaa.com*
Phone: 607/776-2187

◆◆◆◆ ◆◆◆◆

Small-scale Hotel

All Year	1P: $56-$76	2P: $66-$86	XP: $10 F12

Location: I-86, exit 38, just n. 333 W Morris St 14810. Fax: 607/776-3206. **Facility:** 50 one-bedroom standard units. 3 stories (no elevator), interior corridors. **Parking:** on-site. **Terms:** 3 day cancellation notice, [CP] meal plan available. **Amenities:** *Some:* hair dryers. **Guest Services:** valet laundry. **Cards:** AX, CB, DC, DS, MC, VI.

SOME UNITS

[ASK] [icons]

DAYS INN   **Book at aaa.com**
◆◆◆◆ ◆◆◆◆   All Year [ECP]   1P: $75-$84   2P: $80-$89   XP: $5   F18
Small-scale Hotel   **Location:** I-86, exit 38, just n. 330 W Morris St 14810. **Fax:** 607/776-7650. **Facility:** 104 one-bedroom standard
coin laundry. **Business Services:** meeting rooms. Cards: AX, DC, DS, MC, VI.   units, some with whirlpools. 5 stories, interior corridors. **Parking:** on-site, winter plug-ins. **Terms:** 30 day cancellation notice-fee imposed. **Amenities:** safes (fee), hair dryers. **Pool(s):** heated indoor. **Guest Services:**

SOME UNITS

—————— **WHERE TO DINE** ——————

CHAT-A-WHYLE   **Lunch:** $4-$5   **Dinner:** $5-$9   **Phone:** 607/776-8040
◆◆◆◆   **Location:** Center. 28 Liberty St 14810. **Hours:** 5 am-8 pm. Closed major holidays. **Reservations:** accepted.
American   **Features:** Centrally located in the main shopping district, the neat little restaurant always seems busy with hungry diners who come for the generous portions of homemade comfort food and personable service. Casual dress. **Parking:** on-site (fee) and street.

CIELITO LINDO   **Lunch:** $4-$7   **Dinner:** $5-$13   **Phone:** 607/776-8458
◆◆◆◆ ◆◆◆◆   **Location:** 4 mi s. 7500 SR 54 14810. **Hours:** 11 am-8:30 pm; 11:30 am-8 pm in winter. Closed: 11/25, 12/24,
Mexican   12/25; also Sun in winter. **Features:** Mexican and American specialties are made from fresh ingredients at this family-style restaurant decorated in festive colors. Casual dress; cocktails. **Parking:** on-site. Cards: AX, DS, MC, VI.

BAY SHORE pop. 23,852

—————— **WHERE TO STAY** ——————

ECONO LODGE   **Book at aaa.com**   **Phone:** (631)666-6000
◆◆◆ [SAVE]   All Year   1P: $84-$149   2P: $84-$149   XP: $10   F18
◆◆◆   **Location:** Sunrise Hwy, exit 44, 0.8 mi s on Brentwood Rd, then just e. Located in a commercial area. 501 E Main St
Motel   11706. **Fax:** 631/665-7476. **Facility:** 42 one-bedroom standard units. 1 story, exterior corridors. *Bath:* combo or shower only. **Parking:** on-site. **Amenities:** hair dryers. Cards: AX, CB, DC, DS, JC, MC, VI.
Special Amenities: free newspaper and preferred room (subject to availability with advanced reservations).

SOME UNITS

BELLEROSE pop. 1,173

—————— **WHERE TO DINE** ——————

ARTURO'S   **Lunch:** $13-$28   **Dinner:** $14-$30   **Phone:** 516/352-7418
◆◆◆◆   **Location:** Belt Pkwy to Cross Island Pkwy, exit 27, 0.3 mi e on SR 25 (Jericho Tpke). 246-04 Jericho Tpke 11001.
Northern   **Hours:** noon-3 & 5:30-10 pm, Fri-11 pm, Sat 5 pm-11 pm, Sun 3 pm-9:30 pm. Closed major holidays.
Italian   **Reservations:** suggested. **Features:** Guests can savor dinner in the "old school" style. Attentive servers in
semiformal attire deliver Northern Italian cuisine, such as osso buco, grilled veal chops, fine risottos, sole in white wine and garlic, and, of course, pasta preparations. A roving guitarist serenades with song of diners' choosing on most nights. A large bowl of fresh fruit comes to the table before the dessert cart rolls through. This place is good for a nice evening out. Casual dress; cocktails; entertainment. **Parking:** valet. Cards: AX, DC, DS, MC, VI.

CALLA LARGA-NORTHERN ITALIAN   **Lunch:** $10-$24   **Dinner:** $12-$26   **Phone:** 516/775-4388
◆◆◆   **Location:** Cross Island Pkwy, exit 27E, just e. 247-63 Jericho Tpke 11426. **Hours:** noon-3 & 5-10 pm, Fri-11 pm,
Northern   Sat 5 pm-11 pm, Sun 2 pm-9 pm. Closed: 7/4, 12/25; also Mon. **Reservations:** suggested. **Features:** A
Italian   cozy ambience prevails in the intimate dining room, decorated with attractive art. The menu lists a fairly wide assortment of seafood, pasta and meat dishes, including innovative specialties from the Dalmatian coast of the Adriatic. Dressy casual; cocktails. **Parking:** on-site. Cards: AX, DC, MC, VI.

BELLPORT pop. 2,363

—————— **WHERE TO STAY** ——————

THE GREAT SOUTH BAY INN   **Phone:** 631/286-8588
◆◆◆   All Year [BP]   1P: $115-$150   2P: $115-$150   XP: $15
Bed & Breakfast   **Location:** SR 27, exit 56, 2.2 mi s on Station Rd, then just e. Located in a residential area. 160 S Country Rd 11713.
Fax: 631/286-2460. **Facility:** A large parlor, eat-in sunroom, brick patio and gardens create country charm at this late-19th-century shingle-style inn. Smoke free premises. 6 one-bedroom standard units. 2 stories (no elevator), interior corridors. *Bath:* some shared or private, combo or shower only. **Parking:** on-site. **Terms:** 2 night minimum stay - weekends in season, age restrictions may apply, 7 day cancellation notice, small pets only ($15 extra charge).
Amenities: *Some:* hair dryers. Cards: MC, VI.

SOME UNITS

FEE

BEMUS POINT pop. 340

—————— **WHERE TO DINE** ——————

ITALIAN FISHERMAN   **Lunch:** $9-$14   **Dinner:** $15-$22   **Phone:** 716/386-7000
◆◆   **Location:** SR 17, exit 10, 0.7 mi on SR 430 E. 61 Lakeside Dr 14712. **Hours:** Open 5/1-9/30; 11:30 am-10 pm,
American   Fri & Sat-midnight. **Reservations:** accepted. **Features:** The restaurant's outdoor decks, casual gathering
places for families, overlook Lake Chautauqua. The eclectic menu satisfies a wide range of appetites, such as steak, lemon-pepper tuna or pasta. Service is attentive and inquisitive. Casual dress; cocktails.
Parking: street. Cards: AX, DC, DS, MC, VI.

YE HARE N' HOUNDS INN

American

Dinner: $14-$19   **Phone:** 716/386-2181
Location: SR 17, exit 10, 1 mi s. 64 Lakeside Dr 14712. **Hours:** 5 pm-10 pm, Sun 4 pm-9 pm; hours may vary in winter. Closed: 9/6, 12/24, 12/25. **Reservations:** suggested. **Features:** Patrons can enjoy lovely views of Lake Chautauqua from the informal, rustic dining room of the English-style inn. Preparations of seafood, chicken, veal and steak are flavorful. The restaurant is host to the Bemus Bay Pops free open-air concert, as well as specialty theme party nights. Casual dress; cocktails. **Parking:** on-site. **Cards:** AX, MC, VI.

BIG FLATS pop. 2,482

——— WHERE TO STAY ———

ECONO LODGE   *Book at aaa.com*   **Phone:** (607)739-2000
Small-scale Hotel
All Year [CP]   1P: $61-$125   2P: $66-$125   XP: $7   F18
Location: SR 17, exit 51, just s. Located across from a shopping center and mall. 871 Rt 64 14903. Fax: 607/739-3552. **Facility:** 48 one-bedroom standard units, some with whirlpools. 2 stories (no elevator), interior/exterior corridors. **Parking:** on-site. **Amenities:** video library, voice mail, irons, hair dryers. **Guest Services:** coin laundry, area transportation. **Business Services:** fax (fee). **Cards:** AX, CB, DC, DS, JC, MC, VI.
SOME UNITS

BINGHAMTON pop. 47,380

——— WHERE TO STAY ———

BEST WESTERN BINGHAMTON REGENCY HOTEL AND CONFERENCE
CENTER   *Book at aaa.com*   **Phone:** (607)722-7575
Large-scale Hotel
All Year [CP]   1P: $89-$250   2P: $89-$250   XP: $10   F12
Location: SR 17, exit 72 to Front St, 1 mi s, just e on E Clinton, then just s; downtown. 225 Water St 13901. Fax: 607/724-7263. **Facility:** 205 units. 196 one-bedroom standard units. 9 one-bedroom suites ($120-$375), some with whirlpools. 10 stories, interior corridors. **Parking:** on-site. **Terms:** check-in 4 pm. **Amenities:** video games, high-speed Internet, voice mail, irons, hair dryers. **Pool(s):** heated indoor. **Leisure Activities:** saunas, exercise room. **Guest Services:** sundries, valet laundry. **Business Services:** conference facilities, fax (fee). **Cards:** AX, CB, DC, DS, JC, MC, VI. *(See color ad below)*
SOME UNITS

CAROUSEL INN *Book at aaa.com* Phone: (607)724-2412

5/1-10/31 [ECP]	1P: $72-$89	2P: $82-$99	XP: $10	F18
11/1-4/30 [ECP]	1P: $62-$79	2P: $72-$89	XP: $10	F18

Small-scale Hotel **Location:** I-81, exit 5, 2 mi s; SR 17 E, exit 72, 1 mi s. 65 Front St 13905. Fax: 607-724-4000. **Facility:** 124 one-bedroom standard units. 3 stories, interior corridors. **Parking:** on-site. **Terms:** package plans - weekends, pets ($15-$25 fee). **Amenities:** voice mail, irons, hair dryers. **Pool(s):** heated indoor. **Leisure Activities:** saunas. **Guest Services:** valet laundry. **Business Services:** meeting rooms. **Cards:** AX, CB, DC, DS, JC, MC, VI. **Special Amenities:** free expanded continental breakfast and free local telephone calls. *(See color ad p 8)*

SOME UNITS

COMFORT INN *Book at aaa.com* Phone: (607)722-5353

5/1-6/30	1P: $69-$199	2P: $69-$199	XP: $10	F18
7/1-8/31	1P: $79-$159	2P: $79-$159	XP: $10	F18
9/1-10/31	1P: $79-$139	2P: $79-$139		
11/1-4/30	1P: $69-$89	2P: $69-$89		

Small-scale Hotel **Location:** I-81, exit 6, just n of Broome Community College. 1156 Front St 13905. Fax: 607/722-1823. **Facility:** 67 one-bedroom standard units, some with efficiencies. 2 stories, interior corridors. *Bath:* combo or shower only. **Parking:** on-site. **Terms:** cancellation fee imposed, [CP] meal plan available, pets (in designated units). **Amenities:** irons, hair dryers. **Leisure Activities:** exercise room. **Guest Services:** valet and coin laundry. **Business Services:** meeting rooms. **Cards:** AX, CB, DC, DS, JC, MC, VI. **Special Amenities:** free expanded continental breakfast and free local telephone calls.

SOME UNITS

DAYS INN *Book at aaa.com* Phone: (607)724-3297

All Year [ECP]	1P: $80-$90	2P: $90-$100	XP: $10	F17

Small-scale Hotel **Location:** I-81, exit 5, 1 mi n on US 11 (Front St). 1000 Front St 13905. Fax: 607/771-0206. **Facility:** 105 units. 104 one-bedroom standard units. 1 one-bedroom suite ($150-$175). 4 stories, interior corridors. **Parking:** on-site. **Terms:** pets ($10 fee, in smoking units). **Amenities:** irons, hair dryers. **Pool(s):** outdoor. **Leisure Activities:** basketball. **Guest Services:** valet and coin laundry. **Business Services:** meeting rooms. **Cards:** AX, DC, DS, JC, MC, VI.

SOME UNITS

FAIRFIELD INN BY MARRIOTT-BINGHAMTON *Book at aaa.com* **Phone:** (607)651-1000
▼▼▼▼ All Year [ECP] 1P: $89-$109
Small-scale Hotel **Location:** I-81, exit 5, just n on US 11 (Front St). Located across from Broome Community College. 864 Front St 13905. Fax: 607/651-1022. **Facility:** 82 one-bedroom standard units. 4 stories, interior corridors. *Bath:* combo or shower only. **Parking:** on-site. **Amenities:** video library (fee), video games, high-speed Internet, dual phone lines, voice mail, irons, hair dryers. **Pool(s):** small heated indoor. **Leisure Activities:** whirlpool, exercise room. **Guest Services:** valet laundry. **Business Services:** meeting rooms. **Cards:** AX, DC, DS, MC, VI.

SOME UNITS

HOLIDAY INN ARENA *Book at aaa.com* **Phone:** (607)722-1212
▼▼▼ All Year 1P: $79-$300 2P: $89-$300
Large-scale Hotel **Location:** Downtown. 2-8 Hawley St 13901. Fax: 607/722-6063. **Facility:** 240 units. 230 one-bedroom standard units. 10 one-bedroom suites ($129-$300), some with whirlpools. 9 stories, interior corridors. **Parking:** on-site. **Terms:** check-in 4 pm, cancellation fee imposed, [AP] meal plan available, package plans, pets ($25 extra charge). **Amenities:** video library (fee), video games, irons, hair dryers. *Some:* high-speed Internet. **Pool(s):** heated indoor. **Leisure Activities:** exercise room. **Guest Services:** gift shop, valet and coin laundry, beauty salon. **Business Services:** conference facilities, business center. **Cards:** AX, CB, DC, DS, MC, VI. *(See color ad p 231)*

SOME UNITS
FEE FEE FEE

MOTEL 6 - 1222 *Book at aaa.com* **Phone:** 607/771-0400
▼▼▼ 5/27-9/5 1P: $39-$49 2P: $45-$55 XP: $3 F17
9/6-4/30 1P: $36-$46 2P: $42-$52 XP: $3 F17
Small-scale Hotel 5/1-5/26 1P: $35-$45 2P: $41-$51 XP: $3 F17
Location: I-81, exit 6 southbound, 2 mi s on US 11 (Front St); exit 5 northbound, 1 mi n on US 11 (Front St). Located in a light-commercial area. 1012 Front St 13905. Fax: 607/773-4781. **Facility:** 99 one-bedroom standard units. 2 stories (no elevator), interior corridors. *Bath:* combo or shower only. **Parking:** on-site. **Terms:** small pets only. **Guest Services:** coin laundry. **Cards:** AX, CB, DC, DS, MC, VI.

SOME UNITS

SUPER 8 MOTEL-BINGHAMTON *Book at aaa.com* **Phone:** (607)773-8111
ΔΔΔ SAVE 5/1-10/31 [CP] 1P: $39-$49 2P: $49-$54 XP: $5 F16
11/1-4/30 [CP] 1P: $39-$49 2P: $45-$49 XP: $5 F16
▼▼▼ **Location:** I-81, exit 5, to access road. 650 Old Front St 13905. Fax: 607/773-8111. **Facility:** 63 one-bedroom standard units. 2 stories (no elevator), interior corridors. **Parking:** on-site. **Terms:** 3 day cancellation notice, Small-scale Hotel weekly rates available, package plans - seasonal & weekdays, pets ($35 deposit). **Cards:** AX, CB, DC, DS, JC, MC, VI. **Special Amenities:** free continental breakfast and free newspaper.

SOME UNITS
FEE

——— WHERE TO DINE ———

ARGO RESTAURANT **Lunch:** $4-$7 **Dinner:** $6-$12 **Phone:** 607-724-4692
ΔΔΔ **Location:** Center. 117 Court St 13901. **Hours:** 6 am-3 pm, Tues-Sat to 8 pm. Closed: 1/1, 11/25, 12/25.
▼ **Features:** Rustic decor adds to the charm of the simple, casual restaurant, which offers counter and table seating. The broad menu includes Greek, Italian and fresh seafood dishes, as well as lunch specials and sandwiches. Breakfast items are served all day. Casual dress; beer & wine only. **Parking:** street.
Greek **Cards:** AX, DS, MC, VI.

THE COPPER CRICKET **Lunch:** $6-$8 **Dinner:** $9-$19 **Phone:** 607-729-5620
▼▼ **Location:** I-81, exit 5, 1 mi s on Front St, then 1 mi w on Main St; SR 17, exit 71, 0.5 mi s on Airport Rd, 0.5 mi s on Glenwood Ave, then w. 266 Main St 13905. **Hours:** 11:30 am-2 & 5-9 pm, Sat from 5 pm. Closed: 1/1, 7/4,
Continental 12/25; also Sun. **Reservations:** suggested. **Features:** Old hats hang along the walls and wine bottles line the sills of crank windows in the dining room. Representative of menu selections are baked brie with almonds, pork barbecue and cream of mushroom and amaretto soup. Service is informal but attentive. Casual dress; beer & wine only. **Parking:** on-site. **Cards:** AX, MC, VI.

CORTESE RESTAURANT **Lunch:** $3-$13 **Dinner:** $3-$25 **Phone:** 607-723-6477
ΔΔΔ **Location:** SR 17/I-81, exit 4S, s to Robinson St exit, then e. 117 Robinson St 13904. **Hours:** 11 am-11 pm, Fri & Sat-midnight. Closed: 3/27, 11/25, 12/24, 12/25. **Reservations:** suggested, weekends.
▼▼ **Features:** Family-operated since 1947, the family-oriented restaurant boasts a convivial, upbeat atmosphere. The tempting scents of aromatic steak, chops and pizza hang in the air of the dining room.
Italian Italian desserts are homemade. Casual dress; cocktails. **Parking:** on-site. **Cards:** AX, CB, DC, DS, MC, VI.

LITTLE VENICE **Lunch:** $4-$7 **Dinner:** $7-$16 **Phone:** 607-724-2513
▼▼▼ **Location:** Downtown. 111 Chenango St 13901. **Hours:** 11:30 am-11 pm. Closed: 11/25, 12/24, 12/25.
Reservations: suggested. **Features:** An area institution since 1946, the restaurant is known for tasty
Italian Italian and American cuisine, particularly pasta and spaghetti sauce. Dining room walls are covered with original artwork, some of which dates back to the 1800s. Casual dress; cocktails. **Parking:** on-site.
Cards: DS, MC, VI.

LOST DOG CAFE/COFFEEHOUSE **Lunch:** $5-$7 **Dinner:** $10-$15 **Phone:** 607-771-6063
▼▼▼ **Location:** I-81, exit 5 to E Clinton; SR 17 (New York), exit 72, 1 mi s on Front St, just e on E Clinton, then just s; across from Best Western Binghamton Regency Hotel and Conference Center. 222 Water St 13901. **Hours:** 11
American am-10 pm. Closed major holidays. **Features:** Appointed in a mix of Americana furnishings, the trendy bistro has a cafe-style ambience. Health-conscious diners appreciate the creative menu, which focuses on nouvelle cuisine and features many vegetarian dishes. Creative salads, pasta, sandwiches and homemade desserts are complemented by freshly-brewed specialty coffees, lattes, cappuccinos and herbal teas. Casual dress; beer & wine only. **Parking:** on-site. **Cards:** AX, DC, DS, MC, VI.

NUMBER 5 Historic
Dinner: $16-$35
Phone: 607/723-0555
Location: I-81, exit 4S to SR 434, just over bridge. 33 S Washington St 13903. **Hours:** 5 pm-10 pm, Fri & Sat-11 pm, Sun-9 pm. Closed: 12/25. **Reservations:** suggested. **Features:** An extensive wine list complements traditional preparations of steak, fish, veal, pasta and chicken, as well as many Greek entrees. Many antiques and old photographs decorate the restored fire station. The atmosphere is warm and comfortable.
American
Casual dress; cocktails. **Parking:** on-site. **Cards:** AX, DC, DS, MC, VI.

SPOT DINER RESTAURANT
Lunch: $5-$12
Dinner: $8-$20
Phone: 607/723-8149
Location: I-81, exit 5 and 6, on US 11 and 12. 1062 Front St 13905. **Hours:** 24 hours. **Reservations:** accepted. **Features:** Greek and Italian dishes, such as gyros and lasagna, are among selections on the casual restaurant's extensive menu. As diners enter, they're tempted by an appealing display of freshly-baked pastries, fluffy cheesecake and luscious Greek desserts. Casual dress; cocktails. **Parking:** on-site.
American
Cards: AX, DC, DS, MC, VI.

WHOLE IN THE WALL RESTAURANT
Lunch: $3-$6
Dinner: $6-$18
Phone: 607/722-5138
Location: I-81, exit 4S to SR 434, just over the bridge. 43 S Washington St 13903. **Hours:** 11:30 am-9 pm. Closed major holidays; also Sun & Mon. **Reservations:** accepted. **Features:** The menu incorporates many non-dairy vegetarian dishes, such as miso soup, tempura with tofu and stir-fried vegetables, as well as chicken and seafood. Salads contain hydroponically grown, pesticide-free lettuce. The owner/chef has cooked for many famous people, such as Bob Dylan, Kenny G, Busta Rhymes and members of the band Phish. Casual dress.
Vegetarian
Parking: on-site. **Cards:** DS, MC, VI.

BLASDELL —See Buffalo p. 248.

BLOOMFIELD —See Finger Lakes & New York p. 451.

BOLTON LANDING —See also ADIRONDACK MOUNTAINS.

——— **WHERE TO STAY** ———

BONNIE VIEW RESORT
Phone: 518/644-5591

7/24-9/6	1P: $110-$161	2P: $110-$161	XP: $8
6/26-7/23	1P: $90-$132	2P: $90-$132	XP: $8
5/14-6/25 & 9/7-9/20	1P: $61-$80	2P: $61-$80	XP: $3

Motel
Location: 1.5 mi s on SR 9N. Located on lake. 4654 Lake Shore Dr 12814-0330 (PO Box 330). **Facility:** 50 units. 22 one-bedroom standard units, some with efficiencies. 28 cottages ($108-$202). 1 story, exterior corridors. **Bath:** combo or shower only. **Parking:** on-site. **Terms:** open 5/14-9/20, 3-7 night minimum stay - 7/1-8/31, 28 day cancellation notice, weekly rates available. **Pool(s):** heated outdoor. **Leisure Activities:** fishing, tennis court, playground, basketball, horseshoes, shuffleboard. **Fee:** paddleboats, boat dock. **Cards:** DS, MC, VI.

SOME UNITS

MELODY MANOR RESORT
Phone: 518/644-9750

6/25-9/6	1P: $150-$200	2P: $150-$200	XP: $20	D
5/8-6/24 & 9/7-10/30	1P: $100-$150	2P: $100-$150	XP: $15	D

Motel
Location: 1.8 mi s on SR 9N. Located on lake. 4610 Lake Shore Dr 12814 (PO Box 366). Fax: 518/644-9750. **Facility:** 40 one-bedroom standard units. 2 stories (no elevator), exterior corridors. **Parking:** on-site. **Terms:** open 5/8-10/30, 2-3 night minimum stay - seasonal, 30 day cancellation notice-fee imposed, weekly rates available. **Dining:** Villa Napoli, see separate listing. **Pool(s):** heated outdoor. **Leisure Activities:** paddleboats, fishing, rowboats, tennis court, lawn games, playground. **Fee:** boat dock. **Business Services:** meeting rooms. **Cards:** AX, MC, VI. **Special Amenities:** free local telephone calls and preferred room (subject to availability with advanced reservations).

THE SAGAMORE *Book at aaa.com*
Phone: (518)644-9400

6/1-10/16	1P: $269-$708	2P: $269-$708	
5/1-5/31	1P: $209-$515	2P: $209-$515	
10/17-4/30	1P: $275-$420	2P: $275-$420	

Resort
Large-scale Hotel
Location: I-87 N, exit 22, 0.3 mi e. Located on a private island known as Green Island. 110 Sagamore Rd 12814 (PO Box 450). Fax: 518/743-6036. **Facility:** This sprawling resort sits on a 72-acre private island. It offers traditional decor in its hotel units and Adirondack-style furnishings in the lodges. 30 day cancellation notice 7/1-8/31. 350 units. 176 one-bedroom standard units. 174 one-bedroom suites, some with efficiencies. 2-3 stories, interior/exterior corridors. **Bath:** combo or shower only. **Parking:** on-site. **Terms:** check-in 4 pm, 2-3 night minimum stay - weekends & summer, 14 day cancellation notice-fee imposed, [AP], [BP], [CP] & [MAP] meal plans available, $6 service charge. **Amenities:** video games (fee), dual phone lines, voice mail, safes, irons, hair dryers. **Dining:** 4 restaurants, 7 am-midnight, cocktails, also, The Trillium, see separate listing, entertainment. **Pool(s):** heated indoor. **Leisure Activities:** whirlpool, steamrooms, rental boats, fishing, miniature golf, cross country skiing, ice skating, snowshoeing, recreation programs, carriage rides, bicycles, playground, spa, basketball. **Fee:** saunas, sailboats, marina, waterskiing, charter fishing, charter sailboats, parasailing, kayaks, lunch & dinner cruises, golf-18 holes, 6 tennis courts (1 indoor, 5 lighted), racquetball court. **Guest Services:** gift shop, valet laundry, area transportation-within 3 mi, beauty salon. **Business Services:** conference facilities, business center. **Cards:** AX, CB, DC, MC, VI. *(See ad p 326)*

FEE
SOME UNITS

VICTORIAN VILLAGE RESORT MOTEL
Phone: 518/644-9401

6/28-9/7 [CP]	1P: $82-$90	2P: $82-$90	XP: $25	D12
5/1-6/27 & 9/8-10/15 [CP]	1P: $75-$78	2P: $75-$78	XP: $25	D12

Motel
Location: 0.8 mi s on SR 9N. Located on lake. 4818 Lake Shore Dr 12814 (PO Box 12). Fax: 518/644-9401. **Facility:** 30 one-bedroom standard units. 1 story, exterior corridors. **Bath:** combo or shower only. **Parking:** on-site. **Terms:** open 5/1-10/15, 3-4 night minimum stay - seasonal, 7 day cancellation notice. **Leisure Activities:** canoeing, fishing, tennis court, shuffleboard. **Cards:** MC, VI.

SOME UNITS

——— WHERE TO DINE ———

ALGONQUIN RESTAURANT **Lunch:** $7-$17 **Dinner:** $17-$23 **Phone:** 518/644-9442
▼▼/▼▼
American
Location: 1 mi s on SR 9N. 4770 Lake Shore Dr 12814. **Hours:** Open 5/1-1/1 & 2/1-4/30; 11:30 am-10 pm. Closed: 11/25, 12/25; also 3/1-3/31. **Reservations:** suggested, for Topside. **Features:** Overlooking Lake George, the casual restaurant is especially popular in summer, when diners gather in the Topside room and on the patio to enjoy great views and good food. Salmon, veal and steak are among well-prepared choices. Vegetarian selections are also available. Casual dress; cocktails. **Parking:** on-site. **Cards:** AX, DC, DS, MC, VI.
🍸 ✕

CATE'S ITALIAN GARDEN RESTAURANT AND BAR **Lunch:** $5-$10 **Dinner:** $11-$22 **Phone:** 518/644-2041
▼▼ ◆◆
Italian
Location: Corner of Congress Point Way; center. 4952 Main St 12814. **Hours:** Open 5/1-2/28 & 4/16-4/30; noon-11 pm. **Reservations:** accepted. **Features:** At the bustling little bistro, mom and dad can opt for a glass of wine and sea bass encrusted with basil pesto and leave the kids to enjoy delicious homemade pizza. Patio seating is an option. Casual dress; cocktails. **Parking:** street. **Cards:** AX, DS, MC, VI.
🍸 ✕

THE TRILLIUM **Dinner:** $23-$30 **Phone:** 518/644-9400
◆◆◆
▼▼▼ ◆◆
American
Location: I-87 N, exit 22, 0.3 mi e; in The Sagamore. 110 Sagamore Rd 12814. **Hours:** 6 pm-9:30 pm; Sunday brunch 10 am-3 pm. Closed: for dinner Sun. **Reservations:** required. **Features:** An impressive selection of wine complements such innovative entrees as sugar-cured salmon and delightful desserts, including the banana phyllo tower. Bathed in a luxurious, sophisticated ambience, the dining room affords lovely views of Lake George. Service is refined, smooth and pampering. Men must wear a jacket and collared shirt. Semi-formal attire; cocktails. **Parking:** on-site. **Cards:** AX, CB, DC, DS, MC, VI.
✕

VILLA NAPOLI **Dinner:** $16-$24 **Phone:** 518/644-9047
◆◆◆
▼▼▼
Italian
Location: 1.8 mi s on SR 9N; in Melody Manor Resort. 4610 Lake Shore Dr 12814. **Hours:** Open 5/16-10/13; 8 am-11:30 & 5-10 pm; weekends only 5/16-6/22 & 9/1-10/13. **Reservations:** suggested. **Features:** A hand-carved marble fireplace and European artwork lend to the charm of the pleasant dining room, on the property of a former estate. Braised veal shanks and a layered dish of spinach, eggplant, peppers and cheese are examples of flavorful entrees. Dishes made from home-grown herbs and original recipes aren't typical tourist food. Casual dress; cocktails. **Parking:** on-site. **Cards:** AX, MC, VI.
🍸 ✕

BOONVILLE pop. 2,138

——— WHERE TO STAY ———

HEADWATERS MOTOR LODGE **Phone:** 315/942-4493
◆◆◆ SAVE
▼▼
Motel

All Year [CP]	1P: $49-$55	2P: $59-$65	XP: $8	F12

Location: Jct SR 12 and 120, 0.7 mi n. 13524 Rt 12 13309 (PO Box 337). Fax: 315/942-4626. **Facility:** 37 one-bedroom standard units, some with kitchens. 1-2 stories (no elevator), interior corridors. **Parking:** on-site, winter plug-ins. **Terms:** 3 day cancellation notice-fee imposed, small pets only. **Leisure Activities:** Fee: game room. **Business Services:** fax (fee). **Cards:** AX, DC, MC, VI.
SOME UNITS
🅂🄳 🐾 🎯 🖥 / ✕ /

BOWMANSVILLE —See Buffalo p. 248.

BRENTWOOD pop. 53,917

——— WHERE TO STAY ———

——— The following lodging was either not evaluated or did not ———
meet AAA rating requirements but is listed for your information only.

WINGATE INN **Phone:** 631/434-1818
(fyi)
Small-scale Hotel

5/1-9/30	1P: $164	2P: $164	XP: $10	F12
1/1-4/30	1P: $159	2P: $159	XP: $10	F12
10/1-12/31	1P: $154	2P: $154	XP: $10	F12

Too new to rate. **Location:** I-495, exit 52 eastbound; exit 53 westbound. 801 Crooked Hill Rd 11717. Fax: 631/434-1919. **Amenities:** 111 units, coffeemakers, microwaves, refrigerators. **Cards:** AX, DC, DS, JC, MC, VI.

BREWERTON pop. 3,453

——— WHERE TO STAY ———

BEL AIR MOTEL **Phone:** (315)699-5991
◆◆◆ SAVE
▼▼
Motel

6/15-9/15 [CP]	1P: $65-$75	2P: $65-$75	XP: $5
5/1-6/14 [CP]	1P: $60-$65	2P: $65-$75	XP: $5
9/16-10/31	1P: $60-$70	2P: $60-$70	XP: $5
11/1-4/30	1P: $55-$65	2P: $55-$70	XP: $5

Location: I-81, exit 30, just w on SR 31 W to SR 11, then 2.1 mi n. Located in a rural setting. 8961 Rt 11 13029. Fax: 315/699-6083. **Facility:** 14 one-bedroom standard units. 1 story, exterior corridors. **Parking:** on-site, winter plug-ins. **Terms:** 3 day cancellation notice. **Business Services:** fax. **Cards:** AX, DS, MC, VI.
SOME UNITS
🎯 / ✕ /

HOLIDAY INN EXPRESS *Book at aaa.com* Phone: (315)676-3222

All Year [ECP] 1P: $89-$99 2P: $89-$99 XP: $10 F19

Small-scale Hotel **Location:** I-81, exit 31 (Bartell Rd), just w. 5552 Bartell Rd 13029 (PO Box 589). Fax: 315/676-7497. **Facility:** 64 one-bedroom standard units. 2 stories, interior corridors. *Bath:* combo or shower only. **Parking:** on-site, winter plug-ins. **Amenities:** irons, hair dryers. **Leisure Activities:** limited exercise equipment. **Guest Services:** valet and coin laundry. **Business Services:** meeting rooms. **Cards:** AX, DC, DS, MC, VI.

SOME UNITS

(A$K) (&M) (⊗) (⌖) (📷) (DATA PORT) (💻) / (✕) (🛏) (🖥) /

BRIDGEHAMPTON pop. 1,381

─── WHERE TO STAY ───

THE ENCLAVE INN Phone: 631/537-2900

6/16-9/30	1P: $129-$269	2P: $149-$289
5/1-6/15	1P: $79-$229	2P: $99-$254
10/1-12/31	1P: $79-$209	2P: $99-$239
1/1-4/30	1P: $74-$89	2P: $99-$114

Motel **Location:** Just w of town. Located in a quiet area. 2668 Montauk Hwy 11932 (PO Box 623). Fax: 631/537-5436. **Facility:** Smoke free premises. 10 one-bedroom standard units. 1 story, exterior corridors. *Bath:* shower only. **Parking:** on-site. **Amenities:** irons, hair dryers. **Pool(s):** heated outdoor. **Leisure Activities:** bocci, horseshoes. **Cards:** AX, MC, VI.

(🏊) (✕) (🛏)

BRIGHTON pop. 35,584 (See map and index starting on p. 550)

─── WHERE TO STAY ───

COURTYARD BY MARRIOTT BRIGHTON *Book at aaa.com* Phone: (585)292-1000 **18**

All Year 1P: $99-$134

Small-scale Hotel **Location:** I-390, exit 16B southbound (E Henrietta Rd); exit 16 northbound, just e. 33 Corporate Woods 14623. Fax: 585/292-0905. **Facility:** 149 units. 137 one-bedroom standard units. 12 one-bedroom suites. 3 stories, interior corridors. **Parking:** on-site. **Amenities:** video library (fee), video games, high-speed Internet, dual phone lines, voice mail, irons, hair dryers. **Pool(s):** small heated outdoor. **Leisure Activities:** whirlpool, exercise room. **Guest Services:** valet and coin laundry. **Business Services:** meeting rooms. **Cards:** AX, DC, DS, MC, VI.

SOME UNITS

(S/D) (✈) (🏊) (⌖) (DATA PORT) (💻) / (✕) (🛏) (🖥) /

HAMPTON INN-ROCHESTER SOUTH *Book at aaa.com* Phone: (585)272-7800 **16**

All Year 1P: $104-$124 2P: $104-$164 XP: $10 F18

Small-scale Hotel **Location:** I-390, exit 16B southbound (E Henrietta Rd); exit 16 northbound. 717 E Henrietta Rd 14623 (717 E Henrietta Rd, ROCHESTER). Fax: 585/272-1211. **Facility:** 112 one-bedroom standard units. 5 stories, interior corridors. *Bath:* combo or shower only. **Parking:** on-site. **Terms:** [CP] meal plan available. **Amenities:** video library (fee), video games, voice mail, irons, hair dryers. **Guest Services:** valet laundry, area transportation-local business. **Business Services:** meeting rooms. **Cards:** AX, CB, DC, DS, MC, VI.

SOME UNITS

(S/D) (✈) (🍴) (⌖) (📷) (🔌) (📶) (DATA PORT) (💻) / (✕) (🛏) /

TOWPATH MOTEL Phone: (585)271-2147 **19**

5/1-11/1 [CP]	1P: $50-$65	2P: $65-$85	XP: $10	F16
11/2-4/30 [CP]	1P: $40-$50	2P: $50-$65	XP: $5	F16

Motel **Location:** I-590, exit 2 (Monroe Ave), just w; exit 2A southbound. 2323 Monroe Ave (US 31) 14618 (2323 Monroe Ave (US 31), ROCHESTER). Fax: 585/271-2147. **Facility:** 20 one-bedroom standard units. 2 stories (no elevator), exterior corridors. *Bath:* combo or shower only. **Parking:** on-site. **Amenities:** irons, hair dryers. **Business Services:** fax. **Cards:** AX, DC, DS, MC, VI. **Special Amenities:** free continental breakfast.

(S/D) (🍴) (✕) (⌖) (🛏) (🖥)

WELLESLEY INN (ROCHESTER/SOUTH) *Book at aaa.com* Phone: (585)427-0130 **17**

All Year 1P: $55-$105 XP: $10

Small-scale Hotel **Location:** I-390, exit 16 northbound; exit 16B (Henrietta Rd) southbound, just s on SR 15A S. 797 E Henrietta Rd 14623. Fax: 585/427-0903. **Facility:** 96 one-bedroom standard units. 4 stories, interior corridors. *Bath:* combo or shower only. **Parking:** on-site. **Terms:** [ECP] meal plan available. **Amenities:** video library (fee), video games, voice mail, irons, hair dryers. **Business Services:** fax (fee). **Cards:** AX, DC, DS, JC, MC, VI. **Special Amenities:** free expanded continental breakfast and free newspaper. *(See color ad p 553)*

SOME UNITS

(S/D) (🐾) (🍴) (⌖) (📷) (🔌) (📶) (DATA PORT) (💻) / (✕) (🛏) /

─── WHERE TO DINE ───

BAZIL Lunch: $6-$9 Dinner: $8-$18 Phone: 585/427-7420 **13**

Italian **Location:** I-390, exit 16B (Henrietta Rd) southbound; exit 16 northbound. 749 E Henrietta Rd 14623. **Hours:** 11:30 am-2:30 & 5-10 pm, Fri-11 pm, Sat noon-11 pm, Sun noon-9 pm. Closed major holidays. **Features:** The huge lunch buffet incorporates traditional pasta dishes, as well as meat, chicken and seafood specialties. Casual dress; cocktails. **Parking:** on-site. **Cards:** AX, DC, DS, MC, VI.

(🍽) (✕)

MARIO'S VIA ABRUZZI Dinner: $13-$26 Phone: 585/271-1111 **11**

Italian **Location:** I-590, exit 2 (Monroe Ave), just w. 2740 Monroe Ave 14618. **Hours:** 5 pm-10 pm, Fri-11 pm, Sat 4 pm-11 pm, Sun 10 am-3 & 4:30-9 pm. Closed major holidays. **Reservations:** suggested. **Features:** A warm welcome and attentive service mark the dining experience at this Italian restaurant. On the menu are pleasing appetizers from antipasto to ravioli, a wide variety of pasta dishes, and house-designed specials including rabbit, seafood, veal shanks and duck. Among delectable desserts are classic cannoli and tiramisu. Dressy casual; cocktails. **Parking:** on-site. **Cards:** AX, DC, DS, MC, VI.

(🍽) (✕)

(See map and index starting on p. 550)

MUNDO GRILL

American

Lunch: $6-$10   **Dinner:** $13-$19   **Phone:** 585/442-2840   (15)

Location: I-590, exit 2 (Monroe Ave), just w. 2833 Monroe Ave 14618. **Hours:** 11:30 am-3 & 5-10 pm, Fri-11 pm, Sat 5 pm-11 pm, Sun 4 pm-9 pm. Closed major holidays. **Features:** New cuisine offerings reflect the influences of many countries. The casually upscale setting includes a seasonal patio. Casual dress; cocktails. **Parking:** on-site. **Cards:** AX, MC, VI.

PHILLIPS EUROPEAN RESTAURANT

Continental

Dinner: $9-$25   **Phone:** 585/272-9910   (12)

Location: I-390, exit 16B (Henrietta Rd) southbound; exit 16N northbound. 26 Corporate Woods 14623. **Hours:** 11 am-midnight. Closed: 11/25, 12/25; also Sun. **Reservations:** suggested. **Features:** Continental cuisine has been carefully prepared to order for more than 16 years. The on-premises bakery churns out 30 European pastries and desserts daily. Casual dress; cocktails. **Parking:** on-site. **Cards:** AX, CB, DC, DS, MC, VI.

BRISTOL CENTER —*See also FINGER LAKES.*

——— **WHERE TO STAY** ———

ACORN INN

Historic Bed
& Breakfast

Phone: (585)229-2834

All Year [BP]   1P: $130-$230   2P: $140-$230

Location: Center. 4508 SR 64 S 14424-9309 (4508 SR 64 S, CANANDAIGUA). Fax: 585/229-2834. **Facility:** A former stagecoach inn dating from 1795, this Finger Lakes B&B is near many wineries and features four-poster beds and rooms with fireplaces. Smoke free premises. 4 one-bedroom standard units, some with whirlpools. 2 stories (no elevator); interior corridors. **Parking:** on-site. **Terms:** 2 night minimum stay - weekends 5/1-11/31, age restrictions may apply, 14 day cancellation notice-fee imposed, weekly rates available, [CP] meal plan available, package plans - seasonal. **Amenities:** video library, CD players, hair dryers. **Leisure Activities:** whirlpool. **Business Services:** fax. **Cards:** AX, DS, MC, VI. **Special Amenities:** free full breakfast and free local telephone calls.

BROCKPORT pop. 8,103

——— **WHERE TO STAY** ———

ECONO LODGE OF BROCKPORT

Motel

Book at aaa.com

Phone: (585)637-3157

All Year [ECP]   1P: $50-$100   2P: $50-$100   F18

Location: Jct SR 19, just w on SR 31. 6575 Fourth Section Rd 14420. Fax: 585/637-0434. **Facility:** 39 one-bedroom standard units. 2 stories (no elevator); exterior corridors. **Parking:** on-site. **Terms:** cancellation fee imposed, weekly rates available, package plans. **Pool(s):** outdoor. **Leisure Activities:** playground. **Guest Services:** coin laundry. **Cards:** AX, DC, DS, MC, VI. **Special Amenities:** free expanded continental breakfast and preferred room (subject to availability with advanced reservations).

SOME UNITS

HOLIDAY INN EXPRESS

Small-scale Hotel

Book at aaa.com

Phone: (585)395-1000

All Year [ECP]   1P: $89-$139   2P: $89-$139   XP: $10   F14

Location: Just s of jct SR 31 and 19. 4908 Lake Rd S 14420. Fax: 585/395-9492. **Facility:** 41 one-bedroom standard units, some with whirlpools. 2 stories, interior corridors. **Parking:** on-site. **Terms:** pets ($15 fee). **Amenities:** dual phone lines, voice mail, irons, hair dryers. **Cards:** AX, DC, DS, MC, VI. **Special Amenities:** free expanded continental breakfast and free local telephone calls.

SOME UNITS

FEE

——— **WHERE TO DINE** ———

TWO BROTHERS

American

Lunch: $3-$5   **Dinner:** $6-$9   **Phone:** 585/637-7280

Location: Jct SR 31 and 19. 6305 Spencerport Rd (SR 31) 14220. **Hours:** 6 am-9 pm, Fri-10 pm. Closed: 1/1, 12/25. **Features:** The popular, college-town diner offers some upscale appointments, friendly service and ample portions of comfort food. Casual dress. **Parking:** on-site. **Cards:** AX, DS, MC, VI.

——— *The following restaurant has not been evaluated by AAA* ———
but is listed for your information only.

THE APPLE TREE INN

[fyi]

Phone: 585/637-6440

Not evaluated. **Location:** On SR 104. 7407 Ridge Rd W 14420. **Features:** Fine dining can be found in this chic country restaurant, including specialty pasta dishes accented by light wine sauces and intriguing ingredients; seafoods, chicken, steaks and chops are also good choices.

BRONX —*See New York p. 438.*

BROOKLYN —*See New York p. 438.*

Destination Buffalo
pop. 292,648

*O*ften described as a European-looking city, Buffalo has been sculpted by the hands of architectural greats.

*F*rom the bucolic city park system designed by Frederick Law Olmsted and the handful of Frank Lloyd Wright masterpieces, to Henry Hobson Richardson's Psychiatric Center and the Louis Sullivan Guaranty Building, Buffalo offers a varied palette of architectural styles.

© R. Stockton Robertstock

Buffalo skyline.
The old and the not-so-old blend for an architecturally interesting cityscape.

Buffalo Niagara CVB and Angel Art Ltd.

Buffalo waterfront.
For a different perspective, take a harbor cruise and an extended excursion to Lake Erie and beyond.

Buffalo Niagara CVB and Angel Art Ltd.

City Hall, Buffalo.
The 28th-floor observation deck is a great place to begin a self-guiding sight-seeing tour of the city.

See Vicinity map page 238

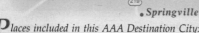

(map showing Buffalo area: Tonawanda, Grand Island, Amherst, East Amherst, Kenmore, Williamsville, Clarence, Bowmansville, Cheektowaga, Depew, West Seneca, Blasdell, Hamburg, East Aurora, Springville)

Buffalo Niagara CVB and Jim Fink

A Taste of Buffalo.
Wings and other things to please the palate attract throngs of tasters to the streets each July.

*P*laces included in this AAA Destination City:

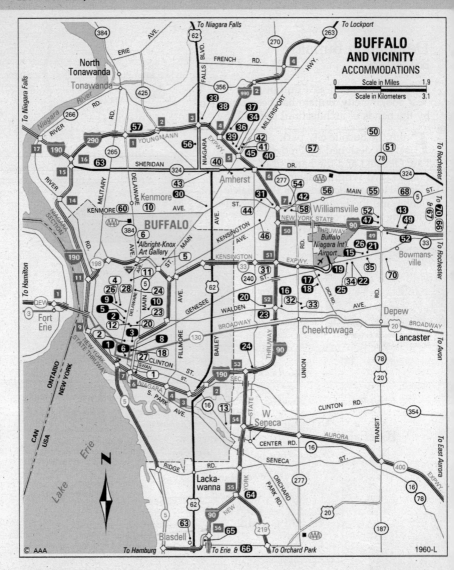

Airport Accommodations

Spotter/Map Page Number	OA	BUFFALO NIAGARA INTERNATIONAL	Diamond Rating	Rate Range High Season	Listing Page
52 / above	AAA	Red Roof Inn-Buffalo Airport, 3 mi e of terminal	◊◊	$53-$81 SAVE	248
21 / above	AAA	Best Western-Norstar Inn, 0.8 mi e of terminal	◊◊	$89-$125 SAVE	249
17 / above	AAA	Comfort Suites-Buffalo Airport, 0.7 mi w of west terminal	◊◊◊	$104-$144 SAVE	249
23 / above	AAA	Hampton Inn-Airport/Galleria, 3.5 mi w of west terminal entrance	◊◊◊	$104-$149 SAVE	249

Spotter/Map Page Number	OA	BUFFALO NIAGARA INTERNATIONAL (continued)	Diamond Rating	Rate Range High Season	Listing Page
15 / p. 238	AAA	Holiday Inn-Buffalo Airport, 0.8 mi e of terminal	▽▽▽	$99-$129 SAVE	249
18 / p. 238		Homewood Suites by Hilton, 0.9 mi w of west terminal	▽▽▽	$109-$199	250
22 / p. 238	AAA	Park Plaza Hotel Buffalo Airport, facing terminal entrance	▽▽▽	$95 SAVE	250
25 / p. 238		Quality Inn-Buffalo Airport, facing terminal entrance	▽▽	$49-$99	250
26 / p. 238		Sleep Inn & Suites, just e of terminal	▽▽	$69-$109	250
47 / p. 238	AAA	Clarion Hotel-Buffalo Airport, 2.5 mi ne of terminal	▽▽▽	$79-$99 SAVE	255

Buffalo and Vicinity

This index helps you "spot" where approved accommodations and restaurants are located on the corresponding detailed maps. Lodging rate ranges are for comparison only and show the property's high season; rates are per night, unless only weekly (W) rates are available. Restaurant rate range is for dinner, unless only lunch (L) is served. Turn to the listing page for more detailed rate information and consult display ads for special promotions.

Spotter/Map Page Number	OA	BUFFALO - Lodgings	Diamond Rating	Rate Range High Season	Listing Page
1 / p. 238	AAA	Adam's Mark Buffalo-Niagara Hotel - see color ad p 242	▽▽▽	$107-$134 SAVE	242
2 / p. 238		The Mansion on Delaware Ave	▽▽▽▽	$145-$185	244
3 / p. 238		Radisson Suite Hotel Buffalo - see color ad p 413	▽▽▽	$109-$169	244
5 / p. 238	AAA	Best Western Inn-On The Avenue	▽▽▽	$99-$159 SAVE	242
6 / p. 238		Hampton Inn & Suites-Downtown	▽▽▽	$109-$209	243
8 / p. 238	AAA	Hyatt Regency Buffalo	▽▽▽	$89-$160 SAVE	243
9 / p. 238	AAA	Holiday Inn-Downtown	▽▽▽	$89-$149 SAVE	243
10 / p. 238		Doubletree Club Buffalo Downtown - see color ad p 243	▽▽▽	$109-$199	242
		BUFFALO - Restaurants			
1 / p. 238		Chef's	▽▽	$4-$16	244
2 / p. 238		Rue Franklin	▽▽▽	$19-$25	245
4 / p. 238		Just Pasta	▽▽	$12-$25	245
5 / p. 238		Anchor Bar & Restaurant	▽▽	$7-$17	244
6 / p. 238		Oliver's Restaurant	▽▽▽	$19-$29	245
10 / p. 238		The Hourglass Restaurant	▽▽▽	$20-$30	244
11 / p. 238		The Park Lane Tavern & Oyster Bar	▽▽▽	$16-$20	245
12 / p. 238		Lord Chumley's	▽▽▽	$18-$39	245
13 / p. 238		The Blackthorn	▽▽	$11-$16	244
18 / p. 238		E B Greens Steakhouse	▽▽▽	$18-$55	244
20 / p. 238		Fiddle Heads Restaurant	▽▽	$14-$25	244
23 / p. 238		Hemingway's	▽▽	$10-$11	244
24 / p. 238		Hutch's	▽▽▽	$12-$26	244
26 / p. 238		Left Bank	▽▽	$8-$19	245
27 / p. 238		Pettibone's Grille	▽	$12-$20	245
28 / p. 238		Roseland	▽▽	$10-$22	245

Spotter/Map Page Number	OA	CHEEKTOWAGA - Lodgings	Diamond Rating	Rate Range High Season	Listing Page
15 / p. 238	AAA	Holiday Inn-Buffalo Airport	◆◆◆	$99-$129 SAVE	249
16 / p. 238		Four Points by Sheraton-Buffalo Airport - see color ad p 210	◆◆◆	$109-$154	249
17 / p. 238	AAA	Comfort Suites-Buffalo Airport	◆◆◆	$104-$144 SAVE	249
18 / p. 238		Homewood Suites by Hilton	◆◆◆	$109-$199	250
19 / p. 238	AAA	Holiday Inn Express Hotel & Suites-Buffalo Airport	◆◆◆	$110-$160 SAVE	250
20 / p. 238		Residence Inn by Marriott	◆◆◆	$99-$179	250
21 / p. 238	AAA	Best Western-Norstar Inn	◆◆	$89-$125 SAVE	249
22 / p. 238	AAA	Park Plaza Hotel Buffalo Airport	◆◆◆	$95 SAVE	250
23 / p. 238	AAA	Hampton Inn-Airport/Galleria	◆◆◆	$104-$149 SAVE	249
24 / p. 238	AAA	Holiday Inn Express Hotel & Suites	◆◆◆	$100-$140 SAVE	249
25 / p. 238		Quality Inn-Buffalo Airport	◆◆	$49-$99	250
26 / p. 238		Sleep Inn & Suites	◆◆	$69-$109	250
		CHEEKTOWAGA - Restaurants			
31 / p. 238		Danny's	◆◆	$7-$9	251
32 / p. 238		Holiday Showcase Restaurant	◆	$6-$11	251
33 / p. 238		Alton's Restaurant	◆	$8-$12	250
34 / p. 238		Pranzo Ristorante	◆◆◆	$23-$32	251
35 / p. 238		Olympic Family Restaurant	◆	$3-$9	251
		AMHERST - Lodgings			
30 / p. 238	AAA	Travelodge	◆◆	$60-$90 SAVE	247
31 / p. 238	AAA	Lord Amherst Motor Hotel	◆◆	$69-$109 SAVE	246
33 / p. 238	AAA	Holiday Inn Buffalo-Amherst	◆◆◆	$100-$160 SAVE	246
34 / p. 238	AAA	Buffalo Marriott-Niagara	◆◆◆	$129-$189 SAVE	246
35 / p. 238		Extended Stay America	◆◆	$85-$105	246
36 / p. 238	AAA	Red Roof Inn	◆◆	$54-$89 SAVE	247
37 / p. 238		Super 8 Motel-Amherst/Buffalo/Niagara Falls	◆◆	$59-$74	247
38 / p. 238		Sleep Inn	◆◆	$79-$109	247
39 / p. 238	AAA	Hampton Inn-Buffalo/Amherst	◆◆◆	$109-$129 SAVE	246
40 / p. 238		Buffalo/Amherst Courtyard By Marriott	◆◆◆	$59-$250	246
		AMHERST - Restaurants			
40 / p. 238		Duff's Famous Wings	◆	$7-$10	247
41 / p. 238		Santora's-Phase II	◆	$4-$20	247
42 / p. 238		Dakota Grill	◆◆	$14-$20	247
43 / p. 238		Taste of India	◆◆	$10-$15	248
44 / p. 238		Siena	◆◆◆	$10-$27	248
46 / p. 238		San Marco	◆◆◆	$14-$21	247
		WILLIAMSVILLE - Lodgings			
42 / p. 238		Hampton Inn at Williamsville	◆◆◆	$145-$199	256
43 / p. 238	AAA	Microtel-Lancaster	◆◆	$49-$79 SAVE	256
45 / p. 238		Residence Inn by Marriott Buffalo/Amherst	◆◆◆	$144-$169	256

Spotter/Map Page Number	OA	WILLIAMSVILLE - Lodgings (continued)	Diamond Rating	Rate Range High Season	Listing Page
47 / p. 238	AAA	**Clarion Hotel-Buffalo Airport** - see color ad p 242	◆◆◆	$79-$99 [SAVE]	255
49 / p. 238		Fairfield Inn-Lancaster	◆◆	$59-$109	255
		WILLIAMSVILLE - Restaurants			
50 / p. 238	AAA	**Kabab & Curry**	◆◆	$6-$15	256
51 / p. 238		Joe Mata's	◆◆	$4-$17	256
52 / p. 238		Protocol	◆◆	$11-$21	257
54 / p. 238		ZuZon American Grille	◆◆	$9-$18	257
55 / p. 238	AAA	**Tandoori's**	◆◆	$10-$20	257
56 / p. 238		Eagle House Restaurant	◆◆	$10-$20	256
57 / p. 238		Daffodil's	◆◆◆	$16-$27	256
58 / p. 238		The Original Pancake House	◆	$4-$8	256
		BOWMANSVILLE - Lodgings			
52 / p. 238	AAA	**Red Roof Inn-Buffalo Airport**	◆◆	$53-$81 [SAVE]	248
		TONAWANDA - Lodgings			
56 / p. 238	AAA	**Days Inn**	◆◆	$60-$125 [SAVE]	255
57 / p. 238	AAA	**Microtel-Tonawanda**	◆◆	$53-$75 [SAVE]	255
		KENMORE - Lodgings			
63 / p. 238		Super 8-Buffalo/Niagara Falls	◆◆	$60-$75	254
		KENMORE - Restaurant			
60 / p. 238		Tsunami	◆◆◆	$14-$22	254
		WEST SENECA - Lodgings			
64 / p. 238		Hampton Inn Buffalo-South/I-90	◆◆◆	$79-$175	255
		BLASDELL - Lodgings			
65 / p. 238	AAA	**Econo Lodge South** - see ad p 243	◆◆	$45-$99 [SAVE]	248
66 / p. 238	AAA	**McKinley's Hotel & Banquet**	◆◆	$74-$159 [SAVE]	248
		BLASDELL - Restaurant			
63 / p. 238	AAA	**Ilio DiPaolo's Restaurant**	◆◆	$7-$18	248
		CLARENCE - Lodgings			
70 / p. 238	AAA	**Asa Ransom House**	◆◆◆	$89-$175 [SAVE]	251
		CLARENCE - Restaurants			
66 / p. 238		Rita's Palermo	◆◆	$9-$18	251
67 / p. 238	AAA	**Asa Ransom House Dining Room**	◆◆◆	$12-$34	251
68 / p. 238		Old Red Mill Inn	◆◆	$12-$25	251
		DEPEW - Restaurant			
70 / p. 238	AAA	**Salvatore's Italian Gardens**	◆◆◆	$19-$45	252

BUFFALO pop. 292,648   (See map and index starting on p. 238)

──────── WHERE TO STAY ────────

ADAM'S MARK BUFFALO-NIAGARA HOTEL   *Book at aaa.com*   Phone: (716)845-5100   **1**
(AAA) (SAVE)   5/1-10/31   1P: $107-$134   2P: $107-$134   XP: $15   F17
♦♦♦   11/1-4/30   1P: $94-$121   2P: $94-$121   XP: $15   F17
Location: I-490, exit 7, at Church and Lower Terrace sts; downtown. 120 Church St 14202. Fax: 716/845-5377.
Facility: 486 units. 480 one-bedroom standard units, some with whirlpools. 6 one-bedroom suites. 9 stories,
Large-scale Hotel interior corridors. **Bath:** combo or shower only. **Parking:** on-site (fee) and valet. **Terms:** cancellation fee imposed, package plans. **Amenities:** video games, voice mail, irons, hair dryers. **Dining:** 24 hours, cocktails.
Pool(s): heated indoor. **Leisure Activities:** sauna. **Guest Services:** gift shop, valet and coin laundry, area transportation-downtown. **Business Services:** conference facilities, business center. **Cards:** AX, CB, DC, DS, JC, MC, VI.
(See color ad below)

SOME UNITS
🅢🅓 ✈ ❲❳ 24⁺ 🍽 ⚓ ♨ 🛎 ⊶ 📠 📶 [DATA PORT] 💻 / ✕ [VCR] 🖨 🖥 /
                                                                                FEE FEE FEE

BEST WESTERN INN-ON THE AVENUE   *Book at aaa.com*   Phone: (716)886-8333   **5**
(AAA) (SAVE)   All Year   1P: $99-$149   2P: $109-$159   XP: $8   F16
♦♦♦   **Location:** Between Virginia and Allen sts; downtown. 510 Delaware Ave 14202. Fax: 716/884-3070. **Facility:** 61 one-bedroom standard units, some with whirlpools. 5 stories, interior corridors. **Bath:** combo or shower only.
Parking: on-site. **Terms:** small pets only. **Amenities:** irons, hair dryers. **Guest Services:** valet laundry. **Business Services:** meeting rooms. **Cards:** AX, CB, DC, DS, JC, MC, VI. **Special Amenities:** free continental
Small-scale Hotel breakfast and free newspaper.

SOME UNITS
🅢🅓 🐾 ❲❳⁺ ⚓ 🛎 📠 [DATA PORT] 💻 / ✕ [VCR] 🖨 🖥 /

DOUBLETREE CLUB BUFFALO DOWNTOWN   *Book at aaa.com*   Phone: (716)845-0112   **10**
♦♦♦   All Year   1P: $109-$189   2P: $119-$199   XP: $10   F18
Small-scale Hotel **Location:** I-90, exit 51W to Buffalo; I-90 W to SR 33 W, exit Locust St to Michigan Ave, 0.4 mi n to High St, then just w.
125 High St 14203. Fax: 716/845-0125. **Facility:** 100 units. 88 one-bedroom standard units. 12 one-bedroom suites ($159-$229). 8 stories, interior corridors. **Bath:** combo or shower only. **Parking:** on-site (fee) and valet.
Amenities: video library, video games, high-speed Internet, dual phone lines, voice mail, irons, hair dryers. **Leisure Activities:** exercise room. **Guest Services:** valet and coin laundry, area transportation. **Business Services:** meeting rooms, business center. **Cards:** AX, CB, DC, DS, JC, MC, VI. *(See color ad p 243)*

SOME UNITS
[ASK] 🅢🅓 ✈ ❲❳ ⚓ 📠 [DATA PORT] 🖨 🖥 💻 / ✕ [VCR] /
           FEE

(See map and index starting on p. 238)

HAMPTON INN & SUITES-DOWNTOWN   *Book at aaa.com*   Phone: (716)855-2223   **6**
All Year [ECP]   1P: $109-$199   2P: $119-$209   XP: $10   F18
Small-scale Hotel   **Location:** At Chippewa St; downtown. 220 Delaware Ave 14202. Fax: 716/856-5221. **Facility:** 137 units. 106 one-bedroom standard units, some with whirlpools. 31 one-bedroom suites ($139-$350), some with efficiencies and/or whirlpools. 6 stories, interior corridors. *Bath:* combo or shower only. **Parking:** on-site.
Amenities: video games, high-speed Internet, dual phone lines, voice mail, irons, hair dryers. **Leisure Activities:** whirlpool, exercise room. **Guest Services:** sundries, valet and coin laundry. **Business Services:** meeting rooms, business center. **Cards:** AX, DC, DS, MC, VI.

SOME UNITS

HOLIDAY INN-DOWNTOWN   *Book at aaa.com*   Phone: 716/886-2121   **9**
4/1-4/30	1P: $89-$139	2P: $99-$149	XP: $10	F12
5/1-8/31	1P: $79-$129	2P: $89-$139	XP: $10	F12
9/1-10/31	1P: $79-$99	2P: $79-$99	XP: $10	F12
11/1-3/31	1P: $69-$89	2P: $69-$89	XP: $10	F12

Small-scale Hotel   **Location:** Between Allen and North sts; downtown. Located in a historic district. 620 Delaware Ave 14202. Fax: 716/886-7942. **Facility:** 168 one-bedroom standard units. 8 stories, interior corridors. **Parking:** on-site. **Terms:** small pets only ($30 fee). **Amenities:** voice mail, irons, hair dryers. **Dining:** 6:30 am-10 pm, cocktails. **Pool(s):** heated outdoor. **Leisure Activities:** exercise room. **Guest Services:** valet and coin laundry, area transportation-bus & train station. **Business Services:** meeting rooms, fax (fee). **Cards:** AX, CB, DC, DS, JC, MC, VI. **Special Amenities:** free newspaper and early check-in/late check-out.

SOME UNITS
FEE   FEE

HYATT REGENCY BUFFALO   *Book at aaa.com*   Phone: (716)856-1234   **8**
All Year   1P: $89-$160   2P: $89-$160   XP: $25   F18
Location: On Pearl St at W Huron St; downtown. 2 Fountain Plaza 14202. Fax: 716/852-6157. **Facility:** 395 units. 384 one-bedroom standard units, some with whirlpools. 11 one-bedroom suites. 16 stories, interior corridors. Large-scale Hotel   *Bath:* combo or shower only. **Parking:** on-site (fee). **Terms:** cancellation fee imposed. **Amenities:** voice mail, irons, hair dryers. *Some:* CD players, fax. **Dining:** 2 restaurants, 6:30 am-10 pm, cocktails, also, E B Greens Steakhouse, see separate listing. **Leisure Activities:** exercise room. **Guest Services:** gift shop, valet laundry. **Business Services:** conference facilities, business center. **Cards:** AX, CB, DC, DS, JC, MC, VI.

SOME UNITS

(See map and index starting on p. 238)

THE MANSION ON DELAWARE AVE *Book at aaa.com*   **Phone:** (716)886-3300   **②**
▼▼▼▼ ▼▼▼▼ All Year [ECP]   1P: $145-$185   2P: $145-$185   XP: $20   F16
     Location: Jct Edward St; downtown. 414 Delaware Ave 14202. Fax: 716/883-3923. **Facility:** Meticulous renovation
Historic   details combine old world elegance with contemporary style and modern amenities including butler service.
Small-scale Hotel   Smoke free premises. 28 units. 25 one-bedroom standard units, some with whirlpools. 3 one-bedroom suites
($250) with whirlpools. 4 stories, interior corridors. *Bath:* combo or shower only. **Parking:** on-site and valet.
Terms: check-in 4 pm, [BP] meal plan available, package plans - seasonal. **Amenities:** high-speed Internet, dual phone lines,
voice mail, hair dryers. **Leisure Activities:** exercise room. *Fee:* massage. **Guest Services:** complimentary evening beverages,
valet laundry, area transportation. **Business Services:** meeting rooms, administrative services, PC. **Cards:** AX, CB, DC, DS,
MC, VI.

SOME UNITS

🚻 ⊠ 📷 📠 📶 / 🖨 /

RADISSON SUITE HOTEL BUFFALO *Book at aaa.com*   **Phone:** (716)854-5500   **③**
▼▼▼▼ ▼▼▼▼ All Year   1P: $109-$159   2P: $109-$169   XP: $10   F18
     Location: Between Main and Washington sts, at Chippewa St; downtown. Located in the theater district. 601 Main St
Small-scale Hotel   14203. Fax: 716/854-4836. **Facility:** 146 one-bedroom suites. 7 stories, interior corridors. **Parking:** no self-
parking. **Terms:** 3 day cancellation notice-fee imposed. **Amenities:** voice mail, irons, hair dryers. **Leisure
Activities:** exercise room. **Guest Services:** valet laundry, area transportation. **Business Services:** meeting rooms. **Cards:** AX,
CB, DC, DS, MC, VI. *(See color ad p 413)*

SOME UNITS

(ASK) 🅂 ✈ 🍴 🍸 📷 📠 🖥 📶 / ⊠ /

FEE

——— WHERE TO DINE ———

ANCHOR BAR & RESTAURANT   **Lunch:** $4-$7   **Dinner:** $7-$17   **Phone:** 716/886-8920   **⑤**
▼▼▼ ▼▼▼   **Location:** Jct Main and North sts; downtown. 1047 Main St 14209. **Hours:** 11 am-11 pm, Fri-1 am, Sat noon-1
am, Sun noon-11 pm. Closed: 11/25, 12/25. **Features:** The self-proclaimed "home of the original buffalo
American   chicken wings," the family-owned restaurant first served buffalo chicken wings in 1964. Open since 1935,
this place also prepares salads, subs, hot and cold sandwiches and pasta dishes. Casual dress; cocktails.
Parking: on-site. **Cards:** AX, DC, DS, MC, VI.   🍸 ⊠

THE BLACKTHORN   **Lunch:** $6-$8   **Dinner:** $11-$16   **Phone:** 716/825-9327   **⑬**
▼▼▼ ▼▼▼   **Location:** I-90, exit 54, 1.5 mi n on SR 16 N; at Seneca and Cazenovia. 2134 Seneca St 14210.
Hours: noon-midnight. Closed major holidays. **Features:** Since 1968, the attractive, nicely-decorated
Steak & Seafood   restaurant has welcomed the neighborhood crowd to enjoy an extensive array of snacks, sandwiches,
soup and entrees. Lunch patrons can sample the buffet. The Friday fish fry and weekend prime rib
specials are popular. Casual dress; cocktails. **Parking:** on-site. **Cards:** AX, DS, MC, VI.   🍸 ⊠

CHEF'S   **Lunch:** $4-$9   **Dinner:** $4-$16   **Phone:** 716/856-9187   **①**
▼▼▼ ▼▼▼   **Location:** Jct Chicago St. 291 Seneca St 14204. **Hours:** 11 am-9 pm. Closed major holidays; also Sun.
Features: This casual spot has been an understandable choice for traditional fine dining for 75 years.
Italian   Delicious homemade sauce is the element that keeps western New Yorkers coming back. Casual dress;
cocktails. **Parking:** on-site. **Cards:** AX, DC, MC, VI.   ⊠

E B GREENS STEAKHOUSE   **Dinner:** $18-$55   **Phone:** 716/855-4870   **⑱**
▼▼▼ ▼▼▼   **Location:** On Pearl St at W Huron St; downtown; in Hyatt Regency Buffalo. 2 Fountain Plaza 14202. **Hours:** 5
pm-11 pm. Closed: 12/25. **Features:** Consistency is the key to success at the
Steak & Seafood   no-nonsense, high-quality steakhouse. Among enduring favorites are the 48-ounce porterhouse, 32-ounce
prime rib and two- to three-pound lobsters. Enormous portions, including steak fries and baked sweet
potatoes, are a challenge for meat-lovers. Dressy casual; cocktails. **Parking:** valet. **Cards:** AX, DC, DS, MC, VI.   🍸 ⊠

FIDDLE HEADS RESTAURANT   **Dinner:** $14-$25   **Phone:** 716/883-4166   **⑳**
▼▼▼ ▼▼▼   **Location:** Corner of Franklin St. 62 Allen St 14202. **Hours:** 5 pm-10 pm. Closed: 11/25, 12/25; also Sun & Mon.
Reservations: suggested. **Features:** The tiny restaurant presents an interesting menu of innovative,
American   well-prepared dishes which are served with unusual sides that complement. Two offerings to try are the
pizza made from real fiddleheads and the steamed sea bass. Servers are friendly. Casual dress; beer &
wine only. **Parking:** street. **Cards:** DS, MC, VI.

HEMINGWAY'S   **Lunch:** $5-$7   **Dinner:** $10-$11   **Phone:** 716/852-1937   **㉓**
▼▼▼ ▼▼▼   **Location:** In the heart of the theater district. 492 Pearl St 14202. **Hours:** 11:30 am-11 pm, Fri & Sat-1 am, Sun 4
pm-10 pm. Closed: 3/27, 11/25, 12/25. **Features:** Well-aged brick walls act as a backdrop for stained glass
American   windows, wooden Indians, brass and wood carvings and guns to create an eclectic atmosphere, a favorite
spot of the theater-going crowd. The menu dabbles in sandwiches and salads, as well as burgers and full
entrees. Chocolate cheesecake is a sinful temptation. Cocktails. **Parking:** on-site. **Cards:** AX, DC, MC, VI.

THE HOURGLASS RESTAURANT   **Dinner:** $20-$30   **Phone:** 716/877-8788   **⑩**
▼▼▼ ▼▼▼   **Location:** 0.8 mi e of SR 384; Kenmore at Hiler. 981 Kenmore Ave 14217. **Hours:** 4 pm-9:30 pm. Closed major
holidays; also Sun, Mon & 6/25-7/14. **Reservations:** suggested. **Features:** Informality characterizes the
Continental   unimposing setting. The freshest seafood preparations are featured, as are rack of lamb and varied
selections of other meats and poultry. Freshly baked desserts, especially creme brulee, highlight the talents
of the owner's wife. Dressy casual; cocktails. **Parking:** on-site. **Cards:** AX, MC, VI.   ⊠

HUTCH'S   **Dinner:** $12-$26   **Phone:** 716/885-0074   **㉔**
▼▼▼ ▼▼▼   **Location:** 1 blk from Gates Cir. 1375 Delaware Ave 14209. **Hours:** 5 pm-10 pm, Fri & Sat-midnight, Sun 4 pm-9
pm. Closed major holidays. **Reservations:** suggested. **Features:** Patrons can savor prime steak, lamb
American   chops and fresh seafood, such as sesame-crusted tuna. Innovative appetizers include Thai calamari and
ceviche. Leopard-skin rugs and a brick-walled bar stand out in the dining room. Dressy casual; cocktails.
Parking: no self-parking. **Cards:** AX, DC, MC, VI.   🍸 ⊠

(See map and index starting on p. 238)

JUST PASTA   Lunch: $5-$9   Dinner: $12-$25   Phone: 716/881-1888   ④
Italian
Location: Jct Bryant St and Elmwood Ave, just w, then 0.3 mi w of Delaware Ave; uptown. 307 Bryant St 14222. **Hours:** 11:30 am-4 & 5-10 pm, Fri-11 pm, Sat 5 pm-11 pm. Closed major holidays; also Sun. **Reservations:** suggested. **Features:** Large oil paintings accented with gold columns and local artist prints set the mood for Northern Italian preparations of pasta. A pronounced use of seasonings wakes the senses. For dessert, choose from a list of irresistible homemade selections. Dressy casual; cocktails. **Parking:** street. **Cards:** AX, DC, MC, VI.

LEFT BANK   Dinner: $8-$19   Phone: 716/882-3509   ㉖
American
Location: Near Kleinhans Music Hall. 511 Rhode Island St 14213. **Hours:** 5 pm-11 pm, Fri & Sat-midnight, Sun 11 am-3 & 4-10 pm. Closed: 7/4, 11/25, 12/24, 12/25. **Reservations:** suggested. **Features:** The comfortable, bistro-like restaurant offers many tempting and unusual items, such as its signature eggplant, a large, thick slice of breaded eggplant "steak" sandwiched with ricotta and grilled veggies and topped with fresh mozzarella. Casual dress. **Parking:** street. **Cards:** AX, DS, MC, VI.

LORD CHUMLEY'S   Historic   Dinner: $18-$39   Phone: 716/886-2220   ⑫
Continental
Location: Just n of jct Virginia St; downtown. 481 Delaware Ave 14202. **Hours:** 5 pm-10 pm, Fri & Sat-11 pm. Closed major holidays. **Reservations:** suggested. **Features:** The turn-of-the-20th-century townhouse reflects the cozy ambience of a cobblestone-street sidewalk cafe. Menu selections are prepared with premium ingredients. Turtle cheesecake is representative of the delicious desserts. Dressy casual; cocktails. **Parking:** street. **Cards:** DC, DS, MC, VI.

OLIVER'S RESTAURANT   Dinner: $19-$29   Phone: 716/877-9662   ⑥
Continental
Location: SR 384, 0.5 mi n of jct SR 198 at Delaware and Amherst aves; uptown. 2095 Delaware Ave 14216. **Hours:** 5 pm-10 pm, Fri & Sat-midnight, Sun 4:30 pm-9:30 pm. Closed: 5/31, 7/4, 9/6. **Reservations:** suggested, weekends. **Features:** Elegant table appointments add to the contemporary sophistication of the informal dining room. International influences punctuate innovative, creatively presented dishes. The food and wine sampler menu, available Tuesday through Friday, is a treat. Dressy casual; cocktails. **Parking:** on-site. **Cards:** AX, MC, VI.

THE PARK LANE TAVERN & OYSTER BAR   Lunch: $6-$11   Dinner: $16-$20   Phone: 716/881-2603   ⑪
American
Location: Delaware Ave at Gates Cir. 33 Gates Cir 14209. **Hours:** 11:30 am-3 & 6-10 pm, Fri & Sat-10:30 pm, Sun 10:30 am-2 pm. Closed: 12/25. **Reservations:** accepted. **Features:** A stylish and upscale aura is provided by the solid background of classic Tudor architecture. Brick, wood, brocades, stained glass, fireplaces and black wrought iron offer timeless style. The menu presents cuisine with a Mediterranean flair, including homemade pasta and other dishes made with fresh ingredients. Desserts are delicious. Casual dress; cocktails. **Parking:** on-site and valet. **Cards:** AX, MC, VI.

PETTIBONE'S GRILLE   Lunch: $5-$10   Dinner: $12-$20   Phone: 716/846-2100   ㉗
American
Location: At Swan and Washington sts; I-190, exit 6, Seneca St ramp to Swan St to Washington St; at Dunn Tire Park. 275 Washington St 14203. **Hours:** 11:30 am-3 pm. Closed major holidays. **Reservations:** suggested, during games. **Features:** Perched above the baseball park, the casual restaurant lays out a menu of such dishes as steak, chops, seafood and pasta. The grilled portobello sandwich is particularly tasty. Plaques commemorate players being inducted in the local Hall of Fame. Casual dress; cocktails. **Parking:** no self-parking. **Cards:** AX, DS, MC, VI.

ROSELAND   Dinner: $10-$22   Phone: 716/882-3328   ㉘
Italian
Location: Near Kleinhans Music Hall. 490 Rhode Island St 14213. **Hours:** 5 pm-10 pm, Sat-11 pm, Sun.3 pm-9 pm. Closed: 5/31, 7/4, 9/6. **Reservations:** suggested. **Features:** The "dinner for two" option is a popular, budget-conscious choice at the intimate restaurant, which focuses on Italian and American fare. Fresh bread and tiramisu are fitting brackets to a meal of lasagna or homemade manicotti topped with sauteed rock shrimp. The atmosphere is cozy. Patio seating is also available. Casual dress; cocktails. **Parking:** on-site. **Cards:** AX, DS, MC, VI.

RUE FRANKLIN   Dinner: $19-$25   Phone: 716/852-4416   ②
French
Location: Just n of Tupper St. 341 Franklin St 14202. **Hours:** Open 5/1-8/22 & 9/11-4/30; 5:30 pm-10 pm. Closed major holidays; also Sun & Mon. **Reservations:** suggested. **Features:** Summer dining with a view of the landscaped courtyard or the Provencal-inspired dining room provides an atmosphere of sophistocated grace. The limited, seasonal menu unveils such interesting, contemporary French-inspired cuisine, such as Muscovy duck breast, squab breasts with b'steeya or lamb loin chops with green lentils. Irresistible housemade desserts are served with panache and are as rich as Trump. The espresso is made the old-fashioned way. Dressy casual; cocktails. **Parking:** on-site. **Cards:** AX, CB, MC, VI.

The Buffalo Vicinity

AMHERST pop. 116,510 (See map and index starting on p. 238)

------ WHERE TO STAY ------

BUFFALO/AMHERST COURTYARD BY MARRIOTT *Book at aaa.com* **Phone:** (716)626-2300 **40**
All Year 1P: $59-$250 2P: $59-$250
Location: I-290, exit 6, just ne. 4100 Sheridan Dr 14221. Fax: 716/626-2322. **Facility:** 108 units. 101 one-
bedroom standard units. 7 one-bedroom suites. 4 stories, interior corridors. **Bath:** combo or shower only.
Small-scale Hotel **Parking:** on-site. **Terms:** [BP] meal plan available. **Amenities:** video library (fee), video games, dual phone
lines, voice mail, irons, hair dryers. **Pool(s):** small heated indoor. **Leisure Activities:** whirlpool, exercise room. **Guest Services:**
valet and coin laundry. **Business Services:** meeting rooms. **Cards:** AX, CB, DC, DS, JC, MC, VI. SOME UNITS

BUFFALO MARRIOTT-NIAGARA *Book at aaa.com* **Phone:** (716)689-6900 **34**
All Year 1P: $129-$189 2P: $129-$189 XP: $20 F18
Location: I-290, exit 5B, 0.5 mi n on SR 263 (Millersport Hwy). Located across from the University of Buffalo, North
Campus. 1340 Millersport Hwy 14221. Fax: 716/689-0483. **Facility:** 356 units. 350 one-bedroom standard units.
6 one-bedroom suites ($250-$300). 10 stories, interior corridors. **Bath:** combo or shower only. **Parking:** on-
Large-scale Hotel site, winter plug-ins. **Terms:** cancellation fee imposed, pets ($50 fee). **Amenities:** video library (fee), voice
mail, honor bars, irons, hair dryers. **Some:** Fee: high-speed Internet. **Dining:** 6:30 am-10 pm, cocktails.
Pool(s): heated indoor/outdoor. **Leisure Activities:** sauna, whirlpool. **Fee:** game room. **Guest Services:** gift shop, valet laundry,
area transportation-within 1.5 mi. **Business Services:** conference facilities, business center. **Cards:** AX, CB, DC, DS, JC,
MC, VI. **Special Amenities:** free newspaper. SOME UNITS
FEE FEE

EXTENDED STAY AMERICA *Book at aaa.com* **Phone:** (716)564-0620 **35**
6/28-4/30 1P: $85 2P: $105
5/1-6/27 1P: $65-$85 2P: $70-$85
Small-scale Hotel **Location:** I-290, exit 3, just n on Niagara Falls Blvd (US 62) to access road. 125 Inn Keepers Ln 14228.
Fax: 716/564-0630. **Facility:** 119 one-bedroom standard units with efficiencies. 3 stories, interior corridors.
Bath: combo or shower only. **Parking:** on-site. **Amenities:** voice mail. **Some:** Fee: high-speed Internet. **Guest Services:** coin
laundry. **Cards:** AX, DC, DS, MC, VI. SOME UNITS

HAMPTON INN-BUFFALO/AMHERST *Book at aaa.com* **Phone:** (716)689-4414 **39**
5/1-8/28 1P: $109-$119 2P: $119-$129
8/29-4/30 1P: $99-$109 2P: $109-$119
Location: I-290, exit 5B, 0.5 mi n on SR 263 (Millersport Hwy). 10 Flint Rd 14226. Fax: 716/689-4382. **Facility:** 196
units. 194 one-bedroom standard units. 2 one-bedroom suites ($139-$179) with efficiencies. 4 stories, inte-
Small-scale Hotel rior corridors. **Parking:** on-site. **Terms:** [CP] meal plan available. **Amenities:** video library (fee), voice mail,
irons, hair dryers. **Pool(s):** heated indoor. **Leisure Activities:** whirlpool. **Guest Services:** valet laundry, area
transportation-within 5 mi. **Business Services:** meeting rooms. **Cards:** AX, CB, DC, DS, MC, VI. **Special Amenities:** early
check-in/late check-out and free room upgrade (subject to availability with advanced reservations). SOME UNITS
FEE FEE

HOLIDAY INN BUFFALO-AMHERST *Book at aaa.com* **Phone:** (716)691-8181 **33**
All Year 1P: $100-$150 2P: $100-$160 XP: $10 F18
Location: I-290, exit 3 on US 62. Located in a retail area. 1881 Niagara Falls Blvd 14228. Fax: 716/691-4965.
Facility: 199 one-bedroom standard units. 2 stories (no elevator), interior corridors. **Parking:** on-site.
Terms: 7 day cancellation notice, [AP] meal plan available. **Amenities:** video library (fee), voice mail, irons,
Small-scale Hotel hair dryers. **Dining:** 6:30 am-11 pm, Sat & Sun from 7 am, cocktails. **Pool(s):** heated indoor. **Leisure Activi-
ties:** whirlpool, exercise room. **Guest Services:** valet and coin laundry, area transportation-within 2 mi. **Busi-
ness Services:** conference facilities. **Cards:** AX, CB, DC, DS, JC, MC. **Special Amenities:** free newspaper and early check-
in/late check-out. SOME UNITS
FEE FEE

LORD AMHERST MOTOR HOTEL *Book at aaa.com* **Phone:** (716)839-2200 **31**
5/1-9/5 [ECP] 1P: $69-$99 2P: $79-$109 XP: $7 F18
9/6-4/30 [ECP] 1P: $65-$89 2P: $75-$99 XP: $7 F18
Location: I-290, exit 7A, just w on SR 5. 5000 Main St 14226. Fax: 716/839-1538. **Facility:** 99 one-bedroom standard units, some with efficiencies. 2 stories (no elevator), interior/exterior corridors. **Parking:** on-site.
Motel **Terms:** weekly rates available, small pets only. **Amenities:** hair dryers. **Dining:** 11 am-10 pm, cocktails.
Pool(s): heated outdoor. **Leisure Activities:** exercise room. **Guest Services:** valet and coin laundry. **Busi-
ness Services:** meeting rooms. **Cards:** AX, CB, DC, DS, MC, VI. **Special Amenities:** free expanded continental breakfast
and early check-in/late check-out. SOME UNITS
FEE FEE

(See map and index starting on p. 238)

RED ROOF INN *Book at aaa.com* Phone: (716)689-7474 36

AAA [SAVE]

5/24-9/1	1P: $54-$82	2P: $61-$89	XP: $7	F18
5/1-5/23	1P: $42-$54	2P: $49-$61	XP: $7	F18
9/2-10/18	1P: $43-$52	2P: $50-$59	XP: $7	F18
10/19-4/30	1P: $40-$46	2P: $47-$53	XP: $7	F18

Motel   **Location:** I-290, exit 5B, 0.5 mi n on SR 263 (Millersport Hwy). Located across from the University of Buffalo, North Campus. 42 Flint Rd 14226. Fax: 716/689-2051. **Facility:** 108 one-bedroom standard units. 2 stories, exterior corridors. **Parking:** on-site. **Amenities:** video games, voice mail. **Cards:** AX, CB, DC, DS, MC, VI. **Special Amenities:** free local telephone calls and free newspaper.

SOME UNITS

🐕 🍴➜ 🔥M 📶 🐾 DATA PORT / ✕ 📦 📷 /
FEE   FEE FEE

SLEEP INN *Book at aaa.com* Phone: (716)691-6510 38

▼▼ ▼▼

9/2-4/30 [ECP]	1P: $79-$99	2P: $89-$109	XP: $8	F18
5/1-9/1 [ECP]	1P: $72-$79	2P: $82-$89	XP: $8	F18

Small-scale Hotel   **Location:** I-290, exit 3, just n on Niagara Falls Blvd (US 62) to access road. 75 Inn Keepers Ln 14228. Fax: 716/691-3454. **Facility:** 92 one-bedroom standard units. 5 stories, interior corridors. *Bath:* combo or shower only. **Parking:** on-site. **Terms:** 2 night minimum stay - seasonal, [CP] meal plan available. **Amenities:** video library (fee), video games, high-speed Internet, dual phone lines, voice mail, irons, hair dryers. **Pool(s):** small heated indoor. **Leisure Activities:** whirlpool, exercise room. **Guest Services:** valet laundry. **Cards:** AX, DC, DS, MC, VI.

SOME UNITS

A$K S📶 🔥 ⛵ 🐾 DATA PORT 📦 / ✕ 📦 📷
FEE

SUPER 8 MOTEL-AMHERST/BUFFALO/NIAGARA FALLS *Book at aaa.com* Phone: (716)688-0811 37

▼▼ ▼▼

7/1-8/31	1P: $59-$69	2P: $64-$74	XP: $5	F12
5/1-6/30	1P: $49-$59	2P: $54-$64	XP: $5	F12
9/1-4/30	1P: $39-$59	2P: $44-$64	XP: $5	F12

Small-scale Hotel   **Location:** I-290, exit 5B, 0.5 mi n on SR 263 (Millersport Hwy), just w. 1 Flint Rd 14226. Fax: 716/688-2365. **Facility:** 103 one-bedroom standard units. 4 stories, interior corridors. **Parking:** on-site. **Terms:** cancellation fee imposed, [CP] meal plan available, small pets only ($10 extra charge). **Amenities:** hair dryers. *Some: Fee:* high-speed Internet. **Guest Services:** valet laundry. **Business Services:** fax (fee). **Cards:** AX, DC, DS, MC, VI.

SOME UNITS

A$K S📶 🐕 🍴➜ 🐾 DATA PORT / ✕ 📦 📷 /
FEE   FEE FEE

TRAVELODGE *Book at aaa.com* Phone: 716/837-3344 30

AAA [SAVE]

▼▼ ▼▼

5/1-9/30	1P: $60	2P: $90	XP: $5	F4
10/1-4/30	1P: $50	2P: $80	XP: $5	F4

Motel   **Location:** Jct US 62, just w on SR 5. Located across from the University of Buffalo. 3612 Main St 14226. Fax: 716/834-6246. **Facility:** 37 one-bedroom standard units, some with whirlpools. 2 stories (no elevator), exterior corridors. *Bath:* combo or shower only. **Parking:** on-site, winter plug-ins. **Terms:** cancellation fee imposed. **Amenities:** voice mail, safes. **Cards:** AX, DC, MC, VI.

SOME UNITS

S📶 🍴➜ 🐾 DATA PORT ☕ / ✕ 📦 📷 /

—— WHERE TO DINE ——

DAKOTA GRILL Lunch: $6-$12   Dinner: $14-$20   Phone: 716/834-6600 42

▼▼▼▼   **Location:** At Sweethome and Maple rds; in Maple Ridge Plaza. 4224 Maple Rd 14226. **Hours:** 11:30 am-10 pm, Fri & Sat 4 pm-11 pm, Sun 4 pm-10 pm. Closed major holidays. **Reservations:** suggested. **Features:** The modern, bistro-style bar serves grilled cuisine with a creative flair. Specials include grilled empire chicken breast with ginger soy, certified Angus steak filets and fresh seafood dishes, each accented with seasoned crust and special sauce. Among other choices are sloppy tender ribs, unusual pasta creations and bountiful, meal-size salads. Dressy casual; cocktails. **Parking:** on-site. **Cards:** AX, DC, DS, MC, VI.

American

🍸 ✕

DUFF'S FAMOUS WINGS Lunch: $5-$8   Dinner: $7-$10   Phone: 716/834-6234 40

▼▼▼   **Location:** Corner of Sheridan Dr and Millersport Hwy. 3651 Sheridan Dr 14226. **Hours:** 11 am-11 pm, Fri & Sat-midnight, Sun noon-11 pm. Closed major holidays; also Super Bowl Sun. **Features:** An area fixture for more than 50 years, the eatery serves some of the city's best wings. Hot wings come with a warning to "eat at your own risk." On the menu are great sandwiches, dinner salads and finger food. Casual dress; beer & wine only. **Parking:** on-site. **Cards:** AX, DS, MC, VI.

American

✕

SAN MARCO Dinner: $14-$21   Phone: 716/839-5876 46

▼▼▼▼   **Location:** I-290, exit Main St W, 1.2 mi sw. 2082 Kensington Ave 14226. **Hours:** 5:30 pm-10:30 pm. Closed major holidays; also Mon. **Reservations:** suggested. **Features:** Northern Italian cuisine is individually prepared to each guest's palate by the owner/chef. Renown for their wild game creations with venison tenderloin, wild boar, rabbit and quail are a few choices accompanied by creative sauces using porcini mushrooms, truffles, balsamic vinagrette, red peppercorns and other exotic ingredients. Personal attention by doting professional staff is the norm. Dressy casual; beer & wine only. **Parking:** on-site. **Cards:** AX, MC, VI.

Northern
Italian

✕

SANTORA'S-PHASE II Lunch: $4-$20   Dinner: $4-$20   Phone: 716/688-3081 41

▼   **Location:** I-290, exit 5B, 0.5 mi n on SR 263 (Millersport Hwy). 1402 Millersport Hwy 14221. **Hours:** 10 am-midnight, Fri & Sat-1 am, Sun noon-11 pm. Closed major holidays. **Features:** Prepared as ordered for eat-in or take-out, the restaurant's dishes include traditional and gourmet pizzas, salads, subs, wings, calzones, wraps, burritos, soups and pasta dinners. Casual dress. **Parking:** on-site. **Cards:** AX, MC, VI.

Italian

(See map and index starting on p. 238)

SIENA

▼▽▽▽▼

Italian

Lunch: $7-$12   **Dinner:** $10-$27   **Phone:** 716/839-3108   ㊹
Location: I-290, exit 7A, just w on SR 5 (Main St). 4516 Main St 14226. **Hours:** 11:30 am-3 & 5-10 pm, Fri & Sat-11 pm, Sun 4:30 pm-9 pm. Closed major holidays. **Reservations:** accepted, for lunch.
Features: Italian fare with a Northern slant is prepared in the trendy bistro-style restaurant. Specialty pizzas cooked in a wood-burning oven are popular, as are grilled dishes, delicious antipasto and daily
traditional specials. Dressy casual; cocktails. **Parking:** on-site. **Cards:** AX, MC, VI.   ⓨ ⓧ

TASTE OF INDIA

▽▽ ▽▽

Indian

Lunch: $5-$8   **Dinner:** $10-$15   **Phone:** 716/837-0460   ㊸
Location: In Northtown Plaza. 3093 Sheridan Dr 14226. **Hours:** 11:30 am-2:30 & 4:30-10 pm. **Features:** The simple, casual Indian restaurant is open for lunch and dinner. Casual dress; beer & wine only. **Parking:** on-site. **Cards:** AX, DC, DS, MC, VI.   ⓖⓜ ⓧ

BLASDELL pop. 2,718   (See map and index starting on p. 238)

———— **WHERE TO STAY** ————

ECONO LODGE SOUTH

ⒶⒶ SAVE

▼▽▽▼

Motel

Book at aaa.com   **Phone:** (716)825-7530   ㉖㊄
All Year   1P: $45-$70   2P: $54-$99   XP: $7   F18
Location: I-90, exit 56, just e on SR 179. 4344 Milestrip Rd 14219. **Fax:** 716/825-7530. **Facility:** 85 one-bedroom standard units. 1-2 stories (no elevator), exterior corridors. **Parking:** on-site, winter plug-ins. **Terms:** pets (in designated units). **Amenities:** *Some:* irons, hair dryers. **Guest Services:** coin laundry. **Cards:** AX, CB, DC, DS, JC, MC, VI. **Special Amenities: free continental breakfast and free local telephone calls.**
(See ad p 243)

SOME UNITS
Ⓢ🄳 🐾 🚭 🖧 / ⓧ 🛗 ⚊ /
FEE

MCKINLEY'S HOTEL & BANQUET

ⒶⒶ SAVE

▽▽ ▽▽

Small-scale Hotel

Phone: (716)648-5700   ㊅㊅
5/1-8/31   1P: $74-$159   2P: $74-$159   XP: $5   F12
9/1-11/30   1P: $74-$154   2P: $74-$154   XP: $5   F12
12/1-4/30   1P: $74-$134   2P: $74-$134   XP: $5   F12
Location: I-90, exit 56, 0.4 mi e on SR 179, then 0.8 mi s. S 3950 McKinley Pkwy 14219. **Fax:** 716/648-5700. **Facility:** 78 one-bedroom standard units, some with whirlpools. 2 stories (no elevator), interior corridors. *Bath:* combo or shower only. **Parking:** on-site. **Terms:** 3 day cancellation notice-fee imposed, [ECP] meal plan available, pets ($5 extra charge). **Amenities:** irons, hair dryers. **Leisure Activities:** exercise room. **Guest Services:** coin laundry. **Business Services:** conference facilities. **Cards:** AX, DC, DS, MC, VI. **Special Amenities: free local telephone calls and free newspaper.**

SOME UNITS
Ⓢ🄳 🐾 🖐 🎥 ⚊ / ⓧ 🖧 🛗 ⚊ /
FEE

———— **WHERE TO DINE** ————

THE DOCK AT THE BAY

▽▽ ▽▽

American

Lunch: $7-$12   **Dinner:** $10-$25   **Phone:** 716/823-8247
Location: I-90, exit 56, follow SR 179 W to SR 5 W, then just w. 3800 Hoover Rd 14219. **Hours:** 11:30 am-10 pm, Fri & Sat-11 pm. Closed: 12/24, 12/25. **Features:** Overlooking Lake Erie, the waterfront restaurant serves fresh seafood, certified Angus beef, Australian lobster tails, steaks, prime rib and a huge selection of appetizers. Outside seating is a popular request on warm summer evenings. Casual dress; cocktails.
Parking: on-site. **Cards:** AX, DC, DS, MC, VI.   ⓨ ⓧ

ILIO DIPAOLO'S RESTAURANT

ⒶⒶ

▽▽ ▽▽

Italian

Lunch: $6-$10   **Dinner:** $7-$18   **Phone:** 716/825-3675   ㊿㉓
Location: I-90, exit 56 on US 62, 0.3 mi n of jct SR 179 and 90. 3785 S Park Ave 14219. **Hours:** 11:30 am-10 pm, Fri-midnight, Sat 2 pm-midnight, Sun 1 pm-10 pm. Closed: 3/27, 11/25, 12/25. **Reservations:** suggested. **Features:** Guests dine among memorabilia honoring the restaurant's founder, a former wrestling champion, and among many other photographs of sports legends. The family eatery is casual. On the impressive menu of amply portioned Italian selections are veal saltimbocca, cannelloni Florentine and other preparations of homemade pasta. Also available are steak, chops and seafood. Casual dress; cocktails.
Parking: on-site. **Cards:** AX, DC, DS, MC, VI.   ⓨ ⓧ

BOWMANSVILLE   (See map and index starting on p. 238)

———— **WHERE TO STAY** ————

RED ROOF INN-BUFFALO AIRPORT

ⒶⒶ SAVE

▼▽▽▼

Motel

Book at aaa.com   **Phone:** (716)633-1100   ㊉㉒
6/23-9/7   1P: $53-$76   2P: $58-$81   XP: $5   F18
9/8-11/2   1P: $45-$69   2P: $50-$74   XP: $5   F18
5/1-6/22   1P: $47-$66   2P: $52-$71   XP: $5   F18
11/3-4/30   1P: $38-$55   2P: $43-$60   XP: $5   F18
Location: Just e of SR 78, just n of entrance to I-90 (New York Thruway), exit 49. Located behind Bob Evans Restaurant. 146 Maple Dr 14026. **Fax:** 716/633-2297. **Facility:** 109 one-bedroom standard units. 2 stories (no elevator), exterior corridors. **Parking:** on-site. **Terms:** small pets only. **Amenities:** video games, voice mail. **Cards:** AX, CB, DC, DS, MC, VI. **Special Amenities: free local telephone calls and free newspaper.**

SOME UNITS
🐾 🍴 🚭 🖐 🎥 🖧 / ⓧ /
FEE

CHEEKTOWAGA pop. 79,988 (See map and index starting on p. 238)

———— WHERE TO STAY ————

BEST WESTERN-NORSTAR INN   *Book at aaa.com*   Phone: (716)631-8966   **21**

7/1-9/6	1P: $89-$119	2P: $95-$125	XP: $6	F16
5/1-6/30	1P: $79-$109	2P: $85-$120	XP: $6	F16
9/7-4/30	1P: $69-$99	2P: $69-$99	XP: $6	F16

Small-scale Hotel **Location:** Jct SR 78, 1 mi w on SR 33. 4630 Genesee St 14225. Fax: 716/631-8977. **Facility:** 77 one-bedroom standard units. 4 stories, interior corridors. *Bath:* combo or shower only. **Parking:** on-site. **Terms:** cancellation fee imposed, [ECP] meal plan available. **Amenities:** video library (fee), video games, voice mail, irons, hair dryers. **Leisure Activities:** exercise room. **Guest Services:** area transportation-Amtrak station. **Cards:** AX, DC, DS, MC, VI. **Special Amenities: free continental breakfast and free newspaper.**

SOME UNITS

[S/D] [✈] [▯+] [&M] [&'] [▧] [DATA PORT] [▭] /[✕]/

COMFORT SUITES-BUFFALO AIRPORT   *Book at aaa.com*   Phone: (716)633-6000   **17**

6/25-9/5 [ECP]	1P: $104-$134	2P: $114-$144
9/6-12/31 [ECP]	1P: $99-$114	2P: $109-$124
5/1-6/24 [ECP]	1P: $94-$114	2P: $104-$124
1/1-4/30 [ECP]	1P: $89-$109	2P: $99-$119

Small-scale Hotel **Location:** SR 33, exit Dick Rd, just sw. 901 Dick Rd 14225. Fax: 716/633-6858. **Facility:** 100 one-bedroom standard units, some with whirlpools. 2 stories (no elevator), interior corridors. **Parking:** on-site. **Terms:** package plans. **Amenities:** video library (fee), video games, dual phone lines, voice mail, safes, irons, hair dryers. **Pool(s):** small heated indoor. **Leisure Activities:** whirlpool, exercise room. **Guest Services:** valet and coin laundry, area transportation-within 5 mi. **Business Services:** meeting rooms. **Cards:** AX, CB, DC, DS, JC, MC, VI.

SOME UNITS

[S/D] [✈] [&M] [▱] [▰] [▧] [DATA PORT] [❚] [▭] /[✕]/

FOUR POINTS BY SHERATON-BUFFALO AIRPORT   *Book at aaa.com*   Phone: (716)681-2400   **16**

7/7-9/2	1P: $109-$154	2P: $109-$154	XP: $10	F18
5/1-7/6 & 9/3-4/30	1P: $99-$144	2P: $99-$144	XP: $10	F18

Large-scale Hotel **Location:** I-90, exit 52E, 0.3 mi e. Located adjacent to Walden Galleria Mall. 2040 Walden Ave 14225. Fax: 716/681-8067. **Facility:** 292 one-bedroom standard units. 2-8 stories, interior/exterior corridors. **Parking:** on-site. **Amenities:** video library (fee), dual phone lines, voice mail, irons, hair dryers. **Pool(s):** heated indoor. **Leisure Activities:** saunas, exercise room. **Fee:** game room. **Guest Services:** valet laundry, area transportation. **Business Services:** meeting rooms. **Cards:** AX, CB, DC, DS, MC, VI. *(See color ad p 210)*

SOME UNITS

[ASK] [S/D] [✈] [▯] [Y] [▱] [▰] [✕] [▧] [DATA PORT] [▭] /[✕]/ FEE

HAMPTON INN-AIRPORT/GALLERIA   *Book at aaa.com*   Phone: (716)894-8000   **23**

6/25-9/5 [ECP]	1P: $104-$139	2P: $114-$149
5/1-6/24 [ECP]	1P: $99-$129	2P: $109-$139
9/6-10/30 [ECP]	1P: $99-$119	2P: $109-$129
10/31-4/30 [ECP]	1P: $89-$119	2P: $99-$129

Small-scale Hotel **Location:** I-90, exit 52W, just w. 1745 Walden Ave 14225. Fax: 716/894-3554. **Facility:** 133 one-bedroom standard units, some with whirlpools. 5 stories, interior corridors. *Bath:* combo or shower only. **Parking:** on-site. **Amenities:** video library (fee), video games, voice mail, irons, hair dryers. **Pool(s):** heated indoor. **Leisure Activities:** whirlpool, exercise room, sports court. **Guest Services:** valet and coin laundry, area transportation-within 5 mi. **Business Services:** meeting rooms. **Cards:** AX, CB, DC, DS, JC, MC, VI. **Special Amenities: free expanded continental breakfast and free local telephone calls.**

SOME UNITS

[S/D] [✈] [▯+] [&'] [▰] [✕] [▧] [DATA PORT] [▭] /[✕] [❚] [▭] / FEE

HOLIDAY INN-BUFFALO AIRPORT   *Book at aaa.com*   Phone: (716)634-6969   **15**

7/1-9/1	1P: $99	2P: $129	XP: $10	F18
5/1-6/30 & 9/2-4/30	1P: $89	2P: $109	XP: $10	F18

Small-scale Hotel **Location:** I-90, exit 51E, 1 mi e on SR 33. 4600 Genesee St 14225. Fax: 716/634-0920. **Facility:** 207 units. 205 one-bedroom standard units, some with whirlpools. 2 one-bedroom suites ($139-$189). 2 stories (no elevator), interior corridors. **Parking:** on-site. **Amenities:** voice mail, irons, hair dryers. **Dining:** 6:30 am-11 pm, Sat from 7 am, Sun 7 am-10 pm, cocktails. **Pool(s):** heated outdoor. **Leisure Activities:** whirlpool, exercise room. **Guest Services:** valet and coin laundry, area transportation-within 5 mi. **Business Services:** meeting rooms, administrative services. **Cards:** AX, CB, DC, DS, JC, MC, VI. **Special Amenities: free newspaper and early check-in/late check-out.**

SOME UNITS

[S/D] [✈] [▯] [Y] [▰] [✕] [DATA PORT] [▭] /[✕] [❚] [▭] /

HOLIDAY INN EXPRESS HOTEL & SUITES   *Book at aaa.com*   Phone: (716)896-2900   **24**

All Year [ECP]	1P: $100-$140	2P: $100-$140	XP: $10	F19

Small-scale Hotel **Location:** I-190, exit 1, just ne; I-90, exit 53. 601 Dingens St 14206. Fax: 716/896-3765. **Facility:** 117 units. 116 one-bedroom standard units. 1 one-bedroom suite ($110-$150) with efficiency and whirlpool. 2 stories (no elevator), interior corridors. *Bath:* combo or shower only. **Parking:** on-site. **Amenities:** dual phone lines, voice mail, irons, hair dryers. **Fee:** video library, high-speed Internet. **Dining:** 11 am-11 pm, Sat from 4 pm; hours vary off season, cocktails. **Pool(s):** heated outdoor. **Leisure Activities:** whirlpool, exercise room. **Guest Services:** valet and coin laundry, area transportation-bus & train station. **Business Services:** meeting rooms. **Cards:** AX, CB, DC, DS, JC, MC, VI. **Special Amenities: free local telephone calls and free newspaper.**

SOME UNITS

[S/D] [✈] [▯+] [Y] [&'] [▰] [✕] [▧] [DATA PORT] [▭] /[✕] [❚] [▭] /

(See map and index starting on p. 238)

HOLIDAY INN EXPRESS HOTEL & SUITES-BUFFALO AIRPORT
Book at aaa.com

Phone: (716)631-8700 ⑲

AAA SAVE

5/1-10/31 [ECP]	1P: $110-$160	2P: $110-$160	XP: $10	F18
11/1-4/30 [ECP]	1P: $100-$150	2P: $100-$150	XP: $10	F18

Location: I-90, exit 33 E. Located across from Buffalo Airport. 131 Buell Ave 14225. Fax: 716/631-8787. **Facility:** 110 units. 101 one-bedroom standard units. 9 one-bedroom suites ($160-$200) with whirlpools. 4 stories, interior corridors. *Bath:* combo or shower only. **Parking:** on-site. **Terms:** pets ($30 fee). **Amenities:** high-speed Internet (fee), dual phone lines, voice mail, irons, hair dryers. **Pool(s):** outdoor, heated indoor. **Leisure Activities:** whirlpool, exercise room. *Fee:* game room. **Guest Services:** valet laundry, area transportation-within 5 mi. **Business Services:** meeting rooms. **Cards:** AX, DC, DS, MC, VI.

Small-scale Hotel

SOME UNITS

HOMEWOOD SUITES BY HILTON
Book at aaa.com

Phone: 716/685-0700 ⑱

All Year 1P: $109-$199

Location: SR 33, exit Dick Rd, 0.3 mi sw. 760 Dick Rd 14225. Fax: 716/685-2034. **Facility:** 77 units. 68 one- and 9 two-bedroom suites with kitchens, some with whirlpools. 3 stories, interior corridors. *Bath:* combo or shower only. **Parking:** on-site. **Terms:** cancellation fee imposed. [ECP] meal plan available, small pets only ($85-$100 fee). **Amenities:** video library (fee), video games, high-speed Internet, dual phone lines, voice mail, irons, hair dryers. **Pool(s):** heated indoor. **Leisure Activities:** whirlpool, exercise room. **Guest Services:** complimentary evening beverages: Mon-Thurs, valet and coin laundry, area transportation. **Business Services:** meeting rooms, business center. **Cards:** AX, CB, DC, DS, JC, MC, VI.

Small-scale Hotel

SOME UNITS

PARK PLAZA HOTEL BUFFALO AIRPORT
Book at aaa.com

Phone: (716)634-2300 ㉒

AAA SAVE

All Year 1P: $95 2P: $95

Location: Jct SR 78, 1.7 mi w on SR 33. Located across from Buffalo Airport. 4243 Genesee St 14225. Fax: 716/632-2387. **Facility:** 274 one-bedroom standard units, some with whirlpools. 2-4 stories, interior corridors. **Parking:** on-site. **Terms:** 3 day cancellation notice. **Amenities:** dual phone lines, voice mail, irons, hair dryers. **Dining:** 2 restaurants, 6 am-10 pm, cocktails, also, Pranzo Ristorante, see separate listing. **Pool(s):** heated indoor. **Leisure Activities:** saunas, whirlpool, steamroom, lifeguard on duty, exercise room. **Guest Services:** valet laundry, area transportation-train station. **Business Services:** meeting rooms, fax (fee). **Cards:** AX, CB, DC, DS, JC, MC, VI. **Special Amenities:** early check-in/late check-out and preferred room (subject to availability with advanced reservations).

Large-scale Hotel

SOME UNITS

FEE FEE

QUALITY INN-BUFFALO AIRPORT
Book at aaa.com

Phone: (716)633-5500 ㉕

All Year [ECP] 1P: $49-$99 2P: $49-$99 XP: $5 F18

Location: Jct SR 78, 1.8 mi e on SR 33. 4217 Genesee St 14225. Fax: 716/633-4231. **Facility:** 104 one-bedroom standard units, some with whirlpools. 1-2 stories (no elevator), interior corridors. *Bath:* combo or shower only. **Parking:** on-site. **Terms:** 5 day cancellation notice. **Amenities:** irons, hair dryers. **Pool(s):** heated indoor. **Leisure Activities:** whirlpool, limited exercise equipment. *Fee:* game room. **Guest Services:** valet laundry, area transportation. **Business Services:** meeting rooms. **Cards:** AX, CB, DC, DS, MC, VI.

Small-scale Hotel

SOME UNITS

FEE FEE

RESIDENCE INN BY MARRIOTT
Book at aaa.com

Phone: (716)892-5410 ⑳

All Year 1P: $99-$179 2P: $99-$179

Location: I-90, exit 52 westbound, stay to the left off exit ramp. Located across from the Galleria Mall. 107 Anderson Rd 14225. Fax: 716/892-5409. **Facility:** 113 units. 49 one-bedroom standard units, some with efficiencies or kitchens. 45 one- and 19 two-bedroom suites, some with efficiencies or kitchens. 3 stories, interior corridors. *Bath:* combo or shower only. **Parking:** on-site. **Terms:** [BP] meal plan available, pets ($200 fee, $20 extra charge). **Amenities:** video library, dual phone lines, voice mail, irons, hair dryers. *Some:* DVD players. **Pool(s):** small heated indoor. **Leisure Activities:** whirlpool, exercise room, sports court. **Guest Services:** complimentary evening beverages: Mon-Thurs, valet and coin laundry. **Business Services:** meeting rooms. **Cards:** AX, DC, DS, MC, VI.

Small-scale Hotel

SOME UNITS

FEE

SLEEP INN & SUITES
Book at aaa.com

Phone: (716)626-4000 ㉖

5/1-9/3	1P: $69-$99	2P: $79-$109	XP: $10	F
9/4-4/30	1P: $49-$79	2P: $59-$89	XP: $10	F

Location: I-90, exit 51E, 1.1 mi e on SR 33, then just n. 100 Hotlz Rd 14225. Fax: 716/626-3370. **Facility:** 86 one-bedroom standard units, some with whirlpools. 3 stories, interior corridors. *Bath:* combo or shower only. **Parking:** on-site. **Terms:** check-in 3:30 pm. **Amenities:** voice mail. *Some:* dual phone lines, irons, hair dryers. **Leisure Activities:** whirlpool, exercise room. **Guest Services:** valet and coin laundry, area transportation. **Business Services:** meeting rooms. **Cards:** AX, DC, DS, MC, VI.

Small-scale Hotel

SOME UNITS

———— WHERE TO DINE ————

ALTON'S RESTAURANT
Lunch: $5-$6 **Dinner:** $8-$12 **Phone:** 716/681-7055 ㉝

Location: I-90, exit 52 eastbound, jct Union Rd. 2250 Walden Ave 14225. **Hours:** 24 hours. Closed major holidays; also Sun 11 pm-6 am. **Features:** Since 1982, the restaurant has offered fast, friendly service and breakfast made all day. Greek specialties such as souvlaki and gyros—as well as steaks, seafood, burgers, beef on weck, chicken wings, large salads and hearty sandwiches—are served in generous portions. The dessert selection is varied. Casual dress; beer & wine only. **Parking:** on-site. **Cards:** AX, DS, MC, VI.

American

(See map and index starting on p. 238)

DANNY'S   **Lunch:** $5-$7   **Dinner:** $7-$9   **Phone:** 716/634-1780   ③①

American   **Location:** I-90, exit 52W, just w. 3715 Genesee St 14225. **Hours:** 11 am-11 pm; seasonal hours vary. Closed: 12/25; also Sun before Memorial Day. **Reservations:** accepted. **Features:** Prompt service and an abundant salad bar with five breads and two homemade soups make the airport-area restaurant a popular choice. Casual dress. **Parking:** on-site. **Cards:** AX, DC, MC, VI.

HOLIDAY SHOWCASE RESTAURANT   **Lunch:** $4-$8   **Dinner:** $6-$11   **Phone:** 716/684-3382   ③②

American   **Location:** I-90, exit 52 westbound, Galleria Dr to Union Rd; exit eastbound, just n. 3765 Union Rd (Rt 277) 14225. **Hours:** 7 am-11 pm, Fri & Sat-midnight. Closed: 12/25. **Features:** The classic all-American diner prepares American food. The dining room has an interesting appeal. Casual dress; beer & wine only. **Parking:** on-site. **Cards:** AX, DS, MC, VI.

OLYMPIC FAMILY RESTAURANT   **Lunch:** $3-$9   **Dinner:** $3-$9   **Phone:** 716/839-4022   ③⑤

Greek   **Location:** Jct SR 78, 1 mi w on SR 33. 4611 Genesee St 14225. **Hours:** 7 am-midnight. Closed: 12/25. **Features:** Near the airport, the casual restaurant presents a menu of Greek and American fare. The friendly staff serves good food fast. Casual dress; beer & wine only. **Parking:** on-site. **Cards:** AX, DS, MC, VI.

PRANZO RISTORANTE   **Dinner:** $23-$32   **Phone:** 716/634-2300   ③④

Nouvelle Italian   **Location:** Jct SR 78, 1.7 mi w on SR 33; in Park Plaza Hotel Buffalo Airport. 4243 Genesee St 14225. **Hours:** 5 pm-11 pm. Closed major holidays; also Sun. **Reservations:** suggested. **Features:** The Pranzo chef creates sumptuous Northern Italian fare, an area favorite for upscale dining. Exquisite and well-presented cuisine such as grilled tiger shrimp, tenderloin of buffalo, rack of lamb and fresh seafoods and pasta complemented by a varied wine list. All breads and luscious desserts are baked in-house. Dressy casual; cocktails. **Parking:** on-site. **Cards:** AX, CB, DC, DS, JC, MC, VI.

CLARENCE pop. 26,123   (See map and index starting on p. 238)

—— WHERE TO STAY ——

ASA RANSOM HOUSE   **Phone:** (716)759-2315   ⑦⓪

(AAA) (SAVE)   All Year [BP]   1P: $89-$135   2P: $98-$175   XP: $20   F8

Historic Country Inn   **Location:** Jct SR 78 (Transit Rd), 5.3 mi e on SR 5 (Main St). 10529 Main St 14031. Fax: 716/759-2791. **Facility:** Built in 1853, this property maintains its Colonial feel with finely furnished suites, a community library and picturesque gardens with a waterfall. Smoke free premises. 9 units. 7 one-bedroom standard units. 2 one-bedroom suites, some with whirlpools. 2 stories (no elevator); interior corridors. **Parking:** on-site. **Terms:** 7 day cancellation notice, [MAP] meal plan available, package plans, pets ($50 deposit, in designated units). **Amenities:** irons, hair dryers. *Some:* CD players. **Dining:** dining room, see separate listing. **Leisure Activities:** pool privileges, bike trail, hiking trails. **Guest Services:** gift shop. **Business Services:** meeting rooms. **Cards:** DC, MC, VI. **Special Amenities:** free full breakfast and free room upgrade (subject to availability with advanced reservations).

—— WHERE TO DINE ——

ASA RANSOM HOUSE

DINING ROOM   Country Inn   **Lunch:** $9-$15   **Dinner:** $12-$34   **Phone:** 716/759-2315   ⑥⑦

American   **Location:** Jct SR 78 (Transit Rd), 5.3 mi e on SR 5 (Main St); in Asa Ransom House. 10529 Main St 14031. **Hours:** Open 5/1-12/31 & 2/7-4/30; 4 pm-8 pm, Wed 11:30 am-2 pm; Fri & Sat 5:30 pm-7:30 pm limited seating. Closed: 12/25; also Mon. **Reservations:** suggested. **Features:** Intimate dining at 1853 inn, with seating fireside or on the veranda, pleases all the senses in any season. Chef Robb Perrott prepares country cuisine with a gourmet flair. Seasonal vegetables and fruits lay the basis for inspiring dishes that change seasonally. The devoted local following gives raves to savory dishes such as raspberry mint rack of lamb, corn-crusted catfish or Riesling salmon with asparagus sabayon. The dessert tray can't be missed if only to admire the baker's work of art. Dressy casual; cocktails. **Parking:** on-site. **Cards:** DS, MC, VI.

OLD RED MILL INN   **Dinner:** $12-$25   **Phone:** 716/633-7878   ⑥⑧

American   **Location:** Jct SR 78 (Transit Rd), 0.5 mi e on SR 5 (Main St). 8326 Main St 14221. **Hours:** 4 pm-9 pm, Fri & Sat-10 pm, Sun 11 am-9 pm. Closed: 12/25. **Features:** Built in 1858, the bright red grist mill is appointed in a rustic theme with antique farm tools and railroad motifs prevailing. Meat and seafood selections show subtle, International influences. Warm apple pie is just one great choice from an array of fresh dessert. Casual dress; cocktails. **Parking:** on-site. **Cards:** AX, DC, DS, MC, VI.

RITA'S PALERMO   **Dinner:** $9-$18   **Phone:** 716/759-8923   ⑥⑥

Italian   **Location:** Jct SR 78 (Transit Rd), 3.7 mi e on SR 5 (Main St). 9780 Main St 14031. **Hours:** 4 pm-10 pm, Fri & Sat-11 pm, Sun 3 pm-9 pm. Closed major holidays. **Reservations:** accepted. **Features:** The spiffy, little place has a traditional Sicilian menu with such specialties as sausage cacciatore with homemade sausage, pasta con sarde and tripe. A "small appetite" section of the menu caters to those who can't handle the plentiful portions. Casual dress; cocktails. **Parking:** on-site. **Cards:** MC, VI.

DEPEW pop. 16,629 (See map and index starting on p. 238)

──── WHERE TO DINE ────

SALVATORE'S ITALIAN GARDENS
AAA
◆◆◆◆
American

Dinner: $19-$45   **Phone:** 716/683-7990 [70]
Location: Jct SR 33, just s on SR 78. 6461 Transit Rd 14043. **Hours:** 5 pm-10 pm, Fri & Sat-11 pm, Sun 3 pm-10 pm. Closed: 12/24, 12/25. **Reservations:** suggested. **Features:** Diners can step into another world, where crystal chandeliers, etched glass, classic sculptures, Remington bronzes and marble define elegant, elaborate, Italian-style architecture. The attentive, pampering wait staff serves rack of lamb, chateaubriand, shrimp scampi, veal steak and prime rib, as well as pasta favorites. This truly is a place for special occasions, where everything is overdone except the food. Dressy casual; cocktails. **Parking:** on-site.
Cards: AX, CB, DC, DS, MC, VI.

EAST AMHERST

──── WHERE TO DINE ────

ARCOBALENO
◆◆◆
Northern
Italian

Dinner: $18-$28   **Phone:** 716/639-7394
Location: Just s of jct Millersport Hwy. 8485 Transit Rd 14051. **Hours:** 5 pm-10 pm. Closed: 7/4, 11/25, 12/25; also Sun & Mon. **Reservations:** suggested. **Features:** Tuscan-influenced fare is served in a romantic atmosphere. A family native to Italy cooks fresh ingredients to order. Tuscan Cornish hen, lamb with coriander seed, risotto with squid ink and other unusual pasta creations are tempting. Service is personable. Guests are treated to Monet-inspired garden views in season. Dressy casual; beer & wine only. **Parking:** on-site. **Cards:** AX, DC, DS, MC, VI.

EAST AURORA pop. 6,673

──── WHERE TO STAY ────

HAMPTON INN EAST AURORA & OAKWOOD EVENT CENTER *Book at aaa.com*   **Phone:** (716)655-3300
◆◆◆
Small-scale Hotel

All Year [CP]   1P: $99-$189   2P: $99-$189   XP: $10   F18
Location: Just s of Main St. 49 Olean St 14052. Fax: 716/655-4740. **Facility:** 80 units. 64 one-bedroom standard units. 16 one-bedroom suites, some with whirlpools. 4 stories, interior corridors. **Parking:** on-site. **Amenities:** video games, CD players, high-speed Internet (fee), dual phone lines, voice mail, irons, hair dryers. **Pool(s):** heated indoor. **Leisure Activities:** whirlpool, exercise room. *Fee:* game room. **Guest Services:** sundries, valet and coin laundry. **Business Services:** conference facilities, business center. **Cards:** AX, CB, DC, DS, JC, MC, VI.
SOME UNITS

THE ROYCROFT INN *Book at aaa.com*   **Phone:** (716)652-5552
◆◆◆
Historic
Country Inn

All Year [ECP]   1P: $120-$280   2P: $120-$280   XP: $20   F12
Location: Just s of jct US 20A and SR 16; downtown. Located adjacent to The Roycroft Colony Buildings. 40 S Grove St 14052. Fax: 716/655-5345. **Facility:** This 1905 mansion features original and reproduction furniture and fixtures from the arts and crafts movement. Smoke free premises. 29 one-bedroom standard units, some with whirlpools. 2-3 stories (no elevator), interior corridors. *Bath:* combo or shower only. **Parking:** on-site, winter plug-ins. **Terms:** check-in 4 pm. **Amenities:** dual phone lines, irons, hair dryers. **Dining:** dining room, see separate listing. **Guest Services:** valet laundry. **Business Services:** meeting rooms. **Cards:** AX, DC, DS, MC, VI. *(See color ad below)*
SOME UNITS

——— WHERE TO DINE ———

OLD ORCHARD INN Historic **Lunch:** $8-$14 **Dinner:** $14-$22 **Phone:** 716/652-4664
▼▼ ▼▼ **Location:** Jct US 20A, 2.4 mi s on old SR 16, go under SR 400 to Blakeley Corners, then 0.4 mi w, follow signs. 2095
Blakeley Corners Rd 14052. **Hours:** 11:30 am-2:30 & 5-9 pm, Sat-10 pm, Sun noon-9 pm. Closed: 12/25;
American also Mon & Tues 1/1-3/31. **Reservations:** suggested. **Features:** On manicured grounds overlooking a
lake, the restored lodge has a convivial, rustic appeal. Homemade rolls and desserts—particularly the
luscious lemon angel—make mouths water. In season, terrace seating is a nice alternative to the dining room. Dressy casual;
cocktails. **Parking:** on-site. **Cards:** AX, DS, MC, VI. 🗙

THE ROYCROFT INN DINING ROOM Historic **Lunch:** $7-$11 **Dinner:** $12-$24 **Phone:** 716/652-5552
▼▼▼▼ **Location:** Just s of jct US 20A and SR 16; downtown; in The Roycroft Inn. 40 S Grove St 14052. **Hours:** 11:30
am-2 & 5-9 pm, Fri & Sat-10 pm. **Reservations:** suggested. **Features:** Reflections of the arts and crafts
American movement—including pictures dating back to the inn's 1900s origin—are evident in the cozy dining room.
The restaurant is known for its fresh sunflower seed bread, lamb chops with mustard demi-glace and
spectacularly displayed desserts made with the freshest seasonal fruits. Dressy casual; cocktails. **Parking:** on-site. **Cards:** AX,
DC, DS, MC, VI. 🍸 🗙

GRAND ISLAND pop. 18,621

——— WHERE TO STAY ———

BUDGET MOTEL **Phone:** (716)773-3902
🅰🅰🅰 SAVE All Year 1P: $35-$69 2P: $45-$79 XP: $5 F12
▼▼ **Location:** I-190, exit 20 northbound, 2 mi se on SR 324; exit 20B southbound, just e on SR 324. 3080 Grand Island Blvd
14072. Fax: 716/773-4972. **Facility:** 22 one-bedroom standard units. 2 stories (no elevator), exterior corri-
Motel dors. **Parking:** on-site, winter plug-ins. **Terms:** 3 day cancellation notice, weekly rates available. **Leisure
Activities:** gas grills. **Cards:** AX, DC, MC, VI.

SOME UNITS
🆘 🛢 / 🗙 📶 /

CHATEAU MOTOR LODGE **Phone:** (716)773-2868
🅰🅰🅰 SAVE 6/1-9/8 1P: $49-$79 2P: $49-$79 XP: $5 F7
5/1-5/31 1P: $35-$49 2P: $39-$69 XP: $5 F7
▼▼ 9/9-4/30 1P: $32-$39 2P: $35-$59 XP: $5 F7
Location: I-190, exit 18A northbound, 0.5 mi w on SR 324 W. 1810 Grand Island Blvd 14072. Fax: 716/773-5173.
Motel **Facility:** 17 one-bedroom standard units. 1 story, exterior corridors. *Bath:* combo or shower only. **Parking:**
on-site, winter plug-ins. **Terms:** 3 day cancellation notice-fee imposed, weekly rates available, pets ($8 extra
charge). **Business Services:** fax (fee). **Cards:** AX, DS, MC, VI.

SOME UNITS
🆘 🐕 🔧 🎬 🛢 / 🗙 DATA PORT /
FEE

CINDERELLA MOTEL **Phone:** (716)773-2872
▼▼ 5/1-10/31 1P: $52-$69 2P: $57-$75 XP: $4 F
11/1-4/30 1P: $42-$48 2P: $46-$52 XP: $4 F
Motel **Location:** I-190, exit 19 northbound, 1.3 mi w on SR 324; exit 20B southbound, just e on SR 324. 2797 Grand Island
Blvd 14072-1210. **Facility:** 16 units. 15 one-bedroom standard units, some with whirlpools. 1 two-bedroom
suite with kitchen. 1 story, exterior corridors. *Bath:* combo or shower only. **Parking:** on-site, winter plug-ins. **Terms:** 3 day cancellation notice, small pets only. **Guest Services:** coin laundry. **Cards:** DS, MC, VI.

SOME UNITS
🐕 🔧 🛡 🛢 / 🗙 🛢 📟 /

HOLIDAY INN GRAND ISLAND RESORT *Book at aaa.com* **Phone:** (716)773-1111
🅰🅰🅰 SAVE 6/26-9/7 1P: $105-$159 2P: $105-$159 XP: $10 F18
5/1-6/25 1P: $82-$139 2P: $82-$139 XP: $10 F18
▼▼▼▼ 9/8-10/29 1P: $82-$119 2P: $82-$119 XP: $10 F18
10/30-4/30 1P: $75-$99 2P: $75-$99 XP: $10 F18
Resort **Location:** I-190, exit 19, 4 mi e. 100 Whitehaven Rd 14072. Fax: 716/773-1229. **Facility:** Extensive conference fa-
Large-scale Hotel cilities are featured at this activity-oriented, family-friendly riverfront resort. 261 units. 257 one-bedroom standard units. 4 one-bedroom suites with whirlpools. 4-6 stories, interior corridors. *Bath:* combo or shower only.
Parking: on-site, winter plug-ins. **Terms:** cancellation fee imposed, [AP], [BP] & [CP] meal plans available, package plans.
Amenities: video games, dual phone lines, voice mail, irons, hair dryers. **Dining:** 7 am-2 & 6-10 pm; hours vary off season,
cocktails. **Pool(s):** heated outdoor, heated indoor, wading, lap. **Leisure Activities:** sauna, whirlpool, boat dock, fishing, Grand
Lady boat cruises, 2 lighted tennis courts. *Fee:* golf-18 holes, massage. **Guest Services:** gift shop, valet and coin laundry. **Business Services:** conference facilities, fax (fee). **Cards:** AX, CB, DC, DS, JC, MC, VI.

SOME UNITS
🆘 🍽 🍸 ♿ 🍳 🐕 🔧 🗙 🎬 📟 📺 / 🗙 VCR 🛢 📶 /
FEE FEE FEE

HAMBURG pop. 10,116

——— WHERE TO STAY ———

COMFORT INN & SUITES *Book at aaa.com* **Phone:** (716)648-2922
🅰🅰🅰 SAVE 6/1-9/8 1P: $99-$189 2P: $99-$189 XP: $10 F18
5/1-5/31 & 9/9-10/31 1P: $89-$159 2P: $89-$159 XP: $10 F18
▼▼▼▼ 11/1-4/30 1P: $74-$139 2P: $74-$139 XP: $10 F18
Small-scale Hotel **Location:** I-90, exit 57, just w. Located in a quiet, secluded area. 3615 Commerce Pl 14075. Fax: 716/648-2904.
Facility: 61 one-bedroom standard units, some with efficiencies (no utensils) and/or whirlpools. 2 stories (no
elevator), interior corridors. *Bath:* combo or shower only. **Parking:** on-site. **Terms:** [CP] meal plan available,
pets ($10 fee). **Amenities:** voice mail, safes, irons, hair dryers. **Pool(s):** heated indoor. **Leisure Activities:** exercise room. **Busi-
ness Services:** meeting rooms, PC, fax. **Cards:** AX, DC, DS, MC, VI. **Special Amenities:** free expanded continental breakfast and free local telephone calls.

SOME UNITS
🆘 🐕 🆖M 🍳 🍳 🎬 DATA PORT 📶 / 🗙 🛢 📶 /
FEE

HOLIDAY INN HAMBURG   *Book at aaa.com*   **Phone:** (716)649-0500

AAA (SAVE)
5/28-9/7	1P: $85-$109	2P: $85-$109
5/1-5/27	1P: $80-$94	2P: $80-$94
9/8-10/31	1P: $70-$89	2P: $70-$89
11/1-4/30	1P: $65-$85	2P: $65-$85

Small-scale Hotel **Location:** I-90, exit 57, 0.3 mi e se on SR 75. 5440 Camp Rd 14075. **Fax:** 716/648-2278. **Facility:** 129 one-bedroom standard units. 2 stories (no elevator), interior corridors. *Bath:* combo or shower only. **Parking:** on-site. **Terms:** check-in 4 pm, [CP] meal plan available, small pets only ($10 extra charge). **Amenities:** video games, voice mail, irons, hair dryers. **Dining:** 6:30 am-2 & 5-9 pm, Sat-10 pm; closed for dinner Sun, cocktails. **Pool(s):** heated outdoor. **Leisure Activities:** exercise room. **Guest Services:** valet and coin laundry. **Business Services:** meeting rooms, fax (fee). **Cards:** AX, CB, DC, DS, JC, MC, VI.

RED ROOF INN   *Book at aaa.com*   **Phone:** (716)648-7222

AAA (SAVE)
6/18-9/4	1P: $50-$80	2P: $56-$80	XP: $6	F18
9/5-10/23	1P: $45-$66	2P: $51-$66	XP: $6	F18
10/24-4/30	1P: $37-$63	2P: $43-$63	XP: $6	F18
5/1-6/17	1P: $42-$60	2P: $48-$60	XP: $6	F18

Motel **Location:** I-90, exit 57, just se on SR 75. 5370 Camp Rd 14075. **Fax:** 716/648-7324. **Facility:** 108 one-bedroom standard units. 2 stories (no elevator), exterior corridors. **Parking:** on-site. **Terms:** small pets only. **Amenities:** voice mail. **Cards:** AX, CB, DC, DS, MC, VI. **Special Amenities:** free local telephone calls and free newspaper.

TALLYHO-TEL   **Phone:** (716)648-2000

AAA (SAVE)
| All Year | 1P: $25-$125 | 2P: $25-$125 | XP: $7 | F18 |

Motel **Location:** I-90, exit 57, just nw on SR 75. 5245 Camp Rd 14075. **Fax:** 716/648-9718. **Facility:** 117 one-bedroom standard units, some with efficiencies. 1 story, exterior corridors. **Parking:** on-site. **Terms:** check-in 4 pm, weekly rates available, pets ($15 deposit). **Pool(s):** outdoor. **Guest Services:** coin laundry. **Cards:** AX, DS, MC, VI.

——— **WHERE TO DINE** ———

DANIEL'S   **Dinner:** $16-$26   **Phone:** 716/648-6554

American   **Location:** On US 62 (Buffalo St); across from Hamburg Village Plaza. 174 Buffalo St 14075. **Hours:** 5 pm-9 pm, Sat-9:30 pm. Closed major holidays; also Sun & Mon. **Reservations:** suggested. **Features:** Rich sauces and many wines complement lavish dishes of fresh seafood, meat and pasta. The former house is cozy and inviting, with piped-in classical music. The experience is understated, elegant and intimate. Dressy casual; cocktails. **Parking:** on-site. **Cards:** AX, MC, VI.

NEW MANCHURIAN HOUSE   **Lunch:** $4-$9   **Dinner:** $4-$12   **Phone:** 716/648-7173

Chinese   **Location:** I-90, exit 57, 2 mi s on SR 75 (Camp Rd), jct of SR 62. 16 Pierce Ave 14075. **Hours:** 11 am-10 pm, Fri & Sat-11 pm, Sun 1 pm-10 pm. Closed: 11/25. **Features:** Extensive selections of freshly-made dishes are made to order for the dining room or to go. The staff is friendly and polite. Casual dress. **Parking:** on-site. **Cards:** AX, DS, MC, VI.

ROMANELLO'S SOUTH   **Dinner:** $12-$25   **Phone:** 716/649-0450

Italian   **Location:** Jct US 20 and 62, 1.7 mi s. 5793 S Park Ave 14075. **Hours:** 4 pm-10 pm, Sun 3 pm-9 pm. Closed: 12/25. **Reservations:** suggested. **Features:** A sophisticated, yet casually friendly, presence is accented by a fireplace set in brick. Bookcases and a variety of plants complete the setting. The competent wait staff serves nicely presented Italian/American cuisine. Dressy casual; cocktails. **Parking:** on-site. **Cards:** AX, DS, MC, VI.

KENMORE pop. 16,426   (See map and index starting on p. 238)

——— **WHERE TO STAY** ———

SUPER 8-BUFFALO/NIAGARA FALLS   *Book at aaa.com*   **Phone:** (716)876-4020   63

6/1-9/2 [CP]	1P: $60-$66	2P: $66-$75
5/1-5/31 & 9/3-10/31 [CP]	1P: $50-$55	2P: $55-$60
11/1-4/30 [CP]	1P: $42-$50	2P: $48-$52

Small-scale Hotel **Location:** I-190, exit 15, 1.5 mi e. 1288 Sheridan Dr 14217. **Fax:** 716/876-4729. **Facility:** 59 one-bedroom standard units. 2 stories (no elevator), interior corridors. **Parking:** on-site, winter plug-ins. **Terms:** cancellation fee imposed. **Amenities:** dual phone lines, voice mail. **Business Services:** meeting rooms. **Cards:** AX, DS, MC, VI.

——— **WHERE TO DINE** ———

TSUNAMI   **Dinner:** $14-$22   **Phone:** 716/447-7915   60

Nouvelle Pacific Rim   **Location:** Just w of Colvin Ave. 1141 Kenmore Ave 14217. **Hours:** 5 pm-10 pm, Fri & Sat-11 pm. Closed: 1/1, 11/25, 12/25; also Sun. **Reservations:** suggested. **Features:** Fresh, distinctive seafood, meats and vegetables are prepared at this culinary oasis for Pacific Rim cuisine. Complex ingredients and imagination create artistic presentations. The staff is knowledgeable and helpful. Dressy casual; cocktails. **Parking:** on-site. **Cards:** AX, DS, MC, VI.

SPRINGVILLE pop. 4,252

------- WHERE TO STAY -------

MICROTEL INN & SUITES   *Book at aaa.com*   Phone: (716)592-3141

AAA (SAVE) 5/1-8/31 & 10/1-10/31 [CP]   1P: $49-$79   2P: $49-$79   XP: $5   F16
            9/1-9/30 & 11/1-4/30 [CP]   1P: $44-$74   2P: $44-$74   XP: $5   F16

Location: On SR 219 S (Cascade Dr). Located in the business district. 270 S Cascade Dr 14141. Fax: 716/592-2565.

Small-scale Hotel   **Facility:** 60 one-bedroom standard units. 2 stories, interior corridors. *Bath:* combo or shower only. **Parking:** on-site. **Terms:** 30 day cancellation notice, package plans, pets ($10 extra charge). **Amenities:** voice mail. *Some:* hair dryers. **Business Services:** meeting rooms. **Cards:** AX, CB, DC, DS, MC, VI.

Special Amenities: free continental breakfast and free local telephone calls.

SOME UNITS

TONAWANDA pop. 61,729   (See map and index starting on p. 238)

------- WHERE TO STAY -------

DAYS INN   *Book at aaa.com*   Phone: (716)835-5916   56

AAA (SAVE) 7/1-8/31   1P: $60-$125   2P: $60-$125   XP: $5   F12
            5/1-6/30 & 1/1-4/30   1P: $45-$99   2P: $45-$99   XP: $5   F12
Motel   9/1-12/31   1P: $45-$75   2P: $45-$75   XP: $5   F12

Location: I-290, exit 3 (Niagara Falls Blvd), 1.3 mi s on US 62. Located across from a shopping mall. 1120 Niagara Falls Blvd 14150. Fax: 716/835-6030. **Facility:** 51 one-bedroom standard units, some with whirlpools. 2 stories (no elevator), exterior corridors. **Parking:** on-site. **Terms:** small pets only. **Amenities:** voice mail, safes, hair dryers. **Cards:** AX, DC, DS, MC, VI. **Special Amenities:** free continental breakfast and free local telephone calls.

SOME UNITS

MICROTEL-TONAWANDA   *Book at aaa.com*   Phone: (716)693-8100   57

AAA (SAVE) 6/1-10/31   1P: $53-$70   2P: $58-$75   XP: $5   F16
            5/1-5/31   1P: $47-$60   2P: $47-$60   XP: $5   F16
            1/1-4/30   1P: $43-$60   2P: $43-$60   XP: $5   F16
            11/1-12/31   1P: $43   2P: $43   XP: $5   F16

Small-scale Hotel   **Location:** I-290, exit 1B; I-290 E, exit 1, 0.5 mi e on Crestmount Ave, just n on SR 384 (Delaware St). 1 Hospitality Centre Way 14150. Fax: 716/693-8750. **Facility:** 100 one-bedroom standard units. 2 stories (no elevator), interior corridors. **Parking:** on-site. **Terms:** 3 day cancellation notice, pets ($10 fee). **Amenities:** video library (fee), video games, safes. **Cards:** AX, DC, DS, MC, VI. **Special Amenities:** free continental breakfast and early check-in/late check-out.

SOME UNITS

WEST SENECA pop. 45,943   (See map and index starting on p. 238)

------- WHERE TO STAY -------

HAMPTON INN BUFFALO-SOUTH/I-90   *Book at aaa.com*   Phone: (716)824-2030   64

            All Year [CP]   1P: $79-$169   2P: $85-$175

Location: I-90, exit 55 (Ridge Rd E), just n. 1750 Ridge Rd 14224. Fax: 716/821-9213. **Facility:** 105 units. 100 one-bedroom standard units. 5 one-bedroom suites, some with whirlpools. 5 stories, interior corridors. *Bath:* combo or shower only. **Parking:** on-site. **Amenities:** video library (fee), video games, high-speed Internet, dual phone lines, voice mail, irons, hair dryers. **Pool(s):** small heated indoor. **Leisure Activities:** whirlpool, exercise room. **Guest Services:** valet laundry. **Business Services:** meeting rooms. **Cards:** AX, CB, DC, DS, JC, MC, VI.

Small-scale Hotel

SOME UNITS

WILLIAMSVILLE pop. 5,573   (See map and index starting on p. 238)

------- WHERE TO STAY -------

CLARION HOTEL-BUFFALO AIRPORT   *Book at aaa.com*   Phone: (716)634-7500   47

AAA (SAVE) 5/1-8/31 [ECP]   1P: $79-$99   2P: $79-$99   XP: $10   F18
            9/1-10/31 [ECP]   1P: $69-$89   2P: $69-$89   XP: $10   F18
            11/1-4/30 [ECP]   1P: $59-$79   2P: $59-$79   XP: $10   F18

Location: I-90, exit 49 (SR 78 N), 0.3 mi n on SR 78. 6700 Transit Rd 14221. Fax: 716/634-7502. **Facility:** 80 one-bedroom standard units. 2 stories (no elevator), interior corridors. **Parking:** on-site. **Amenities:** dual phone lines, voice mail, irons, hair dryers. **Pool(s):** heated indoor. **Leisure Activities:** whirlpool, exercise room. **Guest Services:** complimentary evening beverages: Mon-Thurs, valet and coin laundry, area transportation-within 5 mi. **Business Services:** meeting rooms, business center. **Cards:** AX, CB, DC, DS, JC, MC, VI. **Special Amenities:** free expanded continental breakfast and free local telephone calls. *(See color ad p 242)*

Small-scale Hotel

SOME UNITS

FAIRFIELD INN-LANCASTER   *Book at aaa.com*   Phone: (716)626-1500   49

            All Year [CP]   1P: $59-$109   2P: $59-$109

Location: I-90, exit 49 (SR 78 N), just e. 52 Freeman Dr 14221. Fax: 716/626-1500. **Facility:** 135 one-bedroom standard units. 3 stories, interior/exterior corridors. **Parking:** on-site. **Amenities:** voice mail, irons. **Pool(s):** heated outdoor. **Guest Services:** valet laundry. **Business Services:** fax (fee). **Cards:** AX, DC, DS, JC, MC, VI.

Motel

SOME UNITS

(See map and index starting on p. 238)

HAMPTON INN AT WILLIAMSVILLE   *Book at aaa.com*   Phone: (716)632-0900   **42**
 ▼▼◆▼▼   5/1-10/31 [ECP]   1P: $145-$189   2P: $155-$199   XP: $10   F18
              11/1-4/30 [ECP]   1P: $109-$159   2P: $119-$169   XP: $10   F18
Small-scale Hotel   **Location:** I-290, exit 7B, 0.7 mi e on SR 5 (Main St). 5455 Main St 14221. Fax: 716/632-1300. **Facility:** 80 units. 76 one-bedroom standard units, some with whirlpools. 4 one-bedroom suites ($139-$199) with whirlpools. 4 stories, interior corridors. *Bath:* combo or shower only. **Parking:** on-site. **Terms:** package plans - seasonal. **Amenities:** high-speed Internet, dual phone lines, voice mail, irons, hair dryers. **Pool(s):** small heated indoor. **Leisure Activities:** whirlpool, exercise room. **Guest Services:** valet and coin laundry, area transportation. **Business Services:** meeting rooms. **Cards:** AX, DC, DS, MC, VI.

SOME UNITS

MICROTEL-LANCASTER   *Book at aaa.com*   Phone: (716)633-6200   **43**
 🅰🅰🅰 [SAVE]   6/25-9/6 [CP]   1P: $49-$69   2P: $54-$79
               9/7-4/30 [CP]   1P: $37-$49   2P: $42-$69
 ▼▼◆▼▼   5/1-6/24 [CP]   1P: $44-$54   2P: $49-$59
Small-scale Hotel   **Location:** I-90, exit 49 (SR 78 N), just n, then just e. 50 Freeman Rd 14221. Fax: 716/633-1329. **Facility:** 100 one-bedroom standard units. 2 stories, interior corridors. *Bath:* combo or shower only. **Parking:** on-site, winter plug-ins. **Terms:** 3 day cancellation notice, small pets only ($5 extra charge). **Amenities:** video games, safes. **Guest Services:** valet laundry. **Cards:** AX, CB, DC, DS, JC, MC, VI. **Special Amenities:** free continental breakfast and free newspaper.

SOME UNITS

RESIDENCE INN BY MARRIOTT BUFFALO/AMHERST   *Book at aaa.com*   Phone: (716)632-6622   **45**
 ▼▼◆▼▼   7/1-8/31 [ECP]   1P: $144-$159   2P: $153-$169
              5/1-6/30 [ECP]   1P: $99-$119   2P: $99-$159
Motel   9/1-12/31 [ECP]   1P: $104-$109   2P: $104-$109
              1/1-4/30 [ECP]   1P: $99-$109   2P: $99-$109
Location: I-290, exit 5B, just e on Maple Rd from jct SR 263 (Millersport Hwy). 100 Maple Rd 14221. Fax: 716/632-5247. **Facility:** 112 units. 84 one-bedroom standard units with kitchens. 28 two-bedroom suites with kitchens. 2 stories (no elevator), exterior corridors. **Parking:** on-site. **Terms:** cancellation fee imposed, pets ($50 fee, $6 extra charge). **Amenities:** video library, voice mail, irons, hair dryers. **Pool(s):** heated outdoor. **Leisure Activities:** exercise room, sports court. **Guest Services:** complimentary evening beverages: Mon-Thurs, valet and coin laundry, area transportation. **Business Services:** business center. **Cards:** AX, CB, DC, DS, JC, MC, VI.

SOME UNITS

─────── **WHERE TO DINE** ───────

DAFFODIL'S   **Lunch:** $7-$11   **Dinner:** $16-$27   **Phone:** 716/688-5413   **57**
 ▼▼◆▼▼   **Location:** Jct SR 263 (Millersport Hwy), 1.8 mi e. 930 Maple Rd 14221. **Hours:** 11:30 am-2:30 & 5-11 pm, Fri-midnight, Sat 5 pm-midnight, Sun 4 pm-10 pm. Closed: 5/31, 7/4, 9/6; also Super Bowl Sun.
Steak & Seafood   **Reservations:** accepted. **Features:** Contributing to the restaurant's traditional style are well-worn leather, warm-toned wood, fireplaces and intimate candlelit tables—some of which are in library-like settings. Of renown is the tender, juicy rack of lamb accompanied by decorative fresh vegetables and nouveau potato creations. Trendy American and Continental choices with luscious homemade desserts make for a truly fine dining experience. Dressy casual; cocktails. **Parking:** on-site. **Cards:** AX, DC, MC, VI.

EAGLE HOUSE RESTAURANT   Historic   **Lunch:** $7-$10   **Dinner:** $10-$20   **Phone:** 716/632-7669   **56**
 ▼▼◆▼ ▼▼◆▼ ▼   **Location:** I-290, exit 7, 1 mi e on SR 5; downtown. 5578 Main St 14221. **Hours:** 11 am-10 pm, Fri & Sat-11 pm, Sun 3 pm-9 pm. Closed: 12/25; also Sun 7/1-8/31. **Reservations:** accepted, except Fri night.
American   **Features:** Built in 1827, Eagle House was a hostel, historic tavern and stagecoach mid-station. The dining room is decorated in aged wood, brass and brick. Menu items include homey comfort foods and a tray full of luscious desserts. Casual dress; cocktails. **Parking:** on-site. **Cards:** AX, CB, DS, MC, VI.

JOE MATA'S   **Lunch:** $4-$8   **Dinner:** $4-$17   **Phone:** 716/565-6970   **51**
 ▼▼◆▼▼   **Location:** I-90, exit 49, 2 mi n on SR 78 (Transit Rd). 5063 Transit Rd 14221. **Hours:** 11 am-9 pm, Fri & Sat-10 pm. Closed: 11/25, 12/25. **Features:** Healthy and deliciously fresh sandwiches, wood-fired oven pizzas
Italian   made with tender crust, calzones, soups, salads and tempting desserts make up the menu. The setting is casually upscale. Casual dress; beer & wine only. **Parking:** on-site. **Cards:** AX, CB, DC, DS, MC, VI.

KABAB & CURRY   **Lunch:** $4-$9   **Dinner:** $6-$15   **Phone:** 716/565-3822   **50**
 🅰🅰🅰   **Location:** I-90, exit 49, 2.3 mi n on SR 78 (Transit Rd). 5185 Transit Rd 14221. **Hours:** 11:30 am-2:30 & 5-10 pm, Sat & Sun-3 pm. **Features:** An expanded selection of Indian cuisine, including many vegetarian dishes and
 ▼▼ ▼▼   exclusive preparations such as dhosas and karahi, is prepared daily. Brunch is served on the weekends.
Indian   Casual dress; beer & wine only. **Parking:** on-site. **Cards:** MC, VI.

THE ORIGINAL PANCAKE HOUSE   **Lunch:** $4-$8   **Dinner:** $4-$8   **Phone:** 716/634-5515   **58**
 ▼▼◆▼   **Location:** I-290, exit 7B, 0.8 mi e on SR 5 (Main St). 5479 Main St 14221. **Hours:** 6:30 am-9 pm. Closed: 12/25.
              Features: Originating in 1953, the restaurant has endured due to its use of high-quality ingredients in award-winning recipes. Representative of breakfast fare are classic omelets, wonderful waffles and
American   incredible crepes accompanied by freshly squeezed orange juice, the eatery's own blend of coffee, made-to-order sausage and old-fashioned, dry-cured, hickory-smoked hams and bacons. Casual dress. **Parking:** on-site. **Cards:** AX, MC, VI.

(See map and index starting on p. 238)

PROTOCOL   **Lunch:** $6-$11   **Dinner:** $11-$21   **Phone:** 716/632-9556   52
Seafood

Location: I-90, exit 49, 0.5 mi n on SR 78 (Transit Rd). 6766 Transit Rd 14221. **Hours:** 11 am-11:30 pm. Closed: Sun. **Reservations:** suggested. **Features:** Family-owned since 1972, the restaurant prepares fresh Boston seafood with originality. Sesame-crusted tuna is only one of the most popular dishes. Also tempting are the stuffed filet, baby back ribs, steaks and chicken Protocol. The feel is casual and friendly. Casual dress; cocktails. **Parking:** on-site. **Cards:** AX, MC, VI.

TANDOORI'S   **Lunch:** $8-$9   **Dinner:** $10-$20   **Phone:** 716/632-1112   55
Indian

Location: Jct Sheridan and SR 78 (Transit Rd). 7740 Transit Rd 14221. **Hours:** 11 am-2:30 & 5-11 pm, Sat from 5 pm. Closed: 12/25. **Reservations:** accepted. **Features:** Carefully chosen exotic spices and herbal seasonings are used to create delicious vegetarian and non-vegetarian gourmet dishes. The culinary experience is memorable. Dressy casual; cocktails. **Parking:** on-site. **Cards:** AX, DC, DS, MC, VI.

ZUZON AMERICAN GRILLE   **Lunch:** $7-$12   **Dinner:** $9-$18   **Phone:** 716/634-6123   54
American

Location: I-290, exit 7B on SR 5 (Main St), just e; in Walker Center. 5110 Main St 14221. **Hours:** 11:30 am-10 pm, Sun from 4 pm. Closed: 12/25. **Reservations:** accepted. **Features:** A California bistro in both style and flavor, the restaurant features an open-view kitchen and pizza hearth. Unusual twists mark some old favorites. "Vertical" salads are piled dangerously high, while margherita pizza, Maryland crab pizza, Caribbean chicken and flying shrimp stimulate the senses. The specialty, ZuZon meat loaf with peas, carrots and great mashed potatoes, is a local favorite. Save room for one of the fabulous homemade dessert creations, served with flair. Casual dress; cocktails. **Parking:** on-site. **Cards:** AX, DS, MC, VI.

This ends listings for the Buffalo Vicinity.
The following page resumes the alphabetical listings of
cities in New York.

CALLICOON pop. 216

——— WHERE TO DINE ———

——— *The following restaurant has not been evaluated by AAA* ———
but is listed for your information only.

VILLA ROMA   Phone: 845/887-4880
[fyi]   Not evaluated. **Location:** In Villa Roma Resort. 356 Villa Roma Rd 12723. **Features:** Open for breakfast, lunch
and dinner, this relaxed dining room offers guests Italian-American cuisine.

CAMILLUS pop. 1,249   (See map and index starting on p. 577)

——— WHERE TO DINE ———

INN BETWEEN RESTAURANT   **Dinner:** $18-$23   **Phone:** 315/672-3166   [40]
▽▽▽   **Location:** 2.3 mi w on SR 5; 10 mi w of Syracuse and 10 mi e of Skaneatles. 2290 W Genesee St 13031. **Hours:** 5
pm-10 pm, Sun 2 pm-8 pm. Closed: 1/1, 12/25; also Mon. **Reservations:** required, weekends.
American   **Features:** The 19th-century Victorian manor house has a sophisticated feel, with crisp linens and elegant
table settings. Beef Wellington and roast duckling are among well-prepared entrees of beef, poultry, veal
and seafood. Desserts are delicately presented. Dressy casual; cocktails. **Parking:** on-site. **Cards:** AX, MC, VI.   ⚏ ⊠

CANANDAIGUA pop. 11,264—*See also FINGER LAKES.*

——— WHERE TO STAY ———

1885 SUTHERLAND HOUSE   Phone: 585/396-0375
▽▽▽   All Year [BP]   2P: $105-$350   XP: $25
Location: I-90, exit 44 (Canandaigua); SR 332 S into city, 1.5 mi w on Bristol (SR 21 S). 3179 SR 21 S 14424.
Bed & Breakfast Fax: 585/396-9281. **Facility:** Original woodwork adds charm to this 1885 Victorian home. The hilly grounds
feature gardens and a 200-year-old copper beech tree. Smoke free premises. 5 one-bedroom standard units,
some with whirlpools. 2 stories (no elevator), interior corridors. **Bath:** combo or shower only. **Parking:** on-site. **Terms:** 2 night
minimum stay - 5/1-12/31, age restrictions may apply, cancellation fee imposed, weekly rates available, package plans, no pets
allowed (owner's pet on premises). **Amenities:** video library, CD players, hair dryers. **Guest Services:** gift shop. **Cards:** AX, DS,
MC, VI.   SOME UNITS
⊠ 📺 [VCR] 🕴 / ☎ /

CANANDAIGUA INN ON THE LAKE   *Book at aaa.com*   Phone: (585)394-7800
(AAA) [SAVE]   5/1-10/31   1P: $139   2P: $144   XP: $10   F18
▽▽▽   11/1-4/30   1P: $89   2P: $94   XP: $10   F18
Location: I-90, exit 44, jct SR 332, just s across US 20 and SR 5. 770 S Main St 14424. Fax: 585/394-5003.
Small-scale Hotel **Facility:** 134 units. 88 one-bedroom standard units. 46 one-bedroom suites ($129-$304), some with whirlpools. 2 stories, interior corridors. **Bath:** combo or shower only. **Parking:** on-site. **Terms:** 3 day cancellation
notice, package plans, pets ($5 extra charge). **Amenities:** video library (fee), video games, voice mail, irons.
Some: hair dryers. **Dining:** 6:30 am-9 pm, Fri & Sat-10 pm, cocktails. **Pool(s):** heated outdoor, small heated indoor. **Leisure Activities:** whirlpool, boat dock, fishing, exercise room. **Guest Services:** valet and coin laundry. **Business Services:** conference
facilities, fax (fee). **Cards:** AX, CB, DC, DS, MC, VI.   SOME UNITS
$🄳 🐾 🍴 ⚏ &M 🐕 📷 🔁 ⊠ 📹 [DATA PORT] 💻 / ⊠ 🛄 🍽 /
FEE   FEE FEE

CANANDAIGUA MOTEL   *Book at aaa.com*   Phone: 585/394-4140
(AAA) [SAVE]   6/1-8/31 [CP]   2P: $79-$85   XP: $10   F16
▽▽   9/1-11/30 [CP]   2P: $55-$75   XP: $10   F16
12/1-4/30 [CP]   2P: $45-$65   XP: $10   F16
5/1-5/31 [CP]   2P: $65   XP: $10   F16
Small-scale Hotel **Location:** 1 mi e of jct SR 332. 4232 Rt 5 & 20 14424. Fax: 585/394-5484. **Facility:** 30 one-bedroom standard
units, some with efficiencies and/or whirlpools. 2 stories (no elevator), interior/exterior corridors. **Parking:** on-
site. **Terms:** package plans - seasonal & weekends. **Amenities:** voice mail, irons, hair dryers. **Cards:** AX, DS, MC, VI.
Special Amenities: free continental breakfast and free local telephone calls.
SOME UNITS
📷 [DATA PORT] / ⊠ 🛄 🍽 💻 /

ECONO LODGE CANANDAIGUA   *Book at aaa.com*   Phone: (585)394-9000
(AAA) [SAVE]   5/1-10/31 [CP]   1P: $64-$104   2P: $69-$109   XP: $5   F18
▽▽   11/1-4/30 [CP]   1P: $44-$64   2P: $49-$69   XP: $5   F18
Location: Jct SR 332, 5 and US 20, 0.5 mi e. Located next to Roseland Water Park. 170 Eastern Blvd 14424.
Small-scale Hotel Fax: 585/396-2560. **Facility:** 65 one-bedroom standard units. 2 stories (no elevator), interior corridors.
Parking: on-site. **Terms:** 3 day cancellation notice, package plans. **Amenities:** video library (fee). **Guest
Services:** coin laundry. **Cards:** AX, CB, DC, DS, MC, VI. **Special Amenities:** free continental breakfast
and free newspaper.
SOME UNITS
$🄳 🐾 🍴 📷 [DATA PORT] / ⊠ [VCR] 🛄 🍽 💻 /
FEE FEE FEE

MORGAN-SAMUELS INN

Phone: (585)394-9232

◆◆◆ (SAVE)

9/21-11/20 [BP]	1P: $149-$229	2P: $159-$335	XP: $50
5/26-9/20 [BP]	1P: $139-$199	2P: $159-$295	XP: $50
5/1-5/25 & 11/21-4/30 [BP]	1P: $89-$129	2P: $139-$255	XP: $50

Location: I-90, exit 43, 4.1 mi s on SR 21, just e on SR 488 to East Ave/Smith Rd, then 2 mi s. 2920 Smith Rd 14424.
Bed & Breakfast   Fax: 585/394-8044. **Facility:** Mixing modern conveniences with fine antiques, this 1810 mansion sits on a 46-acre estate eminating an aura of Victorian elegance. Smoke free premises. 6 one-bedroom standard units, some with whirlpools. 2 stories (no elevator), interior/exterior corridors. *Bath:* combo or shower only. **Parking:** on-site. **Terms:** 2 night minimum stay - seasonal weekends, age restrictions may apply, cancellation fee imposed, weekly rates available, [AP] meal plan available. **Amenities:** video library, hair dryers. **Leisure Activities:** whirlpool, tennis court, cross country skiing, bicycles, hiking trails, exercise room. **Business Services:** fax (fee). **Cards:** AX, MC, VI. **Special Amenities:** free full breakfast and free local telephone calls.

SOME UNITS
(X) (X) (Z) / (PW) (VCR) (DATA PORT) (1) /

SUPER 8   *Book at aaa.com*

Phone: 585-396-7224

◆◆◆ (SAVE)

7/1-8/31 [CP]	1P: $80-$102	2P: $85-$107	XP: $5	F12
5/1-6/30 [CP]	1P: $64-$89	2P: $69-$94	XP: $5	F12
9/1-10/31 [CP]	1P: $55-$84	2P: $60-$89	XP: $5	F12
11/1-4/30 [CP]	1P: $49-$65	2P: $54-$70	XP: $5	F12

Small-scale Hotel   **Location:** Jct SR 332, 5 and US 20, 0.5 mi e. 350 Eastern Blvd 14424. Fax: 585/396-7333. **Facility:** 50 one-bedroom standard units, some with whirlpools. 2 stories (no elevator), interior corridors. **Parking:** on-site. **Business Services:** meeting rooms. **Cards:** AX, DC, DS, MC, VI. **Special Amenities:** free continental breakfast and free local telephone calls.

SOME UNITS
(SD) (🎥) / (X) /

―――――― **WHERE TO DINE** ――――――

AKROPOLIS FAMILY RESTAURANT

Lunch: $3-$6   **Dinner:** $6-$8   **Phone:** 585-394-8721

◆
American
Location: 2.7 mi e on SR 5 and US 20. 4025 Rt 5 & 20 14424. **Hours:** 6 am-10 pm. Closed: 12/25. **Features:** Family-owned since 1985, the family-style restaurant serves up Greek and Italian specialties as well as steaks and seafood, as well as a fabulous famous fish fry on Fridays. Casual dress; cocktails. **Parking:** on-site. **Cards:** AX, DS, MC, VI.

CASA DE PASTA

Dinner: $9-$19   **Phone:** 585-394-3710

◆◆
Italian
Location: Downtown. 125 Bemis St 14424. **Hours:** 5 pm-9 pm, Fri & Sat-10 pm. Closed: 11/25, 12/25; also Mon. **Features:** Quality ingredients go into traditional dishes of pasta, seafood, veal and beef. An established local clientele frequents the restaurant—in a mid-19th-century house—for its friendly atmosphere. Soft lighting and background music enhance the ambience. Casual dress; cocktails. **Parking:** on-site. **Cards:** MC, VI.

(Y) (X)

KOOZINA'S RESTAURANT

Lunch: $5-$12   **Dinner:** $6-$13   **Phone:** 585-396-0360

◆◆
Mediterranean
Location: Jct SR 322 and US 20, just e. 699 S Main St 14424. **Hours:** 11 am-10 pm. Closed: 11/25, 12/25. **Reservations:** accepted. **Features:** The eclectic bistro prepares Mediterranean cuisine, as well as pizzas made in a wood-fired oven, in an open kitchen. Fresh market-priced fish and an impressive choice of pastas also add to the menu. Casual dress; cocktails. **Parking:** on-site. **Cards:** AX, DC, DS, MC, VI.

(LM) (Y) (X)

LINCOLN HILL INN   Historic

Dinner: $14-$26   **Phone:** 585-394-8254

◆
◆◆◆
American
Location: 1.3 mi s on SR 364. 3365 E Lake Rd 14424. **Hours:** 5 pm-9 pm, Fri & Sat-10 pm. Closed: 12/25; also Mon, Sun-Thur 1/1-4/1. **Reservations:** suggested. **Features:** The restored 1804 farmhouse exudes a warm, casual ambience in the dining room, as well as on three decks. Such dishes as shrimp scampi and onion soup are flavorful and aesthetically pleasing. Top the meal with dessert or gourmet coffee. Casual dress; cocktails. **Parking:** on-site. **Cards:** AX, MC, VI.

(Y) (X)

STEAMBOAT LANDING

Lunch: $7-$12   **Dinner:** $10-$23   **Phone:** 585-396-7350

◆◆◆
Continental
Location: In the resort area. 205 Lakeshore Dr 14424. **Hours:** 11:30 am-2:30 & 5-9 pm, Fri & Sat-10 pm, Sun 10 am-9 pm. Closed: 1/1, 12/25. **Reservations:** accepted. **Features:** Continental cuisine is prepared and presented with flair at the new lakefront restaurant. Two-story windows take advantage of the vista at every turn. Warm contemporary accents and such rustic touches as exposed beams lend to the relaxed appeal of the dining room. Casual dress; cocktails. **Parking:** on-site. **Cards:** AX, DS, MC, VI.

(Y) (X)

THENDARA INN & RESTAURANT

Dinner: $16-$32   **Phone:** 585-394-4868

◆◆◆
American
Location: 4 mi s on SR 364. 4356 E Lake Rd 14424. **Hours:** Open 5/1-1/1; 5 pm-9 pm, Sun 4 pm-8 pm. Closed: Mon & Tues 5/1-5/31 & 9/1-10/31; Mon-Thurs 11/1-12/31. **Reservations:** suggested. **Features:** The handsome lakefront property offers seating in the cozy, old great room and on the enclosed porch, which looks out over the water. Carefully prepared dishes, such as chicken with prosciutto and mozzarella in a phyllo pastry, are nicely presented. Casual dress; cocktails. **Parking:** on-site. **Cards:** AX, DS, MC, VI.

(Y) (X)

CANASTOTA pop. 4,425

―――――― **WHERE TO STAY** ――――――

DAYS INN   *Book at aaa.com*

Phone: (315)697-3309

◆◆

5/1-8/31 [CP]	1P: $69-$99	2P: $69-$129	XP: $10	F18
9/1-4/30 [CP]	1P: $59-$99	2P: $59-$99	XP: $10	F18

Small-scale Hotel   **Location:** I-90, exit 34, on SR 13. Across from the International Boxing Hall of Fame. N Peterboro St 13032 (PO Box 655). Fax: 315/697-5541. **Facility:** 60 one-bedroom standard units. 2 stories (no elevator), interior corridors. **Parking:** on-site, winter plug-ins. **Amenities:** hair dryers. **Guest Services:** coin laundry. **Business Services:** meeting rooms, fax (fee). **Cards:** AX, CB, DC, DS, JC, MC, VI.

SOME UNITS
(ASK) (SD) (🛏) (🍴) (🎥) / (X) (VCR) (1) (📷) /

CANTON pop. 5,882

——— **WHERE TO STAY** ———

BEST WESTERN UNIVERSITY INN
(AAA) (SAVE)
▼▼◇▼▼
Small-scale Hotel
All Year   1P: $89-$119   2P: $89-$119   Phone: (315)386-8522
Location: Jct US 11, 68 and 310, 1 mi e on US 11. 90 E Main St 13617-1452. Fax: 315/386-1025. **Facility:** 99 one-bedroom standard units. 2-3 stories (no elevator), interior corridors. *Bath:* combo or shower only. **Parking:** on-site, winter plug-ins. **Terms:** 3 day cancellation notice, package plans. **Amenities:** voice mail, irons, hair dryers. **Dining:** 6:30 am-2 & 4:30-9 pm, Sun from 7 am, cocktails. **Pool(s):** small heated outdoor. **Leisure Activities:** exercise room. **Business Services:** meeting rooms. **Cards:** AX, CB, DC, DS, MC, VI.

SOME UNITS
(S/D) ⓘ 𝖄 ⓚ ⚊ 🐾 📷 [DATA PORT] 💻 / ✕ 🛏 🖼 /

CANTON/POTSDAM COMFORT SUITES   *Book at aaa.com*
▼▼◇▼▼
Small-scale Hotel
All Year [ECP]   1P: $99-$199   2P: $99-$199   XP: $10   F18
Location: Jct US 11, 68 and 310, just e. 6000 US 11 13617. Fax: 315/386-2515. **Facility:** 69 one-bedroom standard units, some with whirlpools. 3 stories, interior corridors. *Bath:* combo or shower only. **Parking:** on-site, winter plug-ins. **Amenities:** irons, hair dryers. **Pool(s):** heated indoor. **Leisure Activities:** sauna, whirlpool, exercise room. *Fee:* game room. **Guest Services:** sundries, coin laundry. **Business Services:** meeting rooms. **Cards:** AX, CB, DC, DS, MC, VI.

SOME UNITS
(ASK) (S/D) ⓚ ⚊ ✕ 📷 [DATA PORT] 🛏 💻 / ✕ [VCR] 🖼 /
FEE

CARLE PLACE pop. 5,247

——— **WHERE TO STAY** ———

HOLIDAY INN-WESTBURY   *Book at aaa.com*
(AAA) (SAVE)
▼▼◇▼▼
Small-scale Hotel
All Year [ECP]   1P: $169   XP: $15   F18
Location: Meadow Brook Pkwy, exit M1, 0.5 mi e. Located across from a shopping mall. 369 Old Country Rd 11514. Fax: 516/997-3623. **Facility:** 152 units. 150 one-bedroom standard units. 2 one-bedroom suites ($250-$285). 3 stories, interior corridors. *Bath:* combo or shower only. **Parking:** on-site. **Amenities:** video games (fee), dual phone lines, voice mail, irons, hair dryers. **Dining:** 6:30 am-10 pm, Sat & Sun from 7 am, cocktails. **Pool(s):** outdoor. **Leisure Activities:** exercise room. **Guest Services:** coin laundry. **Business Services:** meeting rooms. **Cards:** AX, CB, DS, JC, MC, VI. **Special Amenities:** free expanded continental breakfast and early check-in/late check-out. (See color ad p 294)

SOME UNITS
(S/D) ⓘ 𝖄 ⓚ 🎮 ⚊ 📷 [DATA PORT] 💻 / ✕ [VCR] 🛏 /
FEE

CARMEL —*See New York p. 451.*

CASTILE pop. 1,051

——— **WHERE TO DINE** ———

GLEN IRIS INN
◇▼▼
American
Lunch: $7-$9   Dinner: $17-$21   Phone: 585/493-2622
Location: 1 mi n off SR 19A and 436; in Letchworth State Park. 7 Letchworth State Park 14427. **Hours:** Open 5/1-11/2 & 3/25-4/30; 8 am-10, noon-2 & 5:30-8 pm, Fri & Sat-9 pm. **Reservations:** suggested. **Features:** Victorian furnishings decorate the former country estate, near a waterfall. Although the steaks, seafood and chicken are well-prepared and tasty, what guests remember is the berry hill dessert, made tableside. Casual dress; cocktails. **Parking:** on-site. **Cards:** AX, DS, MC, VI.

✕

Look For Savings   ⓐⓐⓐ

W hen you pick up a AAA TourBook® guide, look for establishments that display a bright red AAA logo, (SAVE) icon, and Diamond rating in their listing. These AAA Official Appointment establishments place a high value on the patronage they receive from AAA members. And, by offering members great room rates*, they are willing to go the extra mile to get your business.

So, when you turn to the AAA TourBook guide to make your travel plans, look for the establishments that will give you the special treatment you deserve.

* *See TourBook Navigator section, page 14, for complete details.*

CASTLETON-ON-HUDSON pop. 1,619

—— WHERE TO STAY ——

RODEWAY INN   *Book at aaa.com*   Phone: (518)477-2606

AAA SAVE

5/1-7/1 [CP]	1P: $59-$79	2P: $59-$89	XP: $8 D14
7/2-9/1 [CP]	1P: $79	2P: $87	XP: $8 D14
9/2-4/30 [CP]	1P: $49	2P: $59	XP: $8 D14

Motel

Location: I-90, exit 11W, just nw on SR 9 and US 20. 1666 Columbia Tpke 12033. **Fax:** 518/479-4660. **Facility:** 22 one-bedroom standard units, some with whirlpools. 1 story, exterior corridors. **Parking:** on-site, winter plug-ins. **Terms:** 3 day cancellation notice. **Cards:** AX, DC, DS, MC, VI. **Special Amenities:** free continental breakfast and free local telephone calls.

SOME UNITS

CATSKILL pop. 4,392

—— WHERE TO STAY ——

QUALITY INN & CONFERENCE CENTER   *Book at aaa.com*   Phone: (518)943-5800

AAA SAVE

All Year   1P: $69-$249   2P: $69-$249   XP: $10   F18

AAA AAA

Small-scale Hotel

Location: I-87, exit 21, just w. 704 Rt 23B 12414 (PO Box 548). **Fax:** 518/943-7084. **Facility:** 71 one-bedroom standard units, some with kitchens (no utensils) and/or whirlpools. 2 stories (no elevator), interior corridors. **Parking:** on-site. **Terms:** check-in 4 pm, pets ($20 extra charge). **Amenities:** safes, irons, hair dryers. **Dining:** 6 am-10 & 5-10 pm, cocktails. **Pool(s):** outdoor. **Guest Services:** coin laundry. **Business Services:** meeting rooms. **Cards:** AX, CB, DC, DS, MC, VI. **Special Amenities:** free local telephone calls and free newspaper.

SOME UNITS

FEE

RED RANCH MOTEL   Phone: (518)678-3380

AAA SAVE

6/11-9/6	1P: $50-$78	2P: $50-$78	XP: $10 F14
11/25-4/30	1P: $48-$75	2P: $48-$75	XP: $10 F14
9/7-11/24	1P: $45-$60	2P: $45-$60	XP: $10 F14
5/1-6/10	1P: $45-$55	2P: $45-$55	XP: $10 F14

Motel

Location: I-87 New York Thruway, exit 20, 9 mi n; jct SR 23A, 0.5 mi s. 4555 Rt 32 12414. **Facility:** 39 units. 38 one- and 1 two-bedroom standard units, some with kitchens. 1-2 stories, exterior corridors. **Bath:** combo or shower only. **Parking:** on-site, winter plug-ins. **Terms:** 2 night minimum stay - weekends in summer, weekly rates available. **Amenities:** *Some:* hair dryers. **Pool(s):** outdoor. **Leisure Activities:** kiddie pool, playground. *Fee:* game room. **Cards:** AX, CB, DC, DS, MC, VI.

SOME UNITS

—— WHERE TO DINE ——

LA CONCA D'ORO   **Lunch:** $4-$9   **Dinner:** $9-$25   Phone: 518/943-3549

AAA

AAA AAA

Italian

Location: Center. 440 Main St 12414. **Hours:** 11:30 am-10 pm, Fri-11 pm, Sat 3 pm-11 pm, Sun 2 pm-10 pm. **Closed:** 12/25; also Tues. **Reservations:** suggested. **Features:** Representative of tasty choices is the lobster tail Contidinia, which is served with shrimp and clams in a mushroom marinara sauce over fresh linguine. Specials include contemporary American cuisine. Homemade desserts, such as cheesecake, bread pudding, tarts and tiramisu quiet the sweet tooth. Casual dress; cocktails. **Parking:** street. **Cards:** MC, VI.

CAYUGA HEIGHTS pop. 3,273—*See also FINGER LAKES.*

——— WHERE TO DINE ———

THE HEIGHTS CAFE & GRILL   **Lunch:** $8-$12   **Dinner:** $15-$30   **Phone:** 607/257-4144
▼▼▼   **Location:** SR 13, exit Triphammer Rd, 0.9 mi e to Community Corners Plaza. 903 Hanshaw Rd 14850. **Hours:** 11:30
          am-2:30 & 5-9 pm, Fri-10 pm, Sat 5 pm-10 pm. Closed major holidays; also Sun.
American   **Reservations:** suggested. **Features:** An award-winning wine list complements sophisticated cuisine, which
          is prepared with fresh ingredients and imagination. Much attention is paid to artful plate presentation.
Tasteful jazz music plays in the background of the art deco dining room. Dressy casual; cocktails. **Parking:** on-site.
Cards: AX, DC, DS, MC, VI.

CAZENOVIA pop. 2,614

——— WHERE TO STAY ———

BRAE LOCH INN   **Phone:** 315/655-3431
(AAA) (SAVE)   5/1-12/31 [CP]   1P: $65-$150   2P: $85-$150   XP: $15   F12
          1/1-4/30 [CP]   1P: $65-$140   2P: $85-$140   XP: $15   F12
▼▼▼   **Location:** On US 20. 5 Albany St 13035. **Fax:** 315/655-4844. **Facility:** Tartan plaids, stained glass and Scottish
          heirlooms define the Scottish theme of this property which has been family-owned and operated since 1946.
Country Inn   12 one-bedroom standard units, some with whirlpools. 2 stories (no elevator), interior corridors. **Parking:** on-
          site. **Terms:** 10 day cancellation notice, [MAP] meal plan available, package plans - seasonal.
Amenities: hair dryers. **Dining:** restaurant, see separate listing. **Leisure Activities:** lake & golf privileges. *Fee:* massage. **Guest**
Services: gift shop. **Business Services:** meeting rooms, fax. **Cards:** AX, DS, MC, VI. **Special Amenities:** free continental
breakfast and free local telephone calls.

SOME UNITS

——— WHERE TO DINE ———

BRAE LOCH INN   Country Inn   **Dinner:** $15-$21   **Phone:** 315/655-3431
▼▼▼   **Location:** On US 20; in Brae Loch Inn. 5 Albany St 13035. **Hours:** 5 pm-9 pm, Fri & Sat-10 pm, Sun 11 am-2 &
          4-9 pm; hours may vary off season. Closed: 12/24, 12/25. **Reservations:** suggested. **Features:** The prime
Continental   minister—prime rib served in natural juices with a side of Yorkshire pudding—stands out on a menu of
          steak, lamb and seafood choices. A Scottish influence shows in the memorabilia and tartan carpets of the
warm, intimate dining room. Dressy casual; cocktails. **Parking:** on-site. **Cards:** AX, DS, MC, VI.

THE BREWSTER INN DINING ROOM   Country Inn   **Dinner:** $19-$24   **Phone:** 315/655-9232
▼▼▼   **Location:** On US 20, 0.5 mi w; in The Brewster Inn. 6 Ledyard Ave 13035. **Hours:** 5 pm-9 pm, Sat from 6 pm,
          Sun 11 am-2 & 5-9 pm. Closed major holidays. **Reservations:** suggested. **Features:** On Cazenovia Lake,
Continental   the Victorian mansion exudes an upscale charm. Particularly well-prepared is veal Atlantis, a sauteed cut
          of veal topped with lobster, served on a bed of wild greens and finished with tarragon beurre blanc sauce.
Dessert changes daily. Dressy casual; cocktails. **Parking:** on-site. **Cards:** DC, MC, VI.

CHAPPAQUA —*See New York p. 451.*

CHEEKTOWAGA —*See Buffalo p. 249.*

CHESTERTOWN pop. 3,614—*See also ADIRONDACK MOUNTAINS.*

——— WHERE TO STAY ———

FRIENDS LAKE INN   **Phone:** (518)494-4751
(AAA) (SAVE)   All Year [MAP]   1P: $250-$380   2P: $295-$425   XP: $75
          Location: I-87, exit 25, 3.5 mi w on SR 8, then 3.2 mi s. Located in a rural area. 963 Friends Lake Rd 12817.
▼▼▼ ▼▼▼   **Fax:** 518/494-4616. **Facility:** This rural inn offers pleasantly-decorated guest rooms, some with fireplaces.
          The lake is only a short walk away. Smoke free premises. 17 units. 16 one-bedroom standard units, some
Historic   with whirlpools. 1 one-bedroom suite with whirlpool. 3 stories (no elevator), interior corridors. *Bath:* combo or
Country Inn   shower only. **Parking:** on-site. **Terms:** office hours 8 am-11:30 pm, 14 day cancellation notice, [BP] meal plan
          available, package plans, no pets allowed (owner's pet on premises). **Amenities:** irons, hair dryers. *Some:*
CD players, honor bars. **Dining:** restaurant, see separate listing. **Pool(s):** heated outdoor. **Leisure Activities:** sauna, canoeing,
paddleboats, kayaks, cross country skiing, hiking trails. *Fee:* cross country equipment & snowshoes. **Guest Services:** complimentary evening beverages: Fri & Sat. **Cards:** AX, CB, DC, MC, VI. **Special Amenities:** free full breakfast and free local telephone calls.

SOME UNITS

——— WHERE TO DINE ———

FRIENDS LAKE INN   **Lunch:** $6-$12   **Dinner:** $18-$29   **Phone:** 518/494-4751
(AAA)   **Location:** Jct US 9 and SR 8, 2 mi w on SR 8, 1.5 mi s on Friends Lake Rd, then 0.8 mi w; follow signs; in Friends
▼▼▼   Lake Inn. 963 Friends Lake Rd 12817. **Hours:** 8 am-10:30 & 5:30-9:30 pm, Sun 8 am-noon & 5-8:30 pm.
          Reservations: required. **Features:** The dining room invites relaxed, upscale dining. To pair with gourmet
Nouvelle   American cuisine, guests can choose any wine from the award-winning, 21,000-bottle collection or let the
American   sommelier do the work. Those who fall in love with a wine will more than likely be able to buy it at the
          on-site wine shop. Casual dress; cocktails. **Parking:** on-site. **Cards:** AX, CB, DC, MC, VI.

MAIN STREET ICE CREAM PARLOR　　　　**Lunch:** $4-$10　　　　**Dinner:** $10-$15　　　　**Phone:** 518/494-7940

　　　　▼▼▼　　　　**Location:** Center. 6369 Main St 12817. **Hours:** 10 am-10 pm; to 6 pm, Fri & Sat-9 pm, Sun-4 pm 9/15-6/25.

American　　　Closed major holidays. **Features:** An air of nostalgia drifts through the 1950s soda fountain, decorated with Coca-Cola antiques and Adirondack memorabilia. The menu focuses on home-style lighter fare: delicious soups, hearty delicatessen sandwiches and ice cream sundaes made the old-fashioned way. Dinner entrees are served on weekends. Casual dress. **Parking:** street. **Cards:** DS, MC, VI.　　　　　　　　　　　　　　　　☒

CHILDS

———— **WHERE TO STAY** ————

FAIRHAVEN INN　　　　　　　　　　　　　　　　　　　　　　　　　　　　　　**Phone:** 585/589-9151

⬥⬥⬥ SAVE　　　All Year　　　　　　　　1P: $50　　　　　2P: $60　　　　　　XP: $10　　　F12

▼▼▼ ▼　　　**Location:** Jct SR 104 and 98. 14369 Ridge Rd 14411 (14369 Ridge Rd, ALBION). **Fax:** 585/589-7341.

Motel　　　**Facility:** Smoke free premises. 8 one-bedroom standard units. 1-2 stories (no elevator), exterior corridors. *Bath:* combo or shower only. **Parking:** on-site. **Terms:** cancellation fee imposed. **Dining:** Tillman's Village Inn, see separate listing. **Guest Services:** gift shop. **Business Services:** meeting rooms. **Cards:** AX, DC, DS, MC, VI. **Special Amenities:** free local telephone calls and preferred room (subject to availability with advanced reservations).　　　　　　　　　　　　　　　🍽 ☒ 🖥 📼

———— **WHERE TO DINE** ————

TILLMAN'S VILLAGE INN　　　　**Lunch:** $4-$8　　　　**Dinner:** $9-$18　　　　**Phone:** 585/589-9151

▼▼▼ ▼　　　**Location:** Jct SR 104 and 98; in Fairhaven Inn. 14369 Ridge Rd 14411. **Hours:** noon-9 pm. Closed: 12/24, 12/25.

　　　　Reservations: accepted. **Features:** The former stagecoach stop offers prime rib, steaks, seafood and

American　　　home-style comfort foods, including barbecue ribs and roast turkey with stuffing. Casual dress; cocktails. **Parking:** on-site. **Cards:** AX, DC, DS, MC, VI.　　　　　　　　　　　　　　　　🍸 ☒

CICERO pop. 27,982

———— **WHERE TO STAY** ————

BUDGET INN　　　　　　　　　　　　　　　　　　　　　　　　　　　　　**Phone:** (315)458-3510

▼▼▼　　　7/1-9/10　　　　　　　1P: $60-$110　　　2P: $65-$120　　　XP: $10　　　F16

　　　　5/1-6/30 & 9/11-12/31　　1P: $55-$90　　　2P: $60-$100　　　XP: $10　　　F16

Motel　　　1/1-4/30　　　　　　　1P: $50-$85　　　2P: $55-$90　　　XP: $10　　　F16

　　　　Location: I-481, exit 10, just s. 901 S Bay Rd 13039. **Fax:** 315/452-9488. **Facility:** 36 units. 35 one-bedroom standard units, some with efficiencies (no utensils) and/or whirlpools. 1 cottage ($175-$350) with whirlpool. 2 stories (no elevator), exterior corridors. **Parking:** on-site, winter plug-ins. **Terms:** 2-3 night minimum stay - seasonal, weekly rates available, pets (in designated units). **Amenities:** *Some:* hair dryers. **Leisure Activities:** playground. **Cards:** AX, DC, DS, MC, VI.

　　　　　　　　　　　　　　　　　　　　　　　　　　　　SOME UNITS

　　　　　　　　　　　ASK S☉ 🐾 🐾 / ☒ 🖥 🛢 📼 /

———— **WHERE TO DINE** ————

PLAINVILLE FARMS RESTAURANT　　　**Lunch:** $4-$7　　　　**Dinner:** $6-$10　　　　**Phone:** 315/699-3852

⬥⬥⬥　　　**Location:** I-81, exit 30, 0.3 mi n on US 11. 8450 Brewerton Rd 13039. **Hours:** 11 am-9 pm. Closed: 12/25.

　　　　Reservations: suggested, major holidays. **Features:** Hand-painted murals, antique platters and turkey

▼▼▼ ▼　　　memorabilia decorate the cozy dining room of the friendly, family restaurant. The clear specialty is

American　　　home-style turkey, which is freshly roasted and prepared in a variety of flavorful dishes. Deep dish apple pie and bread pudding with vanilla sauce end a perfect home-style meal. Casual dress. **Parking:** on-site. **Cards:** DS, MC, VI.　　　　　　　　　　　　　　　　　　　　　　　☒

CLARENCE —See Buffalo p. 251.

CLAY pop. 58,805

———— **WHERE TO STAY** ————

FAIRFIELD INN-SYRACUSE/CLAY　　*Book at aaa.com*　　　　　　　　　　　**Phone:** (315)622-2576

▼▼▼▼　　　6/1-8/31 [ECP]　　　　1P: $93-$150　　　2P: $93-$150

　　　　1/1-4/30 [ECP]　　　　1P: $92-$150　　　2P: $92-$150

Small-scale Hotel　5/9-5/31 & 9/1-12/31 [ECP]　1P: $91-$150　　　2P: $91-$150

　　　　Location: Jct SR 481, exit 12, just w. (3979 Rt 31, LIVERPOOL, 13090). **Fax:** 315/622-2576. **Facility:** 63 one-bedroom standard units. 3 stories, interior corridors. *Bath:* combo or shower only. **Parking:** on-site. **Terms:** open 5/9-4/30, 2 night minimum stay - weekends, cancellation fee imposed, [AP], [BP], [CP] & [MAP] meal plans available. **Amenities:** irons, hair dryers. **Pool(s):** small heated indoor. **Leisure Activities:** whirlpool. **Guest Services:** valet laundry. **Cards:** AX, DC, DS, MC, VI.

　　　　　　　　　　　　　　　　　　　　　　　　　　SOME UNITS

　　ASK S☉ 🍽 🔒M 📶 ⚡ 🐾 📼 / ☒ 🛢 📼 📼 /

　　　　　　　　　　　　　　　　　　FEE　FEE

———— **WHERE TO DINE** ————

EUCLID RESTAURANT　　　　　**Lunch:** $5-$7　　　　**Dinner:** $10-$12　　　　**Phone:** 315/622-2750

⬥⬥⬥　　　**Location:** Jct SR 31 and Morgan Rd. 4285 Rt 31 13041. **Hours:** 11:30 am-10:30 pm; closed Sun in summer.

▼▼▼ ▼　　　Closed major holidays. **Reservations:** accepted. **Features:** Friendly service is the hallmark at the busy restaurant. Daily specials focus on delicious comfort food. A $2 children's meal is available. Hearty

American　　　helpings are served in a casual setting. Casual dress; cocktails. **Parking:** on-site. **Cards:** AX, CB, DC, DS, MC, VI.　　　　　　　　　　　　　　　　　　　　　　🍸 ☒

CLAYTON pop. 1,821

———— **WHERE TO STAY** ————

BERTRAND'S MOTEL   **Phone: (315)686-3641**

♦   6/25-9/30   1P: $59-$69   2P: $79-$89   XP: $5   F13
           5/1-6/24 & 10/1-4/30   1P: $44-$54   2P: $54-$64   XP: $5   F13
Motel   **Location:** Jct SR 12E and 12, 0.5 mi n. 229 James St 13624. **Fax:** 315/686-3641. **Facility:** 28 one-bedroom standard units. 1-2 stories (no elevator), exterior corridors. **Parking:** on-site, winter plug-ins. **Terms:** 2 night minimum stay - seasonal weekends. **Cards:** DS, MC, VI.

SOME UNITS

(ASK) (S/D) (Y+) / (X) (▤) (▣) /

FAIR WIND MOTEL & COTTAGES   **Phone: (315)686-5251**

AAA (SAVE)   6/18-9/6   1P: $45-$60   2P: $55-$85   XP: $5   D12
♦♦   5/1-6/17 & 9/7-10/1   1P: $40-$50   2P: $45-$60   XP: $5   D12
Motel   **Location:** 1.5 mi sw. Located in a quiet area. 38201 NYS Rt 12 E 13624. **Fax:** 315/686-5384. **Facility:** 18 units. 9 one- and 1 two-bedroom standard units. 2 cabins and 6 cottages ($350-$675). 1 story, exterior corridors. *Bath:* combo or shower only. **Parking:** on-site. **Terms:** open 5/1-10/1, office hours 8 am-10 pm, 2 night minimum stay - weekends in season. **Pool(s):** heated outdoor. **Leisure Activities:** boat dock, fishing.
Cards: AX, DS, MC, VI. **Special Amenities:** free local telephone calls and free room upgrade (subject to availability with advanced reservations).

SOME UNITS

(S/D) (~) (☎) / (X) (K) (DATA PORT) (▤) (▣) (▣) /

———— **WHERE TO DINE** ————

HARBOR INN & RESTAURANT   **Lunch: $4-$8**   **Dinner: $12-$17**   **Phone:** 315/686-2293

♦   **Location:** Center; across from Antique Boat Museum and public docks. 625 Mary St 13624. **Hours:** 6 am-9 pm; hours may vary seasonally. Closed major holidays. **Reservations:** accepted, for dinner. **Features:** After a
American   tour of the Antique Boat Museum, guests can stop across the street to the casual dining spot for a light snack, such as fresh cinnamon rolls or doughnuts, or heartier fare, including red pepper soup or scallops with French white wine sauce. Casual dress; beer & wine only. **Parking:** street. **Cards:** AX, DS, MC, VI.

THOUSAND ISLANDS INN   **Lunch: $4-$9**   **Dinner: $10-$27**   **Phone:** 315/686-3030

AAA   **Location:** On St. Lawrence Riverfront. 335 Riverside Dr 13624. **Hours:** Open 5/16-9/15; 7 am-3 & 5:30-9 pm, Fri
♦♦   & Sat-10 pm. **Reservations:** suggested. **Features:** This family restaurant delivers such tasty fare as
American   homemade beef vegetable soup, fillet of Lake Ontario walleye and Grenadier Island chicken. Thousand Island salad dressing first was served here. Friendly, prompt servers are adept at follow-up. Casual dress; cocktails. **Parking:** on-site. **Cards:** CB, DC, DS, MC, VI.

(Y) (X)

CLIFTON PARK pop. 32,995

———— **WHERE TO STAY** ————

COMFORT INN   *Book at aaa.com*   **Phone: (518)373-0222**

AAA (SAVE)   7/21-9/6 [CP]   1P: $99-$199   2P: $99-$199   XP: $10   F18
♦♦♦   5/1-7/20 & 9/7-4/30 [CP]   1P: $69-$129   2P: $69-$129   XP: $10   F18
           Location: I-87, exit 9 northbound; exit 9E southbound. 41 Fire Rd, Old Rt 146 12065. **Fax:** 518/373-0278. **Facility:** 60
Small-scale Hotel   one-bedroom standard units, some with whirlpools. 2 stories (no elevator), interior corridors. **Parking:** on-site. **Amenities:** voice mail, irons, hair dryers. **Pool(s):** small heated outdoor. **Leisure Activities:** limited exercise equipment. **Guest Services:** valet laundry. **Business Services:** meeting rooms. **Cards:** AX, DC, DS, MC, VI. **Special Amenities:** free continental breakfast and free local telephone calls.

SOME UNITS

(S/D) (~) (₹) (DATA PORT) (▣) / (X) (VCR) (▤) (▣)
                             FEE   FEE

COMFORT SUITES   *Book at aaa.com*   **Phone: (518)373-2255**

AAA (SAVE)   7/21-8/31   1P: $159-$239   2P: $159-$239
♦♦♦   5/1-7/20 & 9/1-4/30   1P: $89-$159   2P: $89-$159
           Location: I-87, exit 9 southbound; exit 9E northbound. 7 Northside Dr 12065. **Fax:** 518/373-7888. **Facility:** 75 units.
Small-scale Hotel   72 one-bedroom standard units, some with whirlpools. 3 one-bedroom suites with kitchens, some with whirlpools. 4 stories, interior corridors. *Bath:* combo or shower only. **Parking:** on-site. **Terms:** [ECP] meal plan available. **Amenities:** dual phone lines, voice mail, safes, irons, hair dryers. **Pool(s):** heated indoor. **Leisure Activities:** exercise room. **Guest Services:** valet and coin laundry. **Business Services:** conference facilities. **Cards:** AX, DC, DS, MC, VI. **Special Amenities:** free expanded continental breakfast and free local telephone calls.

SOME UNITS

(S/D) (Y+) (~) (₹) (DATA PORT) (▤) (▣) (▣) / (X) /

HAMPTON INN   *Book at aaa.com*   **Phone: (518)373-2345**

AAA (SAVE)   All Year [ECP]   1P: $99-$259   2P: $109-$259
♦♦♦   **Location:** I-87, exit 9E southbound; exit 9 northbound, just e. 620 Plank Rd 12065. **Fax:** 518/373-0775. **Facility:** 80
           one-bedroom standard units. 4 stories, interior corridors. *Bath:* combo or shower only. **Parking:** on-site.
Small-scale Hotel   **Amenities:** video library (fee), video games, high-speed Internet, dual phone lines, voice mail, irons, hair dryers. **Pool(s):** small heated indoor. **Leisure Activities:** whirlpool, exercise room. **Guest Services:** valet and coin laundry. **Business Services:** meeting rooms. **Cards:** AX, CB, DC, DS, MC, VI. **Special Amenities:** free expanded continental breakfast and free local telephone calls.

SOME UNITS

(S/D) (Y+) (&M) (&) (⌂) (~) (₹) (DATA PORT) (▤) (▣) (▣) / (X) /

—————— WHERE TO DINE ——————

MANGIA CAFE

Italian

Lunch: $6-$12   **Dinner:** $8-$17   **Phone:** 518/383-6666
Location: I-87, exit 9, just w; in Shopper's World Plaza. 15 Park Ave 12065. **Hours:** 11 am-9 pm, Fri & Sat-10 pm. Closed major holidays; also Sun. **Features:** Italian specialties, including varieties of pasta, are prepared in an open kitchen. Try a wood-fired oven gourmet pizza with a choice of more than 30 toppings. Casual dress; beer & wine only. **Parking:** on-site. **Cards:** AX, DS, MC, VI.

CLINTON pop. 727

—————— WHERE TO STAY ——————

THE ARTFUL LODGER

Historic Bed & Breakfast

Phone: 315/853-3672
All Year [BP]   1P: $89-$130   2P: $99-$140   XP: $15
Location: I-90, exit 32, SR 233 S to SR 412 E, 0.7 mi e on SR 12B N, then just n. Located on the village green. 7 E Park Row 13323. Fax: 315/853-1489. **Facility:** Themed art exhibits, which are changed seasonally, enhance this cozy inn located on the village green. Smoke free premises. 5 one-bedroom standard units. 2 stories (no elevator), interior corridors. *Bath:* combo or shower only. **Parking:** on-site. **Terms:** check-in 4 pm, 7 day cancellation notice. **Amenities:** hair dryers. **Guest Services:** TV in common area, gift shop. **Business Services:** fax. **Cards:** AX, CB, DC, DS, MC, VI.

THE HEDGES

Bed & Breakfast

Phone: 315/853-3031
All Year [BP]   1P: $95-$150   2P: $120-$150   XP: $10   F3
Location: College St, 0.3 mi n on Elm St. Located in a residential area. 180 Sanford Ave 13323. Fax: 315/853-5705. **Facility:** The bed and breakfast is in a quiet residential neighborhood within walking distance of the town center. Smoke free premises. 5 units. 2 one-bedroom standard units, some with whirlpools. 2 one-bedroom suites. 1 cottage. 2 stories (no elevator), interior corridors. *Bath:* combo or shower only. **Parking:** on-site. **Terms:** check-in 4 pm, 5 day cancellation notice-fee imposed, weekly rates available, pets (owner's pet on premises). **Amenities:** video library, hair dryers. *Some:* CD players. **Pool(s):** outdoor. **Leisure Activities:** Fee: massage. **Business Services:** PC, fax. **Cards:** AX, MC.

SOME UNITS

—————— WHERE TO DINE ——————

O'CONNOR'S ALEXANDER HAMILTON INN   Historic   **Lunch:** $9-$16   **Dinner:** $20-$29   **Phone:** 315/853-2061
Continental
Location: Center. 21 W Park Row 13323. **Hours:** 11:30 am-2 & 5-10 pm, Sat from 5 pm, Sun 4 pm-9 pm. Closed major holidays; also 12/24. **Reservations:** suggested. **Features:** An elegant fine dining atmosphere and attentive service are the hallmarks that distinguish the beautifully restored inn. Dressy casual; cocktails. **Parking:** street. **Cards:** AX, DS, MC, VI.

COBLESKILL pop. 4,533

—————— WHERE TO STAY ——————

BEST WESTERN INN OF COBLESKILL   *Book at aaa.com*   **Phone:** (518)234-4321

Small-scale Hotel

7/1-9/8   1P: $139-$179   2P: $139-$179
5/1-6/30 & 9/9-10/31   1P: $99-$149   2P: $99-$149
11/1-4/30   1P: $74-$94   2P: $74-$94
Location: I-88, exit 21 eastbound on SR 7, 0.8 mi e of jct SR 10; exit 22 westbound. 121 Burgin Dr 12043. Fax: 518/234-3869. **Facility:** 76 one-bedroom standard units. 2 stories (no elevator), interior corridors. **Parking:** on-site, winter plug-ins. **Terms:** cancellation fee imposed, pets ($15 deposit). **Amenities:** irons, hair dryers. **Dining:** 8 am-8 pm, Fri & Sat-9 pm; 7 am-10 pm in summer, cocktails. **Pool(s):** heated indoor, wading. **Leisure Activities:** exercise room. *Fee:* bowling. **Business Services:** meeting rooms. **Cards:** AX, CB, DC, DS, MC, VI. **Special Amenities:** free local telephone calls and free newspaper. *(See color ad below)*

SOME UNITS

COLONIE pop. 7,916   (See map and index starting on p. 215)

──── WHERE TO STAY ────

ALBANY MARRIOTT   *Book at aaa.com*   **Phone:** (518)458-8444   **18**
▼▼▼▼   All Year   1P: $184   2P: $184
Large-scale Hotel   **Location:** I-87, exit 4, 0.3 mi se. 189 Wolf Rd 12205. **Fax:** 518/458-7365. **Facility:** 360 units. 357 one-bedroom standard units. 3 one-bedroom suites ($350). 8 stories, interior corridors. **Parking:** on-site. **Terms:** check-in 4 pm. **Amenities:** video games, high-speed Internet (fee), voice mail, irons, hair dryers. *Some:* CD players. **Pool(s):** heated outdoor, heated indoor. **Leisure Activities:** sauna, whirlpool, exercise room. **Guest Services:** gift shop, valet and coin laundry. **Business Services:** conference facilities, business center. **Cards:** AX, CB, DC, DS, JC, MC, VI.

SOME UNITS
(ASK) (SD) (🛁) (🍽️) (🍸) (🔊M) (🅿️) (🏊) (🏋️) (🐾) (DATA PORT) (💻) / (🍽️) (🔒) /

ALBANY SUPER 8 MOTEL   *Book at aaa.com*   **Phone:** (518)869-8471   **26**
▼▼ ▼   7/1-8/31   1P: $72-$79   2P: $75-$85   XP: $5   F12
        9/1-10/31   1P: $55-$70   2P: $72-$75   XP: $5   F12
Motel   5/1-6/30   1P: $58-$65   2P: $65-$75   XP: $5   F12
        11/1-4/30   1P: $55-$60   2P: $60-$65   XP: $5   F12
Location: I-87, exit 2W, just nw on SR 5 W. 1579 Central Ave 12205 (1579 Central Ave, ALBANY). **Fax:** 518/464-4010. **Facility:** 59 one-bedroom standard units. 2 stories (no elevator), exterior corridors. **Parking:** on-site. **Terms:** small pets only. **Amenities:** video library (fee). **Cards:** AX, CB, DC, DS, MC, VI.

SOME UNITS
(ASK) (SD) (🐾) (🍽️) (📷) (DATA PORT) / (🍽️) (🔒) /

AMBASSADOR MOTOR INN   **Phone:** 518/456-8982   **11**
▼   Property failed to provide current rates
Motel   **Location:** I-87, exit 2W, 0.8 mi w; on SR 5, then 5.4 mi w. 1600 Central Ave 12205 (1600 Central Ave, ALBANY). **Fax:** 518/456-8982. **Facility:** 56 one-bedroom standard units. 2 stories (no elevator), exterior corridors. **Parking:** on-site, winter plug-ins. **Terms:** pets ($50 deposit).

SOME UNITS
(🛏️) (🍽️+) (📷) / (🍽️) /
FEE

BEST WESTERN ALBANY AIRPORT INN   *Book at aaa.com*   **Phone:** (518)458-1000   **20**
(AAA) (SAVE)   All Year [ECP]   1P: $89-$149   2P: $99-$159   XP: $10   F18
▼▼▼ ▼   **Location:** I-87, exit 4, just se to Wolf Rd, then just sw. 200 Wolf Rd 12205. **Fax:** 518/458-2807. **Facility:** 153 one-bedroom standard units. 2 stories (no elevator), interior corridors. **Parking:** on-site, winter plug-ins. **Terms:** small pets only ($35 deposit). **Amenities:** voice mail, irons, hair dryers. **Dining:** 4 pm-midnight, cock-
Small-scale Hotel   tails. **Pool(s):** heated indoor. **Guest Services:** valet and coin laundry, area transportation-mall & local restaurants. **Business Services:** meeting rooms. **Cards:** AX, CB, DC, DS, MC, VI. **Special Amenities:** free expanded continental breakfast and free room upgrade (subject to availability with advanced reservations).

SOME UNITS
(SD) (🛁) (🐾) (🍽️) (🍸) (🅿️) (🏊) (🐾) (DATA PORT) (💻) / (🍽️) (🔒) (🖨️) /
FEE   FEE

COMFORT INN & SUITES   *Book at aaa.com*   **Phone:** (518)869-5327   **12**
(AAA) (SAVE)   All Year [CP]   1P: $69-$350   2P: $69-$350   XP: $6   F18
▼▼▼▼   **Location:** I-87, exit 2W, 0.8 mi w. 1606 Central Ave 12205. **Fax:** 518/456-8971. **Facility:** 109 units. 108 one-bedroom standard units, some with whirlpools. 1 one-bedroom suite ($89-$350) with whirlpool. 2-3 stories, interior/exterior corridors. *Bath:* combo or shower only. **Parking:** on-site, winter plug-ins. **Amenities:** video
Small-scale Hotel   games, voice mail, irons, hair dryers. **Pool(s):** small heated indoor. **Leisure Activities:** whirlpool, exercise room. **Guest Services:** valet and coin laundry. **Business Services:** meeting rooms, business center. **Cards:** AX, CB, DC, DS, JC, MC, VI. **Special Amenities:** free continental breakfast and free local telephone calls.

SOME UNITS
(SD) (🛁) (🍽️+) (🔊M) (🅿️) (🏊) (🐾) (DATA PORT) (💻) / (🍽️) (🔒) (🖨️) /
FEE

COURTYARD BY MARRIOTT   *Book at aaa.com*   **Phone:** (518)482-8800   **23**
▼▼▼▼   All Year   1P: $69-$239   2P: $69-$239
Small-scale Hotel   **Location:** I-87, exit 4, 0.4 mi se. 168 Wolf Rd 12205. **Fax:** 518/482-0001. **Facility:** 78 one-bedroom standard units. 3 stories, interior corridors. *Bath:* combo or shower only. **Parking:** on-site. **Terms:** [BP] meal plan available. **Amenities:** video games, high-speed Internet, dual phone lines, voice mail, irons, hair dryers. **Pool(s):** small heated indoor. **Leisure Activities:** whirlpool, exercise room. **Guest Services:** valet and coin laundry. **Business Services:** meeting rooms. **Cards:** AX, CB, DC, DS, JC, MC, VI.

SOME UNITS
(ASK) (SD) (🛁) (♿M) (🍸) (🔊) (🅿️) (📷) (DATA PORT) (💻) / (🍽️) (🔒) /

THE DESMOND HOTEL   *Book at aaa.com*   **Phone:** (518)869-8100   **22**
(AAA) (SAVE)   All Year   1P: $99-$169
▼▼▼▼   **Location:** I-87, exit 4. 660 Albany Shaker Rd 12211. **Fax:** 518/869-7659. **Facility:** 324 units. 306 one-bedroom standard units. 18 one-bedroom suites ($199-$219), some with whirlpools. 3-4 stories, interior corridors. *Bath:* combo or shower only. **Parking:** on-site. **Terms:** check-in 4 pm, [AP] meal plan available, package
Small-scale Hotel   plans - weekends. **Amenities:** voice mail, irons, hair dryers. *Some:* CD players, high-speed Internet, dual phone lines, safes. **Dining:** 3 restaurants, 6:30 am-midnight, cocktails, also Scrimshaw, see separate listing. **Pool(s):** 2 heated indoor. **Leisure Activities:** saunas, billiards, exercise room. **Guest Services:** gift shop, valet laundry, airport transportation-Albany Airport. **Business Services:** conference facilities, business center. **Cards:** AX, DC, DS, MC, VI. **Special Amenities:** free newspaper.

SOME UNITS
(SD) (🛁) (🍽️) (🍸) (🔊) (🅿️) (🏊) (🐾) (🐾) (DATA PORT) (💻) / (🍽️) (🔒) (🖨️) /
FEE

(See map and index starting on p. 215)

HAMPTON INN WOLF ROAD *Book at aaa.com* Phone: (518)438-2822 🔢16

(AAA) (SAVE)

7/24-9/2 [ECP]	1P: $139-$159	2P: $149-$169
5/1-7/23 [ECP]	1P: $112-$129	2P: $122-$139
9/3-4/30 [ECP]	1P: $99-$129	2P: $109-$139

Small-scale Hotel

Location: I-87, exit 4, just se on Wolf Rd, then just e. 10 Ulenski Dr 12205. Fax: 518/438-2931. **Facility:** 154 one-bedroom standard units. 5 stories, interior corridors. **Parking:** on-site. **Amenities:** video library (fee), video games, voice mail, irons, hair dryers. **Pool(s):** small outdoor. **Guest Services:** valet and coin laundry. **Business Services:** meeting rooms. **Cards:** AX, DC, DS, MC, VI.

SOME UNITS

HILTON GARDEN INN-ALBANY AIRPORT *Book at aaa.com* Phone: (518)464-6666 🔢25

(AAA) (SAVE)

All Year 1P: $99-$189 2P: $99-$189 XP: $10 F18

Small-scale Hotel

Location: I-87, exit 4, 1.8 mi nw. Located opposite the terminal. 800 Albany Shaker Rd 12211. Fax: 518/464-9400. **Facility:** 155 one-bedroom standard units. 6 stories, interior corridors. **Parking:** on-site. **Terms:** check-in 4 pm, cancellation fee imposed. **Amenities:** video library (fee), video games, high-speed Internet, dual phone lines, voice mail, irons, hair dryers. **Dining:** 6 am-1 & 5-11 pm, Fri-Sun 7 am-1 & 5-10 pm, wine/beer only. **Pool(s):** small heated indoor. **Leisure Activities:** whirlpool, exercise room. **Guest Services:** sundries, valet and coin laundry. **Business Services:** meeting rooms, business center. **Cards:** AX, CB, DC, DS, MC, VI. **Special Amenities:** free newspaper. *(See color ad p 220)*

SOME UNITS

HOLIDAY INN TURF ON WOLF ROAD *Book at aaa.com* Phone: (518)458-7250 🔢17

All Year 1P: $169-$209 2P: $169-$209

Small-scale Hotel

Location: I-87, exit 4, 0.3 mi se. 205 Wolf Rd 12205. Fax: 518/458-7377. **Facility:** 309 units. 301 one-bedroom standard units, some with whirlpools. 8 one-bedroom suites. 2-6 stories, interior corridors. *Bath:* combo or shower only. **Parking:** on-site. **Terms:** check-in 4 pm, 3 day cancellation notice. **Amenities:** video library (fee), dual phone lines, voice mail, irons, hair dryers. *Some:* safes. **Pool(s):** outdoor, heated indoor. **Leisure Activities:** sauna, whirlpool, exercise room. *Fee:* game room. **Guest Services:** gift shop, valet and coin laundry, area transportation. **Business Services:** conference facilities, business center. **Cards:** AX, CB, DC, DS, MC, VI.

SOME UNITS

QUALITY INN-ALBANY AIRPORT *Book at aaa.com* Phone: (518)456-8811 🔢21

(AAA) (SAVE)

All Year [ECP] 1P: $69-$199 2P: $69-$199 XP: $8 F18

Small-scale Hotel

Location: I-87, exit 2W, 0.8 mi w, just off SR 5. 1632 Central Ave 12205. Fax: 518/456-0811. **Facility:** 100 one-bedroom standard units. 2 stories (no elevator), interior corridors. *Bath:* combo or shower only. **Parking:** on-site, winter plug-ins. **Amenities:** high-speed Internet, voice mail, irons, hair dryers. **Pool(s):** small heated indoor. **Leisure Activities:** whirlpool, exercise room. **Guest Services:** coin laundry. **Business Services:** meeting rooms, PC. **Cards:** AX, CB, DC, DS, MC, VI. **Special Amenities:** free expanded continental breakfast and free local telephone calls.

SOME UNITS

RAMADA LIMITED *Book at aaa.com* Phone: (518)456-0222 🔢24

(AAA) (SAVE)

8/1-9/1 [ECP]	1P: $89-$130	2P: $99-$140	XP: $10 F18
9/2-9/30 [ECP]	1P: $79-$120	2P: $89-$130	XP: $10 F18
5/1-7/31 & 10/1-4/30 [ECP]	1P: $69-$110	2P: $79-$120	XP: $10 F18

Motel

Location: I-87, exit 2W, 0.8 mi w, then 5.5 mi w on SR 5. Located in a busy, commercial area. 1630 Central Ave 12205 (1630 Central Ave, ALBANY). Fax: 518/452-1376. **Facility:** 101 one-bedroom standard units, some with whirlpools. 2 stories (no elevator), exterior corridors. **Parking:** on-site, winter plug-ins. **Terms:** pets ($10 extra charge, in designated units). **Amenities:** voice mail, irons, hair dryers. **Leisure Activities:** exercise room. **Business Services:** meeting rooms. **Cards:** AX, DC, DS, MC, VI. **Special Amenities:** free expanded continental breakfast and free newspaper.

SOME UNITS

FEE

RED ROOF INN *Book at aaa.com* Phone: (518)459-1971 🔢15

(AAA) (SAVE)

7/18-9/2	1P: $88-$92	2P: $88-$92	
9/3-10/30	1P: $64-$68	2P: $69-$73	XP: $5 F18
5/1-7/17	1P: $60-$64	2P: $65-$69	XP: $5 F18
10/31-4/30	1P: $54-$56	2P: $56-$59	XP: $5 F18

Motel

Location: I-87, exit 4, just se to Wolf Rd, then just sw. 188 Wolf Rd 12205. Fax: 518/459-2374. **Facility:** 115 one-bedroom standard units. 3 stories, exterior corridors. **Parking:** on-site. **Terms:** small pets only. **Amenities:** video games, voice mail. **Business Services:** meeting rooms. **Cards:** AX, CB, DC, DS, MC, VI. **Special Amenities:** free local telephone calls and free newspaper.

SOME UNITS

FEE FEE

—— WHERE TO DINE ——

BANGKOK THAI RESTAURANT Lunch: $6-$8 Dinner: $10-$17 Phone: 518/435-1027 🔢14

Thai

Location: I-87, exit 2E (SR 5), just n; opposite Colonie Shopping Mall. 8 Wolf Rd 12205. **Hours:** 11:30 am-10:30 pm, Fri & Sat-11 pm. **Closed:** 11/25, 12/25. **Reservations:** accepted. **Features:** Teak statues and pretty table settings add to the warmth and friendly aura of the relaxed dining room. The menu centers on flavorful preparations of pork, beef, chicken and seafood. Kanom geep—pork and shrimp dumplings—is a nice appetizer choice. Try the specialty dessert: fried ice cream. Casual dress; cocktails. **Parking:** on-site. **Cards:** AX, DC, MC, VI.

(See map and index starting on p. 215)

BUTCHER BLOCK STEAK &
  SEAFOOD RESTAURANT   **Lunch:** $8-$12   **Dinner:** $13-$19   **Phone:** 518/456-1653   16
  Location: I-87, exit 2W, 0.8 mi w. **Hours:** 11:30 am-10 pm, Sun 3 pm-9 pm. Closed: 11/25, 12/25.
  Reservations: accepted. **Features:** As its name might suggest, the restaurant centers the menu on
Steak & Seafood   seafood and steak, particularly the succulent prime rib. The atmosphere of the dining room is rustic and
  cozy, welcoming to families. Decadent dessert appeals to both eyes and palate. Casual dress; cocktails.
Parking: on-site. **Cards:** AX, CB, DC, DS, MC, VI.

DELMONICO'S ITALIAN STEAKHOUSE   **Lunch:** $8   **Dinner:** $18   **Phone:** 518/456-5656   18
  Location: I-87, exit 2W, just w. 1553 Central Ave 12205. **Hours:** 4 pm-10:30 pm, Fri-11:30 pm, Sat 3 pm-11:30
  pm, Sun noon-10 pm. Closed: 11/25, 12/25. **Reservations:** accepted. **Features:** Touted as the "best deal
Steak & Seafood   in town" is the 24-ounce choice Delmonico steak from Midwestern aged beef. Also on the menu are other
  choice cuts, veal specials, seafood and pasta dishes and signature chicken entrees with an Italian accent.
Patrons can dine among life-size caricatures of Italian notables. Casual dress; cocktails. **Parking:** on-site. **Cards:** AX, DC, DS,
MC, VI.

GARCIA'S MEXICAN RESTAURANT   **Lunch:** $5-$6   **Dinner:** $7-$14   **Phone:** 518/456-4116   19
  Location: I-87, exit 2W, 1 mi w, 6 mi w on SR 5. 1614 Central Ave 12205. **Hours:** 1l:30 am-10 pm, Fri & Sat-11
  pm, Sun noon-9 pm. Closed: 11/25, 12/25. **Reservations:** suggested, weekends. **Features:** Popular
Mexican   choices on a menu of mostly Tex-Mex fare are ultimate fajitas, Olivia's sampler and quesadillas. The
  atmosphere is lively and energetic, enhanced by colorful decorations and upbeat music. A varied lunch
buffet is laid out on weekdays. Casual dress; cocktails. **Parking:** on-site. **Cards:** AX, CB, DC, DS, MC, VI.

GRANDMA'S COUNTRY RESTAURANT   **Lunch:** $5-$10   **Dinner:** $8-$15   **Phone:** 518/459-4585   15
  Location: I-87, exit 2E, 1 mi e. 1273 Central Ave 12205. **Hours:** 6 am-11:30 pm, Fri & Sat-midnight. Closed:
  12/24, 12/25. **Features:** Home-style flavors characterize such tried-and-true favorites as turkey soup and
  meatloaf with mashed potatoes and gravy. The challenge at dessert is to choose from more than 25
  varieties of homemade pies, including a delicious lemon meringue. Casual dress; beer & wine only.
American   **Parking:** on-site. **Cards:** AX, CB, DC, DS, MC, VI.

RALPH'S TAVERN   **Lunch:** $5-$13   **Dinner:** $5-$13   **Phone:** 518/489-8290   20
  Location: I-87, exit 2E, 0.6 mi e. 1328 Central Ave 12205. **Hours:** 11 am-midnight, Fri & Sat-2 am, Sun
  noon-midnight. Closed: 3/27, 11/25, 12/25. **Features:** Guests can come early or wait with other diners
American   hungry for great food at a good price. On the no-frills menu are delicious Italian favorites, finger foods,
  steaks and prime rib. Casual dress; cocktails. **Parking:** on-site. **Cards:** AX, DC, DS, MC, VI.

REAL SEAFOOD CO   **Lunch:** $6-$10   **Dinner:** $14-$28   **Phone:** 518/458-2068   11
  Location: I-87, exit 4, 0.3 mi e. 195 Wolf Rd 12205. **Hours:** 11 am-10:30 pm, Fri-11:30 pm, Sat 3 pm-11:30 pm,
  Sun 3 pm-9:30 pm. Closed: 11/25, 12/25. **Reservations:** suggested. **Features:** The freshest, best-quality
Seafood   seafood is prepared in abundance. The attentive staff serves palate-tempting creations. Dressy casual;
  cocktails. **Parking:** on-site. **Cards:** AX, DC, MC, VI.

SCRIMSHAW   **Dinner:** $18-$30   **Phone:** 518/869-8100   17
  Location: I-87, exit 4; in The Desmond Hotel. 660 Albany Shaker Rd 12211. **Hours:** 5:30 pm-10 pm. Closed major
  holidays; also Sun. **Reservations:** suggested. **Features:** A Colonial theme weaves through the upscale
  dining room, where professionals and couples gather to enjoy a sophisticated atmosphere. Seafood is the
Continental   specialty, with such well-prepared dishes as citrus-grilled lobster over artichoke hearts. Dressy casual;
cocktails. **Parking:** on-site. **Cards:** AX, CB, DC, DS, MC, VI.

SMOKEY BONES BARBECUE & GRILL RESTAURANT   **Lunch:** $4-$9   **Dinner:** $8-$17   **Phone:** 518/464-9971   13
  Location: I-87, exit 2W, 0.5 mi w. 1557 Central Ave 12205. **Hours:** 11 am-11 pm, Fri & Sat-midnight. Closed:
  11/25, 12/25. **Features:** The lively sports bar serves up a specialty of delicious, tender baby back ribs in a
American   tangy sauce. Barbecue chicken, hand-pulled pork, catfish and salmon also top menu choices. Service is
  friendly and casual, and guests can view televisions from every seat. Casual dress; cocktails. **Parking:**
on-site. **Cards:** AX, DC, DS, MC, VI.

COMMACK pop. 36,367

------ **WHERE TO STAY** ------

HAMPTON INN   *Book at aaa.com*
  All Year [ECP]   1P: $150-$170   2P: $150-$170   **Phone:** (631)462-5700
  Location: I-495, exit 52 eastbound; exit 53 westbound, just n on CR 4. Located in a commercial area. 680 Commack Rd
Small-scale Hotel   11725. Fax: 631/462-9735. **Facility:** 143 one-bedroom standard units. 5 stories, interior corridors. **Parking:**
  on-site. **Amenities:** video games (fee), voice mail, irons, hair dryers. **Guest Services:** valet laundry, area
transportation. **Business Services:** meeting rooms. **Cards:** AX, CB, DC, DS, MC, VI.

SOME UNITS
FEE   FEE

CONGERS —*See New York p. 451.*

COOPERSTOWN pop. 2,032—*See also HARTWICK SEMINARY, INDEX & SPRINGFIELD CENTER.*

—— **WHERE TO STAY** ——

DIASTOLE BED & BREAKFAST

All Year [BP]   1P: $125-$225   2P: $125-$225   XP: $10   F5

Phone: (607)547-2665

Bed & Breakfast

Location: From Main St, continue e through town to CR 31 2.8 mi n, then 0.6 mi ne on Van Yahres (dirt road). Overlooking Lake Ostego. 276 Van Yahres Rd 13326. **Facility:** Smoke free premises. 4 one-bedroom standard units, some with whirlpools. 2 stories (no elevator), interior corridors. *Bath:* some combo or shower only. **Parking:** on-site. **Terms:** 2 night minimum stay - weekends, 7 day cancellation notice-fee imposed. **Amenities:** video library. *Some:* hair dryers.

SOME UNITS

[ASK] [S⬤] [✕] [☎] / [ⓅⓌ] [VCR] /

Lake 'N Pines Motel

C O O P E R S T O W N

*"Discover Baseball's History While Having the Comfort
of a Country Setting Nestled in the Pines on Otsego Lake"*

INDOOR HEATED POOL, SAUNA, WHIRLPOOL • LARGE HEATED OUTDOOR POOL

Small Refrigerator Included • Open March through November

• Family Game Room • Color Cable TV • HBO •

• FREE Paddleboats & Rowboats • Picnic Area with Grills •

• Continental Breakfast • Balconies overlooking Lake • Conference Room •

FOR RESERVATIONS ONLY, CALL TOLL FREE 1-800-615-5253

For information, Call 607-547-2790 / 607-547-5671, 8 AM - 10 PM

www.cooperstown.net/lake-n-pines

7102 St. Hwy. 80, Cooperstown, New York 13326

Best Western Inn & Suites Cooperstown

• Minutes from the Baseball Hall of Fame and Museums
• Heated Indoor Swimming Pool & Spa
• Complimentary Continental Breakfast
• Fitness Room • Game Room• Conference Room
• Gift Shop • Guest Laundry
• Microwaves & Refrigerators • Coffee Makers
• Hair Dryers • Iron & Ironing Boards
• Picnic Pavilion
• Restaurants Within Walking Distance
• 63 Year-round Rooms-36 Seasonal Junior Suites
• Located 4 miles south of Cooperstown on Route 28 in the
  Hartwick Commons Shopping Plaza – I-88 Exit 17

50 Commons Drive, Route 28
Cooperstown, NY 13326

For reservations call: 607.547.9439

www.bwcooperstown.com

Bay Side Inn Marina & Cottages

• Minutes to Hall of Fame, Museums & Shopping
• 4 Scenic Acres on Lake Otsego
• Beach, Marina, Picnic Area w/Grills
• Air Conditioned Rooms & Cottages
• HBO - Cable TV • In-Room Phones • Refrigerators
• Family Game Room • Free Paddle Boats, Canoes,
  and Row Boats

7090 St. Hwy. 80 Cooperstown, NY 13326

Toll Free-1-866-547-2371 • Fax 607-547-5856

Website: www.cooperstown.net/bayside • Email: bayside @juno.com

For Rate Information, see our listing under Springfield Center

LAKE FRONT MOTEL

♦♦ ◆◆

Motel

	1P:	2P:
7/1-9/6	$115-$190	$115-$190
9/7-10/31	$85-$150	$85-$150
5/1-6/30	$80-$150	$80-$150
11/1-4/30	$65-$150	$65-$150

Phone: 607/547-9511

Location: Just n of center. 10 Fair St 13326. Fax: 607/547-2792. **Facility:** 44 one-bedroom standard units. 1-2 stories (no elevator), exterior corridors. *Bath:* combo or shower only. **Parking:** on-site. **Terms:** 3 day cancellation notice-fee imposed. **Amenities:** voice mail. **Dining:** Lake Front Restaurant, see separate listing. **Leisure Activities:** Fee: marina. **Cards:** MC, VI.

SOME UNITS

⟨ 🍴 📷 DATA PORT / ⊠ / ⟩

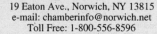

THE OTESAGA HOTEL
Phone: (607)547-9931

5/31-10/11 [MAP]	1P: $310-$345	2P: $365-$400	XP: $90	F18
4/22-4/30 [MAP]	1P: $290-$325	2P: $345-$380	XP: $90	F18
5/1-5/30 & 10/12-11/28 [MAP]	1P: $280-$315	2P: $335-$370	XP: $90	F18

Historic
Large-scale Hotel
Location: On SR 80 E; center. 60 Lake St 13326 (PO Box 311). Fax: 607/547-9675. **Facility:** Guests will find fine craftsmanship within and sweeping views of Lake Otsego from the front porch of this recently restored 1910 hotel. 136 units. 126 one-bedroom standard units. 10 one-bedroom suites, some with whirlpools. 5 stories, interior corridors. *Bath:* combo or shower only. **Parking:** on-site and valet. **Terms:** open 5/1-11/28 & 4/22-4/30, 2 night minimum stay - weekends, 7 day cancellation notice-fee imposed, package plans. **Amenities:** dual phone lines, voice mail, safes, irons, hair dryers. **Pool(s):** heated outdoor. **Leisure Activities:** rental canoes, boat dock, 2 tennis courts, exercise room. *Fee:* golf-18 holes. **Guest Services:** gift shop, valet laundry. **Business Services:** meeting rooms, business center. **Cards:** AX, MC, VI. SOME UNITS

ROSE AND THISTLE B & B
Phone: (607)547-5345

5/1-10/31 [BP]	1P: $145-$165	2P: $145-$165	XP: $25	F6
11/1-12/31 & 2/1-4/30 [BP]	1P: $115-$125	2P: $115-$125	XP: $25	F6

Bed & Breakfast
Location: On SR 28, south end of town. 132 Chestnut St 13326. Fax: 607/547-5917. **Facility:** Smoke free premises. 4 one-bedroom standard units. 2 stories (no elevator), interior corridors. *Bath:* combo or shower only. **Parking:** on-site. **Terms:** open 5/1-12/31 & 2/1-4/30, 2 night minimum stay - 6/1-10/31, age restrictions may apply, 14 day cancellation notice-fee imposed, no pets allowed (owner's cat on premises). **Amenities:** video library, hair dryers. **Cards:** AX, DS, MC, VI. SOME UNITS

——— **WHERE TO DINE** ———

THE BLUE MINGO GRILL
Lunch: $5-$8   Dinner: $18-$25   Phone: 607/547-7496

Continental
Location: 2.5 mi n. 6098 Hwy 80 13326. **Hours:** Open 5/15-9/1; 11:30 am-2:30 & 5-10 pm. **Reservations:** suggested. **Features:** Whether guests are boaters, sightseers or travelers, the attentive service, delectable entrees and lakefront setting of the marina-centered eatery will delight. Chef Joe Ford chooses fresh seasonal ingredients in an ever-changing menu. Desserts start with light passion fruit sorbet and move to Cuban chocolate cake, which is something between bread pudding and chocolate ecstasy. Casual dress; cocktails. **Parking:** on-site. **Cards:** AX, DS, MC, VI.

THE DOUBLEDAY CAFE
Lunch: $3-$10   Dinner: $6-$20   Phone: 607/547-5468

American
Location: Center. 93 Main St 13326. **Hours:** 7 am-9 pm, Fri & Sat-10 pm; hours vary. Closed: 11/25, 12/25. **Features:** Wholesome familiar fare—steaks, salads, sandwiches, burgers and daily specials—makes up the restaurant's menu. Savory soups and desserts are particularly noteworthy. Baseball memorabilia decorates the walls of the popular family spot. Casual dress; beer & wine only. **Parking:** street. **Cards:** DS, MC, VI.

HOFFMAN LANE BISTRO
Lunch: $5-$7   Dinner: $12-$19   Phone: 607/547-7055

Continental
Location: Downtown. 2 Hoffman Ln 13326. **Hours:** 11:30 am-2:30 & 5-9 pm. Closed: 3/27, 11/25, 12/25; also Sun. **Reservations:** required. **Features:** Eclectic decor and such menu items as tuna au poivre and pan-seared salmon make the bistro lively in taste and color. Casual dress; cocktails. **Parking:** street. **Cards:** AX, MC, VI.

LAKE FRONT RESTAURANT
Lunch: $7-$13   Dinner: $13-$18   Phone: 607/547-8188

American
Location: Just n of center; in Lake Front Motel. 10 Fair St 13326. **Hours:** Open 5/1-10/31; 7 am-9 pm. **Reservations:** accepted. **Features:** Two blocks from downtown, the lakefront setting includes plenty of windows for viewing, as well as tables on the seasonal patio. Service has a casual, hometown charm. Menu selections are tasty. Casual dress; cocktails. **Parking:** on-site. **Cards:** MC, VI.

THE PEPPER MILL
Dinner: $8-$17   Phone: 607/547-8550

American
Location: 0.5 mi s. 5418 State Hwy 28 S 13326. **Hours:** Open 5/1-12/31 & 4/2-4/30; 4 pm-10 pm; 11 am-4 pm 6/1-9/2. Closed: 12/24, 12/25. **Reservations:** suggested. **Features:** Baseball Hall of Fame pictures on the wall set the scene for casual dining that is far from ballpark style. Wonderful house sauces flavor preparations of steak and chicken. To top off the meal, enjoy a cup of robust coffee with cinnamon bread pudding. Casual dress; cocktails. **Parking:** on-site. **Cards:** DS, MC, VI.

——— *The following restaurant has not been evaluated by AAA* ———
but is listed for your information only.

CAFE MILANO
Phone: 607/544-1222

[fyi]
Not evaluated. **Location:** Jct Main St. 22 Chestnut St 13326. **Features:** Warm tones, dark wood accents and a fireplace set the tone for a romantic dining experience; the restaurant uses the freshest of ingredients with an emphasis on healthy cooking techniques.

CORNING pop. 10,842—*See also FINGER LAKES.*

——— **WHERE TO STAY** ———

COMFORT INN   *Book at aaa.com*
Phone: (607)962-1515

5/1-10/31 [ECP]	1P: $80-$165	2P: $80-$165	XP: $10	F18
11/1-4/30 [ECP]	1P: $70-$165	2P: $70-$165	XP: $10	F18

Small-scale Hotel
Location: SR 17, exit 46, just s on SR 414, then 0.5 mi w on SR 415 (Pulteney St). 66 W Pulteney St 14830. Fax: 607/962-1899. **Facility:** 62 one-bedroom standard units, some with whirlpools. 2 stories (no elevator), interior corridors. **Parking:** on-site, winter plug-ins. **Amenities:** voice mail, irons, hair dryers. **Pool(s):** heated indoor. **Leisure Activities:** exercise room. **Guest Services:** valet laundry. **Cards:** AX, CB, DC, DS, MC, VI. SOME UNITS

CORNING DAYS INN   *Book at aaa.com*
Phone: 607/936-9370

5/1-10/31 [CP]	1P: $69-$129	2P: $79-$139	XP: $10	F17
11/1-4/30 [CP]	1P: $59-$89	2P: $69-$99	XP: $10	F17

Small-scale Hotel
Location: Corner of Ferris St and Riverside Dr; just w of Corning Glass Center; center. 23 Riverside Dr 14830. Fax: 607/936-0513. **Facility:** 56 one-bedroom standard units, some with efficiencies and/or whirlpools. 3 stories, interior corridors. *Bath:* combo or shower only. **Parking:** on-site. **Terms:** age restrictions may apply. **Amenities:** voice mail, irons, hair dryers. **Pool(s):** heated indoor. **Leisure Activities:** whirlpool. **Guest Services:** valet laundry. **Cards:** AX, DC, DS, MC, VI.

SOME UNITS

FAIRFIELD INN BY MARRIOTT CORNING/RIVERSIDE   *Book at aaa.com*
Phone: (607)937-9600

All Year   1P: $82-$104

Small-scale Hotel
Location: SR 17, exit 45 eastbound, just e on SR 352, then just n; exit 45 westbound, just e on Pulteney St, then just s. 3 S Buffalo St 14830. Fax: 607/937-3155. **Facility:** 63 one-bedroom standard units. 3 stories, interior corridors. *Bath:* combo or shower only. **Parking:** on-site. **Terms:** [ECP] meal plan available. **Amenities:** video games, high-speed Internet, dual phone lines, irons, hair dryers. **Pool(s):** small heated indoor. **Guest Services:** valet laundry. **Cards:** AX, DC, DS, MC, VI.

SOME UNITS

GATE HOUSE MOTEL
Phone: (607)936-4131

5/1-11/30	1P: $42-$50	2P: $49-$66	XP: $6	F18
12/1-4/30	1P: $37-$49	2P: $45-$56	XP: $6	F18

Motel
Location: I-86 (SR 17 E), exit 47 (SR 352), 0.8 mi e; I-86 (SR 17 W), exit 48 (SR 352), 1.5 mi w. 11409 E LPGA Dr (SR 352) 14830-3663. Fax: 607/936-8730. **Facility:** 20 one-bedroom standard units. 1 story, interior/exterior corridors. *Bath:* combo or shower only. **Parking:** on-site, winter plug-ins. **Terms:** 10 day cancellation notice. **Guest Services:** coin laundry. **Cards:** AX, MC, VI. **Special Amenities:** free local telephone calls and preferred room (subject to availability with advanced reservations).

SOME UNITS

RADISSON HOTEL CORNING   *Book at aaa.com*
Phone: (607)962-5000

4/1-4/30	1P: $120-$150	2P: $130-$160	XP: $10	F18
5/1-10/31	1P: $110-$140	2P: $120-$150	XP: $10	F18
11/1-3/31	1P: $100-$130	2P: $110-$140	XP: $10	F18

Small-scale Hotel
Location: On SR 17; center. 125 Denison Pkwy E 14830-2786. Fax: 607/962-4166. **Facility:** 177 one-bedroom standard units, some with whirlpools. 3 stories, interior corridors. *Bath:* combo or shower only. **Parking:** on-site. **Terms:** [AP] meal plan available, small pets only (must be attended). **Amenities:** video games, voice mail, hair dryers. *Some:* high-speed Internet, dual phone lines, safes, honor bars, irons. **Pool(s):** heated indoor. **Leisure Activities:** whirlpool, exercise room. **Guest Services:** valet laundry. **Business Services:** conference facilities, business center. **Cards:** AX, CB, DC, DS, MC, VI.
(See color ad p 413)

SOME UNITS

ROSEWOOD INN
Phone: 607/962-3253

5/1-10/31 [BP]	2P: $125-$185	XP: $50
11/1-4/30 [BP]	2P: $95-$165	XP: $50

Historic Bed & Breakfast
Location: Just off SR 352; corner of 1st and Chemung sts. 134 E 1st St 14830. **Facility:** This seven-room, English Tudor-style 1855 mansion features art-glass chandeliers and numerous antiques. Smoke free premises. 7 one-bedroom standard units, some with kitchens. 2 stories (no elevator), interior/exterior corridors. *Bath:* combo or shower only. **Parking:** on-site. **Terms:** age restrictions may apply, 3 day cancellation notice-fee imposed, package plans. **Amenities:** *Some:* hair dryers. **Cards:** AX, CB, DC, DS, MC, VI.

SOME UNITS

STAYBRIDGE SUITES BY HOLIDAY INN   *Book at aaa.com*
Phone: 607/936-7800

All Year [ECP]   1P: $119-$199   2P: $119-$199

Small-scale Hotel
Location: SR 17, exit 46, just s. 201 Townley Ave 14830. Fax: 607/936-7900. **Facility:** 115 units. 59 one-bedroom standard units with efficiencies. 38 one- and 18 two-bedroom suites with efficiencies. 3 stories, interior corridors. *Bath:* combo or shower only. **Parking:** on-site. **Terms:** pets ($75 fee). **Amenities:** high-speed Internet, dual phone lines, voice mail, irons, hair dryers. **Pool(s):** heated indoor. **Leisure Activities:** whirlpool, exercise room, sports court. **Guest Services:** sundries. **Business Services:** meeting rooms, business center. **Cards:** AX, CB, DC, DS, JC, MC, VI.

SOME UNITS

——— WHERE TO DINE ———

LONDON UNDERGROUND CAFE
Lunch: $5-$10   **Dinner:** $13-$26   **Phone:** 607/962-2345

Continental
Location: Just n of SR 17; downtown. 69 E Market St 14830. **Hours:** 11:30 am-9 pm, Fri & Sat-9:30 pm. Closed: 11/25, 12/25; also Sun. **Reservations:** suggested. **Features:** Palate-pleasing flavors are consistent characteristics of the cafe's gourmet Continental cuisine. Favorites include the memorable Wixon's fall flower honey-pecan-crusted rack of lamb and halibut with Finger Lakes wine butter sauce. The casual, three-level dining room is decorated in a British theme. A pianist entertains on Saturday evenings. Dressy casual; cocktails. **Parking:** street. **Cards:** AX, DC, DS, MC, VI.

SORGE'S RESTAURANT
Lunch: $4-$6   **Dinner:** $7-$20   **Phone:** 607/937-5422

Italian
Location: Historic downtown. 66-68 W Market St 14830. **Hours:** 7 am-10 pm. Closed: 3/27, 11/25, 12/25. **Reservations:** suggested, weekends. **Features:** Operated by the same family since 1951, the restaurant is a local favorite for steak, seafood and pasta. The downstairs dining room is bright and casual; upstairs, the feeling is more romantic and subdued. The friendly staff provides timely follow-up. Casual dress; cocktails. **Parking:** on-site. **Cards:** AX, DS, MC, VI.

SPENCER'S RESTAURANT & MERCANTILE Lunch: $4-$7 Dinner: $6-$16 Phone: 607/936-9196

▼▼▼ ▼▼▼

American

Location: SR 352, just n on Conhocton St to Market St Ext, then just e. 359 E Market St Ext 14830. **Hours:** 11 am-10 pm. Closed: 11/25, 12/25. **Reservations:** accepted. **Features:** In a semi-commercial neighborhood near downtown, the popular family restaurant delivers a wide array of made-to-order pasta selections, as well as well-prepared steaks, chicken and chops. Patrons can dine next to one of four fireplaces in winter. Prices are moderate, and the food tastes great. Casual dress; cocktails. **Parking:** on-site. **Cards:** AX, DS, MC, VI. 🍽 ☒

CORNWALL

―――― **WHERE TO STAY** ――――

CROMWELL MANOR INN Phone: (845)534-7136

▼▼▼▼ ▼▼

Bed & Breakfast

All Year [BP] 1P: $185-$390 2P: $185-$390 XP: $35 D10
Location: Jct US 9W and SR 94, 5.5 mi s on US 9W, then 0.5 mi w. 174 Angola Rd 12518. **Facility:** A natural setting overlooking the valley, complemented by spacious, upscale rooms in the main building, makes this brick Colonial mansion stand out. Smoke free premises. 12 one-bedroom standard units, some with whirlpools. 1-2 stories (no elevator), interior/exterior corridors. **Parking:** on-site. **Terms:** check-in 4 pm, 2 night minimum stay - seasonal, age restrictions may apply, 14 day cancellation notice, weekly rates available, package plans - seasonal. **Amenities:** CD players, hair dryers. **Cards:** MC, VI.

(ASK) (⑤M) (☒) (🎬) (☎)

CORTLAND pop. 18,740

―――― **WHERE TO STAY** ――――

COMFORT INN *Book at aaa.com* Phone: (607)753-7721

▼▼▼ ▼▼▼

Small-scale Hotel

All Year [ECP] 1P: $89-$189 2P: $89-$189 XP: $10 F18
Location: I-81, exit 11, just e. 2 1/2 Locust Ave 13045. Fax: 607/753-7608. **Facility:** 66 one-bedroom standard units, some with whirlpools. 2 stories (no elevator), interior corridors. **Parking:** on-site. **Terms:** small pets only ($10 fee, in smoking units). **Amenities:** irons, hair dryers. **Leisure Activities:** exercise room. *Fee:* game room. **Guest Services:** valet laundry. **Business Services:** fax. **Cards:** AX, CB, DC, DS, MC, VI.

SOME UNITS
(ASK) (⑤D) (📶) (🍴) (DATA PORT) (💻) / ☒ 🛏 📷 /
FEE

ECONO LODGE *Book at aaa.com* Phone: 607/756-2856

(AAA) (SAVE)

▼▼▼

Motel

5/1-8/31 1P: $65-$155 2P: $65-$155 XP: $10 F16
10/1-11/16 1P: $59-$119 2P: $59-$119 XP: $10 F16
9/1-9/30 1P: $55-$105 2P: $55-$105 XP: $10 F16
11/17-4/30 1P: $52-$89 2P: $52-$89 XP: $12 F16
Location: I-81, exit 11, 0.8 mi s on US 11. 10 Church St 13045. Fax: 607/758-7555. **Facility:** 42 one-bedroom standard units. 2 stories (no elevator), exterior corridors. **Parking:** on-site. **Terms:** 2 night minimum stay - seasonal, cancellation fee imposed, [CP] meal plan available, pets ($10 extra charge, in designated units). **Amenities:** video library (fee). *Some:* DVD players (fee). **Cards:** AX, DC, DS, MC, VI. **Special Amenities: free continental breakfast and free local telephone calls.**

SOME UNITS
(⑤D) (🛏) (🍴) (🎬) / ☒ (VCR) 🛏 📷 /
FEE FEE

HAMPTON INN *Book at aaa.com* Phone: 607/662-0007

▼▼▼ ▼▼

Small-scale Hotel

All Year 1P: $89-$199
Location: I-81, exit 11, just s on SR 13, then just e. 26 River St 13045. Fax: 607/662-0678. **Facility:** 68 one-bedroom standard units, some with whirlpools. 3 stories, interior corridors. **Bath:** combo or shower only. **Parking:** on-site. **Amenities:** high-speed Internet, dual phone lines, voice mail, irons, hair dryers. **Pool(s):** heated indoor. **Leisure Activities:** exercise room. **Guest Services:** valet and coin laundry. **Business Services:** meeting rooms, business center. **Cards:** AX, DC, DS, MC, VI.

SOME UNITS
(ASK) (⑤D) (🍴) (🔥) (🏊) (🎬) (DATA PORT) 🛏 📷 💻 / ☒ /

2 River Street
Cortland, NY 13045

Cortland

• 147 Tastefully Renovated Rooms • Full Service Restaurant & Lounge
• Gateway to Fingerlakes Wine Region • Shopping & Local Ski Areas
• Centrally Located: Cornell U., Syracuse U., & SUNY Cortland
• Priority Club® Rewards Program
• Indoor Heated Pool & Fitness Center
• Banquet & Conference Facilities
• Conveniently Located Off I-81, Exit 11

SPECIAL AAA RATES AVAILABLE

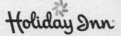 Holiday Inn

For Reservations Call 1-607-756-4431 or 1-800-HOLIDAY
Restrictions apply. Call for details. **www.holiday-inn.com**

HOLIDAY INN CORTLAND   *Book at aaa.com*   Phone: (607)756-4431
▽▽ ▽▽   All Year   1P: $100
Location: I-81, exit 11. 2 River St 13045. Fax: 607/753-3511. Facility: 148 units. 147 one-bedroom standard
Small-scale Hotel   units, some with whirlpools. 1 one-bedroom suite ($120). 2 stories (no elevator), interior corridors. Parking:
on-site. Terms: cancellation fee imposed, [BP] meal plan available. Amenities: video library (fee), video
games, irons, hair dryers. Pool(s): small heated indoor. Leisure Activities: exercise room. Fee: game room. Guest Services:
valet laundry. Business Services: conference facilities. Cards: AX, CB, DC, DS, MC, VI. *(See color ad p 274)*

SOME UNITS
(ASK) (S/D) (Ⅱ) (▽) (🏊) (📷) (DATA PORT) (💻) / (✕) (🛢) (🖨) /

QUALITY INN CORTLAND   *Book at aaa.com*   Phone: (607)756-5622
▽▽ ▽▽▽▽   All Year [ECP]   1P: $79-$179   2P: $79-$179   XP: $10   F18
Location: I-81, exit 11, just n. 188 Clinton St 13045. Fax: 607/753-6171. Facility: 56 one-bedroom standard units.
Small-scale Hotel   2 stories (no elevator), interior corridors. Parking: on-site. Terms: pets ($10 extra charge). Amenities: irons,
hair dryers. Leisure Activities: limited exercise equipment. Guest Services: valet laundry. Cards: AX, CB,
DC, DS, MC, VI.

SOME UNITS
(ASK) (S/D) (🛏) (Ⅱ+) (💻) / (✕) (VCR) (DATA PORT)
FEE   FEE FEE

─────── *The following lodging was either not evaluated or did not* ───────
meet AAA rating requirements but is listed for your information only.

COUNTRY INN & SUITES   Phone: 607/753-8300
(fyi)   All Year   1P: $89-$129   2P: $89-$129   XP: $10   F18
Too new to rate, opening scheduled for December 2003. Location: I-81, exit 12, 3 mi s on SR 281. 3707 Rt 281
Small-scale Hotel   13045. Fax: 607/753-8301. Amenities: 1 unit, pool. Cards: AX, DC, DS, MC, VI.

─────── **WHERE TO DINE** ───────

COMMUNITY RESTAURANT   Lunch: $5-$7   Dinner: $9-$14   Phone: 607/756-5441
(AAA)   Location: Downtown. 10 Main St 13045. Hours: 7 am-9 pm, Fri-Sun to 10 pm. Closed: 1/1, 12/25.
▽▽▽   Features: Serving since 1929, this Main Street mainstay maintains remnants of it past "soda fountain"
appeal. Traditionally prepared comfort food, such as creamy rice pudding, contributes to the restaurant's
American   success. Casual dress; cocktails. Parking: street. Cards: AX, DS, MC, VI.   (✕)

DOUG'S FISH FRY   Lunch: $4-$10   Dinner: $4-$10   Phone: 607/753-9184
▽▽▽   Location: I-81, exit 12, 3 mi s on SR 281 (West Rd). 206 West Rd 13045. Hours: 11 am-9 pm, Fri & Sat-10 pm.
Closed: 3/27, 11/25, 12/25. Features: Fresh fried fish and seafoods are served up fast and friendly.
Seafood   Generous portions of fish, fries, onion rings and other finger foods are served hot and made while you
wait. Casual dress; beer & wine only. Parking: on-site. Cards: AX, MC, VI.   (✕)

HOLLYWOOD RESTAURANT   Lunch: $5-$8   Dinner: $5-$14   Phone: 607/753-3242
▽▽▽   Location: Just n of Main St; downtown. 27 Groton Ave 13045. Hours: 11:30 am-10 pm, Sat from noon, Sun
noon-9 pm. Closed major holidays. Features: The popular Hollywood-themed restaurant displays a
American   life-size statue of Marilyn Monroe as its centerpiece. Movie star pictures line the walls of the retro '50s
MC, VI.   diner, appointed in shiny chrome, black and red. Casual dress; cocktails. Parking: on-site. Cards: AX, DS,
(&M) (▽) (✕)

PITA GOURMET   Lunch: $3-$6   Dinner: $5-$9   Phone: 607/756-4442
▽▽   Location: Center. 41 Main St 13045. Hours: 11 am-9 pm. Closed major holidays; also Sun. Features: Middle
Eastern cuisine and traditional American food, including vegetarian and daily specials and a Friday fish fry,
Lebanese   are prepared from natural fresh ingredients. Casual dress. Parking: street.   (✕)

COXSACKIE pop. 2,895

─────── **WHERE TO DINE** ───────

RED'S RESTAURANT   Lunch: $5-$8   Dinner: $10-$25   Phone: 518/731-8151
(AAA)   Location: 1.5 mi s of New York Thruway, exit 21B. 12005 Rt 9 W 12192. Hours: 11:30 am-9 pm, Fri & Sat-9:30
▽▽ ▽▽   pm, Sun 10:30 am-8 pm. Closed: 1/1, 12/25; also Mon. Features: Established in 1945, the restaurant is
decorated in a roadside country style, with knotty pine, pictures of 1950s and '60s movies and lots of
American   plants. Traditional American preparations of seafood and meat combine with soups, salads and
sandwiches. Casual dress; cocktails. Parking: on-site. Cards: AX, CB, DC, DS, MC, VI.   (▽) (✕)

CROTON-ON-HUDSON —*See New York p. 451.*

CUBA pop. 1,633

─────── **WHERE TO STAY** ───────

CUBA COACHLIGHT MOTEL   Phone: (585)968-1992
(AAA) (SAVE)   All Year   1P: $44-$59   2P: $49-$59   XP: $5   F12
▽▽ ▽▽   Location: US 86, exit 28, n to N Branch Rd, then e. 1 N Branch Rd 14727 (PO Box 103). Fax: 585/968-3826.
Facility: 27 one-bedroom standard units. 1 story, interior corridors. Parking: on-site, winter plug-ins.
Motel   Terms: pets ($5 fee). Amenities: Some: hair dryers. Business Services: meeting rooms. Cards: AX, DC,
DS, MC, VI. Special Amenities: free continental breakfast and free local telephone calls.

SOME UNITS
(S/D) (🛏) (DATA PORT) / (✕) (🛢) /
FEE   FEE

——— WHERE TO DINE ———

MOONWINKS
American

Lunch: $4-$10   **Dinner:** $11-$30   **Phone:** 585/968-1232
Location: I-86, exit 28, 1 mi n. Rt 305 14727. **Hours:** 5 pm-9 pm, Tues noon-2:30 & 5-9 pm, Wed & Thurs noon-2:30 & 5-9:30 pm, Fri noon-2:30 & 4:30-10 pm, Sat noon-10 pm, Sun 11 am-8 pm. Closed: 12/25. **Reservations:** suggested. **Features:** The pleasant, rural atmosphere welcomes diners to relax over entrees of pasta, chicken, veal, pork, seafood and beef. Rack of lamb stands out as a particularly flavorful selection. Wonderful desserts are made on the premises. Servers are attentive. Casual dress; cocktails. **Parking:** on-site.
Cards: AX, DS, MC, VI.

THE STONE HOUSE RESTAURANT
American

Lunch: $4-$9   **Dinner:** $10-$17   **Phone:** 585/968-9773
Location: I-86, exit 28, 0.5 mi s. 46 Genesee St 14727. **Hours:** 11:30 am-9:30 pm, Tues from 4 pm, Sun 1 pm-7 pm. Closed: 1/1, 12/25; also Mon. **Reservations:** accepted. **Features:** The 1800s farmhouse has been transformed into a eclectic restaurant that also offers dinner shows and special entertainment. The on-premises meat house explains the best cuts and richest stocks for soups and sauces. Only the freshest vegetables and ingredients are considered. The delicious desserts are homemade. Casual dress; cocktails. **Parking:** on-site.
Cards: AX, DS, MC, VI.

DANSVILLE pop. 4,832—See FINGER LAKES.

DARIEN CENTER

——— WHERE TO STAY ———

SIX FLAGS HOTEL LODGE ON THE LAKE
Small-scale Hotel

Phone: 585-599-5500
5/7-10/31   2P: $145-$210   XP: $25
Location: I-90, exit 48A, 5 mi s on SR 77. 9993 Alleghney Rd 14040 (PO Box 91). Fax: 585/599-5521. **Facility:** Smoke free premises. 163 units. 161 one-bedroom standard units. 2 one-bedroom suites ($290-$340). 3 stories, interior corridors. *Bath:* combo or shower only. **Parking:** on-site. **Terms:** open 5/7-10/31, 2 night minimum stay - seasonal, cancellation fee imposed, package plans - seasonal. **Amenities:** hair dryers. **Pool(s):** heated outdoor, wading. **Cards:** AX, DS, MC, VI.

SOME UNITS

——— WHERE TO DINE ———

BEACHY'S PIZZA & WING CAFE
American

Lunch: $3-$5   **Dinner:** $5-$10   **Phone:** 585/547-9339
Location: Just e of jct SR 77 and 20 (Broadway). 1415 Broadway 14040. **Hours:** 8 am-10 pm; hours vary in winter. Closed: 1/1, 11/25, 12/25. **Features:** Bright white walls and red-checked tablecloths accent the neat-as-a-pin drive-in. A short drive from Six Flags Darien Lake, this spot is popular for ice cream and fast food, such as subs, pizza, burgers and salads. Casual dress. **Parking:** on-site.

DELHI pop. 2,583

——— WHERE TO STAY ———

BUENA VISTA MOTEL
Motel

Phone: 607/746-2135
All Year   1P: $59-$69   2P: $72-$85   XP: $7   F12
Location: Jct SR 10, 0.8 mi e. Located next to the Susquehannah River. 18718 State Hwy 28 13753. Fax: 607/746-6008. **Facility:** 33 one-bedroom standard units, some with whirlpools. 1-2 stories (no elevator), exterior corridors. *Bath:* combo or shower only. **Parking:** on-site, winter plug-ins. **Terms:** [CP] meal plan available, pets ($7 deposit). **Cards:** AX, DC, DS, MC, VI. **Special Amenities:** free continental breakfast.

SOME UNITS
FEE   FEE FEE

DEPEW —See Buffalo p. 252.

DE WITT pop. 24,071 (See map and index starting on p. 577)

——— WHERE TO STAY ———

ECONO LODGE   *Book at aaa.com*
Motel

Phone: (315)446-3300   40
5/1-10/31   1P: $62-$110   2P: $70-$120   XP: $10   F
11/1-2/28   1P: $60-$99   2P: $65-$99   XP: $10   F
3/1-4/30   1P: $57-$99   2P: $65-$99   XP: $10   F
Location: I-481, exit 3W, 1.2 mi w on SR 5 W. Across from Shoppingtown Mall. 3400 Erie Blvd E 13214. Fax: 315/449-3606. **Facility:** 44 one-bedroom standard units, some with whirlpools. 1 story, exterior corridors. **Parking:** on-site. **Terms:** 3 day cancellation notice, [CP] meal plan available, pets ($10 fee).
Amenities: irons, hair dryers. **Cards:** AX, CB, DC, DS, MC, VI. **Special Amenities:** free continental breakfast.

SOME UNITS
FEE

——— WHERE TO DINE ———

DELMONICO'S ITALIAN STEAKHOUSE
Steak & Seafood

Dinner: $9-$15   **Phone:** 315/445-1111   37
Location: Just w of intersection of Thompson Rd and SR 5 (Erie Blvd). 2950 Erie Blvd E 13224. **Hours:** 4 pm-10:30 pm, Fri-11:30 pm, Sat 3 pm-11:30 pm, Sun noon-10 pm. Closed: 11/25, 12/25. **Features:** As the name implies, the restaurant prides itself on its popular 24-ounce Delmonico steak, they like to call the "best deal in town." Sharing menu space are Italian dishes and meat and seafood choices. The friendly spot invites dining or just meeting with friends. Casual dress; cocktails. **Parking:** on-site. **Cards:** AX, DC, DS, MC, VI.

(See map and index starting on p. 577)

SARATOGA STEAKS AND SEAFOOD
Lunch: $6-$11   **Dinner:** $13-$30   **Phone:** 315/445-1976   (35)

American

Location: I-481, exit 2 (Jamesville), just n, w on Nottingham Rd to 1st stop sign, then right. 200 Waring Rd 13224. **Hours:** 11:30 am-2 & 5-10 pm, Sat from 5 pm, Sun 4 pm-9 pm. Closed: 1/1, 12/25. **Reservations:** accepted. **Features:** Sit by a raised brick fireplace or overlook the golf putting green in a glass-enclosed porch to enjoy this popular restaurant. Try the tender scrod with Italian-seasoned breadcrumbs or one of the hand-cut steaks complemented with a warm loaf of braided egg bread. A doting staff will then serve one of their in-house made desserts such as creme brulee or warmed pecan pie. Casual dress; cocktails. **Parking:** on-site. **Cards:** AX, CB, DC, DS, MC, VI.

SCOTCH N' SIRLOIN
Dinner: $13-$40   **Phone:** 315/446-1771   (36)

Steak & Seafood

Location: 5.5 mi e on SR 5; in Shoppingtown Mall. 3687 Erie Blvd E 13214. **Hours:** 5 pm-10:30 pm, Fri & Sat-11:30 pm, Sun 10:30 am-1:30 & 5-9 pm. Closed major holidays; also Sun 7/1-8/31. **Reservations:** suggested. **Features:** Since 1967, this popular eatery has served USDA choice beef, aged and hand-cut on-premises and fresh seafood shipped in daily from Boston. Professional servers will make this a pleasant dining experience. Casual dress; cocktails. **Parking:** on-site. **Cards:** AX, CB, DC, DS, MC, VI.

DIAMOND POINT —*See also ADIRONDACK MOUNTAINS.*

——— WHERE TO STAY ———

CAPRI VILLAGE
Phone: 518/668-4829

Motel

7/3-9/5	1P: $100-$140	2P: $100-$140	XP: $10 F9
5/21-7/2	1P: $65-$125	2P: $65-$125	XP: $10 F9
9/6-10/11	1P: $65-$100	2P: $65-$100	XP: $10 F9

Location: I-87, exit 22, 4.5 mi n on SR 9N. 3926 Lake Shore Dr 12824. Fax: 518/668-4918. **Facility:** 58 units. 20 one- and 38 two-bedroom standard units, some with kitchens. 1-2 stories (no elevator), interior/exterior corridors. **Parking:** on-site. **Terms:** open 5/21-10/11, 3 night minimum stay - seasonal, 56 day cancellation notice-fee imposed, package plans. **Amenities:** voice mail. **Pool(s):** outdoor. **Leisure Activities:** fishing, playground, volleyball, game room. *Fee:* boat dock. **Cards:** MC, VI.

SOME UNITS

CHELKA LODGE
Phone: 518/668-4677

Motel

6/25-9/5 [ECP]	1P: $139-$165	2P: $139-$165	XP: $15
5/14-6/24 & 9/6-10/17	1P: $99-$135	2P: $99-$135	XP: $10

Location: I-87, exit 22, 5.8 mi n on SR 9N. 4204 Lake Shore Dr 12824. Fax: 518/668-3496. **Facility:** 25 units. 23 one- and 2 two-bedroom standard units, some with efficiencies or kitchens. 1-2 stories (no elevator), interior/exterior corridors. **Parking:** on-site. **Terms:** open 5/14-10/17, 3 night minimum stay - weekends 6/25-9/5, 15 day cancellation notice-fee imposed, weekly rates available, no pets allowed (owner's pet on premises). **Leisure Activities:** canoeing, fishing, kayaks, rowboats, ping pong, badminton, basketball, shuffleboard. *Fee:* boat dock. **Cards:** MC, VI. **Special Amenities:** free expanded continental breakfast and free local telephone calls.
(See color ad p 319)

SOME UNITS

GOLDEN SANDS RESORT
Phone: 518/668-2203

Motel

7/15-9/6		2P: $120-$170
6/24-7/14		2P: $105-$145
5/28-6/23 & 9/7-9/13		2P: $75-$110

Location: I-87, exit 22, 3.3 mi n on SR 9N. 3654 Lake Shore Dr 12824 (PO Box 11). **Facility:** 26 units. 18 one- and 8 two-bedroom standard units, some with kitchens. 1-2 stories (no elevator), exterior corridors. *Bath:* shower only. **Parking:** on-site. **Terms:** open 5/28-9/13, 3 night minimum stay - weekends, 30 day cancellation notice-fee imposed. **Amenities:** video library (fee), CD players. **Pool(s):** small heated outdoor. **Leisure Activities:** fishing, playground, basketball. *Fee:* boat dock. **Cards:** MC, VI.

HILLVIEW COTTAGES
Phone: 518/668-5787

Cottage

7/3-9/13	1P: $89-$99	2P: $89-$99	XP: $10 F12
5/15-7/2	1P: $65-$70	2P: $65-$70	XP: $10 F12

Location: I-87, exit 22, 3.3 mi n on SR 9N. 3647 Lake Shore Dr 12824 (PO Box 65). Fax: 518/668-5787. **Facility:** 14 units. 8 one-bedroom standard units, some with efficiencies. 6 cottages ($100-$225). 1 story, exterior corridors. *Bath:* combo or shower only. **Parking:** on-site. **Terms:** open 5/15-9/13, 2 night minimum stay - seasonal, 30 day cancellation notice-fee imposed, weekly rates available, small pets only. **Pool(s):** heated outdoor, wading. **Leisure Activities:** whirlpool, fishing, miniature golf, playground. **Guest Services:** coin laundry. **Cards:** MC, VI.

TREASURE COVE RESORT MOTEL & COTTAGES
Phone: 518/668-5334

Motel

7/1-9/6		2P: $140-$165	XP: $10 F3
5/1-6/30 & 9/7-10/15		2P: $70-$80	XP: $8 F3

Location: I-87, exit 22, 5 mi n on SR 9N. 3940 Lake Shore Dr 12824. Fax: 518/668-9027. **Facility:** Designated smoking area. 50 units. 33 one-bedroom standard units, some with efficiencies. 3 one-bedroom suites ($1495-$1900) with efficiencies. 14 cottages ($1630-$1780). 1-2 stories (no elevator), exterior corridors. *Bath:* combo or shower only. **Parking:** on-site. **Terms:** open 5/1-10/15, 2 night minimum stay - seasonal, 21 day cancellation notice, weekly rates available. **Amenities:** voice mail. **Pool(s):** outdoor, heated outdoor. **Leisure Activities:** rental boats, fishing, rowboats, grills, picnic tables, playground, basketball. *Fee:* boat dock, game room.

SOME UNITS

------ WHERE TO DINE ------

MCGOWANS

American

Lunch: $4-$8   **Dinner:** $9-$10   **Phone:** 518/668-4800

Location: Center. 3712 Lakeshore Dr 12845. **Hours:** 7 am-2 pm; Wed-Sun also 4:30 pm-9 pm 5/1-10/31. Closed: 3/27, 12/25. **Features:** The casual restaurant is a local favorite for generously portioned breakfasts, from simple eggs with toast to the McGowan special breakfast sandwich, as well as hearty brunches and hot and cold lunch sandwiches. Service is quiet and attentive. Casual dress. **Parking:** on-site. **Cards:** AX, DS, MC, VI.

⊠

DOVER PLAINS pop. 1,996

------ WHERE TO STAY ------

OLD DROVERS INN   *Book at aaa.com*

Historic
Country Inn

All Year   1P: $125-$375   2P: $150-$475   XP: $80   **Phone:** (845)832-9311

Location: 3 mi s of SR 22 on Old Rt 22 (CR 6). 196 E Duncan Hill Rd 12522 (PO Box 100). Fax: 845/832-6356. **Facility:** The Old Drovers Inn was established in 1750, and the rooms are pleasantly appointed with bright fabrics and plush bedding. Designated smoking area. 4 one-bedroom standard units. 2 stories (no elevator), interior corridors. *Bath:* combo or tub only. **Parking:** on-site. **Terms:** age restrictions may apply, 14 day cancellation notice-fee imposed, [BP], [CP] & [MAP] meal plans available, pets ($25 extra charge). **Dining:** Old Drovers Inn, see separate listing. **Guest Services:** TV in common area. **Business Services:** fax. **Cards:** AX, DC, MC, VI.

🈺 🍴 ⊠ 🅿 🖭
FEE

------ WHERE TO DINE ------

OLD DROVERS INN   Country Inn

American

Lunch: $12-$33   **Dinner:** $14-$38   **Phone:** 845/832-9311

Location: 3 mi s of SR 22 on Old Rt 22 (CR 6); in Old Drovers Inn. 196 E Duncan Hill Rd 12522. **Hours:** 5:30 pm-9 pm, Thurs & Fri noon-3 & 5:30-10 pm, Sat noon-10 pm, Sun noon-9 pm. Closed: 12/25; also Wed & 3 weeks in Jan. **Reservations:** suggested. **Features:** The tavern-turned-restaurant reflects an 1800s ambience, much as the state's early herd drovers would have experienced. With seasonally created menus, the contemporary cuisine centers on meats, fowl and seafood. Desserts range from decadent cakes and ice creams to the homey sticky toffee pudding. Dressy casual; cocktails. **Parking:** on-site. **Cards:** AX, CB, DC, MC, VI.

⊠

DUNKIRK pop. 13,131

------ WHERE TO STAY ------

BEST WESTERN DUNKIRK/FREDONIA   *Book at aaa.com*

Small-scale Hotel

5/1-9/15 [ECP]	1P: $89-$139	2P: $89-$139	XP: $10	F16
3/16-4/30 [ECP]	1P: $69-$129	2P: $69-$129	XP: $10	F16
9/16-12/31 [ECP]	1P: $69-$110	2P: $69-$110	XP: $10	F16
1/1-3/15 [ECP]	1P: $69-$89	2P: $69-$89	XP: $10	F16

Phone: (716)366-7100

Location: I-90, exit 59, just w. 3912 Vineyard Dr 14048. Fax: 716/366-1606. **Facility:** 61 one-bedroom standard units, some with whirlpools. 2 stories (no elevator), interior corridors. *Bath:* combo or shower only. **Parking:** on-site. **Terms:** pets ($5-$10 extra charge). **Amenities:** irons, hair dryers. **Pool(s):** small heated indoor. **Leisure Activities:** whirlpool, limited exercise equipment. **Cards:** AX, CB, DC, DS, MC, VI. **Special Amenities:** free expanded continental breakfast and free local telephone calls.

SOME UNITS

🆂🅳 🛏 🍴 🐾 🛟 📷 🅳🅰🆃🅰/PORT 🖭 / ⊠ 🆅🅲🆁 🔌 🖥 /
FEE

COMFORT INN   *Book at aaa.com*

Small-scale Hotel

5/1-9/15 [ECP]	1P: $69-$139	2P: $69-$139	XP: $10	F16
3/16-4/30 [ECP]	1P: $69-$129	2P: $69-$129	XP: $10	F16
9/16-12/31 [ECP]	1P: $69-$110	2P: $69-$110	XP: $10	F16
1/1-3/15 [ECP]	1P: $59-$89	2P: $59-$89	XP: $10	F16

Phone: (716)672-4450

Location: I-90, exit 59, just w of jct SR 60. 3925 Vineyard Dr 14048. Fax: 716/672-4446. **Facility:** 61 one-bedroom standard units, some with whirlpools. 2 stories (no elevator), interior corridors. *Bath:* combo or shower only. **Parking:** on-site, winter plug-ins. **Terms:** pets ($5-$10 extra charge). **Amenities:** irons, hair dryers. **Guest Services:** valet laundry. **Cards:** AX, CB, DC, DS, MC, VI. **Special Amenities:** free expanded continental breakfast and free local telephone calls.

SOME UNITS

🆂🅳 🛏 🍴 🐾 🛟 🅳🅰🆃🅰/PORT 🖭 / ⊠ 🆅🅲🆁 🔌 🖥 /
FEE

DAYS INN DUNKIRK-FREDONIA   *Book at aaa.com*

Small-scale Hotel

5/1-9/15 [ECP]	1P: $75-$115	2P: $85-$125	XP: $10	F17
9/16-12/31 [ECP]	1P: $53-$95	2P: $63-$105	XP: $10	F17
3/16-4/30 [ECP]	1P: $54-$84	2P: $64-$94	XP: $10	F17
1/1-3/15 [ECP]	1P: $50-$80	2P: $60-$90	XP: $10	F17

Phone: (716)673-1351

Location: I-90, exit 59, just s on SR 60. 10455 Bennett Rd 14063 (10455 Bennett Rd, FREDONIA). Fax: 716/672-6909. **Facility:** 134 one-bedroom standard units, some with whirlpools. 2 stories, interior/exterior corridors. **Parking:** on-site. **Terms:** pets (in designated units). **Amenities:** high-speed Internet (fee), hair dryers. *Some:* irons. **Dining:** 5 pm-10 pm; closed Sun. **Pool(s):** small heated indoor. **Leisure Activities:** whirlpool, grills, picnic tables. **Guest Services:** valet and coin laundry. **Business Services:** meeting rooms. **Cards:** AX, DC, DS, MC, VI. **Special Amenities:** free expanded continental breakfast and free newspaper.

SOME UNITS

🆂🅳 🛏 🍴 🍸 🛟 📷 🅳🅰🆃🅰/PORT 🖭 / ⊠ 🔌 🖥 /
FEE FEE

RAMADA INN & CONFERENCE CENTER   *Book at aaa.com*   Phone: (716)366-8350

(AAA) [SAVE]

5/1-9/6	1P: $109-$199	2P: $109-$199	XP: $10 F18
9/7-4/30	1P: $99-$169	2P: $99-$169	XP: $10 F18

Location: Jct SR 60, 0.3 mi w on SR 5. 30 Lake Shore Dr E 14048. Fax: 716/366-8899. **Facility:** 132 one-bedroom standard units, some with whirlpools. 4 stories, interior corridors. **Parking:** on-site. **Terms:** cancellation fee imposed, [AP] meal plan available, small pets only ($10 fee, $10 extra charge). **Amenities:** voice mail, irons, hair dryers. **Dining:** 6:30 am-10 pm, cocktails. **Pool(s):** heated outdoor, heated indoor/outdoor. **Leisure Activities:** saunas, whirlpool. **Guest Services:** valet laundry. **Business Services:** conference facilities. **Cards:** AX, DC, DS, MC, VI. *(See color ad p 8)*

Small-scale Hotel

SOME UNITS

[icons] FEE   [icons] FEE

——— **WHERE TO DINE** ———

DEMETRI'S ON THE LAKE   **Lunch:** $3-$7   **Dinner:** $8-$10   Phone: 716/366-4187

Greek

Location: Jct SR 60, 0.4 mi w on SR 5. 6-8 Lake Shore Dr W 14048. **Hours:** 6 am-11 pm. **Closed:** 12/25. **Features:** In business at the lakeside location for 13 years, the busy restaurant serves tasty Greek and American fare. The seasonal patio and upstairs lounge and restaurant allow for nice views of Lake Erie. Casual dress; cocktails. **Parking:** on-site. **Cards:** AX, MC, VI.

[icons]

EAGLE BAY

——— **WHERE TO DINE** ———

BIG MOOSE INN   **Dinner:** $15-$42   Phone: 315/357-2042

American

Location: Located on Big Moose Lake. 1510 Big Moose Rd 13331. **Hours:** 5 pm-9 pm, Fri & Sat-9:30 pm, Sun 2 pm-9 pm. **Closed:** 11/1-12/26 (except 1st 2 weekends in Nov). **Reservations:** suggested. **Features:** The casual Adirondack-style inn, built in the early 1900s and resting on the edge of Big Moose Lake, is open seasonally and features seafood and prime beef. Nightly specials, an extensive wine list and casual, friendly service are trademarks. The inn is nestled in the Adirondacks of upstate New York. Guests can request patio seating overlooking the lake. Casual dress; cocktails. **Parking:** on-site. **Cards:** AX, MC, VI.

[icons]

EAST AMHERST —*See Buffalo p. 252.*

EAST AURORA —*See Buffalo p. 252.*

EAST CHATHAM

——— **WHERE TO STAY** ———

THE INN AT SILVER MAPLE FARM   Phone: 518/781-3600

11/1-4/30 [BP]	1P: $105-$290	2P: $105-$290	XP: $20
5/1-10/31 [BP]	1P: $90-$250	2P: $90-$250	XP: $20

Bed & Breakfast

Location: Jct SR 22 and 295, 3.2 mi w on SR 295. 1871 CR 295 12060. Fax: 518/781-3883. **Facility:** A large fireplace adds simple charm to the common space of this former barn, which offers comfortable and cozy country-style rooms. Smoke free premises. 11 units. 10 one-bedroom standard units. 1 one-bedroom suite ($230-$290). 1-2 stories (no elevator), interior/exterior corridors. *Bath:* combo or shower only. **Parking:** on-site. **Terms:** 2-4 night minimum stay - seasonal, age restrictions may apply, 14 day cancellation notice-fee imposed. **Amenities:** high-speed Internet (fee), irons, hair dryers. **Leisure Activities:** hiking trails. **Business Services:** meeting rooms. **Cards:** AX, DS, MC, VI.

SOME UNITS

[icons]

EAST DURHAM

——— **WHERE TO STAY** ———

THE CARRIAGE HOUSE BED AND BREAKFAST   Phone: 518/634-2284

(AAA) [SAVE]

5/1-11/15 [BP]	1P: $91-$106	2P: $91-$106	XP: $20 F3

Bed & Breakfast

Location: 1.5 mi w. 2946 Rt 145 12423 (Box 12A, Rt 145). Fax: 518/634-2284. **Facility:** Designated smoking area. 5 one-bedroom standard units. 2 stories (no elevator), interior corridors. *Bath:* combo or shower only. **Parking:** on-site. **Terms:** open 5/1-11/15, 7 day cancellation notice-fee imposed, package plans. **Leisure Activities:** swimming hole, hiking trails. **Guest Services:** gift shop. **Cards:** AX, CB, DC, DS, MC, VI. **Special Amenities:** free full breakfast.

[icons]

GAVIN'S GOLDEN HILL RESORT   Phone: 518/634-2582

5/1-10/31	1P: $150-$160	2P: $200-$220	

Small-scale Hotel

Location: Jct SR 145 and Golden Hill Rd, 0.5 mi w. 118 Golden Hill Rd 12423 (PO Box 6). Fax: 518/634-2531. **Facility:** 61 units. 60 one-bedroom standard units. 1 vacation home. 2-3 stories (no elevator), exterior corridors. *Bath:* combo or shower only. **Parking:** on-site. **Terms:** open 5/1-10/31, 14 day cancellation notice, weekly rates available. **Pool(s):** outdoor. **Leisure Activities:** recreation programs, horseshoes, shuffleboard, volleyball. **Guest Services:** area transportation. **Cards:** MC, VI.

SOME UNITS

[icons]

EAST GREENBUSH pop. 4,085   (See map and index starting on p. 215)

──── WHERE TO STAY ────

ECONO LODGE   *Book at aaa.com*   Phone: (518)472-1360   **39**
(AAA) (SAVE)   All Year   1P: $59-$129   2P: $69-$149   XP: $8   F12
▼▼▼   **Location:** I-787, exit 3, 1.5 mi on US 9 S and 20 E; I-90, exit 9, 2 mi on US 4 S, 2.5 mi n on US 9 N and 20 W. 110 Columbia Tpke 12144. Fax: 518/427-2924. **Facility:** 54 one-bedroom standard units, some with whirlpools. 54
Motel   one-bedroom suites ($89-$169). 1-2 stories (no elevator), interior/exterior corridors. *Bath:* combo or shower only. **Parking:** on-site, winter plug-ins. **Terms:** [ECP] meal plan available. **Amenities:** high-speed Internet, voice mail, hair dryers. *Some:* irons. **Pool(s):** outdoor. **Guest Services:** coin laundry. **Business Services:** fax (fee). **Cards:** AX, CB, DC, DS, JC, MC, VI. **Special Amenities:** free continental breakfast and free local telephone calls.

SOME UNITS
(S🄳) (▢🛏✦) (🌊) (🚭) (DATA PORT) (🖥) (🍽) / (✕) (VCR) /

FAIRFIELD INN BY MARRIOTT-ALBANY/EAST GREENBUSH   *Book at aaa.com*   Phone: (518)477-7984   **40**
(AAA) (SAVE)   All Year [ECP]   1P: $79-$139   2P: $79-$139   XP: $10   F17
▼▼▼▼   **Location:** I-90, exit 9, just s on SR 45 (Troy Rd). 124 Troy Rd 12061. Fax: 518/477-2382. **Facility:** 105 one-bedroom standard units. 4 stories, interior corridors. **Parking:** on-site. **Amenities:** video games, voice mail, irons, hair dryers. *Fee:* video library, high-speed Internet. **Pool(s):** outdoor. **Guest Services:** coin laundry.
Small-scale Hotel   **Cards:** AX, CB, DC, DS, JC, MC, VI. **Special Amenities:** free expanded continental breakfast and free local telephone calls.

SOME UNITS
(S🄳) (▢🛏✦) (🌊) (🚭✦) (🚭) (DATA PORT) / (✕) (🖥) (🍽) /

HOLIDAY INN EXPRESS HOTEL & SUITES   *Book at aaa.com*   Phone: 518/286-1011   **38**
(AAA) (SAVE)   6/1-10/31 [ECP]   1P: $116-$125   XP: $10   F21
▼▼▼▼   5/1-5/31 & 11/1-4/30 [ECP]   1P: $99-$116   XP: $10   F21
Location: I-90, exit 9, just n. 8 Empire Dr 12061 (8 Empire Dr, RENSSELAER, 12144). Fax: 518/286-3952.
Small-scale Hotel   **Facility:** 82 one-bedroom standard units, some with whirlpools. 3 stories, interior corridors. *Bath:* combo or shower only. **Parking:** on-site. **Terms:** 21 day cancellation notice. **Amenities:** video library (fee), video games, high-speed Internet, dual phone lines, voice mail, irons, hair dryers. **Pool(s):** small heated indoor.
Leisure Activities: whirlpool, exercise room. **Guest Services:** sundries, valet laundry. **Business Services:** meeting rooms, business center. **Cards:** AX, DC, DS, MC, VI. **Special Amenities:** free expanded continental breakfast and free newspaper.

SOME UNITS
(S🄳) (▢🛏✦) (♿M) (⬆) (🌊) (🚭) (DATA PORT) (🖥) / (✕) (🖥) (🍽) /

──── The following lodging was either not evaluated or did not meet AAA rating requirements but is listed for your information only. ────

COMFORT INN & SUITES-ALBANY/EAST GREENBUSH   Phone: 518/479-3217
(fyi)   All Year   1P: $79-$350   2P: $79-$350   XP: $10   F19
Too new to rate, opening scheduled for February 2004. **Location:** I-90, exit 10 (Schodack-Miller Rd). 99 Miller Rd 12033. Fax: 518/479-3167. **Amenities:** 89 units, coffeemakers, microwaves, refrigerators, pool. **Terms:** office hours noon-noon. **Cards:** AX, DC, DS, MC, VI.

──── WHERE TO DINE ────

BENNIGAN'S GRILL & TAVERN   **Lunch:** $5-$8   **Dinner:** $6-$17   Phone: 518/283-8397   **30**
▼▼▼   **Location:** I-90, exit 9, just n. 4 Middle Mannix Rd 12144. **Hours:** 11 am-midnight, Fri & Sat-1 am. Closed: 11/25, 12/25. **Features:** The restaurant offers casual dining in a pub-like atmosphere with dark woods, brass and
American   etched glass, including lots of American, Mexican and light food favorites; convenient late-night dining is available. Casual dress; cocktails. **Parking:** on-site. **Cards:** AX, DC, DS, MC, VI.   (✕)

EAST HAMPTON pop. 1,334

──── WHERE TO STAY ────

DUTCH MOTEL & COTTAGES   Phone: 631/324-4550
▼▼▼   7/1-9/5   1P: $155-$285   2P: $155-$285   XP: $10   F12
5/1-6/30 & 9/6-10/31   1P: $95-$215   2P: $95-$215   XP: $10   F12
11/1-4/30   1P: $70-$125   2P: $70-$125   XP: $10   F12
Motel   **Location:** 1.3 mi e on SR 27 E (Montauk Hwy). Located in a commercial area. 488 Montauk Hwy 11937.
Fax: 631/324-2619. **Facility:** 28 units. 17 one-bedroom standard units, some with efficiencies (no utensils) and/or whirlpools. 10 one- and 1 two-bedroom suites with efficiencies (no utensils), some with whirlpools. 2 stories (no elevator), exterior corridors. **Parking:** on-site. **Terms:** 2-3 night minimum stay - weekends in summer, 60 day cancellation notice-fee imposed, small pets only ($10 extra charge). **Amenities:** voice mail. **Cards:** AX, DC, DS, JC, MC, VI.

(🛏🐾) (▢🛏✦) (DATA PORT) (🖥)
FEE

EAST HAMPTON VILLAGE BED & BREAKFAST   Phone: 731/324-1858
▼▼▼   7/1-8/31 [ECP]   1P: $175-$325   2P: $175-$325   XP: $80
9/1-11/30 [ECP]   1P: $145-$325   2P: $145-$325   XP: $50
5/1-6/30 [ECP]   1P: $155-$245   2P: $155-$245   XP: $50
Bed & Breakfast   4/1-4/30 [ECP]   1P: $155-$185   2P: $155-$185   XP: $40
Location: Jct SR 114, 0.5 mi e on SR 27, then 0.6 mi n. 172 Newtown Ln 11937. Fax: 631/329-0762. **Facility:** Designated smoking area. 4 one-bedroom standard units. 2 stories (no elevator), interior corridors. *Bath:* combo or shower only. **Parking:** on-site. **Terms:** open 5/1-11/30 & 4/1-4/30, off-site registration, 2-4 night minimum stay - weekends, 30 day cancellation notice-fee imposed, weekly rates available. **Amenities:** hair dryers. **Cards:** AX, DC, MC, VI.

(ASK) (✕) (🅆) (Ⓩ)

---------- **WHERE TO DINE** ----------

THE PALM IN HUNTTING INN   Country Inn   **Dinner:** $16-$36   **Phone:** 631/324-0411
▼▼▼   **Location:** Center; in Huntting Inn. 94 Main St 11937. **Hours:** 5 pm-10 pm, Fri & Sat-11 pm; hours may vary in
            winter. Closed: 11/25, 12/25. **Reservations:** accepted. **Features:** On the grounds of Huntting Inn, the Early
Steak & Seafood   American landmark is a respected steakhouse, known for succulent porterhouse steaks and huge lobster.
            Dark wood accents decorate the rustic though commanding dining room. Servers in white aprons are
prompt and attentive. Casual dress; cocktails. **Parking:** valet. **Cards:** AX, DC, DS, MC, VI.

EAST MEADOW pop. 37,461

---------- **WHERE TO STAY** ----------

COLISEUM MOTOR INN   **Phone:** (516)794-2100
AAA SAVE   All Year   1P: $95   2P: $110   XP: $10   F12
▼▼ ▼▼   **Location:** Meadowbrook Pkwy, exit M5, 0.3 mi e. Located in a commercial area. 1650 Hempstead Tpke 11554.
            Fax: 516/794-2278. **Facility:** 110 one-bedroom standard units. 2 stories (no elevator), interior/exterior corri-
Motel   dors. *Bath:* combo or shower only. **Parking:** on-site. **Terms:** package plans. **Pool(s):** outdoor. **Business
            Services:** meeting rooms. **Cards:** AX, CB, DC, DS, MC, VI. *(See color ad p 344)*

SOME UNITS

---------- **WHERE TO DINE** ----------

ARTHUR AVE RESTAURANT   **Lunch:** $7-$10   **Dinner:** $6-$16   **Phone:** 516/520-9447
▼▼ ▼▼   **Location:** Meadowbrook Pkwy, exit M5, 1.5 mi e. 2367 Hempstead Tpke 11554. **Hours:** 11:45 am-10 pm, Fri &
            Sat-11 pm, Sun 2 pm-9 pm. Closed: 7/4, 11/25, 12/25. **Reservations:** suggested. **Features:** The
Italian   restaurant is named for the "Little Italy" section of the Bronx, which is depicted by a mural. Relax in the
            comfortable, laid-back setting and enjoy home-style Italian fare, including pasta, traditional and gourmet
pizza, and even hero sandwiches. Outdoor patio dining is also available. Casual dress; cocktails. **Parking:** on-site. **Cards:** AX,
CB, DC, DS, MC, VI.

EAST NORWICH pop. 2,675

---------- **WHERE TO STAY** ----------

EAST NORWICH INN   *Book at aaa.com*   **Phone:** (516)922-1500
AAA SAVE   All Year [ECP]   1P: $122   2P: $137   XP: $15   F12
▼▼ ▼▼   **Location:** SR 25A (N Hempstead Tpke), jct SR 106 (Oyster Bay Rd), just nw. Located in a commercial area. 6321
            Northern Blvd 11732. Fax: 516/922-1089. **Facility:** 72 units. 66 one-bedroom standard units, some with effi-
Small-scale Hotel   ciencies. 5 one-bedroom suites ($260). 1 vacation home. 2 stories (no elevator), interior corridors. *Bath:*
            combo or shower only. **Parking:** on-site. **Amenities:** voice mail, irons, hair dryers. **Pool(s):** small outdoor.
rooms. **Leisure Activities:** sauna, exercise room. **Guest Services:** valet laundry. **Business Services:** meeting
rooms. **Cards:** AX, CB, DC, DS, MC, VI. **Special Amenities:** free expanded continental breakfast and free newspaper.

SOME UNITS
FEE FEE

EAST QUOGUE pop. 4,265

---------- **WHERE TO STAY** ----------

CAROLE'S BED & BREAKFAST   **Phone:** (631)653-5152
▼▼ ▼▼   5/1-10/1 [BP]   1P: $125-$180   2P: $125-$180   XP: $40   F8
            10/2-4/30 [BP]   1P: $100-$150   2P: $100-$150
Bed & Breakfast   **Location:** Just s of St. Rosalie's Church; center. Located in a residential area. 7 Walnut Ave 11942 (PO Box 1646).
            Facility: Smoke free premises. 5 units. 4 one-bedroom standard units. 1 one-bedroom suite. 2 stories (no
elevator), interior corridors. *Bath:* combo or shower only. **Parking:** on-site. **Terms:** 2 night minimum stay - seasonal weekends,
7 day cancellation notice. **Pool(s):** outdoor. **Cards:** AX, MC, VI.

EAST SYRACUSE pop. 3,178   (See map and index starting on p. 577)—See also SYRACUSE.

---------- **WHERE TO STAY** ----------

CANDLEWOOD SUITES SYRACUSE   *Book at aaa.com*   **Phone:** (315)432-1684   16
▼▼▼▼   5/1-11/30   1P: $89
            12/1-4/30   1P: $79
Small-scale Hotel   **Location:** I-90, exit 35 (Carrier Cir) to SR 298 E to Old Collamer Rd, just n. 6550 Baptist Way 13057.
            Fax: 315/433-9959. **Facility:** 92 units. 74 one-bedroom standard units with efficiencies. 12 one- and 6 two-
bedroom suites with efficiencies. 3 stories, interior corridors. *Bath:* combo or shower only. **Parking:** on-site, winter plug-ins.
Terms: office hours 7 am-11 pm, cancellation fee imposed. **Amenities:** video library, CD players, dual phone lines, voice mail,
irons, hair dryers. **Leisure Activities:** exercise room. **Guest Services:** sundries. **Business Services:** fax. **Cards:** AX, DC, DS,
MC, VI.

SOME UNITS

(See map and index starting on p. 577)

COMFORT INN-CARRIER CIRCLE *Book at aaa.com*
Phone: (315)437-0222 25

All Year [ECP]   1P: $85-$109

Location: I-90, exit 35 (Carrier Cir). 6491 Thompson Rd 13206. Fax: 315/437-4510. Facility: 109 units. 107 one-bedroom standard units, some with whirlpools. 2 one-bedroom suites with whirlpools. 4 stories, interior/exterior corridors. Parking: on-site. Amenities: irons, hair dryers. Leisure Activities: exercise room.

Small-scale Hotel   Guest Services: valet laundry. Business Services: meeting rooms. Cards: AX, DC, DS, JC, MC, VI. Special Amenities: free expanded continental breakfast and free local telephone calls.

SOME UNITS

COURTYARD BY MARRIOTT *Book at aaa.com*
Phone: (315)432-0300 14

All Year   1P: $79-$159   2P: $79-$159

Location: I-90, exit 35 (Carrier Cir) to SR 298 E, just e to Old Collamer Rd, then 0.5 mi n. 6415 Yorktown Cir 13057.

Small-scale Hotel   Fax: 315/432-9950. Facility: 149 units. 137 one-bedroom standard units. 12 one-bedroom suites. 3 stories, interior corridors. Bath: combo or shower only. Parking: on-site. Terms: [BP] meal plan available. Amenities: voice mail, irons, hair dryers. Pool(s): small heated indoor. Leisure Activities: whirlpool, exercise room. Guest Services: valet and coin laundry. Business Services: meeting rooms, PC, fax (fee). Cards: AX, CB, DC, DS, JC, MC, VI.

SOME UNITS

CRESTHILL SUITES *Book at aaa.com*
Phone: (315)432-5595 24

1/2-4/30   1P: $129-$259   2P: $129-$259
5/1-1/1   1P: $119-$249   2P: $119-$249

Location: I-90, exit 35 (Carrier Cir) to SR 298 E, just s. 6410 New Venture Gear Dr 13057. Fax: 315/432-5686.

Small-scale Hotel   Facility: 86 units. 14 one-bedroom standard units with kitchens. 60 one- and 12 two-bedroom suites with kitchens. 2 stories, interior corridors. Bath: combo or shower only. Parking: on-site. Terms: [BP] meal plan available, pets ($150 fee). Amenities: video library, high-speed Internet, dual phone lines, voice mail, irons, hair dryers. Pool(s): heated outdoor. Leisure Activities: exercise room. Guest Services: sundries, complimentary evening beverages: Mon-Thurs, area transportation. Business Services: business center. Cards: AX, CB, DC, DS, MC, VI.

SOME UNITS

FEE

EAST SYRACUSE SUPER 8 *Book at aaa.com*
Phone: (315)432-5612 18

All Year [CP]   1P: $45-$75   2P: $50-$80   XP: $5   F13

Location: I-90, exit 35 (Carrier Cir), just e on SR 298, then just n. 6620 Old Collamer Rd 13057. Fax: 315/432-5620.

Small-scale Hotel   Facility: 53 one-bedroom standard units. 2 stories (no elevator), interior corridors. Bath: combo or shower only. Parking: on-site. Terms: pets ($10 fee). Amenities: irons, hair dryers. Guest Services: valet and coin laundry. Cards: AX, DC, DS, MC, VI.

SOME UNITS

FEE

EMBASSY SUITES HOTEL *Book at aaa.com*
Phone: (315)446-3200 19

5/1-11/20 & 3/4-4/30 [BP]   1P: $129-$209   2P: $149-$229   XP: $20   F18
11/21-3/3 [BP]   1P: $109-$189   2P: $129-$209   XP: $20   F18

Large-scale Hotel   Location: I-90, exit 35 (Carrier Cir) to SR 298 E to College Pl. 6646 Old Collamer Rd 13057. Fax: 315/437-3302. Facility: 215 units. 213 one- and 2 two-bedroom suites ($300-$700). 5 stories, interior corridors. Parking: on-site. Terms: check-in 4 pm, cancellation fee imposed. Amenities: video library (fee), video games, voice mail, irons, hair dryers. Pool(s): heated indoor. Leisure Activities: sauna, whirlpool, exercise room. Fee: game room. Guest Services: gift shop, complimentary evening beverages, valet and coin laundry, area transportation. Business Services: conference facilities, fax. Cards: AX, DC, DS, MC, VI. (See ad p 581)

SOME UNITS

FEE

FAIRFIELD INN SYRACUSE *Book at aaa.com*
Phone: (315)432-9333 23

All Year   1P: $65-$85   2P: $65-$85

Location: I-90, exit 35 (Carrier Cir) to SR 298 E. 6611 Old Collamer Rd 13057. Fax: 315/432-9197. Facility: 135 one-bedroom standard units. 3 stories, interior/exterior corridors. Parking: on-site. Amenities: voice mail, irons, hair dryers. Pool(s): heated outdoor. Guest Services: valet laundry. Cards: AX, DC, DS, MC, VI.

Small-scale Hotel   Special Amenities: free expanded continental breakfast and free newspaper.

SOME UNITS

HAMPTON INN-CARRIER CIRCLE *Book at aaa.com*
Phone: (315)463-6443 22

5/1-10/28 [ECP]   1P: $89-$135   2P: $94-$135
10/29-4/30 [ECP]   1P: $84-$99   2P: $89-$99

Location: I-90, exit 35 (Carrier Cir), just e on SR 298, just n. 6605 Old Collamer Rd 13057. Fax: 315/432-1080. Facility: 115 one-bedroom standard units. 4 stories, interior corridors. Bath: combo or shower only. Parking: on-site. Amenities: video library (fee), video games, dual phone lines, voice mail, irons, hair dryers. Guest Services: valet and coin laundry. Business Services: meeting rooms. Cards: AX, CB, DC, DS, JC, MC, VI.

Small-scale Hotel

Special Amenities: free expanded continental breakfast and free local telephone calls.

SOME UNITS

FEE   FEE

HILTON GARDEN INN-SYRACUSE *Book at aaa.com*
Phone: (315)431-4800 12

All Year   1P: $62-$161

Location: I-90, exit 35 (Carrier Cir) to SR 298 E, 0.7 mi to New Venture Gear Dr, just e into Pioneer Business Park. 6004 Fair Lakes Rd 13057. Fax: 315/431-4999. Facility: 100 units. 94 one-bedroom standard units, some with whirlpools. 6 one-bedroom suites. 3 stories, interior corridors. Bath: combo or shower only. Parking: on-site.

Small-scale Hotel   Terms: [AP] meal plan available. Amenities: video library (fee), video games, high-speed Internet, dual phone lines, voice mail, irons, hair dryers. Pool(s): small heated indoor. Leisure Activities: whirlpool, exercise room. Guest Services: sundries, valet and coin laundry. Business Services: meeting rooms, business center. Cards: AX, CB, DC, DS, JC, MC, VI. Special Amenities: free local telephone calls and free newspaper.

SOME UNITS

(See map and index starting on p. 577)

HOLIDAY INN EAST-CARRIER CIRCLE   Book at aaa.com
Phone: (315)437-2761   **17**

▼▼▼▼
5/1-10/31 & 3/1-4/30   1P: $89-$109   2P: $89-$109
11/1-2/28   1P: $79-$99   2P: $79-$99
Small-scale Hotel   **Location:** I-90, exit 35 (Carrier Cir) to SR 298 E to Collamer Rd, just n. 6555 Old Collamer Rd 13057. Fax: 315/463-0028. **Facility:** 203 one-bedroom standard units. 2-3 stories (no elevator), interior/exterior corridors. **Parking:** on-site, winter plug-ins. **Terms:** cancellation fee imposed, [AP] meal plan available, small pets only ($25 fee). **Amenities:** video library (fee), video games, voice mail, irons, hair dryers. **Pool(s):** heated indoor. **Leisure Activities:** whirlpool, exercise room. **Fee:** game room. **Guest Services:** valet and coin laundry. **Business Services:** conference facilities, fax. **Cards:** AX, CB, DC, DS, JC, MC, VI.

SOME UNITS
(ASK) (SD) 🐾 🍽 🍸 📶 ➿ ⊠ 📽 (DATA PORT) 💻 / ⊠ 🛄 /
FEE   FEE FEE

MICROTEL INN SYRACUSE   Book at aaa.com
Phone: 315/437-3500   **20**

(AAA) (SAVE)   All Year   1P: $40-$80   2P: $43-$83
▼▼▼▼   **Location:** I-90, exit 35 (Carrier Cir). 6608 Old Collamer Rd 13057. Fax: 315/437-0111. **Facility:** 99 one-bedroom standard units. 2 stories (no elevator), interior corridors. Bath: combo or shower only. **Parking:** on-site, winter plug-ins. **Terms:** small pets only ($5 fee). **Amenities:** video games. **Fee:** video library, safes.
Small-scale Hotel   **Guest Services:** valet laundry. **Cards:** AX, CB, DC, DS, MC, VI. **Special Amenities:** free continental breakfast and free local telephone calls.

SOME UNITS
(SD) 🐾 🍽 👤M 📶 📽 (DATA PORT) / ⊠ /
FEE

RESIDENCE INN BY MARRIOTT   Book at aaa.com
Phone: 315/432-4488   **15**

▼▼▼▼   Property failed to provide current rates
Location: I-90, exit 35 (Carrier Cir) to SR 298 E, just e to Old Collamer Rd, 0.5 mi n. 6420 Yorktown Cir 13057.
Small-scale Hotel   Fax: 315/432-1042. **Facility:** 102 units. 78 one-bedroom standard units with kitchens. 24 two-bedroom units with kitchens. 2 stories (no elevator), exterior corridors. Bath: combo or shower only. **Parking:** on-site. **Terms:** pets ($50 fee). **Amenities:** video library (fee), voice mail, irons, hair dryers. **Pool(s):** small heated outdoor. **Leisure Activities:** whirlpool, exercise room, sports court. **Guest Services:** complimentary evening beverages: Mon-Thurs, valet and coin laundry. **Business Services:** meeting rooms.

SOME UNITS
🐾 🍽 👤M 📶 📶 ➿ ⊠ 📽 (DATA PORT) 🛄 🛄 💻 / ⊠ /
FEE

WYNDHAM SYRACUSE   Book at aaa.com
Phone: (315)432-0200   **21**

(AAA) (SAVE)   8/19-4/30   1P: $145-$155   2P: $155-$165   XP: $10   F17
5/1-8/18   1P: $139-$149   2P: $149-$159   XP: $10   F17
▼▼▼▼   **Location:** I-90, exit 35 (Carrier Cir), just e. 6301 Rt 298 13057. Fax: 315/433-1210. **Facility:** 250 units. 248 one-bedroom standard units. 2 one-bedroom suites ($179-$300). 4-7 stories, interior corridors. **Parking:** on-site.
Large-scale Hotel   **Terms:** cancellation fee imposed. **Amenities:** video games, dual phone lines, voice mail, irons, hair dryers. **Fee:** video library, high-speed Internet. Some: CD players. **Dining:** 6:30 am-10 pm, cocktails. **Pool(s):** heated outdoor, heated indoor. **Leisure Activities:** sauna, whirlpool, exercise room. **Guest Services:** valet and coin laundry. **Business Services:** conference facilities, PC. **Cards:** AX, CB, DC, DS, JC, MC, VI. Not Affiliated with the Wyndham Hotel in Manhattan.

SOME UNITS
(SD) 🍽 🍽 🍸 📶 ➿ ⊠ 📽 (DATA PORT) 💻 / ⊠ 🛄 /
FEE

------- WHERE TO DINE -------

JUSTIN'S GRILL   Lunch: $7-$11   Dinner: $16-$29
Phone: 315/437-1461   **20**

▼▼▼▼   **Location:** I-90, exit 35 (Carrier Cir), to SR 298 E, just n. 6400 Yorktown Cir 13057. **Hours:** 11:30 am-2:30 & 5:30-9:30 pm, Fri & Sat-10:30 pm. Closed major holidays; also Sun. **Reservations:** suggested.
Steak & Seafood   **Features:** The restaurant, which builds its menu around USDA prime meats, sustains a stylish, casual elegance. Dressy casual; cocktails. **Parking:** on-site. **Cards:** AX, DC, DS, MC, VI.

🍸 ⊠

EAST WINDHAM

------- WHERE TO DINE -------

FALVEY'S ON THE MOUNTAIN   Lunch: $3-$10   Dinner: $12-$22
Phone: 518/622-8744

(AAA)   **Location:** On SR 23. SR 23 12405. **Hours:** 11 am-3 & 4-10 pm, Fri & Sat-11 pm; hours may vary off season. Closed: 12/25. **Reservations:** accepted. **Features:** This restaurant features true all-American fare,
▼▼ ▼▼   including a salad bar and homemade desserts, in a secluded mountaintop location overlooking a valley. Casual dress; cocktails. **Parking:** on-site. **Cards:** AX, DS, MC, VI.
Steak & Seafood

🍸 ⊠

ELIZABETHTOWN pop. 1,315—See also ADIRONDACK MOUNTAINS.

------- WHERE TO STAY -------

PARK MOTOR INN
Phone: (518)873-2233

(AAA) (SAVE)   6/18-10/17   1P: $59-$69   2P: $59-$69   XP: $8
5/1-6/17 & 10/18-4/30   1P: $44-$49   2P: $44-$49   XP: $8
▼▼ ▼▼   **Location:** I-87, exit 31, 5 mi s on SR 9N. 7529 Court St 12932 (PO Box 786). **Facility:** 8 one-bedroom standard units. 1 story, exterior corridors. **Parking:** on-site, winter plug-ins. **Terms:** 4 day cancellation notice.
Motel   **Cards:** MC, VI.

(SD) 🍽 ⊠ 🛄

ELLICOTTVILLE pop. 472

——— WHERE TO STAY ———

ILEX INN

Phone: 716/699-2002

(AAA) (SAVE)

◆◆◆◆

Bed & Breakfast

12/1-3/31 [BP]	2P: $130-$275
4/1-4/30 [BP]	2P: $90-$160
5/1-11/30 [BP]	2P: $85-$160

Location: Eastern jct US 219 and SR 242, just w; western jct US 219 and SR 242, 0.6 mi e. 6416 E Washington St 14731-0775 (PO Box 775). Fax: 716/699-8790. **Facility:** This country-casual B&B offers luxury guest-room appointments such as bathrobes, French matelasse bedspreads and fine antiques. Smoke free premises. 7 units. 5 one-bedroom standard units. 1 one-bedroom suite. 1 cottage. 1-2 stories (no elevator), interior corridors. **Bath:** combo or shower only. **Parking:** on-site, winter plug-ins. **Terms:** check-in 4 pm, age restrictions may apply, 30 day cancellation notice-fee imposed, package plans. **Amenities:** video library, hair dryers. *Some:* CD players. **Pool(s):** heated outdoor. **Leisure Activities:** whirlpool. **Business Services:** PC, fax. **Cards:** AX, DS, MC, VI. **Special Amenities: free full breakfast and free room upgrade (subject to availability with advanced reservations).**

SOME UNITS

⊠ ☒ ☏ / (VCR) ☐ ☐ ☐ /

THE INN AT HOLIDAY VALLEY RESORT

Phone: (716)699-2345

(AAA) (SAVE)

◆◆◆◆

Resort
Small-scale Hotel

12/26-3/13 [ECP]	1P: $138-$295	2P: $138-$295	XP: $20	F17
3/14-4/30 [ECP]	1P: $99-$175	2P: $99-$175	XP: $20	F17
5/1-10/23 [ECP]	1P: $113-$169	2P: $113-$169	XP: $20	F17
10/24-12/25 [ECP]	1P: $95-$162	2P: $95-$162	XP: $20	F17

Location: Jct SR 242 and US 219, 0.6 mi e. Rt 219 and Holiday Valley Rd 14731 (PO Box 370). Fax: 716/699-5861. **Facility:** The resort features mountain views from many guest rooms; several rooms have patios or balconies. 102 units. 97 one-bedroom standard units, some with whirlpools. 5 one-bedroom suites ($152-$375) with whirlpools. 2 stories (no elevator), interior/exterior corridors. **Bath:** combo or shower only. **Parking:** on-site, winter plug-ins. **Terms:** 2 night minimum stay - weekends, 14 day cancellation notice-fee imposed, package plans. **Amenities:** voice mail, irons, hair dryers. **Dining:** 11:30 am-2:30 & 5-9 pm; hours may vary off season, cocktails. **Pool(s):** 2 outdoor, heated indoor/outdoor, wading. **Leisure Activities:** sauna, whirlpool, 52 ski trails & slopes for skiing with 12 lifts, extensive recreational facilities, hiking trails, exercise room. *Fee:* golf-18 holes, downhill & cross country skiing, bicycles, massage. **Guest Services:** coin laundry. **Business Services:** meeting rooms. **Cards:** AX, CB, DC, DS, MC, VI.

SOME UNITS

⊩ ⊤ ⅏ ⊡ ⊠ ☒ [DATA PORT] ☐ ☐ / ☒ ☐

THE JEFFERSON INN OF ELLICOTTVILLE

Phone: 716/699-5869

(AAA) (SAVE)

◆◆◆◆

Bed & Breakfast

12/21-3/15	2P: $109-$199
5/1-12/20 & 3/16-4/30	2P: $89-$139

Location: Western jct US 219 and SR 242, just n; eastern jct US 219 and 242, 0.8 mi w. Located in a quiet area. 3 Jefferson St 14731 (PO Box 1566). Fax: 716/699-5758. **Facility:** Smoke free premises. 7 units. 6 one-bedroom standard units. 1 one-bedroom suite ($129-$199). 1-2 stories (no elevator), interior/exterior corridors. **Parking:** on-site, winter plug-ins. **Terms:** 2-3 night minimum stay - seasonal weekends, age restrictions may apply, 30 day cancellation notice-fee imposed, [BP] meal plan available, pets (in designated units, owner's dog on premises). **Amenities:** video library, hair dryers. **Leisure Activities:** whirlpool. **Business Services:** meeting rooms, fax. **Cards:** AX, DC, MC, VI.

SOME UNITS

🐾 ⊩ ⊞ ☒ [DATA PORT] ☐ / ⊮ (VCR) ☐ ☐ /

——— WHERE TO DINE ———

THE BARN

◆◆◆

American

Dinner: $10-$20

Phone: 716/699-4600

Location: Center. 7 Monroe St 14731. **Hours:** 5 pm-10 pm, Fri & Sat from 4 pm, Sun 3 pm-9 pm. Closed: 11/25, 12/25. **Reservations:** accepted. **Features:** A fireplace accents the relaxed, rustic dining room. The ski-town restaurant's menu covers many popular dishes. The staff is friendly. Casual dress; cocktails. **Parking:** on-site. **Cards:** AX, DS, MC, VI.

⊤ ☒

DINA'S

◆◆◆

American

Lunch: $5-$8   **Dinner:** $8-$21   Phone: 716/699-5330

Location: On US 219; center. 15 Washington St 14731. **Hours:** 7 am-10 pm. Closed: 11/25, 12/25. **Features:** In a restored 1840 building, the restaurant has the ambience of a cozy bistro. Stop by for breakfast, lunch or dinner selections, many of which exhibit Italian and Mexican influences. Homemade pastries are among tempting dessert choices. Casual dress; cocktails. **Parking:** on-site. **Cards:** AX, DS, MC, VI.

☒

TIPS UP-CAFE

▼▼ ▼▼
Italian

Dinner: $8-$22   **Phone:** 716/699-2136
Location: On SR 242; center. 32 Washington St (Rt 242/219) 14731. **Hours:** 4 pm-11 pm, Sun-10 pm. Closed: 3/27, 11/25, 12/24, 12/25; also 3 weeks during Easter. **Features:** Popular with the locals, the often-busy restaurant is in a restored historical building that's loaded with friendly charm. The limited menu of well-prepared dishes features Italian and American offerings. The wait staff provides prompt, pleasant service. Casual dress; cocktails. **Parking:** street. **Cards:** MC, VI. ⓨ ⊠

ELMIRA pop. 30,940

────── WHERE TO STAY ──────

COACHMAN MOTOR LODGE   **Phone:** 607/733-5526

AAA [SAVE]
▼▼ ▼▼
Motel

All Year   1P: $55   2P: $70   XP: $5   F12
Location: SR 17, exit 56 (Church St), 0.5 mi w, 0.5 mi s on Madison Ave, then 1.4 mi s. (908 Pennsylvania Ave). Fax: 607/733-0961. **Facility:** 18 one-bedroom suites with efficiencies. 2 stories (no elevator), exterior corridors. **Parking:** on-site, winter plug-ins. **Terms:** 3 day cancellation notice, weekly rates available, small pets only. **Amenities:** *Some:* irons. **Guest Services:** coin laundry. **Cards:** AX, DS, MC, VI.

[S/D] 🐾 🎣 📷 🖥 📦 💻

HOLIDAY INN-ELMIRA RIVERVIEW   *Book at aaa.com*   **Phone:** (607)734-4211

▼▼ ▼▼
Small-scale Hotel

All Year   1P: $85-$225   2P: $85-$225
Location: SR 17, exit 56 (Water St), 0.5 mi s. 760 E Water St 14901. Fax: 607/734-3549. **Facility:** 149 units. 148 one-bedroom standard units. 1 one-bedroom suite. 2 stories, interior/exterior corridors. *Bath:* combo or shower only. **Parking:** on-site, winter plug-ins. **Terms:** 2-3 night minimum stay - seasonal, 7 day cancellation notice-fee imposed. **Amenities:** irons, hair dryers. *Some:* dual phone lines. **Pool(s):** outdoor, heated indoor, wading. **Leisure Activities:** saunas, exercise room. **Guest Services:** valet and coin laundry. **Business Services:** conference facilities. **Cards:** AX, DC, DS, JC, MC, VI.

SOME UNITS
[ASK] 🍴 📺 🍽 📷 [DATA PORT] 💻 / ⊠ [VCR] 🖥 📦 /
                                  FEE   FEE

────── WHERE TO DINE ──────

BEIJING GARDEN   **Lunch:** $4-$6   **Dinner:** $7-$14   **Phone:** 607/732-7464

▼▼ ▼▼
Chinese

Location: SR 17, exit 56 (Water St), 1 mi w on SR 352, s on Main St, then just e. 145 W Gray St 14901. **Hours:** 11:30 am-10 pm, Fri & Sat-10:30 pm. Closed major holidays. **Reservations:** accepted. **Features:** The friendly staff serves traditional Chinese food prepared with fresh, tender ingredients. Owned by the same family for 14 years, the downtown restaurant is next to Clemens Center. Casual dress; cocktails. **Parking:** street. **Cards:** AX, CB, DC, DS, MC, VI. ⊠

HILL TOP INN

▼▼ ▼▼
American

Dinner: $8-$20   **Phone:** 607/732-6728
Location: SR 17, exit 17, 0.5 mi to top of hill. 171 Jerusalem Hill Rd 14901. **Hours:** Open 5/1-12/31 & 3/1-4/30; 5 pm-8:30 pm. Closed major holidays; also Sun. **Reservations:** accepted. **Features:** As the name implies, the rustic restaurant is set atop a hill, from which it affords a panoramic view of the Chemung Valley and Elmira. The family-owned spot has been serving diners for more than 70 years. The atmosphere is casual and friendly. The patio opens seasonally. Casual dress; cocktails. **Parking:** on-site. **Cards:** AX, DC, DS, MC, VI. ⓨ

MORETTI'S RESTAURANT   Historic   **Dinner:** $8-$32   **Phone:** 607/734-1535

▼▼
Italian

Location: 0.5 mi n, 0.3 mi e on E Washington Ave, then just s. 800 Hatch St 14901. **Hours:** 5 pm-10 pm. Closed: 3/27, 11/25, 12/24, 12/25. **Reservations:** suggested. **Features:** A regional favorite since 1917, the restaurant delivers many Italian staples, as well as traditional American preparations of veal, steak, chicken and chops. Dining rooms are decorated in a local nostalgic theme. Fish is a popular choice on Friday and Saturday. Casual dress; cocktails. **Parking:** on-site. **Cards:** AX, DS, MC, VI. ⓨ ⊠

PIETRO & SON PIZZERIA & RESTAURANT   **Lunch:** $4-$8   **Dinner:** $6-$13   **Phone:** 607/733-4400

▼▼
Italian

Location: Corner of Washington St and Davis. 400 W Washington St 14901. **Hours:** 11 am-10 pm, Fri & Sat-11 pm, Sun 3 pm-9 pm. Closed: 3/27, 11/25, 12/25; also Mon. **Reservations:** accepted. **Features:** Traditional fare makes up the menu at the friendly, family-owned restaurant. Guests can eat in either of two dining rooms or request food for takeout or delivery. The popular, casual spot is near Elmira College. Casual dress; beer & wine only. **Parking:** on-site. **Cards:** AX, DS, MC, VI. ⊠

ELMIRA HEIGHTS pop. 4,170

────── WHERE TO DINE ──────

PIERCE'S 1894 RESTAURANT   **Dinner:** $15-$26   **Phone:** 607/734-2022

AAA
▼▼ ▼▼
American

Location: 2.5 mi n; jct 14th St and Oakwood Ave; 2.5 mi s of jct SR 14, 17 and 328, just w of SR 14. 228 Oakwood Ave 14903. **Hours:** 5 pm-9 pm; Sun hours vary off season. Closed: 12/24, 12/25; also Mon. **Reservations:** accepted. **Features:** Gourmet dishes, as well as varied American entrees, pepper the innovative menu. Selections in the wine cellar are extensive. Distinctive, well-appointed dining rooms contribute to a sophisticated and relaxing experience. Whiskey macaroon torte is delightful. Casual dress; cocktails. **Parking:** on-site. **Cards:** AX, DS, MC, VI. ⓨ ⊠

ELMSFORD —*See New York p. 452.*

ENDICOTT pop. 13,038

———— WHERE TO STAY ————

KINGS INN *Book at aaa.com* Phone: (607)754-8020

AAA SAVE

WWW WWW

Motel

5/1-8/31 [ECP]	1P: $71-$125	2P: $71-$125	XP: $8 F12
9/1-10/31 [ECP]	1P: $60-$89	2P: $60-$89	XP: $8 F12
11/1-4/30 [ECP]	1P: $57-$75	2P: $57-$75	XP: $8 F12

Location: SR 17 W, exit 69, 2.4 mi w on SR 17C; SR 17 E, exit 67N, 1.3 mi e. 2603 E Main St 13760. Fax: 607/754-6768. **Facility:** 60 one-bedroom standard units. 2 stories (no elevator), exterior corridors. **Parking:** on-site, winter plug-ins. **Terms:** package plans, pets ($5 fee, in designated unit). **Amenities:** video library. **Pool(s):** small heated indoor. **Leisure Activities:** sauna. **Guest Services:** valet laundry. **Business Services:** meeting rooms, PC, fax (fee). **Cards:** AX, CB, DS, MC, VI.

SOME UNITS

[icons] FEE / VCR FEE

———— WHERE TO DINE ————

RUSSELL'S STEAK & SEAFOOD HOUSE Dinner: $6-$22 Phone: 607/754-2333

WWW WWW

Steak & Seafood

Location: Jct SR 17C and 26, 1.2 mi w on SR 17C (Main St). 1001 W Main St 13760. **Hours:** 4 pm-9 pm, Fri & Sat-10 pm. Closed: 1/1, 11/25, 12/24, 12/25; also Mon. **Reservations:** suggested, weekends. **Features:** Diners can treat themselves to tender, juicy steaks that are prepared to order. Seafood lovers won't be disappointed with dishes that bring out robust flavors in shrimp, scallops and lobster. Friendly servers contribute to the pleasant atmosphere. Casual dress; cocktails. **Parking:** on-site. **Cards:** AX, DC, DS, MC, VI.

[icons]

FAIRPORT pop. 5,740 (See map and index starting on p. 550)

———— WHERE TO STAY ————

THE LODGE AT WOODCLIFF *Book at aaa.com* Phone: 585/381-4000 [29]

WWW WWW

Small-scale Hotel

All Year	1P: $118-$155	2P: $118-$155	XP: $8 F16

Location: I-490, exit 28, just s on SR 96S. 199 Woodcliff Dr 14450 (PO Box 22850, ROCHESTER, 14692). Fax: 585/381-2673. **Facility:** 244 units. 237 one-bedroom standard units, some with whirlpools. 7 one-bedroom suites with whirlpools. 6 stories, interior corridors. **Bath:** combo or shower only. **Parking:** on-site. **Amenities:** video library (fee), high-speed Internet, dual phone lines, voice mail, irons, hair dryers. *Some:* honor bars. **Pool(s):** heated indoor/outdoor. **Leisure Activities:** saunas, whirlpool, cross country skiing, recreation programs, jogging. *Fee:* golf-9 holes, massage. **Guest Services:** gift shop, valet laundry, area transportation. **Business Services:** meeting rooms, business center. **Cards:** AX, DC, DS, MC, VI.

SOME UNITS

[icons] / VCR FEE

FALCONER pop. 2,540

———— WHERE TO STAY ————

RED ROOF INN JAMESTOWN/FALCONER *Book at aaa.com* Phone: (716)665-3670

AAA SAVE

WWW WWW

Small-scale Hotel

5/1-9/1	1P: $62-$72	2P: $68-$78	XP: $6 F18
9/2-4/30	1P: $48-$59	2P: $54-$65	XP: $6 F18

Location: I-86, exit 13, just w. 1980 E Main St 14733. Fax: 716/664-7651. **Facility:** 80 one-bedroom standard units. 2 stories (no elevator), interior corridors. **Bath:** combo or shower only. **Parking:** on-site. **Amenities:** video library (fee), video games, voice mail. **Cards:** AX, CB, DC, DS, MC, VI. **Special Amenities:** free local telephone calls and free newspaper.

SOME UNITS

[icons] /

———— WHERE TO DINE ————

HULTMAN'S RESTAURANT & LOUNGE Lunch: $4-$7 Dinner: $9-$20 Phone: 716/665-6837

WWW WWW

American

Location: I-86, exit 13, 1 mi w on SR 394. 232 W Main St 14733. **Hours:** 5 pm-9 pm, Wed-Fri also 11:45 am-1:30 pm. Closed major holidays; also 12/24 & Sun. **Reservations:** accepted. **Features:** Victorian tables and antiques decorate the casual restaurant, a family favorite for comfortable dining. A variety of seafood, beef, chicken and pasta preparations lines the menu. Casual dress; cocktails. **Parking:** on-site. **Cards:** AX, DS, MC, VI.

[icons]

FARMINGTON pop. 10,585—See also FINGER LAKES.

———— WHERE TO STAY ————

BUDGET INN Phone: (585)924-5020

AAA SAVE

WWW WWW

Motel

All Year	1P: $43-$59	2P: $54-$79	XP: $5 F8

Location: I-90, exit 44, 1 mi s on SR 332, then just e. 6001 Rt 96 14425. Fax: 585/924-5020. **Facility:** 20 one-bedroom standard units. 1 story, exterior corridors. **Parking:** on-site. **Terms:** 3 day cancellation notice, small pets only ($5 extra charge). **Cards:** AX, DC, DS, MC, VI.

SOME UNITS

[icons] FEE / [icons]

FARMINGVILLE

─────── WHERE TO STAY ───────

HAMPTON INN BROOKHAVEN *Book at aaa.com* **Phone:** (631)732-7300
(AAA) (SAVE) All Year 1P: $179-$329 2P: $179-$329
▼▼▼ **Location:** I-495, exit 63, just n. 2000 N Ocean Ave 11738. Fax: 631/732-5522. **Facility:** 161 units. 154 one-bedroom standard units. 7 one-bedroom suites with whirlpools. 6 stories, interior corridors. *Bath:* combo or shower only. **Parking:** on-site. **Terms:** [ECP] meal plan available. **Amenities:** video games (fee), high-speed
Small-scale Hotel Internet, dual phone lines, voice mail, irons, hair dryers. **Pool(s):** heated indoor. **Leisure Activities:** exercise room. **Guest Services:** valet and coin laundry, area transportation. **Business Services:** meeting rooms.
Cards: AX, CB, DC, DS, MC, VI. **Special Amenities:** free expanded continental breakfast and free local telephone calls.

SOME UNITS

FAYETTEVILLE pop. 4,190

─────── WHERE TO STAY ───────

CRAFTSMAN INN *Book at aaa.com* **Phone:** (315)637-8000
▼▼▼ All Year 1P: $95-$125 2P: $105-$135
Small-scale Hotel **Location:** Located across from Fayetteville Towne Center. 7300 E Genesee St (SR 5) 13066. Fax: 315/637-2440. **Facility:** Smoke free premises. 90 one-bedroom standard units, some with whirlpools. 2 stories, interior corridors. *Bath:* combo or shower only. **Parking:** on-site, winter plug-ins. **Terms:** cancellation fee imposed, [CP] meal plan available. **Amenities:** voice mail, irons, hair dryers. *Some:* high-speed Internet, dual phone lines. **Guest Services:** valet laundry. **Business Services:** meeting rooms. **Cards:** AX, CB, DC, DS, MC, VI.

SOME UNITS

FEE

─────── WHERE TO DINE ───────

ARAD EVANS INN Historic **Dinner:** $17-$24 **Phone:** 315/637-2020
▼▼▼ **Location:** 1.5 mi e of SR 481 S, 0.5 mi w of Lower Fayetteville. 7206 Genesee St 13066. **Hours:** 5 pm-11 pm, Sun
4:30 pm-9 pm. Closed major holidays. **Reservations:** suggested. **Features:** Period furniture and Oriental
Continental rugs decorate the renovated 1840s Federal-style country house. Upscale fusion cuisine blends French, Italian and nouveau influences. The signature New Zealand rack of lamb is memorable, as are such showy
homemade desserts as the chocolate tower. Dressy casual; cocktails. **Parking:** on-site. **Cards:** AX, MC, VI.

KYOKO JAPANESE RESTAURANT **Dinner:** $8-$22 **Phone:** 315/637-9000
▼▼▼ **Location:** SR 5, 2.5 mi e of jct SR 481. 111 Brooklea Dr 13066. **Hours:** 5 pm-9 pm, Fri & Sat-10 pm. Closed
major holidays. **Reservations:** suggested. **Features:** Relaxed dining in the intimate feel of a garden tea
Japanese house with pleasantly arrayed Japanese artwork is found at Kyoko. The friendly staff offers a wide variety of sushi, tempura and teriyaki preparations. Gyoza—steamed and fried meat-filled dumplings—are perfect
to start. Beautifully arrayed sushi, grilled shrimp or chicken stir-fry and all dishes are prepared to order. Each is an art piece intended to satisfy the eye and palate. Casual dress; beer & wine only. **Parking:** on-site. **Cards:** AX, DC, DS, MC, VI.

FILLMORE

─────── WHERE TO STAY ───────

JUST A "PLANE" BED & BREAKFAST **Phone:** 585/567-8338
▼▼▼ 5/1-11/30 & 3/1-4/30 1P: $55 2P: $70 XP: $15
Location: Jct SR 19 and 19A, just n. Located in a rural area, next to grass airstrip. 11152 Rt 19A 14735.
Bed & Breakfast **Facility:** Smoke free premises. 4 one-bedroom standard units. 3 stories (no elevator), interior corridors. *Bath:* combo or shower only. **Parking:** on-site. **Terms:** open 5/1-11/30 & 3/1-4/30, check-in 4:30 pm, 2 night
minimum stay - weekends 9/15-10/31, age restrictions may apply, 14 day cancellation notice-fee imposed. **Amenities:** hair dryers. **Leisure Activities:** hiking trails. **Business Services:** meeting rooms. **Cards:** AX, MC, VI.

FINDLEY LAKE

─────── WHERE TO STAY ───────

HOLIDAY INN EXPRESS HOTEL & SUITES *Book at aaa.com* **Phone:** (716)769-7900
(AAA) (SAVE) 6/8-8/31 & 1/1-4/30 [ECP] 1P: $99-$129 2P: $99-$129 XP: $10 F18
▼▼▼ 5/1-6/7 & 9/1-12/31 [ECP] 1P: $79-$109 2P: $79-$109 XP: $10 F18
Location: I-86, exit 4. 3025 Rt 426 14736. Fax: 716/769-7903. **Facility:** 87 one-bedroom standard units. 3 stories, interior corridors. *Bath:* combo or shower only. **Parking:** on-site. **Terms:** weekly rates available.
Small-scale Hotel **Amenities:** video library, dual phone lines, voice mail, irons, hair dryers. *Some:* video games, CD players. **Dining:** I-86 Express, see separate listing. **Pool(s):** heated indoor. **Leisure Activities:** exercise room. **Guest Services:** valet laundry. **Business Services:** meeting rooms. **Cards:** AX, CB, DC, DS, JC, MC, VI. **Special Amenities:** free expanded continental breakfast and free newspaper.

SOME UNITS

PEEK'N PEAK RESORT & CONFERENCE CENTER

Phone: (716)355-4141

AAA SAVE

12/17-4/30	1P: $160-$260	2P: $160-$260		
5/28-10/14	1P: $165-$185	2P: $165-$185	XP: $20	F18
10/15-12/16	1P: $120-$135	2P: $120-$135	XP: $20	F18
5/1-5/27	1P: $115-$130	2P: $115-$130	XP: $20	F18

Resort
Small-scale Hotel **Location:** I-86, exit 4, 5 mi s via SR 426, follow signs. 1405 Olde Rd 14736 (1405 Olde Rd, PO Box 360). Fax: 716/355-4542. **Facility:** This European-style lodge has Tudor architecture and features some guest rooms with lofts, fireplaces and balconies. 144 units. 72 one-bedroom standard units. 72 one-bedroom suites, some with kitchens. 2 stories (no elevator), interior/exterior corridors. *Bath:* combo or shower only. **Parking:** on-site. **Terms:** check-in 5 pm, 2 night minimum stay - weekends, 7 day cancellation notice-fee imposed. **Amenities:** irons, hair dryers. **Dining:** 2 restaurants, 6:30 am-9 pm, Fri & Sat-10 pm, Sun 6:30 am-2 & 5-9 pm, cocktails. **Pool(s):** heated outdoor, heated indoor. **Leisure Activities:** sauna, whirlpool, waterslide, lifeguard on duty, winter tubing, recreation programs, child care in winter, bicycles, playground, exercise room, sports court, horseshoes, shuffleboard, volleyball. *Fee:* golf-36 holes, miniature golf, indoor tennis court, downhill & cross country skiing, game room. **Guest Services:** gift shop, coin laundry. **Business Services:** conference facilities. **Cards:** AX, DC, DS, MC, VI.

SOME UNITS

——— WHERE TO DINE ———

I-86 EXPRESS

American
MC, VI.

Lunch: $5-$14   **Dinner:** $5-$14   Phone: 716/769-7950

Location: I-86, exit 4; in Holiday Inn Express Hotel & Suites. 3025 Rt 426 14736. **Hours:** 11 am-11 pm. **Features:** Everything is made fresh on the premises. Among selections are rotisserie chicken and ribs, tossed salad, potato salad, spaghetti and meatballs, pizza, hot stuffed sandwiches and subs. Travelers appreciate the easy-off, easy-on interstate access. Casual dress. **Parking:** on-site. **Cards:** AX, DC, DS,

---

Finger Lakes Area

FINGER LAKES —See AUBURN, AVON, BATH, BRISTOL CENTER, CANANDAIGUA, CORNING, DANSVILLE, FARMINGTON, GENESEO, GENEVA, GLENORA, GROTON, HAMMONDSPORT, HONEOYE FALLS, HORNELL, HORSEHEADS, ITHACA, MANCHESTER, MONTOUR FALLS, NAPLES, PAINTED POST, ROMULUS, SKANEATELES, TRUMANSBURG, VICTOR, WATERLOO, WATKINS GLEN & WEEDSPORT.

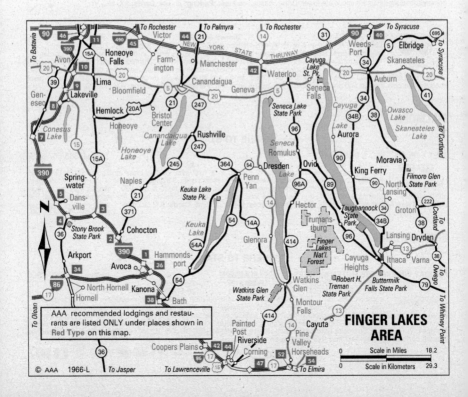

© AAA 1966-L

Expect more value at Hilton Garden Inn. Centrally located to wineries, shopping and attractions. Enjoy our indoor pool, whirlpool and fitness center. Each guest room offers refrigerator, microwave and coffee maker. Just make advance reservations with a call to Hilton's dedicated AAA number, **1-800-916-2221**, or your local AAA travel office. Visit us online at **hiltongardeninn.com**.

35 Arnot Road
Horseheads, NY 14845
607-795-1111

Hilton Garden Inn
Elmira/Corning

Hilton HHonors
Points & Miles

I ♥ NY®

Seneca County
Finger Lakes Region

❖

Cruise the Cayuga-Seneca canal.

Sip a perfectly aged wine along our wine trails. Enjoy a unique shopping experience. Visit the Women's Rights National Historical Park and Hall of Fame.

❖

Seneca County Tourism
One DiPronio Drive, Waterloo, NY 13165
1-800-732-1848
www.visitsenecany.net

LOOK FOR THE RED

*N*ext time you pore over a AAA TourBook® guide in search of a lodging establishment, take note of the vibrant red AAA logo, [SAVE] icon, and Diamond rating just under a select group of property names! These Official Appointment properties place a high value on the business they receive from dedicated AAA travelers and offer members great room rates*.

* See TourBook Navigator section, page 14, for complete details.

FISHKILL pop. 1,735

—— WHERE TO STAY ——

COURTYARD BY MARRIOTT   *Book at aaa.com*   Phone: (845)897-2400
All Year   2P: $169-$219
Location: I-84, exit 13, just n. 17 Westage Dr 12524. Fax: 845/897-2274. **Facility:** 152 units. 140 one-bedroom
Small-scale Hotel   standard units. 12 one-bedroom suites ($199-$239). 4 stories, interior corridors. *Bath:* combo or shower only.
Parking: on-site, winter plug-ins. **Terms:** package plans - seasonal. **Amenities:** high-speed Internet, voice
mail, irons, hair dryers. **Pool(s):** heated indoor. **Leisure Activities:** whirlpool, exercise room. **Guest Services:** sundries, valet
and coin laundry. **Business Services:** meeting rooms, business center. **Cards:** AX, CB, DC, DS, JC, MC, VI.

SOME UNITS

HAMPTON INN FISHKILL   *Book at aaa.com*   Phone: (845)896-4000
All Year [ECP]   1P: $129-$149   2P: $129-$149
Location: I-84, exit 13, just n; behind the Holiday Inn. 544 Rt 9 12524. Fax: 845/896-2799. **Facility:** 99 one-
bedroom standard units. 4 stories, interior corridors. *Bath:* combo or shower only. **Parking:** on-site.
Terms: cancellation fee imposed. **Amenities:** video games, voice mail, irons, hair dryers. **Pool(s):** small
Small-scale Hotel   heated indoor. **Guest Services:** valet laundry. **Cards:** AX, DC, DS, MC, VI. **Special Amenities:** free ex-
panded continental breakfast and free local telephone calls. *(See color ad below)*

SOME UNITS

HILTON GARDEN INN   *Book at aaa.com*   Phone: (845)896-7100
All Year   1P: $119-$199   2P: $119-$199   XP: $10   F18
Location: I-84, exit 13, just n, then just w. Located in a commercial area. 25 Westage Dr 12524. Fax: 845/896-7111.
Small-scale Hotel   **Facility:** 111 one-bedroom standard units. 4 stories, interior corridors. *Bath:* combo or shower only. **Parking:**
on-site. **Terms:** cancellation fee imposed. **Amenities:** dual phone lines, voice mail, irons, hair dryers.
Pool(s): small heated indoor. **Leisure Activities:** whirlpool, exercise room. **Guest Services:** sundries, coin laundry. **Business
Services:** meeting rooms, business center. **Cards:** AX, DC, DS, MC, VI.

SOME UNITS

HOMESTEAD STUDIO SUITES HOTEL-FISHKILL *Book at aaa.com* **Phone:** (845)897-2800
All Year   1P: $113-$122   2P: $118-$127   XP: $5   F17
Location: I-84, exit 13, just n. 25 Merritt Blvd 12524. Fax: 845/897-2616. **Facility:** 106 units. 82 one-bedroom
Small-scale Hotel standard units with efficiencies. 24 one-bedroom suites with efficiencies. 3 stories, interior corridors. *Bath:*
combo or shower only. **Parking:** on-site. **Terms:** pets ($25 extra charge, after 6 days $75 deposit).
Amenities: video games (fee), dual phone lines, voice mail, irons, hair dryers. **Leisure Activities:** limited exercise equipment,
sports court. **Guest Services:** sundries, complimentary evening beverages, valet and coin laundry. **Cards:** AX, CB, DC, DS, JC,
MC, VI.

SOME UNITS

(ASK) (SD) [icons] / (X) /
FEE

RESIDENCE INN BY MARRIOTT *Book at aaa.com* **Phone:** (845)896-5210
All Year [ECP]   1P: $139-$179   2P: $139-$179
Location: I-84, exit 13, just n. 14 Schuyler Blvd 12524. Fax: 845/896-9689. **Facility:** 139 units. 105 one- and 34
Small-scale Hotel two-bedroom standard units with kitchens. 2 stories (no elevator), exterior corridors. **Parking:** on-site.
Terms: pets ($200 fee, $20 extra charge). **Amenities:** video games, dual phone lines, voice mail, irons, hair
dryers. **Pool(s):** outdoor. **Leisure Activities:** whirlpool, exercise room, sports court. **Guest Services:** complimentary evening
beverages: Mon-Thurs, valet and coin laundry. **Business Services:** meeting rooms, fax. **Cards:** AX, DC, DS, MC, VI.

SOME UNITS

(ASK) (SD) [icons] / (X) /
FEE

WELLESLEY INN (FISHKILL) *Book at aaa.com* **Phone:** (845)896-4995
(AAA) (SAVE)   All Year [ECP]   1P: $103   2P: $103
Location: I-84, exit 13, just n. 20 Schuyler Blvd & Rt 9 12524. Fax: 845/896-6631. **Facility:** 82 one-bedroom stan-
dard units. 4 stories, interior corridors. *Bath:* combo or shower only. **Parking:** on-site, winter plug-ins.
Terms: small pets only (with prior approval). **Amenities:** video games, high-speed Internet (fee), voice mail,
Small-scale Hotel irons, hair dryers. *Some:* dual phone lines. **Guest Services:** valet and coin laundry. **Business Services:**
meeting rooms, fax (fee). **Cards:** AX, CB, DC, DS, MC, VI. **Special Amenities:** free expanded continental
breakfast and free newspaper. (See color ad p 291)

SOME UNITS

(SD) [icons] / (X) /

──────── WHERE TO DINE ────────

HUDSON'S RIBS & FISH   **Dinner:** $15-$26   **Phone:** 845/297-5002
Location: I-84, exit 13, 3 mi n. 1099 Rt 9 12524. **Hours:** 4 pm-10 pm, Fri & Sat-11 pm, Sun 2 pm-9 pm.
Closed: 1/1, 11/25, 12/25. **Features:** Baby back ribs, prime rib and fresh fish are the focus of the menu.
Steak & Seafood Lacquered tables with maps of New York riverways contribute to the nautical decor. Delicious popovers are
served with strawberry honey butter. Service is pleasant and prompt. Casual dress; cocktails. **Parking:**
on-site. **Cards:** AX, CB, DC, DS, MC, VI.

(Y) (X)

NORTH STREET GRILL   **Lunch:** $6-$10   **Dinner:** $12-$22   **Phone:** 845/896-1000
Location: I-84, exit 13, 0.9 mi n on SR 9, then just w on SR 52. 1111 Main St 12524. **Hours:** 11:30 am-10 pm, Fri
& Sat-11 pm, Sun 4 pm-9 pm. Closed major holidays. **Features:** The friendly staff welcomes patrons to the
American casual atmosphere in the historic building. Locals and families find the variety of Italian-influenced
American dishes to be just right for hearty appetites. The specialty penne Louisiana with shrimp and tasso
ham in cream sauce and filet mignon with rosemary sauce are good choices. Finish with rich tiramisu or light zabaglione over
fresh fruit. Casual dress; cocktails. **Parking:** on-site. **Cards:** AX, DC, DS, MC, VI.

(X)

FLORAL PARK pop. 15,967 (See map and index starting on p. 373)

──────── WHERE TO STAY ────────

FLORAL PARK MOTOR LODGE *Book at aaa.com* **Phone:** (516)775-7777 (153)
All Year   1P: $200-$244   2P: $220-$270   XP: $15   F18
Location: Cross Island Pkwy (Belt Pkwy), exit 27E, 0.8 mi e on SR 25. 30 Jericho Tpke 11001. Fax: 516/775-0451.
Facility: 107 one-bedroom standard units. 3 stories, interior corridors. *Bath:* combo or shower only. **Parking:**
on-site, winter plug-ins. **Terms:** [ECP] meal plan available. **Amenities:** voice mail, irons, hair dryers. **Guest**
Motel **Services:** valet laundry. **Business Services:** meeting rooms, fax (fee). **Cards:** AX, DC, DS, JC, MC, VI.
Special Amenities: free expanded continental breakfast and free newspaper. (See color ad p 444)

SOME UNITS

(SD) [icons] / (X) (VCR) [icon]
FEE   FEE

──────── WHERE TO DINE ────────

POPPY'S PLACE   **Lunch:** $7-$11   **Dinner:** $10-$22   **Phone:** 516/358-2705 (197)
Location: Tulip Ave and Railroad Station, just e. 12 Verbena Ave 11001. **Hours:** 11 am-3 & 5-10 pm, Fri & Sat-11
pm, Sun 4 pm-9 pm. Closed major holidays; also Mon. **Features:** The unpretentious neighborhood
Italian restaurant is a local favorite for made-from-scratch American and Italian food. Reasonably priced dishes,
such as poached calamari with pasta, are served in generous portions. A few specials are always
available. Casual dress; cocktails. **Parking:** street. **Cards:** AX, DC, DS, MC, VI.

(Y) (X)

FORT MONTGOMERY pop. 1,418

──── WHERE TO STAY ────

HOLIDAY INN EXPRESS HOTEL & SUITES   *Book at aaa.com*   **Phone:** (845)446-4277
▽◇◇◇▽   All Year [ECP]   1P: $130-$140   2P: $130-$140   XP: $10   F17
          Location: Jct US 6 and 9W, 1.5 mi n. 1106 Rt 9W 10922. **Fax:** 845/446-4288. **Facility:** 86 one-bedroom standard
Small-scale Hotel   units, some with whirlpools. 3 stories, interior corridors. **Parking:** on-site. **Terms:** 30 day cancellation
          notice-fee imposed. **Amenities:** dual phone lines, voice mail, irons, hair dryers. **Leisure Activities:** exercise
room. *Fee:* game room. **Guest Services:** valet and coin laundry. **Business Services:** meeting rooms, business center.
Cards: AX, DC, DS, JC, MC, VI. *(See color ad p 202)*

SOME UNITS
(ASK) (⑤⑥) (📶) (🎥) (DATA PORT) (💻) / (✕) (📶) (🖥) (🖵) /

FRANKFORT pop. 2,537

──── WHERE TO DINE ────

KITLAS RESTAURANT   **Lunch:** $3-$6   **Dinner:** $8-$14   **Phone:** 315/732-9616
▽◇◇▽   **Location:** SR 5 S, exit Turner Rd, then n. 2242 Broad St 13340. **Hours:** 11:30 am-2 & 4:30-8:30 pm, Sat from
          4:30 pm. Closed major holidays; also Sun & for dinner Mon. **Reservations:** accepted. **Features:** Owned
American   by the same family since 1939, the restaurant delivers classic fare, including the slow-roasted pork loin
          over herbed mashed potatoes and lemon-horseradish-crusted haddock. The atmosphere is casual and
comfy, making the place popular with families. Casual dress; cocktails. **Parking:** on-site. **Cards:** AX, DS, MC, VI.
(🍽) (✕)

FREDONIA pop. 10,706

──── WHERE TO STAY ────

THE WHITE INN   *Book at aaa.com*   **Phone:** (716)672-2103
(AAA) (SAVE)   All Year [BP]   1P: $79-$179   2P: $79-$179   XP: $10   F12
▽◇◇◇▽   **Location:** Jct SR 60, 1.3 mi sw on US 20; center. 52 E Main St 14063. **Fax:** 716/672-2107. **Facility:** Guest rooms
          appointed with antiques give the inn a pampered atmosphere; accommodations vary from spacious to com-
Historic   pact. 24 units. 19 one-bedroom standard units. 5 one-bedroom suites, some with kitchens and/or whirlpools.
Country Inn   3 stories, interior corridors. *Bath:* combo or shower only. **Parking:** on-site. **Terms:** [MAP] meal plan available.
          Amenities: voice mail, irons, hair dryers. **Dining:** dining room, see separate listing. **Business Services:**
          meeting rooms. **Cards:** AX, DC, DS, MC, VI. **Special Amenities:** free full breakfast and free local tele-
phone calls.

SOME UNITS
(🍽) (🍽) (🎥) (DATA PORT) / (✕) (📶) (🖥) (💻) /

──── WHERE TO DINE ────

BARKER BREW COMPANY   **Lunch:** $5-$10   **Dinner:** $8-$18   **Phone:** 716/679-3435
(AAA)   **Location:** Jct SR 60 on US 20, 1.5 mi sw; center. 34 W Main St 14063. **Hours:** noon-9 pm, Fri & Sat-10 pm, Sun
▽◇◇▽   3 pm-9 pm. Closed major holidays. **Reservations:** accepted. **Features:** The restaurant and microbrewery
          serves hand-crafted ales, stouts, porters and ambers with authentic Mexican and Cajun specialties. Also
American   on the menu are such vegetarian dishes as eggplant parmigiana and vegetarian chicken wings. Casual
          dress; cocktails. **Parking:** on-site. **Cards:** AX, DS, MC, VI.
(🍽) (✕)

THE WHITE INN DINING ROOM   Historic   **Lunch:** $6-$10   **Dinner:** $15-$22   **Phone:** 716/672-2103
▽◇◇◇▽   **Location:** Jct SR 60, 1.3 mi sw on US 20; center; in The White Inn. 52 E Main St 14063. **Hours:** 7-10 am, 11:30-2
          & 5-8:30 pm, Fri & Sat-9 pm, Sun 8 am-11 & 12:30-8 pm. **Reservations:** suggested. **Features:** Casual
American   dining with an elegant flair, soft candlelight and attentive service make for a relaxing evening in a finely
          appointed dining room. The cozy veranda welcomes diners to unwind. Neatly attired servers are prompt
and friendly. Dressy casual; cocktails. **Parking:** on-site. **Cards:** AX, DC, DS, MC, VI.
(🍽) (✕)

FREEHOLD

──── WHERE TO DINE ────

FREEHOLD COUNTRY INN RESTAURANT   **Lunch:** $7-$9   **Dinner:** $14-$32   **Phone:** 518/634-2705
▽◇◇◇▽   **Location:** Jct CR 32 and 67; town center. Rt 32 & 67 12431. **Hours:** noon-3 & 4-9 pm, Sun noon-9 pm. **Closed:**
          12/25; also 1/7-1/21. **Reservations:** suggested, weekends. **Features:** The house dates from the late
American   1700s but has been fully renovated to a fresh and light farmhouse style. Ample-size portions,
          well-garnished courses and homemade desserts will appeal to many travelers. Casual dress; cocktails.
Parking: on-site. **Cards:** AX, MC, VI.
(🍽) (✕)

FREEPORT pop. 39,900

——— WHERE TO STAY ———

FREEPORT MOTOR INN & BOATEL   **Phone:** (516)623-9100
(AAA) (SAVE)   All Year [CP]   1P: $93-$105   2P: $105-$115   XP: $7   F10
                Location: 1 mi s from SR 27 (Sunrise Hwy). Located in a residential area, adjacent to a marina. 445 S Main St 11520.
Motel   **Fax:** 516/546-5739. **Facility:** 60 one-bedroom standard units. 2 stories (no elevator), exterior corridors. *Bath:* combo or shower only. **Parking:** on-site. **Cards:** AX, CB, DC, DS, MC, VI. **Special Amenities:** free continental breakfast and preferred room (subject to availability with advanced reservations).
                (See color ad p 344)

SOME UNITS
[Y+] [cassette] [DATA PORT] / [X] [VCR] [fridge] [microwave] /
     FEE   FEE FEE

FULTON pop. 11,855

——— WHERE TO STAY ———

RIVERSIDE INN   **Phone:** (315)593-2444
            5/1-11/1   1P: $59-$109   2P: $59-$109   XP: $10   F12
            11/2-4/30   1P: $59-$99   2P: $59-$99   XP: $10   F12
Small-scale Hotel **Location:** On SR 481. 930 S First St 13069. **Fax:** 315/593-1730. **Facility:** 69 one-bedroom standard units. 2 stories (no elevator), interior corridors. **Parking:** on-site, winter plug-ins. **Terms:** 2 night minimum stay - seasonal, 7 day cancellation notice, [MAP] meal plan available, pets ($100 deposit). **Amenities:** *Some:* hair dryers. **Pool(s):** outdoor. **Guest Services:** valet laundry. **Business Services:** meeting rooms. **Cards:** AX, DC, DS, MC, VI.

SOME UNITS
[ASK] [S/D] [Y1] [Y] [~] [++] [X] [DATA PORT] / [X] [fridge] [microwave] /
         FEE

——— WHERE TO DINE ———

THE LOCK III RESTAURANT   **Lunch:** $4-$7   **Dinner:** $14-$18   **Phone:** 315/598-6900
                Location: Center. 24 S 1st St 13069. **Hours:** 11:30 am-2:30 & 4:30-10:30 pm, Sun noon-9 pm. Closed major
Continental   holidays. **Reservations:** suggested. **Features:** On the Oswego River overlooking the barge canal at Lock 3, the casual restaurant welcomes a diverse clientele. Specialties of steak and fresh seafood mingle with soups, sandwiches and burgers on the lengthy menu. Decor is cohesive and attractive. Casual dress; cocktails. **Parking:** on-site. **Cards:** AX, DC, DS, MC, VI.

[Y] [X]

GARDEN CITY pop. 21,672

——— WHERE TO STAY ———

WINGATE INN   *Book at aaa.com*   **Phone:** (516)705-9000
            All Year [ECP]   1P: $179-$299   2P: $179-$299   XP: $10   F18
            Location: Meadowbrook Pkwy, exit 3W, 0.5 mi w. 821 Stewart Ave 11530. **Fax:** 516/705-9100. **Facility:** 130 one-
Small-scale Hotel bedroom standard units. 5 stories, interior corridors. *Bath:* combo or shower only. **Parking:** on-site.
            Amenities: video games (fee), high-speed Internet, dual phone lines, voice mail, safes, irons, hair dryers.
Leisure Activities: whirlpool, exercise room. **Guest Services:** valet laundry. **Business Services:** meeting rooms, business center. **Cards:** AX, CB, DC, DS, JC, MC, VI.

SOME UNITS
[ASK] [S/D] [Y] [&M] [&] [cassette] [DATA PORT] [microwave] / [X] [fridge] [microwave] /

——— WHERE TO DINE ———

WALK STREET   **Lunch:** $8-$13   **Dinner:** $14-$24   **Phone:** 516/746-2592
                Location: Just w of Franklin Ave. 176 Seventh St 11530. **Hours:** noon-3 & 5-10 pm, Fri-11 pm, Sat 5 pm-11 pm,
American   Sun 5 pm-9 pm. Closed: 12/25. **Reservations:** suggested. **Features:** Spacious and comfortable with a modern decor and an eclectic menu of tempting dishes, the restaurant invites guests to come with friends. Yellowfin tuna tartare with yuzu-mustard dressing, chilled lobster salad with basil dressing and three-mushroom risotto with herbs, Parmigiano-Reggiano and truffle oil are a sample of the starters. Marinated hanger steak with old bay fries and soft shell crab tempura with warm lemon soy vinaigrette show the range in entrees. Casual dress; cocktails. **Parking:** on-site. **Cards:** AX, DS, MC, VI.

[&M] [X]

GARDINER pop. 856

——— **WHERE TO STAY** ———

MINNEWASKA LODGE   Phone: (845)255-1110
(AAA) [SAVE]   All Year [ECP]   1P: $125-$219   2P: $125-$219   XP: $15   F5
▼▼▼▼   **Location:** Jct SR 299 and US 44/SR 55, just e. 3116 Rt 44/55 12525. Fax: 845/255-5069. **Facility:** Designated
          smoking area. 26 units. 25 one-bedroom standard units. 1 one-bedroom suite ($275-$319). 3 stories (no el-
Small-scale Hotel   evator), interior corridors. **Parking:** on-site. **Terms:** 2 night minimum stay - weekends in summer & fall, 30
          day cancellation notice-fee imposed, weekly rates available. **Amenities:** dual phone lines, voice mail, hair
          dryers. **Leisure Activities:** exercise room. **Guest Services:** gift shop. **Cards:** AX, MC, VI.
**Special Amenities: free expanded continental breakfast and free room upgrade (subject to availability with advanced
reservations).**

SOME UNITS
[S D] [†¶+] [✕] [DATA PORT] / [VCR] [🔒] /

GATES pop. 29,275   (See map and index starting on p. 550)

——— **WHERE TO STAY** ———

COMFORT INN CENTRAL   _Book at aaa.com_   Phone: (585)436-4400   [14]
▼▼ ▼▼   5/1-10/31 [ECP]   1P: $74-$79   2P: $89-$94   XP: $8   F18
          11/1-4/30 [ECP]   1P: $64-$69   2P: $79-$84   XP: $8   F18
Small-scale Hotel   **Location:** I-390, exit 18B (SR 204), 0.3 mi w; opposite entrance to Rochester-Monroe County Airport. 395 Buell Rd
          14624. Fax: 585/436-6496. **Facility:** 73 one-bedroom standard units. 2 stories (no elevator), interior corridors.
Parking: on-site. **Terms:** 3 day cancellation notice, package plans, pets ($25 deposit). **Amenities:** video library (fee), video
games, irons, hair dryers. **Guest Services:** valet laundry, area transportation. **Business Services:** fax. **Cards:** AX, CB, DC, DS,
MC, VI.

SOME UNITS
[ASK] [S D] [✈] [🛏] [†¶+] [📞] [▶] [DATA PORT] [💻] / [✕] [🔒] [▭] /
FEE

HOLIDAY INN-ROCHESTER AIRPORT   _Book at aaa.com_   Phone: 585/328-6000   [13]
(AAA) [SAVE]   5/1-11/1   1P: $131-$141
▼▼▼▼   2/2-4/30   1P: $119-$131
          11/2-2/1   1P: $109-$129
Small-scale Hotel   **Location:** I-390, exit 18A (SR 204), just e. 911 Brooks Ave 14624 (911 Brooks Ave, ROCHESTER). Fax: 585/328-1012.
          Facility: 280 one-bedroom standard units, some with whirlpools. 2 stories (no elevator), interior corridors. **Parking:** on-site. **Terms:** small pets only ($20 deposit). **Amenities:** video library (fee), voice mail, irons, hair
dryers. _Some:_ dual phone lines. **Dining:** 6 am-10 pm, Sat & Sun from 6:30 am, cocktails. **Pool(s):** heated indoor. **Leisure Ac-
tivities:** sauna, whirlpool, exercise room. **Guest Services:** valet and coin laundry, area transportation-within 5 mi. **Business
Services:** meeting rooms, business center. **Cards:** AX, CB, DC, DS, MC, VI. **Special Amenities: free room upgrade (subject
to availability with advanced reservations).** _(See color ad p 554)_

SOME UNITS
[✈] [🛏] [†¶] [Y] [📞] [🏊] [✕] [▶] [DATA PORT] [💻] / [✕] [🔒] /
FEE

MOTEL 6 ROCHESTER-AIRPORT #1221   _Book at aaa.com_   Phone: 585/436-2170   [12]
▼▼   All Year   1P: $38-$60   2P: $41-$66   XP: $3   F
          Location: Just s. 155 Buell Rd 14624. Fax: 585/436-4814. **Facility:** 96 one-bedroom standard units. 2 stories
Small-scale Hotel   (no elevator), interior corridors. _Bath:_ combo or shower only. **Parking:** on-site. **Guest Services:** coin laundry.
          Cards: AX, CB, DC, DS, JC, MC, VI.

SOME UNITS
[S D] [🛏] [👶] [▶] / [✕] /

GENESEO pop. 7,579

——— **WHERE TO STAY** ———

DAYS INN   _Book at aaa.com_   Phone: (585)243-0500
(AAA) [SAVE]   7/1-8/31   1P: $72   2P: $80   XP: $10   F17
▼▼▼▼   5/1-6/30 & 9/1-10/31   1P: $65-$67   2P: $70-$72   XP: $10   F17
          11/1-4/30   1P: $63-$65   2P: $68-$69   XP: $10   F17
Small-scale Hotel   **Location:** I-390, exit 8, 3.4 mi w on SR 20A. 4242 Lakeville Rd 14454. Fax: 585/243-9007. **Facility:** 76 one-
          bedroom standard units. 2 stories (no elevator), interior corridors. _Bath:_ combo or shower only. **Parking:** on-
site. **Terms:** check-in 4 pm, [ECP] meal plan available. **Amenities:** hair dryers. **Pool(s):** outdoor. **Business
Services:** meeting rooms. **Cards:** AX, CB, DC, DS, JC, MC, VI.

SOME UNITS
[S D] [†¶+] [Y] [👶] [📞] [🏊] [▶] [💻] / [✕] /

GENEVA pop. 13,617—_See also FINGER LAKES._

——— **WHERE TO STAY** ———

BELHURST CASTLE   Phone: 315/781-0201
▼▼▼   5/1-10/31   2P: $105-$315   XP: $30
          11/1-4/30   2P: $70-$245   XP: $30
Historic   **Location:** 2 mi s. Rt 14 S 14456 (PO Box 609). Fax: 315/781-0201. **Facility:** This lakefront property was built in
Country Inn   1885 and offers spacious, castlelike common areas accented with massive, original, carved woodwork. 13
          one-bedroom standard units, some with whirlpools. 3 stories (no elevator), interior corridors. _Bath:_ combo or
shower only. **Parking:** on-site. **Terms:** 7 day cancellation notice. **Amenities:** voice mail, irons, hair dryers. _Some:_ CD players,
honor bars. **Leisure Activities:** boat dock, fishing. **Guest Services:** valet laundry. **Business Services:** conference facilities.
Cards: MC, VI. _(See color ad p 289)_

SOME UNITS
[†¶] [Y] [▶] [DATA PORT] [💻] / [VCR] /

CLARK'S MOTEL
Motel

Phone: 315-789-0780

| 5/1-11/30 & 4/1-4/30 | 1P: $42-$48 | 2P: $42-$48 | XP: $3 |

Location: Jct SR 14 and US 20/SR 5, 2.3 mi w. 824 Canandaigua Rd 14456. **Facility:** 10 one-bedroom standard units. 1 story, exterior corridors. **Parking:** on-site, winter plug-ins. **Terms:** open 5/1-11/30 & 4/1-4/30. **Cards:** MC, VI.

SOME UNITS

GENEVA-ON-THE-LAKE *Book at aaa.com*
Historic
Country Inn

Phone: (315)789-7190

6/1-11/13 [ECP]	1P: $216-$352	2P: $226-$362	XP: $40	F6
5/1-5/31 & 4/1-4/30 [ECP]	1P: $171-$280	2P: $181-$290	XP: $40	F6
11/14-3/31 [ECP]	1P: $126-$207	2P: $136-$217	XP: $40	F6

Location: 1.5 mi s on SR 14. 1001 Lochland Rd 14456. Fax: 315/789-0322. **Facility:** Within the Finger Lakes area, the inn offers manicured lawns, an upscale restaurant and some rooms with Stickley furniture. Smoke free premises. 29 units. 6 one-bedroom standard units with kitchens. 13 one- and 10 two-bedroom suites ($356-$770) with kitchens, some with whirlpools. 3 stories (no elevator), interior corridors. *Bath:* combo or shower only. **Parking:** on-site. **Terms:** 2-3 night minimum stay - seasonal, 14 day cancellation notice-fee imposed, [BP] & [MAP] meal plans available, package plans - weekends. **Amenities:** irons, hair dryers. *Some:* CD players. **Dining:** 8 am-10 & 6-9 pm; noon-2 pm in season, cocktails. **Pool(s):** outdoor. **Leisure Activities:** rental canoes, rental paddleboats, boat dock, fishing, lawn games, bicycles, limited exercise equipment, horseshoes. *Fee:* sailboats, windsurfing, pontoon boat, massage. **Guest Services:** gift shop, valet laundry. **Business Services:** meeting rooms. **Cards:** AX, DS, MC, VI. **Special Amenities:** free expanded continental breakfast and free newspaper. *(See color ad p 289)*

SOME UNITS

RAMADA INN GENEVA LAKEFRONT *Book at aaa.com*
Small-scale Hotel

Phone: (315)789-0400

| 5/1-11/1 | 1P: $120-$160 | 2P: $130-$170 |
| 11/2-4/30 | 1P: $89-$119 | 2P: $99-$129 |

Location: I-90, exit 42, 8 mi s on SR 14. 41 Lakefront Dr 14456. Fax: 315/789-4351. **Facility:** 148 one-bedroom standard units, some with whirlpools. 6 stories, interior corridors. *Bath:* combo or shower only. **Parking:** on-site. **Terms:** cancellation fee imposed, pets ($10 extra charge). **Amenities:** video games, voice mail, irons, hair dryers. **Dining:** 6:30 am-3 & 5-10 pm, Sat & Sun 7 am-3 & 5-11 pm, cocktails. **Pool(s):** small heated indoor. **Leisure Activities:** exercise room. **Guest Services:** valet and coin laundry. **Business Services:** meeting rooms. **Cards:** AX, CB, DC, DS, JC, MC, VI. **Special Amenities:** free newspaper. *(See color ad p 8)*

SOME UNITS

── WHERE TO DINE ──

NONNA'S TRATTORIA
Italian

Lunch: $5-$9   Dinner: $8-$20   Phone: 315-789-1638

Location: Just e off Exchange St (SR 14); center. 1 Railroad Pl 14456. **Hours:** 11 am-3 & 4:30-9:30 pm, Fri-10 pm, Sat 4:30 pm-10 pm, Sun 4 pm-9 pm. Closed major holidays. **Reservations:** accepted. **Features:** Patrons can nosh on classic fare either inside or on the seasonal patio. The daily lunch buffet is a local favorite, along with Uncle Joe's Pizzeria for eat-in or take-out. Casual dress; cocktails. **Parking:** on-site. **Cards:** AX, DS, MC, VI.

PASTA ONLY'S COBBLESTONE
Italian

Lunch: $6-$8   Dinner: $10-$22   Phone: 315-789-8498

Location: Jct US 20 and SR 5, 1.5 mi w. 3610 Pre-Emption Rd at 5 & 20 14456. **Hours:** 11:30 am-2 & 5-9 pm; Fri & Sat-10 pm. Closed: 1/1, 12/25; also Mon off season. **Reservations:** suggested. **Features:** Although the restored 1825 farmhouse delivers a menu of Italian cuisine, wood-grilled steak, chops and fresh seafood, this place is known for its exquisite dessert. The pastry chef whips up outstanding creations, including the sunken chocolate souffle. Casual dress; cocktails. **Parking:** on-site. **Cards:** AX, DS, MC, VI.

WING TAI ORIENTAL RESTAURANT
Chinese

Lunch: $4-$5   Dinner: $6-$9   Phone: 315/789-8892

Location: Just off SR 14. 164 Castle St 14456. **Hours:** 11 am-9:30 pm, Fri & Sat-10:30 pm, Sun & Mon 5 pm-9:30 pm. Closed major holidays. **Reservations:** suggested, weekends. **Features:** In business since the late 1970s, the restaurant is decorated in an Oriental style, with Chinese lanterns and painted wallpaper. Seven star around the moon, a seafood, beef and chicken dish for two is popular, as is the irresistible flaming cherry dessert. Casual dress; beer & wine only. **Parking:** on-site. **Cards:** AX, DC, DS, MC, VI.

GHENT pop. 586

── WHERE TO DINE ──

RED BARN LUNCHEONETTE
American

Lunch: $3-$18   Dinner: $8-$26   Phone: 518/828-6677

Location: Jct SR 66 and 9-H, 2.5 mi n. 47 Old Post Rd/Rt 9-H 12075. **Hours:** noon-8 pm, Sat & Sun 7:30 am-9 pm; hours may vary. Closed: 11/25. **Features:** An old-fashioned atmosphere lends to the quaint, homespun charm of the converted barn. Patrons can relax in the smoke-free dining room and enjoy selections including sandwiches and daily specials. When it's time for dessert, opt for the delicious, homemade ice cream. Casual dress. **Parking:** on-site.

GLEN COVE pop. 26,622

── WHERE TO DINE ──

LA PACE
Northern
Italian

Lunch: $12-$18   Dinner: $17-$31   Phone: 516/671-2970

Location: Jct Glen Cove Rd, 0.5 mi e. 51 Cedar Swamp Rd 11542. **Hours:** noon-2:30 & 6-10 pm, Fri-11 pm, Sat 6 pm-11 pm, Sun 4 pm-10 pm. Closed: 3/27, 12/25. **Reservations:** suggested. **Features:** A Gold Coast tradition since the late 1970s, the restaurant exudes a sophisticated European ambience that is reflective of an earlier time. The specialty veal chop with wild mushrooms is well-prepared and flavorful. Service is reserved and professional. Semi-formal attire; cocktails. **Parking:** valet and street. **Cards:** AX, DC, MC, VI.

GLENORA —See also FINGER LAKES.

———— WHERE TO STAY ————

THE INN AT GLENORA WINE CELLARS
▼▼▼▼   5/1-10/31   2P: $139-$235   XP: $10   F12
          11/1-4/30   2P: $99-$210   XP: $10   F12

Phone: (607)243-9500

Small-scale Hotel **Location:** On SR 14. Overlooking Seneca Lake and vineyards. 5435 Rt 14 14837. Fax: 607/243-9595. **Facility:** Smoke free premises. 30 one-bedroom standard units, some with whirlpools. 2 stories (no elevator), interior corridors. *Bath:* combo or shower only. **Parking:** on-site. **Terms:** 2-3 night minimum stay - weekends in summer, [AP], [ECP] & [MAP] meal plans available, package plans - seasonal. **Amenities:** dual phone lines, voice mail, irons, hair dryers. **Dining:** Veraisons, see separate listing. **Business Services:** meeting rooms. **Cards:** AX, DS, MC, VI.

(ASK) (SD) (TI) (占) (X) (DATA PORT) (⬜) (⬛)

SOUTH GLENORA TREE FARM BED & BREAKFAST
▼▼▼   5/1-12/5 & 4/16-4/30 [BP]   1P: $123-$149   2P: $123-$149   XP: $25
        12/6-4/15 [BP]   1P: $98-$119   2P: $98-$119   XP: $25

Phone: 607/243-7414

Bed & Breakfast **Location:** SR 14, 1 mi w via S Glenora Rd, follow signs. Located in a quiet area. 546 S Glenora Rd 14837. **Facility:** Originally a barn, this renovated B&B offers country-themed rooms and plenty of acreage in which to explore and bird-watch. Smoke free premises. 5 one-bedroom standard units. 1 story, interior/exterior corridors. *Bath:* combo or shower only. **Parking:** on-site. **Terms:** 2 night minimum stay - weekends in season, 14 day cancellation notice. **Amenities:** video library, hair dryers. **Leisure Activities:** fishing, hiking trails. **Business Services:** fax. **Cards:** DS, MC, VI.

SOME UNITS
(X) / (PW) (VCR) (☎) (⬜) /

———— WHERE TO DINE ————

VERAISONS
▼▼▼   **Lunch:** $7-$14   **Dinner:** $18-$25   **Phone:** 607/243-9500

Continental **Location:** On SR 14; in The Inn at Glenora Wine Cellars. 5435 SR 14 14837. **Hours:** 8-10 am, 11:30-3 & 5-9 pm, Fri & Sat 5-9 pm; hours vary off season. Closed: 12/25. **Reservations:** suggested. **Features:** Panoramic views of Seneca Lake and vineyards are the focal point of the winery restaurant. Nicely presented creations are made from seasonal local ingredients. Casual dress; beer & wine only. **Parking:** on-site. **Cards:** AX, DS, MC, VI.

(X)

GLENS FALLS pop. 14,354—See also ADIRONDACK MOUNTAINS & SOUTH GLENS FALLS.

———— WHERE TO STAY ————

QUEENSBURY HOTEL   *Book at aaa.com*
(AAA) (SAVE)   7/28-9/4   1P: $149-$179   2P: $149-$179
        5/1-7/27   1P: $109-$119   2P: $109-$119
▼◆▼   9/5-4/30   1P: $89-$119   2P: $89-$119

Phone: (518)792-1121

Historic **Location:** Corner of Maple St; center. 88 Ridge St 12801. Fax: 518/792-9259. **Facility:** Traditional Victorian decor
Small-scale Hotel and furnishings enhance this red brick downtown hotel overlooking a park. 125 units. 114 one-bedroom standard units. 11 one-bedroom suites. 5 stories, interior corridors. *Bath:* combo or shower only. **Parking:** on-site, winter plug-ins. **Terms:** [AP] meal plan available. **Dining:** 6:30 am-11 & 5-9:30 pm. **Pool(s):** heated indoor. **Leisure Activities:** whirlpool, exercise room. *Fee:* massage. **Guest Services:** valet laundry. **Business Services:** conference facilities. **Cards:** AX, DC, DS, MC, VI.

SOME UNITS
(SD) (TI) (Y) (占) (♨) (➷) (X) / (X) (DATA PORT) (⬜) /
FEE

———— WHERE TO DINE ————

DAVIDSON BROTHERS RESTAURANT & BREWERY   **Lunch:** $6-$9   **Dinner:** $11-$20   Phone: 518/743-9026
(AAA)   **Location:** Center. 184 Glen St 12801. **Hours:** 11:30 am-10 pm, Fri-11 pm, Sat noon-11 pm, Sun noon-9 pm.
▼▼   Closed: 3/27, 11/25, 12/25; also Sun 10/1-5/31. **Features:** This two-story English brewhouse offers the
American typical "pub fare" which is well-complemented by a selection of hand-crafted ales made on the premises. Both levels are decorated using a variety of odd pieces of machinery from the city's industrial past. Upstairs holds a game room and dining outdoors is popular, weather permitting. Casual dress; cocktails. **Parking:** street. **Cards:** AX, DC, MC, VI.

(Y) (K) (X)

FIDDLEHEADS   **Lunch:** $6-$15   **Dinner:** $15-$26   **Phone:** 518/793-5789
▼▼▼   **Location:** I-87, exit 18, follow signs toward hospital 2 mi, just beyond to 2nd traffic light, bear left on SR 9L. 21 Ridge
        St 12801. **Hours:** 11:30 am-3 & 5-9 pm. Closed major holidays; also 12/24; also Sun & Mon.
Continental **Reservations:** suggested. **Features:** A country ambience is pervasive in the charming restaurant. Maryland crab cakes stand out on a menu of beef, lamb, fowl and seafood preparations, all thoughtfully arranged by the owner-chef. In addition to being delicious, desserts have great eye appeal. Casual dress; cocktails. **Parking:** street. **Cards:** DS, MC, VI.

(X)

GRAND ISLAND —See Buffalo p. 253.

GREAT NECK pop. 9,538

———— WHERE TO STAY ————

THE ANDREW HOTEL *Book at aaa.com*   Phone: (516)482-2900

△△△ SAVE   6/2-8/31 [ECP]   1P: $215   2P: $215
     5/1-6/1 & 9/1-11/30 [ECP]   1P: $175   2P: $175
▽▽▽▽   12/1-4/30 [ECP]   1P: $165   2P: $165

Small-scale Hotel   **Location:** Jct SR 25A, 0.8 mi n on Middle Neck Rd, then just e. Located in a commercial/residential area. 75 N Station Plaza 11021. Fax: 516/482-4643. **Facility:** 62 units. 59 one-bedroom standard units. 3 one-bedroom suites. 4 stories, interior corridors. **Parking:** valet. **Terms:** package plans - weekends, pets ($150 fee). **Amenities:** video library (fee), DVD players, CD players, high-speed Internet, dual phone lines, voice mail, safes, honor bars, hair dryers. **Dining:** noon-midnight, Fri-4 pm, Sat 4 pm-midnight, cocktails. **Guest Services:** valet laundry. **Business Services:** meeting rooms. **Cards:** AX, DC, JC, MC, VI. **Special Amenities: free expanded continental breakfast and free newspaper.**

SOME UNITS
[⑤Ⓓ] [🛏] [🍽] [🍸] [📶] [DATA PORT] / [✕] [📱] [🖨] /
FEE

INN AT GREAT NECK *Book at aaa.com*   Phone: (516)773-2000

▽▽▽▽   All Year   1P: $219-$259   2P: $219-$259   XP: $20   F16

Small-scale Hotel   **Location:** Jct SR 25A, 0.8 mi n on Middle Neck Rd, then just w. Located in a commercial area. 30 Cutter Mill Rd 11021. Fax: 516/773-2020. **Facility:** 85 units. 79 one-bedroom standard units, some with whirlpools. 6 one-bedroom suites ($319-$369). 5 stories, interior corridors. *Bath:* combo or shower only. **Parking:** valet. **Terms:** pets (with prior approval). **Amenities:** video library, CD players, high-speed Internet, dual phone lines, voice mail, safes, honor bars, irons, hair dryers. **Leisure Activities:** exercise room. **Guest Services:** valet laundry. **Business Services:** meeting rooms, business center. **Cards:** AX, DC, DS, MC, VI.

SOME UNITS
[A$K] [⑤Ⓓ] [🔕] [🛏] [🍽] [🍸] [📷] [📹] [VCR] [📶] [DATA PORT] [📱] / [✕] [📱] [🖨] /
FEE

———— WHERE TO DINE ————

PETER LUGER   **Lunch:** $7-$20   **Dinner:** $16-$32   Phone: 516/487-8800

▽▽▽   **Location:** I-495, exit 33 (Lakeville Rd), 0.8 mi n, then 0.6 mi w. 255 Northern Blvd 11021. **Hours:** 11:45 am-10 pm, Fri & Sat-11 pm, Sun from 1 pm. **Reservations:** required. **Features:** Succulent prime porterhouse steak,

Steak House   which are dry-aged on premise, are this sophisticated restaurant's specialty and they are exceptional. Many by-the-glass selections line the excellent wine list. The dining room exudes an elegant, Old World charm. Casual dress; cocktails. **Parking:** valet and street.

[🍸] [✕]

GREECE pop. 14,614   (See map and index starting on p. 550)

———— WHERE TO STAY ————

COMFORT INN-WEST *Book at aaa.com*   Phone: (585)621-5700   ㉑

△△△ SAVE   5/1-10/31 [ECP]   1P: $64   2P: $84   XP: $8   F18
     11/1-4/30 [ECP]   1P: $54   2P: $84   XP: $8   F18
▽▽▽▽   **Location:** Jct SR 390 and 104 (Ridge Rd), 0.5 mi e. 1501 W Ridge Rd 14615. Fax: 585/621-8446. **Facility:** 83 one-bedroom standard units, some with whirlpools. 5 stories, interior corridors. **Parking:** on-site. **Terms:** 3 day

Small-scale Hotel   cancellation notice, pets ($10 fee, $10 deposit). **Amenities:** video games, dual phone lines, voice mail, safes, irons, hair dryers. **Guest Services:** valet laundry. **Business Services:** fax (fee). **Cards:** AX, CB, DC, DS, MC, VI. **Special Amenities: free expanded continental breakfast and free newspaper.**

SOME UNITS
[⑤Ⓓ] [🛏] [🍽] [📷] [DATA PORT] [📱] / [✕] [📱] [🖨] /
FEE

COURTYARD BY MARRIOTT-ROCHESTER WEST *Book at aaa.com*   Phone: (585)621-6050   ⑳

▽▽▽▽   All Year   1P: $99-$129

Small-scale Hotel   **Location:** I-390, exit 24A, just e on SR 104 (Ridge Rd), just s on Hoover Dr, then just w. 400 Paddy Creek Cir 14615 (400 Paddy Creek Cir, ROCHESTER). Fax: 585/621-6115. **Facility:** 78 units. 70 one-bedroom standard units. 8 one-bedroom suites. 3 stories, interior corridors. *Bath:* combo or shower only. **Parking:** on-site. **Pool(s):** small heated indoor. **Leisure Activities:** whirlpool, exercise room. **Guest Services:** valet and coin laundry, area transportation. **Business Services:** meeting rooms, fax. **Cards:** AX, CB, DC, DS, MC, VI.

SOME UNITS
[⑤Ⓓ] [🔕] [🍽] [&] [📹] [🏊] [📷] [DATA PORT] [📱] / [✕] [📱] [🖨] /

HAMPTON INN-ROCHESTER NORTH *Book at aaa.com*   Phone: (585)663-6070   ㉔

▽▽▽▽   5/1-11/19   1P: $99-$104   2P: $104-$109
     11/20-4/30   1P: $89-$104   2P: $94-$99
     Location: I-390, exit 24A, just e on SR 104 (Ridge Rd), then just n on Buckman Rd. 500 Center Place Dr 14615.
Small-scale Hotel   Fax: 585/663-9158. **Facility:** 118 units. 116 one-bedroom standard units. 2 one-bedroom suites ($125-$149) with whirlpools. 4 stories, interior corridors. *Bath:* combo or shower only. **Parking:** on-site. **Terms:** 7 day cancellation notice. **Amenities:** high-speed Internet, voice mail, irons, hair dryers. **Leisure Activities:** exercise room. **Guest Services:** valet laundry. **Business Services:** meeting rooms. **Cards:** AX, CB, DC, DS, MC, VI.

SOME UNITS
[A$K] [⑤Ⓓ] [🛏] [&M] [&] [📷] [DATA PORT] [📱] / [✕] [📱] [🖨] /
FEE   FEE

MARRIOTT AIRPORT HOTEL *Book at aaa.com*   Phone: (585)225-6880   ㉒

▽▽▽▽   5/1-11/7   1P: $94-$180
     11/8-4/30   1P: $89-$180
Small-scale Hotel   **Location:** I-390, exit 24B, just w on SR 104 (Ridge Rd); 3.5 mi n of I-490. Located close to malls and shopping. 1890 Ridge Rd W 14615. Fax: 585/225-8188. **Facility:** 210 units. 208 one-bedroom standard units. 2 one-bedroom suites. 7 stories, interior corridors. **Parking:** on-site. **Amenities:** video library (fee), video games, high-speed Internet, dual phone lines, voice mail, irons, hair dryers. **Pool(s):** heated indoor. **Leisure Activities:** sauna, whirlpool, exercise room. **Guest Services:** valet laundry. **Business Services:** conference facilities, business center. **Cards:** AX, DC, DS, JC, MC, VI.

SOME UNITS
[A$K] [✈] [🍽] [24H] [🍸] [🏊] [✕] [📷] [DATA PORT] [📱] / [✕] [📱] [🖨] /

(See map and index starting on p. 550)

RESIDENCE INN BY MARRIOTT-WEST   *Book at aaa.com*   Phone: (585)865-2090   ㉕

All Year [ECP]   1P: $109-$219   2P: $109-$219

Location: I-390, exit 24A, just e on SR 104 (Ridge Rd), then just s on Hoover Dr, then just w. 500 Paddy Creek Cir 14615 Small-scale Hotel (500 Paddy Creek Cir, ROCHESTER). Fax: 585/865-2990. **Facility:** 90 units. 51 one-bedroom standard units with kitchens. 26 one- and 13 two-bedroom suites with kitchens. 3 stories, interior corridors. *Bath:* combo or shower only. **Parking:** on-site. **Terms:** pets ($150 fee, $10 extra charge). **Amenities:** video library (fee), video games, high-speed Internet, dual phone lines, voice mail, irons, hair dryers. **Pool(s):** small heated indoor. **Leisure Activities:** whirlpool, exercise room, sports court. **Guest Services:** complimentary evening beverages: Mon-Thurs, valet and coin laundry. **Business Services:** meeting rooms. **Cards:** AX, CB, DC, DS, JC, MC, VI.

SOME UNITS

🛏 ✈ 🐾 🍴 ⬚ 🐕 ✕ 🏋 DATA PORT 🛢 📷 💻 / ✕ VCR / FEE

WELLESLEY INN (ROCHESTER/NORTH)   *Book at aaa.com*   Phone: (585)621-2060   ㉓

AAA SAVE   All Year   1P: $55-$105   XP: $10

Location: I-390, exit 24A, just e on SR 104 (Ridge Rd). 1635 W Ridge Rd 14615. Fax: 585/621-7102. **Facility:** 97 one-bedroom standard units. 4 stories, interior corridors. *Bath:* combo or shower only. **Parking:** on-site. Small-scale Hotel **Terms:** [ECP] meal plan available, pets ($10 fee). **Amenities:** video library (fee), video games, voice mail, irons, hair dryers. **Guest Services:** valet laundry. **Cards:** AX, DC, DS, JC, MC, VI. **Special Amenities:** free expanded continental breakfast and free newspaper. *(See color ad p 553)*

SOME UNITS

🛏 ✈ 🍴 ⬚M 🐕 🐾 🏋 DATA PORT 💻 / ✕ 🛢 📷 / FEE

GREENE pop. 1,701

——— **WHERE TO STAY** ———

SERENITY FARMS   Phone: (607)656-4659

All Year [BP]   1P: $69-$89   2P: $69-$89

Location: I-81, exit 8, 1.2 mi s, 11 mi e on SR 206, 4.1 mi n on SR 12 to King Rd, 2.7 mi n, then 1.5 mi e. Located in a rural area. 386 Pollard Rd 13778. Fax: 253/423-3526. **Facility:** Designated smoking area. 6 one-bedroom stan-Bed & Breakfast dard units. 2 stories (no elevator), interior corridors. *Bath:* some shared or private, shower only. **Parking:** on-site. **Terms:** office hours 9 am-9 pm, 7 day cancellation notice-fee imposed, package plans - seasonal. **Amenities:** hair dryers. *Some:* DVD players. **Pool(s):** heated outdoor. **Leisure Activities:** whirlpool. **Business Services:** PC, fax (fee). **Cards:** AX, MC, VI.

SOME UNITS

ASK 🛏 🐾 🐕 ✕ 📺 🏋 ☎ / 🏋 🛢 💻 /

GREENPORT pop. 4,180

——— **WHERE TO STAY** ———

THE BARTLETT HOUSE INN   Phone: 631/477-0371

5/1-10/31 [ECP]   2P: $125-$215   XP: $35
11/1-12/31 [ECP]   2P: $120-$215   XP: $35
1/1-4/30 [ECP]   2P: $110-$215   XP: $35

Bed & Breakfast **Location:** SR 25 (Front St), just w of town. 503 Front St 11944. **Facility:** Smoke free premises. 10 one-bedroom standard units. 3 stories (no elevator), interior corridors. *Bath:* combo or shower only. **Parking:** on-site. **Terms:** age restrictions may apply, 7 day cancellation notice-fee imposed. **Amenities:** voice mail. *Some:* CD players. **Cards:** AX, MC, VI.

SOME UNITS

✕ �W DATA PORT / 🛢 💻 /

——— *The following lodging was either not evaluated or did not* ———
meet AAA rating requirements but is listed for your information only.

SILVER SANDS MOTEL   Phone: 631/477-0011

[fyi]   Did not meet all AAA rating requirements for locking devices in some guest rooms at time of last evaluation on 05/15/2003. **Location:** SR 25, 1 mi w. Silvermere Rd 11944 (PO Box 285). Facilities, services, and decor charac-Motel terize a basic property.

——— **WHERE TO DINE** ———

CLAUDIO'S RESTAURANT   Historic   Lunch: $9-$14   Dinner: $16-$28   Phone: 631/477-0627

Location: SR 25 to corner of Main and Front sts SE, just s to water. 111 Main St 11944. **Hours:** Open 5/1-11/20; 11:30 am-10 pm, Fri & Sat-11 pm. Closed: Tues 9/6-5/30. **Reservations:** suggested. Steak & Seafood **Features:** Overlooking the marina and fishing harbor, the established restaurant has been operated by generations of the same family since 1870. Traditional preparations of mostly seafood are wholesome and flavorful. A nautical theme weaves through the dining areas. Casual dress; cocktails. **Parking:** on-site. **Cards:** MC, VI.

🍽 ✕

SUSHI AT ALDO'S   Lunch: $10-$25   Dinner: $10-$25   Phone: 631/477-1699

Location: Center. 103-105 Front St 11944. **Hours:** Open 5/15-11/15; noon-3 & 5-10 pm, Tues-9:30 pm, Thurs 5 pm-10 pm, Fri & Sat noon-3 & 5-10:30 pm. Closed: Wed. **Reservations:** accepted. **Features:** Offering a large selection of special rolls, tempura and teriyaki. Casual dress; beer & wine only. **Parking:** street. Sushi **Cards:** AX, MC, VI.

✕

GREENWICH pop. 1,902

——— WHERE TO STAY ———

SUNSHINE INN
Phone: 518/692-2997

Motel

All Year — 1P: $55-$125 — 2P: $55-$125
Location: 0.5 mi n. Located in a rural area. 2624 SR 40 12834. Fax: 518/692-2601. **Facility:** 10 one-bedroom standard units, some with efficiencies. 1 story, exterior corridors. *Bath:* combo or shower only. **Parking:** on-site, winter plug-ins. **Terms:** office hours 9 am-10 pm, 7 day cancellation notice. **Amenities:** voice mail.
Cards: AX, DS, MC, VI.

SOME UNITS

GROTON pop. 2,470—See also FINGER LAKES.

——— WHERE TO DINE ———

BENN CONGER INN Historic
Dinner: $16-$26 — **Phone:** 607/898-5817

Mediterranean

Location: Just w of SR 38. 206 W Cortland St 13073. **Hours:** 5:30 pm-9 pm, Sun from 5 pm. Closed: Mon & Tues. **Reservations:** required. **Features:** The 1919 Southern Revival mansion is elegantly appointed with upscale table settings that include signature china. A delicious menu choice is scallops over spinach fettuccine. Among outstanding desserts are profiterole and blueberry creme brulee. Dressy casual; cocktails. **Parking:** on-site. **Cards:** AX, DC, MC, VI.

GUILDERLAND pop. 32,688 (See map and index starting on p. 215)

——— WHERE TO STAY ———

HOLIDAY INN EXPRESS TURF ON WESTERN AVE *Book at aaa.com*
Phone: (518)438-0001 — **45**

Small-scale Hotel

7/9-8/28 [ECP]	1P: $99-$159	2P: $99-$159	XP: $10	F19
8/29-4/30 [ECP]	1P: $69-$159	2P: $69-$159	XP: $10	F19
5/1-7/8 [ECP]	1P: $89-$149	2P: $89-$149	XP: $10	F19

Location: I-87/90, exit 24, 0.5 mi e on US 20 (Western Ave). 1442 Western Ave 12203 (1442 Western Ave, ALBANY). Fax: 518/438-0690. **Facility:** 121 units. 117 one-bedroom standard units. 4 one-bedroom suites ($99-$179). 4 stories, interior corridors. *Bath:* combo or shower only. **Parking:** on-site. **Terms:** check-in 4 pm, 3 day cancellation notice. **Amenities:** video games, voice mail, safes, irons, hair dryers. **Pool(s):** small heated indoor. **Leisure Activities:** exercise room. **Guest Services:** sundries, valet and coin laundry. **Business Services:** meeting rooms, business center. **Cards:** AX, CB, DC, DS, JC, MC, VI. **Special Amenities:** free local telephone calls and free newspaper.

SOME UNITS
FEE

——— WHERE TO DINE ———

BAVARIAN CHALET
Dinner: $10-$17 — **Phone:** 518/355-8005 — **36**

German

Location: I-87, exit US 20, 5.8 mi w; center. 5060 Western Tpke 12009. **Hours:** 4 pm-9 pm, Sat-10 pm, Sun 3 pm-8 pm. Closed: 7/4, 12/24-12/26; also Mon & Tues. **Reservations:** suggested, weekends. **Features:** German selections, such as soup with potatoes, ham and cabbage, are particularly tasty on a menu of veal, game, black Angus steak and seafood. Bavarian decor lends to the authenticity of the setting. Many imported and microbrewed beers are offered. Casual dress; cocktails. **Parking:** on-site. **Cards:** AX, DS, MC, VI.

LONDONDERRY CAFE
Lunch: $6-$8 — **Dinner:** $8-$17 — **Phone:** 518/489-4288 — **37**

American

Location: Jct US 20 and Northway. Stuyvesant Plaza 12203. **Hours:** 11 am-9 pm, Sun 10:30 am-3 pm. Closed major holidays. **Reservations:** suggested, weekends. **Features:** Guests can choose either to dine outside during warm weather or inside in a cozy dining room. Hearty soups with an unusual bases, crisp salads and innovative "American-style" entrees make up the menu. For dessert, lemon macaroon pie is worth the calories. Service is friendly and casual. Casual dress; wine only. **Parking:** on-site. **Cards:** AX, CB, DC, DS, MC, VI.

METRO 20 DINER
Lunch: $5-$8 — **Dinner:** $9-$16 — **Phone:** 518/456-3876 — **35**

American

DC, DS, MC, VI.

Location: I-87/90, exit 24, at US 20 (Western Ave). 1709 Western Ave 12203. **Hours:** 6 am-midnight, Fri & Sat-1 am. **Features:** It's hard to miss the chrome-laden, '50s-style diner. On the large menu are sandwiches galore, steaks, chops, Italian and Greek items, chicken and platter specials and all-day breakfast foods. Service in the cool surroundings is fast and friendly. Casual dress; cocktails. **Parking:** on-site. **Cards:** AX,

HAGUE pop. 854

——— WHERE TO STAY ———

TROUT HOUSE VILLAGE RESORT
Phone: (518)543-6088

Cabin

All Year — 1P: $59-$450 — 2P: $59-$450
Location: Jct SR 9N and 8, just n; center. 9117 Lake Shore Dr (SR 9N) 12836 (PO Box 510). Fax: 518/543-6124. **Facility:** 27 units. 8 one-bedroom standard units, some with kitchens. 1 two- and 1 three-bedroom suites with kitchens. 14 cabins and 3 cottages, some with whirlpools. 2 stories (no elevator), interior/exterior corridors. *Bath:* combo or shower only. **Parking:** on-site. **Terms:** 2-3 night minimum stay - seasonal, 30 day cancellation notice-fee imposed, weekly rates available, package plans - in summer. **Amenities:** voice mail, hair dryers. *Some:* DVD players, irons. **Leisure Activities:** boating, canoeing, paddleboats, fishing, putting green, bicycles, basketball, horseshoes, shuffleboard, volleyball, game room. *Fee:* marina. **Business Services:** fax (fee). **Cards:** AX, DC, MC, VI.

SOME UNITS

———— WHERE TO DINE ————

THE VIEW AT INDIAN KETTLE **Lunch:** $7-$11 **Dinner:** $14-$30 **Phone:** 518/543-8038

Location: 2 mi n of jct SR 9N and 8, on SR 9N. 9580 Lake Shore Dr 12836. **Hours:** Open 5/1-10/18; 11:30 am-10 pm, Sat & Sun from 7:30 am. Closed: Tues-Thurs 5/1-5/31 & 9/5-10/18. **Reservations:** accepted.
Features: The eatery takes its name from the site where Native Americans used holes formed during the Ice Age for cooking. Its location on the lake allows for beautiful views from outdoor tables. While the lunch
American   menu centers on such simple fare as sandwiches and wraps, the dinner menu lists hearty items, including preparations of chicken, steak and pasta. Casual dress; cocktails. **Parking:** on-site. **Cards:** AX, DS,
MC, VI.

HALFMOON pop. 18,474

———— WHERE TO DINE ————

GRECIAN GARDENS PIZZA & RESTAURANT **Lunch:** $4-$9 **Dinner:** $16 **Phone:** 518/373-9950
Location: Jct SR 146 and 9, 0.9 mi s. 1612 Rt 9 12065. **Hours:** 11 am-11 pm. Closed: 11/25, 12/25.
Reservations: accepted. **Features:** A fountain is the centerpiece of the family-style restaurant's laid-back
Italian   dining room. The menu dabbles in Greek, Italian and American cuisine, including particularly tasty pizza. Tables with colorful umbrellas dot the breezy, seasonal patio. Casual dress; cocktails. **Parking:** on-site.
Cards: AX, DC, MC, VI.

TAI-PAN **Lunch:** $6-$7 **Dinner:** $8-$14 **Phone:** 518/383-8581
Location: On SR 9. 1519 Halfmoon Pkwy 12065. **Hours:** 11 am-10 pm, Sat-11 pm. Closed: 11/25.
Reservations: suggested, weekends. **Features:** Next to Clifton Park, the comfortable restaurant has a
Chinese   moderately sophisticated ambience that's welcoming to professionals. The menu centers on Thai and Hong Kong cuisine, such as chili lamb curry. A wonderful dim sum brunch is served on the weekend. Casual
dress; cocktails. **Parking:** on-site. **Cards:** AX, DC, DS, MC, VI.

HAMBURG —See Buffalo p. 253.

HAMMONDSPORT pop. 731—See also FINGER LAKES.

———— WHERE TO STAY ————

HAMMONDSPORT MOTEL **Phone:** (607)569-2600
⊕⊕⊕ [SAVE]   5/1-11/8 & 4/1-4/30 1P: $66-$73 2P: $66-$73 XP: $10 F6
Location: Just n of SR 54A on Keuka Lake; downtown. Located in Keuka Lakefront Village. William St & Water St 14840
(PO Box 311). Fax: 607/569-2699. **Facility:** 17 one-bedroom standard units. 1 story, exterior corridors.
Parking: on-site. **Terms:** open 5/1-11/8 & 4/1-4/30, 7 day cancellation notice. **Amenities:** voice mail. **Leisure**
Motel   **Activities:** fishing. *Fee:* boat dock. **Cards:** MC, VI. **Special Amenities:** free local telephone calls and preferred room (subject to availability with advanced reservations).
SOME UNITS

PARK INN **Phone:** (607)569-9387
5/1-11/9 1P: $69-$79 2P: $79-$89 XP: $10
11/10-4/30 1P: $49-$59 2P: $59-$69 XP: $10
Historic   **Location:** Center; on town square. 37-39 Shethar St 14840. **Facility:** Historic hotel overlooking the town square.
Country Inn   5 one-bedroom standard units. 2 stories (no elevator), interior corridors. **Bath:** combo or shower only.
Parking: street. **Terms:** 7 day cancellation notice-fee imposed. **Amenities:** hair dryers. **Cards:** DS,
MC, VI.
SOME UNITS

VILLAGE TAVERN INN **Phone:** 607/569-2528
⊕⊕⊕ [SAVE]   10/1-1/3 2P: $79-$169
5/21-9/30 2P: $89-$159
5/1-5/20 & 2/3-4/30 2P: $79-$139
Historic   **Location:** On SR 54A. Located in village square. 30 Mechanic St 14840 (PO Box 92). Fax: 607/569-3560.
Country Inn   **Facility:** Walking distance of Keuka Lake. 8 units. 6 one-bedroom standard units, some with efficiencies (no utensils). 1 one- and 1 two-bedroom suites ($120-$159) with kitchens (no utensils). 2 stories (no elevator),
interior corridors. **Bath:** combo or shower only. **Parking:** street. **Terms:** open 5/1-1/3 & 2/3-4/30, 2 night
minimum stay - seasonal weekends, 11 day cancellation notice-fee imposed, weekly rates available. **Amenities:** hair dryers.
Some: irons. **Dining:** restaurant, see separate listing. **Cards:** AX, DC, MC, VI.
SOME UNITS

———— WHERE TO DINE ————

VILLAGE TAVERN **Lunch:** $5-$10 **Dinner:** $10-$22 **Phone:** 607/569-2528
Location: On SR 54A; in Village Tavern Inn. 30 Mechanic St 14840. **Hours:** Open 5/1-1/1 & 2/1-4/30; 11:30 am-3
& 5-9:30 pm, Fri & Sat-10 pm. Closed: 11/25, 12/25; also Mon-Wed 1/1-3/31. **Reservations:** suggested.
American   **Features:** An extensive selection of wine and exotic beer matches well with thoughtfully prepared steak, seafood and pasta dishes. Airplane photographs hang on the walls of the comfortable, tavern-style dining
room. Casual dress; cocktails. **Parking:** street. **Cards:** AX, DS, MC, VI.

HANCOCK pop. 3,449

─── WHERE TO STAY ───

SMITH'S COLONIAL MOTEL   Phone: 607/637-2989

5/1-9/7	1P: $50-$105	2P: $60-$105	XP: $10 F13
9/8-12/31	1P: $50-$85	2P: $60-$80	XP: $10 F13
1/1-4/30	1P: $50-$65	2P: $60-$65	XP: $10 F13

Motel   **Location:** SR 17, exit 87. Located in a quiet area. 23085 State Hwy 97 13783. Fax: 607/637-2989. **Facility:** 16 one-bedroom standard units. 1 story, exterior corridors. *Bath:* shower only. **Parking:** on-site, winter plug-ins. **Terms:** 2 night minimum stay - weekends 7/1-8/31, pets ($5 extra charge). **Leisure Activities:** rental canoes, fishing. **Cards:** AX, DS, MC, VI.

FEE

HARTSDALE —*See New York p. 452.*

HARTWICK SEMINARY —*See also COOPERSTOWN.*

─── WHERE TO STAY ───

BEST WESTERN INN & SUITES AT THE COMMONS   *Book at aaa.com*   Phone: (607)547-9439

6/11-9/5	1P: $165-$275	2P: $175-$285	XP: $10 F12
1/1-4/30	1P: $80-$220	2P: $90-$230	XP: $10 F12
5/1-6/10 & 9/6-12/31	1P: $80-$210	2P: $90-$220	XP: $10 F12

Small-scale Hotel   **Location:** On SR 28; center. 50 Commons Dr (Rt 28) 13326 (50 Commons Dr, COOPERSTOWN). Fax: 607/547-7082. **Facility:** 99 one-bedroom standard units. 2 stories, interior corridors. *Bath:* combo or shower only. **Parking:** on-site, winter plug-ins. **Terms:** cancellation fee imposed, [ECP] meal plan available. **Amenities:** voice mail, safes, irons, hair dryers. **Pool(s):** small heated indoor. **Leisure Activities:** whirlpool, picnic pavilion with grills, exercise room. *Fee:* game room. **Guest Services:** gift shop, coin laundry. **Business Services:** meeting rooms. **Cards:** AX, DC, DS, MC, VI. **Special Amenities:** free continental breakfast and free local telephone calls. *(See color ad p 269)*

SOME UNITS

FEE

Savings at Your Fingertips

W hen you have a AAA TourBook® guide in your hand, you have a world of savings right at your fingertips. AAA Official Appointment lodgings that display the bright-red AAA logo, [SAVE] icon and Diamond rating in their listing want business from AAA Members, and many offer discounts and special amenities to them*.

So, when planning your next vacation, be sure to consult your AAA TourBook for the familiar red [SAVE] icon.

[SAVE]   *See TourBook Navigator, page 14, for details.*

HAUPPAUGE pop. 20,100

---------- WHERE TO STAY ----------

HOLIDAY INN EXPRESS   *Book at aaa.com*   **Phone:** (631)348-1400

(AAA) (SAVE) | 7/1-12/31 [ECP] | 1P: $159
| 1/1-4/30 [ECP] | 1P: $139-$149
▽▽▽ | 5/1-6/30 [ECP] | 1P: $149

Small-scale Hotel **Location:** I-495, exit 56 (SR 111), just s to Central Ave, then just w. Located in a commercial area. 2050 Express Dr S 11788. Fax: 631/348-1411. **Facility:** 133 units. 131 one-bedroom standard units. 2 one-bedroom suites with whirlpools. 7 stories, interior corridors. *Bath:* combo or shower only. **Parking:** on-site. **Amenities:** video games (fee), dual phone lines, voice mail, irons, hair dryers. **Pool(s):** small heated indoor. **Leisure Activities:** sauna, exercise room. **Business Services:** valet and coin laundry, airport transportation-Islip MacArthur Airport, area transportation-within 5 mi. **Guest Services:** meeting rooms. **Cards:** AX, CB, DC, DS, JC, MC, VI. **Special Amenities: free expanded continental breakfast and free local telephone calls.**

SOME UNITS

 FEE   FEE

RESIDENCE INN BY MARRIOTT   *Book at aaa.com*   **Phone:** (631)724-4188

▽▽▽ | 5/1-12/31 [BP] | 1P: $189-$299 | 2P: $189-$299 | XP: $10 | F21
| 1/1-4/30 [BP] | 1P: $179-$299 | 2P: $179-$299 | XP: $10 | F21

Small-scale Hotel **Location:** I-495, exit 57, 1.2 mi nw. Located close to business park. 850 Veterans Memorial Hwy 11788. Fax: 631/724-4186. **Facility:** 100 units. 44 one-bedroom standard units, some with efficiencies or kitchens. 44 one- and 12 two-bedroom suites ($179-$299), some with efficiencies or kitchens. 3 stories, interior corridors. *Bath:* combo or shower only. **Parking:** on-site. **Terms:** cancellation fee imposed, small pets only ($100 fee, $10 extra charge). **Amenities:** high-speed Internet (fee), voice mail, irons, hair dryers. *Some:* dual phone lines. **Pool(s):** small heated indoor. **Leisure Activities:** whirlpool, exercise room. **Guest Services:** complimentary evening beverages: Mon-Thurs, coin laundry, area transportation. **Business Services:** meeting rooms. **Cards:** AX, DC, DS, MC, VI.

SOME UNITS

(ASK)  FEE

SHERATON LONG ISLAND HOTEL SMITHTOWN   *Book at aaa.com*   **Phone:** (631)231-1100

(AAA) (SAVE) | All Year | 1P: $166 | 2P: $166 | XP: $10 | F18

▽▽▽ | **Location:** I-495, exit 53 (Wicks Rd), 0.3 mi e. Located in a commercial area. 110 Vanderbilt Motor Pkwy 11788.
Large-scale Hotel | Fax: 631/231-1143. **Facility:** 209 units. 200 one-bedroom standard units. 9 one-bedroom suites. 6 stories, interior corridors. *Bath:* combo or shower only. **Parking:** on-site. **Amenities:** video games (fee), dual phone lines, voice mail, irons, hair dryers. *Some:* fax. **Dining:** 2 restaurants, 6:30 am-11 pm, Sat & Sun from 7 am, cocktails. **Pool(s):** heated indoor. **Leisure Activities:** sauna, whirlpool, steamroom, exercise room. **Guest Services:** gift shop, valet laundry, airport transportation-MacArthur Airport, area transportation-within 5 mi. **Business Services:** conference facilities. **Cards:** AX, DC, DS, MC, VI. **Special Amenities: free newspaper and preferred room (subject to availability with advanced reservations).** *(See ad below)*

SOME UNITS

 FEE

WYNDHAM WIND WATCH HOTEL & HAMLET GOLF CLUB   *Book at aaa.com*   **Phone:** (631)232-9800

(AAA) (SAVE) | All Year | 1P: $159-$189 | 2P: $174-$204 | XP: $15 | F17

▽▽▽ | **Location:** I-495, exit 57, just n to Motor Pkwy, 1.3 mi ne. Located adjacent to golf course. 1717 Motor Pkwy 11788.
Large-scale Hotel | Fax: 631/232-9853. **Facility:** 360 units. 356 one-bedroom standard units. 4 one-bedroom suites ($500-$2000). 10 stories, interior corridors. **Parking:** on-site. **Terms:** cancellation fee imposed, small pets only ($50 fee). **Amenities:** dual phone lines, voice mail, irons, hair dryers. *Fee:* video games, high-speed Internet. *Some:* CD players. **Dining:** 6:30 am-2:30 & 5-11 pm, Sat & Sun 7 am-11 pm, cocktails. **Pool(s):** heated outdoor, heated indoor. **Leisure Activities:** saunas, whirlpool, 2 lighted tennis courts, playground, basketball, volleyball. *Fee:* golf-18 holes, driving range, massage, game room. **Guest Services:** valet laundry, airport transportation-MacArthur Airport, area transportation-train station. **Business Services:** conference facilities, business center. **Cards:** AX, CB, DC, DS, JC, MC, VI. Not Affiliated with the Wyndham Hotel in Manhattan.

SOME UNITS

 FEE

——— WHERE TO DINE ———

KOTOBUKI

◆◆

Japanese

Lunch: $6-$18 **Dinner:** $8-$25 **Phone:** 631/360-3969

Location: Jct SR 111, just w; in Hauppauge Shopping Center. 377 Nesconset Hwy 11787. **Hours:** noon-2:30 & 5:30-10 pm, Sat 5 pm-10:30 pm, Sun 5 pm-9:30 pm. Closed major holidays; also Mon. **Features:** Drive up to the unpretentious restaurant, and you'll see "sushi" before you see the name. Among other selections are regionally-inspired rolls, sashimi, and nigiri, as well as a variety of savory cooked dishes, such as teriyaki, yakitori and tempura. Casual dress; beer & wine only. **Parking:** on-site. **Cards:** AX, CB, DC, DS, JC, MC, VI.

⊠

SEMPRE VIVOLO

◆◆◆

Italian

Lunch: $14-$22 **Dinner:** $19-$24 **Phone:** 631/435-1737

Location: I-495, exit 55, just n. 696 Motor Pkwy 11788. **Hours:** noon-2:30 & 5-9:30 pm. Closed major holidays; also Sun. **Reservations:** suggested. **Features:** A knowledgeable and attentive wait staff serves diners in the upscale, elegant setting. Sophisticated Italian dishes include delicious roasted salmon and a pasta dish with pancetta and fresh and sun-dried tomatoes. Roman artwork decorates the dining room. Dressy casual; cocktails. **Parking:** on-site and valet. **Cards:** AX, DC, DS, MC, VI.

⊼ ⊠

HAWTHORNE —*See New York p. 452.*

HECTOR pop. 4,854

——— WHERE TO DINE ———

THE BISTRO AT RED NEWT CELLARS

◆◆◆

Regional American

Lunch: $7-$10 **Dinner:** $17-$23 **Phone:** 607/546-4100

Location: Off SR 414. 3675 Tichenor Rd 14841. **Hours:** Open 5/31-12/12 & 2/13-4/29; noon-9 pm. Closed: Wed 11/1-4/30 & Mon & Tues. **Reservations:** suggested. **Features:** The winery-restaurant offers sumptuous and innovative regional cuisine made from ingredients sold by local producers. Prix fixe, vegan and vegetarian choices also are offered. Casual dress; beer & wine only. **Parking:** on-site. **Cards:** AX, MC, VI.

⊠

HEMPSTEAD pop. 56,544

——— WHERE TO STAY ———

QUALITY HOTEL

◆◆◆ SAVE
◆◆◆ ◆◆

Small-scale Hotel

Book at aaa.com

Phone: (516)486-4100

6/16-9/7	2P: $99-$149	XP: $10	F18
5/1-6/15	2P: $99-$129	XP: $10	F18
9/8-4/30	2P: $89-$109	XP: $10	F18

Location: Meadowbrook Pkwy, exit M5, then 2.3 mi w on SR 24. Located in a commercial area. 80 Clinton St 11550. **Fax:** 516/565-0745. **Facility:** 182 one-bedroom standard units. 8 stories, interior corridors. **Parking:** on-site. **Terms:** cancellation fee imposed, [CP] meal plan available. **Amenities:** video games (fee), voice mail, irons, hair dryers. **Leisure Activities:** exercise room. **Fee:** game room. **Guest Services:** coin laundry. **Business Services:** conference facilities. **Cards:** AX, CB, DC, DS, JC, MC, VI. **Special Amenities:** free continental breakfast and free local telephone calls.

SOME UNITS

Ⓢ🅓 📺 🖧 🖵 / ⊠ 🗍 / FEE

HENRIETTA pop. 39,028 (See map and index starting on p. 550)—*See also WEST HENRIETTA.*

——— WHERE TO STAY ———

COMFORT SUITES OF ROCHESTER

◆◆◆◆ ◆◆

Small-scale Hotel

Book at aaa.com

Phone: (585)334-6620 ㊲

5/1-7/31 [ECP]	1P: $89-$109	2P: $89-$109
8/1-10/31 [ECP]	1P: $79-$109	2P: $79-$109
2/1-4/30 [ECP]	1P: $69-$99	2P: $69-$99
11/1-1/31 [ECP]	1P: $69-$89	2P: $69-$89

Location: I-390, exit 13, just e. 2085 Hylan Dr 14623. **Fax:** 585/334-9649. **Facility:** 66 one-bedroom standard units. 3 stories, interior corridors. *Bath:* combo or shower only. **Parking:** on-site. **Amenities:** irons, hair dryers. **Pool(s):** heated indoor. **Leisure Activities:** whirlpool. **Guest Services:** valet laundry. **Business Services:** fax (fee). **Cards:** AX, DC, DS, MC, VI.

SOME UNITS

ASK Ⓢ🅓 🍽🕂 🖐M 🖥 🛏 🏊 🐾 📺 🖧 🗍 🖼 🖵 / ⊠ /

COUNTRY INN & SUITES BY CARLSON

◆◆◆ SAVE
◆◆◆

Small-scale Hotel

Book at aaa.com

Phone: (585)486-9000 ㊳

5/1-10/31 [ECP]	1P: $99-$189	2P: $99-$189	XP: $10	F17
11/1-4/30 [ECP]	1P: $89-$189	2P: $89-$189	XP: $10	F17

Location: I-390, exit 12 northbound; exit 12A southbound, 0.5 mi w on SR 253, then just n on SR 15 (W Henrietta Rd). 4635 W Henrietta Rd 14467. **Fax:** 585/486-9010. **Facility:** 79 units. 57 one-bedroom standard units, some with whirlpools. 22 one-bedroom suites ($99-$199). 2 stories, interior corridors. *Bath:* combo or shower only. **Parking:** on-site. **Amenities:** video library (fee), video games, voice mail, irons, hair dryers. **Pool(s):** small heated indoor. **Leisure Activities:** whirlpool, exercise room. **Guest Services:** coin laundry. **Business Services:** meeting rooms, business center. **Cards:** AX, CB, DC, DS, MC, VI. **Special Amenities:** free expanded continental breakfast and free local telephone calls. *(See color ad p 554)*

SOME UNITS

Ⓢ🅓 🍽🕂 🏊 📺 🖧 🖵 / ⊠ 🗍 🖼 🖵 /

ECONO LODGE-ROCHESTER SOUTH

◆◆ ◆

Small-scale Hotel

Book at aaa.com

Phone: (585)427-2700 ㉝

5/1-10/31 [ECP]	1P: $54	2P: $82	XP: $8	F18
11/1-4/30 [ECP]	1P: $49	2P: $82	XP: $8	F18

Location: I-390, exit 14A southbound; exit 14 northbound, just w on SR 252 (Jefferson Rd). 940 Jefferson Rd 14623. **Fax:** 585/427-8504. **Facility:** 101 one-bedroom standard units, some with whirlpools. 3 stories, interior corridors. *Bath:* combo or shower only. **Parking:** on-site. **Terms:** 3 day cancellation notice. **Amenities:** video games. **Fee:** video library, safes. *Some:* hair dryers. **Guest Services:** valet and coin laundry, area transportation. **Business Services:** meeting rooms. **Cards:** AX, CB, DC, DS, MC, VI.

SOME UNITS

ASK Ⓢ🅓 🕂 🐾 🍽🕂 🖥 📺 🖧 / ⊠ 🗍 🖼 🖵 /

(See map and index starting on p. 550)

FAIRFIELD INN BY MARRIOTT-ROCHESTER/SOUTH Book at aaa.com   Phone: 585/334-3350 39

▼▼▼

3/2-4/30 [ECP]	1P: $94-$104	2P: $94-$104
5/1-11/1 [ECP]	1P: $104	2P: $104
11/2-3/1 [ECP]	1P: $89-$94	2P: $89-$94

Small-scale Hotel   **Location:** I-90, jct of SR 253 and 15. 4695 W Henrietta Rd 14467. Fax: 585/334-2295. **Facility:** 63 one-bedroom standard units. 3 stories, interior corridors. *Bath:* combo or shower only. **Parking:** on-site. **Amenities:** video library (fee), video games, high-speed Internet, irons, hair dryers. **Pool(s):** small heated indoor. **Guest Services:** valet laundry. **Cards:** AX, DC, DS, MC, VI.

SOME UNITS

HOLIDAY INN SOUTH Book at aaa.com   Phone: (585)475-1510 34

▼▼▼   All Year   1P: $89-$122

Small-scale Hotel   **Location:** I-390, exit 14, on SR 252 (Jefferson Rd). 1111 Jefferson Rd 14623. Fax: 585/427-8673. **Facility:** 250 units. 248 one-bedroom standard units. 2 one-bedroom suites ($190). 6 stories, interior corridors. *Bath:* combo or shower only. **Parking:** on-site. **Terms:** [AP], [BP], [CP] & [ECP] meal plans available. **Amenities:** video library (fee), voice mail, irons, hair dryers. **Pool(s):** heated indoor. **Leisure Activities:** whirlpool, exercise room. *Fee:* game room. **Guest Services:** gift shop, valet laundry. **Business Services:** conference facilities, PC, fax. **Cards:** AX, CB, DC, DS, MC, VI.

SOME UNITS
FEE FEE

HOMEWOOD SUITES BY HILTON-ROCHESTER/HENRIETTA Book at aaa.com   Phone: (585)334-9150 36

▼▼▼   All Year   1P: $119-$135   2P: $119-$135

Small-scale Hotel   **Location:** I-390, exit 13, just e. 2095 Hylan Dr 14623. Fax: 585/334-1226. **Facility:** 90 units. 85 one- and 5 two-bedroom suites with efficiencies. 3 stories, interior corridors. *Bath:* combo or shower only. **Parking:** on-site. **Terms:** [BP] meal plan available, pets ($75 fee). **Amenities:** video library (fee), dual phone lines, voice mail, irons, hair dryers. **Pool(s):** small heated indoor. **Leisure Activities:** exercise room. **Guest Services:** sundries, complimentary evening beverages: Mon-Thurs, valet and coin laundry. **Business Services:** meeting rooms, business center. **Cards:** AX, DC, DS, MC, VI.

SOME UNITS
FEE

MICROTEL-ROCHESTER Book at aaa.com   Phone: (585)334-3400 42

5/1-10/31 & 3/1-4/30 [CP]	1P: $49-$69	2P: $49-$69	XP: $5	F17
11/1-2/28 [CP]	1P: $37-$49	2P: $37-$49	XP: $5	F17

Small-scale Hotel   **Location:** I-390, exit 12 northbound; exit 12A southbound, just w on SR 253. 905 Lehigh Station Rd 14467. Fax: 585/334-5042. **Facility:** 98 one-bedroom standard units. 2 stories (no elevator), interior corridors. *Bath:* combo or shower only. **Parking:** on-site. **Terms:** small pets only. **Amenities:** video library (fee), video games, safes. **Guest Services:** valet laundry. **Cards:** AX, DC, DS, MC, VI. **Special Amenities:** free continental breakfast and free local telephone calls.

SOME UNITS

RADISSON HOTEL ROCHESTER AIRPORT Book at aaa.com   Phone: (585)475-1910 30

5/1-10/31 & 4/1-4/30	1P: $89	2P: $89	XP: $10	F18
11/1-3/31	1P: $79	2P: $79	XP: $10	F18

Small-scale Hotel   **Location:** I-390, exit 14A southbound; exit 14 northbound, 3 mi w on SR 252 (Jefferson Rd). 175 Jefferson Rd 14623. Fax: 585/475-9633. **Facility:** 171 one-bedroom standard units. 4 stories, interior corridors. *Bath:* combo or shower only. **Parking:** on-site. **Terms:** [AP], [BP], [CP], [ECP] & [MAP] meal plans available. **Amenities:** video library (fee), video games, high-speed Internet, voice mail, irons, hair dryers. **Dining:** 6:30 am-10 pm, Sat & Sun from 7 am, cocktails. **Pool(s):** heated indoor. **Leisure Activities:** exercise room. **Guest Services:** valet laundry, area transportation-within 5 mi. **Business Services:** conference facilities. **Cards:** AX, CB, DC, DS, MC, VI. **Special Amenities:** free newspaper and early check-in/late check-out. *(See color ad below & p 413)*

SOME UNITS

(See map and index starting on p. 550)

RAMADA INN ROCHESTER   *Book at aaa.com*   Phone: (585)475-9190 **32**

(AAA) (SAVE)   All Year [ECP]   1P: $79   2P: $79   XP: $5   F18

Location: I-390, exit 14A southbound; exit 14 northbound, 0.5 mi w on SR 252 (Jefferson Rd). Located in a light commercial area. 800 Jefferson Rd 14623. Fax: 585/424-2138. **Facility:** 144 one-bedroom standard units. 3 stories, interior corridors. **Parking:** on-site. **Amenities:** irons, hair dryers. **Dining:** 11:30 am-10 pm, cocktails.

Small-scale Hotel **Pool(s):** heated indoor. **Leisure Activities:** exercise room. **Guest Services:** valet and coin laundry, area transportation-within 5 mi. **Business Services:** meeting rooms. **Cards:** AX, DC, DS, MC, VI.

Special Amenities: free expanded continental breakfast and free newspaper. *(See color ad p 8)*

SOME UNITS

RED ROOF INN-HENRIETTA   *Book at aaa.com*   Phone: (585)359-1100 **41**

(AAA) (SAVE)   6/19-9/3   1P: $52-$70   2P: $57-$75   XP: $5   F18

           5/1-6/18   1P: $47-$70   2P: $52-$75   XP: $5   F18

           9/4-10/18   1P: $50-$63   2P: $55-$68   XP: $5   F18

Motel   10/19-4/30   1P: $43-$52   2P: $48-$57   XP: $5   F18

Location: I-390, exit 12 northbound; exit 12A southbound, 0.5 mi w on SR 253, then just s on SR 15 (W Henrietta Rd). 4820 W Henrietta Rd 14467. Fax: 585/359-1121. **Facility:** 108 one-bedroom standard units. 2 stories (no elevator), exterior corridors. *Bath:* combo or shower only. **Parking:** on-site. **Amenities:** video library (fee), video games, voice mail. **Cards:** AX, CB, DC, DS, MC, VI. **Special Amenities:** free local telephone calls and free newspaper.

SOME UNITS

FEE   FEE

RESIDENCE INN BY MARRIOTT   *Book at aaa.com*   Phone: (585)272-8850 **35**

All Year   1P: $116-$126   2P: $179-$189

Motel   **Location:** I-390, exit 14A southbound, 0.5 mi e on SR 252 (Jefferson Rd); exit 14 northbound, just n on 15A, then 0.5 mi e on SR 252 (Jefferson Rd). 1300 Jefferson Rd 14623. Fax: 585/272-7822. **Facility:** 112 units. 70 one-bedroom standard units with efficiencies. 14 one- and 28 two-bedroom suites ($179-$189). 2 stories (no elevator), interior corridors. *Bath:* combo or shower only. **Parking:** on-site. **Terms:** cancellation fee imposed, [BP] meal plan available, pets ($125 fee). **Amenities:** voice mail, irons, hair dryers. **Pool(s):** small outdoor. **Leisure Activities:** whirlpool, exercise room, sports court. **Guest Services:** complimentary evening beverages: Mon-Thurs, valet and coin laundry. **Business Services:** meeting rooms. **Cards:** AX, CB, DC, DS, MC, VI.

SOME UNITS

FEE

R I T INN & CONFERENCE CENTER   Phone: (585)359-1800 **43**

All Year   1P: $85-$115   2P: $85-$115

Location: I-390, exit 12 northbound; exit 12A southbound, 0.5 mi w on SR 253, then 0.7 mi s. 5257 W Henrietta Rd

Small-scale Hotel 14586 (PO Box 20551, ROCHESTER, 14602). Fax: 585/359-1349. **Facility:** 305 one-bedroom standard units. 5 stories, interior corridors. **Parking:** on-site. **Terms:** pets ($50 deposit). **Amenities:** video games, high-speed Internet, dual phone lines, voice mail, irons, hair dryers. **Pool(s):** heated outdoor, heated indoor. **Leisure Activities:** sauna, whirlpool, exercise room. **Guest Services:** gift shop, valet and coin laundry. **Business Services:** conference facilities, business center. **Cards:** AX, DC, DS, MC, VI.

SOME UNITS

FEE   FEE

——— WHERE TO DINE ———

BUGABOO CREEK STEAK HOUSE   **Lunch:** $5-$12   **Dinner:** $6-$18   Phone: 585/292-5800 **17**

Location: I-390, exit 14A, just w on SR 252 (Jefferson Rd). 935 Jefferson Rd 14623. **Hours:** 11:30 am-10 pm, Fri

American & Sat-10:30 pm, Sun noon-9 pm. Closed: 11/25, 12/25. **Features:** The rustic Canadian Rockies lodge is decorated with all the fixings of the outdoor life. A fun place for families and special gatherings, this place hides a surprise around every corner. Casual dress; cocktails. **Parking:** on-site. **Cards:** AX, DC, DS,

MC, VI.

HERKIMER pop. 7,498

——— WHERE TO STAY ———

HERKIMER MOTEL   Phone: (315)866-0490

(AAA) (SAVE)   All Year   1P: $59-$64   2P: $68-$88   XP: $7   F12

Location: I-90, exit 30, just n on SR 28. 100 Marginal Rd 13350. Fax: 315/866-0416. **Facility:** 60 units. 56 one-bedroom standard units, some with kitchens (no utensils). 4 two-bedroom suites ($99-$125) with kitchens. 2

Motel   stories (no elevator), interior/exterior corridors. *Bath:* combo or shower only. **Terms:** [CP] meal plan available, small pets only. **Amenities:** voice mail, hair dryers. *Some:* irons. **Pool(s):** heated outdoor. **Leisure Activities:** exercise room. **Guest Services:** coin laundry. **Cards:** AX, DS, MC, VI.

Special Amenities: free continental breakfast and free local telephone calls.   SOME UNITS

INN TOWNE MOTEL   Phone: (315)866-1101

(AAA) (SAVE)   All Year   1P: $40-$150   2P: $45-$150   XP: $10   F12

Location: 1 mi n on SR 28, just w; downtown. 227 N Washington St 13350. Fax: 315/866-1101. **Facility:** 33 one-bedroom standard units. 2 stories (no elevator), exterior corridors. **Parking:** on-site, winter plug-ins.

Motel   **Terms:** small pets only ($8 extra charge). **Cards:** AX, DS, MC, VI. **Special Amenities:** early check-in/late check-out and preferred room (subject to availability with advanced reservations).

SOME UNITS

FEE

PUTNAM MANOR HOUSE   Phone: 315/866-6738

▼▲▼▲▼ 5/1-10/31   1P: $125-$135   2P: $125-$135   XP: $20
        11/1-4/30   1P: $85-$115   2P: $85-$115   XP: $20
Bed & Breakfast **Location:** SR 5 and SR 28, 0.4 mi n on N Caroline, then 0.4 mi e. Located in a residential area. 112 W German St 13350. Fax: 315/866-3102. **Facility:** Oak floors, thick pocket doors, mahogany woodwork and oriental carpets accent this 1901 Italianate mansion. Smoke free premises. 5 one-bedroom standard units, some with whirlpools. 2 stories (no elevator), interior corridors. *Bath:* combo or shower only. **Parking:** on-site. **Terms:** 3 day cancellation notice, weekly rates available. **Amenities:** voice mail, hair dryers. **Business Services:** fax. **Cards:** AX, MC, VI.

⊠ VCR DATA PORT

─────── **WHERE TO DINE** ───────

BABY BOOMERS COOKERY & LOUNGE   **Lunch:** $4-$6   **Dinner:** $9-$12   **Phone:** 315/866-3183
▼▲▼   **Location:** SR 5, just n on Albany St, then just e. 527 E Albany St 13350. **Hours:** 11 am-9 pm, Fri & Sat-10 pm. Closed major holidays. **Features:** Baby boomer or not, anyone will enjoy the food prepared and served at
American the casual restaurant. Somewhere between a diner and a cafe, this place has booths and tables that set the scene for hearty eating. For a regional sandwich with a twist, try the veggie spiedie. A large variety of appetizers, burgers, steak and chicken dishes, along with Tex-Mex options, satisfy any kind of hunger. Dessert choices range from mountain berry flan to homemade raisin cookies. Casual dress; cocktails. **Parking:** on-site. **Cards:** AX, DS, MC, VI.

⊤ ⊠

CRYSTAL CHANDELIER RESTAURANT   **Dinner:** $10-$17   **Phone:** 315/891-3366
▼▲▼ ▼▲▼   **Location:** Jct SR 28 and 29/169, 1 mi s. 4579 SR 28 13350. **Hours:** Open 5/1-11/3; 5 pm-9:30 pm, Fri & Sat-10 pm, Sun 1 pm-8 pm. Closed: 1/1, 12/24, 12/25; also Tues. **Reservations:** accepted. **Features:** Smoked
American baby back ribs stand out on a menu of well-prepared beef, seafood and poultry selections. Flowers and fine artwork decorate the moderately upscale dining room. The restaurant caters to a diverse clientele, ranging from families to professionals. Casual dress; cocktails. **Parking:** on-site. **Cards:** AX, CB, DC, DS, MC, VI.

⊤ ⊠

HICKSVILLE pop. 41,260

─────── **WHERE TO STAY** ───────

ECONO LODGE   *Book at aaa.com*   **Phone:** (516)433-3900
ⒶⒶ SAVE   All Year [CP]   1P: $85-$119   2P: $85-$119   XP: $10   F16
▼▲▼   **Location:** I-495, exit 41S, 1.3 mi s on SR 106, then 1.2 mi w on Old Country Rd. Located in a commercial area. 429 Duffy Ave 11801. Fax: 516/433-3909. **Facility:** 82 one-bedroom standard units. 2 stories (no elevator), interior
Small-scale Hotel corridors. *Bath:* combo or shower only. **Parking:** on-site. **Amenities:** voice mail. **Guest Services:** valet laundry. **Cards:** AX, CB, DC, DS, JC, MC, VI. **Special Amenities: free continental breakfast.**

SOME UNITS
S D ⊤↕ ⌖ 📺 DATA PORT / ⊠ 🛏 📠 💻 /

─────── **WHERE TO DINE** ───────

ISLAND INDO-PAK CUISINE   **Lunch:** $8-$15   **Dinner:** $8-$15   **Phone:** 516/681-9834
▼▲▼   **Location:** 0.5 mi s of train station. 128 Broadway 11801. **Hours:** 11:30 am-3:30 & 5-10 pm. Closed major holidays; also Mon. **Reservations:** accepted. **Features:** The clay tandoor oven creates wonderful broiled
Indian meat and seafood, as well as great bread, including naan and roh. The menu also lists other specialties: bicyanis and vegetarian dishes. Selections on the lunch buffet are laid out in copper kettles. Casual dress. **Parking:** on-site. **Cards:** AX, CB, DC, DS, MC, VI.

⊠

HIGH FALLS pop. 627

─────── **WHERE TO DINE** ───────

DEPUY CANAL HOUSE Historic   **Lunch:** $12-$24   **Dinner:** $20-$45   **Phone:** 845/687-7700
▼▲▼▲▼   **Location:** Center. 103 Main St 12440. **Hours:** Open 5/1-1/22 & 2/14-4/30; 5:30 pm-10 pm, Sun 11:30 am-2 & 4:30-9 pm. Closed: 12/25; also Mon-Wed. **Reservations:** suggested. **Features:** Along the historic
American Delaware and Hudson Canal, the 1797 landmark has been meticulously restored and is appointed in antiques. Whole lobster taken out of the shell and presented encrusted with panko crumbs and steamed claws is one example of the creative, Internationally influenced cuisine. Casual dress; cocktails. **Parking:** on-site. **Cards:** AX, MC, VI.

⊤ ⊠

THE EGG'S NEST   **Lunch:** $6-$10   **Dinner:** $8-$14   **Phone:** 845/687-7255
▼▲▼ ▼▲▼   **Location:** Center. 1300 Rt 213 12440. **Hours:** 11:30 am-11 pm, Fri & Sat-midnight. Closed: 11/25, 12/24, 12/25. **Features:** Inventive overstuffed sandwiches—such as the "Thanksgiving feast," which stacks turkey,
American stuffing and melted cheese on egg-battered bread—are as wonderful as the decor, which brims with such funky finds as toaster lamps and three-dimensional art. Casual dress; cocktails. **Parking:** on-site.

HIGHLAND pop. 5,060

──────── WHERE TO STAY ────────

ROCKING HORSE RANCH RESORT
▽▼▽▼▽ 5/29-9/6 [MAP]   1P: $185-$215   2P: $370-$430   XP: $95   F4
   5/1-5/28 & 9/7-4/30 [MAP]   1P: $120-$200   2P: $240-$400   XP: $75   F4

Phone: (845)691-2927

Resort Ranch   **Location:** Jct US 9W and US 44/SR 55, 4 mi w. Located in a quiet area. 600 Rt 44-55 12528. Fax: 845/691-6434. **Facility:** Extensive recreational facilities are one of the highlights of this family-oriented ranch resort. Designated smoking area. 119 one-bedroom standard units. 2 stories, interior/exterior corridors. **Parking:** on-site, winter plug-ins. **Terms:** check-in 4 pm, 28 day cancellation notice, weekly rates available. **Pool(s):** heated outdoor, heated indoor, wading. **Leisure Activities:** saunas, whirlpool, waterslide, paddleboats, waterskiing, fishing, miniature golf, 2 lighted tennis courts, downhill skiing, ice skating, recreation programs, hiking trails, horseback riding, playground, exercise room, basketball, horseshoes, shuffleboard, volleyball. **Fee:** massage. **Guest Services:** gift shop. **Business Services:** meeting rooms, fax (fee). **Cards:** AX, CB, DC, DS, MC, VI.

SOME UNITS
🍽 🏇 🏊 ✕ ✕ DATA PORT / 📞 🖥 /
FEE

HIGHLAND FALLS pop. 3,678

──────── WHERE TO DINE ────────

SCHADES RESTAURANT   **Lunch:** $5-$9   **Dinner:** $9-$20   **Phone:** 845/446-2626
◆◆◆
   Location: Downtown. 457 Main St 10928. **Hours:** 11 am-9 pm, Fri & Sat-10 pm. Closed: 11/25, 12/25.
American   **Features:** Near the West Point front gates, the eatery is perfect for a casual family dinner. On the varied menu are Mexican and Italian entrees, sandwich wraps and basket dinners, but the highlight is pizza. Specialty pizzas—such as Mexican, steak and cheese, Hawaiian and seafood—are popular, as are the "rolled" pizzas, which (more accurately) are stuffed. Casual dress; cocktails. **Parking:** street. **Cards:** AX, DS, MC, VI.   ✕

HILLSDALE pop. 1,744

──────── WHERE TO DINE ────────

AUBERGINE   Country Inn   **Dinner:** $25-$30   **Phone:** 518/325-3412
▽▼▽◆ ▽▼▽◆
   Location: Jct SR 22 and 23, northwest corner. Intersection Rts 22 & 23 12529. **Hours:** 5:30 pm-9 pm. Closed:
French   1/1, 12/25; also Mon & Tues. **Reservations:** suggested. **Features:** The owner-chef prepares superior American country dishes, which are clearly influenced by contemporary French cuisine. The smoke-free dining rooms have an elegant, but casual atmosphere, with fireplaces and some intimate areas. Innovative desserts include flavored souffles ordered ahead of the meal and molten bittersweet chocolate cake. Dressy casual; cocktails. **Parking:** on-site. **Cards:** AX, CB, DC, MC, VI.   🍽 ✕

HOLBROOK pop. 27,512

──────── WHERE TO DINE ────────

MAMMA LOMBARDI'S   **Lunch:** $9-$15   **Dinner:** $13-$22   **Phone:** 631/737-0774
◆◆ ◆◆◆
   Location: I-495, exit 61, 0.8 mi s, then just w. 400 Furrows Rd 11741. **Hours:** 11:30 am-10 pm, Fri & Sat-11:30
Italian   pm, Sun 1 pm-10 pm. Closed: 11/25, 12/25. **Features:** Burgundy tones and gilded artwork lend an air of sophistication to the cozy dining room. Bow tie pasta with gorgonzola sauce is representative of the well-prepared offerings, which are served in abundant portions. Service is professional and attentive. Casual dress; cocktails. **Parking:** on-site. **Cards:** AX, DC, DS, MC, VI.   🍽 ✕

HONEOYE —See also FINGER LAKES.

──────── WHERE TO STAY ────────

GREENWOODS BED & BREAKFAST INN   *Book at aaa.com*   **Phone:** (585)229-2111
▽▼▽◆
   All Year [BP]   1P: $89-$169   2P: $99-$179   XP: $20
   Location: 2.5 mi e on SR 20A, just n. 8136 Quayle Rd 14471. Fax: 585/229-0034. **Facility:** Quality appointments are the signature of this Adirondack-themed B&B overlooking a scenic valley; three rooms have fireplaces, Bed & Breakfast   all have feather beds. Smoke free premises. 5 units. 3 one-bedroom standard units. 2 one-bedroom suites. 2 stories (no elevator), interior/exterior corridors. **Parking:** on-site. **Terms:** 2 night minimum stay - weekends 5/1-11/30, age restrictions may apply, 14 day cancellation notice-fee imposed. **Amenities:** video library, CD players, hair dryers. **Leisure Activities:** whirlpool, hiking trails, game room. **Business Services:** PC, fax. **Cards:** AX, DS, MC, VI.

SOME UNITS
✕ ✕ VCR ☎ / DATA PORT 📞 /

HONEOYE FALLS pop. 2,595—See FINGER LAKES.

HORNELL pop. 9,019—See also FINGER LAKES.

──────── WHERE TO STAY ────────

COMFORT INN   *Book at aaa.com*   **Phone:** (607)324-4300
▽▼▽◆
   5/1-10/1 [CP]   1P: $89-$125   2P: $89-$125   XP: $5   F18
   10/2-4/30 [CP]   1P: $79-$99   2P: $79-$99   XP: $5   F18
Small-scale Hotel   **Location:** Jct US 36 and SR 17, 3 mi s. 1 Canisteo Sq 14843. Fax: 607/324-4311. **Facility:** 62 one-bedroom standard units, some with whirlpools. 2 stories (no elevator), interior corridors. *Bath:* combo or shower only. **Parking:** on-site, winter plug-ins. **Amenities:** high-speed Internet, voice mail, irons, hair dryers. **Pool(s):** small heated indoor. **Leisure Activities:** exercise room. **Guest Services:** valet and coin laundry. **Business Services:** meeting rooms. **Cards:** AX, CB, DC, DS, JC, MC, VI.

SOME UNITS
ASK 🅂 🍽 ♿M 📶 🏊 🏋 DATA PORT 🖥 / ✕ 📞 🖥 /
FEE FEE

HORSEHEADS pop. 6,452—See also FINGER LAKES.

———— WHERE TO STAY ————

COUNTRY INN & SUITES-BIG FLATS   **Book at aaa.com**   Phone: (607)739-9205
▼▼▼▼ All Year [ECP]   1P: $99-$125   2P: $99-$125   XP: $5   F
Small-scale Hotel **Location:** SR 17, exit 51A westbound; exit 51 eastbound. 105 E Mall Rd 14845. Fax: 607/739-9205. **Facility:** 70 units. 50 one-bedroom standard units. 19 one- and 1 two-bedroom suites. 3 stories, interior corridors. *Bath:* combo or shower only. **Parking:** on-site. **Terms:** cancellation fee imposed. **Amenities:** voice mail, irons, hair dryers. **Pool(s):** small heated indoor. **Leisure Activities:** whirlpool, exercise room. **Guest Services:** valet and coin laundry. **Business Services:** meeting rooms. **Cards:** AX, CB, DC, DS, MC, VI. *(See color ad p 554)*

SOME UNITS
(ASK) (S/D) (⊙) (⊠) (📠) (DATA PORT) (💻) / (✕) (🛏) /

HILTON GARDEN INN ELMIRA/CORNING   **Book at aaa.com**   Phone: (607)795-1111
▼▼▼▼ All Year   1P: $99-$150   2P: $99-$150   XP: $20   F18
Small-scale Hotel **Location:** SR 17, exit 51A westbound; exit 51 eastbound. Located across from shopping mall. 35 Arnot Rd 14845. Fax: 607/795-4103. **Facility:** 119 one-bedroom standard units, some with whirlpools. 4 stories, interior corridors. *Bath:* combo or shower only. **Parking:** on-site. **Terms:** 3 day cancellation notice-fee imposed, pets ($20 extra charge). **Amenities:** video games, high-speed Internet, dual phone lines, voice mail, irons, hair dryers. **Pool(s):** heated indoor. **Leisure Activities:** whirlpool, exercise room. **Guest Services:** valet and coin laundry. **Business Services:** meeting rooms, business center. **Cards:** AX, CB, DC, DS, JC, MC, VI. *(See color ad p 290)*

SOME UNITS
(ASK) (S/D) (🐾) (🍴) (🍸) (♿) (🏊) (📺) (DATA PORT) (🛏) (📠) (💻) / (✕) /
FEE

HOLIDAY INN HORSEHEADS   **Book at aaa.com**   Phone: 607/739-3681
▼▼▼▼ 7/1-8/31   1P: $99-$159
   5/1-6/30   1P: $93-$129
Small-scale Hotel 9/1-10/31   1P: $99-$124
   11/1-4/30   1P: $93-$109
Location: Jct SR 14, 17 and 328, exit 52 off SR 17. 2666 Corning Rd 14845. Fax: 607/796-6927. **Facility:** 100 one-bedroom standard units. 2 stories (no elevator), interior/exterior corridors. *Bath:* combo or shower only. **Parking:** on-site. **Terms:** cancellation fee imposed. **Amenities:** video games, irons, hair dryers. *Some:* dual phone lines. **Pool(s):** outdoor. **Leisure Activities:** exercise room. **Guest Services:** valet and coin laundry. **Business Services:** conference facilities. **Cards:** AX, DC, DS, MC, VI.

SOME UNITS
(ASK) (✈) (🍴) (🍸) (♿) (🏊) (📺) (DATA PORT) (💻) / (✕) (VCR) (🛏) (📠) /

———— WHERE TO DINE ————

SUGAR & SPICE RESTAURANT   **Lunch:** $4-$6   **Dinner:** $8   Phone: 607/739-5303
(AAA) **Location:** Just n of Hanover Sq; center. 300 Watkins Rd 14845. **Hours:** 6 am-3 pm, Fri-7:30 pm, Sat & Sun 7 am-1 pm. Closed major holidays. **Features:** Daily specials coordinate with fresh seasonal fruits and vegetables in the popular little diner. Old-fashioned comfort food is made on the premises. Casual dress. **Parking:** on-site. **Cards:** AX, DS, MC, VI.
▼
American   (✕)

HOUGHTON pop. 1,748

———— WHERE TO STAY ————

THE INN AT HOUGHTON CREEK   Phone: (585)567-8400
▼▼▼▼ All Year   1P: $64   2P: $69   XP: $5   F12
Small-scale Hotel **Location:** On CR 19; center. Located next to the college. 9722 Genesee St 14744-8773. Fax: 585/567-4842. **Facility:** Smoke free premises. 17 one-bedroom standard units. 2 stories (no elevator), interior corridors. *Bath:* combo or shower only. **Parking:** on-site. **Terms:** cancellation fee imposed. **Amenities:** high-speed Internet (fee), irons, hair dryers. **Business Services:** PC. **Cards:** AX, DS, MC, VI.

SOME UNITS
(ASK) (S/D) (♿M) (♿) (🛁) (✕) / (VCR) /
FEE

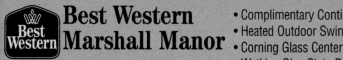

HOWES CAVE

——— WHERE TO STAY ———

HOWE CAVERNS MOTEL
Phone: 518/296-895C

(AAA) [SAVE]

	7/1-9/6	1P: $85-$160	2P: $85-$160
	5/1-6/30 & 9/7-10/31	1P: $60-$140	2P: $60-$140
	11/1-4/30	1P: $45-$100	2P: $45-$100

Motel **Location:** I-88, exit 22, 1.2 mi e on SR 7, 1.3 mi n on CR 8, then e, follow signs. 255 Discovery Dr 12092 **Fax:** 518/296-8958. **Facility:** 21 one-bedroom standard units, some with whirlpools. 1 story, exterior corridors. **Bath:** combo or shower only. **Parking:** on-site. **Terms:** cancellation fee imposed, [CP] meal plan available, package plans. **Amenities:** hair dryers. **Dining:** 7:30 am-8 pm, Fri from 4 pm; weekends only 5/1-6/30 & 9/7-10/11; close 10/12-4/30, cocktails. **Pool(s):** outdoor. **Leisure Activities:** Fee: cavern tours, gem stone mining. **Business Services:** fax **Cards:** AX, DS, MC, VI. **Special Amenities:** free continental breakfast and free local telephone calls.
(See color ad p 271)

SOME UNITS

HUNTER pop. 490

——— WHERE TO STAY ———

HUNTER INN
Phone: (518)263-3777

(AAA) [SAVE]

| | 11/24-4/10 [BP] | 1P: $79-$295 | 2P: $79-$295 | XP: $25 | F1(|
| | 7/2-11/23 [BP] | 1P: $79-$135 | 2P: $79-$135 | XP: $20 | F1(|

Small-scale Hotel **Location:** Jct SR 296, 1.9 mi e. Rt 23A 12442 (PO Box 355). **Fax:** 518/263-3981. **Facility:** 40 one-bedroom standard units, some with whirlpools. 3 stories (no elevator), interior corridors. **Parking:** on-site. **Terms:** oper 7/2-4/10, 2 night minimum stay - seasonal weekends, 14 day cancellation notice-fee imposed, [ECP] meal plan available, package plans, pets ($20 extra charge). **Amenities:** video library, hair dryers. **Leisure Activities:** whirlpool, exercise room, game room. **Guest Services:** coin laundry. **Business Services:** fax (fee). **Cards:** AX, DS, MC, VI **Special Amenities:** free local telephone calls.

SOME UNITS

FEE   FEE   FEE

SCRIBNER HOLLOW LODGE
Phone: (518)263-4211

| | All Year [MAP] | 1P: $150-$300 | 2P: $220-$700 | XP: $75 | D1(|

Small-scale Hotel **Location:** 0.5 mi e. Rt 23A 12442 (PO Box 156). **Fax:** 518/263-5266. **Facility:** 37 one-bedroom standard units some with whirlpools. 2-3 stories (no elevator), interior corridors. **Parking:** on-site. **Terms:** 2-3 night minimum stay - weekends, [BP] & [ECP] meal plans available. **Amenities:** hair dryers. **Dining:** The Prospect Restaurant, see separate listing. **Pool(s):** outdoor, small heated indoor. **Leisure Activities:** saunas, whirlpool, tennis court, cross country skiing, recreation programs. **Fee:** massage, game room. **Guest Services:** area transportation. **Business Services:** meeting rooms. **Cards:** AX, DC, MC, VI.

SOME UNITS

——— WHERE TO DINE ———

MOUNTAIN BROOK DINING AND SPIRITS **Dinner:** $12-$29 **Phone:** 518/263-5351

American **Location:** Town center. 625 Main St 12442. **Hours:** 5 pm-9 pm, Fri & Sat-10 pm; seasonal hours may vary **Reservations:** suggested, weekends. **Features:** Perched along the creek side at the entrance to the ski area, the casual eatery offers warm ambience, attentive service and a selection of foods made with the freshest ingredients, from delicate seafood to veal, fowl and beef. Casual dress; cocktails. **Parking:** street

Cards: MC, VI.

THE PROSPECT RESTAURANT **Dinner:** $18-$27 **Phone:** 518/263-4211

American **Location:** 0.5 mi e; in Scribner Hollow Lodge. Rt 23A 12442. **Hours:** 8 am-10 & 5-10 pm, Fri & Sat-11 pm, Su 8 am-11 & 5-11 pm. **Reservations:** suggested. **Features:** Wide windows offer views to the ski area from every table. The friendly and competent staff brings pleasant selections from the kitchen, including poultry fish and beef items. The wine list is extensive. Casual dress; cocktails. **Parking:** on-site. **Cards:** AX, DS

MC, VI.

HUNTINGTON STATION pop. 29,910

——— WHERE TO STAY ———

WHITMAN MOTOR LODGE
Phone: (631)271-280(

(AAA) [SAVE]

| | All Year [CP] | 1P: $99-$108 | 2P: $99-$108 | XP: $20 | F1(|

Motel **Location:** On SR 25 (Jericho Tpke), 0.6 mi e of SR 110. Located in a commercial area. 295 E Jericho Tpke 11746 **Fax:** 631/271-2804. **Facility:** 44 units. 36 one-bedroom standard units. 8 one-bedroom suites ($125-$150) some with efficiencies or kitchens. 1-2 stories (no elevator), interior/exterior corridors. **Bath:** combo or shower only. **Parking:** on-site. **Terms:** weekly rates available. **Cards:** AX, DC, DS, MC, VI. **Special Amenities:** free continental breakfast.

SOME UNITS

FEE   FEE

——— WHERE TO DINE ———

PANAMA HATTIE'S **Dinner:** $65 **Phone:** 631/351-1727

American **Location:** Between SR 110 and Deer Park. 872 E Jericho Tpke 11746. **Hours:** 5:30 pm-10 pm. Closed: 12/25 **Reservations:** required. **Features:** The three-course, prix fixe menu centers on eclectic cuisine, which i prepared with gourmet ingredients, as well as rare delicacies. Sophisticated dining rooms are appointed i the art deco style. Dessert is not only decadent, but also artful. Dressy casual; cocktails. **Parking:** on-site

Cards: AX, DC, DS, MC, VI.

HYDE PARK pop. 20,851

------- **WHERE TO STAY** -------

GOLDEN MANOR MOTEL
Phone: 845/229-2157

Motel

All Year   1P: $40-$65   2P: $50-$75   XP: $10   F5
Location: Jct CR 41, 1.5 mi s. 522 Albany Post Rd (US Rt 9) 12538. Fax: 845/229-6127. **Facility:** 38 units. 37 one-bedroom standard units, some with efficiencies. 1 one-bedroom suite ($65-$115). 1 story, exterior corridors. **Parking:** on-site, winter plug-ins. **Terms:** weekly rates available. **Cards:** AX, DS, MC, VI.

SOME UNITS

THE ROOSEVELT INN
Phone: 845/229-2443

Motel

Property failed to provide current rates
Location: Jct CR 41 and US 9, just s. 4360 Albany Post Rd. Fax: 845/229-0026. **Facility:** 26 units. 25 one-bedroom standard units. 1 one-bedroom suite. 1-2 stories (no elevator), exterior corridors. *Bath:* combo or shower only. **Parking:** on-site. **Business Services:** fax (fee).

SOME UNITS

SUPER 8 MOTEL
Phone: (845)229-0088

Motel

All Year   1P: $60-$115   2P: $70-$140   XP: $8   F12
Location: Jct CR 41, 1.3 mi s. 4142 Albany Post Rd (US Rt 9) 12538. Fax: 845/229-8088. **Facility:** 61 one-bedroom standard units. 2 stories (no elevator), interior corridors. **Parking:** on-site. **Terms:** [CP] meal plan available. **Amenities:** hair dryers. *Some:* irons. **Cards:** AX, DC, DS, MC, VI. **Special Amenities: free continental breakfast and free newspaper.**

SOME UNITS

FEE FEE

------- **WHERE TO DINE** -------

AMERICAN BOUNTY
Lunch: $12-$18   **Dinner:** $18-$24   **Phone:** 845/471-6608

Regional American

Location: 3 mi n of Poughkeepsie on US 9; in the Culinary Institute. 1946 Campus Dr 12538-1499. **Hours:** 11:30 am-1 & 6:30-8:30 pm. Closed major holidays; also Sun, Mon & 2 weeks in July & Dec. **Reservations:** suggested. **Features:** In Roth Hall, the restaurant prepares diverse cuisine that reflects the country's rich heritage via homegrown ingredients. A few tables face the open kitchen, where tempting desserts come to life. Dressy casual; cocktails. **Parking:** on-site. **Cards:** AX, CB, DC, DS, MC, VI.

THE APPLE PIE BAKERY CAFE
Lunch: $5-$6   **Phone:** 845/905-4500

Deli/Subs
Sandwiches

Location: 3 mi n of Poughkeepsie on US 9; in the Culinary Institute. 1946 Campus Dr 12538-1499. **Hours:** 8 am-6:30 pm. Closed major holidays; also Sat, Sun & 2 weeks in July & Dec. **Features:** In Roth Hall, the restaurant blends organic and fresh ingredients in offerings of coffee, tea, salad, delicatessen-style sandwiches and baked goods. Casual dress; beer & wine only. **Parking:** on-site. **Cards:** AX, CB, DC, DS, MC, VI.

THE BRASS ANCHOR
Lunch: $8-$12   **Dinner:** $17-$28   **Phone:** 845/452-3232

Seafood

Location: Jct CR 41, 3.7 mi s on US 9, then 0.5 mi sw. 31 River Point Rd 12601. **Hours:** 11:30 am-10 pm. Closed: 1/1, 12/25. **Reservations:** accepted. **Features:** Green awnings decorate the front of the blue, wood-sided building, while nautical decor brightens the dining room, which overlooks the Hudson River. The menu centers on seafood, with such choices as fried clams and fish and chips. Service is responsive both inside and on the seasonal patio. Casual dress; cocktails. **Parking:** on-site. **Cards:** AX, DC, DS, MC, VI.

CATERINA LE MEDICI
Lunch: $9-$19   **Dinner:** $9-$19   **Phone:** 845/471-6608

Regional
Italian

Location: 3 mi n of Poughkeepsie on US 9; in the Culinary Institute. 1946 Campus Dr 12538-1499. **Hours:** 11:30 am-1 & 6:30-8 pm. Closed major holidays; also Sat, Sun & 2 weeks in July & Dec. **Reservations:** suggested. **Features:** In Colavita Center, the restaurant lets patrons escape to the Old World and indulge in rich, hearty Italian flavors. Dressy casual; cocktails. **Parking:** on-site. **Cards:** AX, DC, DS, MC, VI.

COPPOLA'S ITALIAN AMERICAN BISTRO
Lunch: $6-$14   **Dinner:** $7-$18   **Phone:** 845/229-9113

Italian

Location: Jct CR 41 on US 9, 1 mi s. 4167 Albany Post Rd 12538. **Hours:** 11:30 am-9:30 pm, Fri & Sat-10 pm, Sun 10:30 am-9 pm. Closed: 11/25, 12/25. **Reservations:** suggested, for dinner. **Features:** Traditional preparations of American and Italian foods, including lots of pasta and pizzas, are well-presented and flavorful. The menu also offers a selection of lighter fare. The casual, laid-back atmosphere makes the restaurant a favorite of families. Casual dress; cocktails. **Parking:** on-site. **Cards:** AX, DC, DS, MC, VI.

ESCOFFIER
Lunch: $17-$25   **Dinner:** $24-$28   **Phone:** 845/471-6608

French

Location: 3 mi n of Poughkeepsie on US 9; in the Culinary Institute. 1946 Campus Dr 12538-1499. **Hours:** 11:30 am-1 & 6:30-8:30 pm. Closed major holidays; also Sun, Mon & 2 weeks in July & Dec. **Reservations:** suggested. **Features:** In Roth Hall, the restaurant mixes high elegance with traditional Provencal flavors and the upscale tastes of Paris. Dressy casual; cocktails. **Parking:** on-site. **Cards:** AX, CB, DC, DS, MC, VI.

ST. ANDREW'S CAFE
WWW
American

Lunch: $14-$18   **Dinner:** $16-$24   **Phone:** 845/471-6608
Location: 3 mi n of Poughkeepsie on US 9; in the Culinary Institute. 1946 Campus Dr 12538-1499. **Hours:** 11:30 am-1 & 6:30-8:30 pm. Closed major holidays; also Sat, Sun & 2 weeks in July & Dec. **Reservations:** suggested. **Features:** In the General Foods Nutrition Center, the restaurant hints at an Asian influence in some preparations, which are offered along with wood-fired pizza and other chicken and seafood dishes. Formal service is the norm in what could pass as an exclusive country-club dining room. Casual dress; cocktails. **Parking:** on-site. **Cards:** AX, CB, DC, DS, MC, VI.

INDEX —See also COOPERSTOWN.

─── **WHERE TO STAY** ───

RED CARPET INN & SUITES/LEATHERSTOCKING LODGE   **Book at aaa.com**   **Phone:** 607/544-1000
AAA [SAVE]
WWW
Motel

6/11-9/5	1P: $120-$155	2P: $120-$155
5/1-6/10 & 9/6-10/24	1P: $85-$130	2P: $85-$130

Location: Jct SR 80 and 28, 2.9 mi s. 4909 State Hwy 28 13326 (4909 State Hwy 28, COOPERSTOWN). Fax: 607/547-8251. **Facility:** Smoke free premises. 36 one-bedroom standard units. 1-2 stories (no elevator), exterior corridors. **Parking:** on-site. **Terms:** open 5/1-10/24, 30 day cancellation notice-fee imposed. **Amenities:** voice mail. **Cards:** AX, DC, DS, MC, VI. **Special Amenities:** free local telephone calls.

─── **WHERE TO DINE** ───

THE 1819 HOUSE RESTAURANT & TAVERN   Historic   **Dinner:** $11-$23   **Phone:** 607/547-1819
WW
Continental

Location: SR 28 on CR 11, just w. **Hours:** 5 pm-9 pm. Closed: 1/1, 12/25; also Sun, Mon & Tues seasonal. **Reservations:** accepted. **Features:** The unusual, historic, countryside setting welcomes diners to relax in a casually sophisticated environment. Veal and seafood, particularly fresh fish, stand out on a menu that also delivers a good array of lighter fare. Service is professional and attentive. Casual dress; cocktails. **Parking:** on-site. **Cards:** AX, MC, VI.

INLET pop. 406—See also ADIRONDACK MOUNTAINS.

─── **WHERE TO STAY** ───

MARINA MOTEL   **Phone:** 315/357-3883
AAA [SAVE]
WWW
Motel

All Year	1P: $69-$129	2P: $69-$149 XP: $10 F10

Location: Center. Located across from Fourth Lake. 6 S Shore Rd 13360 (PO Box 480). **Facility:** 16 one-bedroom standard units. 1 story, exterior corridors. **Parking:** on-site, winter plug-ins. **Terms:** office hours 9 am-9 pm, 14 day cancellation notice-fee imposed, package plans - in winter. **Leisure Activities:** adjacent to cross country & snowmobile trails. *Fee:* game room. **Cards:** MC, VI.

SOME UNITS
FEE

IRONDEQUOIT pop. 52,354

─── **WHERE TO STAY** ───

HOLIDAY INN EXPRESS-IRONDEQUOIT   **Book at aaa.com**   **Phone:** (585)342-0430
WWW
Small-scale Hotel

6/1-8/31	1P: $109
5/1-5/31	1P: $89
9/1-4/30	1P: $79

Location: SR 104, exit Goodman St, just n. Located adjacent to Irondequoit Mall. 2200 Goodman St N 14609. Fax: 585/342-0430. **Facility:** 66 one-bedroom standard units. 3 stories, interior corridors. *Bath:* combo or shower only. **Parking:** on-site. **Terms:** [CP] meal plan available. **Amenities:** dual phone lines, voice mail, irons, hair dryers. **Pool(s):** small heated indoor. **Leisure Activities:** whirlpool, exercise room. **Business Services:** business center. **Cards:** AX, DC, DS, JC, MC, VI.

SOME UNITS

ISLANDIA pop. 3,057

─── **WHERE TO STAY** ───

HAMPTON INN   **Book at aaa.com**   **Phone:** (631)234-0400
WWW
Small-scale Hotel

4/2-4/30 [ECP]	1P: $149-$179	2P: $149-$179
5/1-10/1 [ECP]	1P: $139-$169	2P: $139-$169
10/2-4/1 [ECP]	1P: $119-$149	2P: $119-$149

Location: I-495, exit 57, just e on south service road. Located in a commercial area. 1600 Veterans Memorial Hwy 11749. Fax: 631/234-0415. **Facility:** 121 one-bedroom standard units, some with whirlpools. 4 stories, interior corridors. **Parking:** on-site. **Amenities:** voice mail, irons, hair dryers. **Leisure Activities:** exercise room. **Guest Services:** valet laundry, area transportation. **Cards:** AX, CB, DC, DS, JC, MC, VI.

SOME UNITS
FEE FEE

ISLANDIA MARRIOTT LONG ISLAND   **Book at aaa.com**   **Phone:** (631)232-3000
WWW
Small-scale Hotel

All Year	1P: $249	2P: $249

Location: I-495, exit 58, 0.3 mi w on north service road. Located in a commercial area. 3635 Express Dr N 11749. Fax: 631/232-3029. **Facility:** 278 one-bedroom standard units. 10 stories, interior corridors. *Bath:* combo or shower only. **Parking:** on-site. **Terms:** [AP] meal plan available. **Amenities:** voice mail, irons, hair dryers. *Fee:* video games, high-speed Internet. **Pool(s):** heated indoor. **Leisure Activities:** whirlpool, exercise room. **Guest Services:** gift shop, valet laundry, area transportation. **Business Services:** conference facilities, business center. **Cards:** AX, DC, DS, MC, VI.

SOME UNITS

ITHACA pop. 29,287—See also *FINGER LAKES.*

———— **WHERE TO STAY** ————

COMFORT INN   *Book at aaa.com*   **Phone:** (607)272-0100

6/1-8/31	1P: $109-$269	2P: $109-$269	XP: $10 F18
5/1-5/31	1P: $99-$179	2P: $99-$179	XP: $10 F18
9/1-4/30	1P: $79-$159	2P: $79-$159	XP: $10 F18

Small-scale Hotel   **Location:** Jct SR 96, 89 and 79, 1.5 mi sw on SR 13. Located in a light-commercial area. 356 Elmira Rd 14850. Fax: 607/272-2405. **Facility:** 79 one-bedroom standard units, some with whirlpools. 2 stories (no elevator), interior/exterior corridors. **Parking:** on-site, winter plug-ins. **Amenities:** voice mail, irons, hair dryers. **Leisure Activities:** exercise room. **Guest Services:** valet laundry. **Business Services:** meeting rooms. **Cards:** AX, DC, DS, MC, VI.

SOME UNITS

HOLIDAY INN-EXECUTIVE TOWER   *Book at aaa.com*   **Phone:** (607)272-1000

All Year	1P: $126-$135	2P: $126-$135	XP: $10 F19

Small-scale Hotel   **Location:** Just n from SR 96B. 222 S Cayuga St 14850. Fax: 607/277-1275. **Facility:** 181 units. 179 one-bedroom standard units. 2 one-bedroom suites with whirlpools. 2-10 stories (no elevator), interior corridors. **Bath:** combo or shower only. **Parking:** on-site. **Terms:** 1-3 night minimum stay - seasonal, 30 day cancellation notice, small pets only ($15 fee). **Amenities:** voice mail, irons, hair dryers. **Dining:** 6:30 am-10 pm, Sat & Sun from 7 am, cocktails. **Pool(s):** heated indoor. **Leisure Activities:** exercise room. **Guest Services:** valet laundry, area transportation-bus station & colleges. **Business Services:** meeting rooms. **Cards:** AX, CB, DC, DS, JC, MC, VI. **Special Amenities:** free newspaper and early check-in/late check-out.

SOME UNITS   FEE   FEE FEE

LA TOURELLE COUNTRY INN   **Phone:** (607)273-2734

All Year	1P: $99-$299	2P: $99-$299

Country Inn   **Location:** 2.7 mi s on SR 96B. Adjacent to Buttermilk Falls State Park. 1150 Danby Rd 14850. Fax: 607/273-4821. **Facility:** On a hill overlooking Cayuga Lake, the inn offers distinctively-furnished rooms in a quiet country setting. 35 units. 34 one-bedroom standard units, some with whirlpools. 1 one-bedroom suite. 1-3 stories (no elevator), interior corridors. **Bath:** combo or shower only. **Parking:** on-site. **Terms:** cancellation fee imposed, [CP] meal plan available, pets (in designated units). **Amenities:** video library, high-speed Internet, voice mail, safes, irons, hair dryers. **Dining:** John Thomas Steakhouse, see separate listing. **Leisure Activities:** fishing, 4 tennis courts (2 lighted), hiking trails. **Guest Services:** valet laundry. **Business Services:** meeting rooms. **Cards:** AX, DC, MC, VI.

SOME UNITS

MEADOW COURT INN   **Phone:** (607)273-3885

5/1-11/30	1P: $50-$195	2P: $60-$195	XP: $10 F12
12/1-4/30	1P: $40-$95	2P: $50-$95	XP: $10 F12

Motel   **Location:** 1.5 mi s on SR 13 and 96. Located in a commercial area. 529 S Meadow St 14850. Fax: 607/277-0758. **Facility:** 75 one-bedroom standard units, some with whirlpools. 1-2 stories, interior/exterior corridors. **Parking:** on-site. **Terms:** cancellation fee imposed, pets ($10 fee, in designated units). **Amenities:** hair dryers. *Some:* high-speed Internet. **Dining:** 7 am-9 pm, Sat from 5 pm; closed Sun, cocktails. **Business Services:** meeting rooms. **Cards:** AX, DC, DS, MC, VI. **Special Amenities:** early check-in/late check-out and free room upgrade (subject to availability with advanced reservations).

SOME UNITS   FEE   FEE FEE

THE STATLER HOTEL AT CORNELL UNIVERSITY   *Book at aaa.com*   **Phone:** (607)257-2500

All Year	1P: $175-$395	2P: $195-$425	XP: $10 F18

Small-scale Hotel   **Location:** On the campus of Cornell University. 11 East Ave 14853. Fax: 607/257-6432. **Facility:** 150 units. 138 one-bedroom standard units. 12 one-bedroom suites ($275-$500), some with whirlpools. 9 stories, interior corridors. **Bath:** combo or shower only. **Parking:** on-site. **Amenities:** CD players, high-speed Internet, dual phone lines, voice mail, irons, hair dryers. *Some:* safes. **Fee:** DVD players. **Leisure Activities:** exercise room. **Guest Services:** gift shop, valet laundry, area transportation. **Business Services:** conference facilities. **Cards:** AX, DC, MC, VI.

SOME UNITS   FEE FEE

SUPER 8 MOTEL   *Book at aaa.com*   **Phone:** (607)273-8088

All Year [CP]	1P: $70-$190	2P: $76-$190	XP: $6 F12

Small-scale Hotel   **Location:** Jct SR 96B and 13, just s. 400 S Meadow St 14850. Fax: 607/273-4832. **Facility:** 63 one-bedroom standard units. 2 stories (no elevator), interior corridors. **Parking:** on-site. **Terms:** 90 day cancellation notice. **Amenities:** *Some:* hair dryers. **Leisure Activities:** exercise room. **Cards:** AX, DC, DS, MC, VI.

SOME UNITS

———— *The following lodging was either not evaluated or did not*
meet AAA rating requirements but is listed for your information only. ————

HAMPTON INN   **Phone:** 607/277-5500

7/1-11/7 [BP]	1P: $109-$159	2P: $109-$169
5/1-6/30 [BP]	1P: $99-$139	2P: $99-$149
11/8-4/30 [BP]	1P: $89-$129	2P: $99-$129

Small-scale Hotel   Too new to rate, opening scheduled for December 2003. **Location:** On SR 13 (Elmira Rd). 337 Elmira Rd 14850. **Amenities:** 66 units, coffeemakers, microwaves, refrigerators, pool. **Terms:** 2-4 night minimum stay - seasonal & weekends. **Cards:** AX, DC, DS, MC, VI.

——— WHERE TO DINE ———

BOATYARD GRILL
American
and American fare.
Lunch: $6-$11   **Dinner:** $12-$21   **Phone:** 607/256-2628
Location: Just off SR 89. 525 Taughannock Blvd 14850. **Hours:** noon-4 & 5-10 pm, Fri & Sat-11 pm; call for seasonal lunch hours. Closed: 1/1, 11/25, 12/25. **Features:** The waterside restaurant affords great views from every seat. Although this place is newly built, it displays suspended antique wooden boats and canoes along with other nautical decor. The menu centers on fresh seafood and other popular Continental and American fare. Phone-ahead seating is accepted. Casual dress; cocktails. **Parking:** on-site. **Cards:** AX, DC, DS, MC, VI.

GLENWOOD PINES
American
Lunch: $3-$16   **Dinner:** $3-$16   **Phone:** 607/273-3709
Location: 4 mi n on SR 89. 1213 Taughannock Blvd 14850. **Hours:** 11 am-11 pm. Closed major holidays; also 4/4. **Features:** Perched atop a slope overlooking Cayuga Lake, the restaurant caters to families. Tasty food is reasonably priced and traditionally prepared with simple ingredients. Casually-dressed servers capably handle the generally busy business. Casual dress; cocktails. **Parking:** on-site. **Cards:** MC, VI.

JOHN THOMAS STEAKHOUSE
American
provides a fitting complement.
Dinner: $13-$36   **Phone:** 607/273-3464
Location: 3 mi s on SR 96B; in La Tourelle Country Inn. 1152 Danby Rd 14850. **Hours:** 5:30 pm-10 pm, Fri & Sat-11 pm. Closed major holidays. **Reservations:** required, college events. **Features:** Prime, dry-aged beef, such as the specialty porterhouse steak for two—and fresh seafood are what the restaurant is all about. The mid-1800s farmhouse has beam ceilings and wide-plank floors. An extensive selection of wines provides a fitting complement. Dressy casual; cocktails. **Parking:** on-site. **Cards:** AX, CB, DC, DS, MC, VI.

LOST DOG CAFE/COFFEEHOUSE
International
teas.
Lunch: $7-$10   **Dinner:** $14-$17   **Phone:** 607/277-9143
Location: Center. 106-112 S Cayuga St 14850. **Hours:** 11:30 am-3 & 5-10 pm, Sat 11:30 am-10 pm, Sun 11:30 am-9 pm. Closed major holidays; also Mon. **Features:** Eclectic, Bohemian-inspired decor sets a relaxing atmosphere for health-conscious diners. The nouvelle cuisine with an international flair also features many vegetarian dishes, all complemented by fresh specialty brewed coffees, lattes, cappuccinos and herbal teas. Casual dress; cocktails. **Parking:** street. **Cards:** AX, MC, VI.

MOOSEWOOD RESTAURANT
American
draws on many inspirations,
Lunch: $5-$6   **Dinner:** $10-$13   **Phone:** 607/273-9610
Location: Downtown; in Dewitt Mall (old Ithaca High School). 215 N Cayuga St 14850. **Hours:** 11:30 am-2 & 5:30-8:30 pm, Fri & Sat-9 pm; hours vary in summer. Closed major holidays; also for lunch Sun. **Features:** Celebrating 30 years, the restaurant is acclaimed as a driving force in the world of creative vegetarian cooking. Organic ingredients are used whenever possible. The innovative daily changing menu draws on many inspirations, ranging from regional American to many ethnicities. The atmosphere is casual and relaxed. Casual dress; cocktails. **Parking:** on-site (fee). **Cards:** AX, DS, MC, VI.

SIMEON'S
Continental
dress; cocktails.
Lunch: $6-$8   **Dinner:** $15-$24   **Phone:** 607/272-2212
Location: Corner of State and Aurora sts; on The Commons. 224 E State St 14854. **Hours:** 11 am-midnight. Closed: 1/1, 11/25, 12/25. **Features:** Since 1975, the restaurant has prepared Continental dishes with a Mediterranean flair. The full menu—which includes monstrous healthy salads, jumbo sandwiches, generous and creative pasta dishes, rack of lamb, duck, tuna and some vegetarian fare—is offered all day. Casual dress; cocktails. **Parking:** street. **Cards:** AX, DC, DS, MC, VI.

STATION RESTAURANT AND SLEEPING CARS Historic
American
Dinner: $12-$24   **Phone:** 607/272-2609
Location: Corner of SR 89 and 96. 806 W Buffalo St 14850. **Hours:** 4 pm-9 pm, Fri & Sat-9:30 pm, Sun noon-8 pm. Closed: 1/1, 12/25; also Mon in off season. **Reservations:** accepted. **Features:** The converted, late-19th-century railroad station and railroad cars provide both fun settings for families or quiet romantic tables with nice views of Cayuga Lake. Menu offerings include well-prepared specialties of beef, seafood and pasta. Casual dress; cocktails. **Parking:** on-site. **Cards:** AX, DS, MC, VI.

THAI CUISINE
Ethnic
piquant to hot.
DC, DS, MC, VI.
Dinner: $9-$15   **Phone:** 607/273-2031
Location: 1.5 mi s on SR 13 and 96. 501 S Meadow St 14850. **Hours:** 5 pm-9:30 pm, Fri-10 pm, Sat 11:30 am-2:30 & 5-10 pm, Sun 11:30 am-2 & 5-9:30 pm. Closed: 11/25, 12/25; also Tues. **Reservations:** suggested. **Features:** Authentic Thai cuisine—including many preparations of beef, chicken, pork and seafood—is made from traditional recipes. Dishes are seasoned to suit your tastes, from mild to piquant to hot. Casual servers exhibit good menu knowledge. Casual dress; beer & wine only. **Parking:** on-site. **Cards:** AX, DC, DS, MC, VI.

VIVA TAQUERIA AND CANTINA
Mexican
Lunch: $6-$8   **Dinner:** $7-$9   **Phone:** 607/277-1752
Location: Corner of State and Aurora sts. 101 N Aurora St 14850. **Hours:** 11 am-10 pm. Closed: 11/25; also 12/25-1/2. **Features:** Patrons can nosh on fast, healthy and reasonably priced food in the lively cantina, on the patio or to go. Generous servings go well with Mexican and local beers, premium tequilas and fresh sangria. Casual dress; cocktails. **Parking:** street. **Cards:** DS, MC, VI.

JAMESTOWN pop. 31,730

——— WHERE TO STAY ———

COMFORT INN   *Book at aaa.com*
Small-scale Hotel
Phone: (716)664-5920

5/1-10/31 [ECP]	1P: $89	2P: $169	XP: $10	F18
11/1-4/30 [ECP]	1P: $59	2P: $149	XP: $10	F18

Location: I-86, exit 12, just s. 2800 N Main St Extension 14701. Fax: 716/664-3068. **Facility:** 101 one-bedroom standard units, some with whirlpools. 2 stories, interior corridors. **Parking:** on-site. **Terms:** cancellation fee imposed, pets ($10 fee, in designated units). **Amenities:** video library (fee), video games, dual phone lines, voice mail, safes, irons, hair dryers. **Guest Services:** valet laundry. **Business Services:** meeting rooms. **Cards:** AX, DC, DS, MC, VI. **Special Amenities:** free expanded continental breakfast and free newspaper.

SOME UNITS

FEE

HOLIDAY INN
AAA **SAVE**

Large-scale Hotel

Book at aaa.com

5/29-9/1	1P: $100-$120	2P: $100-$120
5/1-5/28 & 9/2-4/30	1P: $80-$100	2P: $80-$100

Phone: (716)664-3400

Location: I-86, exit 12, 2 mi s on SR 60; center. 150 W 4th St 14701. **Fax:** 716/484-3304. **Facility:** 146 units. 144 one-bedroom standard units. 2 one-bedroom suites. 8 stories, interior corridors. *Bath:* combo or shower only. **Parking:** on-site. **Amenities:** voice mail, irons, hair dryers. **Dining:** 6:30 am-2 & 5:30-10 pm, Sat & Sun from 7 am, cocktails. **Pool(s):** heated indoor. **Leisure Activities:** exercise room. **Guest Services:** valet and coin laundry. **Business Services:** meeting rooms. **Cards:** AX, CB, DC, DS, MC, VI.

SOME UNITS / FEE

——— WHERE TO DINE ———

MACDUFF'S
Continental

Dinner: $18-$27

Phone: 716/664-9414

Location: Just e of SR 60, at 4th St and Pine; downtown. 317 Pine St 14701. **Hours:** 5:30 pm-9 pm. Closed major holidays; also 12/24 & Sun. **Reservations:** suggested. **Features:** The intimate restaurant boasts a sophisticated verbal menu that changes nightly. Personal service and comfortable surroundings add to the dining experience. Offerings include distinctive signature dishes, more than 40 single-malt scotches, a nice wine list and homemade ice cream. Dressy casual; cocktails. **Parking:** street. **Cards:** AX, MC, VI.

JAMESVILLE (See map and index starting on p. 577)

——— WHERE TO DINE ———

GLEN LOCH RESTAURANT Historic
AAA

Continental

Dinner: $11-$32

Phone: 315/469-6969 **42**

Location: I-481, exit 2, 1.4 mi s. 4626 North St 13078. **Hours:** 4:30 pm-10 pm, Sun 10 am-9 pm. Closed: 12/24, 12/25; also Mon. **Reservations:** suggested. **Features:** Attractive Scots Highland decor in the old rustic feed mill lends to an enjoyable, relaxed evening. Friendly service and Continental entrees combine pleasantly with the lovely view across the mill stream. Outdoor deck seating can be requested from early June through early September. Casual dress; cocktails. **Parking:** on-site. **Cards:** AX, DS, MC, VI.

JEFFERSONVILLE pop. 420

——— WHERE TO STAY ———

THE GRIFFIN HOUSE

Historic Bed & Breakfast

Phone: (845)482-3371

All Year [BP]	1P: $159-$189	2P: $159-$189	XP: $50

Location: Just n; center. 27 Maple Ave 12748. **Facility:** Architecturally pristine features add an ambience of Victorian elegance at this two-acre estate, which claims Franklin Roosevelt as a one-time guest. Smoke free premises. 4 one-bedroom standard units. 2 stories (no elevator), interior corridors. *Bath:* combo or shower only. **Parking:** on-site. **Terms:** 2 night minimum stay - seasonal weekends, age restrictions may apply, 30 day cancellation notice-fee imposed, no pets allowed (owner's pet on premises). **Amenities:** hair dryers. **Business Services:** fax. **Cards:** AX, MC, VI.

JOHNSON CITY pop. 15,535

——— WHERE TO STAY ———

BEST INN & SUITES
Small-scale Hotel

Book at aaa.com

All Year	1P: $44-$64	2P: $55-$105	XP: $8	F18

Phone: (607)770-9333

Location: SR 17, exit 70N, 0.3 mi n. Located opposite Oakdale Mall. 581 Harry L Dr 13790. **Fax:** 607/770-7526. **Facility:** 60 one-bedroom standard units. 4 stories, interior corridors. **Parking:** on-site. **Terms:** 7 day cancellation notice, weekly rates available, [ECP] meal plan available. **Amenities:** irons, hair dryers. **Guest Services:** valet and coin laundry. **Business Services:** meeting rooms. **Cards:** AX, CB, DC, DS, JC, MC, VI.

SOME UNITS

BEST WESTERN OF JOHNSON CITY
AAA **SAVE**

Small-scale Hotel

Book at aaa.com

All Year	1P: $55-$90	2P: $65-$105	XP: $8	F12

Phone: (607)729-9194

Location: SR 17, exit 70N, 0.3 mi n. Located opposite Oakdale Mall. 569 Harry L Dr 13790. **Fax:** 607/729-3205. **Facility:** 102 one-bedroom standard units. 4 stories, interior corridors. **Parking:** on-site, winter plug-ins. **Terms:** [CP] meal plan available, pets ($8 fee, in designated units). **Amenities:** high-speed Internet, voice mail, irons, hair dryers. **Leisure Activities:** pool privileges. **Guest Services:** valet and coin laundry. **Business Services:** meeting rooms. **Cards:** AX, DC, DS, MC, VI. **Special Amenities:** free expanded continental breakfast and free local telephone calls.

SOME UNITS / FEE

HAMPTON INN
Small-scale Hotel

Book at aaa.com

All Year [ECP]	1P: $99-$115	2P: $99-$115	XP: $8	F16

Phone: (607)729-9125

Location: SR 17, exit 70N. Located in a commercial area. 630 Field St 13790. **Fax:** 607/729-9816. **Facility:** 64 one-bedroom standard units. 3 stories, interior corridors. *Bath:* combo or shower only. **Terms:** cancellation fee imposed. **Amenities:** video library (fee), voice mail, irons, hair dryers. **Pool(s):** small heated indoor. **Leisure Activities:** whirlpool. **Business Services:** fax (fee). **Cards:** AX, CB, DC, DS, MC, VI.

SOME UNITS

RED ROOF INN-BINGHAMTON *Book at aaa.com* Phone: (607)729-8940

6/29-9/8	1P: $52-$67	2P: $57-$72	XP: $5	F18
5/1-6/28	1P: $44-$60	2P: $49-$66	XP: $5	F18
9/9-12/31	1P: $44-$60	2P: $49-$60	XP: $5	F18
1/1-4/30	1P: $38-$46	2P: $43-$51	XP: $5	F18

Motel **Location:** SR 17, exit 70N, 0.3 mi n, just n on Reynolds Rd. 590 Fairview St 13790. Fax: 607/729-8949. **Facility:** 107 one-bedroom standard units. 2 stories (no elevator), exterior corridors. **Parking:** on-site. **Terms:** small pets only. **Amenities:** video library (fee), video games, voice mail. **Guest Services:** valet laundry. **Cards:** AX, CB, DC, DS, MC, VI. **Special Amenities:** free local telephone calls and free newspaper.

SOME UNITS

—— WHERE TO DINE ——

CACCIATORE'S **Dinner:** $8-$18 Phone: 607/798-7699

Italian **Location:** SR 17, exit 70N, 0.5 mi e. 365 Harry L Dr E 13790. **Hours:** 4 pm-10 pm. Closed major holidays; also Sun. **Features:** The popular restaurant is tucked away in a small shopping center. Established favorites are dished in abundant servings. Casual dress; cocktails. **Parking:** on-site. **Cards:** AX, DS, MC, VI.

CHRISTIE'S GRILL **Lunch:** $6-$9 **Dinner:** $9-$21 Phone: 607/729-3100

American **Location:** SR 17, exit 70N; in Giant Plaza. 560 Harry L Dr 13790. **Hours:** 11 am-10 pm, Fri & Sat-11 pm, Sun-9 pm. Closed: 11/25, 12/25. **Reservations:** accepted. **Features:** The American grill reflects an Italian flair. Certified Angus beef is used in specialties such as steak au poivre or juicy, slow-roasted prime rib. All soup is made in house and served in bottomless helpings. Among other generous entrees are fresh seafood, pasta favorites, tender chicken and ribs. The family atmosphere is friendly. Casual dress; cocktails. **Parking:** on-site. **Cards:** AX, CB, DC, DS, MC, VI.

DELGADO'S CAFE **Lunch:** $4-$7 **Dinner:** $7-$12 Phone: 607/798-7306

Mexican **Location:** SR 17, exit 70N, just n on SR 201, then 1.1 mi e. 119 Harry L Dr 13790. **Hours:** 11:30 am-11 pm, Sat from 4 pm. Closed major holidays; also Sun. **Features:** Popular with the neighborhood crowd, the casual restaurant is a nice place to take the family for good food. Although the menu centers on Mexican fare—burritos, enchiladas, tacos and nachos—guests also find a number of traditional American choices. Casual dress; cocktails. **Parking:** on-site. **Cards:** DC, DS, MC, VI.

WEST OF BOSTON **Lunch:** $4-$10 **Dinner:** $14-$18 Phone: 607/748-6088

American **Location:** SR 17, exit 69 northbound, 1.7 mi w on SR 17C (Main St). 110 Endwell Plaza 13760. **Hours:** 11 am-3 & 4-9 pm, Fri & Sat-10 pm, Sun 3 pm-8 pm. Closed: 12/25. **Reservations:** accepted. **Features:** A refreshing nautical theme sets the stage for a cozy, relaxed dining experience. The friendly staff serves fresh seafood, pasta, chicken, veal and filet mignon. All dressings and desserts are homemade. Casual dress; cocktails. **Parking:** on-site. **Cards:** AX, DC, DS, MC, VI.

JOHNSTOWN pop. 8,511

—— WHERE TO STAY ——

HOLIDAY INN *Book at aaa.com* Phone: (518)762-4686

8/1-8/31	1P: $132-$145	XP: $10	F19
7/1-7/31	1P: $117-$127	XP: $10	F19
5/1-6/30	1P: $94-$102	XP: $10	F19
9/1-4/30	1P: $96-$100	XP: $10	F19

Small-scale Hotel **Location:** Jct SR 30A and 29 E, 1.3 mi n. 308 N Comrie Ave 12095-1095. Fax: 518/762-4034. **Facility:** 99 one-bedroom standard units. 2-3 stories (no elevator), interior/exterior corridors. *Bath:* combo or shower only. **Parking:** on-site, winter plug-ins. **Terms:** pets ($10 fee, 1st floor units). **Amenities:** video library (fee), irons, hair dryers. **Pool(s):** heated outdoor. **Leisure Activities:** exercise room. **Guest Services:** valet and coin laundry. **Business Services:** meeting rooms. **Cards:** AX, CB, DC, DS, JC, MC, VI.

SOME UNITS

KEENE VALLEY

—— WHERE TO DINE ——

KEENE VALLEY MARKET PLACE **Lunch:** $4-$7 Phone: 518/576-9731

American **Location:** On SR 73; center. 87 Main St 12943. **Hours:** Open 5/1-1/31 & 4/1-4/30; 11 am-3 pm. Closed: 1st 3 weeks of Nov. **Features:** Keene Valley Market Place has very limited indoor seating with only a few tables and some self-service aspects. The menu is made up of a few soups, a good variety of creative sandwiches and home-made casseroles. Casual dress; beer & wine only. **Parking:** on-site. **Cards:** MC, VI.

KEESEVILLE pop. 1,850

—— WHERE TO DINE ——

PLEASANT CORNER RESTAURANT **Lunch:** $3-$9 **Dinner:** $3-$9 Phone: 518/834-7127

American **Location:** I-87, exit 34, just e. 262 Rt 9N 12944. **Hours:** 6 am-9 pm. Closed: 11/25, 12/25. **Features:** There's nothing fancy about the small-town diner, but as its name implies, it is pleasant. The menu mostly comprises burgers and sandwiches, but do ask about the daily specials. Casual dress; beer & wine only. **Parking:** on-site. **Cards:** DS, MC, VI.

KENMORE —*See Buffalo p. 254.*

KINGSTON pop. 23,456

―――― WHERE TO STAY ――――

HOLIDAY INN
(AAA) [SAVE]
◆◆◆◆◆
Small-scale Hotel

Book at aaa.com
5/1-10/31   1P: $139-$179   2P: $139-$179
11/1-4/30   1P: $139-$159   2P: $139-$159
Location: I-87, exit 19, just e of traffic circle. 503 Washington Ave 12401. Fax: 845/340-1908. **Facility:** 212 one-bedroom standard units. 2 stories (no elevator), interior corridors. **Parking:** on-site. **Terms:** 2 night minimum stay - weekends 8/1-10/31, 3 day cancellation notice, [BP] meal plan available. **Amenities:** voice mail, irons, hair dryers. **Dining:** 6:30 am-2 & 5-10 pm, cocktails. **Pool(s):** heated indoor, wading. **Leisure Activities:** sauna, whirlpool. *Fee:* game room. **Guest Services:** coin laundry. **Business Services:** meeting rooms, fax (fee).
Cards: AX, DC, DS, MC, VI.

Phone: (845)338-0400

SOME UNITS

🅢🅓 🍴 🍸 🏊 🛁 ✖ 🎥 ᴰᴬᵀᴬᴾᴼᴿᵀ ▣ / ✖ �📼 🔌 /
               FEE FEE

―――― WHERE TO DINE ――――

ARMADILLO BAR & GRILL   **Lunch:** $6-$8   **Dinner:** $9-$14   **Phone:** 845/339-1550
◆◆ ◆◆
Tex-Mex
Location: Just s of Broadway, 1.8 mi e of jct US 587 and SR 28; in Rondout Historic Region. 97 Abeel St 12401. **Hours:** noon-3 pm, Tues-Thurs 4:30 pm-10 pm, Fri & Sat 5 pm-11 pm, Sun 4 pm-9 pm; hours may vary in winter. Closed major holidays; also Mon. **Features:** Soft colors decorate the dining room, where a wide array of regulars gather to enjoy Southwestern cuisine, particularly Tex-Mex specialties. Frozen margaritas and Mexican beers complement such selections as shrimp stuffed jalapenos and grilled tuna. Casual dress; cocktails. **Parking:** street. **Cards:** AX, DS, MC, VI.

🍸 ✖

THE HOFFMAN HOUSE Historic   **Lunch:** $8-$12   **Dinner:** $16-$22   **Phone:** 845/338-2626
◆◆ ◆◆
American
Location: I-87, exit 19, 0.5 mi e on Washington Ave; left at bus station. 94 N Front St 12401. **Hours:** Open 5/1-2/1 & 3/1-4/29; 11:30 am-9 pm, Fri & Sat-10 pm. Closed major holidays; also Sun. **Reservations:** suggested. **Features:** The late-17th-century, Dutch rubble house exudes historic charm, with three fireplaces and lots of original woodwork. Representative of traditional fare are fish and chips, as well as the Saturday special of prime rib with Yorkshire pudding. Casual dress; cocktails. **Parking:** on-site. **Cards:** AX, CB, DC, DS, MC, VI.

🍸 ✖

LAKE GEORGE pop. 985—See also *ADIRONDACK MOUNTAINS.*

―――― WHERE TO STAY ――――

ADMIRAL MOTEL   **Phone:** 518/668-2097
◆◆ ◆◆
Motel
7/21-9/6   1P: $100-$115 2P: $100-$115 XP: $10 F12
7/1-7/20   1P: $95-$110   2P: $95-$110   XP: $10 F12
5/1-6/30 & 9/7-10/18 1P: $65-$75   2P: $65-$75   XP: $10 F12
Location: I-87, exit 22, 0.5 mi s on US 9. 401 Canada St 12845. Fax: 518/668-3250. **Facility:** 27 one-bedroom standard units. 2 stories (no elevator), exterior corridors. *Bath:* combo or shower only. **Parking:** on-site. **Terms:** open 5/1-10/18, 2-5 night minimum stay - in summer, 10 day cancellation notice-fee imposed. **Pool(s):** heated outdoor. **Cards:** DC, MC, VI.

SOME UNITS

🍴 🏊 / 🔌 /

BALMORAL MOTEL

Phone: (518)668-2673

6/21-9/10	1P: $69-$215	2P: $79-$225	XP: $10	F16
5/1-6/20 & 9/11-10/20	1P: $49-$99	2P: $59-$109	XP: $10	F16
4/23-4/30	1P: $49-$59	2P: $49-$59	XP: $10	F16

Motel

Location: I-87, exit 22, 0.3 mi s on US 9. 444 Canada St 12845. Fax: 518/668-9248. **Facility:** 31 units. 29 one- and 1 two-bedroom standard units, some with efficiencies. 1 one-bedroom suite. 2 stories (no elevator), exterior corridors. *Bath:* combo or shower only. **Parking:** on-site. **Terms:** open 5/1-10/20 & 4/23-4/30, office hours 8 am-11 pm, 2-3 night minimum stay - weekends in season, 14 day cancellation notice-fee imposed, pets ($10 extra charge, in designated units). **Pool(s):** heated outdoor. **Leisure Activities:** Fee: game room. **Guest Services:** coin laundry. **Cards:** DS, MC, VI.

SOME UNITS

FEE

BEST WESTERN OF LAKE GEORGE

Book at aaa.com

Phone: (518)668-5701

6/25-9/5	1P: $149-$179	2P: $149-$179	XP: $15	F12
5/28-6/24 & 9/6-4/30	1P: $94-$124	2P: $94-$124	XP: $15	F12
5/1-5/27	1P: $74-$119	2P: $74-$119	XP: $15	F12

Motel

Location: I-87, exit 21, just e. Rt 9 12845 (48 Canada St). Fax: 518/668-5701. **Facility:** 87 units. 79 one- and 4 two-bedroom standard units. 3 one- and 1 two-bedroom suites ($119-$399), some with kitchens ($119-$399), some with elevator), interior/exterior corridors. **Parking:** on-site, winter plug-ins. **Terms:** 3 day cancellation notice. **Amenities:** voice mail, safes, irons, hair dryers. **Pool(s):** outdoor, small heated indoor, wading. **Leisure Activities:** whirlpool. **Guest Services:** valet laundry. **Cards:** AX, CB, DC, DS, MC, VI. **Special Amenities:** free continental breakfast and early check-in/late check-out.

SOME UNITS

FEE

CHOICE INN & SUITES

Phone: 518/668-2143

6/25-9/6	1P: $89-$149	2P: $109-$179	XP: $10	F18
5/1-6/24	1P: $59-$89	2P: $69-$129	XP: $10	F18
9/7-10/11	1P: $59-$89	2P: $69-$119	XP: $10	F18
10/12-4/30	1P: $45-$89	2P: $49-$119	XP: $10	F18

Motel

Location: I-87, exit 22, 0.3 mi s on US 9. 435 Canada St 12845. Fax: 518/668-3025. **Facility:** 39 one-bedroom standard units. 2 stories, exterior corridors. **Parking:** on-site, winter plug-ins. **Terms:** 2-3 night minimum stay - seasonal, 14 day cancellation notice-fee imposed, weekly rates available. **Amenities:** voice mail. **Pool(s):** heated indoor. **Leisure Activities:** whirlpool, playground, basketball, volleyball. **Business Services:** fax (fee). **Cards:** DS, MC, VI.

SOME UNITS
FEE

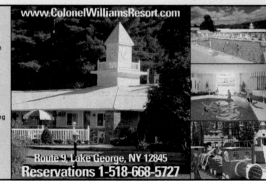

Show your card & Save

Participating members of the Hiltons of New York City will make AAA members feel at home.

For availability and reservations at special AAA rates, call 1-877-NYC-HILT, or visit us online at www.nychilton.com

Classic luxury and timeless elegance at an exclusive Park Avenue address.

301 Park Avenue

Setting the standard for quality and service in the heart of Rockefeller Center.

1335 Avenue of the Americas

A chic haven glittering high atop Times Square.

234 West 42nd Street

Luxurious all suite hotel in the heart of Broadway and Times Square.

47th Street at 7th Avenue

The only upscale all-suite hotel located on the water in downtown Manhattan.

102 North End Avenue

Located in the heart of New York City's Financial District.

55 Church Street

COLONEL WILLIAMS RESORT
Phone: 518/668-5727

♦♦ ◆◆

Motel

6/26-9/15	1P: $95-$120	2P: $95-$120	XP: $10
6/1-6/25	1P: $75-$90	2P: $75-$90	XP: $10

Location: I-87, exit 21, 1.3 mi s on US 9. 1787 Historic Dr 12845 (PO Box 268). Fax: 518/668-2996. **Facility:** Smoke free premises. 45 units. 30 one-bedroom standard units. 9 one- and 6 two-bedroom suites ($150-$185). 1 story, interior/exterior corridors. *Bath:* combo or shower only. **Parking:** on-site. **Terms:** open 6/1-9/15, 3 night minimum stay - seasonal weekends, 14 day cancellation notice-fee imposed. **Amenities:** voice mail. *Some:* irons. **Pool(s):** heated outdoor, heated indoor, wading. **Leisure Activities:** sauna, whirlpools, playground, exercise room. *Fee:* game room. **Guest Services:** coin laundry. **Cards:** AX, DC, MC, VI. *(See color ad p 318)*

SOME UNITS

ECONO LODGE LAKE GEORGE MOTEL *Book at aaa.com*
Phone: (518)668-2689

(AAA) [SAVE]
♦♦ ◆◆

Motel

6/18-9/5	1P: $79-$154	2P: $79-$154	XP: $10	F17
5/1-6/17 & 9/6-10/31	1P: $49-$79	2P: $49-$79	XP: $10	F17

Location: I-87, exit 22, 0.3 mi s on US 9. 439 Canada St 12845. Fax: 518/798-3455. **Facility:** 50 one-bedroom standard units, some with whirlpools. 2-3 stories, interior/exterior corridors. *Bath:* combo or shower only. **Parking:** on-site. **Terms:** open 5/1-10/31, 7 day cancellation notice-fee imposed. **Amenities:** hair dryers. **Pool(s):** outdoor, small heated indoor. **Leisure Activities:** whirlpool, pool table. *Fee:* game room. **Business Services:** meeting rooms. **Cards:** AX, CB, DC, DS, MC, VI. **Special Amenities:** free local telephone calls and free room upgrade (subject to availability with advanced reservations).** *(See color ad below)*

SOME UNITS

GENTLEMAN JOHNNY'S INN
Phone: 518/668-2096

(AAA) [SAVE]
◆

Motel

8/1-9/7	1P: $65-$75	2P: $65-$75	XP: $10	D
7/1-7/31	1P: $60-$70	2P: $60-$70	XP: $10	D
5/1-6/30 & 9/8-10/12	1P: $50-$55	2P: $50-$55	XP: $10	D

Location: I-87, exit 22, 0.5 mi n on SR 9N. 3057 Lake Shore Dr 12845. Fax: 518/668-0168. **Facility:** 17 units. 14 one- and 3 two-bedroom standard units, some with kitchens. 1 story, exterior corridors. *Bath:* combo or shower only. **Parking:** on-site. **Terms:** open 5/1-10/12, 7 day cancellation notice, 30 day for cottages-fee imposed. **Pool(s):** outdoor. **Leisure Activities:** grills, picnic tables, ping pong, basketball, horseshoes. **Cards:** DS, MC, VI. **Special Amenities:** free local telephone calls.

SOME UNITS

THE GEORGIAN

  Small-scale Hotel

Phone: (518)668-5401

5/29-10/11	1P: $99-$279	2P: $99-$279	XP: $10	F5
5/1-5/28 & 10/12-4/30	1P: $79-$199	2P: $79-$199	XP: $10	F5

Location: I-87, exit 22, 0.5 mi s on US 9. 384 Canada St 12845. **Fax:** 518/668-5870. **Facility:** 163 units. 161 one-bedroom standard units, some with whirlpools. 1 one- and 1 two-bedroom suites ($139-$359) with whirlpools. 1-3 stories, exterior corridors. **Parking:** on-site, winter plug-ins. **Terms:** 2-3 night minimum stay - some weekends, 3 day cancellation notice, package plans - seasonal. **Amenities:** voice mail, irons, hair dryers. **Dining:** 6:30 am-midnight, entertainment. **Pool(s):** heated outdoor. **Guest Services:** valet laundry. **Business Services:** meeting rooms. **Cards:** AX, CB, DC, DS, MC, VI. *(See color ad p 321)*

SOME UNITS

  /

GREEN HAVEN

Motel

Phone: 518/668-2489

11/1-4/30 [CP]	2P: $59-$109	XP: $10	D3
5/1-6/30 & 9/6-10/31 [CP]	2P: $54-$109	XP: $10	D3
7/1-9/5 [CP]	2P: $69-$79	XP: $10	D3

Location: I-87, exit 22, 0.8 mi n on SR 9N. 3136 Lake Shore Dr 12845. **Fax:** 518/668-2575. **Facility:** 20 units. 8 one-bedroom standard units. 2 two-bedroom suites ($94-$129) with kitchens. 10 cottages ($94-$129). 1-2 stories (no elevator), exterior corridors. *Bath:* combo or shower only. **Parking:** on-site. **Terms:** 10 day cancellation notice, pets ($10 fee, with prior approval). **Pool(s):** outdoor, wading. **Leisure Activities:** whirlpool, playground, horseshoes, shuffleboard, volleyball. *Fee:* game room. **Cards:** AX, DS, MC, VI.

SOME UNITS

FEE

HERITAGE OF LAKE GEORGE

Motel

Phone: 518/668-3357

6/25-9/6	1P: $90-$180	2P: $90-$180	XP: $15	F16
5/7-6/24	1P: $65-$130	2P: $65-$130	XP: $15	F16
9/7-10/17	1P: $60-$120	2P: $60-$120	XP: $15	F16

Location: I-87, exit 22, 0.3 mi s on US 9. 419 Canada St 12845. **Fax:** 518/668-9784. **Facility:** Designated smoking area. 38 units. 32 one-bedroom standard units. 6 cottages. 1-2 stories (no elevator), exterior corridors. *Bath:* combo or shower only. **Parking:** on-site. **Terms:** open 5/7-10/17, 2-3 night minimum stay - weekends 7/1-8/31, 14 day cancellation notice-fee imposed, weekly rates available. **Pool(s):** heated outdoor. **Leisure Activities:** shuffleboard. **Cards:** AX, DC, MC, VI.

SOME UNITS

HOLIDAY INN LAKE GEORGE-TURF

Book at aaa.com

Phone: (518)668-5781

5/27-10/15	1P: $129-$289	2P: $129-$289	XP: $10	F21
10/16-4/30	1P: $129-$159	2P: $129-$159	XP: $10	F21
5/1-5/26	1P: $129-$139	2P: $129-$139	XP: $10	F21

AAA **SAVE** ◆◆◆

Small-scale Hotel

Location: I-87, exit 21, 0.8 mi n. 2223 Rt 9 (Canada St) 12845 (Rt 9, Box 231). Fax: 518/668-9213. **Facility:** 105 units. 104 one-bedroom standard units. 1 one-bedroom suite ($179-$329). 2 stories, interior corridors. *Bath:* combo or shower only. **Parking:** on-site, winter plug-ins. **Terms:** 3 day cancellation notice. **Amenities:** video games (fee), high-speed Internet, dual phone lines, voice mail, safes, irons, hair dryers. **Dining:** 6:30 am-2 & 5-10 pm, Sun 4 pm-9 pm, cocktails. **Pool(s):** heated outdoor, heated indoor, wading. **Leisure Activities:** sauna, whirlpool, miniature golf, pool table, playground, exercise room, shuffleboard. **Guest Services:** sundries, valet and coin laundry. **Business Services:** meeting rooms. **Cards:** AX, DC, DS, MC, VI. **Special Amenities:** free newspaper.

SOME UNITS

HOWARD JOHNSON TIKI RESORT INN

Book at aaa.com

Phone: (518)668-5744

6/28-9/6	1P: $99-$259	2P: $99-$259	XP: $10	F18
5/1-6/27 & 9/7-10/31	1P: $75-$199	2P: $75-$199	XP: $10	F18

AAA **SAVE** ◆◆◆

Small-scale Hotel

Location: I-87, exit 21, 0.7 mi n on US 9. 2 Canada St 12845. Fax: 518/668-3544. **Facility:** 110 one-bedroom standard units, some with efficiencies (no utensils) and/or whirlpools. 2 stories (no elevator), interior/exterior corridors. **Parking:** on-site. **Terms:** open 5/1-10/31, 7 day cancellation notice-fee imposed. **Amenities:** voice mail, irons, hair dryers. **Dining:** 7 am-noon; dinner theater 7/1-8/31, cocktails. **Pool(s):** outdoor, small heated indoor, wading. **Leisure Activities:** exercise room. **Guest Services:** valet laundry. **Business Services:** meeting rooms. **Cards:** AX, DS, MC, VI. **Special Amenities:** free local telephone calls and free newspaper.

SOME UNITS

INN ON THE HILL

Phone: (518)668-2572

7/1-9/5	1P: $85-$110	2P: $85-$110	XP: $15	F16
5/21-6/30 & 9/6-10/31	1P: $55-$65	2P: $55-$65	XP: $15	F16

◆◆◆

Motel

Location: I-87, exit 22, 1 mi n on SR 9N. 3007 Lake Shore Dr 12845. Fax: 518/668-3728. **Facility:** Smoke free premises. 22 units. 20 one- and 2 two-bedroom standard units. 2 stories (no elevator), exterior corridors. **Parking:** on-site. **Terms:** open 5/21-10/31, office hours 8 am-10 pm, 7 day cancellation notice. **Pool(s):** heated outdoor. **Leisure Activities:** horseshoes, volleyball. **Cards:** MC, VI.

LAKE HAVEN MOTEL

Phone: 518/668-2260

7/19-9/6	1P: $89-$109	2P: $89-$139	XP: $10	F18
7/1-7/18	1P: $84-$99	2P: $84-$129	XP: $10	F18
5/1-6/30 & 9/7-10/20	1P: $49-$89	2P: $49-$99	XP: $5	F18

◆◆◆

Motel

Location: I-87, exit 22, 0.4 mi s on SR 9. 442 Canada St 12845 (PO Box 581). **Facility:** 31 one-bedroom standard units. 2 stories, exterior corridors. *Bath:* combo or shower only. **Parking:** on-site. **Terms:** open 5/1-10/20, 10 day cancellation notice-fee imposed, pets (with prior approval). **Amenities:** *Some:* DVD players, irons, hair dryers. **Pool(s):** heated outdoor. **Guest Services:** area transportation. **Cards:** AX, DS, MC, VI. *(See color ad below)*

SOME UNITS

LYN AIRE MOTEL

Phone: (518)668-4612

6/19-9/7	1P: $99-$159	2P: $119-$189	XP: $10	F12
5/27-6/18	1P: $69-$119	2P: $69-$129	XP: $10	F12

AAA **SAVE** ◆◆◆

Motel

Location: I-87, exit 21, 1 mi s. 1872 US 9 12845. Fax: 518/668-5804. **Facility:** 28 units. 27 one- and 1 two-bedroom standard units. 1 story, exterior corridors. *Bath:* combo or shower only. **Parking:** on-site. **Terms:** open 5/27-9/7, 3 night minimum stay - weekends, 14 day cancellation notice-fee imposed. **Amenities:** voice mail. **Pool(s):** heated outdoor. **Leisure Activities:** whirlpool, game pavilion, barbecue grills, playground, basketball, shuffleboard, volleyball. **Cards:** DS, MC, VI. **Special Amenities:** free local telephone calls and early check-in/late check-out.

SOME UNITS

MARINE VILLAGE RESORT

Phone: (518)668-5478

AAA [SAVE]
◇◇◇◇ ◇◇
Motel

	1P: $125-$209	2P: $125-$209	XP: $10
7/8-9/5	1P: $125-$209	2P: $125-$209	XP: $10
6/18-7/7	1P: $89-$179	2P: $89-$179	XP: $10
5/1-6/17	1P: $69-$130	2P: $69-$130	XP: $10
9/6-10/31	1P: $59-$95	2P: $59-$95	XP: $10

Location: I-87, exit 22, 0.5 mi s; center of village on Lake George. 370 Canada St 12845. Fax: 518/668-5546. **Facility:** 100 units. 95 one-bedroom standard units. 5 one-bedroom suites ($260-$280), some with kitchens. 1-2 stories (no elevator), exterior corridors. **Parking:** on-site. **Terms:** open 5/1-10/31, 3 night minimum stay - weekends, 7 day cancellation notice-fee imposed. **Amenities:** voice mail, safes. **Dining:** 7-11 am. **Pool(s):** heated outdoor. **Leisure Activities:** rental paddleboats, fishing, rowboats, barbecue grills, picnic tables, shuffleboard. *Fee:* boat dock, game room. **Cards:** AX, CB, DC, DS, MC, VI. *(See color ad p 323)*

SOME UNITS

⊞ ➰ ⊠ ⊠ ☀ DATA PORT ⊟ ⊡ / VCR ⊡ /

MOHAWK MOTEL & COTTAGES

Phone: 518/668-2143

◇◇◇◇ ◇◇
Motel

	1P: $89-$149	2P: $119-$179	XP: $10	F18
6/25-9/6	1P: $89-$149	2P: $119-$179	XP: $10	F18
5/1-6/24	1P: $59-$89	2P: $69-$129	XP: $10	F18
9/7-10/11	1P: $59-$89	2P: $69-$119	XP: $10	F18
10/12-4/30	1P: $45-$89	2P: $49-$119	XP: $10	F18

Location: I-87, exit 22, 0.3 mi s on US 9. 435 Canada St 12845. Fax: 518/668-3025. **Facility:** 23 units. 17 one-bedroom standard units, some with efficiencies and/or whirlpools. 6 cottages ($159-$425). 2 stories, exterior corridors. **Parking:** on-site, winter plug-ins. **Terms:** 3 night minimum stay - efficiencies, 7 night cottages, 14 day cancellation notice-fee imposed, weekly rates available. **Amenities:** voice mail. **Pool(s):** heated indoor. **Leisure Activities:** whirlpool, playground, basketball, volleyball. **Cards:** DS, MC, VI. *(See color ad below)*

SOME UNITS

⊞ ➰ ⊠ ☀ DATA PORT / ⊠ ⊟ ⊡ /

MOTEL MONTREAL

Phone: (518)668-5439

AAA [SAVE]
◇◇◇◇ ◇◇
Motel

	1P: $85-$125	2P: $85-$125	XP: $10	F16
7/1-9/6	1P: $85-$125	2P: $85-$125	XP: $10	F16
5/1-6/30	1P: $45-$85	2P: $49-$95	XP: $10	F16
9/7-10/12	1P: $49-$85	2P: $49-$95	XP: $10	F16

Location: I-87, exit 22, 0.3 mi s on SR 9, then just e. 3 Lake Ave 12845. Fax: 518/668-5439. **Facility:** 40 units. 39 one-bedroom standard units. 1 two-bedroom suite ($1150-$1350) with kitchen. 1-2 stories, exterior corridors. *Bath:* combo or shower only. **Parking:** on-site. **Terms:** open 5/1-10/12, 7 day cancellation notice-fee imposed. **Amenities:** voice mail. **Pool(s):** heated outdoor. **Leisure Activities:** grills, picnic tables. **Cards:** DC, DS, MC, VI. **Special Amenities:** early check-in/late check-out and free room upgrade (subject to availability with advanced reservations). *(See color ad below)*

SOME UNITS

S/D ⊞ ➰ DATA PORT / ⊠ ⊟ /
FEE

NASSAU MOTEL

Motel

Phone: 518/668-5356

5/1-10/31	2P: $75-$175	XP: $10	F11
11/1-4/30	2P: $60-$160	XP: $10	F11

Location: I-87, exit 21, 0.8 mi s. 1881 Rt 9 12845. Fax: 518/668-3671. **Facility:** 21 units. 10 one-bedroom standard units, some with efficiencies. 5 one-bedroom suites with efficiencies. 1 vacation home and 5 cabins. 1-2 stories (no elevator), exterior corridors. *Bath:* combo or shower only. **Parking:** on-site. **Terms:** 2 night minimum stay - in summer, 14 day cancellation notice-fee imposed. **Pool(s):** heated outdoor. **Leisure Activities:** playground, basketball, volleyball. *Fee:* game room. **Cards:** MC, VI.

SOME UNITS

🔄 ⊠ ⊠ 📶 📺 / 📟 /

QUALITY INN

Motel

Book at aaa.com

Phone: (518)668-3525

5/21-9/5 [ECP]	1P: $79-$199	2P: $79-$199	XP: $10	F18
9/6-11/21 [ECP]	1P: $59-$159	2P: $59-$159	XP: $10	F18
5/1-5/20 & 4/1-4/30 [ECP]	1P: $59-$139	2P: $59-$139	XP: $10	F18

Location: I-87, exit 21, 1 mi n on US 9. 57 Canada St 12845. Fax: 518/668-3598. **Facility:** 54 one-bedroom standard units. 2 stories (no elevator), exterior corridors. **Parking:** on-site. **Terms:** open 5/1-11/21 & 4/1-4/30, check-in 4 pm, 1-3 night minimum stay - seasonal weekends, 5 day cancellation notice-fee imposed, package plans. **Amenities:** voice mail, irons, hair dryers. **Pool(s):** heated outdoor. **Guest Services:** valet laundry. **Cards:** AX, CB, DC, DS, JC, MC, VI. **Special Amenities:** free expanded continental breakfast and free newspaper.
(See color ad below)

SOME UNITS

🅂/🄳 🔄 📹 📶 🖥 📺 / ⊠ /

ROARING BROOK RANCH & TENNIS RESORT

Resort
Small-scale Hotel

Phone: (518)668-5767

6/25-9/7 [MAP]	2P: $196-$246	XP: $55	D7
5/28-6/24 [MAP]	2P: $170-$220	XP: $55	D7
9/8-10/11 [MAP]	2P: $170-$210	XP: $55	D7

Location: I-87, exit 21, 1 mi s. Rt 9N South 12845 (Lake George 3). Fax: 518/668-4019. **Facility:** This family-oriented resort, a sprawling complex on spacious grounds, is in a mountain setting away from the hubbub of the village. 135 units. 118 one-bedroom standard units. 17 one-bedroom suites. 1-2 stories (no elevator), interior/exterior corridors. **Parking:** on-site. **Terms:** open 5/28-10/11, 2 night minimum stay, 10 day cancellation notice, weekly rates available. **Dining:** 8 am-4 pm, cocktails, entertainment. **Pool(s):** 2 outdoor, heated indoor. **Leisure Activities:** saunas, 5 tennis courts (2 lighted), tennis clinic, pool tables, children's counselor 7/1-8/31, archery, hiking trails, horseback riding, playground, exercise room, basketball, shuffleboard, volleyball. *Fee:* riding instruction, massage, horseshoes, game room. **Guest Services:** gift shop, coin laundry, area transportation-Lake George Bus Station. **Business Services:** conference facilities. **Cards:** AX, MC, VI. *(See color ad p 326)*

SOME UNITS

🍴 🍸 📶 🔄 ⊠ / ⊠ VCR 📶 /
FEE FEE

STILL BAY RESORT

Phone: 518/668-2584

6/25-9/5	2P: $130-$170	XP: $20
5/28-6/24	2P: $85-$120	XP: $10
9/6-10/11	2P: $85-$110	XP: $10

Motel

Location: I-87, exit 22, 3 mi n on SR 9N. Located on the lake. Lake Shore Dr 12845 (PO Box 333, DIAMOND POINT, 12824). Fax: 518/668-3880. **Facility:** 24 units. 19 one- and 3 two-bedroom standard units, some with efficiencies. 1 two-bedroom suite with kitchen. 1 cottage ($1350-$1450). 2 stories (no elevator), exterior corridors. *Bath:* combo or shower only. **Parking:** on-site. **Terms:** open 5/28-10/11, office hours 9 am-9 pm, 10 day cancellation notice, [ECP] meal plan available. **Leisure Activities:** paddleboats, boat dock, fishing, lawn games, grills, picnic tables. **Cards:** MC, VI. **Special Amenities:** free local telephone calls.

SOME UNITS

⊠ ⊠ ☎ 🛇 / 🍴 ⌷ /

Roaring Brook
Ranch & Tennis Resort

Lake George 3, N.Y. 12845 (518) 668-5767
www.roaringbrookranch.com

• Three Pools • One Indoor • Sauna Baths
• 5 Tennis Courts • Horseback Riding
• Dinner And Breakfast Included
• Excellent Food • Choice Of Menu

Reservations: (800) 882-7665

SUPER 8 LAKE GEORGE DOWNTOWN

Book at aaa.com

Phone: 518/668-2470

▼▼▼ ◆◆
Motel

	6/25-9/13	1P: $99-$249	2P: $99-$249	XP: $5	F17
	5/1-6/24	1P: $69-$249	2P: $69-$249	XP: $5	F17
	9/14-4/30	1P: $69-$119	2P: $69-$119	XP: $5	F17

Location: I-87, exit 21, 0.4 mi n. 2159 US 9 (Canada St) 12845 (PO Box 448). Fax: 518/668-5355. **Facility:** 54 one-bedroom standard units, some with efficiencies. 1-2 stories (no elevator), exterior corridors. **Parking:** on-site, winter plug-ins. **Terms:** 1-3 night minimum stay - weekends 7/1-8/31, 3 day cancellation notice-fee imposed. **Amenities:** voice mail. *Some:* hair dryers. **Pool(s):** heated outdoor. **Cards:** AX, DC, MC, VI.

SOME UNITS

(⎘ ⊞) 🛏 🎿 🖥 🖨 / ⊠ 🖨 🖵 /

SURFSIDE ON THE LAKE

Phone: 518/668-2442

◇◇◇ (SAVE)
▼▼▼ ◆◆
Small-scale Hotel

	7/9-9/5	1P: $85-$230	2P: $85-$230	XP: $10	F12
	6/18-7/8	1P: $65-$185	2P: $65-$185	XP: $10	F12
	5/1-6/17 & 9/6-11/1	1P: $45-$155	2P: $45-$155	XP: $10	F12

Location: I-87, exit 22, 0.3 mi s on US 9. Located on the lake. 400 Canada St 12845. Fax: 518/668-3202. **Facility:** 144 units. 117 one-bedroom standard units, some with efficiencies. 11 one-bedroom suites ($90-$235) with efficiencies. 16 cabins. 1-2 stories, interior/exterior corridors. *Bath:* combo or shower only. **Parking:** on-site. **Terms:** open 5/1-11/1, 2-3 night minimum stay - weekends, 10 day cancellation notice-fee imposed, package plans. **Dining:** 7:30-11 am 6/1-9/1, hours vary on weekends. **Pool(s):** heated outdoor. **Leisure Activities:** barbecue grills, playground. **Business Services:** meeting rooms. **Cards:** AX, CB, DC, DS, MC, VI. *(See color ad below)*

SOME UNITS

(⎘) 🛏 🖥 / ⊠ [DATA PORT] 🖨 🖵 /

TALL PINES MOTEL

Phone: 518/668-5122

◇◇◇ (SAVE)
▼▼▼ ◆◆
Motel

	7/23-9/5	1P: $95-$120	2P: $105-$125	XP: $10	F
	6/18-7/22	1P: $85-$105	2P: $95-$110	XP: $10	F
	5/1-6/17 & 9/6-10/11	1P: $50-$75	2P: $55-$85	XP: $10	F

Location: I-87, exit 20, 1.5 mi n; exit 21, 2 mi s. 1747 US 9 12845. Fax: 518/668-5128. **Facility:** 26 one-bedroom standard units. 1-2 stories, exterior corridors. **Parking:** on-site. **Terms:** open 5/1-10/11, office hours 7:30 am-10 pm, 7 day cancellation notice-fee imposed, no pets allowed (owner's pet on premises). **Pool(s):** heated outdoor, wading. **Leisure Activities:** sauna, whirlpools, picnic tables, barbecue grills, playground, basketball. **Cards:** AX, MC, VI. **Special Amenities:** free room upgrade **(subject to availability with advanced reservations).** *(See color ad p 323)*

SOME UNITS

[S/D] 🛏 ⊠ ⊠ 🖥 / 🖨 /

TRAVELODGE OF LAKE GEORGE

Book at aaa.com

Phone: (518)668-5421

◇◇◇ (SAVE)
▼▼▼ ◆◆
Motel

| | 5/21-10/12 | 1P: $74-$164 | 2P: $74-$164 | XP: $15 | F16 |

Location: I-87, exit 21. 2011 SR 9 12845. Fax: 518/668-2696. **Facility:** 100 units. 99 one-bedroom standard units. 1 one-bedroom suite with efficiency. 2 stories, interior/exterior corridors. *Bath:* combo or shower only. **Parking:** on-site. **Terms:** open 5/21-10/12, cancellation fee imposed, [BP] meal plan available, pets (with prior approval). **Amenities:** safes, irons, hair dryers. **Dining:** 6:30 am-11 & 6-10 pm, beer only. **Pool(s):** outdoor. **Leisure Activities:** playground. **Guest Services:** valet laundry. **Cards:** AX, CB, DC, DS, JC, MC, VI. **Special Amenities:** free local telephone calls and free newspaper.

SOME UNITS

[S/D] 🐾 ⎘ 🎿 📷 / ⊠ 🖥 🖨 🖵 /

*——— The following lodgings were either not evaluated or did not ———
meet AAA rating requirements but are listed for your information only.*

FORT WILLIAM HENRY RESORT HOTEL & CONFERENCE CENTER   Phone: (518)668-3081

	6/25-9/5	1P: $169-$229	2P: $169-$229	XP: $15	F12
	5/28-6/24 & 9/6-4/30	1P: $119-$179	2P: $119-$179	XP: $15	F12
	5/1-5/27	1P: $89-$139	2P: $89-$139	XP: $15	F12

Historic
Large-scale Hotel
Under major renovation, scheduled to be completed May 2004. **Last rated:** ▼▼ **Location:** I-87, exit 21, 1 mi n on US 9. 48 Canada St 12845. Fax: 518/668-4926. **Facility:** Overlooking Lake George. 195 units. 98 one-bedroom standard units. 97 one-bedroom suites ($159-$499), some with whirlpools. 2-5 stories, interior/exterior corridors. **Parking:** on-site. **Terms:** 3 day cancellation notice, pets ($15 extra charge, in designated units). **Amenities:** high-speed Internet, voice mail, irons, hair dryers. *Fee:* video games, safes. *Some:* dual phone lines. **Dining:** 4 restaurants, 6:30 am-1 am, cocktails. **Pool(s):** outdoor, heated indoor. **Leisure Activities:** sauna, whirlpool, yoga instruction, horseshoes, shuffleboard, volleyball. **Guest Services:** gift shop, valet and coin laundry. *Fee:* airport transportation-Albany Airport, area transportation. **Business Services:** conference facilities, business center. **Cards:** AX, CB, DC, DS, MC, VI. **Special Amenities:** free newspaper and free room upgrade (subject to availability with advanced reservations).

SOME UNITS

THE QUARTERS AT LAKE GEORGE   Phone: 518/668-4901

[fyi] Not evaluated. **Location:** 1 mi n on SR 9N; 0.3 mi n of I-87 Northway, exit 22. 3014 Lake Shore Dr, Rt 9 N 12845 (RD 2, Box 2367). Facilities, services, and decor characterize a mid-range property.

——— **WHERE TO DINE** ———

EAST COVE RESTAURANT   Dinner: $8-$26   Phone: 518/668-5265

American
Location: 0.8 mi e. 3873 Rt 9L 12845. **Hours:** 5 pm-10 pm, Sun from 11 am. Closed: Mon & Tues 11/1-4/30. **Reservations:** suggested. **Features:** Informal dining in a rustic log cabin, East Cove serves a great American fare. One can enjoy early bird specials such as prime rib and then top it off with a great slice of carrot cake. Casual dress; cocktails. **Parking:** on-site. **Cards:** AX, CB, DC, DS, MC, VI.

THE GEORGIAN DINING ROOM   Lunch: $6-$14   Dinner: $17-$24   Phone: 518/668-5401

American
Location: I-87, exit 22, 0.5 mi se; in The Georgian. 384 Canada St 12845. **Hours:** Open 5/19-10/21; 7:30 am-10 pm; 7:30 am-1 & 5:30-9 pm 5/19-7/1. Closed major holidays. **Reservations:** suggested, in season. **Features:** The attractive dining room, as well as the luncheon patio, overlook Lake George. In addition to tableside-carved chateaubriand and thick-cut prime rib, the restaurant serves tasty breakfast selections. Entertainers perform on summer nights. Dressy casual; cocktails. **Parking:** on-site. **Cards:** AX, DC, DS, MC, VI.

J T KELLY'S   Dinner: $10-$22   Phone: 518/668-3165

Steak & Seafood
Location: I-87, exit 21, 1 mi n; jct US 9 and SR 9N. 50 Canada St 12845. **Hours:** Open 5/15-10/15; 11:30 am-9 pm; to 10 pm 7/1-9/1. Closed: Mon, Tues & 5/15-6/22. **Reservations:** accepted. **Features:** Serving up steak and seafood, J T Kelly's is a great place to have a meal. Families enjoy this local spot because it is only minutes from downtown Lake George where shopping and fun can be had. Casual dress; cocktails. **Parking:** on-site. **Cards:** AX, CB, DC, DS, MC, VI.

MARIO'S RESTAURANT   Dinner: $9-$22   Phone: 518/668-2665

Italian
Location: I-87, exit 22, 0.3 mi s, then 0.3 mi n on US 9 and SR 9N. 429 Canada St 12845. **Hours:** Open 5/1-11/1 & 12/16-4/30; 3:30 pm-11 pm; 8 am-noon 7/1-8/31; also 4:30 pm-close, Sun 3 pm-close 12/15-4/30. Closed: Tues & Wed 12/15-4/30. **Reservations:** suggested. **Features:** A favorite local restaurant that's been family-operated since 1954, Mario's serves a variety of dishes including steak, chicken and seafood. Hearty portions of pasta, veal and chops can also be found on the menu. Casual dress; cocktails. **Parking:** on-site. **Cards:** AX, CB, DC, MC, VI.

SHORELINE RESTAURANT   Lunch: $8-$11   Dinner: $14-$20   Phone: 518/668-2875

American
Location: On lake at foot of Kurosaka Lane; center. 4 Kurosaka Ln 12845. **Hours:** Open 5/1-10/31 & 4/1-4/30; 11 am-10 pm, Fri & Sat-11 pm, Sun 10 am-9 pm; hours may vary off season. **Reservations:** suggested, evenings. **Features:** Overlooking the lake, the contemporary dining room is handsome and casual, while the seasonal terrace is warm and breezy. Among oven-cooked and grilled entrees are inventive chicken selections. The Sunday breakfast buffet is particularly popular. Casual dress; cocktails. **Parking:** on-site. **Cards:** AX, DC, DS, MC, VI.

SOPRANOS   Lunch: $6-$18   Dinner: $6-$18   Phone: 518/668-4379

Italian
Location: On US 9; center. 157 Canada St 12845. **Hours:** 11:30 am-11 pm. Closed: 1/1, 11/25, 12/24-12/26. **Features:** There's a "pasta fa u" on the menu at the casual eatery. For those in the mood for something else, the joint also prepares "fuhgeddaboutit" heroes and New York-style pizza, including the "stuffed trunk," "godfather" and "empty suit." Everyone here is treated like a "goomba.". Casual dress. **Parking:** street. **Cards:** MC, VI.

TASTE OF POLAND   Lunch: $8-$19   Dinner: $8-$19   Phone: 518/668-4386

Polish
Location: I-87, exit 22, 0.4 mi s on US 9. 375 Canada St 12845. **Hours:** 8 am-10 pm; from 5 pm 11/1-4/30. **Features:** With the feel of a cozy cottage, the restaurant presents a large menu of Bavarian-influenced Polish food. Among choices are pierogies, potato pancakes, kielbasa and a variety of soups and salads. A favorite is the "taste of Poland," a sampler of menu selections. Authenticity is seen even in the beverage selections, which include traditional Polish juices. Casual dress; beer & wine only. **Parking:** on-site. **Cards:** AX, DS, MC, VI.

──────── *The following restaurant has not been evaluated by AAA* ────────
but is listed for your information only.

ADIRONDACK PUB & BREWERY   Phone: 518/668-0002
[fyi]   Not evaluated. **Location:** 33 Canada St 12845. **Features:** Renovated building made to look like an
Adirondack lodge. Pub fare and craft-brewed ales on premises.

LAKE LUZERNE pop. 2,240—*See also ADIRONDACK MOUNTAINS.*

──────── **WHERE TO STAY** ────────

LAMPLIGHT INN BED & BREAKFAST   Phone: (518)696-5294
▼▼▼▼   7/22-9/6 [BP]   2P: $139-$249   XP: $35
5/1-7/21 & 9/7-11/1 [BP]   2P: $119-$239   XP: $35
Historic Bed   11/2-4/30 [BP]   2P: $95-$199   XP: $35
& Breakfast   **Location:** I-87, exit 21, 10.2 mi s on SR 9N. 231 Lake Ave 12846 (PO Box 130, 12846-0130). **Facility:** Themed rooms
are featured at this 1890 hilltop home; furnished with antiques, it offers a sunny breakfast room and spacious
traditional parlor area. Smoke free premises. 13 units. 6 one-bedroom standard units. 7 one-bedroom suites, some with whirlpools. 1-2 stories (no elevator), interior corridors. **Bath:** combo or shower only. **Parking:** on-site. **Terms:** age restrictions may
apply, 21 day cancellation notice. **Amenities:** voice mail. *Some:* hair dryers. **Leisure Activities:** cross country skiing, hiking trails.
Guest Services: gift shop. **Cards:** AX, MC, VI.

SOME UNITS

[⊞] [⛧] [✕] [DATA PORT] / [W] /

LUZERNE COURT   Phone: 518/696-2734
[AAA] [SAVE]   5/14-10/4   2P: $66-$195   XP: $15   F10
▼   **Location:** I-87, exit 21, 8.7 mi s on SR 9N. 508 Lake Ave 12846. Fax: 518/696-3204. **Facility:** 10 one-bedroom
Motel   standard units, some with efficiencies. 1 story, exterior corridors. *Bath:* combo or shower only. **Parking:** on-
site. **Terms:** open 5/14-10/4, 2-3 night minimum stay - weekends, 14 day cancellation notice, [BP] meal plan
available. **Dining:** 7:30-11 am 7/1-9/6. **Pool(s):** outdoor. **Cards:** AX, DS, MC, VI.

SOME UNITS

[🛏] [⊞] [🐾] [✕] [Ⓩ] [▤] / [VCR] [🖥] /

PINE POINT COTTAGES & MOTEL   Phone: (518)696-3015
▼▼ ▼▼   6/21-9/3   1P: $65-$72   2P: $65-$72   XP: $5
5/15-6/20 & 9/4-10/15   1P: $59-$65   2P: $59-$65   XP: $5
Cottage   **Location:** I-87, exit 21, 4.9 mi s on SR 9N. Located in a quiet area. 1369 Lake Ave 12846. Fax: 518/696-3015.
Facility: 18 units. 10 one-bedroom standard units. 8 cottages ($72-$102). 1 story, exterior corridors. *Bath:*
shower only. **Parking:** on-site. **Terms:** open 5/15-10/15, 14 day cancellation notice. **Leisure Activities:** paddleboats, boat dock,
fishing, shuffleboard, volleyball. **Cards:** MC, VI.

SOME UNITS

[⊞+] [✕] [Ⓩ] [▤] / [✗] /

──────── **WHERE TO DINE** ────────

PAPA'S ICE CREAM PARLOR RESTAURANT   **Lunch:** $3-$11   **Dinner:** $3-$11   Phone: 518/696-3667
▼▼   **Location:** Center. 29 Main St 12846. **Hours:** Open 5/24-9/1; 8 am-9 pm. **Features:** The classic, old-fashioned
ice cream parlor sits on the banks of the Hudson River and offers outdoor seating on the deck. On the
American   menu is mostly simple fare, such as sandwiches and salads, as well as a few dinner platters. Don't leave
without trying the scrumptious ice cream desserts. Breakfast is served all day, and a barbershop quartet
entertains guests on Thursdays. Casual dress. **Parking:** on-site. **Cards:** MC, VI.   [✕]

THE WATERHOUSE   **Dinner:** $13-$20   Phone: 518/696-3115
▼▼ ▼▼   **Location:** On SR 9N; center. 85 Lake Ave 12846. **Hours:** 4 pm-10 pm, Sun from noon. **Closed:** 11/25, 12/25.
Reservations: accepted. **Features:** Beyond the characterless walls of the exterior, with its neon Michelob
American   sign, hides a magical little room aglow with the sparkle of lights and the charm of walls filled with antique
knick-knacks and pictures. The cozy place prepares good food ranging from the simple to the creative.
Casual dress; cocktails. **Parking:** on-site. **Cards:** MC, VI.   [🍸] [✕]

LAKE PLACID pop. 2,638—See also ADIRONDACK MOUNTAINS.

——— WHERE TO STAY ———

ALPINE AIR MOTEL   Phone: 518/523-9261

AAA SAVE   All Year   1P: $50-$110   2P: $50-$110   XP: $10   F12

Motel   **Location:** 0.5 mi w on SR 86. 99 Saranac Ave 12946. Fax: 518/523-9273. **Facility:** 24 units. 21 one- and 3 two-bedroom standard units. 1-2 stories, exterior corridors. *Bath:* combo or shower only. **Parking:** on-site, winter plug-ins. **Terms:** 14 day cancellation notice-fee imposed. **Pool(s):** heated outdoor. **Leisure Activities:** picnic tables, basketball. **Cards:** MC, VI. **Special Amenities:** free local telephone calls.

SOME UNITS
  /
FEE

ART DEVLIN'S OLYMPIC MOTOR INN, INC   Phone: 518/523-3700

AAA SAVE   6/17-9/13   1P: $68-$148   2P: $68-$148   XP: $8
            5/1-6/16 & 9/14-4/30 1P: $58-$148   2P: $58-$148   XP: $8

Motel   **Location:** 0.5 mi e on SR 86. 350 Main St 12946. Fax: 518/523-3893. **Facility:** 41 one-bedroom standard units. 1-2 stories (no elevator), exterior corridors. **Parking:** on-site. **Terms:** 1-3 night minimum stay - some weekends, 10 day cancellation notice. **Pool(s):** heated outdoor, wading. **Business Services:** meeting rooms. **Cards:** AX, DC, DS, MC, VI. **Special Amenities:** free local telephone calls and early check-in/late check-out. *(See color ad below)*

SOME UNITS
    / /

BEST WESTERN GOLDEN ARROW HOTEL   *Book at aaa.com*   Phone: (518)523-3353

AAA SAVE   6/17-10/19   1P: $129-$189   2P: $139-$199   XP: $10   F12
            12/26-4/30   1P: $89-$199   2P: $99-$199   XP: $10   F12
            10/20-12/25   1P: $89-$199   2P: $99-$199   XP: $10   F12
            5/1-6/16   1P: $89-$149   2P: $99-$159   XP: $10   F12

Small-scale Hotel **Location:** On SR 86; center. 150 Main St 12946. Fax: 518/523-8063. **Facility:** 141 units. 133 one-bedroom standard units, some with efficiencies and/or whirlpools. 8 one-bedroom suites ($139-$399), some with efficiencies, kitchens and/or whirlpools. 2-5 stories, interior corridors. **Parking:** on-site, winter plug-ins. **Terms:** 2 night minimum stay - seasonal weekends, 30 day cancellation notice, [AP], [BP] & [MAP] meal plans available, pets ($50 fee, in designated units). **Amenities:** video games, high-speed Internet, voice mail, irons, hair dryers. *Some:* safes. **Dining:** 7 am-9:30 pm, cocktails, nightclub. **Pool(s):** heated indoor, wading. **Leisure Activities:** saunas, whirlpool, steamroom, canoeing, paddleboats, boat dock, fishing, putting green, downhill & cross country skiing, snowmobiling, ice skating, rowboats. *Fee:* racquetball court, massage, game room. **Guest Services:** gift shop, valet and coin laundry, airport transportation-Saranac Lake Airport, tanning facility. **Business Services:** conference facilities. **Cards:** AX, CB, DC, DS, MC, VI. *(See color ad below)*

SOME UNITS
FEE   FEE   / VCR /

CARRIAGE HOUSE MOTOR INN

▼▼▼ ▼▼▼
Motel

Phone: (518)523-2260

5/28-10/23 & 12/24-4/30	1P: $65-$150	2P: $70-$150	XP: $10	F18
5/1-5/27 & 10/24-12/23	1P: $55-$125	2P: $60-$125	XP: $10	F18

Location: Cascade Rd 12946 (PO Box 527). Fax: 518/523-2817. **Facility:** 17 one-bedroom standard units. 1-2 stories (no elevator), interior/exterior corridors. **Parking:** on-site, winter plug-ins. **Terms:** cancellation fee imposed. **Pool(s):** outdoor. **Cards:** AX, MC, VI.

SOME UNITS
(ASK) (SD) (Tl+) (🏊) (💻) / (✕) (DATA PORT) (🛏) /
FEE

ECONO LODGE

(AAA) (SAVE)
▼▼ ▼▼
Small-scale Hotel

Book at aaa.com

Phone: (518)523-2817

5/28-10/23 & 12/24-4/30	1P: $65-$150	2P: $70-$150	XP: $10	F18
5/1-5/27 & 10/24-12/23	1P: $55-$125	2P: $60-$125	XP: $10	F18

Location: 3 mi s on SR 73 from jct SR 86. Cascade Rd 12946 (PO Box 527). Fax: 518/523-2817. **Facility:** 61 one-bedroom standard units. 2 stories (no elevator), interior/exterior corridors. **Parking:** on-site. **Terms:** cancellation fee imposed. **Pool(s):** heated indoor. **Leisure Activities:** whirlpool. **Guest Services:** coin laundry. **Business Services:** meeting rooms. **Cards:** AX, DC, DS, JC, MC, VI. **Special Amenities:** free local telephone calls and free newspaper.

SOME UNITS
(SD) (🐾) (🏊) (💻) / (✕) (DATA PORT) (🛏) /
FEE

EDGE OF THE LAKE MOTEL

(AAA) (SAVE)
▼▼ ▼▼
Motel

Phone: 518/523-9430

5/1-9/1	1P: $74-$124	2P: $79-$129	XP: $10	F12
12/22-4/1	1P: $64-$124	2P: $69-$129	XP: $10	F12
9/2-12/21	1P: $54-$124	2P: $59-$129	XP: $10	F12
4/2-4/30	1P: $44-$94	2P: $49-$99	XP: $10	F12

Location: 0.5 mi w on SR 86. 56 Saranac Ave 12946. Fax: 518/523-7886. **Facility:** 25 one-bedroom standard units, some with efficiencies. 2-3 stories (no elevator), interior/exterior corridors. **Bath:** combo or shower only. **Parking:** on-site, winter plug-ins. **Terms:** weekly rates available, package plans, pets ($10 extra charge). **Pool(s):** heated outdoor. **Leisure Activities:** canoeing, paddleboats, rowboat, picnic table. **Fee:** boat dock. **Cards:** AX, DS, MC, VI.

SOME UNITS
(🛏) (Tl+) (🏊) (✕) (🐾) (🛏) (💻) / (🖥) /
FEE

HILTON LAKE PLACID RESORT

▼▼▼ ▼▼▼
Small-scale Hotel

Book at aaa.com

Phone: (518)523-4411

7/1-10/10	1P: $159-$289	2P: $159-$289	XP: $15	F18
10/11-4/30	1P: $79-$289	2P: $79-$289	XP: $15	F18
5/1-6/30	1P: $79-$269	2P: $79-$269	XP: $15	F18

Location: 0.3 mi w on SR 86. 1 Mirror Lake Dr 12946. Fax: 518/523-1120. **Facility:** 179 one-bedroom standard units. 2-5 stories, interior corridors. **Bath:** combo or shower only. **Parking:** on-site, winter plug-ins. **Terms:** check-in 4 pm, 2 night minimum stay - weekends, 7 day cancellation notice-fee imposed, [BP] & [MAP] meal plans available, package plans, pets ($25 deposit). **Amenities:** video games (fee), voice mail, irons, hair dryers. **Pool(s):** 2 heated outdoor, 2 heated indoor. **Leisure Activities:** whirlpools, paddleboats, fishing, exercise room. **Fee:** game room. **Guest Services:** valet laundry. **Business Services:** conference facilities. **Cards:** AX, CB, DC, DS, MC, VI.

SOME UNITS
(ASK) (SD) (🐾) (Tl+) (Y) (🔔M) (🖼) (🐾) (🏊) (✕) (🔔) (DATA PORT) (💻) / (✕) (🛏) (🖥) /
FEE   FEE

HOWARD JOHNSON RESORT INN

(AAA) (SAVE)
▼▼ ▼▼
Small-scale Hotel

Book at aaa.com

Phone: (518)523-9555

All Year	1P: $75-$180	2P: $85-$190	XP: $10	F18

Location: 0.5 mi w on SR 86. 90 Saranac Ave 12946. Fax: 518/523-4765. **Facility:** 92 units. 88 one- and 1 two-bedroom standard units. 3 one-bedroom suites ($120-$250), some with kitchens. 1-2 stories (no elevator), interior/exterior corridors. **Parking:** on-site, winter plug-ins. **Terms:** 2-3 night minimum stay - seasonal, [MAP] meal plan available, package plans. **Amenities:** voice mail, irons, hair dryers. **Dining:** 6:15 am-10 pm, Fri & Sat-11 pm, cocktails. **Pool(s):** heated indoor. **Leisure Activities:** whirlpool, canoeing, paddleboats, boat dock, fishing, rowboats, 2 tennis courts, cross country skiing, picnic areas with charcoal grills, hiking trails. **Guest Services:** valet and coin laundry. **Business Services:** conference facilities. **Cards:** AX, CB, DC, DS, MC, VI. **Special Amenities:** free newspaper. *(See color ad p 218)*

SOME UNITS
(SD) (🐾) (Tl+) (🏊) (🐾) (✕) (🔔) (DATA PORT) (💻) / (✕) (VCR) (🛏) (🖥) /

LAKE PLACID RAMADA INN *Book at aaa.com* Phone: (518)523-2587

(AAA) [SAVE]

1/1-4/30 [CP]	1P: $89-$159	2P: $99-$169	XP: $10	F17
10/25-12/31 [CP]	1P: $69-$159	2P: $79-$169	XP: $10	F17
6/19-10/24 [CP]	1P: $129-$149	2P: $139-$159	XP: $10	F17
5/1-6/18 [CP]	1P: $69-$79	2P: $79-$89	XP: $10	F17

Small-scale Hotel **Location:** 0.3 mi w on SR 86. 8-12 Saranac Ave 12946. Fax: 518/523-2328. **Facility:** 54 one-bedroom standard units. 2-3 stories, interior corridors. **Parking:** on-site, winter plug-ins. **Terms:** 2 night minimum stay - weekends in season, 3 day cancellation notice-fee imposed, package plans - seasonal. **Amenities:** voice mail, irons, hair dryers. **Dining:** 7 am-10 & 5-9 pm, Fri & Sat-10 pm, cocktails. **Pool(s):** heated indoor. **Leisure Activities:** whirlpool, exercise room. **Guest Services:** valet and coin laundry. **Business Services:** meeting rooms. **Cards:** AX, CB, DC, DS, MC, VI. **Special Amenities:** free continental breakfast and free room upgrade (subject to availability with advanced reservations).** (See color ad'p 8)

SOME UNITS
FEE   FEE

LAKE PLACID RESORT HOTEL & GOLF CLUB/HOLIDAY INN *Book at aaa.com* Phone: (518)523-2556

All Year	1P: $69-$249	2P: $69-$249	XP: $10	F19

Small-scale Hotel **Location:** Downtown. 1 Olympic Dr 12946. Fax: 518/523-9410. **Facility:** 208 units. 194 one-bedroom standard units. 12 one-bedroom suites with whirlpools. 2 cottages with whirlpools. 2-4 stories, interior/exterior corridors. **Parking:** on-site, winter plug-ins. **Terms:** check-in 4 pm, 30 day cancellation notice-fee imposed, [BP] meal plan available, package plans, pets ($100 deposit). **Amenities:** video games, voice mail, irons, hair dryers. **Dining:** Veranda Restaurant, see separate listing. **Pool(s):** heated indoor. **Leisure Activities:** sauna, whirlpool, paddleboats, 8 tennis courts, cross country skiing, hiking trails, exercise room. **Fee:** golf-45 holes. **Guest Services:** valet and coin laundry. **Business Services:** conference facilities. **Cards:** AX, CB, DC, DS, MC. (See color ad p 332)

SOME UNITS
FEE

MAPLE LEAF INN Phone: 518/523-2471

(AAA) [SAVE]

5/1-10/31 & 12/1-4/1	1P: $75-$400	2P: $75-$400	XP: $25	F10

Motel **Location:** 0.5 mi w on SR 86. 53-55 Saranac Ave 12946. Fax: 518/523-5378. **Facility:** 18 units. 15 one- and 1 two-bedroom standard units, some with efficiencies and/or whirlpools. 2 one-bedroom suites, some with efficiencies and/or whirlpools. 1-2 stories (no elevator), interior/exterior corridors. **Parking:** on-site, winter plug-ins. **Terms:** open 5/1-10/31 & 12/1-4/1, 2-7 night minimum stay - weekends in season, 14 day cancellation notice-fee imposed, weekly rates available, package plans. **Amenities:** irons, hair dryers. **Pool(s):** heated outdoor. **Leisure Activities:** picnic & charcoal grill area. **Cards:** AX, MC, VI. **Special Amenities:** free local telephone calls and early check-in/late check-out.

SOME UNITS

MIRROR LAKE INN RESORT AND SPA *Book at aaa.com* Phone: (518)523-2544

(AAA) [SAVE]

1/3-4/30	1P: $215-$355	2P: $215-$355	XP: $40	D18
12/20-1/2	1P: $270-$350	2P: $270-$350	XP: $40	D18
5/1-10/10	1P: $260-$340	2P: $260-$340	XP: $40	D18
10/11-12/19	1P: $200-$250	2P: $200-$250	XP: $40	D18

Small-scale Hotel **Location:** Just off SR 86, 0.5 mi w. 5 Mirror Lake Dr 12946. Fax: 518/523-2871. **Facility:** Guests can enjoy views of Mirror Lake from the balconies of most guest rooms at this traditional resort. 128 units. 126 one- and 1 two-bedroom standard units, some with whirlpools. 1 two-bedroom suite ($375-$515). 2-4 stories, interior/exterior corridors. **Parking:** on-site, winter plug-ins. **Terms:** 2-4 night minimum stay - weekends, 14 day cancellation notice, [BP] & [MAP] meal plans available, $3 service charge. **Amenities:** voice mail, irons, hair dryers. *Some:* CD players. **Dining:** 2 restaurants, 7:30 am-10 & 5:30-9 pm, Sat & Sun 7:30 am-11 & 5:30-9 pm, also, Averil Conwell Dining Room, see separate listing. **Pool(s):** heated outdoor, heated indoor. **Leisure Activities:** sauna, whirlpool, canoeing, paddleboats, boat dock, fishing, rowboats, tennis court, cross country skiing, ice skating, guided snowshoe hikes, hiking trails, spa. **Guest Services:** gift shop, valet laundry. **Business Services:** conference facilities. **Cards:** AX, DC, DS, MC, VI.

SOME UNITS

MOUNTAIN VIEW INN Phone: (518)523-2439

(AAA) [SAVE]

6/23-10/31 & 12/27-3/31	1P: $105-$160	2P: $105-$160	XP: $10	F12
5/15-6/22 & 11/1-12/26	1P: $75-$105	2P: $75-$105	XP: $10	F12

Motel **Location:** On SR 86; center. 140 Main St 12946. Fax: 518/523-8974. **Facility:** 18 one-bedroom standard units. 2-3 stories (no elevator), interior/exterior corridors. **Parking:** on-site. **Terms:** open 5/15-3/31, 2 night minimum stay - weekends, 30 day cancellation notice, package plans. **Amenities:** hair dryers. **Leisure Activities:** use of Lake Placid Club beach. **Cards:** AX, CB, DC, DS, MC, VI. **Special Amenities:** free local telephone calls and preferred room (subject to availability with advanced reservations).

SOME UNITS

THE NORTHWAY MOTEL

Phone: 518/523-3500

12/16-4/30	1P: $90-$125	2P: $90-$125	XP: $8	F16
6/16-10/23	1P: $75-$125	2P: $75-$125	XP: $8	F16
5/1-6/15 & 10/24-12/15	1P: $55-$90	2P: $55-$90	XP: $8	F16

Motel

Location: On SR 86, 0.5 mi e of jct SR 73. 5 Wilmington Rd 12946. **Facility:** 14 units. 12 one- and 2 two-bedroom standard units. 1-2 stories, exterior corridors. **Parking:** on-site. **Terms:** 2-3 night minimum stay - weekends in winter, 7 day cancellation notice-fee imposed, weekly rates available, package plans. **Pool(s):** outdoor. **Cards:** AX, DS, MC, VI. **Special Amenities:** free local telephone calls and preferred room (subject to availability with advanced reservations).

SOME UNITS

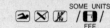

SWISS ACRES INN

Phone: 518/523-3040

All Year 1P: $49-$98 2P: $49-$98 XP: $10 F16

Small-scale Hotel

Location: 1 mi w on SR 86. 189 Saranac Ave 12946. Fax: 518/523-2196. **Facility:** 40 units. 33 one-bedroom standard units, some with efficiencies. 7 one-bedroom suites ($69-$148), some with efficiencies or kitchens. 1-2 stories (no elevator), interior/exterior corridors. *Bath:* some combo or shower only. **Parking:** on-site, winter plug-ins. **Terms:** 2 night minimum stay - weekends in season, 7 day cancellation notice-fee imposed, package plans, pets ($20 fee). **Dining:** 7:30 am-11 & 5-9 pm; hours vary in winter, cocktails. **Pool(s):** outdoor. **Leisure Activities:** sauna, whirlpool, picnic tables, barbecue grill. **Business Services:** meeting rooms. **Cards:** AX, DS, MC, VI. **Special Amenities:** free full breakfast and preferred room (subject to availability with advanced reservations).

SOME UNITS

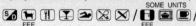

TOWN & COUNTRY MOTOR INN

Phone: 518/523-9268

6/22-10/14 & 12/21-4/30	1P: $69-$98	2P: $69-$98	XP: $10	F10
5/1-6/21 & 10/15-12/20	1P: $52-$69	2P: $52-$69	XP: $10	F10

Motel

Location: 0.5 mi w on SR 86. 67 Saranac Ave 12946. Fax: 518/523-8058. **Facility:** 24 units. 22 one-bedroom standard units. 1 one-bedroom suite ($140-$170) with kitchen. 1 cottage ($140-$170). 2 stories (no elevator), exterior corridors. **Parking:** on-site. **Terms:** 2 night minimum stay - seasonal weekends, 10 day cancellation notice, [CP] meal plan available, package plans. **Pool(s):** heated outdoor. **Leisure Activities:** picnic area with grills. **Cards:** MC, VI. **Special Amenities:** free continental breakfast.

SOME UNITS

TOWN HOUSE LODGE "BY THE LAKE"

Phone: 518/523-2532

6/25-9/6	2P: $78-$135	XP: $10	F12
9/7-4/30	2P: $58-$135	XP: $10	F12
5/1-6/24	2P: $58-$78	XP: $10	F12

Motel

Location: 0.5 mi w on SR 86. 40 Saranac Ave 12946. Fax: 518/523-2533. **Facility:** 25 one-bedroom standard units. 1-2 stories (no elevator), exterior corridors. *Bath:* combo or shower only. **Parking:** on-site, winter plug-ins. **Terms:** 2-5 night minimum stay - some weekends, 15 day cancellation notice-fee imposed. **Amenities:** *Some:* hair dryers. **Pool(s):** heated outdoor, wading. **Leisure Activities:** Fee: game room. **Cards:** AX, MC, VI.

SOME UNITS

The following lodging was either not evaluated or did not meet AAA rating requirements but is listed for your information only.

LAKE PLACID LODGE

Phone: 518/523-1124

[fyi]

Not evaluated. **Location:** 1 mi s on SR 86 to Whiteface Inn Rd, 1.5 mi w, follow signs. Whiteface Inn Rd 12946 (PO Box 550). Facilities, services, and decor characterize an upscale property.

── WHERE TO DINE ──

AVERIL CONWELL DINING ROOM Historic

Dinner: $16-$30 **Phone:** 518/523-2544

Regional American

Location: Just off SR 86, 0.5 mi w; in Mirror Lake Inn Resort and Spa. 5 Mirror Lake Dr 12946. **Hours:** 7:30 am-10 & 5:30-9 pm, Sat & Sun 7:30 am-11 & 5:30-9 pm. **Reservations:** suggested. **Features:** One of the region's most elegant dining rooms is the place for a cozy tete-a-tete or a leisurely meal in the company of good friends. The cuisine here is creative, and even dishes on the spa menu are sure to please any palate. Casual dress; cocktails. **Parking:** on-site. **Cards:** AX, DC, DS, MC, VI.

THE BOAT HOUSE

Dinner: $8-$20 **Phone:** 518/523-4822

Continental

Location: 1.5 mi n of jct SR 86. 89 Mirror Lake Dr 12946. **Hours:** 5 pm-10 pm. **Reservations:** suggested. **Features:** Along with a fine Continental menu, the newcomer to the Lake Placid scene boasts a warm Adirondack ambience, spectacular views and sunsets and a covered deck extending over Mirror Lake. Selections range from juicy hamburgers and filet mignon to pasta and seafood dishes. For dessert, guests can prepare true Adirondack s'mores over an open flame at the table. Casual dress; cocktails. **Parking:** on-site. **Cards:** AX, DC, DS, MC, VI.

THE BROWN DOG CAFE & WINE BAR

Lunch: $6-$8 Dinner: $7-$22 **Phone:** 518/523-3036

American

Location: Downtown. 3 Main St 12946. **Hours:** 11:30 am-9 pm. **Closed:** 3/27, 11/25, 12/25; also last week of Oct & 1st week of Nov. **Reservations:** accepted. **Features:** Don't let the carry-out aspect of the bistro-type establishment throw you. Fine creative dinners are served in the small restaurant portion at the rear, while traditional delicatessen fare is offered during the day. More than 50 wines are available by the glass. Saturday night wine dinners are popular. Casual dress; cocktails. **Parking:** street. **Cards:** AX, MC, VI.

THE CHARCOAL PIT

American

Dinner: $12-$33   **Phone:** 518/523-3050
Location: 1 mi w. 100 Saranac Ave 12946. **Hours:** 5 pm-10 pm. Closed: Mon-Thurs 4/1-4/30 & 11/1-11/30. **Reservations:** accepted. **Features:** Located at the edge of picturesque Lake Placid Village, this restaurant has been family-owned and operated since 1957. The variety of dishes offered assures that any craving will be met. Casual dress; cocktails. **Parking:** on-site. **Cards:** AX, CB, DC, DS, MC, VI.

DESPERADOS

Tex-Mex

Lunch: $6-$10   **Dinner:** $6-$10   **Phone:** 518/523-1507
Location: 0.5 mi w on SR 86. 97 Saranac Ave 12946. **Hours:** 11:30 am-9 pm, Sun-Tues from 4 pm. Closed: 3/27, 11/25, 12/25. **Features:** Hand-made nachos, big fat burritos and hot sauces! Add to this the bright, bold citrus colours of the interior and the rhythmic sounds of salsa and you will no doubt find yourself transported to the fine white sandy beaches and hot tropical sun of Mexico. And, well, if that doesn't do it, try a shot of one of the fifty premium brands of tequila that the owner keeps in stock. Casual dress; cocktails. **Parking:** on-site. **Cards:** MC, VI.

**THE GREAT ADIRONDACK STEAK & SEAFOOD COMPANY &
GREAT ADIRONDACK BREWING CO**

Steak & Seafood

Lunch: $5-$15   **Dinner:** $8-$20   **Phone:** 518/523-1629
Location: Center. 34 Main St 12946. **Hours:** 11:30 am-9:30 pm; to 10 pm 6/15-9/15 & 12/24-3/1. **Features:** In the heart of the village, the casual restaurant offers a little something for everyone, ranging from flavorful French onion soup to exquisite flatbread. An interesting story is behind the name of every beer made at the on-site microbrewery. Casual dress; cocktails. **Parking:** street. **Cards:** AX, CB, DC, DS, MC, VI.

MYKONOS

Greek

Lunch: $7-$13   **Dinner:** $9-$20   **Phone:** 518/523-1164
Location: 0.5 mi w on SR 86. 38 Saranac Ave 12946. **Hours:** Open 5/1-10/31 & 12/1-3/31; 11 am-2 & 5-9:30 pm; from 5 pm 12/1-5/31. Closed: Mon & Tues 12/1-3/31 & 5/1-5/31. **Reservations:** accepted. **Features:** The menu selections at Mykonos are varied and include not only the standard gyro and souflaki but many wonderful traditional appetizers and soups as well. If you're are not sure what to order, try one of the combination platters for a little sampling of their best Greek specialties. But, do come with your appetite, the servings are hardy. Casual dress; beer & wine only. **Parking:** on-site. **Cards:** AX, DS, MC, VI.

TERRACE ROOM RESTAURANT

American

Lunch: $7-$9   **Dinner:** $14-$32   **Phone:** 518/523-4411
Location: In Hilton Lake Placid Resort. 1 Mirror Lake Dr 12946. **Hours:** 7 am-10:30, noon-2 & 5:30-9 pm, Sun 11 am-2 & 5:30-9 pm; Sunday brunch. **Reservations:** suggested, for dinner. **Features:** The Terrace Room offers great American fare with a choice of buffet for breakfast and lunch. Dinner reservations are highly suggested. Casual dress; cocktails. **Parking:** on-site. **Cards:** AX, DC, DS, MC, VI.

VERANDA RESTAURANT

Continental

Dinner: $15-$30   **Phone:** 518/523-3339
Location: Downtown; in Lake Placid Resort Hotel & Golf Club/Holiday Inn. 1 Olympic Dr 12946. **Hours:** 5:30 pm-9:30 pm. Closed: 7/4, 11/25, 12/25; also Mon. **Reservations:** suggested. **Features:** Intimate dining rooms throughout the attractively restored house boast tasteful decor and afford lovely lake views. The casual fine-dining restaurant offers a nice selection of seafood, meat and fowl, along with a few pasta dishes, all thoughtfully presented. Outdoor terrace seating is a seasonal option. Casual dress; cocktails. **Parking:** on-site. **Cards:** AX, CB, DC, DS, MC, VI. *(See color ad p 332)*

LANSING pop. 3,417—*See also FINGER LAKES.*

——— **WHERE TO STAY** ———

THE CLARION UNIVERSITY HOTEL & CONFERENCE CENTER

Small-scale Hotel

All Year	1P: $89-$249	2P: $99-$269	XP: $10	F18

Phone: (607)257-2000
Location: On SR 13, N of Ithaca, exit Triphammer Rd, then just s. (One Sheraton Dr, ITHACA, 14850). Fax: 607/257-3998. **Facility:** 106 one-bedroom standard units. 3 stories, interior corridors. **Parking:** on-site, winter plug-ins. **Terms:** [BP] & [ECP] meal plans available, pets ($20 fee). **Amenities:** voice mail, irons, hair dryers. **Pool(s):** heated indoor. **Leisure Activities:** saunas, lifeguard on duty, exercise room. **Guest Services:** valet laundry, area transportation. **Business Services:** conference facilities, business center. **Cards:** AX, CB, DC, DS, MC, VI.

SOME UNITS

ECONO LODGE   *Book at aaa.com*

Small-scale Hotel

7/1-8/31	1P: $96-$135	2P: $96-$135	XP: $10	F18
5/1-6/30 & 9/1-11/30	1P: $86-$106	2P: $86-$106	XP: $10	F18
12/1-4/30	1P: $66-$81	2P: $66-$81	XP: $10	F18

Phone: (607)257-1400
Location: Intersection of SR 13 and Triphammer Rd. Adjoins Cayuga Mall. 2303 N Triphammer Rd 14850. Fax: 607/257-6359. **Facility:** 72 one-bedroom standard units, some with whirlpools. 2 stories (no elevator), interior corridors. **Parking:** on-site, winter plug-ins. **Terms:** [CP] meal plan available, pets ($10 extra charge). **Guest Services:** valet laundry, airport transportation-Tompkins County Airport. **Business Services:** meeting rooms, fax (fee). **Cards:** AX, CB, DC, DS, JC, MC, VI. **Special Amenities:** free continental breakfast and preferred room (subject to availability with advanced reservations).

SOME UNITS

ITHACA COURTYARD BY MARRIOTT *Book at aaa.com*

Phone: (607)330-1000

All Year   1P: $109-$159

Location: Jct SR 13 N and Warren Rd, just w to Brown Rd, just e. Located next to Tompkins County Airport. 29 Thornwood Dr 14850. Fax: 607/330-1500. **Facility:** 106 units. 99 one-bedroom standard units. 6 one- and 1 two-bedroom suites. 4 stories, interior corridors. *Bath:* combo or shower only. **Parking:** on-site. **Amenities:** video games, high-speed Internet, dual phone lines, voice mail, irons, hair dryers. **Pool(s):** heated indoor. **Leisure Activities:** whirlpool, exercise room. **Guest Services:** valet and coin laundry, area transportation. **Business Services:** meeting rooms, fax (fee). **Cards:** AX, DC, DS, MC, VI.

Small-scale Hotel

SOME UNITS

RAMADA INN-AIRPORT *Book at aaa.com*

Phone: (607)257-3100

All Year   1P: $99-$249   2P: $109-$269   XP: $10   F18

Location: Jct SR 13 and 34, 3.5 mi n on SR 13, exit Triphammer Rd, then just w. 2310 N Triphammer Rd 14850. Fax: 607/257-4425. **Facility:** 121 one-bedroom standard units, some with whirlpools. 2 stories, interior corridors. *Bath:* combo or shower only. **Parking:** winter plug-ins. **Terms:** [AP], [BP], [CP] & [MAP] meal plans available, pets ($20 fee). **Amenities:** video library (fee), voice mail, irons, hair dryers. **Pool(s):** outdoor, heated indoor, wading. **Leisure Activities:** sauna, whirlpool, exercise room. **Guest Services:** valet laundry, area transportation. **Business Services:** conference facilities. **Cards:** AX, CB, DC, DS, MC, VI.

Small-scale Hotel

SOME UNITS

ROGUE'S HARBOR BED & BREAKFAST

Phone: (607)533-3535

5/1-11/30 & 4/1-4/30 [CP]   1P: $125-$150   2P: $125-$150
12/1-3/31 [CP]   1P: $100   2P: $100

Location: SR 34, 6 mi n of Ithaca; corner of SR 34 and 34B. 2079 E Shore Dr 14882 (PO Box 97). Fax: 607/533-9155. **Facility:** Some guest rooms at this 1830s B&B feature brass beds. Smoke free premises. 8 one-bedroom standard units. 3 stories (no elevator), interior corridors. *Bath:* some shared or private, combo or shower only. **Parking:** on-site. **Terms:** 14 day cancellation notice, weekly rates available. **Amenities:** hair dryers. **Dining:** dining room, see separate listing. **Cards:** AX, MC, VI.

Historic Bed & Breakfast

------ **WHERE TO DINE** ------

KYUSHU

Lunch: $5-$9   Dinner: $12-$26   Phone: 607-257-6788

Location: SR 13, exit Triphammer Rd, just w. 2300 Triphammer Rd 14850. **Hours:** 11:30 am-3 & 5-10 pm, Fri & Sat-11 pm, Sun noon-10 pm. Closed: 11/25. **Reservations:** accepted. **Features:** Bright, uncomplicated decor provides the background for the hibachi and sushi bar, at which patrons can sample healthy, fresh and delicious food. Casual dress. **Parking:** on-site. **Cards:** AX, DS, MC, VI.

Sushi

ROGUE'S HARBOR STEAK & ALE INC

Dinner: $8-$20   Phone: 607-533-3535

Location: SR 34, 6 mi n of Ithaca; corner of SR 34 and 34B; in Rogue's Harbor Bed & Breakfast. 2079 East Shore Dr 14882. **Hours:** 4 pm-10 pm, Sat from 11 am, Sun 11 am-9 pm; Saturday & Sunday brunch. Closed: 1/1, 12/25. **Features:** Antiques, local memorabilia and 13 fireplaces add to the ambience of the 19th-century historic landmark. The menu centers on prime rib, fresh seafood and interesting pasta combinations. Seasonal outdoor seating is a warm-weather option. Casual dress; cocktails. **Parking:** on-site. **Cards:** AX, DS, MC, VI.

American

LATHAM pop. 10,100 (See map and index starting on p. 215)

------ **WHERE TO STAY** ------

CENTURY HOUSE RESTAURANT & HOTEL *Book at aaa.com*

Phone: (518)785-0931   **30**

7/22-9/6 [BP]   1P: $129-$225   2P: $129-$225   XP: $15   F12
5/1-7/21 & 9/7-4/30 [BP]   1P: $115-$225   2P: $115-$225   XP: $12   F12

Location: I-87, exit 7 (SR 7), just e; 0.5 mi n on US 9 (New Loudon Rd). 997 New Loudon Rd 12110 (PO Box 1100). Fax: 518/785-3274. **Facility:** 68 units. 64 one-bedroom standard units. 2 one- and 2 two-bedroom suites ($150-$225) with kitchens. 2 stories (no elevator), interior corridors. **Parking:** on-site. **Terms:** pets ($15 extra charge). **Amenities:** dual phone lines, voice mail, irons, hair dryers. **Dining:** restaurant, see separate listing. **Pool(s):** small outdoor. **Leisure Activities:** tennis court, cross country skiing, nature trail, exercise room. **Guest Services:** valet laundry, area transportation-Amtrak station. **Business Services:** conference facilities. **Cards:** AX, CB, DC, DS, MC, VI. **Special Amenities:** free full breakfast and free newspaper.

Small-scale Hotel

SOME UNITS

CLARION INN & SUITES *Book at aaa.com*

Phone: (518)785-5891   **31**

7/1-10/31   1P: $109-$239   2P: $109-$239   XP: $10   F18
5/1-6/30 & 1/1-4/30   1P: $89-$189   2P: $89-$189   XP: $10   F18
11/1-12/31   1P: $79-$179   2P: $79-$179   XP: $10   F18

Location: I-87, exit 6, just w. 611 Troy-Schenectady Rd 12110. Fax: 518/785-5805. **Facility:** 132 units. 119 one-bedroom standard units. 13 one-bedroom suites with efficiencies and whirlpools. 2 stories (no elevator), interior/exterior corridors. *Bath:* combo or shower only. **Parking:** on-site. **Terms:** [ECP] meal plan available. **Amenities:** voice mail, irons, hair dryers. **Pool(s):** outdoor. **Leisure Activities:** exercise room. **Guest Services:** valet laundry, area transportation. **Business Services:** meeting rooms. **Cards:** AX, DC, DS, MC, VI.

Small-scale Hotel

SOME UNITS

COMFORT INN AT ALBANY AIRPORT *Book at aaa.com*

Phone: (518)783-1900   **28**

7/20-8/26   1P: $99-$109   2P: $99-$109   XP: $10   F
5/1-7/19 & 8/27-4/30   1P: $89-$99   2P: $89-$99   XP: $10   F

Location: I-87, exit 4, 2.2 mi nw on Albany Shaker Rd, just se. 20 Airport Park Blvd 12110. Fax: 518/783-4085. **Facility:** 96 one-bedroom standard units, some with whirlpools. 2 stories (no elevator), interior corridors. **Parking:** on-site. **Terms:** [ECP] meal plan available. **Amenities:** voice mail, irons, hair dryers. **Leisure Activities:** exercise room. **Guest Services:** valet and coin laundry. **Business Services:** meeting rooms, business center. **Cards:** AX, DC, DS, MC, VI.

Small-scale Hotel

SOME UNITS

(See map and index starting on p. 215)

HAMPTON INN-LATHAM   *Book at aaa.com*   Phone: 518/785-0000   32
▼▼▼▽

7/18-9/7 [CP]	1P: $134-$164	
5/1-7/17 [CP]	1P: $104-$144	
9/8-4/30 [CP]	1P: $109-$139	

Small-scale Hotel   **Location:** I-87, exit 7 (SR 7), just n on US 9 (New Loudon Rd). 981 New Loudon Rd 12047 (981 New Loudon Rd, CO-HOES). Fax: 518/785-1285. **Facility:** 126 one-bedroom standard units. 4 stories, interior corridors. **Terms:** cancellation fee imposed. **Amenities:** voice mail, irons, hair dryers. **Pool(s):** small outdoor. **Leisure Activities:** exercise room. **Guest Services:** valet laundry, area transportation. **Business Services:** meeting rooms, fax (fee). **Cards:** AX, DC, MC, VI.

SOME UNITS
ASK SD ⊁ 🛏 ¶↑ 🖶M ⊿ 🐾 DATA/PORT 💻 / ✕ 🖪 /

HOLIDAY INN EXPRESS-AIRPORT   *Book at aaa.com*   Phone: (518)783-6161   33
ⒶⒶⒶ [SAVE]
▽▼▽

All Year	1P: $70-$120	2P: $80-$130	XP: $5 F

Small-scale Hotel   **Location:** I-87, exit 7 (SR 7) on US 9 N, then just n. 946 New Loudon Rd 12110. Fax: 518/783-0154. **Facility:** 120 one-bedroom standard units. 2 stories (no elevator), exterior corridors. **Parking:** on-site, winter plug-ins. **Terms:** [ECP] meal plan available, pets ($20 fee). **Amenities:** dual phone lines, voice mail, irons, hair dryers. **Pool(s):** outdoor. **Leisure Activities:** exercise room. **Guest Services:** valet and coin laundry, area transportation-train and bus station. **Business Services:** meeting rooms, fax (fee). **Cards:** AX, DC, DS, MC, VI. **Special Amenities:** free local telephone calls and free newspaper.

SOME UNITS
SD ⊁ 🛏 ¶↑ 🖊 ⊿ 🐾 DATA/PORT 💻 / ✕ VCR 🖪 /
FEE   FEE FEE

MICROTEL INN   *Book at aaa.com*   Phone: 518/782-9161   34
ⒶⒶⒶ [SAVE]
▽▼▽

5/1-10/31 [CP]	1P: $52-$119	2P: $52-$119
11/1-4/30 [CP]	1P: $47-$99	2P: $47-$99

Small-scale Hotel   **Location:** I-87, exit 6, just w. 7 Rensselaer Ave 12110. Fax: 518/782-9162. **Facility:** 100 one-bedroom standard units. 2 stories (no elevator), interior corridors. *Bath:* combo or shower only. **Parking:** on-site. **Amenities:** video library (fee), video games, voice mail, safes. **Guest Services:** valet laundry. **Business Services:** meeting rooms, fax. **Cards:** AX, DC, DS, MC, VI. **Special Amenities:** free continental breakfast.

SOME UNITS
SD 🛏 ¶↑ 🖶M 🖊 🐾 DATA/PORT / ✕ 🖪 💻 /

RESIDENCE INN BY MARRIOTT ALBANY AIRPORT   *Book at aaa.com*   Phone: (518)783-0600   27
▼▼▽

7/1-9/6	1P: $189-$209
9/7-4/30	1P: $159-$189
5/1-6/30	1P: $149-$179

Small-scale Hotel   **Location:** I-87, exit 6, 2 mi w on SR 7. 1 Residence Inn Dr 12110. Fax: 518/783-0709. **Facility:** 112 units. 68 one-bedroom standard units with kitchens. 44 one-bedroom suites with kitchens. 2 stories, exterior corridors. **Parking:** on-site. **Terms:** [BP] meal plan available, pets ($100 fee, $250 deposit, $5 extra charge). **Amenities:** voice mail, irons, hair dryers. **Pool(s):** small outdoor. **Leisure Activities:** whirlpool, exercise room, sports court. **Guest Services:** complimentary evening beverages: Mon-Thurs, valet and coin laundry. **Business Services:** meeting rooms, business center. **Cards:** AX, CB, DC, DS, JC, MC, VI.

SOME UNITS
ASK SD ⊁ 🛏 ¶↑ 🖊 ⊿ ✕ 🐾 DATA/PORT 🖪 🖂 💻 / ✕ VCR /
FEE

WINGATE INN   *Book at aaa.com*   Phone: (518)869-9100   29
▼▼▽

5/1-10/31 [ECP]	1P: $150-$165	2P: $160-$175	XP: $10 F18
11/1-4/30 [ECP]	1P: $125-$140	2P: $135-$150	XP: $10 F18

Small-scale Hotel   **Location:** I-87, exit 4, just w on Albany Shaker Rd. 254 Old Wolf Rd 12110. Fax: 518/869-0114. **Facility:** 107 one-bedroom standard units. 5 stories, interior corridors. *Bath:* combo or shower only. **Parking:** on-site. **Amenities:** video library (fee), video games, high-speed Internet, dual phone lines, voice mail, safes, irons, hair dryers. **Leisure Activities:** sauna, exercise room. **Guest Services:** valet laundry. **Business Services:** meeting rooms, business center. **Cards:** AX, CB, DC, DS, MC, VI.

SOME UNITS
ASK SD ⊁ 🛏 ¶ 🍸 🖶M 🖊 🐾 DATA/PORT 💻 / ✕ 🖪 /

––––––– **WHERE TO DINE** –––––––

CENTURY HOUSE   Lunch: $7-$13   Dinner: $16-$27   Phone: 518/785-0834   25
ⒶⒶⒶ
▽▼▽

Regional American   **Location:** I-87, exit 7 (SR 7), just e, 0.5 mi n on US 9 (New Loudon Rd); in Century House Restaurant & Hotel. 997 New Loudon Rd 12110. **Hours:** 11 am-3 & 4-9 pm, Fri-10 pm, Sat 4 pm-10 pm, Sun 1 pm-9 pm. Closed: 7/4, 12/25. **Reservations:** suggested. **Features:** Early American furnishings decorate the casual dining room of the well-established restaurant. Garlic beef (flaked roast sirloin brushed with garlic butter,) is the specialty on a menu of mostly steak and seafood. Death by chocolate cake is decadent. Casual dress; cocktails. **Parking:** on-site. **Cards:** AX, CB, DC, DS, MC, VI.

🍽 ✕

DAKOTA   Dinner: $9-$18   Phone: 518/786-1234   24
ⒶⒶ
▽▼

Steak & Seafood   **Location:** I-87, exit 6, just e; in Latham Circle Farms. 579 Troy-Schenectady Rd 12110. **Hours:** 4:30-10 pm, Fri & Sat 4 pm-11 pm, Sun 1 pm-9 pm. Closed: 11/25, 12/25. **Reservations:** accepted. **Features:** Hand-cut steak and fresh seafood make up the bulk of the relaxed restaurant's menu. The rustic dining room has the feel of an Adirondack mountain lodge, with wood beams, two fireplaces and American Indian artifacts. Try the yummy mud pie. Casual dress; cocktails. **Parking:** on-site. **Cards:** AX, DC, DS, MC, VI.

🖶M 🍽 ✕

KIRKER'S STEAK & SEAFOOD   Lunch: $6-$10   Dinner: $12-$22   Phone: 518/785-3653   23
▽▼ ▽▼

Steak & Seafood   **Location:** I-87, exit 7 (SR 7), just n on US 9 (New Loudon Rd). 959 New Loudon Rd 12110. **Hours:** 11:30 am-3 & 4-9:30 pm, Sat from 4 pm, Sun 1 pm-8 pm. Closed: 12/24, 12/25. **Reservations:** accepted. **Features:** Serving delicious steak and seafood and other popular American fare for more than 50 years, the well-established restaurant has a warm inviting charm with gracious, friendly hospitality. Reduced portions and healthy choices are available. Casual dress; cocktails. **Parking:** on-site. **Cards:** AX, DS, MC, VI.

🍽 ✕

─── *The following restaurant has not been evaluated by AAA* ───
but is listed for your information only.

TOKYO SUSHI **Phone:** 518/783-7838
[fyi] Not evaluated. **Location:** 571 Watervliet Shaker Rd 12110. **Features:** This casual Japanese restaurant is open for both lunch and dinner.

LEEDS pop. 369

─── **WHERE TO STAY** ───

CARL'S RIP VAN WINKLE MOTOR LODGE **Phone:** 518/943-3303
◇◇◇ (SAVE) 5/1-11/15 & 4/15-4/30 1P: $60-$80 2P: $60-$80 XP: $15
▽▽▽ ▽▽▽ **Location:** New York Thruway, exit 21, 0.3 mi nw. 810 CR 23B 12451. Fax: 518/943-2309. **Facility:** 37 units. 14
Cabin one-bedroom standard units. 23 cabins. 1 story, exterior corridors. *Bath:* combo or shower only. **Parking:** on-site. **Terms:** open 5/1-11/15 & 4/15-4/30, 7 day cancellation notice. **Pool(s):** outdoor, wading. **Leisure Activities:** fishing, hiking trails, playground, shuffleboard. **Business Services:** fax (fee). **Cards:** AX, MC, VI.
Special Amenities: free local telephone calls. *(See ad p 261)*

SOME UNITS
[icons] / FEE

─── **WHERE TO DINE** ───

LOGSIDER CAFE **Dinner:** $10-$20 **Phone:** 518/943-2581
◇◇◇ **Location:** I-87, exit 21, 0.3 mi w of New York Thruway. 800 23B 12451. **Hours:** 4 pm-9 pm, Sun noon-8 pm.
▽▽▽ ▽▽▽ Closed: Mon. **Reservations:** suggested, weekends. **Features:** The 1934 log cabin has an Adirondack
American atmosphere, with timbers, massive stone fireplaces and varied antique appointments. Well-seasoned dishes include traditional preparations of black Angus beef and fresh seafood. The barbecue ribs are outstanding. Casual dress; cocktails. **Parking:** on-site. **Cards:** AX, MC, VI. [icons]

LEONARDSVILLE

─── **WHERE TO DINE** ───

─── *The following restaurant has not been evaluated by AAA* ───
but is listed for your information only.

THE HORNED DORSET INN **Phone:** 315/855-7898
[fyi] Not evaluated. **Location:** Jct SR 8 and 20, 4 mi s; center. Rt 8 13364. **Features:** On a village main street tucked away in the countryside, the hidden restaurant is a bona fide treat. Elaborate wood trim and a heavy stone hearth decorate the upscale dining room. Fish, red meat and fowl are prepared with both care and flair. [icon]

LE ROY pop. 4,462

─── **WHERE TO STAY** ───

EDSON HOUSE BED & BREAKFAST **Phone:** (585)768-8579
▽▽▽ ▽▽▽ All Year [CP] 1P: $79-$109 2P: $79-$109
Bed & Breakfast **Location:** I-90, exit 47, just s on SR 19. 7863 Griswold Circle Rd 14482-0296. Fax: 585/768-2063. **Facility:** Smoke free premises. 4 one-bedroom standard units. 2 stories (no elevator), interior corridors. **Parking:** on-site. **Terms:** 7 day cancellation notice-fee imposed, no pets allowed (owner's cat on premises). **Amenities:** video library. **Cards:** AX, DS, MC, VI.

SOME UNITS
[icon] / (VCR) /

─── **WHERE TO DINE** ───

THE CREEKSIDE INN **Lunch:** $4-$7 **Dinner:** $7-$25 **Phone:** 585/768-7846
▽▽▽ ▽▽▽ **Location:** Center. 1 Main St 14482. **Hours:** 11 am-9 pm, Fri & Sat-10 pm, Sun 1 pm-8 pm. Closed major
American holidays. **Reservations:** suggested. **Features:** The casual, tavern-style restaurant overlooks a mill stream and pretty waterfalls. Among selections on the extensive menu are lots of finger foods as well as seafood, prime rib, pork, chicken, soup, salad and sandwiches. Servers are pleasant. Casual dress; cocktails.
Parking: on-site. **Cards:** AX, CB, DC, DS, MC, VI. [icons]

D & R DEPOT RESTAURANT **Lunch:** $5-$8 **Dinner:** $6-$17 **Phone:** 585/768-6270
◇◇◇ **Location:** Jct SR 5 and 19, just n. 63 Lake St (SR 19) 14482. **Hours:** 7 am-9 pm, Sun from 11:30 am. Closed:
▽▽▽ ▽▽▽ 12/25. **Reservations:** accepted, suggested weekends. **Features:** Near the historic town, the former 1901
American train depot offers a heart-smart menu that incorporates such choices as ostrich meat, fresh seafood, prime rib and chicken pot pie. Casual dress; beer & wine only. **Parking:** on-site. **Cards:** AX, DS, MC, VI. [icon]

L.B. GRAND STEAK AND SPAGHETTI HOUSE **Lunch:** $4-$9 **Dinner:** $7-$20 **Phone:** 585/768-6707
▽▽▽ **Location:** Center. 37-39 Main St 14482. **Hours:** 11 am-9 pm, Fri & Sat-10 pm. Closed major holidays; also
Italian Sun. **Reservations:** accepted, Sat-Thurs. **Features:** The downtown local favorite serves fresh Italian fare, seafood and USDA choice steaks in a friendly, casual atmosphere. Sunday brunch is only by reservation. Casual dress; cocktails. **Parking:** on-site. **Cards:** AX, DC, DS, MC, VI.

PONTILLO'S PIZZA & PASTA   **Lunch:** $5-$7   **Dinner:** $7-$8   **Phone:** 585/768-6660

Italian

Location: Jct SR 19 and 5; downtown. 49 Main St 14482. **Hours:** 11 am-11 pm, Fri & Sat-midnight. Closed: 3/27, 11/25, 12/25. **Features:** The casual downtown eatery lays out a popular lunch buffet and presents a menu of stone-hearth pizza, chicken wings, hot subs and pasta dishes. Casual dress; beer & wine only. **Parking:** on-site. **Cards:** AX, DC, DS, MC, VI.

LEWISTON —*See Niagara Falls p. 480.*

LIBERTY pop. 3,975

──────── **WHERE TO STAY** ────────

DAYS INN   *Book at aaa.com*   **Phone:** (845)292-7600

⚫⚫ SAVE

7/1-9/3	1P: $75-$120	2P: $80-$120	XP: $6	F12
5/1-6/30	1P: $70-$110	2P: $75-$110	XP: $6	F12
1/1-4/30	1P: $72-$85	2P: $77-$90	XP: $6	F12
9/4-12/31	1P: $67-$80	2P: $72-$85	XP: $6	F12

Small-scale Hotel **Location:** SR 17, exit 100, 0.3 mi e. 52 Sullivan Ave 12754. Fax: 845/292-3303. **Facility:** 118 one-bedroom standard units. 2 stories (no elevator), interior corridors. **Parking:** on-site. **Terms:** pets ($100 deposit). **Amenities:** voice mail, hair dryers. **Pool(s):** small outdoor, small heated indoor. **Business Services:** meeting rooms. **Cards:** AX, CB, DC, DS, MC, VI. **Special Amenities:** free continental breakfast and free newspaper.

SOME UNITS

──────── **WHERE TO DINE** ────────

MANNY'S STEAKHOUSE   **Lunch:** $7-$13   **Dinner:** $12-$29   **Phone:** 845/295-3170

Steak & Seafood

Location: SR 17, exit 100, 0.4 mi e. 79 Sullivan Ave 12754. **Hours:** 11:30 am-10 pm. Closed: 1/1, 12/25. **Reservations:** suggested. **Features:** An upscale, refreshing atmosphere makes the restaurant an ideal place to enjoy steaks, prime rib and fresh seafood. The prime rib sandwich layers tender, juicy, thinly-sliced prime rib on a garlic-butter toasted roll au jus. All luscious desserts are made in house. Casual dress; cocktails. **Parking:** on-site. **Cards:** AX, DS, MC, VI.

PICCOLO PAESE   **Lunch:** $17-$23   **Dinner:** $17-$23   **Phone:** 845/292-7210

Northern Italian

MC, VI.

Location: SR 17 westbound, exit 100, just n; exit SR 17 eastbound, just s. 2071 SR 52 12754. **Hours:** noon-10 pm, Fri-11 pm, Sat 4 pm-11 pm, Sun 4 pm-10 pm. Closed major holidays; also Mon 9/1-5/30. **Reservations:** suggested. **Features:** The fine-dining establishment specializes in Northern Italian cuisine made from the freshest quality ingredients. Pastas are made on the premises. An extensive wine list and in-house desserts complement a perfect meal. Casual dress; cocktails. **Parking:** on-site. **Cards:** AX, DS,

LITTLE FALLS pop. 5,188

──────── **WHERE TO STAY** ────────

BEST WESTERN LITTLE FALLS MOTOR INN   *Book at aaa.com*   **Phone:** (315)823-4954

⚫⚫ SAVE

5/1-9/30	1P: $70-$90	2P: $75-$105	XP: $6	F12
10/1-4/30	1P: $60-$80	2P: $65-$85	XP: $6	F12

Small-scale Hotel **Location:** On SR 5 and 167. 20 Albany St 13365. Fax: 315/823-4507. **Facility:** 56 one-bedroom standard units. 2 stories (no elevator), interior corridors. **Parking:** on-site, winter plug-ins. **Terms:** package plans, pets ($10 deposit). **Amenities:** irons, hair dryers. **Dining:** 6:30 am-2 & 5-9 pm, Sun 7 am-1 & 5-9 pm, cocktails. **Leisure Activities:** Fee: movie theaters. **Guest Services:** valet laundry. **Business Services:** meeting rooms. **Cards:** AX, DC, DS, MC, VI. **Special Amenities:** free local telephone calls.

SOME UNITS

──────── **WHERE TO DINE** ────────

BEARDSLEE CASTLE   **Dinner:** $12-$23   **Phone:** 315/823-3000

American

Location: On SR 5; just w of East Canada Creek. 123 Old State Rd 13365. **Hours:** 5 pm-9 pm, Sun 4 pm-8 pm. Closed: 1/1, 12/25; also Mon-Wed. **Reservations:** suggested. **Features:** Guests can read through the written history of the castle as they enjoy the quaint surroundings. Stone walls and fireplaces enhance the atmosphere of the dining room. The innovative, daily changing menu dabbles in steak, seafood and lamb, just to name a few. Appetizers, such as alligator fritters and grilled buffalo satay, are intriguing. Desserts are all made on the premises and are ample enough to share. Dressy casual; cocktails. **Parking:** on-site. **Cards:** AX, DS, MC, VI.

BELLA VISTA RESTAURANT   **Dinner:** $13-$26   **Phone:** 315/823-2861

Italian

Location: Jct SR 167 and 5 S, 1.3 mi s. 3622 SR 167 13365. **Hours:** 5 pm-9 pm, Fri & Sat-10 pm. Closed: 1/1, 12/24, 12/25; also Sun, Mon & Tues. **Reservations:** required. **Features:** Patrons can sample hearty, tasty food—such as the pleasantly presented chicken Christina, a chicken breast stuffed with crabmeat, spinach and cheese—in the casual, friendly restaurant. Look across the street for beautiful views of Shoemaker Mountain. Casual dress; cocktails. **Parking:** on-site. **Cards:** AX, DS, MC, VI.

CANAL SIDE INN   Historic   **Dinner:** $16-$25   **Phone:** 315/823-1170

⚫⚫

French

Location: Just s of SR 5, follow SR 167 S. 395 S Ann St 13365. **Hours:** Open 5/1-2/1 & 3/1-4/30; 5 pm-9 pm, Fri & Sat-10 pm. Closed major holidays; also Sun & Mon. **Reservations:** suggested. **Features:** In the historic area near the Erie Canal Project is a French dining experience waiting to delight. Expert service smooths the way through a pleasing meal of the chef/owner's traditionally prepared cuisine. The house Caesar salad, made tableside, is mouthwatering. Choose from a variety of pates, soup and appetizers. Beef, chicken, seafood and lamb are presented with sauce, garnish and fresh seasonal vegetables. Casual dress; cocktails. **Parking:** on-site. **Cards:** DS, MC, VI.

LIVERPOOL pop. 2,505 (See map and index starting on p. 577)

———— WHERE TO STAY ————

BEST WESTERN INN & SUITES *Book at aaa.com* Phone: **315/701-4400** 🔟 30
AAA SAVE   All Year   1P: $99-$169   2P: $99-$169   XP: $5   F12
▽▽▽▽   **Location:** I-90, exit 37 (Electronics Pkwy), just n; I-81, exit 25 (7th North St), 1.3 mi w, just n on Electronics Pkwy, then
Small-scale Hotel   just w. 136 Transistor Pkwy 13088. Fax: 315/701-2712. **Facility:** 61 one-bedroom standard units, some with whirlpools. 2 stories, interior corridors. **Parking:** on-site. **Terms:** pets ($10 extra charge, small dogs only, must be caged). **Amenities:** voice mail, irons, hair dryers. **Pool(s):** small heated indoor. **Leisure Activities:** whirlpool, exercise room. **Business Services:** meeting rooms. **Cards:** AX, CB, DC, DS, MC, VI.
Special Amenities: free continental breakfast and free newspaper.

SOME UNITS
[S/D] 🐾 ➤ 🎇 DATA/PORT 💻 / ✕ 🖥 🖨 /
FEE

HAMPTON INN *Book at aaa.com* Phone: **(315)457-9900** 🔟 27
▽▽▽▽   6/1-4/30 [ECP]   1P: $89-$99   2P: $89-$99
    5/1-5/31 [ECP]   1P: $85-$94   2P: $85-$94
Small-scale Hotel   **Location:** I-81, exit 25 (7th North St); I-90, exit 36. 417 7th North St 13088. Fax: 315/457-6600. **Facility:** 105 one-bedroom standard units. 3 stories, interior corridors. *Bath:* combo or shower only. **Parking:** on-site.
Amenities: video library (fee), video games, voice mail, irons, hair dryers. **Leisure Activities:** exercise room. **Guest Services:** valet and coin laundry. **Business Services:** meeting rooms. **Cards:** AX, CB, DC, DS, MC, VI.

SOME UNITS
[ASK] [S/D] ✈ 🍽 🔥♿ 🎇 DATA/PORT 💻 / ✕ [VCR] 🖨 /
FEE FEE

HOLIDAY INN SYRACUSE AIRPORT *Book at aaa.com* Phone: **(315)457-1122** 🔟 31
▽▽▽▽   All Year   1P: $114-$139   XP: $10   F
    Location: I-90, exit 37 (Electronics Pkwy); I-81, exit 25 (7th North St), 1.3 mi nw. 441 Electronics Pkwy. 13088.
Large-scale Hotel   Fax: 315/451-1269. **Facility:** 274 units. 272 one-bedroom standard units. 2 two-bedroom suites. 2-8 stories, interior corridors. *Bath:* combo or shower only. **Parking:** on-site. **Terms:** check-in 4 pm, [AP] & [BP] meal plans available, small pets only (in designated units). **Amenities:** video library (fee), video games, voice mail, irons, hair dryers. **Pool(s):** heated indoor. **Leisure Activities:** sauna, whirlpool, exercise room, volleyball. *Fee:* game room. **Guest Services:** valet laundry. **Business Services:** conference facilities, business center. **Cards:** AX, CB, DC, DS, JC, MC, VI.

SOME UNITS
[ASK] [S/D] ✈ 🐾 🍽 🍸 🔥♿ ♿ 🚭 ➤ ✕ 🎇 DATA/PORT 💻 / ✕ /
FEE

HOMEWOOD SUITES *Book at aaa.com* Phone: **315/451-3800** 🔟 28
▽▽▽▽   All Year   1P: $109-$219   2P: $109-$219   XP: $10   F18
    Location: I-81, exit 25 (7th North St), 1 mi w; I-90, exit 36. 275 Elwood Davis Rd 13088. Fax: 315/451-5838.
Small-scale Hotel   **Facility:** 102 units. 98 one- and 4 two-bedroom suites with efficiencies. 3 stories, interior corridors. **Parking:** on-site. **Terms:** [BP] meal plan available, pets ($75 fee). **Amenities:** video library (fee), high-speed Internet, dual phone lines, voice mail, irons, hair dryers. **Pool(s):** outdoor. **Leisure Activities:** exercise room, basketball, game room. **Guest Services:** sundries, complimentary evening beverages: Mon-Thurs, valet and coin laundry. **Business Services:** meeting rooms, business center. **Cards:** AX, DC, DS, MC, VI.

SOME UNITS
[ASK] [S/D] ✈ 🐾 ➤ ✕ [VCR] 🎇 🖨 🖥 💻 / ✕ /
FEE

KNIGHTS INN *Book at aaa.com* Phone: **(315)453-6330** 🔟 32
AAA SAVE   All Year   1P: $44-$109   2P: $44-$129   XP: $6   F17
▽▽▽▽   **Location:** I-90, exit 37 (Electronics Pkwy), just s; I-81, exit 25 (7th North St), 1.3 mi nw, just s. 430 Electronics Pkwy
Motel   13088. Fax: 315/457-9240. **Facility:** 80 one-bedroom standard units. 1 story, exterior corridors. **Parking:** on-site. **Terms:** weekly rates available, [ECP] meal plan available, pets ($8 fee). **Guest Services:** coin laundry. **Cards:** AX, CB, DC, DS, JC, MC, VI. **Special Amenities: free expanded continental breakfast and preferred room (subject to availability with advanced reservations).** *(See color ad p 581)*

SOME UNITS
[S/D] 🐾 🍽 🎇 DATA/PORT / ✕ 🖥 🖨 /
FEE

SUPER 8 MOTEL ROUTE 57 *Book at aaa.com* Phone: **315/451-8550** 🔟 29
AAA SAVE   All Year   1P: $59-$109   2P: $63-$109   XP: $5   F12
▽▽   **Location:** I-90, exit 38, 1 mi n on CR 57. 7360 Oswego Rd 13090. Fax: 315/451-6205. **Facility:** 43 one-bedroom standard units, some with whirlpools. 2 stories (no elevator), interior corridors. **Parking:** on-site. **Amenities:** hair dryers. *Some:* irons. **Cards:** AX, CB, DC, DS, MC, VI. **Special Amenities:**
Small-scale Hotel   **free continental breakfast and free newspaper.**

SOME UNITS
[S/D] 🍽 🎇 DATA/PORT / ✕ 💻 /

SUPER 8 MOTEL SYRACUSE/LIVERPOOL *Book at aaa.com* Phone: **315/451-8888** 🔟 33
▽▽▽   All Year   1P: $59-$99   2P: $69-$99
    Location: I-81, exit 25 (7th North St), just nw; I-90, exit 36. 421 7th North St 13088. Fax: 315/451-0043. **Facility:** 99
Small-scale Hotel   one-bedroom standard units. 4 stories, interior corridors. **Parking:** on-site. **Terms:** [ECP] meal plan available. **Guest Services:** valet laundry. **Cards:** AX, CB, DC, DS, JC, MC, VI.

SOME UNITS
[ASK] [S/D] 🐾 🍽 🎇 / ✕ /

———— WHERE TO DINE ————

ICHIBAN JAPANESE STEAK HOUSE Dinner: $14-$27 Phone: **315/457-0000** 🔟 26
AAA   **Location:** 1 mi nw from SR 370 and Buckley Rd. 302 Old Liverpool Rd 13088-6219. **Hours:** 5 pm-9 pm, Fri &
▽▽   Sat-10 pm, Sun 4 pm-9 pm. Closed major holidays. **Reservations:** suggested. **Features:** Polite service
Japanese   and fresh ingredients are hallmarks of the hibachi-style restaurant. Sushi can be ordered from the sushi bar or off the menu. Meals prepared in front of guests provide for a fun, lively experience. Casual dress. **Parking:** on-site. **Cards:** AX, DC, DS, MC, VI.

🍸 ✕

(See map and index starting on p. 577)

PIER 57

◆◆ ◆◆
American

Lunch: $5-$7   **Dinner:** $10-$15   **Phone:** 315/457-8109 ㉕
Location: I-90, exit 38, 1 mi n on CR 57 (Oswego Rd). 7376 Oswego Rd 13090. **Hours:** 11 am-10 pm, Fri & Sat-11 pm. Closed: 1/1, 11/25, 12/24, 12/25. **Reservations:** accepted. **Features:** The busy favorite serves traditional American fare, including many pasta dishes, seafood, steaks and hearty sandwiches. Casual dress; cocktails. **Parking:** on-site. **Cards:** AX, CB, DC, DS, MC, VI.

⊻ ⊠

LIVINGSTON MANOR pop. 1,355

────── WHERE TO STAY ──────

THE MAGICAL LAND OF OZ B & B

◆◆ ◆◆
Bed & Breakfast

Phone: (845)439-3418
All Year [BP]   1P: $75-$85   2P: $75-$85
Location: SR 17, exit 96, just se, 3.6 mi s. 753 Shandelee Rd (CR 149) 12758. Fax: 845/439-3446. **Facility:** Designated smoking area. 7 one-bedroom standard units. 2 stories (no elevator), interior corridors. *Bath:* some shared, combo or shower only. **Parking:** on-site. **Terms:** 7 day cancellation notice, no pets allowed (owner's pet on premises). **Leisure Activities:** whirlpool, canoeing, paddleboats, fishing. **Guest Services:** TV in common area. **Business Services:** fax. **Cards:** AX, MC, VI.

SOME UNITS
(ASK) (S☎) (⊠) (X) (X) (W) (Z) / (DATA PORT)

LOCKPORT — See NIAGARA FALLS p. 480.

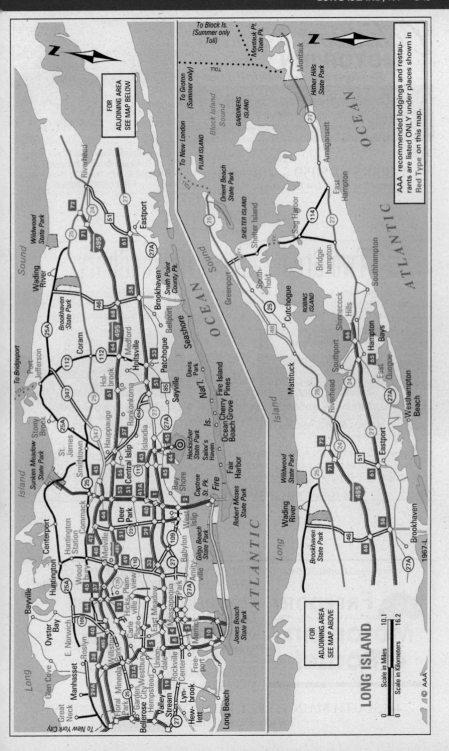

LONG ISLAND CITY —*See New York p. 452.*

LONG LAKE pop. 852—*See also ADIRONDACK MOUNTAINS.*

——— WHERE TO STAY ———

JOURNEY'S END COTTAGES
Phone: 518/624-5381

AAA SAVE

	6/26-9/10 Wkly	2P: $700-$750	XP: $50
	9/11-11/15 Wkly	2P: $650-$700	XP: $25
	5/1-6/25 Wkly	2P: $550-$650	XP: $25

Cottage

Location: On SR 30/28, 1 mi s. Deerland Rd (Rt 30) 12847 (PO Box 96). **Facility:** 4 cottages. 1 story, exterior corridors. **Parking:** on-site. **Terms:** open 5/1-11/15, 3-7 night minimum stay - seasonal, 60 day cancellation notice, pets ($10 fee). **Amenities:** hair dryers. **Leisure Activities:** canoeing, boat dock, fishing, grills & picnic tables. *Fee:* floatboat. **Cards:** DS, MC, VI.

FEE

LONG VIEW LODGE
Phone: (518)624-2862

All Year   2P: $65-$95   XP: $10

Historic Country Inn

Location: On SR 30/28, 2.2 mi s. Deerland Rd (Rt 30) 12847 (HCO1 Box 32). Fax: 518/624-2862. **Facility:** Designated smoking area. 15 units. 9 one- and 4 two-bedroom standard units. 2 cottages ($85-$95). 2 stories (no elevator), interior/exterior corridors. *Bath:* combo or shower only. **Parking:** on-site. **Terms:** check-in 4 pm, 2-4 night minimum stay - seasonal weekends, 7 day cancellation notice-fee imposed, pets (in cottages). **Leisure Activities:** canoeing, boat dock, fishing. **Cards:** DS, MC, VI.

SOME UNITS

MOTEL LONG LAKE & COTTAGES
Phone: 518/624-2613

AAA SAVE

| | 1/1-4/30 | 1P: $80 | 2P: $80 | XP: $10 |
| | 5/1-11/30 | 1P: $80 | 2P: $80 | XP: $10 |

Motel

Location: Just n of jct SR 30, at flashing traffic light. Located in a quiet area. Dock 12847 (PO Box 740). Fax: 518/624-2576. **Facility:** 19 units. 8 one-bedroom standard units. 11 cottages ($500-$990). 1 story, exterior corridors. *Bath:* combo or shower only. **Parking:** on-site. **Terms:** open 5/1-11/30 & 1/1-4/30, 3 night minimum stay - 7/1-8/31, 7 night in cottages, 10 day cancellation notice, 30 day in cottages, weekly rates available. **Amenities:** *Some:* irons. **Leisure Activities:** canoeing, boat dock, fishing. **Cards:** MC, VI.

SOME UNITS

SANDY POINT MOTEL
Phone: (518)624-3871

AAA SAVE

5/1-10/26   1P: $55-$85   2P: $55-$95   XP: $10   F5

Motel

Location: On SR 30/28, 1.3 mi s. Deerland Rd (Rt 30) 12847 (PO Box 8). Fax: 518/624-3348. **Facility:** 11 one-bedroom standard units, some with efficiencies. 2 stories (no elevator), exterior corridors. **Parking:** on-site. **Terms:** open 5/1-10/26, 10 day cancellation notice-fee imposed. **Leisure Activities:** sauna, rental boats, rental canoes, rental paddleboats, boat dock, fishing. **Cards:** AX, DS, MC, VI. **Special Amenities:** free local telephone calls and preferred room (subject to availability with advanced reservations).

SOME UNITS

SHAMROCK MOTEL AND COTTAGES
Phone: (518)624-3861

AAA SAVE

5/1-10/15   1P: $50-$95   2P: $50-$95   XP: $10   D16

Motel

Location: On SR 30/28 N, 0.5 mi s. Located in a quiet area. Deerland Rd (Rt 30) 12847 (PO Box 205). Fax: 518/624-9803. **Facility:** 17 units. 10 one-bedroom standard units, some with efficiencies. 7 cottages ($100). 1 story, exterior corridors. *Bath:* combo or shower only. **Parking:** on-site. **Terms:** open 5/1-10/15, 7 day cancellation notice-fee imposed. **Leisure Activities:** boat dock, fishing, badminton, horseshoes, shuffleboard. **Guest Services:** coin laundry. **Cards:** AX, DC, MC, VI.

SOME UNITS

LOUDONVILLE pop. 10,900   (See map and index starting on p. 215)

——— WHERE TO DINE ———

PEARL OF THE ORIENT
Lunch: $6-$7   **Dinner:** $7-$17   **Phone:** 518/459-0903   40

Chinese

Location: I-87, exit 4 (Kimberly Square); just w of jct Albany Shaker and Osborn rds, 1.7 mi e. 471 Albany Shaker Rd 12211. **Hours:** 11 am-10 pm, Fri-11 pm, Sat noon-11 pm, Sun noon-10 pm. **Closed:** 7/4, 11/25, 12/25. **Reservations:** accepted. **Features:** The variety of regional Chinese dishes includes Hunan, Szechuan and Cantonese preparations. Luncheon buffets and weekend dinner buffets allow for a sampling of some of each of these styles. Shrimp with black bean sauce and vegetables is a standard dish, and there are a number of chef's specials, including empress duck and chow steak kew. Other seafood, beef and poultry options can be ordered to varying degrees of spiciness. Casual dress; cocktails. **Parking:** on-site. **Cards:** AX, DC, DS, MC, VI.

LOWMAN

——— WHERE TO STAY ———

RED JACKET MOTOR INN
Phone: (607)734-1616

AAA SAVE

| | 5/1-11/30 | 1P: $36-$40 | 2P: $45-$65 | XP: $10 | F14 |
| | 12/1-4/30 | 1P: $30-$36 | 2P: $36-$40 | XP: $10 | F14 |

Motel

Location: SR 17, just e from CR 8; between MM 195 and 196. Located in a rural area. Rt 17 14902 (PO Box 709, ELMIRA). Fax: 607/732-0848. **Facility:** 48 one-bedroom standard units. 1 story, exterior corridors. *Bath:* combo or shower only. **Parking:** on-site. **Terms:** 3 day cancellation notice-fee imposed, pets ($10 extra charge, small dogs only). **Amenities:** hair dryers. **Dining:** 8 am-8 pm. **Pool(s):** outdoor. **Guest Services:** coin laundry. **Cards:** AX, CB, DC, DS, JC, MC, VI.

SOME UNITS

FEE   FEE   FEE

LOWVILLE pop. 3,476

—— WHERE TO STAY ——

RIDGE VIEW MOTOR LODGE
Phone: 315/376-2252
▼▼ ▼▼
Motel
All Year   1P: $59-$69   2P: $69-$89   XP: $10   F12
Location: 1.5 mi n. Located in a quiet, rural area. 7491 SR 12 13367. Fax: 315/376-2977. **Facility:** 40 one-bedroom standard units, some with whirlpools. 1 story, interior corridors. **Parking:** on-site, winter plug-ins. **Terms:** 6 day cancellation notice-fee imposed. [CP] meal plan available. **Leisure Activities:** playground. *Fee:* game room. **Business Services:** meeting rooms. **Cards:** AX, MC, VI.

SOME UNITS
🎦 / ⊠ VCR 🛏 📷 /
FEE FEE FEE

LYONS FALLS pop. 591

—— WHERE TO STAY ——

THE EDGE HOTEL
Phone: 315/348-4211
▼▼ ▼▼
Small-scale Hotel
All Year   1P: $79   2P: $79
Location: On SR 12, just n. 3952 SR 12 13368. Fax: 315/348-8111. **Facility:** 51 one-bedroom standard units, some with whirlpools. 2 stories (no elevator), interior corridors. *Bath:* combo or shower only. **Parking:** on-site. **Terms:** cancellation fee imposed. **Amenities:** high-speed Internet, voice mail, hair dryers. **Cards:** AX, DS, MC, VI.

SOME UNITS
🍽→ 🎦 DATA PORT 💻 / ⊠ VCR 🛏 📷
FEE FEE FEE

MALONE pop. 6,075

—— WHERE TO STAY ——

FOUR SEASONS MOTEL
Phone: (518)483-3490
(AAA) SAVE
▼▼ ▼▼
Motel
5/1-10/14   1P: $48-$59   2P: $55-$79   XP: $5   F12
10/15-4/30   1P: $40-$48   2P: $45-$65   XP: $5   F12
Location: 1 mi w on US 11. 236 W Main St 12953. Fax: 518/483-1693. **Facility:** 26 units. 25 one-bedroom standard units. 1 one-bedroom suite with kitchen. 1 story, exterior corridors. *Bath:* combo or shower only. **Parking:** on-site, winter plug-ins. **Terms:** package plans. **Pool(s):** outdoor. **Guest Services:** valet laundry. **Cards:** AX, CB, DC, DS, MC, VI.

SOME UNITS
S/D 🐾 🏊 🎦 DATA PORT / ⊠ 🛏 📷 💻 /

SUNSET INN
Phone: 518/483-3367
▼▼ ▼▼
Motel
10/15-4/30   1P: $45-$65   2P: $50-$75   XP: $5   F16
6/1-10/14   1P: $50   2P: $60   XP: $5   F16
5/1-5/31   1P: $45   2P: $52   XP: $5   F16
Location: 1.5 mi e. 3899 US 11 12953. Fax: 518/481-6172. **Facility:** 27 units. 26 one-bedroom standard units. 1 two-bedroom suite with kitchen. 1 story, exterior corridors. **Parking:** on-site, winter plug-ins. **Terms:** pets (in designated units). **Pool(s):** outdoor. **Cards:** AX, CB, DC, DS, MC, VI.

SOME UNITS
(ASK) S/D 🐾 🏊 🎦 🛏 📷 💻 / ⊠ /

SUPER 8 MOTEL AT JONS   *Book at aaa.com*
Phone: 518/483-8123
(AAA) SAVE
▼▼ ▼▼
Small-scale Hotel
5/17-10/16   1P: $67-$83   2P: $73-$89   XP: $6   F12
3/25-4/30   1P: $63-$79   2P: $68-$84   XP: $5   F12
5/1-5/16 & 10/17-3/24   1P: $62-$78   2P: $67-$83   XP: $5   F12
Location: On SR 30; just s of jct US 11. 42 Finney Blvd 12953. Fax: 518/483-8058. **Facility:** 44 one-bedroom standard units. 2 stories (no elevator), interior corridors. **Parking:** on-site, winter plug-ins. **Terms:** small pets only (in designated units). **Amenities:** video library (fee). **Guest Services:** valet laundry. **Cards:** AX, CB, DC, DS, MC, VI. **Special Amenities:** free local telephone calls.

SOME UNITS
🐾 ♿M 🎦 DATA PORT 🛏 / ⊠ VCR 🛏
FEE

—— WHERE TO DINE ——

JONS FAMILY RESTAURANT   **Lunch:** $2-$10   **Dinner:** $2-$10   **Phone:** 518/483-6230
(AAA)
▼▼
American
Location: Jct US 11/SR 30/37, just s on SR 30 S. 44 Finney Blvd 12953. **Hours:** 5:30 am-8 pm, Fri & Sat-9 pm. Closed: 11/25, 12/25. **Features:** The menu at Jons is all about traditional comfort food that's both tasty and filling,. This simple, casual restaurant offers family-style dining with table, booth and counter seating available. For dessert, choose from a variety of homemade pies; for breakfast, try a homemade donut. Casual dress; cocktails. **Parking:** on-site. **Cards:** AX, DS, MC, VI.
⊠

VILLA FIORE   **Lunch:** $4-$7   **Dinner:** $7-$16   **Phone:** 518/481-6557
▼▼ ▼▼
Italian
Location: On US 11/SR 30; center. 18 E Main St 12953. **Hours:** 11 am-10 pm, Fri & Sat-11 pm, Sun 4 pm-9 pm. Closed: 11/25, 12/25. **Reservations:** accepted. **Features:** The family restaurant serves Italian-American cuisine. In addition to traditional pasta dishes, the dinner menu lists prime rib and seafood selections. Casual dress; cocktails. **Parking:** on-site. **Cards:** AX, MC, VI.
🍽 ⊠

MALTA pop. 13,005

———— WHERE TO DINE ————

THE RIPE TOMATO - AN AMERICAN GRILL   **Lunch:** $4-$7   **Dinner:** $12-$17   **Phone:** 518/581-1530
Location: I-87, exit 13S, 1.9 mi s. 2721 Rt 9 12020. **Hours:** 11:30 am-10 pm, Fri & Sat-11 pm. Closed: 12/25.
Reservations: suggested. **Features:** From 10 pasta dishes to Yankee pot roast, house ribs and spicy
American   wings, the restaurant's presentations are unbeatable. Eclectic art adorns the walls, and memorable food
choices crowd the menu. Chef Tom Clark dishes up ample portions of well-prepared, "all-American" food
culled from the backgrounds of those who settled this country. The bustling, friendly atmosphere appeals to families and is
great for celebrations. Decadent homemade desserts cater to the sweet tooth. Casual dress; cocktails. **Parking:** on-site.
Cards: AX, DC, MC, VI.

MALTA RIDGE

———— WHERE TO DINE ————

CHEZ SOPHIE BISTRO   **Dinner:** $24-$30   **Phone:** 518/583-3538
Location: I-87, exit 13S, just s. 2853 SR 9 12020. **Hours:** 5:30 pm-close; from 5 pm in summer. Closed major
holidays; also Sun & Mon. **Reservations:** suggested. **Features:** Fine dining is the mode in the restored
French   1952 Fodero diner or in either of two elegant dining rooms. With a choice of more than 3,000 French
wines from the cellar, diners are sure to find a delicious match for such entrees as Canadian Moulard duck
breast with apricot and green peppercorn sauce and marinated quail with truffle butter sauce. Local purveyors provide
top-quality organic produce and free-range meats. Professional, courteous staff members can assist with selections. Casual
dress; cocktails. **Parking:** on-site. **Cards:** AX, CB, DC, MC, VI.

MANCHESTER pop. 1,475—See also *FINGER LAKES.*

———— WHERE TO STAY ————

ROADSIDE INN   **Phone:** (585)289-3811

7/1-8/31	1P: $55-$75	2P: $60-$85	XP: $8	F12
9/1-10/31	1P: $50-$70	2P: $60-$85	XP: $8	F12
5/1-6/30	1P: $50-$70	2P: $60-$80	XP: $8	F12
11/1-4/30	1P: $50-$70	2P: $55-$75	XP: $8	F12

Motel   **Location:** I-90, exit 43, jct SR 21, just e. 4078 Rt 96 14504. Fax: 585/289-3811. **Facility:** 38 one-bedroom standard units. 1-2 stories (no elevator), interior/exterior corridors. **Parking:** on-site. **Terms:** office hours 7 am-11 pm. **Cards:** AX, CB, DC, DS, MC, VI. **Special Amenities:** free full breakfast and free newspaper.

SOME UNITS

MARGARETVILLE pop. 643

———— WHERE TO STAY ————

MARGARETVILLE MTN INN B&B & VILLAGE SUITES   **Phone:** 845/586-3933
All Year [BP]   2P: $75-$130   XP: $15   F12
Location: 2 mi n on Walnut St/Margaretville Mountain Rd. 1478 Margaretville Mountain Rd 12455. Fax: 845/586-1699.
Historic Bed   **Facility:** This restored Victorian home, which dates from 1886, features wide porches. Smoke free premises.
& Breakfast   8 units. 5 one- and 1 two-bedroom standard units. 2 two-bedroom suites ($125-$300) with kitchens. 2 stories
(no elevator), interior corridors. *Bath:* combo or shower only. **Parking:** on-site. **Terms:** check-in 4 pm, 2-3
night minimum stay - seasonal weekends, 10 day cancellation notice-fee imposed, weekly rates available, package plans, no
pets allowed (owner's pet on premises). **Amenities:** video library. **Guest Services:** TV in common area. **Cards:** AX, MC, VI.

SOME UNITS

MASSAPEQUA PARK pop. 17,499

———— WHERE TO STAY ————

BEST WESTERN BAR HARBOUR INN   *Book at aaa.com*   **Phone:** (516)541-2000
All Year [CP]   1P: $95-$199   2P: $95-$199   XP: $10   F18
Location: SR 27 E, 2.5 mi e of SR 27 E). Located in a commercial area. 5080 Sunrise Hwy (SR 27 E) 11762.
Fax: 516/541-2004. **Facility:** 51 one-bedroom standard units. 2 stories (no elevator), exterior corridors.
Motel   **Parking:** on-site. **Amenities:** irons, hair dryers. **Pool(s):** outdoor. **Cards:** AX, CB, DC, DS, MC, VI.
Special Amenities: free continental breakfast and free newspaper.

SOME UNITS

MASSENA pop. 11,209

———— WHERE TO STAY ————

ECONO LODGE-MEADOW VIEW MOTEL   *Book at aaa.com*   **Phone:** (315)764-0246
All Year   1P: $70-$90   2P: $72-$99   XP: $10   F18
Location: On SR 37 W, 2.7 mi sw. 15054 SR 37 13662. Fax: 315/764-9615. **Facility:** 52 one-bedroom standard
units. 2 stories (no elevator), interior/exterior corridors. *Bath:* combo or shower only. **Parking:** on-site, winter
Small-scale Hotel   plug-ins. **Terms:** cancellation fee imposed, small pets only ($5 fee, in designated units). **Amenities:** voice
mail, irons, hair dryers. **Dining:** 6 am-10:30 & 5-10 pm, Mon from 5 pm; Sun 7 am-2 pm 5/1-10/31; hours
vary off season, cocktails. **Leisure Activities:** exercise room. **Guest Services:** valet laundry. **Business
Services:** meeting rooms. **Cards:** AX, CB, DC, DS, JC, MC, VI. **Special Amenities:** free local telephone calls and preferred
room (subject to availability with advanced reservations).

SOME UNITS

FEE

SUPER 8 MOTEL   *Book at aaa.com*   Phone: 315/764-1065

5/1-10/31 [CP]	1P: $69-$90	2P: $76-$95	XP: $7	F12
11/1-4/30 [CP]	1P: $62-$72	2P: $69-$79	XP: $7	F12

Location: Jct SR 56, 2 mi e on SR 37. 84 Grove St 13662. Fax: 315/764-9710. **Facility:** 42 units. 41 one-bedroom standard units. 1 two-bedroom suite. 3 stories (no elevator), interior corridors. **Parking:** on-site, winter plug-ins. **Amenities:** irons, hair dryers. **Cards:** AX, DC, DS, MC, VI. **Special Amenities: free continental breakfast and free local telephone calls.**

Small-scale Hotel

MAYVILLE pop. 1,756

WHERE TO DINE

WEBB'S CAPTAINS TABLE   **Lunch:** $7-$10   **Dinner:** $14-$30   Phone: 716/753-3960

American

Location: 1.3 mi s from center on SR 394. 115 W Lake Rd 14757. **Hours:** 11:30 am-11 pm. Closed: 11/25, 12/24, 12/25. **Reservations:** suggested, weekends. **Features:** Many tables in the interestingly decorated dining room overlook Lake Chautauqua. Regional dishes, as well as weekend specials and vegetarian choices, line the menu. Half portions are available. The neatly dressed wait staff provides attentive service. Dressy casual; cocktails. **Parking:** on-site. **Cards:** AX, DS, MC, VI.

The following restaurant has not been evaluated by AAA but is listed for your information only.

THE WATERMARK RESTAURANT   Phone: 716/753-2900

[fyi]

Not evaluated. **Location:** 188 S Erie St 14757. **Features:** The new lakeside restaurant specializes in fresh regional seafood and dry-aged Midwestern beef. Patrons who opt for seating on the Regatta Deck can sample more casual fare, such as burgers and wings.

MCGRAW pop. 1,000

WHERE TO STAY

CORTLAND DAYS INN   *Book at aaa.com*   Phone: (607)753-7594

5/1-10/31	1P: $49-$125	2P: $59-$125	XP: $10	F16
11/1-4/30	1P: $49-$89	2P: $59-$89	XP: $10	F16

Small-scale Hotel

Location: I-81, exit 10 (McGraw/Cortland), just n. 3775 US Rt 11 13101. Fax: 607/753-6508. **Facility:** 72 one-bedroom standard units, some with whirlpools. 2 stories (no elevator), interior corridors. **Parking:** on-site. **Terms:** cancellation fee imposed, [ECP] meal plan available, small pets only ($10 fee, in smoking rooms). **Amenities:** hair dryers. **Cards:** AX, DC, DS, MC, VI. **Special Amenities: free expanded continental breakfast and free local telephone calls.**

MEDFORD pop. 21,985

WHERE TO STAY

THE COMFORT INN   *Book at aaa.com*   Phone: (631)654-3000

5/1-9/30 [CP]	1P: $99-$159	2P: $99-$159	XP: $10	F15
10/1-4/30 [CP]	1P: $89-$129	2P: $89-$129	XP: $10	F15

Small-scale Hotel

Location: I-495, exit 64, just s. Located in a commercial area. 2695 Rt 112 11763. Fax: 631/654-1281. **Facility:** 76 one-bedroom standard units, some with whirlpools. 2 stories (no elevator), interior/exterior corridors. **Parking:** on-site. **Amenities:** video games (fee), high-speed Internet, dual phone lines, voice mail, irons, hair dryers. **Pool(s):** outdoor. **Leisure Activities:** saunas, exercise room. **Guest Services:** valet and coin laundry. **Business Services:** meeting rooms. **Cards:** AX, CB, DC, DS, MC, VI.

MELVILLE pop. 14,533

WHERE TO STAY

HILTON HUNTINGTON   *Book at aaa.com*   Phone: (631)845-1000

All Year	1P: $119-$219		XP: $10	F18

Large-scale Hotel

Location: I-495, exit 49, 1 mi s on SR 110. Located in a business park. 598 Broad Hollow Rd (SR 110) 11747. Fax: 631/845-1223. **Facility:** 305 units. 296 one-bedroom standard units. 9 one-bedroom suites. 5 stories, interior corridors. *Bath:* combo or shower only. **Parking:** on-site. **Terms:** check-in 4 pm, [AP], [BP], [CP], [ECP] & [MAP] meal plans available. **Amenities:** dual phone lines, voice mail, irons, hair dryers. *Fee:* video games, high-speed Internet. **Pool(s):** outdoor, heated indoor. **Leisure Activities:** whirlpool, lighted tennis court, exercise room. *Fee:* massage. **Guest Services:** gift shop, valet and coin laundry. **Business Services:** conference facilities. **Cards:** AX, CB, DC, DS, MC, VI.

MELVILLE MARRIOTT LONG ISLAND   *Book at aaa.com*   Phone: 631/423-1600

All Year	1P: $159-$289	2P: $159-$289

Large-scale Hotel

Location: I-495 E (Long Island Expwy), exit 49S eastbound, just n; exit 49N westbound, off north service road, just w of SR 110. Located in a business park. 1350 Old Walt Whitman Rd 11747. Fax: 631/423-1790. **Facility:** 369 one-bedroom standard units. 4 stories, interior corridors. *Bath:* combo or shower only. **Parking:** on-site. **Amenities:** video games (fee), voice mail, irons, hair dryers. **Pool(s):** heated indoor. **Leisure Activities:** whirlpool, exercise room. **Guest Services:** gift shop, valet laundry. **Business Services:** conference facilities, business center. **Cards:** AX, CB, DC, DS, JC, MC, VI.

MERRICK pop. 22,764

——— WHERE TO STAY ———

GATEWAY INN
(AAA) (SAVE)
▼▼▼
Motel

Phone: (516)378-7100
All Year   1P: $99-$119   2P: $99-$119   XP: $7   F12
Location: Meadowbrook Pkwy, exit M8 E, 0.3 mi e. Located in a commercial area. 1780 Sunrise Hwy 11566. **Fax:** 516/378-5745. **Facility:** 60 units. 59 one-bedroom standard units. 1 one-bedroom suite ($149). 2 stories, interior/exterior corridors. *Bath:* combo or shower only. **Parking:** on-site. **Terms:** cancellation fee imposed, [ECP] meal plan available. **Amenities:** *Some:* safes. **Cards:** AX, CB, DC, DS, MC, VI. **Special Amenities:** free expanded continental breakfast and free newspaper. *(See color ad p 342)*

SOME UNITS
[S][D] [📺] [DATA PORT] / [X] [🛗] / FEE

MIDDLETOWN pop. 25,388

——— WHERE TO STAY ———

HOLIDAY INN
▼▼▼
Small-scale Hotel

Book at aaa.com
Phone: (845)343-1474
All Year   1P: $89-$129   2P: $89-$129   XP: $10   F
Location: SR 17, exit 122, 0.3 mi ne. 68 Crystal Run Rd 10941. Fax: 845/692-7155. **Facility:** 100 one-bedroom standard units. 2 stories, interior corridors. **Parking:** on-site, winter plug-ins. **Terms:** [ECP] meal plan available. **Amenities:** video games (fee), high-speed Internet, dual phone lines, voice mail, irons, hair dryers. **Pool(s):** outdoor, heated indoor. **Leisure Activities:** sauna, exercise room. **Guest Services:** valet and coin laundry. **Business Services:** meeting rooms, business center. **Cards:** AX, CB, DC, DS, JC, MC, VI.

SOME UNITS
[ASK] [S][D] [🍴] [🍸] [🌀] [🏊] [🐾] [DATA PORT] [🛗] [🖥] / [X] /

MIDDLETOWN HAMPTON INN
▼▼▼
Small-scale Hotel

Book at aaa.com
Phone: 845/344-3400
5/1-11/21 [ECP]   1P: $114-$119   2P: $124-$129
1/1-4/30 [ECP]   1P: $94-$119   2P: $104-$129
11/22-12/31 [ECP]   1P: $94-$99   2P: $104-$109
Location: SR 17, exit 122, just ne. 20 Crystal Run Crossing 10941. Fax: 845/344-3403. **Facility:** 127 units. 119 one-bedroom standard units. 8 one-bedroom suites ($145-$165). 4 stories, interior corridors. *Bath:* combo or shower only. **Parking:** on-site. **Terms:** cancellation fee imposed. **Amenities:** dual phone lines, voice mail, irons, hair dryers. **Pool(s):** heated outdoor. **Leisure Activities:** exercise room. **Guest Services:** valet and coin laundry. **Business Services:** meeting rooms, business center. **Cards:** AX, DC, DS, MC, VI.

SOME UNITS
[ASK] [S][D] [♿M] [⌨] [🌀] [🏊] [🐾] [DATA PORT] [🖥] / [X] [VCR] [🛗] [🖥] /

SUPER 8 MOTEL
▼▼
Small-scale Hotel

Book at aaa.com
Phone: (845)692-5828
All Year   1P: $70-$85   2P: $90-$99   XP: $10   F12
Location: I-84, exit 4W, 0.5 mi w on SR 17 to exit 120, then 0.3 mi e. Located next to a shopping mall. 563 Rt 211 E 10940. Fax: 845/692-5828. **Facility:** 82 one-bedroom standard units. 2 stories (no elevator), interior corridors. **Parking:** on-site. **Terms:** 30 day cancellation notice, pets ($25 deposit). **Amenities:** *Some:* hair dryers. **Guest Services:** coin laundry. **Cards:** AX, DC, DS, MC, VI.

SOME UNITS
[ASK] [S][D] [🐾] [🍴] [📺] [DATA PORT] / [X] [🛗] [🖥] / FEE

——— The following lodging was either not evaluated or did not meet AAA rating requirements but is listed for your information only. ———

COURTYARD BY MARRIOTT
(fyi)
Small-scale Hotel

Phone: 845/695-0606
All Year   1P: $139-$189   2P: $139-$189
Too new to rate. **Location:** SR 17, exit 122, just ne. 24 Crystal Run Crossing 10941. Fax: 845/695-0607. **Amenities:** 134 units, coffeemakers, refrigerators, pool. **Cards:** AX, DC, DS, JC, MC, VI.

——— WHERE TO DINE ———

HANA
▼▼ ▼▼
Japanese

Lunch: $8-$17   **Dinner:** $12-$26   **Phone:** 845/342-6634
Location: SR 17, exit 120 westbound; exit 120 W eastbound, 1 mi w on SR 211. 339 Rt 211 E 10940. **Hours:** noon-10 pm, Fri & Sat-10:30 pm, Sun-9:30 pm. Closed: 11/25. **Reservations:** suggested, weekends. **Features:** A red brick base lines the bottom of the attractive, stone-sided building. Soft Japanese music plays in the background as diners enjoy traditional Japanese and Korean cuisine, including a nice array of sushi. The tatami room is available by reservation. Casual dress; cocktails. **Parking:** on-site. **Cards:** AX, MC, VI.

[🍸] [X]

MILTON pop. 1,251

——— WHERE TO DINE ———

SHIP LANTERN INN
(AAA)
▼▼ ▼▼
American

Lunch: $8-$20   **Dinner:** $15-$25   **Phone:** 845/795-5400
Location: Jct US 44 and SR 55, 4.3 mi s on US 9 W; at Mid-Hudson Bridge. 1725 Rt 9 W 12547. **Hours:** noon-2 & 5-9:30 pm, Sat 5 pm-10:30 pm, Sun 1 pm-8 pm. Closed: 12/24, 12/25; also Mon & 1/5-1/20. **Reservations:** suggested. **Features:** Three generations of the Foglia family have hosted guests. Their grandfather was a founding owner of Chef Boyardi, but they style the food served now as "New American." Traditional pasta such as spaghetti con vongole e cozze with mussels and clams. A new chef, Dana Calabrese, conjures up delectable caramelized salmon with braised spinach or filet of beef tenderloin with piquant salsa verde. The nautical decor, including ship models and lanterns, warms the dining room and cozy bar. Cocktails. **Parking:** on-site. **Cards:** AX, DC, DS, MC, VI.

[🍸] [X]

MINEOLA pop. 19,234

─── WHERE TO DINE ───

LA CISTERNA RESTAURANT **Lunch:** $13-$16 **Dinner:** $18-$24 **Phone:** 516/248-2112
▼▼▼
Italian
Location: SR 25, 1 mi s; just n of train station. 109 Mineola Blvd 11501. **Hours:** noon-3:30 & 5:30-10 pm. Closed: 1/1, 7/4, 12/25. **Reservations:** suggested. **Features:** Traditional dishes of pasta, veal, chicken and fish are served in a lovely dining room highlighted by walls of large, Renaissance-style faux oil paintings. Service is unobtrusive. Casual dress; cocktails. **Parking:** street. **Cards:** AX, DC, MC, VI.

MONTAUK pop. 3,851

─── WHERE TO STAY ───

MONTAUK YACHT CLUB RESORT & MARINA *Book at aaa.com* **Phone:** (631)668-3100

6/27-9/2	1P: $249-$459	2P: $249-$459	XP: $25	F
5/1-6/26 & 3/15-4/30	1P: $109-$329	2P: $109-$329	XP: $25	F
9/3-11/28	1P: $99-$319	2P: $99-$319	XP: $25	F

▼▼▼
Resort
Small-scale Hotel
Location: 1 mi e on SR 27, 2 mi n on W Lake Dr (CR 77), then just e. Located on the waterfront. 32 Star Island Rd 11954 (PO Box 5048). Fax: 631/668-6181. **Facility:** Some guests boat to this Star Island resort, where many of the beige-and-white rooms, each with a patio, overlook the marina. 107 units. 105 one-bedroom standard units. 2 one-bedroom suites. 2 stories (no elevator); interior corridors. **Parking:** on-site. **Terms:** open 5/1-11/28 & 3/15-4/30, check-in 4 pm, 2 night minimum stay - weekends & seasonal, cancellation fee imposed, weekly rates available, [AP], [BP], [CP], [ECP] & [MAP] meal plans available. **Amenities:** voice mail, safes, irons, hair dryers. **Pool(s):** 2 heated outdoor, small heated indoor. **Leisure Activities:** saunas, putting green, 9 tennis courts (4 lighted), playground, exercise room. *Fee:* marina, massage, game room. **Guest Services:** gift shop, coin laundry, area transportation. **Business Services:** meeting rooms. **Cards:** AX, DC, MC, VI.

SOME UNITS
[ASK] [❙❙] [Y] [▨] [✕] [DATA PORT] [❚] [▭] / [✕] /

─── WHERE TO DINE ───

GOSMAN'S DOCK **Lunch:** $14-$25 **Dinner:** $14-$25 **Phone:** 631/668-5330
▼▼ ▼▼
Seafood
Location: 1 mi e on SR 27, then 2.5 mi n on CR 77. 500 W Lake Dr 11954. **Hours:** Open 5/1-10/15 & 4/15-4/30; noon-10 pm. Closed: 10/11 & Tues 5/31-9/6. **Features:** From the flower-filled patio to the open dining dock, the setting here is perfect for a summer meal. The menu offers the sea's bounty, particularly excellent local lobster and Long Island produce, in traditional and modern dishes. Casual dress; cocktails.
Parking: on-site. **Cards:** AX, MC, VI. [Y] [✕]

SEA GRILL AT GURNEY'S INN **Dinner:** $18-$35 **Phone:** 631/668-2660
◈◈◈
▼▼▼
Italian
Location: 3 mi w; in Gurney's Inn Resort, Spa & Conference Center. 290 Old Montauk Hwy 11954. **Hours:** 5:30 pm-9 pm, Fri & Sat-10 pm. **Reservations:** suggested, in season. **Features:** Mouthwatering aromas hang in the air as the on-site bakery produces tempting fresh bread. Enjoy breathtaking views of the ocean from the modestly decorated dining room. The menu lists Internationally influenced entrees of fresh seafood and prime meat. Dressy casual; cocktails; entertainment. **Parking:** on-site and valet. **Cards:** AX, DC, DS, MC, VI. [Y] [✕]

MONTICELLO pop. 6,512

─── WHERE TO STAY ───

BEST WESTERN MONTICELLO *Book at aaa.com* **Phone:** (845)796-4000

5/1-9/18 [CP]	1P: $105-$165	2P: $105-$195	XP: $20	F12
9/19-4/30 [CP]	1P: $95-$155	2P: $105-$165	XP: $20	F12

◈◈◈ [SAVE]
▼▼ ▼▼
Small-scale Hotel
Location: SR 17, exit 104, 0.3 mi s on SR 17B. 16 Raceway Rd 12701. Fax: 845/796-4000. **Facility:** 62 one-bedroom standard units, some with whirlpools. 2 stories (no elevator); interior corridors. **Parking:** on-site, winter plug-ins. **Terms:** 2-3 night minimum stay - seasonal weekends. **Amenities:** voice mail, irons, hair dryers. **Pool(s):** small heated indoor. **Leisure Activities:** sauna. **Business Services:** meeting rooms. **Cards:** AX, CB, DC, DS, MC, VI. **Special Amenities:** free continental breakfast and free local telephone calls.

SOME UNITS
[❙❙+] [▨] [✕] [DATA PORT] [▭] / [✕] [❚] [▭] /
FEE FEE

─── WHERE TO DINE ───

HANA RESTAURANT **Lunch:** $5-$14 **Dinner:** $12-$20 **Phone:** 845/794-3700
▼▼▼ ▼▼▼
Japanese
Location: SR 17, exit 106 eastbound; exit 107 westbound. 166 Bridgeville Rd 12701. **Hours:** noon-10 pm, Fri & Sat-10:30 pm, Sun-9:30 pm. **Reservations:** suggested, weekends. **Features:** Deliciously fresh preparations of Japanese and Korean cuisine include sushi, sashimi and tempura. The Asian atmosphere is relaxing. Casual dress; cocktails. **Parking:** on-site. **Cards:** AX, MC, VI. [Y] [✕]

OLD HOMESTEAD RESTAURANT **Dinner:** $19-$38 **Phone:** 845/794-8973
▼▼ ▼▼
American
Location: SR 17, exit 107, 1 mi se. 472 Bridgeville Rd 12701. **Hours:** Open 5/1-3/14 & 4/16-4/30; 4:30 pm-9:30 pm, Fri & Sat-10 pm. Closed: 11/25, 12/25; also Mon & Tues 10/1-10/30. **Features:** For more than 40 years, delicious American fare has been served in a comfortable, homey and country-like setting. Generously plated food is prepared to the guest's liking. Homemade banana cream pie is to die for. Casual dress; cocktails. **Parking:** on-site. **Cards:** AX, DC, DS, MC, VI. [Y] [✕]

MONTOUR FALLS pop. 1,797—*See also FINGER LAKES.*

——— WHERE TO STAY ———

RELAX INN

(AAA) (SAVE)

◇◇◇

Motel

5/1-10/31	1P: $49-$79	2P: $59-$89	XP: $10
11/1-4/30	1P: $39-$49	2P: $39-$49	XP: $5

Phone: (607)535-7183
F10
F10

Location: Jct SR 14 and 224. Located in a residential area. 100 Clawson Blvd 14865. Fax: 607/535-6199. **Facility:** 12 one-bedroom standard units. 1 story, exterior corridors. *Bath:* combo or shower only. **Parking:** on-site. **Terms:** 3 day cancellation notice, weekly rates available, package plans - weekends, pets ($10 extra charge). **Cards:** AX, DC, MC, VI. **Special Amenities:** free local telephone calls and preferred room (subject to availability with advanced reservations).

SOME UNITS

[S/D] [dog] [phone] [icon] / [X] [fridge] /
FEE

——— WHERE TO DINE ———

CHEF'S DINER

◇◇◇

American

Lunch: $4-$7   **Dinner:** $4-$14   **Phone:** 607/535-9975

Location: 1 mi n; 2.4 mi s on SR 14 from Watkins Glen State Park entrance. Rt 14 Montour-Watkins Rd 14865. **Hours:** 6 am-10 pm; to 9 pm off season. Closed: 12/25. **Features:** An area institution since 1949, the family restaurant delivers a diverse menu of traditional favorites, ranging from salads, sandwiches and quiche to meatloaf and pork chops. Big portions and reasonable prices mean excellent value. Casual dress. **Parking:** on-site.

MOUNT KISCO —*See New York p. 453.*

MOUNT MORRIS pop. 3,266

——— WHERE TO STAY ———

COUNTRY INN AND SUITES   *Book at aaa.com*

◇◇◇◇

Small-scale Hotel

All Year	1P: $85	2P: $85-$144	XP: $10

Phone: (585)658-4080
F18

Location: On SR 36; center. 130 N Main St 14510. Fax: 585/658-4020. **Facility:** 60 units. 43 one-bedroom standard units, some with whirlpools. 17 one-bedroom suites. 2 stories, interior corridors. *Bath:* combo or shower only. **Parking:** on-site, winter plug-ins. **Terms:** [ECP] meal plan available. **Amenities:** voice mail, irons, hair dryers. **Pool(s):** small heated indoor. **Leisure Activities:** whirlpool, exercise room. **Guest Services:** coin laundry. **Business Services:** meeting rooms. **Cards:** AX, DC, DS, MC, VI. *(See color ad p 554)*

SOME UNITS

(ASK) [S/D] [phone] [icon] [icon] [icon] [icon] [DATA PORT] [icon] / [X] [fridge] [icon] /

MOUNT TREMPER

——— WHERE TO STAY ———

THE EMERSON INN & SPA   *Book at aaa.com*

◇◇◇ ◇◇◇

Historic
Small-scale Hotel

5/23-4/30 [MAP]	1P: $500-$1000	2P: $600-$1050
5/1-5/22 [MAP]	1P: $450-$1000	2P: $500-$1050

Phone: (845)688-7900

Location: Jct of CR 212, 0.9 mi w on SR 28. 146 Mt Pleasant Rd 12457 (5340 Rt 28). Fax: 845/688-2789. **Facility:** The rooms, themed to five styles of the 19th century, are exquisitely appointed and the well-trained staff are prepared to care for your every need. Designated smoking area. 24 units. 22 one-bedroom standard units, some with whirlpools. 2 one-bedroom suites ($900-$1500). 3 stories, interior corridors. **Parking:** on-site and valet. **Terms:** 2 night minimum stay - weekends, age restrictions may apply, 30 day cancellation notice-fee imposed, package plans - midweek & weekends, 18% service charge. **Amenities:** CD players, dual phone lines, safes, hair dryers. **Dining:** The Emerson, see separate listing. **Pool(s):** small heated indoor. **Leisure Activities:** saunas, whirlpool, steamrooms, exercise room, spa. **Guest Services:** complimentary evening beverages: afternoon tea 3-5 pm, area transportation. **Business Services:** fax. **Cards:** AX, MC, VI.

SOME UNITS

[icon] [icon] [icon] [icon] [X] [X] [DATA PORT] / [W] [VCR] /
FEE

——— WHERE TO DINE ———

THE EMERSON Historic

◇◇◇ ◇◇◇

Continental

Lunch: $14-$22   **Dinner:** $22-$32   **Phone:** 845/688-7900

Location: Jct of CR 212, 0.9 mi w on SR 28; in The Emerson Inn & Spa. 146 Mt Pleasant Rd 12457. **Hours:** 8-10:30 am, 12:30-2 & 6:30-9:30 pm. **Reservations:** suggested. **Features:** Casual elegance combined with accomplished service and exquisitely prepared food bring guests a dining experience unsurpassed in the area. From cocktails in the lounge surrounded by Persian-African inspired decor to succulent entrees such as chargrilled tuna steak nicoise, the restaurant delights at every turn. Dressy casual; cocktails. **Parking:** on-site and valet. **Cards:** AX, DS, MC, VI.

[Y] [X]

MOUNT UPTON

——— WHERE TO DINE ———

THE OLD MILL

◇◇◇

American

Dinner: $12-$25   **Phone:** 607/764-8300

Location: Jct SR 51, 1.5 mi n. Rt 8 13809. **Hours:** Open 5/1-11/28 & 3/29-4/30; 4:30 pm-9 pm, Sun noon-7:30 pm; hours may vary 11/1-11/30. Closed: 12/25; also Mon. **Reservations:** suggested. **Features:** The converted old mill, featuring tables set with hand-painted china, sits alongside the river and affords beautiful views. Such dishes as the signature chicken Old Mill are well-prepared, tasty and served in ample portions. Homemade desserts are a treat. Casual dress; cocktails. **Parking:** on-site. **Cards:** AX, DS, MC, VI.

[X]

NANUET —*See New York p. 453.*

NAPLES pop. 1,072—See also *FINGER LAKES.*

────── WHERE TO DINE ──────

REDWOOD RESTAURANT   **Lunch:** $4-$8   **Dinner:** $10-$15   **Phone:** 585/374-6360
Location: 0.5 mi s on SR 21. 6 Cohocton St 14512. **Hours:** 6 am-8 pm, Fri & Sat-9 pm. Closed: 12/25.
Reservations: suggested, weekends. **Features:** Many windows let in lots of light at the bright,
American   family-oriented restaurant. The menu includes seafood and steak, as well as soup, sandwiches and Italian
entrees. The Friday fish fry is popular, as are the delicious and tempting homemade dessert. Casual dress;
cocktails. **Parking:** on-site. **Cards:** MC, VI.

NEWBURGH pop. 28,259

────── WHERE TO STAY ──────

CLARION HOTEL   *Book at aaa.com*   **Phone:** (845)564-9020

5/1-11/1	1P: $105-$199	2P: $115-$199	XP: $10
11/2-4/30	1P: $95-$199	2P: $105-$199	XP: $10

Location: I-87, exit 17, then w; I-84, exit 6, 2 mi e. 90 Rt 17K 12550. Fax: 845/564-9040. **Facility:** 122 units. 121
one-bedroom standard units. 1 one-bedroom suite. 2 stories (no elevator), interior/exterior corridors.
Small-scale Hotel   **Parking:** on-site, winter plug-ins. **Terms:** cancellation fee imposed. **Amenities:** video games, irons, hair
dryers. **Dining:** 6:30 am-9:30 & 5-9 pm, cocktails. **Pool(s):** outdoor. **Leisure Activities:** exercise room.
Guest Services: valet laundry, airport transportation-Stewart International Airport. **Business Services:** conference facilities,
business center. **Cards:** AX, DS, MC, VI.
SOME UNITS / FEE

COMFORT INN NEWBURGH   *Book at aaa.com*   **Phone:** (845)567-0567

5/25-11/15 & 4/15-4/30 [ECP]	1P: $103-$112	2P: $103-$112	XP: $6	F18
5/1-5/24 [ECP]	1P: $99-$112	2P: $99-$112	XP: $6	F18
11/16-4/14 [ECP]	1P: $99-$109	2P: $99-$109	XP: $6	F18

Location: I-84, exit 6, just w. 5 Lakeside Rd 12550. Fax: 845/567-0582. **Facility:** 130 one-bedroom standard
units, some with whirlpools. 3 stories, interior corridors. **Parking:** on-site, winter plug-ins. **Terms:** cancellation fee imposed.
Amenities: irons, hair dryers. **Pool(s):** outdoor. **Leisure Activities:** exercise room. **Guest Services:** coin laundry. **Business
Services:** meeting rooms, fax (fee). **Cards:** AX, CB, DC, DS, MC, VI.
SOME UNITS / FEE

COURTYARD BY MARRIOTT STEWART/NEWBURGH   *Book at aaa.com*   **Phone:** (845)567-4800
All Year   1P: $104-$150
Location: I-84, exit 6. Located in Stewart International Airport Industrial Park. 4 Governor Dr 12550.
Fax: 845/567-9550. **Facility:** 78 units. 70 one-bedroom standard units. 8 one-bedroom suites. 3 stories, in-
Small-scale Hotel   terior corridors. *Bath:* combo or shower only. **Parking:** on-site. **Amenities:** video games, high-speed Internet,
dual phone lines, voice mail, irons, hair dryers. **Pool(s):** small heated indoor. **Leisure Activities:** whirlpool, exercise room. **Guest
Services:** coin laundry. **Business Services:** meeting rooms, fax. **Cards:** AX, DC, DS, MC, VI.
SOME UNITS

HAMPTON INN-NEWBURGH   *Book at aaa.com*   **Phone:** (845)567-9100
All Year   1P: $99-$249   2P: $99-$249   XP: $6   F12
Location: I-87, exit 17, w to SR 300 (Union Ave), just n; I-84, exit 7S. 1292 SR 300 (Union Ave) 12550.
Small-scale Hotel   Fax: 845/567-6331. **Facility:** 116 one-bedroom standard units. 2 stories, interior corridors. *Bath:* combo or
shower only. **Parking:** on-site. **Terms:** [ECP] meal plan available. **Amenities:** video games, voice mail, irons,
hair dryers. *Some:* DVD players. **Pool(s):** heated indoor. **Leisure Activities:** whirlpool, exercise room. **Guest Services:** valet
laundry. **Business Services:** meeting rooms. **Cards:** AX, CB, DC, DS, MC, VI.
SOME UNITS / FEE

HOWARD JOHNSON INN   _Book at aaa.com_   Phone: (845)564-4000

AAA SAVE   5/1-11/20 [ECP]   1P: $69-$129   2P: $69-$129   XP: $8   F17
▼▼▼   11/21-4/30 [ECP]   1P: $59-$109   2P: $59-$109   XP: $8   F17
         Location: I-87, exit 17, just w; I-84, exit 7S westbound to SR 17K W; exit 6 eastbound, 2 mi e. 95 Rt 17k 12550.
         Fax: 845/564-0620. **Facility:** 74 one-bedroom standard units. 2 stories (no elevator), interior corridors.
Small-scale Hotel **Parking:** on-site, winter plug-ins. **Amenities:** video library (fee), voice mail, irons, hair dryers. **Pool(s):** out-
         door, wading. **Leisure Activities:** tennis court. **Guest Services:** coin laundry, airport transportation-Stewart
International Airport. **Business Services:** meeting rooms, fax. **Cards:** AX, CB, DC, DS, MC, VI. **Special Amenities: free ex-
panded continental breakfast and free local telephone calls.** _(See color ad below & p 218)_

SOME UNITS
[S☐] [✈] [†|] [🍴] [+↑] [⚓] [🎥] [DATA PORT] [💻] / [✕] [VCR] [🛏] [☕] /
                                                          FEE FEE FEE

RAMADA INN & SUITES   _Book at aaa.com_   Phone: (845)564-4500

▼▼▼▼   All Year [ECP]   1P: $95-$99   2P: $95-$99   XP: $10   F18
         Location: I-87, exit 17 via SR 17K W to SR 300 (Union Ave), just n; I-84, exit 7S. 1289 Rt 300 (Union Ave) 12550.
         Fax: 845/564-4524. **Facility:** 164 units. 125 one-bedroom standard units. 39 one-bedroom suites ($135-
Small-scale Hotel $250), some with whirlpools. 2 stories (no elevator), interior corridors. **Parking:** on-site. **Amenities:** voice
mail, irons, hair dryers. **Pool(s):** outdoor. **Leisure Activities:** exercise room. **Guest Services:** coin laundry. **Business Services:**
conference facilities. **Cards:** AX, DS, MC, VI.

SOME UNITS
[ASK] [S☐] [✈] [†|] [🍸] [⚓] [🎥] [DATA PORT] [💻] / [✕] [🛏] /
                                                          FEE

------- **WHERE TO DINE** -------

CENA 2000   **Lunch:** $13-$19   **Dinner:** $15-$24   **Phone:** 845/561-7676
▼▼▼   **Location:** Jct US 9, 0.7 mi e on Broadway, just ne on Washington Pl, then just s. 50 Front St 12550. **Hours:** noon-3
         & 5-10 pm, Fri & Sat-11 pm. **Closed:** 11/25, 12/25. **Reservations:** accepted. **Features:** On the trendy
Italian   waterfront, the eatery serves traditional Tuscan dishes, and daily specials are sure to entice. The patio
         overlooks the Hudson. Casual dress; cocktails. **Parking:** on-site. **Cards:** AX, MC, VI.   [🍸] [✕]

IL CENA'COLO

▼▼▼▼

Northern
Italian

DC, MC, VI.

Lunch: $10-$22   **Dinner:** $15-$26   **Phone:** 845/564-4494

Location: Jct SR 300 and 52, just w on SR 52. 228 S Plank Rd (SR 52) 12550. **Hours:** noon-2:30 & 5-9 pm, Fri & Sat 6 pm-11 pm, Sun 4 pm-9 pm. Closed major holidays; also Tues. **Reservations:** suggested. **Features:** An outstanding example of true Tuscan cuisine is the ravioli, which is stuffed with cheese and spinach, with pureed mushrooms in cream sauce. The wine list concentrates exclusively on Italian selections. Melt-in-your-mouth dessert is homemade. Casual dress; cocktails. **Parking:** on-site. **Cards:** AX,

---

TORCHES ON THE HUDSON

▼▼▼▼

American

Lunch: $8-$14   **Dinner:** $12-$21   **Phone:** 845/568-0100

Location: Jct US 9, 0.7 mi e on Broadway, just ne on Washington Pl, then just n. 120 Front St 12550. **Hours:** 11 am-4 & 4:30-10 pm, Fri & Sat noon-4 & 4:30-11 pm, Sun noon-10 pm. Closed: 12/25. **Reservations:** required. **Features:** Guests can come by car or boat—dockage is available—to the fresh and popular riverfront restaurant. Contemporary dishes, such as panko-encrusted crab cakes and oak-fired chicken breast, are complemented by friendly and efficient service. Entertainers perform on weekends. Dressy casual; cocktails; entertainment. **Parking:** on-site. **Cards:** AX, CB, DC, DS, JC, MC, VI.

YOBO ORIENTAL RESTAURANT

▼▼▼▼

Asian

Lunch: $5-$10   **Dinner:** $10-$23   **Phone:** 845/564-3848

Location: I-87, exit 17 to SR 300 via SR 17K W, then just n. 1297 SR 300 12550. **Hours:** 11:30 am-10 pm, Fri-11 pm, Sat 12:30 pm-11 pm, Sun 12:30 pm-10 pm. Closed: 11/25. **Reservations:** accepted. **Features:** Despite covering broad territory, the menu does a good job with cuisines of China, Japan, Thailand, Korea and Indonesia. Among selections are sushi, sashimi, tempura, dim sum and Korean bolgogi. The wait staff provides capable, well-executed service. Casual dress; cocktails. **Parking:** on-site. **Cards:** AX, MC, VI.

NEWFANE —See Niagara Falls p. 481.

NEW HAMPTON

———— WHERE TO STAY ————

DAYS INN

▼▼▼ ▼▼

Motel

Book at aaa.com

All Year [CP]   **Phone:** (845)374-2411

1P: $59-$119   2P: $59-$119   XP: $10   F12

Location: I-84, 0.8 mi e on US 6 and SR 17M. 4939 Rt 17M 10958 (PO Box 279). Fax: 845/374-0011. **Facility:** 45 one-bedroom standard units. 1-2 stories (no elevator), interior/exterior corridors. *Bath:* combo or shower only. **Parking:** on-site, winter plug-ins. **Terms:** pets (in designated units). **Amenities:** hair dryers. *Some:* irons. Pool(s): outdoor. **Cards:** AX, CB, DC, DS, MC, VI.

NEW HARTFORD pop. 1,886

———— WHERE TO STAY ————

HOLIDAY INN UTICA

▼▼▼▼

Small-scale Hotel

Book at aaa.com

7/1-10/31	1P: $149-$169	2P: $149-$169
11/1-4/30	1P: $129-$139	2P: $129-$139
5/1-6/30	1P: $139	2P: $139

Phone: (315)797-2131

Location: I-90 (New York Thruway), exit 31, 4.5 mi w on SR 5 W and 12 S, exit Burrstone Rd, then 1 mi nw. 1777 Burrstone Rd 13413. Fax: 315/797-5817. **Facility:** 100 units. 96 one-bedroom standard units. 4 one-bedroom suites ($159-$229) with kitchens. 2 stories (no elevator), interior/exterior corridors. *Bath:* combo or shower only. **Parking:** on-site, winter plug-ins. **Terms:** small pets only. **Amenities:** video games, high-speed Internet, irons, hair dryers. Pool(s): outdoor. **Leisure Activities:** whirlpool, exercise room. *Fee:* game room. **Guest Services:** sundries, valet and coin laundry. **Business Services:** conference facilities. **Cards:** AX, CB, DC, DS, JC, MC, VI.

RAMADA INN

AAA SAVE

▼▼ ▼▼

Small-scale Hotel

(See color ad p 8)

Book at aaa.com

5/1-10/31	1P: $103-$139	2P: $110-$139	XP: $7	F16
11/1-4/30	1P: $84-$129	2P: $89-$129	XP: $7	F16

Phone: (315)735-3392

Location: SR 8, 12 and 5, exit New York Mills. 141 New Hartford St 13413. Fax: 315/738-7642. **Facility:** 104 units. 102 one-bedroom standard units. 2 one-bedroom suites. 2 stories (no elevator), interior corridors. **Parking:** on-site. **Terms:** cancellation fee imposed, [AP], [BP], [CP], [ECP] & [MAP] meal plans available. **Amenities:** voice mail, irons, hair dryers. **Dining:** 6:30 am-1 & 5-10 pm, Sun 7 am-1 pm, cocktails. Pool(s): heated outdoor. **Guest Services:** valet laundry. **Business Services:** meeting rooms. **Cards:** AX, DC, DS, MC, VI. **Special Amenities:** free newspaper and free room upgrade (subject to availability with advanced reservations).

———— WHERE TO DINE ————

CARMELLA'S CAFE

▼▼▼ ▼▼▼

American

Lunch: $5-$11   **Dinner:** $6-$14   **Phone:** 315/797-3350

Location: 0.5 mi w on SR 5. 8530 Seneca Tpke 13413. **Hours:** 11 am-1 am, Sun from 9 am. Closed: 11/25, 12/25. **Reservations:** accepted. **Features:** A festive mood prevails in the energized dining room, which is decorated with eclectic antiques. Chicken riggies, which blends rigatoni noodles, charbroiled chicken, mushrooms, peppers, olives and onions, has long been a favorite dinner selection. Casual dress; cocktails. **Parking:** on-site. **Cards:** AX, CB, DC, DS, MC, VI.

HOOK, LINE & SINKER PUB

Seafood

Lunch: $5-$7   **Dinner:** $11-$16   **Phone:** 315/732-3636

Location: SR 12 and 5 W, 0.8 mi w on SR 5. 8471 Seneca Tpke 13413. **Hours:** 11:30 am-3 & 4:30-10 pm, Sun 1 pm-9 pm. **Closed:** 11/25, 12/25. **Reservations:** suggested, weekends. **Features:** Casual dining is the bait for families, groups and those looking for hearty meals and tasty desserts, all served with a smile. Although the fish displayed on the walls might subtly lead you to choose a seafood entree, at least consider the beef, chicken, vegetarian and pasta choices. The grilled portobello sandwich is a delectable, juicy "two-napkin" selection. Choose prime rib in servings from a half-pound up to a full pound. Crispy salad and tummy-warming soup fill out any meal. Casual dress; cocktails. **Parking:** on-site. **Cards:** AX, CB, DC, DS, MC, VI.

MICHAEL T'S

Italian

Dinner: $7-$15   **Phone:** 315/724-4882

Location: Jct SR 12 and 5 W, 1 mi w on SR 5. 8390 Seneca Tpke 13413. **Hours:** 4 pm-9 pm, Fri & Sat-10 pm, Sun 3 pm-9 pm. Closed major holidays. **Reservations:** accepted. **Features:** Representative of regional Italian specialties are "greens," which are not salads but tasty blends of cooked escarole with spicy Italian meats. Haddock delivered fresh daily along with certified Angus beef make options in the casual atmosphere a delight. Friendly, familiar service place diners at ease to enjoy any number of traditional pasta, seafood, chicken and beef dishes. Casual dress; cocktails. **Parking:** on-site. **Cards:** AX, DS, MC, VI.

THE PHOENICIAN RESTAURANT

Lebanese

Lunch: $4-$7   **Dinner:** $7-$16   **Phone:** 315/733-2709

Location: I-90 (New York Thruway), exit 31, 4.5 mi w on SR 5 W and 12 S, exit Burrstone Rd, just ne. 623 French Rd 13413. **Hours:** 11 am-10 pm. **Closed:** 11/25, 12/24, 12/25; also Sun. **Reservations:** accepted. **Features:** The restaurant offers authentic Lebanese fare made with only the freshest ingredients - no canned or preserved foods. Exotic spices bring out the full flavor of meats and fish. Casual dress; beer & wine only. **Parking:** on-site. **Cards:** AX, MC, VI.

NEW LEBANON pop. 2,454

———— WHERE TO DINE ————

MARIO'S RESTAURANT

Northern Italian

Dinner: $14-$22   **Phone:** 518/794-9495

Location: Jct US 20 and SR 22, just n on SR 22. **Hours:** 4 pm-9:30 pm, Fri & Sat-10 pm, Sun-9 pm. **Closed:** 11/25, 12/25; also Tues. **Reservations:** suggested. **Features:** The restaurant's pleasant wait staff serves a fine selection of traditional and seasonal Northern Italian dishes, including preparations of pasta, veal, seafood and chicken. Enjoy the serene mountain setting and the elegant surroundings. Casual dress; cocktails. **Parking:** on-site. **Cards:** AX, CB, DC, DS, MC, VI.

———— *The following restaurant has not been evaluated by AAA* ———— *but is listed for your information only.*

FRESCO'S

fyi

Phone: 518/794-9339

Not evaluated. **Location:** Jct SR 20 and 22. **Features:** Famous for their wood-fired pizza, this casual restaurant also offers all popular Italian favorites.

NEW PALTZ pop. 6,034

——— WHERE TO STAY ———

ECONO LODGE *Book at aaa.com* Phone: 845/255-6200
(AAA) SAVE
▼▼▼ ▼▼▼
Motel

| 5/1-10/31 [CP] | 1P: $71-$129 | 2P: $71-$129 | XP: $6 | F17 |
| 11/1-4/30 [CP] | 1P: $61-$99 | 2P: $61-$99 | XP: $6 | F17 |

Location: I-87, exit 18, 0.5 mi e on SR 299. 530 Main St 12561. Fax: 845/256-0675. **Facility:** 34 one-bedroom standard units. 2 stories (no elevator), interior/exterior corridors. *Bath:* combo or shower only. **Parking:** on-site, winter plug-ins. **Pool(s):** outdoor. **Business Services:** fax (fee). **Cards:** AX, DC, DS, MC, VI. **Special Amenities:** free continental breakfast.

SOME UNITS

⌂ 🏊 ⊕ DATA PORT / ✕ 🖥 /

SUPER 8 MOTEL OF NEW PALTZ Phone: 845/255-8865
▼▼▼ ▼▼▼
Motel

| All Year | 1P: $50-$175 | 2P: $50-$175 |

Location: I-87, exit 18, just w. 7 Terwilliger Ln 12561. Fax: 845/255-1629. **Facility:** 69 one-bedroom standard units, some with whirlpools. 2 stories (no elevator), interior corridors. **Parking:** on-site, winter plug-ins. **Amenities:** voice mail, hair dryers. **Cards:** AX, DC, DS, MC, VI.

SOME UNITS

ASK ⌂ ⊕ DATA PORT 🖥 / ✕ 🖥 /

The following lodging was either not evaluated or did not meet AAA rating requirements but is listed for your information only.

MOHONK MOUNTAIN HOUSE Phone: 845/255-1000
[fyi] Not evaluated. **Location:** 1000 Mountain Rest Rd 12561. Facilities, services, and decor characterize a mid-range property.

——— WHERE TO DINE ———

RISTORANTE LOCUST TREE Historic **Dinner:** $15-$28 Phone: 845/255-7888
▼▼▼ ▼▼▼
Italian

Location: I-87, exit 18, 1.5 mi w on SR 299, n just before bridge, then 1.3 mi on Huguenot St; on public golf course. 215 Huguenot St 12561. **Hours:** 5:30 pm-10 pm, Sun-9 pm. Closed: 1/1, 11/25, 12/25; also Mon & Tues. **Reservations:** suggested. **Features:** A new chef-owner has melded a pleasant combination of contemporary Italian cuisine and charming atmosphere. The 1759 stone house has a summer patio for leisurely dining and intimate rooms with fireplaces and flower-filled windows. Accomplished servers bring eye-catching dishes from Chef Vanoli's kitchen. Dressy casual; cocktails. **Parking:** on-site. **Cards:** AX, DC, MC, VI.

✕

NEW ROCHELLE —*See New York p. 454.*

NEW WINDSOR pop. 9,077

——— WHERE TO STAY ———

DAYS INN NEWBURGH *Book at aaa.com* Phone: (845)564-7550
(AAA) SAVE
▼▼▼ ▼▼▼
Small-scale Hotel

| 5/1-11/15 [CP] | 1P: $77-$102 | 2P: $77-$102 | XP: $6 | F12 |
| 11/16-4/30 [CP] | 1P: $65-$85 | 2P: $65-$85 | XP: $6 | F12 |

Location: On SR 300, just s, follow signs for Stewart International Airport; I-84, exit 7 southbound; I-87, exit 17 via SR 17K W to SR 300, 1 mi s. 915 Union Ave (SR 300) 12553. Fax: 845/564-7560. **Facility:** 97 one-bedroom standard units. 2 stories, interior corridors. *Bath:* combo or shower only. **Parking:** on-site, winter plug-ins. **Amenities:** voice mail, hair dryers. **Pool(s):** heated indoor. **Guest Services:** coin laundry. **Business Services:** fax (fee). **Cards:** AX, DC, DS, MC, VI. **Special Amenities:** free continental breakfast and free newspaper. *(See ad p 352)*

SOME UNITS

⌂ 🍴 ♿ 🏊 ⊕ / ✕ 🖥 /
FEE

WINDSOR MOTEL Phone: (845)562-7777
(AAA) SAVE
▼▼▼ ▼▼▼
Motel

5/1-11/15 [ECP]	1P: $49-$149	2P: $49-$149	XP: $10	F12
3/2-4/30 [ECP]	1P: $49-$99	2P: $49-$99	XP: $10	F12
11/16-3/1 [ECP]	1P: $45-$99	2P: $45-$119	XP: $10	F12

Location: Jct SR 17K and 32, 2.4 mi s. 2976 Rt 9W 12553. Fax: 845/562-7889. **Facility:** 30 one-bedroom standard units. 1 story, exterior corridors. *Bath:* combo or shower only. **Parking:** on-site. **Terms:** 2-5 night minimum stay - seasonal, 14 day cancellation notice-fee imposed, weekly rates available. **Amenities:** *Some:* high-speed Internet. **Business Services:** fax. **Cards:** AX, DS, MC, VI. **Special Amenities:** free expanded continental breakfast and early check-in/late check-out. *(See ad p 353)*

SOME UNITS

⌂ ⊕ DATA PORT 🖥 / ✕ VCR 🖥 /
FEE

——— WHERE TO DINE ———

JOHNNY D'S **Lunch:** $4-$8 **Dinner:** $7-$19 Phone: 845/567-1600
▼▼▼ ▼▼▼
American
DC, DS, MC, VI.

Location: I-87, exit 17 via SR 17K, w to SR 300, 2 mi s. 909 Union Ave (SR 300) 12553. **Hours:** 24 hours. **Features:** The charming 1950s-style diner is all chrome and neon, with Coca Cola memorabilia and lots of windows that overlook the lake. The 15-page menu includes a little bit of everything, from eggs to lobster tail. Tempting desserts are made on the premises. Casual dress; cocktails. **Parking:** on-site. **Cards:** AX,

🍸 ✕

SCHLESINGER'S STEAK HOUSE **Lunch:** $7-$23 **Dinner:** $14-$33 Phone: 845/561-1762
▼▼▼ ▼▼▼
Steak & Seafood

Location: 2 mi s on SR 300. 475 Temple Hill Rd 12553. **Hours:** 11:30 am-9 pm, Fri-10 pm, Sat 4:30 pm-10 pm, Sun 3 pm-9 pm. Closed major holidays. **Reservations:** accepted. **Features:** Casual dining in the steakhouse's historic atmosphere makes for a relaxed evening. The house, dating from 1762, has picturesque stone walls and beam ceilings. Steak and ribs are house specialties, as are the Rocky Mountain mashed potatoes. Seafood and pasta choices cater to diverse taste buds. Lighter fare is offered at lunch, along with the steaks. Casual dress; cocktails. **Parking:** on-site. **Cards:** AX, CB, DC, DS, MC, VI.

🍸 ✕

Look for the Signs of Approval

When you're on the road, look for lodgings that display the AAA Approved sign. It's your sign that the property works hard to win AAA member business. In fact, these properties offer AAA members great room rates*.

When you see AAA Approved signs, you know you've arrived.

* See TourBook Navigator, page 14, for complete details.

Destination New York City
pop. 8,008,278

Skyline.
A sax and a skyline suggest a New York state of mind.

From pastrami and corned beef on rye to spicy Indian curry, the Big Apple dishes up varied cuisine.

Take a bite out of New York and visit Little Italy for eggplant, *parmigiana*, or Chinatown for dim sum. While in Harlem, stop for some soul food, or grab a slice of pizza at one of the city's many pizzerias. Don't forget about New York's favorite street fare—jumbo hot dogs, giant soft pretzels and bags of roasted chestnuts—all served from pushcarts.

Spring Valley

Suffern

© NYC & Company, Inc.

Dining, New York-style.
There's a place to suit any pace or taste—inside and elegant, outside and casual, or curbside on-the-run.

Places included in this AAA Destination City:

Ice skating, Central Park.
Wollman Rink is one of two
places in the park where
skaters can glide across
sparkling ice day or night.
(See mention page 143)

© Michael S. Yamashita
Corbis

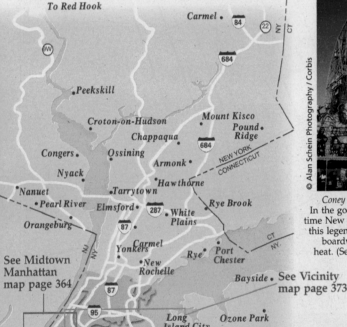

To Red Hook

Carmel

84

22

NY
CT

684

Peekskill

Croton-on-Hudson

Mount Kisco
Pound
Ridge

Chappaqua

684

Congers

Ossining

Armonk

NEW YORK
CONNECTICUT

Nyack

Hawthorne

Nanuet

Tarrytown

Pearl River

Elmsford

287

Rye Brook

White
Plains

Orangeburg

87

Carmel

CT
NY

See Midtown
Manhattan
map page 364

Yonkers

Rye

Port
Chester

New
Rochelle

Bayside

See Vicinity
map page 373

87

Long
Island City

Ozone Park

95

495

New York City

678

278

See Lower Manhattan
map page 360

© Alan Schein Photography / Corbis

Coney Island, Brooklyn.
In the good ole summer-
time New Yorkers head to
this legendary beach and
boardwalk to beat the
heat. (See mention page
143)

© Julie Lemberger / Corbis

Performing arts.
The art of dance finds many forms of
expression in New York City, from classical ballet to performances by imaginative, avant-garde troupes.

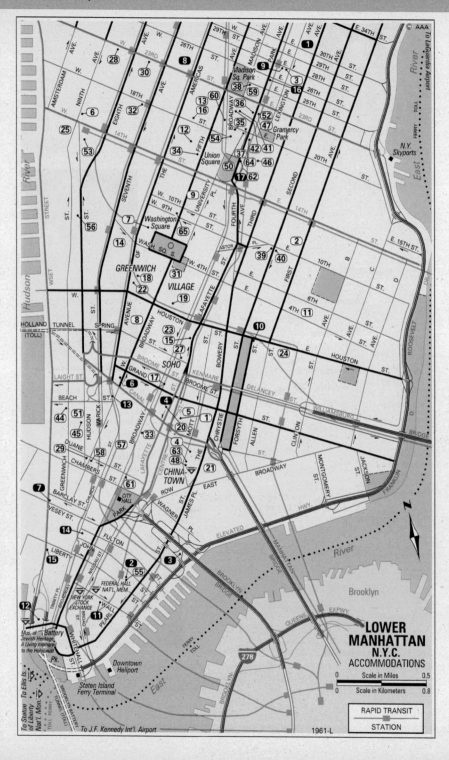

© AAA

To LaGuardia Airport

LOWER
MANHATTAN
N.Y.C.
ACCOMMODATIONS

Scale in Miles
0   0.5

Scale in Kilometers
0   0.8

RAPID TRANSIT

STATION

1961-L

Lower Manhattan

This index helps you "spot" where approved accommodations and restaurants are located on the corresponding detailed maps. Lodging rate ranges are for comparison only and show the property's high season; rates are per night, unless only weekly (W) rates are available. Restaurant rate range is for dinner, unless only lunch (L) is served. Turn to the listing page for more detailed rate information and consult display ads for special promotions.

Spotter/Map Page Number	OA	LOWER MANHATTAN - Lodgings	Diamond Rating	Rate Range High Season	Listing Page
1 / p. 360		Ramada Inn Eastside	2	$169-$199	379
2 / p. 360		Holiday Inn Wall Street Hotel	3	$249-$369	378
3 / p. 360	AAA	**Best Western Seaport Inn, New York** - see color ad p 376	3	$209-$240 SAVE	376
4 / p. 360		Holiday Inn Downtown	3	$229-$279	376
6 / p. 360		The SoHo Grand Hotel	3	Failed to provide	379
7 / p. 360		Embassy Suites Hotel New York - see color ad card insert	3	$179-$359	376
8 / p. 360	AAA	**Hampton Inn Chelsea** - see color ad p 401	3	$196-$224 SAVE	376
9 / p. 360		Park South Hotel	3	$255	379
10 / p. 360	AAA	**Howard Johnson Express Inn** - see color ad p 218	2	$109-$219 SAVE	378
11 / p. 360		The Regent Wall Street	4	$550	379
12 / p. 360	AAA	**The Ritz-Carlton New York, Battery Park**	5	$475 SAVE	379
13 / p. 360		Tribeca Grand Hotel	3	Failed to provide	379
14 / p. 360	AAA	**Millenium Hilton** - see color ad card insert	4	$179-$499 SAVE	378
15 / p. 360		Marriott Financial Center Hotel	3	$259-$349	378
16 / p. 360		Hotel Giraffe	3	$365-$425	378
17 / p. 360		W New York-Union Square	4	$599-$1900	379
		LOWER MANHATTAN - Restaurants			
1 / p. 360		Il Cortile	3	$15-$24	382
2 / p. 360		Cyclo	2	$8-$15	381
3 / p. 360		I Trulli	3	$19-$32	382
4 / p. 360		Sweet-n-Tart Cafe	1	$3-$9	386
5 / p. 360		Sal Anthony's S P Q R	2	$16-$25	385
6 / p. 360		The Old Homestead	2	$21-$38	384
7 / p. 360		Babbo	4	$16-$28	380
8 / p. 360		Montrachet	3	$24-$30	383
9 / p. 360		Gotham Bar & Grill	4	$28-$41	382
11 / p. 360		Mamlouk	2	$30	383
12 / p. 360		AZ	3	$45	380
13 / p. 360		Periyali	3	$18-$29	385
14 / p. 360		One If By Land, Two If By Sea	4	$59	384
15 / p. 360		Savoy Restaurant	2	$18-$26	385
16 / p. 360		City Bakery	1	$8-$16	381
17 / p. 360		L'Ecole, the Restaurant of the French Culinary Institute	3	$30	383
18 / p. 360	AAA	**Monte's Restaurant**	2	$8-$22	383
19 / p. 360		Il Mulino	3	$25-$45	382
20 / p. 360		Pacifica	2	$15-$25	384
21 / p. 360		Canton	2	$20-$45	381

Spotter/Map Page Number	OA	LOWER MANHATTAN - Restaurants (continued)	Diamond Rating	Rate Range High Season	Listing Page
㉒ / p. 360	AAA	**Villa Mosconi Restaurant**	♦♦	$11-$27	386
㉓ / p. 360	AAA	**Zoe Restaurant**	♦♦	$18-$29	387
㉔ / p. 360		Katz Deli	♦	$8-$16	382
㉕ / p. 360		Pastis	♦♦	$11-$34	384
㉗ / p. 360		Balthazar	♦♦♦	$15-$24	380
㉘ / p. 360		Chelsea Bistro & Bar	♦♦♦	$18-$25	381
㉙ / p. 360		Danube	♦♦♦♦	$28-$35	381
㉚ / p. 360		El Quijote Restaurant	♦♦	$10-$30	382
㉛ / p. 360		Bond St.	♦♦♦♦	$18-$26	381
㉜ / p. 360		le Madri	♦♦♦	$16-$30	383
㉝ / p. 360		Layla	♦♦	$18-$26	382
㉞ / p. 360		Mesa Grill	♦♦♦	$18-$32	383
㉟ / p. 360		Old Town Bar & Restaurant	♦	$7-$10	384
㊱ / p. 360		Patria	♦♦♦	$20-$32	384
㊲ / p. 360		Veritas	♦♦♦	$68	386
㊳ / p. 360		Tabla	♦♦♦	$23-$35	386
㊴ / p. 360		Rectangles	♦♦	$11-$16	385
㊵ / p. 360		Second Avenue Kosher Deli	♦	$15-$23	385
㊶ / p. 360		Beppe	♦♦♦	$17-$29	380
㊷ / p. 360		Tamarind	♦♦♦	$13-$23	386
㊹ / p. 360		Tribeca Grill	♦♦♦	$17-$29	386
㊺ / p. 360		Chanterelle	♦♦♦♦	$84-$95	381
㊻ / p. 360		Verbena	♦♦♦	$18-$29	386
㊼ / p. 360		Novita	♦♦	$12-$21	384
㊽ / p. 360		Ping's	♦♦	$20-$40	385
㊿ / p. 360		Gramercy Tavern	♦♦♦♦	$68-$95	382
(51) / p. 360		Nobu	♦♦♦♦	$12-$25	384
(52) / p. 360		Union Pacific	♦♦♦♦	$68	386
(53) / p. 360		Meet	♦♦♦	$16-$28	383
(54) / p. 360		Pipa	♦♦	$10-$25	385
(55) / p. 360		L'Orto Ristorante Elegante	♦♦	$18-$23	383
(56) / p. 360	AAA	**Alfama, Fine Portuguese Cuisine**	♦♦♦	$18-$26	380
(57) / p. 360		66	♦♦♦	$19-$38	380
(58) / p. 360		Bouley	♦♦♦♦	$34-$38	381
(59) / p. 360		Eleven Madison Park	♦♦♦♦	$22-$28	381
(60) / p. 360		Fleur de Sel	♦♦♦	$28-$33	382
(61) / p. 360		NAM	♦♦	$10-$16	383
(62) / p. 360		Olives	♦♦♦	$22-$29	384
(63) / p. 360		Peking Duck House	♦♦	$12-$34	385
(64) / p. 360		SushiSamba Park	♦♦	$17-$26	385
(65) / p. 360		Washington Park	♦♦♦	$26-$29	386

USED   CERTIFIED PRE-OWNED

When you purchase a Ford Quality Checked Certified Pre-owned vehicle, Lincoln Premier

Certified Pre-owned vehicle or a Mercury Certified Pre-owned vehicle, you'll get more than

a great deal. You'll get up to 141 points of inspection by certified technicians, a vehicle history

report, 24-hour roadside assistance and 6-year/75,000-mile limited warranty coverage.*

All backed by Ford Motor Company. Why risk it? Visit your Ford or Lincoln-Mercury

Dealer today for a Certified Pre-owned vehicle. It's really the safe choice.

**For a Certified Pre-owned dealer and special financing options,
visit www. fordcpo.com or call 866-222-6798.**

IF IT'S NOT CERTIFIED, IT'S JUST USED.
*See dealer for warranty details.

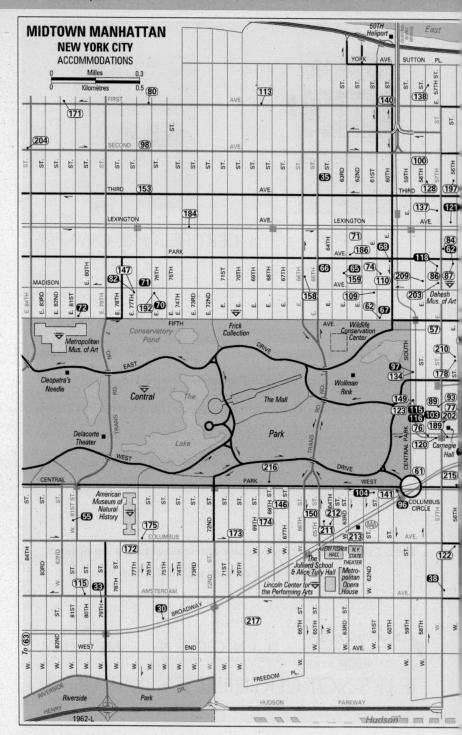

MIDTOWN MANHATTAN
NEW YORK CITY
ACCOMMODATIONS

Miles 0 — 0.3
Kilomètres 0 — 0.5

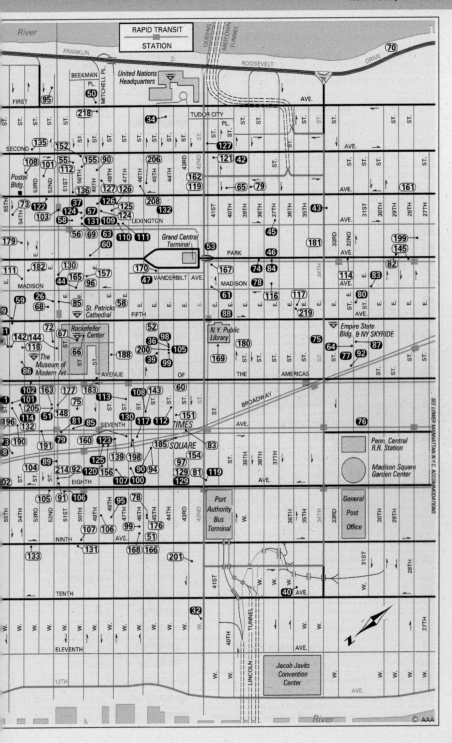

Midtown Manhattan

This index helps you "spot" where approved accommodations and restaurants are located on the corresponding detailed maps. Lodging rate ranges are for comparison only and show the property's high season; rates are per night, unless only weekly (W) rates are available. Restaurant rate range is for dinner, unless only lunch (L) is served. Turn to the listing page for more detailed rate information and consult display ads for special promotions.

Spotter/Map Page Number	OA	MIDTOWN MANHATTAN - Lodgings	Diamond Rating	Rate Range High Season	Listing Page
26 / p. 364		Omni Berkshire Place	▽▽▽▽	$479-$519	410
30 / p. 364	AAA	Hotel Beacon - see color ad p 403	▽▽	$180-$225 SAVE	403
31 / p. 364		The Shoreham Hotel	▽▽▽	$169-$1500	415
32 / p. 364	AAA	Travel Inn - see color ad p 416	▽▽	$120-$230 SAVE	416
33 / p. 364	AAA	Hotel Lucerne - see color ad p 404	▽▽▽	$190-$280 SAVE	403
34 / p. 364	AAA	Millennium UN Plaza Hotel New York - see color ad p 389	▽▽▽	$269-$418 SAVE	409
35 / p. 364		Lyden Gardens Hotel	▽▽	$309-$329	406
36 / p. 364	AAA	Sofitel New York - see color ad p 414	▽▽▽▽	$289 SAVE	415
37 / p. 364		Plaza Fifty Hotel	▽▽	$314-$419	411
38 / p. 364	.	Holiday Inn Midtown-57th Street	▽▽	$219-$239	403
39 / p. 364		Super 8 Hotel-Times Square	▽▽	$89-$329	415
40 / p. 364	AAA	Comfort Inn	▽▽	$109-$169 SAVE	396
41 / p. 364		Le Parker Meridien New York	▽▽▽▽	$475-$505	406
42 / p. 364		Eastgate Tower Hotel	▽▽	$279-$324	397
43 / p. 364		Dumont Plaza Suite Hotel	▽▽▽	$399-$424	397
44 / p. 364	AAA	The New York Palace	▽▽▽▽	$595-$770 SAVE	410
45 / p. 364		Shelburne Murray Hill Hotel	▽▽▽	$309-$334	414
46 / p. 364		Sheraton Russell Hotel	▽▽▽	$189-$399	415
47 / p. 364	AAA	The Roosevelt Hotel	▽▽▽	$349-$369 SAVE	413
49 / p. 364	AAA	The St. Regis-New York	▽▽▽▽▽	$690-$6000 SAVE	415
50 / p. 364		Beekman Tower Hotel	▽▽▽	$275-$299	389
51 / p. 364		The Flatotel	▽▽▽	$349-$369	399
53 / p. 364	AAA	Grand Hyatt New York	▽▽▽	$159-$325 SAVE	401
55 / p. 364		The Excelsior Hotel	▽▽▽	$159-$299	397
57 / p. 364		The Benjamin Hotel	▽▽▽▽	$394-$479	392
58 / p. 364		The Metropolitan	▽▽▽	$299-$339	408
59 / p. 364	AAA	The Peninsula New York	▽▽▽▽▽	$500-$640 SAVE	411
60 / p. 364		The Waldorf-Astoria - see color ad card insert	▽▽▽▽	$199-$599	417
61 / p. 364		Library Hotel	▽▽▽	$335-$415	406
62 / p. 364		Swissotel The Drake, New York	▽▽▽	$290	416
63 / p. 364		InterContinental The Barclay New York	▽▽▽	Failed to provide	405
64 / p. 364		La Quinta Manhattan Hotel	▽▽▽	$109-$329	405
65 / p. 364		The Lowell Hotel	▽▽▽	$465-$585	406
66 / p. 364		Hotel Plaza Athenee	▽▽▽▽	$495-$675	403
67 / p. 364		The Pierre New York - A Four Seasons Hotel	▽▽▽▽	$475-$905	411

Spotter/Map Page Number	OA	MIDTOWN MANHATTAN - Lodgings (continued)	Diamond Rating	Rate Range High Season	Listing Page
68 / p. 364	AAA	The Regency Hotel	◇◇◇◇	$339-$419 SAVE	412
70 / p. 364		Surrey Hotel	◇◇◇	$394-$479	416
71 / p. 364		The Carlyle	◇◇◇◇	$510-$610	393
72 / p. 364	AAA	The Stanhope Park Hyatt New York	◇◇◇◇	$279-$499 SAVE	415
73 / p. 364		The Majestic	◇◇◇	$199-$2500	406
74 / p. 364		70 Park Avenue Hotel	fyi	$225-$425	417
75 / p. 364	AAA	Comfort Inn-Manhattan - see color ad p 393	◇◇	$159-$169 SAVE	396
76 / p. 364		Southgate Tower Suite Hotel	◇◇◇	$279-$334	415
77 / p. 364	AAA	Hotel Stanford	◇◇	$149-$165 SAVE	404
78 / p. 364		Jolly Hotel Madison Towers	◇◇◇	$265	405
79 / p. 364		Sheraton Manhattan Hotel	◇◇◇	$169-$389	414
80 / p. 364	AAA	Avalon Hotel - see color ad p 390	◇◇◇	$220-$300 SAVE	389
81 / p. 364		Sheraton New York Hotel & Towers	◇◇◇	$169-$389	414
82 / p. 364		The Mark, New York	◇◇◇◇	$570-$2500	406
83 / p. 364		The Roger Williams Hotel	◇◇◇	$330	413
84 / p. 364	AAA	The Kitano New York Hotel	◇◇◇◇	$430-$2100 SAVE	405
85 / p. 364		The Michelangelo	◇◇◇◇	$395-$1200	408
86 / p. 364		The Warwick New York	◇◇◇	$395-$475	417
87 / p. 364		Red Roof Inn	◇◇	$119-$299	412
88 / p. 364		Clarion Hotel Fifth Avenue	◇◇◇	$385	396
89 / p. 364	AAA	Novotel New York - see color ad p 410	◇◇◇	$239-$369 SAVE	410
90 / p. 364		New York Marriott Marquis	◇◇◇	$199-$700	409
92 / p. 364	AAA	The Holiday Inn Martinique on Broadway - see color ad p 402	◇◇◇	$249-$299 SAVE	402
95 / p. 364	AAA	Belvedere Hotel - see color ad p 392	◇◇	$170-$230 SAVE	389
96 / p. 364		Trump International Hotel & Tower	◇◇◇◇	$575-$625	416
97 / p. 364	AAA	The Ritz-Carlton New York, Central Park	◇◇◇◇◇	$550-$875 SAVE	412
98 / p. 364		The Mansfield	◇◇◇	$330-$350	406
99 / p. 364		Iroquois Hotel	◇◇◇	$329-$379	405
100 / p. 364		Hotel Edison	◇◇	$160-$190	403
101 / p. 364	AAA	The Gorham Hotel - see color ad p 400	◇◇◇	$225-$440 SAVE	400
102 / p. 364		Hilton New York - see color ad card insert	◇◇◇	$169-$529	401
103 / p. 364		Salisbury Hotel	◇◇	$249-$309	414
104 / p. 364	AAA	The Mayflower Hotel On The Park	◇◇	$205-$270 SAVE	408
105 / p. 364		Royalton	◇◇◇	$225-$495	413
106 / p. 364	AAA	Howard Johnson Plaza Hotel - see color ad p 218	◇◇	$149-$279 SAVE	404
107 / p. 364	AAA	Best Western President Hotel	◇◇	$149-$369 SAVE	393
108 / p. 364	AAA	The Muse	◇◇◇◇	$449 SAVE	409
109 / p. 364		New York Marriott Eastside	◇◇◇	$199-$375	409
110 / p. 364	AAA	Radisson Lexington Hotel New York - see color ad p 413	◇◇◇	$279-$379 SAVE	412

Spotter/Map Page Number	OA	MIDTOWN MANHATTAN - Lodgings (continued)	Diamond Rating	Rate Range High Season	Listing Page
111 / p. 364	AAA	The Roger Smith Hotel	♦♦	$215-$255 SAVE	413
112 / p. 364	AAA	Millennium Broadway - see color ad p 389	♦♦♦	$389-$479 SAVE	409
113 / p. 364		Quality Hotel Times Square	♦♦	$170-$350	411
114 / p. 364		RIHGA Royal Hotel	♦♦♦♦	$269-$800	412
115 / p. 364		The Essex House-A Westin Hotel	♦♦♦♦	$509-$559	397
116 / p. 364		Inter-Continental Central Park South New York	♦♦♦♦	$265-$615	404
117 / p. 364	AAA	Doubletree Guest Suites Times Square/New York City - see color ad card insert	♦♦♦	$189-$499 SAVE	396
118 / p. 364		Four Seasons Hotel, New York	♦♦♦♦♦	$575-$675	399
119 / p. 364		Hilton Times Square - see color ad card insert	♦♦♦	$179-$449	401
120 / p. 364		The Time	♦♦♦	$199-$429	416
121 / p. 364	AAA	Fitzpatrick Manhattan Hotel - see color ad p 399	♦♦♦	$285-$485 SAVE	399
122 / p. 364		New York Midtown East Courtyard by Marriott	♦♦♦	$219-$349	409
123 / p. 364	AAA	Renaissance New York Hotel Times Square	♦♦♦	$269-$369 SAVE	412
124 / p. 364	AAA	The Kimberly A Boutique Hotel	♦♦♦	$259-$399 SAVE	405
125 / p. 364		Crowne Plaza Times Square Manhattan	♦♦♦	$229	396
126 / p. 364	AAA	Best Western Hospitality House - see color ad p 393	♦♦	$249-$349 SAVE	393
127 / p. 364		Crowne Plaza at the United Nations	♦♦♦	$319-$369	396
128 / p. 364	AAA	Park Central New York - see color ad p 411	♦♦♦	$319-$349 SAVE	411
129 / p. 364		The Westin	♦♦♦	$199-$519	417
130 / p. 364		W New York Times Square	♦♦♦	$489-$539	417
131 / p. 364		W New York	♦♦♦	$509	417
132 / p. 364		Fitzpatrick Grand Central Hotel	♦♦♦	$375-$495	397
		MIDTOWN MANHATTAN - Restaurants			
51 / p. 364		Yum Yum Bangkok	♦	$8-$14	435
52 / p. 364		Bread From Beirut	♦	$5-$10	421
55 / p. 364		Amma	♦♦	$17-$24	419
56 / p. 364		Mr. K's	♦♦♦♦	$18-$38	429
57 / p. 364		Brasserie 8 1/2	♦♦♦	$22-$34	421
58 / p. 364		Kuruma Zushi	♦♦♦	$18-$200	427
59 / p. 364		La Caravelle	♦♦♦♦	$46-$72	427
60 / p. 364		SushiZen	♦♦♦	$19-$31	433
61 / p. 364	AAA	San Domenico	♦♦♦♦	$19-$30	432
62 / p. 364	AAA	Cafe Pierre	♦♦♦♦	$18-$36	422
63 / p. 364		Docks Oyster Bar & Seafood Grill	♦♦	$20-$30	424
65 / p. 364		Docks Oyster Bar & Seafood Grill	♦♦	$16-$22	424
66 / p. 364		Rock Center Cafe	♦♦	$17-$25	431
67 / p. 364		The Sea Grill	♦♦♦	$22-$32	432
68 / p. 364		La Grenouille	♦♦♦♦	$45-$49	427
69 / p. 364		Terrance Brennans Seafood & Chop House	♦♦♦	$20-$39	434

Spotter/Map Page Number	OA	MIDTOWN MANHATTAN - Restaurants (continued)	Diamond Rating	Rate Range High Season	Listing Page
70 / p. 364	AAA	The Water Club	◈◈◈	$26-$35	435
71 / p. 364		Jo Jo	◈◈◈◈	$18-$34	426
72 / p. 364		21 Club	◈◈◈	$27-$41	418
73 / p. 364		Shun Lee Palace	◈◈◈	$14-$39	432
74 / p. 364		Aureole	◈◈◈◈◈	$69	420
75 / p. 364	AAA	Cite	◈◈◈	$20-$33	423
76 / p. 364		Petrossian	◈◈◈	$27-$32	430
77 / p. 364		Norma's	◈◈◈	$8-$22(L)	429
78 / p. 364		Orso	◈◈	$18-$24	429
79 / p. 364		Byblos	◈◈	$9-$19	421
80 / p. 364		Canyon Road	◈◈	$13-$21	422
81 / p. 364		Above	◈◈	$21-$45	418
82 / p. 364		Brasserie Les Halles	◈◈◈	$13-$28	421
83 / p. 364		The Manhattan Chili Co	◈◈	$6-$17	428
84 / p. 364		pazo	◈◈◈	$24-$30	430
85 / p. 364		Il Menestrello	◈◈◈	$17-$35	425
86 / p. 364		Fifty-Seven Fifty-Seven Restaurant & Bar	◈◈◈◈	$28-$34	425
87 / p. 364		Q 56	◈◈◈	$17-$27	431
89 / p. 364		Plaza Espana Restaurant	◈	$13-$23	431
90 / p. 364	AAA	San Martin Restaurant	◈◈	$14-$24	432
91 / p. 364	AAA	Siam Inn	◈◈	$10-$17	432
92 / p. 364		Victor's Cafe 52	◈◈	$10-$32	434
93 / p. 364	AAA	Angelo's Pizza	◈	$9-$17	419
94 / p. 364		The View	◈◈	$25-$55	435
95 / p. 364	AAA	Le Perigord	◈◈◈	$62	428
96 / p. 364	AAA	Giambelli 50th	◈◈	$20-$35	425
97 / p. 364		Sardi's	◈◈◈	$19-$30	432
98 / p. 364		Il Monello	◈◈◈	$16-$25	426
99 / p. 364	AAA	Barbetta	◈◈◈	$27-$30	420
100 / p. 364		Felidia	◈◈◈	$18-$32	425
101 / p. 364		Il Nido	◈◈◈	$19-$35	426
102 / p. 364		Cinnabar Asian Grill & Restaurant	◈◈◈	$12-$24	423
103 / p. 364		Restaurant Nippon	◈◈	$32-$45	431
104 / p. 364		Sugiyama	◈◈◈	$45-$150	433
105 / p. 364		Bangkok Cuisine	◈◈	$7-$16	420
106 / p. 364	AAA	Churrascaria Plataforma	◈◈	$43	423
107 / p. 364		Costa del Sol Restaurant	◈◈	$11-$25	423
108 / p. 364		Vong Restaurant	◈◈◈	$21-$35	435
109 / p. 364		Fred's at Barney's	◈◈◈	$20-$28	425
110 / p. 364		RM	◈◈◈◈	$58	431

Spotter/Map Page Number	OA	MIDTOWN MANHATTAN - Restaurants (continued)	Diamond Rating	Rate Range High Season	Listing Page
111 / p. 364		Oceana	◇◇◇◇	$68	429
112 / p. 364		Ess-a-Bagel	◇	$2-$10	424
113 / p. 364		Evergreen Cafe	◇◇	$7-$16	424
114 / p. 364		Artisanal	◇◇◇	$17-$25	419
115 / p. 364		Sarabeth's	◇◇	$12-$20	432
116 / p. 364		Asia de Cuba	◇◇◇	$18-$36	419
117 / p. 364		Toledo Restaurant	◇◇◇	$17-$36	434
118 / p. 364		Aquavit	◇◇◇◇	$69-$115	419
119 / p. 364		Sushi Yasuda	◇◇◇	$18-$29	433
120 / p. 364		Cafe Europa	◇◇	$7-$13	422
121 / p. 364		Cibo	◇◇◇	$15-$35	423
122 / p. 364		Bello Restaurant	◇◇	$11-$24	420
123 / p. 364		Cafe Botanica	◇◇◇	$28-$42	421
124 / p. 364		AVRA Estiatorio	◇◇◇	$14-$25	420
125 / p. 364		Diwan	◇◇	$13-$24	424
126 / p. 364		Chiam	◇◇◇	$16-$25	422
127 / p. 364		Chin Chin	◇◇◇	$18-$22	422
128 / p. 364		dawat	◇◇◇	$13-$23	423
129 / p. 364		John's Pizzeria-Times Square	◇◇	$8-$15	426
130 / p. 364		Fresco by Scotto	◇◇	$15-$30	425
131 / p. 364		Uncle Nick's Greek Cuisine	◇	$10-$25	434
132 / p. 364		Estiatorio Milos	◇◇◇	$24-$40	424
133 / p. 364	◬◬◬	**Julian's Cuisine**	◇◇	$10-$28	427
134 / p. 364		Atelier	◇◇◇◇◇	$28-$44	419
135 / p. 364		La Mangeoire	◇◇	$15-$29	427
136 / p. 364		al BUSTAN	◇◇	$20-$28	419
137 / p. 364		Le Colonial	◇◇◇	$13-$20	428
138 / p. 364		March	◇◇◇◇	$68-$126	428
139 / p. 364	◬◬◬	**Foley's Restaurant & Bar**	◇◇◇	$25-$39	425
140 / p. 364		East River Cafe	◇◇	$12-$20	424
141 / p. 364		Jean Georges Restaurant	◇◇◇◇◇	$87-$118	426
142 / p. 364		Michael's	◇◇◇	$25-$38	429
143 / p. 364		District	◇◇◇	$25-$35	424
144 / p. 364		Bombay Palace Restaurant	◇◇	$9-$30	421
145 / p. 364		Park Bistro	◇◇	$18-$28	430
146 / p. 364		Cafe des Artistes	◇◇◇	$27-$37	422
147 / p. 364		Mark's	◇◇◇◇	$24-$38	428
148 / p. 364		Le Bernardin	◇◇◇◇	$84	427
149 / p. 364		Alain Ducasse at the Essex House	◇◇◇◇◇	$145-$280	419
150 / p. 364		Shun Lee	◇◇◇	$12-$26	432

Spotter/Map Page Number	OA	MIDTOWN MANHATTAN - Restaurants (continued)	Diamond Rating	Rate Range High Season	Listing Page
151 / p. 364		Virgil's Real Barbecue	◈	$8-$25	435
152 / p. 364		Zarela	◈◈	$14-$19	435
153 / p. 364		Atlantic Grill	◈◈◈	$19-$25	419
154 / p. 364		Pasta Break	◈	$6-$9	430
155 / p. 364		Lutece	◈◈◈	$59	428
156 / p. 364		Noche	◈◈◈	$17-$22	429
157 / p. 364		Cinquanta Ristorante	◈◈◈	$13-$25	423
158 / p. 364		Restaurant Daniel	◈◈◈◈◈	$85-$140	431
159 / p. 364		The Post House	◈◈◈	$22-$43	431
160 / p. 364		Raku	◈	$9-$30	431
161 / p. 364		Vatan	◈◈	$22	434
162 / p. 364		Malika	◈◈	$11-$16	428
163 / p. 364		Ben Benson's Steak House	◈◈◈	$16-$33	420
165 / p. 364	▲▲▲	**Le Cirque 2000**	◈◈◈◈◈	$23-$43	427
166 / p. 364		Zen Palate	◈◈	$11-$18	435
167 / p. 364		Pershing Square Cafe	◈◈	$20-$26	430
168 / p. 364		Becco	◈◈	$25-$30	420
169 / p. 364		Bryant Park Grill	◈◈	$17-$28	421
170 / p. 364		Cafe Centro	◈◈◈	$20-$27	422
171 / p. 364		Cafe Trevi	◈◈	$15-$24	422
172 / p. 364		Spazzia	◈◈	$10-$21	433
173 / p. 364		Metsovo	◈◈	$15-$25	428
174 / p. 364		La Boite en Bois	◈◈◈	$19-$25	427
175 / p. 364		Isabella's	◈◈	$14-$23	426
176 / p. 364		Joe Allen	◈	$10-$25	426
177 / p. 364		Judson Grill	◈◈◈	$23-$35	426
178 / p. 364		Bay Leaf Indian Brasserie	◈◈	$12-$25	420
179 / p. 364		Korea Palace	◈◈	$19-$35	427
180 / p. 364		I Lo	◈◈◈	$22-$40	426
181 / p. 364		Sushi Sen-nin	◈◈◈	$18-$48	433
182 / p. 364		The Steakhouse at Monkey Bar	◈◈◈	$22-$32	433
183 / p. 364		Citarella the Restaurant	◈◈◈	$25-$32	423
184 / p. 364		Payard Patisserie & Bistro	◈◈◈	$25-$33	430
185 / p. 364		Ollie's	◈	$9-$18	429
186 / p. 364		Park Avenue Cafe	◈◈◈	$20-$34	429
188 / p. 364		Shaan	◈◈◈	$30-$40	432
189 / p. 364		Trattoria Dell'Arte	◈◈	$16-$28	434
190 / p. 364		Carnegie Delicatessen & Restaurant	◈	$9-$17	422
191 / p. 364		Lindy's	◈	$8-$19	428
192 / p. 364		Cafe Boulud	◈◈◈	$22-$35	421

Spotter/Map Page Number	OA	**MIDTOWN MANHATTAN -** **Restaurants (continued)**	Diamond Rating	Rate Range High Season	Listing Page
(196) / p. 364		Molyvos	▽▽▽	$20-$29	429
(197) / p. 364		Bill Hong's	▽▽▽	$13-$32	420
(198) / p. 364		Blue Fin	▽▽▽	$19-$28	421
(199) / p. 364		Blue Smoke	▽▽	$9-$24	421
(200) / p. 364		db bistro moderne	▽▽▽▽	$26-$32	423
(201) / p. 364		Esca	▽▽▽	$24-$28	424
(202) / p. 364		Fontana di Trevi	▽▽▽	$9-$26	425
(203) / p. 364		The Four Seasons	▽▽▽▽	$30-$45	425
(204) / p. 364		Jasmine	▽▽	$8-$17	426
(205) / p. 364		Moda	▽▽	$21-$29	429
(206) / p. 364		Patroon	▽▽▽	$28-$38	430
(208) / p. 364		Spark's Steak House	▽▽	$25-$38	433
(209) / p. 364		Tao	▽▽▽	$16-$28	433
(210) / p. 364		Town	▽▽▽	$22-$36	434
(211) / p. 364		Cafe Fiorello	▽▽	$15-$34	422
(212) / p. 364		Picholine	▽▽▽▽	$28-$38	430
(213) / p. 364		Rosa Mexicano	▽▽▽	$17-$27	431
(214) / p. 364	(AAA)	**Gallagher's Steak House**	▽▽	$20-$50	425
(215) / p. 364		Patsy's Italian Restaurant	▽▽	$18-$28	430
(216) / p. 364		Tavern on the Green	▽▽▽	$18-$39	434
(217) / p. 364		Compass	▽▽▽	$18-$34	423
(218) / p. 364		Verderame Ristorante	▽▽	$12-$25	434
(219) / p. 364		Steve's Metro Fish	▽▽	$21-$28	433

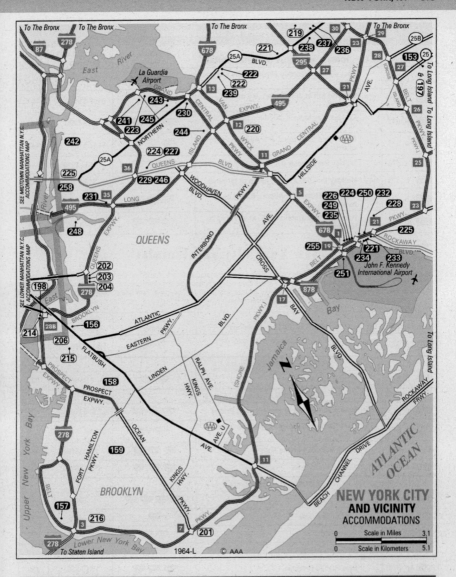

NEW YORK CITY AND VICINITY ACCOMMODATIONS

Scale in Miles 0 — 3.1
Scale in Kilometers 0 — 5.1

1964-L   © AAA

✈ Airport Accommodations

Spotter/Map Page Number	OA	LA GUARDIA	Diamond Rating	Rate Range High Season	Listing Page
223 / above	AAA	**Clarion Hotel at La Guardia Airport, opposite airport**	▽▽▽	$175-$285 SAVE	442
241 / above		Courtyard by Marriott New York/La Guardia Airport, opposite airport	▽▽▽	$89-$259	443
245 / above		Crowne Plaza Hotel and Resort La Guardia, 0.4 mi from entrance	▽▽▽	$109-$259	443
243 / above		New York La Guardia Airport Marriott, opposite terminal	▽▽▽	$149-$229	445
239 / above		Sheraton La Guardia East Hotel, 3 mi se of terminal	▽▽▽	$145-$245	447

✈ Airport Accommodations

Spotter/Map Page Number	OA	JOHN F. KENNEDY INTERNATIONAL	Diamond Rating	Rate Range High Season	Listing Page
233 / p. 373		Best Western Kennedy Airport, 0.5 mi e of airport	◆◆	$119-$159	442
234 / p. 373	◆◆◆	Comfort Inn at JFK Airport, 0.5 mi e of terminal	◆◆	$109-$149 SAVE	442
224 / p. 373		Courtyard by Marriott JFK Airport, 1 mi n of terminal	◆◆◆	$99-$399	442
225 / p. 373	◆◆◆	Doubletree Club Hotel JFK Airport, 1.5 mi w of entrance	◆◆◆	$149-$199 SAVE	443
231 / p. 373		Holiday Inn Express, 0.5 mi e of terminal	◆◆◆	$139-$179	444
249 / p. 373	◆◆◆	Holiday Inn-JFK Airport, just n of terminal	◆◆◆	$199 SAVE	445
235 / p. 373	◆◆◆	Radisson Hotel-JFK Airport, 0.5 mi ne of terminal	◆◆◆	$129-$139 SAVE	446
251 / p. 373	◆◆◆	Ramada Plaza Hotel at JFK, at entrance to terminal	◆◆◆	$129 SAVE	446

New York City and Vicinity

This index helps you "spot" where approved accommodations and restaurants are located on the corresponding detailed maps. Lodging rate ranges are for comparison only and show the property's high season; rates are per night, unless only weekly (W) rates are available. Restaurant rate range is for dinner, unless only lunch (L) is served. Turn to the listing page for more detailed rate information and consult display ads for special promotions.

Spotter/Map Page Number	OA	FLORAL PARK - Lodgings	Diamond Rating	Rate Range High Season	Listing Page
153 / p. 373	◆◆◆	Floral Park Motor Lodge - see color ad p 444	◆◆	$200-$270 SAVE	292
		FLORAL PARK - Restaurant			
197 / p. 373		Poppy's Place	◆◆	$10-$22	292
		BROOKLYN - Lodgings			
156 / p. 373	◆◆◆	New York Marriott at the Brooklyn Bridge	◆◆◆	$239-$319 SAVE	439
157 / p. 373	◆◆◆	Best Western Gregory Hotel - see color ad p 438	◆◆	$179-$189 SAVE	438
158 / p. 373		Bed & Breakfast on the Park	◆◆◆	$125-$195	438
159 / p. 373		Avenue Plaza Hotel	◆◆◆	$149-$169	438
		BROOKLYN - Restaurants			
198 / p. 373		River Cafe	◆◆◆◆	$70	440
201 / p. 373		Ocean View Cafe	◆	$7-$15	439
202 / p. 373		Peter Luger's	◆◆	$45-$55	439
203 / p. 373		Blue Ribbon Sushi	◆◆	$12-$27	439
204 / p. 373		Blue Ribbon Brooklyn	◆◆◆	$13-$36	439
206 / p. 373		Gage and Tollner	◆◆◆	$14-$29	439
214 / p. 373		Grimaldi's Pizzeria	◆	$12-$18	439
215 / p. 373		Aunt Suzie's Restaurant	◆◆	$9-$15	439
216 / p. 373		Tommaso's	◆◆	$8-$27	440
		QUEENS - Lodgings			
221 / p. 373	◆◆◆	Holiday Inn Express - see color ad p 444	◆◆	$159-$169 SAVE	445
222 / p. 373	◆◆◆	Best Western Queens Court Hotel	◆◆◆	$119-$149 SAVE	442
223 / p. 373	◆◆◆	Clarion Hotel at La Guardia Airport	◆◆◆	$175-$285 SAVE	442
224 / p. 373		Courtyard by Marriott JFK Airport - see color ad p 442	◆◆◆	$99-$399	442

Spotter/Map Page Number	OA	QUEENS - Lodgings (continued)	Diamond Rating	Rate Range High Season	Listing Page
225 / p. 373	AAA	**Doubletree Club Hotel JFK Airport**	◆◆◆	$149-$199 [SAVE]	443
226 / p. 373	AAA	**Hampton Inn**	◆◆◆	$129-$199 [SAVE]	444
227 / p. 373		Howard Johnson Express Inn - see color ad p 218	◆◆	$99-$159	445
228 / p. 373		Howard Johnson Express Inn	◆◆	$109-$149	445
229 / p. 373		Metro Motel	◆◆	Failed to provide	445
230 / p. 373		Ramada Plaza La Guardia	◆◆◆	$159-$239	447
231 / p. 373		Holiday Inn Express	◆◆◆	$139-$179	444
232 / p. 373	AAA	**Crowne Plaza JFK Airport** - see color ad p 443	◆◆◆	$259 [SAVE]	443
233 / p. 373		Best Western Kennedy Airport	◆◆	$119-$159	442
234 / p. 373	AAA	**Comfort Inn at JFK Airport**	◆◆	$109-$149 [SAVE]	442
235 / p. 373	AAA	**Radisson Hotel-JFK Airport** - see color ad p 413	◆◆◆	$129-$139 [SAVE]	446
236 / p. 373	AAA	**Adria Hotel and Conference Center**	◆◆	$129-$169 [SAVE]	440
237 / p. 373	AAA	**Ramada Inn Adria**	◆◆	$129-$169 [SAVE]	446
238 / p. 373	AAA	**Anchor Motor Inn** - see color ad p 440	◆◆	$124-$164 [SAVE]	440
239 / p. 373		Sheraton La Guardia East Hotel	◆◆◆	$145-$245	447
241 / p. 373		Courtyard by Marriott New York/La Guardia Airport	◆◆◆	$89-$259	443
242 / p. 373	AAA	**Super 8 Motel**	◆◆	$95-$105 [SAVE]	447
243 / p. 373		New York La Guardia Airport Marriott	◆◆◆	$149-$229	445
244 / p. 373	AAA	**Best Western Eden Park Hotel** - see color ad p 441	◆◆◆	$139-$159 [SAVE]	441
245 / p. 373		Crowne Plaza Hotel and Resort La Guardia	◆◆◆	$109-$259	443
246 / p. 373	AAA	**Pan American Hotel** - see color ad p 446	◆◆	$109-$169 [SAVE]	445
248 / p. 373	AAA	**Best Western City View** - see color ad p 441	◆◆	$149-$179 [SAVE]	441
249 / p. 373	AAA	**Holiday Inn-JFK Airport**	◆◆◆	$199 [SAVE]	445
250 / p. 373	AAA	**Executive Motor Inn**	◆	$85-$98 [SAVE]	444
251 / p. 373	AAA	**Ramada Plaza Hotel at JFK**	◆◆◆	$129 [SAVE]	446
255 / p. 373		Econo Lodge	◆	$99-$159	443
		QUEENS - Restaurants			
219 / p. 373	AAA	**First Edition Bistro**	◆	$8-$16	447
220 / p. 373		Lailla Turkish Restaurant	◆◆	$11-$15	447
221 / p. 373		Mythos Authentic Helenic Cuisine	◆◆	$10-$20	447
222 / p. 373		Penang	◆	$6-$18	447
224 / p. 373		Jaiya Thai-Oriental Restaurant	◆	$6-$17	447
225 / p. 373	AAA	**Water's Edge**	◆◆◆◆	$58-$78	447
		LONG ISLAND CITY - Lodgings			
258 / p. 373		Comfort Inn	◆◆	$109-$209	452

LOWER MANHATTAN (See map and index starting on p. 360)

——— WHERE TO STAY ———

BEST WESTERN SEAPORT INN, NEW YORK   *Book at aaa.com*   Phone: (212)766-6600   **3**

AAA SAVE
▽▽▽▽
Historic
Small-scale Hotel

All Year   1P: $209-$240   2P: $209-$240   XP: $10   F17
Location: North end of South St Seaport. 33 Peck Slip 10038. Fax: 212/766-6615. **Facility:** This 19th-century guest house features some units with terraces overlooking the seaport. 72 one-bedroom standard units, some with whirlpools. 7 stories, interior corridors. **Parking:** no self-parking. **Terms:** [ECP] meal plan available. **Amenities:** video games (fee), dual phone lines, voice mail, irons, hair dryers. *Some:* safes. **Leisure Activities:** exercise room. **Guest Services:** valet laundry. **Business Services:** meeting rooms, fax. **Cards:** AX, CB, DC, DS, MC, VI. **Special Amenities:** free expanded continental breakfast and free local telephone calls. *(See color ad below)*

SOME UNITS
⟨SD⟩ ⟨†⎮⟩ ⟨🛀⟩ ⟨VCR⟩ ⟨✦⟩ ⟨DATA PORT⟩ ⟨▤⟩ ⟨▱⟩ / ⟨✕⟩ /

EMBASSY SUITES HOTEL NEW YORK   *Book at aaa.com*   Phone: (212)945-0100   **7**

▽▽▽▽
Large-scale Hotel

5/1-6/25 & 9/5-12/16 [BP]   1P: $179-$359   2P: $179-$359   XP: $20   F18
12/17-4/30 [BP]   1P: $159-$359   2P: $159-$359   XP: $20   F18
6/26-9/4 [BP]   1P: $159-$329   2P: $159-$329   XP: $20   F18
Location: Between Murray and Vesey sts. 102 N End Ave 10282. Fax: 212/945-3012. **Facility:** 463 units. 462 one- and 1 two-bedroom suites. 15 stories, interior corridors. *Bath:* combo or shower only. **Parking:** valet. **Terms:** check-in 4 pm, weekly rates available, pets (small dogs only). **Amenities:** video games (fee), high-speed Internet, dual phone lines, voice mail, safes, honor bars, irons, hair dryers. *Some:* CD players, fax. **Guest Services:** gift shop, complimentary evening beverages, valet and coin laundry. **Business Services:** conference facilities, business center. **Cards:** AX, DC, DS, MC, VI. *(See color ad card insert)*

SOME UNITS
⟨🛏⟩ ⟨†⎮⟩ ⟨Y⟩ ⟨&⟩ ⟨✦⟩ ⟨✦⟩ ⟨DATA PORT⟩ ⟨▤⟩ ⟨▱⟩ / ⟨✕⟩ ⟨VCR⟩ ⟨▤⟩ /

HAMPTON INN CHELSEA   *Book at aaa.com*   Phone: (212)414-1000   **8**

AAA SAVE
▽▽▽▽
Small-scale Hotel

10/1-12/18 [CP]   1P: $196-$224   XP: $10   F18
12/19-4/30 [CP]   1P: $179-$209   XP: $10   F18
7/1-9/30 [CP]   1P: $177-$197   XP: $10   F18
5/1-6/30 [CP]   1P: $169-$194   XP: $10   F18
Location: Between 6th (Ave of the Americas) and 7th aves. 108 W 24th St 10011. Fax: 212/647-1511. **Facility:** 144 one-bedroom standard units. 20 stories, interior corridors. *Bath:* combo or shower only. **Parking:** no self-parking. **Terms:** pets ($20 fee). **Amenities:** high-speed Internet, dual phone lines, voice mail, irons, hair dryers. *Some:* DVD players, CD players. **Leisure Activities:** exercise room. **Guest Services:** valet and coin laundry. **Business Services:** fax (fee). **Cards:** AX, DC, DS, MC, VI. **Special Amenities:** free continental breakfast and free local telephone calls. *(See color ad p 401)*

SOME UNITS
⟨SD⟩ ⟨🛏⟩ ⟨&⟩ ⟨🛀⟩ ⟨✦⟩ ⟨DATA PORT⟩ ⟨▱⟩ / ⟨✕⟩ ⟨VCR⟩ ⟨▤⟩ ⟨▤⟩ /
FEE

HOLIDAY INN DOWNTOWN   *Book at aaa.com*   Phone: (212)966-8898   **4**

▽▽▽▽
Small-scale Hotel

9/1-12/31   1P: $229-$279   2P: $229-$279   XP: $20   F18
5/1-6/30   1P: $209-$259   2P: $209-$259   XP: $20   F18
7/1-8/31   1P: $179-$229   2P: $179-$229   XP: $20   F18
1/1-4/30   1P: $169-$219   2P: $169-$219   XP: $20   F18
Location: Corner of Howard St, just n of Canal St. Located in Chinatown. 138 Lafayette St 10013. Fax: 212/966-3933. **Facility:** 227 one-bedroom standard units. 14 stories, interior corridors. *Bath:* combo or shower only. **Parking:** valet. **Terms:** cancellation fee imposed. **Amenities:** CD players, dual phone lines, voice mail, irons, hair dryers. **Dining:** Pacifica, see separate listing. **Guest Services:** valet laundry. **Business Services:** meeting rooms, fax (fee). **Cards:** AX, DC, DS, JC, MC, VI.

SOME UNITS
⟨ASK⟩ ⟨SD⟩ ⟨†⎮⟩ ⟨Y⟩ ⟨&⟩ ⟨✦⟩ ⟨✦⟩ ⟨DATA PORT⟩ ⟨▱⟩ / ⟨✕⟩ ⟨VCR⟩ ⟨▤⟩ /
FEE FEE

IF YOU HAVEN'T SEEN DOWNTOWN, YOU HAVEN'T SEEN NEW YORK.

It's the birthplace of the nation. It's Wall Street, the South Street Seaport and the Brooklyn Bridge. It's breathtaking views of the harbor and Statue of Liberty. It's narrow winding streets and skyscraper canyons. It's parks, plazas and esplanades. It's museums, concerts and outdoor sculpture. It's diverse shopping, superb dining and world-class hotels. Best of all, it's a short walk from one great attraction to the next.

DOWNTOWN NEW YORK

Downtown
ALLiANCE

For more information call 1-800-377-1083
or visit www.DowntownNY.com

(See map and index starting on p. 360)

HOLIDAY INN WALL STREET HOTEL *Book at aaa.com* Phone: (212)232-7700
Large-scale Hotel

9/6-12/31	1P: $249-$369	2P: $249-$369	XP: $25	F19
5/1-6/30	1P: $249-$329	2P: $249-$329	XP: $25	F19
7/1-9/5 & 1/1-4/30	1P: $199-$299	2P: $199-$299	XP: $25	F19

Location: Corner of Gold and Platt sts. 15 Gold St 10038. Fax: 212/425-0330. Facility: 138 one-bedroom standard units. 18 stories, interior corridors. Bath: combo or shower only. Parking: on-site (fee). Terms: cancellation fee imposed, small pets only ($50 deposit). Amenities: CD players, dual phone lines, voice mail, safes, honor bars, irons, hair dryers. Fee: video games, high-speed Internet. Leisure Activities: exercise room. Guest Services: valet laundry. Business Services: meeting rooms, business center. Cards: AX, CB, DC, DS, JC, MC, VI.

HOTEL GIRAFFE *Book at aaa.com* Phone: (212)685-7700 16
Small-scale Hotel

9/7-12/31 [ECP]	1P: $365-$425
5/1-6/30 & 1/1-4/30 [ECP]	1P: $345-$365
7/1-9/6	1P: $325-$345

Location: At E 26th St. 365 Park Ave S 10016. Fax: 212/685-7771. Facility: 73 units. 52 one-bedroom standard units. 21 one-bedroom suites ($425-$525). 12 stories, interior corridors. Bath: combo or shower only. Parking: valet. Terms: cancellation fee imposed, package plans. Amenities: video library, CD players, high-speed Internet, dual phone lines, voice mail, safes, honor bars, irons, hair dryers. Guest Services: valet laundry. Business Services: meeting rooms, administrative services, PC. Cards: AX, CB, DC, MC, VI.

HOWARD JOHNSON EXPRESS INN *Book at aaa.com* Phone: (212)358-8844 10
Small-scale Hotel

5/1-11/1 & 3/1-4/30 [CP]	1P: $109-$209	2P: $119-$219	XP: $10	F12
11/2-2/28 [CP]	1P: $99-$209	2P: $109-$219	XP: $10	F12

Location: Jct Forsythe, between 1st and 2nd aves. 135 E Houston St 10002. Fax: 212/473-3500. Facility: 46 one-bedroom standard units. 6 stories, interior corridors. Parking: no self-parking. Terms: cancellation fee imposed. Amenities: voice mail, hair dryers. Guest Services: valet laundry. Business Services: fax (fee). Cards: AX, DC, DS, MC, VI. Special Amenities: free continental breakfast and free newspaper.
(See color ad p 218)

FEE   FEE   FEE

MARRIOTT FINANCIAL CENTER HOTEL *Book at aaa.com* Phone: (212)385-4900 15
Large-scale Hotel

All Year	1P: $259-$349	2P: $259-$349

Location: Between Albany and Carlyle sts. 85 West St 10006. Fax: 212/227-8136. Facility: 500 units. 493 one-bedroom standard units. 7 one-bedroom suites ($500-$1100). 38 stories, interior corridors. Parking: valet. Terms: check-in 4 pm. Amenities: dual phone lines, voice mail, safes, honor bars, irons, hair dryers. Fee: video games, high-speed Internet. Some: fax. Pool(s): heated indoor. Leisure Activities: exercise room. Guest Services: gift shop, valet laundry. Business Services: conference facilities, business center. Cards: AX, CB, DC, DS, JC, MC, VI.

MILLENIUM HILTON *Book at aaa.com* Phone: (212)693-2001 14
Large-scale Hotel

All Year	1P: $179-$499	2P: $179-$499	XP: $30	F18

Location: Between Dey and Fulton sts. 55 Church St 10007. Fax: 212/571-2316. Facility: This hotel offers magnificent views of the city, including some river views. 565 units. 464 one-bedroom standard units. 97 one- and 4 two-bedroom suites. 55 stories, interior corridors. Parking: on-site (fee) and valet. Terms: cancellation fee imposed, pets ($250 deposit). Amenities: CD players, dual phone lines, voice mail, safes, honor bars, irons, hair dryers. Fee: video games, high-speed Internet. Dining: 6:30 am-11, noon-2:30 & 5-10:30 pm, cocktails. Pool(s): heated indoor. Leisure Activities: sauna, exercise room. Guest Services: gift shop, valet laundry. Business Services: meeting rooms, business center. Cards: AX, CB, DC, DS, JC, MC, VI. *(See color ad card insert)*

FEE   FEE

(See map and index starting on p. 360)

PARK SOUTH HOTEL   *Book at aaa.com*   Phone: (212)448-0888   **9**
▼▼▽▽▽▽
	9/8-12/15 [ECP]	1P: $255	2P: $255	XP: $25	F12
	5/1-6/15 [ECP]	1P: $225	2P: $225	XP: $25	F12
	6/16-9/7 & 12/16-4/30 [ECP]	1P: $199	2P: $199	XP: $25	F12

Small-scale Hotel   **Location:** Between Park and Lexington aves. 124 E 28th St 10016. Fax: 212/448-0811. **Facility:** 143 one-bedroom standard units. 8 stories, interior corridors. *Bath:* combo or shower only. **Parking:** no self-parking. **Terms:** 24 day cancellation notice-fee imposed, package plans - weekends. **Amenities:** video library, DVD players, high-speed Internet, dual phone lines, voice mail, fax, safes, irons, hair dryers. *Some:* CD players. **Leisure Activities:** exercise room, **Guest Services:** valet laundry. **Business Services:** meeting rooms, business center. **Cards:** AX, DC, JC, MC, VI.

SOME UNITS

(ASK) (S/D) (¶) (Y) (⌐) (📷) (DATA PORT) / (✕) (🔌) (💻) /

RAMADA INN EASTSIDE   *Book at aaa.com*   Phone: (212)545-1800   **1**
▼▼▽▽ ▼▼▽▽
	10/1-12/31 [CP]	1P: $169-$189	2P: $179-$199	XP: $10	F14
	6/1-9/30 [CP]	1P: $129-$149	2P: $139-$159	XP: $10	F14
	5/1-5/31 [CP]	1P: $109-$129	2P: $119-$139	XP: $10	F14
	1/1-4/30 [CP]	1P: $99-$119	2P: $109-$129	XP: $10	F14

Small-scale Hotel   **Location:** At 30th St. 161 Lexington Ave 10016. Fax: 212/481-7270. **Facility:** 95 one-bedroom standard units. 12 stories, interior corridors. **Parking:** no self-parking. **Terms:** $2 service charge. **Amenities:** video games (fee), voice mail, irons, hair dryers. **Leisure Activities:** exercise room. **Business Services:** meeting rooms, business center. **Cards:** AX, DC, DS, JC, MC, VI.

SOME UNITS

(ASK) (S/D) (📷) (🐾) (DATA PORT) (💻) / (✕) /

THE REGENT WALL STREET   *Book at aaa.com*   Phone: (212)845-8600   **11**
▼▼▽▽▽▽ ▼▼▽▽▽▽
| | 9/1-4/30 | 1P: $550 | 2P: $550 | XP: $50 | F12 |
| | 5/1-8/31 | 1P: $525 | 2P: $525 | XP: $50 | F12 |

Historic
Small-scale Hotel   **Location:** Corner of William and Wall sts. 55 Wall St 10005. Fax: 212/845-8601. **Facility:** This boutique hotel is a historic landmark built in 1842 featuring both Greek Revival and Italian Renaissance elements. 144 units. 97 one-bedroom standard units. 47 one-bedroom suites. 9 stories, interior corridors. **Parking:** valet. **Terms:** cancellation fee imposed, [AP], [BP] & [CP] meal plans available. **Amenities:** video library, DVD players, CD players, high-speed Internet, dual phone lines, voice mail, fax, safes, honor bars, hair dryers. **Leisure Activities:** steamrooms, exercise room, spa. **Guest Services:** valet laundry. **Business Services:** conference facilities, business center. **Cards:** AX, CB, DC, DS, JC, MC, VI.

SOME UNITS

(ASK) (🛏) (¶) (24¶) (🔒) (📷) (✕) (🐾) (DATA PORT) / (✕) /

THE RITZ-CARLTON NEW YORK, BATTERY PARK   *Book at aaa.com*   Phone: (212)344-0800   **12**
(AAA) (SAVE)
| | 9/2-12/31 | 1P: $475 | 2P: $475 | XP: $40 | F18 |
▼▼▽▽▽▽ | 5/1-6/30 & 1/1-4/30 | 1P: $395 | 2P: $395 | XP: $40 | F18 |
| | 7/1-9/1 | 1P: $350 | 2P: $350 | XP: $40 | F18 |

Small-scale Hotel   **Location:** Jct Battery Pl. Located opposite Battery Park. Two West St 10004. Fax: 212/877-6465. **Facility:** This luxury waterfront hotel features telescopes in some rooms and offers sweeping views of the Statue of Liberty and Ellis Island. 298 units. 254 one-bedroom standard units. 44 one-bedroom suites, some with whirlpools. 14 stories, interior corridors. *Bath:* combo or shower only. **Parking:** valet. **Terms:** cancellation fee imposed, [AP], [BP] & [CP] meal plans available, small pets only ($30 extra charge). **Amenities:** video library, video games, CD players, high-speed Internet (fee), dual phone lines, voice mail, safes, honor bars, irons, hair dryers. *Some:* DVD players. **Dining:** 6:30 am-11 pm; Sunday brunch, cocktails. **Leisure Activities:** spa. **Guest Services:** gift shop, valet laundry, area transportation-lower Manhattan. **Business Services:** conference facilities, business center. **Cards:** AX, CB, DC, DS, JC, MC, VI. **Special Amenities:** free newspaper and free room upgrade (subject to availability with advanced reservations).

SOME UNITS

(🛏) (¶) (24¶) (Y) (🔒) (⌐M) (🔒) (📷) (🐾) (🐾) (DATA PORT) / (✕) (VCR) (🔌) (💻) /
FEE

THE SOHO GRAND HOTEL   *Book at aaa.com*   Phone: 212/965-3000   **6**
▼▼▽▽▽▽
Property failed to provide current rates
Location: Jct Grand St; in SoHo District. 310 W Broadway 10013. Fax: 212/965-3200. **Facility:** 366 units. 364 one-
Small-scale Hotel   bedroom standard units. 2 one-bedroom suites. 17 stories, interior corridors. *Bath:* combo or shower only. **Parking:** valet. **Amenities:** CD players, dual phone lines, voice mail, safes, honor bars, hair dryers. **Leisure Activities:** exercise room. **Guest Services:** valet laundry. **Business Services:** meeting rooms, fax.

(🛏) (¶) (24¶) (Y) (VCR) (🐾) (DATA PORT)

TRIBECA GRAND HOTEL   *Book at aaa.com*   Phone: 212/519-6600   **13**
▼▼▽▽▽▽
Property failed to provide current rates
Location: 6th Ave (Ave of the Americas) and White St. 2 Ave of the Americas 10013. Fax: 212/519-6700.
Small-scale Hotel   **Facility:** 203 units. 195 one-bedroom standard units. 8 one-bedroom suites. 8 stories, interior corridors. *Bath:* combo or shower only. **Parking:** valet. **Amenities:** CD players, high-speed Internet, dual phone lines, voice mail, fax, safes, honor bars, irons, hair dryers. **Leisure Activities:** exercise room. **Guest Services:** valet laundry. **Business Services:** meeting rooms, business center.

SOME UNITS

(🛏) (¶) (24¶) (Y) (🔒) (VCR) (🐾) (DATA PORT) / (✕) /

W NEW YORK-UNION SQUARE   *Book at aaa.com*   Phone: (212)253-9119   **17**
▼▼▽▽▽▽
| | 8/29-4/30 | 1P: $599-$1900 | 2P: $599-$1900 | XP: $25 | F |
| | 5/1-8/28 | 1P: $579-$1800 | 2P: $579-$1800 | XP: $25 | F |

Small-scale Hotel   **Location:** At 17th St. 201 Park Ave S 10003. Fax: 212/253-9229. **Facility:** Surfaces reminiscent of mother-of-pearl give the lobby a glittering ambience while guest rooms are handsomely outfitted and luxurious. 270 units. 252 one-bedroom standard units. 16 one- and 2 two-bedroom suites ($850-$1900), some with whirlpools. 21 stories, interior corridors. *Bath:* combo or shower only. **Parking:** valet. **Terms:** cancellation fee imposed, pets ($100 fee, $25 extra charge). **Amenities:** CD players, high-speed Internet (fee), dual phone lines, voice mail, safes, honor bars, irons, hair dryers. **Leisure Activities:** exercise room. *Fee:* massage. **Guest Services:** valet laundry. **Business Services:** conference facilities, business center. **Cards:** AX, CB, DC, DS, JC, MC, VI.

SOME UNITS

(ASK) (S/D) (🛏) (¶) (24¶) (Y) (⌐M) (🔒) (📷) (VCR) (🐾) (DATA PORT) (💻) / (✕) (🔌) (💻) /
FEE

(See map and index starting on p. 360)

─────── *The following lodgings were either not evaluated or did not* ───────
meet AAA rating requirements but are listed for your information only.

CLARION HOTEL PARK AVENUE   **Phone: 212/532-4860**
[fyi]   Not evaluated. **Location:** 429 Park Ave S 10016. Facilities, services, and decor characterize a mid-range property.

FOUR POINTS BY SHERATON MANHATTAN CHELSEA   **Phone: 212/627-1888**

[fyi]	9/7-12/31	1P: $269-$299	2P: $269-$299	XP: $10	F18
	1/1-4/30	1P: $189-$249	2P: $189-$249	XP: $10	F18
	5/1-6/30	1P: $189-$229	2P: $189-$229	XP: $10	F18
	7/1-9/6	1P: $145-$199	2P: $145-$199	XP: $10	F18

Too new to rate, opening scheduled for November 2003. **Location:** Between 6th (Ave of the Americas) and 7th aves. 160 W 25th St 10011. **Amenities:** 148 units. **Cards:** AX, CB, DC, DS, JC, MC, VI. *(See color ad p 378)*

HAMPTON INN MANHATTAN/FINANCIAL DISTRICT   **Phone: 212/571-4400**
[fyi]   All Year   1P: $169-$229   2P: $179-$239
Too new to rate, opening scheduled for May 2004. **Location:** 320 Pearl St 10038. Fax: 212/571-4400.
Amenities: 65 units, pets. **Cards:** AX, CB, DC, DS, JC, MC, VI.

THE INN AT IRVING PLACE   **Phone: 212/533-4600**
[fyi]   Not evaluated. **Location:** Between 17th and 18th sts. 56 Irving Pl 10003. Facilities, services, and decor characterize an
upscale property.

─────── **WHERE TO DINE** ───────

66   **Lunch:** $6-$19   **Dinner:** $19-$38   **Phone:** 212/925-0202   (57)
▽▼▽▼▽   **Location:** In TriBeCa; between Worth and Leonard sts. 241 Church St 10013. **Hours:** noon-3 & 6-midnight, Fri &
Chinese   Sat-1 am, Sun noon-3 & 5:30-10:30 pm. **Reservations:** suggested. **Features:** A highly polished and
minimally embellished series of rooms includes a large tropical fish tank with a through-kitchen view. It's
easy to order a lot from a menu of either small tastes or slightly larger ones. Some of the familiar-sounding
dishes are stellar, with rich, clear flavors. Stir-fried shrimp, chive dumplings, beef short ribs and steamed cod with caramelized
onion, ginger and scallion look spectacular. Tapioca fruit parfait is texture-filled and fun. Dressy casual; cocktails. **Parking:** no
self-parking. **Cards:** AX, DC, MC, VI.   &M X

ALFAMA, FINE PORTUGUESE CUISINE   **Dinner:** $18-$26   **Phone:** 212/645-2500   (56)
(AAA)   **Location:** At Perry St. 551 Hudson St 10014. **Hours:** 6 pm-10:30 pm, Fri & Sat-11:30 pm. Closed: 12/25.
Reservations: suggested. **Features:** The cozy dining room is pleasant and fresh looking with pressed
▽▼▽▼▽   linen and a charming blue and white Portuguese theme. The menu is reflective of the fish and shellfish so
Portuguese   abundant in Portugal but there is also a selection of meats like braised chicken with smoked ham or
roasted skewered lamb with garlic. The menu changes but always offers homey hearty dishes though
prepared with a somewhat delicate touch. The selection of Portuguese wines is considerable. Dressy
casual; cocktails. **Parking:** no self-parking. **Cards:** AX, DC, DS, MC, VI.   X

AZ   **Dinner:** $45   **Phone:** 212/691-8888   (12)
▽▼▽▼▽   **Location:** Between 5th and 6th (Ave of the Americas) aves. 21 W 17th St 10011. **Hours:** 5:30 pm-11 pm,
Asian   Thurs-Sat to 11:30 pm, Sun-10 pm. Closed: 12/24, 12/25. **Reservations:** suggested. **Features:** Follow the
delicate sounds of a stone waterfall up the glass elevator to the airy glass-roofed dining room to settle in
and watch the stars while sampling Patricia Yeo's much-acclaimed modern Asian cuisine. The menu is
ever-changing so even frequent diners are surprised by the flavor mixtures they encounter and the wine list ascribes attributes
of the I-Ching to its numerous offerings. Dressy casual; cocktails. **Parking:** no self-parking. **Cards:** AX, DC, DS, MC, VI.
                                                                                                                    Y X

BABBO   **Dinner:** $16-$28   **Phone:** 212/777-0303   (7)
▽▼▽▼▽   **Location:** Between 6th Ave (Ave of the Americas) and MacDougal St; just w of Washington Square Park. 110 Waverly
Italian   Pl 10011. **Hours:** 5:30 pm-11:30 pm, Sun 5 pm-11 pm. Closed: 11/25, 12/25. **Reservations:** suggested.
Features: The hard-to-get Village favorite has received a lot of press for showcasing innovative, new
Italian cuisine. Mario Batali uses only fresh global products in designing a most discerning and modern
menu. Black tagliatelle with charred corn, rock shrimp and budding chives, along with foie gras ravioli with balsamic vinegar
reduction, take the place of traditional fare. The seven-course and pasta-tasting menus are worth their weight in calories.
Dressy casual; cocktails. **Parking:** street. **Cards:** AX, DC, MC, VI.   Y X

BALTHAZAR   **Lunch:** $11-$23   **Dinner:** $15-$24   **Phone:** 212/965-1414   (27)
▽▼▽▼▽   **Location:** In SoHo; between Broadway and Lafayette St. 80 Spring St 10012. **Hours:** 7:30 am-11:30, noon-5 &
French   6-midnight, Sat & Sun 10 am-4 & 6-midnight. Closed: 12/25. **Reservations:** required. **Features:** The
trendy hot spot is still a favorite hangout in which to see and be seen. Styled as a traditional brasserie, it
feels warm and authentic, with large depressed mirrors, decorative microtile floors, a pressed-tin ceiling
towering over the cavernous space and delightful art deco touches. Savory, flavorful and textural dishes—such as brandade,
steak frites, duck confit, duck shepherd's pie and skate—span the range from traditional to modern and would delight any
Frenchman. Casual dress; cocktails. **Parking:** no self-parking. **Cards:** AX, MC, VI.   Y X

BEPPE   **Lunch:** $17-$29   **Dinner:** $17-$29   **Phone:** 212/982-8422   (41)
▽▼▽▼▽   **Location:** Between Broadway and Park Ave S. 45 E 22nd St 10010. **Hours:** noon-2:30 & 5:30-10:30 pm, Fri &
Italian   Sat-11:30 pm. Closed major holidays; also Sun. **Reservations:** required. **Features:** A pleasant dining room
manages to be both modern and provincial with dark woods, beautiful burnt hues, warm brick walls and
shelves of grain and bean filled mason jars. Utterly charming and comfortable. Fine country cooking from
Tuscany means all house-made pastas, sausages, and custom farm grown produce. Simple cooking methods leave nothing to
be desired but more, more, more. Dressy casual; cocktails. **Parking:** no self-parking. **Cards:** AX, DC, DS, MC, VI.   Y X

(See map and index starting on p. 360)

BOND ST.
Japanese

Dinner: $18-$26   Phone: 212/777-2500   ③1

Location: In NoHo; between Broadway and Lafayette sts. 6 Bond St 10012. **Hours:** 6 pm-midnight, Sun-11 pm. Closed major holidays. **Reservations:** required. **Features:** In a non-descript brick townhouse, the restaurant exudes style and sophistication from every corner and every plate. Patrons can experience some of the finest modern Japanese cuisine around, from duck pho to fantastic sushi—both classic and innovative. Dressy casual; cocktails. **Parking:** no self-parking. **Cards:** AX, DC, MC, VI.

BOULEY
French

Lunch: $32-$36   Dinner: $34-$38   Phone: 212/964-2525   ⑤8

Location: At Duane St. 120 W Broadway 10013. **Hours:** 11:30 am-3 & 5:30-11:30 pm. Closed: for lunch 1/1 & 12/25. **Reservations:** required. **Features:** Two glorious dining rooms—one a rich red, the other a silvery white—are architecturally sophisticated and as romantic as could be, with elaborate flowers, flickering candlelight, the scent of warm apple and bedecked mantels. This also happens to be food nirvana. Dishes are lovely to behold, and preparatory skill is evident from the first glance to the last dab with a pristine linen napkin. A meal here is a dining event for sure. Semi-formal attire; cocktails. **Parking:** no self-parking. **Cards:** AX, DC, MC, VI.

CANTON
Chinese

Lunch: $20-$45   Dinner: $20-$45   Phone: 212/226-4441   ②1

Location: In Chinatown; between Bowery and Market sts. 45 Division St 10002. **Hours:** Open 5/1-7/5 & 8/16-4/30; noon-9:30 pm, Fri & Sat-10:30 pm. Closed: Mon & Tues. **Reservations:** suggested. **Features:** Subdued lighting gives the moderately upscale restaurant—a well-established local favorite—an air of romance. The seasonal menu centers on creative preparations of Cantonese cuisine, bathed in piquant, distinctive sauces. Servers are knowledgeable. Casual dress; beer & wine only. **Parking:** no self-parking.

CHANTERELLE
French

Lunch: $19-$25   Dinner: $84-$95   Phone: 212/966-6960   ④5

Location: In TriBeCa; at Hudson St. 2 Harrison St 10013. **Hours:** noon-2:30 & 5:30-11 pm. Closed major holidays; also 7/1-7/14, for lunch Sun & Mon. **Reservations:** suggested. **Features:** Elaborate architecture distinguishes the sophisticated dining room which seems to glitter with wine glasses under the soft lights. Window alcoves are charming. The menu changes monthly and showcases fresh seasonal produce and innovative combinations, which are complemented by an extensive wine book. The specialty seafood sausage with beurre blanc sauce is worth a try. Semi-formal attire; cocktails. **Parking:** street. **Cards:** AX, DC, DS, MC, VI.

CHELSEA BISTRO & BAR
French

Dinner: $18-$25   Phone: 212/727-2026   ②8

Location: Between 8th and 9th aves. 358 W 23rd St 10011. **Hours:** 5 pm-11 pm, Fri & Sat-11:30 pm, Sun-10:30 pm. Closed: 7/4, 9/6. **Reservations:** suggested. **Features:** The classic Parisian bistro focuses on delivering modernized classics, from leg of lamb to the famed goat cheese tart. Warm tones and an inviting brick hearth lend to the cozy atmosphere of the relaxed dining room. The glass-enclosed Garden Terrace Room has a more romantic appeal. The wine book is comprehensive. Dressy casual; cocktails. **Parking:** no self-parking. **Cards:** AX, DS, MC, VI.

CITY BAKERY
Bakery/Desserts

Lunch: $8-$16   Dinner: $8-$16   Phone: 212/366-1414   ⑯

Location: Between 5th and 6th (Ave of the Americas) aves. 3 W 18th St 10011. **Hours:** 7:30 am-7 pm, Sat 7 am-6 pm, Sun 9 am-6 pm. Closed major holidays. **Features:** Sample New York's most creative salad bar with dishes wide-ranging in inspiration, from Asian rice noodle salad to cornmeal crusted catfish. Alternatively, grab a seat at the soda fountain for hot items like mac n' cheese, ice creams or the best hot cocoa with homemade marshmallows. Don't forget to save room for dessert; cookies, cakes, tarts and the famed pretzel croissant are the specialties that originally made this spot a favorite. Casual dress. **Parking:** no self-parking. **Cards:** MC, VI.

CYCLO
Vietnamese

Dinner: $8-$15   Phone: 212/673-3957   ②

Location: Between 12th and 13th sts. 203 1st Ave 10003. **Hours:** 5 pm-11 pm, Fri & Sat-midnight. **Reservations:** suggested. **Features:** A rickshaw sits in front of the upbeat restaurant, which offers sidewalk or open air seating in good weather. Light and flavorful dishes, carefully prepared, are highlighted by fresh mint, cilantro, basil and savory sauces. Specialties include crispy snapper with spicy chili-lime sauce, grilled marinated pork over angel hair rice noodles and ginger chicken baked in a clay pot with shiitake mushrooms and scallion. It's hard to go wrong. Casual dress; beer & wine only. **Parking:** no self-parking. **Cards:** AX, DS, MC, VI.

DANUBE
Hungarian

Dinner: $28-$35   Phone: 212/791-3771   ②9

Location: Between Duane and Reade sts. 30 Hudson St 10013. **Hours:** 5:30 pm-11 pm. Closed major holidays; also Sun. **Reservations:** required. **Features:** A hint of Eastern European mystique is evident at this grand and enchanting TriBeCa fantasy. Dangling fringed lanterns softly illuminate the jewel tones, eccentric portraits, mosaic wall murals and accents of gold leaf. The deep banquette seats and throne-like chairs are color-rich, plush and velvety. David Bouley breathes new life into traditional Austro-Hungarian dishes, as the selections are contemporary and beguiling. What began as a whisper, is now a steady murmur around town. Dressy casual; cocktails. **Parking:** no self-parking. **Cards:** AX, DC, DS, MC, VI.

ELEVEN MADISON PARK
American

Lunch: $18-$23   Dinner: $22-$28   Phone: 212/889-0905   ⑤9

Location: At 24th St. 11 Madison Ave 10010. **Hours:** 11:30 am-2 & 5:30-10:30 pm, Fri & Sat-11 pm, Sun 5:30 pm-10 pm. Closed major holidays; also 12/24. **Reservations:** suggested. **Features:** Another Danny Meyer restaurant devoted to service but delivering culinary hits using fine ingredients and perfect dish pairings, thus ensuring continued popularity. The dining room itself, a reclaimed grand bank lobby, is something to behold in all its elegance and glory. This place seems to have it all: food, service and decor. Dressy casual; cocktails. **Parking:** no self-parking. **Cards:** AX, DC, DS, MC, VI.

(See map and index starting on p. 360)

EL QUIJOTE RESTAURANT **Lunch:** $7-$12   **Dinner:** $10-$30   **Phone:** 212/929-1855   ③⓪
▼▼ ▼▼
Spanish
Location: In Chelsea; between 7th and 8th aves. 226 W 23rd St 10011. **Hours:** noon-midnight, Fri & Sat-1 am. **Reservations:** accepted. **Features:** This place is the city's oldest Spanish restaurant, and little has changed since its inception. Older decor is accentuated with colorful murals and windmills. Lobster is brought in straight from the owner's fishing fleet. Paella and sangria are divine. Casual dress; cocktails. **Parking:** no self-parking. **Cards:** AX, DC, DS, MC, VI.   ☨ ☒

FLEUR DE SEL **Lunch:** $25-$33   **Dinner:** $28-$33   **Phone:** 212/460-9100   ⑥⓪
▼▼▼
French
Location: Between 5th Ave and Broadway. 5 E 20th St 10003. **Hours:** noon-2 & 5:30-10:30 pm, Fri & Sat-11 pm, Sun 5 pm-9 pm. **Closed:** 1/1, 12/25. **Reservations:** suggested. **Features:** This gem, with casual refinement serves French food with flair and civility. Seating is tight, other conversations easy to hear but no one seems to care as they focus on lovely dishes prepared with skill and wisdom. Crisp baby chicken with chanterelles and a foie gras emulsion, olive marinated lamb loin with a fennel and rosemary lamb jus, and seared sea scallops with honey sherry wine gastric and sage shine. The chef is not only master in the kitchen but his original art is on display. Dressy casual; cocktails. **Parking:** no self-parking. **Cards:** AX, DC, MC, VI.   ☒

GOTHAM BAR & GRILL **Lunch:** $16-$22   **Dinner:** $28-$41   **Phone:** 212/620-4020   ⑨
▼▼▼ ▼▼▼
American
Location: Between 5th Ave and University Pl. 12 E 12th 10003. **Hours:** noon-2:15 & 5:30-10 pm, Fri-11 pm, Sat 5 pm-11 pm, Sun 5 pm-10 pm. **Closed:** 1/1, 12/25. **Reservations:** suggested. **Features:** New York sophisticates have kept this bastion of Gotham chic busy from opening. The music, the black and white art photos, tall ceilings with enormous fabric hung lights, the deep mahogany bar and soft jazz in the background suit the city just fine. The food, creative and beautiful and decadently good, is the work of a master chef who all who have eaten here revere. Desserts are no less marvelous. Many say this is among the best. Dressy casual; cocktails. **Parking:** no self-parking. **Cards:** AX, DC, DS, MC, VI.   ☨ ☒

GRAMERCY TAVERN **Lunch:** $21-$68   **Dinner:** $68-$95   **Phone:** 212/477-0777   ⑤⓪
▼▼▼ ▼▼▼
Continental
Location: Between Park Ave S and Broadway. 42 E 20th St 10003. **Hours:** noon-2 & 5:30-10 pm, Fri & Sat 5:30 pm-11 pm, Sun 5:30 pm-10 pm. Closed major holidays. **Reservations:** suggested. **Features:** A rustic, yet first-class event; patrons of the traditional American tavern never had it so good. The use of the finest ingredients, linens and tableware, in contrast to wooden floors, copper enhancements, fresh flowers and trellised vines evoke the atmosphere of old New England with all the best of New World refinement. This NYC institution bestows true hospitality as an accent to its flawless pioneering approach to food. Semi-formal attire; cocktails. **Parking:** no self-parking. **Cards:** AX, DC, DS, MC, VI.   ♿Ⓜ ☨ ☒

IL CORTILE **Lunch:** $15-$24   **Dinner:** $15-$24   **Phone:** 212/226-6060   ①
▼▼▼ ▼▼▼
Italian
Location: Between Canal and Hester sts; in Little Italy. 125 Mulberry St 10013. **Hours:** noon-midnight, Fri & Sat-1 am. **Closed:** 11/25, 12/24, 12/25. **Reservations:** suggested. **Features:** The restaurant, in the bustling heart of Little Italy, has the inviting feel of a terrace garden, with open skylights, natural wood tables and brick walls. Specialties center on seafood, veal and homemade pasta. Seating is available on the seasonal patio. Casual dress; cocktails. **Parking:** no self-parking. **Cards:** AX, DC, DS, MC, VI.   ☨ ☒

IL MULINO **Lunch:** $25-$45   **Dinner:** $25-$45   **Phone:** 212/673-3783   ⑲
▼▼▼
Italian
Location: In Greenwich Village; between Sullivan and Thompson sts. 86 W Third St 10012. **Hours:** Open 5/1-6/30 & 8/1-4/30; noon-2:30 & 5-11:30 pm, Sat from 5 pm. Closed major holidays; also Sun. **Reservations:** required. **Features:** If you hope to dine here, call well in advance. The charming haven is quite small and extremely popular. The magnificent cuisine is pure Old World Italian—rich, bountiful and among the city's finest. The specialty rack of lamb is accented by fresh sage. Semi-formal attire; cocktails. **Parking:** no self-parking. **Cards:** AX, DC, MC, VI.   ☨ ☒

I TRULLI **Lunch:** $17-$28   **Dinner:** $19-$32   **Phone:** 212/481-7372   ③
▼▼▼
Provincial Italian
Location: Between Park and Lexington aves. 122 E 27th St 10016. **Hours:** noon-3 & 5:30-10:30 pm, Sat 5:30 pm-11 pm. Closed major holidays; also Sun. **Reservations:** suggested. **Features:** Distinct Mediterranean style makes for a charming setting for creative and savory dishes, some prepared on the rotisserie or in the wood-burning oven. Warm-weather dining in the walled garden, which has a rush-mat roof and lovely waterfall, has a hide-away appeal. Casual dress; cocktails. **Parking:** no self-parking. **Cards:** AX, DC, MC, VI.   ☨ ☒

KATZ DELI **Lunch:** $8-$16   **Dinner:** $8-$16   **Phone:** 212/254-2246   ㉔
▼
Deli/Subs
Sandwiches
Location: At Ludlow St; on the Lower East Side. 205 E Houston 10002. **Hours:** 8 am-10 pm, Wed & Thurs-11 pm, Fri & Sat-3 am. **Features:** Katz's has been the quintessential New York deli for over 113 years now; serving up heaping portions of great Kosher food such as steaming pastrami sandwiches, knishes, and more. If it looks familiar, a scene from "Harry Met Sally" was filmed here. Casual dress. **Parking:** no self-parking. **Cards:** AX, MC, VI.   ☒

LAYLA **Dinner:** $18-$26   **Phone:** 212/431-0700   ㉝
▼▼ ▼▼
Mediterranean
Location: In SoHo; jct W Franklin St. 211 W Broadway 10013. **Hours:** 5:30 pm-10:30 pm, Fri & Sat-11:30 pm. Closed major holidays; also Sun. **Reservations:** suggested. **Features:** The setting is rich and exotic, with mosaics and pottery shards creating swirls overhead and on the walls; belly dancers sway through the maze of tables later in the evening. The menu offers modern takes on traditional cuisine from Middle-Eastern countries. A popular choice is the mezze, in which appetizers are grouped hot and cold for a whole meal. Casual dress; cocktails. **Parking:** street. **Cards:** AX, DC, DS, MC, VI.   ☨ ☒

(See map and index starting on p. 360)

L'ECOLE, THE RESTAURANT OF THE FRENCH CULINARY INSTITUTE — **Lunch:** $20 — **Dinner:** $30 — **Phone:** 212/219-3300 ⑰

◆◆◆ Nouvelle French

Location: In SoHo; at Grand St. 462 Broadway 10013. **Hours:** 12:15 pm-2:30 & 6-9 pm, Thurs-Sat 12:15 pm-2:30 & 5:30-9 pm. Closed major holidays; also Sun. **Reservations:** suggested, for dinner. **Features:** Students of the institute prepare the innovative, daily changing menu, which includes a prix-fixe lunch as well as four- and five-course prix fixe menus at dinner. Set in the trendy SoHo environment, the restaurant displays an elegant simplicity. Casual dress; cocktails. **Parking:** no self-parking. **Cards:** AX, DC, DS, MC, VI. ⊠

LE MADRI — **Lunch:** $13-$22 — **Dinner:** $16-$30 — **Phone:** 212/727-8022 ㉜

◆◆◆ Northern Italian

Location: At 7th Ave. 168 W 18th St 10011. **Hours:** noon-3 & 6-10:30 pm, Sun from 6 pm. Closed major holidays. **Reservations:** required. **Features:** The warm, roomy dining room is appointed with Tuscan decor. Osso buco, roasted salmon and the specialty baby artichoke salad are outstanding menu selections. The wine list emphasizes imported Italian varieties. The homemade tiramisu is light and fluffy. Off-site validated parking is offered. Dressy casual; cocktails. **Parking:** on-site. **Cards:** AX, DC, DS, MC, VI. 🍸 ⊠

L'ORTO RISTORANTE ELEGANTE — **Lunch:** $18-$23 — **Dinner:** $18-$23 — **Phone:** 212/742-8524 (55)

◆◆ Italian

Location: Between Maiden Ln and Platt St. 5 Gold St 10038. **Hours:** 11:30 am-10 pm, Sat from 5 pm. Closed: 1/1, 11/25, 12/25; also Sun. **Reservations:** required. **Features:** Hidden on a side street, this unpretentious restaurant serves up classic Italian cuisine. The menu offers many favorite dishes, with some having slight variations. After a hearty dinner, relax in the comfortable dining room, enjoying a flavored grappa. Dressy casual; cocktails. **Parking:** no self-parking. **Cards:** AX, DC, DS, MC, VI. ⊠

MAMLOUK — **Dinner:** $30 — **Phone:** 212/529-3477 ⑪

◆◆ Middle Eastern

Location: Between Aves A and B. 211 E 4th St 10009. **Hours:** 7 pm-10 pm. Closed: Mon. **Reservations:** suggested. **Features:** A narrow little restaurant where diners sit at low tables in short inlaid chairs and enjoy multi-dish courses of what the chef has prepared. There is no room for disappointment with the fragrantly seasoned tenderly cooked food that emerges. Salads, dips, breads, olives, meats and braised and stewed vegetables are followed by dessert. For large groups, reserve a couple of couches and ottomans below and follow the meal with the houka whose long pipe can reach easily around the table. Casual dress; cocktails. **Parking:** no self-parking. **Cards:** AX, DC, MC, VI. ⊠

MEET — **Dinner:** $16-$28 — **Phone:** 212/242-0990 (53)

◆◆◆ American

Location: In the meat-packing district; between 9th Ave and Washington St. 71-73 Gansevoort St 10014. **Hours:** 4 pm-2 am, Fri & Sat-4 am. Closed: 9/6, 11/25, 12/25. **Reservations:** suggested. **Features:** This restaurant offers a cozy respite. Rich velvet draperies, a lit curving catwalk, and a Feng Shui consulation conceal this spot's history as a meat locker. The menu offers comforting bistro fare as wide-ranging as seared duck, butternut squash ravioli and foie gras terrine, showing a creativity that never overwhelms. Casual dress; cocktails. **Parking:** street. **Cards:** AX, MC, VI. ⊠

MESA GRILL — **Lunch:** $10-$18 — **Dinner:** $18-$32 — **Phone:** 212/807-7400 ㉞

◆◆◆ Regional American

Location: Between 15th and 16th sts. 102 5th Ave 10011. **Hours:** noon-2:30 & 5:30-10:30 pm, Fri-11 pm, Sat 11:30 am-2:30 & 5-11 pm, Sun 11:30 am-3 & 5:30-10:30 pm. Closed: 12/25. **Reservations:** required. **Features:** Among the chef's piquant, Southwest-inspired creations are spice-crusted black Angus steak, tuna steak with pineapple/green chile glaze, red chile-rubbed rabbit, ancho-rubbed chicken and yellow corn-crusted chiles rellenos filled with eggplant and goat cheese. Flavors burst from every dish. Weekend brunch is a tasty experience. Dressy casual; cocktails. **Parking:** no self-parking. **Cards:** AX, DC, DS, MC, VI. ⊠

MONTE'S RESTAURANT — **Lunch:** $8-$22 — **Dinner:** $8-$22 — **Phone:** 212/228-9194 ⑱

AAA ◆◆ Italian

Location: In Greenwich Village; between Bleeker and W 3rd sts. 97 MacDougal St 10012. **Hours:** noon-11 pm, Fri & Sat-11:30 pm. Closed: 11/25, 12/25; also Tues. **Reservations:** suggested. **Features:** The charming owner-host delights in welcoming every guest to the family-oriented restaurant, in an old New York setting. Representative of home-cooking like Mama made are traditional pasta, veal and seafood dishes. Walls are lined with maps and celebrity pictures. Casual dress; cocktails. **Parking:** no self-parking. **Cards:** AX, DC, DS, MC, VI. 🍸 ⊠

MONTRACHET — **Lunch:** $16-$22 — **Dinner:** $24-$30 — **Phone:** 212/219-2777 ⑧

◆◆◆ French

Location: In TriBeCa; between White St and Walker. 239 W Broadway 10013. **Hours:** 5:30 pm-10 pm, Fri noon-2:15 & 5:30-10:30 pm, Sat 5:30 pm-10:30 pm. Closed major holidays; also Sun. **Reservations:** suggested. **Features:** The non-descript entrance, painted red, marks the spot. Settle in at the unpretentious bistro to enjoy modern French cuisine and excellent wines. The dining room is small and intimate, the perfect place to begin a romantic night on the town. The wait staff is focused and professional. Casual dress; cocktails. **Parking:** no self-parking. **Cards:** AX, DC, DS, MC, VI. ⊠

NAM — **Lunch:** $8-$15 — **Dinner:** $10-$16 — **Phone:** 212/267-1777 (61)

◆◆ Vietnamese

Location: Between Church St and W Broadway. 110 Reade St 10013. **Hours:** noon-2 & 5:30-10:30 pm, Fri-11 pm, Sat 5:30 pm-11 pm, Sun 5:30 pm-10:30 pm. Closed: 1/1, 11/25, 12/25. **Reservations:** accepted. **Features:** Casual and attractive with a serene, grown-up refinement, the restaurant is a great place to come for not-so-typical, but still traditional, Vietnamese cooking. Wok-seared chopped monkfish with herbs, grilled eggplant with ginger and lime sauce and crispy spring rolls are popular starters, while crispy red snapper in chili-lime sauce, caramelized shrimp and pork in light pepper sauce are popular main courses. Respectful servers are pleased to offer menu advice. Casual dress; cocktails. **Parking:** no self-parking. **Cards:** AX, MC, VI. ⊠

(See map and index starting on p. 360)

NOBU   Lunch: $12-$20   Dinner: $12-$25   Phone: 212/219-0500   ⑤⑴
Japanese   Location: In TriBeCa; at Franklin St. 105 Hudson St 10013. Hours: 11:45 am-2:15 & 5:45-10:15 pm, Sat & Sun from 5:45 pm. Closed major holidays. Reservations: suggested. Features: Continually voted one of New York's best and for good reason. The menu is a melange of flavors and textures, featuring mainly finest quality fish and seafood, best experienced "family-style", sharing with the table so as to experience a range of exquisite dishes with explosive flavors. The server will expertly guide you through the menu and you will find yourself on the edge of your seat with anticipation. Casual dress; cocktails. Parking: no self-parking. Cards: AX, DC, MC, VI.   ✕

NOVITA   Lunch: $12-$21   Dinner: $12-$21   Phone: 212/677-2222   ④⑺
Northern Italian   Location: In Gramercy Park; between Park Ave S and Lexington. 102 E 22nd St 10010. Hours: noon-3 & 6-11 pm, Fri & Sat-midnight, Sun 5 pm-10 pm. Closed major holidays. Reservations: suggested. Features: Polished wood floors, crisp linen and butter-yellow walls lend a soothing hand to the tailored decor. Pappardelle with lamb ragu and porcini mushrooms, pan-roasted sea bass with artichoke fricassee and roasted breast of duck with Barolo wine sauce are among modern dishes on a menu of Northern Italian fare. Casual dress; cocktails. Parking: no self-parking. Cards: AX, DC, MC, VI.   ✕

THE OLD HOMESTEAD   Lunch: $12-$25   Dinner: $21-$38   Phone: 212/242-9040   ⑹
Steak House   Location: Between 14th and 15th sts. 56 9th Ave 10011. Hours: noon-3:30 & 4-10:45 pm, Sat 1 pm-11:45 pm, Sun 1 pm-9:45 pm. Reservations: suggested. Features: In the historic Chelsea meat market district, the restaurant has specialties that range from succulent prime sirloin steak, filet mignon and prime rib to creamed spinach and cottage fries. The restaurant has been operated by the same family since 1954. Casual dress; cocktails. Parking: no self-parking. Cards: AX, CB, DC, MC, VI.   ⓨ ✕

OLD TOWN BAR & RESTAURANT Historic   Lunch: $7-$9   Dinner: $7-$10   Phone: 212/529-6732   ③⑸
American   Location: Between Park Ave and Broadway. 45 E 18th St 10003. Hours: noon-midnight. Closed major holidays. Features: Housed in an 1892 structure, the old, New York establishment still features many of historic architectural elements, including a pressed-tin ceiling, magnificent bar and beveled glass mirrors. Expect generous portions of hearty tavern food. Casual dress; cocktails. Parking: no self-parking. Cards: AX, MC, VI.   ⓨ ✕

OLIVES   Lunch: $17-$28   Dinner: $22-$29   Phone: 212/353-8345   ⑥⑵
American   Location: In W New York-Union Square at 17th St. 201 Park Ave S 10003. Hours: 7 am-10:30, noon-2:30 & 6-10:30 pm, Fri-11 pm, Sat 10 am-2 & 6-11 pm, Sun 10 am-2 & 5:30-9:30 pm. Reservations: suggested. Features: The mesmerizing space—with loud, rhythmic music, suave warmth, blown glass shaded light fixtures and energy wafting in from the bar—exudes style. The more important half of the equation is the superb food. Plate envy could be a problem, but there are flexible tasting menus and knowledgeable servers to assist. The dishes, which merge time-tested flavor combinations and scrumptious textures, are the brainchild of skilled staffers who must, themselves, love to eat. Dressy casual; cocktails. Parking: no self-parking. Cards: AX, MC, VI.   ♿Ⓜ ⓨ ✕

ONE IF BY LAND, TWO IF BY SEA   Dinner: $59   Phone: 212/228-0822   ①⑷
American   Location: Between W 4th St and 7th Ave; just off 7th Ave. 17 Barrow St 10014. Hours: 5:30 pm-11:15 pm. Closed: 5/31, 9/6. Reservations: suggested. Features: Overlooking a small courtyard garden, the beautifully restored, 18th-century carriage house once owned by Aaron Burr offers candlelight dining in a room filled with the sounds of piano music. Beef Wellington and souffles are specialties on a menu of classic and creative cuisine. Parking across the street. Semi-formal attire; cocktails; entertainment. Parking: no self-parking. Cards: AX, DC, DS, MC, VI.   ⓨ ✕

PACIFICA   Lunch: $10-$20   Dinner: $15-$25   Phone: 212/966-8898   ②⓪
Chinese   Location: In Chinatown; corner of Howard St, just n of Canal St; in Holiday Inn Downtown. 138 LaFayette St 10013. Hours: 6:30 am-10:30 pm. Reservations: suggested. Features: Enjoy many exotic alternatives to "American Chinese" cuisine at the relaxing, second-floor restaurant, which overlooks the bustling street. The menu centers on Cantonese-style preparations. Oriental paintings in lacquered frames hang on the walls. Casual dress; cocktails. Parking: no self-parking. Cards: AX, DC, DS, JC, MC, VI.   ♿Ⓜ ⓨ ✕

PASTIS   Lunch: $9-$16   Dinner: $11-$34   Phone: 212/929-4844   ②⑸
French   Location: Corner of Little W 12th St and Ninth Ave. 9 Ninth Ave 10014. Hours: 9 am-5 & 6-2 am, Fri & Sat-3 am. Closed: 12/25. Reservations: accepted. Features: This very French brasserie on the cusp of the trendy meat packing district is a hit with locals eager for the charm of this old converted storage space. Beautiful fanned tile and older rustic wood floors, walls accented with old tile and hung with giant tarnished mirrors, and fans whirling above add rustic charm. The menu is big on French comfort food such as pissaladiere, grilled sardines, croque monsieur or madame, steak frites, leg of lamb, skate and more. Casual dress; cocktails. Parking: no self-parking. Cards: AX, MC, VI.   ⓨ ✕

PATRIA   Lunch: $14-$19   Dinner: $20-$32   Phone: 212/777-6211   ③⑹
Ethnic   Location: 20th St, southwest corner. 250 Park Ave S 10003. Hours: noon-3 & 5:30-11 pm, Fri & Sat-midnight, Sun 5:30 pm-10:30 pm. Closed: 11/25. Reservations: suggested, strongly advise. Features: The trend-setting spot offers nuevo Latino cuisine, which blends unusual ingredients, vibrant flavors and stunning presentations. Seviches and empanadas—including tasting menus for each—are a great way to start the meal. The multilevel dining room is charged with high energy. Premium wines from Spain, Chile and Argentina are featured. Dressy casual; cocktails. Parking: no self-parking. Cards: AX, DC, DS, MC, VI.   ⓨ ✕

(See map and index starting on p. 360)

PEKING DUCK HOUSE   **Lunch:** $12-$34   **Dinner:** $12-$34   **Phone:** 212/227-1810   ⑥③
Chinese
Location: In Chinatown; between Chatam Square and Pell St. 28 Mott St 10013. **Hours:** 11:30 am-10:30 pm, Fri & Sat-11:30 pm. Closed major holidays. **Reservations:** suggested. **Features:** Guests walk past the heavy green curtain into a stylishly simple pair of dining rooms. The menu shows a heavy emphasis on seafood, as well as the signature Peking duck. The duck, which is crisp, moist and tender, is brought to the table; the chef follows, deftly cutting the bird to produce a beautiful platter of slices that are expertly folded into soft, warm pancakes with plum sauce, scallions and crispy skin. Virtually every table orders a duck. Casual dress; beer & wine only. **Parking:** no self-parking. **Cards:** AX, MC, VI.

PERIYALI   **Lunch:** $17-$26   **Dinner:** $18-$29   **Phone:** 212/463-7890   ①③
Greek
Location: Between 5th and 6th (Ave of the Americas) aves. 35 W 20th St 10011. **Hours:** noon-3 & 5:30-11 pm, Fri-11:30 pm, Sat 5:30 pm-11:30 pm. Closed major holidays; also Sun. **Reservations:** suggested. **Features:** Long a local favorite, the relaxed, gentrified Mediterranean dining room serves flavorful fresh dishes prepared by skilled hands. Of particular interest are the many appetizers, such as octopus, fava beans with garlic sauce, cheese and spinach phyllo packets and taramasalata. Sauteed sweetbreads, barbecue quail, moussaka and rabbit stew are among other menu items, and there is a lengthy list of Greek wines. Homemade desserts are delicious. Garden seating is a pleasure if available. Dressy casual; cocktails. **Parking:** no self-parking. **Cards:** AX, DC, MC, VI.

PING'S   **Lunch:** $10-$20   **Dinner:** $20-$40   **Phone:** 212/602-9988   ④⑧
Chinese
Location: In Chinatown; just beyond Bayard St. 22 Mott St 10013. **Hours:** 10 am-midnight. **Reservations:** accepted. **Features:** The restaurant is popular with locals and uptowners in search of a Chinese meal. Large, clear tanks of shrimp and fish guide up to the brightly lit, crowded, no-nonsense room. As dishes go by and heads turn, guests might mutter: "I should have ordered that." Numerous dishes cater to the wary and the adventurous alike. Casual dress; beer & wine only. **Parking:** no self-parking. **Cards:** MC, VI.

PIPA   **Lunch:** $8-$20   **Dinner:** $10-$25   **Phone:** 212/677-2233   ⑤④
Spanish
Location: Between Broadway and Park Ave. 38 E 19th St 10003. **Hours:** noon-3 & 6-11 pm, Fri noon-3 & 5:30-midnight, Sat 5:30 pm-midnight, Sun 11 am-3:30 & 5:30-10 pm. Closed major holidays. **Reservations:** accepted. **Features:** Despite the storefront setting, including brick walls, a myriad of carpets and fabrics draped about and assorted chandeliers of every style imaginable, there's an attic feel to this spot. You can spend as much or as little you like here with the Spanish tapas style menu of tiny plates of seafood bites, marinated items, savory sausages and especially the flatbreads, with which the weirder the topping combinations sound, the better the taste. Casual dress; cocktails. **Parking:** no self-parking. **Cards:** AX, MC, VI.

RECTANGLES   **Lunch:** $8-$16   **Dinner:** $11-$16   **Phone:** 212/677-8410   ③⑨
Mediterranean
Location: Corner of 10th St. 159 2nd Ave 10003. **Hours:** 11:30 am-midnight, Fri & Sat-1 am. Closed: Passover week. **Reservations:** suggested. **Features:** In the exciting East Village, the casual, often tightly packed restaurant is popular with a young Israeli crowd. Among the assorted salads are hummus, tahini, baba ghanoush, baked or marinated eggplant and other selections that can easily be a meal when paired with a warm pita. Lamb, chicken and kafta kebabs also are good, and with choices such as beef goulash and roast lamb shank, diners face difficult choices. Casual dress; cocktails. **Parking:** no self-parking. **Cards:** AX, DC, DS, MC, VI.

SAL ANTHONY'S S P Q R   **Lunch:** $13   **Dinner:** $16-$25   **Phone:** 212/925-3120   ⑤
Italian
Location: In Little Italy; between Hester and Grand sts. 133 Mulberry St 10013. **Hours:** noon-11 pm, Fri & Sat-midnight. **Reservations:** suggested. **Features:** In the center of Little Italy, with neighboring restaurants on either side, something for everyone can be found on the traditional menu. The room is large, wide open and bright though surrounded by dark wood paneled walls. Fresh flowers, artwork and an attractive wall mural add a bit of cheer. Casual dress; cocktails. **Parking:** no self-parking. **Cards:** AX, DC, MC, VI.

SAVOY RESTAURANT   **Lunch:** $9-$14   **Dinner:** $18-$26   **Phone:** 212/219-8570   ①⑤
American
Location: In SoHo; corner of Prince and Crosby sts. 70 Prince St 10012. **Hours:** noon-3 & 6-10:30 pm, Fri & Sat-11 pm, Sun 6 pm-10 pm. Closed major holidays. **Reservations:** suggested. **Features:** The small storefront is unassuming from the outside and pleasant on the inside with a small stone fireplace, wood floors, tables and chairs, and varnished particle-wood walls lined with decorative plates at ceiling height. The menu reflects seasonings and cooking methods from various regions around the world, resulting in colorful offerings with unusual ingredients that may surprise. If available, a side order of fava bean tahini with grilled bread deserves a try. Casual dress; cocktails. **Parking:** no self-parking. **Cards:** AX, MC, VI.

SECOND AVENUE KOSHER DELI   **Lunch:** $8-$23   **Dinner:** $15-$23   **Phone:** 212/677-0606   ④⓪
Kosher
Location: At 10th St. 156 2nd Ave 10003. **Hours:** 7:30 am-midnight, Fri & Sat-3 am. Closed: Jewish holidays. **Features:** In the East Village neighborhood of Manhattan, this old family deli is surprisingly warm and comfortable. The menu centers on outstanding kosher food, including magnificent chopped liver and tasty chicken soup. The thick and chewy chocolate bagka is sure to please. Casual dress; beer & wine only. **Parking:** street. **Cards:** AX, DC, DS, MC, VI.

SUSHISAMBA PARK   **Lunch:** $15-$29   **Dinner:** $17-$26   **Phone:** 212/475-9377   ⑥④
Japanese
Location: Between 19th and 20th sts. 245 Park Ave S 10003. **Hours:** 11:45 am-1 am, Thurs-Sat to 2 am, Sun 1 pm-midnight. **Reservations:** suggested. **Features:** Vibrant colors of mango, red, lime and gold celebrate Brazil's Carnival. Bubble-shaped lights add another jolt of fun. The food is lively, making use of Brazilian, Japanese and Peruvian cuisines in creative fusion, furiously flavorful. The tuna sashimi seviche with orange, ginger, yuzu and white soy, octopus sashimi seviche with sweet sake and mustard, sushi combinations, grilled meats with farofa and chimichurri are examples of cuisines worked together. Cocktails are wild and wonderful. Casual dress; cocktails. **Parking:** no self-parking. **Cards:** AX, MC, VI.

(See map and index starting on p. 360)

SWEET-N-TART CAFE **Lunch:** $3-$9 **Dinner:** $3-$9 **Phone:** 212/334-8088 ④

Chinese

Location: Jct Canal St. 76 Mott St 10013. **Hours:** 9 am-10 pm. **Features:** Hidden beneath Mott Street, this small cafe is typically filled to capacity; be prepared to wait in the street. Once inside, the wonderful authentic Chinese dishes eclipse the basic, straightforward approach to decor and service. For the first-timer, try the special suggestions and one of the wonderful health tonics. Casual dress. **Parking:** no self-parking.

TABLA **Lunch:** $14-$23 **Dinner:** $23-$35 **Phone:** 212/889-0667 ㊳

Indian

Location: At 25th St. 11 Madison Ave 10010. **Hours:** noon-2 & 5:30-10:30 pm, Sat from 5:30 pm, Sun 5:30 pm-10 pm. Closed major holidays. **Reservations:** suggested. **Features:** Eye catching and visually appealing with hints of art-deco once you ascend the spiral staircase which leads from the very popular lively scene of the Bread Bar downstairs to the more subdued polished scene upstairs. Aroma of spice and herbs vitually waft up from the menu as you read. Some ingredients are exotic but the servers can explain. Dishes arrive full of flavor and wonderful texture. The tasting menu is a great way to sample. Dressy casual; cocktails. **Parking:** no self-parking. **Cards:** AX, DC, DS, MC, VI.

TAMARIND **Lunch:** $13-$23 **Dinner:** $13-$23 **Phone:** 212/674-7400 ㊷

Indian

Location: Between Lexington and Park aves. 41-43 E 22nd St 10010. **Hours:** 11:30 am-2:45 & 5:30-11:30 pm. Closed: 1/1. **Reservations:** suggested. **Features:** A very lovely dining room with silk lanterns, gentle lights, soft fabric walls, and a display of old calf bells, sets the mood for the exotic meal. Food is prepared in a exhibition kitchen by masters. Dishes like lotus root dumplings in a spicy sauce, shrimp in aromatic coconut sauce, roasted mint and ginger marinated leg of lamb, and oven roasted cornish game hen are but a few of the anything- but-ordinary selections. Service is gracious and will help with difficult decisions! Dressy casual; cocktails. **Parking:** no self-parking. **Cards:** AX, DC, DS, MC, VI.

TRIBECA GRILL **Lunch:** $12-$22 **Dinner:** $17-$29 **Phone:** 212/941-3900 ㊹

American

Location: In TriBeCa; at Franklin St. 375 Greenwich St 10013. **Hours:** 11:30 am-3 & 5:30-11 pm, Fri & Sat-11:30 pm, Sun-10 pm. Closed major holidays; also for lunch Sat. **Reservations:** required. **Features:** Many celebrities enjoy the famous spot, which is owned by Robert DeNiro in partnership with noted restaurateur Drew Nieporent. The unpretentious setting radiates energy, and a down-to-earth mood punctuates the renovated warehouse, which has brick walls hung with original art and high ceilings traversed by large painted pipes. Contemporary cuisine is on the menu. Casual dress; cocktails. **Parking:** no self-parking. **Cards:** AX, DC, DS, MC, VI.

UNION PACIFIC **Lunch:** $20 **Dinner:** $68 **Phone:** 212/995-8500 (52)

American

Location: In Gramercy Park; between Park Ave S and Lexington Ave. 111 E 22nd St 10010. **Hours:** noon-2 & 5:30-10 pm, Sat 5:15 pm-10:30 pm. Closed major holidays; also Sun. **Reservations:** suggested. **Features:** Famed chef Rocco Dispirito, trained in Europe but inspired by the Far East, merges the two in this stylish spot. A rock garden and a trickling curtain of water provide the Eastern influence to the setting and spices from fresh wasabi to Thai basil flavor the creative dishes on a seasonally changing menu. Dressy casual; cocktails. **Parking:** street. **Cards:** AX, DC, DS, MC, VI.

VERBENA **Dinner:** $18-$29 **Phone:** 212/260-5454 ㊻

American

Location: In Gramercy Park; between 17th and 18th sts. 54 Irving Pl 10003. **Hours:** 5:30 pm-10:30 pm, Sat-11 pm, Sun 11:30 am-2:30 & 5-10 pm. Closed major holidays. **Reservations:** required. **Features:** In a Federal-style townhouse, the dining room is appointed with sleek, simple stylings, and the candlelit courtyard has an inviting, relaxed charm. Mediterranean influences infuse preparations of contemporary American cuisine. Griddled rainbow trout with roasted fennel and onions, grilled brown-sugar-cured pork chop with sweet corn cake, and spice-lacquered duck with pea shoots, yucca and wild huckleberries are examples of creative cuisine made from seasonal ingredients. Wines are distinctive. Dressy casual; cocktails. **Parking:** no self-parking. **Cards:** AX, DC, MC, VI.

VERITAS **Dinner:** $68 **Phone:** 212/353-3700 ㊲

American

Location: Between Park Ave S and Broadway. 43 E 20th St 10003. **Hours:** 5:30 pm-10:30 pm, Sun 5 pm-9:30 pm. Closed major holidays. **Reservations:** required. **Features:** The intimate dining room, modern and hip, with illuminated art glass and original art on red brick walls, soft track lighting and flickering candle light, is perfect for an un-assuming quiet night out with a well prepared dinner of upscale comfort food, beautifully presented. For wine lovers, this is Mecca. Dressy casual; cocktails. **Parking:** no self-parking. **Cards:** AX, DC, DS, MC, VI.

VILLA MOSCONI RESTAURANT **Lunch:** $10-$22 **Dinner:** $11-$27 **Phone:** 212/673-0390 ㉒

AAA

Italian

Location: In Greenwich Village; between Bleeker and Houston sts. 69 MacDougal St 10012. **Hours:** noon-11 pm. Closed: 12/25; also Sun. **Reservations:** suggested. **Features:** Special requests are handled expediently at the casual restaurant, which is known for flavorful, traditional preparations of homemade pasta. The down-to-earth atmosphere is reminiscent of an Old World setting. Servers are prompt and efficient. Casual dress; cocktails. **Parking:** no self-parking. **Cards:** AX, DC, DS, MC, VI.

WASHINGTON PARK **Lunch:** $14-$20 **Dinner:** $26-$29 **Phone:** 212/529-4400 (65)

American

Location: At 9th St. 24 Fifth Ave 10011. **Hours:** noon-2:30 & 5:30-11 pm, Sat from 5:30 pm, Sun noon-4 & 5-10 pm. Closed: 1/1. **Reservations:** suggested. **Features:** Although there is an element of sophistication, the manner remains casual and relaxed. Groups gather to have a good time and order from the notable wine list and the menu of both simple and special market-inspired dishes, which the skilled chef dreams up daily. Fritto misto is a heaping pile of light-as-air fried seafood, which is de rigueur at each table. Chicken and fries have become somewhat of a signature dish for the chef's groupies. Dressy casual; cocktails. **Parking:** no self-parking. **Cards:** AX, MC, VI.

(See map and index starting on p. 360)

ZOE RESTAURANT   **Lunch:** $10-$15   **Dinner:** $18-$29   **Phone:** 212/966-6722   ㉓

American

Location: In SoHo; between Broadway and Mercer St. 90 Prince St 10012. **Hours:** noon-3 & 6-10:30 pm, Fri-11 pm, Sat-11:30 pm, Sun 11:30 am-3 & 5:30-10 pm; Saturday & Sunday brunch. Closed: 12/25; also Mon. **Reservations:** suggested. **Features:** Crispy calamari with Vietnamese dipping sauce and the grilled tuna club with wasabi mayonnaise are representative of flavorful dishes on the varied menu. Terra cotta columns and tile work in the cast-iron building date back to the 1890s. Casual dress; cocktails. **Parking:** no self-parking. **Cards:** AX, CB, DC, MC, VI.

--------- ***The following restaurants have not been evaluated by AAA*** ---------
but are listed for your information only.

71 CLINTON FRESH FOOD   **Phone:** 212/614-6960

[fyi]   Not evaluated. **Location:** Between Rivington and Stanton sts. 71 Clinton St 10002. **Features:** Creative dishes that pique interest and taste buds with layered flavors, sometimes sweet and savory together, prepared by a skilled hand. Crowded, close-knit seating but few mind.

BLUE WATER GRILL   **Phone:** 212/675-9500

[fyi]   Not evaluated. **Location:** At 16th St. 31 Union Square W. **Features:** Seafood restaurant located in a former bank. Open for lunch and dinner.

CAFE LEBOWITZ   **Phone:** 212/219-2399

[fyi]   Not evaluated. **Location:** At Elizabeth St. 14 Spring St 10010. **Features:** Ultra-relaxed may describe the attitude of the nifty neighborhood cafe, which serves favorites such as duck confit, croque monsieur, artichoke vinaigrette and steak frites. The charcuterie platter—which displays thinly sliced cured meats, pate, pickles, confit and grilled bread—can make a meal itself.

CANDELA RESTAURANT   **Phone:** 212/254-1600

[fyi]   Not evaluated. **Location:** Between Park Ave and Irving Pl. 116 E 16th St. **Features:** Open for dinner, the restaurant offers an upscale romantic atmosphere.

CAPITALE   **Phone:** 212/334-5500

[fyi]   Not evaluated. **Location:** At Grand St. 130 Bowery 10013. **Features:** Having been a bank designed by the likes of Stanford White, the restaurant sports a massive interior with opulent decor reminiscent of the ancient Greeks. The food manages to refocus the diner's attention away from the room. Plates, which sometimes show unexpected food pairings, brim with eye appeal, creativity and robust flavor.

CHEZ ES SAADA   **Phone:** 212/777-5617

[fyi]   Not evaluated. **Location:** 42 E First St 10003. **Features:** Moroccan cuisine with a French twist is a good thing at the restaurant, which is hard to find due to lack of signage.

CHINATOWN ICE CREAM FACTORY   **Phone:** 212/608-4170

[fyi]   Not evaluated. **Location:** In Chinatown; jct Mott St. 65 Bayard St 10013. **Features:** If you are looking for a cool treat, look no further. And you can choose from 42 flavors of ice cream, from the traditional to exotic such as green tea, red bean, lychee and ginger. They close 30 minutes earlier in the fall and winter.

FERRARA PASTICCERIA BAKERY & CAFE   **Phone:** 212/226-6150

[fyi]   Not evaluated. **Location:** In Little Italy; just e of jct Mulberry St. 195 Grand St 10013. **Features:** Since 1892, this cafe has served baked goods and sweet treats.

JOE'S GINGER   **Phone:** 212/966-6613

[fyi]   Not evaluated. **Location:** 113 Mott St 10013. **Features:** Shanghai-style food gives a nod to Hong Kong in its preparation. The restaurant is in the heart of Chinatown. Prices are reasonable, and dishes such as soup dumplings, sauteed eel with yellow chives, smoked fish, braised duck and fried quail are delightfully savory. Only cash is accepted.

JOHN'S PIZZERIA   **Phone:** 212/243-1680

[fyi]   Not evaluated. **Location:** Just e of jct 6th Ave (Ave of the Americas). 278 Bleecker St 10014. **Features:** A Greenwich Village institution for 70 years, John's offers coal-fired pizzas and sweet sausage.

LIMA'S TASTE   **Phone:** 212/228-7900

[fyi]   Not evaluated. **Location:** Between 1st Ave and Ave A. 432 E 13th St. **Features:** Peruvian cuisine has graduated, and preparations are finely turned out with skill and attention to eye appeal, let alone nose appeal. Fresh citrus flavors buoyed by herbs and spices make easy work of fresh seafood and meats on the tantalizing menu.

L'ORANGE BLEUE   **Phone:** 212/226-4999

[fyi]   Not evaluated. **Location:** At Crosby St. 430 Broome St 10013. **Features:** Exotic good looks and comfortable covered outdoor seating in warmer months are only a small part of the appeal. The inspired Mediterranean/Moroccan/French cuisine is the rest.

NOBU NEXT DOOR   **Phone:** 212/334-4445

[fyi]   Not evaluated. **Location:** In TriBeCa; at Franklin St. 105 Hudson. **Features:** A first-come, first-served solution to the hard-to-get tables at the original Nobu is found at this casual offshoot. Many of the same exciting and innovative dishes are available, along with an extensive raw bar, market and sake bar. Whole fish are cooked to order.

OTTO   **Phone:** 212/995-9559

[fyi]   Not evaluated. **Location:** 1 5th Ave 10003. **Features:** The collaboration of four chefs, including Mario Batali and Joseph Bastianich, helped create a pizzeria unlike any other. Pizza with cured salt pork—more a flatbread with savory essences unhampered by tomato products—and other pies, some more traditional, are loved by many. Among appetizers are cauliflower with lemon and garlic, eggplant caponata and fried tidbits, such as chickpea fritters and whitebait. The large menu offers plenty over which to ogle.

(See map and index starting on p. 360)

RHONE   **Phone:** 212/367-8440

fyi   Not evaluated. **Location:** Between Greenwich and Washington sts. 63 Gansevoort St 10014. **Features:** Many
           wines from the Rhone region, including a large selection of by-the-glass choices, are served. Lighter
French specialties, such as grilled octopus, hanger steak and choucroute, are good.

SAGE RESTAURANT   **Phone:** 212/253-8400

fyi   Not evaluated. **Location:** Between 24th and 25th sts. 331 Park Ave S 10010. **Features:** A trip to the Far East
           inspired this new spot which offers dishes in their pure form, as one would have them in their home nation.
One might sample a Vietnamese spring roll, followed by Japanese tuna tartare and end with Thai coconut shrimp; all the
better topped off with cookies and soy milk.   ⊻

STRIP HOUSE   **Phone:** 212/328-0000

fyi   Not evaluated. **Location:** Between 5th Ave and University Pl. 13 E 12th St 10038. **Features:** Upscale steak
           house.   ⊻

UNION SQUARE CAFE   **Phone:** 212/243-4020

fyi   Not evaluated. **Location:** Between 5th Ave and Union Square W. 21 E 16th St 10003. **Features:** Delightful Italian
           cuisine with Tuscan influence. Open for lunch and dinner.

MIDTOWN MANHATTAN   (See map and index starting on p. 364, 372)

―――― **WHERE TO STAY** ――――

AVALON HOTEL   *Book at aaa.com*   Phone: (212)299-7000   ⑧⓪
ⒶⒶⒶ ⓢⒶⓋⒺ   9/16-12/31 [CP]   1P: $220-$300   2P: $220-$300   XP: $25   F12
▽▽◇◇▽▽   5/1-6/30 [CP]   1P: $180-$240   2P: $180-$240   XP: $25   F12
             7/1-9/15 & 1/1-4/30 [CP] 1P: $170-$220   2P: $170-$220   XP: $25   F12
             Location: Between 5th and Madison aves. 16 E 32nd St 10016. Fax: 212/299-7001. **Facility:** 100 units. 80 one-
Small-scale Hotel   bedroom standard units. 20 one-bedroom suites. 12 stories, interior corridors. *Bath:* combo or shower only.
             Parking: valet. **Terms:** cancellation fee imposed. **Amenities:** high-speed Internet (fee), dual phone lines,
voice mail, safes, honor bars, irons, hair dryers. *Some:* fax. **Dining:** 11:30 am-10 pm, cocktails. **Guest Services:** valet laundry.
Business Services: meeting rooms, fax (fee). **Cards:** AX, DC, DS, JC, MC, VI. **Special Amenities:** free continental breakfast
and free newspaper. *(See color ad p 390)*   SOME UNITS

Ⓢⓓ Ⓨ Ⓨ ⓬Ⓜ Ⓔ ⓐ ⓱ ⓧ 〔DATA PORT〕 ⌨ / ⓧ ⟨VCR⟩ /
                                                                                              FEE

BEEKMAN TOWER HOTEL   *Book at aaa.com*   Phone: (212)355-7300   ⑤⓪
▽▽◇◇▽▽   9/1-12/31   1P: $275-$299   2P: $275-$299   XP: $25   F12
             5/1-6/30   1P: $235-$249   2P: $235-$249   XP: $25   F12
Small-scale Hotel   7/1-8/31 & 1/1-4/30   1P: $225-$239   2P: $225-$239   XP: $25   F12
             Location: 49th St and 1st Ave. 3 Mitchell Pl 10017. Fax: 212/753-9366. **Facility:** 174 units. 56 one-bedroom stan-
dard units with efficiencies. 114 one- and 4 two-bedroom suites with kitchens. 25 stories, interior corridors. *Bath:* combo or
shower only. **Parking:** valet. **Terms:** cancellation fee imposed. **Amenities:** video games (fee), dual phone lines, voice mail,
safes, irons, hair dryers. *Some:* fax. **Leisure Activities:** saunas, exercise room. **Guest Services:** valet and coin laundry. **Business Services:** meeting rooms, fax (fee). **Cards:** AX, CB, DC, DS, JC, MC, VI.   SOME UNITS

ⓗ Ⓨ Ⓨ Ⓔ ⓐ ⓱ 〔DATA PORT〕 ⌨ ⊡ ⌨ / ⓧ /

BELVEDERE HOTEL   *Book at aaa.com*   Phone: (212)245-7000   ⑨⑤
ⒶⒶⒶ ⓢⒶⓋⒺ   9/6-12/31   1P: $170-$230   2P: $170-$230   XP: $20   F12
▽▽◇◇▽▽   5/1-6/30   1P: $155-$170   2P: $155-$170   XP: $20   F12
             7/1-9/5 & 1/1-4/30   1P: $140-$150   2P: $140-$150   XP: $20   F12
             Location: Between 8th and 9th aves. 319 W 48th St 10036. Fax: 212/245-4455. **Facility:** 320 one-bedroom stan-
Small-scale Hotel   dard units. 17 stories, interior corridors. *Bath:* combo or shower only. **Parking:** valet. **Terms:** check-in 4 pm.
             Amenities: dual phone lines, voice mail, safes, irons, hair dryers. *Fee:* video library, video games.
Dining: Churrascaria Plataforma, see separate listing. **Guest Services:** gift shop, valet and coin laundry. **Business Services:**
meeting rooms, business center. **Cards:** AX, CB, DC, DS, JC, MC, VI. *(See color ad p 392)*   SOME UNITS

Ⓢⓓ Ⓨ Ⓨ ⓐ ⓱ 〔DATA PORT〕 ⊡ ⌨ ⌨ / ⓧ /

LIKE MOST NEW YORKERS, WE'RE NICER THAN YOU THINK.

Red Roof Inn Manhattan
6 W. 32nd St

La Quinta Manhattan
17 W. 32nd St

Ramada Inn Eastside
161 Lexington Ave

Comfort Inn Midtown
129 W. 46th St

Super 8 Hotel Times Square
59 W. 46th St

Free local calls
Fitness centers
Complimentary breakfast
Laundry and valet services
Web TV Internet access
Telephone with data port
Voice mail
In-room coffee machine
Iron/ironing board
Hair dryer in every room
Weekday newspapers

APPLE CORE HOTELS

BOOK ONLINE OR CALL.   applecorehotels.com   800.567.7720

(See map and index starting on p. 364)

THE BENJAMIN HOTEL   *Book at aaa.com*   **Phone:** (212)715-2500   [57]

▼▼▼ ▼▼▼	9/1-12/31	1P: $394-$479	2P: $394-$479	XP: $25	F12
	5/1-6/30	1P: $364-$444	2P: $364-$444	XP: $25	F12
Small-scale Hotel	7/1-8/31 & 1/1-4/30	1P: $334-$434	2P: $334-$434	XP: $25	F12

Location: Between Lexington and 3rd aves. 125 E 50th St 10022. Fax: 212/715-2525. **Facility:** High-tech amenities meld with Deco-era high style at this 1920s hotel; adorning the exterior are intricate cartouches and pediments. 209 units. 112 one-bedroom standard units. 96 one- and 1 two-bedroom suites. 26 stories, interior corridors. **Parking:** valet. **Terms:** cancellation fee imposed, pets ($500 deposit). **Amenities:** dual phone lines, voice mail, fax, safes, honor bars, irons, hair dryers. *Fee:* video games, high-speed Internet. *Some:* DVD players, CD players. **Dining:** Terrance Brennans Seafood & Chop House, see separate listing. **Leisure Activities:** saunas, exercise room, spa. **Guest Services:** valet laundry. **Business Services:** meeting rooms. **Cards:** AX, CB, DC, DS, JC, MC, VI.

SAVE Yourself From
Paying Full Room Rates

When selecting a AAA Approved lodging, look for the SAVE in TourBook® guide listings, and save money on your travel expenses. These properties actively solicit AAA business and offer members great room rates. See the TourBook Navigator section, pages 14 and 20, for details.

(See map and index starting on p. 364)

BEST WESTERN HOSPITALITY HOUSE   Phone: (212)753-8781   **126**
AAA SAVE   5/1-12/31 & 4/1-4/30   1P: $249-$349   2P: $249-$349   XP: $20   F13
           1/1-3/31   1P: $199-$299   2P: $199-$299   XP: $20   F13
▼▼ ▼▼   **Location:** Between 3rd and Lexington aves. 145 E 49th St 10022. Fax: 212/813-2070. **Facility:** Smoke free prem-
Small-scale Hotel ises. 35 units. 19 one- and 16 two-bedroom suites ($249-$349) with kitchens. 10 stories, interior corridors.
           Parking: no self-parking. **Terms:** cancellation fee imposed. **Amenities:** voice mail, safes, irons, hair dryers.
           Guest Services: coin laundry. **Business Services:** fax (fee). **Cards:** AX, CB, DC, JC, MC, VI.
Special Amenities: free continental breakfast and free newspaper. *(See color ad below)*

BEST WESTERN PRESIDENT HOTEL   *Book at aaa.com*   Phone: (212)246-8800   **107**
AAA SAVE   9/1-12/31   1P: $149-$329   2P: $159-$369   XP: $20   F10
           5/1-8/31   1P: $109-$209   2P: $119-$219   XP: $20   F10
▼▼ ▼▼   1/1-4/30   1P: $79-$139   2P: $89-$149   XP: $20   F10
           Location: Between Broadway and 8th Ave. 234 W 48th St 10036. Fax: 212/974-3922. **Facility:** 334 units. 309 one-
Small-scale Hotel bedroom standard units. 24 one- and 1 two-bedroom suites ($139-$469). 16 stories, interior corridors. *Bath:*
           combo or shower only. **Parking:** no self-parking. **Terms:** cancellation fee imposed. **Amenities:** video library
(fee), dual phone lines, voice mail, safes, irons, hair dryers. *Some:* CD players. **Dining:** 2 restaurants, 7 am-10 pm, cocktails.
Guest Services: gift shop, valet laundry. **Business Services:** fax (fee). **Cards:** AX, CB, DC, DS, JC, MC, VI.
Special Amenities: free local telephone calls and free newspaper.

SOME UNITS

THE CARLYLE   *Book at aaa.com*   Phone: (212)744-1600   **71**
▼▼▼▼ ▼▼▼▼   5/1-6/27 & 9/8-12/31   1P: $510-$610   2P: $510-$610
           6/28-9/7 & 1/1-4/30   1P: $410-$460   2P: $410-$460
Small-scale Hotel **Location:** At Madison Ave. 35 E 76th St 10021. Fax: 212/717-4682. **Facility:** Pantries are featured in the suites
           at this elegant hotel. 179 units. 122 one-bedroom standard units, some with whirlpools. 49 one- and 8 two-
bedroom suites ($900-$3200), some with efficiencies, kitchens and/or whirlpools. 34 stories, interior corridors. **Parking:** valet.
Terms: cancellation fee imposed. **Amenities:** CD players, dual phone lines, voice mail, fax, safes, honor bars, hair dryers. *Some:*
DVD players. **Leisure Activities:** saunas, steamroom. *Fee:* massage. **Guest Services:** gift shop, valet laundry. *Fee:* personal
trainers. **Business Services:** meeting rooms, PC, fax. **Cards:** AX, DC, DS, MC, VI.

SOME UNITS

(See map and index starting on p. 364)

CLARION HOTEL FIFTH AVENUE — *Book at aaa.com* — Phone: (212)447-1500 — **88**

9/4-12/31	1P: $385	2P: $385	XP: $15	F18
5/1-9/3 & 4/1-4/30	1P: $250	2P: $250	XP: $15	F18
1/1-3/31	1P: $199	2P: $199	XP: $15	F18

Small-scale Hotel **Location:** Between Madison and 5th aves. 3 E 40th St 10016. Fax: 212/213-0972. **Facility:** 189 one-bedroom standard units. 30 stories, interior corridors. **Parking:** no self-parking. **Terms:** cancellation fee imposed. **Amenities:** dual phone lines, voice mail, irons, hair dryers. **Fee:** video games, safes. **Guest Services:** valet laundry. **Business Services:** business center. **Cards:** AX, CB, DC, DS, JC, MC, VI.

SOME UNITS

COMFORT INN — *Book at aaa.com* — Phone: (212)714-6699 — **40**

9/1-12/31	1P: $109-$159	2P: $119-$169	XP: $10	F12
5/1-8/31 & 1/1-4/30	1P: $99-$129	2P: $109-$139	XP: $10	F12

Small-scale Hotel **Location:** Between 9th and 10th aves. 442 W 36th St 10018. Fax: 212/714-6681. **Facility:** 56 one-bedroom standard units. 15 stories, interior corridors. **Parking:** no self-parking. **Terms:** cancellation fee imposed, [CP] meal plan available. **Amenities:** dual phone lines, voice mail, irons, hair dryers. **Guest Services:** valet laundry. **Business Services:** fax (fee). **Cards:** AX, CB, DC, DS, JC, MC, VI. **Special Amenities:** free continental breakfast and free newspaper.

SOME UNITS

COMFORT INN-MANHATTAN — *Book at aaa.com* — Phone: (212)947-0200 — **75**

11/16-12/31 [CP]	1P: $159-$169	2P: $159-$169	XP: $15	F18
9/11-11/15 [CP]	1P: $149	2P: $159	XP: $15	F18
5/1-8/31 [CP]	1P: $119	2P: $129	XP: $15	F18
1/1-4/30 [CP]	1P: $109	2P: $119	XP: $15	F18

Small-scale Hotel **Location:** Between 5th and 6th (Ave of the Americas) aves, just e of Herald Square. 42 W 35th 10001. Fax: 212/594-3047. **Facility:** 131 one-bedroom standard units. 13 stories, interior corridors. **Parking:** no self-parking. **Terms:** cancellation fee imposed. **Amenities:** voice mail, safes (fee), irons, hair dryers. **Dining:** 7 am-11 pm. **Guest Services:** valet laundry. **Business Services:** fax (fee). **Cards:** AX, DC, DS, MC, VI. **Special Amenities:** free continental breakfast and free newspaper. *(See color ad p 393)*

SOME UNITS

CROWNE PLAZA AT THE UNITED NATIONS — *Book at aaa.com* — Phone: (212)986-8800 — **127**

8/21-12/11	1P: $319-$369	2P: $319-$369	XP: $35	F14
5/1-6/23	1P: $239-$279	2P: $239-$279	XP: $35	F14
12/12-4/30	1P: $209-$269	2P: $209-$269	XP: $35	F14
6/24-8/20	1P: $219	2P: $259	XP: $35	F14

Historic Large-scale Hotel **Location:** Between 1st and 2nd aves. 304 E 42nd St 10017. Fax: 212/986-1758. **Facility:** The hotel offers smaller, though very charming accommodtions, and has a well-equipped exercise room. 300 units. 286 one-bedroom standard units, some with whirlpools. 14 one-bedroom suites with whirlpools. 17-20 stories, interior corridors. **Bath:** combo or shower only. **Parking:** valet. **Terms:** package plans - seasonal, small pets only ($500 deposit, $50 extra charge). **Amenities:** CD players, high-speed Internet (fee), dual phone lines, voice mail, safes, honor bars, irons, hair dryers. **Leisure Activities:** saunas, exercise room. **Fee:** massage. **Guest Services:** valet laundry. **Business Services:** meeting rooms, business center. **Cards:** AX, DC, DS, JC, MC, VI.

SOME UNITS — FEE — FEE

CROWNE PLAZA TIMES SQUARE MANHATTAN — *Book at aaa.com* — Phone: (212)977-4000 — **125**

10/1-12/15	1P: $229	2P: $229	XP: $30	F17
5/1-6/30	1P: $189	2P: $189	XP: $30	F17
7/1-9/30 & 12/16-4/30	1P: $169	2P: $169	XP: $30	F17

Large-scale Hotel **Location:** 49th St and Broadway. 1605 Broadway 10019. Fax: 212/333-7393. **Facility:** 770 one-bedroom standard units, some with whirlpools. 46 stories, interior corridors. **Bath:** combo or shower only. **Parking:** valet. **Terms:** cancellation fee imposed, package plans, small pets only. **Amenities:** dual phone lines, voice mail, safes, honor bars, irons, hair dryers. **Fee:** video library, video games. **Pool(s):** heated indoor. **Leisure Activities:** saunas, steamrooms. **Fee:** massage. **Guest Services:** gift shop, valet laundry. **Business Services:** conference facilities, business center. **Cards:** AX, DC, DS, MC, VI.

SOME UNITS — FEE

DOUBLETREE GUEST SUITES TIMES SQUARE/NEW YORK CITY — *Book at aaa.com* — Phone: (212)719-1600 — **117**

9/11-12/31	1P: $189-$499	2P: $189-$499	XP: $20	F18
6/27-9/10 & 1/1-4/30	1P: $179-$399	2P: $179-$399	XP: $20	F18
5/1-6/26	1P: $179-$359	2P: $179-$359	XP: $20	F18

Large-scale Hotel **Location:** 47th St and 7th Ave. 1568 Broadway 10036. Fax: 212/921-5212. **Facility:** 460 units. 458 one- and 2 two-bedroom suites. 43 stories, interior corridors. **Bath:** combo or shower only. **Parking:** valet. **Terms:** [AP], [BP] & [CP] meal plans available. **Amenities:** dual phone lines, voice mail, safes, honor bars, irons, hair dryers. **Fee:** video library, video games, high-speed Internet. **Dining:** 6:30 am-11 pm, cocktails. **Leisure Activities:** exercise room. **Guest Services:** valet laundry. **Business Services:** conference facilities, fax (fee). **Cards:** AX, MC, VI. **Special Amenities:** free newspaper. *(See color ad card insert)*

SOME UNITS — FEE

(See map and index starting on p. 364)

DUMONT PLAZA SUITE HOTEL   *Book at aaa.com*   Phone: (212)481-7600   **43**
	9/1-12/31	1P: $399-$424	2P: $399-$424	XP: $25	F12
	5/1-6/30	1P: $334-$364	2P: $334-$364	XP: $25	F12
	7/1-8/31 & 1/1-4/30	1P: $309-$334	2P: $309-$334	XP: $25	F12

Small-scale Hotel   **Location:** Between Lexington and 3rd aves. 150 E 34th St 10016. Fax: 212/889-8856. **Facility:** 252 units. 173 one-bedroom standard units with kitchens. 79 one-bedroom suites with kitchens. 37 stories, interior corridors. *Bath:* combo or shower only. **Parking:** no self-parking. **Terms:** cancellation fee imposed, [ECP] meal plan available. **Amenities:** video games (fee), dual phone lines, voice mail, irons, hair dryers. *Some:* fax. **Leisure Activities:** steamrooms, exercise room, spa. **Guest Services:** valet and coin laundry. **Business Services:** meeting rooms, PC, fax (fee). **Cards:** AX, CB, DC, DS, MC, VI.

SOME UNITS

EASTGATE TOWER HOTEL   *Book at aaa.com*   Phone: (212)687-8000   **42**
| | 9/1-12/31 | 1P: $279-$324 | 2P: $279-$324 | XP: $25 | F12 |
| | 5/1-8/31 & 1/1-4/30 | 1P: $224-$269 | 2P: $224-$269 | XP: $25 | F12 |

Small-scale Hotel   **Location:** Between 2nd and 3rd aves. 222 E 39th St 10016. Fax: 212/490-2634. **Facility:** 187 units. 133 one-bedroom standard units with kitchens. 36 one- and 18 two-bedroom suites with kitchens. 25 stories, interior corridors. *Bath:* combo or shower only. **Parking:** valet. **Terms:** cancellation fee imposed, pets ($250 deposit). **Amenities:** video games (fee), dual phone lines, voice mail, irons, hair dryers. **Leisure Activities:** exercise room. **Guest Services:** valet and coin laundry. **Business Services:** meeting rooms, fax (fee). **Cards:** AX, DC, DS, JC, MC, VI.

SOME UNITS

FEE   FEE

THE ESSEX HOUSE-A WESTIN HOTEL   *Book at aaa.com*   Phone: (212)247-0300   **115**
	8/29-12/31	1P: $509-$559	2P: $509-$559	XP: $25	F17
	5/1-6/30 & 1/1-4/30	1P: $429-$479	2P: $429-$479	XP: $25	F17
	7/1-8/28	1P: $409-$459	2P: $409-$459	XP: $25	F17

Classic   **Location:** Between 6th (Ave of the Americas) and 7th aves. 160 Central Park S 10019. Fax: 212/484-4635.
Large-scale Hotel   **Facility:** Classic Art Deco styling and unobstructed views of Central Park are highlights of this luxury hotel. 605 units. 524 one-bedroom standard units. 81 one-bedroom suites ($750-$4500), some with whirlpools. 40 stories, interior corridors. *Bath:* combo or shower only. **Parking:** valet. **Terms:** cancellation fee imposed. **Amenities:** dual phone lines, voice mail, safes, honor bars, irons, hair dryers. *Fee:* video games, high-speed Internet. *Some:* fax. **Dining:** Cafe Botanica, see separate listing. **Leisure Activities:** saunas, steamrooms, spa. **Guest Services:** gift shop, valet laundry. *Fee:* personal trainers, tanning facility. **Business Services:** conference facilities, business center. **Cards:** AX, DC, DS, JC, MC, VI.

SOME UNITS

THE EXCELSIOR HOTEL   *Book at aaa.com*   Phone: (212)362-9200   **55**
	5/1-5/31 & 9/16-12/30	1P: $159-$299	2P: $159-$299	XP: $20	F14
	12/31-4/30	1P: $129-$299	2P: $129-$299	XP: $20	F14
	6/1-9/15	1P: $129-$229	2P: $129-$229	XP: $20	F14

Small-scale Hotel   **Location:** Between Columbus Ave and Central Park W. Located on the Upper West Side. 45 W 81st St 10024. Fax: 212/580-3972. **Facility:** 199 units. 110 one-bedroom standard units. 89 one-bedroom suites ($179-$399). 16 stories, interior corridors. **Parking:** no self-parking. **Terms:** [BP] & [CP] meal plans available. **Amenities:** video games (fee), voice mail, fax, safes, irons, hair dryers. *Some:* dual phone lines. **Leisure Activities:** exercise room. **Guest Services:** gift shop, valet laundry. **Business Services:** meeting rooms, fax (fee). **Cards:** AX, DC, DS, MC, VI.

SOME UNITS

FEE

FITZPATRICK GRAND CENTRAL HOTEL   *Book at aaa.com*   Phone: (212)351-6800   **132**
| | All Year | 1P: $375-$495 | 2P: $375-$495 | XP: $30 | F12 |

    Location: Between 3rd and Lexington aves. 141 E 44th St 10017. Fax: 212/818-1747. **Facility:** 150 units. 142 one-bedroom standard units. 8 one-bedroom suites. 9 stories, interior corridors. *Bath:* combo or shower only.
Small-scale Hotel   **Parking:** valet. **Terms:** cancellation fee imposed. **Amenities:** video games (fee), dual phone lines, voice mail, safes, irons, hair dryers. *Some:* CD players. **Guest Services:** valet laundry. **Business Services:** meeting rooms, fax (fee). **Cards:** AX, CB, DC, DS, JC, MC, VI.

SOME UNITS

(See map and index starting on p. 364)

FITZPATRICK MANHATTAN HOTEL *Book at aaa.com*   **Phone:** (212)355-0100 **121**

AAA SAVE 9/7-4/30   1P: $285-$485   2P: $285-$485   XP: $30
◇◇◇◇   5/1-9/6   1P: $225-$465   2P: $225-$465   XP: $30
Small-scale Hotel **Location:** Between 56th and 57th sts. 687 Lexington Ave 10022. Fax: 212/355-1371. **Facility:** 93 units. 40 one-bedroom standard units. 53 one-bedroom suites. 16 stories, interior corridors. **Parking:** valet. **Terms:** cancellation fee imposed. **Amenities:** video games (fee), dual phone lines, voice mail, safes, irons, hair dryers. *Some:* CD players. **Dining:** 7 am-10:30 pm, cocktails. **Guest Services:** valet laundry. **Business Services:** meeting rooms, fax (fee). **Cards:** AX, CB, DC, DS, JC, MC, VI. *(See color ad below)*

SOME UNITS

THE FLATOTEL *Book at aaa.com*   **Phone:** (212)887-9400 **51**

◇◇◇   9/1-12/31 [CP]   1P: $349-$369   2P: $349-$369   XP: $20   F12
           1/1-4/30 [CP]   1P: $269-$289   2P: $269-$289   XP: $20   F12
           5/1-8/31 [CP]   1P: $249-$269   2P: $249-$269   XP: $20   F12
Large-scale Hotel **Location:** Between 6th (Ave of the Americas) and 7th aves. 135 W 52nd St 10019. Fax: 212/887-9442. **Facility:** 283 units. 213 one-bedroom standard units, some with efficiencies. 54 one- and 16 two-bedroom suites with kitchens. 46 stories, interior corridors. **Parking:** on-site (fee) and valet. **Terms:** check-in 4 pm, [AP], [BP], [ECP] & [MAP] meal plans available. **Amenities:** dual phone lines, voice mail, irons, hair dryers. *Some:* high-speed Internet (fee), safes. **Dining:** Moda, see separate listing. **Leisure Activities:** exercise room. **Guest Services:** gift shop, valet laundry. **Business Services:** meeting rooms, business center. **Cards:** AX, CB, DC, DS, JC, MC, VI.

SOME UNITS

FOUR SEASONS HOTEL, NEW YORK *Book at aaa.com*   **Phone:** (212)758-5700 **118**

◇◇◇◇◇   All Year   1P: $575-$675   2P: $575-$675
Large-scale Hotel **Location:** Between Park and Madison aves. 57 E 57th St 10022. Fax: 212/758-5711. **Facility:** Said to be the tallest hotel in the city, this lavishly-decorated luxury property sets equally lofty standards for service. 368 units. 307 one-bedroom standard units. 61 one-bedroom suites ($1350-$20,000), some with whirlpools. 52 stories, interior corridors. **Parking:** valet. **Terms:** cancellation fee imposed, [AP] meal plan available, small pets only. **Amenities:** video library, video games, CD players, dual phone lines, voice mail, fax, safes, honor bars, irons, hair dryers. *Fee:* DVD players, high-speed Internet. **Dining:** Fifty-Seven Fifty-Seven Restaurant & Bar, see separate listing. **Leisure Activities:** saunas, whirlpools, spa. **Guest Services:** gift shop, valet laundry, area transportation. **Business Services:** conference facilities, business center. **Cards:** AX, CB, DC, DS, JC, MC, VI.

SOME UNITS

(See map and index starting on p. 364)

THE GORHAM HOTEL *Book at aaa.com*   **Phone:** (212)245-1800   101
AAA SAVE   All Year   1P: $225-$400   2P: $235-$440   XP: $20   F16
◇◇◇   **Location:** Between 6th (Ave of the Americas) and 7th aves. Located across from City Center. 136 W 55th St 10019.
Fax: 212/582-8332. **Facility:** 115 units. 71 one-bedroom standard units. 44 one-bedroom suites ($255). 17
Small-scale Hotel   stories, interior corridors. **Parking:** on-site (fee). **Terms:** 2 night minimum stay - seasonal weekends.
Dining: noon-3 & 5:30-11 pm, Sat from 5:30 pm. **Leisure Activities:** exercise room. **Guest Services:** valet
laundry. **Business Services:** meeting rooms, fax. **Cards:** AX, CB, DC, JC, MC, VI. **Special Amenities:** free newspaper and
preferred room (subject to availability with advanced reservations). *(See color ad below)*   SOME UNITS

(See map and index starting on p. 364)

GRAND HYATT NEW YORK   *Book at aaa.com*   Phone: (212)883-1234   [53]

AAA SAVE
▽▽▽▽
Large-scale Hotel

All Year   1P: $159-$325   2P: $159-$325   XP: $25   F18
Location: Between Lexington and Park aves at E 42nd St. Located adjacent to Grand Central Station. Park Ave at Grand Central 10017 (109 E 42nd St, NEW YORK). Fax: 212/697-3772. **Facility:** 1336 units. 1319 one-bedroom standard units. 16 one- and 1 three-bedroom suites, some with whirlpools. 34 stories, interior corridors. *Bath:* combo or shower only. **Parking:** valet. **Terms:** cancellation fee imposed. **Amenities:** dual phone lines, voice mail, fax, safes, irons. *Some:* CD players, hair dryers. **Dining:** 2 restaurants, 6:30 am-midnight, cocktails. **Guest Services:** gift shop, valet laundry. **Business Services:** conference facilities, business center. **Cards:** AX, CB, DC, DS, JC, MC, VI.

SOME UNITS
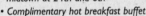

HILTON NEW YORK   *Book at aaa.com*   Phone: (212)586-7000   [102]

▽▽▽▽
Large-scale Hotel

All Year   1P: $169-$499   2P: $199-$529   XP: $30   F18
Location: Between 53rd and 54th sts. 1335 Ave of the Americas 10019-6078. Fax: 212/261-5806. **Facility:** 1980 units. 1925 one-bedroom standard units. 40 one-, 12 two- and 3 three-bedroom suites ($245-$3000), some with whirlpools. 46 stories, interior corridors. *Bath:* combo or shower only. **Parking:** on-site (fee) and valet. **Terms:** cancellation fee imposed. **Amenities:** video games (fee), dual phone lines, voice mail, honor bars, irons, hair dryers. *Some:* safes. *Fee:* high-speed Internet. **Leisure Activities:** spa. **Guest Services:** gift shop, valet laundry. **Business Services:** conference facilities, business center. **Cards:** AX, CB, DC, DS, JC, MC, VI. *(See color ad card insert)*

SOME UNITS

HILTON TIMES SQUARE   *Book at aaa.com*   Phone: (212)840-8222   [119]

▽▽▽▽
Large-scale Hotel

All Year   1P: $179-$449   2P: $179-$449   XP: $30   F18
Location: Between 7th and 8th aves. 234 W 42nd St 10036. Fax: 212/840-5516. **Facility:** 444 units. 429 one-bedroom standard units. 14 one- and 1 two-bedroom suites ($379-$1300) with whirlpools. 44 stories, interior corridors. *Bath:* combo or shower only. **Parking:** on-site (fee) and valet. **Terms:** cancellation fee imposed. [BP] meal plan available, pets ($250 deposit). **Amenities:** video games (fee), CD players, high-speed Internet, dual phone lines, voice mail, safes, honor bars, irons, hair dryers. *Some:* fax. **Leisure Activities:** exercise room. **Guest Services:** valet laundry. **Business Services:** conference facilities, business center. **Cards:** AX, CB, DC, DS, MC, VI. *(See color ad card insert)*

SOME UNITS

(See map and index starting on p. 364)

THE HOLIDAY INN MARTINIQUE ON BROADWAY   *Book at aaa.com*   Phone: (212)736-3800   92

9/5-12/31	1P: $249-$299	2P: $249-$299	XP: $20	F12
5/1-6/30	1P: $229-$279	2P: $229-$279	XP: $20	F12
7/1-9/4 & 1/1-4/30	1P: $199-$249	2P: $199-$249	XP: $20	F12

Location: Corner of Broadway. 49 W 32nd St 10001. Fax: 212/277-2702. **Facility:** 532 units. 528 one-bedroom
Small-scale Hotel standard units. 4 one-bedroom suites. 19 stories, interior corridors. **Parking:** valet. **Terms:** pets ($100 de-
posit, $50 extra charge). **Amenities:** dual phone lines, voice mail, honor bars, irons, hair dryers. *Fee:* video
library, video games, safes. **Dining:** 2 restaurants, 6:30 am-11 pm, cocktails. **Leisure Activities:** exercise room, spa. **Guest
Services:** gift shop, valet laundry. **Business Services:** meeting rooms, business center. **Cards:** AX, DC, DS, MC, VI
Special Amenities: early check-in/late check-out and free room upgrade (subject to availability with advanced reservations). *(See color ad below)*

Near Madison Square Garden, B'way Theatre,
Empire State Bldg., Macy's, 5th Ave. Shopping

Holiday Inn
MARTINIQUE
ON BROADWAY

49 West 32nd Street, New York, NY 10001
Phone 212-736-3800 / 1-800-465-4329

fitness and business center • minibar/personal safe • playstation videos
asian day spa • restaurant/lounge • nearby parking
children under 19 stay free with parents: 12 and younger eat free with parents
WWW.MARTINIQUEONBROADWAY.COM

(See map and index starting on p. 364)

HOLIDAY INN MIDTOWN-57TH STREET *Book at aaa.com*   Phone: (212)581-8100   38

9/1-12/31 & 4/1-4/30	1P: $219-$239	2P: $219-$239	XP: $15	F18
5/1-8/31 & 1/1-3/31	1P: $199-$219	2P: $199-$219	XP: $15	F18

Large-scale Hotel   **Location:** Between 9th and 10th aves. 440 W 57th St 10019. Fax: 212/581-7739. **Facility:** 596 units. 592 one-bedroom standard units. 3 one- and 1 two-bedroom suites. 10-18 stories, interior corridors. **Parking:** on-site (fee) and valet. **Terms:** check-in 4 pm, cancellation fee imposed. **Amenities:** dual phone lines, voice mail, irons, hair dryers. **Pool(s):** outdoor. **Guest Services:** gift shop, valet laundry. **Business Services:** conference facilities, fax (fee). **Cards:** AX, CB, DS, JC, MC, VI.

SOME UNITS / FEE FEE

HOTEL BEACON *Book at aaa.com*   Phone: (212)787-1100   30

All Year   1P: $180-$195   2P: $195-$225   XP: $15   F17

Small-scale Hotel   **Location:** At W 75th St. 2130 Broadway 10023. Fax: 212/724-0839. **Facility:** 241 units. 131 one-bedroom standard units with efficiencies. 110 one-bedroom suites ($250-$500) with kitchens. 25 stories, interior corridors. *Bath:* combo or shower only. **Parking:** on-site (fee). **Amenities:** voice mail, safes, irons, hair dryers. **Guest Services:** valet and coin laundry. **Business Services:** meeting rooms, business center. **Cards:** AX, CB, DC, DS, JC, MC, VI. **Special Amenities:** free newspaper. *(See color ad below)*

SOME UNITS / FEE

HOTEL EDISON *Book at aaa.com*   Phone: (212)840-5000   100

All Year   1P: $160   2P: $190   XP: $15

Large-scale Hotel   **Location:** Between Broadway and 8th Ave. 228 W 47th St 10036. Fax: 212/596-6850. **Facility:** 800 units. 745 one- and 10 two-bedroom standard units. 45 one-bedroom suites ($220-$260). 22 stories, interior corridors. **Parking:** valet. **Amenities:** voice mail. **Leisure Activities:** exercise room. **Business Services:** meeting rooms, fax (fee). **Cards:** AX, CB, DC, DS, JC, MC, VI.

SOME UNITS

HOTEL LUCERNE *Book at aaa.com*   Phone: (212)875-1000   33

9/7-12/31	1P: $190-$280	2P: $190-$280	XP: $20	F16
5/1-9/6 & 3/1-4/30	1P: $150-$235	2P: $150-$235	XP: $20	F16
1/1-2/28	1P: $135-$200	2P: $135-$200	XP: $20	F16

Small-scale Hotel   **Location:** Between Amsterdam and Broadway. 201 W 79th St 10024. Fax: 212/362-7251. **Facility:** 185 units. 143 one-bedroom standard units. 42 one-bedroom suites ($220-$635). 13 stories, interior corridors. **Parking:** on-site (fee). **Terms:** check-in 4 pm. **Amenities:** dual phone lines, voice mail, irons, hair dryers. *Fee:* video games, high-speed Internet. **Dining:** 7 am-midnight, Fri & Sat-1 am, cocktails. **Leisure Activities:** exercise room. **Guest Services:** valet laundry. **Business Services:** meeting rooms, business center. **Cards:** AX, CB, DC, DS, MC, VI. **Special Amenities:** free newspaper. *(See color ad p 404)*

SOME UNITS

HOTEL PLAZA ATHENEE *Book at aaa.com*   Phone: (212)734-9100   66

All Year   1P: $495-$645   2P: $525-$675   XP: $40   F12

Historic Small-scale Hotel   **Location:** Between Madison and Park aves. 37 E 64th St 10021. Fax: 212/772-0958. **Facility:** Old World touches add an elegant ambience to this Upper East Side property, which is walking distance from the designer boutiques of Madison Avenue. 152 units. 117 one-bedroom standard units. 35 one-bedroom suites ($1200-$3600). 17 stories, interior corridors. *Bath:* combo or shower only. **Parking:** on-site (fee) and valet. **Terms:** package plans, small pets only. **Amenities:** CD players, dual phone lines, voice mail, safes, honor bars, hair dryers. *Fee:* video library, high-speed Internet. *Some:* DVD players. **Leisure Activities:** Fee: massage. **Guest Services:** valet laundry. **Business Services:** meeting rooms, PC, fax (fee). **Cards:** AX, CB, DC, DS, JC, MC, VI.

SOME UNITS / FEE

(See map and index starting on p. 364)

HOTEL STANFORD   *Book at aaa.com*   Phone: (212)563-1500   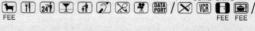 77

AAA SAVE	9/6-12/15 [CP]	1P: $149-$155	2P: $159-$165	XP: $20	F12
	5/1-9/5 [CP]	1P: $129-$135	2P: $139-$145	XP: $20	F12
▼▼▼ ▼▼▼	3/6-4/30 [CP]	1P: $129-$135	2P: $129-$135	XP: $20	F12
	12/16-3/5 [CP]	1P: $119-$125	2P: $129-$135	XP: $20	F12

Small-scale Hotel **Location:** Between 5th Ave and Broadway. 43 W 32nd St 10001. Fax: 212/629-0043. **Facility:** 121 units. 101 one-bedroom standard units. 20 one-bedroom suites. 12 stories, interior corridors. **Parking:** no self-parking. **Terms:** cancellation fee imposed, small pets only (with prior approval). **Amenities:** video library, voice mail, safes, hair dryers. **Dining:** 24 hours, cocktails. **Guest Services:** valet laundry. **Cards:** AX, DC, JC, MC, VI. **Special Amenities:** free continental breakfast and free newspaper.

SOME UNITS

HOWARD JOHNSON PLAZA HOTEL   *Book at aaa.com*   Phone: (212)581-4100   106

AAA SAVE	9/1-12/31	1P: $149-$259	2P: $169-$279	XP: $10	F17
	7/1-8/31	1P: $109-$239	2P: $139-$259	XP: $10	F17
▼▼▼ ▼▼▼	5/1-6/30	1P: $139-$189	2P: $159-$209	XP: $10	F17
	1/1-4/30	1P: $119-$189	2P: $139-$209	XP: $10	F17

Large-scale Hotel **Location:** Between 51st and 52nd sts. 851 8th Ave 10019. Fax: 212/974-7502. **Facility:** 300 one-bedroom standard units. 11 stories, interior corridors. *Bath:* combo or shower only. **Parking:** on-site (fee). **Amenities:** voice mail, safes (fee), irons, hair dryers. **Dining:** 7 am-11 pm, Fri & Sat-11:30 pm. **Guest Services:** gift shop, valet laundry. **Business Services:** fax (fee). **Cards:** AX, CB, DC, DS, JC, MC, VI. **Special Amenities:** free newspaper and early check-in/late check-out. *(See color ad p 218)*

SOME UNITS

INTER-CONTINENTAL CENTRAL PARK SOUTH NEW YORK   *Book at aaa.com*   Phone: (212)757-1900   116

▼▼▼ ▼▼▼	9/3-4/30	1P: $265-$615	2P: $265-$615	XP: $50	F12
	5/1-6/27	1P: $259-$435	2P: $259-$435	XP: $50	F12
	6/28-9/2	1P: $239-$425	2P: $239-$425	XP: $50	F12

Small-scale Hotel **Location:** Between 6th (Ave of the Americas) and 7th aves. Located opposite Central Park. 112 Central Park S 10019. Fax: 212/757-9620. **Facility:** Enhancing the decor at this European-style hotel is lavish artwork and floral pieces. 211 units. 189 one-bedroom standard units. 19 one- and 3 two-bedroom suites ($575-$4500), some with whirlpools. 25 stories, interior corridors. **Parking:** on-site (fee) and valet. **Terms:** cancellation fee imposed, [BP] meal plan available, small pets only ($150 deposit, with prior approval). **Amenities:** dual phone lines, safes, honor bars, irons, hair dryers. *Fee:* video games, high-speed Internet. *Some:* CD players, voice mail. **Leisure Activities:** saunas, exercise room. *Fee:* massage. **Guest Services:** valet laundry. **Business Services:** conference facilities, business center. **Cards:** AX, CB, DC, DS, JC, MC, VI.

SOME UNITS

FEE   FEE   FEE

(See map and index starting on p. 364)

INTERCONTINENTAL THE BARCLAY NEW YORK   Book at aaa.com   Phone: 212/755-5900   63
Property failed to provide current rates
▼▼▼▼   **Location:** Between Park and Lexington aves. 111 E 48th St 10017. Fax: 212/644-0079. **Facility:** 686 units. 622
Large-scale Hotel   one-bedroom standard units. 62 one- and 2 two-bedroom suites, some with whirlpools. 14 stories, interior
corridors. *Bath:* combo or shower only. **Parking:** valet. **Amenities:** high-speed Internet, dual phone lines,
voice mail, safes, honor bars, irons, hair dryers. *Some:* CD players. **Leisure Activities:** sauna, steamroom, exercise room. *Fee:*
massage. **Guest Services:** gift shop, valet laundry. **Business Services:** conference facilities, business center.

SOME UNITS

[🍴] [24] [Y] [&] [✕] [👁] [DATA PORT] [🖥] / [✕] [🔒] [📷] /

IROQUOIS HOTEL   Book at aaa.com   Phone: 212/840-3080   99
9/7-12/31	1P: $329-$379	2P: $329-$379
5/1-6/30	1P: $309-$349	2P: $309-$349
7/1-9/6 & 1/1-4/30	1P: $289-$329	2P: $289-$329

Historic   **Location:** Between 5th and 6th (Ave of the Americas) aves. 49 W 44th St 10036. Fax: 212/398-1754. **Facility:** Inti-
Small-scale Hotel   mate and elegant are the best words to describe this historic hotel; guest rooms and bathrooms tend to be
small but the decor is rich and luxurious. 114 units. 104 one-bedroom standard units. 10 one-bedroom suites ($449-$645) with
whirlpools, some with kitchens. 12 stories, interior corridors. **Terms:** cancellation fee imposed.
Amenities: video library, video games (fee), CD players, high-speed Internet, dual phone lines, voice mail, safes, honor bars,
irons, hair dryers. **Leisure Activities:** sauna, exercise room. **Guest Services:** valet laundry. **Business Services:** meeting
rooms, PC, fax (fee). **Cards:** AX, CB, DC, DS, JC, MC, VI.

SOME UNITS

[ASK] [🍴] [24] [Y] [VCR] [👁] [DATA PORT] / [✕] [🔒] [📷] /

JOLLY HOTEL MADISON TOWERS   Book at aaa.com   Phone: (212)802-0600   78
9/8-12/31 [ECP]	1P: $265	2P: $265	XP: $50	F16
5/1-9/7 & 1/1-4/30 [ECP]	1P: $214	2P: $214	XP: $50	F16

Large-scale Hotel   **Location:** Between Park and Madison aves. 22 E 38th St 10016. Fax: 212/447-0747. **Facility:** 237 units. 230 one-
bedroom standard units. 7 one-bedroom suites. 18 stories, interior corridors. *Bath:* combo or shower only.
Parking: valet. **Terms:** cancellation fee imposed, small pets only. **Amenities:** video games (fee), dual phone lines, voice mail,
honor bars, irons, hair dryers. *Some:* high-speed Internet (fee). **Guest Services:** valet laundry. **Business Services:** conference
facilities, fax (fee). **Cards:** AX, CB, DC, DS, JC, MC, VI.

SOME UNITS

[ASK] [S/D] [🛏] [🍴] [Y] [&] [👥] [👁] [DATA PORT] [VCR] [🔒] /

THE KIMBERLY A BOUTIQUE HOTEL   Book at aaa.com   Phone: (212)755-0400   124
9/1-4/30	1P: $259-$389	2P: $279-$399	XP: $25	F17
5/1-8/31	1P: $249-$379	2P: $269-$379	XP: $25	F17

Small-scale Hotel   **Location:** Between 3rd and Lexington aves. 145 E 50th St 10022. Fax: 212/486-6915. **Facility:** 186 units. 35 one-
bedroom standard units, some with kitchens. 135 one- and 16 two-bedroom suites, some with kitchens
and/or whirlpools. 31 stories, interior corridors. **Parking:** valet. **Terms:** cancellation fee imposed, package
plans. **Amenities:** video games (fee), high-speed Internet, dual phone lines, voice mail, fax, safes, honor
bars, irons, hair dryers. **Dining:** 2 restaurants, 6:30 am-11 pm, cocktails, nightclub, entertainment. **Leisure Activities:** Fee: massage. **Guest Services:** valet laundry. **Business Services:** meeting rooms, business center. **Cards:** AX, CB, DC, DS, JC, MC, VI.
Special Amenities: free newspaper and free room upgrade (subject to availability with advanced reservations).

SOME UNITS

[🍴] [24] [Y] [🎬] [👥] [👁] [DATA PORT] [🔒] [📷] [🖥] / [✕] [VCR]
FEE

THE KITANO NEW YORK HOTEL   Book at aaa.com   Phone: (212)885-7000   84
All Year	1P: $430-$2100	2P: $430-$2100	XP: $25	F12

Small-scale Hotel   **Location:** At 38th St. 66 Park Ave 10016. Fax: 212/885-7100. **Facility:** Warm wood tones and gentle lighting give
this hotel a serene ambience. 149 units. 141 one-bedroom standard units. 8 one-bedroom suites. 18 stories,
interior corridors. **Parking:** on-site (fee) and valet. **Terms:** cancellation fee imposed. **Amenities:** high-speed
Internet (fee), dual phone lines, voice mail, fax, safes, honor bars, hair dryers. **Dining:** 2 restaurants, 7 am-
2:30 & 6-10 pm, cocktails. **Guest Services:** gift shop, valet laundry, area transportation-Wall Street. **Business Services:** meeting rooms, fax (fee). **Cards:** AX, DC, DS, JC, MC, VI. **Special Amenities: free newspaper and preferred
room (subject to availability with advanced reservations).**

SOME UNITS

[🍴] [Y] [👥] [🎬] [DATA PORT] / [✕] [VCR] [🔒] /
FEE

LA QUINTA MANHATTAN HOTEL   Book at aaa.com   Phone: (212)736-1600   64
9/1-12/31	1P: $109-$329	2P: $139-$329	XP: $20	F12
5/1-8/31	1P: $109-$149	2P: $129-$229	XP: $20	F12
3/1-4/30	1P: $109-$129	2P: $159-$189	XP: $20	F12
1/1-2/28	1P: $89-$109	2P: $119-$139	XP: $20	F12

Small-scale Hotel   **Location:** Between 5th Ave and Broadway. 17 W 32nd St 10001. Fax: 212/563-4007. **Facility:** 182 one-bedroom standard units. 12
stories, interior corridors. *Bath:* combo or shower only. **Parking:** valet. **Terms:** 14 day cancellation notice-fee imposed, [ECP]
meal plan available. **Amenities:** video games (fee), high-speed Internet, voice mail, irons, hair dryers. **Leisure Activities:** limited exercise equipment. **Guest Services:** gift shop, valet laundry. **Business Services:** business center. **Cards:** AX, CB, DC,
DS, JC, MC, VI.

SOME UNITS

[ASK] [S/D] [🍴] [🎬] [DATA PORT] [🖥] / [🔒] [📷] /

(See map and index starting on p. 364)

LE PARKER MERIDIEN NEW YORK *Book at aaa.com*   **Phone:** (212)245-5000   **41**

▽▽▽ ▽▽▽	9/7-12/31	1P: $475-$505	2P: $475-$505	XP: $30	F18
	6/25-9/6	1P: $410-$440	2P: $410-$440	XP: $30	F18
	5/1-6/24 & 1/1-4/30	1P: $380-$410	2P: $380-$410	XP: $30	F18

Large-scale Hotel **Location:** Between 6th (Ave of the Americas) and 7th aves; vehicle entrance on 56th St. 118 W 57th St 10019. Fax: 212/307-1776. **Facility:** Characterized by artful accents in stone, cherry and teak, these sleek-lined accommodations include work spaces and swiveling entertainment centers. 731 units. 717 one-bedroom standard units. 14 one-bedroom suites, some with whirlpools. 42 stories, interior corridors. *Bath:* combo or shower only. **Parking:** on-site (fee) and valet. **Terms:** cancellation fee imposed. **Amenities:** DVD players, video games (fee), CD players, high-speed Internet, dual phone lines, voice mail, safes, honor bars, irons, hair dryers. **Pool(s):** heated indoor. **Leisure Activities:** saunas. *Fee:* racquetball courts, massage, basketball. **Guest Services:** gift shop, valet laundry. *Fee:* personal trainer, nutritionist. **Business Services:** meeting rooms, business center. **Cards:** AX, CB, DC, DS, JC, MC, VI.

SOME UNITS
(ASK) 🐕 ❌ 🍽 📶 🛎 📺 🏊 🏋 ❌ VCR 📷 DATA PORT / ❌ 🔒 🍳 /

LIBRARY HOTEL *Book at aaa.com*   **Phone:** (212)983-4500   **61**

▽▽▽	1/1-4/30	1P: $335	2P: $415
	5/1-12/31	1P: $315	2P: $385

Small-scale Hotel **Location:** At 41st St. 299 Madison Ave 10017. Fax: 212/499-9099. **Facility:** 60 one-bedroom standard units. 14 stories, interior corridors. *Bath:* combo or shower only. **Parking:** no self-parking. **Terms:** cancellation fee imposed, [ECP] meal plan available. **Amenities:** video library, CD players, high-speed Internet, dual phone lines, voice mail, safes, honor bars, hair dryers. *Some:* irons. **Leisure Activities:** *Fee:* massage. **Guest Services:** valet laundry. **Business Services:** meeting rooms, business center. **Cards:** AX, DC, MC, VI.

SOME UNITS
🍽 24 ♿ 🛎 VCR 📷 DATA PORT / ❌ /

THE LOWELL HOTEL *Book at aaa.com*   **Phone:** (212)838-1400   **65**

💎💎 💎💎	9/7-4/30	1P: $465	2P: $525-$585	XP: $45	F5
	5/1-9/6	1P: $445	2P: $525-$575	XP: $45	F5

Historic Small-scale Hotel **Location:** Between Park and Madison aves. 28 E 63rd St 10021. Fax: 212/319-4230. **Facility:** Luxurious, intimate lodgings define this charming European-style hotel; some accommodations have fireplaces, and one has an exercise room. 70 units. 23 one-bedroom standard units. 47 one-bedroom suites ($775-$5000) with kitchens. 17 stories, interior corridors. **Parking:** valet. **Terms:** cancellation fee imposed, small pets only. **Amenities:** video library (fee), high-speed Internet, dual phone lines, voice mail, fax, safes, honor bars, hair dryers. *Some:* DVD players, CD players. **Dining:** The Post House, see separate listing. **Leisure Activities:** exercise room. *Fee:* massage. **Guest Services:** valet laundry. **Business Services:** meeting rooms, business center. **Cards:** AX, DC, DS, JC, MC, VI.

SOME UNITS
🐕 🍽 24 📶 VCR 📷 DATA PORT / 🔒 🍳 🖥 /

LYDEN GARDENS HOTEL *Book at aaa.com*   **Phone:** (212)355-1230   **35**

▽▽ ▽	9/1-12/31	1P: $309-$329	2P: $309-$329	XP: $30	F12
	5/1-6/30	1P: $284-$314	2P: $284-$314	XP: $30	F12
	1/1-4/30	1P: $254-$289	2P: $254-$289	XP: $30	F12
	7/1-8/31	1P: $254-$284	2P: $254-$284	XP: $30	F12

Small-scale Hotel **Location:** Between 2nd and 3rd aves. Located in residential area. 215 E 64th St 10021. Fax: 212/758-7858. **Facility:** 132 units. 82 one-bedroom standard units with kitchens. 46 one- and 4 two-bedroom suites with kitchens. 13 stories, interior corridors. *Bath:* combo or shower only. **Parking:** no self-parking. **Terms:** cancellation fee imposed. **Amenities:** video games (fee), voice mail, safes, irons, hair dryers. **Leisure Activities:** exercise room. **Business Services:** fax (fee). **Cards:** AX, CB, DC, DS, JC, MC, VI.

SOME UNITS
🏋 🛎 ♿ 📶 📷 DATA PORT 🔒 🍳 🖥 / ❌ VCR
FEE   FEE

THE MAJESTIC *Book at aaa.com*   **Phone:** (212)247-2000   **73**

▽▽▽	All Year	1P: $199-$2500	2P: $199-$2500

Historic Small-scale Hotel **Location:** Between Broadway and 7th Ave. 210 W 55th St 10019. Fax: 212/581-2248. **Facility:** Original relief detailing still enhances the lobby of this hotel built in the 1920s. 228 units. 227 one-bedroom standard units, some with whirlpools. 1 two-bedroom suite with whirlpool. 14 stories, interior corridors. *Bath:* combo or shower only. **Parking:** valet. **Terms:** cancellation fee imposed, package plans - seasonal. **Amenities:** dual phone lines, voice mail, safes, irons, hair dryers. *Fee:* video games, high-speed Internet. *Some:* DVD players (fee). **Guest Services:** gift shop, valet laundry. **Business Services:** fax. **Cards:** AX, CB, DC, DS, JC, MC, VI.

SOME UNITS
(ASK) 🛡 🛎 ♿ 📶 🏋 📷 DATA PORT 🖥 / ❌ VCR 🔒 🍳
FEE

THE MANSFIELD *Book at aaa.com*   **Phone:** (212)944-6050   **98**

▽▽▽	9/2-12/31 [ECP]	1P: $330-$350	2P: $330-$350	XP: $20	F18
	4/1-4/30 [ECP]	1P: $265-$285	2P: $265-$285	XP: $20	F18
	5/1-9/1 & 1/1-3/31 [ECP]	1P: $245-$265	2P: $245-$265	XP: $20	F18

Small-scale Hotel **Location:** Between 5th and 6th (Ave of the Americas) aves. 12 W 44th St 10036. Fax: 212/764-4477. **Facility:** 124 units. 98 one-bedroom standard units. 25 one- and 1 two-bedroom suites ($330-$410). 13 stories, interior corridors. *Bath:* combo or shower only. **Parking:** valet. **Terms:** package plans. **Amenities:** video games, CD players, dual phone lines, voice mail, safes, hair dryers. **Guest Services:** valet laundry. **Business Services:** meeting rooms, business center. **Cards:** AX, DC, MC, VI.

SOME UNITS
(ASK) 🛡 🐕 🍽 🛎 VCR 📷 DATA PORT / ❌
FEE

THE MARK, NEW YORK *Book at aaa.com*   **Phone:** (212)744-4300   **82**

▽▽▽ ▽▽▽	All Year	1P: $570-$2500	2P: $600-$2500	XP: $30	F12

Small-scale Hotel **Location:** Madison Ave at E 77th St. Located in a residential area. 25 E 77th St 10021. Fax: 212/744-2749. **Facility:** Featuring a small, ornately decorated lobby, the hotel is in a quiet neighborhood just steps from Central Park; some guest rooms have kitchenettes. 176 units. 131 one-bedroom standard units, some with efficiencies (no utensils). 45 one-bedroom suites with kitchens (no utensils). 16 stories, interior corridors. **Parking:** on-site (fee) and valet. **Terms:** cancellation fee imposed, [AP], [CP] & [ECP] meal plans available, package plans - seasonal & weekends, small pets only (dogs only). **Amenities:** video games (fee), high-speed Internet, dual phone lines, voice mail, fax, safes, honor bars, irons, hair dryers. *Some:* CD players. **Dining:** Mark's, see separate listing. **Leisure Activities:** saunas, steamrooms, exercise room. *Fee:* massage. **Guest Services:** valet laundry. **Business Services:** meeting rooms, business center. **Cards:** AX, CB, DC, DS, JC, MC, VI.

SOME UNITS
🐕 🍽 🍷 📶 ❌ VCR 📷 DATA PORT / ❌ 🍳

(See map and index starting on p. 364)

THE MAYFLOWER HOTEL ON THE PARK — *Book at aaa.com*
Phone: (212)265-0060 · 104

AAA SAVE ◇◇ ◇◇ · Small-scale Hotel

| All Year | 1P: $205-$245 | 2P: $230-$270 | XP: $20 | F14 |

Location: At 61st St. 15 Central Park W 10023. Fax: 212/265-5098. **Facility:** 365 units. 175 one-bedroom standard units. 190 one-bedroom suites ($300-$1000). 18 stories, interior corridors. **Parking:** on-site (fee) and valet. **Terms:** small pets only. **Amenities:** video games, voice mail, irons, hair dryers. *Some:* high-speed Internet. **Dining:** 7 am-11:30 pm, cocktails. **Leisure Activities:** exercise room. **Guest Services:** valet laundry. **Business Services:** meeting rooms, fax (fee). **Cards:** AX, DC, DS, JC, MC, VI.

SOME UNITS
[icons] SD · / · VCR · DATA PORT
FEE

THE METROPOLITAN — *Book at aaa.com*
Phone: (212)752-7000 · 58

◇◇◇ · Small-scale Hotel

9/5-12/18	1P: $299-$339	2P: $299-$339
5/1-6/26	1P: $209-$299	2P: $209-$299
6/27-8/26 & 12/19-4/30	1P: $239-$279	2P: $239-$279

Location: At E 51st St. 569 Lexington Ave 10022. Fax: 212/758-6311. **Facility:** 722 units. 692 one-bedroom standard units. 30 one-bedroom suites ($299-$339). 20 stories, interior corridors. *Bath:* combo or shower only. **Parking:** on-site (fee). **Terms:** open 5/1-8/26 & 9/5-4/30, cancellation fee imposed, small pets only. **Amenities:** dual phone lines, voice mail, safes, irons, hair dryers. *Some: Fee:* high-speed Internet. **Leisure Activities:** exercise room. **Guest Services:** gift shop, valet laundry, hair & nail salon. **Business Services:** conference facilities, business center. **Cards:** AX, DC, JC, MC, VI.

SOME UNITS
[icons] ASK · SD · / · DATA PORT · / · VCR
FEE · FEE

THE MICHELANGELO — *Book at aaa.com*
Phone: (212)765-1900 · 85

◇◇◇ ◇◇◇ · Small-scale Hotel

| All Year | 1P: $395-$1200 | 2P: $395-$1200 |

Location: At 7th Ave. 152 W 51st St 10019. Fax: 212/541-6604. **Facility:** The property features an elegant lobby and tailored traditional decor in guest rooms, where generous amenities and marble baths add luxury. 178 units. 163 one-bedroom standard units. 15 one-bedroom suites. 5 stories, interior corridors. **Parking:** valet. **Terms:** cancellation fee imposed. **Amenities:** CD players, dual phone lines, voice mail, fax, honor bars, hair dryers. *Some:* DVD players. **Leisure Activities:** exercise room. *Fee:* massage. **Guest Services:** valet laundry, area transportation. **Business Services:** meeting rooms, fax (fee). **Cards:** AX, CB, DC, DS, JC, MC, VI.

SOME UNITS
[icons] / · DATA PORT · / · VCR · /

(See map and index starting on p. 364)

MILLENNIUM BROADWAY
Book at aaa.com Phone: (212)768-4400 **112**

AAA SAVE

9/7-4/30	1P: $389-$479	2P: $389-$479	
5/1-9/6	1P: $329-$379	2P: $329-$379	

Large-scale Hotel **Location:** Between 6th (Ave of the Americas) and 7th aves. Located in the theater district. 145 W 44th St 10036. **Fax:** 212/768-0847. **Facility:** 750 units. 737 one-bedroom standard units. 13 one-bedroom suites. 52 stories, interior corridors. *Bath:* combo or shower only. **Parking:** valet. **Terms:** check-in 4 pm, cancellation fee imposed. **Amenities:** voice mail, safes, honor bars, irons, hair dryers. *Some:* CD players. **Dining:** noon-2:30 & 5:15-10:30 pm, Sun 10 am-2:30 & 5:15-9:30 pm, cocktails. **Leisure Activities:** exercise room. *Fee:* massage. **Guest Services:** gift shop, valet laundry. **Business Services:** conference facilities, business center. **Cards:** AX, CB, DC, DS, JC, MI, VI.
(See color ad p 389)

SOME UNITS
[icons] / FEE

MILLENNIUM UN PLAZA HOTEL NEW YORK
Book at aaa.com Phone: (212)758-1234 **34**

AAA SAVE

9/1-12/31	1P: $269-$418	XP: $35	F18
1/1-4/30	1P: $199-$309	XP: $35	F18
5/1-8/31	1P: $189-$299	XP: $35	F18

Large-scale Hotel **Location:** Between 1st and 2nd aves. Located across from United Nations Headquarters. One UN Plaza, 44th St 10017-3575. **Fax:** 212/702-5051. **Facility:** 427 units. 383 one-bedroom standard units, some with efficiencies. 34 one- and 10 two-bedroom suites, some with kitchens. 38-40 stories, interior corridors. *Bath:* combo or shower only. **Parking:** on-site (fee) and valet. **Amenities:** voice mail, fax, safes, honor bars, irons, hair dryers. *Some:* CD players. **Dining:** 6:30 am-2:30 & 6-11 pm, cocktails. **Pool(s):** heated indoor. **Leisure Activities:** saunas. *Fee:* indoor tennis court, massage. **Guest Services:** gift shop, valet laundry, area transportation (fee)-theater. **Business Services:** meeting rooms, business center. **Cards:** AX, DC, DS, MC, VI. *(See color ad p 389)*

SOME UNITS
[icons] /

THE MUSE
Book at aaa.com Phone: (212)485-2400 **108**

AAA SAVE

9/2-12/31	1P: $449	2P: $449	XP: $30	F12
1/1-4/30	1P: $369-$399	2P: $369-$399	XP: $30	F12
5/1-6/29	1P: $399	2P: $399	XP: $30	F12
6/30-9/1	1P: $369	2P: $369	XP: $30	F12

Small-scale Hotel **Location:** Between 6th (Ave of the Americas) and 7th aves. 130 W 46th St 10036. **Fax:** 212/485-2900. **Facility:** In the heart of the theater district, The Muse is a sophisticated and elegant small hotel offering fine service with modern style and personality. 200 one-bedroom standard units. 19 stories, interior corridors. *Bath:* combo or shower only. **Parking:** valet. **Terms:** cancellation fee imposed, [AP], [BP] & [CP] meal plans available. **Amenities:** CD players, high-speed Internet (fee), dual phone lines, voice mail, fax, safes, honor bars, irons, hair dryers. *Some:* DVD players. **Dining:** District, see separate listing. **Leisure Activities:** exercise room. **Guest Services:** valet laundry. **Business Services:** meeting rooms, administrative services, fax. **Cards:** AX, CB, DC, DS, MC, VI. **Special Amenities:** free local telephone calls and free newspaper.

SOME UNITS
[icons] /

NEW YORK MARRIOTT EASTSIDE
Book at aaa.com Phone: (212)755-4000 **109**

9/5-12/18	1P: $199-$375	2P: $199-$375	XP: $20	F18
5/1-6/26 & 12/19-4/30	1P: $179-$299	2P: $179-$299	XP: $20	F18
6/27-9/4	1P: $179-$279	2P: $179-$279	XP: $20	F18

Large-scale Hotel **Location:** Between 48th and 49th sts. 525 Lexington Ave 10017. **Fax:** 212/751-3440. **Facility:** 646 units. 629 one-bedroom standard units. 17 one-bedroom suites ($250-$1500), some with whirlpools. 33 stories, interior corridors. *Bath:* some combo or shower only. **Parking:** valet. **Terms:** cancellation fee imposed, package plans - weekends. **Amenities:** dual phone lines, voice mail, safes, honor bars, irons, hair dryers. **Leisure Activities:** exercise room. **Guest Services:** gift shop, valet laundry. **Business Services:** conference facilities, business center. **Cards:** AX, CB, DC, DS, JC, MC, VI.

SOME UNITS
[icons] / FEE

NEW YORK MARRIOTT MARQUIS
Book at aaa.com Phone: 212/398-1900 **90**

1/1-4/30	1P: $199-$700
5/1-12/31	1P: $199-$600

Large-scale Hotel **Location:** Between 45th and 46th sts; motor entrance on 46th St. Located in Times Square. 1535 Broadway 10036. **Fax:** 212/704-8930. **Facility:** 1944 units. 1924 one-bedroom standard units. 20 one-bedroom suites. 48 stories, interior corridors. *Bath:* combo or shower only. **Parking:** on-site (fee) and valet. **Terms:** cancellation fee imposed, small pets only. **Amenities:** dual phone lines, voice mail, safes, honor bars, irons, hair dryers. *Fee:* video library, video games, high-speed Internet. *Some:* fax. **Leisure Activities:** saunas. **Guest Services:** gift shop, valet laundry. **Business Services:** conference facilities, business center. **Cards:** AX, CB, DC, DS, MC, VI.

SOME UNITS
[icons] / FEE

NEW YORK MIDTOWN EAST COURTYARD BY MARRIOTT
Book at aaa.com Phone: (212)644-1300 **122**

9/5-12/11	1P: $219-$349	2P: $219-$349	
3/6-4/30	1P: $199-$299	2P: $199-$299	
5/1-9/4 & 12/12-3/5	1P: $179-$299	2P: $179-$279	

Small-scale Hotel **Location:** Between 52nd and 53rd sts. 866 3rd Ave 10022. **Fax:** 212/317-7940. **Facility:** 307 units. 299 one-bedroom standard units. 8 one-bedroom suites. 31 stories, interior corridors. *Bath:* combo or shower only. **Parking:** valet. **Amenities:** high-speed Internet (fee), dual phone lines, voice mail, safes, irons, hair dryers. **Leisure Activities:** exercise room. **Guest Services:** valet and coin laundry. **Business Services:** meeting rooms, fax (fee). **Cards:** AX, CB, DC, DS, JC, MC, VI.

SOME UNITS
[icons] /

(See map and index starting on p. 364)

THE NEW YORK PALACE   *Book at aaa.com*   Phone: (212)888-7000   **44**

9/2-12/31	1P: $595-$745	2P: $620-$770	XP: $25	F12
1/1-4/30	1P: $545-$660	2P: $570-$685	XP: $25	F12
5/1-6/27	1P: $495-$645	2P: $520-$670	XP: $25	F12
6/28-9/1	1P: $450-$600	2P: $475-$625	XP: $25	F12

Historic
Large-scale Hotel
Location: Between 50th and 51st sts. 455 Madison Ave 10022. Fax: 212/303-6000. **Facility:** A grand staircase and marble fireplace accent the Neo-Italian Renaissance lobby at this hotel, which provides polished service and excellent views. 896 units. 843 one-bedroom standard units. 53 one-bedroom suites ($950-$2100) with kitchens, some with whirlpools. 55 stories, interior corridors. *Bath:* combo or shower only. **Parking:** valet. **Terms:** small pets only. **Amenities:** high-speed Internet (fee), dual phone lines, voice mail, fax, safes, honor bars, irons, hair dryers. *Some:* DVD players, video games, CD players. **Dining:** 2 restaurants, 6:30 am-11 pm, cocktails, also, Le Cirque 2000, see separate listing, entertainment. **Leisure Activities:** steamrooms, spa. **Guest Services:** gift shop, valet laundry, area transportation-Wall Street. **Business Services:** conference facilities, business center. **Cards:** AX, CB, DC, DS, MC, VI.

SOME UNITS

NOVOTEL NEW YORK   Phone: (212)315-0100   **69**

9/6-12/31	1P: $239-$349	2P: $239-$369	XP: $20	F16
5/1-6/30	1P: $199-$269	2P: $199-$289	XP: $20	F16
1/1-4/30	1P: $199-$249	2P: $199-$269	XP: $20	F16
7/1-9/6	1P: $179-$249	2P: $179-$269	XP: $20	F16

Large-scale Hotel **Location:** At Broadway. 226 W 52nd St 10019. Fax: 212/765-5365. **Facility:** 480 one-bedroom standard units. 33 stories, interior corridors. **Parking:** no self-parking. **Terms:** [AP], [BP] & [CP] meal plans available. **Amenities:** voice mail, safes, honor bars, irons, hair dryers. *Fee:* video library, video games. *Some:* dual phone lines. **Dining:** 6:30 am-midnight, cocktails, entertainment. **Leisure Activities:** exercise room. **Guest Services:** gift shop, valet laundry. **Business Services:** meeting rooms, business center. **Cards:** AX, CB, DC, DS, JC, MC, VI. *(See color ad below)*

SOME UNITS

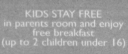

OMNI BERKSHIRE PLACE   *Book at aaa.com*   Phone: (212)753-5800   **26**

9/6-12/31	1P: $479-$519	2P: $479-$519	XP: $30	F12
5/1-6/30	1P: $409-$449	2P: $409-$449	XP: $30	F12
1/1-4/30	1P: $319-$449	2P: $319-$449	XP: $30	F12
7/1-9/5	1P: $319-$359	2P: $319-$359	XP: $30	F12

Large-scale Hotel
Location: Between Madison and 5th aves. 21 E 52nd St 10022. Fax: 212/754-5020. **Facility:** Setting a tone of elegance at this luxury hotel are sparkling chandeliers, 18th-century-inspired carpets and marble finishes. 396 units. 353 one-bedroom standard units. 43 one-bedroom suites ($499-$950), some with whirlpools. 22 stories, interior corridors. *Bath:* combo or shower only. **Parking:** valet. **Terms:** package plans. **Amenities:** video games (fee), CD players, high-speed Internet, dual phone lines, voice mail, fax, safes, honor bars, irons, hair dryers. **Leisure Activities:** exercise room. *Fee:* massage. **Guest Services:** valet laundry, area transportation. **Business Services:** meeting rooms, business center. **Cards:** AX, CB, DC, DS, JC, MC, VI.

SOME UNITS

FEE

(See map and index starting on p. 364)

PARK CENTRAL NEW YORK   *Book at aaa.com*   Phone: (212)247-8000   128

| | 9/1-12/31 | 1P: $319-$349 | 2P: $319-$349 | XP: $25 | F17 |
| | 5/1-8/31 & 1/1-4/30 | 1P: $219-$249 | 2P: $219-$249 | XP: $25 | F17 |

Location: At 56th St. 870 7th Ave 10019. Fax: 212/707-5557. **Facility:** 935 units. 914 one-bedroom standard units. 20 one- and 1 two-bedroom suites ($279-$2500). 25 stories, interior corridors. *Bath:* combo or shower only. **Parking:** valet. **Terms:** check-in 4 pm. **Amenities:** dual phone lines, voice mail, safes, irons, hair dryers. **Fee:** video games, high-speed Internet. *Some:* honor bars. **Dining:** 6 am-11 pm, cocktails. **Leisure Activities:** exercise room. **Guest Services:** gift shop, valet laundry. **Business Services:** conference facilities, fax (fee). **Cards:** AX, CB, DC, DS, JC, MC, VI. **Special Amenities:** free newspaper. *(See color ad below)*

Large-scale Hotel

SOME UNITS

THE PENINSULA NEW YORK   *Book at aaa.com*   Phone: (212)956-2888   59

| | 9/7-12/31 | 1P: $500-$640 | 2P: $500-$640 | XP: $50 | F12 |
| | 5/1-9/6 & 1/1-4/30 | 1P: $440-$560 | 2P: $440-$560 | XP: $50 | F12 |

Location: At 55th St. 700 5th Ave 10019. Fax: 212/903-3949. **Facility:** Distinct grandeur and intricate architecture mark this turn-of-the-20th-century Beaux Arts-style hotel, which offers modern rooms and a rooftop health spa. 239 units. 201 one-bedroom standard units. 37 one- and 1 two-bedroom suites, some with whirlpools. 23 stories, interior corridors. *Bath:* combo or shower only. **Parking:** valet. **Terms:** cancellation fee imposed, small pets only. **Amenities:** video library, high-speed Internet, dual phone lines, voice mail, fax, safes, honor bars, hair dryers. *Some:* DVD players, video games, CD players. **Dining:** 6:30-10:30 am, 11:30-2:30 & 5:30-10 pm, cocktails. **Pool(s):** heated indoor. **Leisure Activities:** saunas, whirlpool, steamrooms, spa. **Guest Services:** valet laundry, area transportation-theater district. **Business Services:** meeting rooms, business center. **Cards:** AX, DC, DS, JC, MC, VI. **Special Amenities:** free local telephone calls and free newspaper.

Large-scale Hotel

SOME UNITS

THE PIERRE NEW YORK - A FOUR SEASONS HOTEL   *Book at aaa.com*   Phone: (212)838-8000   67

| | 5/1-6/24 & 9/7-4/30 | 1P: $475-$905 | 2P: $475-$905 | XP: $50 | F18 |
| | 6/25-9/6 | 1P: $405-$865 | 2P: $405-$865 | XP: $50 | F18 |

Historic Small-scale Hotel

Location: At 5th Ave. 2 E 61st St 10021. Fax: 212/940-8109. **Facility:** White-gloved elevator operators add Old World charm at this grand 1930s hotel, where high tea is served amid Rococo murals in the rotunda. 202 units. 142 one-bedroom standard units. 60 one-bedroom suites ($655-$1180). 39 stories, interior corridors. *Bath:* combo or shower only. **Parking:** valet. **Terms:** [AP] meal plan available, small pets only. **Amenities:** video library (fee), high-speed Internet, dual phone lines, voice mail, safes, honor bars, hair dryers. *Some:* DVD players, video games, CD players, fax, irons. **Dining:** Cafe Pierre, see separate listing. **Leisure Activities:** exercise room. **Fee:** massage. **Guest Services:** gift shop, valet laundry, area transportation. **Business Services:** conference facilities, business center. **Cards:** AX, CB, DC, DS, JC, MC, VI.

SOME UNITS

PLAZA FIFTY HOTEL   *Book at aaa.com*   Phone: (212)751-5710   37

| | 9/1-12/31 | 1P: $314-$419 | 2P: $314-$419 | XP: $25 | F12 |
| | 5/1-8/31 & 1/1-4/30 | 1P: $249-$309 | 2P: $249-$309 | XP: $25 | F12 |

Small-scale Hotel

Location: Between 3rd and Lexington aves. 155 E 50th St 10022. Fax: 212/753-1468. **Facility:** 211 units. 151 one-bedroom standard units, some with kitchens. 57 one- and 3 two-bedroom suites with kitchens. 22 stories, interior corridors. **Parking:** valet. **Terms:** cancellation fee imposed. **Amenities:** video games (fee), dual phone lines, voice mail, safes, irons, hair dryers. **Leisure Activities:** exercise room. **Guest Services:** valet laundry. **Cards:** AX, CB, DC, DS, JC, MC, VI.

SOME UNITS

QUALITY HOTEL TIMES SQUARE   *Book at aaa.com*   Phone: (212)768-3700   113

	9/10-1/1 [CP]	1P: $170-$330	2P: $180-$350	XP: $25	F12
	7/1-9/9 [CP]	1P: $120-$210	2P: $150-$270	XP: $25	F12
	5/1-6/30 & 1/2-4/30 [CP]	1P: $130-$190	2P: $150-$200	XP: $25	F12

Small-scale Hotel

Location: Between 6th (Ave of the Americas) and 7th aves. 157 W 47th St 10036. Fax: 212/768-7573. **Facility:** 160 units. 137 one-bedroom standard units. 23 one-bedroom suites ($170-$400), some with whirlpools. 10 stories, interior corridors. *Bath:* combo or shower only. **Parking:** on-site (fee). **Terms:** 45 day cancellation notice-fee imposed. **Amenities:** voice mail, irons, hair dryers. **Fee:** video library, safes. **Guest Services:** valet laundry. **Business Services:** meeting rooms, fax (fee). **Cards:** AX, CB, DC, DS, MC, VI.

SOME UNITS

(See map and index starting on p. 364)

RADISSON LEXINGTON HOTEL NEW YORK   *Book at aaa.com*   Phone: (212)755-4400   **110**

AAA SAVE

8/26-12/31	1P: $279-$379	2P: $279-$379	XP: $20	F12
6/27-8/25 & 1/1-4/30	1P: $239-$339	2P: $239-$339	XP: $20	F12
5/1-6/26	1P: $219-$319	2P: $219-$319	XP: $20	F12

Location: At E 48th St. 511 Lexington Ave 10017. Fax: 212/751-4091. **Facility:** 701 units. 677 one-bedroom standard units. 24 one-bedroom suites ($339-$850), some with whirlpools. 27 stories, interior corridors. *Bath:* combo or shower only. **Parking:** no self-parking. **Terms:** check-in 4 pm, cancellation fee imposed, $2 service charge. **Amenities:** dual phone lines, voice mail, safes, irons, hair dryers. *Fee:* video games, high-speed Internet. **Dining:** 3 restaurants, 6 am-11 pm, cocktails. **Leisure Activities:** exercise room. **Guest Services:** valet laundry. **Business Services:** meeting rooms, business center. **Cards:** AX, CB, DC, DS, JC, MC, VI. **Special Amenities:** early check-in/late check-out and preferred room (subject to availability with advanced reservations). *(See color ad p 413)*

Large-scale Hotel

SOME UNITS

RED ROOF INN   *Book at aaa.com*   Phone: 212/643-7100   **87**

All Year [CP]   1P: $119-$289   2P: $129-$299   XP: $20   F13

Location: Between Broadway and 5th Ave. 6 W 32nd St 10001. Fax: 212/643-7101. **Facility:** 171 one-bedroom standard units. 17 stories, interior corridors. **Parking:** no self-parking. **Terms:** cancellation fee imposed. **Amenities:** video games (fee), high-speed Internet, voice mail, irons, hair dryers. **Leisure Activities:** exercise room. **Guest Services:** valet laundry. **Business Services:** meeting rooms, fax (fee). **Cards:** AX, DC, DS, MC, VI.

Small-scale Hotel

SOME UNITS

THE REGENCY HOTEL   *Book at aaa.com*   Phone: (212)759-4100   **68**

AAA SAVE

9/13-12/12	1P: $339-$419	2P: $339-$419	XP: $30	F17
5/1-9/12 & 12/13-4/30	1P: $239-$379	2P: $239-$379	XP: $30	F17

Location: At 61st St. 540 Park Ave 10021. Fax: 212/826-5674. **Facility:** Guest rooms at this upscale hotel are done in muted earth tones, wood and granite. 351 units. 265 one-bedroom standard units. 72 one- and 14 two-bedroom suites ($459-$1239). 21 stories, interior corridors. *Bath:* combo or shower only. **Parking:** valet. **Amenities:** video library, CD players, high-speed Internet (fee), dual phone lines, voice mail, safes, honor bars, irons, hair dryers. **Dining:** 7 am-1 am, Fri & Sat-2 am, cocktails. **Leisure Activities:** sauna. **Guest Services:** gift shop, valet laundry, beauty salon. **Business Services:** conference facilities, business center. **Cards:** AX, CB, DC, DS, MC, VI. Affiliated with Loews Hotels.

Large-scale Hotel

SOME UNITS

RENAISSANCE NEW YORK HOTEL TIMES SQUARE   *Book at aaa.com*   Phone: (212)765-7676   **123**

AAA SAVE

5/1-12/31 & 3/1-4/30	1P: $269-$349	2P: $289-$369	XP: $20	F18
1/1-2/28	1P: $229-$349	2P: $249-$369	XP: $20	F18

Location: Broadway and 7th Ave; auto access from 7th Ave, s of W 48th St. 2 Times Square, 7th Ave at W 48th St 10036. Fax: 212/765-1962. **Facility:** This richly decorated luxury hotel offers large guest rooms and central Times Square location. 305 units. 300 one-bedroom standard units. 5 one-bedroom suites ($500-$650). 26 stories, interior corridors. **Parking:** valet. **Terms:** pets ($60 fee). **Amenities:** video games (fee), dual phone lines, voice mail, safes, honor bars, irons, hair dryers. *Some:* CD players, high-speed Internet, fax. **Dining:** Foley's Restaurant & Bar, see separate listing, entertainment. **Leisure Activities:** exercise room. **Guest Services:** valet laundry. **Business Services:** meeting rooms, business center. **Cards:** AX, DC, DS, MC, VI. **Special Amenities:** free newspaper.

Large-scale Hotel

SOME UNITS

FEE

RIHGA ROYAL HOTEL   *Book at aaa.com*   Phone: (212)307-5000   **114**

All Year   1P: $269-$800

Location: Between 6th (Ave of the Americas) and 7th aves. 151 W 54th St 10019. Fax: 212/765-6530. **Facility:** Seating areas and mirrored French doors add charm to the large guest rooms at this modern hotel, which is decorated in rich fabrics and hardwoods. 500 units. 6 one-bedroom standard units. 453 one- and 41 two-bedroom suites. 54 stories, interior corridors. *Bath:* combo or shower only. **Parking:** valet. **Amenities:** video library (fee), CD players, dual phone lines, voice mail, fax, safes, honor bars, irons, hair dryers. *Some: Fee:* high-speed Internet. **Leisure Activities:** saunas, exercise room. *Fee:* massage. **Guest Services:** valet laundry. **Business Services:** meeting rooms, business center. **Cards:** AX, CB, DC, DS, MC, VI. Affiliated with Marriott Hotels, Resorts and Suites.

Large-scale Hotel

SOME UNITS

FEE

THE RITZ-CARLTON NEW YORK, CENTRAL PARK   *Book at aaa.com*   Phone: (212)308-9100   **97**

AAA SAVE

10/31-11/30	1P: $550-$875	2P: $550-$875
8/26-10/30	1P: $550-$825	2P: $550-$825
12/1-4/30	1P: $450-$825	2P: $450-$825
5/1-8/25	1P: $425-$750	2P: $425-$750

Location: Between 5th and 6th (Ave of the Americas) aves. 50 Central Park S 10019. Fax: 212/207-8831. **Facility:** This traditionally elegant property offers a plush lounge, quality appointments, a high standard of service and views of Central Park. 277 units. 237 one-bedroom standard units. 40 one-bedroom suites ($1395-$12,000), some with whirlpools. 22 stories, interior corridors. *Bath:* combo or shower only. **Parking:** valet. **Terms:** cancellation fee imposed. **Amenities:** video library, DVD players, CD players, high-speed Internet, dual phone lines, voice mail, safes, honor bars, hair dryers. *Some: Fee:* high-speed Internet. **Dining:** 6:30 am-10 pm, Fri & Sat-11 pm, cocktails, entertainment. **Leisure Activities:** exercise room, spa. **Guest Services:** gift shop, valet laundry, area transportation-midtown area. **Business Services:** meeting rooms, business center. **Cards:** AX, CB, DC, DS, JC, MC, VI. **Special Amenities:** free newspaper.

Large-scale Hotel

SOME UNITS

(See map and index starting on p. 364)

THE ROGER SMITH HOTEL   *Book at aaa.com*   Phone: (212)755-1400 **111**

9/1-12/31 [ECP]	1P: $215-$255	2P: $215-$255	XP: $20	F16
5/1-6/24 [ECP]	1P: $195-$235	2P: $195-$235	XP: $20	F16
6/25-8/31 & 1/1-4/30 [ECP]	1P: $169-$195	2P: $169-$195	XP: $20	F16

Historic
Small-scale Hotel

Location: Between 47th and 48th sts. 501 Lexington Ave 10017. Fax: 212/758-4061. **Facility:** Rooms are individually decorated at this family run hotel and much of the sculpture in the lobby is the owners own work of art. 134 units. 106 one-bedroom standard units, some with whirlpools. 28 one-bedroom suites ($249-$400), some with whirlpools. 16 stories, interior corridors. **Parking:** valet. **Terms:** cancellation fee imposed. **Amenities:** video library, voice mail, irons, hair dryers. *Some:* CD players, dual phone lines. **Fee:** high-speed Internet. **Dining:** 6 am-10, noon-3 & 5-10 pm, Sat & Sun 7-11 am, cocktails. **Guest Services:** valet laundry. **Business Services:** meeting rooms, fax (fee). **Cards:** AX, CB, DC, DS, JC, MC, VI. **Special Amenities:** free expanded continental breakfast and free local telephone calls.

SOME UNITS

🅂🄳 🐾 🍴 ☕ 🚫 ➕ 🆅🅲🆁 🐾 📶 🔲 💻 /☒ 📺 /
FEE

THE ROGER WILLIAMS HOTEL   *Book at aaa.com*   Phone: (212)448-7000 **83**

9/2-12/31 [ECP]	1P: $330	2P: $330	XP: $20	F18
5/1-6/28 [ECP]	1P: $300	2P: $300	XP: $20	F18
6/29-9/1 & 1/1-4/30 [ECP]	1P: $245	2P: $245	XP: $20	F18

Small-scale Hotel **Location:** Corner of 31st. 131 Madison Ave 10016. Fax: 212/448-7007. **Facility:** 187 units. 185 one-bedroom standard units. 2 one-bedroom suites. 16 stories, interior corridors. *Bath:* some combo or shower only. **Parking:** valet. **Terms:** package plans. **Amenities:** video library, CD players, dual phone lines, voice mail, safes, irons, hair dryers. *Some:* high-speed Internet (fee). **Leisure Activities:** exercise room. **Guest Services:** valet laundry. **Business Services:** business center. **Cards:** AX, DC, DS, JC, MC, VI.

SOME UNITS

🅰🅂 🅂🄳 🆅🅲🆁 🐾 📶 /☒ /

THE ROOSEVELT HOTEL   *Book at aaa.com*   Phone: (212)661-9600 **47**

9/8-12/12	1P: $349-$369	2P: $349-$369	XP: $20	F17
12/13-4/30	1P: $329-$349	2P: $329-$349	XP: $20	F17
5/1-6/30	1P: $269-$289	2P: $269-$289	XP: $20	F17
7/1-9/7	1P: $209-$249	2P: $209-$249	XP: $20	F17

Large-scale Hotel **Location:** Between Madison and Vanderbilt aves. 45 E 45th St 10017. Fax: 212/885-6161. **Facility:** 1014 units. 966 one-bedroom standard units. 35 one-, 10 two- and 3 three-bedroom suites ($450-$750). 19 stories, interior corridors. *Bath:* combo or shower only. **Parking:** valet. **Terms:** cancellation fee imposed. **Amenities:** video games (fee), dual phone lines, voice mail, safes, irons, hair dryers. **Dining:** 6:30 am-11 pm, cocktails. **Leisure Activities:** exercise room. **Guest Services:** gift shop, valet laundry. **Business Services:** conference facilities, business center. **Cards:** AX, CB, DC, DS, JC, MC, VI.

SOME UNITS

🅂🄳 🍴 24 ☕ ♿ 🏊 🚫 🐾 📶 /☒ 🆅🅲🆁 🔲 📺 💻 /
FEE FEE

ROYALTON   *Book at aaa.com*   Phone: (212)869-4400 **105**

All Year	1P: $225-$495

Large-scale Hotel **Location:** Between 5th and 6th (Ave of the Americas) aves. 44 W 44th St 10036. Fax: 212/869-8965. **Facility:** 169 units. 166 one-bedroom standard units. 3 one-bedroom suites. 16 stories, interior corridors. *Bath:* combo or shower only. **Parking:** on-site (fee) and valet. **Terms:** cancellation fee imposed, [BP] meal plan available. **Amenities:** CD players, dual phone lines, voice mail, safes, honor bars, irons, hair dryers. **Fee:** video library, high-speed Internet. **Leisure Activities:** exercise room. **Fee:** massage. **Guest Services:** valet laundry. **Business Services:** meeting rooms, fax (fee). **Cards:** AX, CB, DC, DS, JC, MC, VI.

SOME UNITS

🍴 ☕ 🚫 🆅🅲🆁 🐾 📶 /☒ /

(See map and index starting on p. 364)

THE ST. REGIS-NEW YORK *Book at aaa.com*   Phone: (212)753-4500 **49**

(AAA) SAVE
	1/1-4/30	1P: $690-$6000	2P: $690-$6000
	9/7-12/31	1P: $660-$6000	2P: $660-$6000
	5/1-9/6	1P: $610-$6000	2P: $610-$6000

Historic
Large-scale Hotel

Location: Between Madison and 5th aves. 2 E 55th St 10022. **Fax:** 212/787-3447. **Facility:** A New York landmark since 1904, The St. Regis-New York offers personalized butler service and classic Old World decor. 315 units. 245 one-bedroom standard units. 69 one- and 1 two-bedroom suites, some with whirlpools. 19 stories, interior corridors. **Parking:** on-site (fee) and valet. **Terms:** cancellation fee imposed, [AP], [BP] & [CP] meal plans available, small pets only. **Amenities:** dual phone lines, voice mail, safes, honor bars, hair dryers. *Some:* DVD players, CD players, fax. **Dining:** 7 am-11 pm, entertainment. **Leisure Activities:** steamrooms, exercise room, spa. **Guest Services:** gift shop, valet laundry, personal trainer, beauty salon. **Business Services:** conference facilities, business center. **Cards:** AX, CB, DC, DS, JC, MC, VI. **Special Amenities:** free newspaper.

SOME UNITS

SALISBURY HOTEL *Book at aaa.com*   Phone: (212)246-1300 **103**

| | All Year | 1P: $249-$289 | 2P: $269-$309 | XP: $30 | F15 |

Small-scale Hotel

Location: Between 6th (Ave of the Americas) and 7th aves. 123 W 57th St 10019. **Fax:** 212/977-7752. **Facility:** 200 units. 120 one-bedroom standard units. 80 one-bedroom suites ($229-$499). 17 stories, interior corridors. *Bath:* combo or shower only. **Parking:** no self-parking. **Amenities:** voice mail, safes, irons, hair dryers. **Guest Services:** valet laundry. **Business Services:** meeting rooms, fax (fee). **Cards:** AX, CB, DC, DS, JC, MC, VI.

SOME UNITS

SHELBURNE MURRAY HILL HOTEL *Book at aaa.com*   Phone: (212)689-5200 **45**

| | 9/1-12/31 | 1P: $309-$334 | 2P: $309-$334 | XP: $25 | F12 |
| | 5/1-8/31 & 1/1-4/30 | 1P: $254-$279 | 2P: $254-$279 | XP: $25 | F12 |

Small-scale Hotel

Location: Between 37th and 38th sts. 303 Lexington Ave 10016. **Fax:** 212/779-7068. **Facility:** 264 units. 131 one-bedroom standard units, some with efficiencies. 119 one- and 14 two-bedroom suites with kitchens. 16 stories, interior corridors. *Bath:* combo or shower only. **Parking:** valet. **Terms:** cancellation fee imposed. **Amenities:** video games (fee), dual phone lines, voice mail, safes, honor bars, irons, hair dryers. **Leisure Activities:** saunas, exercise room. **Guest Services:** valet and coin laundry. **Business Services:** meeting rooms, fax (fee). **Cards:** AX, CB, DC, DS, JC, MC, VI.

SOME UNITS

SHERATON MANHATTAN HOTEL *Book at aaa.com*   Phone: (212)581-3300 **79**

| | All Year | | 2P: $169-$389 | XP: $30 | F17 |

Large-scale Hotel

Location: Between 51st and 52nd sts. 790 7th Ave 10019. **Fax:** 212/541-9219. **Facility:** 665 units. 657 one-bedroom standard units. 7 one- and 1 two-bedroom suites ($575-$5000), some with kitchens and/or whirlpools. 22 stories, interior corridors. *Bath:* combo or shower only. **Parking:** on-site (fee). **Terms:** cancellation fee imposed. **Amenities:** dual phone lines, voice mail, safes, honor bars, irons, hair dryers. *Fee:* video library, video games, high-speed Internet. *Some:* fax. **Pool(s):** heated indoor. **Leisure Activities:** saunas, exercise room. *Fee:* massage. **Guest Services:** gift shop, valet laundry. **Business Services:** meeting rooms, business center. **Cards:** AX, CB, DC, DS, JC, MC, VI.

SOME UNITS

(See map and index starting on p. 364)

SHERATON NEW YORK HOTEL & TOWERS   *Book at aaa.com*   Phone: (212)581-1000   **81**
▼▼▽▼▽▼   All Year   1P: $169-$389   2P: $169-$389   XP: $30   F17
Location: At 52nd St. 811 7th Ave 10019. Fax: 212/262-4410. **Facility:** 1749 units. 1714 one-bedroom standard
Large-scale Hotel   units. 35 one-bedroom suites ($575-$5000), some with whirlpools. 50 stories, interior corridors. **Bath:** combo
or shower only. **Parking:** on-site (fee) and valet. **Terms:** cancellation fee imposed. **Amenities:** voice mail,
safes, irons, hair dryers. *Fee:* video library, video games. *Some:* high-speed Internet, dual phone lines, fax, honor bars. **Leisure
Activities:** saunas, steamrooms. *Fee:* massage. **Guest Services:** gift shop, valet laundry. **Business Services:** conference facilities, business center. **Cards:** AX, CB, DC, DS, JC, MC, VI.

SHERATON RUSSELL HOTEL   *Book at aaa.com*   Phone: (212)685-7676   **46**
▼▼▽▼   All Year   2P: $189-$399   XP: $30   F17
Location: At 37th St. Located in a historic district. 45 Park Ave 10016. Fax: 212/889-3193. **Facility:** 146 units. 120
Small-scale Hotel   one-bedroom standard units. 26 one-bedroom suites ($675-$975). 10 stories, interior corridors. **Bath:** combo
or shower only. **Parking:** valet. **Terms:** cancellation fee imposed. **Amenities:** video games (fee), dual phone
lines, voice mail, fax, safes, honor bars, irons, hair dryers. **Guest Services:** valet laundry. **Business Services:** meeting rooms.
Cards: AX, CB, DC, DS, JC, MC, VI.

THE SHOREHAM HOTEL   *Book at aaa.com*   Phone: (212)247-6700   **31**
▼▼▽▼▽   All Year   1P: $169-$1500   2P: $169-$1500   XP: $25   F11
Location: Between 5th and 6th (Ave of the Americas) aves. 33 W 55th St 10019. Fax: 212/765-9741. **Facility:** 174
Small-scale Hotel   units. 135 one-bedroom standard units. 39 one-bedroom suites ($400-$2000). 11 stories, interior corridors.
Bath: combo or shower only. **Parking:** no self-parking. **Amenities:** video library, CD players, voice mail,
safes, irons, hair dryers. **Leisure Activities:** exercise room. **Guest Services:** valet laundry. **Business Services:** meeting rooms,
business center. **Cards:** AX, CB, DC, DS, JC, MC, VI.

SOFITEL NEW YORK   *Book at aaa.com*   Phone: (212)354-8844   **36**
(AAA) (SAVE)   All Year   1P: $289
Location: Between 5th and 6th (Ave of the Americas) aves. 45 W 44th St 10036. Fax: 212/354-2480. **Facility:** The
▼▼▽▼▽▼   lobby of this jewel box is so plush it's like coming home, and guest rooms welcome with the same enveloping
luxury. Attentive and gracious staff. 398 units. 346 one-bedroom standard units. 52 one-bedroom suites
Large-scale Hotel   ($459-$2000). 29 stories, interior corridors. **Bath:** combo or shower only. **Parking:** on-site (fee) and valet.
Terms: cancellation fee imposed, package plans - weekends. **Amenities:** CD players, high-speed Internet
(fee), dual phone lines, voice mail, safes, honor bars, irons, hair dryers. **Dining:** 6 am-midnight. **Leisure Activities:** exercise
room. *Fee:* massage. **Guest Services:** gift shop, valet laundry. **Business Services:** conference facilities, business center.
Cards: AX, CB, DC, DS, JC, MC, VI. *(See color ad p 414)*

SOUTHGATE TOWER SUITE HOTEL   *Book at aaa.com*   Phone: (212)563-1800   **76**
▼▼▽▼▽   9/1-12/31   1P: $279-$334   2P: $279-$334   XP: $25   F12
   5/1-6/30   1P: $254-$294   2P: $254-$294   XP: $25   F12
   1/1-4/30   1P: $244-$284   2P: $244-$284   XP: $25   F12
Large-scale Hotel   7/1-8/31   1P: $224-$269   2P: $224-$269   XP: $25   F12
Location: At 31st St. Located opposite Madison Square Garden. 371 7th Ave 10001-3984. Fax: 212/643-8028. **Facility:** 497 units. 326
one-bedroom standard units with efficiencies. 164 one- and 7 two-bedroom suites with kitchens. 28 stories, interior corridors.
Bath: combo or shower only. **Parking:** valet. **Terms:** cancellation fee imposed. **Amenities:** dual phone lines, voice mail, irons,
hair dryers. *Fee:* video games, high-speed Internet. *Some:* CD players. **Leisure Activities:** exercise room. **Guest Services:**
valet and coin laundry. **Business Services:** conference facilities, business center. **Cards:** AX, CB, DC, DS, JC, MC, VI.

THE STANHOPE PARK HYATT NEW YORK   *Book at aaa.com*   Phone: (212)774-1234   **72**
(AAA) (SAVE)   All Year   1P: $279-$499   2P: $279-$499   XP: $25   F18
Location: At 81st St. Located opposite the Metropolitan Museum of Art. 995 5th Ave 10028. Fax: 212/517-0088.
▼▼▽▼▽ ▼▼▽▼▽   **Facility:** This grand hotel features a recently redecorated lobby; guest rooms are finely appointed. 185 units.
Historic   154 one-bedroom standard units. 31 one-bedroom suites. 16 stories, interior corridors. **Parking:** valet.
Small-scale Hotel   **Terms:** cancellation fee imposed, small pets only ($100 extra charge, with prior approval). **Amenities:** CD
players, dual phone lines, voice mail, fax, safes, honor bars, irons, hair dryers. **Dining:** 6:30 am-10 pm, cock-
tails. **Leisure Activities:** sauna, exercise room. *Fee:* massage. **Guest Services:** valet laundry. **Business
Services:** meeting rooms, business center. **Cards:** AX, CB, DC, DS, JC, MC, VI.

SUPER 8 HOTEL-TIMES SQUARE   *Book at aaa.com*   Phone: (212)719-2300   **39**
▼▽▼▽ ▼▽▼▽   All Year   1P: $89-$329   2P: $89-$329   XP: $10   F18
Location: Between 5th and 6th aves. 59 W 46th St 10036. Fax: 212/768-3477. **Facility:** 206 units. 196 one-
bedroom standard units. 10 one-bedroom suites. 12 stories, interior corridors. **Parking:** no self-parking.
Small-scale Hotel   **Terms:** [ECP] meal plan available. **Amenities:** voice mail, safes, irons, hair dryers. *Fee:* video games, high-
speed Internet. **Leisure Activities:** exercise room. **Guest Services:** valet laundry. **Business Services:** meeting rooms, business
center. **Cards:** AX, DC, DS, MC, VI.

(See map and index starting on p. 364)

SURREY HOTEL — *Book at aaa.com*
Small-scale Hotel

9/1-12/31	1P: $394-$479	2P: $394-$479	XP: $25	F12
5/1-6/30	1P: $354-$439	2P: $354-$439	XP: $25	F12
7/1-8/31 & 1/1-4/30	1P: $334-$414	2P: $334-$414	XP: $25	F12

Phone: (212)288-3700 **70**

Location: E 76th St and Madison Ave. 20 E 76th St 10021. Fax: 212/628-1549. **Facility:** 131 units. 37 one-bedroom standard units, some with efficiencies. 90 one- and 4 two-bedroom suites with kitchens. 16 stories, interior corridors. **Parking:** on-site (fee) and valet. **Terms:** cancellation fee imposed, pets ($200 deposit). **Amenities:** video games (fee), high-speed Internet, dual phone lines, voice mail, safes, irons, hair dryers. **Dining:** Cafe Boulud, see separate listing. **Leisure Activities:** exercise room. **Guest Services:** valet and coin laundry. **Business Services:** meeting rooms, fax (fee). **Cards:** AX, CB, DC, DS, JC, MC, VI.

SOME UNITS

SWISSOTEL THE DRAKE, NEW YORK — *Book at aaa.com*
Small-scale Hotel

9/7-12/31	1P: $290	XP: $30
1/1-4/30	1P: $250	XP: $30
5/1-9/6	1P: $240	XP: $30

Phone: (212)421-0900 **62**

Location: At 56th St; between Park and Madison aves. 440 Park Ave 10022. Fax: 212/371-4190. **Facility:** 495 units. 386 one-bedroom standard units. 95 one- and 1 three-bedroom suites, some with whirlpools. 21 stories, interior corridors. *Bath:* combo or shower only. **Parking:** on-site (fee) and valet. **Terms:** pets (with prior approval). **Amenities:** video games (fee), dual phone lines, voice mail, fax, safes, honor bars, irons, hair dryers. *Some:* CD players. **Leisure Activities:** steamrooms, spa. *Fee:* saunas. **Guest Services:** gift shop, valet laundry. **Business Services:** meeting rooms, business center. **Cards:** AX, CB, DC, DS, JC, MC, VI.

SOME UNITS

THE TIME — *Book at aaa.com*
Small-scale Hotel

8/24-12/20	1P: $199-$429	2P: $199-$429
5/1-6/27	1P: $179-$339	2P: $179-$339
12/21-4/30	1P: $159-$259	2P: $159-$259
6/28-8/23	1P: $159-$209	2P: $159-$209

Phone: (212)246-5252 **120**

Location: Between 8th Ave and Broadway. 224 W 49th St 10019. Fax: 212/245-2305. **Facility:** 193 units. 164 one-bedroom standard units. 29 one-bedroom suites with whirlpools. 17 stories, interior corridors. *Bath:* combo or shower only. **Parking:** no self-parking. **Terms:** cancellation fee imposed. **Amenities:** dual phone lines, voice mail, fax, safes, honor bars, irons, hair dryers. *Some:* CD players. **Leisure Activities:** Fee: massage. **Guest Services:** valet laundry. **Business Services:** meeting rooms, fax (fee). **Cards:** AX, CB, DC, DS, MC, VI.

SOME UNITS

TRAVEL INN — *Book at aaa.com*
Small-scale Hotel

All Year	1P: $120-$200	2P: $135-$230	XP: $15	F16

Phone: (212)695-7171 **32**

Location: Between 10th and 11th aves. 515 W 42nd St 10036. Fax: 212/967-5025. **Facility:** 160 units. 159 one-bedroom standard units. 1 one-bedroom suite. 7 stories, interior corridors. **Parking:** on-site. **Terms:** cancellation fee imposed. **Amenities:** voice mail, irons, hair dryers. *Fee:* video library, video games. **Dining:** 6 am-8 pm, wine/beer only. **Pool(s):** outdoor. **Leisure Activities:** lifeguard on duty, exercise room. **Guest Services:** gift shop. **Business Services:** meeting rooms, fax (fee). **Cards:** AX, DC, DS, MC, VI.
Special Amenities: preferred room (subject to availability with advanced reservations). *(See color ad below)*

SOME UNITS

TRUMP INTERNATIONAL HOTEL & TOWER — *Book at aaa.com*
Small-scale Hotel

1/1-4/30	1P: $575-$625
5/1-12/31	1P: $550-$595

Phone: 212/299-1000 **96**

Location: Jct Central Park S; at Columbus Circle. 1 Central Park W 10023. Fax: 212/299-1150. **Facility:** Like its namesake, this apartment-type high-rise is upscale all the way, combining white-glove service and decked-out decor. 167 units. 36 one-bedroom standard units. 131 one-bedroom suites ($795-$1725) with kitchens. 17 stories, interior corridors. **Parking:** valet. **Terms:** check-in 4 pm, cancellation fee imposed, small pets only ($200 deposit). **Amenities:** video games (fee), DVD players, video games (fee), CD players, high-speed Internet, dual phone lines, voice mail, fax, safes, honor bars, irons, hair dryers. **Dining:** Jean Georges Restaurant, see separate listing. **Pool(s):** heated indoor. **Leisure Activities:** saunas, steamrooms, spa. **Guest Services:** valet laundry. **Business Services:** meeting rooms, business center. **Cards:** AX, CB, DC, DS, JC, MC, VI.

SOME UNITS

(See map and index starting on p. 364)

THE WALDORF-ASTORIA   *Book at aaa.com*   Phone: (212)355-3000   **60**
All Year   1P: $199-$599   2P: $199-$599   XP: $30   F18
▼▼▼▼▼   **Location:** Between E 49th and 50th sts. 301 Park Ave 10022. Fax: 212/872-7272. **Facility:** The well-known hotel,
Classic   which was built in 1932, centers around a grand lobby and offers expectedly elegant accommodations. 1425
Large-scale Hotel   units. 1281 one-bedroom standard units. 139 one-, 4 two- and 1 three-bedroom suites, some with efficien-
cies. 42 stories, interior corridors. *Bath:* combo or shower only. **Parking:** valet. **Terms:** cancellation fee im-
posed. **Amenities:** video games (fee), dual phone lines, voice mail, fax, honor bars, irons, hair dryers. *Some:* CD players, high-
speed Internet, safes. **Leisure Activities:** steamrooms. *Fee:* massage. **Guest Services:** gift shop, valet laundry. **Business
Services:** conference facilities, business center. **Cards:** AX, CB, DC, DS, JC, MC, VI. Affiliated with A Hilton Hotel.
(See color ad card insert)

SOME UNITS

(ASK) (S❖) (📺) (24↑) (🍴) (👤) (🐾) (➕) (🎬) (DATA PORT) (💻) / (✕) (VCR) (🔌) /
FEE   FEE

THE WARWICK NEW YORK   *Book at aaa.com*   Phone: 212/247-2700   **86**
All Year   1P: $395-$475   2P: $395-$475   XP: $25   F12
▼▼▼   **Location:** Corner of 54th St and 6th Ave (Ave of the Americas). 65 W 54th St 10019. Fax: 212/247-2725.
Historic   **Facility:** Built in 1927 by William Randolph Hearst, the property is close to shops and Central Park; some of
Small-scale Hotel   the plush, spacious rooms have a private terrace. 426 units. 359 one-bedroom standard units. 66 one- and
1 two-bedroom suites ($329-$850), some with whirlpools. 33 stories, interior corridors. *Bath:* combo or
shower only. **Parking:** valet. **Terms:** cancellation fee imposed. **Amenities:** video games (fee), dual phone lines, voice mail,
safes, honor bars, irons, hair dryers. *Some:* CD players, fax. **Leisure Activities:** exercise room. **Guest Services:** valet laundry.
Business Services: meeting rooms, business center. **Cards:** AX, DC, JC, MC, VI.

SOME UNITS

(ASK) (S❖) (🛏) (🍴) (24↑) (🍴) (👤M) (👤) (🐾) (🎬) (DATA PORT) / (✕) (VCR) (🔌) /

THE WESTIN   *Book at aaa.com*   Phone: (212)201-2700   **129**
8/28-12/31   1P: $199-$519   2P: $199-$519   XP: $30   F18
▼▼▼   1/1-4/30   1P: $189-$469   2P: $189-$469   XP: $30   F18
5/1-6/29   1P: $189-$449   2P: $189-$449   XP: $30   F18
Large-scale Hotel   6/30-8/27   1P: $179-$359   2P: $179-$359   XP: $30   F18
Location: Corner of 8th Ave. 270 W 43rd St 10036. Fax: 212/201-2701. **Facility:** 863 units. 854 one-bedroom standard units. 4 one-
and 5 two-bedroom suites ($299-$2000). 45 stories, interior corridors. *Bath:* combo or shower only. **Parking:** valet. **Terms:** small
pets only. **Amenities:** dual phone lines, voice mail, safes, honor bars, irons, hair dryers. *Fee:* video games, high-speed Internet.
Some: CD players. **Leisure Activities:** saunas, spa. *Fee:* exercise room. **Guest Services:** gift shop, valet laundry. **Business
Services:** conference facilities, business center. **Cards:** AX, CB, DC, DS, MC, VI.   SOME UNITS

(ASK) (S❖) (🛏) (📺) (24↑) (🍴) (👤) (🐾) (✕) (🎬) (DATA PORT) (💻) / (✕) (VCR) (🔌) /

W NEW YORK   *Book at aaa.com*   Phone: (212)755-1200   **131**
9/7-12/31   1P: $509   2P: $509   XP: $25   F12
▼▼▼▼   1/1-4/30   1P: $449-$499   2P: $449-$499   XP: $25   F12
5/1-6/30   1P: $469   2P: $469   XP: $25   F12
Large-scale Hotel   7/1-9/6   1P: $449   2P: $449   XP: $25   F12
Location: At 49th St. 541 Lexington Ave 10022. Fax: 212/421-3876. **Facility:** 713 units. 659 one-bedroom standard units. 54 one-
bedroom suites. 18 stories, interior corridors. *Bath:* some combo or shower only. **Parking:** valet. **Terms:** cancellation fee imposed, pets ($100 fee, $25 extra charge). **Amenities:** CD players, high-speed Internet (fee), dual phone lines, voice mail, safes,
honor bars, irons, hair dryers. *Some:* fax. **Leisure Activities:** spa. **Guest Services:** valet laundry. **Business Services:** conference facilities, business center. **Cards:** AX, CB, DC, JC, MC, VI.   SOME UNITS

(ASK) (S❖) (🛏) (🍴) (24↑) (🍴) (👤M) (👤) (🐾) (VCR) (🎬) (DATA PORT) (💻) / (✕) (🔌) /
FEE

W NEW YORK TIMES SQUARE   *Book at aaa.com*   Phone: (212)930-7400   **130**
1/1-4/30   1P: $489-$539   2P: $489-$539   XP: $25   F12
▼▼▼   9/7-12/31   1P: $539   2P: $539   XP: $25   F12
5/1-9/6   1P: $489   2P: $489   XP: $25   F12
Large-scale Hotel   **Location:** Corner of 47th St. 1567 Broadway at 47th St 10036. Fax: 212/930-7501. **Facility:** 509 units. 464 one-
bedroom standard units. 43 one- and 2 two-bedroom suites. 57 stories, interior corridors. *Bath:* combo or shower only. **Parking:**
valet. **Terms:** cancellation fee imposed, pets ($100 fee, $25 extra charge). **Amenities:** DVD players, CD players, dual phone
lines, voice mail, safes, honor bars, irons, hair dryers. *Fee:* video games, high-speed Internet. *Some:* fax. **Leisure Activities:** exercise room. *Fee:* massage. **Guest Services:** gift shop, valet laundry. **Business Services:** conference facilities, business center.
Cards: AX, CB, DC, DS, MC, VI.   SOME UNITS

(ASK) (S❖) (🛏) (🍴) (24↑) (🍴) (👤M) (👤) (🐾) (VCR) (🎬) (DATA PORT) (💻) / (✕) (🔌) (📼) /
FEE

──────── *The following lodgings were either not evaluated or did not* ────────
meet AAA rating requirements but are listed for your information only.

70 PARK AVENUE HOTEL   Phone: (212)687-7050   **74**
(fyi)   All Year   1P: $225-$425   2P: $225-$425   XP: $50   F17
Under major renovation, scheduled to be completed July 2004. *Last rated:* ▼▼▼ **Location:** Between 38th
Small-scale Hotel   and 39th sts. 70 Park Ave 10016. Fax: 212/973-2440. **Facility:** 188 units. 185 one-bedroom standard units. 3
one-bedroom suites ($450-$3500). 17 stories, interior corridors. *Bath:* combo or shower only. **Parking:** on-
site (fee) and valet. **Terms:** cancellation fee imposed, [AP] meal plan available, package plans - seasonal, weekends.
Amenities: voice mail, safes, honor bars, irons, hair dryers. **Guest Services:** valet laundry. **Business Services:** meeting rooms,
fax (fee). **Cards:** AX, CB, DC, DS, JC, MC, VI.   SOME UNITS

(ASK) (S❖) (🛏) (🍴) (👤) (🐾) (➕) (🎬) (DATA PORT) / (✕) /

THE ALEX   Phone: 212/867-5100
(fyi)   9/1-4/30   1P: $500-$2000   2P: $500-$2000
5/1-8/31   1P: $480-$1500   2P: $480-$1500
Too new to rate, opening scheduled for November 2003. **Location:** At 3rd Ave. 205 E 45th St 10017.
Amenities: 203 units. **Terms:** cancellation fee imposed. **Cards:** AX, CB, DC, DS, JC, MC, VI. *(See color ad p 390)*

(See map and index starting on p. 364)

ALGONQUIN HOTEL
Phone: 212/840-6800
[fyi] Not evaluated. **Location:** Between 5th and 6th (Ave of the Americas) aves. 59 W 44th St 10036 (3060 Peachtree Rd, Suite 1700, ATLANTA, GA, 30305). Facilities, services, and decor characterize a mid-range property.

BENTLEY HOTEL
Phone: 212/644-6000
[fyi] Not evaluated. **Location:** At York Ave. 500 E 62nd St 10021. Facilities, services, and decor characterize a mid-range property.

THE BRYANT PARK HOTEL
Phone: 212/869-0100
[fyi] Not evaluated. **Location:** Between 5th and 6th (Ave of the Americas) aves. 40 W 40th St 10018 (417 5th Ave 3rd Floor, NEW YORK, 10016). Facilities, services, and decor characterize an upscale property.

CASABLANCA HOTEL
Phone: 212/869-1212
[fyi] Not evaluated. **Location:** Between 6th Ave (Ave of the Americas) and Broadway. 147 W 43rd St 10036. Facilities, services, and decor characterize a mid-range property.

COURTYARD BY MARRIOTT/MANHATTAN-TIMES SQUARE SOUTH
Phone: 212/391-0088
[fyi] Not evaluated. **Location:** Between Broadway and 6th Ave (Ave of the Americas). 114 W 40th St 10018. Facilities, services, and decor characterize a mid-range property.

HAMPTON INN-HERALD SQUARE
[fyi]   Property failed to provide current rates
Too new to rate, opening scheduled for May 2004. **Location:** Between 6th (Ave of the Americas) and 7th aves. 116
Small-scale Hotel W 31st St 10001. **Amenities:** 136 units, pets, coffeemakers.

MANDARIN ORIENTAL, NEW YORK
Phone: 212/805-8800

[fyi]	8/25-4/30	1P: $615-$4500	2P: $615-$4500
	5/1-8/24	1P: $595-$4500	2P: $595-$4500

Large-scale Hotel Too new to rate. **Location:** At 60th St. 80 Columbus Cir 10019. Fax: 212/805-8888. **Amenities:** 251 units, pets, restaurant, pool, exercise facilities. **Terms:** cancellation fee imposed. **Cards:** AX, DC, DS, JC, MC, VI.

MORGANS HOTEL
Phone: 212/686-0300
[fyi] Not evaluated. **Location:** Between 37th and 38th sts. 237 Madison Ave 10016. Facilities, services, and decor characterize a mid-range property.

THE PLAZA
Phone: 212/759-3000
[fyi] Not evaluated. **Location:** 5th Ave at Central Park S 10019. Facilities, services, and decor characterize a mid-range property.

W NEW YORK-THE COURT
Phone: 212/685-1100
[fyi] Not evaluated. **Location:** Between Park and Lexington aves. 130 E 39th St 10016. Facilities, services, and decor characterize an upscale property.

W NEW YORK-THE TUSCANY
Phone: 212/686-1600
[fyi] Not evaluated. **Location:** Between Park and Lexington aves. 120 E 39th St 10016. Facilities, services, and decor characterize an upscale property.

──── WHERE TO DINE ────

21 CLUB   **Lunch:** $24-$39   **Dinner:** $27-$41   **Phone:** 212/582-7200   [72]
♦♥♦♥♦   **Location:** Between 5th and 6th (Ave of the Americas) aves. 21 W 52nd St 10019. **Hours:** noon-2:15 & 5:30-10:15
American   pm, Fri & Sat-11:15 pm. Closed major holidays; also Sun & for lunch Sat. **Reservations:** suggested.
Features: Noticeable from the street by miniature statuary and fancy wrought-iron fencing surrounding the
entrance, the bastion of old New York is still clubby with dark wood, brass-studded leather banquettes and
toys hanging from every corner of the ceiling. Classic "21" dishes have been revived; Senegalese soup, an extraordinary "21"
burger and eye-catching game pot pie are among those choices. Although the food isn't fancy, it's top quality and richly
satisfying. Service is Old World professional. Semi-formal attire; cocktails. **Parking:** no self-parking. **Cards:** AX, CB, DC, DS,
MC, VI.

ABOVE   **Lunch:** $8-$22   **Dinner:** $21-$45   **Phone:** 212/642-2626   [81]
♦♥♦♥♦   **Location:** Between 7th and 8th aves; in Hilton Times Square. 234 W 42nd St 10036. **Hours:** 6:30-11 am,
American   11:30-3:30 & 5:30-10 pm. **Reservations:** suggested. **Features:** The lounge has become a hot post-theater
spot and the view of the lights of theater row below is commanding, but the cuisine is more than an
afterthought. The menu focuses on large and small dishes, so sample as you will from appetizers, salads
and tasty pastas—some accented by savory veal sausage—served in two sizes; dive into the crunchy breadsticks as you
consider your options. Dressy casual; cocktails. **Parking:** on-site (fee) and valet. **Cards:** AX, CB, DC, DS, JC, MC, VI.

(See map and index starting on p. 364)

ALAIN DUCASSE AT THE ESSEX HOUSE
French

Lunch: $65-$250   Dinner: $145-$280   Phone: 212/265-7300   149
Location: Between 6th (Ave of the Americas) and 7th aves. 155 W 58th St 10019. **Hours:** 6:30 pm seating. Closed major holidays; also Sun. **Reservations:** required. **Features:** This notable French chef is renown in Europe and now has come to America. His new creation, within the nostalgic, art deco splendor of the Essex House, is extravagantly appointed with silk-lined walls, Baccarat crystal, Lalique light fixtures and whimsical, sun-splashed red and gold decor. Prix fixe carte du jour reflect the global market. Selections are superbly prepared and flavored with honest French-style presentations. Classic service is top notch, inexhaustible and almost excessive. Formal attire; cocktails. **Parking:** valet. **Cards:** AX, CB, DC, DS, JC, MC, VI.

AL BUSTAN
Lebanese

Lunch: $20-$28   Dinner: $20-$28   Phone: 212/759-8439   136
Location: Between 50th and 51st sts. 827 3rd Ave 10022. **Hours:** noon-3 & 5:30-10 pm. **Reservations:** suggested. **Features:** Well-known for Lebanese cuisine with a flair, the restaurant presents a long list of hot and cold appetizers that could be a great meal. However, diners would miss such entrees as marinated lamb medallions, grilled quail, steamed fish and the specialty spiced lamb tartare. The tranquil dining room is mirrored and best described as neutral. Dressy casual; cocktails. **Parking:** no self-parking. **Cards:** AX, DC, DS, JC, MC, VI.

AMMA
Indian

Lunch: $10-$15   Dinner: $17-$24   Phone: 212/644-8330   55
Location: Between 2nd and 3rd aves. 246 E 51st St 10022. **Hours:** noon-3 & 5-10:30 pm. **Reservations:** accepted. **Features:** India isn't likely to immediately come to mind when diners walk into the neat, contemporary dining room, but then the tamarind-yellow walls, persimmon chairs and otherworldly new-age music may make subtle hints at the distinctly ethnic menu to come. Amma, or "mother," serves home-style cooking from the north and south of India. Lamb shank curry or tandoor and moist, fragrant chicken tikka masala are specialties. Casual dress; cocktails. **Parking:** no self-parking. **Cards:** AX, DC, DS, MC, VI.

ANGELO'S PIZZA
Italian

Lunch: $9-$17   Dinner: $9-$17   Phone: 212/333-4333   93
Location: Between 6th (Ave of the Americas) and 7th aves. 117 W 57th St 10019. **Hours:** 11:30 am-11 pm, Fri & Sat-midnight. Closed: 11/25, 12/25. **Features:** Tried-and-true family recipes are used to create delicious dishes, such as pasta e fagioli and pizza baked in a coal-fired brick oven. Black-and-white photographs of old New York street scenes and celebrities line the walls. Service is efficient. Casual dress; cocktails. **Parking:** no self-parking. **Cards:** AX, MC, VI.

AQUAVIT
Swedish

Lunch: $24-$26   Dinner: $69-$115   Phone: 212/307-7311   118
Location: Between 5th and 6th (Ave of the Americas) aves. 13 W 54th St 10019. **Hours:** noon-2:30 & 5:30-10:30 pm, Sat from 5:30 pm. Closed major holidays. **Reservations:** suggested. **Features:** The stunning dining room features as its focal point a soaring atrium with a soft, two-story waterfall. Scandinavian, mostly Swedish, seafood and meat preparations make up the bulk of the menu. Try an "aquavit," a refreshing house-made drink. Semi-formal attire; cocktails. **Parking:** no self-parking. **Cards:** AX, DC, MC, VI.

ARTISANAL
French

Lunch: $15-$24   Dinner: $17-$25   Phone: 212/725-8585   114
Location: At 32nd St. 2 Park Ave 10016. **Hours:** noon-11 pm, Fri-midnight, Sat 11 am-3 & 5-midnight, Sun 11 am-3 & 5-10 pm. Closed: 1/1, 12/25. **Reservations:** suggested. **Features:** The theme here is cheese—if there was a cheese heaven, this would be it. Guests smell it when they walk into the handsome, sophisticated dining room, and if they breathe deeply enough, they may taste it. Half a dozen fondues such as Stilton and Sauternes are popular. Classic bistro fare is good, and there also is a large selection of fine cheeses displayed for an end-of-meal treat. Dressy casual; cocktails. **Parking:** no self-parking. **Cards:** AX, MC, VI.

ASIA DE CUBA
Cuban

Lunch: $18-$36   Dinner: $18-$36   Phone: 212/726-7755   116
Location: Between 37th and 38th sts. 237 Madison Ave 10016. **Hours:** noon-3 & 5:30-11 pm, Thurs & Fri-12:30 am, Sat 5:30 pm-12:30 am, Sun 5:30 pm-11 pm. Closed: 11/25, 12/25; also for lunch 1/1. **Reservations:** required. **Features:** The scene starts with the upstairs bar, where drinks in elegant glasses ride by on servers' trays. The bar encircles and overlooks diners downstairs seated in plush banquettes or around the common central table—a single, illuminated slab of marble perfect for smaller parties. A two-story waterfall hologram adds interest. Asian and Cuban seasonings spice up dishes such as mai tai lobster, grilled mojito-glazed gaucho rib steak and honey rum-glazed pot roast of pork. Dressy casual; cocktails. **Parking:** no self-parking. **Cards:** AX, DC, MC, VI.

ATELIER
French

Lunch: $22-$34   Dinner: $28-$44   Phone: 212/521-6125   134
Location: Between 5th and 6th (Ave of the Americas) aves. In The Ritz-Carlton New York, Central Park. 50 Central Park S 10019. **Hours:** noon-2 & 5:30-10 pm, Fri & Sat-11 pm. **Reservations:** suggested. **Features:** Highly touted by critics and overjoyed diners, the restaurant affords a highly refined experience. Dishes are beautifully prepared and presented, with a delicacy rare and welcomed. Preparations on the frequently changing menu are expert. Plush, yet tailored, comfort means attention can be focused on the eye-catching original artwork and the meal itself, which is served, again, by experts. Semi-formal attire; cocktails. **Parking:** valet. **Cards:** AX, CB, DC, DS, JC, MC, VI.

ATLANTIC GRILL
Seafood

Lunch: $12-$20   Dinner: $19-$25   Phone: 212/988-9200   153
Location: Between 76th and 77th aves. 1341 3rd Ave 10021. **Hours:** 11:30 am-4 & 5-11:30 pm, Sun 11 am-4 pm. Closed: 12/25. **Reservations:** suggested. **Features:** The restaurant is popular for fresh seafood dishes—such as barbecue-glazed mahi mahi, whole-grain mustard-glazed Nova Scotia halibut, nori-wrapped yellowfin tuna and wild basil couscous-crusted swordfish. An added attraction is the sushi bar. Fish prepared over the wood-burning grill is a specialty, as is the Sunday brunch. The room itself is visual smooth jazz, with sea blue walls, linen-topped tables and interesting abstract photos. Casual dress; cocktails. **Parking:** no self-parking. **Cards:** AX, DS, MC, VI.

(See map and index starting on p. 364)

AUREOLE
Lunch: $20-$27   **Dinner:** $69   **Phone:** 212/319-1660   (74)

American

Location: Between Park and Madison aves. 34 E 61st St 10021. **Hours:** noon-2:30 & 5:30-11 pm, Sat 5 pm-11:30 pm. Closed major holidays; also Sun. **Reservations:** required. **Features:** Chef/owner Charlie Palmer continues to orchestrate a once-in-a-lifetime experience. New American cuisine was founded here. The food is absolutely delectable, and the presentations are unmatched for their distinctive style. Service does not take a back seat and is executed with impeccable precision. The prix fixe late lunch is an outstanding bargain. Semi-formal attire; cocktails. **Parking:** no self-parking. **Cards:** AX, CB, DC, DS, MC, VI.

AVRA ESTIATORIO
Lunch: $10-$20   **Dinner:** $14-$25   **Phone:** 212/759-8550   (124)

Mediterranean

Location: Between Lexington and 3rd aves. 141 E 48th St 10017. **Hours:** noon-11 pm, Sat & Sun 11 am-4 & 5-midnight. **Reservations:** suggested. **Features:** Soaring ceilings are warmly draped in gauzy fabrics to lend a cozier ambience to the large, sophisticated space. The freshest day-catch seafood is the specialty here, served whole and simply grilled with fresh herbs. Dressy casual; cocktails. **Parking:** no self-parking. **Cards:** AX, DC, JC, MC, VI.

BANGKOK CUISINE
Lunch: $7-$15   **Dinner:** $7-$16   **Phone:** 212/581-6370   (105)

Thai

Location: Between 52nd and 53rd sts. 885 8th Ave 10019. **Hours:** noon-11:30 pm, Sun-11 pm. **Reservations:** suggested, weekends. **Features:** The casual storefront restaurant has large fish tanks to distract children, as well as paintings of the Thai countryside, klongs and temples. An all-you-can-eat lunch buffet is laid out weekdays from noon to 3 pm. Green and red curry, masaman curry and spicy Thai-style salad are among the many choices. Vegetarian items are available as well. Casual dress; cocktails. **Parking:** no self-parking. **Cards:** AX, MC, VI.

BARBETTA

Northern
Italian

Lunch: $18-$27   **Dinner:** $27-$30   **Phone:** 212/246-9171   (99)

Location: Between 8th and 9th aves; in theatre district; on Restaurant Row. 321 W 46th St 10036. **Hours:** noon-2:30 & 5-midnight. **Reservations:** suggested. **Features:** Opulence abounds in the sophisticated dining room, which is appointed with 18th-century antiques. The lovely garden is pleasant. Such preparations as swordfish over lentils in a balsamic vinaigrette are unequivocally Italian. A prix fixe pre-theater dinner is featured for $45. The menu includes dishes served since the 1906 opening by the same family still in ownership. Dressy casual; cocktails; entertainment. **Parking:** no self-parking. **Cards:** AX, CB, DC, DS, JC, MC, VI.

BAY LEAF INDIAN BRASSERIE
Lunch: $15   **Dinner:** $12-$25   **Phone:** 212/957-1818   (178)

Northern Indian

Location: Between 5th and 6th (Ave of the Americas) aves. 49 W 56th St 10019. **Hours:** noon-3 & 5:30-11 pm. Closed major holidays. **Reservations:** required. **Features:** Skilled hands with a light touch create dishes from Hydrobad, Kashmir, Bangal, Bombay, Goa and more. Dishes such as grilled jumbo shrimp marinated in olive oil, garlic and herbs, fish simmered in a sauce of yellow chilis, coconut milk and spices, and minced lamb with spices rolled onto skerwers and broiled in the clay oven hold a certain appeal.The almost weightless naan, perfectly charred, goes with melt in your mouth chicken saag. Servers are attentive and the host is a pleasure. Casual dress; cocktails. **Parking:** no self-parking. **Cards:** AX, DC, MC, VI.

BECCO
Lunch: $13-$18   **Dinner:** $25-$30   **Phone:** 212/397-7597   (168)

Regional
Italian

Location: Between 8th and 9th aves. 355 W 46th St 10036. **Hours:** noon-3 & 5-midnight, Wed-Sat noon-3 & 4:30-midnight, Sun noon-10 pm. Closed: 11/25, 12/25. **Reservations:** required. **Features:** Symphony de pasta, a bottomless dish of three daily pastas, is a signature creation on a menu of farmhouse-style, countrified Northern Italian cuisine. Osso buco is another. Portions are ample, flavors hearty and fresh, and prices reasonable. Three dining areas deliver distinct, but altogether pleasant, experiences. The back room is bright with natural light from the glass pyramid ceiling. This place is a neat find. Casual dress; cocktails. **Parking:** no self-parking. **Cards:** AX, DC, DS, MC, VI.

BELLO RESTAURANT
Lunch: $11-$24   **Dinner:** $11-$24   **Phone:** 212/246-6773   (122)

Northern
Italian

Location: At 56th St. 863 9th Ave 10019. **Hours:** 11:30 am-11 pm, Fri-midnight, Sat 3:30 pm-midnight. Closed: 1/1, 7/4, 12/25; also Sun. **Reservations:** suggested. **Features:** Consistently flavorful food brings locals back again and again for fresh marinated anchovies, sauteed portobello mushrooms, stuffed veal chop with cognac sauce and salmon dijon, among other difficult choices. Casual dress; cocktails. **Parking:** no self-parking. **Cards:** AX, DC, DS, MC, VI.

BEN BENSON'S STEAK HOUSE
Lunch: $16-$33   **Dinner:** $16-$33   **Phone:** 212/581-8888   (163)

Steak & Seafood

Location: Between 6th (Ave of the Americas) and 7th aves. 123 W 52nd St 10019. **Hours:** 11:45 am-11 pm, Fri-midnight, Sat 5 pm-midnight, Sun 5 pm-10 pm. Closed major holidays. **Reservations:** suggested. **Features:** Great steak plus famous crab cakes, lobster, veal and lamb. Lunch specials daily. Winter and summer menus. Indoor parking at 31 W 52nd St from 5 pm-midnight. Outdoor cafe, seasonal. Casual dress; cocktails. **Parking:** no self-parking. **Cards:** AX, DC, DS, JC, MC, VI.

BILL HONG'S
Lunch: $13-$18   **Dinner:** $13-$32   **Phone:** 212/751-4048   (197)

Chinese

Location: Between 2nd and 3rd aves. 227 E 56th St 10022. **Hours:** noon-10 pm, Sun from 2 pm. Closed: 11/25. **Reservations:** accepted. **Features:** The restaurant is well-known by locals whose parents and grandparents have dined on fine, well-made traditional dishes. Beef dishes such as steak kew use filet mignon, and shrimp, such as those in Grand Marnier shrimp, are large and sweet. Sauces are rich with flavor and fine in texture. Egg rolls are plump with pork, ribs are lean and tasty, and wonton soup is almost a meal in itself. The staff is professional and attentive. Dressy casual; cocktails. **Parking:** no self-parking. **Cards:** AX, DC, JC, MC, VI.

(See map and index starting on p. 364)

BLUE FIN   **Lunch:** $12-$23   **Dinner:** $19-$28   **Phone:** 212/918-1400   (198)
Location: Corner of 47th St. 1567 Broadway 10036. **Hours:** 7 am-12:30 am, Wed-Sun to 1 am.
Reservations: suggested. **Features:** The "wow" factor is high at the oh-so-cool eye-pleaser, where fresh
flavor comes from the kitchen. Predominantly seafood dishes with relatively simple preparations look
Seafood   beautiful from menu to table, and service leaves a pleasant aftertaste. The sushi bar has a master working
behind. Casual dress; cocktails. **Parking:** no self-parking. **Cards:** AX, DS, MC, VI.

BLUE SMOKE   **Lunch:** $9-$24   **Dinner:** $9-$24   **Phone:** 212/447-7733   (199)
Location: Between Lexington and Park aves. 116 E 27th St 10016. **Hours:** 11:30 am-11 pm, Thurs & Fri-1 am,
Sat noon-1 am, Sun noon-11 pm. Closed major holidays. **Reservations:** suggested. **Features:** The
famous blend in and dig into reasonably priced ribs, pulled pork and beef brisket that keep lines long at the
Barbecue   casual, down-home eatery. More than just barbecue, the menu lists sides and vegetables, as well as
dishes rarely seen since the '50s: iceberg wedges with green goddess dressing, fry bread with chipotle butter and jalapeno
marmalade and chocolate layer cake and milk. Sticky toffee pudding, banana cream pie or a banana split is a perfect
conclusion. Casual dress; cocktails. **Parking:** no self-parking. **Cards:** AX, DC, DS, MC, VI.

BOMBAY PALACE RESTAURANT   **Lunch:** $9-$30   **Dinner:** $9-$30   **Phone:** 212/541-7777   (144)
Location: Between 5th and 6th (Ave of the Americas) aves. 30 W 52nd St 10019. **Hours:** noon-3 & 5:30-11 pm.
Reservations: suggested. **Features:** Tandoori chicken and vegetable curry are representative of Indian
cuisine served here. The daily all-you-can-eat lunch buffet lays out a nice assortment of choices in the
Indian   casual upstairs dining room, which has a large TV showing financial news. Chandeliers and etched glass
lend an upscale feel to the more formal downstairs dining room. Casual dress; cocktails. **Parking:** no self-parking. **Cards:** AX,
DC, DS, MC, VI.

BRASSERIE 8 1/2   **Lunch:** $17-$27   **Dinner:** $22-$34   **Phone:** 212/829-0812   (57)
Location: Between 5th and 6th (Ave of the Americas) aves. 9 W 57th St 10019. **Hours:** 11:30 am-3 & 5:30-11 pm,
Sun 11 am-3:30 & 5:30-9 pm. Closed: Sun 7/1-8/30. **Reservations:** suggested. **Features:** While the
entrance to this upscale restaurant is at street level, diners descend a sweeping semi-circular staircase
American   into the casually elegant dining room and lounge. The menu reflects French and American brasserie
influences. Lunch and dinner have both prix fixe and a la carte offerings. Casual dress; cocktails. **Parking:** no self-parking.
Cards: AX, CB, DC, DS, MC, VI.

BRASSERIE LES HALLES   **Lunch:** $13-$28   **Dinner:** $13-$28   **Phone:** 212/679-4111   (82)
Location: Between 28th and 29th sts. 411 Park Ave S 10016. **Hours:** noon-midnight. **Reservations:** accepted.
Features: It's loud, it's crowded, the air is full of energy and this only adds to the experience of this
brasserie. The dishes are classic hearty French, including top-quality grilled angus beef ribeyes, the
French   famous hanger steak with shallot sauce, tartiflette, duck confit, cassoulet, choucroute garni, steak frites,
lighter salads spiked with meat and other classic much-loved classics. Preparations are tasty and not a single delicious calorie
is spared. Dressy casual; cocktails. **Parking:** no self-parking. **Cards:** AX, DC, DS, MC, VI.

BREAD FROM BEIRUT   **Lunch:** $4-$10   **Dinner:** $5-$10   **Phone:** 212/764-1588   (52)
Location: Between 5th and 6th (Ave of the Americas) aves. 24 W 45th St 10036. **Hours:** 9 am-9 pm, Sat 11 am-6
pm. Closed major holidays; also Sun. **Features:** The small "quick serve" has attracted much attention in
the area by serving some good Middle Eastern eats. Guests can take out grilled kebabs of beef, lamb or
Lebanese   chicken, savory pastries or appetizer salads or carry meals to the tables in the back. Casual dress.
Parking: no self-parking. **Cards:** AX, MC, VI.

BRYANT PARK GRILL   **Lunch:** $13-$22   **Dinner:** $17-$28   **Phone:** 212/840-6500   (169)
Location: Between 5th and 6th (Ave of the Americas) aves. 25 W 40th St 10018. **Hours:** 11:30 am-10 pm, Fri &
Sat-10:30 pm; Saturday & Sunday brunch. **Reservations:** suggested. **Features:** Tempting selections
include succulent filet mignon, lobster salad and pork tenderloin. The large, glorious building, which
American   overlooks the park for which the restaurant is named, offers seasonal seating on the patio. Casual dress;
cocktails. **Parking:** no self-parking. **Cards:** AX, DC, MC, VI.

BYBLOS   **Lunch:** $9-$13   **Dinner:** $9-$19   **Phone:** 212/687-0808   (79)
Location: Jct E 39th St and 3rd Ave. 200 E 39th St 10016. **Hours:** 11:30 am-11 pm. **Reservations:** suggested.
Features: The casual dining spot employs a charming staff and serves authentic Middle Eastern fare. Start
with an appetizer assortment to sample the various tastes, then move on to specialties such as kebabs,
Lebanese   lamb and even vegetarian dishes. Casual dress; cocktails. **Parking:** no self-parking. **Cards:** AX, DC, DS,
MC, VI.

CAFE BOTANICA   **Lunch:** $18-$32   **Dinner:** $28-$42   **Phone:** 212/484-5120   (123)
Location: Between 6th (Ave of the Americas) and 7th aves; in The Essex House-A Westin Hotel. 160 Central Park S
10019. **Hours:** 6:30 am-10:30, noon-2:30 & 5-10:30 pm. **Reservations:** suggested. **Features:** A warm,
relaxed ambience settles in the lush, almost magical, dining room of the upscale restaurant. Enjoy first-rate
French   gourmet cuisine on the prix fixe and pre- and post-theater menus. Set aside time to visit for the Sunday
champagne brunch. Dressy casual; cocktails. **Parking:** no self-parking. **Cards:** AX, DC, DS, MC, VI.

CAFE BOULUD   **Lunch:** $19-$29   **Dinner:** $22-$35   **Phone:** 212/772-2600   (192)
Location: E 76th St and Madison Ave; in Surrey Hotel. 20 E 76th St 10021. **Hours:** noon-2:30 & 5:45-11 pm, Sun
& Mon from 5:45 pm. Closed major holidays. **Reservations:** suggested. **Features:** A smart sophisticated
dining room in subtle hues provides a lovely place for a beautifully prepared meal. The menu features
French   classic French dishes, seasonal market specialties, vegetable garden focused dishes, and dishes
showcasing exotic world flavors. Dressy casual; cocktails. **Parking:** no self-parking. **Cards:** AX, DC, MC, VI.

(See map and index starting on p. 364)

CAFE CENTRO
French
Lunch: $20-$27 **Dinner:** $20-$27 **Phone:** 212/818-1222 (170)
Location: Between Lexington and Vanderbilt aves. 200 Park Ave on 45th 10166. **Hours:** 11:30 am-10:30 pm, Sat from 5 pm. Closed major holidays; also Sun. **Reservations:** suggested. **Features:** A massive stone fireplace encloses eight rotisserie spits laden with roasting chicken, rack of lamb, pork and filet mignon. Strong, sleek lines shape the warm, comfortable dining room, trimmed with beautiful wood, heavy moldings and relief-work. Although dishes are French, they reflect Mediterranean influences. Dressy casual; cocktails. **Parking:** no self-parking. **Cards:** AX, DC, DS, MC, VI.

CAFE DES ARTISTES
French
Lunch: $16-$25 **Dinner:** $27-$37 **Phone:** 212/877-3500 (146)
Location: Between Columbus Ave and Central Park W. One W 67th St 10023. **Hours:** noon-3 & 5:30-midnight, Sat 11 am-3 & 5-midnight, Sun 10 am-3 & 5:30-midnight. Closed: 12/25. **Reservations:** suggested. **Features:** History abounds in the 76-year-old establishment, once a meeting and eating place for artists that lived in apartments above. French food and famous murals of naked nymphs playing in a richly flowered forest remain for the pleasure of a new group of diners, many dressed for the opera or performances at Lincoln Center. Rich flavors punctuate such dishes as steak frites, pan-roasted squab with garlic flan, tea-smoked duck breast, crisp duck confit and Wiener or sturgeon schnitzel. Dressy casual; cocktails. **Parking:** no self-parking. **Cards:** AX, DC, MC, VI.

CAFE EUROPA
American
Lunch: $7-$13 **Dinner:** $7-$13 **Phone:** 212/977-4030 (120)
Location: At 7th Ave. 205 W 57th St 10019. **Hours:** 7 am-1 am. **Features:** The unpretentious bakery sticks to a menu of mostly lighter fare, pasta, sandwiches, salad and pizza, as well as exceptional European pastry and dessert. Bright lighting adds to the energetic, upbeat mood of the dining room. Gourmet coffees are a treat. Casual dress; beer & wine only. **Parking:** no self-parking. **Cards:** AX, DC, MC, VI.

CAFE FIORELLO
Italian
Lunch: $14-$19 **Dinner:** $15-$34 **Phone:** 212/595-5330 (211)
Location: At 64th St; across from Lincoln Center. 1900 Broadway 10023. **Hours:** 8 am-11 pm. **Features:** Settle into the colorful, festive dining room to enjoy award-winning gourmet pizza, delicacies from the antipasto bar, and daily fresh fish selections. The wide sidewalk patio is a delightful spot in good weather. Casual dress; cocktails. **Parking:** street. **Cards:** AX, DC, MC, VI.

CAFE PIERRE
AAA
French
Lunch: $18-$36 **Dinner:** $18-$36 **Phone:** 212/940-8195 (62)
Location: At 5th Ave; in The Pierre New York-A Four Seasons Hotel. 5th Ave at 61st St 10021. **Hours:** 7 am-10:30, noon-2:30 & 6-11 pm. **Reservations:** suggested. **Features:** An old New York style punctuates the richly opulent dining room, in which both creative contemporary and traditional classic entrees are served. Enjoy light lunches and high tea on the trompe l'oeil Queen's Court rotunda. The tasting menu is exquisite. Semi-formal attire; cocktails; entertainment. **Parking:** valet. **Cards:** AX, DC, DS, MC, VI.

CAFE TREVI
Italian
Dinner: $15-$24 **Phone:** 212/249-0040 (171)
Location: Between E 81st and E 82nd sts. 1570 1st Ave 10028. **Hours:** 5:30 pm-midnight. Closed major holidays; also Sun. **Reservations:** suggested. **Features:** Flickering candles, Florentine prints and brick walls enhance the intimate ambience of the neighborhood restaurant. The menu lists honest, simply great food. For dessert, it's tough to choose with such selections as tiramisu and pumpkin cheesecake. Casual dress; cocktails. **Parking:** on-site. **Cards:** AX, DC, MC, VI.

CANYON ROAD
Southwestern
Dinner: $13-$21 **Phone:** 212/734-1600 (80)
Location: Between 76th and 77th sts. 1470 1st Ave 10021. **Hours:** 5 pm-11 pm. Closed: 11/25, 12/25. **Reservations:** required. **Features:** Canyon's Southwestern cuisine is imaginative, slightly nouvelle, and dependably good. This was a new take on the style when the restaurant first opened but now swordfish fajita's, duck burrito's, a killer barbecue skirt steak and shrimp in green garlic chilli sauce are what regulars expect to find and relish at this modern neighborhood haunt. Casual dress; cocktails. **Parking:** no self-parking. **Cards:** AX, DC, DS, MC, VI.

CARNEGIE DELICATESSEN & RESTAURANT
American
Lunch: $9-$17 **Dinner:** $9-$17 **Phone:** 212/757-2245 (190)
Location: At 55th St. 854 7th Ave 10019. **Hours:** 6:30 am-4 am. **Features:** This is the quintessential New York deli, a landmark since 1937. Meat is cured, pickled and smoked "in-house." Portions are immense and the sight alone will put a twinkle in your eye! The menu is a doozy. Start with matzo ball soup, a frank, stuffed derma, pickled herring, chopped liver, blintzes then perhaps brisket, corned beef, hot pastrami, or hard salami, goulash, flanken, chicken paprikash. Then, hold your breath and order dessert. Quarters are tight and service is brisk. Casual dress; beer only. **Parking:** no self-parking.

CHIAM
Chinese
Lunch: $20-$25 **Dinner:** $16-$25 **Phone:** 212/371-2323 (126)
Location: Between Lexington and 3rd aves. 160 E 48th St 10017. **Hours:** 11:30 am-11:30 pm. Closed: 11/25. **Reservations:** suggested. **Features:** Carefully selected wines complement creative preparations of Cantonese food. Diners face hard choices from a long menu that includes hand-shredded chicken in oyster sauce, filet mignon kew, Grand Marnier prawns, salt and pepper prawns and crispy spicy sea bass. Spa and grill options are also available. The restaurant, which got its name from combining Chinese and American, is a favorite for dim sum. Dressy casual; cocktails. **Parking:** no self-parking. **Cards:** AX, DC, DS, MC, VI.

CHIN CHIN
Nouvelle Chinese
Lunch: $15-$18 **Dinner:** $18-$22 **Phone:** 212/888-4555 (127)
Location: Between 2nd and 3rd aves. 216 E 49th St 10017. **Hours:** noon-midnight, Sat from 5 pm, Sun 5 pm-11 pm. Closed: 11/25. **Reservations:** suggested. **Features:** Chinese food is a treat at the modern, sophisticated restaurant, which presents a menu of traditional and familiar dishes. Assorted dumplings and ribs flow from the kitchen, and many patrons can't resist Grand Marnier prawns. Peking duck, tea-smoked duck with scallion bread and boneless duck l'Orange are most popular, although such standards as orange beef and sesame chicken are also excellent. The $20 four-course lunch is one of the best deals in town. Casual dress; cocktails. **Parking:** no self-parking. **Cards:** AX, DC, MC, VI.

(See map and index starting on p. 364)

CHURRASCARIA PLATAFORMA **Lunch:** $30   **Dinner:** $43   **Phone:** 212/245-0505 `106`
AAA **Location:** Between 8th and 9th aves; in Belvedere Hotel. 316 W 49th St 10019. **Hours:** noon-midnight.
▽▽ ▽▽ **Reservations:** required. **Features:** The lively, festive spot allows for a distinctive Brazilian dining
experience. Try not to fill up on the extensive variety of salads and antipasto because the true delights
Brazilian await as servers parade by with sabers filled with savory beef, lamb, pork and poultry. Dressy casual;
cocktails; entertainment. **Parking:** on-site. **Cards:** AX, CB, DC, MC, VI.

CIBO **Lunch:** $15-$30   **Dinner:** $15-$35   **Phone:** 212/681-1616 `121`
▽▽▽▽▽▽ **Location:** At 41st St. 767 2nd Ave 10017. **Hours:** 11:30 am-3 & 5:30-10 pm, Fri & Sat-11 pm.
Reservations: suggested. **Features:** A romantic aura punctuates the modern and casual dining room,
Continental which is accented with floral arrangements and dramatic, freshly cut branches. The seasonal menu centers
on Tuscan-American cuisine. Weekend brunches are popular, as are the pastry chef's decadent creations.
Dressy casual; cocktails. **Parking:** no self-parking. **Cards:** AX, DC, DS, MC, VI.

CINNABAR ASIAN GRILL & RESTAURANT   **Lunch:** $10-$13   **Dinner:** $12-$24   **Phone:** 212/399-1100 `102`
▽▽▽▽▽▽ **Location:** At 8th Ave. 235 W 56th St 10019. **Hours:** noon-midnight. Closed: 11/25, 12/25.
Reservations: suggested. **Features:** Striking contemporary decor with red, ribbon candy-like lights hung
Chinese from very tall ceilings, lively jazz and comfortable chairs provide a pleasant and upbeat backdrop for
dishes prepared in the open kitchen. Dim sum selections, roast pork, salt & pepper shrimp and crispy duck
are all choice starters, then on to the sizeable menu. Dressy casual; cocktails. **Parking:** no self-parking. **Cards:** AX, DC, DS,
MC, VI.

CINQUANTA RISTORANTE   **Lunch:** $12-$22   **Dinner:** $13-$25   **Phone:** 212/759-5050 `157`
▽▽▽▽▽▽ **Location:** Between Madison and Park aves. 50 E 50th St 10022. **Hours:** noon-11:30 pm, Fri & Sat-midnight, Sun
5 pm-11 pm. **Reservations:** suggested. **Features:** The bright dining room has an art deco feel.
Italian Representative of dishes is bass encrusted with shredded potatoes and served in thickened fish broth.
Game is available in season. Outfitted in black-and-white attire, the wait staff delivers old-school,
professional service. Casual dress; cocktails. **Parking:** on-site. **Cards:** AX, CB, DC, DS, MC, VI.

CITARELLA THE RESTAURANT   **Lunch:** $21-$28   **Dinner:** $25-$32   **Phone:** 212/332-1515 `183`
▽▽▽▽▽▽ **Location:** At 49th St. 1240 6th Ave 10020. **Hours:** 11:30 am-2:30 & 5:30-10 pm, Fri-11 pm, Sat 5:30-11 pm.
Closed major holidays; also Sun. **Reservations:** suggested. **Features:** Stately even among towering
Seafood buildings, the red brick townhouse is a subdued and elegant seafood restaurant with four dining floors,
each sophisticated and warm. A hint of whimsy is seen through portholes. Fine ingredients, fresh fish and
chef skill merge in such creative starters as Asian seviche, lobster tempura salad and grilled Portuguese sardines with
Parmesan-lemon crust. Fine sushi offerings are popular. Dressy casual; cocktails. **Parking:** no self-parking. **Cards:** AX, DC,
DS, MC, VI.

CITE **Lunch:** $20-$33   **Dinner:** $20-$33   **Phone:** 212/956-7100 `75`
AAA **Location:** Between 6th (Ave of the Americas) and 7th aves. 120 W 51st 10020. **Hours:** noon-11:30 pm. Closed
▽▽▽▽▽▽ major holidays. **Reservations:** suggested. **Features:** An upscale steakhouse with handsome art deco
decor slightly reminiscent of "nouvelle Paris." The popular wine dinners are a bargain. Dressy casual;
Steak House cocktails. **Parking:** on-site. **Cards:** AX, CB, DC, DS, MC, VI.

COMPASS **Lunch:** $13-$22   **Dinner:** $18-$34   **Phone:** 212/875-8600 `217`
▽▽▽▽▽▽ **Location:** Between Amsterdam and West End aves. 208 W 70th St 10023. **Hours:** noon-2:30 & 5-11:30 pm, Sat
from 5 pm. **Reservations:** suggested. **Features:** The seats are so comfortable guests could sit all night
American amid sophisticated, albeit understated, contemporary surroundings. Representative of the offerings are
yellowtail snapper tapenade, roast guinea hen with chanterelles, steamed black sea bass and pan-seared
hanger steak. Savory dishes reflect a new American flair and creativity. Another selection is the $30 prix fixe meal. Dressy
casual; cocktails. **Parking:** no self-parking. **Cards:** AX, DC, DS, MC, VI.

COSTA DEL SOL RESTAURANT   **Lunch:** $8-$17   **Dinner:** $11-$25   **Phone:** 212/541-8382 `107`
▽▽▽ ▽▽▽ **Location:** Corner of 9th Ave and W 50th St. 369 W 50th St 10019. **Hours:** noon-11 pm, Fri & Sat-midnight.
Reservations: accepted. **Features:** Authentic Spanish cuisine served in a casual setting. Meals start with
Spanish traditional appetizers followed by a large menu of paella, mariscada in hot garlic sauce or green sauce,
shrimp Diablo, chicken with almond sauce, chicken and rice, veal with wine sauce, as well as selection of
daily specials are among the many choices. Casual dress; cocktails. **Parking:** no self-parking. **Cards:** AX, DC, DS, MC, VI.

DAWAT **Lunch:** $13-$23   **Dinner:** $13-$23   **Phone:** 212/355-7555 `128`
▽▽▽▽▽▽ **Location:** Between 2nd and 3rd aves. 210 E 58th St 10022. **Hours:** 11:30 am-2:45 & 5:30-10:45 pm, Fri-11:15
pm, Sun 5:30 pm-10:45 pm. **Reservations:** suggested. **Features:** Reserved formality is evident in every
Indian aspect of the restaurant—from its menu of creatively prepared dishes to its servers in crisp uniform.
Wonderful ground lamb meatballs are served in a thick puree of onions, tomatoes and chilis. Dressy
casual; cocktails. **Parking:** no self-parking. **Cards:** AX, DC, DS, MC, VI.

DB BISTRO MODERNE   **Lunch:** $24-$28   **Dinner:** $26-$32   **Phone:** 212/391-2400 `200`
▽▽▽▽▽▽ **Location:** Between 5th and 6th (Ave of the Americas) aves. 55 W 44th St 10036. **Hours:** noon-2:30 & 5:30-11 pm,
Sun from 5:30 pm. Closed major holidays. **Reservations:** suggested. **Features:** Casual yet sleek, with
French design in mind in every crevice, the dining rooms are handsome and stylish. As for the food, Daniel Boulud
may play around but never misses with his dishes. Artful use of the freshest ingredients mean plates go
back to the kitchen empty. Dressy casual; cocktails. **Parking:** no self-parking. **Cards:** AX, DC, DS, MC, VI.

(See map and index starting on p. 364)

DISTRICT Lunch: $16-$20 Dinner: $25-$35 Phone: 212/485-2999 [143]
American
Location: Between 6th (Ave of the Americas) and 7th aves; in The Muse. 130 W 46th St 10036. **Hours:** 7 am-10:30, noon-2 & 5:30-9:45 pm. **Reservations:** suggested. **Features:** Richly designed to resemble a theater with the open kitchen being center stage. District, just off Broadway, offers an eclectic menu that ranges from luxury box items, including truffle and foie gras selections to seafood tacos and Tokyo roast. Casual dress; cocktails. **Parking:** no self-parking. **Cards:** AX, CB, DC, DS, MC, VI.

DIWAN Lunch: $13 Dinner: $13-$24 Phone: 212/593-5425 [125]
Indian
Location: Between Lexington and 3rd aves. 148 E 48th St 10017. **Hours:** 11:30 am-2:30 & 5-10:30 pm, Fri-11 pm, Sat 11:30 am-3 & 5-11 pm, Sun 11:30 am-3 & 5-10:30 pm. **Reservations:** accepted. **Features:** The seasoned chef prepares not only wonderfully cooked, familiar dishes but also more intriguing choices. Stuffed chicken breast with lemon rice and tamarind sauce, basil chicken, tandoori jhinga, tandoori halibut and wild boar chops are a few lively dishes. Starters of Goan shrimp, crab beggar's purses and crisp vegetable fritters are little prizes. Chai- and cardamom-infused pot de creme, richly creamy and smooth, is a refreshing end to the meal. Casual dress; cocktails. **Parking:** no self-parking. **Cards:** AX, DC, MC, VI.

DOCKS OYSTER BAR & SEAFOOD GRILL Lunch: $14-$22 Dinner: $16-$22 Phone: 212/986-8080 [65]
Seafood
Location: Between 40th and 41st sts. 633 3rd Ave 10017. **Hours:** 11:30 am-11 pm, Fri-midnight, Sat 5 pm-midnight, Sun 11:30 am-2:45 & 5-11 pm. **Closed:** 12/25. **Reservations:** suggested. **Features:** The lively, noisy dining room is not a distraction from the straightforward fresh seafood preparations, which are at the heart of a varied menu that includes some selections of chicken, pasta and steak. The long-running establishment caters to both businessmen and ladies lunching. Generous but not gross portions add to the appeal. The wait staff, in casual dress, delivers knowledgeable service. Casual dress; cocktails. **Parking:** no self-parking. **Cards:** AX, DC, DS, MC, VI.

DOCKS OYSTER BAR & SEAFOOD GRILL Lunch: $15-$18 Dinner: $20-$30 Phone: 212/724-5588 [63]
Seafood
Location: Between W 89th and W 90th sts. 2427 Broadway 10024. **Hours:** 11:30 am-11 pm, Fri & Sat-midnight, Sun 11 am-11 pm. **Closed:** 12/25. **Reservations:** suggested. **Features:** Shellfish are at the heart of a varied menu that includes selections of chicken, pasta, steak and of course seafood. Sconces and artwork add to the appeal of the lively, noisy dining room. The wait staff, in casual dress, delivers knowledgeable service. Casual dress; cocktails. **Parking:** on-site. **Cards:** AX, DC, DS, MC, VI.

EAST RIVER CAFE Lunch: $12-$20 Dinner: $12-$20 Phone: 212/980-3144 [140]
Italian
Location: At 61st St. 1111 1st Ave 10021. **Hours:** noon-4 & 5-11 pm. **Reservations:** suggested. **Features:** Lending to the simple decor are small black-and-white photographs, lanterns on the walls and a handsome copper-topped bar. On the menu are such choices as lobster-stuffed pasta with shrimp in fra diavolo sauce, pasta with grilled sausage, broccoli rabe in garlic and oil, monkfish with lemon-thyme-white wine sauce and pasta stuffed with roasted meat and mushrooms in a sauce of shallots, sage, brandy and cream. Creative and well-prepared dishes all are redolent with flavor. Casual dress; cocktails. **Parking:** no self-parking. **Cards:** AX, DC, MC, VI.

ESCA Lunch: $16-$21 Dinner: $24-$28 Phone: 212/564-7272 [201]
Seafood
Location: 9th Ave; in the theater district. 402 W 43rd St 10036. **Hours:** noon-2:30 & 5-11:30 pm, Sun 4:30 pm-10:30 pm. **Closed:** 11/25, 12/25. **Reservations:** required. **Features:** Celebrity-chef Mario Batali interprets the coastal cuisine of Italy here, which means all manner of fish and shellfish; baked whole, mixed in pasta, or served raw, crudo-style with a little olive oil, spices, and maybe some citrus, this section of the menu is not to be missed and will delight those who thought raw fish began and ended with sushi. Casual dress; cocktails. **Parking:** street. **Cards:** AX, DC, MC, VI.

ESS-A-BAGEL Lunch: $2-$10 Dinner: $2-$10 Phone: 212/980-1010 [112]
American
Location: Between 50th and 51st sts. 831 3rd Ave 10022. **Hours:** 6 am-9 pm, Sat & Sun 7 am-5 pm. Closed major holidays. **Features:** The unpretentious spot is a favorite for classic New York bagels, which are served with spreads, including vegetarian, tofu and such smoked fish as sturgeon, nova lox, sable, whitefish and baked salmon. Also on the menu are reasonably priced salads, smoked meat and fish platters, pastries and cookies. Casual dress. **Parking:** no self-parking. **Cards:** AX, DC, DS, MC, VI.

ESTIATORIO MILOS Lunch: $15-$30 Dinner: $24-$40 Phone: 212/245-7400 [132]
Greek
Location: Between 6th (Ave of the Americas) and 7th aves. 125 W 55th St 10019. **Hours:** noon-2:45 & 5-11:45 pm, Sat from 5:30 pm, Sun 5 pm-10:45 pm. Closed major holidays. **Reservations:** suggested. **Features:** Fresh fish grilled over an open fire with a sprinkle of olive oil and herbs is what's cooking here. Simple preparation does not mean simple flavors. Fish are displayed as if at market and are sold by the pound, so sharing is advised. Larger appetizers also are meant for the table. Dishes are huge, but flocks of devotees will agree they're worth the price. Dressy casual; cocktails. **Parking:** no self-parking. **Cards:** AX, MC, VI.

EVERGREEN CAFE Lunch: $6-$8 Dinner: $7-$16 Phone: 212/744-3266 [113]
Chinese
Location: At 69th St. 1288 1st Ave 10021. **Hours:** 11:30 am-11 pm. **Closed:** 11/25. **Features:** This is a comfortable place to take children, and the menu offers something for everyone. Tempting choices include Beijing pork fillets, pine-nut crispy sea bass, shredded pork with spicy pickle and the exquisite Grand Marnier prawns. Weekends are busy with patrons vying for seats for an exceptional dim sum offering. Casual dress; cocktails. **Parking:** no self-parking. **Cards:** AX, DC, MC, VI.

(See map and index starting on p. 364)

FELIDIA
Northern Italian

Lunch: $18-$27   Dinner: $18-$32   Phone: 212/758-1479   (100)
Location: Between 2nd and 3rd aves. 243 E 58th St 10022. **Hours:** noon-3 & 5-11 pm, Sat from 5 pm. Closed major holidays; also Sun. **Reservations:** suggested. **Features:** This place is a breath of fresh air in hectic Manhattan. Saffron-colored walls soothe the soul and prepare guests for satisfying regional dishes delivered with fine attentive service. Pastas are made in-house daily, and many vegetables and herbs are picked from the owner's garden. The extensive wine list represents several regions of Italy. Dressy casual; cocktails. **Parking:** no self-parking. **Cards:** AX, DC, DS, MC, VI.

FIFTY-SEVEN FIFTY-SEVEN RESTAURANT & BAR
American

Lunch: $17-$26   Dinner: $28-$34   Phone: 212/758-5757   (86)
Location: Between Madison and Park aves; in Four Seasons Hotel, New York. 57 E 57th St 10022. **Hours:** 7 am-10:15 pm; Sunday brunch. **Reservations:** required. **Features:** The warmth and sincerity of the staff overcome the cold nature of the soaring modern marble architecture of the hotel dining room. Ever-changing dishes are of the highest quality and bring out the freshest tastes. Semi-formal attire; cocktails; entertainment. **Parking:** on-site (fee) and valet. **Cards:** AX, CB, DC, DS, JC, MC, VI.

FOLEY'S RESTAURANT & BAR
Seafood

Lunch: $15-$29   Dinner: $25-$39   Phone: 212/261-5200   (139)
Location: Broadway and 7th Ave; auto access from 7th Ave, s of W 48th St; in Renaissance New York Hotel Times Square. 2 Times Square, 7th Ave at W 48th St 10036. **Hours:** 6:30 am-2:30 & 5-10 pm. **Reservations:** suggested. **Features:** Relax and enjoy the feast of lights created by Times Square as you look out from this two-level restaurant. Fin and turf offerings are creatively prepared and served in ample portions. The bread selection is extensive. A pre-theater menu is available. Save plenty of room for one of the decadent desserts. Dressy casual; cocktails. **Parking:** valet. **Cards:** AX, CB, DC, DS, JC, MC, VI.

FONTANA DI TREVI
Italian

Lunch: $8-$25   Dinner: $9-$26   Phone: 212/247-5683   (202)
Location: Between 6th (Ave of the Americas) and 7th aves. 151 W 57th St 10019. **Hours:** noon-4 & 5-11 pm, Fri-11:30 pm, Sat 5 pm-11:30 pm. Closed: 1/1, 11/25, 12/25; also Sun. **Reservations:** required. **Features:** Directly across from Carnegie Hall is this welcoming cucina, opened in 1956, serving traditional dishes such as osso buco, gnocchi with a variety of sauces to choose from and lasagna made with spinach noodles and mushroom ravioli, as well as specials like striped bass oreganata. Dressy casual; cocktails. **Parking:** no self-parking. **Cards:** AX, DC, DS, MC, VI.

THE FOUR SEASONS
American

Lunch: $30-$40   Dinner: $30-$45   Phone: 212/754-9494   (203)
Location: Between Park and Lexington aves. 99 E 52nd St 10022. **Hours:** noon-2 & 5-9:30 pm, Sat 5 pm-11 pm. Closed major holidays; also Sun. **Reservations:** required. **Features:** Designed by architects Mies van der Rohe and Philip Johnson, the restaurant has been a notable landmark and modern classic in New York since 1959. It features contemporary cuisine, several dining rooms, an extensive wine cellar and a renowned art collection. Six menus range from the prix fixe bar lunch to the Pool Room's multifaceted a la carte menu. All feature a good selection of global variety. Semi-formal attire; cocktails. **Parking:** no self-parking. **Cards:** AX, CB, DC, DS, MC, VI.

FRED'S AT BARNEY'S
American

Lunch: $16-$22   Dinner: $20-$28   Phone: 212/833-2200   (109)
Location: Madison Ave at 61st St, 9th floor. 660 Madison Ave 10021. **Hours:** 11:30 am-9 pm, Sat 11 am-8 pm, Sun 11 am-6 pm. Closed major holidays. **Reservations:** suggested. **Features:** On the top level of the ultra-chic Barney's department store, the pleasant, tucked-away cafe serves more than 50 varieties of International cheeses, as well as fresh bakery items, light lunches and more. Casual dress; cocktails. **Parking:** no self-parking. **Cards:** AX, CB, DC, JC, MC, VI.

FRESCO BY SCOTTO
Northern Italian

Lunch: $15-$30   Dinner: $15-$30   Phone: 212/935-3434   (130)
Location: Between Madison and Park aves. 34 E 52nd St 10022. **Hours:** 11:30 am-3 & 5:30-11 pm, Sat from 5 pm. Closed major holidays; also Sun. **Reservations:** suggested. **Features:** Bright-colored frescoes and mirrors enhance the upbeat and friendly mood of this inviting, comfortable, yet small dining room. Modern Tuscan menu selections featuring homemade pasta and bread are cooked to perfection and served by a most accomplished staff. Casual dress; cocktails. **Parking:** no self-parking. **Cards:** AX, DC, MC, VI.

GALLAGHER'S STEAK HOUSE
Steak House

Lunch: $12-$32   Dinner: $20-$50   Phone: 212/245-5336   (214)
Location: Between Broadway and 8th Ave. 228 W 52nd St 10019. **Hours:** noon-midnight. **Reservations:** suggested. **Features:** A New York landmark since 1927, Gallagher's displays its trademark dry-aged prime beef at the entrance. The years melt away as you enter a large dark wood paneled room dominated by photos of famous people and a large old-time bar. The tables are set with red and white checkered cloths and sturdy chairs. Located in the heart of the theater district. Casual dress; cocktails. **Parking:** no self-parking. **Cards:** AX, CB, DC, DS, MC, VI.

GIAMBELLI 50TH
Northern Italian

Lunch: $18-$35   Dinner: $20-$35   Phone: 212/688-2760   (96)
Location: Between Madison and Park aves. 46 E 50th St 10022. **Hours:** noon-midnight. **Reservations:** suggested. **Features:** An interesting collection of art decorates the moderately upscale restaurant. On the menu is a wide variety of selections, ranging from seafood and pasta to veal and beef. Many wines serve as fitting complements. Servers are knowledgeable. Dressy casual; cocktails. **Parking:** no self-parking. **Cards:** AX, CB, DC, DS, MC, VI.

IL MENESTRELLO
Northern Italian

Lunch: $17-$35   Dinner: $17-$35   Phone: 212/421-7588   (85)
Location: Between 5th and Madison aves. 14 E 52nd St 10022. **Hours:** noon-11 pm, Fri & Sat-midnight. Closed major holidays. **Reservations:** suggested. **Features:** Aromatic herbs and spices wake up the flavors in such dishes as Dover sole. The dining room atmosphere is sophisticated and contemporary, with modern artwork and nice flowers. Professional basketball players have been known to frequent the establishment. Dressy casual; cocktails. **Parking:** no self-parking. **Cards:** AX, DC, MC, VI.

(See map and index starting on p. 364)

IL MONELLO
▼▼▼
Northern
Italian

Lunch: $16-$25   **Dinner:** $16-$25   **Phone:** 212/535-9310   98
Location: Between 76th and 77th sts. 1460 2nd Ave 10021. **Hours:** noon-3 & 5-11 pm, Fri & Sat 5 pm-midnight, Sun noon-10 pm. **Closed:** 1/1, 11/25, 12/25. **Reservations:** suggested. **Features:** Elegant table settings and attractive artwork lend to the sophisticated appeal of the comfortably refined dining room. The menu centers on Northern Italian dishes, which are well complemented by an assortment of wines. Desserts are delicious. Dressy casual; cocktails. **Parking:** no self-parking. **Cards:** AX, CB, DC, DS, MC, VI.

IL NIDO
▼▼▼
Northern
Italian

Lunch: $18-$27   **Dinner:** $19-$35   **Phone:** 212/753-8450   101
Location: Between 2nd and 3rd aves. 251 E 53rd St 10022. **Hours:** noon-3 & 5:30-11 pm. Closed major holidays; also Sun. **Reservations:** suggested. **Features:** An extensive selection of Italian wines complements selections of Northern Italian cuisine. Subtle lighting helps to give the quiet, Tuscan-influenced dining room a warm, intimate feel. Among the wonderful desserts are classic tiramisu and zabaglione. Semi-formal attire; cocktails. **Parking:** no self-parking. **Cards:** AX, CB, DC, MC, VI.

I LO
▼▼▼
American

Lunch: $22-$29   **Dinner:** $22-$40   **Phone:** 212/642-2255   180
Location: Between 5th and 6th (Ave of the Americas) aves. 40 W 40th St 10018. **Hours:** 7 am-10, noon-2:30 & 5:30-10:30 pm. **Closed:** 1/1. **Reservations:** suggested. **Features:** The young, old and beautiful give energy to the handsome space, which is wide open yet intimate, hip yet subdued. A grown-up evening out promises refined dishes. An overview of offerings might include roast Atlantic cod with tapenade, whole roasted branzino, sauteed skate with lobster mushrooms and port wine truffle sauce, roast chicken with hen-of-the-woods mushrooms and preserved lemon gravy and a selection of prime steaks. Pre-theater and prix fixe menus make good sense. Dressy casual; cocktails. **Parking:** no self-parking. **Cards:** AX, DC, MC, VI.

ISABELLA'S
▼▼▼
Mediterranean

Lunch: $8-$17   **Dinner:** $14-$23   **Phone:** 212/724-2100   175
Location: At 77th St. 359 Columbus Ave 10024. **Hours:** 11:30 am-12:30 am, Fri-1 am, Sat 11 am-1 am, Sun 10:30 am-midnight. **Closed:** 12/25. **Reservations:** accepted. **Features:** Value and variety are cornerstones of the big sidewalk cafe, which is always bustling. Herb-crusted salmon, marinated seafood salad, striped bass wrapped in prosciutto and well-prepared sirloin are among American dishes that exhibit Mediterranean influences. Casual dress; cocktails. **Parking:** street. **Cards:** AX, DS, MC, VI.

JASMINE
▼▼ ▼▼
Thai

Lunch: $8-$17   **Dinner:** $8-$17   **Phone:** 212/517-8854   204
Location: Corner of 84th St and 2nd Ave. 1619 2nd Ave 10021. **Hours:** 11:30 am-10:30 pm, Fri & Sat-11:30 pm, Sun 1 am-10:30 pm. **Closed:** 11/25. **Features:** This casual storefront favorite has outdoor street dining in warmer weather but is popular all-year-round for the highly flavorful dishes, both traditional and unusual. The lemongrass grilled pork chops are sublime and the ginger chicken and lemongrass shrimp are aromatic and addictive. But these are just a few of the excellent choices. Casual. Casual dress; cocktails. **Parking:** no self-parking. **Cards:** AX, MC, VI.

JEAN GEORGES RESTAURANT
▼▼◆▼▼
French

Lunch: $29-$42   **Dinner:** $87-$118   **Phone:** 212/299-3900   141
Location: Jct Central Park S; at Columbus Circle; in Trump International Hotel & Tower. 1 Central Park W 10023. **Hours:** 7 am-10, noon-2:30 & 5:30-11 pm. Closed major holidays; also Sun. **Reservations:** required. **Features:** The Central Park skyline enhances this serene, center-stage location in the Trump International Hotel and Tower. Once inside, the elaborate open kitchen fuses the imaginative, art deco elements of the formal dining room with the equally appealing, yet less starched, bistro milieu. Enticing, cultivated aromas feed the frenzy for the sumptuous food, which is always presented in remarkable Chef Vongerichten's style. Semi-formal attire; cocktails. **Parking:** valet. **Cards:** AX, DC, MC, VI.

JOE ALLEN
▼
Regional American

Lunch: $10-$25   **Dinner:** $10-$25   **Phone:** 212/581-6464   176
Location: Between 8th and 9th aves. 326 W 46th St 10036. **Hours:** noon-11:45 pm, Fri-midnight, Sat 11:30 am-midnight, Sun & Wed 11:30 am-11:45 pm. **Closed:** 11/25, 12/25. **Reservations:** required. **Features:** A theater district classic, the cheerful pub delivers unpretentious, home-style staples, such as meatloaf, liver and roasted chicken. Apple pie is stuffed full of fruit and served warm. Broadway stars are known to gather here for late night meals. Casual dress; cocktails. **Parking:** no self-parking. **Cards:** MC, VI.

JOHN'S PIZZERIA-TIMES SQUARE
▼▼ ▼
American

Lunch: $8-$15   **Dinner:** $8-$15   **Phone:** 212/391-7560   129
Location: Between 7th and 8th aves. 260 W 44th St 10036. **Hours:** 11:30 am-11:30 pm, Sun-9 pm. **Features:** First established in 1929 and now with four New York City locations, this spacious eatery is situated in an historic landmark church. Although famous for thin crust pizza baked in a coal-fired brick oven, the pasta, sandwiches and homemade dessert is worthy of a return visit. Casual dress; cocktails. **Parking:** no self-parking. **Cards:** AX, MC, VI.

JO JO
▼▼▼ ▼▼▼
French

Lunch: $18-$28   **Dinner:** $18-$34   **Phone:** 212/223-5656   71
Location: Between Lexington and 3rd aves. 160 E 64th St 10021. **Hours:** noon-2:30 & 6-11 pm, Sat noon-2:30 & 5:30-11:30 pm, Sun noon-2:30 & 5:30-11 pm. **Closed:** Sun. **Reservations:** suggested. **Features:** Located in a charming brownstone, a few steps down will bring you into the little hideaway of the intimate dining room, with banquettes along the walls hung with large beveled mirrors and fanciful Venetian glass sconces. Food is creative but firmly French with artful presentation and clear and boastful flavors. Dressy casual; cocktails. **Parking:** no self-parking. **Cards:** AX, DC, MC, VI.

JUDSON GRILL
▼▼▼
American

Lunch: $21-$29   **Dinner:** $23-$35   **Phone:** 212/582-5252   177
Location: Between 6th (Ave of the Americas) and 7th aves. 152 W 52nd St 10019. **Hours:** noon-2:15 & 5:30-10:15 pm, Fri-11 pm, Sat 5 pm-11:30 pm. Closed major holidays; also Sun. **Reservations:** suggested. **Features:** Convenient to the theater district, the dining room is large and impressive. Illuminated by great amber-hued chandeliers, adorned with huge, fresh floral arrangements and trimmed in dark wood, it is, in a word, distinctive. Eclectic contemporary and soul-satisfying dishes, touched by Mediterranean influences, are well complemented by a selection of more than 160 wines. Dressy casual; cocktails. **Parking:** no self-parking. **Cards:** AX, DC, DS, MC, VI.

(See map and index starting on p. 364)

JULIAN'S CUISINE
Italian
Lunch: $6-$13   **Dinner:** $10-$28   **Phone:** 212/262-4800   (133)
Location: Between 53rd and 54th sts. 802 9th Ave 10019. **Hours:** noon-11 pm, Fri-midnight, Sat 11 am-midnight, Sun 11 am-11 pm. **Closed:** 1/1, 7/4. **Reservations:** suggested. **Features:** The menu covers broad territory, with northern and southern Italian dishes and Mediterranean cuisine. Shelves with European decorations line the comfortable but slightly crowded dining room. The seasonal garden and relaxed sidewalk area invite diners to unwind. Casual dress; cocktails. **Parking:** no self-parking. **Cards:** AX, DC, DS, MC, VI.

KOREA PALACE
Korean
Lunch: $11-$18   **Dinner:** $19-$35   **Phone:** 212/832-2350   (179)
Location: Between Park and Lexington aves. 127 E 54th St 10022. **Hours:** 11:30 am-10:30 pm. **Closed:** 11/25. **Reservations:** suggested. **Features:** Each table is equipped with a hot plate for popular Korean barbecue. Among many traditional dishes are Korean pancakes, a large selection of hot pot soups and hot-stone-cooked choices. Stewed cod with garlic and soy, the pa jun seafood pancake, barbecue and sushi are favorites. The relaxed dining room is appropriately appointed in ethnic decor. Servers in black and white uniforms are friendly and efficient. Casual dress; cocktails. **Parking:** no self-parking. **Cards:** AX, DC, MC, VI.

KURUMA ZUSHI
Sushi
Lunch: $18-$200   **Dinner:** $18-$200   **Phone:** 212/317-2802   (58)
Location: Between 5th and Madison aves. 7 E 47th St, 2nd Floor 10017. **Hours:** 11:30 am-2 & 5:30-10 pm. Closed major holidays; also Sun. **Reservations:** suggested. **Features:** No street sign marks this exclusive sushi-only restaurant, located on the second floor of a nondescript building. The understated but bright and spotless dining room is small but there is room at the sushi bar. The menu offers sushi in three different qualities: high, higher and spectacular, as well as special fish flown in from Japan. One orders by quality or price. There is also a menu of various sushi rolls. Service is sweet and demure and ever watchful for the guest's needs. Casual dress; cocktails. **Parking:** no self-parking. **Cards:** AX, JC, MC, VI.

LA BOITE EN BOIS
French
Lunch: $15-$20   **Dinner:** $19-$25   **Phone:** 212/874-2705   (174)
Location: Between Columbus Ave and Central Park W. 75 W 68th St 10023. **Hours:** noon-2:30 & 5:30-10:30 pm, Sun 11:30 am-2:30 & 5-10 pm, Mon 5:30 pm-10 pm. Closed major holidays. **Reservations:** suggested. **Features:** Dressy casual; cocktails. **Parking:** no self-parking.

LA CARAVELLE
French
Lunch: $38   **Dinner:** $46-$72   **Phone:** 212/586-4252   (59)
Location: Between 5th and 6th (Ave of the Americas) aves. 33 W 55th St 10019. **Hours:** noon-2:30 & 5:30-10 pm, Sat from 5:30 pm. Closed major holidays; also Sun & first week of July. **Reservations:** suggested. **Features:** Decorated with vibrant flowers and a charming mural of Parisian scenes, the elegant dining room has a reserved but sunny disposition. High society lunches here, but others are welcomed. Traditional foods are not only pretty to admire but also are expertly prepared and served by doting, professional servers. Jackets are required for gentlemen. Semi-formal attire; cocktails. **Parking:** no self-parking. **Cards:** AX, DC, DS, MC, VI.

LA GRENOUILLE
French
Lunch: $29-$35   **Dinner:** $45-$49   **Phone:** 212/752-1495   (68)
Location: Between 5th and Madison aves. 3 E 52nd St 10022. **Hours:** Open 5/1-8/1 & 9/10-4/30; noon-2:30 & 5:30-10 pm, Fri & Sat-11 pm. Closed major holidays; also Sun. **Reservations:** required. **Features:** An abundance of sophistication is apparent in the food, the room and the guests of this long-standing New York favorite. Classic dishes are served by mature and professional staff who will speak French to you, charm you, and most important, help you with the menu, written entirely in French. Enormous and elaborate floral arrangements and brocade walls are reflected in walls of mirror with stunning effect. No need to fly to Paris for a dose of grandeur. Prix fixe menu available lunch and dinner. Semi-formal attire; cocktails. **Parking:** no self-parking. **Cards:** AX, DC, JC, MC, VI.

LA MANGEOIRE
French
Lunch: $9-$28   **Dinner:** $15-$29.   **Phone:** 212/759-7086   (135)
Location: Between 53rd and 54th sts. 1008 2nd Ave 10022. **Hours:** noon-2:30 & 5:30-10:30 pm, Fri & Sat-11 pm, Sun noon-3 & 5:30-9:30 pm. **Closed:** Sun 7/4-9/2. **Reservations:** suggested. **Features:** Guests step out of New York and into Provence, where bundles of dried herbs and flowers hang from thatched roofs, and hearty cooking with fresh herbs and ingredients makes mealtime special. A charming, rustic appearance prevails inside and out. Fish soup, onion tart, escargot with garlic cream, braised leg of lamb and shepherd's pie all are representative of the dive-right-in menu. The wine list carefully combines French and Californian selections. Dressy casual; cocktails. **Parking:** no self-parking. **Cards:** AX, DC, MC, VI.

LE BERNARDIN
Seafood
Lunch: $47   **Dinner:** $84   **Phone:** 212/489-1515   (148)
Location: Between 6th (Ave of the Americas) and 7th aves; in the Equitable Bldg. 155 W 51st St 10019. **Hours:** noon-2:30 & 5:15-10:30 pm, Fri-11 pm, Sat 5:15 pm-11 pm. Closed major holidays; also Sun. **Reservations:** required. **Features:** Simply put, the menu is a who's who of fish. The scope of seafood choices is exciting to any fish lover, especially to those eager to enjoy the fish itself. The varied accompanying flavors creatively and gracefully spotlight the star of the show. The graceful dining room also pays tribute through large still life paintings of the sea's rich bounty. Many consider this one of New York's premier seafood restaurants. Semi-formal attire; cocktails. **Parking:** no self-parking. **Cards:** AX, DC, DS, MC, VI.

LE CIRQUE 2000   Classic
French
Lunch: $28-$41   **Dinner:** $23-$43   **Phone:** 212/303-7788   (165)
Location: Between 50th and 51st sts; in The New York Palace. 455 Madison Ave 10022. **Hours:** 11:45 am-2:30 & 5:30-10:30 pm, Sun from 5:30 pm. Closed major holidays. **Reservations:** required. **Features:** In the historic 1883 Villard House, the much-lauded restaurant is glorious to see with its grand scale, winding grand staircase, elaborate carved and inlaid woodwork and ornate ceilings and fixtures. Each room is greatly different from the next, but all are equally remarkable. The dignified cuisine, prepared with skill from fresh produce, is offered as grand classics as well as inspired modern dishes. Semi-formal attire; cocktails. **Parking:** valet. **Cards:** AX, DC, DS, MC, VI.

(See map and index starting on p. 364)

LE COLONIAL
Vietnamese

Lunch: $13-$20   **Dinner:** $13-$20   **Phone:** 212/752-0808   (137)
Location: Between Lexington and 3rd aves. 149 E 57th St 10022. **Hours:** noon-2:15 & 5:30-11:30 pm, Fri-midnight, Sat & Sun 5:30 pm-11 pm. Closed: 11/25, 12/25. **Reservations:** suggested. **Features:** Twirling fans, tall ferns and an original tin ceiling painted deep, brick red with a black border give the dining room the feel of 1940s Vietnam. The menu centers on excellent Vietnamese cuisine, all priced reasonably. Servers are gentle and efficient. Dressy casual; cocktails. **Parking:** no self-parking. **Cards:** AX, DC, JC, MC, VI.

LE PAIN QUOTIDIEN
French

Lunch: $7-$13   **Dinner:** $7-$13   **Phone:** 212/327-4900
Location: Between 84th and 85th sts. 1131 Madison Ave 10028. **Hours:** 7:30 am-7 pm. Closed: 12/25. **Features:** Fresh from Belgium comes this small chain sandwich and bake shop. Its very casual manner is typified by a long communal table down the center of one room, though there is individual seating as well. There is no decor to speak of except raw wood floors, unfinished window trim and stripped walls. The sandwiches and baked goods, especially the breakfast pastries, are quality and typically European in nature, thus there are usually many full tables. Casual dress. **Parking:** no self-parking. **Cards:** AX, MC, VI.

LE PERIGORD
French

Lunch: $28   **Dinner:** $62   **Phone:** 212/755-6244   (95)
Location: E of 1st Ave. 405 E 52nd St 10022. **Hours:** noon-3 & 5:30-10:30 pm, Sat from 5:30 pm, Sun 5 pm-10:30 pm. Closed: 1/1, 12/25. **Reservations:** required. **Features:** In a residential area near the United Nations building, the long-established restaurant has welcomed guests with grace and dignity. The staid yet elegant spot employs servers seemingly born ages ago. The broad menu centers on classic dishes, which are nicely complemented by a fine wine list. Semi-formal attire; cocktails. **Parking:** no self-parking. **Cards:** AX, DC, DS, MC, VI.

LINDY'S
American

Lunch: $8-$19   **Dinner:** $8-$19   **Phone:** 212/767-8343   (191)
Location: At 53rd St. 825 7th Ave 10019. **Hours:** 7 am-11 pm. **Features:** This New York institution is the place to go when an urge strikes for authentic New York-style cheesecake. Deli sandwiches are the main bill of fare, but there are plenty of hot items as well. This spot is casual and good for a rest after a day of walking. Breakfast also is served. Casual dress; cocktails. **Parking:** no self-parking. **Cards:** AX, DC, DS, MC, VI.

LUTECE
French

Lunch: $29   **Dinner:** $59   **Phone:** 212/752-2225   (155)
Location: Between 2nd and 3rd aves. 249 E 50th St 10022. **Hours:** noon-2:30 & 5:30-10 pm, Sat from 5:30 pm. Closed major holidays; also Sun. **Reservations:** suggested. **Features:** Subdued elegance in celadon green with high-back leather chairs, a two-story ceiling, vine-like chandeliers and painted brick accents work toward a relaxed dining experience. Fine French preparations, served by a large professional staff, go with the territory. Semi-formal attire; cocktails. **Parking:** no self-parking. **Cards:** AX, DC, DS, MC, VI.

MALIKA
Indian

Lunch: $11   **Dinner:** $11-$16   **Phone:** 212/681-6775   (162)
Location: Between 2nd & 3rd aves. 210 E 43rd St 10017. **Hours:** 11:30 am-3 & 5-11 pm. Closed: 12/25. **Reservations:** suggested. **Features:** Popular with the lunch crowd for its varied and nicely presented buffet, the restaurant offers some of the same well-prepared and fragrant items on the dinner menu. Casual decor makes this place appropriate for kids. Casual dress; cocktails. **Parking:** no self-parking. **Cards:** AX, DC, MC, VI.

THE MANHATTAN CHILI CO
Southwestern

Lunch: $6-$17   **Dinner:** $6-$17   **Phone:** 212/730-8666   (83)
Location: At Broadway and 43rd St; entrance on 43rd St. 1500 Broadway 10036. **Hours:** 11:30 am-11 pm, Fri & Sat-midnight. Closed: 11/25, 12/25. **Features:** Located at Times Square, this family-friendly restaurant has a lively ambiance and colorful decor. Southwestern favorites are on the menu, including 11 types of chili and some vegetarian options. Casual dress; cocktails. **Parking:** no self-parking. **Cards:** AX, DS, MC, VI.

MARCH
American

Lunch: $18-$26   **Dinner:** $68-$126   **Phone:** 212/754-6272   (138)
Location: Between 1st Ave and Sutton Pl. 405 E 58th St 10022. **Hours:** noon-2 & 5:30-11 pm, Sat & Sun from 5:30 pm. Closed major holidays. **Reservations:** required. **Features:** Appointed with elegant, turn-of-the-century decor, this multi-level townhouse features a Degne chandelier, Chinese needlepoint tapestry and a working fireplace. A myriad of dining rooms provide a romantic intimacy. Alfresco dining is available. The menu accommodates a refined level of curiosity and appetite featuring distinguished and exquisitely prepared New World selections. An award-winning wine list complements this warm and comfortable approach to fine dining. Semi-formal attire; cocktails. **Parking:** no self-parking. **Cards:** AX, DC, DS, JC, MC, VI.

MARK'S
Continental

Lunch: $15-$26   **Dinner:** $24-$38   **Phone:** 212/879-1864   (147)
Location: Madison Ave at E 77th St; in The Mark, New York. 25 Madison Ave at E 77th St 10021. **Hours:** 7 am-10 pm. **Reservations:** suggested. **Features:** Roman prints decorate the walls of the plush, terraced dining room. The atmosphere is refined and comfortable, welcoming diners to unwind. The menu presents traditional choices, with the three-course prix fixe meals being a particular deal. Dressy casual; cocktails. **Parking:** no self-parking. **Cards:** AX, CB, DC, DS, JC, MC, VI.

METSOVO
Greek

Dinner: $15-$25   **Phone:** 212/873-2300   (173)
Location: Between Columbus Ave and Central Park W. 65 W 70th St 10023. **Hours:** 5 pm-11 pm. Closed: 1/1, 11/25, 12/25. **Reservations:** accepted. **Features:** The refreshingly different Greek option serves hearty homestyle dishes of fish and lamb with a nice selection of hot and cold mezze to start; don't look for moussaka here. Brick walls and understated but warm decor softly lit by candlelight present a very comfortable atmosphere which is enhanced by lively music. Platters piled high with powdered and nut covered cookies are a nice distraction throughout meal. Casual dress; cocktails. **Parking:** no self-parking. **Cards:** AX, DC, MC, VI.

(See map and index starting on p. 364)

MICHAEL'S
▼▼▼
American

Lunch: $25-$26   **Dinner:** $25-$38   **Phone:** 212/767-0555   142
Location: Between 5th and 6th (Ave of the Americas) aves. 24 W 55th St 10019. **Hours:** 7:30 am-9:30, noon-2:30 & 5:30-10:30 pm, Sat from 5:30 pm. Closed major holidays; also Sun. **Reservations:** suggested. **Features:** Diners are frequently surrounded by live famous faces amid walls of original artwork and two life-size ceramic sheep. Well-prepared dishes are light but savory, designed to keep figures svelte and pampered palates satisfied. Large, colorful floral arrangements add even more interest to an already head-turning room. Dressy casual; cocktails. **Parking:** no self-parking. **Cards:** AX, DC, MC, VI.

MODA
▼▼▼
Continental

Lunch: $18-$26   **Dinner:** $21-$29   **Phone:** 212/887-9880   205
Location: Between 6th (Ave of the Americas) and 7th ave; in The Flatotel. 135 W 52nd St 10019. **Hours:** 7 am-2:30 & 5:30-11 pm, Sat & Sun 7 am-11:30 & 5:30-11 pm. **Reservations:** required. **Features:** Mediterranean and Italian bents are evident in creative and substantial dishes, such as roast rack and slow-cooked leg of lamb white beans and escarole; sauteed skate with fava, artichoke and corn shoots; and grilled pheasant with sage and soft polenta. The food is warm and satisfying, while the room, mainly concrete with candles hung on walls, is a cool space. Dressy casual; cocktails. **Parking:** no self-parking. **Cards:** AX, MC, VI.

MOLYVOS
▼▼▼
Greek

Lunch: $18-$28   **Dinner:** $20-$29   **Phone:** 212/582-7500   196
Location: Between 55th and 56th sts. 871 7th Ave 10019. **Hours:** noon-3 & 5:30-11:30 pm. Closed: 12/25. **Reservations:** suggested. **Features:** Inspired from the memories of their Mediterranean island the Livanos family has created Molyvos as a celebration of its cuisine. Start with a meze assortment of small dishes such as tangy cheese in phyllo, tiny lamb meatballs, or various dips with triangles of pita bread. Then on to delicious Greek dishes such as lamb stewed in a clay pot or grilled whole fish. Dressy casual; cocktails. **Parking:** street. **Cards:** AX, DC, DS, MC, VI.

MR. K'S
▼▼▼ ▼▼▼
Chinese

Lunch: $18-$33   **Dinner:** $18-$38   **Phone:** 212/583-1668   56
Location: At 51st St. 570 Lexington Ave 10022. **Hours:** 11:30 am-11 pm, Sat & Sun from noon. **Reservations:** suggested. **Features:** This is not your typical Chinese restaurant. Located in one of the city's historic landmarks, the magnificent art deco design is in keeping with the old GE building tradition. Design features include high ceilings, quality woodwork, plush fabrics and etched glass. Table tops are adorned with the finest place settings accented by a circle of light from below. The food and service are of equal elegance and combine for a unique dining experience. Dressy casual; cocktails. **Parking:** no self-parking. **Cards:** AX, DC, DS, JC, MC, VI.

NOCHE
▼▼▼
Latino

Lunch: $6-$14   **Dinner:** $17-$22   **Phone:** 212/541-7070   156
Location: Between 48th and 49th aves. 1604 Broadway 10019. **Hours:** 11 am-3 & 5-11 pm, Sat from 5 pm. Closed: 1/1, 12/25; also Sun. **Reservations:** suggested. **Features:** The downstairs bar is loud and energetic with crowds having a collective party, but the multistory dining rooms, each with its own bar tucked into a nook or alcove, are quieter. The menu lists food from not just one Latin nation but many. Flavor is in the air, the music and the food. Casual dress; cocktails. **Parking:** no self-parking. **Cards:** AX, DC, DS, MC, VI.

NORMA'S
▼▼▼
American

Lunch: $8-$22   **Phone:** 212/708-7460   77
Location: Between 6th (Ave of the Americas) and 7th aves; in the Le Parker Meridien New York. 118 W 57th St 10019-3318. **Hours:** 6:30 am-3 pm, Sat & Sun from 7 am. **Features:** If you go here for breakfast or lunch, you will be glad that you did. Menu selections are clever, uniquely over-sized, creative and delectable. The contemporary yet casual atmosphere features European and South American accents and treatments. Casual dress. **Parking:** on-site (fee) and valet. **Cards:** AX, CB, DC, DS, JC, MC, VI.

OCEANA
▼▼▼ ▼▼▼
Seafood

Lunch: $45   **Dinner:** $68   **Phone:** 212/759-5941   111
Location: Between Madison and Park aves. 55 E 54th St 10022. **Hours:** noon-2:30 & 5:30-10:30 pm, Sat from 5 pm. Closed major holidays; also Sun. **Reservations:** suggested. **Features:** The dining room presents what looks like a ship-side view of lush cliffs, seaside villages, and other ships, from windows within a stately ocean vessel's dining room through murals and clever streamlined architectural detail. The entirely seafood menu is enticing and exhibits outstanding visual and vibrant flavor combinations. The staff is welcoming and gracious. Semi-formal attire; cocktails. **Parking:** no self-parking. **Cards:** AX, DC, DS, JC, MC, VI.

OLLIE'S
▼▼▼
Chinese

Lunch: $9-$18   **Dinner:** $9-$18   **Phone:** 212/921-5988   185
Location: Between 7th and 8th aves. 200B W 44th St 10036. **Hours:** 11:30 am-midnight, Fri & Sat-1 am, Sun-11:30 pm. **Reservations:** required. **Features:** Known for dumplings, barbecue and a good variety of Cantonese wonton and Mandarin noodle soups, the casual and usually bustling Times Square restaurant is a favorite for traditional food. No-nonsense servers are efficient. Casual dress; cocktails. **Parking:** no self-parking. **Cards:** AX, MC, VI.

ORSO
▼▼▼
Italian

Lunch: $18-$24   **Dinner:** $18-$24   **Phone:** 212/489-7212   78
Location: Between 8th and 9th aves; on Restaurant Row. 322 W 46th St 10036. **Hours:** noon-11:45 pm, Wed, Sat & Sun from 11:30 am; closing hours may vary Sun & Mon. Closed: 11/25, 12/25. **Reservations:** suggested. **Features:** Guests must look hard for the sign to this quaint Mediterranean hideaway, where well-prepared food is flavorful and fresh and complemented by a carefully selected Italian wine list. Dishes look colorful and appetizing and make good use of fresh herbs. Dressy casual; cocktails. **Parking:** no self-parking. **Cards:** MC, VI.

PARK AVENUE CAFE
▼▼▼
American

Lunch: $16-$28   **Dinner:** $20-$34   **Phone:** 212/644-1900   186
Location: At Park Ave. 100 E 63rd St 10021. **Hours:** 11:30 am-3 & 5:30-10:30 pm, Fri & Sat 5:30 pm-midnight, Sun 11 am-2:30 & 5:30-10:30 pm. Closed: 1/1, 12/25. **Reservations:** suggested. **Features:** Charm and sophistication with a touch of whimsy and the food is excellent. Ingenuity and consistency are the hallmarks of the changing nightly menu which focuses on contemporary cuisine with wide appeal. Bread basket is full of surprises. Side dishes are happy extras. Desserts are both fun and fabulous. Flights of wine are a good option with dinner. Dressy casual; cocktails. **Parking:** no self-parking. **Cards:** AX, DC, DS, JC, MC, VI.

(See map and index starting on p. 364)

PARK BISTRO

Lunch: $15-$22 **Dinner:** $18-$28 **Phone:** 212/689-1360 (145)

French

Location: Between 28th and 29th sts. 414 Park Ave S 10016. **Hours:** noon-3 & 5:30-11 pm, Sat from 5:30 pm, Sun 5:30 pm-10:30 pm. Closed major holidays. **Reservations:** suggested. **Features:** Wonderful food fits the description of bistro cooking: bold, colorful, flavorful and hearty. Meaty hangar steak is topped with seasoned cream sauce, and chicken fricassee is in a rich demi-glace spiked with rosemary, black olives and sun-dried tomatoes. Excellent desserts are prepared on site. The small space gets crowded at night and can be a bit loud, but that's part of the charm. Casual dress; cocktails. **Parking:** no self-parking. **Cards:** AX, DC, MC, VI.

PASTA BREAK

Lunch: $6-$9 **Dinner:** $6-$9 **Phone:** 212/488-2300 (154)

Italian

Location: Between 7th and 8th aves. 235 W 42nd St 10036. **Hours:** 7:40 am-midnight, Fri-2 am, Sat 11 am-2 am, Sun 11 am-midnight. **Features:** One of the better fast food joints around, the eatery uses high-quality ingredients to create homemade taste. Guests can either serve themselves in the front of the store or sit in back for casual table service. The mix-and-match menu lists diverse pasta and sauce varieties. Casual dress; beer & wine only. **Parking:** no self-parking. **Cards:** AX, DC, DS, MC, VI.

PATROON

Dinner: $28-$38 **Phone:** 212/883-7373 (206)

Steak House

Location: Between Lexington and 3rd aves. 160 E 46th St 10017. **Hours:** noon-2:30 & 5:30-11 pm, Sat from 5:30 pm. Closed major holidays; also Sun. **Reservations:** suggested. **Features:** Patroon strikes a pose between an art deco steakhouse and a photo gallery showcasing striking stills in black and white. The menu is mostly American with a touch of a French accent; grilled seafood and a dramatic lobster presentation also make their case; sides such as porcini mashed or garlic roasted potatoes are extra and sized to split so plan accordingly. Dressy casual; cocktails. **Parking:** street. **Cards:** AX, DS, MC, VI.

PATSY'S ITALIAN RESTAURANT

Lunch: $15-$22 **Dinner:** $18-$28 **Phone:** 212/247-3491 (215)

South Italian

Location: Between Broadway and 8th Ave. 236 W 56th St 10019. **Hours:** noon-10 pm, Fri & Sat-11 pm. Closed major holidays. **Reservations:** suggested. **Features:** Open since 1944 and having catered to celebrities like Frank Sinatra, Madonna, David Letterman, George Clooney, and Oprah Winfrey, Patsy's offers traditional Neopolitan-style dishes as well as signature dishes such as calamari stuffed with seafood with garlic sauce, spicy lobster fra diavolo, and stuffed veal chop marsala in a cozy and inviting atmosphere with soft lighting and comfortable booths. Pre-theater menu. Parking at Central Park Systems, 235 W 56th. Dressy casual; cocktails. **Parking:** no self-parking. **Cards:** AX, CB, DC, DS, MC, VI.

PAYARD PATISSERIE & BISTRO

Lunch: $23-$25 **Dinner:** $25-$33 **Phone:** 212/717-5252 (184)

French

Location: Between 73rd and 74th sts. 1032 Lexington Ave 10021. **Hours:** noon-3 & 5:45-10:30 pm, Fri & Sat-11 pm; pastry 7 am-11 pm. Closed major holidays; also Sun. **Reservations:** required. **Features:** Visually impressive with soft lights, tall ceilings, playful wall moldings and a loft dining room, this place exudes style. Bright cases are filled with the gleaming pastries, individual gateaux and tarts, chocolates and confectionaries that have made this place a staple for exquisite desserts. Dinner is popular with the locals, with satisfying changing specials seasoned and sauced by expert hands. Morning pastry and afternoon tea are other fine pleasures. Dressy casual; cocktails. **Parking:** no self-parking. **Cards:** AX, DC, MC, VI.

PAZO

Lunch: $12-$23 **Dinner:** $24-$30 **Phone:** 212/752-7470 (84)

Mediterranean

Location: Between Lexington and Park aves. 106 E 57th St 10022. **Hours:** noon-2:30 & 5:30-11 pm, Sat from 5:30 pm, Sun 5:30 pm-9 pm. Closed: 1/1, 7/4, 12/25. **Reservations:** required. **Features:** "Striking, Moroccan-inspired with Moorish influence" would insufficiently describe a room plush with silky fabrics, filagree screens and savoir faire. The menu, equally posh, is a small yet sublime picture of innovation and skill which comes to beguiling ends with a distinct Mediterranean inflection right on your plate. Though the menu changes daily, wood-oven roasted lamb with eggplant, honey roasted duck breast and black olive braised monkfish with lemon dill orecchiette are samples in style. Semi-formal attire; cocktails. **Parking:** no self-parking. **Cards:** AX, DC, DS, MC, VI.

PERSHING SQUARE CAFE

Lunch: $17-$24 **Dinner:** $20-$26 **Phone:** 212/286-9600 (167)

American

Location: At Park Ave. 90 E 42nd St 10017. **Hours:** 7-11 am, 11:30-3 & 5-10:30 pm, Sat & Sun from 8 am. Closed: 5/31, 9/6, 12/25. **Reservations:** suggested, for dinner. **Features:** Across the street from Grand Central, the lively joint is energized by the sounds of jazz playing and the din of the happy crowd. The handsome room features shaded lanterns that cast light over dark wood tables flanked by brass-studded red leather chairs. Sophisticated comfort food is tasty and hearty, with a measure of refinement. Fried oysters with sesame aioli are popular to start. Good choices include beef short ribs and chicken pot pie topped with a golden puff pastry dome. Casual dress; cocktails. **Parking:** no self-parking. **Cards:** AX, DC, DS, MC, VI.

PETROSSIAN

Lunch: $27-$32 **Dinner:** $27-$32 **Phone:** 212/245-2214 (76)

Continental

Location: At 7th Ave. 182 W 58th St 10019. **Hours:** 11:30 am-3 & 5:30-11 pm, Sun-10 pm. **Reservations:** suggested. **Features:** The restaurant's elegant, streamlined, art deco style—which employs marble floors, rose-tinted mirrors, etched glass, rows of shimmering champagne glasses behind the bar and sleek, bronze sculptures—says chic. Caviar, smoked salmon and foie gras are specialties at this New York institution. Semi-formal attire; cocktails. **Parking:** no self-parking. **Cards:** AX, CB, DC, JC, MC, VI.

PICHOLINE

Lunch: $24-$28 **Dinner:** $28-$38 **Phone:** 212/724-8585 (212)

French

Location: Between Broadway and Central Park W. 35 W 64th St 10023. **Hours:** 5 pm-11 pm, Thur & Fri-11:45 pm, Sat 11:45 am-2 & 5-11:45 pm, Sun 5 pm-9 pm. Closed: 1/1, 11/25, 12/25. **Reservations:** suggested. **Features:** Noted as one of the city's best for good reason. The room is lovely with large gilded oil paintings, plush seating and elaborately set tables with Italian linen and flowers. There is a menu to match. Layers of flavor that tickle the fancy of any true food lover can be found throughout the menu, unusual ingredients peppered here and there among traditional dishes expertly prepared with such happy results. Service is gracious and refined. Don't pass up the cheese tray, one of the best in town. Semi-formal attire; cocktails. **Parking:** no self-parking. **Cards:** AX, DC, MC, VI.

(See map and index starting on p. 364)

PLAZA ESPANA RESTAURANT   Lunch: $13-$23   Dinner: $13-$23   Phone: 212/757-6434   89
Spanish   **Location:** Between 6th (Ave of the Americas) and 7th aves. 130 W 58th St 10019. **Hours:** noon-11 pm, Sun-10 pm. Closed major holidays. **Reservations:** suggested. **Features:** The simple dining room provides an intimate setting in which to savor authentic Spanish dishes, such as paella with assorted seafood, fish prepared Basque-style and veal in sherry wine. The restaurant is frequented by a solid base of regulars.
Casual dress; cocktails. **Parking:** no self-parking. **Cards:** AX, DC, MC, VI.

THE POST HOUSE   Lunch: $16-$29   Dinner: $22-$43   Phone: 212/935-2888   159
Steak & Seafood   **Location:** Between Park and Madison aves; in The Lowell Hotel. 28 E 63rd St 10021. **Hours:** noon-11 pm, Sat & Sun from 5:30 pm. Closed major holidays. **Reservations:** suggested. **Features:** In the bustling, vibrant atmosphere, guests can enjoy a relaxed meal of steak and seafood with a choice of fresh vegetables. Accompany the entree with a selection from the award-winning wine list and a temptation from the dessert menu—banana cream pie perhaps. Dressy casual; cocktails. **Parking:** on-site. **Cards:** AX, CB, DC, DS, JC, MC, VI.

Q 56   Lunch: $16-$21   Dinner: $17-$27   Phone: 212/756-3800   87
American   **Location:** At 56th St; between Park and Madison aves; in Swissotel The Drake, New York. 65 E 56th St 10022-2604. **Hours:** 6:30 am-3 & 5:30-11 pm, Sat & Sun from 7 am. **Reservations:** suggested. **Features:** An exercise in visual and gastronomic contentment, the restaurant's creative, satisfying dishes are prepared by chefs in an open kitchen. Choosing an entree from the menu is difficult; seared scallops with sea urchin vinaigrette and John Dory fish over oyster ragout are two options. Dressy casual; cocktails. **Parking:** on-site (fee). **Cards:** AX, DC, DS, MC, VI.

RAKU   Lunch: $9-$30   Dinner: $9-$30   Phone: 212/719-9055   160
Japanese   **Location:** Between Broadway and 8th Ave. 252 W 47th St 10036. **Hours:** 11:45 am-2:30 & 5-10 pm. Closed major holidays; also Sun. **Features:** Specializing in traditional dishes, the cozy little place is tucked away as a quiet respite from the busy city bustle. "Crazy" rolls and chef's sushi specials made from fresh seafood are offered daily. Casual dress; beer & wine only. **Parking:** no self-parking. **Cards:** MC, VI.

RESTAURANT DANIEL   Dinner: $85-$140   Phone: 212/288-0033   158
French   **Location:** Between Park and Madison aves. 60 E 65th St 10021. **Hours:** 5:45 pm-11 pm, Fri & Sat from 5:30 pm. Closed major holidays; also Sun. **Reservations:** required. **Features:** Daniel Boulud masterfully brings the essences of France to the Upper East Side restaurant. Indirect lighting and warm, coppery hues highlight the architectural accents of the turn-of-the-20th-century building. Superb food, wine and service astound even the most refined foodie. Semi-formal attire; cocktails. **Parking:** valet. **Cards:** AX, DC, MC, VI.

RESTAURANT NIPPON   Lunch: $12-$28   Dinner: $32-$45   Phone: 212/758-0226   103
Japanese   **Location:** Between 3rd and Lexington aves. 155 E 52nd St 10022. **Hours:** noon-2:30 & 5:30-10 pm, Fri & Sat 5:30 pm-10:30 pm. Closed: Sun for dinner. **Reservations:** suggested. **Features:** The dining room is relaxed and tranquil with a few private rooms and tables separated by screens. There is a large menu of homemade soba noodle dishes, which are among fine traditional dishes served beside familiar standbys. The dessert menu includes a wonderful choice of yokan, red bean cake. Service is attentive. Dressy casual; cocktails. **Parking:** no self-parking. **Cards:** AX, DC, JC, MC, VI.

RM   Lunch: $20-$25   Dinner: $58   Phone: 212/319-3800   110
Seafood   **Location:** Between Madison and Park aves. 33 E 60th St 10022. **Hours:** noon-2 & 5:30-10 pm, Sat from 5:30 pm. Closed major holidays; also Sun. **Reservations:** suggested. **Features:** The chef of the new Midtown seafood restaurant knows what he's doing after years at another Midtown seafood institution. Meat is offered, but prices make the seafood dishes most appealing. Semi-formal attire; cocktails. **Parking:** no self-parking. **Cards:** AX, DC, MC, VI.

ROCK CENTER CAFE   Lunch: $15-$25   Dinner: $17-$25   Phone: 212/332-7620   66
American   **Location:** On concourse level, at Rockefeller Center Skating Rink; between 5th and 6th (Ave of the Americas) aves. 20 W 50th 10020. **Hours:** 11:30 am-10 pm, Sat & Sun 11 am-9 pm. **Reservations:** suggested. **Features:** A bright, simply done dining room of beige looks directly at the Rockefeller Center Fountain year-round and the skating rink in winter. A collection of original Andy Warhol lithographs hang above the bar, adding vibrant color. The menu consists of pasta dishes, cioppino, veal chops, roast chicken, fish and steak. A more modest and limited menu is presented at lunch. Casual dress; cocktails. **Parking:** no self-parking. **Cards:** AX, CB, DC, DS, JC, MC, VI.

ROSA MEXICANO   Lunch: $10-$18   Dinner: $17-$27   Phone: 212/977-7700   213
Mexican   **Location:** At 62nd St. 61 Columbus Ave 10023. **Hours:** noon-3 & 5-11:30 pm, Sun & Mon-10:30 pm. Closed: 11/25. **Reservations:** suggested. **Features:** The space is wide open and handsome with sophisticated, comfortable decor and a water wall falling over high diving figures. Meals usually start with the renowned guacamole, prepared tableside from fresh avacados, onion and cilantro. The menu, rich with unusual flavor pairings which please, isn't typical, but refined with dishes like spicy mahi mahi seviche, wild mushroom tamale with an intense mole, or tender aromatic lamb shank braised in banana and avacado leaves. Dressy casual; cocktails. **Parking:** no self-parking. **Cards:** AX, DC, DS, MC, VI.

SAIGON GRILL   Lunch: $5-$6   Dinner: $7-$14   Phone: 212/996-4600
Vietnamese   **Location:** At 88th St. 1700 2nd Ave 10128. **Hours:** 11:30 am-11:30 pm. Closed: 11/25. **Features:** Food that delivers on flavor and spice is served in a space perfect for a casual meal out with the kids. Each dish on the large menu is thoroughly and mouthwateringly described, making it easy to pick dishes to suit any palate. Basil beef, prawns with sate sauce, curry salmon and grilled pork chop with lemongrass are among choices. Portions are ample. Casual dress; beer & wine only. **Parking:** no self-parking. **Cards:** AX, DC, MC, VI.

(See map and index starting on p. 364)

SAN DOMENICO   **Lunch:** $17-$20   **Dinner:** $19-$30   **Phone:** 212/265-5959   ⑥¹
AAA
▼▼ ▼▼
   Italian

Location: W 59th St, between Broadway and 7th Ave. 240 Central Park S 10019. **Hours:** noon-2:30 & 5:30-11 pm, Sat 5 pm-11:30 pm, Sun 5 pm-10 pm. Closed: 1/1, 11/25, 12/25. **Reservations:** suggested. **Features:** A seasonal art collection enhances the sophisticated, contemporary dining room. The building was designed by Italian architects and constructed of Italian materials. Risotto parmigiano with beef glaze is an outstanding choice, and the soft, egg-yolk-filled ravioli in truffle butter is a popular signature dish. Service is relaxed though professional. Semi-formal attire; cocktails. **Parking:** no self-parking. **Cards:** AX, CB, DC, MC, VI.

SAN MARTIN RESTAURANT   **Lunch:** $11-$21   **Dinner:** $14-$24   **Phone:** 212/832-0888   ⑨⁰
AAA
▼▼▼▼
   Italian

Location: Between Lexington and 3rd aves. 143 E 49th St 10017. **Hours:** noon-midnight. **Reservations:** suggested. **Features:** Patrons visit the pleasant Italian stop for a traditional meal without any pomp or circumstance. Specialty dishes please regular guests who come for penne pasta with porcini mushrooms, sun-dried tomatoes, green peas in cream sauce, rosemary-scented baby lamb chops or porcini mushroom ravioli with gorgonzola walnut sauce. The mood is all-around casual and friendly. Casual dress; cocktails. **Parking:** no self-parking. **Cards:** AX, DC, DS, MC, VI.

SARABETH'S   **Lunch:** $8-$12   **Dinner:** $12-$20   **Phone:** 212/496-6280   ⑪⁵
▼▼▼
   American

Location: Between 80th and 81st sts. 423 Amsterdam Ave 10024. **Hours:** 8 am-10:30 pm, Fri-11 pm, Sat 8 am-4 & 5:30-11 pm, Sun 8 am-4 & 5:30-9:30 pm. Closed: 12/25. **Reservations:** accepted, for dinner. **Features:** Menu offerings include goldi lox, which blends smoked salmon and cream cheese; pumpkin waffles; and Popeye eggs, which are served on homemade English muffins. The homelike atmosphere is reminiscent of a country inn. Baked goods are delicious. Casual dress; cocktails. **Parking:** no self-parking. **Cards:** AX, DC, MC, VI.

SARDI'S   Classic   **Lunch:** $14-$24   **Dinner:** $19-$30   **Phone:** 212/221-8440   ⑨⁷
▼▼▼
   Continental

Location: Between Broadway and 8th Ave. 234 W 44th St 10036. **Hours:** 11:30 am-12:30 am, Fri & Sat-1 am, Sun noon-8 pm. Closed: Mon. **Reservations:** suggested. **Features:** A New York institution, located deep in the theatre district, known for the signed caricatures of famous faces which fill the walls. Professional waiters wait in bright red jackets and black tie to tend to you. Come ready for a dose of nostalgia. Its administered as soon as you walk into the dining room. Cannelloni au gratin, shrimp sardi, and crab cakes are old time favorites. Prix fixe pre-theater dinner available. Casual dress; cocktails. **Parking:** no self-parking. **Cards:** AX, DC, MC, VI.

THE SEA GRILL   **Lunch:** $19-$28   **Dinner:** $22-$32   **Phone:** 212/332-7610   ⑥⁷
▼▼▼
   Seafood

Location: On concourse level; at Rockefeller Center Skating Rink. 19 W 49th St 10020. **Hours:** 11:30 am-2:30 & 5-9:45 pm, Sat from 5 pm. Closed major holidays; also Sun. **Reservations:** suggested. **Features:** A quick elevator ride brings guests down level with the Rockefeller Center Fountain and skating rink to a lovely dining room of beige and sea blue hues. There is a din of the crowd enjoying fresh seafood, ordered by the piece for create-your-own platters or raw in ceviche, carpaccio or tartare dishes. Appetizers are enlivened with herbs, light vinaigrettes or sauces, and entrees of fresh fish are prepared as diners like. Also on offer are pre-designed entrees. Dressy casual; cocktails. **Parking:** no self-parking. **Cards:** AX, CB, DC, MC, VI.

SHAAN   **Lunch:** $14-$25   **Dinner:** $30-$40   **Phone:** 212/977-8400   ⑱⁸
▼▼▼▼
   Indian

Location: Between 5th and 6th (Ave of the Americas) aves. 57 W 48th St 10020. **Hours:** noon-3 & 5:30-11 pm. **Reservations:** accepted. **Features:** The vast menu includes many selections prepared in the tandoori oven. Lavish decorating lends the dining room an upscale feel and comfy ambience, which is further enhanced on weekends by live sitar music. A daily lunch buffet presents many fine choices. Casual dress; cocktails. **Parking:** no self-parking. **Cards:** AX, DC, MC, VI.

SHUN LEE   **Lunch:** $10-$24   **Dinner:** $12-$26   **Phone:** 212/595-8895   ⑮⁰
▼▼▼▼
   Chinese

Location: Between Columbus Ave and Central Park W. 43 W 65th St 10023. **Hours:** noon-midnight, Sun-10:30 pm. Closed: 11/25. **Reservations:** suggested. **Features:** Across the street from Lincoln Center, the often-packed restaurant is a neighborhood favorite for pre-theater, ballet or opera dinners. The sleek, black dining room, with red-eyed dragons snaking around the perimeter, is abuzz from the crowd, and some seats are tight. However, traditional preparations of Hunan and Szechuan cuisine are the true draw here. There also is a cafe-like dining room, which is chic, trendy and fun with wild animal lights dangling overhead. Dressy casual; cocktails. **Parking:** no self-parking. **Cards:** AX, DC, DS, MC, VI.

SHUN LEE PALACE   **Lunch:** $12-$24   **Dinner:** $14-$39   **Phone:** 212/371-8844   ⑦³
▼▼▼▼
   Chinese

Location: Between Lexington and 3rd aves. 155 E 55th St 10022. **Hours:** noon-11:30 pm, Sun-11 pm. Closed: 11/25. **Reservations:** suggested. **Features:** A gentle ambience—enhanced by subtle lighting, silk lanterns and frosted-glass art—settles over the elegant rooms. The menu of gourmet Szechuan and Cantonese selections lists such excellent, not-to-be-missed selections as sliced duck with fresh ginger, heavenly sea bass and sole with crisp bones. Semi-formal attire; cocktails. **Parking:** no self-parking. **Cards:** AX, DC, MC, VI.

SIAM INN   **Lunch:** $8-$12   **Dinner:** $10-$17   **Phone:** 212/757-4006   ⑨¹
AAA
▼▼▼
   Ethnic

Location: Between W 51st and W 52nd sts. 854 8th Ave 10019. **Hours:** 11:30 am-11 pm, Sat noon-11:30 pm, Sun noon-10:30 pm. Closed major holidays. **Reservations:** suggested. **Features:** Familiar curried, grilled meat, sauteed and noodle dishes are well-prepared and flavorful, taking advantage of the herbs and spices that make the flavors bright and fresh. Presentations are decorative with a delicate touch. Soft and inviting decor, with a rose on each table, is a cut above though still casual. Casual dress; cocktails. **Parking:** no self-parking. **Cards:** AX, CB, DC, MC, VI.

(See map and index starting on p. 364)

SPARK'S STEAK HOUSE   **Lunch:** $25-$38   **Dinner:** $25-$38   **Phone:** 212/687-4855   `208`
Steak & Seafood   **Location:** Between 2nd and 3rd aves. 210 E 46th St 10017. **Hours:** noon-11 pm, Fri & Sat-11:30 pm. Closed major holidays; also Sun. **Reservations:** suggested. **Features:** The pedestrian New York legend serves ample portions in a boisterous atmosphere. Be prepared to wait even with reservations. Dressy casual; cocktails. **Parking:** no self-parking. **Cards:** AX, DC, DS, MC, VI.

SPAZZIA   **Lunch:** $9-$16   **Dinner:** $10-$21   **Phone:** 212/799-0150   `172`
Mediterranean   **Location:** At 77th St. 366 Columbus Ave 10024. **Hours:** 11:30 am-10 pm, Fri-11 pm, Sat 11 am-11 pm, Sun 11 am-10 pm. **Closed:** 11/25, 12/25. **Reservations:** accepted. **Features:** A location near The Museum of Natural History makes this a great lunch stop. Grilled pizzas with mushrooms and truffle oil, goat cheese or steak and onions or more involved dishes such as pan-seared chicken Marsala, Boursin cheese ravioli, scallop risotto and duck confit pappardelle are typical of the relaxed menu. Casual dress; cocktails. **Parking:** no self-parking. **Cards:** AX, DC, MC, VI.

THE STEAKHOUSE AT MONKEY BAR   **Lunch:** $16-$28   **Dinner:** $22-$32   **Phone:** 212/838-2600   `182`
American   **Location:** Between Madison and Park aves. 60 E 54th St 10022. **Hours:** 11:30 am-2:30 & 5:30-11 pm, Fri-11:30 pm, Sat 5:30 pm-11:30 pm, Sun 6 pm-10 pm. **Closed:** 1/1, 12/25. **Reservations:** suggested. **Features:** Black-and-white photographs of yesteryear's stars and rich velvet fabrics evoke '40s Hollywood glamour. Adding whimsy are a monkey mural and monkey figures that hang from chandeliers and hide among the railings, ready to swing into the jungle leaf pattern of plush banquettes. The bar has served the signature penny martini and banana highball since 1936. Well-prepared food deserves no less a mention and has kept this place in peanuts. Live piano music is performed weekdays and jazz on weekends. Dressy casual; cocktails; entertainment. **Parking:** no self-parking. **Cards:** AX, CB, DC, DS, MC, VI.

STEVE'S METRO FISH   **Lunch:** $16-$18   **Dinner:** $21-$28   **Phone:** 212/683-6444   `219`
Seafood   **Location:** Between 5th Ave and Madison. 8 E 36th St 10016. **Hours:** noon-11 pm. **Closed:** 12/24, 12/25; also Sun. **Reservations:** suggested. **Features:** The upstairs dining room is simple but peaceful, the fresh fish being the star of the show. The fish can be broiled, baked or blackened, served Greek or Bouillabaisse-style or one may choose preparations, none complicated, from the menu. Fish oven-baked with plum tomato, onion, garlic and light spices is a house specialty, but baked shrimp Rockefeller and broiled jumbo Guatemala shrimp with seasoned bread crumbs and drawn butter are a few fine choices. Casual dress; cocktails. **Parking:** no self-parking. **Cards:** AX, DC, DS, MC, VI.

SUGIYAMA   **Dinner:** $45-$150   **Phone:** 212/956-0670   `104`
Japanese   **Location:** Between Broadway and 8th Ave. 251 W 55th St 10019. **Hours:** 5:30 pm-11:45 pm. Closed major holidays; also Sun & Mon. **Reservations:** suggested. **Features:** Not the place for the faint of heart, the restaurant welcomes food-lovers for kaiseki meals, in which the chef prepares a multi-course offering of exotic dishes that are lovely to look at. The food—elegant and amazing in range—may include tiny translucent baby eels or a small fried crab to be eaten whole. The point of all eight, 10 or 12 courses is to be highly aware of the beauty and flavor of the food. Here, it is easy. Casual dress; cocktails. **Parking:** no self-parking. **Cards:** AX, DC, MC, VI.

SUSHI SEN-NIN   **Lunch:** $18-$48   **Dinner:** $18-$48   **Phone:** 212/889-2208   `181`
Japanese   **Location:** Between Park and Madison aves. 49 E 34th St 10016. **Hours:** 11:30 am-10 pm, Fri-11 pm, Sat & Sun 4:45 pm-10 pm. **Closed:** 7/4, 11/25, 12/25. **Reservations:** accepted. **Features:** A babbling fish pond and a warm greeting welcome diners to this unassuming store front. Though casual, it is clear sophisticated folks are here to dine on extravagant sushi dishes, ordering special seasonal fish recommended by knowledgeable servers. Put your faith in their hands and expect beautifully presented delicate dishes with spicy sauce accents. The ginger dressing deserves its own mention. The prices may wow you but so will the food and service is very gracious and competent. Casual dress; cocktails. **Parking:** no self-parking. **Cards:** AX, MC, VI.

SUSHI YASUDA   **Lunch:** $18-$29   **Dinner:** $18-$29   **Phone:** 212/972-1001   `119`
Japanese   **Location:** Between 2nd and 3rd aves. 204 E 43rd St 10017. **Hours:** noon-2:15 & 6-10:15 pm, Sat from 6 pm. Closed major holidays; also Sun. **Reservations:** suggested. **Features:** Typically handsome and simple decor makes use of the large space, and beautifully grained blond wood is everywhere the eye looks. The fine sushi restaurant serves quality fresh fish, well cut and tender. Some fish on the list of available options are unusual. Only one hot dish of grilled sea bass or salmon shares menu space with the sushi, sashimi and rolls. Flexible combination platters give diners variety. Dressy casual; cocktails. **Parking:** no self-parking. **Cards:** AX, DC, MC, VI.

SUSHIZEN   **Lunch:** $19-$24   **Dinner:** $19-$31   **Phone:** 212/302-0707   `60`
Japanese   **Location:** Between Broadway and 6th Ave. 108 W 44th St 10036. **Hours:** noon-2:45 & 5:30-10 pm, Sat from 5 pm. **Closed:** Sun. **Reservations:** suggested. **Features:** A relaxed and well-clad clientele squeeze in to the cozy and serene, if loud, dining room to spoil themselves with the freshest fish, beautifully presented on lacquer trays and attractive pottery dishes. Choose your own meal or leave it to the chef's wise discretion. Dressy casual; cocktails. **Parking:** no self-parking. **Cards:** AX, MC, VI.

TAO   **Lunch:** $16-$28   **Dinner:** $16-$28   **Phone:** 212/888-2288   `209`
Asian   **Location:** Between Madison and Park aves. 42 E 58th St 10022. **Hours:** 11:30 am-midnight, Wed-Fri to 1 am, Sat 5 pm-1 am, Sun 5 pm-midnight. **Closed:** 11/25, 12/25. **Reservations:** suggested. **Features:** Massive carved doors lead into a dark, candlelit sanctuary resembling a temple in a lost city deep in the jungle. Towering brick walls with inset statuary, huge lanterns, banners and a giant Buddha sitting before a fish pond are good conversation starters. The large menu provides an exercise in self-control. Squab lettuce wraps, dragon-tail spare ribs, miso-glazed sea bass, Mongolian filet mignon and Hong Kong XO shrimp are a sample. Offering price fixed lunch January through November at $20.04. Dressy casual; cocktails. **Parking:** no self-parking. **Cards:** AX, DC, MC, VI.

(See map and index starting on p. 364)

TAVERN ON THE GREEN   Lunch: $15-$32   Dinner: $18-$39   Phone: 212/873-3200   216
▼▼▼▼   **Location:** Central Park at W 67th St 10023. **Hours:** 11:30 am-3:30 & 5-11 pm, Fri-11:30 pm, Sat 10 am-3:45 & 5-11:30 pm, Sun 10 am-3:45 & 5-11 pm. **Reservations:** suggested. **Features:** One of New York's most enchanting dining rooms has visual delights around every corner. Inside and out, flowers are draped, walls are mural-covered, and all is dripping with lights and lanterns, creating a festival for the eyes. Dishes suit just about every taste, but whatever guests order is beside the point. Casual dress; cocktails; entertainment. **Parking:** valet. **Cards:** AX, CB, DC, DS, MC, VI.
American

TERRANCE BRENNANS SEAFOOD &
CHOP HOUSE   Lunch: $12-$39   Dinner: $20-$39   Phone: 212/715-2400   69
▼▼▼▼   **Location:** Between Lexington and 3rd aves; in The Benjamin Hotel. 565 Lexington Ave 10022. **Hours:** 7-10 am, 11:30-2 & 5-10 pm, Sat 8-10:30 am, 11:30-2 & 5-10 pm, Sun 8:30-10:30 am, 11:30-2 & 5-9 pm. **Reservations:** suggested. **Features:** Owner/chef Larry Forgione insists on using only choice American ingredients, which are blended in wonderfully innovative interpretations. Among specialties are cedar-planked salmon and pot-roasted Black Angus short ribs. The dining room and showcase kitchen are sleek and stylish. Dessert is not to be missed, nor is the pastry chef's surprise treat at the end of all meals. Casual dress; cocktails. **Parking:** no self-parking. **Cards:** AX, CB, DC, DS, MC, VI.
Steak & Seafood

TOLEDO RESTAURANT   Lunch: $17-$36   Dinner: $17-$36   Phone: 212/696-5036   117
▼▽▽▼   **Location:** Between 5th and Madison aves. 6 E 36th St 10016. **Hours:** noon-10:30 pm, Fri & Sat-11 pm. Closed major holidays; also Sun. **Reservations:** suggested. **Features:** Gracious, attentive service is as pleasant as the handsome room, which displays distinguished still-life paintings softly lit by sconces and a skylight. The menu lists seafood and meats, served with colorful herbs, garlicky sauces and yellow rice. Pitchers of fruit-filled sangria look irresistible. Dishes are brought to the table and served in the traditional style, and then the dessert cart comes by for the finale. Dressy casual; cocktails. **Parking:** no self-parking. **Cards:** AX, DC, DS, MC, VI.
Spanish

TOWN   Lunch: $20   Dinner: $22-$36   Phone: 212/582-4445   210
▼▽▽▼   **Location:** Between 5th and 6th (Ave of the Amercias) aves. 15 W 56th St 10019. **Hours:** 7 am-10:30, noon-2 & 5:30-10:30 pm, Fri & Sat-11 pm, Sun 11 am-2 & 5:30-9:15 pm. Closed: 1/1. **Reservations:** suggested. **Features:** The contemporary dining room is a looker, with soft, neutral colors, fine fabric, wood-veneer walls and a glass waterfall. Diners dress the part and fit right in. Skillfully conceived and carried out, dishes are modern themselves and devilishly good. The upstairs bar overlooks the dining room and has a small but intriguing menu of its own. Dressy casual; cocktails. **Parking:** no self-parking. **Cards:** AX, MC, VI.
American

TRATTORIA DELL'ARTE   Lunch: $16-$28   Dinner: $16-$28   Phone: 212/245-9800   189
▽▽▽ ▽▽▽   **Location:** Between 56th and 57th sts. 900 7th Ave 10019. **Hours:** 11:45 am-2:30 & 5-11:30 pm, Sat 11 am-3 & 5-11:30 pm, Sun 11 am-3 & 5-10:30 pm. **Reservations:** suggested. **Features:** Convenient to Carnegie Hall, the whimsical, artsy restaurant bustles with energy. The extensive vegetable and seafood antipasto bar is a great place to start, but from there the decisions get harder. From great thin-crust lobster pizzas to savory pasta dishes, nothing disappoints. In fine weather, many diners prefer to take a seat on the sidewalk patio. Dressy casual; cocktails. **Parking:** no self-parking. **Cards:** AX, DC, DS, MC, VI.
Northern
Italian

UNCLE NICK'S GREEK CUISINE   Lunch: $8-$10   Dinner: $10-$25   Phone: 212/245-7992   131
▽▽▽   **Location:** Between 50th and 51st sts. 747 9th Ave 10019. **Hours:** noon-11 pm. Closed: 1/1, 12/25. **Reservations:** accepted. **Features:** Quick, no-nonsense Greek cuisine—such as spanakopita, moussaka, kebabs, gyros and monumental salads meant for sharing—is served by a casual clan of staff members. This is a great place to bring children. The tapas dinner menu at the sister restaurant next door is an option, but appetizer variety is plentiful here, too. Casual dress; cocktails. **Parking:** no self-parking. **Cards:** AX, DC, DS, MC, VI.
Greek

VATAN   Dinner: $22   Phone: 212/689-5666   161
▽▽▽ ▽▽   **Location:** Between 28th and 29th sts. 409 3rd Ave 10016. **Hours:** 5:30 pm-9 pm, Fri & Sat-10:30 pm. Closed: Mon. **Reservations:** required. **Features:** There are few like this restaurant in New York. Diners get the sense of being seated in a rural, idyllic Indian village with a leafy tree, village well, thatched-roof huts, fancy doorways and colorful mural scenes. The menu exists only to show what will be served in various courses, but the quantity and level of spice are up to the guest. Aromatic vegetarian dishes, some wonderfully distinctive, provide a brief education in pleasant taste. Casual dress; beer & wine only. **Parking:** on-site. **Cards:** AX, MC, VI.
Indian

VERDERAME RISTORANTE   Lunch: $11-$24   Dinner: $12-$25   Phone: 212/750-1804   218
▽▽▽ ▽▽   **Location:** At 49th St. 883 1st Ave 10022. **Hours:** noon-3 & 5-10:30 pm, Sat & Sun from 5 pm. **Reservations:** accepted. **Features:** Guests won't find red-and-white-checkered tablecloths here. Instead, white linen and a rose bud on each table lend a bit of sweetness to the cozy neighborhood spot. Regular frequent this place for a casual and relaxed meal. Among offerings are veal scaloppine, grilled veal chops with fresh sage, sole oreganata and daily specials, such as orecchiette with broccoli rabe and grilled sweet sausage. Casual dress; cocktails. **Parking:** no self-parking. **Cards:** AX, DC, JC, MC, VI.
Italian

VICTOR'S CAFE 52   Lunch: $8-$19   Dinner: $10-$32   Phone: 212/586-7714   92
▽▽▽ ▽▽   **Location:** Between Broadway and 8th Ave. 236 W 52nd St 10019. **Hours:** noon-midnight, Fri & Sat-1 am. **Reservations:** suggested. **Features:** Wildly colorful wall murals lend energy, boldness and a touch of ethnicity to the upbeat dining room and colorful atrium area. There is no doubt about these Cuban digs when the food arrives—it looks and tastes good. Buttery-soft caramelized plantains, grilled skirt steak with tangy, garlicky chimichurri sauce and, of course, fragrant black beans with fluffy white rice make a lovely meal. Pictures of famous folks who have dined here are on display. Casual dress; cocktails. **Parking:** no self-parking. **Cards:** AX, CB, DC, MC, VI.
Cuban

(See map and index starting on p. 364)

THE VIEW
$\diamond\diamond\diamond$ $\diamond\diamond$
American

Dinner: $25-$55   **Phone:** 212/398-1900 (94)
Location: Between 45th and 46th sts; in Marriott Marquis. 1535 Broadway 10036. **Hours:** 5:30 pm-11 pm, Fri & Sat 5 pm-midnight, Sun 10:30 am-2 & 5:30-11 pm. Closed: Mon. **Reservations:** suggested. **Features:** The city's only revolving rooftop restaurant, The View got its name for obvious reasons. Chilean sea bass and seared veal chop are among appetizing dishes on a menu of creative fare. In addition to being tasty, desserts are showy and fun. Dressy casual; cocktails; entertainment. **Parking:** on-site. **Cards:** AX, DC, DS, MC, VI.
🅜 𝕐 ✕

VIRGIL'S REAL BARBECUE
$\diamond\diamond$
Barbecue

Lunch: $8-$25   **Dinner:** $8-$25   **Phone:** 212/921-9494 (151)
Location: Between Broadway and 6th (Ave of the Americas) Ave. 152 W 44th St 10036. **Hours:** 11:30 am-midnight, Sun & Mon-11 pm. **Reservations:** accepted. **Features:** It's a good thing there are lots of tables because crowds flock here for smoky, meaty, succulent, finger-licking, gooey barbecue ribs, brisket, shrimp and pulled pork, which are served in generous portions with mustard slaw and other sides. Free tea refills might make guests forget they're in New York City. There are no napkins, but towels—clean and dry before the meal and hot and damp after—are plentiful. Service is brisk and friendly. Casual dress; cocktails. **Parking:** no self-parking. **Cards:** AX, DC, DS, MC, VI.
𝕐 ✕

VONG RESTAURANT
$\diamond\diamond\diamond$ $\diamond\diamond$
Thai

Lunch: $20-$35   **Dinner:** $21-$35   **Phone:** 212/486-9592 (108)
Location: Between 2nd and 3rd aves. 200 E 54th St 10022. **Hours:** noon-2:30 & 5:30-11 pm, Sat 5 pm-11:15 pm, Sun 5:30 pm-10 pm. Closed major holidays. **Reservations:** suggested. **Features:** Tiki lights at the entrance welcome guests to a memorable room with fabric-covered walls, a shimmering gold-leaf ceiling, softly whirring fans and nooks nestled in the shadows. An elaborate display of spices hints at the flavor of the food. French accents infuse dishes, including the delicious lobster, with Thai herbs. Foremost, however, is the black plate special: a sampling of five appetizers. The prix fixe lunch is a bargain. Dressy casual; cocktails. **Parking:** no self-parking. **Cards:** AX, DC, MC, VI.
𝕐 ✕

THE WATER CLUB
AAA
$\diamond\diamond\diamond$ $\diamond\diamond$
American

Lunch: $16-$22   **Dinner:** $26-$35   **Phone:** 212/683-3333 (70)
Location: On east end of 23rd St to FDR service road, n. 500 E 30th St 10016. **Hours:** noon-3 & 5:30-10 pm, Fri & Sat-11 pm, Sun 11 am-3 & 5:45-10 pm. **Reservations:** suggested. **Features:** A fresh-looking, nautical-themed dining room with a casually sophisticated air and river views makes this a lovely place to enjoy a seafood meal. Preparations are not complex or cutting-edge creative, but fresh seafood is well-seasoned and sauced and served with tasty side dishes. Prix fixe lunch and dinner are an excellent value. Semi-formal attire; cocktails; entertainment. **Parking:** valet. **Cards:** AX, CB, DC, DS, JC, MC, VI.
🅜 ✕

YUM YUM BANGKOK
$\diamond\diamond$
Thai

Lunch: $7-$10   **Dinner:** $8-$14   **Phone:** 212/262-7244 (51)
Location: Between 45th and 46th sts. 650 9th Ave 10036. **Features:** If you're in the neighborhood and need a quick and savory meal, this most casual store front has a good selection of traditional noodles and currys. The mix and match menu allows diners to select from a list of sauces and a list of meats to create their own dish. Casual dress. **Parking:** no self-parking. **Cards:** AX, MC, VI.
✕

ZARELA
$\diamond\diamond$ $\diamond\diamond$
Mexican

Lunch: $10-$15   **Dinner:** $14-$19   **Phone:** 212/644-6740 (152)
Location: Between 50th and 51st sts. 953 2nd Ave 10022. **Hours:** noon-3 & 5-11 pm, Fri-11:30 pm, Sat 5 pm-11:30 pm, Sun 5 pm-10 pm. Closed major holidays. **Reservations:** suggested. **Features:** Guests who step inside the lively restaurant might feel as though they're inside a pinata. Wild colors and "stuff" are everywhere, live Mexican music is played on the steps for lack of space anywhere else, and the bar is hopping. Creative, well-prepared choices include duck in "tablecloth stainer" sauce, red snapper hash and a killer hanger steak fajita. Black beans with rice and plantains are great side dishes. Traditional Mexican dishes also are listed. Casual dress; cocktails. **Parking:** no self-parking. **Cards:** AX, DC, MC, VI.
𝕐 ✕

ZEN PALATE
$\diamond\diamond$ $\diamond\diamond$
Vegetarian

Lunch: $7-$9   **Dinner:** $11-$18   **Phone:** 212/582-1669 (166)
Location: At 46th St, southwest corner. 663 9th Ave 10036. **Hours:** 11:30 am-11 pm, Sun noon-10:30 pm. Closed: 7/4, 11/25. **Reservations:** suggested, pre-theater. **Features:** The restaurant affords diners a moment of calm in the midst of the Midtown rush. Warm sconce lighting and skylights are among features of the soothing decor. Dishes creatively blend Asian and Western influences. The Key lime pie is satisfying. BYOB. Dressy casual. **Parking:** no self-parking. **Cards:** AX, DC, MC, VI.
✕

The following restaurants have not been evaluated by AAA but are listed for your information only.

GRAY'S PAPAYA
[fyi]

                                            Phone: 212/799-0243
Not evaluated. **Location:** Jct 72nd St. 2090 Broadway 10023. **Features:** The corner counter offers grilled hot dogs and fresh tropical juice.

GRAY'S PAPAYA
[fyi]

                                            Phone: 212/260-3532
Not evaluated. **Location:** Jct 8th St. 402 Ave of the Americas 10011. **Features:** The corner counter offers grilled hot dogs and fresh tropical juice.

ISTANA
[fyi]

                                            Phone: 212/303-6032
Not evaluated. **Location:** Between 50th and 51st (valet parking access on 50th); in The New York Palace. 455 Madison Ave 10022. **Features:** Casually elegant restaurant offering Mediterranean cuisine. Open for breakfast, lunch and dinner.
𝕐

JOHN'S PIZZERIA EAST
[fyi]

                                            Phone: 212/935-2895
Not evaluated. **Location:** Between 1st and York aves. 408 E 64th St 10021. **Features:** First established in 1929 and now with four New York City locations. Famous for their thin crust pizza.

(See map and index starting on p. 364)

L'IMPERO
[fyi] Not evaluated. **Location:** Between 42nd and 43rd sts. 95 Tudor City Pl 10017. **Features:** People are talking about this newcomer from star chef Scott Conant. The menu successfully delivers sophisticated high Italian dishes.

Phone: 212/599-5045

OSTERIA DEL CIRCO
[fyi] Not evaluated. **Location:** Between 6th (Ave of the Americas) and 7th aves. 120 W 55th St 10019. **Features:** Whimsy takes on new meaning at the fantastical eatery, which is devoted to the fun of fine dining. The circus atmosphere is serious, and so is the food, which can be pizza or the signature brick-pressed chicken, but it generally reflects Tuscan sensibilities.

Phone: 212/265-3636

OUEST
[fyi] Not evaluated. **Location:** Between 83rd and 84th sts. 2315 Broadway. **Features:** Open only for dinner, this popular restaurant offers a new twist on American cooking.

Phone: 212/580-8700

OYSTER BAR
[fyi] Not evaluated. **Location:** Lower level of Grand Central Station. 42nd St 10017. **Features:** The extensive seafood menu includes more than 50 kinds of fresh fish.

Phone: 212/490-6650

PASHA
[fyi] Not evaluated. **Location:** Between Columbus Ave and Central Park W. 70 W 71st St. **Features:** Locals are loyal to this jewel-red Turkish delight, where fragrant and flavorful dishes are prepared by a chef who knows flavor. The selection of appetizers shouldn't be bypassed, notably manti, a tender steamed dumpling filled with ground lamb and fresh mint drizzled with a light garlic yogurt sauce. Lamb dishes, especially those with eggplant in the mix, are a standout. A prix fixe menu and outdoor sidewalk seating are available.

Phone: 212/579-8751

RUBY FOO'S DIM SUM & SUSHI PALACE
[fyi] Not evaluated. **Location:** At 77th St. 2182 Broadway. **Features:** A work of Asian art in itself, serving a lot of delightful sushi and also dishes such as green curry chicken with eggplant, basil-crusted salmon, and 7-flavor beef in a sprawling 3-story space with eye catching over-the-top Asian decor.

Phone: 212/724-6700

UPPER MANHATTAN

———— WHERE TO STAY ————

THE FRANKLIN HOTEL
♦♦ ♦♦ All Year [CP] 1P: $259-$299 2P: $259-$299 XP: $20 F12
Phone: (212)369-1000
Small-scale Hotel **Location:** Between 3rd and Lexington aves. 164 E 87th St 10128. Fax: 212/369-8000. **Facility:** 48 one-bedroom standard units. 9 stories, interior corridors. **Parking:** on-site (fee). **Amenities:** CD players, dual phone lines, voice mail, safes, hair dryers. **Guest Services:** valet laundry. **Business Services:** fax (fee). **Cards:** AX, DC, DS, JC, MC, VI.

SOME UNITS
(ASK) (S/D) (Y|→) (🛉🛉) (VCR) (🖐) (DATA PORT) (🗙) (🖥) /
FEE

HOTEL NEWTON
[AAA] [SAVE] *Book at aaa.com*
♦♦ ♦♦ All Year 1P: $99-$160 2P: $109-$175 XP: $15 F16
Small-scale Hotel **Location:** Between 94th and 95th sts. 2528 Broadway 10025. Fax: 212/678-6758. **Facility:** 110 units. 90 one-bedroom standard units. 20 one-bedroom suites. 9 stories, interior corridors. *Bath:* combo or shower only. **Parking:** on-site (fee). **Terms:** cancellation fee imposed. **Amenities:** voice mail, irons, hair dryers. **Cards:** AX, DC, DS, MC, VI. **Special Amenities:** preferred room (subject to availability with advanced reservations). *(See color ad below)*

Phone: (212)678-6500

SOME UNITS
(S/D) (Y|→) (🌀) / (🗙) (🖥) (🖥) /
FEE FEE

HOTEL WALES *Book at aaa.com*
▽▽▽▽

Phone: (212)876-6000

| 1/1-4/30 | | 2P: $249-$745 | XP: $20 | F17 |
| 7/1-8/31 | | 2P: $239-$450 | XP: $20 | F17 |

Historic
Small-scale Hotel

Location: Between 92 E and 93 E sts. 1295 Madison Ave 10128. **Fax:** 212/860-7000. **Facility:** This historic hotel retains its charm with carved wood trim, renovated baths in pre-War style, and a parlor featuring a harpist in the afternoon. 87 units. 85 one-bedroom standard units, some with efficiencies. 2 one-bedroom suites. 10 stories, interior corridors. *Bath:* combo or shower only. **Parking:** valet. **Terms:** open 7/1-8/31 & 1/1-4/30, cancellation fee imposed, small pets only ($75 deposit). **Amenities:** video library, CD players, dual phone lines, voice mail, safes, hair dryers. *Some:* irons. **Leisure Activities:** Fee: massage. **Guest Services:** valet laundry. **Business Services:** meeting rooms, business center. **Cards:** AX, DC, DS, JC, MC, VI.

SOME UNITS

(ASK) (S⊂) (🐾) (🍴) (⊘) (♿) (VCR) (☂) (DATA PORT) / (✕) (🛡) (🖥) /
    FEE   FEE

---------- **WHERE TO DINE** ----------

LEMONGRASS GRILL
▽▽ ▽▽

| **Lunch:** $6-$9 | **Dinner:** $6-$14 | Phone: 212/666-0888 |

Thai

Location: Between 94th and 95th sts. 2534 Broadway 10025. **Hours:** noon-11 pm, Fri & Sat-midnight, Sun 1 pm-11 pm. Closed: 11/25. **Features:** Pleasant ethnic music, Asian lanterns, ceiling fans and bamboo accents gently put diners in the Thai frame of mind. Representative of sumptuous choices are zesty chicken and lemongrass soup, grilled beef salad with lime-chili-mint dressing, vibrant, flavorful rich curries with coconut milk, grilled lemongrass pork chops, deep-fried duck with tamarind sauce, noodles of all sorts and many other fish, duck, seafood, meat and vegetarian selections. Locations are citywide. Casual dress; cocktails. **Parking:** no self-parking. **Cards:** AX, MC, VI.

(✕)

SAIGON GRILL
▽▽

| **Lunch:** $4-$8 | **Dinner:** $7-$14 | Phone: 212/875-9072 |

Vietnamese

Location: Corner of 90th St. 620 Amsterdam Ave 10024. **Hours:** 11 am-midnight. Closed: 11/25. **Features:** A formidable menu offers unusual and familiar dishes, each replete with vibrant flavor and colors. Fragrant seasonings perfume the air, and you'll find your head turning as dishes go by. Red curries, spicy soup and seafood dishes are excellent, and the grilled pork chop marinated in lemon grass is a must. Casual dress; beer only. **Parking:** street. **Cards:** AX, DC, DS, MC, VI.

(✕)

SARABETH'S
▽▽ ▽▽

| **Lunch:** $8-$15 | **Dinner:** $16-$25 | Phone: 212/410-7335 |

American

Location: At E 92nd St; on the Upper East Side. 1295 Madison Ave 10128. **Hours:** 8 am-3:30 & 5:30-10:30 pm, Sun-9:30 pm; afternoon tea 3:30 pm-5:30 pm. Closed: 12/25. **Reservations:** accepted. **Features:** Crowded with "ladies who lunch" and their well-heeled offspring, Sarabeth's became famous first for her sweet preserves, and now also for creative egg and brunch dishes, homemade granola, and of course cookies and milk. Casual dress; cocktails. **Parking:** no self-parking. **Cards:** AX, DC, MC, VI.

(✕)

YORK GRILL
▽▽ ▽▽

| **Dinner:** $15-$23 | Phone: 212/772-0261 |

American

Location: Between 88th and 89th aves. 1690 York Ave 10128. **Hours:** 4 pm-11:30 pm. Closed: 12/25. **Reservations:** accepted. **Features:** A neighborhood go-to spot for a nice yet casual evening out for a good meal. Decor is vibrant with yellows and blues and a wall-sized mural of a crowd having fun. Food is creative American with flavorful seasonings and sauces. A very comfortable bar area is also a local draw. Casual dress; cocktails. **Parking:** no self-parking. **Cards:** AX, DC, MC, VI.

(Ⴤ) (✕)

---------- *The following restaurants have not been evaluated by AAA but are listed for your information only.* ----------

AIX
(fyi)

Phone: 212/874-7400

Not evaluated. **Location:** At 88th St. 2398 Broadway 10024. **Features:** The restaurant offers guests innovative French cuisine in a truly elegant setting.

BARNEY'S GREENGRASS
(fyi)

Phone: 212/724-4707

Not evaluated. **Location:** Upper West Side, by 86th and 87th sts. 541 Amsterdam Ave 10024. **Features:** Since 1908, the "sturgeon king" has offered varieties of smoked fish including sable, lob, nova, and pickled herring. A popular breakfast spot, it serves eggs and bagels, as well deli sandwiches and salad. Very popular, so a wait can be expected. No credit cards accepted.

BRONX pop. 1,332,650

——— WHERE TO STAY ———

ECONO LODGE
(AAA) (SAVE)
▼▼▼▼
Small-scale Hotel

Book at aaa.com
All Year [CP]   1P: $95-$150   2P: $110-$175
Location: I-95, exit 13 northbound, just s on Tillotson Ave; southbound, e over bridge, then s on Tillotson Ave. 1000 Baychester Ave 10475. Fax: 718/862-3090. **Facility:** 40 one-bedroom standard units, some with whirlpools. 2 stories, interior corridors. **Parking:** on-site. **Terms:** cancellation fee imposed. **Amenities:** voice mail, hair dryers. **Business Services:** fax (fee). **Cards:** AX, CB, DC, DS, MC, VI. **Special Amenities:** free continental breakfast.

Phone: (718)862-2000

SOME UNITS
(S) (D) (✦) (DATA PORT) / (✕) (�) /

BROOKLYN pop. 2,465,326   (See map and index starting on p. 373)

——— WHERE TO STAY ———

AVENUE PLAZA HOTEL
▼▼▼▼
Small-scale Hotel

All Year   1P: $149-$169   2P: $149-$169   XP: $20
Location: Belt Pkwy W, exit 7N to Ocean Pkwy, 3.4 mi n on 18th Ave, 0.4 mi w to 47th, then 0.7 mi n. 4624 13th Ave 11219. Fax: 718/552-3201. **Facility:** Smoke free premises. 52 units. 51 one-bedroom standard units. 1 one-bedroom suite ($290-$449) with whirlpool. 8 stories, interior corridors. *Bath:* combo or shower only. **Parking:** on-site. **Terms:** [BP] meal plan available. **Amenities:** voice mail, safes, irons, hair dryers. **Guest Services:** valet laundry. **Business Services:** meeting rooms, fax (fee). **Cards:** AX, DC, MC, VI.

Phone: 718/552-3200   159
                             F5

(ASK) (¶) (⟨) (✕) (DATA PORT) (■) (▣)

BED & BREAKFAST ON THE PARK
▼▼▼▼
Historic Bed
& Breakfast

All Year   2P: $125-$195   XP: $35
Location: Between 6th and 7th sts. Located opposite Prospect Park. 113 Prospect Park W 11215. Fax: 718/499-1385. **Facility:** This opulent Victorian brownstone features stained-glass windows and abundant artwork. Smoke free premises. 7 units. 6 one- and 1 two-bedroom standard units. 4 stories (no elevator), interior corridors. *Bath:* some shared or private, combo or shower only. **Parking:** street. **Terms:** 2 night minimum stay, 11 day cancellation notice. **Amenities:** voice mail, hair dryers. **Cards:** AX, MC, VI.

Phone: 718/499-6115   158
                             F6

SOME UNITS
(✕) / (VCR) /

BEST WESTERN GREGORY HOTEL
(AAA) (SAVE)
▼▼▼▼
Small-scale Hotel

Book at aaa.com
5/1-11/15 [ECP]   1P: $179-$189   2P: $185-$189   XP: $10   F18
11/16-12/31 [ECP]   1P: $175-$189   2P: $179-$189   XP: $10   F18
1/1-4/30 [ECP]   1P: $165-$179   2P: $169-$189   XP: $10   F18
Location: I-278 (Brooklyn-Queens Expwy), exit 86th St southbound; exit 92nd St northbound, w to 4th Ave, then 0.4 mi n; between 83rd and 84th sts. Located in a commercial area. 8315 4th Ave 11209. Fax: 718/680-0827. **Facility:** 70 units. 64 one-bedroom standard units. 6 one-bedroom suites ($259-$299), some with whirlpools. 4 stories, interior corridors. *Bath:* combo or shower only. **Parking:** valet. **Terms:** cancellation fee imposed. **Amenities:** video games (fee), voice mail, safes, irons, hair dryers. **Guest Services:** valet laundry. **Business Services:** meeting rooms, fax (fee). **Cards:** AX, DC, DS, JC, MC, VI. *(See color ad below)*

Phone: (718)238-3737   157

SOME UNITS
(S) (D) (⟨) (🐕) (✦) (DATA PORT) (■) / (✕) (■) (▣) /

(See map and index starting on p. 373)

NEW YORK MARRIOTT AT THE BROOKLYN BRIDGE   *Book at aaa.com*   Phone: 718/246-7000   156

(AAA) (SAVE)
▽▽▽▽▽▽

Large-scale Hotel

All Year   1P: $239-$319   2P: $239-$319
Location: I-278 (Brooklyn-Queens Expwy), exit Tillary St, just s, then just e. 333 Adams St 11201. Fax: 718/246-0563. **Facility:** 376 units. 362 one-bedroom standard units. 12 one- and 2 two-bedroom suites ($399-$499). 7 stories, interior corridors. *Bath:* combo or shower only. **Parking:** on-site (fee) and valet. **Terms:** check-in 4 pm, [BP] meal plan available, package plans. **Amenities:** dual phone lines, voice mail, safes, honor bars, irons, hair dryers. *Fee:* video games, high-speed Internet. **Dining:** 6:30 am-midnight, cocktails. **Pool(s):** heated indoor. **Leisure Activities:** whirlpool. **Guest Services:** gift shop, valet laundry. **Business Services:** conference facilities, business center. **Cards:** AX, CB, DC, DS, JC, MC, VI.

SOME UNITS

⊟ 🍴 🛎 ㊎ ✉ 📷 🏊 ✈ 🐾 😊 DATA PORT 💻 / ✕ VCR 🔌 /
FEE

─── WHERE TO DINE ───

AUNT SUZIE'S RESTAURANT   Dinner: $9-$15   Phone: 718/788-2868   215
▽▽ ▽▽

South Italian

Location: Between Carroll St and Garfield Pl. 247 5th Ave 11215. **Hours:** 5 pm-10:30 pm, Fri & Sat-11:30 pm. Closed: 11/25, 12/25. **Features:** The neighborhood restaurant delivers one of the best bargains in the metro area, with its enormous portions of hearty, reasonably priced food. The tasty penne is served in a rich, satisfying pink sauce studded with dried tomatoes and peppercorns. Pasta or salad comes with most entrees. Casual dress; beer & wine only. **Parking:** street. **Cards:** MC, VI.   ✕

BLUE RIBBON BROOKLYN   Dinner: $13-$36   Phone: 718/840-0404   204
▽▽ ▽▽▽

American

Location: In Park Slope; between Garfield Pl and 1st St. 280 5th Ave 11215. **Hours:** 6 pm-2 am, Fri-4 am, Sat 4 pm-4 am, Sun noon-midnight. Closed major holidays. **Features:** Comfortable, modern, smart and suitable for well-behaved kids, this restaurant has a menu at once adult yet familiar and homey. The menu goes on and on, making choices difficult but it seems as though you can't go wrong. A long list of varied appetizers from herring in cream sauce and steak tartare to caviar is a schizophrenic marvel. The menu, while comforting with familiar fried chicken, hanger steak and BBQ pulled pork, shows off with skate and roast duck. Delectible refined fun for everyone. Casual dress; cocktails. **Parking:** street. **Cards:** AX, MC, VI.   🛎 ⊟ ✕

BLUE RIBBON SUSHI   Dinner: $12-$27   Phone: 718/840-0408   203
▽▽ ▽▽

Japanese

Location: In Park Slope; between Garfield Pl and 1st Ave. 278 Fifth Ave 11215. **Hours:** 5 pm-midnight, Fri & Sat-2 am. Closed: Mon. **Features:** The entrance is soft and candlelit but the dining room, with blue painted cement walls, dark grain wood benches and boothes, rafter ceilings and overall hip design, is colder. A large appetizer and salad selection, like warm broiled wild mushrooms with tamari butter, offer satisfaction while the large, mainly sushi and sashimi menu, with a few hot-broiled entrees, is varied with specific Pacific and Atlantic selections. The crowd and the especially eager-to-please service warm this place up. Casual dress; beer & wine only. **Parking:** street. **Cards:** AX, MC, VI.   ✕

GAGE AND TOLLNER   Lunch: $12-$25   Dinner: $14-$29   Phone: 718/875-5181   206
▽▽ ▽▽▽

Seafood

Location: On Fulton Pedestrian Mall, between Red Hook Ln and Boerum Pl. 372 Fulton St 11201. **Hours:** 11:30 am-3:30 & 4:30-11 pm, Fri from 4:30 pm, Sat from 3:30 pm. Closed: 12/25; also Sun. **Reservations:** suggested. **Features:** Opened in 1880, the venerable restaurant was host to Diamond Jim Brady, Lillian Russell and other socials. Recently restored to Victorian grace are the polished mahogany, red brocade walls, large arched mirrors and original gas lights. Among classic dishes are seafood and lobster Newburg, fried or broiled soft clam bellies, pan-roasted oysters in sherry cream and crabmeat Virginia with delicate garlic bread crumbs and beurre blanc sauce. Service is old-fashioned, in a good way. Casual dress; cocktails. **Parking:** valet. **Cards:** AX, DC, DS, MC, VI.   ⊟ ✕

GRIMALDI'S PIZZERIA   Lunch: $12-$18   Dinner: $12-$18   Phone: 718/858-4300   214
▽▽

American

Location: Between Water and Front sts; adjacent to base of Brooklyn Bridge. 19 Old Fulton St 11201. **Hours:** 11:30 am-11 pm, Fri-midnight, Sat noon-midnight, Sun noon-11 pm. Closed: 3/27, 11/25, 12/25. **Features:** Although the lively, tightly packed restaurant serves calzones, antipasto and pasta, it is known for great brick-oven pizzas. There are no salads, and only one starter is served. The dessert menu tempts with such selections as cannoli, spumoni, tortoni and tartufo. Casual dress; beer & wine only. **Parking:** no self-parking.   ✕

OCEAN VIEW CAFE   Lunch: $5-$12   Dinner: $7-$15   Phone: 718/332-1900   201
▽▽

Russian

Location: Corner of 3rd and Brighton St. 290 Brighton Beach Ave 11235. **Hours:** 10 am-10 pm, Sat-11:30 pm. Closed: Yom Kippur. **Reservations:** accepted. **Features:** The small storefront is casual and frequently busy, serving Russian dishes to locals who come for richly flavored Ukrainian borscht with garlic popovers, herring with potato, stuffed cabbage, beef stew, a variety of blintzes and truly terrific potato vareniki with onion. Casual dress; beer & wine only. **Parking:** no self-parking. **Cards:** AX, DS, MC, VI.   ✕

PETER LUGER'S   Lunch: $15-$30   Dinner: $45-$55   Phone: 718/387-7400   202
▽▽ ▽▽

Steak House

Location: From Manhattan, outside lane of Williamsburg Bridge, 1st exit, then sharp right. 178 Broadway 11211. **Hours:** 11:45 am-9:45 pm, Fri & Sat-10:45 pm, Sun & major holidays 1 pm-9:45 pm. **Reservations:** suggested. **Features:** A star-studded dining room filled with business professionals hungry for dry-aged prime porterhouse steaks attests to the reputation for excellence that has been the restaurant's hallmark for decades. A tomato and onion salad and side dishes of creamed spinach and potatoes are most typically ordered. The rustic, old dining rooms—with bulky wood tables, plank wood floors, pressed-tin ceilings and little else to distract from dinner—are classic Brooklyn, classic Peter Luger's. Casual dress; cocktails. **Parking:** on-site.   ⊟ ✕

(See map and index starting on p. 373)

RIVER CAFE   **Lunch:** $18-$30   **Dinner:** $70   **Phone:** 718/522-5200   198

American

Location: At base of Brooklyn Bridge. 1 Water St 11201. **Hours:** noon-3 & 5:30-11 pm, Sun 11:30 am-2:30 & 6-11 pm. **Reservations:** required, for dinner. **Features:** At the base of the Brooklyn Bridge, a cobblestone drive leads to a wall festooned with flowers in warmer months and to the fragrant garden entrance of the floating restaurant. Walk over an enclosed gangplank to a lovely flower-filled dining room with a spectacular Manhattan view. A glance at the menu reveals such seafood choices as clams, oyster stew, tuna carpaccio, lump crab cakes and other excellent preparations. Semi-formal attire; cocktails. **Parking:** valet. **Cards:** AX, DC, DS, JC, MC, VI.

TOMMASO'S   **Lunch:** $8-$27 ·   **Dinner:** $8-$27   **Phone:** 718/236-9883   216

Italian

Location: Belt Pkwy, exit 4 (Bay 8th St), 0.6 mi ne. 1464 86th St 11228. **Hours:** noon-midnight, Sun 1 pm-10 pm. Closed: 12/25. **Reservations:** suggested. **Features:** A relaxed and mildly sophisticated mood pervades the friendly neighborhood restaurant. The menu lists traditional pasta, chicken and fish dishes, as well as well-prepared quail, veal and lamb. An assortment of cold antipasto is displayed to awaken the appetite. Casual dress; cocktails. **Parking:** valet. **Cards:** AX, DC, MC, VI.

The following restaurants have not been evaluated by AAA but are listed for your information only.

AL DI LA   **Phone:** 718/783-4565

[fyi]   Not evaluated. **Location:** In Park Slope; at Carroll St. 248 Fifth Ave 11215. **Features:** In a neighborhood experiencing a restaurant rebirth, the small jewel is popular for reliably excellent food. Dishes are fresh, and flavors distinctly scrumptious. The daily changing menu keeps patrons returning.

LA BOUILLABAISE   **Phone:** 718/522-8275

[fyi]   Not evaluated. **Location:** 145 Atlantic Ave 11201. **Features:** The cozy, casual restaurant serves French fare.

QUEENS pop. 2,229,379   (See map and index starting on p. 373)

—— WHERE TO STAY ——

ADRIA HOTEL AND CONFERENCE CENTER   **Phone:** (718)631-5900   236

All Year   1P: $129-$159   2P: $139-$169   XP: $10   F12

Small-scale Hotel

Location: In Bayside; Cross Island Pkwy, exit 31W (SR 25A). 220-33 Northern Blvd 11361. Fax: 718/279-9080. **Facility:** 57 one-bedroom standard units. 4 stories, interior corridors. **Parking:** on-site. **Terms:** [ECP] meal plan available. **Amenities:** voice mail, irons, hair dryers. **Guest Services:** valet laundry. **Business Services:** meeting rooms, fax (fee). **Cards:** AX, CB, DC, DS, MC, VI. **Special Amenities:** free continental breakfast and free newspaper.

SOME UNITS

ANCHOR MOTOR INN   *Book at aaa.com*   **Phone:** (718)428-8000   238

All Year [CP]   1P: $124-$159   2P: $124-$164   XP: $10   F18

Small-scale Hotel

Location: In Bayside; 0.8 mi w of Cross Island Pkwy, exit 31 W. 215-34 Northern Blvd SR 25A 11361. Fax: 718/428-7001. **Facility:** 66 one-bedroom standard units, some with efficiencies and/or whirlpools. 2 stories, interior corridors. **Parking:** on-site. **Terms:** weekly rates available. **Amenities:** video library (fee), voice mail, safes, hair dryers. *Some:* irons. **Guest Services:** valet laundry. **Business Services:** fax (fee). **Cards:** AX, CB, DC, DS, MC, VI. **Special Amenities:** free continental breakfast and free room upgrade **(subject to availability with advanced reservations).** *(See color ad below)*

SOME UNITS

(See map and index starting on p. 373)

BEST WESTERN CITY VIEW *Book at aaa.com* Phone: (718)392-8400 **248**
[AAA] [SAVE] All Year 1P: $149-$179 2P: $149-$179 XP: $12 F12
[WWW WWW] **Location:** In Long Island City; Long Island Expwy, exit Greenpoint Ave westbound, just s; exit Borden Ave eastbound. 33-17 Greenpoint Ave 11101. Fax: 718/392-2110. **Facility:** 71 one-bedroom standard units, some with whirlpools. 5 stories, interior corridors. **Parking:** on-site. **Terms:** weekly rates available. **Amenities:** video library
Small-scale Hotel (fee), irons, hair dryers. **Leisure Activities:** limited exercise equipment. **Guest Services:** valet laundry, airport transportation-La Guardia Airport, area transportation-nearby restaurants. **Business Services:** fax (fee). **Cards:** AX, CB, DC, DS, JC, MC, VI. **Special Amenities:** free continental breakfast and free newspaper. *(See color ad below)*

SOME UNITS
[S/D] [icons] [VCR] [icon] [DATA PORT] [icon] / [X] [icon] /

BEST WESTERN EDEN PARK HOTEL *Book at aaa.com* Phone: (718)699-4500 **244**
[AAA] [SAVE] 5/1-8/22 [CP] 1P: $139-$159 2P: $139-$159 XP: $5 F12
[WWW WWW] 8/23-4/30 [CP] 1P: $129-$149 2P: $129-$149 XP: $5 F12
Location: In Flushing; Grand Central Pkwy, exit 10, just w via north service road for Long Island Expwy; Long Island Expwy, exit 22A eastbound; exit 108th St westbound. 113-10 Horace Harding Expwy 11368. Fax: 718/760-3916.
Small-scale Hotel **Facility:** 74 one-bedroom standard units. 5 stories, interior corridors. **Parking:** on-site. **Terms:** [MAP] meal plan available. **Amenities:** voice mail, irons, hair dryers. **Dining:** 6 am-11 & 6-11 pm, cocktails. **Leisure Activities:** limited exercise equipment. **Guest Services:** valet laundry, airport transportation-John F Kennedy International & La Guardia airports, area transportation-mall & subway. **Business Services:** meeting rooms, fax (fee). **Cards:** AX, CB, DC, DS, MC, VI. **Special Amenities:** free continental breakfast and free local telephone calls. *(See color ad below)*

SOME UNITS
[S/D] [icons] [icon] [icon] [VCR] [icon] [DATA PORT] [icon] / [X] [icon] [icon] /

(See map and index starting on p. 373)

BEST WESTERN KENNEDY AIRPORT   *Book at aaa.com*   Phone: (718)977-2100   233
◆◆ ◆◆
5/1-8/31 [ECP]   1P: $119-$149   2P: $129-$159   XP: $10   F12
9/1-4/30 [ECP]   1P: $109-$139   2P: $119-$149   XP: $10   F12
Small-scale Hotel **Location:** In Jamaica; Van Wyck Expwy S, exit 1E to Belt Pkwy E, exit S Conduit Ave, then just e; Belt Pkwy E, exit 20; Belt Pkwy W, exit 21A, s at 150th Ln, then e on S Conduit Ave. 144-25 153rd Ln 11434. Fax: 718/977-2200.
Facility: 88 one-bedroom standard units, some with whirlpools. 4 stories, interior corridors. *Bath:* combo or shower only.
Parking: on-site. **Terms:** cancellation fee imposed, [CP] meal plan available. **Amenities:** high-speed Internet, voice mail, irons, hair dryers. **Leisure Activities:** limited exercise equipment. **Guest Services:** valet laundry. **Business Services:** fax. **Cards:** AX, CB, DC, DS, JC, MC, VI.

SOME UNITS
(A$K) (S/D) ✈ (&) (▥) (DATA PORT) (⌨) / (⊠) /

BEST WESTERN QUEENS COURT HOTEL   *Book at aaa.com*   Phone: (718)888-1900   222
(AAA) (SAVE)
◆◆ ◆◆
All Year [CP]   1P: $119-$139   2P: $129-$149   XP: $10   F12
Small-scale Hotel **Location:** In Flushing; Grand Central Pkwy s to Northern Blvd E, 1 mi s to Main St, 0.3 mi s to 39th Ave, then just w. 133-51 39th Ave 11354. Fax: 718/888-1141. **Facility:** 59 one-bedroom standard units, some with whirlpools. 8 stories, interior corridors. *Bath:* combo or shower only. **Parking:** no self-parking. **Terms:** cancellation fee imposed. **Amenities:** voice mail, irons, hair dryers. **Guest Services:** valet laundry. **Business Services:** meeting rooms, fax (fee). **Cards:** AX, CB, DC, DS, MC, VI. **Special Amenities:** early check-in/late check-out.

SOME UNITS
(S/D) (¶¶) (&) (▥) (DATA PORT) (⌨) / (⊠) /

CLARION HOTEL AT LA GUARDIA AIRPORT   *Book at aaa.com*   Phone: 718/335-1200   223
(AAA) (SAVE)
◆◆ ◆◆
8/21-12/1 [CP]   1P: $175-$275   2P: $185-$285   XP: $10   F
5/1-8/20 & 4/1-4/30 [CP] 1P: $150-$250   2P: $160-$260   XP: $10   F
12/2-3/31 [CP]   1P: $125-$225   2P: $135-$235   XP: $10   F
Small-scale Hotel **Location:** In East Elmhurst; Grand Central Pkwy, exit 6 (94th St). 9400 Ditmars Blvd 11369. Fax: 718/458-1239. **Facility:** 169 units. 159 one-bedroom standard units. 10 one-bedroom suites ($175-$325), some with whirlpools. 3 stories, interior corridors. *Bath:* combo or shower only. **Parking:** on-site (fee). **Terms:** cancellation fee imposed, package plans. **Amenities:** voice mail, irons, hair dryers. **Dining:** 5 pm-11 pm. **Leisure Activities:** exercise room. **Guest Services:** valet laundry, airport transportation-La Guardia Airport. **Business Services:** meeting rooms, business center. **Cards:** AX, DC, DS, MC, VI.

SOME UNITS
(S/D) ✈ (¶¶) (&) (⊘) (▥) (DATA PORT) / (⊠) (▯) (⌷) /

COMFORT INN AT JFK AIRPORT   *Book at aaa.com*   Phone: (718)977-0001   234
(AAA) (SAVE)
◆◆ ◆◆
5/1-8/31 [ECP]   1P: $109-$139   2P: $119-$149   XP: $10   F12
9/1-4/30 [ECP]   1P: $99-$129   2P: $109-$139   XP: $10   F12
Small-scale Hotel **Location:** In Jamaica; Van Wyck Expwy S to exit 1E to Belt Pkwy E, exit S Conduit Ave, then just e; Belt Pkwy E, exit 20; Belt Pkwy W, exit 21A, s at 150th St, then left on S Conduit Ave. 144-36 153rd Ln 11434. Fax: 718/977-9166. **Facility:** 59 one-bedroom standard units. 4 stories, interior corridors. *Bath:* combo or shower only. **Parking:** on-site. **Terms:** cancellation fee imposed. **Amenities:** voice mail, hair dryers. **Guest Services:** valet laundry, airport transportation-John F Kennedy International Airport. **Business Services:** fax. **Cards:** AX, CB, DC, DS, JC, MC, VI. **Special Amenities:** free expanded continental breakfast and free newspaper.

SOME UNITS
(S/D) ✈ (&) (▥) (DATA PORT) / (⊠) /

COURTYARD BY MARRIOTT JFK AIRPORT   *Book at aaa.com*   Phone: (718)848-2121   224
◆◆ ◆◆
All Year   1P: $99-$399   2P: $99-$399
Small-scale Hotel **Location:** In Jamaica; Van Wyck Expwy, s to exit 2 (Rockaway Blvd), just e to Rockaway Blvd, then just w. 145-11 N Conduit Ave 11436. Fax: 718/848-0888. **Facility:** 166 units. 164 one-bedroom standard units. 2 one-bedroom suites ($299-$499). 14 stories, interior corridors. *Bath:* combo or shower only. **Parking:** valet. **Terms:** [BP] meal plan available, package plans. **Amenities:** video games (fee), dual phone lines, voice mail, irons, hair dryers. **Leisure Activities:** exercise room. **Guest Services:** sundries, valet and coin laundry. **Business Services:** meeting rooms, fax (fee). **Cards:** AX, DC, DS, JC, MC, VI. *(See color ad below)*

SOME UNITS
(A$K) (S/D) ✈ (¶¶) (▼) (&M) (&) (⊘) (▥) (DATA PORT) (▯) (⌨) / (⊠) (⌷) /

(See map and index starting on p. 373)

COURTYARD BY MARRIOTT NEW YORK/ LA GUARDIA AIRPORT   *Book at aaa.com*

Phone: (718)446-4800   **241**

All Year   1P: $89-$259

Location: In East Elmhurst; Grand Central Pkwy, exit 6 (94th St) eastbound; exit 7 westbound, 0.5 mi s on 94th St to 23rd Ave, then just w to 90th St. 90-10 Grand Central Pkwy 11369. Fax: 718/446-5733. **Facility:** 288 units. 283 one-bedroom standard units. 5 one-bedroom suites. 1-6 stories, interior corridors. *Bath:* combo or shower only. **Parking:** on-site (fee). **Terms:** package plans - weekends & seasonal. **Amenities:** high-speed Internet (fee), voice mail, irons, hair dryers. **Pool(s):** outdoor. **Leisure Activities:** whirlpool, exercise room. **Guest Services:** gift shop, valet and coin laundry. **Business Services:** meeting rooms, business center. **Cards:** AX, CB, DC, DS, JC, MC, VI.

Large-scale Hotel

SOME UNITS

CROWNE PLAZA HOTEL AND RESORT LA GUARDIA   *Book at aaa.com*

Phone: (718)457-6300   **245**

All Year   1P: $109-$249   2P: $119-$259   XP: $10   F16

Location: In East Elmhurst; Grand Central Pkwy, exit 7 eastbound to 94th St, then 0.5 mi e; exit 6 (94th St) westbound, 0.5 mi e. 104-04 Ditmars Blvd 11369. Fax: 718/899-9768. **Facility:** 358 units. 342 one-bedroom standard units. 16 one-bedroom suites ($295-$300), some with whirlpools. 7 stories, interior corridors. *Bath:* some combo or shower only. **Parking:** on-site (fee). **Terms:** [BP] & [CP] meal plans available. **Amenities:** video games (fee), CD players, dual phone lines, voice mail, irons, hair dryers. **Pool(s):** heated indoor. **Leisure Activities:** sauna, whirlpool, exercise room. **Guest Services:** gift shop, valet and coin laundry. **Business Services:** conference facilities, business center. **Cards:** AX, DC, DS, MC, VI.

Large-scale Hotel

SOME UNITS

CROWNE PLAZA JFK AIRPORT   *Book at aaa.com*

Phone: (718)489-1000   **232**

5/1-10/31   1P: $259   2P: $259   XP: $20   F17
11/1-4/30   1P: $249   2P: $249   XP: $20   F17

Location: In Jamaica; Belt Pkwy E to Farmer's Blvd exit, just n to N Conduit, then just w to Baisley Blvd; Van Wyck Expwy S, exit 2, then e on Rockaway Blvd to Baisley Blvd. 151-20 Baisley Blvd 11434. Fax: 718/276-8212. **Facility:** 184 units. 171 one-bedroom standard units. 13 one-bedroom suites, some with whirlpools. 5 stories, interior corridors. *Bath:* combo or shower only. **Parking:** valet. **Amenities:** video games (fee), dual phone lines, voice mail, irons, hair dryers. **Dining:** 6 am-10 pm, cocktails. **Leisure Activities:** patio, exercise room. **Guest Services:** valet laundry, airport transportation-John F Kennedy International Airport. **Business Services:** conference facilities, fax (fee). **Cards:** AX, DC, DS, MC, VI. **Special Amenities:** free newspaper and free room upgrade (subject to availability with advanced reservations).** *(See color ad below)*

Small-scale Hotel

SOME UNITS

DOUBLETREE CLUB HOTEL JFK AIRPORT   *Book at aaa.com*

Phone: (718)276-2188   **225**

5/1-10/31 & 3/1-4/30   1P: $149-$199
11/1-2/28   1P: $129-$159

Location: In Jamaica; Belt Pkwy E, exit 20, 1 mi e to 156th St; Belt Pkwy W, exit 21B (Rockaway Blvd), left at 1st light, then just s. 156-08 Rockaway Blvd 11434. Fax: 718/276-0255. **Facility:** 110 one-bedroom standard units. 5 stories, interior corridors. *Bath:* combo or shower only. **Parking:** on-site. **Terms:** [AP] & [BP] meal plans available. **Amenities:** video games (fee), dual phone lines, voice mail, irons, hair dryers. **Dining:** 6 am-2 & 4-11 pm, cocktails. **Leisure Activities:** exercise room. **Guest Services:** valet laundry, airport transportation-John F Kennedy International Airport. **Business Services:** meeting rooms, business center. **Cards:** AX, CB, DC, DS, JC, MC, VI.

Small-scale Hotel

SOME UNITS

ECONO LODGE   *Book at aaa.com*

Phone: (718)843-4300   **255**

5/1-9/30   1P: $99-$159   2P: $99-$159
10/1-4/30   1P: $89-$139   2P: $89-$139

Location: In Queens; Van Wyck Expwy, exit 2 (Rockaway Blvd), 1 mi w to 114th St. 113-18 Rockaway Blvd 11420. Fax: 718/843-0161. **Facility:** 38 one-bedroom standard units, some with whirlpools. 2 stories (no elevator), interior/exterior corridors. *Bath:* combo or shower only. **Parking:** on-site. **Terms:** weekly rates available. **Cards:** AX, CB, DC, DS, MC, VI.

Small-scale Hotel

SOME UNITS

(See map and index starting on p. 373)

EXECUTIVE MOTOR INN

AAA [SAVE]
Motel

All Year [CP]   1P: $85-$98   2P: $85-$98   **Phone: 718/341-0800** [250]

Location: In Jamaica; Belt Pkwy, exit 21A (Rockaway Blvd), just w on north service road (Conduit Ave); Belt Pkwy E, exit 21. 151-67 N Conduit Ave 11434. Fax: 718/712-2079. **Facility:** 44 one-bedroom standard units. 3 stories, interior corridors. **Parking:** on-site. **Amenities:** hair dryers. **Cards:** AX, DS, MC, VI. **Special Amenities:** free continental breakfast and free newspaper.

HAMPTON INN   *Book at aaa.com*

AAA [SAVE]
◆◆◆
Small-scale Hotel

All Year   1P: $129-$189   2P: $139-$199   **Phone: (718)322-7500** [226]

Location: In Jamaica; Belt Pkwy W, exit Rockaway Blvd to N Conduit Ave; Belt Pkwy E, exit 20 to 150th St, cross over Belt Pkwy, then just w. 144-10 135th Ave 11436. Fax: 718/322-7933. **Facility:** 216 one-bedroom standard units. 12 stories, interior corridors. *Bath:* combo or shower only. **Parking:** on-site (fee). **Terms:** [ECP] meal plan available, package plans. **Amenities:** video games (fee), dual phone lines, voice mail, irons, hair dryers. **Pool(s):** heated indoor. **Leisure Activities:** limited exercise equipment. **Guest Services:** valet laundry, airport transportation-John F Kennedy International & La Guardia airports. **Business Services:** meeting rooms, fax (fee). **Cards:** AX, CB, DC, DS, MC, VI. **Special Amenities:** free expanded continental breakfast and free local telephone calls.

SOME UNITS

FEE

HOLIDAY INN EXPRESS   *Book at aaa.com*

◆◆◆
Small-scale Hotel

5/1-8/31 [ECP]   1P: $139-$169   2P: $149-$179   XP: $10   **Phone: (718)977-3100** [231]
9/1-4/30 [ECP]   1P: $129-$159   2P: $139-$169   XP: $10   F

Location: In Jamaica; Van Wyck Expwy S, exit 1E to Belt Pkwy, exit S Conduit Ave, then just e; Belt Pkwy E, exit 20; Belt Pkwy W, exit 21A (Rockaway Blvd), s at 150th Ln, then e. 153-70 S Conduit Ave 11434. Fax: 718/977-6100. **Facility:** 128 one-bedroom standard units. 5 stories, interior corridors. *Bath:* combo or shower only. **Parking:** on-site. **Terms:** cancellation fee imposed. **Amenities:** high-speed Internet, dual phone lines, voice mail, irons, hair dryers. **Leisure Activities:** exercise room. **Guest Services:** valet laundry. **Business Services:** business center. **Cards:** AX, CB, DC, DS, JC, MC, VI.

SOME UNITS

(See map and index starting on p. 373)

HOLIDAY INN EXPRESS   *Book at aaa.com*   Phone: (718)706-6700   221

(AAA) [SAVE]

◊◊◊◊

Small-scale Hotel

9/1-10/31 [ECP]	1P: $159-$169	2P: $159-$169
5/1-8/31 [ECP]	1P: $149-$169	2P: $149-$169
11/1-4/30 [ECP]	1P: $149-$159	2P: $149-$159

Location: In Long Island City; I-278, exit I-495 (Midtown tunnel) eastbound, exit 15 (Van Dam St), just n to Hunters Point Blvd, w on Greenpoint Ave, n at 39th St; I-278 westbound, exit 35 (Greenpoint Ave), n on Greenpoint Ave, then e on 39th St. 3805 Hunters Point Ave 11101. Fax: 718/784-8532. **Facility:** 79 one-bedroom standard units. 3 stories, interior corridors. *Bath:* combo or shower only. **Parking:** on-site. **Terms:** cancellation fee imposed, small pets only ($5 extra charge). **Amenities:** dual phone lines, voice mail, irons, hair dryers. **Guest Services:** valet laundry. **Business Services:** fax (fee). **Cards:** AX, DC, DS, MC, VI. *(See color ad p 444)*

SOME UNITS
[S/D] [🐾] [🔽] [⚙] [DATA PORT] [💻] / [✕] [📱] [🖨] /
FEE

HOLIDAY INN-JFK AIRPORT   *Book at aaa.com*   Phone: (718)659-0200   249

(AAA) [SAVE]

◊◊◊◊

Large-scale Hotel

All Year   1P: $199   2P: $199

Location: In Jamaica; Van Wyck Expwy, exit 2 (Rockaway Blvd), just e to 143rd St, then just s. 144-02 135th Ave 11436. Fax: 718/322-2533. **Facility:** 360 units. 349 one-bedroom standard units. 11 one-bedroom suites ($250). 12 stories, interior corridors. **Parking:** on-site. **Terms:** package plans. **Amenities:** video games (fee), dual phone lines, voice mail, irons, hair dryers. **Dining:** 6 am-10 pm. **Pool(s):** heated indoor. **Leisure Activities:** whirlpool, exercise room. **Guest Services:** gift shop, valet and coin laundry, airport transportation-John F Kennedy International & La Guardia airports. **Business Services:** conference facilities, business center. **Cards:** AX, CB, DC, DS, JC, MC, VI. **Special Amenities: early check-in/late check-out and preferred room (subject to availability with advanced reservations).**

SOME UNITS
[S/D] [✈] [🍴] [🍸] [🏊] [🐾] [DATA PORT] [💻] / [✕] [📱] /

HOWARD JOHNSON EXPRESS INN   *Book at aaa.com*   Phone: (718)723-6700   228

◊◊◊◊

Small-scale Hotel

5/1-8/31 [ECP]	1P: $109-$139	2P: $119-$149
9/1-4/30 [ECP]	1P: $99-$129	2P: $109-$139

Location: In Jamaica; Belt Pkwy, exit 20, 0.4 mi e on service road, then just n; Van Wyck Expwy, s to exit 2 (Rockaway Blvd) service road, then just n. 153-95 Rockaway Blvd 11434. Fax: 718/527-6300. **Facility:** 72 one-bedroom standard units, some with whirlpools. 3 stories, interior corridors. *Bath:* combo or shower only. **Parking:** on-site. **Terms:** cancellation fee imposed. **Amenities:** dual phone lines, voice mail, safes (fee), irons, hair dryers. **Guest Services:** valet laundry. **Cards:** AX, CB, DC, DS, MC, VI.

SOME UNITS
[ASK] [S/D] [✈] [🔽] [🐾] [DATA PORT] [💻] / [✕] /

HOWARD JOHNSON EXPRESS INN   Phone: (718)426-6200   227

◊◊◊◊

Small-scale Hotel

8/1-9/30	1P: $99-$159	2P: $99-$159	XP: $10 F18
10/1-12/31	1P: $99-$149	2P: $99-$149	XP: $10 F18
5/1-7/31	1P: $99-$119	2P: $99-$119	XP: $10 F18
1/1-4/30	1P: $89-$119	2P: $89-$119	XP: $10 F18

Location: In Woodside; Brooklyn-Queens Expwy, exit 36 to Queens Blvd. 65-09 Queens Blvd 11377. Fax: 718/426-6373. **Facility:** 44 one-bedroom standard units. 3 stories, interior corridors. *Bath:* combo or shower only. **Parking:** on-site. **Terms:** [CP] meal plan available. **Amenities:** voice mail, irons, hair dryers. **Guest Services:** valet laundry. **Business Services:** fax (fee). **Cards:** AX, DC, DS, MC, VI. *(See color ad p 218)*

SOME UNITS
[ASK] [S/D] [♿] [🐾] [DATA PORT] [💻] / [✕] [📱] /

METRO MOTEL   *Book at aaa.com*   Phone: 718/457-5000   229

◊◊

Motel

Property failed to provide current rates

Location: In Woodside; I-278, exit 36, 0.4 mi e. 73-00 Queens Blvd 11377. Fax: 718/457-0717. **Facility:** 120 one-bedroom standard units, some with whirlpools. 2 stories (no elevator), interior/exterior corridors. *Bath:* combo or shower only. **Parking:** on-site. **Amenities:** voice mail. **Leisure Activities:** limited exercise equipment. **Business Services:** meeting rooms.

SOME UNITS
[✈] [🔽] [🐾] [DATA PORT] / [✕] [📱] /

NEW YORK LA GUARDIA AIRPORT MARRIOTT   *Book at aaa.com*   Phone: (718)565-8900   243

◊◊◊◊

Large-scale Hotel

8/14-12/31	1P: $149-$229	2P: $149-$229
5/1-8/13	1P: $139-$219	2P: $139-$219
1/1-4/30	1P: $118-$199	2P: $118-$199

Location: In East Elmhurst; Grand Central Pkwy, exit 6 (94th St), 0.3 mi e. 102-05 Ditmars Blvd 11369. Fax: 718/898-4955. **Facility:** 438 units. 436 one-bedroom standard units. 2 one-bedroom suites ($400-$600). 9 stories, interior corridors. *Bath:* combo or shower only. **Parking:** on-site (fee). **Amenities:** video games (fee), dual phone lines, voice mail, irons, hair dryers. **Pool(s):** heated indoor. **Leisure Activities:** saunas, whirlpool, exercise room. **Guest Services:** gift shop, valet laundry. **Business Services:** conference facilities, business center. **Cards:** AX, CB, DC, DS, MC, VI.

SOME UNITS
[ASK] [S/D] [✈] [🍴] [🍸] [⚙M] [♿] [🐾] [🏊] [✕] [🐾] [DATA PORT] [💻] / [✕] [VCR] [📱] [🖨] /
FEE FEE

PAN AMERICAN HOTEL   *Book at aaa.com*   Phone: (718)446-7676   246

(AAA) [SAVE]

◊◊◊◊

Small-scale Hotel

All Year   1P: $109-$169   2P: $109-$169   XP: $10 F12

Location: I-278, exit 36, 1 mi e. 79-00 Queens Blvd 11373. Fax: 718/446-7991. **Facility:** 216 one-bedroom standard units. 7 stories, interior corridors. **Parking:** on-site. **Amenities:** voice mail, hair dryers. **Dining:** 7 am-midnight, Fri & Sat-4 am, cocktails. **Guest Services:** valet laundry, airport transportation-John F Kennedy International & La Guardia airports. **Business Services:** meeting rooms, fax (fee). **Cards:** AX, CB, DC, DS, MC, VI. *(See color ad p 446)*

SOME UNITS
[S/D] [✈] [🍴] [🍸] [🐾] [🐾] [DATA PORT] / [✕] [📱] /

(See map and index starting on p. 373)

RADISSON HOTEL-JFK AIRPORT *Book at aaa.com* Phone: (718)322-2300 235

AAA (SAVE)

5/1-10/31 1P: $129-$139 2P: $129-$139 XP: $20 F18
11/1-4/30 1P: $109-$119 2P: $109-$119 XP: $20 F18

Large-scale Hotel

Location: In Jamaica; Van Wyck Expwy, exit 2 (Rockaway Blvd), just e to 140th St, then s. 135-30 140th St 11436. **Fax:** 718/322-6894. **Facility:** 386 one-bedroom standard units. 12 stories, interior corridors. *Bath:* combo or shower only. **Parking:** on-site. **Terms:** cancellation fee imposed. **Amenities:** video games (fee), dual phone lines, voice mail, irons, hair dryers. *Some:* high-speed Internet (fee). **Dining:** 5:30 am-11 pm, cocktails. **Leisure Activities:** exercise room. **Guest Services:** gift shop, valet laundry, airport transportation-John F Kennedy International Airport. **Business Services:** conference facilities, business center. **Cards:** AX, DC, DS, JC, MC, VI. *(See color ad p 413)*

SOME UNITS

RAMADA INN ADRIA *Book at aaa.com* Phone: (718)631-4900 237

AAA (SAVE)

All Year 1P: $129-$159 2P: $139-$169 XP: $20 F12

Small-scale Hotel

Location: In Bayside; Laurelton Belt Pkwy, exit 25A (Northern Blvd); just w of Cross Island Pkwy, exit 31W. 220-33 Northern Blvd 11361. **Fax:** 718/631-7501. **Facility:** 48 one-bedroom standard units. 4 stories, interior corridors. **Parking:** on-site. **Amenities:** voice mail, irons, hair dryers. **Guest Services:** valet laundry. **Business Services:** meeting rooms, fax. **Cards:** AX, CB, DC, DS, MC, VI. **Special Amenities: free newspaper and free room upgrade (subject to availability with advanced reservations).**

SOME UNITS

RAMADA PLAZA HOTEL AT JFK *Book at aaa.com* Phone: (718)995-9000 251

AAA (SAVE)

All Year 1P: $129 2P: $129 XP: $20 F12

Large-scale Hotel

Location: In Jamaica; Van Wyck Expwy at Belt Pkwy; southwest corner. Bldg 144/JFK International Airport 11430-1613. **Fax:** 718/224-8962. **Facility:** 478 units. 473 one-bedroom standard units. 5 one-bedroom suites. 6 stories, interior corridors. *Bath:* combo or shower only. **Parking:** on-site. **Terms:** cancellation fee imposed. **Amenities:** voice mail, irons, hair dryers. **Dining:** 5:30 am-11, noon-3 & 6:30-12:30 am, cocktails. **Leisure Activities:** pool table, exercise room. *Fee:* game room. **Guest Services:** gift shop, valet laundry. **Business Services:** conference facilities, business center. **Cards:** AX, CB, DC, DS. **Special Amenities: free local telephone calls and early check-in/late check-out.**

SOME UNITS

(See map and index starting on p. 373)

RAMADA PLAZA LA GUARDIA   *Book at aaa.com*   Phone: (718)651-2100   [230]
All Year   1P: $159-$239   2P: $159-$239
Location: In Flushing; Grand Central Pkwy W, exit 9 W (Northern Blvd W), s on 114th St, then just s; exit 8 (111th St) eastbound, 111th St, e at stop sign, e at 1st light, then just s on Astoria Blvd (turns into 114th St). 37-10 114th St 11368.
Large-scale Hotel   Fax: 718/651-2222. **Facility:** 214 units. 211 one-bedroom standard units. 3 one-bedroom suites ($249-$299). 8 stories, interior corridors. **Parking:** on-site. **Amenities:** video games (fee), dual phone lines, voice mail, safes, irons, hair dryers. **Pool(s):** heated indoor. **Leisure Activities:** exercise room. **Guest Services:** gift shop, valet laundry. **Business Services:** meeting rooms, business center. **Cards:** AX, CB, DC, DS, JC, MC, VI.

SOME UNITS
FEE

SHERATON LA GUARDIA EAST HOTEL   *Book at aaa.com*   Phone: (718)460-6666   [239]
All Year [BP]   1P: $145-$230   2P: $156-$245   XP: $11   F5
Location: In Flushing; Grand Central Pkwy to Northern Blvd E, 1 mi e to Main St, 0.3 mi s to 39th Ave, then just w. 135-20 39th Ave 11354. Fax: 718/445-2655. **Facility:** 173 units. 165 one-bedroom standard units. 8 one-bedroom
Large-scale Hotel   suites ($275-$290), some with whirlpools. 16 stories, interior corridors. **Parking:** valet. **Amenities:** dual phone lines, voice mail, irons, hair dryers. *Some:* fax, safes. **Leisure Activities:** exercise room. **Guest Services:** gift shop, valet laundry. **Business Services:** conference facilities, business center. **Cards:** AX, DC, DS, JC, MC, VI.

SOME UNITS

SUPER 8 MOTEL   *Book at aaa.com*   Phone: (718)932-2100   [242]
All Year   1P: $95-$105   2P: $95-$105   F16
Location: In Astoria; Grand Central Pkwy, exit 3 (Hoyt Ave), 0.7 mi s on 31st, then 0.5 mi w on Broadway. 31-62 14th St 11106. Fax: 718/932-0954. **Facility:** 29 units. 23 one- and 6 two-bedroom standard units. 2 stories (no elevator), interior corridors. **Parking:** on-site. **Amenities:** *Some:* hair dryers. **Cards:** AX, CB, DC, DS, MC, VI.
Small-scale Hotel   **Special Amenities:** free continental breakfast and free local telephone calls.

SOME UNITS

——— **WHERE TO DINE** ———

FIRST EDITION BISTRO   Lunch: $8-$16   Dinner: $8-$16   Phone: 718/428-8522   [219]
Location: In Bayside; between 41st and 42nd aves. 41-08 Bell Blvd 11361. **Hours:** 11:30 am-midnight, Fri & Sat-2 am. Closed: 11/25, 12/25. **Reservations:** accepted. **Features:** This pub has a separate dining room on the second floor, away from the bustle of the bar but fully equipped with TVs. Typical burgers, create your own
American   pizzas, pastas as well as wraps and a few more complex dinner specials are served up in most casual fashion. Casual dress; cocktails. **Parking:** street. **Cards:** MC, VI.

JAIYA THAI-ORIENTAL RESTAURANT   Lunch: $5-$9   Dinner: $6-$17   Phone: 718/651-1330   [224]
Location: In East Elmhurst; 81st St and Broadway. 81-11 Broadway 11373. **Hours:** 11:30 am-midnight, Sat & Sun from noon. **Reservations:** accepted. **Features:** In the heart of the Chinatown area of Queens, the cozy
Thai   restaurant delivers piquant Thai dishes that employ seafood, tropical fruits and spices, chili peppers and vegetables. The atmosphere is casual and relaxed, while servers are friendly and efficient. Casual dress;
cocktails. **Parking:** street. **Cards:** AX, DC, MC, VI.

LAILLA TURKISH RESTAURANT   Lunch: $4-$6   Dinner: $11-$15   Phone: 718/225-2904   [220]
Location: In Bayside; between 42nd and 43rd aves. 42-24 Bell Blvd 11361. **Hours:** 11:30 am-10:30 pm, Fri-midnight, Sat & Sun noon-midnight. **Reservations:** accepted. **Features:** This casual Turkish restaurant
Turkish   offers patrons a delicious and delightful meal with attentive and friendly service. Casual dress; cocktails. **Parking:** street. **Cards:** AX, DC, DS, MC, VI.

MYTHOS AUTHENTIC HELENIC CUISINE   Lunch: $6-$12   Dinner: $10-$20   Phone: 718/357-6596   [221]
Location: In Flushing; on 25A/Northwestern Blvd, just w of Cross Island Expwy. 196-29 Northern Blvd 11358.
Hours: 11:30 am-midnight. **Reservations:** accepted. **Features:** Enjoy regional Greek cuisine from Cephalunia Island, including a good selection of fish and meat dishes, which are prepared daily. Many
Greek   interesting, authentic appetizers and salad, and traditional Greek dessert, such as yummy baklava, grace the menu. The ethnic staff is gracious. Casual dress; beer & wine only. **Parking:** street. **Cards:** MC, VI.

PENANG   Lunch: $4-$18   Dinner: $6-$18   Phone: 718/321-2078   [222]
Location: In Flushing; Grand Central Pkwy to Northern Blvd E, 1 mi e to Main St, 0.3 mi to 39th Ave, then just w. 38-04 Prince St 11354. **Hours:** 11 am-midnight. Closed: Chinese New Year. **Features:** A sea of foreign faces
Asian   assures you of authentic food, and if you stay, you'll be rewarded. The very large and varied menu is full of surprises, such as the outstanding Indian pancake with curry chicken dipping sauce—a must for starters.
The satays are also good. Vivid menu descriptions make a decision difficult. Portions are large, nice to look at and even better to eat. This place is sure to please the adventurous diner. Casual dress. **Parking:** street.

WATER'S EDGE   Lunch: $29   Dinner: $58-$78   Phone: 718/482-0033   [225]
Location: In Long Island City; from Manhattan, 59th St Queensborough Bridge upper level to 21st St exit, left on 21st to 44th Dr, 2nd light, then right to river. 44th Dr at the East River 11101. **Hours:** noon-3 & 6-11 pm, Sat 6
pm-11:30 pm. Closed: Sun. **Reservations:** suggested. **Features:** At Water's Edge, the view of Manhattan rivals most others. An extensive selection of wine complements the well-prepared and artfully-presented
American   dishes. Showcase desserts are displayed on a cart to temp those with a sweet tooth. A free water taxi leaves from the 34th Street marina from 6 pm. Seasonal outdoor seating on the deck is pleasant. Dressy
casual; cocktails; entertainment. **Parking:** valet. **Cards:** AX, DC, DS, MC, VI.

(See map and index starting on p. 373)

——— *The following restaurants have not been evaluated by AAA* ———
but are listed for your information only.

NO 1 PEOPLE'S & PEOPLE

Phone: 718/460-8686

[fyi] Not evaluated. **Location:** In Flushing. 38-06 Prince St 11354. **Features:** The name may seem confusing, but the eatery is popular among locals. Exotic dishes—including fish head casserole, salt and pepper frog and duck tongue with basil—may cause a little hesitation, but diners looking for the real McCoy will accomplish their objective here. Also sharing space on the huge menu are such recognizable choices as Mongolian beef with scallion sauce, orange chicken and shrimp with lobster sauce.

PEARSON'S TEXAS BARBECUE

Phone: 718/779-7715

[fyi] Not evaluated. **Location:** In Jackson Heights; at 71st St. 71-04 35th Ave. **Features:** A wood-burning pit helps make the meat "slow and low," hickory-roasted, tender, moist and flavorful. Beef ribs, brisket and pork shoulder are the most popular choices, but all is good. Don't forget the slaw and the beer at this casual, bustling eatery.

STATEN ISLAND pop. 443,728

——— **WHERE TO STAY** ———

HILTON GARDEN INN STATEN ISLAND   *Book at aaa.com*

Phone: (718)477-2400

▼▼▼▼ All Year   1P: $139-$159   2P: $139-$159   XP: $10   F18
Location: I-278 westbound, exit 6 (South Ave), then just s; I-278 eastbound, exit 5 to SR 440 S, exit South Ave, 1 mi n
Small-scale Hotel to Lois Ln, then just w. 1100 South Ave 10314. Fax: 718/477-5620. **Facility:** 148 units. 136 one-bedroom standard units. 12 one-bedroom suites with whirlpools. 6 stories, interior corridors. *Bath:* combo or shower only.
Parking: on-site. **Terms:** cancellation fee imposed, weekly rates available, small pets only ($35 extra charge). **Amenities:** dual phone lines, voice mail, irons, hair dryers. *Fee:* video games, high-speed Internet. **Pool(s):** heated indoor. **Leisure Activities:** whirlpool, hiking trails, exercise room, spa. **Guest Services:** sundries, valet and coin laundry, area transportation. **Business Services:** conference facilities, business center. **Cards:** AX, CB, DC, DS, MC, VI.

SOME UNITS
(ASK) (S) (×) (🐕) (⌂) (¶) (🏊) (🏊) (⊗) (✦) (DATA PORT) (🔌) (▭) (◨) / (⊗) (VCR) /
FEE   FEE

THE STATEN ISLAND HOTEL   *Book at aaa.com*

Phone: (718)698-5000

▼▼▼ All Year   1P: $154   2P: $154   XP: $5   F
Location: I-278, exit Richmond Ave, 0.5 mi se. 1415 Richmond Ave 10314. Fax: 718/354-7071. **Facility:** 187 units.
Large-scale Hotel 186 one-bedroom standard units. 1 one-bedroom suite ($375-$575). 10 stories, interior corridors. *Bath:* combo or shower only. **Parking:** on-site. **Terms:** small pets only. **Amenities:** video games (fee), dual phone lines, voice mail, safes, irons, hair dryers. **Leisure Activities:** exercise room. **Guest Services:** valet and coin laundry. **Business Services:** meeting rooms, fax (fee). **Cards:** AX, DC, MC, VI.

SOME UNITS
(ASK) (S) (🐕) (¶) (🍽) (✦) (DATA PORT) (▭) / (⊗) /
FEE

——— **WHERE TO DINE** ———

——— *The following restaurant has not been evaluated by AAA* ———
but is listed for your information only.

THE OLD BERMUDA INN

Phone: 718/948-7600

[fyi] Not evaluated. **Location:** SR 440, exit 4, just sw. 2512 Arthur Kill Rd 10309. **Features:** The 1830s mansion, restored to resemble a Henry VIII pub, has a cozy, intimate ambience. Eggplant Napoleon and chicken chasseur stand out on a menu of well-prepared choices. Bananas Hamilton, served on a bed of creme anglaise, is exquisite.

(Ⓨ)

The New York City Vicinity

ARMONK pop. 3,461

──── WHERE TO STAY ────

WELLESLEY INN   _Book at aaa.com_   Phone: (914)273-9090

All Year   1P: $179-$199   2P: $179-$199   XP: $10   F18
Location: I-684, exit 3S northbound; exit 3 southbound, 0.3 mi s on SR 22 to Business Park Dr. 94 Business Park Dr 10504. Fax: 914/273-4105. **Facility:** 140 one-bedroom standard units. 2 stories (no elevator), interior corridors. _Bath:_ combo or shower only. **Parking:** on-site. **Terms:** [ECP] meal plan available. **Amenities:** video

Small-scale Hotel   games (fee), voice mail, irons, hair dryers. **Dining:** 6:30 am-11 pm, cocktails. **Pool(s):** outdoor. **Leisure Activities:** exercise room, volleyball. **Guest Services:** valet and coin laundry, airport transportation-Westchester County Airport, area transportation-local businesses. **Business Services:** conference facilities. **Cards:** AX, CB, DC, DS, JC, MC, VI. **Special Amenities:** free expanded continental breakfast and free newspaper.   SOME UNITS

BLOOMFIELD pop. 1,267

——— WHERE TO DINE ———

THE ORIGINAL HOLLOWAY HOUSE Historic **Lunch:** $8-$14 **Dinner:** $15-$30 **Phone:** 585/657-7120
American
Location: Jct SR 332 on US 20 and SR 5, 8 mi w. 29 State St 14443. **Hours:** Open 5/1-12/15 & 4/1-4/30; 11:30 am-2 & 5-9 pm, Sun noon-7:30 pm. **Closed:** Mon except 9/2. **Reservations:** suggested. **Features:** The quaint 1808 country inn is decorated in the Early American style, with lace curtains, wreaths and country accents. Home-style favorites, such as roast turkey dinner with gravy and mashed potatoes, fresh seafood and steak, mingle with fresh house-baked bread and sumptuous dessert. Casual dress; cocktails. **Parking:** on-site. **Cards:** AX, DS, MC, VI.

CARMEL pop. 5,560

——— WHERE TO DINE ———

CUTILLO'S RESTAURANT **Lunch:** $7-$12 **Dinner:** $13-$30 **Phone:** 845/225-8903
Italian
Location: I-84, exit 17, 1 mi e on SR 52, then just s. 1196 Farmers Mill Rd 10512. **Hours:** noon-10 pm, Fri & Sat-10:30 pm. Closed major holidays; also Mon. **Reservations:** suggested. **Features:** The Cutillo family home of stucco and stone is set back among tall trees on a hill and is decorated with many family furnishings and pictures. You may sit on the enclosed porch, in the sitting room, the living room or den. On the menu are many dishes named after family members, such as clams Camille, chicken Lucille, shrimp Patricia and cavatelli Pasquale. Homemade cheesecake is decadent. Dressy casual; cocktails. **Parking:** on-site. **Cards:** DS, MC, VI.

CHAPPAQUA pop. 9,468

——— WHERE TO DINE ———

CRABTREES KITTLE HOUSE **Lunch:** $10-$19 **Dinner:** $18-$32 **Phone:** 914/666-8044
American
Location: Saw Mill Pkwy, exit 33, 0.9 mi se on Readers Digest and Roaring Brook rds, then 0.5 mi n on CR 117. 11 Kittle Rd 10514. **Hours:** noon-2:30 & 5:30-9:30 pm, Fri-10:30 pm, Sat 5:30 pm-10:30 pm, Sun noon-2:30 & 3-9 pm. **Closed:** 12/25. **Reservations:** suggested. **Features:** An award-winning list of wines complements such colorfully prepared choices as seafood stew and free-range chicken with couscous, vegetables and rice vermici. A woodsy setting and large, white pillars distinguish the stately, Colonial-style building. Semi-formal attire; cocktails. **Parking:** on-site. **Cards:** AX, CB, DC, DS, MC, VI.

CONGERS pop. 8,303

——— WHERE TO DINE ———

RESTAURANT X **Lunch:** $10-$15 **Dinner:** $17-$25 **Phone:** 845/268-6555
American
Location: Jct US 9 W, 1 mi s; I-87/287, exit 12, 4 mi n. 117 N SR 303 10920. **Hours:** noon-2:30 & 5:30-10 pm, Fri-10:30 pm, Sat 5 pm-11 pm, Sun noon-2:30 & 6-8 pm. **Closed:** 1/1, 12/24, 12/25; also Mon. **Reservations:** suggested. **Features:** Upscale country charm envelops the restaurant, which offers serene views of a country landscape. Grilled squab and crispy salmon roll tempura stand out on a menu of contemporary American cuisine. For dessert, savor warm coconut cake or rum raisin ice cream. Dressy casual; cocktails. **Parking:** on-site and valet. **Cards:** AX, MC, VI.

ROMOLO'S **Lunch:** $11-$14 **Dinner:** $12-$26 **Phone:** 845/268-3770
Italian
Location: I-87/287, exit 12, 3 mi n. 77 Rt 303 10920. **Hours:** 11:30 am-2:30 & 5-9:30 pm, Fri-10:30 pm, Sat 5 pm-10:30 pm, Sun 3 pm-8:30 pm. Closed major holidays; also Mon. **Reservations:** suggested. **Features:** Excellently seasoned dishes include ravioli stuffed with goat cheese and grilled chicken salad with endive and arugula leaves. Photographs of celebrities line the entry area. Polished servers exhibit solid menu knowledge and timely follow-up. Casual dress; cocktails. **Parking:** on-site. **Cards:** AX, CB, DC, DS, MC, VI.

CROTON-ON-HUDSON pop. 7,606

——— WHERE TO STAY ———

ALEXANDER HAMILTON HOUSE **Phone:** (914)271-6737
All Year [BP] 1P: $85-$150 2P: $100-$250 XP: $25 D15
Historic Bed & Breakfast
Location: US 9, exit SR 129, e to light, n on Riverside, e on Grand, then n on Hamilton. 49 Van Wyck St 10520. Fax: 914/271-3927. **Facility:** Victorian hats and shadowboxes accent the eclectic decor at this quiet inn offering fireplaces, a gazebo and a fishpond. Designated smoking area. 8 one-bedroom standard units, some with whirlpools. 3 stories (no elevator), interior corridors. **Bath:** combo or shower only. **Parking:** on-site. **Terms:** 2 night minimum stay - weekends, 7 day cancellation notice-fee imposed, weekly-rates available. **Amenities:** high-speed Internet, hair dryers. Some: DVD players, CD players, irons. **Pool(s):** outdoor. **Business Services:** meeting rooms. **Cards:** AX, DC, DS, MC, VI.

FEE

SOME UNITS

ELMSFORD pop. 4,676

---- WHERE TO STAY ----

HAMPTON INN WHITE PLAINS/TARRYTOWN *Book at aaa.com*   Phone: (914)592-5680

(AAA) (SAVE)   All Year [ECP]   1P: $159-$229   2P: $159-$229   XP: $10   F17

Small-scale Hotel   **Location:** I-287, exit 1; I-87, exit 8, just w. 200 Tarrytown Rd 10523. Fax: 914/592-6727. **Facility:** 156 one-bedroom standard units. 7 stories, interior corridors. *Bath:* combo or shower only. **Parking:** on-site. **Amenities:** video games (fee), voice mail, irons, hair dryers. **Pool(s):** outdoor. **Leisure Activities:** exercise room. **Guest Services:** valet and coin laundry. **Business Services:** meeting rooms. **Cards:** AX, CB, DC, DS, JC, MC, VI. **Special Amenities:** free expanded continental breakfast and free newspaper. *(See color ad p 459)*

SOME UNITS

WELLESLEY INN (ELMSFORD) *Book at aaa.com*   Phone: (914)592-3300

(AAA) (SAVE)   All Year   1P: $119-$159   XP: $10   F18

Small-scale Hotel   **Location:** SR 9A, 1.5 mi n of SR 119; 1 mi n of I-287, exit 2 westbound; exit 1 eastbound, jct SR 100C. 540 Saw Mill River Rd 10523. Fax: 914/592-3381. **Facility:** 101 one-bedroom standard units. 4 stories, interior corridors. *Bath:* combo or shower only. **Parking:** on-site. **Terms:** cancellation fee imposed. **Amenities:** video games (fee), dual phone lines, voice mail, irons, hair dryers. **Dining:** 7 am-10 pm, cocktails. **Pool(s):** heated indoor. **Leisure Activities:** exercise room. **Guest Services:** valet laundry. **Business Services:** meeting rooms, fax. **Cards:** AX, CB, DC, DS, JC, MC, VI. **Special Amenities:** free expanded continental breakfast and free newspaper. *(See color ad p 8)*

SOME UNITS

---- WHERE TO DINE ----

ICHI RIKI RESTAURANT   **Lunch:** $9-$19   **Dinner:** $15-$25   Phone: 914/592-2220

Japanese   **Location:** Jct SR 119 (Main St or Tarrytown Rd) and SR 9A, just e on SR 119; downtown. 1 E Main St 10523. **Hours:** 11:45 am-2:30 & 5:30-10 pm, Fri-11 pm, Sat noon-2:30 & 5-11 pm, Sun 5 pm-9:30 pm. Closed major holidays; also Mon. **Reservations:** suggested. **Features:** Japanese music and art, tatami rooms and servers in kimonos lend to the authentic feel of the comfortable restaurant. The menu lists varied sushi and sashimi, as well as seasoned preparations of seafood, beef, pork and chicken. Casual dress; cocktails. **Parking:** on-site. **Cards:** AX, CB, DC, MC, VI.

HARTSDALE pop. 9,830

---- WHERE TO DINE ----

CAFE MEZE'   **Lunch:** $6-$15   **Dinner:** $16-$24   Phone: 914/428-2400

Mediterranean   **Location:** Jct Hartsdale and Central Park aves, just n. 20 N Central Park Ave 10530. **Hours:** noon-2:30 & 5:30-9:30 pm, Fri & Sat-10:30 pm, Sun-9:30 pm. Closed: 7/4, 12/25. **Reservations:** suggested, weekends. **Features:** Varnished wood panel walls below numerous Mediterranean pictures and glasses shimmering against votives creates a warm intimate room in which to enjoy upscale comfort food, full flavored and hearty. The menu changes seasonally but you can count on creative dishes, a few of which are bound to intrigue you. Casual dress; cocktails. **Parking:** on-site. **Cards:** AX, DC, DS, MC, VI.

HAWTHORNE pop. 5,083

---- WHERE TO STAY ----

COMFORT INN & SUITES *Book at aaa.com*   Phone: (914)592-8600

(AAA) (SAVE)   All Year   1P: $150-$250   2P: $150-$250   XP: $10   F18

Small-scale Hotel   **Location:** Saw Mill River Pkwy, exit 25 northbound; exit 23 (Eastview) southbound, 1 mi e on Old Saw Mill River Rd, then 1 mi n on SR 9A. 20 Saw Mill River Rd 10532. Fax: 914/592-7457. **Facility:** 86 units. 72 one-bedroom standard units, some with whirlpools. 12 one- and 2 two-bedroom suites with efficiencies (no utensils). 3 stories, interior corridors. *Bath:* combo or shower only. **Parking:** on-site. **Terms:** check-in 3:30 pm, [ECP] meal plan available, package plans. **Amenities:** video games (fee), dual phone lines, voice mail, safes, irons, hair dryers. **Pool(s):** heated indoor. **Leisure Activities:** sauna, patio, exercise room. **Guest Services:** coin laundry. **Business Services:** meeting rooms. **Cards:** AX, CB, DC, DS, MC, VI. **Special Amenities:** free continental breakfast and free local telephone calls.

SOME UNITS

LONG ISLAND CITY (See map and index starting on p. 373)

---- WHERE TO STAY ----

COMFORT INN *Book at aaa.com*   Phone: (718)303-3700   (258)

5/1-9/30 & 3/1-4/30 [CP]	1P: $109-$189	2P: $119-$209	XP: $10 F12
10/1-12/31 [CP]	1P: $99-$189	2P: $109-$209	XP: $10 F12
1/1-2/28 [CP]	1P: $89-$159	2P: $99-$179	XP: $10 F12

Small-scale Hotel   **Location:** Between 24th and 27th sts. 42-24 Crescent St 11101. Fax: 718/303-3800. **Facility:** 80 one-bedroom standard units, some with whirlpools. 8 stories, interior corridors. **Parking:** no self-parking. **Terms:** cancellation fee imposed. **Amenities:** voice mail, hair dryers. **Guest Services:** valet laundry. **Business Services:** meeting rooms. **Cards:** AX, DC, DS, MC, VI.

SOME UNITS

MOUNT KISCO pop. 9,983

──────── WHERE TO STAY ────────

HOLIDAY INN
AAA SAVE
◆◆◆
Small-scale Hotel

Book at aaa.com
All Year   1P: $119-$149   2P: $119-$149   **Phone:** (914)241-2600
Location: Saw Mill River Pkwy, exit 37, just e. 1 Holiday Inn Dr 10549. Fax: 914/241-4742. **Facility:** 122 one-bedroom standard units, some with whirlpools. 2 stories (no elevator), interior corridors. *Bath:* combo or shower only. **Terms:** cancellation fee imposed. **Amenities:** dual phone lines, voice mail, irons, hair dryers. *Fee:* video games, high-speed Internet. **Dining:** 6:30 am-2 & 5-10 pm, Sat from 7 am, Sun 11:30 am-2:30 & 5-10 pm, cocktails. **Pool(s):** heated outdoor. **Guest Services:** valet and coin laundry. **Business Services:** meeting rooms. **Cards:** AX, CB, DC, DS, JC, MC, VI. **Special Amenities:** free newspaper.

SOME UNITS
[icons] FEE ... FEE

NANUET pop. 16,707

──────── WHERE TO STAY ────────

CANDLEWOOD SUITES
◆◆◆
Small-scale Hotel

Book at aaa.com
All Year   1P: $139-$179   2P: $139-$179   **Phone:** 845/371-4445
Location: I-287/87, exit 14 (SR 59 W) to New Clarkstown Rd. 20 Overlook Blvd 10954. Fax: 845/371-4446. **Facility:** 124 units. 100 one-bedroom standard units with efficiencies. 24 one-bedroom suites with efficiencies. 3 stories, interior corridors. *Bath:* combo or shower only. **Parking:** on-site. **Terms:** pets ($15 extra charge). **Amenities:** video library, CD players, dual phone lines, voice mail, irons, hair dryers. **Leisure Activities:** exercise room. **Guest Services:** sundries. **Business Services:** fax. **Cards:** AX, CB, DC, DS, JC, MC, VI.

SOME UNITS
[icons] FEE

COMFORT INN & SUITES
AAA SAVE
◆◆◆
Small-scale Hotel

Book at aaa.com
All Year   1P: $98-$159   2P: $108-$169   XP: $10   F18
Phone: (845)623-6000
Location: Palisades Pkwy, exit 8W, jct SR 59/304, then just e. 425 E Rt 59 10954. Fax: 845/623-9338. **Facility:** 150 units. 144 one-bedroom standard units, some with efficiencies (no utensils) and/or whirlpools. 6 one-bedroom suites ($150-$199) with efficiencies (no utensils) and whirlpools. 2-4 stories, interior corridors. *Bath:* combo or shower only. **Parking:** on-site. **Terms:** [ECP] meal plan available. **Amenities:** voice mail, irons, hair dryers. *Fee:* video games, high-speed Internet. **Dining:** 6:30 am-11 & 5-10 pm, Sun 7-11 am, cocktails. **Pool(s):** heated indoor. **Leisure Activities:** exercise room. **Guest Services:** valet and coin laundry, area transportation (fee). **Business Services:** meeting rooms, business center. **Cards:** AX, CB, DC, DS, JC, MC, VI. **Special Amenities:** free continental breakfast and free local telephone calls.

SOME UNITS
[icons]

DAYS INN NANUET
AAA SAVE
◆◆◆
Small-scale Hotel

Book at aaa.com
5/1-9/30 [CP]   1P: $88-$129   2P: $88-$129   XP: $10   F17
10/1-4/30 [CP]   1P: $79-$119   2P: $79-$119   XP: $10   F17
Phone: (845)623-4567
Location: I-287/87, exit 14 (SR 59 W), just w. 367 W Rt 59 10954. Fax: 845/623-0190. **Facility:** 70 one-bedroom standard units, some with whirlpools. 2 stories (no elevator), interior/exterior corridors. **Terms:** pets ($8 fee). **Amenities:** safes, irons, hair dryers. **Pool(s):** heated outdoor. **Guest Services:** valet and coin laundry. **Cards:** AX, CB, DC, DS, MC, VI. **Special Amenities:** free continental breakfast and free newspaper.

SOME UNITS
[icons] FEE

──────── *The following lodging was either not evaluated or did not* ────────
meet AAA rating requirements but is listed for your information only.

HILTON GARDEN INN
fyi

                                  All Year   1P: $115-$199   2P: $125-$199   XP: $10   F16
Phone: 845/623-0600
Too new to rate. **Location:** I-287/87, exit 14. 260 W Rt 59 10954. Fax: 845/623-6500. **Amenities:** 88 units, restaurant, coffeemakers, microwaves, refrigerators. **Cards:** AX, CB, DC, DS, JC, MC, VI.

NEW ROCHELLE pop. 72,182

———— WHERE TO STAY ————

RADISSON HOTEL   Phone: (914)576-3700
(AAA) (SAVE)   All Year   1P: $154-$161   2P: $163-$170   XP: $10   F18
◆◆◆◆ ◆◆◆◆   **Location:** I-95, exit 16, via Cedar St. 1 Ramada Plaza 10801. **Fax:** 914/576-5864. **Facility:** 130 units. 127 one-
Small-scale Hotel   bedroom standard units. 3 one-bedroom suites. 10 stories, interior corridors. **Parking:** on-site. **Terms:** 10 day
cancellation notice-fee imposed. **Amenities:** video games (fee), voice mail, irons, hair dryers. **Dining:** 6:30
am-10 pm, cocktails. **Pool(s):** outdoor. **Leisure Activities:** exercise room. **Guest Services:** valet laundry.
Business Services: meeting rooms. **Cards:** AX, CB, DC, DS, JC, MC, VI. **Special Amenities:** free newspaper and early check-in/late check-out. (See color ad below)

SOME UNITS

NYACK pop. 6,737

———— WHERE TO STAY ————

BEST WESTERN NYACK ON HUDSON   *Book at aaa.com*   Phone: (845)358-8100
(AAA) (SAVE)   5/1-11/28   1P: $109-$119   2P: $109-$119   XP: $5   F17
◆◆◆◆ ◆◆◆◆   11/29-4/30   1P: $89-$99   2P: $89-$99   XP: $5   F17
Motel   **Location:** I-87/287, exit 11, just e. 26 Rt 59 10960. **Fax:** 845/358-3644. **Facility:** 80 one-bedroom standard units.
2 stories, exterior corridors. **Parking:** on-site, winter plug-ins. **Amenities:** dual phone lines, voice mail, irons,
hair dryers. **Dining:** 6 am-1 am, cocktails. **Business Services:** meeting rooms. **Cards:** AX, CB, DC, DS,
MC, VI. **Special Amenities:** free newspaper and early check-in/late check-out.

SOME UNITS

SUPER 8 MOTEL   *Book at aaa.com*   Phone: 845/353-3880
(AAA) (SAVE)   All Year   1P: $69-$149   2P: $69-$149   XP: $10   F17
◆◆◆◆ ◆◆◆◆   **Location:** I-87/287, exit 11 eastbound; exit 11 westbound, 0.5 mi w. 47 Rt 59 10960. **Fax:** 845/353-0271. **Facility:** 43
one-bedroom standard units. 2 stories (no elevator), interior corridors. **Parking:** on-site. **Terms:** [CP] meal
Small-scale Hotel   plan available. **Amenities:** irons, hair dryers. **Cards:** AX, CB, DC, DS, JC, MC, VI. **Special Amenities:** free
continental breakfast.

SOME UNITS

———— WHERE TO DINE ————

THE HUDSON HOUSE OF NYACK   **Lunch:** $7-$9   **Dinner:** $18-$21   **Phone:** 845/353-1355
◆◆◆ ◆◆◆   **Location:** Jct Franklin and Main sts, just e; downtown. 134 Main St 10960. **Hours:** 11:30 am-2:30 & 5:30-10 pm,
American   Fri & Sat-11 pm, Sun 11:30 am-3 & 4:30-9:30 pm. Closed: 11/25, 12/25; also Mon.
Reservations: suggested, Fri & Sat. **Features:** The restaurant delivers complex cuisine, such as
blackened catfish over artichoke hearts, radicchio, Belgian endive, mesclun, red potatoes and orange
slices. The restored storefront building exudes a quaint, comfortable charm. Homemade desserts are a must. Casual dress;
cocktails. **Parking:** street. **Cards:** AX, MC, VI.

ICHI RIKI   **Lunch:** $8-$15   **Dinner:** $15-$25   **Phone:** 845/358-7977
◆◆◆ ◆◆◆   **Location:** On continuation of SR 59; downtown. 110 Main St 10960. **Hours:** noon-2:30 & 5:30-10 pm, Fri-11 pm,
Japanese   Sat 5 pm-11 pm, Sun 5 pm-9:30 pm. Closed: 11/25, 12/25; also Mon. **Reservations:** suggested,
weekends. **Features:** Japanese music and art, tatami rooms and servers in kimonos lend to the authentic
feel of the comfortable restaurant. The menu lists varied sushi and sashimi, as well as wonderfully
seasoned preparations of seafood, beef, pork and chicken. Casual dress; cocktails. **Parking:** street. **Cards:** AX, CB, DC,
MC, VI.

LANTERNA TUSCAN BISTRO   **Lunch:** $8-$15   **Dinner:** $12-$25   **Phone:** 845/353-8361
(AAA)   **Location:** Downtown. 3 S Broadway 10960. **Hours:** 11:30 am-3:30 & 4:30-10 pm, Fri & Sat-11 pm. Closed:
◆◆◆ ◆◆◆   1/1, 11/25, 12/25. **Reservations:** required. **Features:** This upscale, lively bistro-style restaurant offers
Italian   authentic Tuscan style cuisine. Careful preparation of the best quality ingredients are served by friendly,
efficient staff. Casual dress; cocktails. **Parking:** street. **Cards:** AX, DC, MC, VI.

ORANGEBURG pop. 3,388

———— WHERE TO STAY ————

ORANGEBURG HOLIDAY INN & REGISTRY HOTEL   *Book at aaa.com*   **Phone:** (845)359-7000
All Year   1P: $135-$164   XP: $10   F
Location: I-87/287, exit 12, 4 mi s on SR 303; 1 mi n of Palisades Interstate Pkwy, exit 5N northbound; 1 mi e of exit 6E.
Small-scale Hotel   329 Rt 303 10962. Fax: 845/359-7196. **Facility:** 167 one-bedroom standard units, some with whirlpools. 2-3
stories, interior corridors. *Bath:* some combo or shower only. **Parking:** on-site. **Amenities:** video games
(fee), voice mail, irons, hair dryers. **Pool(s):** outdoor. **Leisure Activities:** sauna, exercise room. **Guest Services:** valet laundry,
area transportation. **Business Services:** meeting rooms. **Cards:** AX, CB, DC, DS, JC, MC, VI.
SOME UNITS

(ASK) (SD) (╎╎) (Y) (&) (🖉) (➾) (📺) (DATA PORT) (💻) / (✕) (🔒) /
FEE

OSSINING pop. 24,010

———— WHERE TO DINE ————

BRASSERIE SWISS   **Lunch:** $8-$15   **Dinner:** $16-$27   **Phone:** 914/941-0319
Location: SR 133, between US 9 and 9A. 118 Croton Ave 10562. **Hours:** noon-2:30 & 5:30-10:30 pm, Sun 4
pm-9 pm. Closed: Mon. **Reservations:** accepted. **Features:** Continental Swiss cuisine, featuring
Swiss   appetizers such as pate and a variety of schnitzel entrees and gracious service are to be enjoyed at
Brasserie Swiss. Casual dress; cocktails. **Parking:** on-site. **Cards:** AX, CB, DC, DS, MC, VI.   (Y) (✕)

GUIDA'S   **Lunch:** $10-$15   **Dinner:** $20-$30   **Phone:** 914/941-2662
Location: Corner of US 9 and Main St; downtown. 199 Main St 10562. **Hours:** 11:30 am-10 pm, Fri & Sat-11 pm,
Sun 1 pm-10 pm. Closed: 11/25, 12/25. **Reservations:** suggested. **Features:** Soft sconce lighting on
Italian   yellow walls hung with ornately framed mirrors and upscale table settings enhance the sophisticated
appeal of the downtown restaurant. The menu is traditional and brings in a loyal local crowd. Homemade
pastas, veal, filet mignon, chicken and fish are done many ways and if you don't see it, ask. Casual dress; cocktails. **Parking:**
street. **Cards:** AX, MC, VI.   (✕)

PEARL RIVER pop. 15,553

———— WHERE TO STAY ————

HILTON PEARL RIVER   *Book at aaa.com*   **Phone:** (845)735-9000
All Year   1P: $109-$259   2P: $109-$279   F19
Location: Palisades Interstate Pkwy, exit 6W, 2.5 mi w on CR 20 W (Veterans Memorial Dr). 500 Veterans Memorial Dr
Small-scale Hotel   10965. Fax: 845/735-9005. **Facility:** 150 units. 148 one-bedroom standard units. 2 one-bedroom suites. 5
stories, interior corridors. **Parking:** on-site. **Terms:** cancellation fee imposed, [AP] meal plan available.
Amenities: video games (fee), dual phone lines, voice mail, irons, hair dryers. **Pool(s):** heated indoor. **Leisure Activi-
ties:** saunas, whirlpool, exercise room. *Fee:* massage. **Guest Services:** valet and coin laundry, area transportation. **Business
Services:** conference facilities. **Cards:** AX, CB, DC, DS, JC, MC, VI.
SOME UNITS

(ASK) (╎╎) (Y) (&M) (🖉) (➾) (✕) (📺) (DATA PORT) (💻) / (✕) (🔒) /

PEEKSKILL pop. 22,441

———— WHERE TO STAY ————

PEEKSKILL INN   **Phone:** (914)739-1500
(AAA) (SAVE)   All Year [ECP]   1P: $117-$130
Location: Jct US 6 and 9, e to top of Main St. 634 Main St 10566. Fax: 914/739-7067. **Facility:** 53 units. 52 one-
bedroom standard units. 1 one-bedroom suite ($179-$209). 2 stories, exterior corridors. **Parking:** on-site.
Motel   **Terms:** small pets only. **Amenities:** voice mail, hair dryers. *Some:* irons. **Dining:** 11:30 am-9:30 pm, cock-
tails. **Pool(s):** outdoor. **Cards:** AX, DC, DS, MC, VI. **Special Amenities:** free expanded continental breakfast and free newspaper.
SOME UNITS

(SD) (✦) (🐾) (╎╎) (Y) (➾) (📺) (DATA PORT) / (✕) (🔒) (🍴) /
FEE

———— WHERE TO DINE ————

MONTEVERDE AT OLDSTONE   **Lunch:** $10-$23   **Dinner:** $17-$27   **Phone:** 914/739-5000
Location: On US 6 and 202; 2.5 mi se of Bear Mountain Bridge. 28 Bear Mountain Bridge Rd 10566.
Hours: noon-2:30 & 5:30-9:30 pm, Fri-10 pm, Sat-11 pm, Sun noon-8:30 pm. Closed major holidays; also
Continental   Tues & for lunch Sat. **Features:** Overlooking the Hudson River, the 18th-century mansion features a
DC, MC, VI.   Continental menu and formally dressed servers. Dressy casual; cocktails. **Parking:** on-site. **Cards:** AX,   (Y) (✕)

PORT CHESTER pop. 27,867

———— WHERE TO DINE ————

THE WILLETT HOUSE   **Lunch:** $9-$27   **Dinner:** $26-$48   **Phone:** 914/939-7500
Location: Corner of Willett and Abendroth aves. 20 Willett Ave 10573. **Hours:** 11:45 am-10 pm, Sat noon-11 pm,
Sun 4 pm-9 pm. **Reservations:** suggested. **Features:** The large and attractive red-brick restaurant
Steak & Seafood   welcomes families to enjoy well-prepared selections of prime steak, plus lobster and grilled seafood.
Lighter lunch fare includes such tasty sandwiches as the BLT, which comes with homemade potato chips.
Casual dress; cocktails. **Parking:** on-site (fee). **Cards:** AX, DC, DS, MC, VI.   (Y) (✕)

POUND RIDGE pop. 4,726

──── WHERE TO DINE ────

THE INN AT POUND RIDGE   Historic   **Lunch:** $10-$14   **Dinner:** $19-$30   **Phone:** 914/764-5779
▼▼▼▼   **Location:** Jct SR 172, SR 137, just n; in the Hamlet. 258 Westchester Ave (SR 137) 10576. **Hours:** noon-3 & 6-9
American   pm, Sat 6 pm-10 pm, Sun noon-3 & 5-9 pm. Closed: 1/1, 12/25; also Mon. **Reservations:** suggested.
Features: Nestled amid beautifully landscaped grounds, the historic inn features extensive accents of
wood and stone. The downstairs dining room faces a lovely picture window garden. Rack of lamb is the
signature dish on a menu of contemporary American cuisine. An accomplished pianist performs on Saturday nights. Dressy
casual; cocktails. **Parking:** on-site. **Cards:** AX, MC, VI.   🍸 ✕

RED HOOK pop. 1,805

──── WHERE TO DINE ────

CAPPUCINO BY COPPOLA'S   **Lunch:** $6-$14   **Dinner:** $7-$18   **Phone:** 845/876-1331
◉◉◉   **Location:** Jct SR 199, 3.4 mi n. 4604 Rt 9G 12571. **Hours:** 11:30 am-9:30 pm, Fri & Sat-10 pm, Sun 10:30
▼▼▼   am-9 pm. Closed: 11/25, 12/25. **Reservations:** accepted. **Features:** Offering a wide variety of classic
Italian   Italian dishes as well as pizza, this roadside eatery is popular with locals and the college crowd. Casual
dress; cocktails. **Parking:** on-site. **Cards:** AX, CB, DC, DS, JC, MC, VI.   🍸 ✕

RYE pop. 14,955

──── WHERE TO STAY ────

COURTYARD BY MARRIOTT   *Book at aaa.com*   **Phone:** (914)921-1110
▼▼▼▼   All Year   1P: $89-$149   2P: $89-$149
Small-scale Hotel   **Location:** I-95 (New England Thruway), exit 22 northbound, 0.3 mi n; exit 21 southbound, just s; I-287 (Cross
Westchester Exwy), exit 11 eastbound, 0.4 mi s on US 1, 0.4 mi e on Peck Ave, then just n. 631 Midland Ave 10580.
Fax: 914/921-2446. **Facility:** 145 units. 133 one-bedroom standard units. 12 one-bedroom suites. 4 stories,
interior corridors. *Bath:* combo or shower only. **Parking:** on-site. **Terms:** cancellation fee imposed. **Amenities:** dual phone lines,
voice mail, irons, hair dryers. **Pool(s):** heated indoor. **Leisure Activities:** whirlpool, exercise room. **Guest Services:** valet and
coin laundry. **Business Services:** meeting rooms. **Cards:** AX, DC, DS, MC, VI.

SOME UNITS
🅰ⓈⓀ Ⓢ🄳 ➕ 🍽 🍸 🚻 🔌 🛜 ➿ 📷 🖥 / ✕ 🛢 📺 /
FEE

──── WHERE TO DINE ────

CAFE LIVORNO   **Lunch:** $10-$15   **Dinner:** $17-$33   **Phone:** 914/967-1909
▼▼▼   **Location:** Jct US 1, 0.3 mi n; downtown. 92 Purchase St 10580. **Hours:** noon-2 & 5:30-10 pm, Sat 5:30
Northern   pm-10:30 pm. Closed major holidays; also Sun. **Reservations:** suggested. **Features:** The established
Italian   bistro serves authentic food in a cozy atmosphere perfect for an intimate dinner. Casual dress; cocktails.
Parking: street. **Cards:** AX, DC, MC, VI.   ✕

LA PANETIERE   **Lunch:** $17-$27   **Dinner:** $28-$45   **Phone:** 914/967-8140
▼▼▼▼   **Location:** I-95 (New England Thruway), exit 19, 0.8 mi e on Playland Pkwy, then 0.5 mi s. 530 Milton Rd 10580.
French   **Hours:** noon-2:30 & 6-9:30 pm, Sat from 6 pm, Sun 1 pm-3 & 5-8:30 pm. Closed: 1/1.
Reservations: suggested. **Features:** This lovely dining room is replete with Provincial charm from the
stenciled stucco walls, imported fabrics, beamed ceilings, to the delightful dishes and the chicken/rooster
salt and pepper shakers. Cheerful flower bouquets on each table further brighten the intimate room. Delicate portions of fine,
traditionally prepared dishes attract locals again and again. Gracious service is de rigueur. Semi-formal attire; cocktails.
Parking: on-site and valet. **Cards:** AX, CB, DC, DS, MC, VI.   🍸 ✕

RYE BROOK pop. 8,602

──── WHERE TO STAY ────

DORAL ARROWWOOD RESORT & GOLF CLUB   *Book at aaa.com*   **Phone:** 914/939-5500
▼▼▼   Property failed to provide current rates
Resort   **Location:** Hutchinson River Pkwy, exit 28, 1 mi nw on Lincoln Ave, then 0.7 mi n. 975 Anderson Hill Rd 10573.
Large-scale Hotel   Fax: 914/935-6617. **Facility:** Featuring complete conference facilities, this resort on 114 rolling acres also offers extensive recreational facilities. 374 units. 372 one-bedroom standard units. 2 one-bedroom suites. 5
stories, interior corridors. **Terms:** check-in 5 pm. **Amenities:** video games (fee),
dual phone lines, voice mail, safes, irons, hair dryers. *Some:* DVD players, CD players, high-speed Internet (fee). **Pool(s):** heated
indoor/outdoor. **Leisure Activities:** saunas, whirlpool, steamrooms, racquetball courts, jogging, basketball, volleyball. *Fee:* golf-9
holes, 2 indoor tennis courts. **Guest Services:** gift shop, valet laundry. **Business Services:** conference facilities, business
center.

SOME UNITS
➕ 🍽 24✎ 🍸 ➿ 🚹 ✕ 📷 🔌 🖥 / ✕ /
FEE

HILTON RYE TOWN   *Book at aaa.com*   **Phone:** (914)939-6300
◉◉◉ Ⓢ🄰🅅🄴   All Year   1P: $119-$299   2P: $139-$319   XP: $20   F18
▼▼▼   **Location:** I-287 (cross the Westchester Expwy), exit 10 eastbound, 0.6 mi ne on SR 120A; westbound, 0.3 mi n on Webb
Large-scale Hotel   Ave, then 0.4 mi ne on SR 120A. 699 Westchester Ave 10573. Fax: 914/939-5328. **Facility:** 437 units. 426 one-
bedroom standard units. 5 one- and 6 two-bedroom suites. 4 stories, interior corridors. *Bath:* combo or
shower only. **Parking:** on-site and valet. **Terms:** cancellation fee imposed. **Amenities:** dual phone lines,
voice mail, honor bars, irons, hair dryers. *Fee:* video games, high-speed Internet. **Dining:** 2 restaurants, 6:30
am-11 pm, cocktails. **Pool(s):** outdoor, heated indoor. **Leisure Activities:** saunas, whirlpool, exercise room, basketball, shuffleboard. *Fee:* 3 lighted indoor tennis courts. **Guest Services:** gift shop, valet laundry. **Business Services:** conference facilities,
business center. **Cards:** AX, DC, DS, JC, MC, VI.

SOME UNITS
Ⓢ🄳 🍽 🍸 🚻 🔌 🛜 ➿ ✕ 📷 🔌 🖥 / ✕ 🛢 /

SPRING VALLEY pop. 25,464

——— WHERE TO STAY ———

FAIRFIELD INN BY MARRIOTT   *Book at aaa.com*   **Phone:** (845)426-2000
▼▼▼▼   All Year   1P: $99-$119
Location: I-87/287, exit 14 (SR 59 W) to New Clarkstown Rd, just e. 100 Spring Valley Marketplace 10977.
Small-scale Hotel   Fax: 845/426-2008. **Facility:** 105 one-bedroom standard units. 4 stories, interior corridors. *Bath:* combo or
shower only. **Terms:** [ECP] meal plan available. **Amenities:** video games (fee), voice mail,
irons, hair dryers. **Pool(s):** outdoor. **Leisure Activities:** exercise room. **Guest Services:** valet and coin laundry. **Business Serv-**
ices: fax (fee). **Cards:** AX, CB, DC, DS, MC, VI.

SOME UNITS

(ASK) (S/D) (&) (≈) (※) (DATA PORT) / (✕) /

——— WHERE TO DINE ———

——— *The following restaurant has not been evaluated by AAA*
but is listed for your information only. ———

SUSHI & STEAK   **Phone:** 845/426-5472
[fyi]   Not evaluated. **Location:** I-87/287, exit 14 (SR 59 W) to New Clarkstown Rd, just e; in Spring Valley Marketplace.
100 Spring Valley Marketplace 10977. **Features:** Sushi, tempura and teriyaki are traditionally made from fresh
ingredients. Many healthy and vegetarian choices.

SUFFERN pop. 11,006

——— WHERE TO STAY ———

HOLIDAY INN-SUFFERN   *Book at aaa.com*   **Phone:** (845)357-4800
(AAA) (SAVE)   All Year [CP]   1P: $108-$159   2P: $108-$159
▼▼▼   **Location:** I-87/287, exit 14B, just n. 3 Executive Blvd 10901. Fax: 845/918-1475. **Facility:** 243 units. 238 one-
bedroom standard units. 5 one-bedroom suites ($150-$225) with whirlpools. 3 stories, interior corridors.
Small-scale Hotel   **Parking:** on-site. **Terms:** check-in 4 pm, [BP] meal plan available. **Amenities:** dual phone lines, voice mail,
irons, hair dryers. **Dining:** 6:30 am-10:30 & 5-10 pm, Fri & Sat-11 pm, cocktails. **Pool(s):** heated indoor.
Leisure Activities: sauna, whirlpool, exercise room. *Fee:* game room. **Guest Services:** sundries, valet and
coin laundry, area transportation-within 5 mi. **Business Services:** conference facilities, business center. **Cards:** AX, DC, DS,
MC, VI. **Special Amenities:** free continental breakfast and early check-in/late check-out.

SOME UNITS

(S/D) (¶¶) (Y) (≈) (≈) (✕) (※) (DATA PORT) (▭) / (✕) (▤) /

WELLESLEY INN (SUFFERN)   *Book at aaa.com*   **Phone:** (845)368-1900
(AAA) (SAVE)   All Year [ECP]   1P: $79-$119   XP: $10   F17
▼▼ ▼▼   **Location:** I-87/287, exit 14B, just s. 17 N Airmont Rd 10901. Fax: 845/368-1927. **Facility:** 95 one-bedroom stan-
dard units. 4 stories, interior corridors. *Bath:* combo or shower only. **Parking:** on-site. **Amenities:** video
Small-scale Hotel   games (fee), voice mail, irons, hair dryers. *Some:* dual phone lines. **Guest Services:** valet and coin laundry.
Cards: AX, DC, DS, JC, MC, VI. **Special Amenities:** free expanded continental breakfast and free
newspaper. *(See color ad p 449)*

SOME UNITS

(S/D) (🐾) (¶¶) (&M) (&) (◢) (※) (DATA PORT) (▭) / (✕) (▤) (▣) /

——— WHERE TO DINE ———

MARCELLO'S OF SUFFERN   **Lunch:** $11-$16   **Dinner:** $17-$27   **Phone:** 845/357-9108
(AAA)   **Location:** Between Orange and Chestnut aves; center. 21 Lafayette Ave 10901. **Hours:** noon-2 & 5-9:30 pm, Sat
▼▼▼   noon-2:30 & 5-10 pm, Sun 3 pm-8:30 pm. Closed major holidays. **Reservations:** suggested.
Features: The chef-owned ristorante uses quality, hand-selected ingredients in traditional Italian dishes
Italian   such as tangy eggplant caponata, rack of lamb, grilled ostrich with spicy Mediterranean salsa and salmon
with mustard and mushroom sauce. Pastas are handmade, as are the scrumptious desserts. A
professionally trained staff accommodates every whim. Dressy casual; cocktails. **Parking:** valet and street.
Cards: AX, CB, DS, MC, VI.

(Y) (✕)

ORIENTAL GARDEN   **Lunch:** $6-$14   **Dinner:** $8-$14   **Phone:** 845/368-0011
▼▼ ▼▼   **Location:** Between Orange and Chestnut aves; center. 25 Lafayette Ave (Rt 59) 10901. **Hours:** 11:30 am-10 pm,
Fri-11 pm, Sat noon-11 pm, Sun 2 pm-10 pm. Closed: 11/25. **Features:** Simple to look at and unassuming
Chinese   from the outside, the restaurant treats locals to well-prepared dishes, including such standouts as lace
shrimp and lobster lover. Ribs and Peking duck are some of the best around. Service is extra-friendly.
Casual dress; cocktails. **Parking:** street. **Cards:** AX, DS, MC, VI.

(✕)

TARRYTOWN pop. 11,090

——— WHERE TO STAY ———

THE CASTLE AT TARRYTOWN   *Book at aaa.com*   **Phone:** (914)631-1980
▼▼▼ ▼▼▼   All Year   1P: $295-$315   2P: $295-$315   XP: $25   F12
Location: I-287 (cross the Westchester Expwy), exit 1, 0.3 mi w on SR 119, then 0.6 mi n on Benedict Ave; opposite
Historic   entrance to Hackley School. 400 Benedict Ave 10591. Fax: 914/631-4612. **Facility:** Views of the river and, on clear
Country Inn   days, the Manhattan skyline, are a feature of this luxurious Gothic-style stone castle set on lush grounds.
Smoke free premises. 31 units. 26 one-bedroom standard units. 5 one-bedroom suites ($435-$800). 3-4 sto-
ries, interior corridors. **Parking:** valet. **Terms:** check-in 4 pm, 7 day cancellation notice, package plans - seasonal.
Amenities: video library, DVD players, CD players, dual phone lines, voice mail, safes, irons, hair dryers. *Some:* video games.
Dining: Equus, see separate listing. **Pool(s):** heated outdoor. **Leisure Activities:** whirlpool, tennis court, hiking trails, jogging,
exercise room. *Fee:* bicycles, massage. **Guest Services:** valet laundry. **Business Services:** meeting rooms, administrative services (fee), fax. **Cards:** AX, DC, DS, MC, VI.

(¶¶) (&M) (◢) (≈) (✕) (✕) (VCR) (※) (DATA PORT) (▤)

COURTYARD BY MARRIOTT   *Book at aaa.com*   Phone: 914/631-1122

All Year   1P: $89-$189   2P: $89-$189

Small-scale Hotel

Location: I-287 (cross the Westchester Exwy), exit 1, 1 mi w on SR 119. 475 White Plains Rd 10591. Fax: 914/631-1357. **Facility:** 139 units. 125 one-bedroom standard units. 14 one-bedroom suites ($199-$219). 3 stories, interior corridors. *Bath:* combo or shower only. **Parking:** on-site. **Terms:** cancellation fee imposed, [BP] meal plan available. **Amenities:** high-speed Internet (fee), dual phone lines, voice mail, irons, hair dryers. **Pool(s):** heated indoor. **Leisure Activities:** whirlpool, exercise room. **Guest Services:** valet laundry. **Business Services:** meeting rooms. **Cards:** AX, DC, DS, JC, MC, VI.

SOME UNITS / FEE

DOLCE TARRYTOWN HOUSE   *Book at aaa.com*   Phone: (914)591-8200

All Year   1P: $229

Large-scale Hotel

Location: I-87, exit 9, 0.9 mi s on US 9, then just e: I-287 (cross the Westchester Expwy), exit 1, 1.7 mi w on SR 119, 1.1 mi s on US 9, then just e. 49 E Sunnyside Ln 10591 (PO Box 222). Fax: 914/591-3131. **Facility:** 212 units. 206 one-bedroom standard units. 6 one-bedroom suites. 5 stories, interior corridors. **Parking:** on-site. **Terms:** check-in 4 pm, cancellation fee imposed, [BP] meal plan available, package plans - weekends. **Amenities:** video games (fee), high-speed Internet, dual phone lines, voice mail, irons, hair dryers. *Some:* CD players. **Dining:** 7 am-9, noon-2 & 6-9 pm, cocktails. **Pool(s):** outdoor, heated indoor. **Leisure Activities:** sauna, whirlpool, 2 tennis courts, racquetball court, 1 lane bowling alley, billiards, bocci, spa, basketball, horseshoes, shuffleboard, volleyball. **Guest Services:** sundries, valet laundry. **Business Services:** conference facilities, business center. **Cards:** AX, CB, DC, DS, MC, VI.

SOME UNITS / FEE

HILTON OF TARRYTOWN   *Book at aaa.com*   Phone: (914)631-5700

All Year   1P: $99-$209   2P: $119-$229   XP: $20   F18

Large-scale Hotel

Location: I-287/87 (New York Thruway), exit 9, then just s on US 9. 455 S Broadway 10591. Fax: 914/631-0075. **Facility:** 246 units. 242 one-bedroom standard units. 4 one-bedroom suites. 2 stories, interior corridors. **Parking:** on-site. **Terms:** cancellation fee imposed. **Amenities:** dual phone lines, voice mail, honor bars, irons, hair dryers. *Fee:* video games, high-speed Internet. **Pool(s):** heated outdoor, heated indoor, wading. **Leisure Activities:** saunas, whirlpool, 2 lighted tennis courts, jogging, playground, exercise room, basketball. **Guest Services:** valet laundry. **Business Services:** conference facilities, business center. **Cards:** AX, CB, DC, DS, MC, VI.

SOME UNITS / FEE

WESTCHESTER MARRIOTT HOTEL   *Book at aaa.com*   Phone: (914)631-2200

9/12-11/20   1P: $214   2P: $214
5/1-6/24   1P: $204   2P: $204
6/25-9/11 & 11/21-4/30   1P: $199   2P: $199

Large-scale Hotel

Location: I-87 (New York Thruway), exit 9 northbound, 0.8 mi e on SR 119; southbound, just n on US 9, then 1 mi e on SR 119. 670 White Plains Rd 10591. Fax: 914/631-7819. **Facility:** 444 units. 439 one-bedroom standard units. 5 one-bedroom suites. 10 stories, interior corridors. *Bath:* combo or shower only. **Parking:** on-site. **Amenities:** dual phone lines, voice mail, irons, hair dryers. *Fee:* video games, high-speed Internet. **Pool(s):** heated indoor. **Leisure Activities:** saunas, whirlpool. *Fee:* massage. **Guest Services:** gift shop, valet and coin laundry, beauty salon. **Business Services:** conference facilities, business center. **Cards:** AX, DC, DS, MC, VI.

SOME UNITS /

──── *The following lodging was either not evaluated or did not* ────
meet AAA rating requirements but is listed for your information only.

SPRINGHILL SUITES BY MARRIOTT TARRYTOWN/GREENBURGH   Phone: 914/366-4600

[fyi]

1/1-4/30   1P: $169-$189   2P: $169-$189
9/6-12/31   1P: $149-$169   2P: $149-$169

Small-scale Hotel   5/1-9/5   1P: $129-$169   2P: $129-$169

Too new to rate. **Location:** I-287 (cross the Westchester Expwy), exit 1, just w; New York Thruway, exit 9, just n on US 9, then e on SR 119. 480 White Plains Rd 10523. Fax: 914/366-4601. **Amenities:** 145 units, coffeemakers, microwaves, refrigerators, pool. **Terms:** cancellation fee imposed. **Cards:** AX, CB, DC, DS, JC, MC, VI.

──── **WHERE TO DINE** ────

EQUUS   Lunch: $22-$35   Dinner: $64-$84   Phone: 914/631-3646

French

Location: I-287, exit 1, I-287 (cross the Westchester Expwy), exit 1, 0.3 mi w on SR 119, then 0.6 mi n; opposite entrance to Hackley School; in The Castle at Tarrytown. 400 Benedict Ave 10591. **Hours:** 7 am-10, noon-2:30 & 6-10 pm. **Closed:** 1/2-1/18. **Reservations:** suggested. **Features:** In a veritable stone castle atop a hill overlooking the Hudson River, the restaurant is as noted for its setting as for its impressive contemporary French cuisine. Grilled salmon, for example, is simply superb—perfectly seasoned, yet moist and opaque. Semi-formal attire; cocktails. **Parking:** valet. **Cards:** AX, DC, MC, VI.

HORSEFEATHERS   Lunch: $7-$12   Dinner: $16-$29   Phone: 914/631-6606

American

Location: Downtown. 94 N Broadway (SR 9) 10591. **Hours:** 11:30 am-10 pm, Sun-9 pm. Closed major holidays. **Reservations:** suggested, weekends. **Features:** Decor is reflective of the 1700s in this quaint, casual restaurant. A literary theme, with books and murals of authors, ties it all together. The menu centers on wholesome, home-style fare, such as burgers, steak and pasta. Weekend brunch is popular. Casual dress; cocktails. **Parking:** on-site. **Cards:** AX, DS, MC, VI.

WHITE PLAINS pop. 53,077

——— WHERE TO STAY ———

CROWNE PLAZA WHITE PLAINS   *Book at aaa.com*   **Phone:** (914)682-0050

▽▼▽ ▼▽
5/1-6/30 & 10/1-12/31   1P: $159-$269   2P: $159-$269
7/1-9/30 & 1/1-4/30   1P: $139-$259   2P: $139-$259
Large-scale Hotel   **Location:** I-287, exit 8 westbound; exit 8W eastbound, just e on Bloomingdale Rd, then just s on Maple Ave. Located next to a mall. 66 Hale Ave 10601. Fax: 914/682-0405. **Facility:** 400 units. 396 one-bedroom standard units. 4 one-bedroom suites, some with whirlpools. 14 stories, interior corridors. *Bath:* combo or shower only. **Parking:** on-site and valet. **Amenities:** CD players, dual phone lines, voice mail, safes, honor bars, irons, hair dryers. **Pool(s):** heated indoor. **Leisure Activities:** whirlpool, exercise room. **Guest Services:** gift shop, valet and coin laundry, area transportation. **Business Services:** conference facilities, business center. **Cards:** AX, CB, DC, DS, JC, MC, VI.

SOME UNITS
(ASK) 🔊 ⊹ 🍽 🍸 🅼 ▧ 🏊 🛥 ⚡ [DATA PORT] 💻 / ⊠ ☎ /
FEE

RENAISSANCE WESTCHESTER HOTEL   *Book at aaa.com*   **Phone:** (914)694-5400

▽▼▽ ▼▽
5/1-9/4   1P: $129-$221   2P: $129-$221
9/5-4/30   1P: $119-$215   2P: $119-$215
Large-scale Hotel   **Location:** I-287 (Cross Westchester Exwy), exit 9N-S eastbound, 0.5 mi e on Westchester Ave, just n on Kenilworth Rd, then 0.7 mi w on Westchester Ave; westbound, 0.8 mi w on Westchester Ave. 80 W Red Oak Ln 10604. Fax: 914/694-5616. **Facility:** 350 units. 343 one-bedroom standard units. 7 one-bedroom suites. 6 stories, interior corridors. **Parking:** on-site. **Terms:** small pets only ($60 extra charge). **Amenities:** video games, high-speed Internet (fee), dual phone lines, voice mail, honor bars, irons, hair dryers. *Some:* CD players. **Pool(s):** heated indoor. **Leisure Activities:** saunas, whirlpool, exercise room, horseshoes, volleyball. *Fee:* 2 lighted indoor tennis courts, game room. **Guest Services:** gift shop, valet laundry. **Business Services:** conference facilities, business center. **Cards:** AX, CB, DC, DS, MC, VI.

SOME UNITS
(ASK) ⊹ 🍽 24🍸 🍸 🅼 ▧ 🏊 ⚡ ⊠ ⚡ [DATA PORT] 💻 / ⊠ [VCR] ☎ /
FEE FEE   FEE

SUMMERFIELD SUITES BY WYNDHAM-WESTCHESTER   *Book at aaa.com*   **Phone:** (914)251-9700

▽▼▽
All Year   1P: $109-$329   2P: $109-$329
Small-scale Hotel   **Location:** I-287 (Cross Westchester Exwy), exit 9A eastbound, 0.6 mi e on Westchester Ave, then 0.3 mi n; exit 9N-S westbound, 0.9 mi w on Westchester Ave. 101 Corporate Park Dr 10604. Fax: 914/251-1699. **Facility:** 159 units. 104 one- and 55 two-bedroom suites ($109-$329), some with efficiencies or kitchens. 4 stories, interior corridors. *Bath:* combo or shower only. **Parking:** on-site. **Terms:** check-in 4 pm, cancellation fee imposed, [BP] meal plan available, pets ($50-$250 fee). **Amenities:** dual phone lines, voice mail, irons, hair dryers. *Fee:* video library, high-speed Internet. **Pool(s):** heated outdoor. **Leisure Activities:** whirlpool, exercise room, sports court. **Guest Services:** sundries, complimentary evening beverages: Mon-Thurs, valet and coin laundry. **Business Services:** meeting rooms, business center. **Cards:** AX, CB, DC, JC, MC, VI. Not Affiliated with the Wyndham Hotel in Manhattan.

SOME UNITS
(ASK) 🔊 🐾 ▧ 🏊 ⊠ [VCR] ⚡ [DATA PORT] ☎ 🖨 💻 / ⊠ /
FEE

——— WHERE TO DINE ———

DAWAT   **Lunch:** $11   **Dinner:** $8-$25   **Phone:** 914/428-4411
▽▼ ▽▼▽
Indian   **Location:** Jct Mamaroneck Ave and E Post Rd, just ne; downtown. 230 E Post Rd 10601. **Hours:** 11:30 am-2:45 & 5-10 pm, Fri & Sat-10:30 pm, Sun-9:30 pm. Closed: 12/25; also Mon. **Reservations:** suggested. **Features:** Indian music plays in the background of the dining room, which is decorated with artwork of carved wood and painted faces. The daily luncheon buffet lays out piquant selections of beef, chicken, rice and lamb. Service is consistent and thorough. Cocktails. **Parking:** on-site. **Cards:** AX, CB, DC, MC, VI.   🍸 ⊠

REKA'S THAI RESTAURANT   **Lunch:** $10   **Dinner:** $10-$20   **Phone:** 914/949-1440
AAA
▽▼▽   **Location:** Southeast corner of Main St and SR 22 (N Broadway). 2 Westchester Ave 10601. **Hours:** noon-10 pm. Closed major holidays; also Mon. **Reservations:** suggested, weekends. **Features:** A favorite with the locals, the inviting, vibrant restaurant is a great spot in which to enjoy piquant dishes of authentic Thai cuisine. The atmosphere is warm and casual. Particularly popular are the prix fixe lunch and the Sunday champagne brunch. Dressy casual; cocktails. **Parking:** street. **Cards:** AX, CB, DC, MC, VI.   🍸 ⊠
Thai

SPORTS PAGE PUB　　　　Lunch: $5-$14　　　　Dinner: $5-$14　　　　Phone: 914/761-6697

American

Location: Jct Hutchison River Pkwy, just n. 1205 Mamaroneck Ave 10605. **Hours:** 11:30 am-11 pm, Sat from noon, Sun noon-10 pm; from 5 pm weekends in summer. Closed major holidays. **Reservations:** accepted. **Features:** This place is jock nirvana—if it has to do with sports, you'll find it here. Not only can diners enjoy a menu that includes Southwestern, Tex-Mex, barbecue, steak and pasta choices, but they also can play all kinds of games and watch events on 50 TVs. Casual dress; cocktails. **Parking:** on-site. **Cards:** AX, DC, MC, VI.

YONKERS pop. 196,086

———— WHERE TO STAY ————

HOLIDAY INN　　*Book at aaa.com*

Small-scale Hotel

All Year　　　　Phone: (914)476-3800

Location: I-87, exit 6, just w. 125 Tuckahoe Rd 10710. Fax: 914/423-3555. **Facility:** 103 units. 100 one-bedroom standard units. 3 one-bedroom suites. 3 stories, interior/exterior corridors. *Bath:* combo or shower only. **Parking:** on-site. **Amenities:** video games (fee), voice mail, irons, hair dryers. **Pool(s):** outdoor. **Leisure Activities:** exercise room. **Guest Services:** valet laundry. **Business Services:** meeting rooms, fax (fee). **Cards:** AX, DC, DS, MC, VI. Affiliated with Holiday Inns.

1P: $138-$195　　　2P: $138-$195

SOME UNITS

ROYAL REGENCY HOTEL & CONFERENCE CENTER　　*Book at aaa.com*　　　Phone: (914)476-6200

Small-scale Hotel

All Year [ECP]　　　1P: $114　　　2P: $124　　　XP: $10　　　F16

Location: I-87, exit 6W, just w. 165 Tuckahoe Rd 10710. Fax: 914/375-7017. **Facility:** 91 units. 90 one-bedroom standard units, some with whirlpools. 1 one-bedroom suite ($225-$450) with whirlpool. 3 stories, interior/exterior corridors. *Bath:* combo or shower only. **Parking:** on-site. **Amenities:** voice mail. **Dining:** 4 pm-11 pm; closed Sun, cocktails. **Leisure Activities:** exercise room. **Guest Services:** valet laundry. **Business Services:** conference facilities. **Cards:** AX, DS, MC, VI. **Special Amenities:** free expanded continental breakfast and free newspaper.

SOME UNITS

———— WHERE TO DINE ————

HUNAN VILLAGE　　　　Lunch: $12-$25　　　　Dinner: $12-$25　　　　Phone: 914/779-2272

Chinese

Location: I-87, exit 6E southbound; exit 6 northbound, 1.5 mi e on Tuckahoe Rd, then just n. 1828 Central Park Ave (SR 100) 10710. **Hours:** noon-11 pm, Fri & Sat-midnight. Closed: 11/25. **Reservations:** suggested, weekends. **Features:** The established local favorite delivers a broad range of cuisines: Hunan, Cantonese, Hong Kong, Mandarin and Szechuan. An emphasis is placed on fresh produce and seafood. Attentive servers and a soothing atmosphere make your experience a memorable one. Casual dress; cocktails. **Parking:** on-site. **Cards:** AX, DC, MC, VI.

Statue of Liberty / © Lester Lefkowitz / Corbis

This ends listings for the New York City Vicinity.
The following page resumes the alphabetical listings of cities in New York.

Destination Niagara Falls
pop. 55,593

Welcome to Niagara Falls, where the mesmerizing cataracts will capture your heart forever. The Honeymoon Capital attracts some 50,000 newlyweds yearly.

There are more ways than one to view the plunging water. Take an evening stroll along the river, when the spectacle of colored lights offers an enchanting experience. Capture the aura of the rolling water with a romantic picnic overlooking the marvelous falls. Or treat yourself to a guided tour.

© W. Bertsch / Robertstock

Dining, Niagara Falls. Goat Island restaurants offer a two-for-one dining experience: dinner and a spectacular view.

© Gibson Stock Photography

Seneca Niagara Casino, Niagara Falls. Downtown's Las Vegas-style casino offers a glitzy diversion from the natural spectacle just minutes away. (See listing page 164)

Niagara Falls

CANADA
USA

Youngstown

See Vicinity map page 462

Lewiston

Newfane

Lockport
Sanborn

Niagara Falls

Niagara Falls

Wheatfield

See Vicinity map page 464

ON NY

© Earl W. Brydges ArtPark

Arts and entertainment, Lewiston. The muses lure visitors to Earl W. Brydges ArtPark to enjoy theater, concerts and dance performances. (See listing page 166)

Places included in this AAA Destination City:

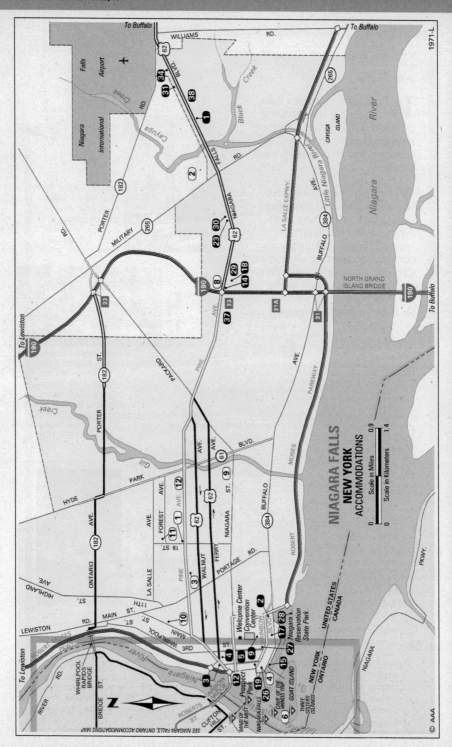

NIAGARA FALLS
NEW YORK
ACCOMMODATIONS

Scale in Miles
0   0.9

Scale in Kilometers
0   1.4

1971-L

© AAA

Niagara Falls, New York

This index helps you "spot" where approved accommodations and restaurants are located on the corresponding detailed maps. Lodging rate ranges are for comparison only and show the property's high season; rates are per night, unless only weekly (W) rates are available. Restaurant rate range is for dinner, unless only lunch (L) is served. Turn to the listing page for more detailed rate information and consult display ads for special promotions.

Spotter/Map Page Number	OA	NIAGARA FALLS, NEW YORK - Lodgings	Diamond Rating	Rate Range High Season	Listing Page
❶ / p. 462		Travelers Budget Inn	◈	$45-$135	478
❷ / p. 462	ⒶⒶⒶ	Rodeway Inn at the Falls	◈ ◈	$109-$199 SAVE	477
❸ / p. 462	ⒶⒶⒶ	Howard Johnson Inn at the Falls - see color ad p 473, p 218	◈ ◈	$89-$175 SAVE	473
❹ / p. 462	ⒶⒶⒶ	Days Inn at the Falls - see color ad p 470	◈ ◈	$89-$219 SAVE	470
❺ / p. 462	ⒶⒶⒶ	Holiday Inn Select-Niagara Falls	◈ ◈ ◈	$125-$175 SAVE	473
❾ / p. 462	ⒶⒶⒶ	Ramada Inn By the Falls - see color ad p 476, p 8	◈ ◈	$79-$179 SAVE	476
⓬ / p. 462	ⒶⒶⒶ	Comfort Inn The Pointe - see color ad p 469	◈ ◈	$65-$169 SAVE	470
⓮ / p. 462	ⒶⒶⒶ	Howard Johnson Inn-Niagara - see color ad p 474, p 218	◈ ◈	$69-$169 SAVE	474
⓯ / p. 462	ⒶⒶⒶ	Four Points by Sheraton - see color ad p 210	◈ ◈ ◈	$109-$209 SAVE	471
⓱ / p. 462	ⒶⒶⒶ	Hampton Inn-Niagara Falls - see color ad p 472	◈ ◈ ◈	$79-$159 SAVE	472
⓲ / p. 462	ⒶⒶⒶ	Budget Host Inn	◈	$49-$149 SAVE	469
⓳ / p. 462		Quality Hotel and Suites "At the Falls" - see color ad p 475	◈ ◈	$99-$299	474
㉓ / p. 462	ⒶⒶⒶ	Super 8 Motel - see color ad p 477	◈ ◈	$49-$139 SAVE	477
㉖ / p. 462	ⒶⒶⒶ	The Red Coach Inn - see color ad p 476	◈ ◈ ◈	$139-$179 SAVE	477
㉗ / p. 462	ⒶⒶⒶ	Holiday Inn at the Falls - see color ad p 472	◈ ◈ ◈	$99-$199 SAVE	473
㉘ / p. 462		Holley Rankine House	◈ ◈	$70-$135	473
㉙ / p. 462	ⒶⒶⒶ	Swiss Cottage Inn	◈	$32-$169 SAVE	478
㉚ / p. 462		Quality Inn Niagara - see color ad p 475	◈ ◈	$39-$189	475
㉛ / p. 462	ⒶⒶⒶ	Bel Aire Motel	◈	$58-$128 SAVE	468
㉞ / p. 462	ⒶⒶⒶ	Best Western Summit Inn - see color ad p 468	◈ ◈	$79-$159 SAVE	468
㉟ / p. 462	ⒶⒶⒶ	Econo Lodge at the Falls - see color ad p 471	◈ ◈	$50-$185 SAVE	470
㊳ / p. 462	ⒶⒶⒶ	Thriftlodge - see color ad p 478	◈	$36-$199 SAVE	478
		NIAGARA FALLS, NEW YORK - Restaurants			
① / p. 462	ⒶⒶⒶ	Como Restaurant & Deli	◈ ◈	$7-$18	479
② / p. 462		John's Flaming Hearth	◈ ◈	$12-$19	479
③ / p. 462		Pete's Market House Restaurant	◈	$4-$18	479
④ / p. 462	ⒶⒶⒶ	The Red Coach Inn Restaurant	◈ ◈ ◈	$7-$20	479
⑥ / p. 462		Top of the Falls Restaurant	◈	$7-$20	479
⑧ / p. 462		Timber Lodge Steakhouse	◈ ◈	$9-$22	479
⑨ / p. 462		Koban's	◈	$8-$12	479
⑩ / p. 462	ⒶⒶⒶ	Chu's Dining Lounge-Chinese Food	◈ ◈	$6-$11	479
⑪ / p. 462		Fortuna's	◈ ◈	$6-$15	479
⑫ / p. 462		Michael's	◈	$7-$9	479

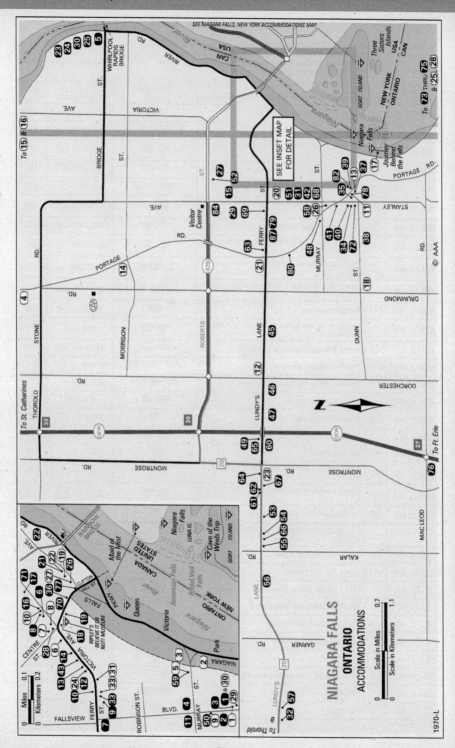

SEE NIAGARA FALLS, NEW YORK ACCOMMODATIONS MAP

NIAGARA FALLS
ONTARIO
ACCOMMODATIONS

Scale in Miles
Scale in Kilometers

1970-L

© AAA

Niagara Falls, Ontario

This index helps you "spot" where approved accommodations and restaurants are located on the corresponding detailed maps. Lodging rate ranges are for comparison only and show the property's high season; rates are per night, unless only weekly (W) rates are available. Restaurant rate range is for dinner, unless only lunch (L) is served. Turn to the listing page for more detailed rate information and consult display ads for special promotions.

Spotter/Map Page Number	OA	NIAGARA FALLS, ONTARIO - Lodgings	Diamond Rating	Rate Range High Season	Listing Page
1 / p. 464		The Oakes Hotel Overlooking the Falls - see color ad p 494	◇◇	$139-$569	508
2 / p. 464	CAA	Renaissance Fallsview Hotel - see color ad p 517	◇◇◇◇	$169-$499 SAVE	516
3 / p. 464		Ramada Plaza Hotel Fallsview - see color ad starting on p 514	◇◇◇	$169-$349	516
4 / p. 464	CAA	Holiday Inn By The Falls - see color ad p 503, p 527	◇◇◇	$110-$245 SAVE	504
5 / p. 464	CAA	Hampton Inn North of the Falls - see color ad p 498	◇◇◇	$89-$249 SAVE	501
6 / p. 464	CAA	Niagara Family Inn	◇	$55-$95 SAVE	508
7 / p. 464	CAA	Cadillac Motel	◇	$50-$120 SAVE	486
8 / p. 464		Chalet Inn and Suites	◇◇◇	$89-$229	489
9 / p. 464	CAA	Travelodge Near The Falls - see color ad p 523	◇◇	$89-$269 SAVE	523
10 / p. 464	CAA	Quality Hotel-Near the Falls - see color ad p 511	◇◇◇	$129-$309 SAVE	513
11 / p. 464	CAA	Best Western Fallsview - see color ad p 486	◇◇	$149-$299 SAVE	486
12 / p. 464	CAA	Days Inn Near the Falls - see color ad p 497	◇◇	$89-$299 SAVE	496
13 / p. 464	CAA	Howard Johnson By The Falls	◇◇◇	$99-$369 SAVE	504
14 / p. 464	CAA	Imperial Hotel and Suites - see color ad p 506	◇◇◇	$79-$359 SAVE	506
15 / p. 464	CAA	Camelot Inn - see color ad p 488	◇◇	$49-$199 SAVE	487
16 / p. 464		The Days Inn Clifton Hill Casino - see color ad p 494	◇◇	$89-$429	490
17 / p. 464	CAA	Hampton Inn at the Falls - see color ad p 501	◇◇◇	$129-$329 SAVE	501
18 / p. 464	CAA	Comfort Inn Clifton Hill - see color ad starting on p 491	◇◇◇	$79-$279 SAVE	489
19 / p. 464	CAA	Quality Inn Clifton Hill - see color ad starting on p 491	◇◇	$69-$269 SAVE	513
21 / p. 464	CAA	Brock Plaza Hotel - see color ad p 487	◇◇◇	$149-$699 SAVE	486
22 / p. 464	CAA	Aston Michael's Inn-By the Falls - see color ad p 525, p 484	◇◇◇	$88-$288 SAVE	484
23 / p. 464	CAA	Comfort Inn North of the Falls - see color ad p 498	◇◇	$79-$249 SAVE	490
24 / p. 464	CAA	Days Inn North of the Falls - see color ad p 498	◇◇	$78-$228 SAVE	496
25 / p. 464		Crystal Motel	◇◇	$79-$189	490
26 / p. 464	CAA	Sheraton on the Falls - see color ad p 487	◇◇◇◇	$169-$1199 SAVE	518
27 / p. 464	CAA	Red Carpet Inn and Suites, Fallsway	◇◇	$49-$199 SAVE	516
28 / p. 464	CAA	Days Inn & Suites by the Falls	◇◇	$79-$299 SAVE	490
29 / p. 464	CAA	Sunset Inn - see color ad p 488	◇◇	$79-$199 SAVE	518
30 / p. 464	CAA	Best Western Fireside Hotel - see color ad p 498	◇◇◇	$89-$249 SAVE	486
31 / p. 464	CAA	Fallsview Inn - see color ad p 499	◇◇◇	$79-$209 SAVE	499
32 / p. 464	CAA	Melody Motel	◇	$48-$98 SAVE	508
33 / p. 464	CAA	Courtyard by Marriott Niagara Falls	◇◇◇	$99-$399 SAVE	490
34 / p. 464	CAA	Vacation Inn - see color ad inside front cover	◇◇◇	$99-$250 SAVE	523
35 / p. 464	CAA	Horseshoe Falls Motor Inn - see color ad p 505	◇◇	$69-$229 SAVE	504
36 / p. 464	CAA	Travelodge Clifton Hill - see color ad p 522	◇◇◇	$99-$389 SAVE	521

Spotter/Map Page Number	OA	NIAGARA FALLS, ONTARIO - Lodgings (continued)	Diamond Rating	Rate Range High Season	Listing Page
37 / p. 464	CAA	**Sheraton Fallsview Hotel & Conference Centre** - see color ad p 519	◆◆◆◆	$159-$349 SAVE	517
38 / p. 464		Aurora Motel	◆	$59-$179	485
39 / p. 464	CAA	**Niagara Falls Marriott Fallsview** - see color ad card insert	◆◆◆◆	$189-$599 SAVE	508
40 / p. 464	CAA	**The President Motor Inn** - see color ad p 509	◆	$79-$175 SAVE	510
41 / p. 464	CAA	**Lincoln Motor Inn** - see color ad p 507	◆◆	$89-$189 SAVE	507
42 / p. 464	CAA	**Stanley Motor Inn**	◆◆	$70-$150 SAVE	518
43 / p. 464	CAA	**A Victoria Motor Inn**	◆	$89-$199 SAVE	485
45 / p. 464	CAA	**Best Western Cairn Croft Hotel** - see color ad p 485, card insert	◆◆◆	$99-$249 SAVE	485
46 / p. 464	CAA	**Knights Inn** - see color ad card insert	◆◆	$79-$249 SAVE	507
47 / p. 464		Days Inn-Lundy's Lane - see color ad p 494, card insert	◆◆	$79-$269	496
48 / p. 464	CAA	**Knights Inn-By The Falls**	◆◆	$84-$254 SAVE	507
49 / p. 464		Ramada Suites Hotel - see color ad p 513, card insert	◆◆◆	$90-$230	516
50 / p. 464	CAA	**Hilton Niagara Falls** - see color ad p 502	◆◆◆◆	$129-$499 SAVE	502
51 / p. 464		Econo Lodge Near the Falls	◆◆	$75-$195	496
53 / p. 464	CAA	**Best Inn**	◆◆	$89-$149 SAVE	485
54 / p. 464	CAA	**Carriage House Motor Lodge** - see color ad p 488, card insert	◆◆	$69-$130 SAVE	488
55 / p. 464	CAA	**Howard Johnson Express Inn** - see color ad card insert	◆◆	$60-$200 SAVE	506
56 / p. 464	CAA	**Americana Resort & Spa** - see color ad p 483, card insert	◆◆◆	$99-$249 SAVE	483
57 / p. 464	CAA	**A Gardens Inn**	◆◆	$69-$129 SAVE	482
58 / p. 464	CAA	**Clarion President Hotel & Suites, By The Falls** - see color ad p 489	◆◆◆	$99-$299 SAVE	489
59 / p. 464		Old Stone Inn	◆◆◆	$129-$349	508
60 / p. 464	CAA	**Comfort Inn Lundy's Lane** - see color ad card insert	◆◆	$99-$269 SAVE	489
61 / p. 464	CAA	**Advantage Inn**	◆	$48-$118 SAVE	482
62 / p. 464	CAA	**Travelodge Bonaventure** - see color ad p 521, card insert	◆◆◆	$79-$199 SAVE	521
63 / p. 464	CAA	**Park Plaza** - see color ad p 510	◆◆◆	$89-$169 SAVE	510
64 / p. 464	CAA	**Flamingo Motor Inn** - see color ad p 500, card insert	◆◆	$69-$179 SAVE	500
65 / p. 464	CAA	**Ramada Coral Resort Hotel** - see color ad p 513, card insert	◆◆◆	$90-$200 SAVE	515
66 / p. 464	CAA	**Villager Lodge** - see color ad card insert	◆◆	$69-$219 SAVE	523
67 / p. 464		Rodeway Inn & Suites	◆◆	$65-$150	516
68 / p. 464	CAA	**Days Inn Fallsview District** - see color ad p 496	◆◆	$75-$275 SAVE	490
69 / p. 464		Kings Inn Near the Falls	◆◆	$79-$199	506
70 / p. 464	CAA	**Thriftlodge Clifton Hill**	◆	$79-$369 SAVE	521
71 / p. 464	CAA	**Skyline Inn** - see color ad p 520	◆◆	$129-$329 SAVE	518
72 / p. 464	CAA	**Rodeway Inn Fallsview** - see color ad p 518	◆◆◆	$79-$259 SAVE	516
73 / p. 464	CAA	**Niagara Parkway Court Motel**	◆	$49-$199 SAVE	508
74 / p. 464	CAA	**Surfside Inn**	◆◆	$69-$229 SAVE	520
75 / p. 464	CAA	**Niagara Falls Motor Lodge**	◆◆	$59-$129 SAVE	508
76 / p. 464	CAA	**Peninsula Inn & Resort**	◆◆	$99-$209 SAVE	510
77 / p. 464		Pilgrim Motor Inn	◆	$99-$149	510
78 / p. 464		Radisson Hotel & Suites Fallsview - see color ad starting on p 514	◆◆◆	$149-$249	514

Spotter/Map Page Number	OA	NIAGARA FALLS, ONTARIO - Lodgings (continued)	Diamond Rating	Rate Range High Season	Listing Page
79 / p. 464	Ⓐ	**Super 8 Hotel** - see color ad p 520	◈◈◈	$59-$289 ⓢⓐⓥⓔ	519
80 / p. 464		Victorian Charm Bed and Breakfast	◈◈	$100-$190	523
82 / p. 464		Embassy Suites Niagara Falls Fallsview	◈◈◈	$189-$599	497
84 / p. 464	Ⓐ	**Glengate Hotel** - see color ad p 500	◈◈◈	$110-$300 ⓢⓐⓥⓔ	501
87 / p. 464		Continental Inn	◈	$59-$119	490
		NIAGARA FALLS, ONTARIO - Restaurants			
① / p. 464		Minolta Tower Centre/Pinnacle Restaurant	◈◈◈	$19-$48	526
② / p. 464	Ⓐ	**Victoria Park Restaurant**	◈◈	$20-$40	528
③ / p. 464	Ⓐ	**The Skylon Tower Dining Rooms** - see color ad p 175	◈◈◈	$36-$84	527
④ / p. 464		Fine Kettle 'O' Fish Inc	◈◈	$8-$30	524
⑤ / p. 464		The Millery Dining Room	◈◈◈	$19-$48	526
⑥ / p. 464	Ⓐ	**Hard Times**	◈◈	$10-$23	525
⑦ / p. 464	Ⓐ	**The Beef Baron**	◈◈	$11-$35	524
⑧ / p. 464	Ⓐ	**Mama Mia's**	◈◈	$7-$22	526
⑨ / p. 464		The Watermark - see color ad p 502	◈◈◈	$25-$65	528
⑩ / p. 464	Ⓐ	**Monticello Grille House & Wine Bar** - see ad p 526	◈◈◈	$15-$35	526
⑪ / p. 464		Outback Steakhouse	◈◈	$12-$25	526
⑫ / p. 464		Frank's Tomato Pie	◈◈	$10-$28	525
⑬ / p. 464		Fallsview Dining Room	◈◈◈	$20-$45	524
⑭ / p. 464		Delduca's	◈◈	$13-$22	524
⑮ / p. 464	Ⓐ	**Whirlpool Restaurant**	◈◈	$6-$20	528
⑯ / p. 464	Ⓐ	**Queenston Heights Restaurant**	◈◈◈	$20-$29	527
⑰ / p. 464	Ⓐ	**Table Rock Restaurant**	◈◈	$20-$35	527
⑱ / p. 464		The Love Boat II	◈◈	$8-$35	525
⑲ / p. 464		Twenty One Club	◈◈◈◈	$16-$61	528
⑳ / p. 464	Ⓐ	**Capri Restaurant**	◈◈◈	$10-$35	524
㉑ / p. 464		La Hacienda Restaurant	◈	$7-$20	525
㉒ / p. 464		The Rainbow Grille Fallsview Steakhouse	◈◈◈	$25-$50	527
㉓ / p. 464	Ⓐ	**Mick and Angelo's Eatery and Bar**	◈◈	$7-$20	526
㉔ / p. 464		Casa d'Oro Dining Lounge	◈◈◈	$19-$60	524
㉕ / p. 464		Betty's Restaurant	◈	$7-$14	524
㉖ / p. 464		Happy Wanderer	◈	$10-$25	525
㉗ / p. 464		Penthouse Restaurant	◈◈◈	$20-$40	526
㉘ / p. 464		Legends on the Niagara	◈◈	$8-$22	525
㉙ / p. 464	Ⓐ	**Terrapin Grille**	◈◈◈	$26-$69	528
㉚ / p. 464		Rooftop Fallsview Dining Room	◈◈◈	$22-$55	527
㉛ / p. 464		Sparks Steak and Seafood	◈◈◈	$15-$39	527
㉝ / p. 464		The Keg Steakhouse and Bar	◈◈	$20-$55	525

NIAGARA FALLS pop. 55,593   (See map and index starting on p. 462)

Accommodations for the Canadian side are listed under Niagara Falls, Ontario.

——— **WHERE TO STAY** ———

BEL AIRE MOTEL   Phone: 716/297-2250   **31**

6/19-9/6	1P: $58-$118	2P: $62-$128	XP: $8
5/1-6/18	1P: $38-$120	2P: $44-$120	XP: $5
9/7-10/13	1P: $38-$80	2P: $44-$80	XP: $6
10/14-4/30	1P: $36-$60	2P: $36-$70	XP: $5

Motel   **Location:** I-190, exit 22, 2 mi e. 9470 Niagara Falls Blvd 14304. **Fax:** 716/297-8712. **Facility:** 22 units. 19 one-bedroom standard units. 3 one-bedroom suites. 1 story, exterior corridors. *Bath:* combo or shower only.
Parking: on-site. **Terms:** 3 day cancellation notice-fee imposed, weekly rates available. **Pool(s):** heated outdoor. **Cards:** AX, MC, VI.

SOME UNITS

BEST WESTERN SUMMIT INN   *Book at aaa.com*   Phone: (716)297-5050   **34**

5/1-9/5 [ECP]	1P: $79-$159	2P: $79-$159	XP: $10 F17
9/6-4/30 [ECP]	1P: $59-$109	2P: $59-$109	XP: $10 F17

Location: I-190, exit 22, 2.1 mi e on US 62 S. 9500 Niagara Falls Blvd 14304. **Fax:** 716/297-0802. **Facility:** 88 one-bedroom standard units, some with whirlpools. 2 stories (no elevator), interior corridors. **Parking:** on-site.
Small-scale Hotel   **Terms:** small pets only ($8 fee, with prior approval). **Amenities:** video library, irons, hair dryers. **Pool(s):** heated indoor. **Leisure Activities:** sauna. **Guest Services:** coin laundry. **Business Services:** meeting rooms, PC. **Cards:** AX, DC, DS, MC, VI. **Special Amenities:** free expanded continental breakfast. *(See color ad below)*

SOME UNITS

(See map and index starting on p. 462)

BUDGET HOST INN   *Book at aaa.com*   Phone: (716)283-3839   **18**
AAA SAVE   7/1-8/31   1P: $49-$119   2P: $59-$149   XP: $8   F8
              5/1-6/30 & 9/1-10/31   1P: $39-$89   2P: $49-$109   XP: $8   F8
              11/1-4/30   1P: $39-$69   2P: $49-$89   F8
Motel   **Location:** I-190, exit 22, just e on US 62 S. 6621 Niagara Falls Blvd 14304. Fax: 716/236-0586. **Facility:** 30 one-
              bedroom standard units, some with efficiencies. 1 story, exterior corridors. **Parking:** on-site. **Terms:** cancel-
              lation fee imposed, pets ($8 deposit). **Pool(s):** small outdoor. **Cards:** AX, DS, MC, VI. **Special Amenities:**
free local telephone calls and early check-in/late check-out.

(See map and index starting on p. 462)

COMFORT INN THE POINTE *Book at aaa.com*   Phone: (716)284-6835   [12]

6/11-9/5	1P: $65-$159	2P: $75-$169	XP: $10 F18
5/1-6/10 & 10/24-4/30	1P: $55-$129	2P: $65-$139	XP: $10 F18
9/6-10/23	1P: $69-$102	2P: $79-$112	XP: $10 F18

Location: I-290 W to I-190, exit 21 (Robert Moses Pkwy) to State Reservation Park entrance. 1 Prospect Pointe 14303.
Small-scale Hotel **Fax:** 716/284-5177. **Facility:** 118 units. 116 one-bedroom standard units, some with whirlpools. 2 one-bedroom suites ($129-$295) with whirlpools. 6 stories, interior corridors. **Parking:** on-site. **Amenities:** video games, voice mail, irons, hair dryers. **Dining:** 7 am-11 pm; hours vary off season, cocktails. **Leisure Activities:** exercise room. **Guest Services:** gift shop, valet laundry. **Business Services:** meeting rooms. **Cards:** AX, CB, DC, DS, JC, MC, VI. **Special Amenities:** free expanded continental breakfast and free local telephone calls. *(See color ad p 469)*

SOME UNITS

DAYS INN AT THE FALLS *Book at aaa.com*   Phone: (716)284-8801   [4]

5/1-9/30	1P: $89-$219	2P: $89-$219	XP: $10 F17
10/1-4/30	1P: $49-$99	2P: $49-$99	XP: $10 F17

Location: On SR 104; downtown; facing entrance to Rainbow Bridge to Canada. 443 Main St 14301.
Small-scale Hotel **Fax:** 716/284-8633. **Facility:** 168 one-bedroom standard units, some with whirlpools. 9 stories, interior corridors. **Parking:** on-site. **Terms:** cancellation fee imposed. **Amenities:** video games, hair dryers. *Some:* irons. **Dining:** 24 hours, cocktails. **Pool(s):** heated indoor. **Leisure Activities:** sauna, exercise room. **Guest Services:** valet and coin laundry. **Business Services:** meeting rooms. **Cards:** AX, DC, DS, MC, VI. *(See color ad below)*

SOME UNITS

ECONO LODGE AT THE FALLS *Book at aaa.com*   Phone: (716)283-1100   [37]

7/1-8/31	1P: $50-$180	2P: $55-$185	XP: $5 F16
5/1-6/30	1P: $35-$149	2P: $40-$149	XP: $5 F16
11/1-4/30	1P: $35-$80	2P: $55-$80	XP: $5 F16
9/1-10/31	1P: $35-$80	2P: $35-$80	XP: $5 F16

Motel **Location:** I-190, exit 22, 0.3 mi n on US 62 N. 5919 Niagara Falls Blvd 14304. Fax: 716/283-2150. **Facility:** 56 one-bedroom standard units, some with whirlpools. 2 stories (no elevator), exterior corridors. **Parking:** on-site. **Terms:** cancellation fee imposed, [ECP] meal plan available. **Amenities:** voice mail. *Some:* irons, hair dryers. **Pool(s):** heated outdoor. **Leisure Activities:** playground. *Fee:* game room. **Guest Services:** coin laundry. **Cards:** AX, DS, MC, VI. **Special Amenities:** free continental breakfast and free newspaper. *(See color ad p 471)*

SOME UNITS

FEE FEE

(See map and index starting on p. 462)

FOUR POINTS BY SHERATON *Book at aaa.com* Phone: (716)285-2521 **15**

5/21-9/6	1P: $109-$199	2P: $119-$209	XP: $10 F
5/1-5/20 & 9/7-4/30	1P: $69-$129	2P: $79-$139	XP: $10 F

Large-scale Hotel **Location:** I-190, exit 21 (Robert Moses Pkwy); exit City Traffic, just w on Rainbow Blvd. 114 Buffalo Ave 14303. Fax: 716/285-0963. **Facility:** 189 units. 183 one-bedroom standard units. 6 one-bedroom suites ($129-$259) with efficiencies, some with whirlpools. 7 stories, interior corridors. *Bath:* combo or shower only. **Parking:** on-site. **Terms:** [BP] meal plan available. **Amenities:** video library (fee), dual phone lines, voice mail, irons, hair dryers. **Dining:** 6:30 am-11 pm; hours vary off season, cocktails. **Pool(s):** heated indoor. **Leisure Activities:** sauna, whirlpool, indoor children's playground, exercise room. *Fee:* game room. **Guest Services:** gift shop, valet and coin laundry. **Business Services:** meeting rooms, PC, fax (fee). **Cards:** AX, CB, DC, DS, JC, MC, VI. *(See color ad p 210)*

(See map and index starting on p. 462)

HAMPTON INN-NIAGARA FALLS Book at aaa.com Phone: (716)285-6666 [17]

Small-scale Hotel

5/1-9/1 [ECP]	1P: $79-$149	2P: $89-$159	
9/2-12/31 [ECP]	1P: $59-$119	2P: $69-$129	
1/1-4/30 [ECP]	1P: $49-$109	2P: $59-$119	

Location: I-190, exit 21 (Robert Moses Pkwy), exit City Traffic; just w. 501 Rainbow Blvd 14303. Fax: 716/285-1423. **Facility:** 100 one-bedroom standard units, some with whirlpools. 5 stories, interior corridors. **Bath:** combo or shower only. **Parking:** on-site. **Terms:** check-in 4 pm, package plans. **Amenities:** video games, voice mail, irons, hair dryers. **Pool(s):** small heated indoor. **Leisure Activities:** whirlpool, exercise room. **Guest Services:** valet and coin laundry. **Business Services:** meeting rooms. **Cards:** AX, DC, DS, MC, VI. **Special Amenities:** free expanded continental breakfast and free local telephone calls. *(See color ad below)*

SOME UNITS

(See map and index starting on p. 462)

HOLIDAY INN AT THE FALLS   *Book at aaa.com*   **Phone:** (716)282-2211   27

AAA [SAVE]   6/25-9/5   1P: $99-$199   2P: $99-$199
     5/1-6/24 & 9/6-4/30   1P: $59-$179   2P: $59-$179

◆◆◆◆   **Location:** Just s of Rainbow Mall, 2 blks from the falls; downtown. 231 Third St 14303. Fax: 716/282-2748.
Small-scale Hotel   **Facility:** 161 one-bedroom standard units, some with whirlpools. 8 stories, interior corridors. **Parking:** on-site. **Terms:** package plans. **Amenities:** video games, voice mail, irons, hair dryers. **Dining:** 24 hours, cocktails. **Pool(s):** heated indoor. **Leisure Activities:** sauna, whirlpool, playground, exercise room. *Fee:* game room. **Guest Services:** valet and coin laundry. **Business Services:** meeting rooms. **Cards:** AX, CB, DC, DS, JC, MC, VI.
(See color ad p 472)

SOME UNITS

🆂🅳 🍴 🍸 🛗 🚭 🏊 ⛔ ✂ 🖥️ 📶 💻 / ⊠ 🛄 /

HOLIDAY INN SELECT-NIAGARA FALLS   *Book at aaa.com*   **Phone:** (716)285-3361   5

AAA [SAVE]   7/2-9/5   1P: $125-$175   2P: $125-$175   XP: $10   F18
     5/1-7/1 & 9/6-10/31   1P: $95-$145   2P: $95-$145   XP: $10   F18
◆◆◆◆   11/1-4/30   1P: $65-$95   2P: $65-$95   XP: $10   F18

Location: Third and Niagara sts; downtown. Located across from the Seneca Niagara Casino. 300 Third St 14303.
Small-scale Hotel   Fax: 716/285-3900. **Facility:** 397 units. 369 one-bedroom standard units. 28 one-bedroom suites. 6 stories, interior corridors. **Parking:** on-site. **Terms:** [BP] & [CP] meal plans available, package plans. **Amenities:** video library (fee), video games, dual phone lines, voice mail, irons, hair dryers. **Dining:** 6:30 am-10 pm; to 11 pm in summer; hours may vary in winter, cocktails. **Pool(s):** heated indoor. **Leisure Activities:** sauna, whirlpool, exercise room. *Fee:* game room. **Guest Services:** gift shop, valet and coin laundry. **Business Services:** conference facilities, fax (fee). **Cards:** AX, CB, DC, DS, JC, MC, VI.

SOME UNITS

🆂🅳 🍴 🍸 🛗 🚭 🏊 ⛔ ✂ 📶 💻 / ⊠ 🛄 📠 /
                                       FEE FEE

HOLLEY RANKINE HOUSE   **Phone:** 716/285-4790   28

◆◆   All Year [BP]   1P: $70-$80   2P: $125-$135

Location: I-190, exit 21 (Robert Moses Pkwy), just w on Buffalo Ave, then just s. Located in a residential area. 525 Riverside Dr 14303. **Facility:** This stately stone house was built in 1955. Smoke free premises. 5 one-bedroom
Historic Bed & Breakfast   standard units. 2 stories (no elevator), interior corridors. *Bath:* some shared or private, combo or shower only. **Parking:** on-site. **Terms:** age restrictions may apply. **Amenities:** hair dryers. **Business Services:** PC.
Cards: MC, VI.

SOME UNITS

[ASK] ⊠ 📺 ☎ / 🍴 📺 /

HOWARD JOHNSON INN AT THE FALLS   *Book at aaa.com*   **Phone:** (716)285-5261   3

AAA [SAVE]   6/19-9/5 [ECP]   1P: $89-$150   2P: $105-$175   XP: $10   F18
     9/6-10/31 [ECP]   1P: $65-$100   2P: $75-$115   XP: $10   F18
◆◆◆   5/1-6/18 [ECP]   1P: $59-$100   2P: $65-$109   XP: $10   F18
     11/1-4/30 [ECP]   1P: $49-$89   2P: $55-$105   XP: $10   F18

Small-scale Hotel   **Location:** I-190, exit 21 (Robert Moses Pkwy), 2 mi e, just n to Rainbow Blvd, then just s. Located adjacent to Rainbow Bridge. 454 Main St 14301. Fax: 716/285-8536. **Facility:** 80 one-bedroom standard units, some with whirlpools. 5 stories, interior corridors. **Parking:** on-site. **Terms:** check-in 4 pm, small pets only ($10 extra charge). **Amenities:** irons, hair dryers. **Pool(s):** heated indoor. **Leisure Activities:** sauna. *Fee:* game room. **Guest Services:** coin laundry. **Business Services:** fax (fee). **Cards:** AX, CB, DC, DS, JC, MC, VI. *(See color ad below & p 218)*

SOME UNITS

🆂🅳 🛏 🍴 🛗 🐕 🚭 📶 💻 / ⊠ 🛄 📠 /
       FEE   FEE FEE

(See map and index starting on p. 462)

HOWARD JOHNSON INN-NIAGARA   *Book at aaa.com*   **Phone:** (716)283-8791   **14**

	6/22-9/10	1P: $69-$159	2P: $79-$169	XP: $10	F17
	9/11-12/31	1P: $59-$69	2P: $69-$79	XP: $10	F17
	5/1-6/21	1P: $49-$59	2P: $69-$79	XP: $10	F17
	1/1-4/30	1P: $49-$59	2P: $59-$69	XP: $10	F17

Small-scale Hotel   **Location:** I-190, exit 22, just e. 6505 Niagara Falls Blvd 14304. Fax: 716/283-9313. **Facility:** 88 one-bedroom standard units, some with whirlpools. 2 stories (no elevator), interior corridors. **Parking:** on-site. **Terms:** cancellation fee imposed. **Amenities:** irons, hair dryers. **Pool(s):** outdoor. **Guest Services:** coin laundry. **Business Services:** meeting rooms. **Cards:** AX, CB, DC, DS, JC, MC, VI. **Special Amenities:** free newspaper and early check-in/late check-out.
(See color ad below & p 218)

SOME UNITS

QUALITY HOTEL AND SUITES "AT THE FALLS"   *Book at aaa.com*   **Phone:** (716)282-1212   **19**

	6/15-9/15	1P: $99-$299	2P: $99-$299	XP: $15	F17
	5/1-6/14 & 9/16-12/31	1P: $79-$299	2P: $79-$299	XP: $15	F17
	1/1-4/30	1P: $89-$299	2P: $89-$299	XP: $15	F17

Small-scale Hotel   **Location:** Downtown. Adjoins Rainbow Shopping Center. 240 Rainbow Blvd 14303. Fax: 716/282-0051. **Facility:** 199 units. 192 one-bedroom standard units, some with whirlpools. 7 one-bedroom suites ($134-$299). 4 stories, interior corridors. **Parking:** on-site. **Terms:** cancellation fee imposed, [BP] meal plan available, pets ($20 extra charge). **Amenities:** voice mail, irons, hair dryers. **Pool(s):** small heated indoor. **Leisure Activities:** whirlpool. **Guest Services:** gift shop, valet laundry. **Business Services:** meeting rooms. **Cards:** AX, DC, DS, JC, MC, VI. *(See color ad p 475)*

SOME UNITS

(See map and index starting on p. 462)

QUALITY INN NIAGARA   *Book at aaa.com*   Phone: (716)283-0621 **30**
▽▽▽ ▽▽▽   All Year   1P: $39-$169   2P: $45-$189   XP: $10   F16
Small-scale Hotel   **Location:** I-190, exit 22, 0.8 mi e. 7708 Niagara Falls Blvd 14304. Fax: 716/283-2121. **Facility:** 94 one-bedroom
standard units, some with whirlpools. 2 stories (no elevator), interior corridors. **Parking:** on-site. **Terms:** [BP],
[ECP] & [MAP] meal plans available, package plans - seasonal. **Amenities:** irons, hair dryers. *Some:* high-
speed Internet. **Pool(s):** indoor. **Business Services:** conference facilities. **Cards:** AX, CB, DC, DS, JC, MC, VI.
(See color ad below)

SOME UNITS

(A$K) (S🛏) (🍽) (🏊) (📷) (DATA PORT) (💻) / (⊠) (📶) (🖥) /
                                            FEE FEE

(See map and index starting on p. 462)

RAMADA INN BY THE FALLS   *Book at aaa.com*   Phone: (716)282-1734

6/12-9/5	1P: $79-$179	2P: $79-$179	XP: $10	F18
5/1-6/11	1P: $49-$139	2P: $49-$139	XP: $10	F18
9/6-10/11	1P: $49-$129	2P: $49-$129	XP: $10	F18
10/12-4/30	1P: $39-$129	2P: $39-$129	XP: $10	F18

Small-scale Hotel   **Location:** I-190, exit 21 (Robert Moses Pkwy), 3.5 mi w; just s of Rainbow Mall. 219 4th St 14303. Fax: 716/282-1881. **Facility:** 112 one-bedroom standard units, some with whirlpools. 2 stories, interior corridors. **Parking:** on-site. **Terms:** 2 night minimum stay - weekends in season, [AP] meal plan available. **Amenities:** voice mail, irons, hair dryers. **Dining:** 6:30 am-11 pm, cocktails. **Pool(s):** heated indoor. **Leisure Activities:** whirlpool. **Guest Services:** valet and coin laundry. **Business Services:** meeting rooms. **Cards:** AX, DS, MC, VI. **Special Amenities:** free newspaper. *(See color ad below & p 8)*

(See map and index starting on p. 462)

THE RED COACH INN
Phone: (716)282-1459

Historic
Country Inn

	6/28-9/6 [ECP]	1P: $139-$179	2P: $139-$179	XP: $19
	5/1-6/27 & 9/7-10/31 [ECP]	1P: $109-$139	2P: $109-$139	XP: $19
	11/1-4/30 [ECP]	1P: $89-$129	2P: $89-$129	XP: $19

Location: Downtown. 2 Buffalo Ave 14303. **Fax:** 716/282-2650. **Facility:** Views of the rapids are a draw at this inn, which offers 18th-century furnishings and distinctively decorated suites, two with laundry machines. Smoke free premises. 15 units. 2 one-bedroom standard units with whirlpools. 8 one- and 5 two-bedroom suites ($129-$339) with whirlpools, some with kitchens. 3 stories (no elevator), interior/exterior corridors.
Parking: on-site. **Terms:** 14 day cancellation notice-fee imposed, package plans. **Amenities:** CD players, voice mail, irons, hair dryers. **Dining:** restaurant, see separate listing. **Guest Services:** valet laundry. **Business Services:** meeting rooms. **Cards:** DS, MC, VI. **Special Amenities:** free expanded continental breakfast and free newspaper. *(See color ad p 476)*

SOME UNITS

RODEWAY INN AT THE FALLS   *Book at aaa.com*
Phone: (716)284-9778 **2**

Small-scale Hotel

	7/2-9/5	1P: $109-$189	2P: $119-$199	XP: $10	F17
	9/6-10/13	1P: $79-$89	2P: $89-$99	XP: $10	F17
	10/14-4/30	1P: $49-$69	2P: $59-$79	XP: $10	F17
		1P: $49-$59	2P: $59-$69	XP: $10	F17

Location: Robert Moses Pkwy, exit city, just n at Rainbow Blvd. Located near the falls. 795 Rainbow Blvd 14303. **Fax:** 716/284-5252. **Facility:** 39 one-bedroom standard units. 2 stories (no elevator), interior corridors.
Parking: on-site. **Terms:** cancellation fee imposed. **Cards:** AX, CB, DC, DS, JC, MC, VI.

SOME UNITS

SUPER 8 MOTEL   *Book at aaa.com*
Phone: (716)283-3151 **23**

Small-scale Hotel

	5/1-9/30	1P: $49-$139	2P: $49-$139	XP: $10	F12
	10/1-12/31	1P: $49-$69	2P: $49-$69	XP: $10	F12
	1/1-4/30	1P: $39-$59	2P: $39-$59	XP: $10	F12

Location: I-190, exit 22, 0.6 mi e. 7680 Niagara Falls Blvd 14304. **Fax:** 716/283-2638. **Facility:** 73 one-bedroom standard units, some with whirlpools. 1-3 stories (no elevator), interior corridors. *Bath:* combo or shower only.
Parking: on-site. **Terms:** cancellation fee imposed, [ECP] meal plan available. **Amenities:** voice mail, hair dryers. **Pool(s):** heated outdoor. **Guest Services:** area transportation-Seneca Niagara Casino. **Cards:** AX, CB, DC, DS, MC, VI.
Special Amenities: free continental breakfast and free local telephone calls. *(See color ad below)*

SOME UNITS

(See map and index starting on p. 462)

SWISS COTTAGE INN

Phone: (716)283-8142

Motel

All Year   1P: $32-$169   2P: $35-$169   XP: $10   F14
Location: I-190, exit 22, 0.5 mi e. 6831 Niagara Falls Blvd 14304. Fax: 716/283-2420. **Facility:** 31 one-bedroom standard units. 1 story, exterior corridors. *Bath:* combo or shower only. **Parking:** on-site. **Terms:** cancellation fee imposed, weekly rates available. **Pool(s):** small outdoor. **Cards:** AX, DS, MC, VI. **Special Amenities: early check-in/late check-out and preferred room (subject to availability with advanced reservations).**

SOME UNITS

THRIFTLODGE

Book at aaa.com
Phone: (716)297-2660

Motel

5/16-9/5   1P: $36-$139   2P: $39-$199   XP: $5   F12
5/1-5/15 & 9/6-4/30   1P: $28-$69   2P: $32-$69   XP: $5   F12
Location: I-190, exit 22, 1.8 mi e. 9401 Niagara Falls Blvd 14304. Fax: 716/297-7675. **Facility:** 45 one-bedroom standard units, some with whirlpools. 1 story, exterior corridors. **Parking:** on-site. **Terms:** 3 day cancellation notice-fee imposed, [CP] meal plan available, small pets only ($10 fee). **Pool(s):** outdoor. **Cards:** AX, DC, DS, MC, VI. **Special Amenities: free continental breakfast.** *(See color ad below)*

SOME UNITS

FEE

TRAVELERS BUDGET INN
Phone: (716)297-3228

Motel

5/1-9/7   1P: $45-$99   2P: $55-$135   XP: $10   F3
9/8-12/31   1P: $40-$45   2P: $49-$59   XP: $10   F3
1/1-4/30   1P: $35-$39   2P: $45-$55   XP: $10   F3
Location: I-190, exit 22, 1.7 mi e. 9001 Niagara Falls Blvd 14304. Fax: 716/236-0208. **Facility:** 24 one-bedroom standard units, some with whirlpools. 1 story, exterior corridors. **Parking:** on-site. **Terms:** cancellation fee imposed, package plans - weekly, seasonal, pets ($6 fee). **Cards:** AX, CB, DC, DS, MC, VI.

SOME UNITS

FEE   FEE FEE

(See map and index starting on p. 462)

———— WHERE TO DINE ————

CHU'S DINING LOUNGE-CHINESE FOOD   **Lunch:** $5-$11   **Dinner:** $6-$11   **Phone:** 716/285-7278   ⑩
   Location: Jct US 62A and SR 104, 0.4 mi ne. 1019 Main St 14301. **Hours:** 11 am-11 pm. Closed: 12/25.
Features: Abundant servings of familiar Chinese choices are prepared individually and served piping hot. Only the freshest and best ingredients are used to produce the most flavorful offerings. Friendly, fast service is the norm in the family-owned and operated restaurant. Casual dress; cocktails. **Parking:** street.
Chinese   **Cards:** AX, DS, MC, VI.

COMO RESTAURANT & DELI   **Lunch:** $4-$8   **Dinner:** $7-$18   **Phone:** 716/285-9341   ①
   Location: Jct SR 104, 1 mi s of US 62A. 2220 Pine Ave 14301. **Hours:** 11:30 am-10 pm, Fri & Sat-11 pm. Closed: 5/31, 7/4, 12/25. **Reservations:** suggested. **Features:** Family-owned since 1927, the restaurant consistently delivers tasty homemade pasta and traditional American dishes. Generous portions and reasonable prices make this a good choice for the value-conscious diner. Casual dress; cocktails. **Parking:** on-site. **Cards:** AX, DS, MC, VI.
Italian

FORTUNA'S   **Lunch:** $5-$8   **Dinner:** $6-$15   **Phone:** 716/282-2252   ⑪
   Location: Jct 19th St and Forest. 827 19th St 14301. **Hours:** 4 pm-9:30 pm, Fri 11:30 am-10 pm, Sat 4 pm-10:30 pm, Sun noon-8:30 pm. Closed: 7/4, 11/25, 12/24, 12/25; also Mon & Tues. **Features:** Classic Italian fare made from the freshest ingredients available and served by the friendly staff in a casual, subdued setting distinguish this restaurant. Longtime favorites include handmade gnocchi and ravioli made from secret family recipes. Casual dress; cocktails. **Parking:** on-site. **Cards:** AX, DC, DS, MC, VI.
Italian

JOHN'S FLAMING HEARTH   **Lunch:** $5-$9   **Dinner:** $12-$19   **Phone:** 716/297-1414   ②
   Location: I-190, exit 22, 1.2 mi e on US 62, then 0.5 mi n on SR 265. 1965 Military Rd 14304. **Hours:** 11:30 am-3 & 4-10 pm, Fri & Sat-11 pm, Sun noon-9 pm. Closed: Mon. **Reservations:** suggested. **Features:** Chicken Marsala, New York strip steak and Polynesian chicken are representative of tried-and-true menu selections. The dining room is formally cozy. Desserts, such as the specialty pumpkin ice cream pie and homemade apple pie, melt in the mouth. Casual dress; cocktails. **Parking:** on-site. **Cards:** AX, DC, DS, MC, VI.
American

KOBAN'S   **Dinner:** $8-$12   **Phone:** 716/282-5151   ⑨
   Location: 2 mi e from center. 3045 Niagara St 14301. **Hours:** 5 pm-10 pm, Sun 4 pm-9 pm. Closed major holidays; also Mon & Tues. **Features:** Specialties at the tavern restaurant include steak, prime rib, seafood and great French onion soup. Casual dress; cocktails. **Parking:** on-site.
American

MICHAEL'S   **Lunch:** $5-$7   **Dinner:** $7-$9   **Phone:** 716/282-4043   ⑫
   Location: Downtown. 3011 Pine Ave 14301. **Hours:** 11 am-11:30 pm, Fri & Sat-1:30 am. Closed: 3/27, 11/25, 12/25. **Features:** The small diner offers generous portions of Italian and American comfort foods at reasonable prices. Servers are friendly and efficient. Casual dress; beer & wine only. **Parking:** on-site.
Italian   **Cards:** MC, VI.

PETE'S MARKET HOUSE RESTAURANT   **Lunch:** $3-$6   **Dinner:** $4-$18   **Phone:** 716/282-7225   ③
   Location: Jct SR 104, 0.8 mi s of US 62A. 1701 Pine Ave 14301. **Hours:** 11:15 am-2:15 & 4:30-10:30 pm, Fri 11:15 am-10:30 pm, Sat 3:30 pm-11 pm, Sun 1 pm-10 pm. **Features:** The casual, popular dining spot occupies an 1800s-style building with original tin-type ceilings. The menu centers on all-American favorites, such as thick sandwiches, homemade soups, juicy steaks, prime rib and lobster. Expect a friendly, hometown atmosphere and service to match. Casual dress; cocktails. **Parking:** on-site.
Traditional Steak & Seafood

THE RED COACH INN RESTAURANT   **Lunch:** $4-$9   **Dinner:** $7-$20   **Phone:** 716/282-1459   ④
   Location: Downtown; in The Red Coach Inn. 2 Buffalo Ave 14303. **Hours:** 11:30 am-10 pm, Fri & Sat-11 pm, Sun noon-10 pm; 11:30 am-2:30 & 5-9 pm, Fri & Sat 11:30 am-10 pm, Sun 1 pm-9 pm 11/1-4/30. Closed: 12/25. **Reservations:** suggested. **Features:** The Tudor-style, tavernlike dining room has an Old World feel. Selections on the varied menu display creative preparation and nice presentation. The house specialty is succulent prime rib. Servers exhibit good menu knowledge and timely follow-up. Casual dress; cocktails. **Parking:** on-site. **Cards:** DS, MC, VI.
American

TIMBER LODGE STEAKHOUSE   **Dinner:** $9-$22   **Phone:** 716/283-2548   ⑧
   Location: I-190, exit 22, just e. 6560 Niagara Falls Blvd 14304. **Hours:** 4 pm-10 pm, Fri-11 pm, Sat 3 pm-11 pm, Sun 3 pm-10 pm. Closed: 11/25, 12/25. **Features:** The casual steak house is decorated in a lodge-like motif of antler chandeliers and knotty pine furniture. The emphasis is on plentiful portions and value prices. In addition to numerous selections of quality beef, the menu includes chicken, shrimp and fresh fish choices. Come with a healthy appetite. Casual dress; cocktails. **Parking:** on-site. **Cards:** AX, DC, DS, MC, VI.
Steak House

TOP OF THE FALLS RESTAURANT   **Lunch:** $5-$8   **Dinner:** $7-$20   **Phone:** 716/278-0348   ⑥
   Location: On Goat Island; at Terrapin Point, overlooking Horseshoe Falls. Goat Island-American Falls Park 14302. **Hours:** Open 5/28-10/1; 11 am-7 pm, Fri-Sun to 10 pm. **Reservations:** accepted. **Features:** The stark decor of the second floor dining room serves to accentuate all the more the excellent Horseshoe Falls views, which are afforded from every table. Simple menu offerings include sandwiches, burgers, salad and finger foods. Servers are pleasant. Casual dress; cocktails. **Parking:** on-site (fee). **Cards:** AX, DS, MC, VI.
American

The Niagara Falls Vicinity

LEWISTON pop. 2,781

------ WHERE TO STAY ------

PORTAGE HOUSE MOTEL   Phone: 716/754-8295
▼▼▼   5/1-10/31   1P: $57-$75   2P: $64-$99   XP: $7   F18
              11/1-4/30   1P: $42   2P: $49   XP: $7   F18
Motel   **Location:** 0.3 mi w from jct SR 18F and Robert Moses Pkwy; opposite entrance to Artpark. 280 Portage Rd 14092
on-site. **Cards:** AX, DC, MC, VI. **Fax:** 716/754-1613. **Facility:** 21 one-bedroom standard units. 2 stories, interior/exterior corridors. **Parking:**
                                                                              SOME UNITS
                                                    (A$K) 🍴 ☎ / ⊠ 📠 /

------ WHERE TO DINE ------

CLARKSON HOUSE   Historic   **Lunch:** $5-$10   **Dinner:** $15-$50   Phone: 716/754-4544
(AAA)   **Location:** 0.4 mi w on SR 104 from jct Robert Moses Pkwy. 810 Center St 14092. **Hours:** 11:30 am-2:30 &
▼▼▼ ▼▼▼   5-10:30 pm, Sat from 5 pm, Sun 4 pm-9 pm. **Closed:** 1/1, 9/6, 12/25. **Reservations:** suggested
American   weekends. **Features:** Since the 1940s, the restaurant has listed steak, live lobster and baked Alaska on its
              traditional menu. Over the years, such dishes as swordfish with lime salsa, thickly cut lamb chops and
              cherries jubilee have become welcomed additions. Casual dress; cocktails. **Parking:** on-site. **Cards:** AX
              DC, MC, VI.   🍸 ⊠

VILLA FORTUNATA'S   **Lunch:** $5-$12   **Dinner:** $6-$12   Phone: 716/754-4904
▼▼▼ ▼▼▼   **Location:** Center. 490 Center St 14092. **Hours:** 5 pm-11 pm, Thurs & Fri from noon. Closed major holidays.
              Reservations: suggested, weekends. **Features:** The friendly staff serves traditional Italian dishes made
Italian   with the freshest, quality ingredients. The dining room is comfortable; patio dinnig is available in season
              Casual dress; cocktails. **Parking:** on-site. **Cards:** AX, DC, MC, VI.
                                                                                  ⊠

LOCKPORT pop. 22,279

------ WHERE TO STAY ------

COMFORT INN   *Book at aaa.com*   Phone: (716)434-4411
▼▼▼ ▼▼▼   5/1-9/15 [ECP]   1P: $79-$129   2P: $79-$129   XP: $10   F16
              9/16-4/30 [ECP]   1P: $69-$119   2P: $69-$119   XP: $10   F16
Small-scale Hotel **Location:** 1 mi s on SR 78. 551 S Transit St 14094. **Fax:** 716/434-9649. **Facility:** 50 one-bedroom standard units
seasonal. **Amenities:** irons, hair dryers. **Leisure Activities:** exercise room. **Guest Services:** valet laundry. **Cards:** AX, CB,
DS, MC, VI. *(See color ad p 469)*
                                                                              SOME UNITS
                    (A$K) (S🄳) 🍴 (&M) 🎦 (DATA PORT) 💻 / ⊠ 📠 /
                                                                                    FEE

HOLIDAY INN LOCKPORT INN   *Book at aaa.com*   Phone: (716)434-6151
▼▼▼ ▼▼▼   5/1-9/15   1P: $79-$129   2P: $79-$129   XP: $10   F16
              9/16-4/30   1P: $69-$119   2P: $69-$119   XP: $10   F16
Motel   **Location:** 1 mi s on SR 78. 515 S Transit St 14094. **Fax:** 716/434-5117. **Facility:** 95 one-bedroom standard units
some with efficiencies. 2 stories, interior corridors. **Parking:** on-site. **Terms:** [MAP] meal plan available
package plans - seasonal, pets ($5 fee, $25 deposit). **Amenities:** video library (fee), irons, hair dryers. **Pool(s):** heated indoor
Guest Services: valet and coin laundry. **Business Services:** conference facilities. **Cards:** AX, CB, DC, DS, MC, VI.
(See color ad p 468)
                                                                              SOME UNITS
              (A$K) (S🄳) 🐾 🍴 🍸 🛥 🎦 (DATA PORT) 💻 / ⊠ (VCR) 📠 📠
                            FEE   FEE FEE FEE

------ WHERE TO DINE ------

FIELDSTONE COUNTRY INN RESTAURANT   **Lunch:** $5-$7   **Dinner:** $8-$17   Phone: 716/625-6193
▼▼▼ ▼▼▼   **Location:** 1.5 mi s on SR 78. 5986 S Transit Rd 14094. **Hours:** 11 am-9 pm, Fri-10 pm, Sat 4 pm-10 pm, Sur
              noon-8 pm. **Closed:** 12/24, 12/25. **Features:** Recognized by its rounded fieldstone exterior, the casua
American   restaurant is popular for the salad bar, fast service and good, cooked-to-order food. The baby back ribs
              specialty is tender, smoky and delicious. Casual dress; cocktails. **Parking:** on-site. **Cards:** AX, DC, DS
MC, VI.
                                                                                  🍸 ⊠

GARLOCK'S   **Dinner:** $11-$30   Phone: 716/433-5559
▼▼▼ ▼▼▼   **Location:** Jct SR 78 and 31; on Erie Canal. 35 S Transit Rd 14094. **Hours:** 4:30 pm-11:30 pm, Fri-midnight, Sat
              5 pm-midnight, Sun 3:30 pm-10 pm. **Closed:** 11/25, 12/25. **Features:** Serving delicious steaks, lamb chops
Steak & Seafood prime rib, lobster, seafood and more for more than 55 years, the cozy spot has a rustic feel. Friendly
              hometown service can be expected. Casual dress; cocktails. **Parking:** on-site. **Cards:** AX, DS, MC, VI.
                                                                                  🍸 ⊠

VILLAGE EATERY ITALIAN BISTRO   **Lunch:** $5-$9   **Dinner:** $7-$15   Phone: 716/433-0688
(AAA)   **Location:** 0.8 mi s of jct SR 31. 429 Davison Road Sq 14094. **Hours:** 11 am-11 pm, Sun 1 pm-9 pm; Sun 4
▼▼▼ ▼▼▼   pm-11 pm 6/2-9/7. Closed major holidays. **Features:** The contemporary, casual dining and upscale bistro
              bar offered at Village Eatery spotlight abundant, delicious traditional Italian dishes of pasta, steak, veal and
Italian   chicken. Pizzas have a gourmet. Casual dress; cocktails. **Parking:** on-site. **Cards:** AX, DS, MC, VI.
                                                                                  ⊠

NEWFANE pop. 3,129

——— WHERE TO STAY ———

LAKE ONTARIO MOTEL
◆◆ Motel

			Phone: 716/778-5004
7/1-10/31	1P: $39-$45	2P: $52-$65	XP: $7	F12
5/1-6/30 & 4/21-4/30	1P: $37	2P: $49-$58	XP: $7	F12

Location: 2.5 mi n of jct SR 104 on SR 78. 3330 Lockport-Olcott Rd 14108. **Facility:** 11 one-bedroom standard units. 2 stories (no elevator), interior corridors. *Bath:* shower only. **Parking:** on-site. **Terms:** open 5/1-10/31 & 4/21-4/30, weekly rates available, pets ($5 extra charge). **Cards:** AX, DS, MC, VI. *(See ad p 474)*

SOME UNITS
(ASK) 🛏 ⁺ / ⊠ 🖥 /

——— WHERE TO DINE ———

GORDIE HARPER'S BAZAAR
◆◆ American

Lunch: $4-$8	**Dinner:** $6-$12	**Phone:** 716/778-8048

Location: 2.5 mi n of jct SR 104 on SR 78. 3333 Lockport-Olcott Rd 14108. **Hours:** 8 am-8 pm, Fri & Sat-9 pm. Closed: 11/25, 12/25. **Features:** Although the experience at the casual roadside bazaar of arts and crafts is unusual, the comfort food tastes great and is served in ample portions. Bakery items are made on the premises. Casual dress; cocktails. **Parking:** on-site. **Cards:** DS, MC, VI.

⊠

RIB HOUSE RESTAURANT
◆◆ American

Dinner: $9-$20	**Phone:** 716/778-7910

Location: Jct SR 104 on SR 78, 3.4 mi n. 2990 Lockport-Olcott Rd (NY Rt 78) 14108. **Hours:** 4 pm-9 pm, Fri & Sat-10 pm, Sun-8 pm. Closed: 1/1, 11/25, 12/25; also Mon. **Reservations:** suggested, weekends. **Features:** The rustic country dining room at this restaurant is charming. Prime rib and the signature ribs— which actually are only a small portion of the menu—stand out among selections of seafood, poultry, steak and pork. Casual dress; cocktails. **Parking:** on-site. **Cards:** AX, DS, MC, VI.

🍸 ⊠

SANBORN

——— WHERE TO DINE ———

THE NEW SCHIMSCHACK'S RESTAURANT
◆◆◆ American

Dinner: $12-$35	**Phone:** 716/731-4111

Location: 1.3 mi n from jct SR 425 and 31, 2.3 mi w. 2943 Upper Mountain Rd 14132. **Hours:** 4 pm-9 pm, Sat-10 pm, Sun noon-8 pm. Closed: 12/24, 12/25; also Mon 11/1-3/31. **Reservations:** suggested. **Features:** Charbroiled baby back ribs stand out on a menu of traditional favorites. The three-tiered dining room, which affords lovely panoramic views of the vineyards, exudes an informal, romantic ambience. Tempting dessert is prepared on the premises. Marilyn Monroe and Joe DiMaggio dined here during the filming of "Niagara". Casual dress; cocktails. **Parking:** on-site. **Cards:** AX, CB, DC, DS, MC, VI.

⊠

WHEATFIELD pop. 14,086

——— WHERE TO STAY ———

BORDER INN
AAA (SAVE)
◆◆ Motel

			Phone: (716)743-9224
5/21-9/5	1P: $39-$149	2P: $59-$199	
5/1-5/20 & 9/6-4/30	1P: $39-$59	2P: $59-$79	

Location: I-190, exit 22, 5.5 mi s on US 62; I-290, exit 3, 7.5 mi n on US 62. 2821 Niagara Falls Blvd 14304 (2821 Niagara Falls Blvd, NIAGARA FALLS). Fax: 716/695-6161. **Facility:** 20 one-bedroom standard units, some with efficiencies and/or whirlpools. 1 story, exterior corridors. *Bath:* combo or shower only. **Parking:** on-site. **Terms:** cancellation fee imposed, weekly rates available. **Amenities:** voice mail, hair dryers. **Pool(s):** outdoor. **Guest Services:** coin laundry. **Business Services:** fax. **Cards:** AX, DC, MC, VI. **Special Amenities:** free local telephone calls.

SOME UNITS
🅂🄳 📶 🏊 🎥 DATA PORT 🖥 🖨 / ⊠ (VCR) ⊑ /

DRIFTWOOD MOTEL
AAA (SAVE)
◆ Motel

			Phone: (716)692-6650
5/1-9/30	1P: $45-$85	2P: $55-$99	
10/1-4/30	1P: $35-$49	2P: $39-$65	

Location: I-190, exit 22, 5 mi e on US 62 S. 2754 Niagara Falls Blvd 14304. Fax: 716/695-6928. **Facility:** 20 one-bedroom standard units. 1 story, exterior corridors. **Parking:** on-site. **Terms:** 5 day cancellation notice-fee imposed, weekly rates available, [CP] meal plan available, small pets only ($8 fee). **Pool(s):** outdoor. **Cards:** AX, DC, DS, MC, VI. **Special Amenities:** early check-in/late check-out and preferred room (subject to availability with advanced reservations).

SOME UNITS
🅂🄳 🛏 ⁺ 🏊 🎥 / ⊠ 🖥 🖨 /

——— WHERE TO DINE ———

SUZANNE'S FINE DINING
◆◆ American

Dinner: $14-$22	**Phone:** 716/694-6562

Location: I-90, exit 22, 5.5 mi s on US 62; I-290, exit 3, 7.6 mi n on US 62. 2843 Niagara Falls Blvd 14304. **Hours:** 3 pm-10 pm. Closed: 7/4, 12/25; also Sun & Mon. **Reservations:** accepted. **Features:** Soothing, soft peach colors set the mood for relaxed dining. A sophisticated flair punctuates such delectable menu offerings as chicken Oscar, pork tenderloin and steak Bradley, each embraced by rich sauces and fresh ingredients. It's worth leaving room for one of the homemade desserts. Fine wine offerings, espresso and cappuccino complete a fine-dining experience. Casual dress; cocktails. **Parking:** on-site. **Cards:** AX, DS, MC, VI.

🍸 ⊠

YOUNGSTOWN pop. 1,957

——— WHERE TO STAY ———

CAMEO MANOR BED & BREAKFAST
Phone: 716/745-3034
▼▼▼ ▼▼▼ All Year [BP]   1P: $85-$140   2P: $85-$140   XP: $25
Bed & Breakfast   **Location:** North from jct Robert Moses Pkwy and SR 104, SR 18F N (Seaway Tr), 4.5 mi n. 3881 Lower River Rd 14174. Fax: 716/745-3034. **Facility:** Smoke free premises. 4 one-bedroom standard units. 2 stories (no elevator), interior corridors. *Bath:* some shared or private. **Parking:** on-site. **Terms:** 2 night minimum stay - seasonal weekends, age restrictions may apply, 14 day cancellation notice-fee imposed, package plans. **Leisure Activities:** bicycles, hiking trails. **Business Services:** meeting rooms. **Cards:** DS, MC, VI.

SOME UNITS
⊠ ☎ / 📺 VCR /

Nearby Ontario

NIAGARA FALLS pop. 78,815 (See map and index starting on p. 464)

——— WHERE TO STAY ———

ADVANTAGE INN   *Book at aaa.com*   **Phone:** 905/374-4442   **61**
CAA SAVE   6/26-9/6   1P: $48-$98   2P: $58-$118   XP: $10   F14
▼▼▼   5/1-6/25   1P: $38-$78   2P: $48-$98   XP: $10   F14
Motel   9/7-4/30   1P: $38-$58   2P: $44-$78   XP: $10   F14
Location: QEW, exit Hwy 20, 4.6 km w. 7797 Lundy's Ln L2H 1H3. Fax: 905/357-1854. **Facility:** 35 one-bedroom standard units, some with efficiencies, kitchens (no utensils) and/or whirlpools. 1-2 stories (no elevator), exterior corridors. *Bath:* combo or shower only. **Parking:** on-site, winter plug-ins. **Terms:** 3 day cancellation notice-fee imposed. **Pool(s):** heated outdoor. **Leisure Activities:** barbecue, playground. **Guest Services:** area transportation (fee)-falls & casino. **Business Services:** fax (fee). **Cards:** AX, DS, MC, VI. **Special Amenities:** free local telephone calls and early check-in/late check-out.

SOME UNITS
🛜 🏊 🎥 🛗 / ⊠ 🖥 /

A GARDENS INN   **Phone:** (905)227-0891   **57**
CAA SAVE   6/27-9/1   1P: $69-$119   2P: $79-$129   XP: $10   F12
▼▼▼ ▼▼▼   5/1-6/26   1P: $59-$89   2P: $69-$99   XP: $10   F12
Motel   9/2-4/30   1P: $45-$79   2P: $55-$89   XP: $5   F12
Location: 9.2 km w on Hwy 20. 13055 Lundy's Ln L2E 6S4. Fax: 905/227-3720. **Facility:** 28 one-bedroom standard units, some with whirlpools. 1 story, exterior corridors. **Parking:** on-site. **Terms:** 2 night minimum stay - weekends, 3 day cancellation notice-fee imposed, [BP] meal plan available, package plans - 7. **Pool(s):** heated outdoor. **Leisure Activities:** playground. **Cards:** AX, DC, JC, MC, VI. **Special Amenities:** free local telephone calls and preferred room (subject to availability with advanced reservations).

SOME UNITS
🅂🄳 🏊 📺 🎥 / ⊠ 🛗 /

(See map and index starting on p. 464)

AMERICANA RESORT & SPA   *Book at aaa.com*   Phone: (905)356-8444   **56**

CAA SAVE	6/18-9/5	2P: $99-$249	XP: $10	F16
	9/6-10/11	2P: $99-$199	XP: $10	F16
	5/1-6/17 & 10/12-4/30	2P: $69-$159	XP: $10	F16

Location: QEW, exit Hwy 20 W, 5.5 km w. 8444 Lundy's Ln L2H 1H4. Fax: 905/356-8576. **Facility:** 211 units. 192 one-bedroom standard units, some with whirlpools. 19 one-bedroom suites ($99), some with whirlpools. 2-3 stories (no elevator), interior corridors. **Parking:** on-site. **Terms:** cancellation fee imposed. **Amenities:** voice mail, hair dryers. **Dining:** 7 am-11 pm, Fri & Sat-midnight, cocktails. **Pool(s):** heated outdoor, heated indoor. **Leisure Activities:** saunas, whirlpool, lighted tennis court, squash court, playground, exercise room, basketball, shuffleboard, volleyball. **Guest Services:** gift shop, valet and coin laundry, area transportation (fee). **Business Services:** conference facilities, business center. **Cards:** AX, DC, DS, MC, VI. **Special Amenities:** preferred room (subject to availability with advanced reservations).
(See color ad below & card insert)   SOME UNITS

Large-scale Hotel

Hungry? Look for the RED AAA Logo

Next time you look through a AAA/CAA TourBook® guide in search of a place to dine, take note of the bright red AAA logo just under a select group of restaurant names! These Official Appointment restaurants place a high value on the business they receive from dedicated AAA/CAA travelers.

As a member, you already turn to TourBooks for quality travel information. Now look for restaurants that display the bright red AAA logo in their listing for dining experiences you'll long remember!

(See map and index starting on p. 464)

ASTON MICHAEL'S INN-BY THE FALLS   *Book at aaa.com*   Phone: (905)354-2727   22

(CAA) (SAVE)

6/11-9/12 [CP]	1P: $88-$288	2P: $88-$288
5/1-6/10 & 9/13-10/31 [CP]	1P: $58-$178	2P: $58-$178
11/1-4/30 [CP]	1P: $48-$158	2P: $48-$158

Small-scale Hotel

Location: Just n of Rainbow Bridge and QEW. 5599 River Rd L2E 3H3. Fax: 905/374-7706. **Facility:** 130 units. 129 one- and 1 two-bedroom standard units, some with whirlpools. 4 stories, interior corridors. **Parking:** on-site. **Terms:** package plans. **Amenities:** video games, voice mail, irons, hair dryers. **Dining:** 7 am-11 pm; 8 am-9 pm 11/1-4/30, cocktails. **Pool(s):** heated indoor, wading. **Leisure Activities:** sauna, whirlpool, exercise room. *Fee:* game room. **Guest Services:** gift shop, valet laundry. **Business Services:** meeting rooms. **Cards:** AX, CB, DC, DS, JC, MC, VI. **Special Amenities:** free continental breakfast and free newspaper. *(See color ad p 525 & below)*

SOME UNITS

(See map and index starting on p. 464)

AURORA MOTEL   **Phone:** 905/356-4490 **38**

6/21-9/5	1P: $59-$169	2P: $69-$179	XP: $10	F10
5/1-6/20 & 9/6-4/30	1P: $39-$79	2P: $49-$89	XP: $10	F10

Motel   **Location:** Just w of Minolta Tower. Located in a residential area. 5630 Dunn St L2G 2N7. Fax: 905/357-9631. **Facility:** 29 one-bedroom standard units. 2 stories (no elevator), exterior corridors. **Parking:** on-site. **Pool(s):** heated outdoor. **Cards:** MC, VI.

SOME UNITS

(ASK) 🏊 / ✕ /

A VICTORIA MOTOR INN   **Phone:** (905)374-6522 **43**

6/15-9/6	1P: $89-$129	2P: $99-$199	XP: $10	F16
9/7-9/30	1P: $69-$99	2P: $99-$139	XP: $10	F16
5/1-6/14 & 10/1-4/30	1P: $59-$79	2P: $79-$99	XP: $10	F16

Motel   **Location:** Just w on Victoria Ave from Clifton St. Located in a commercial area. 5869 Victoria Ave L2G 3L6. Fax: 905/374-3038. **Facility:** 33 one-bedroom standard units, some with whirlpools. 3 stories (no elevator), exterior corridors. **Parking:** on-site. **Terms:** 3 day cancellation notice-fee imposed. **Dining:** 7 am-noon. **Pool(s):** heated outdoor. **Cards:** AX, DC, DS, MC.

SOME UNITS

(S/D) 🍽 🏊 ✆ / ✕ /

BEST INN   *Book at aaa.com*   **Phone:** (905)356-8280 **53**

5/1-9/30	1P: $89-$129	2P: $99-$149	XP: $10	F12
10/1-4/30	1P: $59-$99	2P: $59-$99	XP: $10	F12

Motel   **Location:** QEW, exit Hwy 20 W, 4.6 km w. 7800 Lundy's Ln L2H 1H1. Fax: 905/356-6948. **Facility:** 69 units. 68 one-bedroom standard units, some with whirlpools. 1 three-bedroom suite. 2 stories (no elevator), interior corridors. **Parking:** on-site. **Terms:** cancellation fee imposed. **Dining:** 6 am-11 pm; 24 hours 6/1-10/31. **Pool(s):** heated outdoor. **Special Amenities:** free continental breakfast and free local telephone calls.

SOME UNITS

(S/D) 🍽 🏊 / ✕ 🔌 /

BEST WESTERN CAIRN CROFT HOTEL   *Book at aaa.com*   **Phone:** (905)356-1161 **45**

6/18-9/5	1P: $99-$249	2P: $99-$249	XP: $10	F16
5/1-6/17 & 9/6-4/30	1P: $69-$189	2P: $69-$189	XP: $10	F16

Small-scale Hotel   **Location:** 2.4 km w on Hwy 20. 6400 Lundy's Ln L2G 1T6. Fax: 905/356-8664. **Facility:** 165 one-bedroom standard units, some with whirlpools. 2-5 stories, interior/exterior corridors. **Parking:** on-site, winter plug-ins. **Terms:** package plans. **Amenities:** video games, irons, hair dryers. **Dining:** 7 am-2 & 5-10 pm; to 9 pm off season except weekends, cocktails. **Pool(s):** heated indoor. **Leisure Activities:** whirlpools, indoor children's play area. *Fee:* game room. **Guest Services:** valet laundry, area transportation (fee)-casino & falls. **Business Services:** meeting rooms. **Cards:** AX, DC, DS, MC, VI. *(See color ad below & card insert)*

SOME UNITS

(S/D) 🍽 🍸 🏊 ✕ 📷 (DATA PORT) 🖥 / ✕ 🔌 📠 /
FEE FEE

(See map and index starting on p. 464)

BEST WESTERN FALLSVIEW

(CAA) (SAVE)

Phone: (905)356-0551   **11**

	6/25-9/5	1P: $149-$299	2P: $149-$299	XP: $10	F12
	9/6-10/10	1P: $119-$249	2P: $119-$249	XP: $10	F12
	10/11-4/30	1P: $89-$199	2P: $89-$199	XP: $10	F12
	5/1-6/24	1P: $79-$199	2P: $79-$199	XP: $10	F12

Small-scale Hotel **Location:** Jct Niagara Pkwy, just n on Murray St. 6289 Fallsview Blvd L2G 3V7. Fax: 905/356-7773. **Facility:** Smoke free premises. 243 one-bedroom standard units, some with whirlpools. 4-6 stories, interior/exterior corridors. **Parking:** on-site. **Terms:** 3 day cancellation notice-fee imposed, package plans - 9/1-4/6, small pets only. **Amenities:** video games, voice mail, irons, hair dryers. **Dining:** 7 am-10 & 5-10 pm, Sat & Sun 8 am-9 pm; 8 am-9 pm 5/15-10/12, cocktails. **Pool(s):** heated indoor. **Leisure Activities:** sauna, whirlpool, playground. *Fee:* game room. **Guest Services:** gift shop. **Business Services:** meeting rooms. **Cards:** AX, CB, DC, DS, JC, MC, VI. *(See color ad below)*

BEST WESTERN FIRESIDE HOTEL   *Book at aaa.com*

(CAA) (SAVE)

Phone: (905)374-2027   **30**

| | 6/18-9/5 | 1P: $89-$249 | 2P: $89-$249 | XP: $10 | F12 |
| | 5/1-6/17 & 9/6-4/30 | 1P: $69-$199 | 2P: $69-$199 | XP: $10 | F12 |

Location: 3 km n of Rainbow Bridge. 4067 River Rd L2E 3E5. Fax: 905/374-7746. **Facility:** 96 one-bedroom standard units, some with whirlpools. 4 stories, interior corridors. **Parking:** on-site. **Terms:** 3 day cancellation notice, package plans. **Amenities:** video library (fee), irons, hair dryers. **Dining:** 7 am-noon, cocktails. **Pool(s):** heated indoor. **Leisure Activities:** sauna, whirlpool, exercise room. **Guest Services:** area transportation-casino & falls. **Cards:** AX, DC, DS, MC, VI. **Special Amenities:** early check-in/late check-out and free room upgrade (subject to availability with advanced reservations). *(See color ad p 498)*

SOME UNITS / FEE

BROCK PLAZA HOTEL   *Book at aaa.com*

(CAA) (SAVE)

Phone: (905)374-4444   **21**

	8/1-10/15	1P: $149-$699	2P: $149-$699	XP: $10	F18
	6/1-7/31	1P: $129-$599	2P: $129-$599	XP: $10	F18
	5/1-5/31	1P: $119-$529	2P: $119-$529	XP: $10	F18
	10/16-4/30	1P: $99-$529	2P: $99-$529	XP: $10	F18

Historic
Large-scale Hotel **Location:** Entrance to Rainbow Bridge on Hwy 20, just n from the falls. Located next to a casino. 5685 Falls Ave L2E 6W7. Fax: 905/371-8347. **Facility:** This grand hotel, built in 1929, offers many rooms overlooking the falls; accommodations are cozy and well-appointed with modern amenities. 234 units. 221 one- and 6 two-bedroom standard units, some with whirlpools. 5 one- and 2 two-bedroom suites ($329-$699). 12 stories, interior corridors. *Bath:* combo or shower only. **Parking:** on-site (fee). **Terms:** cancellation fee imposed. **Amenities:** video games, voice mail, hair dryers. *Some:* irons. **Dining:** The Rainbow Grille Fallsview Steakhouse, see separate listing. **Pool(s):** heated indoor. **Leisure Activities:** sauna, whirlpool, limited exercise equipment. **Guest Services:** gift shop, valet laundry. **Business Services:** conference facilities. **Cards:** AX, DC, DS, JC, MC, VI. *(See color ad p 487)*

SOME UNITS / FEE

CADILLAC MOTEL

(CAA) (SAVE)

Phone: (905)356-0830   **7**

| | 6/21-9/1 | 1P: $50-$100 | 2P: $70-$120 | XP: $10 | F12 |
| | 5/1-6/20, 9/2-10/31 & 3/1-4/30 | 1P: $40-$60 | 2P: $50-$80 | XP: $10 | F12 |

Motel **Location:** On Hwy 20, 0.6 km from the falls. Located in a commercial area. 5342 Ferry St L2G 1R7. Fax: 905/356-5624. **Facility:** 23 one-bedroom standard units. 1 story, exterior corridors. **Parking:** on-site. **Terms:** open 5/1-10/31 & 3/1-4/30, cancellation fee imposed. **Cards:** AX, DS, JC, MC, VI.

SOME UNITS

(See map and index starting on p. 464)

CAMELOT INN   **Phone:** (905)354-3754   **15**

Motel

6/19-9/5	1P: $49-$179	2P: $49-$199	XP: $10	F12
5/1-6/18 & 9/6-4/30	1P: $39-$129	2P: $39-$149	XP: $10	F12

Location: Just n of Hwy 20; just s of Hwy 420. 5640 Stanley Ave L2G 3X5. Fax: 905/354-6683. **Facility:** 53 one-bedroom standard units, some with whirlpools. 2 stories (no elevator), exterior corridors. **Parking:** on-site. **Terms:** office hours 8 am-2 am, weekly rates available, [BP] meal plan available, package plans - seasonal, small pets only ($10 extra charge). **Pool(s):** outdoor. **Cards:** AX, DS, MC, VI. *(See color ad p 488)*

SOME UNITS

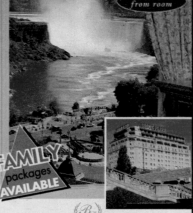

(See map and index starting on p. 464)

CARRIAGE HOUSE MOTOR LODGE

Phone: (905)356-7799 [54]

	6/18-9/5	1P: $69-$130	2P: $69-$130	XP: $10	F12
	5/1-6/17 & 9/6-10/31	1P: $49-$99	2P: $49-$99	XP: $10	F12
	11/1-4/30	1P: $45-$89	2P: $45-$89	XP: $10	F12

CAA SAVE

Small-scale Hotel

Location: QEW, exit Hwy 20 W, 4.9 km w. 8004 Lundy's Ln L2H 1H1. Fax: 905/358-6431. **Facility:** 120 one-bedroom standard units, some with whirlpools. 2 stories (no elevator), interior/exterior corridors. **Parking:** on-site. **Terms:** package plans. **Dining:** 7 am-noon; closed 11/1-4/30. **Pool(s):** heated outdoor, heated indoor. **Leisure Activities:** whirlpool. **Guest Services:** gift shop, area transportation (fee)-casino & falls. **Business Services:** meeting rooms. **Cards:** AX, DS, MC, VI. *(See color ad below & card insert)*

SOME UNITS

(See map and index starting on p. 464)

CHALET INN AND SUITES   **Phone: 905/374-1921** **8**

6/15-9/4	1P: $89-$149	2P: $99-$229	XP: $10 F12
9/5-9/30	1P: $69-$109	2P: $99-$149	XP: $10 F12
5/1-6/14 & 10/1-4/30	1P: $59-$89	2P: $79-$129	XP: $10 F12

Small-scale Hotel   **Location:** 0.6 km from the falls, n on Clifton, then just e. 5577 Ellen Ave L2G 3P5. **Fax:** 905/374-1868. **Facility:** 73 units. 66 one- and 7 two-bedroom standard units, some with whirlpools. 3-5 stories, interior/exterior corridors. **Parking:** on-site. **Terms:** office hours 7 am-2 am, 3 day cancellation notice-fee imposed, package plans. **Pool(s):** heated outdoor, heated indoor. **Cards:** AX, CB, DC, DS, JC, MC, VI.

SOME UNITS

CLARION PRESIDENT HOTEL & SUITES, BY THE FALLS   *Book at aaa.com*   **Phone: (905)374-4142** **58**

CAA SAVE

5/1-9/30	1P: $99-$199	2P: $99-$299	XP: $12 F18
10/1-4/30	1P: $69-$199	2P: $99-$299	

Small-scale Hotel   **Location:** 1.2 km w on Hwy 20, then s. 6045 Stanley Ave L2G 3Y3. **Fax:** 905/358-3430. **Facility:** 192 one-bedroom standard units, some with whirlpools. 8 stories, interior corridors. **Parking:** on-site (fee). **Terms:** cancellation fee imposed, [BP] & [MAP] meal plans available, package plans. **Amenities:** video games, voice mail, irons, hair dryers. *Some:* dual phone lines. **Dining:** 7 am-noon & 5-10 pm, cocktails. **Pool(s):** heated indoor. **Leisure Activities:** limited exercise equipment. **Guest Services:** valet laundry, area transportation (fee). **Business Services:** meeting rooms. **Cards:** AX, CB, DC, DS, MC, VI. **Special Amenities:** free newspaper. *(See color ad below)*

SOME UNITS

COMFORT INN CLIFTON HILL   *Book at aaa.com*   **Phone: (905)358-3293** **18**

CAA SAVE

5/1-10/31 [ECP]	1P: $79-$279	2P: $79-$279	XP: $12 F18
11/1-4/30 [ECP]	1P: $49-$189	2P: $49-$189	XP: $12 F18

Small-scale Hotel   **Location:** Jct Victoria Ave and Clifton Hill, just s. 4960 Clifton Hill L2E 6S8 (PO Box 60, NIAGARA FALLS, ON). **Fax:** 905/358-3818. **Facility:** 185 units. 173 one- and 12 two-bedroom standard units, some with whirlpools. 3 stories (no elevator), interior corridors. **Parking:** on-site. **Terms:** package plans - 9/1-6/30. **Amenities:** *Some:* irons, hair dryers. **Dining:** 11 am-2 am, cocktails. **Pool(s):** heated outdoor, heated indoor. **Leisure Activities:** whirlpool. *Fee:* miniature golf. **Guest Services:** valet laundry. **Cards:** AX, CB, DC, DS, JC, MC, VI. **Special Amenities:** free expanded continental breakfast and free local telephone calls. *(See color ad starting on p 491)*

SOME UNITS

COMFORT INN LUNDY'S LANE   *Book at aaa.com*   **Phone: (905)354-1849** **60**

CAA SAVE

6/18-9/5 [CP]	1P: $99-$269	2P: $99-$269	XP: $10 F18
5/1-6/17 & 9/6-10/10 [CP]	1P: $79-$189	2P: $79-$189	XP: $10 F18
10/11-4/30 [CP]	1P: $59-$189	2P: $59-$189	XP: $10 F18

Small-scale Hotel   **Location:** QEW, exit Hwy 20 (Lundy's Ln); 5 km of downtown. 7514 Lundy's Ln L2H 1G8. **Fax:** 905/354-6619. **Facility:** 148 one-bedroom standard units. 2-5 stories, interior/exterior corridors. **Parking:** on-site, winter plug-ins. **Amenities:** video games, voice mail, hair dryers. **Pool(s):** heated indoor. **Leisure Activities:** sauna, whirlpool, exercise room. *Fee:* game room. **Business Services:** meeting rooms. **Cards:** AX, DC, DS, MC, VI. **Special Amenities:** free continental breakfast and free local telephone calls. *(See color ad card insert)*

SOME UNITS

(See map and index starting on p. 464)

COMFORT INN NORTH OF THE FALLS   *Book at aaa.com*   Phone: (905)356-0131   23

CAA (SAVE)

6/18-9/5	1P: $79-$249	2P: $79-$249	XP: $10 F12
5/1-6/17	1P: $59-$199	2P: $59-$199	XP: $10 F12
9/6-4/30	1P: $49-$169	2P: $49-$169	XP: $10 F12

Motel

Location: 3 km n Rainbow Bridge. 4009 River Rd L2E 3E5. **Fax:** 905/356-3306. **Facility:** 66 one-bedroom standard units, some with whirlpools. 2 stories (no elevator), exterior corridors. **Parking:** on-site. **Terms:** 3 day cancellation notice, package plans. **Amenities:** video library (fee). **Dining:** 7 am-10 pm 5/15-10/15. **Pool(s):** outdoor. **Guest Services:** area transportation-casino & falls. **Cards:** AX, DC, DS, MC, VI. **Special Amenities:** free local telephone calls and early check-in/late check-out. *(See color ad p 498)*

SOME UNITS

CONTINENTAL INN   Phone: (905)356-2449   87

6/26-9/6 [ECP]	1P: $59-$99	2P: $69-$119	XP: $10 F12
5/1-6/25 [ECP]	1P: $49-$79	2P: $59-$99	XP: $10 F12
9/7-4/30 [ECP]	1P: $39-$69	2P: $49-$89	XP: $10 F12

Motel

Location: On Hwy 20, 1.5 km w from the falls. 5756 Ferry St L2G 1S7. **Fax:** 905/371-8202. **Facility:** 51 one-bedroom standard units, some with whirlpools. 2 stories (no elevator), exterior corridors. **Parking:** on-site. **Terms:** 2-3 night minimum stay - weekends, cancellation fee imposed. **Pool(s):** heated outdoor. **Cards:** AX, DS, MC, VI.

SOME UNITS

COURTYARD BY MARRIOTT NIAGARA FALLS   *Book at aaa.com*   Phone: (905)358-3083   33

CAA (SAVE)

6/16-9/2	1P: $99-$399	2P: $99-$399	XP: $10 F18
5/1-6/15 & 9/3-4/30	1P: $79-$299	2P: $79-$299	XP: $10 F18

Large-scale Hotel

Location: Jct of Ferry St. 5950 Victoria Ave L2G 3L7. **Fax:** 905/358-8720. **Facility:** 258 one-bedroom standard units, some with whirlpools. 10 stories, interior corridors. *Bath:* combo or shower only. **Parking:** on-site (fee). **Terms:** 3 day cancellation notice, package plans. **Amenities:** video games, dual phone lines, voice mail, safes, irons, hair dryers. **Dining:** 6:30 am-11 pm. **Pool(s):** outdoor, heated indoor. **Leisure Activities:** sauna, whirlpool, sun deck, exercise room. *Fee:* game room. **Guest Services:** gift shop, valet and coin laundry, area transportation (fee)-casino. **Business Services:** meeting rooms. **Cards:** AX, DC, DS, JC, MC, VI.

SOME UNITS

CRYSTAL MOTEL   Phone: (905)354-0460   25

6/26-9/5	1P: $79-$159	2P: $89-$189	XP: $10 F12
5/1-6/25 & 9/6-10/31	1P: $49-$99	2P: $59-$119	XP: $10 F12
11/1-4/30	1P: $49-$89	2P: $49-$109	XP: $10 F12

Motel

Location: 2.8 km n of falls on Niagara River Pkwy. 4267 River Rd L2E 3E7. **Fax:** 905/374-4972. **Facility:** 38 one-bedroom standard units, some with whirlpools. 2 stories (no elevator), exterior corridors. **Parking:** on-site. **Terms:** 3 day cancellation notice-fee imposed. **Pool(s):** heated outdoor. **Cards:** AX, DS, MC, VI.

SOME UNITS

DAYS INN & SUITES BY THE FALLS   Phone: (905)357-2550   28

CAA (SAVE)

6/26-9/5 [CP]	1P: $79-$299	2P: $79-$299	XP: $10 F16
5/1-6/25 & 9/6-4/30 [CP]	1P: $59-$179	2P: $59-$179	XP: $10 F16

Small-scale Hotel

Location: Jct Ellen Ave. 5068 Centre St L2G 3N9. **Fax:** 905/357-7771. **Facility:** 152 units. 142 one-bedroom standard units, some with whirlpools. 10 one-bedroom suites. 3-6 stories, interior corridors. *Bath:* combo or shower only. **Parking:** on-site. **Terms:** 3 day cancellation notice. **Amenities:** voice mail, irons, hair dryers. **Pool(s):** heated indoor. **Leisure Activities:** sauna, whirlpool, exercise room. **Guest Services:** coin laundry. **Business Services:** meeting rooms. **Cards:** AX, DS, MC, VI. **Special Amenities:** free continental breakfast and free newspaper.

SOME UNITS

THE DAYS INN CLIFTON HILL CASINO   *Book at aaa.com*   Phone: 905/356-2461   16

6/25-9/5	1P: $89-$429	2P: $89-$429	XP: $10 F16
9/6-4/30	1P: $49-$329	2P: $49-$329	XP: $10 F16
5/1-6/24	1P: $49-$229	2P: $49-$229	XP: $10 F16

Small-scale Hotel

Location: Just e on Hwy 20. 5657 Victoria Ave L2G 3L5. **Fax:** 905/356-2467. **Facility:** 138 units. 136 one- and 2 two-bedroom standard units, some with whirlpools. 2-7 stories, interior/exterior corridors. **Parking:** on-site. **Terms:** cancellation fee imposed. **Amenities:** safes, hair dryers. *Some:* voice mail, irons. **Pool(s):** heated indoor. **Leisure Activities:** sauna, whirlpool. **Guest Services:** gift shop, area transportation (fee). **Cards:** AX, CB, DC, DS, JC, MC, VI. *(See color ad p 494)*

SOME UNITS

DAYS INN FALLSVIEW DISTRICT   *Book at aaa.com*   Phone: (905)356-5877   68

CAA (SAVE)

6/18-9/5	1P: $75-$275	2P: $75-$275	XP: $10 F12
9/6-4/30	1P: $65-$195	2P: $65-$195	XP: $10 F12
5/1-6/17	1P: $55-$195	2P: $55-$195	XP: $10 F12

Motel

Location: Between Minolta and Skylon Towers, just w of the falls via Murray St. 6408 Stanley Ave L2G 3Y5. **Fax:** 905/356-9452. **Facility:** 100 units. 98 one- and 2 two-bedroom standard units. 3 stories, interior/exterior corridors. **Parking:** on-site. **Terms:** 3 day cancellation notice, package plans. **Amenities:** hair dryers, irons. **Pool(s):** heated indoor. **Leisure Activities:** sauna. **Guest Services:** area transportation-casino. **Cards:** AX, DC, DS, MC, VI. **Special Amenities:** free local telephone calls and free room upgrade (subject to availability with advanced reservations). *(See color ad p 496)*

SOME UNITS

(See map and index starting on p. 464)

DAYS INN-LUNDY'S LANE   *Book at aaa.com*   Phone: 905/358-3621   **47**

6/25-9/5	1P: $79-$269	2P: $79-$269	XP: $10	F16
9/6-4/30	1P: $45-$269	2P: $45-$269	XP: $10	F16
5/1-6/24	1P: $45-$189	2P: $45-$189	XP: $10	F16

Small-scale Hotel **Location:** QEW, exit Hwy 20 W, 3.8 km w. 7280 Lundy's Ln L2G 1W2. Fax: 905/356-7693. **Facility:** 135 one-bedroom standard units, some with whirlpools. 2-5 stories, interior/exterior corridors. **Parking:** on-site (fee). **Terms:** cancellation fee imposed. **Amenities:** *Some:* irons, hair dryers. **Pool(s):** heated indoor. **Leisure Activities:** sauna, whirlpool, miniature golf, playground. **Guest Services:** area transportation (fee). **Cards:** AX, CB, DC, DS, JC, MC, VI.
(See color ad p 494 & card insert)

SOME UNITS
(ASK) (†) (Y) (≈) (⊠) (🎥) / (⊠) (🖥) /

DAYS INN NEAR THE FALLS   *Book at aaa.com*   Phone: (905)374-3333   **12**

5/1-9/30	1P: $89-$299	2P: $89-$299	XP: $20	F12
10/1-4/30	1P: $79-$279	2P: $79-$279	XP: $20	F12

Location: On Hwy 20, 0.6 km from the falls. 5943 Victoria Ave L2G 3L8. Fax: 905/374-0669. **Facility:** 117 one-bedroom standard units, some with whirlpools. 7 stories, interior corridors. **Parking:** on-site (fee).
Small-scale Hotel **Terms:** cancellation fee imposed. **Amenities:** hair dryers. *Some:* irons. **Pool(s):** heated indoor. **Leisure Activities:** sauna, whirlpool. *Fee:* game room. **Guest Services:** gift shop. **Cards:** AX, DS, MC, VI.
(See color ad p 497)

SOME UNITS
(S/D) (††+) (≈) (⊠) (🎥) / (⊠) /

DAYS INN NORTH OF THE FALLS   *Book at aaa.com*   Phone: (905)356-6666   **24**

6/18-9/5	1P: $78-$228	2P: $78-$228	XP: $10	F12
5/1-6/17 & 9/6-4/30	1P: $48-$168	2P: $48-$168	XP: $10	F12

Location: 3 km n of Rainbow Bridge. 4029 River Rd L2E 3E5. Fax: 905/356-1800. **Facility:** 94 one-bedroom standard units, some with whirlpools. 4 stories (no elevator), interior/exterior corridors. **Parking:** on-site. **Terms:** 3
Small-scale Hotel day cancellation notice, package plans. **Amenities:** video library (fee). *Some:* irons, hair dryers. **Dining:** noon-10 pm; from 5 pm 10/15-5/14, cocktails. **Pool(s):** heated indoor. **Leisure Activities:** sauna, whirlpool. **Guest Services:** area transportation-casino & falls. **Cards:** AX, DC, DS, MC, VI. **Special Amenities:** free local telephone calls and early check-in/late check-out. *(See color ad p 498)*

SOME UNITS
(S/D) (†) (≈) (🎥) (🖥) / (⊠) (VCR) /
FEE

ECONO LODGE NEAR THE FALLS   *Book at aaa.com*   Phone: (905)358-6243   **51**

6/21-8/17	1P: $75-$195	2P: $75-$195	XP: $10	F16
8/18-4/30	1P: $60-$145	2P: $60-$145	XP: $10	F16
5/1-6/20	1P: $50-$120	2P: $50-$120	XP: $10	F16

Motel **Location:** 1.3 km w on Hwy 20, just s. 6000 Stanley Ave L2G 3Y1. Fax: 905/358-1864. **Facility:** 80 one-bedroom standard units, some with whirlpools. 2 stories (no elevator), interior/exterior corridors. **Parking:** on-site. **Terms:** small pets only ($10 extra charge, limit 1). **Pool(s):** outdoor. **Business Services:** fax (fee). **Cards:** AX, CB, DC, DS, JC, MC, VI.

SOME UNITS
(ASK) (S/D) (🐾) (††+) (≈) (DATA PORT) / (⊠) (📶) /
FEE

(See map and index starting on p. 464)

EMBASSY SUITES NIAGARA FALLS FALLSVIEW   *Book at aaa.com*   Phone: (905)356-3600   82

	7/1-8/31 [BP]	1P: $189-$599	2P: $189-$599
	5/1-6/30 [BP]	1P: $129-$599	2P: $129-$599
	9/1-4/30 [BP]	1P: $119-$599	2P: $119-$599

Large-scale Hotel **Location:** Adjacent to the Minolta Tower. 6700 Fallsview Blvd L2G 3W6. Fax: 905/356-0472. **Facility:** 512 one-bedroom suites ($179-$799), some with whirlpools. 42 stories, interior corridors. **Parking:** on-site (fee) and valet. **Terms:** 3 day cancellation notice-fee imposed, package plans. **Amenities:** video games, dual phone lines, voice mail, safes, honor bars, irons, hair dryers. **Pool(s):** heated indoor. **Leisure Activities:** whirlpool, exercise room. **Guest Services:** sundries, valet and coin laundry, area transportation (fee). **Business Services:** meeting rooms. **Cards:** AX, CB, DC, DS, JC, MC, VI.

SOME UNITS

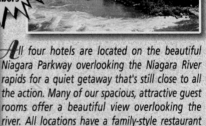

(See map and index starting on p. 464)

FALLSVIEW INN

				Phone: (905)374-4244	31
CAA SAVE	5/1-9/5	1P: $79-$209	2P: $79-$209	XP: $10	F18
	9/6-4/30	1P: $49-$199	2P: $49-$199	XP: $10	F18

Location: 1.2 km w on Hwy 20, just s. 6170 Stanley Ave L2G 3Y4. Fax: 905/374-6142. **Facility:** 65 one-bedroom standard units, some with whirlpools. 5 stories, interior corridors. **Parking:** on-site. **Terms:** cancellation fee imposed, [BP] meal plan available, package plans. **Amenities:** hair dryers. **Dining:** 7 am-11 & 5-9 pm, cocktails. **Pool(s):** heated indoor. **Leisure Activities:** sauna, whirlpool. *Fee:* game room. **Guest Services:** area transportation-casino. **Cards:** AX, DC, MC, VI. *(See color ad below)*

Small-scale Hotel

SOME UNITS

🍽 🍷 🛋 ⊠ 🎞 / ⊠ 📠 📶 / FEE

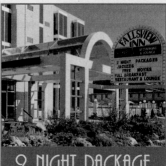

(See map and index starting on p. 464)

FLAMINGO MOTOR INN

			Phone: (905)356-4646	64
6/25-8/28	1P: $69-$139	2P: $79-$179	XP: $10	F
5/1-6/24 & 8/29-10/9	1P: $49-$99	2P: $56-$109	XP: $10	F
10/10-4/30	1P: $45-$69	2P: $49-$79	XP: $10	F

CAA SAVE

Motel

Location: QEW, 3.4 km w on Hwy 20. 7701 Lundy's Ln L2H 1H3. **Fax:** 905/356-9373. **Facility:** 93 one-bedroom standard units, some with whirlpools. 2 stories (no elevator), exterior corridors. **Parking:** on-site, winter plug-ins. **Terms:** 7 day cancellation notice, small pets only ($10 extra charge). **Amenities:** voice mail. **Pool(s):** heated outdoor. **Cards:** AX, CB, DC, DS, MC, VI. **Special Amenities:** free local telephone calls and free newspaper.
(See color ad below & card insert)

SOME UNITS
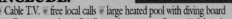

(See map and index starting on p. 464)

GLENGATE HOTEL   *Book at aaa.com*   **Phone:** (905)357-1333   ⟨84⟩

	6/1-9/30	1P: $110-$250	2P: $135-$300	XP: $15	F12
	5/1-5/31	1P: $80-$165	2P: $80-$165
	10/1-12/31	1P: $70-$150	2P: $70-$150
	1/1-4/30	1P: $65-$125	2P: $65-$125

Small-scale Hotel **Location:** Jct Hwy 420. 5534 Stanley Ave L2G 3X2. Fax: 905/357-1341. **Facility:** 60 units. 57 one-bedroom standard units, some with whirlpools. 3 one-bedroom suites, some with whirlpools. 3 stories, interior corridors. **Parking:** on-site. **Terms:** package plans, pets ($50 fee). **Amenities:** voice mail, irons, hair dryers. **Guest Services:** valet laundry. **Business Services:** meeting rooms. **Cards:** AX, CB, DC, DS, MC, VI. **Special Amenities: free continental breakfast.** *(See color ad p 500)*

SOME UNITS

HAMPTON INN AT THE FALLS   *Book at aaa.com*   **Phone:** (905)357-1626   ⟨17⟩

	6/1-9/30	1P: $129-$329	2P: $129-$329	XP: $10	F18
	10/1-10/31	1P: $99-$249	2P: $99-$249	XP: $10	F18
	5/1-5/31	1P: $89-$219	2P: $89-$219	XP: $10	F18
	11/1-4/30	1P: $69-$199	2P: $69-$199	XP: $10	F18

Small-scale Hotel **Location:** At top of Clifton Hill; ne of the falls. 5591 Victoria Ave L2G 3L4. Fax: 905/357-5869. **Facility:** 127 units. 105 one- and 22 two-bedroom standard units, some with whirlpools. 6 stories, interior corridors. **Parking:** on-site. **Amenities:** video games, voice mail, irons. *Some:* hair dryers. **Pool(s):** heated indoor. **Leisure Activities:** sauna, whirlpool. **Guest Services:** gift shop, valet laundry. **Cards:** AX, DC, DS, MC, VI. *(See color ad below)*

SOME UNITS

HAMPTON INN NORTH OF THE FALLS   *Book at aaa.com*   **Phone:** (905)358-5555   ⟨5⟩

	6/18-9/5 [CP]	1P: $89-$249	2P: $89-$249	XP: $10	F12
	5/1-6/17 & 9/6-4/30 [CP]	1P: $69-$199	2P: $69-$199	XP: $10	F12

Small-scale Hotel **Location:** 2.8 km n of the falls. 4357 River Rd L2E 3E8. Fax: 905/358-0140. **Facility:** 105 one-bedroom standard units, some with whirlpools. 5 stories, interior corridors. **Parking:** on-site. **Terms:** 3 day cancellation notice, package plans. **Amenities:** voice mail, irons, hair dryers. **Dining:** 6-10 am. **Pool(s):** heated indoor. **Leisure Activities:** sauna, whirlpool, sun deck. **Guest Services:** area transportation-casino. **Cards:** AX, DC, DS, MC, VI. **Special Amenities: free local telephone calls and early check-in/late check-out.** *(See color ad p 498)*

SOME UNITS

(See map and index starting on p. 464)

HILTON NIAGARA FALLS   *Book at aaa.com*   Phone: (905)354-7887   50

(CAA) (SAVE)   6/18-9/5   1P: $129-$499   2P: $129-$499   XP: $20   F12
               5/1-6/17 & 9/6-4/30   1P: $99-$299   2P: $99-$299   XP: $20   F12

▼▼▼▼ ▼▼▼▼   **Location:** Hwy 20, just s. 6361 Fallsview Blvd L2G 3V9. Fax: 905/357-9300. **Facility:** Good views of the falls are
offered from many of the hotel's rooms as well as from its rooftop restaurant; a waterslide is featured. 516
Large-scale Hotel one-bedroom standard units, some with whirlpools. 34 stories, interior corridors. **Parking:** on-site (fee) and
valet. **Terms:** check-in 4 pm, 3 day cancellation notice, package plans. **Amenities:** video games, dual phone
lines, voice mail, irons, hair dryers. **Dining:** 7 am-10:30 pm, cocktails, also, The Watermark, see separate listing. **Pool(s):** heated
indoor. **Leisure Activities:** sauna, whirlpool, steamroom, waterslide. **Guest Services:** gift shop, valet laundry, area transportation (fee)-casino. **Business Services:** meeting rooms. *Fee:* administrative services, fax. **Cards:** AX, DC, DS, MC, VI.
Special Amenities: free newspaper and free room upgrade (subject to availability with advanced reservations).
(See color ad below)

SOME UNITS

⬛ 🍴 🍸 🏊 🏋 ✂ 📷 DATA PORT 🖥 / ✂ 📶 /

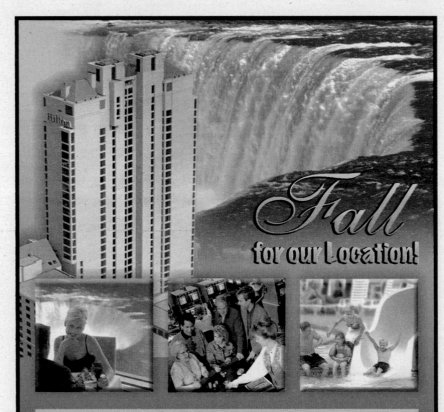

Holiday Inn By The Falls

In Niagara, why stay anywhere else?

Why indeed when one location offers it all… quality, comfort and convenience. Just 220 yds. from the Falls, next to the famous Skylon Tower, and right beside the magnificent new Casino. Plus free on-site parking. ★ Spacious well-appointed guest rooms with King or Queen-size bed and private balcony… or a luxury suite with whirl-pool bath for two.

★ **Coco's Terrace Steakhouse** offers superb dining by an open-hearth grill in a smart but casual indoor/outdoor setting… breakfast, lunch and dinner. Children's menu. In season, nightly entertainment on the patio. Plus a **gourmet pizza bar** with authentic woodfire oven and a unique cocktail lounge.

★ Unwind at our luxury **Nordic Spa** with large sparkling indoor pool, relaxing sauna and invigorating whirlpool. In summer, our 50 ft. outdoor pool awaits.

★ Plus… **special value rates for AAA/CAA members**. Special package rates October thru May. So why stay anywhere else? Experience it all at Holiday Inn By The Falls!

5339 Murray St. (cor. Fallsview Blvd.), Niagara Falls, Ontario, Canada L2G 2J3

(905) 356-1333 • 1-800-263-9393   res@holidayinn.com   www.holidayinn.com

(See map and index starting on p. 464)

HOLIDAY INN BY THE FALLS

Phone: (905)356-1333　

CAA SAVE

	6/18-9/5	1P: $110-$245	2P: $110-$245	XP: $10	F14
	9/6-10/10	1P: $85-$225	2P: $85-$225	XP: $10	F14
	5/1-6/17	1P: $75-$225	2P: $75-$225	XP: $10	F14
	10/11-4/30	1P: $69-$185	2P: $69-$185	XP: $5	F14

Small-scale Hotel **Location:** Just w from the falls, directly across from the new casino. Located adjacent to Skylon Tower. 5339 Murray St L2G 2J3. Fax: 905/356-7128. **Facility:** 122 one-bedroom standard units, some with whirlpools. 6 stories, interior corridors. **Parking:** on-site. **Terms:** cancellation fee imposed, package plans - 10/1-5/31. **Amenities:** video games, dual phone lines, voice mail, irons, hair dryers. **Dining:** 8 am-10 pm; 7 am-11 pm 6/14-10/15, cocktails. **Pool(s):** heated outdoor, heated indoor. **Leisure Activities:** sauna, whirlpool. **Guest Services:** gift shop. **Cards:** AX, CB, DC, DS, JC, MC, VI. **Special Amenities:** free newspaper and free room upgrade (subject to availability with advanced reservations). *(See color ad p 503 & p 527)*

SOME UNITS

HORSESHOE FALLS MOTOR INN

Phone: (905)358-9353　**35**

CAA SAVE

	6/18-9/6	1P: $69-$229	2P: $69-$229	XP: $10	F12
	9/7-10/11	1P: $49-$179	2P: $49-$179	XP: $7	F12
	5/1-6/17	1P: $49-$169	2P: $49-$169	XP: $7	F12
	10/12-4/30	1P: $39-$129	2P: $39-$129	XP: $7	F12

Small-scale Hotel **Location:** Opposite Minolta Tower. 5481 Dunn St L2G 2N6. Fax: 905/356-7298. **Facility:** 64 one-bedroom standard units, some with whirlpools. 2-4 stories, interior corridors. **Parking:** on-site. **Terms:** 4 day cancellation notice-fee imposed, [AP], [BP] & [MAP] meal plans available, package plans - seasonal. **Dining:** 8 am-midnight; closed 11/30-3/15, cocktails. **Pool(s):** heated outdoor. **Leisure Activities:** whirlpool. **Cards:** AX, CB, DC, DS, JC, MC, VI. **Special Amenities:** free local telephone calls and early check-in/late check-out. *(See color ad p 505)*

SOME UNITS

FEE

HOWARD JOHNSON BY THE FALLS

Book at aaa.com

Phone: 905/357-4040　**13**

CAA SAVE

| | 6/25-9/6 | 1P: $99-$369 | 2P: $99-$369 | XP: $10 | F16 |
| | 5/1-6/24 & 9/7-4/30 | 1P: $69-$369 | 2P: $69-$369 | XP: $10 | F16 |

Location: On Hwy 20, 0.6 km from the falls. 5905 Victoria Ave L2G 3L8. Fax: 905/357-6202. **Facility:** 199 units. 186 one- and 13 two-bedroom standard units, some with whirlpools. 7 stories, interior corridors. **Parking:** on-site

Small-scale Hotel (fee). **Terms:** check-in 4 pm, package plans. **Amenities:** voice mail, hair dryers. *Some:* irons. **Pool(s):** heated indoor/outdoor. **Leisure Activities:** sauna, whirlpool. *Fee:* game room. **Guest Services:** valet and coin laundry, area transportation-casino. **Business Services:** meeting rooms. **Cards:** AX, DS, MC, VI.

SOME UNITS

(See map and index starting on p. 464)

HOWARD JOHNSON EXPRESS INN *Book at aaa.com* Phone: (905)358-9777 ⑤⑤

(CAA) (SAVE)
7/1-9/4 1P: $60-$200 2P: $60-$200 XP: $10 F17
5/1-6/30 & 9/5-4/30 1P: $40-$150 2P: $40-$150 XP: $10 F17
Location: QEW, exit Hwy 20 W, 5 km w. 8100 Lundy's Ln L2H 1H1. Fax: 905/358-0575. **Facility:** 84 one-bedroom standard units, some with whirlpools. 2 stories (no elevator), exterior corridors. **Parking:** on-site, winter plug-ins. **Terms:** cancellation fee imposed, [CP] meal plan available. **Pool(s):** heated outdoor. **Guest Services:** area transportation (fee)-casino. **Cards:** AX, DC, DS, JC, MC, VI. **Special Amenities:** free continental breakfast and free local telephone calls. *(See color ad card insert)*

Motel

SOME UNITS
🅂🄳 🏊 📷 🖥 /✕ 🔌 /
FEE

IMPERIAL HOTEL AND SUITES Phone: (905)356-2648 ⑭

(CAA) (SAVE)
5/1-9/30 [BP] 1P: $79-$359 2P: $79-$359 XP: $15 F12
10/1-4/30 [BP] 1P: $69-$299 2P: $69-$299 XP: $15 F12
Location: Hwy 20, 0.5 km from the falls. 5851 Victoria Ave L2G 3L6. Fax: 905/356-4068. **Facility:** 104 one-bedroom standard units, some with whirlpools. 10 stories, interior corridors. **Parking:** on-site. **Terms:** check-in 4 pm, cancellation fee imposed. **Amenities:** voice mail. *Some:* irons, hair dryers. **Dining:** 7-11 am in season. **Pool(s):** heated indoor. **Leisure Activities:** whirlpool. *Fee:* game room. **Guest Services:** gift shop, coin laundry. **Business Services:** meeting rooms, fax (fee). **Cards:** AX, DC, DS, MC, VI. *(See color ad below)*

Small-scale Hotel

SOME UNITS
🅂🄳 🍴 🏊 📷 🖥 🔌 🖥 /✕ 📞 /

KINGS INN NEAR THE FALLS Phone: (905)356-1233 ⑥⑨

🌊🌊 🌊🌊
6/20-9/6 1P: $79-$199 2P: $79-$199 XP: $15 D12
5/1-6/19 & 9/7-9/30 1P: $49-$149 2P: $49-$149 XP: $10 D12
10/1-4/30 1P: $44-$89 2P: $44-$89 XP: $10 D12
Motel
Location: On Hwy 20, 1 km from the falls. Located in a commercial area. 5525 Ferry St L2G 1S3. Fax: 905/374-6412. **Facility:** 44 one-bedroom standard units, some with whirlpools. 3 stories (no elevator), exterior corridors. **Parking:** on-site. **Terms:** office hours 8 am-2 am, 3 day cancellation notice. **Pool(s):** heated outdoor. **Leisure Activities:** *Fee:* game room. **Cards:** AX, CB, DC, DS, JC, MC, VI.

SOME UNITS
🍴 🏊 📷 /✕ /

(See map and index starting on p. 464)

KNIGHTS INN *Book at aaa.com*   Phone: (905)354-6939 **46**
(CAA) (SAVE)
6/27-9/3	1P: $79-$249	2P: $79-$249	XP: $5	F18
5/1-6/26	1P: $55-$199	2P: $55-$199	XP: $5	F18
9/4-4/30	1P: $49-$199	2P: $49-$199	XP: $5	F18

Motel **Location:** 3.4 km w on Hwy 20. Located in a commercial area. 7034 Lundy's Ln L2G 1V9. Fax: 905/354-3699. **Facility:** 64 one-bedroom standard units. 2 stories (no elevator), exterior corridors. **Parking:** on-site. **Pool(s):** heated outdoor. **Guest Services:** area transportation (fee)-casino. **Business Services:** fax (fee). **Cards:** AX, DC, DS, MC, VI. **Special Amenities:** free local telephone calls and free newspaper. *(See color ad card insert)*

SOME UNITS

[S/D] [icons] / [X] [icons] /
FEE FEE

KNIGHTS INN-BY THE FALLS *Book at aaa.com*   Phone: (905)358-8132 **48**
(CAA) (SAVE)
6/27-9/3	1P: $84-$254	2P: $84-$254	XP: $5	F18
5/1-6/26	1P: $59-$205	2P: $59-$205	XP: $5	F18
9/4-4/30	1P: $54-$205	2P: $54-$205	XP: $5	F18

Motel **Location:** Jct of Murray St. 6276 Main St L2G 6A4. Fax: 905/358-2777. **Facility:** 47 one-bedroom standard units, some with efficiencies and/or whirlpools. 1-2 stories (no elevator), exterior corridors. *Bath:* combo or shower only. **Parking:** on-site. **Pool(s):** heated outdoor, wading. **Leisure Activities:** whirlpool. **Cards:** AX, DC, MC, VI. **Special Amenities:** free local telephone calls and free newspaper.

SOME UNITS

[S/D] [icons] / [X] [icons] /

LINCOLN MOTOR INN   Phone: (905)356-1748 **41**
(CAA) (SAVE)
| 6/25-9/5 | 1P: $89-$189 | 2P: $89-$189 | XP: $10 | F12 |
| 5/1-6/24 & 9/6-4/30 | 1P: $49-$149 | 2P: $49-$149 | XP: $10 | F12 |

Motel **Location:** By Minolta Tower; 0.3 mi w of the falls via Murray St. 6417 Main St L2G 5Y3. Fax: 905/356-7531. **Facility:** 60 units. 59 one- and 1 two-bedroom standard units, some with whirlpools. 2 stories (no elevator), exterior corridors. **Parking:** on-site. **Terms:** office hours 7:50 am-11:50 pm, 2 night minimum stay - weekends, [BP] & [MAP] meal plans available, package plans. **Amenities:** hair dryers. **Dining:** 7:30 am-noon. **Pool(s):** heated outdoor. **Leisure Activities:** whirlpool. **Cards:** AX, DC, DS, MC, VI. **Special Amenities:** free local telephone calls and free newspaper. *(See color ad below)*

SOME UNITS

[S/D] [icons] / [X] /

(See map and index starting on p. 464)

MELODY MOTEL   Phone: 905/227-1023   32

(CAA) (SAVE)

6/28-9/3	1P: $48-$88	2P: $58-$98	XP: $10	F12
5/1-6/27 & 9/4-4/30	1P: $38-$48	2P: $48-$58	XP: $10	F12

Motel   **Location:** 9.2 km w on Hwy 20. 13065 Lundy's Ln L2E 6S4. Fax: 905/227-3712. **Facility:** 19 one-bedroom standard units, some with whirlpools. 1 story, exterior corridors. **Parking:** on-site, winter plug-ins. **Terms:** office hours 9 am-midnight, 3 day cancellation notice-fee imposed. **Pool(s):** heated outdoor. **Cards:** AX, DC, DS, MC, VI. **Special Amenities:** free local telephone calls and preferred room (subject to availability with advanced reservations).

SOME UNITS

NIAGARA FALLS MARRIOTT FALLSVIEW   *Book at aaa.com*   Phone: (905)357-7300   39

(CAA) (SAVE)

7/1-8/31	1P: $189-$599	2P: $189-$599	
5/1-6/30 & 9/1-4/30	1P: $129-$599	2P: $129-$599	

Large-scale Hotel   **Location:** Next to Minolta Tower. 6740 Fallsview Blvd L2G 3W6. Fax: 905/357-0490. **Facility:** On a hilltop, the hotel offers good views of the falls from many of its guest rooms and common areas. 427 units. 394 one-bedroom standard units, some with whirlpools. 33 one-bedroom suites ($179-$849), some with whirlpools. 20 stories, interior corridors. **Parking:** on-site (fee) and valet. **Terms:** 3 day cancellation notice-fee imposed, package plans. **Amenities:** video games, high-speed Internet, dual phone lines, voice mail, safes, honor bars, irons, hair dryers. **Dining:** Terrapin Grille, see separate listing. **Pool(s):** heated indoor. **Leisure Activities:** saunas, whirlpools, steamroom, exercise room, spa. *Fee:* game room. **Guest Services:** gift shop, valet laundry, area transportation (fee)-casino. **Business Services:** meeting rooms, business center. **Cards:** AX, CB, DC, DS, JC, MC, VI. *(See color ad card insert)*

SOME UNITS

NIAGARA FALLS MOTOR LODGE   Phone: (905)295-3569   75

(CAA) (SAVE)

6/18-9/7	1P: $59-$129	2P: $59-$129	XP: $10	F12
5/1-6/17 & 9/8-4/30	1P: $49-$79	2P: $49-$79	XP: $10	F12

Motel   **Location:** 2 km s of Horseshoe Falls, on Niagara Pkwy to Portage Rd S, just to the right; 1.2 km s of Marineland. Located in a residential area. 7950 Portage Rd S L2G 5Y8. Fax: 905/295-0022. **Facility:** 20 one-bedroom standard units. 2 stories (no elevator), exterior corridors. **Parking:** on-site. **Terms:** office hours 7 am-midnight, 3 day cancellation notice. **Pool(s):** heated outdoor. **Business Services:** fax (fee). **Cards:** AX, MC, VI. **Special Amenities:** free local telephone calls and free newspaper.

SOME UNITS

NIAGARA FAMILY INN   Phone: 905/354-9844   6

(CAA) (SAVE)

6/25-9/5	1P: $55-$95	2P: $69-$95	XP: $10	F12
5/1-6/24	1P: $39-$59	2P: $49-$79	XP: $10	F12
9/6-4/30	1P: $39-$59	2P: $49-$69	XP: $10	F12

Motel   **Location:** Jct Clifton Ave, just e. 5612 Ellen Ave L2G 7V5. Fax: 905/354-6691. **Facility:** 36 one-bedroom standard units. 2 stories (no elevator), interior/exterior corridors. *Bath:* combo or shower only. **Parking:** on-site. **Terms:** 5 day cancellation notice-fee imposed. **Dining:** noon-midnight, cocktails. **Pool(s):** heated outdoor. **Business Services:** meeting rooms. **Cards:** AX, DS, MC, VI. **Special Amenities:** early check-in/late check-out and preferred room (subject to availability with advanced reservations).

SOME UNITS

NIAGARA PARKWAY COURT MOTEL   Phone: (905)295-3331   73

(CAA) (SAVE)

6/18-9/30 [CP]	1P: $49-$129	2P: $49-$199	XP: $10	F14
5/1-6/17 [BP]	1P: $49-$79	2P: $49-$129	XP: $10	F14
10/1-4/30 [BP]	1P: $39-$69	2P: $39-$99	XP: $10	F14

Motel   **Location:** 2.5 km s of the falls on the Niagara Pkwy. Located in a quiet area. 3708 Main St L2G 6B1. Fax: 905/295-3331. **Facility:** 19 one-bedroom standard units, some with efficiencies and/or whirlpools. 2 stories (no elevator), exterior corridors. **Parking:** on-site. **Terms:** package plans, small pets only ($10 extra charge, in designated units). **Cards:** AX, DC, DS, JC, MC, VI. **Special Amenities:** free continental breakfast.

FEE   SOME UNITS

THE OAKES HOTEL OVERLOOKING THE FALLS   *Book at aaa.com*   Phone: (905)356-4514   1

6/23-9/7	1P: $139-$569	XP: $10	F18
5/1-6/22 & 9/8-4/30	1P: $79-$429	XP: $10	F18

Small-scale Hotel   **Location:** By Minolta Tower, adjacent to the new casino. 6546 Fallsview Blvd L2G 3W2. Fax: 905/356-3651. **Facility:** 167 one-bedroom standard units, some with whirlpools. 2-12 stories, interior/exterior corridors. **Parking:** on-site (fee). **Terms:** 3 day cancellation notice. **Amenities:** hair dryers. *Some:* irons. **Pool(s):** heated indoor. **Leisure Activities:** sauna, whirlpool, exercise room. **Guest Services:** gift shop, valet laundry, area transportation (fee). **Business Services:** meeting rooms, fax (fee). **Cards:** AX, DC, DS, JC, MC, VI. *(See color ad p 494)*

SOME UNITS

OLD STONE INN   *Book at aaa.com*   Phone: (905)357-1234   59

7/1-9/5	1P: $129-$349	2P: $129-$349	XP: $20	F12
10/24-4/30	1P: $99-$309	2P: $99-$309	XP: $20	F12
9/6-10/23	1P: $109-$289	2P: $109-$289	XP: $20	F12
5/1-6/30	1P: $99-$289	2P: $99-$289	XP: $20	F12

Small-scale Hotel   **Location:** Just w via Murray St, then just n on Buchanan Ave. Located adjacent to Skylon Tower. 5425 Robinson St L2G 7L6. Fax: 905/357-9299. **Facility:** 114 one-bedroom standard units, some with whirlpools. 3 stories, interior/exterior corridors. **Parking:** on-site, winter plug-ins. **Terms:** check-in 4 pm, cancellation fee imposed, package plans. **Amenities:** video games, voice mail, hair dryers. **Dining:** The Millery Dining Room, see separate listing. **Pool(s):** heated outdoor, heated indoor. **Leisure Activities:** whirlpool. **Guest Services:** valet laundry, area transportation. **Business Services:** meeting rooms. **Cards:** AX, CB, DC, DS, JC, MC, VI.

SOME UNITS

(See map and index starting on p. 464)

PARK PLAZA Phone: (905)353-1010 63

CAA SAVE

6/18-9/5		2P: $89-$169	XP: $10	F16
5/1-6/17 & 9/6-4/30		2P: $59-$89	XP: $10	F16

Location: Jct Main and Ferry sts, just s. 5807 Ferry St L2G 1S8. Fax: 905/358-7131. **Facility:** 145 one-bedroom standard units, some with whirlpools. 2-11 stories, interior/exterior corridors. *Bath:* combo or shower only. **Parking:** on-site. **Terms:** package plans. **Amenities:** voice mail, hair dryers. *Some:* honor bars. **Dining:** 7 am-2 am, cocktails. **Pool(s):** heated outdoor, heated indoor. **Leisure Activities:** sauna, whirlpool, exercise room. *Fee:* massage. **Guest Services:** area transportation-casino & falls. **Business Services:** meeting rooms. **Cards:** AX, DC, DS, MC, VI. **Special Amenities:** free local telephone calls and early check-in/late check-out. *(See color ad below)*

Large-scale Hotel

SOME UNITS

PENINSULA INN & RESORT Phone: (905)354-8812 76

CAA SAVE

7/1-9/6		2P: $99-$209	XP: $10	F12
5/1-6/30		2P: $79-$189	XP: $10	F12
9/7-10/31		2P: $79-$159	XP: $10	F12
11/1-4/30		2P: $59-$159	XP: $10	F12

Location: QEW, exit McLeod Rd, just w. Located in a quiet area. 7373 Niagara Square Dr L2E 6S5. Fax: 905/354-7174. **Facility:** 95 units. 93 one-bedroom standard units, some with whirlpools. 2 one-bedroom suites ($159-$349). 5 stories, interior corridors. **Parking:** on-site. **Terms:** cancellation fee imposed, pets ($10 fee, with prior approval). **Amenities:** dual phone lines, voice mail, hair dryers. **Dining:** 7 am-11 & 5:30-9 pm, Mon-11 am, cocktails. **Pool(s):** heated indoor. **Leisure Activities:** sauna, whirlpool, exercise room, spa. **Guest Services:** gift shop, coin laundry, area transportation-casino & falls. **Business Services:** meeting rooms. **Cards:** AX, DC, MC, VI.

Small-scale Hotel

SOME UNITS

PILGRIM MOTOR INN Phone: 905/374-7777 77

7/1-8/31	1P: $99-$149	2P: $99-$149	XP: $10	F
5/1-6/30 & 9/1-12/31	1P: $68-$129	2P: $68-$129	XP: $10	F
1/1-4/30	1P: $58-$129	2P: $58-$129	XP: $10	F

Location: Just s of jct Victoria Ave. 4955 Clifton Hill L2G 3N5. Fax: 905/354-8086. **Facility:** 40 one-bedroom standard units, some with whirlpools. 3 stories (no elevator), interior corridors. *Bath:* combo or shower only. **Parking:** on-site. **Terms:** package plans. **Cards:** AX, MC, VI.

Motel

THE PRESIDENT MOTOR INN Phone: 905/358-7272 40

CAA SAVE

7/1-8/21	1P: $79-$175	2P: $79-$175	XP: $10	F11
8/22-9/2	1P: $59-$150	2P: $59-$150	XP: $10	F11
9/3-10/30	1P: $49-$150	2P: $59-$150	XP: $10	F11
5/1-6/30	1P: $49-$150	2P: $49-$150	XP: $10	F11

Location: Just w of Minolta Tower, corner of Stanley and Dixon aves. 6503 Stanley Ave L2G 7L2. Fax: 905/356-0392. **Facility:** 42 one-bedroom standard units. 2 stories (no elevator), exterior corridors. **Parking:** on-site. **Terms:** open 5/1-10/30, cancellation fee imposed, package plans. **Pool(s):** heated outdoor. **Cards:** AX, DS, MC, VI. **Special Amenities:** free room upgrade and preferred room (each subject to availability with advanced reservations). *(See color ad p 509)*

Motel

SOME UNITS

See Why They Call It America The Beautiful.

*T*rafalgar's exciting selection of escorted tours lets you discover the magnificence and grandeur of the USA. These vacations include first-class accommodations, touring by luxury motorcoach, many meals and the services of a professional tour director.

AAA members who book an escorted motorcoach tour of the USA with a AAA Travel Agency also receive an exclusive AAA member benefit value of at least $35. See your AAA Travel professional for details.

TRAFALGAR
The Company of Choice

For more information, contact your AAA Travel Office or log on to www.aaa.com.

Travel

Travel With Someone You Trust®

* Discount vouchers available on select motorcoach tours only. Ask your AAA Travel Agency for details.

(See map and index starting on p. 464)

QUALITY HOTEL-NEAR THE FALLS *Book at aaa.com* Phone: (905)356-2842 🔟
CAA SAVE
5/29-8/28	1P: $129-$309	2P: $129-$309	XP: $25	F16
8/29-4/30	1P: $69-$289	2P: $69-$289	XP: $25	F16
5/1-5/28	1P: $69-$249	2P: $69-$249	XP: $25	F16

Location: On Hwy 20, 0.7 km from the falls. 5257 Ferry St L2G 1R6. Fax: 905/356-6629. **Facility:** 120 one-
Small-scale Hotel bedroom standard units, some with whirlpools. 11 stories, interior corridors. **Parking:** on-site.
Terms: package plans - 10/1-4/30. **Amenities:** video games, irons, hair dryers. **Dining:** 7 am-noon; hours
may vary off season. **Pool(s):** heated indoor, wading. **Leisure Activities:** sauna, whirlpool, sun deck. **Guest Services:** gift shop.
Business Services: meeting rooms. **Cards:** AX, CB, DC, DS, JC, MC, VI. *(See color ad p 511)*

SOME UNITS

🛎️ 🍴 🛥️ 🚫 📷 📹 💻 / 🚫 📠 /

QUALITY INN CLIFTON HILL *Book at aaa.com* Phone: (905)358-3601 🔟9️⃣
CAA SAVE
| 5/1-10/31 | 1P: $69-$269 | 2P: $69-$269 | XP: $12 | F18 |
| 11/1-4/30 | 1P: $49-$179 | 2P: $49-$179 | XP: $12 | F18 |

Location: Jct Victoria Ave and Clifton Hill, just s. 4946 Clifton Hill L2E 6S8 (PO Box 60, NIAGARA FALLS, ON).
Small-scale Hotel Fax: 905/358-3818. **Facility:** 263 units. 255 one- and 8 two-bedroom standard units, some with whirlpools.
2-3 stories (no elevator), interior/exterior corridors. **Parking:** on-site. **Terms:** package plans - 9/1-6/30.
Dining: 6:30 am-11 pm; hours may vary off season, cocktails. **Pool(s):** heated outdoor, heated indoor,
wading. **Leisure Activities:** whirlpool, playground. **Guest Services:** gift shop, valet laundry. **Cards:** AX, CB, DC, DS, JC, MC, VI.
Special Amenities: free local telephone calls and free newspaper. *(See color ad starting on p 491)*

SOME UNITS

🛎️ 🍴 🛥️ 💻 / 🚫 /

(See map and index starting on p. 464)

RADISSON HOTEL & SUITES FALLSVIEW   *Book at aaa.com*   Phone: (905)356-1944   [78]

6/18-9/7	1P: $149-$249	2P: $149-$249	XP: $10	F18
5/1-6/17 & 9/8-4/30	1P: $89-$149	2P: $89-$149	XP: $10	F18

Large-scale Hotel **Location:** Corner of Stanley Ave and Dunn St. Located across from Minolta Tower. 6733 Fallsview Blvd L2G 3W7. Fax: 905/374-2555. **Facility:** 227 units. 206 one-bedroom standard units, some with whirlpools. 21 one-bedroom suites ($149-$299) with whirlpools. 16 stories, interior corridors. **Parking:** on-site (fee) and valet. **Terms:** [BP] meal plan available, package plans. **Amenities:** video games, high-speed Internet, dual phone lines, voice mail, irons, hair dryers. *Some:* safes. **Dining:** Outback Steakhouse, see separate listing. **Pool(s):** heated indoor. **Leisure Activities:** whirlpool, exercise room. *Fee:* massage. **Guest Services:** gift shop, valet laundry, area transportation (fee). **Business Services:** meeting rooms, business center. **Cards:** AX, DC, DS, MC, VI. *(See color ad starting below)*

SOME UNITS

(ASK) (SD) (⛏) (Y) (&) (⇌) (✕) (🐕) (DATA PORT) (▭) / (✕) (▯) (▭) /

(See map and index starting on p. 464)

RAMADA CORAL RESORT HOTEL   *Book at aaa.com*   Phone: (905)356-6116 65

6/19-9/5	1P: $90-$200	2P: $90-$200	XP: $10	F18
5/1-6/18 & 9/6-4/30	1P: $70-$160	2P: $70-$160	XP: $10	F18

Small-scale Hotel

Location: QEW, exit Hwy 20 W (Lundy's Ln); from downtown, 4 km w. 7429 Lundy's Ln L2H 1G9. Fax: 905/356-5201. **Facility:** 129 one-bedroom standard units, some with whirlpools. 4 stories, interior corridors. **Parking:** on-site, winter plug-ins. **Terms:** cancellation fee imposed. **Amenities:** video games, voice mail, irons, hair dryers. **Dining:** 7 am-9 pm; to 2 pm 11/1-5/1, cocktails. **Pool(s):** heated outdoor, heated indoor. **Leisure Activities:** sauna, whirlpool, playground. *Fee:* game room. **Guest Services:** gift shop, valet laundry, area transportation (fee)-attractions & casino. **Business Services:** meeting rooms, administrative services (fee). **Cards:** AX, DC, DS, JC, MC, VI. **Special Amenities:** free newspaper and early check-in/late check-out. *(See color ad p 513 & card insert)*

SOME UNITS

(See map and index starting on p. 464)

RAMADA PLAZA HOTEL FALLSVIEW *Book at aaa.com*   **Phone:** (905)356-1501   **3**

6/18-9/5	1P: $169-$349	2P: $169-$349
5/1-6/17	1P: $119-$249	2P: $119-$249
9/6-4/30	1P: $99-$229	2P: $99-$229

Large-scale Hotel   **Location:** In the Minolta Tower Centre. 6732 Fallsview Blvd L2G 3W6. Fax: 905/356-8245. **Facility:** 42 one-bedroom standard units, some with whirlpools. 30 stories, interior corridors. *Bath:* combo or shower only. **Parking:** on-site (fee) and valet. **Terms:** check-in 4 pm, [BP] meal plan available, package plans. **Amenities:** voice mail, safes, irons, hair dryers. **Dining:** Minolta Tower Centre/Pinnacle Restaurant, see separate listing. **Guest Services:** gift shop, valet laundry, area transportation (fee). **Cards:** AX, CB, DC, DS, MC, VI. *(See color ad starting on p 514)*

SOME UNITS
(ASK) (SD) (†1) (DATA PORT) ⊟ 🖼 ⬜ / (✕) /

RAMADA SUITES HOTEL *Book at aaa.com*   **Phone:** (905)356-6119   **49**

6/19-9/5	1P: $90-$230	2P: $90-$230	XP: $10 F18
5/1-6/18 & 9/6-4/30	1P: $90-$180	2P: $90-$180	XP: $10 F18

Small-scale Hotel   **Location:** QEW, exit Hwy 20 W (Lundy's Ln); from downtown, 4 km w. 7389 Lundy's Ln L2H 2W9. Fax: 905/356-5201. **Facility:** 73 units. 4 one-bedroom standard units with whirlpools. 69 one-bedroom suites, some with whirlpools. 6 stories, interior corridors. **Parking:** on-site. **Terms:** cancellation fee imposed. **Amenities:** video games, voice mail, irons, hair dryers. **Pool(s):** heated indoor. **Leisure Activities:** whirlpool, steamroom, exercise room. **Guest Services:** valet laundry, area transportation (fee). **Business Services:** conference facilities, business center. **Cards:** AX, DC, DS, JC, MC, VI. *(See color ad p 513 & card insert)*

SOME UNITS
(ASK) (SD) (†1) (Y) (🏊) (✕) (📹) (DATA PORT) ⊟ ⬜ / (✕) /

RED CARPET INN AND SUITES, FALLSWAY *Book at aaa.com*   **Phone:** (905)374-7666   **27**

(CAA) (SAVE)   5/1-10/31 & 4/1-4/30   1P: $49-$199   2P: $49-$199   F4

Motel   **Location:** Just s of Hwy 420 and Stanley Ave, then just e. Located in a residential area. 5334 Kitchener St L2G 1B5. Fax: 905/358-8221. **Facility:** 100 one-bedroom standard units, some with whirlpools. 2 stories (no elevator), interior/exterior corridors. **Parking:** on-site. **Terms:** open 5/1-10/31 & 4/1-4/30, 7 day cancellation notice-fee imposed. **Pool(s):** heated outdoor. **Leisure Activities:** saunas. **Guest Services:** coin laundry. **Business Services:** fax (fee). **Cards:** AX, MC, VI. **Special Amenities:** early check-in/late check-out and free room upgrade (subject to availability with advanced reservations).

SOME UNITS
(SD) (🏊) / (Z) ⊟ /
FEE

RENAISSANCE FALLSVIEW HOTEL *Book at aaa.com*   **Phone:** (905)357-5200   **2**

7/1-10/15	1P: $169-$499	2P: $169-$499	XP: $10 F18
5/1-6/30 & 10/16-12/31	1P: $99-$299	2P: $99-$299	XP: $10 F18
1/1-4/30	1P: $89-$199	2P: $89-$199	XP: $10 F18

Large-scale Hotel   **Location:** Just n of Minolta Tower, corner of Fallsview Blvd and Dixon Ave. 6455 Fallsview Blvd L2G 3V9. Fax: 905/357-3422. **Facility:** This centrally located hotel with distinctive contemporary decor throughout guest rooms and public areas is convenient to the area's attractions. 262 one-bedroom standard units, some with whirlpools. 18 stories, interior corridors. **Parking:** on-site (fee) and valet. **Terms:** cancellation fee imposed. **Amenities:** video games, dual phone lines, voice mail, irons, hair dryers. **Dining:** 6:30 am-midnight, cocktails, also, Rooftop Fallsview Dining Room, see separate listing. **Pool(s):** heated indoor. **Leisure Activities:** saunas, whirlpool. *Fee:* racquetball court, squash court, massage. **Guest Services:** gift shop, valet laundry, area transportation (fee)-casino. **Business Services:** conference facilities, business center. **Cards:** AX, CB, DC, DS, JC, MC, VI. *(See color ad p 517)*

SOME UNITS
(†1) (Y) (🍸) (🏊) (✦) (✕) (📹) (DATA PORT) ⬜ / (✕) /

RODEWAY INN & SUITES   **Phone:** 905/358-9833   **67**

5/1-9/30 [CP]	1P: $65-$150	2P: $65-$150	XP: $5 F
10/1-12/31 [CP]	1P: $50-$125	2P: $50-$125	XP: $5 F
1/1-4/30 [CP]	1P: $50-$75	2P: $50-$75	XP: $5 F

Small-scale Hotel   **Location:** QEW, 4 km w on Hwy 20. 7720 Lundy's Ln L2H 1H1. Fax: 905/358-3090. **Facility:** 90 one-bedroom standard units, some with whirlpools. 2-3 stories, interior/exterior corridors. **Parking:** on-site. **Terms:** cancellation fee imposed. **Pool(s):** outdoor, heated indoor. **Leisure Activities:** whirlpool. **Guest Services:** area transportation (fee). **Business Services:** fax (fee). **Cards:** AX, MC, VI.

SOME UNITS
(ASK) (†1+) (🏊) (DATA PORT) ⬜ / (✕) /

RODEWAY INN FALLSVIEW *Book at aaa.com*   **Phone:** (905)354-2322   **72**

7/1-9/5	1P: $79-$259	2P: $79-$259	XP: $10 F17
5/1-6/30 & 9/6-4/30	1P: $59-$189	2P: $59-$189	XP: $10 F17

Small-scale Hotel   **Location:** Jct Dunn St. 6663 Stanley Ave L2G 3Y9. Fax: 905/354-4955. **Facility:** 61 one-bedroom standard units, some with whirlpools. 2-3 stories (no elevator), interior/exterior corridors. **Parking:** on-site. **Terms:** cancellation fee imposed, [BP] & [CP] meal plans available, package plans - weekends. **Amenities:** voice mail, irons, hair dryers. **Dining:** 2 restaurants, 7 am-midnight, cocktails. **Pool(s):** heated outdoor. **Leisure Activities:** playground. **Guest Services:** gift shop. **Cards:** AX, DC, DS, MC, VI. **Special Amenities:** free local telephone calls and free newspaper. *(See color ad p 518)*

SOME UNITS
(SD) (†1) (🏊) (📹) (DATA PORT) ⬜ / (✕) ⊟ /
FEE

(See map and index starting on p. 464)

SHERATON FALLSVIEW HOTEL & CONFERENCE CENTRE   Book at aaa.com   Phone: (905)374-1077   **37**

(CAA) (SAVE)	6/11-9/30	1P: $159-$349	2P: $159-$349	XP: $20	F17
	5/1-6/10 & 10/1-10/31	1P: $129-$229	2P: $129-$229	XP: $20	F17
▼▼▼ ▼▼▼	11/1-4/30	1P: $99-$229	2P: $99-$229	XP: $20	F17

Large-scale Hotel

Location: Near Minolta Tower. 6755 Fallsview Blvd L2G 3W7. Fax: 905/374-6224. **Facility:** Guest rooms in this high-rise have modern, well-appointed decor; many offer very good views of the falls. 402 units. 376 one- and 8 two-bedroom standard units, some with whirlpools. 18 one-bedroom suites ($249-$639) with whirlpools. 32 stories, interior corridors. **Parking:** on-site (fee). **Terms:** cancellation fee imposed, [AP] meal plan available, package plans, small pets only (with prior approval). **Amenities:** video games, dual phone lines, voice mail, irons, hair dryers. *Some:* safes. **Dining:** 7 am-1 am, also, Fallsview Dining Room, see separate listing. **Pool(s):** heated indoor. **Leisure Activities:** sauna, whirlpool, exercise room. **Guest Services:** gift shop, valet laundry, area transportation (fee)-casino. **Business Services:** conference facilities, business center. **Cards:** AX, CB, DC, DS, JC, MC, VI. *(See color ad p 519)*

(See map and index starting on p. 464)

SHERATON ON THE FALLS   *Book at aaa.com*   Phone: (905)374-4445   **26**

8/1-10/15	1P: $169-$1199	2P: $169-$1199	XP: $10	F18
6/1-7/31	1P: $149-$999	2P: $149-$999	XP: $10	F18
5/1-5/31	1P: $129-$899	2P: $129-$899	XP: $10	F18
10/16-4/30	1P: $99-$799	2P: $99-$799	XP: $10	F18

Large-scale Hotel   **Location:** Entrance to Rainbow Bridge on Hwy 20. 5875 Falls Ave L2E 6W7. Fax: 905/371-0157. **Facility:** This large hotel offers a hard-to-beat location; adjacent to casino and directly across the street from the falls. Many units offer stunning views. 670 units. 659 one-bedroom standard units, some with whirlpools. 11 one-bedroom suites ($329-$1199) with whirlpools. 24 stories, interior corridors. **Parking:** on-site (fee) and valet. **Terms:** cancellation fee imposed. **Amenities:** video games, dual phone lines, voice mail, irons, hair dryers. *Some:* CD players. **Dining:** 6 am-midnight, cocktails, also, Penthouse Restaurant, see separate listing. **Pool(s):** heated outdoor, heated indoor. **Leisure Activities:** exercise room, spa. **Guest Services:** gift shop, valet laundry. **Business Services:** conference facilities, business center. **Cards:** AX, DC, JC, MC, VI. *(See color ad p 487)*

SOME UNITS

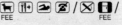
FEE

SKYLINE INN   *Book at aaa.com*   Phone: (905)374-4444   **71**

8/1-10/15	1P: $129-$329	2P: $129-$329	XP: $10	F18
6/1-7/31	1P: $99-$299	2P: $99-$299	XP: $10	F18
5/1-5/31	1P: $99-$249	2P: $99-$249	XP: $10	F18
10/16-4/30	1P: $79-$229	2P: $79-$229	XP: $10	F18

Small-scale Hotel   **Location:** At the Ontario end of the Rainbow Bridge. 4800 Bender Hill L2E 6W7. Fax: 905/374-0800. **Facility:** 206 one-bedroom standard units. 3 stories, interior/exterior corridors. **Parking:** on-site (fee). **Terms:** cancellation fee imposed. **Amenities:** video games, voice mail. **Dining:** 7 am-midnight; to 9 pm 12/1-3/31. **Leisure Activities:** shared recreational facilities with Brock Plaza Hotel. **Guest Services:** gift shop, valet laundry. **Business Services:** fax (fee). **Cards:** AX, DC, DS, MC, VI. *(See color ad p 520)*

SOME UNITS

STANLEY MOTOR INN   Phone: (905)358-9238   **42**

6/25-9/25	1P: $70-$120	2P: $90-$150	XP: $10	D12
5/1-6/24	1P: $60-$70	2P: $70-$85	XP: $10	D12
9/26-4/30	1P: $50-$60	2P: $60-$70	XP: $10	D12

Motel   **Location:** 2 blks from the falls, w of Skylon Tower. 6220 Stanley Ave L2G 3Y4. Fax: 905/358-2840. **Facility:** 49 one-bedroom standard units, some with whirlpools. 2 stories (no elevator), interior/exterior corridors. **Bath:** combo or shower only. **Parking:** on-site. **Terms:** office hours 7 am-midnight, pets ($10 extra charge). **Pool(s):** outdoor. **Guest Services:** coin laundry. **Cards:** AX, DC, DS, JC, MC, VI. **Special Amenities:** free local telephone calls and preferred room (subject to availability with advanced reservations).

SOME UNITS

FEE   FEE

SUNSET INN   *Book at aaa.com*   Phone: 905-354-7513   **29**

6/21-9/1	1P: $79-$199	2P: $79-$199	XP: $10	F12
5/1-6/20 & 9/2-9/30	1P: $49-$149	2P: $49-$149	XP: $10	F12
10/1-4/30	1P: $39-$99	2P: $39-$99	XP: $10	F12

Motel   **Location:** 1.2 km w on Hwy 20, just n, then s of Hwy 420. 5803 Stanley Ave L2G 3X8. Fax: 905/354-4766. **Facility:** 32 one-bedroom standard units, some with whirlpools. 2 stories (no elevator), exterior corridors. **Parking:** on-site, winter plug-ins. **Terms:** office hours 8 am-midnight, cancellation fee imposed. **Pool(s):** heated outdoor. **Cards:** AX, DC, DS, MC, VI. **Special Amenities:** early check-in/late check-out and free room upgrade (subject to availability with advanced reservations). *(See color ad p 488)*

SOME UNITS

FEE

(See map and index starting on p. 464)

SUPER 8 HOTEL
CAA SAVE   ▽▽▽▽▽
Small-scale Hotel

All Year   1P: $59-$289   2P: $59-$289   **Phone:** (905)356-0052   **79**   XP: $5   F12
Location: On Hwy 20, 1.5 km from the falls. 5706 Ferry St L2G 1S7. Fax: 905/356-7760. **Facility:** 190 units. 181 one-bedroom standard units, some with whirlpools. 9 one-bedroom suites ($99-$439). 7 stories, interior corridors. **Parking:** on-site, winter plug-ins. **Terms:** package plans. **Amenities:** video games (fee), voice mail, hair dryers. Some: irons. **Dining:** 6 am-3 pm, cocktails. **Pool(s):** heated outdoor, heated indoor. **Leisure Activities:** sauna, whirlpool, exercise room. Fee: game room. **Guest Services:** gift shop, coin laundry, area transportation (fee)-casino. **Business Services:** meeting rooms. **Cards:** AX, CB, DC, DS, JC, MC, VI. **Special Amenities:** free local telephone calls. (See color ad p 520)

SOME UNITS

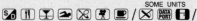   /
FEE

(See map and index starting on p. 464)

SURFSIDE INN

(CAA) (SAVE)

♦♦♦ ◊

Motel

6/19-8/31	2P: $69-$229	XP: $10	F12
5/1-6/18	2P: $59-$189	XP: $10	F12
9/1-4/30	2P: $55-$139	XP: $10	F12

Phone: (905)295-4354   **74**

Location: 3.5 km s of Horseshoe Falls on Niagara River Pkwy. Located in a quiet area. 3665 Macklem St L2G 6C8. Fax: 905/295-4374. **Facility:** 31 one-bedroom standard units, some with efficiencies and/or whirlpools. 1 story, exterior corridors. **Parking:** on-site. **Terms:** cancellation fee imposed. **Amenities:** hair dryers. **Pool(s):** heated outdoor. **Guest Services:** area transportation (fee)-falls & casino. **Cards:** AX, CB, DC, DS, JC, MC, VI.

SOME UNITS

⬛

(See map and index starting on p. 464)

THRIFTLODGE CLIFTON HILL   *Book at aaa.com*

CAA SAVE

Motel

				Phone: (905)357-4330	**70**
5/1-9/7	1P: $79-$369	2P: $79-$369	XP: $10	F16
10/13-12/31	1P: $59-$369	2P: $59-$369	XP: $10	F16
1/1-4/30	1P: $69-$359	2P: $69-$359	XP: $10	F16
9/8-10/12	1P: $69-$349	2P: $69-$349	XP: $10	F16

Location: Just s on jct Victoria Ave. 4945 Clifton Hill L2G 3N5. Fax: 905/357-2223. **Facility:** 38 one-bedroom standard units. 2 stories (no elevator), exterior corridors. **Parking:** on-site. **Terms:** 1-2 night minimum stay - with Saturday stayover, cancellation fee imposed, [MAP] meal plan available. **Leisure Activities:** pool privileges. **Guest Services:** coin laundry. **Cards:** AX, MC, VI. **Special Amenities:** free local telephone calls and free newspaper.

SOME UNITS

TRAVELODGE BONAVENTURE

CAA SAVE

Small-scale Hotel

				Phone: (905)374-7171	**62**
6/25-8/28	1P: $79-$189	2P: $89-$199	XP: $10	F17
5/1-6/24 & 8/29-10/9	1P: $59-$129	2P: $64-$149	XP: $10	F17
10/10-4/30	1P: $49-$99	2P: $54-$119	XP: $10	F17

Location: QEW, exit Hwy 20 W, 4.5 km w. 7737 Lundy's Ln L2H 1H3. Fax: 905/374-1151. **Facility:** 118 one-bedroom standard units, some with whirlpools. 3 stories, interior/exterior corridors. **Parking:** on-site, winter plug-ins. **Amenities:** video games, voice mail. **Dining:** 7:30-11:30 am; weekends only off season. **Pool(s):** heated outdoor, heated indoor. **Leisure Activities:** sauna, whirlpool. **Guest Services:** area transportation (fee)-casino & falls. **Business Services:** meeting rooms. **Cards:** AX, CB, DC, DS, MC, VI. **Special Amenities:** free local telephone calls and free newspaper. *(See color ad below & card insert)*

SOME UNITS

TRAVELODGE CLIFTON HILL   *Book at aaa.com*

CAA SAVE

Small-scale Hotel

				Phone: (905)357-4330	**36**
5/1-9/7	1P: $99-$389	2P: $99-$389	XP: $10	F16
10/13-12/31	1P: $69-$389	2P: $69-$389	XP: $10	F16
1/1-4/30	1P: $79-$379	2P: $79-$379	XP: $10	F16
9/8-10/12	1P: $89-$369	2P: $89-$369	XP: $10	F16

Location: Just s on jct Victoria Ave. 4943 Clifton Hill L2G 3N5. Fax: 905/357-2223. **Facility:** 68 units. 67 one- and 1 two-bedroom standard units, some with kitchens and/or whirlpools. 2 stories (no elevator), interior/exterior corridors. **Parking:** on-site. **Terms:** 1-2 night minimum stay - with Saturday stayover, cancellation fee imposed, [MAP] meal plan available. **Amenities:** voice mail. **Dining:** 11 am-1 am, cocktails. **Pool(s):** heated outdoor. **Business Services:** meeting rooms. **Cards:** AX, MC, VI. **Special Amenities:** free local telephone calls and free newspaper. *(See color ad p 522)*

SOME UNITS

(See map and index starting on p. 464)

TRAVELODGE NEAR THE FALLS   *Book at aaa.com*   Phone: (905)374-7771   **9**

	6/16-8/31	1P: $89-$269	2P: $89-$269
	9/1-12/31	1P: $79-$249	2P: $79-$249
	5/1-6/15	1P: $59-$249	2P: $59-$249
	1/1-4/30	1P: $59-$229	2P: $59-$229

Small-scale Hotel **Location:** Jct of Victoria Ave. 5234 Ferry St L2G 1R5. Fax: 905/374-1996. **Facility:** 87 one-bedroom standard units, some with whirlpools. 2-4 stories, interior/exterior corridors. *Bath:* combo or shower only. **Parking:** on-site (fee). **Terms:** package plans - seasonal. **Amenities:** hair dryers. **Dining:** 7 am-2 pm; 8 am-12:30 pm 10/1-6/30. **Pool(s):** heated indoor. **Leisure Activities:** sauna, whirlpool. **Cards:** AX, DC, MC, VI. **Special Amenities:** free local telephone calls and free newspaper. *(See color ad below)*

SOME UNITS

⛶ 🍴 🏊 🐾 / ⊗ /

VACATION INN   Phone: (905)356-1722   **34**

| | 6/30-9/5 | 1P: $99-$250 | 2P: $99-$250 | XP: $10 | F11 |
| | 5/1-6/29, 9/6-11/30 & 4/1-4/30 | 1P: $89-$225 | 2P: $89-$225 | XP: $10 | F11 |

Small-scale Hotel **Location:** Corner of Dixon, 2 blks from Minolta Tower. 6519 Stanley Ave L2G 7L2. Fax: 905/356-0392. **Facility:** 95 one-bedroom standard units, some with whirlpools. 3 stories (no elevator), interior corridors. **Parking:** on-site. **Terms:** open 5/1-11/30 & 4/1-4/30, cancellation fee imposed, package plans. **Dining:** 7:30 am-11:30 & 4:30-8:30 pm, cocktails. **Pool(s):** heated outdoor. **Business Services:** meeting rooms, fax (fee). **Cards:** AX, DS, MC, VI. **Special Amenities:** free local telephone calls and preferred room (subject to availability with advanced reservations).** *(See color ad inside front cover)*

SOME UNITS

⛶ 🍴 🏊 📠 / ⊗ /

VICTORIAN CHARM BED AND BREAKFAST   Phone: 905/357-4221   **80**

| | All Year [BP] | 1P: $100-$120 | 2P: $150-$190 | XP: $25 | F10 |

Bed & Breakfast **Location:** Between Main St and Drummond. 6028 Culp St L2G 2B7. Fax: 905/357-9115. **Facility:** Smoke free premises. 4 one-bedroom standard units, some with whirlpools. 2 stories (no elevator), interior corridors. **Parking:** on-site. **Terms:** office hours 7 am-11 pm, 2 night minimum stay - weekends, 3 day cancellation notice-fee imposed, package plans. **Amenities:** video library. **Cards:** DC, MC, VI.

ASK ⛶ ⊗ VCR 🕿 🖥

VILLAGER LODGE   *Book at aaa.com*   Phone: (905)354-3162   **66**

	6/25-9/6 [BP]	1P: $69-$219	2P: $69-$219	XP: $10	F12
	5/1-6/24 [BP]	1P: $49-$179	2P: $49-$179	XP: $5	F12
	9/7-4/30 [BP]	1P: $39-$179	2P: $39-$179	XP: $5	F12

Motel **Location:** QEW, exit Hwy 20 W (Lundy's Ln), 5 km w. 8054 Lundy's Ln L2H 1H1. Fax: 905/354-8422. **Facility:** 32 one-bedroom standard units, some with efficiencies and/or whirlpools. 2 stories, exterior corridors. **Parking:** on-site, winter plug-ins. **Terms:** cancellation fee imposed, weekly rates available, [AP] meal plan available, package plans. **Amenities:** voice mail. **Pool(s):** heated outdoor. **Leisure Activities:** barbecue grills, playground. **Guest Services:** area transportation (fee)-casino. **Cards:** AX, CB, DC, DS, MC, VI. **Special Amenities:** free local telephone calls and free newspaper. *(See color ad card insert)*

SOME UNITS

⛶ 🍴 🏊 📶 / ⊗ 🖨 🖥 /

(See map and index starting on p. 464)

——— *The following lodgings were either not evaluated or did not* ———
meet AAA/CAA rating requirements but are listed for your information only.

ASTORIA HOTEL   **Phone: 905/358-1676**
[fyi]   Property failed to provide current rates
              Too new to rate, opening scheduled for September 2004. **Location:** QEW to Niagara Falls, exit 420, 5 km to
Small-scale Hotel   Stanley Ave, right on Stanby to Ferry St, turn right. 5685 Ferry St L2G 1S5. Fax: 905/354-1656. **Amenities:** 43 units, coffeemakers, microwaves, refrigerators, pool.

DOUBLETREE RESORT LODGE & SPA FALLSVIEW   **Phone: 905/358-3817**

[fyi]	6/18-9/5	1P: $129-$329	2P: $129-$329	XP: $10	F18
	5/1-6/17 & 9/6-10/30	1P: $99-$249	2P: $99-$249	XP: $10	F18
Large-scale Hotel	10/31-4/30	1P: $79-$189	2P: $79-$189	XP: $10	F18

              Too new to rate, opening scheduled for February 2004. **Location:** Adjacent to Skylon Tower, just w via Murray St,
n on Fallsview Blvd. 6039 Fallsview Blvd L2G 3V6. Fax: 905/358-3680. **Amenities:** 224 units, restaurant, coffeemakers, refrigerators, pool. **Terms:** off-site registration. **Cards:** AX, DC, DS, JC, MC, VI. *(See color ad p 499)*

NIAGARA FALLSVIEW CASINO RESORT
[fyi]   Property failed to provide current rates
              Too new to rate, opening scheduled for April 2004. **Location:** 6380 Fallsview Blvd L2G 7X5. **Amenities:** 368
Large-scale Hotel   units, coffeemakers, pool.

——— **WHERE TO DINE** ———

THE BEEF BARON   **Lunch: $7-$10**   **Dinner: $11-$35**   **Phone: 905-356-6110**   (7)
(CAA)   **Location:** Top of Clifton Hill. 5019 Centre St L2G 3N5. **Hours:** 4 pm-midnight, Sat & Sun noon-11:30 pm;
▽▽▽   noon-11:30 pm 6/15-9/15. **Closed:** 12/24, 12/25. **Reservations:** suggested, in season. **Features:** Hungry?
Steak House   Really hungry? Order Baron's 26 oz. porterhouse. Prime rib and seafood are two more house favorites.
              Three dining rooms, trimmed in cherry wood, brass and Italian prints, mix well in the bustling summer atmosphere and quieter ambience of winter. Casual dress; cocktails. **Parking:** on-site (fee). **Cards:** AX, CB, DC, DS, JC, MC, VI.

BETTY'S RESTAURANT   **Lunch: $4-$9**   **Dinner: $7-$14**   **Phone: 905/295-4436**   (25)
▽▽▽   **Location:** In Chippawa District; Niagara Pkwy S to Main St, just w. 8921 Sodom Rd L2E 6S6. **Hours:** 8 am-9 pm.
              Closed: 12/25, 12/26. **Features:** Betty's pleasantly appointed, spacious dining room highlights the
Seafood   good-value home cooking served here. Seafood and fish are what they do best, but many other tasty dishes are offered. The fish and chips keeps regular patrons coming back for more. Casual dress; cocktails. **Parking:** on-site. **Cards:** AX, MC, VI.

CAPRI RESTAURANT   **Lunch: $6-$14**   **Dinner: $10-$35**   **Phone: 905/354-7519**   (20)
(CAA)   **Location:** Hwy 20, 1 km from the falls. 5438 Ferry St L2G 1S1. **Hours:** 11 am-11 pm, Sat & Sun from 4 pm.
▽▽▽   Closed: 12/24-12/26. **Reservations:** accepted. **Features:** The dining room offers an elegant, yet relaxed
Italian   atmosphere for special occasion or family dining. The menu emphasizes Southern Italian cuisine and features a wide selection of homemade pasta as well as a full array of steak, seafood and poultry selections. Casual dress; cocktails. **Parking:** on-site. **Cards:** AX, CB, DC, JC, MC, VI.

CASA D'ORO DINING LOUNGE   **Lunch: $10-$15**   **Dinner: $19-$60**   **Phone: 905-356-5646**   (24)
▽▽▽   **Location:** Just e of jct Ferry St; jct w of Clifton Hill. 5875 Victoria Ave L2G 3L7. **Hours:** noon-10:30 pm, Sat 4
              pm-11 pm. Closed: 12/25, 12/26. **Reservations:** suggested. **Features:** The restaurant, a popular choice
Italian   with locals and tourists alike, offers a unique ambience created by elaborate wall murals of Italian and European themes as well as the pleasant outdoor patio area in season. The menu highlights include all the traditional favorites for that special occasion dining including shrimp cocktail, French onion soup, prime rib, steak, lobster and of course the excellent selection of fine Italian fare and pastas. Dressy casual; cocktails. **Parking:** street. **Cards:** AX, MC, VI.

DELDUCA'S   **Dinner: $13-$22**   **Phone: 905/357-3638**   (14)
▽▽▽   **Location:** Hwy 420, just n on Stanley Ave, just w on Morrison St. 4781 Portage Rd L2E 6B1. **Hours:** 5 pm-10 pm.
              Closed major holidays; also Sun. **Reservations:** suggested. **Features:** Enjoy the spacious, modern
Italian   bistro-style atmosphere and featured fare of homemade pasta, ravioli, seafood, steak, veal and savory appetizers. Large portions are prepared fresh and presented attractively. Pleasant Mediterranean background music adds to the European ambience. Casual dress; cocktails. **Parking:** on-site. **Cards:** AX, MC, VI.

FALLSVIEW DINING ROOM   **Lunch: $8-$16**   **Dinner: $20-$45**   **Phone: 905/374-1077**   (13)
▽▽▽   **Location:** Near Minolta Tower; in Sheraton Fallsview Hotel & Conference Centre. 6755 Fallsview Blvd L2G 3W7.
              Hours: 7 am-10 pm. **Reservations:** suggested. **Features:** Diners are awed by the spectacular views
Continental   overlooking the falls and upper river—that and the wonderful selection of salad, appetizer, entree and dessert on the daily buffet. A full a la carte menu is also offered with creative International items. Casual dress; cocktails. **Parking:** on-site. **Cards:** AX, DC, DS, JC, MC, VI.

FINE KETTLE 'O' FISH INC   **Lunch: $6-$9**   **Dinner: $8-$30**   **Phone: 905/357-3474**   (4)
▽▽▽   **Location:** Jct of Huggins; in far back section of strip mall. 3641 Portage Rd L2J 2K8. **Hours:** 11:30 am-10 pm.
              Closed: 12/25, 12/26. **Features:** The casual, nautical setting at this popular eatery is enhanced by cozy
Seafood   corners and fish aquariums throughout. Good menu selections offer a wide range of fresh seafood—from fish and chips to lobster as well as steak, chicken and stir-fry options. Casual dress; cocktails. **Parking:** on-site. **Cards:** AX, MC, VI.

(See map and index starting on p. 464)

FRANK'S TOMATO PIE **Lunch:** $7-$10 **Dinner:** $10-$28 **Phone:** 905/371-9111 ⑫
Italian
Location: Jct of Dorchester Rd. 6889 Lundy's Ln L2G 1V7. **Hours:** 11 am-midnight, Fri & Sat-1 am. Closed: 12/25. **Reservations:** suggested. **Features:** Located in a converted bank building, Frank's Tomato Pie is a favorite of locals and tourists alike. The atmosphere is casual but the food is certainly gourmet. You can experience the sounds and smells of the chefs at work through the open concept kitchen. Inside you will find a funky decor of brick walls and mosaic tiles. In summer, the large outdoor patio is a main draw. Whatever the season, you will find fresh pasta, specialty pizza, veal, seafood and poultry. Cocktails. **Parking:** on-site. **Cards:** AX, DC, MC, VI. ✕

HAPPY WANDERER **Lunch:** $5-$12 **Dinner:** $10-$25 **Phone:** 905/354-9825 ㉖
German
Location: Near Minolta Tower. 6405 Stanley Ave L2G 3Y6. **Hours:** 8 am-11 pm. Closed: 12/24. **Reservations:** accepted. **Features:** If you're looking for a fun, casual restaurant with a European atmosphere, this place is for you. Come hungry as you will be served heaping portions of homemade German cuisine. Choose from traditional favorites such as bratwurst, schnitzel, smoked pork or rolled beef rolls with homemade dumplings. The atmosphere is set by servers in traditional costumes and distinctive Bavarian decor. Saving room for dessert will be a challenge but well worth it. Casual dress; cocktails. **Parking:** on-site. **Cards:** AX, MC, VI. ✕

HARD TIMES **Lunch:** $5-$8 **Dinner:** $10-$23 **Phone:** 905/374-3650 ⑥
(CAA)
American
Location: Top of Clifton Hill. 5759 Victoria Ave L2G 3L6. **Hours:** noon-midnight; 4 pm-10 pm 11/1-12/31. Closed: 12/24, 12/25. **Reservations:** suggested, weekends/summer. **Features:** Large dining room featuring a mock ship as decorative centerpiece. Menu features huge portions with many fully inclusive meals featured. Select from prime rib, steak, ribs, chicken and seafood or the daily pasta special. Casual dress; cocktails. **Parking:** street. **Cards:** AX, DC, DS, JC, MC, VI. ✕ ✕

THE KEG STEAKHOUSE AND BAR **Lunch:** $10-$20 **Dinner:** $20-$55 **Phone:** 905/353-4022 ㉝
Steak House
Location: Jct of Ferry St. 5950 Victoria Ave L2G 3L7. **Hours:** 11 am-1:30 am; to midnight 11/1-4/30. Closed: 12/25. **Features:** Well-known for its Mesquite-grilled steaks and fun, laid back atmosphere, this steakhouse is a long time favorite with the local crowd. In addition to the great beef, the traditional menu features seafood, grilled chicken, hickory ribs and pasta offering. All meals come with a hot loaf or sourdough bread. Try the tasty cheesecake or the specialty coffees for the perfect ending. Casual dress; cocktails. **Parking:** on-site. **Cards:** AX, MC, VI. ✕ ✕

LA HACIENDA RESTAURANT **Dinner:** $7-$20 **Phone:** 905/356-8051 ㉑
American
Location: QEW, exit Hwy 20 (Lundy's Ln), 1.6 km e. 5991 Lundy's Ln L2G 1T2. **Hours:** 4 pm-midnight. Closed major holidays; also Wed & 4/1-4/30 & 6/1-6/30. **Reservations:** accepted. **Features:** La Hacienda offers the best of two worlds: Tex-Mex and Italian fare. So don't be surprised to find veal parmigiana on one side of the menu and fajitas-for-two on the other. And what a wonderful way to blend both cuisines—in a creative Mexican cannoli. Casual dress; cocktails. **Parking:** on-site. **Cards:** AX, DC, MC, VI. ✕

LEGENDS ON THE NIAGARA **Lunch:** $8-$13 **Dinner:** $8-$22 **Phone:** 905/295-9595 ㉘
American
Location: 5 km s of the falls, on the Niagara Pkwy. 9233 Niagara River Pkwy L2E 6T2. **Hours:** Open 5/1-10/31 & 4/1-4/30; 6 am-10 pm. **Reservations:** suggested. **Features:** Diners enjoy a wonderful view of the golf course through the large panoramic windows or from the large patio. Casual fare—along the lines of wings, burgers and sandwiches—is available for breakfast, lunch and lighter meals, while larger entrees are served after 4 p.m. Casual dress; cocktails. **Parking:** on-site. **Cards:** AX, DC, JC, MC, VI. ✕

THE LOVE BOAT II **Lunch:** $8-$35 **Dinner:** $8-$35 **Phone:** 905/358-0660 ⑱
Seafood
Location: 1.1 km w of Minolta Tower. 6130 Dunn St L2G 2P1. **Hours:** 11:30 am-9 pm, Sat from 3 pm, Sun 11:30 am-8 pm. Closed: 12/25; also Mon-Thurs. **Reservations:** accepted. **Features:** A collection of seafaring articles such as anchors, portholes and nets adds to this eatery's pleasant nautical ambience. Very extensive menu selection offering traditional favorites such as surf and turf or fish and chips as well as land lovers specials. Hearty portions. Friendly service. Casual dress; cocktails. **Parking:** on-site. **Cards:** AX, DC, MC, VI. ✕ ✕

(See map and index starting on p. 464)

MAMA MIA'S   Lunch: $5-$9   Dinner: $7-$22   Phone: 905/354-7471   ⑧

Italian
Location: Top of Clifton Hill. 5719 Victoria Ave L2G 3L5. **Hours:** 11:30 am-11 pm; hours vary seasonally. Closed: 12/23-12/25. **Features:** What would an Italian eatery be without a good menu selection of lasagna, manicotti and cannelloni? You'll never find out because Mama Mia's serves all these house specialties and more in this quaint dining room. Steak and seafood also make an appearance. Casual dress; cocktails. **Parking:** on-site (fee). **Cards:** AX, DC, DS, JC, MC, VI.   ✕

MICK AND ANGELO'S EATERY AND BAR   Lunch: $5-$10   Dinner: $7-$20   Phone: 905/357-6543   ㉓
Italian
Location: QEW, exit Lundy's Ln, corner of Lundy's Ln and Montrose Rd. 7600 Lundy's Ln L2H 1H1. **Hours:** 11 am-12:30 am. Closed: 12/25. **Reservations:** accepted. **Features:** A diverse crowd patronizes this popular eatery and bar where an extensive menu, large portions and reasonable prices prevail. The specialty white pizza (sans tomato sauce) consists of oil, garlic and three cheeses. Entertainment is offered in season. Casual dress; cocktails. **Parking:** on-site. **Cards:** AX, MC, VI.   🍸 ✕

THE MILLERY DINING ROOM   Lunch: $8-$12   Dinner: $19-$48   Phone: 905/357-1234   ⑤
Continental
Location: Just w via Murray St, then just n on Buchanan Ave; in Old Stone Inn. 5425 Robinson St L2G 7L6. **Hours:** 7 am-3 & 4:30-10 pm. Closed: for dinner 12/24. **Reservations:** suggested. **Features:** Located in a wonderfully converted flour mill, the Millery Dining Room provides upscale dining in an elegant country setting. The dining room features high beam cathedral ceilings and accent stone walls from the original structure of the early 1900s. The innovative menu features fine Continental cuisine with an emphasis on creativity in presentation and freshness of ingredients. It is the perfect choice for special occasion or business dining. Casual dress; cocktails. **Parking:** on-site. **Cards:** AX, DC, DS, JC, MC, VI.   ✕

**MINOLTA TOWER CENTRE/PINNACLE
RESTAURANT**   Lunch: $10-$27   Dinner: $19-$48   Phone: 905/356-1501   ①
Continental
Location: In the Minolta Tower Centre; in Ramada Plaza Hotel Fallsview. 6732 Fallsview Blvd L2G 3W6. **Hours:** 7 am-midnight. **Reservations:** suggested. **Features:** Diners can enjoy a bird's-eye view of the falls from atop the Minolta Tower while relaxing in an upscale, yet relaxed, atmosphere. The menu lists traditional fare served in ample portions and with attractive plate presentations. Full a la carte and prix fixe specials are served. Casual dress; cocktails. **Parking:** on-site. **Cards:** AX, DC, DS, JC, MC, VI.   ✕

MONTICELLO GRILLE HOUSE & WINE BAR   Lunch: $9-$35   Dinner: $15-$35   Phone: 905/357-4888   ⑩
American
Location: Just e of jct Clifton Hill and Victoria Ave. 5645 Victoria Ave L2G 3L5. **Hours:** noon-10:30 pm. Closed: 12/24, 12/25. **Reservations:** accepted. **Features:** The brick and wood-beamed steak and seafood restaurant gives a nod to New Orleans with such menu items as spicy gumbo. Also offered are more traditional items. The wine list is extensive, and food portions are large. Specialty desserts such as bread pudding add to the theme. Cocktails. **Parking:** on-site. **Cards:** AX, CB, DC, JC, MC, VI. *(See ad below)*   🍸 ✕

OUTBACK STEAKHOUSE   Dinner: $12-$25   Phone: 905/357-6284   ⑪
Steak House
Location: Corner of Stanley Ave and Dunn St; in Radisson Hotel & Suites Fallsview. 6733 Fallsview Blvd L2G 3W7. **Hours:** 4 pm-11 pm, Sun-10 pm. Closed: 12/25. **Features:** The restaurant sustains a fun, casual mood in a loud and bustling Aussie atmosphere. Huge portions of freshly grilled and barbecued foods—including well-spiced steaks, chicken and ribs dinners—are a challenge to finish but are too good to leave. Fresh bread, tasty salads and the ever-popular bloomin' onion starter bring back locals and tourists alike. Service is friendly. Casual dress; cocktails. **Parking:** on-site. **Cards:** AX, DC, DS, JC, MC, VI.   ✕

PENTHOUSE RESTAURANT   Lunch: $10-$20   Dinner: $20-$40   Phone: 905/374-4444   ㉗
American
Location: Entrance to Rainbow Bridge on Hwy 20; in Sheraton on the Falls. 5875 Falls Ave L2E 6W7. **Hours:** 7-11 am, 11:30-2 & 5-9:30 pm. **Reservations:** suggested. **Features:** There's always something to tempt all tastes on the all-you-can-eat breakfast, lunch and dinner buffet. Besides a spectacular view of the falls, the Penthouse offers daily entertainment in season; weekends off season. An a la carte menu is also available. Casual dress; cocktails. **Parking:** on-site (fee). **Cards:** AX, CB, DC, DS, JC, MC, VI.   🍸 ✕

(See map and index starting on p. 464)

QUEENSTON HEIGHTS RESTAURANT   Lunch: $13-$18   Dinner: $20-$29   Phone: 905/262-4274   16

Continental
Location: 10.4 km n of Rainbow Bridge, on scenic route. 14276 Niagara Pkwy L2E 6T2. **Hours:** Open 5/1-12/31 & 4/1-4/30; noon-3 & 5-9 pm; from 11:30 am, Sat-9:30 pm 7/1-8/31. Closed: 12/25, 12/26; also for dinner Sun-Fri 10/1-12/31. **Reservations:** suggested. **Features:** Enjoy a panoramic view of the lower Niagara River and surrounding fruit lands from your table, while scanning a varied menu of such specialties as Atlantic salmon, Black Angus prime rib and seasonal fruit dessert. Patio lounge dining is offered in season. Cocktails. **Parking:** on-site. **Cards:** AX, DC, DS, MC, VI.

THE RAINBOW GRILLE FALLSVIEW STEAKHOUSE   Lunch: $8-$16   Dinner: $25-$50   Phone: 905/374-4444   22
American
Location: Entrance to Rainbow Bridge on Hwy 20, just n from the falls; in Brock Plaza Hotel. 5685 Falls Ave L2E 6W7. **Hours:** 7-10 am, 11-2 & 5-10 pm. **Reservations:** suggested. **Features:** Creative food presentation and good menu variety are hallmarks at the casually elegant restaurant. Poultry, beef, seafood, fresh vegetables and decadent desserts keep excellent company in the upscale dining room, which affords a fine view of the falls. Casual dress; cocktails. **Parking:** on-site (fee). **Cards:** AX, CB, DC, DS, JC, MC, VI.

ROOFTOP FALLSVIEW DINING ROOM   Dinner: $22-$55   Phone: 905/375-5200   30
Continental
Location: Just n of Minolta Tower, corner of Fallsview Blvd and Dixon Ave; in Renaissance Fallsview Hotel. 6455 Fallsview Blvd L2G 3V9. **Hours:** 5 pm-10 pm; to 11 pm 5/1-10/31. **Reservations:** suggested. **Features:** Diners here enjoy a fine menu of traditional Continental fare with a Niagara touch, including a wine list featuring selections from the local wineries. Staff offer warm, personable service to ensure a memorable dining experience. Views of the Niagara Falls add to the atmosphere, and are particularly enjoyed during the nightly illumination schedule. A perfect choice for a fine meal, personable service and a relaxed setting away from the hustle and bustle of the main tourist area. Dressy casual; cocktails. **Parking:** on-site. **Cards:** AX, DC, DS, JC, MC, VI.

THE SKYLON TOWER DINING ROOMS   Lunch: $24-$31   Dinner: $36-$84   Phone: 905/356-2651   3

American
Location: In Skylon Tower. 5200 Robinson St L2G 2A3. **Hours:** 11:30 am-3 & 4:30-10 pm. **Reservations:** suggested. **Features:** Affording spectacular, panoramic views of Niagara Falls from its large windows, the revolving restaurant features a traditional menu of Continental fare. The cost to ascend the tower is $2, and diners are welcomed to visit the viewing area after dinner to capture some great photographs. More casual buffet dining is available at the Summit, one floor up. Casual dress; cocktails. **Parking:** on-site (fee). **Cards:** AX, DC, DS, JC, MC, VI. *(See color ad p 175)*

SPARKS STEAK AND SEAFOOD   Lunch: $15-$39   Dinner: $15-$39   Phone: 905/354-8561   31
Steak & Seafood
Location: Just e of jct Ferry St. 5930 Victoria Ave L2G 3L7. **Hours:** noon-11 pm. Closed: 12/24, 12/25. **Reservations:** suggested. **Features:** A upbeat bistro atmosphere and a fine menu of traditional fare set the tone. Menu highlights include crab-stuffed mushrooms, shrimp cocktail or French onion soup to start, followed by prime rib, steak, surf and turf or seafood specialties. Full-course set menus appeal to those with hearty appetites. The dining room is sophisticated and modern, and servers are professional and personable. Dressy casual; cocktails. **Parking:** street. **Cards:** AX, DC, MC, VI.

TABLE ROCK RESTAURANT   Lunch: $10-$15   Dinner: $20-$35   Phone: 905/354-3631   17
Continental
Location: At Canadian Horseshoe Falls. 6400 Niagara Pkwy L2E 6T2. **Hours:** 11:30 am-9:30 pm, Sat-10 pm; 9 am-11 & 11:30-9:30 pm 7/1-8/31; hours may vary off season. Closed: 12/25. **Reservations:** accepted. **Features:** It's difficult to take your eyes off the outstanding view of Horseshoe Falls and the upper rapids long enough to make a choice from the menu featuring traditional fare and some Canadian dishes. Attentive and friendly service is the norm. Casual dress; cocktails. **Parking:** street. **Cards:** AX, DC, MC, VI.

(See map and index starting on p. 464)

TERRAPIN GRILLE   Lunch: $14-$45   Dinner: $26-$69   Phone: 905/357-7300 29
ⓐ
♦♦♦
Continental
Location: Next to Minolta Tower; in Niagara Falls Marriott Fallsview. 6740 Fallsview Blvd L2G 3W6. **Hours:** 6 am-11 pm. **Reservations:** suggested. **Features:** The Terrapin Grille features a good selection of fine Continental cuisine. The dining room is dimly lit at dinner, providing a romantic atmosphere with a stunning backdrop of Niagara Falls seen through its panoramic windows. It is spectacular during the lighting up of the falls each evening. Staff members have good menu knowledge and provide professional, attentive service. Casual dress; cocktails. **Parking:** on-site. **Cards:** AX, CB, DC, DS, MC, VI. 🍸 ✕

TWENTY ONE CLUB   Lunch: $10-$20   Dinner: $16-$61   Phone: 905/374-3598 19
♦♦♦ ♦♦♦
Steak House
Location: Just n of Rainbow Bridge; in Casino Niagara, 2nd Floor. 5705 Falls Ave L2G 7M9. **Hours:** 11:30 am-4 & 6-11 pm, Fri & Sat-midnight. **Reservations:** required, weekends. **Features:** Pianist entertainment, elaborate floral arrangements and cozy booths await diners at the sophisticated restaurant, on the second floor of Casino Niagara. The a la carte menu specializes in huge, tender cuts of beef and prime rib with accompaniments such as steaming baked potatoes, sizzling mushrooms and steamed asparagus. A wide selection of pasta dishes is also offered. Casual dress; cocktails. **Parking:** valet. **Cards:** AX, CB, DS, MC, VI. ✕

VICTORIA PARK RESTAURANT   Lunch: $10-$17   Dinner: $20-$40   Phone: 905/356-2217 2
ⓐ
♦♦
Continental
Location: In Queen Victoria Park; on scenic route. 6345 Niagara Pkwy L2E 6T2. **Hours:** Open 5/1-10/15; 11:30 am-10 pm; to 9 pm 5/1-6/18 & 9/5-10/15. **Features:** What better way to enjoy a breathtaking view of the falls than from an open air balcony while dining on an array of items, including some Canadian fare, prepared with fresh ingredients. A year round cafeteria with more formal dining in season. Casual dress; cocktails. **Parking:** street. **Cards:** AX, MC, VI. 🍴 ✕

THE WATERMARK   Lunch: $10-$25   Dinner: $25-$65   Phone: 905/354-7887 9
♦♦♦
Continental
Location: Hwy 20, just s; in Hilton Niagara Falls. 6361 Fallsview Blvd L2G 3V9. **Hours:** 7 am-10:30 pm. **Reservations:** required, for dinner. **Features:** The contemporary dining room carries out a distinct water theme, thanks in part to its rooftop location at the Hilton Niagara. Large windows offer spectacular, panoramic views of the falls. The menu features a nice mix of traditional Continental fare prepared with market-fresh vegetables. At lunch, lighter options include burgers, sandwiches and pasta. Dressy casual; cocktails. **Parking:** on-site (fee) and valet. **Cards:** AX, CB, DC, DS, JC, MC, VI. *(See color ad p 502)* 🍸 ✕

WHIRLPOOL RESTAURANT   Lunch: $6-$20   Dinner: $6-$20   Phone: 905/356-7221 15
ⓐ
♦♦
American
Location: 5.3 km n of Rainbow Bridge, on scenic route; in Public Whirlpool Golf Complex. 3351 Whirlpool Golf Complex L2E 6T2. **Hours:** Open 5/1-11/1 & 4/1-4/30; 6 am-9 pm. **Reservations:** suggested. **Features:** Canadian dishes, snacks and daily seasonal featured fare are served in this casual, golf-course-view restaurant across from a whirlpool gorge. Try the very good chicken teriyaki atop angel hair pasta and an eye appealing fruit plate for dessert. Casual dress; cocktails. **Parking:** on-site. **Cards:** AX, MC, VI. 🍸 ✕

This ends listings for the Niagara Falls Vicinity.
The following page resumes the alphabetical listings of
cities in New York.

NORTH CREEK —*See also ADIRONDACK MOUNTAINS.*

——— WHERE TO STAY ———

COPPERFIELD INN
(AAA) SAVE

▼▼▼ ▼▼▼

Country Inn

Phone: (518)251-2500

5/1-10/30 & 12/17-4/30 [BP]   1P: $145-$380   2P: $145-$380   XP: $25   F12
Location: Just e of SR 28; center. 307 Main St 12853 (PO Box 28). Fax: 518/251-4143. **Facility:** Traditionally furnished rooms are offered at this contemporary country inn convenient to dining and shopping. 31 units. 29 one-bedroom standard units, some with whirlpools. 2 one-bedroom suites with whirlpools. 2 stories, interior corridors. **Parking:** on-site. **Terms:** open 5/1-10/30 & 12/17-4/30, 2-3 night minimum stay - seasonal & weekends, 14 day cancellation notice-fee imposed, [CP] & [MAP] meal plans available. **Amenities:** DVD players, video games (fee), voice mail, safes, honor bars, irons, hair dryers. *Some:* CD players, fax. **Dining:** Gardens, see separate listing. **Pool(s):** heated outdoor. **Leisure Activities:** saunas, whirlpool, lighted tennis court, exercise room. *Fee:* massage. **Guest Services:** gift shop, valet laundry, area transportation-ski area, beauty salon, tanning facility. **Business Services:** meeting rooms, fax (fee). **Cards:** AX, CB, DC, DS, MC, VI.

🍽 ⛤ ✕ ✕ 🎥 DATA/PORT

GOOSE POND INN

▼▼▼

Historic Bed & Breakfast

Phone: (518)251-3434

All Year [BP]   1P: $75-$95   2P: $95-$150   XP: $20
Location: SR 28, 1 mi e, then 0.9 mi n. 196 Main St 12853 (PO Box 273). Fax: 518/251-3434. **Facility:** Antiques and individually decorated rooms distinguish this residential-area inn dating from 1894; rooms vary in size. Designated smoking area. 4 one-bedroom standard units. 2 stories (no elevator), interior corridors. *Bath:* combo or shower only. **Parking:** on-site. **Terms:** 2-3 night minimum stay - seasonal weekends, age restrictions may apply, 14 day cancellation notice-fee imposed, no pets allowed (owner's pets on premises). **Amenities:** hair dryers. **Guest Services:** TV in common area, area transportation.

✕ 🅦 ☎

——— WHERE TO DINE ———

CASEY'S NORTH
(AAA)

▼▼ ▼▼

American

Lunch: $6-$16   **Dinner:** $6-$16   **Phone: 518/251-5836**
Location: On SR 28, 5 mi s. 3195 SR 28 12853. **Hours:** 11:30 am-9:30 pm, Sat & Sun-10 pm. **Features:** Adirondack brew pub offering a variety of sandwiches, burgers, appetizers and full entrees. Casual dress; cocktails. **Parking:** on-site. **Cards:** AX, DC, DS, MC, VI.

♿M 🍸 🎮 ✕

GARDENS Country Inn

▼▼▼

American

Dinner: $11-$25   **Phone: 518/251-2500**
Location: Just e of SR 28; center; in Copperfield Inn. 307 Main St 12853. **Hours:** Open 6/25-10/11 & 12/24-4/30; 7 am-11 & 5:30-9 pm, Fri & Sat 5:30 pm-11 pm. Closed: Mon-Thurs 3/28-4/30. **Reservations:** suggested. **Features:** In the heart of the Adirondack Mountains one can still enjoy fine dining in an elegant atmosphere at the Garden. Serving gourmet dishes of chicken, lamb, steak and pasta, this restaurant will delight all. Casual dress; cocktails. **Parking:** on-site. **Cards:** AX, CB, DC, DS, MC, VI.

♿M 🍸 ✕

NORTH HORNELL pop. 851—*See also FINGER LAKES.*

——— WHERE TO STAY ———

ECONO LODGE
(AAA) SAVE

▼▼▼ ▼▼▼

Motel

Book at aaa.com

Phone: (607)324-0800

All Year   1P: $39-$59   2P: $44-$69   XP: $3   F18
Location: Jct I-86 and SR 36, exit 34, just s to SR 21, just e to Seneca Rd, then just s. 7462 Seneca Rd 14843 (PO Box 486, HORNELL). Fax: 607/324-0905. **Facility:** 67 one-bedroom standard units. 2 stories (no elevator), interior/exterior corridors. **Parking:** on-site, winter plug-ins. **Terms:** [CP] meal plan available, pets ($7 fee). **Amenities:** *Some:* hair dryers. **Dining:** 5 pm-11 pm, Sun from 10 am; closed Mon, cocktails. **Leisure Activities:** *Fee:* miniature golf, driving range. **Guest Services:** airport transportation-Hornell Airport. **Business Services:** meeting rooms. **Cards:** AX, DC, DS, MC, VI. **Special Amenities:** free continental breakfast and free newspaper.

SOME UNITS

S🅓 ✈ 🐾 🍽 🍸 DATA/PORT / 🏋 🛁 📺 /
　　　　FEE

NORTH SYRACUSE pop. 6,862 (See map and index starting on p. 577)—*See also SYRACUSE.*

——— WHERE TO STAY ———

BEST WESTERN SYRACUSE AIRPORT INN
(AAA) SAVE

▼▼ ▼▼

Small-scale Hotel

Book at aaa.com   **Phone: (315)455-7362**   **36**

All Year   1P: $74-$105   2P: $79-$115   XP: $10   F12
Location: I-81, exit 27 (Hancock Airport). Hancock Airport 13212. Fax: 315/455-6840. **Facility:** 95 units. 91 one-bedroom standard units. 4 one-bedroom suites. 2 stories (no elevator), interior corridors. *Bath:* combo or shower only. **Parking:** on-site. **Terms:** 7 day cancellation notice. **Amenities:** irons, hair dryers. **Dining:** 7 am-2 & 5-10 pm, cocktails. **Pool(s):** outdoor. **Guest Services:** valet laundry. **Business Services:** meeting rooms. **Cards:** AX, CB, DC, DS, MC, VI. **Special Amenities:** free newspaper and free room upgrade (subject to availability with advanced reservations).

SOME UNITS

S🅓 ✈ 🍽 🍸 ⛤ ✕ DATA/PORT 📺 / 📼 /
　　　　　　　　　　　　　FEE

DOUBLETREE CLUB HOTEL/SYRACUSE AIRPORT

▼▼▼ ▼▼▼

Small-scale Hotel

Book at aaa.com   **Phone: (315)457-4000**   **34**

All Year   1P: $75-$139
Location: I-81, exit 25 (7th North St), 0.8 mi w; I-90, exit 36. 6701 Buckley Rd 13212. Fax: 315/453-7877. **Facility:** 187 one-bedroom standard units. 2 stories (no elevator), interior corridors. **Parking:** on-site. **Terms:** small pets only. **Amenities:** video library (fee), video games, voice mail, irons. **Pool(s):** heated indoor. **Leisure Activities:** sauna, whirlpool, exercise room. **Guest Services:** valet and coin laundry. **Business Services:** conference facilities, business center. **Cards:** AX, DS, MC, VI.

SOME UNITS

ASK S🅓 ✈ 🐾 🍽 🍸 🎮 ⛤ ✕ 🎥 DATA/PORT 📺 / ✕ 🛁 /
　　　　　　　　　　　　　　　　　　　　　FEE

(See map and index starting on p. 577)

QUALITY INN NORTH *Book at aaa.com*   Phone: (315)451-1212   37

  (AAA) (SAVE)   5/1-10/31   1P: $79-$139   2P: $79-$139   XP: $10   F17
          11/1-4/30   1P: $69-$139   2P: $69-$139   XP: $10   F17
 ▽▽▽ ▽   **Location:** I-81, exit 25 (7th North St), 0.3 mi w, then just n. 1308 Buckley Rd 13212. Fax: 315/453-8050. **Facility:** 142
    Motel   units.* 141 one-bedroom standard units. 1 one-bedroom suite ($175-$275) with whirlpool. 1-3 stories (no elevator), interior/exterior corridors. **Parking:** on-site. **Terms:** cancellation fee imposed, [CP] meal plan available, pets ($10 extra charge). **Amenities:** irons, hair dryers. *Some:* CD players. **Dining:** 4:30 pm-9:30 pm,
Fri & Sat-10 pm, cocktails. **Pool(s):** outdoor, wading. **Leisure Activities:** whirlpool, exercise room. **Guest Services:** coin laundry, airport transportation-Syracuse Hancock International Airport, area transportation-train & bus station. **Business Services:** meeting rooms. **Cards:** AX, DC, DS, MC, VI. **Special Amenities: free continental breakfast and free local telephone calls.**

SOME UNITS

[S🅓] [✈] [🛏] [🍴] [Ⓨ] [🖈] [🎥] [DATA PORT] [💻] / [✕] [VCR] [🔒] [🖨] /
            FEE

RAMADA INN *Book at aaa.com*   Phone: (315)457-8670   35

  (AAA) (SAVE)   All Year [BP]   1P: $99   2P: $99
 ▽▽▽▽   **Location:** I-81, exit 25 (7th North St), just nw; I-90, exit 36. 1305 Buckley Rd 13212. Fax: 315/457-8633. **Facility:** 150
             units. 149 one-bedroom standard units. 1 one-bedroom suite with whirlpool. 2 stories (no elevator), interior
             corridors. *Bath:* combo or shower only. **Parking:** on-site, winter plug-ins. **Amenities:** voice mail, irons, hair
Small-scale Hotel   dryers. **Dining:** 6 am-2 & 5-9 pm, Fri-10 pm, Sat 6 am-1 & 5-10 pm, cocktails. **Pool(s):** heated outdoor.
             Leisure Activities: exercise room. **Guest Services:** valet laundry. **Business Services:** conference facilities,
business center. **Cards:** AX, DC, DS, MC, VI. **Special Amenities: free full breakfast and free local telephone calls.**
(See color ad p 581)

SOME UNITS

[S🅓] [✈] [🍴] [Ⓨ] [🖥] [🏊] [🖈] [🎥] [DATA PORT] [💻] / [✕] [VCR] [🔒] [🖨] /

> *The following lodging was either not evaluated or did not meet AAA rating requirements but is listed for your information only.*

CANDLEWOOD SUITES SYRACUSE AIRPORT   Phone: 315/454-8999

  [fyi]   5/1-12/31   1P: $89-$129   2P: $99-$139
         1/1-4/30   1P: $79-$109   2P: $89-$119
        Too new to rate, opening scheduled for December 2003. **Location:** I-90, exit 36; I-81, exit Mattydale. 5414 South
Bay Rd 13212. Fax: 315/455-1173. **Amenities:** 124 units, pets, coffeemakers, microwaves, refrigerators. **Cards:** AX, DS, MC, VI.

WHERE TO DINE

THE CLAM BAR   **Lunch:** $5-$6   **Dinner:** $10-$12   Phone: 315/458-1662   30

 ▽▽▽   **Location:** I-81, exit Mattydale, 2 mi n. 3914 SR 11 13212. **Hours:** 11:30 am-10 pm, Fri-11 pm, Sat noon-11 pm,
          Sun noon-9 pm. Closed: 1/1, 12/24, 12/25. **Features:** The rustic decor welcomes any hunter or angler to
Steak & Seafood   feel at home. The freshest seafood is prepared in delectable ways. A lively atmosphere makes this place
          like the "Cheers" of the seafood scene. Casual dress; cocktails. **Parking:** on-site. **Cards:** AX, DS, MC, VI.

[Ⓨ]

COLORADO MINE COMPANY STEAKHOUSE   **Lunch:** $3-$6   **Dinner:** $10-$19   Phone: 315/451-6956   29

 ▽▽▽ ▽▽▽   **Location:** I-81, exit 25 (7th North St); I-90, exit 36, 0.6 mi w. 1333 Buckley Rd 13212. **Hours:** 11 am-11 pm, Sun
          from noon. Closed: 11/25, 12/25. **Features:** Servers in Western apparel traverse the rustic dining room,
Steak House   which is decorated with oak and brass accents and mounted animals. Steaks are clearly the focus of the
          menu although pasta, chicken and seafood also are offered. Some dishes are flavored with savory
barbecue sauce. Casual dress; cocktails. **Parking:** on-site. **Cards:** AX, DS, MC, VI.

[Ⓨ] [✕]

HUNAN EMPIRE   **Lunch:** $4-$7   **Dinner:** $6-$14   Phone: 315/455-9900   31

 ▽▽ ▽▽   **Location:** I-81, exit 26 (US 11). Northern Lights Mall 13212. **Hours:** 11:30 am-9:30 pm, Fri-10:30 pm, Sat
          noon-10:30 pm, Sun noon-9 pm. Closed: 7/4, 11/25, 12/25. **Reservations:** accepted. **Features:** As people
Chinese   might surmise from the name, the restaurant focuses on Hunan cuisine, such as wonton soup and beef
          and snow pea pods. Oriental landscape paintings add an attractive touch to the otherwise simple decor.
Servers are efficient and direct. Casual dress; cocktails. **Parking:** on-site. **Cards:** AX, CB, DC, DS, MC, VI.

[✕]

NORWICH pop. 7,355

WHERE TO STAY

SUPER 8 MOTEL OF NORWICH   *Book at aaa.com*   Phone: (607)336-8880

 ▽▽▽ ▽▽▽   5/1-9/1 [CP]   1P: $65-$75   2P: $105-$115   XP: $10   F
          9/2-12/1 [CP]   1P: $65-$85   2P: $75-$95   XP: $10   F
          12/2-4/30 [CP]   1P: $55-$65   2P: $65-$75   XP: $10   F
Small-scale Hotel   **Location:** On SR 12, 0.9 mi n. 6067 SR 12 13815. Fax: 607/336-2076. **Facility:** 42 one-bedroom standard units.
3 stories (no elevator), interior corridors. **Parking:** on-site. **Terms:** 7 day cancellation notice. **Cards:** AX, DC, DS, MC, VI.

SOME UNITS

[ASK] [S🅓] [🛏] [🍴] [🖈] [DATA PORT] / [✕] /

OGDENSBURG pop. 12,364

WHERE TO STAY

QUALITY INN GRAN-VIEW   *Book at aaa.com*   Phone: (315)393-4550

AAA SAVE

7/1-8/31 [ECP]	1P: $93-$142	2P: $104-$169	XP: $10		F18
5/1-6/30 & 9/1-10/31 [ECP]	1P: $81-$135	2P: $93-$158	XP: $10		F18
11/1-4/30 [ECP]	1P: $72-$116	2P: $80-$126	XP: $10		F18

Motel

Location: On SR 37 W, 3 mi sw. 6765 State Hwy 37 13669. Fax: 315/393-3520. **Facility:** 47 units. 44 one-bedroom standard units, some with whirlpools. 2 two-bedroom suites ($104-$220). 1 cottage. 1-2 stories (no elevator), interior/exterior corridors. **Parking:** on-site, winter plug-ins. **Terms:** package plans - weekends, pets ($10 extra charge, in designated units). **Amenities:** voice mail, irons, hair dryers. *Some:* dual phone lines. **Dining:** Gran-View, see separate listing. **Pool(s):** outdoor. **Leisure Activities:** boat dock, fishing, lawn games, exercise room, shuffleboard, volleyball. **Guest Services:** coin laundry. **Business Services:** meeting rooms. **Cards:** AX, CB, DC, DS, JC, MC, VI. **Special Amenities: free expanded continental breakfast and free local telephone calls.**

SOME UNITS

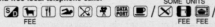

THE STONEFENCE RESORT & MOTEL   Phone: 315/393-1545

AAA SAVE

6/15-9/5	1P: $77-$119	2P: $82-$132	XP: $10		F11
5/1-6/14 & 9/6-4/30	1P: $66-$79	2P: $77-$99	XP: $8		F11

Motel

Location: Jct SR 68 W, 0.5 mi w. 7191 SR 37 13669. Fax: 315/393-1749. **Facility:** 50 units. 44 one-bedroom standard units, some with whirlpools. 6 one-bedroom suites ($119-$189) with kitchens. 1-2 stories (no elevator), interior/exterior corridors. **Bath:** combo or shower only. **Parking:** on-site, winter plug-ins. **Terms:** [AP] & [BP] meal plans available, small pets only ($25 fee, in designated units). **Amenities:** voice mail, irons, hair dryers. **Dining:** Stone Fence Dining Room, see separate listing. **Pool(s):** heated outdoor. **Leisure Activities:** paddleboats, marina, fishing, putting green, tennis court, playground, exercise room, basketball, horseshoes, shuffleboard, volleyball. **Guest Services:** coin laundry. **Business Services:** meeting rooms. **Cards:** AX, DC, DS, MC, VI. **Special Amenities: free local telephone calls and free newspaper.** *(See color ad below)*

SOME UNITS

WHERE TO DINE

GRAN-VIEW   **Lunch:** $5-$12   **Dinner:** $8-$19   Phone: 315/393-4550

Continental

Location: On SR 37 W, 3 mi sw; in Quality Inn Gran-View. 6765 State Hwy 37 13669. **Hours:** 6 am-10 pm, Sun 8 am-9 pm; Fri & Sat 6 am-11 pm in summer. Closed: 12/24, 12/25. **Reservations:** accepted. **Features:** Overlooking the St. Lawrence River, the restaurant affords stunning views of the Canadian sunset. Italian influences touch selections of Continental cuisine, such as chicken cordon bleu with burgundy currant sauce. The chocolate cheesecake is decadent. Casual dress; cocktails. **Parking:** on-site. **Cards:** AX, CB, DC, DS, JC, MC, VI.

STONE FENCE DINING ROOM   **Lunch:** $4-$10   **Dinner:** $8-$17   Phone: 315/393-1545

American

Location: Jct SR 68 W, 0.5 mi w; in The Stonefence Resort & Motel. 7191 State Hwy 37 13669. **Hours:** 7 am-2:30 & 4:30-9 pm; winter hours may vary. Closed: 1/1, 12/24, 12/25. **Reservations:** accepted. **Features:** The inviting, seasonal patio—as well as both levels of the dining room—overlooks beautifully landscaped grounds and the waterway. London broil is representative of traditionally prepared menu selections. Service is attentive throughout the meal. Casual dress. **Parking:** on-site. **Cards:** AX, DC, DS, MC, VI. *(See color ad below)*

OLD FORGE —*See also ADIRONDACK MOUNTAINS.*

───── **WHERE TO STAY** ─────

19TH GREEN MOTEL
Phone: 315/369-3575

6/26-10/15	2P: $55-$105	XP: $5	F4
12/25-4/30	2P: $50-$105	XP: $10	F4
5/1-6/25	2P: $50-$75	XP: $5	F4
10/16-12/24	2P: $45-$75	XP: $5	F4

Motel

Location: 0.3 mi s. 2761 SR 28 13420 (PO Box 37). **Fax:** 315/369-4437. **Facility:** 13 one-bedroom standard units. 1 story, exterior corridors. *Bath:* combo or shower only. **Parking:** on-site, winter plug-ins. **Terms:** 14 day cancellation notice-fee imposed, weekly rates available, package plans. **Amenities:** hair dryers. **Pool(s):** heated outdoor. **Leisure Activities:** cross country skiing. **Cards:** AX, CB, DC, DS, JC, MC, VI. **Special Amenities:** free local telephone calls and early check-in/late check-out.

SOME UNITS

BEST WESTERN SUNSET INN   *Book at aaa.com*
Phone: (315)369-6836

6/27-10/25 [ECP]	1P: $89-$239	2P: $89-$239	XP: $10	F12
12/26-4/30 [ECP]	1P: $49-$239	2P: $49-$239	XP: $10	F12
5/1-6/26 [ECP]	1P: $49-$139	2P: $49-$139		
10/26-12/25 [ECP]	1P: $49-$119	2P: $49-$119		

Motel

Location: 0.3 mi s. 2752 SR 28 13420 (PO Box 261). **Fax:** 315/369-2607. **Facility:** 52 one-bedroom standard units, some with whirlpools. 1-2 stories (no elevator), interior/exterior corridors. **Parking:** on-site, winter plug-ins. **Terms:** 7 day cancellation notice-fee imposed, pets (in smoking units, dogs only). **Amenities:** irons, hair dryers. **Pool(s):** heated indoor. **Leisure Activities:** sauna, whirlpool, tennis court. **Guest Services:** coin laundry. **Cards:** AX, DS, MC, VI.

SOME UNITS

BLUE SPRUCE MOTEL
Phone: 315/369-3817

7/1-10/31	2P: $65-$120	XP: $5
11/1-4/30	2P: $50-$90	XP: $5
5/1-6/30	2P: $45-$75	XP: $5

Motel

Location: Just s of town center. 2898 SR 28 13420 (PO Box 604). **Facility:** 13 one-bedroom standard units. 1 story, exterior corridors. **Parking:** on-site, winter plug-ins. **Terms:** 7 day cancellation notice-fee imposed. **Pool(s):** heated outdoor. **Cards:** AX, DS, MC, VI.

SOME UNITS

COUNTRY CLUB MOTEL
Phone: 315/369-6340

6/25-9/6	1P: $80-$90	2P: $80-$90	XP: $5	F12
5/1-6/24 & 9/7-4/30	1P: $50-$90	2P: $50-$90	XP: $5	F12

Motel

Location: 0.3 mi s. 2747 SR 28 13420 (PO Box 419). **Fax:** 315/369-6550. **Facility:** 27 one-bedroom standard units. 1 story, exterior corridors. **Parking:** on-site. **Terms:** 2 night minimum stay - seasonal weekends, 14 day cancellation notice. **Pool(s):** heated outdoor. **Cards:** AX, DS, MC, VI.

SOME UNITS

WATER'S EDGE INN & CONFERENCE CENTER
Phone: 315/369-2484

6/19-9/1	1P: $65-$225	2P: $65-$225	XP: $10	F12
10/19-4/30	1P: $35-$225	2P: $35-$225	XP: $10	F12
9/2-10/18	1P: $45-$195	2P: $45-$195	XP: $10	F12
5/1-6/18	1P: $35-$110	2P: $35-$110	XP: $10	F12

Small-scale Hotel

Location: On SR 28; center. Located opposite the Enchanted Forest. 3188 SR 28 13420 (PO Box 1141). **Fax:** 315/369-6782. **Facility:** 74 units. 66 one-bedroom standard units. 8 one-bedroom suites ($79-$225). 2-3 stories (no elevator), interior corridors. *Bath:* combo or shower only. **Parking:** on-site. **Terms:** office hours 8 am-11 pm, 2 night minimum stay - weekends, 7 day cancellation notice-fee imposed, [CP] meal plan available. **Amenities:** irons, hair dryers. **Pool(s):** heated indoor. **Leisure Activities:** sauna, boat dock, fishing. **Business Services:** meeting rooms. **Cards:** AX, MC, VI.

SOME UNITS

───── **WHERE TO DINE** ─────

THE OLD MILL RESTAURANT
Dinner: $12-$20   **Phone:** 315/369-3662

American

Location: 0.3 mi sw. 2888 SR 28 13420. **Hours:** Open 5/10-11/1 & 12/26-3/15; 4:30 pm-9:30 pm, Fri & Sat-10 pm, Sun 1 pm-9 pm; hours may vary in winter. **Closed:** 3/27, 11/25, 12/25. **Features:** Resembling a rustic, Adirondack log cabin, the dining room is a casual spot for cozy family dining. Patrons can expect large portions of everything from salad to steak. The restaurant often is packed, and it's not unusual to have to wait during peak times. Casual dress; cocktails. **Parking:** on-site. **Cards:** MC, VI.

WILDWOOD CAFE
Lunch: $4-$8   **Dinner:** $4-$8   **Phone:** 315/369-2300

American

Location: Center. 3063 Main St 13420. **Hours:** 8 am-7 pm; to 3:30 pm off season. **Closed:** 12/25. **Features:** The Internet coffee shop serves delicious homemade soups, salads, sandwiches and baked goods, as well as delectable desserts. The patio opens seasonally. Casual dress. **Parking:** street. **Cards:** AX, DS, MC, VI.

OLEAN pop. 15,347

———— WHERE TO STAY ————

HAMPTON INN   *Book at aaa.com*   Phone: (716)375-1000

All Year   1P: $79-$168   2P: $89-$168
Location: I-86, exit 26, on Main St at Union St (SR 16). 101 Main St 14760. Fax: 716/375-1279. **Facility:** 76 one-
Small-scale Hotel   bedroom standard units, some with whirlpools. 3 stories, interior corridors. *Bath:* combo or shower only.
Parking: on-site. **Terms:** [ECP] meal plan available. **Amenities:** dual phone lines, voice mail, irons, hair
dryers. **Pool(s):** small heated indoor. **Leisure Activities:** exercise room. **Guest Services:** valet and coin laundry. **Business
Services:** meeting rooms, fax (fee). **Cards:** AX, CB, DC, DS, MC.

SOME UNITS
(ASK) (S/D) (TI+) (&M) (⟳) (⇆) (✷) (DATA PORT) (▯) / (✕) (VCR) (▮) (▭) /
FEE   FEE

OLD LIBRARY INN BED & BREAKFAST   Phone: 716/373-9804

All Year   1P: $65-$75   XP: $20   F10
Location: I-86, exit 26, 1.4 mi s on SR 16 (Union St), just s of jct SR 417; downtown. 120 S Union St 14760.
Historic Bed   Fax: 716/373-2462. **Facility:** Hand-carved oak woodwork distinguishes this restored 1895 Victorian home;
& Breakfast   furnishings include numerous antiques. Smoke free premises. 8 one-bedroom standard units. 2 stories (no
elevator), interior corridors. *Bath:* combo or shower only. **Parking:** on-site. **Dining:** Old Library Restaurant,
see separate listing. **Guest Services:** complimentary evening beverages: Mon-Thurs, valet laundry. **Business Services:**
meeting rooms, fax (fee). **Cards:** AX, MC, VI.

SOME UNITS
(ASK) (S/D) (TI) (⊞+⊞) (✕) (✷) (DATA PORT) / (VCR) /
FEE

———— WHERE TO DINE ————

BEEF N' BARREL RESTAURANT   Lunch: $5-$8   Dinner: $6-$17   Phone: 716/372-2985

Location: Jct SR 16 (Union St) and 417; downtown. 146 N Union St 14760. **Hours:** 11 am-10 pm. Closed major
holidays; also Sun. **Features:** The restaurant is popular and with good reason. Selections of choice-grade
beef, especially hand-carved roast beef, are succulent and well-prepared. All dressings—as well as such
American   aromatic baked goods as bread, rolls, pastries, cakes and the like—are made on the premises. Casual
dress; cocktails. **Parking:** on-site. **Cards:** AX, DC, DS, MC, VI.   (Y) (✕)

CENTURY MANOR GRILLHOUSE   Dinner: $13-$24   Phone: 716/372-1864

Location: I-86, exit 26, just s of jct SR 16 (Union St) and 417. 401 E State St 14760. **Hours:** 4:30 pm-10:30 pm,
Sun-9:30 pm. Closed: 12/24, 12/25. **Reservations:** suggested. **Features:** The fine dining establishment
Steak & Seafood   nurtures a relaxed atmosphere. On the menu are certified Angus beef, seafood, meat and pasta dishes,
some prepared on the open pit grill. Mix-and-match items help diners who can't decide among the
delicious entrees. Casual dress; cocktails. **Parking:** on-site. **Cards:** AX, DS, MC, VI.   (Y) (✕)

OLD LIBRARY RESTAURANT   Historic   Lunch: $5-$10   Dinner: $8-$26   Phone: 716/372-2226

Location: I-86, exit 26, 1.4 mi s on SR 16 (Union St), just s of jct SR 417; downtown; in Old Library Inn Bed &
Breakfast. 116 S Union St 14760. **Hours:** 11 am-11 pm. Closed: 12/25. **Reservations:** accepted.
Features: The renovated 1909 library serves as a finely appointed yet casually relaxed setting in which to
enjoy such creatively prepared dishes as pasta Louis, antelope and steak. Chicken, veal and seafood
American   entrees also share menu space. Patrons can choose an appropriate wine from the impressive selection
carefully stored in the on-premises cellar. Servers show good menu knowledge. Casual dress; cocktails.
Parking: on-site. **Cards:** AX, DC, DS, MC, VI.   (Y) (✕)

ONEIDA pop. 10,987

———— WHERE TO STAY ————

ONEIDA COMMUNITY MANSION HOUSE   Phone: 315/363-0745

All Year [CP]   1P: $100-$125   2P: $100-$125   XP: $10   F
Location: I-90, exit 33, 4 mi s on SR 365 to SR 5, to Sherrill Rd, then 1 mi s. 170 Kenwood Ave 13421.
Historic   Fax: 315/361-4580. **Facility:** A historically significant mansion, the property offers communal dining and com-
Small-scale Hotel   fortable, spacious accommodations with a homey style. 8 one-bedroom standard units. 1 story, interior cor-
ridors. **Parking:** on-site. **Amenities:** voice mail, honor bars, irons, hair dryers. **Business Services:** meeting
rooms. **Cards:** AX, DS, MC, VI.

SOME UNITS
/ (✕) (▮) /

SUPER 8 MOTEL-ONEIDA   *Book at aaa.com*   Phone: (315)363-5168

All Year [CP]   1P: $45-$80   2P: $50-$85   XP: $5   F12
Location: I-90, exit 33, 4 mi s on SR 365 to SR 5, then 0.5 mi w. 215 Genesee St 13421. Fax: 315/363-4628.
Small-scale Hotel   **Facility:** 40 units. 39 one-bedroom standard units. 1 one-bedroom suite ($79-$110). 2 stories (no elevator),
interior corridors. **Parking:** on-site. **Amenities:** hair dryers. **Cards:** AX, DC, DS, MC, VI.

SOME UNITS
(ASK) (S/D) (TI+) (✷) (▮) (▭) / (✕) /

ONEONTA pop. 13,292

——— WHERE TO STAY ———

CLARION HOTEL *Book at aaa.com* Phone: (607)432-7500

▽▽▽ ▽▽▽

| 5/1-8/31 [ECP] | 1P: $149-$299 | 2P: $149-$299 | XP: $10 | F18 |
| 9/1-4/30 [ECP] | 1P: $99-$199 | 2P: $109-$199 | XP: $10 | F18 |

Small-scale Hotel **Location:** I-88, exit 15 to Main St; downtown. 55 Market St 13820. Fax: 607/433-2202. **Facility:** 78 one-bedroom standard units, some with whirlpools. 5 stories, interior corridors. *Bath:* combo or shower only. **Parking:** on-site. **Terms:** 2 night minimum stay - weekends 5/1-11/20, 3 day cancellation notice, $2 service charge. **Amenities:** dual phone lines, voice mail, irons, hair dryers. **Pool(s):** small heated indoor. **Leisure Activities:** sauna, whirlpool, exercise room. **Guest Services:** valet and coin laundry. **Business Services:** meeting rooms, business center. **Cards:** AX, CB, DC, DS, MC, VI.

SOME UNITS

(ASK) [S/D] [㊅] [➲] [✕] [DATA PORT] [▤] [▯] / [✕] /

HOLIDAY INN ONEONTA/COOPERSTOWN AREA *Book at aaa.com* Phone: (607)433-2250

(AAA) (SAVE)

7/1-8/31	1P: $139-$189	2P: $139-$189
5/1-6/30 & 9/1-11/22	1P: $99-$149	2P: $99-$149
11/23-4/30	1P: $79-$119	2P: $79-$119

▽▽▽ ▽▽▽

Small-scale Hotel **Facility:** 120 one-bedroom standard units. 2 stories (no elevator), interior corridors. *Bath:* combo or shower only. **Parking:** on-site. **Terms:** cancellation fee imposed, small pets only (in smoking units). **Amenities:** voice mail, irons, hair dryers. **Dining:** 6:30 am-2 & 5-10 pm; to 9 pm weekdays in winter, cocktails. **Pool(s):** outdoor, wading. **Leisure Activities:** soccer, grill, playground, exercise room, basketball, shuffleboard, volleyball. **Guest Services:** valet and coin laundry. **Business Services:** conference facilities. **Cards:** AX, CB, DC, DS, MC, VI. **Special Amenities:** free local telephone calls and free room upgrade (subject to availability with advanced reservations).** *(See color ad p 271)*

Location: I-88, exit 15 (SR 23 and 28), 1.5 mi e. 5206 State Hwy 23 13820-0634 (PO Box 634). Fax: 607/432-7028.

SOME UNITS

[S/D] [🐾] [🍴] [Y] [㊅] [⌖] [➲] [✕] [✦] [DATA PORT] [▯] / [✕] [VCR] [▤] [▯] /
FEE

KOUNTRY LIVING-THE SISTERS B & B Phone: 607/432-0186

▽▽▽▽

| All Year | 1P: $95 | 2P: $95 |

Historic Bed & Breakfast **Location:** I-88, exit 14 eastbound, just s; exit 15 (SR 23 and 28) westbound, 1 mi s. 576 SR 28 13820. **Facility:** Casual decor and handcrafted accents bring a country ambience to this near-town B&B. 4 one-bedroom standard units. 2 stories (no elevator), interior corridors. *Bath:* shared. **Parking:** on-site. **Terms:** age restrictions may apply, 30 day cancellation notice-fee imposed.

SOME UNITS

[✕] / [☎] /

RAINBOW INN ONEONTA/COOPERSTOWN AREA Phone: (607)432-1280

(AAA) (SAVE)

6/25-9/4	1P: $99-$175	2P: $129-$250	XP: $10
5/1-6/24	1P: $79-$129	2P: $89-$168	XP: $10
9/5-4/30	1P: $79-$109	2P: $89-$168	XP: $10

▽▽ ▽▽

Motel **Location:** I-88, exit 16 (Emmons/Davenport), 0.3 mi e. 5690 SR 7 13820. Fax: 607/433-2972. **Facility:** 28 one-bedroom standard units, some with whirlpools. 1 story, interior/exterior corridors. **Parking:** on-site, winter plug-ins. **Terms:** 30 day cancellation notice-fee imposed. **Amenities:** voice mail, hair dryers. **Pool(s):** heated outdoor. **Guest Services:** coin laundry. **Cards:** AX, CB, DC, DS, MC, VI.

SOME UNITS

[S/D] [🍴] [➲] [DATA PORT] [▯] / [✕] [VCR] [▤] /

SUPER 8 MOTEL *Book at aaa.com* Phone: (607)432-9505

▽▽ ▽▽

6/13-9/4	1P: $94-$140	2P: $94-$150	XP: $10	F12
9/5-11/27	1P: $71-$110	2P: $71-$131	XP: $10	F12
5/1-6/12	1P: $71-$90	2P: $71-$109	XP: $10	F12
11/28-4/30	1P: $62-$79	2P: $62-$79	XP: $10	F12

Small-scale Hotel **Location:** I-88, exit 15 (SR 23 and 28), 0.3 mi e. 4973 SR 23 13820. Fax: 607/432-9505. **Facility:** 60 one-bedroom standard units. 2 stories (no elevator), interior corridors. **Parking:** on-site, winter plug-ins. **Terms:** 3 day cancellation notice. **Amenities:** video library (fee). **Guest Services:** coin laundry. **Cards:** AX, CB, DC, DS, MC, VI.

SOME UNITS

(ASK) [S/D] [🐾] [🍴] [㊉M] / [✕] [VCR] [DATA PORT] [▯] [▤] /
FEE

——— WHERE TO DINE ———

AUTUMN CAFE Lunch: $5-$9 Dinner: $9-$16 Phone: 607/432-6845

▽▽▽

American **Location:** Center. 244 Main St 13820. **Hours:** 11 am-9 pm; Sunday brunch 10:30 am-2:30 pm. Closed major holidays; also Mon. **Features:** Since 1980, the cafe has featured daily-changing specials in addition to its tasty sandwiches, omelets, seafood, poultry, Mexican and vegetarian entrees. Most soups, breads and desserts are made on the premises. Patio seating, entertainment and an ever-changing artwork display make this a favorite gathering place. Casual dress; beer & wine only. **Parking:** street. **Cards:** AX, DS, MC, VI.

[Y] [✕]

BROOKS HOUSE OF BAR-B-Q Lunch: $4-$8 Dinner: $5-$15 Phone: 607/432-1782

(AAA)

▽▽▽

American **Location:** I-88, exit 16 (Emmons/Davenport), 0.3 mi w, then 2 mi e. 5560 State Hwy 7 13820. **Hours:** 11 am-9 pm. Closed: 1/1, 11/25, 12/24, 12/25; also 12/31, Mon except Memorial Day & Labor Day, also Tues after Labor Day. **Features:** Delicious chicken, ribs, pork, beef and seafood are prepared over a charcoal pit barbecue. The family-oriented restaurant is large and open, while the summer picnic areas encourage guests to kick back and enjoy time among friends. Servers are pleasant. Casual dress. **Parking:** on-site. **Cards:** DS, MC, VI.

[✕]

CORFU DINER Lunch: $3-$9 Dinner: $9-$13 Phone: 607/643-0232

▽▽▽

International **Location:** Center. 139 Main St 13820. **Hours:** 7 am-9 pm, Fri & Sat-10 pm. Closed: 12/25. **Reservations:** accepted, Fri & Sat. **Features:** The corner diner is alive and well. Delicious freshly prepared dishes are served from breakfast to dinner. Italian and Thai choices are offered along with the Mediterranean and American. Also available is a long list of hot and cold sandwiches. Casual dress. **Parking:** on-site. **Cards:** AX, DS, MC, VI.

[✕]

FARMHOUSE Historic
American

Dinner: $11-$29
Phone: 607/432-7374
Location: I-88, exit 16 (Emmons/Davenport), just n. SR 1 13820. **Hours:** 3 pm-9 pm, Fri & Sat-9:30 pm, Sun noon-8 pm; Sunday brunch. Closed: 12/25. **Reservations:** accepted. **Features:** Traditional steaks, chops, seafood, chicken and vegetarian choices are the fare in the century-old farmhouse. Guests can enjoy fireside dining under a plethora of stained-glass lamps, under a billowy ceiling in the blue room or on a covered patio in the company of hanging geraniums. The abundant salad bar features peel-and-eat shrimp, soups, salads, homemade breads and pasta. Casual dress; cocktails. **Parking:** on-site. **Cards:** AX, DC, MC, VI.

IANNELLI'S RISTORANTE
Regional
Italian

Lunch: $4-$7   **Dinner:** $5-$18   **Phone:** 607/433-5230
Location: SR 7 and 23, 0.4 mi w of jct Main St. 99 Chestnut St 13820. **Hours:** 11:30 am-10 pm, Sun 2 pm-9 pm. Closed major holidays. **Reservations:** suggested. **Features:** The popular restaurant deserves its popularity for distinctive cuisine. Ample, reasonably priced meals are prepared in the nouveau style—affording diners a refreshing change from typical Italian fare. Tiramisu and cheesecake are good dessert choices. Casual dress; cocktails. **Parking:** on-site. **Cards:** AX, DS, MC, VI.

JOE RUFFINO'S PIZZERIA & RESTAURANT
Italian

Lunch: $2-$9   **Dinner:** $4-$9   **Phone:** 607/432-7400
Location: I-88, exit 14, just n; downtown. 224 Main St 13820. **Hours:** 11 am-10 pm. Closed major holidays; also Sun. **Features:** Since 1972, the Ruffino family has served great prepared-to-order Italian food. Among offerings are weekly specials, pasta dinners, cold and hot submarine sandwiches and salads, as well as pizza and wings. The pizzeria offers free delivery in the city limits from 5 pm until closing. Casual dress; beer & wine only. **Parking:** street.

NEPTUNE DINER
American

Lunch: $5-$7   **Dinner:** $9-$18   **Phone:** 607/432-8820
Location: I-88, exit 15 (SR 23 and 28), 0.5 mi e. 5001 SR 23 13820. **Hours:** 24 hours. **Features:** Diners can enjoy their favorite American, Greek and Italian comfort foods in this throwback to a '50s diner. Contributing to the decor are a jukebox, neon signs, chrome accents and unusual tropical fish tanks flanking the spare dining room. Casual dress; cocktails. **Parking:** on-site. **Cards:** AX, MC, VI.

SABATINI'S LITTLE ITALY
Italian

Lunch: $7-$8   **Dinner:** $11-$18   **Phone:** 607/432-3000
Location: I-88, exit 15 (SR 23 and 28), just s, then just w. Rt 23 Southside 13820. **Hours:** 11:30 am-9:30 pm, Fri-10 pm, Sat 4 pm-10 pm, Sun 1:30 pm-9:30 pm. Closed: 12/25. **Reservations:** accepted. **Features:** The charming dining room is set up to remind diners of old Italy. Wrought-iron lamps and a suspended ceiling add to the look. The menu centers on large portions of pasta, veal, beef, chicken and seafood, as well as flavorful brick-oven pizza. Casual dress; cocktails. **Parking:** on-site. **Cards:** AX, MC, VI.

STELLA LUNA STAZIONE
Italian

Dinner: $10-$24   **Phone:** 607/433-7646
Location: Downtown. 58-60 Market St 13820. **Hours:** 5 pm-9 pm, Thurs-Sat to 10 pm. Closed: 11/25, 12/25; also Mon. **Reservations:** required, weekends. **Features:** The renovated 1892 train station has been transformed with soft tones into an outdoor courtyard, cantina-type atmosphere. The "sky" room is divine. Among examples of traditional fare are Chilean sea bass, veal chops, homemade ravioli and preparations of certified Angus beef. Desserts are made on the premises, and wine can be selected from a temperature-controlled room. Casual dress; cocktails. **Parking:** on-site. **Cards:** AX, DS, MC, VI.

VINES
Continental

Lunch: $4-$8   **Dinner:** $8-$19   **Phone:** 607/433-9895
Location: I-88, exit 14; center. 214 Main St 13820. **Hours:** 11 am-10 pm, Sun-3 pm. Closed: 11/25, 12/25. **Features:** Summer people-watching is easy from patio doors or on the patio at the downtown bistro. The friendly staff serves delicious Continental fare, including offerings of tapas. Casual dress; cocktails. **Parking:** street. **Cards:** AX, DS, MC, VI.

ORANGEBURG —See New York p. 455.

OSSINING —See New York p. 455.

OSWEGO pop. 17,954

——— **WHERE TO STAY** ———

BEST WESTERN CAPTAIN'S QUARTERS   *Book at aaa.com*
Small-scale Hotel

			Phone: (315)342-4040	
1/1-4/30 [ECP]	1P: $84-$94	2P: $96-$106	XP: $12	F18
5/1-12/31 [ECP]	1P: $82-$92	2P: $94-$104	XP: $12	F18

Location: Just n on SR 481. 26 E 1st St 13126. Fax: 315/342-5454. **Facility:** 93 units. 90 one-bedroom standard units. 3 one-bedroom suites. 4 stories, interior corridors. *Bath:* combo or shower only. **Parking:** on-site. **Amenities:** video games, honor bars, irons, hair dryers. **Pool(s):** heated indoor. **Leisure Activities:** sauna, whirlpool, steam-room. **Guest Services:** complimentary evening beverages, valet laundry. **Business Services:** meeting rooms. **Cards:** AX, CB, DC, DS, MC, VI.

SOME UNITS

ECONO LODGE RIVERFRONT HOTEL
Small-scale Hotel

			Phone: (315)343-1600	
All Year	1P: $62-$125	2P: $74-$138	XP: $12	F18

Location: Just n on SR 481. 70 E 1st St 13126. Fax: 315/343-1222. **Facility:** 93 units. 81 one-bedroom standard units. 12 one-bedroom suites, some with kitchens. 5 stories, interior corridors. *Bath:* combo or shower only. **Parking:** on-site, winter plug-ins. **Terms:** [CP] meal plan available. **Amenities:** voice mail. **Guest Services:** valet laundry. **Business Services:** meeting rooms. **Cards:** AX, CB, DC, DS, JC, MC, VI.

SOME UNITS

OSWEGO INN LTD
Phone: 315/342-6200

▽▽▽ ▽▽▽   5/1-10/31 & 4/1-4/30 [CP]   1P: $55-$105   2P: $60-$115   XP: $15   F12
           11/1-3/31 [CP]   1P: $40   2P: $45-$55   XP: $5   F12
Small-scale Hotel   **Location:** Jct 10th St and SR 104; center. 180 E 10th St 13126. **Fax:** 315/343-6234. **Facility:** Smoke free premises. 13 one-bedroom standard units. 2 stories (no elevator), interior corridors. **Parking:** on-site. **Terms:** 14 day cancellation notice, weekly rates available. **Cards:** AX, CB, DC, DS, MC, VI.

─────── **WHERE TO DINE** ───────

CANALE'S RISTORANTE   **Lunch:** $5-$7   **Dinner:** $7-$18   **Phone:** 315/343-3540

▽▽▽ ▽▽   **Location:** Jct Utica and Herrick sts; jct SR 481, 0.8 mi w. 156 W Utica St 13126. **Hours:** 11:30 am-10 pm, Fri & Sat-11 pm; closed for lunch Sat & Sun in summer. Closed: 3/27, 11/25, 12/25. **Reservations:** suggested.
Italian   **Features:** Vintage artwork, overhead lighting and lots of windows add to the casual warmth of the informal dining room. Diners enjoy good-size portions of steak, veal, pizza, sandwiches and seafood. Servers in attractive uniforms are pleasant and prompt. Casual dress; cocktails. **Parking:** on-site. **Cards:** AX, CB, DC, DS, MC, VI.

COLEMAN'S   **Lunch:** $6-$8   **Dinner:** $8-$18   **Phone:** 315/343-1433

▽▽▽ ▽▽   **Location:** Bayfront at W Seneca St and W 1st St; center. W Seneca St 13126. **Hours:** 11:30 am-10 pm, Thurs-Sat to 11 pm. Closed: 12/25. **Reservations:** accepted. **Features:** Overlooking the harbor and Lake Ontario,
Irish   the cozy pub presents a menu of traditional Irish fare and American favorites. Casual dress; cocktails. **Parking:** on-site. **Cards:** AX, MC, VI.

OTEGO pop. 1,052

─────── **WHERE TO DINE** ───────

GUS'S DINER   **Lunch:** $3-$7   **Dinner:** $5-$13   **Phone:** 607/988-9818

▽   **Location:** I-88, exit 12, just s. 202 County Hwy 48 13825. **Hours:** 6 am-9 pm. **Features:** The new, family-owned diner offers easy access to the interstate. Friendly servers deliver good American comfort food, including
American   daily specials. Casual dress. **Parking:** on-site. **Cards:** AX, DC, DS, MC, VI.

OWEGO pop. 20,365

─────── **WHERE TO STAY** ───────

HOLIDAY INN EXPRESS   *Book at aaa.com*
Phone: (607)687-9000

▽▽▽ ▽   All Year [ECP]   1P: $89-$129   XP: $10   F18
          Location: SR 17, exit 65, at foot of ramp. 20 Hickory Park Rd 13827. **Fax:** 607/687-3034. **Facility:** 74 one-bedroom
Small-scale Hotel   standard units, some with efficiencies. 2 stories, interior corridors. **Parking:** on-site. **Terms:** check-in 4 pm. **Amenities:** dual phone lines, voice mail, irons, hair dryers. **Leisure Activities:** fishing. **Guest Services:** valet and coin laundry. **Business Services:** meeting rooms. **Cards:** AX, CB, DC, DS, MC, VI.

SOME UNITS

OWEGO TREADWAY INN & SUITES   *Book at aaa.com*
Phone: (607)687-4500

▽▽▽ ▽   All Year   1P: $84-$109   XP: $10   F18
          Location: SR 17, exit 65. 1100 SR 17C 13827. **Fax:** 607/687-2456. **Facility:** 92 units. 88 one-bedroom standard
Small-scale Hotel   units, some with whirlpools. 4 one-bedroom suites ($114-$139) with efficiencies. 2 stories, interior corridors. *Bath:* combo or shower only. **Parking:** on-site. **Terms:** check-in 4 pm. **Amenities:** irons, hair dryers. *Some:* safes. **Pool(s):** small heated indoor. **Leisure Activities:** fishing, exercise room. **Guest Services:** valet laundry. **Business Services:** conference facilities. **Cards:** AX, CB, DC, DS, MC, VI.

SOME UNITS

SUNRISE MOTEL
Phone: (607)687-5667

◭◭◭ [SAVE]   All Year [CP]   1P: $47-$51   2P: $51-$55   XP: $8   F12
▽▽▽ ▽   **Location:** SR 17, exit 64 (SR 96 N) across river w to SR 17C, then 2 mi s. 3778 Waverly Rd 13827 (14 Courtley Cir).
Motel   Fax: 607/687-5666. **Facility:** 20 one-bedroom standard units. 1 story, exterior corridors. *Bath:* combo or shower only. **Parking:** on-site, winter plug-ins. **Terms:** pets ($5 extra charge, in designated units, small dogs only). **Cards:** AX, CB, DC, DS, MC, VI. **Special Amenities:** free continental breakfast and free local telephone calls.

SOME UNITS
FEE

PAINTED POST pop. 1,842—See also FINGER LAKES.

─────── **WHERE TO STAY** ───────

BEST WESTERN LODGE ON THE GREEN   *Book at aaa.com*
Phone: (607)962-2456

◭◭◭ [SAVE]   5/24-10/19 [ECP]   1P: $80-$100   2P: $80-$100   XP: $8   F18
▽▽▽ ▽   5/1-5/23 & 10/20-4/30 [ECP]   1P: $50-$70   2P: $50-$70   XP: $8   F18
Motel   **Location:** SR 17, exit 44, s to Gang Mills exit, then n. 3171 Canada Rd 14870. **Fax:** 607/962-1769. **Facility:** 135 one-bedroom standard units. 1-2 stories (no elevator), interior corridors. **Parking:** on-site, winter plug-ins. **Terms:** check-in 4 pm. **Amenities:** voice mail, irons, hair dryers. **Dining:** 11:30 am-2 & 5-9 pm, cocktails. **Pool(s):** heated outdoor. **Guest Services:** valet and coin laundry. **Business Services:** meeting rooms.
Cards: AX, CB, DC, DS, JC, MC, VI. **Special Amenities:** free room upgrade (subject to availability with advanced reservations).

SOME UNITS
FEE   FEE

ECONO LODGE *Book at aaa.com*

Phone: (607)962-4444

5/1-10/31	1P: $65-$110	2P: $95-$120	XP: $10	F13
11/1-12/30	1P: $40-$75	2P: $45-$80	XP: $5	F13
12/31-4/30	1P: $40-$45	2P: $45-$50	XP: $5	F13

Small-scale Hotel **Location:** Jct US 15 and SR 17, exit 44, s to Gang Mills exit. 200 Robert Dann Dr 14870. Fax: 607/937-5397. **Facility:** 62 units. 61 one-bedroom standard units, some with whirlpools. 1 one-bedroom suite ($85-$120) with kitchen. 2 stories (no elevator), interior corridors. **Parking:** on-site. **Terms:** cancellation fee imposed, [ECP] meal plan available, pets ($10 fee). **Amenities:** voice mail, irons, hair dryers. **Business Services:** PC. **Cards:** AX, DC, DS, MC, VI.

SOME UNITS

ASK SD 🐄 &M 🖨 ➕ 🖥 DATA PORT 🖥 🖨 / ✕ 🖥 /
FEE

ERWIN MOTEL

Phone: 607/962-7411

5/1-10/20	1P: $44-$52	2P: $59-$79	XP: $10	F12
10/21-11/30	1P: $39-$47	2P: $49-$69	XP: $7	F12
12/1-4/30	1P: $36-$42	2P: $42-$59	XP: $5	F12

Motel **Location:** US 15, exit Erwin Addison, 0.5 mi e. Rt 417 14870 (806 Addison Rd). Fax: 607/962-6373. **Facility:** 25 one-bedroom standard units, some with efficiencies. 1 story, exterior corridors. *Bath:* combo or shower only. **Parking:** on-site. **Terms:** 3 day cancellation notice, [CP] meal plan available, pets ($5 fee, in designated units). **Pool(s):** heated outdoor. **Leisure Activities:** barbecue grill, picnic table. **Guest Services:** coin laundry. **Cards:** AX, DS, MC, VI. **Special Amenities:** free continental breakfast and free local telephone calls.

SOME UNITS

🐄 🖥 ➡ / ✕ 🖥 🖨 /
FEE

HAMPTON INN *Book at aaa.com*

Phone: (607)936-3344

5/1-10/31 & 4/1-4/30 [ECP]	1P: $84-$169	2P: $84-$169	
11/1-3/31 [ECP]	1P: $69-$129	2P: $69-$129	

Small-scale Hotel **Location:** I-86, exit 43, just w. 9775 Victory Hwy 14870. Fax: 607/936-3393. **Facility:** 67 one-bedroom standard units, some with whirlpools. 3 stories, interior corridors. *Bath:* combo or shower only. **Parking:** on-site, winter plug-ins. **Amenities:** voice mail, irons, hair dryers. **Pool(s):** small heated indoor. **Leisure Activities:** exercise room. **Guest Services:** valet laundry. **Business Services:** meeting rooms. **Cards:** AX, DC, DS, MC, VI.

SOME UNITS

ASK SD 🖥 &M 🖥 🖨 ➡ 🖥 DATA PORT 🖥 / ✕ VCR 🖥 🖨 /

HOLIDAY INN *Book at aaa.com*

Phone: (607)962-5021

7/9-10/10	1P: $81-$100	2P: $81-$100
5/1-7/8 & 10/11-4/30	1P: $81-$95	2P: $81-$95

Small-scale Hotel **Location:** Just s on US 15 to Gang Mills exit, then s. Located in a light-commercial area. 3101 S Hamilton St 14870. Fax: 607/937-4080. **Facility:** 105 one-bedroom standard units. 2 stories (no elevator), interior corridors. *Bath:* combo or shower only. **Parking:** on-site. **Amenities:** video games, irons, hair dryers. **Dining:** 7 am-1:30 & 5-9 pm, cocktails. **Pool(s):** heated outdoor, wading. **Leisure Activities:** exercise room. **Guest Services:** valet and coin laundry. **Business Services:** conference facilities. **Cards:** AX, DC, DS, MC, VI. **Special Amenities:** free local telephone calls and free newspaper.

SOME UNITS

SD 🖥 🖥 &M 🖨 🖥 ➡ 🖥 DATA PORT 🖥 / ✕ VCR 🖥 🖨 /

SUPER 8 MOTEL

Phone: (607)937-5383

5/1-9/30 [CP]	1P: $55-$70	2P: $60-$75	XP: $5	F12
10/1-4/30 [CP]	1P: $45-$65	2P: $50-$70	XP: $5	F12

Small-scale Hotel **Location:** SR 17, exit 44 on US 15 s to Gang Mills exit. 255 S Hamilton St 14870. Fax: 607/962-7115. **Facility:** 61 one-bedroom standard units. 2 stories (no elevator), interior corridors. *Bath:* combo or shower only. **Parking:** on-site, winter plug-ins. **Cards:** AX, DC, DS, MC, VI. **Special Amenities:** free continental breakfast and free local telephone calls.

SOME UNITS

SD &M 🖨 🖥 / ✕ /

-------- **WHERE TO DINE** --------

JELLY BEANS

Lunch: $5-$7 **Dinner:** $8-$10 **Phone:** 607/936-2290

American **Location:** SR 17, exit 44 (US 15 S), just s to Gang Mills exit, then just s. 319 S Hamilton St 14870. **Hours:** 6 am-10 pm. Closed: 12/25. **Features:** Bright primary colors surround patrons of the casual restaurant. Generous portions of breakfast, lunch and dinner are served all day. Complimentary Jelly Belly jelly beans accompany every bill and can be bought separately. Casual dress; beer & wine only. **Parking:** on-site. **Cards:** AX, DS, MC, VI.

✕

PIERI'S CENTRAL RESTAURANT

Lunch: $4-$6 **Dinner:** $5-$25 **Phone:** 607/962-6917

American **Location:** Center; in Village Square. 104 Village Square 14870. **Hours:** 6 am-8:30 pm, Sat from 7 am. Closed major holidays; also Sun. **Features:** From hearty soups, burgers and sandwiches to steaks and lobster tail, the busy restaurant has it all. Lots of popular appetizers and Italian fare, as well as children's items, are offered all day. Casual dress; cocktails. **Parking:** on-site. **Cards:** AX, DS, MC, VI.

✕

PALENVILLE pop. 1,120

-------- **WHERE TO STAY** --------

CATSKILL MOUNTAIN LODGE

Phone: 518/678-3101

All Year	1P: $80-$200	2P: $85-$200	XP: $15	F5

Small-scale Hotel **Location:** Jct SR 32, 1 mi nw. 334 Rt 32A 12463. Fax: 518/678-3103. **Facility:** 42 units. 37 one-bedroom standard units. 3 cabins and 2 cottages ($795-$895). 1-2 stories, interior/exterior corridors. *Bath:* combo or shower only. **Parking:** on-site, winter plug-ins. **Terms:** 2-3 night minimum stay - weekends in season, 14 day cancellation notice-fee imposed, weekly rates available. **Amenities:** *Some:* hair dryers. **Dining:** 7 am-3 & 5-9 pm, Mon & Tues-3 pm, cocktails. **Pool(s):** heated outdoor, wading. **Leisure Activities:** lawn games, playground, basketball, horseshoes, shuffleboard, volleyball. **Guest Services:** coin laundry. **Cards:** AX, CB, DC, DS, MC, VI.

SOME UNITS

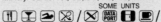
🖥 🖥 ➡ ✕ / ✕ DATA PORT 🖥 🖨 /
FEE

PEARL RIVER —See New York p. 455.

PEEKSKILL —See New York p. 455.

PEMBROKE pop. 4,530

——— WHERE TO STAY ———

DARIEN LAKES ECONO LODGE   *Book at aaa.com*   Phone: (585)599-4681
▼▼▼ ▼▼▼
6/18-9/6   1P: $79-$119   2P: $79-$119   XP: $5   F18
5/1-6/17   1P: $50-$75   2P: $50-$80   XP: $5   F18
Small-scale Hotel 9/7-10/31   1P: $50-$75   2P: $50-$75   XP: $5   F18
11/1-4/30   1P: $44-$65   2P: $44-$70   XP: $5   F18
Location: I-90, exit 48A, exit s. 8493 SR 77 14036. Fax: 585/599-3040. **Facility:** 73 one-bedroom standard units. 2 stories (no elevator), interior corridors. **Parking:** on-site. **Leisure Activities:** Fee: game room. **Guest Services:** coin laundry. **Cards:** AX, DC, DS, MC, VI.

SOME UNITS
(A$K) (S🐾) (🛏) (🎥) / (✕) (VCR) (DATA PORT) (🔌) (▢) /
FEE   FEE

PENFIELD pop. 34,645   (See map and index starting on p. 550)

——— WHERE TO STAY ———

COURTYARD BY MARRIOTT   *Book at aaa.com*   Phone: (585)385-1000   46
▼▼▼▼
All Year   1P: $99-$134
Small-scale Hotel **Location:** I-490, exit 23 (SR 441 E), 1.7 mi to Washington St exit, then just s to Linden Park. Located in a quiet area. 1000 Linden Park 14625. Fax: 585/385-1005. **Facility:** 95 one-bedroom standard units, some with whirlpools. 5 stories, interior corridors. *Bath:* combo or shower only. **Parking:** on-site. **Amenities:** video games, high-speed Internet, dual phone lines, voice mail, irons, hair dryers. **Pool(s):** small heated indoor. **Leisure Activities:** whirlpool, exercise room. **Guest Services:** valet and coin laundry. **Business Services:** meeting rooms, fax (fee). **Cards:** AX, DC, DS, MC, VI.

SOME UNITS
(S🐾) (✈) (🍴) (🎥) (🏊) (🏊) (🏋) (DATA PORT) (▢) / (✕) (🔌) /

——— WHERE TO DINE ———

DAISY FLOUR MILL   Historic   **Dinner:** $9-$25   Phone: 585/381-1880   19
▼▼▼▼
Location: I-590, exit 6 (Blossom Rd), 1.4 mi e; in Ellison Park. 1880 Blossom Rd 14625. **Hours:** 5 pm-9 pm, Fri & Sat-9 pm, Sun 4 pm-8 pm. Closed: 12/25. **Reservations:** suggested. **Features:** The 1848 restored grist
American   mill is decorated with lots of wood and interesting furnishings, including a 1919 Ford Model T Huckster in the foyer. Beef, seafood and game dishes are the focus of the menu. Delicious desserts are prepared with the mill's flour. Casual dress; cocktails. **Parking:** on-site. **Cards:** AX, CB, DC, DS, MC, VI.

(🍸) (✕)

PENN YAN pop. 5,219—See also FINGER LAKES.

——— WHERE TO STAY ———

MERRITT HILL MANOR BED & BREAKFAST   Phone: 315/536-7682
▼▼▼▼
All Year [BP]   1P: $130-$150   2P: $130-$150   XP: $25
Location: 3 mi s on SR 54A, then 1 mi w on Merritt Hill Rd. 2756 Coates Rd 14527. **Facility:** A peaceful ambience
Historic Bed   characterizes the sprawling grounds of this hilltop, Federal-style, 1822 farmhouse, which offers views of lakes
& Breakfast   Keuka and Seneca. Smoke free premises. 5 one-bedroom standard units. 2 stories (no elevator), interior corridors. *Bath:* combo or shower only. **Parking:** on-site. **Terms:** 2 night minimum stay - weekends 5/1-12/31, age restrictions may apply, 7 day cancellation notice. **Amenities:** hair dryers. **Guest Services:** TV in common area. **Cards:** AX, MC, VI.

(✕) (🅦) (🖙)

TRIMMER HOUSE BED AND BREAKFAST   Phone: 315/536-8304
▼▼▼▼
All Year [BP]   1P: $75-$150   2P: $99-$199   XP: $25
Location: Jct SR 54 and Main St, 0.6 mi e. 145 E Main St 14527. Fax: 315/536-8304. **Facility:** Guests can walk
Historic Bed   to town from this restored 1891 Victorian house, which has nicely appointed rooms and modern baths.
& Breakfast   Smoke free premises. 5 one-bedroom standard units. 2 stories (no elevator), interior corridors. **Parking:** on-site. **Terms:** check-in 4 pm, 2 night minimum stay - weekends, 14 day cancellation notice-fee imposed.
Amenities: video library, CD players, dual phone lines, hair dryers. **Leisure Activities:** whirlpool. **Guest Services:** valet laundry. **Business Services:** fax. **Cards:** AX, MC, VI.

(✈) (✕) (VCR) (🎥) (DATA PORT)

——— WHERE TO DINE ———

MILLER'S ESSENHAUS   **Lunch:** $3-$8   **Dinner:** $7-$19   Phone: 315/531-8260
(AAA)
▼▼ ▼▼
American
Location: 2 mi n. 1300 SR 14A 14527. **Hours:** 8-11 am, 11:30-3 & 4-9 pm, Sun 10 am-3 pm. Closed major holidays. **Reservations:** accepted. **Features:** The restaurant serves wholesome dishes—such as sauerbraten and orange-glazed roast pork—that the bakers and chefs make from scratch. Casual dress; beer & wine only. **Parking:** on-site. **Cards:** AX, DS, MC, VI.

(♿M) (✕)

PERTH pop. 3,638

——— WHERE TO DINE ———

RAINDANCER STEAK PARLOUR   **Lunch:** $5-$10   **Dinner:** $12-$25   **Phone:** 518/842-2606
▼▼▼▼ ▼▼▼▼   **Location:** I-90, exit 27, 4.5 mi n; jct SR 67, 3.8 mi n. 4582 SR 30 12010. **Hours:** 11:30 am-10 pm, Sun 12:30
Steak & Seafood   pm-8 pm. Closed: 12/24, 12/25. **Reservations:** suggested. **Features:** Prime rib and Alaskan king crab legs
are specialties on a menu of mostly steak, seafood and pasta dishes, which are served in generous
portions. Fireplaces and antiques decorate the rustic dining room. The casual atmosphere is welcoming to
families. Casual dress; cocktails. **Parking:** on-site. **Cards:** AX, DS, MC, VI.   🍽 ✕

PERU pop. 1,514

——— WHERE TO DINE ———

——— *The following restaurant has not been evaluated by AAA* ———
but is listed for your information only.

CRICKET'S CASUAL FOOD & SPIRITS   **Phone:** 518/643-2433
[fyi]   Not evaluated. **Location:** Bear Swamp Rd 12972. **Features:** Pleasant family restaurant open for lunch and
dinner.

PINE VALLEY

——— WHERE TO STAY ———

BEST WESTERN MARSHALL MANOR   *Book at aaa.com*   **Phone:** (607)739-3891
🅐🅐🅐 [SAVE]   6/29-10/18   1P: $63-$82   2P: $72-$87   XP: $5   F17
▼▼◆▼▼   5/1-6/28 & 10/19-11/23   1P: $52-$69   2P: $59-$78   XP: $5   F17
Motel   11/24-4/30   1P: $46-$60   2P: $50-$68   XP: $5   F17
Location: SR 17, exit 52, 5 mi n on SR 14. Located in a quiet area. 3527 Watkins Rd 14845. Fax: 607/739-3892.
Facility: 40 one-bedroom standard units. 1 story, exterior corridors. **Parking:** on-site. **Terms:** [ECP] meal
plan available, pets ($4 extra charge). **Amenities:** irons, hair dryers, safes (fee), irons. **Pool(s):** heated outdoor. **Cards:** AX,
CB, DC, DS, MC, VI. **Special Amenities:** free continental breakfast and early check-in/late check-out.
(See color ad p 309)

SOME UNITS
🆂 🐾 🍽 🏊 🎥 📠 🛗 💻 / ✕ 📼 📶 /
FEE

PITTSFORD pop. 27,212   (See map and index starting on p. 550)

——— WHERE TO STAY ———

BROOKWOOD INN ROCHESTER/PITTSFORD   *Book at aaa.com*   **Phone:** (585)248-9000   [26]
▼▼◆▼▼   5/1-10/31 [BP]   1P: $89   2P: $139   XP: $10   F18
Small-scale Hotel   11/1-4/30 [BP]   1P: $79   2P: $139   XP: $10   F18
Location: I-490, exit 27 (Bushnell's Basin SR 96 N), just n. 800 Pittsford/Victor Rd 14534. Fax: 585/248-8569.
Facility: 108 one-bedroom standard units, some with whirlpools. 5 stories, interior corridors. **Parking:** on-
site. **Terms:** 3 day cancellation notice, package plans. **Amenities:** video games, dual phone lines, voice mail, safes (fee), irons,
hair dryers. **Pool(s):** heated indoor. **Leisure Activities:** sauna, whirlpool, exercise room. *Fee:* bicycles. **Guest Services:** valet
laundry. **Business Services:** meeting rooms. **Cards:** AX, CB, DC, DS, MC, VI.

SOME UNITS
🆂🆂 🆓 ➡ 🍽 🍽 🛎 🏊 ✕ 🎥 📠 💻 / ✕ 🛗 📶 /

THE DEL MONTE LODGE A RENAISSANCE HOTEL   *Book at aaa.com*   **Phone:** (585)381-9900   [28]
▼▼◆▼▼   All Year   1P: $179-$194
Small-scale Hotel   **Location:** I-90, exit 45 westbound, 2 mi w on SR 31, then just n on SR 96; exit 46 eastbound, 5 mi n on I-390, 3 mi n
I-590, 3 mi e on SR 31, then just n on SR 96. Located next to Erie Canal path. 41 N Main St 14534. Fax: 585/381-9825.
Facility: 99 units. 97 one-bedroom standard units. 2 one-bedroom suites, some with whirlpools. 3 stories,
interior corridors. *Bath:* combo or shower only. **Parking:** on-site. **Amenities:** video games, high-speed Internet, dual phone lines,
voice mail, safes, honor bars, irons, hair dryers. **Pool(s):** heated indoor. **Leisure Activities:** whirlpool, exercise room. *Fee:* massage. **Guest Services:** valet laundry, area transportation. **Business Services:** conference facilities, PC. **Cards:** AX, DC, DS,
MC, VI.

SOME UNITS
🆂 🆓 🍽 🍽 🎮 🏊 ✕ 🎥 📠 💻 / ✕ 🛗 📶 /

——— WHERE TO DINE ———

RICHARDSON'S CANAL HOUSE Historic   **Lunch:** $8-$12   **Dinner:** $18-$28   **Phone:** 585/248-5000   [16]
▼▼◆▼▼   **Location:** I-490, exit 27 (Bushnell's Basin SR 96 N), just n; in Oliver Loud's Inn. 1474 Marsh Rd 14534.
American   **Hours:** 11:30 am-2 & 5:30-10 pm, Mon from 5:30 pm, Sat 5 pm-10 pm. Closed: 1/1, 3/27, 12/25; also Sun.
Reservations: suggested. **Features:** Sophisticated furnishings decorate the refurbished 1818 Erie Canal
tavern, a favorite romantic spot for couples. Freshly-prepared American country and French regional
cuisine is complex and flavorful. The focus is on fresh seafood and tantalizing preparations of meats, such as rack of lamb,
roasted duck or osso buco. Dressy casual; cocktails. **Parking:** on-site. **Cards:** AX, DS, MC, VI.   🍽 ✕

PLAINVIEW pop. 25,637

------- WHERE TO STAY -------

HOLIDAY INN
Small-scale Hotel

Book at aaa.com

All Year   1P: $109-$169   2P: $109-$169   XP: $15   F19

Location: I-495, exit 46N, northeast corner. Located in a commercial area. 215 Sunnyside Blvd 11803. **Fax:** 516/349-7491. **Facility:** 125 one-bedroom standard units, some with whirlpools. 2 stories, interior corridors. *Bath:* combo or shower only. **Parking:** on-site. **Amenities:** video games (fee), dual phone lines, voice mail, irons, hair dryers. **Pool(s):** outdoor. **Leisure Activities:** exercise room. *Fee:* game room. **Guest Services:** valet and coin laundry. **Business Services:** meeting rooms. **Cards:** AX, CB, DC, DS, JC, MC, VI.

Phone: (516)349-7400

SOME UNITS

RESIDENCE INN BY MARRIOTT
Small-scale Hotel

Book at aaa.com

5/1-11/20 & 4/1-4/30 [BP]   1P: $219-$375   2P: $229-$375
1/1-3/31 [BP]   1P: $209-$365   2P: $219-$365
11/21-12/31 [BP]   1P: $199-$355   2P: $209-$355

Location: I-495, exit 44, 1.6 mi s on SR 135, exit 10, then just e on Old Country Rd. Located opposite North Shore University Hospital. 9 Gerhard Rd 11803. **Fax:** 516/433-2569. **Facility:** 170 units. 112 one-bedroom standard units with efficiencies. 48 one- and 10 two-bedroom suites with kitchens, some with whirlpools. 2-3 stories, interior corridors. *Bath:* combo or shower only. **Parking:** on-site. **Terms:** check-in 4 pm, cancellation fee imposed, pets ($150 fee, $10 extra charge). **Amenities:** high-speed Internet (fee), dual phone lines, voice mail, irons, hair dryers. **Pool(s):** outdoor, lap. **Leisure Activities:** saunas, whirlpool, putting green, recreation programs, exercise room, basketball, shuffleboard. *Fee:* massage, game room. **Guest Services:** sundries, complimentary evening beverages: Mon-Thurs, coin laundry. **Business Services:** meeting rooms, business center. **Cards:** AX, CB, DC, DS, JC, MC, VI.

Phone: 516/433-6200

SOME UNITS

FEE

PLATTSBURGH pop. 18,816

------- WHERE TO STAY -------

BAYMONT INN & SUITES PLATTSBURGH
Small-scale Hotel

Book at aaa.com

5/1-10/31   1P: $70-$90   2P: $70-$90   XP: $10   F
11/1-4/30   1P: $60-$80   2P: $60-$80   XP: $10   F

Location: I-87, exit 37, just w. 16 Plaza Blvd 12901-6439. **Fax:** 518/561-3234. **Facility:** 103 units. 100 one-bedroom standard units, some with kitchens. 3 one-bedroom suites ($99). 4 stories, interior corridors. *Bath:* combo or shower only. **Parking:** on-site, winter plug-ins. **Terms:** [ECP] meal plan available, pets (on 1st floor, in smoking units). **Amenities:** video games (fee), voice mail, irons, hair dryers. **Pool(s):** heated indoor. **Leisure Activities:** whirlpool. **Guest Services:** coin laundry. **Cards:** AX, CB, DC, DS, MC, VI. **Special Amenities:** free local telephone calls and free newspaper. *(See color ad below)*

Phone: (518)562-4000

SOME UNITS

FEE FEE

BEST WESTERN THE INN AT SMITHFIELD
Small-scale Hotel

Book at aaa.com

7/2-9/4 [ECP]   1P: $88-$104   2P: $88-$104   XP: $5   F
5/1-7/1 & 9/5-4/30 [ECP]   1P: $69-$99   2P: $69-$99   XP: $5   F

Location: I-87, exit 37, just w. 446 Rt 3 12901. **Fax:** 518/561-9431. **Facility:** 118 units. 116 one-bedroom standard units. 2 one-bedroom suites with whirlpools. 2 stories (no elevator), interior corridors. **Parking:** on-site, winter plug-ins. **Terms:** package plans. **Amenities:** video games (fee), high-speed Internet, dual phone lines, voice mail, irons, hair dryers. **Dining:** 2 restaurants, 11:30 am-11 pm, Fri & Sat-midnight, cocktails. **Pool(s):** heated indoor. **Leisure Activities:** small playground area, exercise room. *Fee:* game room. **Guest Services:** valet and coin laundry. **Business Services:** meeting rooms. **Cards:** AX, CB, DC, DS, MC, VI. **Special Amenities:** free expanded continental breakfast and free newspaper.

Phone: (518)561-7750

SOME UNITS

COMFORT INN

Book at aaa.com

▼▼▼▼▼ All Year

Small-scale Hotel

| | 1P: $55-$154 | 2P: $65-$164 | XP: $10 | F18 |

Phone: (518)562-2730

Location: I-87, exit 37, 0.5 mi e. 411 Rt 3 12901. **Fax:** 518/563-1562. **Facility:** 111 units. 85 one-bedroom standard units, some with whirlpools. 26 one-bedroom suites, some with efficiencies (no utensils) and/or whirlpools. 2 stories (no elevator), interior corridors. **Parking:** on-site, winter plug-ins. **Terms:** [ECP] meal plan available. **Amenities:** high-speed Internet, voice mail, irons, hair dryers. **Pool(s):** heated indoor. **Leisure Activities:** sauna, whirlpool, steamroom, waterslide, racquetball courts, playground. **Fee:** miniature golf, game room. **Guest Services:** valet and coin laundry. **Fee:** tanning facility. **Business Services:** meeting rooms, business center. **Cards:** AX, DC, DS, MC, VI.

SOME UNITS

(A$K) (S🄳) ⊗ ⊗ ⊗ ⊗ ⊗ ⊗ ⊗ (DATA PORT) ⊗ ⊗ ⊗ / ⊗ (VCR) / FEE

DAYS INN & SUITES

Book at aaa.com

▼▼▼ 6/18-10/16 [ECP]
5/1-6/17 & 10/17-4/30 [ECP]

Small-scale Hotel

| | 1P: $69 | 2P: $79 | XP: $10 | F17 |
| | 1P: $67 | 2P: $77 | XP: $10 | F17 |

Phone: (518)561-0403

Location: I-87, exit 37, just w. 8 Everleth Dr 12901. **Fax:** 518/561-4192. **Facility:** 106 units. 100 one-bedroom standard units, some with efficiencies. 6 one-bedroom suites ($158-$198) with whirlpools. 3 stories, interior corridors. **Parking:** on-site, winter plug-ins. **Terms:** 3 day cancellation notice-fee imposed, package plans - seasonal. **Amenities:** video games (fee), high-speed Internet, dual phone lines, irons, hair dryers. **Pool(s):** outdoor, heated indoor. **Leisure Activities:** whirlpool, exercise room. **Guest Services:** valet and coin laundry. **Business Services:** meeting rooms. **Cards:** AX, CB, DC, DS, JC, MC, VI.

SOME UNITS

(A$K) (S🄳) (Y+) ⊗ ⊗ (DATA PORT) / ⊗ ⊗ ⊗ ⊗ /

HOLIDAY INN

Book at aaa.com

▼▼▼ All Year

Small-scale Hotel

| | 1P: $95 | 2P: $95 | XP: $10 | F18 |

Phone: 518/561-5000

Location: I-87, exit 37, 0.5 mi e. 412 Rt 3 12901. **Fax:** 518/562-2974. **Facility:** 102 one-bedroom standard units. 4 stories, interior corridors. **Bath:** combo or shower only. **Parking:** on-site, winter plug-ins. **Terms:** [BP] meal plan available, package plans - seasonal. **Amenities:** video games (fee), high-speed Internet, dual phone lines, voice mail, irons, hair dryers. **Pool(s):** heated indoor, wading. **Leisure Activities:** exercise room. **Fee:** game room. **Guest Services:** valet and coin laundry. **Business Services:** meeting rooms. **Cards:** AX, DC, DS, MC, VI.

SOME UNITS

(A$K) ⊗ ⊗ ⊗ ⊗ ⊗ ⊗ (DATA PORT) ⊗ / ⊗ ⊗ ⊗ / FEE FEE

POINT AU ROCHE LODGE AND BED & BREAKFAST

▼▼▼ All Year [BP]

Bed & Breakfast

| | | 2P: $85-$135 | XP: $20 | D |

Phone: (518)563-8714

Location: I-87, exit 40, 0.5 mi e on SR 456, 0.5 mi s on US 9, then 2.2 mi e. Located next to Point Au Roche State Park. 463 Point Au Roche Rd 12901. **Fax:** 518/561-0332. **Facility:** This B&B offers attractive, individually themed guest rooms; TV's are available on request. Smoke free premises. 9 one-bedroom standard units, some with whirlpools. 2 stories (no elevator), interior corridors. **Bath:** combo or shower only. **Parking:** on-site. **Terms:** 7 day cancellation notice-fee imposed. **Leisure Activities:** Fee: cross country skiing. **Cards:** AX, DC, MC, VI.

SOME UNITS

(A$K) ⊗ ⊗ / ⊗ ⊗ (VCR) /

QUALITY INN

Book at aaa.com

▼▼ 5/1-10/1 [ECP]
10/2-4/30 [ECP]

Motel

| | 1P: $69-$79 | 2P: $69-$79 | | |
| | 1P: $59-$69 | 2P: $59-$69 | | |

Phone: (518)563-0222

Location: I-87, exit 37, just w. 19 Booth Dr 12901. **Fax:** 518/563-5807. **Facility:** 102 units. 101 one- and 1 two-bedroom standard units, some with kitchens and/or whirlpools. 2 stories (no elevator), exterior corridors. **Parking:** on-site, winter plug-ins. **Amenities:** voice mail, irons, hair dryers. **Some:** high-speed Internet. **Pool(s):** outdoor. **Guest Services:** coin laundry. **Cards:** AX, DC, DS, JC, MC, VI.

SOME UNITS

(A$K) (S🄳) (Y+) ⊗ ⊗ (DATA PORT) ⊗ / ⊗ ⊗ ⊗ /

─────── **WHERE TO DINE** ───────

ANTHONY'S RESTAURANT & BISTRO

ⒶⒶⒶ

▼▼▼

Continental

Lunch: $6-$13   **Dinner:** $16-$26   **Phone:** 518/561-6420

Location: I-87, exit 37, just w. 538 Rt 3 12901. **Hours:** 11:30 am-2:30 & 5-9 pm, Fri-10 pm, Sat 5 pm-10 pm, Sun 5 pm-9 pm. Closed major holidays. **Reservations:** suggested. **Features:** Dinner in the cozy and creatively remodeled 150 year old farmhouse may be mustard and herb-crusted salmon, duckling with figs and pears or a choice of steak broiled to your order. Appetizer, soup and salad blend Continental and American cuisine styles. Imaginatively presented dessert such as cheesecake souffle or Belgium chocolate torte are sure to please. Live entertainment in lounge and bistro menu. Dressy casual; cocktails. **Parking:** on-site. **Cards:** AX, CB, DC, DS, MC, VI.

⊗ ⊗

BUTCHER BLOCK STEAK & SEAFOOD

ⒶⒶⒶ

▼▼▼

Steak & Seafood

Lunch: $6-$8   **Dinner:** $11-$20   **Phone:** 518/563-0920

Location: I-87, exit 37. 15 Booth Dr 12901. **Hours:** 11:30 am-3 & 4:30-9:30 pm, Fri & Sat-10 pm. Closed: 11/25, 12/25. **Reservations:** suggested. **Features:** As its name might suggest, the restaurant centers the menu on seafood and steak, particularly succulent prime rib. The atmosphere of the dining room is rustic and cozy, and welcoming to families. Decadent desserts appeal to both eyes and palate. Casual dress; cocktails. **Parking:** on-site. **Cards:** AX, DC, DS, MC, VI.

⊗ ⊗

DOMENIC'S RESTAURANT & LOUNGE

ⒶⒶⒶ

▼▼

Italian

Dinner: $9-$25   **Phone:** 518/563-6980

Location: I-87, exit 39, 0.5 mi s. 7081 Rt 9 N 12901. **Hours:** 4 pm-9 pm, Fri & Sat-10 pm. Closed: 11/25, 12/25. **Reservations:** suggested. **Features:** Bold shades of red, white and green in the dining room give the place a festive atmosphere. Homemade Italian-American fare centers heavily on "surf and turf." Spumoni and tiramisu satisfy a sweet tooth. Casual dress; cocktails. **Parking:** on-site. **Cards:** AX, CB, DC, DS, MC, VI.

⊗ ⊗

IRISES CAFE AND WINE BAR   **Lunch:** $5-$10   **Dinner:** $10-$20   **Phone:** 518/566-7000
American
Location: Corner of Court St; downtown. 20-22 City Hall Pl 12901. **Hours:** 11:30 am-9:30 pm, Fri-10 pm, Sat 4:30 pm-10 pm. Closed: 5/31, 9/6, 12/25; also Sun. **Reservations:** suggested. **Features:** Perhaps the trendiest city eatery, the cafe is a good place for those who want a little something out of the ordinary. The menu is eclectic, with pronounced Mediterranean and Asian influences. A wonderful variety of by-the-glass wines can be had along with a good selection of microbrewed beers. Casual dress; cocktails; entertainment. **Parking:** street. **Cards:** AX, DC, DS, MC, VI.

PORT CHESTER —See New York p. 455.

PORT JEFFERSON pop. 7,837

——— **WHERE TO DINE** ———

25 EAST AMERICAN BISTRO   Country Inn   **Lunch:** $8-$17   **Dinner:** $17-$32   **Phone:** 631/928-5200
American
Location: In village center; adjacent to ferry dock; in Danford's Inn Marina and Conference Center. 25 E Broadway 11777. **Hours:** 7 am-10:30 & 11:30-10 pm, Sat & Sun 8 am-10:30 & 11:30-11 pm. **Reservations:** suggested. **Features:** Overlooking the marina and ferry terminal, the restaurant is decorated with lots of ship memorabilia and nautical accents. Seafood is clearly the focus, with such choices as clams and broiled fish. The casual dining dock has a relaxed, comfortable feel. Casual dress; cocktails. **Parking:** on-site. **Cards:** AX, DC, DS, MC, VI.

PORT JERVIS pop. 8,860

——— **WHERE TO STAY** ———

COMFORT INN   *Book at aaa.com*   **Phone:** (845)856-6611
Small-scale Hotel

5/1-10/31	1P: $90-$180	2P: $90-$180	XP: $8 F18
11/1-4/30	1P: $70-$140	2P: $70-$140	XP: $8 F18

Location: I-84, exit 1, just se. 2247 Greenville Tpke 12771. Fax: 845/856-5299. **Facility:** 103 one-bedroom standard units. 2 stories (no elevator), interior corridors. **Parking:** on-site. **Terms:** 2 night minimum stay - seasonal weekends, [AP], [BP] & [MAP] meal plans available, package plans - seasonal, pets ($20 fee, $50 deposit). **Amenities:** voice mail, irons, hair dryers. **Pool(s):** outdoor. **Leisure Activities:** video games. **Guest Services:** coin laundry. **Business Services:** meeting rooms. **Cards:** AX, CB, DC, DS, JC, MC, VI. **Special Amenities:** free continental breakfast and free local telephone calls. *(See color ad below)*

SOME UNITS

FEE

PORTVILLE pop. 1,024

——— **WHERE TO DINE** ———

SPRAGUE'S MAPLE FARMS PANCAKE
HOUSE & RESTAURANT   **Lunch:** $5-$8   **Dinner:** $8-$16   **Phone:** 716/933-6637
American
Location: I-86, exit 28, 15 mi s; 1 mi n on SR 305; center. 1048 Rt 305 14770. **Hours:** 7 am-8 pm, Fri & Sat-9 pm. Closed: 12/25. **Features:** The new country restaurant's signature recipes are created from maple syrup harvested on the working maple farm. Breakfast is served all day, so a taste of the 100 percent pure maple syrup can be sampled on fluffy pancakes served with double-smoked bacon, country ham or its own recipe of maple sausage patties. Premium, free-range roast turkey from its own farm is used in all dishes. The Friday night buttermilk-battered fish fry is a local favorite. Casual dress; cocktails. **Parking:** on-site. **Cards:** DS, MC, VI.

POTSDAM pop. 9,425

—— WHERE TO STAY ——

THE CLARKSON INN   Phone: 315/265-3050
All Year   1P: $90-$139   2P: $99-$149   XP: $10
Location: Jct US 11 and SR 56; center. 1 Main St 13676. **Fax:** 315/265-5848. **Facility:** Smoke free premises. 40
one-bedroom standard units. 2 stories (no elevator), interior corridors. **Parking:** on-site, winter plug-ins.
Small-scale Hotel **Terms:** 30 day cancellation notice-fee imposed. **Amenities:** voice mail, irons, hair dryers. **Guest Services:**
valet laundry. **Business Services:** meeting rooms. **Cards:** AX, MC, VI.

SOME UNITS

  / VCR /

NORTHERN FAMILY MOTEL   Phone: (315)265-4640
    All Year [ECP]   1P: $46-$49   2P: $55-$59   XP: $5   F5
Location: 2.3 mi n. 6775 State Hwy 56 13676. **Fax:** 315/265-4614. **Facility:** 15 one-bedroom standard units. 1
Motel   story, exterior corridors. **Parking:** on-site, winter plug-ins. **Pool(s):** outdoor. **Cards:** AX, DS, MC, VI.

SOME UNITS

(ASK) (SD) (PORT) / (D) /

THE SMALLING MOTEL SOUTH   Phone: 315/265-0709
All Year [CP]   1P: $51-$54   2P: $56-$61   XP: $5   F6
Location: On US 11 S, 0.5 mi s. 7518 State Hwy 11 13676. **Fax:** 315/265-0709. **Facility:** 16 one-bedroom stan-
Motel   dard units. 1 story, exterior corridors. **Parking:** on-site, winter plug-ins. **Cards:** AX, DS, MC, VI.

SOME UNITS

(ASK) (SD) (PORT) / (X) (D) /

—— WHERE TO DINE ——

CACTUS GRILL AND CANTINA   Dinner: $5-$12   Phone: 315/265-0240
Location: Center. 11 Raymond St 13676. **Hours:** 5 pm-9 pm, Fri & Sat-10 pm. **Closed:** 1/1, 11/25, 12/25.
Reservations: accepted. **Features:** Freshly made Mexican favorites are plated in abundant servings.
Mexican   Festive, sunny decor brightens the dining room and lounge. The staff is friendly and casual. Casual dress;
cocktails. **Parking:** street. **Cards:** AX, MC, VI.

THE LOBSTER HOUSE   Lunch: $5-$8   Dinner: $11-$20   Phone: 315/353-2366
Location: 3 mi n on SR 56. 95 S Main St 13668. **Hours:** 11 am-9:30 pm, Fri & Sat-10:30 pm. **Closed:** 11/25,
12/25. **Reservations:** suggested, weekends. **Features:** Locally famous for fresh seafoods, delicious pasta
Seafood   creations and abundant combination platters. Baby back ribs and prime rib are also favorites served by
friendly wait staff. Casual dress; cocktails. **Parking:** on-site. **Cards:** AX, CB, DS, MC, VI.

MAMA LUCIA   Dinner: $12-$14   Phone: 315/265-0475
Location: Center. 1 Constitution Ave 13676. **Hours:** 5 pm-9 pm, Fri & Sat-10 pm. Closed major holidays.
Reservations: suggested. **Features:** Family-style Italian cuisine is served in this renovated train station.
Italian   Bright, fresh decor is fun and trendy. Wood-oven pizzas and traditional pastas choices are plated in ample
portions and served pass-the-dish, family style. Casual dress; cocktails. **Parking:** on-site. **Cards:** AX,
MC, VI.

MAXFIELDS   Lunch: $6-$9   Dinner: $12-$20   Phone: 315/265-3796
Location: Center. 5-7 Market St 13676. **Hours:** 11:30 am-2:30 & 5-9 pm, Fri & Sat-9:30 pm. Closed major
holidays; also Sun. **Reservations:** accepted. **Features:** Patio diners at the historic brick building can watch
American   the Raquette River lull by while dining on fresh, quality Continental cuisine. Servers are pleasant and
helpful. Casual dress; cocktails. **Parking:** street. **Cards:** AX, MC, VI.

POUGHKEEPSIE pop. 29,871—*See also RED OAKS MILL.*

────── **WHERE TO STAY** ──────

BEST INN *Book at aaa.com* Phone: (845)454-1010
All Year   1P: $80-$120   2P: $90-$140   XP: $6   F12
Location: 2 mi e of Mid-Hudson Bridge on US 44 and SR 55. 536 Haight Ave 12603. Fax: 845/454-0127. **Facility:** 41 one-bedroom standard units. 1-2 stories (no elevator), exterior corridors. *Bath:* combo or shower only. **Parking:** on-site, winter plug-ins. **Terms:** 7 day cancellation notice, [ECP] meal plan available. **Amenities:** voice mail. **Business Services:** meeting rooms, fax (fee). **Cards:** AX, DC, DS, MC, VI. **Special Amenities:** free continental breakfast and free newspaper.
Motel

SOME UNITS

BEST WESTERN INN & CONFERENCE CENTER *Book at aaa.com* Phone: (845)462-4600
All Year   1P: $90-$130   2P: $90-$130   XP: $10   F16
Location: Jct US 44 and SR 55, 4.7 mi s. 2170 South Rd (US 9) 12601. Fax: 845/462-3228. **Facility:** 153 one-bedroom standard units, some with whirlpools. 3 stories (no elevator), interior corridors. **Parking:** on-site. **Terms:** weekly rates available, [ECP] & [MAP] meal plans available, package plans. **Amenities:** voice mail, irons, hair dryers. *Some:* high-speed Internet, fax. **Dining:** 6:30 am-10 & 5-10 pm, Sat 8 am-11 & 5-10 pm, Sun 8 am-noon & 5-10 pm, cocktails. **Pool(s):** outdoor. **Guest Services:** valet and coin laundry. **Business Services:** conference facilities, fax (fee). **Cards:** AX, CB, DC, DS, MC, VI. *(See color ad below)*
Small-scale Hotel

SOME UNITS

HOLIDAY INN EXPRESS *Book at aaa.com* Phone: (845)473-1151
All Year [ECP]   1P: $99-$219   2P: $99-$219   XP: $10   F18
Location: Jct US 44 and SR 55, 1.8 mi s; 1.5 mi s of Mid-Hudson Bridge. 2750 South Rd (US Rt 9) 12601. Fax: 845/485-8127. **Facility:** 121 units. 119 one-bedroom standard units. 2 one-bedroom suites ($250) with whirlpools. 4 stories, interior corridors. *Bath:* combo or shower only. **Parking:** on-site, winter plug-ins. **Terms:** cancellation fee imposed. **Amenities:** video games (fee), voice mail, irons, hair dryers. **Pool(s):** outdoor. **Leisure Activities:** exercise room. **Guest Services:** complimentary laundry. **Business Services:** meeting rooms, fax. **Cards:** AX, CB, DC, DS, JC, MC, VI.
Small-scale Hotel

SOME UNITS

POUGHKEEPSIE GRAND HOTEL AND CONFERENCE CENTER *Book at aaa.com* Phone: (845)485-5300
5/1-10/31   1P: $119-$179   2P: $119-$179   XP: $10   F16
11/1-4/30   1P: $99-$159   2P: $99-$159   XP: $10   F16
Location: Jct US 44 and SR 55 E, just n on Market St. 40 Civic Center Plaza 12601. Fax: 845/485-4720. **Facility:** 200 units. 198 one-bedroom standard units, some with whirlpools. 2 one-bedroom suites ($185-$600) with whirlpools. 10 stories, interior corridors. **Parking:** on-site. **Terms:** check-in 4 pm, [BP] meal plan available. **Amenities:** voice mail, irons, hair dryers. *Fee:* video games, high-speed Internet. *Some:* fax, safes. **Guest Services:** gift shop, valet and coin laundry, area transportation, beauty salon. **Business Services:** conference facilities, business center. **Cards:** AX, DC, DS, MC, VI.
Small-scale Hotel

SOME UNITS

────── **WHERE TO DINE** ──────

CAPPUCINO BY COPPOLA'S Lunch: $5-$12   Dinner: $7-$18   Phone: 845/462-4545
Location: Jct US 44 and SR 55, 3.7 mi s. 2373 South Rd (US 9) 12601. **Hours:** 11:30 am-10 pm, Fri-11 pm, Sat 9 am-11 pm, Sun 10 am-9 pm. Closed: 11/25, 12/25. **Reservations:** suggested. **Features:** In operation since the late 1960s, the casual restaurant is a favorite for home-style, bistro fare. Six small dining rooms offer warmth and cozy comfort. The extensive menu includes several lighter items. Sunday brunch draws a hungry crowd. Casual dress; cocktails. **Parking:** on-site. **Cards:** AX, DC, DS, MC, VI.
Italian

THE HAYMAKER

▼▼▼▼

American

Lunch: $8-$16   **Dinner:** $14-$22   **Phone:** 845/486-9454

Location: Jct US 9 and US 44/SR 55, 4.5 mi e on US 44; in Arlington Plaza. 718 Dutchess Tpke 12603. **Hours:** 11 am-2:30 & 5-9 pm, Fri & Sat-10 pm, Sun 5 pm-9 pm. Closed major holidays. **Reservations:** required. **Features:** The intimate restaurant has a bright, modern look. On the menu is a diverse selection of contemporary American dishes that fuse Southwestern and Asian influences. Portobello fries and grilled flat-iron steak are popular. Casual dress; cocktails. **Parking:** on-site. **Cards:** AX, DC, DS, MC, VI.

O'SHO JAPANESE STEAKHOUSE

▼▼ ▼▼

Japanese

Lunch: $7-$16   **Dinner:** $14-$26   **Phone:** 845/297-0540

Location: Jct US 44 and SR 55, 5.8 mi s; across from Poughkeepsie Galleria Mall. 763 South Rd (US 9) 12601. **Hours:** 11:30 am-2:30 & 5-10 pm, Sat & Sun 3:30 pm-10 pm. Closed: 11/25. **Reservations:** accepted. **Features:** From grill table to yakitori to sushi, the food is fresh and delightful to the taste buds. The country inn exterior changes to Japanese tea house upon entry. The staff is pleasant. Casual dress; cocktails. **Parking:** on-site. **Cards:** AX, DC, DS, MC, VI.

POUND RIDGE —See New York p. 456.

PULASKI pop. 2,398

——— **WHERE TO STAY** ———

REDWOOD MOTEL

AAA SAVE

▼

Motel

Phone: (315)298-4717

	1P: $42-$49	2P: $55-$59	XP: $5	F10
8/30-10/31	1P: $40-$46	2P: $53-$57	XP: $5	F10
7/1-8/29	1P: $39-$45	2P: $52-$56	XP: $5	F10
5/1-6/30 & 11/1-4/30				

Location: I-81, exit 36, just e. 3723 SR 13 13142. Fax: 315/298-4717. **Facility:** 50 units. 49 one-bedroom standard units. 1 one-bedroom suite ($96-$97) with kitchen. 1 story, interior/exterior corridors. **Bath:** combo or shower only. **Parking:** on-site. **Terms:** [CP] meal plan available, pets ($20 deposit). **Dining:** 11 am-9 pm, Fri-10 pm, Sat 8 am-10 pm, Sun 8 am-9 pm. **Pool(s):** outdoor. **Guest Services:** coin laundry. **Business Services:** meeting rooms. **Cards:** AX, MC, VI. **Special Amenities:** free continental breakfast and free local telephone calls.

SOME UNITS

🐾 🍴 🏊 ✕ 🛗 🖼 /   FEE   FEE FEE

——— **WHERE TO DINE** ———

C & M DINER

▼

American

Lunch: $3-$6   **Dinner:** $5-$10   **Phone:** 315/298-5443

Location: I-81, exit 36, just e. 3739 Rome Rd 13142. **Hours:** 5 am-9 pm. Closed: 1/1, 12/25. **Features:** The easily accessible old-fashioned diner is great for a delicious, quick bite. Daily homemade specials and traditional American fare make up the offerings. Casual dress. **Parking:** on-site. **Cards:** DS, MC, VI.

QUEENS —See New York p. 440.

QUEENSBURY pop. 25,441—See also ADIRONDACK MOUNTAINS.

——— **WHERE TO STAY** ———

BROWN'S WELCOME INN MOTEL

AAA SAVE

▼▼ ▼▼

Motel

Phone: 518/792-9576

	1P: $99-$120	2P: $110-$130	XP: $10	
6/21-9/2	1P: $59-$90	2P: $59-$95	XP: $10	
5/16-6/20	1P: $59-$90	2P: $59-$90	XP: $10	
9/3-10/25				

Location: I-87, exit 19, 0.8 mi ne. 932 US 9 Lake George Rd 12804. Fax: 518/792-8072. **Facility:** 20 one-bedroom standard units. 1 story, exterior corridors. **Bath:** combo or shower only. **Parking:** on-site. **Terms:** open 5/16-10/25, 7 day cancellation notice-fee imposed. **Pool(s):** heated outdoor. **Leisure Activities:** gazebo, playground. **Business Services:** fax. **Cards:** AX, DC, DS, MC, VI. *(See color ad p 318)*

SOME UNITS

🅢 🍴 🏊 🛗 💻 / ✕

DAYS INN OF LAKE GEORGE   *Book at aaa.com*

▼▼ ▼▼

Small-scale Hotel

Phone: (518)793-3196

	1P: $116-$186	2P: $116-$186	XP: $10	F16
6/25-9/5	1P: $69-$116	2P: $69-$116	XP: $10	F16
5/1-6/24 & 9/6-4/30				

Location: I-87, exit 20, just n. Located in a commercial area. 1454 US 9 12845. Fax: 518/793-6028. **Facility:** 104 units. 101 one- and 3 two-bedroom standard units. 2 stories, interior/exterior corridors. **Parking:** on-site. **Terms:** 2-5 night minimum stay - seasonal weekends, 21 day cancellation notice-fee imposed. **Amenities:** hair dryers. **Dining:** The Meeting Place, see separate listing. **Pool(s):** heated indoor. **Leisure Activities:** whirlpool. **Guest Services:** valet laundry. **Business Services:** meeting rooms, fax (fee). **Cards:** AX, CB, DC, DS, MC, VI. *(See color ad p 320)*

SOME UNITS

ASK 🅢 🍴 🏊 💈 / ✕ DATA PORT 🛗 /   FEE

DUNHAM'S BAY LODGE

AAA SAVE

▼▼ ▼▼

Motel

Phone: (518)656-9242

	1P: $200	2P: $200	XP: $20	F
5/26-9/3	1P: $100	2P: $100	XP: $20	F
5/1-5/25 & 9/4-10/5				

Location: Jct US 9, 5 mi ne. 2999 SR 9L 12845. Fax: 518/656-9250. **Facility:** 50 units. 38 one- and 2 two-bedroom standard units. 2 one- and 8 two-bedroom suites ($125-$295) with kitchens. 1-3 stories (no elevator), exterior corridors. **Parking:** on-site. **Terms:** open 5/1-10/5, 14 day cancellation notice-fee imposed, weekly rates available. **Amenities:** voice mail, hair dryers. **Dining:** 7 am-11 & 5-9 pm, cocktails. **Pool(s):** heated indoor, wading. **Leisure Activities:** whirlpool, tennis court, lawn games, ping pong, hiking trails, jogging, playground, shuffleboard. **Fee:** game room. **Business Services:** meeting rooms, fax (fee). **Cards:** AX, MC, VI.

SOME UNITS

🅢 🍴 🍸 🏊 🐾 DATA PORT / ✕ VCR 🛗 🖼 💻 /   FEE

ECONO LODGE & SUITES OF GLENS FALLS/LAKE GEORGE
Book at aaa.com **Phone:** 518/793-3700

6/30-9/3	1P: $60-$140	2P: $60-$150	XP: $10 F16
5/1-6/29 & 9/4-4/30	1P: $35-$89	2P: $35-$99	XP: $10 F16

Motel **Location:** I-87, exit 19, just e. 543 Aviation Rd 12804. **Fax:** 518/793-8678. **Facility:** 48 units. 44 one-bedroom standard units. 4 two-bedroom suites ($99-$299) with efficiencies. 2 stories (no elevator), exterior corridors. **Parking:** on-site. **Terms:** cancellation fee imposed. **Amenities:** voice mail, irons, hair dryers. **Cards:** AX, DC, DS, MC, VI.

SOME UNITS

GRAYCOURT MOTEL
Phone: 518/792-0223

6/20-9/20	1P: $85-$98	2P: $110-$125	XP: $5
5/20-6/19	1P: $75-$90	2P: $85-$95	XP: $5

Motel **Location:** I-87, exit 19, 1.3 mi ne. 1082 US 9 12804. **Fax:** 518/792-2003. **Facility:** 25 units. 20 one-bedroom standard units. 5 cottages ($115-$150). 1 story, exterior corridors. *Bath:* combo or shower only. **Parking:** on-site. **Terms:** open 5/20-9/20, 2 night minimum stay - in cottages, 7 day cancellation notice-fee imposed. **Pool(s):** heated outdoor. **Leisure Activities:** picnic area with barbecue grill, playground. **Business Services:** fax. **Cards:** AX, DS, MC, VI. *(See color ad p 320)*

SOME UNITS

MOHICAN MOTEL
Phone: 518/792-0474

6/25-9/6	1P: $105-$145	2P: $105-$145	XP: $10
5/28-6/24	1P: $78-$105	2P: $78-$105	XP: $10
5/1-5/27 & 9/7-10/24	1P: $58-$88	2P: $68-$88	XP: $10

Motel **Location:** I-87, exit 20, 3.5 mi s. (1545 US 9, LAKE GEORGE, 12845). **Fax:** 518/761-4089. **Facility:** 44 units. 14 one- and 22 two-bedroom standard units, some with efficiencies, kitchens and/or whirlpools. 8 two-bedroom suites ($98-$245) with whirlpools. 1-2 stories, exterior corridors. **Parking:** on-site. **Terms:** open 5/1-10/24, 3 night minimum stay - seasonal for suites, 21 day cancellation notice-fee imposed. **Amenities:** voice mail. *Some:* hair dryers. **Pool(s):** outdoor, heated indoor, 2 wading. **Leisure Activities:** sauna, whirlpools, playground, sports court. *Fee:* game room. **Guest Services:** coin laundry. **Business Services:** fax. **Cards:** AX, MC, VI. *(See color ad p 323)*

SOME UNITS

RAMADA INN GLENS FALLS
Book at aaa.com **Phone:** (518)793-7701

7/22-9/5	1P: $159-$169	2P: $169-$179	XP: $10 F
6/1-7/21	1P: $69-$89	2P: $79-$99	XP: $10 F
9/6-4/30	1P: $69-$84	2P: $79-$94	XP: $10 F
5/1-5/31	1P: $59-$79	2P: $69-$79	XP: $10 F

Small-scale Hotel **Location:** I-87, exit 19, just w. 1 Abby Ln 12804. **Fax:** 518/792-5463. **Facility:** 110 one-bedroom standard units. 2 stories (no elevator), interior corridors. **Parking:** on-site, winter plug-ins. **Amenities:** voice mail, irons, hair dryers. **Dining:** 6:30 am-1 & 5-10 pm, cocktails. **Pool(s):** heated indoor. **Business Services:** valet laundry. **Business Services:** meeting rooms. **Cards:** AX, DC, DS, JC, MC, VI. **Special Amenities:** free local telephone calls and free newspaper. *(See color ad p 8)*

SOME UNITS
FEE

RODEWAY INN LAKE GEORGE
Phone: (518)792-5904

7/1-9/7	1P: $89-$99	2P: $129-$149	XP: $10 F12
6/1-6/30	1P: $49-$59	2P: $109-$119	XP: $10 F12
9/8-4/30	1P: $45-$55	2P: $89-$99	XP: $10 F12
5/1-5/31	1P: $39-$89	2P: $49-$99	XP: $10 F12

Motel **Location:** I-87, exit 20, just n; just US 149 and US 9. 1449 US 9 12845. **Fax:** 518/761-6014. **Facility:** 27 units. 22 one-bedroom standard units. 5 one-bedroom suites ($129-$159), some with efficiencies. 1-2 stories (no elevator), exterior corridors. *Bath:* combo or shower only. **Parking:** on-site. **Terms:** 3 day cancellation notice. **Amenities:** voice mail. **Pool(s):** outdoor. **Business Services:** fax (fee). **Cards:** AX, DS, MC, VI.

SOME UNITS

SLEEP INN & SUITES
Book at aaa.com **Phone:** (518)955-3000

All Year [ECP]	1P: $69-$139	XP: $5 F18

Location: I-87, exit 19, 0.3 mi e on Aviation Rd, then 0.5 mi n. 906 Lake George Rd (SR 9) 12804. **Fax:** 518/955-3008. **Facility:** 78 one-bedroom standard units, some with whirlpools. 3 stories, interior corridors. *Bath:* combo or shower only. **Parking:** on-site. **Amenities:** voice mail. *Some:* irons, hair dryers. **Pool(s):** heated indoor. **Leisure Activities:** exercise room, game room. **Guest Services:** coin laundry. **Business Services:** meeting rooms. **Cards:** AX, CB, DC, DS, JC, MC, VI. **Special Amenities:** free expanded continental breakfast and free newspaper.

Small-scale Hotel

SOME UNITS
FEE

WAKITA COURT MOTEL
Phone: (518)792-0326

7/2-9/6	1P: $79-$109	2P: $99-$149	
5/21-7/1	1P: $59-$89	2P: $69-$109	

Cabin **Location:** I-87, exit 19, 1.9 mi ne. 1130 US 9 12804. **Fax:** 518/792-0326. **Facility:** 28 units. 13 one-bedroom standard units. 15 cabins ($79-$179). 1 story, exterior corridors. *Bath:* combo or shower only. **Parking:** on-site. **Terms:** open 5/21-9/6, 7 day cancellation notice-fee imposed. **Pool(s):** heated outdoor. **Leisure Activities:** whirlpool, playground, basketball. **Guest Services:** coin laundry. **Business Services:** fax. **Cards:** AX, DS, MC, VI. **Special Amenities:** free local telephone calls and early check-in/late check-out.

SOME UNITS
FEE

——— WHERE TO DINE ———

THE ADIRONDACK COACH HOUSE   Lunch: $5-$10   Dinner: $13-$24   Phone: 518/743-1575
AAA   **Location:** 4 mi n on US 9. Lake George Rd 12804. **Hours:** 11:30 am-9 pm, Sun from 4 pm; hours may vary
          seasonally. Closed: 12/24, 12/25. **Reservations:** suggested. **Features:** You'll enjoy casual dining in a
          charming rustic atmosphere, complete with a cozy fireplace for winter evenings. The eatery also boasts a
          popular salad bar. Casual dress; cocktails. **Parking:** on-site. **Cards:** AX, CB, DC, DS, MC, VI.
American

CARL R'S CAFE   Lunch: $5-$10   Dinner: $9-$12   Phone: 518/793-7676
AAA   **Location:** I-87, exit 18. 124 Corinth Rd 12804. **Hours:** 7 am-11 pm; to 9 pm, Wed & Thurs-10 pm, Fri & Sat-11
          pm 10/2-5/31; hours may vary. Closed: 11/25, 12/25. **Reservations:** accepted. **Features:** Sombreros are
          not needed to enjoy the Mexican/American flavors at Carl R's. A bustling, casual atmosphere and oversize
American   portions are served everyday from 7 am to late. Complimentary chips and salsa to start and then move on
          to dishes such as chicken fajitas with your choice of toppings, buffalo burgers or steak. Close with a
          selection of dessert from fried ice cream to apple bread pudding. Casual dress; cocktails. **Parking:** on-site.
Cards: AX, CB, DC, DS, MC, VI.

FISHTALES   Lunch: $6-$18   Dinner: $6-$18   Phone: 518/761-7101
          Location: I-87, exit 19, 1.3 mi n. 1036 Rt 9 12804. **Hours:** Open 5/1-12/31 & 3/1-4/30; 11 am-9 pm.
          Features: Steamers, hand-battered seafood and slow-cooked barbecue baby back ribs are just some of
Seafood   the house specialties. Patrons should find room for one of the many delicious flavors of homemade hard
          ice cream. Deck seating is a plus. Casual dress; beer & wine only. **Parking:** on-site. **Cards:** AX, DC, DS,
MC, VI.

FLOWER DRUM SONG RESTAURANT   Lunch: $4-$8   Dinner: $6-$18   Phone: 518/798-0455
          Location: I-87, exit 19, 0.3 mi e on US 9, then 0.5 mi n. 909 SR 9 12804. **Hours:** 11 am-10 pm, Fri & Sat-10:30
          pm, Sun noon-9:30 pm. Closed: 3/27, 11/25, 12/25. **Reservations:** accepted. **Features:** Encounter the
Asian   Orient with the variety of Asian cuisines offered here - traditional Chinese, Szechuan and a few Thai and
          Japanese dishes. The friendly and relaxed service in the pleasant tea house surroundings will delight you.
Casual dress; cocktails. **Parking:** on-site. **Cards:** AX, DC, DS, MC, VI.

GAMBLE'S BAKERY & COFFEE SHOP   Lunch: $3-$8   Phone: 518/793-5384
          Location: I-87, exit 19, 0.3 mi e, then 0.6 mi n. 920 Rt 9 12804. **Hours:** 7 am-3 pm, Sun-2 pm. Closed: 1/1,
          11/25, 12/25. **Features:** Great spot for breakfast, limited seating. Soup and sandwiches also available for
A'merican   lunch. Casual dress. **Parking:** on-site. **Cards:** MC, VI.

LOG JAM   Lunch: $6-$10   Dinner: $13-$22   Phone: 518/798-1155
          Location: Jct US 9 and 149. 1484 US 9 12845. **Hours:** 11:30 am-2:30 & 5-9 pm, Fri & Sat-9:30 pm, Sun 11:30
          am-2:30 & 4:30-9 pm. Closed: 11/25, 12/25. **Reservations:** suggested. **Features:** This restaurant is
American   located in the midst of many popular shopping outlets. Wood floors and beamed ceilings lend to the feeling
          that you're dining in a rustic, Adirondack log cabin. Memorabilia of the logging industry is spread
throughout the dining room. Portions are hearty and the service friendly. Casual dress; cocktails. **Parking:** on-site. **Cards:** AX,
CB, DC, DS, MC, VI.

THE MEETING PLACE   Lunch: $4-$7   Dinner: $12-$20   Phone: 518/792-9565
          Location: I-87, exit 20, just n; in Days Inn of Lake George. 1454 SR 9 12845. **Hours:** 7 am-10 pm. Closed: 11/25,
          12/24, 12/25. **Features:** Pizza from a wood-fired brick oven and well-prepared specials are favorites at the
American   casual, cafe-style restaurant. A glassed atrium on each side of the dining room lends warmth. Homemade
          dessert and gourmet coffee are fitting toppers to any meal. Casual dress; cocktails. **Parking:** on-site.
Cards: AX, CB, DC, DS, MC, VI.

SUTTON'S COUNTRY CAFE   Lunch: $4-$8   Dinner: $9-$16   Phone: 518/798-1188
          Location: I-87, exit 19, 1.3 mi ne. 1066 Rt 9 (Lake George Rd) 12804. **Hours:** 7:30 am-3 pm, Fri also 5 pm-8:30
          pm. Closed major holidays. **Features:** Knickknacks and dishes line the shelves around the cozy dining
American   room, which has the aura of a friendly country cafe. The menu revolves around home-style dishes, such as
          chicken pot pie and pot roast. Particularly tempting are the fresh bread and pie. Casual dress; cocktails.
Parking: on-site. **Cards:** AX, DC, DS, MC, VI.

RANDOLPH pop. 1,316

——— WHERE TO DINE ———

R & M RESTAURANT   Lunch: $5-$6   Dinner: $7-$10   Phone: 716/358-5141
          Location: I-87, exit 16, just n. 265 Main St 14772. **Hours:** 6 am-10 pm; hours vary in winter. Closed: 1/1, 3/27,
          12/25. **Features:** Comfort food is no exaggeration at the neat-as-a-pin diner. Easy-on, easy-off access
American   makes this place a convenient spot for a satisfying meal. Casual dress. **Parking:** on-site. **Cards:** AX, DS,
          MC, VI.

RAY BROOK

——— WHERE TO DINE ———

TAIL O' THE PUP   Lunch: $5-$15   Dinner: $5-$15   Phone: 518/891-0777
          Location: Center. SR 86. **Hours:** Open 5/1-10/25; 10 am-10:30 pm. **Reservations:** not accepted.
          Features: Locals and visitors alike flock here to savor the famous smokehouse-barbecued chicken and
Barbecue   ribs. It's a "roll up your sleeves and dig in" type of place. Casual dress; cocktails; entertainment. **Parking:**
          on-site. **Cards:** MC, VI.

RED CREEK pop. 521

─────── **WHERE TO STAY** ───────

BLACK CREEK FARM B & B
6/2-9/10 & 12/16-4/30 [BP]　　　1P: $85　　　　2P: $90　　　　　　**Phone:** (315)947-5282
5/1-6/1 & 9/11-12/15 [BP]　　　　1P: $75　　　　2P: $80　　　　　　XP: $25
XP: $25
Bed & Breakfast　**Location:** 0.8 mi w of SR 104A. Located in a quiet, secluded area. 13615 Mixer Rd 13143 (PO Box 390, FAIR HAVEN, 13064). Fax: 315/947-5282. **Facility:** Secluded grounds and a stocked pond enhance this 1888 farmhouse filled with antique collections including Victorian-style dolls and tea sets. Smoke free premises. 4 one-bedroom standard units. 2 stories (no elevator), interior corridors. *Bath:* some shared or private, combo or shower only. **Parking:** on-site. **Terms:** 2-3 night minimum stay - weekends & seasonal, age restrictions may apply, 14 day cancellation notice-fee imposed, weekly rates available. **Amenities:** video library, hair dryers. **Leisure Activities:** fishing, hiking trails. **Guest Services:** TV in common area. **Business Services:** fax. **Cards:** MC, VI.

⊠ 🕮 💈 ☎

RED HOOK —See New York p. 456.

RED OAKS MILL pop. 4,930—See also POUGHKEEPSIE.

─────── **WHERE TO STAY** ───────

INN AT THE FALLS
All Year [ECP]　　　　　　　　　　　2P: $170-$205　　　　XP: $10　　　　　**Phone:** (845)462-5770
F18
Location: Jct SR 376 and CR 113, just se. 50 Red Oaks Mill Rd (CR 44) 12603 (50 Red Oaks Mill Rd (CR 44), POUGH-KEEPSIE), Fax: 845/462-5943. **Facility:** 36 units. 24 one-bedroom standard units. 12 one-bedroom suites with whirlpools. 2 stories, interior corridors. **Parking:** on-site. **Amenities:** voice mail, safes, irons, hair dryers.
Small-scale Hotel　**Leisure Activities:** fishing, exercise room. *Fee:* game room. **Guest Services:** complimentary evening beverages: Sun-Thurs. **Business Services:** meeting rooms, business center. **Cards:** AX, DC, DS, MC, VI.
Special Amenities: free expanded continental breakfast and free local telephone calls.

SOME UNITS
[S/D] ⊠ [VCR] 💈 [DATA PORT] / ⊠ 🖃 /

RHINEBECK pop. 3,077

─────── **WHERE TO STAY** ───────

BEEKMAN ARMS & DELAMATER INN AND CONFERENCE CENTER　　　　　　**Phone:** 845/876-7077
All Year [ECP]　　　　　　1P: $115-$250　　　　2P: $115-$250　　　　XP: $15
Location: Jct US 9 and SR 308. 6387 Mill St (Rt 9) 12572. Fax: 845/876-7077. **Facility:** The property's well-furnished accommodations, some with fireplaces, occupy a main inn as well as several guest houses. 63
Historic　units. 57 one-bedroom standard units. 6 one-bedroom suites. 1-3 stories (no elevator), interior/exterior corri-
Country Inn　dors. *Bath:* combo or shower only. **Parking:** on-site. **Terms:** 2 night minimum stay - weekends in season, 7 day cancellation notice-fee imposed, pets (in designated units). **Amenities:** voice mail, hair dryers. **Dining:** The Traphagen Restaurant, see separate listing. **Business Services:** meeting rooms, fax (fee). **Cards:** AX, DC, DS, MC, VI.

SOME UNITS
🐏 🍴 🍸 🖧 💈 [DATA PORT] / ⊠ 🖃 🖃 🖃 /
FEE

─────── **WHERE TO DINE** ───────

THE TRAPHAGEN RESTAURANT　Historic　　　**Lunch:** $7-$12　　　**Dinner:** $19-$26　　**Phone:** 845/876-1766
Location: Jct US 9 and SR 308; in Beekman Arms & Delamater Inn and Conference Center. 6387 Mill St 12572.
Hours: 11:30 am-3 & 5:30-9 pm, Fri & Sat-9:30 pm, Sun 10:30 am-2 & 4-8:30 pm.
Regional American　**Reservations:** suggested, weekends. **Features:** A wide selection of seafood, duck, pork and chicken is offered, and the Traphagen filet is popular. The 1766 inn has the feel of a cozy tavern, with Colonial furnishings and a charming pewter room. The creative menu changes seasonally. Casual dress; cocktails. **Parking:** on-site.
Cards: AX, CB, DC, DS, MC, VI.

🍸 ⊠

─────── The following restaurant has not been evaluated by AAA ───────
but is listed for your information only.

TERRAPIN　　　　　　　　　　　　　　　　　　　　　　　　　　　**Phone:** 845/876-3330
[fyi]　　　Not evaluated. **Location:** Jct Montgomery St (US 9) and Livingston. 6426 Montgomery St 12572. **Features:** After a drive in the countryside, settle in to choose from 100-plus wines and a wide range of food offerings prepared by Chef Kroner. Dishes distinctively blend classical French with Southwestern, Italian and Asian influences.

🍸

RICHFIELD SPRINGS pop. 1,255

─────── **WHERE TO STAY** ───────

FOUNTAIN VIEW MOTEL　　　　　　　　　　　　　　　　　　　　　　**Phone:** 315/858-1360
6/11-9/6　　　　　　1P: $72-$95　　　　2P: $72-$95　　　　XP: $6
9/7-12/1　　　　　　1P: $49-$72　　　　2P: $49-$72　　　　XP: $6
5/1-6/10 & 4/1-4/30　1P: $49-$59　　　　2P: $49-$59　　　　XP: $6
Location: 1 mi e. 3607 US 20 13439. **Facility:** Smoke free premises. 16 one-bedroom standard units. 1 story,
Motel　exterior corridors. **Parking:** on-site. **Terms:** open 5/1-12/1 & 4/1-4/30, office hours 7 am-10:30 pm, 3 day cancellation notice-fee imposed. **Cards:** DS, MC, VI. **Special Amenities:** free local telephone calls.
(See color ad p 270)

⊠ 🖃 🖃

STONY BROOK MOTEL

Phone: (315)858-9929

[AAA] [SAVE]

6/13-9/5	1P: $75-$90	2P: $85-$95	XP: $5	F18
5/1-6/12 & 9/6-4/30	1P: $55-$75	2P: $60-$80	XP: $5	F18

Motel

Location: 0.5 mi e on US 20. 232 Main St (Rt 20) 13439 (PO Box 1849). Fax: 607/547-5671. **Facility:** 7 one-bedroom standard units. 1 story, exterior corridors. *Bath:* shower only. **Parking:** on-site, winter plug-ins. **Terms:** 5 day cancellation notice. **Cards:** AX, DC, MC, VI. **Special Amenities:** free local telephone calls and free room upgrade (subject to availability with advanced reservations).

SOME UNITS

[S] [H+] [icons] / [X] /

VILLAGE MOTEL

Phone: (315)858-1540

[AAA] [SAVE]

6/13-9/6	1P: $90-$95	2P: $100-$110	XP: $6
9/7-10/31	1P: $55-$65	2P: $65-$75	XP: $6
5/1-6/12	1P: $55-$60	2P: $59-$75	XP: $6
11/1-4/30	1P: $55-$65	2P: $59-$70	XP: $6

Motel

Location: Center. 168 Main St (Rt 20) 13439 (PO Box 766). 1 story, exterior corridors. **Parking:** on-site, winter plug-ins. **Terms:** 5 day cancellation notice-fee imposed. **Cards:** AX, DS, MC, VI. **Special Amenities:** free local telephone calls and free room upgrade (subject to availability with advanced reservations).

SOME UNITS

[S] [H+] [icons] / [X] /

——— **WHERE TO DINE** ———

TALLY-HO RESTAURANT

Lunch: $5-$7   **Dinner:** $7-$11   **Phone:** 315/858-0180

American

Location: On US 20; center. 156 Main St 13439. **Hours:** 5 am-7:30 pm, Fri-8:30 pm, Sat-8 pm, Sun-3 pm; winter hours vary. Closed: 1/1, 12/25. **Features:** In the center of town, the casual eatery makes delicious hot and cold sandwiches to order. All-American favorites, along with daily specials, make up the menu. Casual dress. **Parking:** on-site. **Cards:** DS, MC, VI.

[X]

RICHMONDVILLE pop. 786

——— **WHERE TO STAY** ———

ECONO LODGE COBLESKILL/RICHMONDVILLE

Book at aaa.com   **Phone:** (518)294-7739

7/1-9/4	1P: $99-$175	2P: $99-$175	XP: $10	F
9/5-4/30	1P: $59-$99	2P: $59-$99	XP: $10	F
5/1-6/30	1P: $59-$80	2P: $59-$80	XP: $10	F

Motel

Location: I-88, exit 20, just e on SR 7, then just s. 555 Ploss Rd 12149 (PO Box 119). Fax: 518/294-3286. **Facility:** 28 one-bedroom standard units, some with kitchens. 2 stories (no elevator), exterior corridors. *Bath:* combo or shower only. **Parking:** on-site. **Terms:** cancellation fee imposed, pets ($10 extra charge, with prior approval, in designated units). **Cards:** AX, DC, DS, MC, VI.

SOME UNITS

[ASK] [S] [icons] [DATA PORT] [icons] / [X] /
                    FEE

RIVERHEAD pop. 10,513

——— **WHERE TO STAY** ———

BEST WESTERN EAST END

Book at aaa.com   **Phone:** (631)369-2200

5/1-9/30 [ECP]	1P: $149-$229	2P: $149-$229	
10/1-4/30 [ECP]	1P: $139-$169	2P: $139-$169	

Small-scale Hotel

Location: I-495, exit 72 (SR 25 E). Located in a commercial area. 1830 SR 25 11901. Fax: 631/369-1202. **Facility:** 100 units. 99 one-bedroom standard units. 1 one-bedroom suite with whirlpool. 2 stories, interior corridors. *Bath:* combo or shower only. **Parking:** on-site. **Terms:** cancellation fee imposed, small pets only ($50 fee). **Amenities:** video games (fee), voice mail, irons, hair dryers. **Pool(s):** outdoor. **Leisure Activities:** exercise room. **Guest Services:** valet laundry. **Business Services:** meeting rooms. **Cards:** AX, DC, DS, MC, VI.

SOME UNITS

[ASK] [S] [icons] [icons] [DATA PORT] [icons] / [X] [icons] /
                    FEE   FEE FEE

——— **WHERE TO DINE** ———

DIGGER'S FINE FOOD & SPIRITS

Lunch: $5-$20   **Dinner:** $5-$20   **Phone:** 631/369-3200

American

Location: Jct Griffing Ave. 58 W Main St 11901. **Hours:** 11:30 am-10 pm. Closed: 11/25, 12/25. **Features:** A mixed menu, generous portions and efficient, friendly, casual service keep locals returning to the restaurant, which at times fosters a boisterous atmosphere. Casual dress; cocktails. **Parking:** on-site. **Cards:** AX, DS, MC, VI.

[Y] [X]

STAR CONFECTIONERY

Lunch: $5-$10   **Phone:** 631/727-9873

American

Location: Jct Roanoke Ave. 4 E Main St 11901. **Hours:** 7 am-3 pm. Closed major holidays. **Features:** The original pressed-tin ceiling, wooden booths and soda counter with stools create a unique atmosphere of a bygone era. Diners can enjoy a hearty breakfast from the open grill or simply indulge in a sundae topped the way they like it. Casual dress. **Parking:** street.

[X]

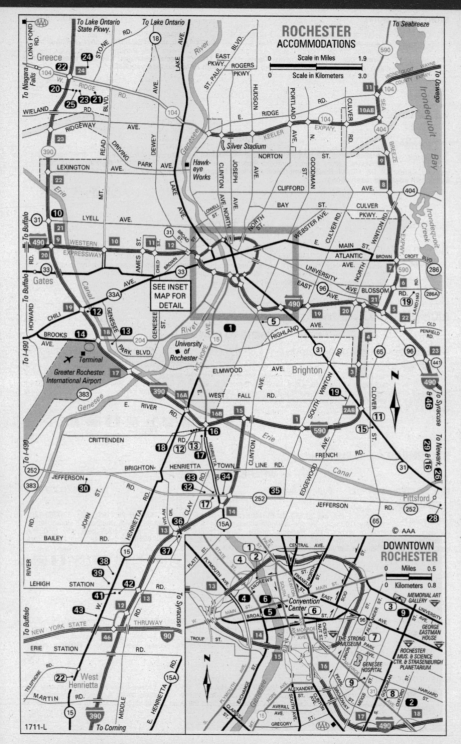

ROCHESTER
ACCOMMODATIONS

DOWNTOWN
ROCHESTER

© AAA

1711-L

✈ Airport Accommodations

Spotter/Map Page Number	OA	GREATER ROCHESTER INTERNATIONAL	Diamond Rating	Rate Range High Season	Listing Page
14 / p. 550		Comfort Inn Central, across from terminal	◆◆	$74-$94	295
13 / p. 550	AAA	**Holiday Inn-Rochester Airport, 0.3 mi e of terminal**	◆◆◆	$131-$141 SAVE	295

Rochester and Vicinity

This index helps you "spot" where approved accommodations and restaurants are located on the corresponding detailed maps. Lodging rate ranges are for comparison only and show the property's high season; rates are per night, unless only weekly (W) rates are available. Restaurant rate range is for dinner, unless only lunch (L) is served. Turn to the listing page for more detailed rate information and consult display ads for special promotions.

Spotter/Map Page Number	OA	ROCHESTER - Lodgings	Diamond Rating	Rate Range High Season	Listing Page
1 / p. 550		428 Mt. Vernon	◆◆◆	$110-$125	553
2 / p. 550		A Bed and Breakfast at Dartmouth House	◆◆◆	$95-$150	553
4 / p. 550	AAA	**Crowne Plaza Hotel and Resort Rochester**	◆◆◆	$69-$139 SAVE	553
5 / p. 550		Clarion Riverside Hotel	◆◆	$71-$139	553
6 / p. 550	AAA	**Hyatt Regency Rochester**	◆◆◆	$89-$189 SAVE	554
9 / p. 550		Strathallan	◆◆◆	$179-$325	554
10 / p. 550	AAA	**The Best Western Diplomat Hotel**	◆◆	$75-$105 SAVE	553
		ROCHESTER - Restaurants			
① / p. 550		Tapas 177	◆◆	$9-$24	555
② / p. 550		Sienna Contemporary Grill and Bar	◆◆◆	$18-$30	555
③ / p. 550		Cutler's Restaurant at the Gallery	◆◆	$16-$25	554
④ / p. 550		Triphammer Grill	◆◆	$17-$25	555
⑤ / p. 550		India House Restaurant	◆	$8-$16	555
⑥ / p. 550	AAA	**The Grill at Strathallan**	◆◆◆◆	$19-$30	555
⑦ / p. 550		The Rio Bamba	◆◆◆◆	$23-$28	555
⑧ / p. 550		Alladin's Natural Eatery	◆	$4-$8	554
⑨ / p. 550		Raj Mahal	◆	$9-$17	555
		GATES - Lodgings			
12 / p. 550		Motel 6 Rochester-Airport #1221	◆	$38-$66	295
13 / p. 550	AAA	**Holiday Inn-Rochester Airport** - see color ad p 554	◆◆◆	$131-$141 SAVE	295
14 / p. 550		Comfort Inn Central	◆◆	$74-$94	295
		BRIGHTON - Lodgings			
16 / p. 550	AAA	**Hampton Inn-Rochester South**	◆◆◆	$104-$164 SAVE	235
17 / p. 550	AAA	**Wellesley Inn (Rochester/South)** - see color ad p 553	◆◆	$55-$105 SAVE	235
18 / p. 550		Courtyard by Marriott Brighton	◆◆◆	$99-$134	235
19 / p. 550	AAA	**Towpath Motel**	◆	$50-$85 SAVE	235
		BRIGHTON - Restaurants			
⑪ / p. 550		Mario's Via Abruzzi	◆◆◆	$13-$26	235
⑫ / p. 550	AAA	**Phillips European Restaurant**	◆◆◆	$9-$25	236
⑬ / p. 550		Bazil	◆◆	$8-$18	235

Spotter/Map Page Number	OA	BRIGHTON - Restaurants (continued)	Diamond Rating	Rate Range High Season	Listing Page
⑮ / p. 550		Mundo Grill	◆◆	$13-$19	236
		GREECE - Lodgings			
⑳ / p. 550		Courtyard by Marriott-Rochester West	◆◆◆	$99-$129	298
㉑ / p. 550	AAA	**Comfort Inn-West**	◆◆	$64-$84 SAVE	298
㉒ / p. 550		Marriott Airport Hotel	◆◆◆	$94-$180	298
㉓ / p. 550	AAA	**Wellesley Inn (Rochester/North) -** see color ad p 553	◆◆	$55-$105 SAVE	299
㉔ / p. 550		Hampton Inn-Rochester North	◆◆◆	$99-$109	298
㉕ / p. 550		Residence Inn by Marriott-West	◆◆◆	$109-$219	299
		PITTSFORD - Lodgings			
㉖ / p. 550		Brookwood Inn Rochester/Pittsford	◆◆◆	$89-$139	539
㉘ / p. 550		The Del Monte Lodge A Renaissance Hotel	◆◆◆	$179-$194	539
		PITTSFORD - Restaurant			
⑯ / p. 550		Richardson's Canal House	◆◆◆	$18-$28	539
		FAIRPORT - Lodgings			
㉙ / p. 550		The Lodge At Woodcliff	◆◆◆	$118-$155	286
		HENRIETTA - Lodgings			
㉚ / p. 550	AAA	**Radisson Hotel Rochester Airport -** see color ad p 305, p 413	◆◆◆	$89 SAVE	305
㉜ / p. 550	AAA	**Ramada Inn Rochester -** see color ad p 8	◆◆	$79 SAVE	306
㉝ / p. 550		Econo Lodge-Rochester South	◆◆	$54-$82	304
㉞ / p. 550		Holiday Inn South	◆◆◆	$89-$122	305
㉟ / p. 550		Residence Inn by Marriott	◆◆◆	$116-$189	306
㊱ / p. 550		Homewood Suites by Hilton-Rochester/Henrietta	◆◆◆	$119-$135	305
㊲ / p. 550		Comfort Suites of Rochester	◆◆◆	$89-$109	304
㊳ / p. 550	AAA	**Country Inn & Suites By Carlson -** see color ad p 554	◆◆◆	$99-$189 SAVE	304
㊴ / p. 550		Fairfield Inn by Marriott-Rochester/South	◆◆◆	$94-$104	305
㊶ / p. 550	AAA	**Red Roof Inn-Henrietta**	◆◆	$52-$75 SAVE	306
㊷ / p. 550	AAA	**Microtel-Rochester**	◆◆	$49-$69 SAVE	305
㊸ / p. 550		R I T Inn & Conference Center	◆◆◆	$85-$115	306
		HENRIETTA - Restaurant			
⑰ / p. 550		Bugaboo Creek Steak House	◆◆	$6-$18	306
		PENFIELD - Lodgings			
㊻ / p. 550		Courtyard By Marriott	◆◆◆	$99-$134	538
		PENFIELD - Restaurant			
⑲ / p. 550		Daisy Flour Mill	◆◆◆	$9-$25	538
		WEST HENRIETTA - Restaurant			
㉒ / p. 550	AAA	**The Cartwright Inn**	◆◆	$13-$20	596

ROCHESTER pop. 219,773   (See map and index starting on p. 550)

——— WHERE TO STAY ———

428 MT. VERNON

▼▼▼

Historic Bed & Breakfast

All Year [BP]   1P: $110   2P: $125   XP: $15

Phone: (585)271-0792   **1**

Location: I-490, exit 15 eastbound, 1 mi s on South Ave, just e on Rockingham, then just s on Doctor's Rd; exit 17 westbound, 0.6 mi s on Goodman St, 0.3 mi w on Rockingham, then just s on Mt. Vernon to Doctor's Rd. Located next to University Rochester Medical & Highland Park. 428 Mt Vernon Ave 14620. Fax: 585/271-0946. **Facility:** On two wooded acres next to a large park, this 1917 home has attractive, individually decorated rooms. 7 one-bedroom standard units. 3 stories (no elevator), interior corridors. *Bath:* combo or shower only. **Parking:** on-site. **Terms:** 2 night minimum stay - weekends 1/1-11/30, age restrictions may apply, package plans - 12/1-3/31. **Amenities:** hair dryers. **Cards:** AX, DC, MC, VI.

SOME UNITS
[DATA PORT] / [⊠] /

A BED AND BREAKFAST AT DARTMOUTH HOUSE

▼▼▼

Historic Bed & Breakfast

5/1-12/28 & 3/31-4/30 [BP]   1P: $95-$115   2P: $125-$150   XP: $25

Phone: (585)271-7872   **2**

Location: I-490, exit 18, just w on SR 31 W (Monroe Ave), then just n. 215 Dartmouth St 14607. Fax: 585/473-0778. **Facility:** The five-course, gourmet, candlelight breakfast is a highlight at this 1905 English Tudor home, part of a Victorian neighborhood near several museums. Smoke free premises. 4 units. 3 one- and 1 two-bedroom standard units. 3 stories (no elevator), interior corridors. *Bath:* combo or shower only. **Parking:** on-site. **Terms:** open 5/1-12/28 & 3/31-4/30, age restrictions may apply. **Amenities:** video library, irons, hair dryers. **Business Services:** PC, fax. **Cards:** AX, CB, DC, DS, MC, VI.

[⊠] [VCR] [🎥] [DATA PORT]

THE BEST WESTERN DIPLOMAT HOTEL   *Book at aaa.com*

(AAA) (SAVE)

▼▼▼

Small-scale Hotel

All Year   1P: $75-$95   2P: $85-$105   XP: $10

Phone: 585/254-1000   **10**
F16

Location: I-390, exit 21, just e on SR 31. 1956 Lyell Ave 14606. Fax: 585/254-1510. **Facility:** 90 one-bedroom standard units, some with whirlpools. 5 stories, interior corridors. **Parking:** on-site. **Terms:** 1-2 night minimum stay - seasonal, cancellation fee imposed, [CP] meal plan available. **Amenities:** voice mail, irons, hair dryers. **Business Services:** meeting rooms, fax (fee). **Cards:** AX, DC, DS, MC, VI. **Special Amenities:** free continental breakfast.

SOME UNITS
[S/D] [🍴+] [🛎+] [🎥] [DATA PORT] [🖥] / [⊠] [🛏] [🖨] /
FEE

CLARION RIVERSIDE HOTEL   *Book at aaa.com*

▼▼▼▼

Large-scale Hotel

All Year   1P: $71-$139   2P: $71-$139

Phone: (585)546-6400   **5**

Location: Downtown. Located opposite the convention center. 120 E Main St 14604. Fax: 585/546-1341. **Facility:** 466 units. 458 one-bedroom standard units. 8 one-bedroom suites ($175-$999). 15 stories, interior corridors. *Bath:* some combo or shower only. **Parking:** on-site (fee). **Terms:** cancellation fee imposed, [AP], [BP], [CP] & [MAP] meal plans available. **Amenities:** *Some:* voice mail, safes, irons, hair dryers. **Pool(s):** heated outdoor. **Leisure Activities:** sauna, exercise room. *Fee:* massage. **Guest Services:** gift shop, valet and coin laundry, area transportation. **Business Services:** conference facilities, business center. **Cards:** AX, CB, DC, DS, JC, MC, VI.

SOME UNITS
[ASK] [S/D] [✈] [🍴] [24🍴] [⊡] [♿M] [🏃] [🏊] [⊠] [🎥] / [⊠] [🐕] [📺] [DATA PORT] [🗄] [🛏] [🖨] [🖥] /

CROWNE PLAZA HOTEL AND RESORT ROCHESTER   *Book at aaa.com*

(AAA) (SAVE)

▼▼▼▼

Large-scale Hotel

All Year   1P: $69-$139   2P: $69-$139   XP: $10

Phone: (585)546-3450   **4**
F

Location: Downtown. 70 State St 14614. Fax: 585/546-8712. **Facility:** 362 units. 356 one-bedroom standard units. 5 one- and 2 two-bedroom suites. 7 stories, interior corridors. **Parking:** on-site (fee). **Amenities:** voice mail, irons, hair dryers. *Fee:* video library, video games. *Some:* CD players, dual phone lines. **Dining:** 6 am-2 & 4-11 pm, cocktails. **Pool(s):** heated outdoor. **Leisure Activities:** sauna, exercise room. **Guest Services:** gift shop, valet laundry, area transportation-train & bus stations. **Business Services:** conference facilities, business center. **Cards:** AX, DC, DS, MC, VI.

SOME UNITS
[S/D] [✈] [🍴] [24🍴] [⊡] [🏃] [🏊] [🎥] [DATA PORT] [🖥] / [⊠] [🛏] [🖨] /

(See map and index starting on p. 550)

HYATT REGENCY ROCHESTER   *Book at aaa.com*   **Phone:** (585)546-1234   **6**
AAA SAVE   All Year   1P: $89-$189   2P: $89-$189   XP: $25   F18
VVVV   **Location:** Downtown. Located next to the convention center, connected by skywalk. 125 E Main St 14604.
Large-scale Hotel   **Fax:** 585/546-6777. **Facility:** 336 one-bedroom standard units. 25 stories, interior corridors. *Bath:* combo or shower only. **Parking:** on-site (fee). **Terms:** cancellation fee imposed. **Amenities:** voice mail, irons, hair dryers. *Some:* fax. **Dining:** 6:30 am-10 pm, cocktails. **Pool(s):** heated indoor. **Leisure Activities:** whirlpool, accessible pool lift, exercise room. **Guest Services:** sundries, valet laundry. **Business Services:** conference facilities, business center. **Cards:** AX, CB, DC, DS, JC, MC, VI.

SOME UNITS
🛬 🍴 🍸 🕭M 🐕 🕬 🏊 ✕ 🛒 📠 📷 / ✕ VCR 🔌 /
                                                              FEE FEE

STRATHALLAN   *Book at aaa.com*   **Phone:** (585)461-5010   **9**
VVVV   All Year   1P: $179-$325   2P: $189-$325
Small-scale Hotel   **Location:** I-490, exit 17, 0.8 mi n on Goodman, then just w. 550 East Ave 14607. **Fax:** 585/461-3387. **Facility:** 156 units. 80 one-bedroom standard units. 73 one- and 3 two-bedroom suites, some with efficiencies. 9 stories, interior corridors. **Parking:** on-site. **Amenities:** video games, dual phone lines, voice mail, safes (fee), irons, hair dryers. **Dining:** The Grill at Strathallan, see separate listing. **Leisure Activities:** sauna, exercise room. **Guest Services:** valet and coin laundry. **Business Services:** conference facilities. **Cards:** AX, CB, DC, DS, MC, VI.

SOME UNITS
ASK 🔒 🛬 🍴 🍸 📷 📠 🔌 🖨 📷 📷 / ✕ /

——— WHERE TO DINE ———

ALLADIN'S NATURAL EATERY   **Lunch:** $4-$8   **Dinner:** $4-$8   **Phone:** 585/442-5000   **8**
VV   **Location:** Between Oxford and Goodman. 646 Monroe Ave 14607. **Hours:** 11 am-10 pm, Fri & Sat-11 pm, Sun
Greek   noon-10 pm. Closed: 3/27, 11/25, 12/25. **Features:** Generous servings of fresh, healthy Greek/Mediterranean meals from an extensive list of choices are tempting and delicious. Casual dress; beer & wine only. **Parking:** on-site. **Cards:** AX, DS, MC, VI.
✕

CUTLER'S RESTAURANT AT THE GALLERY   **Lunch:** $8-$11   **Dinner:** $16-$25   **Phone:** 585/473-6380   **3**
VV   **Location:** I-490, exit University Ave/Main St, 1.8 mi ne. 500 University Ave 14607. **Hours:** 11:30 am-2:30 pm, Sun
American   11 am-2 pm, Tues & Sat also 5 pm-8:30 pm. Closed major holidays; also Mon. **Reservations:** suggested.
Features: In the Memorial Art Gallery, the two-tiered restaurant offers a creative menu of popular American entrees served in an elegant atmosphere amid lovely artwork. Casual dress; cocktails. **Parking:** on-site.
Cards: AX, DC, MC, VI.
✕

(See map and index starting on p. 550)

THE GRILL AT STRATHALLAN   **Lunch:** $6-$14   **Dinner:** $19-$30   **Phone:** 585/454-1880   6
AAA
▼▼▼▼ ▼▼▼▼
Nouvelle
American

Location: I-490, exit 17, 0.8 mi n on Goodman, then just w; in Strathallan. 550 East Ave 14607. **Hours:** 6:30-10:30 am, 11:30-2:30 & 5-11 pm, Fri & Sat-midnight, Sun 6:30 am-2:30 & 5-11 pm. **Reservations:** suggested. **Features:** The lush, downtown restaurant offers a casually elegant atmosphere accompanied by impeccable service. The view across the canal competes with Chef Jason Soul's dishes, which delight both the eye and palate. Appetizers appear as art forms, and entrees include such delectable preparations as mustard-crusted salmon, filets of venison and giant scallops wrapped in leeks. Desserts made to entice include mocha creme brulee and three-berry shortcake. The wine list is extensive. Dressy casual; cocktails. **Parking:** on-site and valet. **Cards:** AX, CB, DC, DS, MC, VI.   ⦿ ⦻

INDIA HOUSE RESTAURANT   **Lunch:** $8-$9   **Dinner:** $8-$16   **Phone:** 585/461-0880   5
▼▼▼
Indian

Location: I-490, exit 17, sw to Clinton Ave, then just s. 998 S Clinton Ave 14620. **Hours:** 11:30 am-2:30 & 5-9:30 pm, Fri & Sat-10 pm. Closed: 7/4, 11/25, 12/25. **Reservations:** suggested. **Features:** Piquant flavors, pungent aromas and distinctive spices combine in delicious dishes, such as aloo samosa and curried lamb. Tapestries, paintings and carvings are examples of Indian art in the large but intimate dining room. Servers are attentive. Casual dress; cocktails. **Parking:** on-site. **Cards:** AX, DC, DS, MC, VI.   ⦻

RAJ MAHAL   **Lunch:** $8   **Dinner:** $9-$17   **Phone:** 585/546-2315   9
▼▼▼
Indian

Location: I-490, exit 18, 0.5 mi e. 324 Monroe Ave 14607. **Hours:** 11:30 am-2:30 & 5-10 pm. Closed major holidays. **Reservations:** suggested, weekends. **Features:** Patrons can feel like an Indian raja as they dine on well-seasoned curry, brightly colored chicken tandoori, beef samosa, lamb or one of a large selection of vegetarian dishes. Homemade ice cream in such flavors as mango and pistachio will cool down diners if the chutneys were overly "warm." Relaxed service and a warm, casual atmosphere make for a pleasant meal. Casual dress; cocktails. **Parking:** on-site. **Cards:** AX, DC, DS, MC, VI.   ⦻

THE RIO BAMBA   **Dinner:** $23-$28   **Phone:** 585/244-8680   7
▼▼▼ ▼▼▼
Continental

Location: Downtown. 282 Alexander St 14607. **Hours:** 5:30 pm-10 pm. Closed major holidays; also Sun. **Reservations:** suggested. **Features:** An exotic, romantic atmosphere surrounds you as you enjoy French-inspired Mediterranean cuisine. A favorite is the Crab Louis salad, so fresh and nicely presented. Two tasting menus are offered daily for a sampling of the chef's expertise. Dressy casual; cocktails. **Parking:** valet. **Cards:** AX, DC, DS, MC, VI.   ⦿ ⦻

SIENNA CONTEMPORARY GRILL AND BAR   **Dinner:** $18-$30   **Phone:** 585/546-4070   2
▼▼▼
Continental

Location: Corner of St. Paul St and South Ave; downtown. 151 St. Paul St 14604. **Hours:** 5 pm-10 pm, Fri & Sat-11 pm, Sun 4 pm-9 pm. Closed: 11/25, 12/25. **Reservations:** suggested. **Features:** Near downtown businesses and hotels, the metropolitan-style restaurant serves contemporary, trendy dishes, as well as established favorites. Good choices include seared foie gras, perfectly prepared steaks and an impressive selection of fresh seafood. The professional staff spoils patrons. Dressy casual; cocktails. **Parking:** on-site. **Cards:** AX, DC, DS, MC, VI.   ⦿ ⦻

TAPAS 177   **Dinner:** $9-$24   **Phone:** 585/262-2090   1
▼▼
Mediterranean

Location: Off Inner Loop of I-490, exit 13; downtown. 177 St. Paul St 14604. **Hours:** 5 pm-midnight. Closed: 1/1, 11/25, 12/25; also Sun. **Reservations:** accepted. **Features:** The funky little basement bistro features subdued candlelight and intimate table dining. A diverse menu of tapas and full entrees focuses on fusion-style cuisine incorporating almost every ethnic background. Check for the monthly wine tasting. Casual dress; cocktails. **Parking:** on-site (fee) and valet. **Cards:** AX, DS, MC, VI.   ⦿ ⦻

TRIPHAMMER GRILL   **Lunch:** $8-$13   **Dinner:** $17-$25   **Phone:** 585/262-2700   4
▼▼▼
Nouvelle American

Location: Downtown; in the Center Brown's Race Historic District. 60 Brown's Race 14614. **Hours:** 11:30 am-2:30 & 5-10 pm, Sat from 5 pm. Closed: Sun. **Reservations:** suggested. **Features:** Built as a forge in 1816, the Triphammer Building has been home to its namesake restaurant since 1993. Fresh quality ingredients are the hallmark of all courses served in the bistro-like atmosphere. Patio seating is available in season. Dressy casual; cocktails. **Parking:** on-site. **Cards:** AX, DC, DS, MC, VI.   ♿Ⓜ ⦻

ROCK HILL pop. 1,056

——— **WHERE TO STAY** ———

THE LODGE AT ROCK HILL   *Book at aaa.com*   **Phone:** (845)796-3100
AAA SAVE
▼▼▼
Small-scale Hotel

6/21-9/7	1P: $149-$189
9/8-4/30	1P: $99-$129
5/1-6/20	1P: $99-$119

Location: SR 17, exit 109, just e. 283 Rock Hill Dr 12775 (PO Box 858). **Fax:** 845/796-3130. **Facility:** 78 one-bedroom standard units, some with whirlpools. 1-2 stories (no elevator), interior corridors. *Bath:* combo or shower only. **Parking:** on-site. **Terms:** cancellation fee imposed, pets ($25 fee). **Amenities:** high-speed Internet, dual phone lines, voice mail, irons, hair dryers. *Some:* CD players. **Pool(s):** heated indoor. **Leisure Activities:** steamroom, exercise room. **Guest Services:** valet laundry. **Business Services:** meeting rooms, business center. **Cards:** AX, DC, DS, MC, VI. **Special Amenities:** free continental breakfast.

SOME UNITS

⒮ 🛏 🍴 🎣 📷 ➡ 📺 📠 💻 / ⦻ 📼 📞 /
FEE   FEE

THE DODGE INN
▼▼ ▼▼
American

Lunch: $6-$12 **Dinner:** $16-$28 **Phone:** 845/794-5376
Location: SR 17, exit 110, just n. 227 Lake Marie Louise Rd 12775. **Hours:** noon-10 pm, Sun-9 pm; 4 pm-9 pm, Sat noon-4 pm, Sun noon-8 pm 10/1-5/1. **Closed:** 1/1, 11/25, 12/25; also Wed in winter & Tues. **Reservations:** accepted. **Features:** Hickory-smoked barbecue ribs, chicken and brisket are the specialty, and they come highly recommended. Pasta, chicken and seafood dishes are also intelligent choices. Guests can unwind in the casual lounge dining or in the rustic, fireside setting. Casual dress; cocktails. **Parking:** on-site.
Cards: AX, MC, VI.

⎚ ✕

ROCKVILLE CENTRE pop. 24,568

——— WHERE TO STAY ———

HOLIDAY INN
AAA SAVE
▼▼ ▼▼
Small-scale Hotel

Book at aaa.com
All Year 1P: $159 **Phone:** (516)678-1300
Location: On SR 27, between N Village and N Centre aves. Located adjacent to a train station. 173 Sunrise Hwy 11570. Fax: 516/678-5657. **Facility:** 100 one-bedroom standard units. 5 stories, exterior corridors. *Bath:* combo or shower only. **Parking:** on-site. **Terms:** pets ($15 extra charge). **Amenities:** video games (fee), dual phone lines, voice mail, irons, hair dryers. **Dining:** 6 am-2 & 5-10 pm, cocktails. **Pool(s):** outdoor. **Leisure Activities:** exercise room. **Guest Services:** coin laundry. **Business Services:** meeting rooms, fax (fee).
Cards: AX, CB, DC, DS, JC, MC, VI. **Special Amenities:** free local telephone calls and free newspaper.

SOME UNITS
[S/D] [🛏] [🍴] [⎚] [&M] [♿] [🗑] [🏊] [📽] [DATA PORT] [▭] / [✕] [🔋] /
FEE   FEE

——— WHERE TO DINE ———

TAIKO
▼▼ ▼▼
Japanese

Lunch: $6-$10 **Dinner:** $11-$15 **Phone:** 516/678-6149
Location: Just s of jct Sunrise Hwy. 15 S Village Ave 11570. **Hours:** noon-2:30 & 5:30-10:30 pm, Fri-11 pm, Sat 5:30 pm-11 pm. Closed major holidays. **Features:** Rice paper screens and tatami tables decorate the simple dining room. Sushi and sashimi choices are excellent, and more timid palates will find plenty of cooked choices, such as teriyaki, tempura and noodle dishes. Ice cream flavors are exquisite. Casual dress; cocktails. **Parking:** street. **Cards:** AX, CB, DC, MC, VI.

✕

TOMATOES
▼▼ ▼▼
American

Dinner: $15-$25 **Phone:** 516/594-2977
Location: Between N Park and N Village aves; center. 242 Sunrise Hwy 11570. **Hours:** 5 pm-10 pm, Fri & Sat-11 pm, Sun 3 pm-9:30 pm. **Closed:** 11/25, 12/25. **Features:** Sesame-crusted, seared ahi tuna and penne with shrimp arrabbiata are two shining examples of interesting, California-Italian cuisine, but there are also wood-grilled fish selections and creative daily specials. Dishes exhibit interesting and complex flavors. The energized dining room has a bright, contemporary and upbeat mood. Casual dress; cocktails. **Parking:** street. **Cards:** AX, DS, MC, VI.

✕

ROME pop. 34,950

——— WHERE TO STAY ———

ADIRONDACK THIRTEEN PINES MOTEL
▼
Motel

5/1-10/1 1P: $40-$50 2P: $45-$60 XP: $5 F18 **Phone:** (315)337-4930
Location: Jct SR 49, 0.5 mi e on SR 365. Located in a rural area. 7353 River Rd 13440. **Facility:** 10 one-bedroom standard units. 1 story, exterior corridors. *Bath:* combo or shower only. **Parking:** on-site, winter plug-ins. **Terms:** open 5/1-10/1, 3 day cancellation notice. **Pool(s):** heated outdoor. **Leisure Activities:** putting green, playground, basketball, horseshoes, shuffleboard, volleyball. **Cards:** AX, CB, DC, DS, JC, MC, VI.

SOME UNITS
[ASK] [S/D] [🛏] [🍴+] [🏊] [✕] / [🔋] /

GREEN LANTERN MOTOR COURT
▼
Motel

All Year 1P: $50 2P: $60 XP: $5 **Phone:** 315/336-5200
Location: Jct SR 46, 2.9 mi n on SR 26 (Turin Rd). 8189 Turin Rd 13440. Fax: 315/336-5203. **Facility:** 11 one-bedroom standard units. 1 story, exterior corridors. *Bath:* combo or shower only. **Parking:** on-site, winter plug-ins. **Terms:** 3 day cancellation notice. **Amenities:** hair dryers. **Cards:** AX, DS, MC, VI.

SOME UNITS
[🔋] [▭] / [✕] [📺] /

INN AT THE BEECHES
AAA SAVE
▼▼ ▼▼
Motel

Book at aaa.com
All Year 1P: $73-$89 2P: $79-$125 XP: $10 F16 **Phone:** (315)336-1776
Location: Jct SR 46, 2 mi n on SR 26 (Turin Rd). 7900 Turin Rd 13440. Fax: 315/339-2636. **Facility:** 66 units. 65 one-bedroom standard units. 1 one-bedroom suite ($165-$250) with whirlpool. 1 story, exterior corridors. *Bath:* combo or shower only. **Parking:** on-site. **Terms:** cancellation fee imposed, [BP] meal plan available, small pets only ($5 extra charge). **Dining:** 6 am-10 & 11:30-10 pm, Sat 8 am-noon, Sun 8 am-2 pm; closed Mon, cocktails. **Pool(s):** outdoor. **Guest Services:** valet laundry. **Business Services:** conference facilities.
Cards: AX, DC, DS, MC, VI.

SOME UNITS
[S/D] [🛏] [🍴] [⎚] [🏊] / [✕] [🔋] [📺] /
FEE

——— WHERE TO DINE ———

SAVOY RESTAURANT
AAA
▼▼ ▼▼
Italian

Lunch: $4-$7 **Dinner:** $6-$15 **Phone:** 315/339-3166
Location: Jct SR 26 and 46, just s. 255 E Dominick St 13440. **Hours:** 11:30 am-10 pm, Fri-11 pm, Sat 5 pm-11 pm, Sun 4 pm-9 pm. **Closed:** 11/25, 12/25. **Reservations:** suggested. **Features:** In operation since 1908, the family restaurant has a warm, casual atmosphere. El cicco—a seasoned steak with wine, garlic and spices—is particularly flavorful on a menu of mostly Italian choices. Some American specialties also are offered. Casual dress; cocktails. **Parking:** on-site. **Cards:** AX, CB, DC, DS, MC, VI.

⎚ ✕

ROMULUS pop. 2,036

——— WHERE TO DINE ———

KNAPP WINERY & RESTAURANT **Lunch:** $8-$9 **Dinner:** $18-$24 **Phone:** 607/869-9271
▼▼▼
Continental
Location: 2 mi s on SR 96, then just w on CR 128 (Ernsberger Rd). 2770 County Road 128 14541. **Hours:** Open 5/30-11/1 & 4/1-4/29; 11 am-3:30 pm, Thurs-Sun also 5 pm-8 pm. **Reservations:** accepted. **Features:** Patrons can dine indoors or on the lovely patio, surrounded by the vineyards and sounds of nature. Fresh local fruits and vegetables complement fresh seafood, chicken and pasta dishes for a memorable lunch. Choose a locally produced wine to enhance the occasion. Casual dress; beer & wine only. **Parking:** on-site.
Cards: AX, MC, VI. ⊠

RONKONKOMA pop. 20,029

——— WHERE TO STAY ———

COURTYARD BY MARRIOTT LONG ISLAND MACARTHUR AIRPORT *Book at aaa.com* **Phone:** (631)612-5000
▼▼▼ All Year 1P: $149-$159
Small-scale Hotel
Location: I-495, exit 60 (Express Dr S), 0.5 mi e. Located in a commercial area. 5000 Express Dr S 11779. Fax: 631/612-5008. **Facility:** 154 units. 146 one-bedroom standard units, some with whirlpools. 8 one-bedroom suites ($159-$189) with whirlpools. 7 stories, interior corridors. *Bath:* combo or shower only. **Parking:** on-site. **Amenities:** high-speed Internet (fee), dual phone lines, voice mail, irons, hair dryers. **Pool(s):** small heated indoor. **Leisure Activities:** whirlpool, exercise room. **Guest Services:** valet and coin laundry, area transportation. **Business Services:** meeting rooms. **Cards:** AX, CB, DC, DS, MC, VI.
SOME UNITS
(ASK) 〔S🄳〕 ✚ 🍽 ▼ 🐾 ➢ 🐾 (DATA PORT) 🔌 🖥 💻 / ⊠ /

ECONO LODGE LONG ISLAND ISLIP MACARTHUR AIRPORT *Book at aaa.com* **Phone:** (631)588-6800
ⒶⒶⒶ (SAVE) All Year 1P: $85-$165 2P: $85-$165 XP: $8 F18
▼▼▼
Motel
Location: I-495, exit 57, 3 mi se. Located in a commercial area. 3055 Veterans Memorial Hwy 11779. Fax: 631/588-6815. **Facility:** 59 one-bedroom standard units. 1-2 stories (no elevator), interior/exterior corridors. *Bath:* combo or shower only. **Parking:** on-site. **Amenities:** *Some:* hair dryers. **Cards:** AX, CB, DC, DS, JC, MC, VI. **Special Amenities:** free continental breakfast and free newspaper.
SOME UNITS
〔S🄳〕 🐾 🐾 (DATA PORT) / ⊠ /

HOLIDAY INN *Book at aaa.com* **Phone:** (631)585-9500
▼▼▼ All Year 1P: $179 2P: $179
Small-scale Hotel
Location: I-495, exit 57, 4.5 mi se, follow signs to MacArthur Airport. Located in a commercial area. 3845 Veterans Memorial Hwy 11779. Fax: 631/585-9550. **Facility:** 287 one-bedroom standard units, some with whirlpools. 2 stories, interior corridors. *Bath:* combo or shower only. **Parking:** on-site. **Terms:** [BP] meal plan available. **Amenities:** voice mail, honor bars, irons, hair dryers. **Pool(s):** outdoor. **Leisure Activities:** exercise room. **Guest Services:** valet and coin laundry, area transportation. **Business Services:** conference facilities. **Cards:** AX, CB, DC, DS, JC, MC, VI.
SOME UNITS
(ASK) ✚ 🍽 ▼ 🛗 &M 🐾 🐾 ➢ 🐾 (DATA PORT) 💻 / ⊠ 🔌 /
FEE

ROSCOE pop. 597

——— WHERE TO STAY ———

ROSCOE MOTEL **Phone:** 607/498-5220
ⒶⒶⒶ (SAVE) All Year 1P: $50 2P: $55-$65 XP: $10 D5
▼▼ ▼▼
Motel
Location: SR 17, exit 94, 0.5 mi n on SR 206, then just w. Located in a quiet area. 2054 Old Rt 17 12776 (PO Box 609). Fax: 607/498-4643. **Facility:** 18 units. 16 one-bedroom standard units. 2 cottages. 1 story, exterior corridors. *Bath:* combo or shower only. **Parking:** on-site. **Terms:** small pets only ($10 extra charge). **Leisure Activities:** fishing, barbecue grills. **Cards:** AX, MC, VI.
SOME UNITS
🐾 / 🔌 💻 /
FEE

——— WHERE TO DINE ———

RAIMONDO'S RESTAURANT & PIZZERIA **Lunch:** $5-$8 **Dinner:** $11-$25 **Phone:** 607/498-4702
▼
Italian
Location: SR 17, exit 94; corner of SR 206 and Main St; downtown. Main St 12776. **Hours:** Open 5/1-1/31 & 2/23-4/30; 11 am-11 pm; to 10 pm in winter. Closed: 3/27, 11/25, 12/25. **Reservations:** accepted. **Features:** Family-owned for 22 years, the popular restaurant offers carefully prepared Northern Italian dishes that are promptly served. Casual dress; cocktails. **Parking:** on-site. **Cards:** AX, DS, MC, VI.
▼ ⊠

ROSCOE DINER **Lunch:** $4-$9 **Dinner:** $8-$25 **Phone:** 607/498-4405
▼
American
MC, VI.
Location: SR 17, exit 94, just se. 1908 Old Rt 17 12776. **Hours:** 6 am-midnight. Closed: 12/24, 12/25. **Features:** Decorated with chrome and teal accents, the casual, '50s-style diner seats up to 300 guests in its three dining rooms. The on-premises bakery offers a showy display of its creations. American and Greek favorites are dished in generous portions. Casual dress; cocktails. **Parking:** on-site. **Cards:** AX, DS,
⊠

ROSLYN pop. 2,750

——— WHERE TO DINE ———

BRYANT & COOPER STEAKHOUSE **Lunch:** $10-$18 **Dinner:** $17-$35 **Phone:** 516/627-7270
▼▼▼▼ **Location:** I-495, exit 36 (Searingtown), n to Northern Blvd (SR 25A), 0.3 mi e, then just n. 2 Middle Neck Rd 11576.
Hours: noon-3:30 & 5-10 pm, Fri-11 pm, Sat 5 pm-midnight, Sun 3 pm-10 pm. Closed: 12/25.
Steak House **Reservations:** suggested. **Features:** Hardwood floors, earth tones and paneling add to the rich, clublike ambience of the upscale dining room. A comprehensive selection of wines complements preparations of prime rib, chicken, seafood and ribeye steak. Servers are knowledgeable. Dressy casual; cocktails. **Parking:** on-site and valet. **Cards:** AX, DC, MC, VI.

🍽 ✕

ROTTERDAM pop. 20,536

——— WHERE TO STAY ———

MALLOZZI'S BELVEDERE HOTEL *Book at aaa.com* **Phone:** (518)630-4020
Ⓐ Ⓐ Ⓐ ⓈⓐⓥⒺ
7/13-9/8	1P: $132-$148	2P: $132-$148	XP: $10	F10
9/9-12/31	1P: $125-$132	2P: $125-$132	XP: $10	F10
5/1-7/12	1P: $120-$132	2P: $120-$132	XP: $10	F10
1/1-4/30	1P: $115-$125	2P: $115-$125	XP: $10	F10

Small-scale Hotel **Location:** I-890, exit 9 (Curry Rd), 1.8 mi w; I-90, exit 25. 1926 Curry Rd 12303. Fax: 518/630-4055. **Facility:** 31 units. 29 one-bedroom standard units. 2 one-bedroom suites ($145-$178) with whirlpools. 2 stories, interior corridors. **Parking:** on-site. **Terms:** cancellation fee imposed, [CP] meal plan available. **Amenities:** video library (fee), dual phone lines, voice mail, safes, irons, hair dryers. **Dining:** Mallozzi's Restaurant, see separate listing. **Guest Services:** valet laundry. **Cards:** AX, DS, MC, VI. **Special Amenities: free continental breakfast and free newspaper.** (See color ad p 567)

SOME UNITS
Ⓢ/D 🍴 🕸 🛜 Ⓥ🄲🅁 🅟🅞🅡🅣 ▣ / ✕ 🖬 /
FEE

SUPER 8 SCHENECTADY *Book at aaa.com* **Phone:** (518)355-2190
▼▼ ◆◆
6/1-8/31	1P: $65-$70	2P: $75-$80	XP: $10	F10
5/1-5/31 & 9/1-10/31	1P: $50-$55	2P: $60-$65	XP: $10	F10
11/1-4/30	1P: $45-$55	2P: $55-$65	XP: $10	F10

Small-scale Hotel **Location:** I-890, exit 9 (Curry Rd), 0.4 mi w; I-90, exit 25. 3083 Carman Rd 12303. Fax: 518/355-3843. **Facility:** 99 one-bedroom standard units. 2 stories (no elevator), interior corridors. **Parking:** on-site. **Terms:** 5 day cancellation notice, pets ($10 extra charge). **Cards:** AX, CB, DC, DS, MC, VI.

SOME UNITS
🄰🅂🄺 Ⓢ/D 🛏 🍴 📹 / ✕ /
FEE

——— WHERE TO DINE ———

MALLOZZI'S RESTAURANT **Dinner:** $11-$18 **Phone:** 518/355-0340
▼▼▼ **Location:** I-890, exit 9 (Curry Rd), 1.8 mi w; I-90, exit 25; in Mallozzi's Belvedere Hotel. 1930 Curry Rd 12303.
Hours: 4:30 pm-9 pm, Sat from 5 pm. Closed: 7/4, 12/25; also Sun & Mon. **Reservations:** suggested.
Italian **Features:** Well-prepared offerings include steak, chops, veal and such tempting seafood selections as the fisherman's delight platter—a combination of fresh clams, New Zealand mussels, lobster tail, shrimp and scallops over linguine in marinara sauce. Casual dress; cocktails. **Parking:** on-site. **Cards:** AX, DC, DS, MC, VI.
(See color ad p 567)

🄼 🍽 ✕

ROUND LAKE pop. 604

——— WHERE TO DINE ———

LAKE RIDGE **Lunch:** $5-$8 **Dinner:** $13-$18 **Phone:** 518/899-6000
▼▼▼ **Location:** I-87, exit 11, just e on Round Lake Rd. 35 Burlington Ave 12151. **Hours:** 11:30 am-2:30 & 5-9 pm.
Closed: 11/25, 12/25; also Sun. **Reservations:** suggested. **Features:** The intimate restaurant offers fine
American dining in an unpretentious atmosphere either fireside or on the patio. Top-quality ingredients are incorporated into such dishes as the popular crab cakes with garlic citrus aioli and veal Jacqueline with shallots, shiitake mushrooms and king crab meat in garlic sherry cream sauce. The friendly staff is helpful in recommending good wines to accompany all choices. Desserts made in house are a perfect end to the feast. Casual dress; cocktails. **Parking:** on-site. **Cards:** AX, DS, MC, VI.

✕

RYE —See New York p. 456.

RYE BROOK —See New York p. 456.

SACKETS HARBOR pop. 1,386

——— WHERE TO STAY ———

ONTARIO PLACE HOTEL *Book at aaa.com* **Phone:** (315)646-8000
▼▼ ◆◆
5/1-10/15	1P: $79-$150	2P: $79-$150	XP: $10	F16
10/16-4/30	1P: $69-$135	2P: $69-$135	XP: $10	F16

Small-scale Hotel **Location:** Center. 103 General Smith Dr 13685 (PO Box 540). Fax: 315/646-2506. **Facility:** 38 units. 37 one-bedroom standard units, some with whirlpools. 1 two-bedroom suite ($375) with kitchen and whirlpool. 2-3 stories (no elevator), interior corridors. *Bath:* combo or shower only. **Parking:** on-site. **Terms:** 3 day cancellation notice, pets ($10 fee, in designated units). **Amenities:** *Some:* DVD players (fee), hair dryers. **Guest Services:** gift shop. **Business Services:** meeting rooms. **Cards:** AX, CB, DC, DS, MC, VI.

SOME UNITS
🛏 🍴 🅟🅞🅡🅣 / ✕ Ⓥ🄲🅁 🖬 🖨 ▣ /
FEE FEE

─────── **WHERE TO DINE** ───────

1812 STEAK AND SEAFOOD COMPANY　　　**Dinner:** $9-$30　　　　**Phone:** 315/646-2041

▼▼ ▼▼　　**Location:** Center. 212 W Main St 13685. **Hours:** 4 pm-10 pm; hours vary off season. Closed: 11/25, 12/25.
Reservations: accepted. **Features:** Seafood is the forte at the casual downtown restaurant in a historic
American　　village. The Thursday night special is all-you-can-eat Alaskan snow crab clusters. Guests also can opt for
traditional Italian dishes. Freshly-made omelets are part of the Sunday breakfast buffet. Casual dress;
cocktails. **Parking:** on-site. **Cards:** AX, DC, DS, MC, VI.　　　　　　　　　　　　　　　　 ▯Ⅺ ✕

SACKETS HARBOR BREWING CO　　**Lunch:** $6-$7　　　**Dinner:** $9-$22　　　**Phone:** 315/646-2739

▼▼ ▼▼　　**Location:** Center. 212 W Main St 13685. **Hours:** call for hours. Closed: 3/27, 11/25, 12/25.
Reservations: suggested. **Features:** In a former train station, the waterfront brew pub offers seating in the
American　　bi-level dining room and on the patio. The eclectic menu puts a new spin on old favorite dishes, such as
chicken pasta pilaf. Custom-prepared microbrewed beers are a nice touch. Casual dress; cocktails.
Parking: on-site. **Cards:** AX, DS, MC, VI.　　　　　　　　　　　　　　　　　　　　　　　 ▯Ⅺ ✕

SAG HARBOR pop. 2,313

─────── **WHERE TO DINE** ───────

B SMITH'S　　　　　**Lunch:** $10-$28　　　　**Dinner:** $13-$35　　　**Phone:** 631/725-5858

▼▼ ▼▼　　**Location:** At end of Bay St, just s of bridge to North Haven. Long Wharf Promenade 11963. **Hours:** Open
5/15-10/15; noon-4 & 6-10 pm; Fri & Sat-11 pm in season. Closed major holidays; also Mon-Fri 5/15-5/28
Seafood　　& 9/7-10/15. **Reservations:** accepted. **Features:** Relax in the brightly lit dining room and enjoy views of
yachts and boats sailing into and out of the harbor. Mediterranean and southern influences infuse
preparations of new American cuisine, such as caramelized diver scallops over orrechiette pasta. Casual dress; cocktails.
Parking: street. **Cards:** AX, DC, DS, MC, VI.　　　　　　　　　　　　　　　　　　　　　 ▯Ⅺ ✕

SEN　　　　　　　**Dinner:** $14-$28　　　　　　　　　　**Phone:** 631/725-1774

▼▼ ▼▼　　**Location:** Just w of SR 114 from south side of bridge; center. 23 Main St 11963. **Hours:** 6 pm-11 pm, Fri &
Sat-midnight; hours may vary seasonally. Closed: 11/25, 12/25. **Features:** Expect ultra-modern, sparse
Sushi　　decor and a bustling atmosphere at the highly popular spot. The menu delivers sushi, a wide assortment of
traditional and unusual rolls, fun appetizers, noodle soup and steamed fish. Saki varieties are extensive.
Casual dress; cocktails. **Parking:** street. **Cards:** AX, MC, VI.　　　　　　　　　　　　　　　　 ✕

ST. JAMES pop. 13,268

─────── **WHERE TO DINE** ───────

MIRABELLE　　　　　**Lunch:** $14-$23　　　　**Dinner:** $23-$39　　　**Phone:** 631/584-5999

▼▼ ▼▼▼　　**Location:** 1.6 mi on SR 25A (N Country Rd) from jct SR 25. 404 N Country Rd (SR 25A) 11780. **Hours:** noon-2 &
6-10 pm, Sat from 6 pm, Sun 5 pm-10 pm. Closed: 1/1, 11/25, 12/25; also Mon. **Reservations:** suggested.
French　　**Features:** In a small house in a small town, the trendy dining room has bright yellow walls, low ceilings
and a large painting that is reprinted on the menu cover. Foie gras mousse roulade and eggplant-goat
cheese terrine are representative appetizers. Casual dress; cocktails. **Parking:** on-site. **Cards:** AX, DC, DS, MC, VI.　 ▯Ⅺ ✕

ST. JOHNSVILLE pop. 1,685

─────── **WHERE TO STAY** ───────

INN BY THE MILL　　　　　　　　　　　　　　　　　　　　　　　　**Phone:** (518)568-2388

▼▼ ▼▼▼　　All Year [ECP]　　　　　1P: $110-$350　　　　2P: $110-$350　　　XP: $30
Location: 1 mi w on SR 5, then 0.5 mi n. 1679 Mill Rd 13452. Fax: 518/568-6060. **Facility:** An 1835 gristmill fea-
Historic Bed　　turing a self-service soda fountain shares these grounds with a cascading creek, a waterfall, and a cottage
& Breakfast　　with an outdoor spa. Smoke free premises. 5 units. 3 one-bedroom standard units. 2 one-bedroom suites
($165-$350), some with whirlpools. 2 stories (no elevator), interior corridors. Bath: combo or shower only.
Parking: on-site. **Terms:** 2 night minimum stay - weekends, age restrictions may apply, 14 day cancellation notice-fee imposed.
Amenities: video library, hair dryers. Some: CD players, irons. **Leisure Activities:** recreation programs. **Guest Services:** gift
shop, area transportation. **Cards:** AX, MC, VI.

SOME UNITS

✕ / �📶 ⃞ VCR ⃞ DATA PORT ⃞ ⊘ 🛏 ▣ 🖵 /

SALAMANCA pop. 6,097

─────── **WHERE TO STAY** ───────

HOLIDAY INN EXPRESS HOTEL & SUITES　*Book at aaa.com*　　　　**Phone:** (716)945-7600

▼▼ ▼▼　　12/15-4/14 [CP]　　　　1P: $139-$179　　　2P: $139-$179　　XP: $10　　F16
5/1-12/14 & 4/15-4/30 [CP]　　1P: $104-$149　　　2P: $104-$149　　XP: $10　　F16
Small-scale Hotel　　**Location:** I-86, exit 20, just n. 779 Broad St 14779. Fax: 716/945-7200. **Facility:** 68 units. 66 one-bedroom standard units, some with whirlpools. 2 one-bedroom suites with efficiencies. 2 stories, interior corridors. Bath:
combo or shower only. **Parking:** on-site. **Terms:** cancellation fee imposed, small pets only ($50 deposit). **Amenities:** dual phone
lines, voice mail, irons, hair dryers. **Pool(s):** heated indoor. **Leisure Activities:** whirlpool, exercise room. **Guest Services:** sundries, complimentary laundry. **Business Services:** meeting rooms. **Cards:** AX, DC, DS, MC, VI.

SOME UNITS

ASK ⃞ S/D ⃞ 🍽 ⃞ FEE ⃞ 🐾 ⃞ DATA PORT ⃞ 🖵 / ✕ 🛏 ▣ /

SANBORN —See Niagara Falls p. 481.

SARANAC LAKE pop. 5,041—See also ADIRONDACK MOUNTAINS.

—— WHERE TO STAY ——

ADIRONDACK MOTEL

(AAA) [SAVE]   All Year   1P: $55-$160   2P: $55-$160   XP: $7   Phone: 518/891-2116   F10
◊   **Location:** 0.7 mi e on SR 86. 248 Lake Flower Ave 12983. Fax: 518/891-0380. **Facility:** 13 units. 11 one-bedroom
Motel   standard units, some with efficiencies. 2 one-bedroom suites ($110-$160) with kitchens. 1-2 stories, exterior
corridors. *Bath:* combo or shower only. **Parking:** on-site, winter plug-ins. **Terms:** [CP] meal plan available,
pets ($7 extra charge additional pets). **Leisure Activities:** canoeing, paddleboats, boat dock, fishing, kayak,
rowboat, gazebo. **Cards:** DS, MC, VI. **Special Amenities:** free continental breakfast and preferred room
(subject to availability with advanced reservations).

SOME UNITS

BEST WESTERN MOUNTAIN LAKE INN   *Book at aaa.com*   Phone: (518)891-1970
(AAA) [SAVE]   6/25-10/10   1P: $85-$150   2P: $85-$150   XP: $5   F17
◊◊   12/24-4/30   1P: $70-$140   2P: $70-$140   XP: $5   F17
5/1-6/24 & 10/11-12/23   1P: $70-$95   2P: $70-$95   XP: $5   F17
Small-scale Hotel   **Location:** 0.8 mi e on SR 86. 487 Lake Flower Ave 12983. Fax: 518/891-6195. **Facility:** 69 one-bedroom standard
units. 2 stories (no elevator), interior corridors. **Parking:** on-site, winter plug-ins. **Terms:** [BP] meal plan available, pets ($20 extra charge, in smoking units). **Amenities:** irons, hair dryers. **Dining:** 6 am-2 pm, cocktails.
Pool(s): heated indoor. **Leisure Activities:** sun deck. **Guest Services:** coin laundry. **Business Services:** meeting rooms.
Cards: AX, CB, DC, DS, MC, VI. **Special Amenities:** free local telephone calls and free newspaper. *(See color ad below)*

SOME UNITS

THE HOTEL SARANAC OF PAUL SMITH'S COLLEGE   *Book at aaa.com*   Phone: (518)891-2200
(AAA) [SAVE]   All Year   1P: $99-$140   2P: $99-$140   XP: $10   F18
◊◊◊   **Location:** Center. 101 Main St 12983. Fax: 518/891-5664. **Facility:** This restored 1927 hotel is a training facility
for hotel-management students. 88 one-bedroom standard units, some with whirlpools. 6 stories, interior cor-
Historic   ridors. **Parking:** on-site. **Terms:** 2-3 night minimum stay - weekends in season, 3 day cancellation notice,
Small-scale Hotel   [AP], [BP], [CP], [ECP] & [MAP] meal plans available, package plans - seasonal, pets ($15 extra charge, in
designated units). **Amenities:** video library, voice mail, hair dryers. **Dining:** A.P. Smith Restaurant, see separate listing. **Guest Services:** gift shop, valet laundry. **Business Services:** meeting rooms. **Cards:** AX, CB,
DC, DS, MC, VI. **Special Amenities:** free newspaper and free room upgrade (subject to availability with advanced reservations).

SOME UNITS

LAKE FLOWER INN

◆ Motel

All Year   1P: $48-$108   2P: $48-$108   XP: $10   F16

Phone: 518/891-2310

Location: 0.6 mi e on SR 86. 234 Lake Flower Ave 12983. **Fax:** 518/891-0399. **Facility:** 14 one-bedroom standard units. 1 story, exterior corridors. *Bath:* combo or shower only. **Parking:** on-site, winter plug-ins. **Terms:** 2 night minimum stay - weekends in season, 14 day cancellation notice-fee imposed, package plans, pets (dogs only, with prior approval). **Pool(s):** outdoor. **Leisure Activities:** canoeing, boat dock, fishing. **Cards:** MC, VI.

SOME UNITS

🐾 🛶 ⊠ 🎥 [DATA PORT] / ✕ 🖥 /

LAKE SIDE MOTEL

AAA [SAVE]
◆◆◆ Motel

All Year [CP]   2P: $59-$109   XP: $10   F12

Phone: (518)891-4333

Location: 0.6 mi e on SR 86. 256 Lake Flower Ave 12983. **Facility:** 22 one-bedroom standard units, some with efficiencies. 1 story, exterior corridors. *Bath:* combo or shower only. **Parking:** on-site. **Terms:** 7 day cancellation notice-fee imposed, pets ($10 deposit, with prior approval). **Amenities:** *Some:* irons. **Pool(s):** outdoor. **Leisure Activities:** canoeing, paddleboats, boat dock, fishing, rowboat. **Cards:** AX, DS, MC, VI. **Special Amenities:** free continental breakfast and early check-in/late check-out.

SOME UNITS

[SD] [FEE] 🐾 🛶 ⊠ 🎥 [DATA PORT] / ✕ 🖥 🖨 /

SARA-PLACID MOTOR INN

AAA [SAVE]
◆◆◆ Motel

All Year   1P: $58-$99   2P: $58-$109   XP: $10

Phone: (518)891-2729

Location: 0.8 mi e on SR 86. 120 Lake Flower Ave 12983. **Fax:** 518/891-5624. **Facility:** 19 units. 13 one- and 3 two-bedroom standard units, some cottages. 3 cottages ($150-$295), some with whirlpools. 1-2 stories, exterior corridors. **Parking:** on-site, winter plug-ins. **Terms:** 3 day cancellation notice-fee imposed, weekly rates available, package plans. **Amenities:** *Some:* DVD players. **Leisure Activities:** paddleboats, fishing, ice skating. *Fee:* boats. **Guest Services:** valet laundry. **Cards:** AX, CB, DC, DS, JC, MC, VI.

(See color ad p 333 & p 560)

SOME UNITS

[SD] 🍴 ⊠ ✕ 🎥 [DATA PORT] 🖥 🖨 🖥 / [VCR] /

The following lodging was either not evaluated or did not meet AAA rating requirements but is listed for your information only.

THE POINT

[fyi]

Phone: 518/891-5674

Not evaluated. **Location:** SR 3. HCR 1, Box 65 12983. Facilities, services, and decor characterize an upscale property.

--- **WHERE TO DINE** ---

A.P. SMITH RESTAURANT

AAA
◆◆ American

Lunch: $6-$12   Dinner: $15-$21   Phone: 518/891-2200

Location: Center; in The Hotel Saranac of Paul Smith's College. 101 Main St 12983. **Hours:** 7 am-1:30 & 5-9 pm. **Reservations:** suggested, for dinner. **Features:** A.P. Smith's offers a good spot for a leisurely afternoon lunch in the company of friends. The dining room is pleasant and the atmosphere casually busy. Light fare is offered at lunch with a more elaborate menu in the evenings. Service is afforded by students in training. Overall, decent food at reasonable prices. Casual dress; cocktails. **Parking:** on-site. **Cards:** AX, CB, DC, DS, MC, VI.

🍽 ✕

CASA DEL SOL

◆ Mexican

Dinner: $4-$13   Phone: 518/891-0977

Location: 0.8 mi e on SR 86. 154 Lake Flower Ave 12983. **Hours:** 4:30 pm-10 pm. Closed: 11/25, 12/24, 12/25; also Easter week. **Features:** Located between Saranac Lake and Lake Placid, this restaurant serves up some genuine Mexican fare. With six choices of sauces on the table to chose from, every taste is met from mild to fire-breathing hot. Casual dress; cocktails. **Parking:** on-site.

🍽 🍸 ✕

SARATOGA SPRINGS pop. 26,186

——— WHERE TO STAY ———

ADELPHI HOTEL

Phone: 518/587-4688

Historic
Small-scale Hotel

7/21-8/31	1P: $195-$475	2P: $195-$475
7/1-7/20	1P: $165-$275	2P: $165-$275
5/15-6/30 & 9/1-10/15	1P: $120-$225	2P: $120-$225

Location: Between Division and Washington sts; center. 365 Broadway 12866. Fax: 518/587-0851. **Facility:** Period pieces furnish the individually decorated rooms at this 1877 Victorian inn. 39 units. 32 one- and 7 two-bedroom standard units. 4 stories, interior corridors. *Bath:* combo or shower only. **Parking:** street. **Terms:** open 5/15-10/15, check-in 4 pm, 2-3 night minimum stay - weekends, 14 day cancellation notice, [ECP] meal plan available. **Amenities:** safes, hair dryers. **Pool(s):** small heated outdoor. **Business Services:** meeting rooms. **Cards:** MC, VI.

CARRIAGE HOUSE INN

Phone: 518/584-4220

Small-scale Hotel

7/21-9/6	2P: $229-$269
5/1-7/20 & 9/7-10/31	2P: $99-$149
11/1-4/30	2P: $99-$129

Location: I-87, exit 13 N, 3.7 mi n on US 9. 198 Broadway 12866. Fax: 518/584-3620. **Facility:** 14 units. 12 one-bedroom standard units, some with efficiencies. 2 one-bedroom suites ($189-$399) with efficiencies and whirlpools. 2 stories (no elevator), interior/exterior corridors. **Parking:** on-site. **Amenities:** voice mail. **Leisure Activities:** bicycles. **Cards:** AX, DS, MC, VI. **Special Amenities:** early check-in/late check-out and preferred room (subject to availability with advanced reservations).

FOX N' HOUND B & B

Phone: (518)584-5959

Bed & Breakfast

7/15-9/4 [BP]	2P: $270-$345
5/1-7/14 [BP]	2P: $150-$220
9/5-4/30 [BP]	2P: $135-$195

Location: I-87, exit 15 (downtown), 1.6 mi w, then 0.3 mi e on SR 29. 142 Lake View 12866. Fax: 518/584-2594. **Facility:** 5 one-bedroom standard units, some with whirlpools. 2 stories, interior corridors. *Bath:* combo or shower only. **Parking:** on-site. **Terms:** 2 night minimum stay - weekends, age restrictions may apply, 14 day cancellation notice-fee imposed, package plans. **Amenities:** video library, irons, hair dryers. **Pool(s):** outdoor. **Cards:** AX, DS, MC, VI.

HILTON GARDEN INN-SARATOGA SPRINGS   *Book at aaa.com*

Phone: (518)587-1500

Small-scale Hotel

7/28-9/5	1P: $199-$399	2P: $199-$399	XP: $10	F18
5/1-7/27 & 9/6-10/30	1P: $109-$229	2P: $109-$229	XP: $10	F18
10/31-4/30	1P: $99-$199	2P: $99-$199	XP: $10	F18

Location: I-87, exit 13 N, 3.4 mi n on US 9. 125 S Broadway 12866. Fax: 518/587-7800. **Facility:** 112 one-bedroom standard units. 4 stories, interior corridors. *Bath:* combo or shower only. **Parking:** on-site. **Terms:** 3 day cancellation notice. **Amenities:** video games (fee), high-speed Internet, dual phone lines, voice mail, safes, irons, hair dryers. **Pool(s):** heated indoor. **Leisure Activities:** whirlpool, exercise room. **Guest Services:** coin laundry. **Business Services:** meeting rooms, business center. **Cards:** AX, CB, DC, DS, JC, MC, VI.

HOLIDAY INN   *Book at aaa.com*

Phone: (518)584-4550

Small-scale Hotel

7/29-9/6	1P: $289-$499	2P: $289-$499	XP: $10	F19
5/1-7/28 & 9/7-11/20	1P: $159-$319	2P: $159-$319	XP: $10	F19
11/21-4/30	1P: $125-$229	2P: $125-$229	XP: $10	F19

Location: On US 9, jct SR 50. 232 Broadway 12866. Fax: 518/584-4417. **Facility:** 168 units. 162 one-bedroom standard units. 6 one-bedroom suites ($199-$499) with whirlpools. 4 stories, interior corridors. **Parking:** on-site, winter plug-ins. **Terms:** 2-3 night minimum stay - seasonal & weekends. **Amenities:** voice mail, irons, hair dryers. *Some:* dual phone lines, safes. **Pool(s):** heated outdoor, heated indoor. **Leisure Activities:** exercise room. **Guest Services:** sundries, valet and coin laundry. **Business Services:** conference facilities. **Cards:** AX, DC, MC, VI.

THE INN AT SARATOGA   *Book at aaa.com*

Phone: (518)583-1890

Historic
Small-scale Hotel

7/28-9/5 [BP]	1P: $269-$319	2P: $269-$319	XP: $15	F12
5/1-7/27 [BP]	1P: $134-$169	2P: $134-$169	XP: $15	F12
9/6-10/31 [BP]	1P: $134-$149	2P: $134-$149	XP: $15	F12
11/1-4/30 [BP]	1P: $109-$129	2P: $109-$129	XP: $15	F12

Location: Jct SR 50 and US 9. 231 Broadway 12866. Fax: 518/583-2543. **Facility:** This restored inn dating from 1890 offers well-appointed rooms with Victorian decor. 38 units. 36 one-bedroom standard units. 2 one-bedroom suites ($149-$599). 3 stories, interior corridors. *Bath:* combo or shower only. **Parking:** on-site. **Terms:** 30 day cancellation notice. **Amenities:** high-speed Internet, voice mail, irons, hair dryers. **Business Services:** meeting rooms. **Cards:** AX, CB, DC, DS, MC, VI.

LONGFELLOWS INN AND RESTAURANT   *Book at aaa.com*

Phone: (518)587-0108

Country Inn

7/24-9/1 [CP]	1P: $275-$495	2P: $275-$495	XP: $10	F
5/1-7/23 & 9/2-10/31 [CP]	1P: $115-$495	2P: $115-$495	XP: $10	F
11/1-4/30 [CP]	1P: $95-$495	2P: $95-$495	XP: $10	F

Location: I-87, exit 14, 1.4 mi s on SR 9P. 500 Union Ave 12866. Fax: 518/587-6649. **Facility:** Once part of a 1,000-acre dairy farm, this converted barn is now home to modern, stylish guest rooms and charming public areas. Designated smoking area. 50 units. 46 one- and 4 two-bedroom standard units with whirlpools. 3 stories, interior corridors. **Parking:** on-site. **Terms:** 14 day cancellation notice. **Amenities:** high-speed Internet, voice mail, irons, hair dryers. **Dining:** restaurant, see separate listing. **Leisure Activities:** exercise room. **Guest Services:** valet laundry. **Business Services:** meeting rooms. **Cards:** AX, DC, DS, MC, VI.

THE PRIME HOTEL & CONFERENCE CENTER *Book at aaa.com* Phone: (518)584-4000

7/28-9/5	1P: $259-$375	XP: $15 F17
9/6-11/20	1P: $134	XP: $15 F17
5/1-7/27	1P: $129	XP: $15 F17
11/21-4/30	1P: $99	XP: $15 F17

Small-scale Hotel **Location:** I-87, exit 15, on SR 50. 534 Broadway 12866. Fax: 518/584-7430. **Facility:** 240 units. 235 one-bedroom standard units, some with whirlpools. 5 one-bedroom suites. 5 stories, interior corridors. *Bath:* combo or shower only. **Parking:** on-site. **Amenities:** video games (fee), high-speed Internet, dual phone lines, voice mail, irons, hair dryers. **Dining:** 7 am-10 pm, cocktails. **Pool(s):** small heated indoor. **Leisure Activities:** sauna, exercise room. **Guest Services:** gift shop, valet laundry. **Business Services:** conference facilities, business center. **Cards:** AX, CB, DC, DS, MC, VI.
(See color ad below)

SOME UNITS
🔲 🍴 🍸 🛗 📶 🖧 ➰ 🐾 📠 💻 / ✕ 🔌 🛗 /

SARATOGA BED & BREAKFAST Phone: 518/584-0920

All Year [BP]	1P: $99-$239	2P: $99-$239
		XP: $25 F

Historic Bed & Breakfast **Location:** 2.3 m w on SR 9N. 434 Church St 12866. Fax: 518/584-7177. **Facility:** This rambling, wood-frame farmhouse, which dates from 1860, offers guest rooms furnished with antiques and quilts; some rooms have a fireplace. Smoke free premises. 5 one-bedroom standard units. 2 stories (no elevator), interior corridors. *Bath:* combo or shower only. **Parking:** on-site. **Terms:** check-in 4 pm, 2 night minimum stay - weekends 4/1-10/31, age restrictions may apply, 14 day cancellation notice-fee imposed. **Amenities:** voice mail, hair dryers. **Cards:** AX, MC, VI.

ASK 🔌 ✕ 📠 🔌

SARATOGA DOWNTOWNER MOTEL Phone: (518)584-6160

7/28-9/5 [CP]	1P: $175-$209	2P: $175-$209 XP: $15 F18
5/1-7/27 & 9/6-10/31 [CP]	1P: $89-$99	2P: $89-$99 XP: $10 F18
11/1-4/30 [CP]	1P: $69-$79	2P: $69-$79 XP: $10 F18

Motel **Location:** On US 9, corner of Division St. 413 Broadway 12866. Fax: 518/584-2907. **Facility:** 42 one-bedroom standard units. 2 stories (no elevator), interior/exterior corridors. **Parking:** on-site. **Terms:** cancellation fee imposed. **Pool(s):** heated indoor. **Cards:** AX, DC, DS, MC, VI. **Special Amenities:** free continental breakfast and free newspaper.

SOME UNITS
🔲 🍴 ➰ 📠 / ✕ 🔌 /

SARATOGA MOTEL Phone: 518/584-0920

All Year	1P: $69-$189	2P: $69-$189 XP: $25

Motel **Location:** On SR 9N, 2.3 mi w of jct US 9/SR 50. Located in a rural area. 440 Church St 12866. Fax: 518/584-7177. **Facility:** 9 one-bedroom standard units, some with efficiencies. 1 story, exterior corridors. *Bath:* combo or shower only. **Parking:** on-site. **Terms:** check-in 4 pm, 14 day cancellation notice-fee imposed, small pets only. **Amenities:** voice mail. **Cards:** AX, MC, VI.

SOME UNITS
ASK 🔲 🐾 ✕ 📠 🔌 / 🛗 💻 /

THE SPRINGS MOTEL

Phone: (518)584-6336

AAA SAVE

	7/28-9/6	1P: $190	2P: $190	XP: $10 F18
	5/1-7/27 & 9/7-10/31	1P: $80	2P: $90	XP: $10 F18
	11/1-4/30	1P: $60	2P: $70	XP: $10 F18

Motel

Location: I-87, exit 13 N, 3.6 mi n on US 9. 189 Broadway 12866. **Fax:** 518/587-8164. **Facility:** 28 one-bedroom standard units. 2 stories (no elevator), exterior corridors. **Parking:** on-site, winter plug-ins. **Terms:** 2-3 night minimum stay - seasonal weekends, 20 day cancellation notice. **Amenities:** irons, hair dryers. **Pool(s):** outdoor. **Cards:** AX, DS, MC, VI. **Special Amenities: free local telephone calls.**

TURF AND SPA MOTEL

Phone: 518/584-2550

AAA SAVE

	7/28-9/5 [CP]	1P: $150-$170	2P: $150-$170	XP: $10 F18
	5/1-7/27, 9/6-11/1 & 4/1-4/30 [CP]	1P: $50-$85	2P: $55-$85	XP: $5 F18

Motel

Location: I-87, exit 13 N, 3.4 mi n on US 9. 176 Broadway 12866. **Fax:** 518/587-8162. **Facility:** 43 one-bedroom standard units. 2 stories (no elevator), exterior corridors. **Parking:** on-site. **Terms:** open 5/1-11/1 & 4/1-4/30, 14 day cancellation notice. **Amenities:** voice mail. **Pool(s):** heated outdoor. **Leisure Activities:** 2 mineral water whirlpools, barbecue & picnic area. *Fee:* massage. **Cards:** AX, CB, DC, DS, MC, VI. **Special Amenities: free continental breakfast and free local telephone calls.** *(See color ad below)*

UNION GABLES BED & BREAKFAST

Phone: 518/584-1558

AAA SAVE

	7/28-9/5	2P: $275-$300
	5/1-7/27 & 9/6-10/31	2P: $160-$175
	11/1-4/30	2P: $130-$145

Historic Bed & Breakfast

Location: I-87, exit 14, 1.5 mi w. 55 Union Ave 12866. **Fax:** 518/583-0649. **Facility:** This B&B, built in 1901, has been restored and offers well-decorated guest rooms. Designated smoking area. 12 units, 11 one- and 1 two-bedroom standard units. 3 stories (no elevator), interior corridors. *Bath:* combo or shower only. **Parking:** on-site. **Terms:** 14 day cancellation notice-fee imposed, [ECP] meal plan available, pets (owner's pet on premises). **Amenities:** irons, hair dryers. **Leisure Activities:** bicycles, exercise room. **Cards:** AX, DS, MC, VI.

THE WESTCHESTER HOUSE BED & BREAKFAST

Phone: (518)587-7613

AAA SAVE

	7/27-9/7 [ECP]	1P: $235-$350	2P: $235-$350
	5/1-7/26, 9/8-11/30 & 4/1-4/30 [ECP]	1P: $105-$210	2P: $105-$210

Historic Bed & Breakfast

Location: I-87, exit 13 N, 3.5 mi n on US 9, then 0.3 mi e. 102 Lincoln Ave 12866 (PO Box 944). **Fax:** 518/583-9562. **Facility:** This Queen Anne-style inn, built in 1885, is characterized by an Old World ambience yet offers up-to-date amenities. Smoke free premises. 7 one-bedroom standard units. 2 stories (no elevator), interior corridors. *Bath:* combo or shower only. **Parking:** on-site. **Terms:** open 5/1-11/30 & 4/1-4/30, check-in 4 pm, 2-4 night minimum stay - weekends, age restrictions may apply, 14 day cancellation notice. **Amenities:** CD players, voice mail. **Cards:** AX, CB, DC, DS, MC, VI. **Special Amenities: free local telephone calls and preferred room (subject to availability with advanced reservations).**

—————— **WHERE TO DINE** ——————

43 PHILA BISTRO

Dinner: $20-$30

Phone: 518/584-2720

American

Location: Between Caroline and Spring sts; center. 43 Phila St 12866. **Hours:** 5 pm-10 pm. Closed: 5/31, 12/25. **Reservations:** suggested. **Features:** The gaiety of the city's summer life is reflected in the animated conversations that take place around tables at the upscale bistro. Expect creative cuisine, capable service and an excellent wine list. Dressy casual; cocktails. **Parking:** street. **Cards:** AX, DC, DS, MC, VI.

BEVERLY'S

Lunch: $4-$9

Phone: 518/583-2755

American

Location: Between Caroline and Spring sts. 47 Phila St 12866. **Hours:** 8 am-3 pm. Closed: 3/27, 11/25, 12/25. **Features:** The restaurant serves breakfast and light lunches and also will pack picnics for patrons who want them. Casual dress. **Parking:** on-site. **Cards:** AX, DC, DS, MC, VI.

THE BREAD BASKET
Lunch: $3-$6 **Phone:** 518/587-4233
Location: Between Henry St and Circular Dr; center. 65 Spring St 12866. **Hours:** 6 am-6 pm, Sat & Sun-4 pm. Closed: 3/27, 11/25, 12/25; also Mon. **Features:** This small bakery offers a variety of soups and desserts. Limited indoor seating is available. Casual dress. **Parking:** on-site.
Bakery/Desserts

CHIANTI IL RISTORANTE
Dinner: $13-$20 **Phone:** 518/580-0025
Location: 0.5 mi n on US 9. 208 S Broadway 12866. **Hours:** 5:30 pm-10 pm. Closed major holidays. **Features:** A warm and intimate ambience accompanied by attentive and accomplished service set the scene for the simply wonderful food at Chianti's. Salads have unique accompaniments such as roasted eggplant. A great seafood choice is angel hair pasta with shrimp in a lobster, cream and grappa sauce. The classic tiramisu almost floats off the plate, even with a cup of robust espresso. Casual dress; cocktails.
Northern Italian
Parking: on-site. **Cards:** AX, MC, VI.

FOUR SEASONS NATURAL FOODS STORE & CAFE
Lunch: $5-$10 **Dinner:** $5-$10 **Phone:** 518/584-4670
Location: Corner of Putnam St; center. 33 Phila St 12866. **Hours:** 11:30 am-8 pm. Closed major holidays. **Features:** The city's only vegetarian restaurant also boasts a well-stocked natural foods/products store. Choices at the self-serve cafe are limited and the food is basic and functional. Among offerings are a salad bar, soups and several choices of hot meals. Try one of the many delicious made-to-order shakes and smoothies. Casual dress. **Parking:** street. **Cards:** AX, DC, DS, MC, VI.
Vegetarian

HATTIE'S
Dinner: $13-$18 **Phone:** 518/584-4790
Location: Between Caroline and Spring sts; center. 45 Phila St 12866. **Hours:** 5 pm-10 pm. Closed major holidays; also Mon & Tues 9/1-7/15. **Reservations:** accepted, except 7/1-8/31. **Features:** The restaurant is a part of city history, and the newest owners have done a remarkable job keeping its past alive in the countless photographs and reviews that adorn the walls and, more importantly, in faithful re-creations of some of Hattie's original recipes. Representative of fine down-home cooking are such dishes as Hattie's southern-fried chicken and Creole jambalaya. Chef Alexander also prepares more creative takes on Southern cuisine. Casual dress; cocktails. **Parking:** street. **Cards:** AX, DC, DS, MC, VI.
Southern

HIBACHI RESTAURANT
Lunch: $8-$10 **Dinner:** $14-$20 **Phone:** 518/580-9343
Location: I-87, exit 13, 1.8 mi n on US 9. 3310 S Broadway 12866. **Hours:** 11:30 am-10 pm, Fri & Sat-11 pm. **Reservations:** accepted. **Features:** Sushi, steak table fare, tempura and teriyaki - all can be found at the Hibachi Restaurant. The charm of a warm, Japanese-style tea house welcomes you to a relaxed and casual lunch or dinner. You will enjoy smooth service with touches of the Orient. A separate sushi menu is offered. A special machine to warm your saki to the correct temperature and dishes prepared to order. A house dessert combines east and west in the fried hibachi split - a fried banana and ice cream. Casual dress. **Parking:** on-site. **Cards:** AX, DC, MC, VI.
Japanese

LILLIAN'S
Lunch: $7-$10 **Dinner:** $15-$20 **Phone:** 518/587-7766
Location: Center. 408 Broadway 12866. **Hours:** 11:30 am-10 pm, Fri & Sat-11 pm, Sun noon-9 pm; 11:30 am-11 pm 6/1-9/30. Closed: 11/25, 12/25. **Reservations:** suggested, weekends. **Features:** Located on the main street, this restaurant which is named after actress Lillian Russell, is appointed in turn-of-the-20th-century decor, with Tiffany-style lamps, stained glass and Victorian accents. Prime rib and grilled salmon stand out on a menu of steak and seafood selections. Seasonal outdoor dining is available, weather permitting. Casual dress; cocktails. **Parking:** street. **Cards:** AX, CB, DC, MC, VI.
American

LONGFELLOWS RESTAURANT
Dinner: $15-$30 **Phone:** 518/587-0108
Location: I-87, exit 14, 1.4 mi s on SR 9P; in Longfellows Inn and Restaurant. 500 Union Ave 12866. **Hours:** 5 pm-10 pm, Fri & Sat-11 pm, Sun 4 pm-9 pm. Closed: 5/31, 12/24, 12/25. **Reservations:** suggested. **Features:** The warmth of an old inn combines with attentive service to make any evening memorable. Thick, creamy lobster bisque and Southwestern chicken strudel are two of several tempting appetizers. Entrees range from Kentucky bourbon-glazed salmon to slow-roasted prime rib. Pasta and vegetarian dishes have rich sauces and are served in ample portions. Dressy casual; cocktails. **Parking:** on-site. **Cards:** AX, CB, DC, DS, MC, VI.
Continental

MORRISSEY'S RESTAURANT
Lunch: $8-$12 **Dinner:** $8-$19 **Phone:** 518/584-8200
Location: I-87, exit 13N, 0.5 mi n on US 9. 3246 S Broadway 12866. **Hours:** 11 am-10 pm, Fri & Sat-11 pm. Closed: 1/1, 12/25. **Features:** Located just south of Saratoga Springs, the restaurant has a great lunch menu and a wonderful dinner menu. Wood-fired pizza is their specialty and you can watch it being made; on the dinner menu the crab cakes are a must. There is also a lounge area for a more casual atmosphere. Casual dress; cocktails. **Parking:** on-site. **Cards:** AX, DC, MC, VI.
American

THE OLDE BRYAN INN Historic
Lunch: $7-$10 **Dinner:** $11-$20 **Phone:** 518/587-2990
Location: I-87, exit 15 (downtown), 1.5 mi s on SR 50. 123 Maple Ave 12866. **Hours:** 11 am-10 pm, Fri & Sat-11 pm. Closed: 5/31, 11/25, 12/25; also for dinner 12/24. **Features:** Originally established as an inn in 1773, the Victorian restaurant is quaintly decorated with red globe lamps and wood accents. Menu selections are tried and true—prime rib, old-fashioned turkey dinner, homemade apple crisp and chocolate chip pie. Casual dress; cocktails. **Parking:** on-site. **Cards:** AX, DC, DS, MC, VI.
American

PANZA'S RESTAURANT
Dinner: $15-$25 **Phone:** 518/584-6882
Location: SR 9P, south end of Saratoga Lake. 510 Rt 9P 12866. **Hours:** 5 pm-10 pm, Fri & Sat-11 pm; hours vary off season. Closed: 11/25, 12/25; also Mon & Tues. **Reservations:** suggested. **Features:** Family-owned since 1938, the restaurant is decorated in the art deco style, with purple linens and striking artwork. Chicken Tuscany and shrimp Sorrentino, which blends shrimp, eggplant, mozzarella cheese and butter, are outstanding choices. Casual dress; cocktails. **Parking:** on-site. **Cards:** AX, CB, DS, MC, VI.
Continental

RAVENOUS
Continental

Lunch: $7-$9   **Dinner:** $7-$9   **Phone:** 518/581-0560

Location: Between Spring and Caroline sts; center. 21 Phila St 12866. **Hours:** 11:30 am-8 pm, Fri & Sat-9 pm; Saturday & Sunday brunch 10 am-3 pm. Closed: Mon & 12/25-1/2. **Features:** The small, funky, contemporary-style cafe has the feel of a local hang-out and offers a nice alternative to a heavy lunch or dinner. Savory luncheon and dinner crepes are served with organic lettuces, and lip-smacking, mouthwatering dessert crepes are made with nothing but the freshest, finest ingredients. Guests often are tempted by the pommes frites, Belgian-style fries, as well as by the delicious iced Moroccan mint tea. Casual dress; beer & wine only. **Parking:** street. **Cards:** MC, VI.

SARGO'S AT SARATOGA NATIONAL GOLF CLUB
Continental

Lunch: $9-$24   **Dinner:** $19-$44   **Phone:** 518/583-4653

Location: I-87, exit 14, 1 mi w on SR 9P. 458 Union Ave 12866. **Hours:** 11:30 am-4 & 5-10 pm, Fri & Sat-11 pm. Closed: 12/25. **Reservations:** required. **Features:** The restaurant boasts a very tempting Continental menu and an excellent wine list to go with it. The menu features such favorites as wood-grilled wild king salmon, seared Maine hand-dived scallops, and veal and lobster Lorenzo. With its high ceilings and great lighting, the dining room offers scenic views of the golf course, but if you prefer, you can sit in the lounge for a more casual atmosphere. Dressy casual; cocktails. **Parking:** on-site. **Cards:** AX, DC, DS, MC, VI.

SPRING WATER INN Historic
American

Dinner: $18-$26   **Phone:** 518/584-6440

Location: I-87, exit 14, 1.5 mi w; corner of Union Ave and Nelson. 139 Union Ave 12866. **Hours:** 5:30 pm-9:30 pm. Closed: 1/1, 11/25, 12/25; also Tues. **Reservations:** suggested. **Features:** For Saratoga racing season dining or anytime of year, the ambience of a private library and relaxed, friendly service at Spring Water Inn is sure to please. The variety of appetizers ranges from pate to crab cakes. Steak is a specialty but dishes such as veal with shrimp are tempting choices. The house dessert is a "not to be missed" frozen chocolate mousse with chunks of white chocolate and nuts. Valet parking is available 8/1-8/31. Casual dress; cocktails. **Parking:** on-site. **Cards:** AX, DC, MC, VI.

THE STADIUM CAFE
American

Lunch: $5-$15   **Dinner:** $5-$15   **Phone:** 518/226-4437

Location: Center. 389 Broadway 12866. **Hours:** 11:30 am-10 pm, Sat & Sun-midnight. Closed: 11/25, 12/25. **Features:** If you have to watch a baseball or football game, this is the place to watch it. There are so many televisions around the restaurant that any seat is a good seat. A list of appetizers will keep you busy and make it hard to choose one of the many sandwiches, wraps or burgers they offer. Outdoor dining in the summer offers views of Broadway. Casual dress; cocktails. **Parking:** street. **Cards:** AX, DS, MC, VI.

SUSHI THAI GARDEN
Asian

Lunch: $6-$12   **Dinner:** $8-$20   **Phone:** 518/580-0900

Location: Between Spring and Caroline sts; center. 44-46 Phila St 12866. **Hours:** 11:30 am-3 & 5-10 pm, Fri & Sat-10:30 pm. Closed: 11/25, 12/25. **Reservations:** accepted. **Features:** The restaurant offers diners a choice between the milder cuisine of Japan and the spicier foods of Thailand. Opt for teriyaki or tempura, or spice it up with a curry dish. Sushi is another good bet. Casual dress; beer & wine only. **Parking:** street. **Cards:** AX, DS, MC, VI.

WEATHERVANE SEAFOOD RESTAURANT
Seafood

Lunch: $4-$10   **Dinner:** $4-$18   **Phone:** 518/584-8157

Location: I-87, exit 13 N, 2.5 mi n, then 1.5 mi s on US 9. 3368 S Broadway 12866. **Hours:** 11 am-9:30 pm; to 9 pm in winter. Closed: 11/25, 12/24, 12/25. **Features:** This casual family-oriented restaurant is located on the edge of town. There are several large dining rooms which offer a light nautical decor. The wait staff is very casual but pleasant. The menu offers a variety of seafood items which can be broiled, baked or fried. Casual dress; cocktails. **Parking:** on-site. **Cards:** MC, VI.

WHEATFIELDS
Italian

Lunch: $7-$8   **Dinner:** $8-$19   **Phone:** 518/587-0534

Location: Center. 440 Broadway 12866. **Hours:** noon-10 pm; hours may vary off season. Closed: 11/25, 12/25. **Features:** This moderately upscale restaurant delivers an excellent variety of homemade pasta dishes, as well as preparations of fresh veal and seafood. The inviting dining room, with candlelit tables, is a nice contrast to the more casual patio overlooking the main street. Casual dress; cocktails. **Parking:** street. **Cards:** AX, DS, MC, VI.

THE WINE BAR
California

Dinner: $9-$21   **Phone:** 518/584-8777

Location: On US 9; center. 417 Broadway 12866. **Hours:** 4 pm-midnight. Closed: 11/25, 12/24, 12/25; also Sun & Mon. **Reservations:** suggested. **Features:** The environment is perfect for sharing a casual evening with friends. Among offerings are lighter fare, including a selection of gourmet cheeses, a full bar with an extensive by-the-glass list, a cigar lounge and an outdoor patio. Dressy casual; cocktails. **Parking:** street. **Cards:** AX, DC, DS, MC, VI.

The following restaurants have not been evaluated by AAA but are listed for your information only.

BRINDISI'S RESTAURANT & BAR
fyi

Phone: 518/587-6262

Not evaluated. **Location:** 390 Broadway 12866. **Features:** Lunch, dinner and late-night dancing are what to expect. Innovative cuisine blends Italian and Continental flavors.

ONE CAROLINE STREET BISTRO
fyi

Phone: 518/587-2026

Not evaluated. **Location:** 1 Caroline St 12866. **Features:** The intimate little bistro offers a lively international menu and nightly live jazz. The premises are entirely smoke-free.

SAUGERTIES pop. 4,955

------- WHERE TO STAY -------

COMFORT INN
AAA [SAVE]
◇◇◇◇ ◇◇◇◇
Small-scale Hotel

Book at aaa.com
All Year [ECP]   1P: $76-$159   2P: $76-$159   XP: $6   F18
Phone: (845)246-1565
Location: I-87, exit 20, just n. 2790 SR 32 12477. Fax: 845/246-1631. **Facility:** 65 one-bedroom standard units, some with efficiencies and/or whirlpools. 2 stories (no elevator), interior corridors. **Parking:** on-site, winter plug-ins. **Terms:** 14 day cancellation notice-fee imposed. **Amenities:** irons, hair dryers. **Leisure Activities:** exercise room. **Business Services:** meeting rooms. **Cards:** AX, CB, DC, DS, MC, VI.
Special Amenities: free expanded continental breakfast and free local telephone calls.

SOME UNITS
[S] [D] [🍴] [▦] / [✕] [DATA PORT] [🔌] [🖼] /
FEE   FEE

------- WHERE TO DINE -------

CAFE TAMAYO   Historic
◇◇ ◇◇
Regional American
Dinner: $14-$22
Phone: 845/246-9371
Location: On SR 32 and US 9W S; center. 89 Partition St 12477. **Hours:** 5 pm-9 pm, Fri & Sat-10 pm, Sun 11:30 am-3 & 5-8 pm. Closed: 1/1, 7/4, 12/25; also Mon-Wed. **Reservations:** suggested. **Features:** The attractively restored 1864 building has an original walnut bar, belt-driven paddle fans and plaster on canvas ceilings. Representative of complex preparations is the confit of duck, which is served with wild rice and red onion marmalade. Casual dress; cocktails. **Parking:** on-site. **Cards:** DS, MC, VI.
[✕]

EMILIANI RISTORANTE
◇◇ ◇◇
Italian
Dinner: $14-$20
Phone: 845/246-6169
Location: I-87, exit 20, 0.7 mi s on SR 32. 147-149 Ulster Ave 12477. **Hours:** 4:30 pm-10 pm, Sun 3 pm-9 pm. Closed: 11/25, 12/25; also Wed. **Reservations:** suggested, weekends. **Features:** Stenciled and decorated by the owner, the cozy restaurant has a quaint, homey atmosphere. The menu is undeniably sophisticated, with thoughtful preparations of chicken, veal, steak, seafood and pasta. The breads and desserts will make your mouth water. Casual dress; cocktails. **Parking:** on-site. **Cards:** AX, DS, MC, VI.
[✕]

NEW WORLD HOME COOKING CO.
◇◇ ◇◇
American
Lunch: $7-$16   Dinner: $8-$23   Phone: 845/246-0900
Location: I-87, exit 20, just w to SR 32, just n to CR 212, then 4.5 mi w. 1411 Rt 212 12477. **Hours:** 5 pm-10 pm, Fri-Mon also noon-3 pm. Closed: 12/25. **Reservations:** suggested. **Features:** Between Woodstock and Saugerties, the country eatery is bright with artful decorations and palate-pleasing dishes. Chef-owner Ric Orlando's creative menu combines flavors and styles from around the world. Locally produced foods factor heavily in dishes. Casual dress; cocktails. **Parking:** on-site. **Cards:** AX, CB, DC, DS, JC, MC, VI.
[⊻] [✕]

SCHENECTADY pop. 61,821

------- WHERE TO STAY -------

DAYS INN
◇◇◇ ◇◇◇
Small-scale Hotel
Book at aaa.com
5/1-8/31   1P: $54-$89   2P: $64-$99   XP: $10   F12
9/1-4/30   1P: $49-$89   2P: $54-$94   XP: $5   F12
Phone: (518)370-3297
Location: Jct State St (SR 5) and Nott Terrace, 2 blks e; downtown. 167 Nott Terrace 12308. Fax: 518/370-5948. **Facility:** 68 one-bedroom standard units, some with whirlpools. 3 stories, interior corridors. **Parking:** on-site, winter plug-ins. **Terms:** cancellation fee imposed, weekly rates available, small pets only ($10 extra charge, in designated units). **Amenities:** hair dryers. *Some:* irons. **Guest Services:** valet and coin laundry. **Cards:** AX, DC, MC, VI.

SOME UNITS
[ASK] [S] [D] [🐾] [🍴+] [⊘] [🍴] / [✕] [DATA PORT] [🔌] [🖼] [▦] /
FEE   FEE FEE

HOLIDAY INN-DOWNTOWN SCHENECTADY
◇◇◇ ◇◇◇
Small-scale Hotel
Book at aaa.com
All Year   1P: $109-$129   2P: $109-$129   XP: $16   F18
Phone: (518)393-4141
Location: Jct State St (SR 5) and Nott Terrace, 2 blks e; center. 100 Nott Terrace 12308. Fax: 518/393-4174. **Facility:** 184 one-bedroom standard units. 4 stories, interior corridors. **Parking:** on-site. **Terms:** small pets only (1st floor units). **Amenities:** video library (fee), video games, high-speed Internet, voice mail, irons, hair dryers. **Pool(s):** heated indoor. **Leisure Activities:** whirlpool, putting green, exercise room. *Fee:* game room. **Guest Services:** valet and coin laundry, area transportation. **Business Services:** conference facilities, fax (fee). **Cards:** AX, CB, DC, DS, JC, MC, VI.

SOME UNITS
[ASK] [S] [D] [✈] [🐾] [🍴] [⊻] [🛏] [✕] [📷] [DATA PORT] [▦] / [✕] [🔌] /

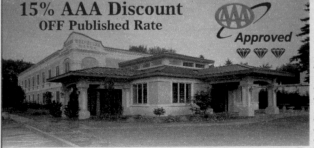

THE PARKER INN *Book at aaa.com* **Phone: (518)688-1001**
▽▽▽▽ All Year [CP] 1P: $145-$155 2P: $145-$155 XP: $15 F12
Location: Center. Located next to the Proctor Theater. 434 State St 12305. Fax: 518/688-1002. **Facility:** 23 units.
Small-scale Hotel 22 one-bedroom standard units. 1 one-bedroom suite ($175-$275). 8 stories, interior corridors. *Bath:* combo or shower only. **Parking:** on-site. **Terms:** cancellation fee imposed, package plans. **Amenities:** high-speed Internet (fee), dual phone lines, voice mail, irons, hair dryers. **Guest Services:** valet laundry. **Business Services:** meeting rooms, business center. **Cards:** AX, DC, DS, MC, VI.

SOME UNITS

(ASK) (S/D) (TI+) (Y) (X) (R) (DATA PORT) (▭) / (▯) /

QUALITY INN & SUITES **Phone: (518)355-1111**
(AAA) (SAVE) 6/1-10/31 [CP] 1P: $85-$95 2P: $95-$105 XP: $10 F12
5/1-5/31 & 11/1-12/31 [CP] 1P: $75-$85 2P: $85-$95 XP: $10 F12
▽▽▽ ▽▽▽ 1/1-4/30 [CP] 1P: $65-$75 2P: $75-$85 XP: $10 F12
Small-scale Hotel **Location:** I-890, exit 9 (Curry Rd); jct SR 7 and 146, 0.5 mi ne. 2788 Hamburg St 12303. Fax: 518/356-3817. **Facility:** 50 one-bedroom standard units, some with whirlpools. 2 stories (no elevator). **Parking:** on-site. **Terms:** 3 day cancellation notice. **Amenities:** irons. **Dining:** 11:30 am-3 & 5-10 pm, Fri & Sat-11 pm, cocktails. **Pool(s):** small heated outdoor. **Business Services:** conference facilities. **Cards:** AX, DC, MC, VI. **Special Amenities:** free continental breakfast and free local telephone calls.

SOME UNITS

(S/D) (TI) (Y) (≈) (R) (▭) / (X) (▯) /

——— **WHERE TO DINE** ———

PARISI'S **Lunch: $6-$10** **Dinner: $14-$33** **Phone: 518/374-0100**
▽▽▽ ▽▽▽ **Location:** Jct Union and Liberty St. 11 N Broadway 12305. **Hours:** 11 am-10 pm, Sat & Sun from 4 pm. Closed major holidays. **Features:** Known locally for its cut-to-order steaks, the restaurant also makes comparably Steak & Seafood delicious pasta and seafood dishes. An impressive list of mouthwatering appetizers and specialty salads makes decisions difficult. Dining rooms have an exotic look. Casual dress; cocktails. **Parking:** on-site.
Cards: AX, CB, DC, DS, MC, VI.

(Y) (X)

SCHOHARIE pop. 1,030

——— **WHERE TO STAY** ———

HOLIDAY INN EXPRESS HOTEL & SUITES SCHOHARIE *Book at aaa.com* **Phone: (518)295-6088**
▽▽▽ ▽▽▽ 7/5-9/6 [CP] 1P: $122-$167 XP: $10 F18
5/1-7/4 & 9/7-10/31 [CP] 1P: $104-$149 XP: $10 F18
Small-scale Hotel 11/1-4/30 [CP] 1P: $89-$134 XP: $10 F18
Location: I-88, exit 23, just e to Park Pl, then just s. 160 Holiday Way 12157. Fax: 518/295-6099. **Facility:** 56 units. 54 one-bedroom standard units, some with whirlpools. 2 one-bedroom suites ($130-$240) with whirlpools. 3 stories, interior corridors. *Bath:* combo or shower only. **Parking:** on-site. **Amenities:** dual phone lines, voice mail, irons, hair dryers. **Leisure Activities:** exercise room. *Fee:* game room. **Guest Services:** valet and coin laundry. **Business Services:** conference facilities, fax. **Cards:** AX, CB, DC, DS, JC, MC, VI.

SOME UNITS

(ASK) (S/D) (&) (Z) (R) (DATA PORT) (▭) / (X) (▯) (▤) /

——— **WHERE TO DINE** ———

GEORGE MANN'S TORY TAVERN Historic **Dinner: $30-$35** **Phone: 518/295-7128**
(AAA) **Location:** I-88, exit 23, 2.2 mi s on SR 30, then just e on SR 443. 104 Vrooman Cross Rd 12157. **Hours:** Open 5/1-1/1 & 2/2-4/30; 5 pm-9 pm, Sun 1 pm-7 pm. Closed: Mon & Tues. **Reservations:** suggested.
▽▽▽ ▽▽▽ **Features:** Colonial furnishings decorate the restored 1700s tavern. The daily-changing menu might include American such dishes as veal-mushroom pate, rabbit-white bean soup and flavorful veal gruyere with fresh, al dente vegetables. Desserts are almost irresistible. Casual dress; cocktails. **Parking:** on-site. **Cards:** AX, MC, VI.

(X)

THE PARROTT HOUSE Historic **Lunch: $4-$8** **Dinner: $9-$16** **Phone: 518/295-7111**
▽▽▽ **Location:** On SR 30; downtown. 294 Main St 12157. **Hours:** 11 am-2 & 5-9 pm, Sat from noon. Closed major holidays; also Sun. **Reservations:** suggested, weekends. **Features:** There are no talking birds or pirates American here, just ample servings of good food in a casual family atmosphere. The 1870s tavern specializes in seafood, steak and game. Great soups and hearty sandwiches fill the lunch bill as well. The restaurant is adjacent to other historic buildings in town. Casual dress; cocktails. **Parking:** on-site. **Cards:** AX, CB, DC, DS, MC, VI.

(Y) (X)

SCHROON LAKE —See also ADIRONDACK MOUNTAINS.

——— **WHERE TO STAY** ———

BLUE RIDGE MOTEL **Phone: (518)532-7521**
(AAA) (SAVE) 5/19-9/5 1P: $68-$78 2P: $79-$89 XP: $10 F18
Location: I-87, exit 28, 4 mi n. 2455 US Rt 9 12870. Fax: 518/532-9235. **Facility:** 17 one-bedroom standard units.
▽▽▽ 1 story, interior/exterior corridors. *Bath:* combo or shower only. **Parking:** on-site. **Terms:** open 5/19-9/5, 2 Motel night minimum stay - weekends in season, 14 day cancellation notice-fee imposed, weekly rates available, pets ($5 fee). **Pool(s):** heated outdoor. **Leisure Activities:** recreation programs, playground. **Business Services:** fax. **Cards:** AX, MC, VI. **Special Amenities:** free expanded continental breakfast and free local telephone calls.

SOME UNITS

(S/D) (ਦ) (≈) (Z) (▭) / (X) (▯) (▤) /
FEE

------- **WHERE TO DINE** -------

DRAKE'S RESTAURANT   **Lunch:** $4-$7   **Dinner:** $8-$18   **Phone:** 518/532-9040
△△△
Location: I-87, exit 28, 1 mi s; in Drakes Motel. US 9 12870. **Hours:** Open 5/23-10/12; 11:30 am-3 & 4:30-9 pm;
7:30 am-3 & 4:30-9 pm 7/1-9/1. **Reservations:** suggested, for dinner. **Features:** In a seasonal resort town,
the cheerful restaurant is appointed with nautical decor. Reasonably priced selections of standard
American   American favorites make this place popular with families. Breakfasts and light lunches also are served.
Service is friendly. Casual dress; cocktails. **Parking:** on-site. **Cards:** AX, DS, MC, VI.   ⓨ ☒

SCOTIA pop. 7,957

------- **WHERE TO DINE** -------

GLEN SANDERS MANSION Historic   **Lunch:** $7-$14   **Dinner:** $17-$34   **Phone:** 518/374-7262
▽▽▽
Location: Just sw on Glen Ave from SR 5, 1 mi from I-890. 1 Glen Ave 12302. **Hours:** 11:30 am-2 & 5-10 pm, Sat
Continental   from 5 pm, Sun 10:30 am-1:30 & 4-9 pm. **Reservations:** suggested. **Features:** Built in the late 1600s, the
elegantly renovated mansion houses a restaurant where accomplished and deft service brings guests a
delightful meal. The setting is fitting for sweet corn and crab cake, salmon, roasted sea bass,
maple-marinated sirloin, chocolate gooey cake and fine liquors. Dressy casual; cocktails. **Parking:** on-site. **Cards:** AX, CB,
DC, DS, MC, VI.   ⓨ ☒

SENECA FALLS pop. 6,861—See also FINGER LAKES.

------- **WHERE TO STAY** -------

BARRISTER'S BED & BREAKFAST   **Phone:** (315)568-0145
▽▽▽
All Year [BP]   1P: $110-$155   2P: $110-$155
Location: I-90, exit 41, 4 mi s on SR 414, then 2 mi e on SR 5 and 20 (Cayuga St). 56 Cayuga St 13148. **Facility:** 1888
Bed & Breakfast Colonial revival with carved fireplaces, stained glass windows within walking distance to museums, canal and
shops. Smoke free premises. 5 units. 4 one-bedroom standard units, some with whirlpools. 1 one-bedroom
suite ($235-$255). 2 stories (no elevator); interior corridors. **Bath:** combo or shower only. **Parking:** on-site. **Terms:** 2 night
minimum stay - weekends, 7 day cancellation notice-fee imposed. **Amenities:** Some: CD players. **Guest Services:** TV in
common area. **Cards:** AX, DS, MC, VI.

SOME UNITS

(ASK) 🖼 ☒ 🅦 ☎ / (VCR) 🔲 💻 /

------- **WHERE TO DINE** -------

HENRY B'S   **Dinner:** $12-$30   **Phone:** 315/568-1600
▽▽▽
Location: Center. 84 Fall St 13148. **Hours:** 4:30 pm-10 pm. Closed: Sun & Mon. **Reservations:** suggested.
Italian   **Features:** Authentic Italian cuisine is carefully prepared from quality ingredients and proudly presented by
friendly, professional staff who can assist you in your selection. The shared dining concept offers generous
portions for two or more in an intimate, upscale but unpretentious atmosphere. Casual dress; cocktails.
Parking: street. **Cards:** AX, DC, DS, MC, VI.   🔊 ⓨ ☒

SHELTER ISLAND HEIGHTS pop. 981

------- **WHERE TO STAY** -------

DERING HARBOR INN   **Phone:** (331)749-0900
▽▽▽ ▽▽▽
5/29-9/5   1P: $200-$425   XP: $20   F12
5/14-5/28 & 9/6-10/17   1P: $170-$370   XP: $20   F12
Small-scale Hotel **Location:** North ferry, 0.5 mi s on SR 114; jct SR 114 and Winthrop Rd, just e. Located on waterfront. 13 Winthrop Rd
11965 (PO Box 3028). Fax: 631/749-2045. **Facility:** 20 units. 4 one-bedroom standard units. 13 one- and 3
two-bedroom suites with kitchens. 2 stories (no elevator); exterior corridors. **Parking:** on-site. **Terms:** open 5/14-10/17, 2 night
minimum stay - weekends, 14 day cancellation notice-fee imposed. **Amenities:** voice mail, hair dryers.
Pool(s): outdoor. **Leisure Activities:** fishing, 2 tennis courts, basketball, volleyball. *Fee:* boat dock. **Guest Services:** valet and
coin laundry. **Business Services:** meeting rooms. **Cards:** AX, DS, MC, VI.

SOME UNITS

🍴 ⓨ ⇌ ☒ 🔲 💻 / ☒ (VCR) 💻 /

SHERRILL pop. 3,147

------- **WHERE TO DINE** -------

COLOSSEO ITALIAN & AMERICAN RESTAURANT   **Lunch:** $3-$5   **Dinner:** $6-$12   **Phone:** 315/363-9076
▽▽▽
Location: SR 5 13461. **Hours:** 11 am-10 pm, Fri & Sat-11 pm. Closed major holidays.
Reservations: suggested. **Features:** A casual ease is evident in the relaxed dining room of the
Italian   family-oriented restaurant. Traditional entrees are split among American and Italian selections. Manicotti is
particularly tasty, as is the scrumptious blueberry pie, served a la mode. Casual dress; cocktails. **Parking:**
on-site. **Cards:** AX, DC, DS, MC, VI.   ⓨ ☒

ROSS'S GINGERBREAD HOUSE FAMILY RESTAURANT   **Lunch:** $4-$7   **Dinner:** $7-$14   **Phone:** 315/363-6644
▽▽ ▽▽
Location: On SR 5, just e of Main St. Rt 5 & Betsinger Rd 13461. **Hours:** 11 am-9 pm, Fri & Sat-9:30 pm, Sun
noon-6 pm. Closed: 1/1, 11/25, 12/25; also Mon. **Reservations:** accepted. **Features:** Country crafts and
American   Victorian appointments decorate the inviting dining room in the no-smoking restaurant. Chicken in lemon
butter and haddock with white wine sauce are tasty choices, as are the splendid homemade desserts.
Casual dress; cocktails. **Parking:** on-site. **Cards:** AX, DC, DS, MC, VI.   ⓨ ☒

SHINNECOCK HILLS pop. 1,749

——— WHERE TO STAY ———

OCEAN VIEW TERRACE MOTEL

Phone: (631)728-4036

| | 5/21-9/14 | 1P: $150-$250 | 2P: $150-$250 | XP: $30 | F12 |
| | 5/1-5/20, 9/15-1/3 & 4/1-4/30 | 1P: $135-$210 | 2P: $135-$210 | XP: $30 | F12 |

Motel **Location:** SR 27, exit 65 S (Hampton Bays), just s, then 2.5 mi e on SR 80. 285 E Montauk Hwy 11946 (285 E Montauk Hwy, HAMPTON BAYS). Fax: 631/723-3287. **Facility:** 16 units. 13 one-bedroom standard units, some with efficiencies. 2 one- and 1 two-bedroom suites ($210-$320), some with kitchens and/or whirlpools. 1-2 stories (no elevator), exterior corridors. *Bath:* combo or shower only. **Parking:** on-site. **Terms:** open 5/1-1/3 & 4/1-4/30, 2 night minimum stay - weekends in season, 10 day cancellation notice-fee imposed, weekly rates available, package plans. **Amenities:** voice mail. **Pool(s):** outdoor. **Guest Services:** valet laundry. **Cards:** AX, CB, DC, DS, MC, VI.

SKANEATELES pop. 2,616—See also FINGER LAKES.

——— WHERE TO STAY ———

ARBOR HOUSE INN

Phone: 315/685-8966

| | 5/1-10/31 [BP] | | 2P: $150-$195 | XP: $10 | |
| | 11/1-4/30 [BP] | | 2P: $75-$195 | XP: $10 | |

Bed & Breakfast **Location:** Downtown. 41 Fennell St 13152. Fax: 315/685-7841. **Facility:** This circa 1850 Federal style home offers all modern amenities including private baths. Tastefully renovated and furnished with antiques. Smoke free premises. 5 units. 4 one-bedroom standard units, some with whirlpools. 1 one-bedroom suite ($195) with whirlpool. 2 stories, interior corridors. **Parking:** on-site. **Terms:** age restrictions may apply, 10 day cancellation notice-fee imposed. **Cards:** AX, DS, MC, VI.

HI-WAY HOST MOTEL

Phone: 315/685-7633

| | All Year | 1P: $60-$65 | 2P: $60-$65 | XP: $5 | D10 |

Motel **Location:** 0.8 mi w on US 20. 834 W Genesee St 13152. **Facility:** 12 one-bedroom standard units. 1 story, exterior corridors. **Parking:** on-site. **Terms:** office hours 7 am-9 pm. **Cards:** MC, VI.

HOBBIT HOLLOW FARM BED AND BREAKFAST

Phone: 315/685-2791

| | 5/1-1/1 [BP] | 1P: $120-$270 | 2P: $120-$270 | XP: $25 | |
| | 1/2-4/30 [BP] | 1P: $100-$250 | 2P: $100-$250 | XP: $25 | |

Historic Bed & Breakfast **Location:** 1.7 mi s on SR 41A from US 20. Located in a quiet, rural area. 3061 W Lake Rd 13152. Fax: 315/685-3426. **Facility:** A lake and 320 acres of rolling hills provide a scenic backdrop to this finely furnished B&B; an adjacent barn houses horses. Smoke free premises. 5 one-bedroom standard units, some with whirlpools. 2 stories (no elevator), interior corridors. *Bath:* combo or shower only. **Parking:** on-site. **Terms:** age restrictions may apply, 10 day cancellation notice. **Amenities:** video library, hair dryers. **Leisure Activities:** cross country skiing, recreation programs. *Fee:* massage. **Guest Services:** TV in common area, complimentary evening beverages. **Business Services:** PC, fax. **Cards:** AX, DS, MC, VI.

HUMMINGBIRD'S HOME BED & BREAKFAST

Phone: (315)685-5075

| | All Year [BP] | 1P: $75-$130 | 2P: $89-$145 | | |

Bed & Breakfast **Location:** From center, 1.5 mi w on US 20. 4273 W Genesee St 13152. **Facility:** Cozy, inviting rooms with hospitality to match make it easy to relax in this restored 1803 farmhouse; full gourmet breakfast served. 4 one-bedroom standard units. 2 stories, interior corridors. *Bath:* combo or shower only. **Parking:** on-site. **Terms:** 2 night minimum stay - weekends 5/1-9/30, 14 day cancellation notice-fee imposed, no pets allowed (owner's dog on premises). **Amenities:** hair dryers. **Cards:** AX, DS, MC, VI.

SKANEATELES HOTEL

Phone: (315)685-2333

| | 6/1-9/30 [CP] | 1P: $125-$195 | 2P: $125-$195 | XP: $15 | F12 |
| | 5/1-5/31 & 10/1-4/30 [CP] | 1P: $95-$195 | 2P: $95-$195 | XP: $15 | |

Small-scale Hotel **Location:** Off Jordon St; center. 12 Fennell St 13152 (PO Box 912). Fax: 315/685-7223. **Facility:** Smoke free premises. 5 one-bedroom standard units. 2 stories (no elevator), interior corridors. *Bath:* combo or shower only. **Parking:** on-site. **Terms:** 2 night minimum stay - with Saturday night stayover, 10 day cancellation notice-fee imposed, weekly rates available, package plans. **Amenities:** voice mail, hair dryers. **Guest Services:** complimentary laundry. **Cards:** AX, DC, DS, MC, VI.

SKANEATELES SUITES

Phone: (315)685-7568

| | 5/1-5/31 & 10/1-4/30 [CP] | 1P: $95-$195 | 2P: $95-$195 | XP: $15 | F12 |
| | 6/1-9/30 [CP] | 1P: $125 | 2P: $195 | XP: $15 | F12 |

Motel **Location:** On US 20, 2 mi w. 4114 W Genesee St 13152 (PO Box 912). Fax: 315/685-1021. **Facility:** Smoke free premises. 9 units. 7 one-bedroom standard units, some with whirlpools. 1 one- and 1 three-bedroom suites ($1600-$4500) with kitchens. 2 stories (no elevator), exterior corridors. *Bath:* combo or shower only. **Parking:** on-site. **Terms:** 2 night minimum stay - with Saturday night stayover, 10 day cancellation notice-fee imposed, weekly rates available, package plans, pets ($35 fee). **Amenities:** video library, CD players, irons, hair dryers. **Leisure Activities:** gas grill, hiking trails. **Guest Services:** valet laundry. **Cards:** AX, DC, DS, MC, VI. **Special Amenities:** free local telephone calls and free room upgrade (subject to availability with advanced reservations).

————— WHERE TO DINE —————

BLUEWATER GRILL
Lunch: $5-$9   **Dinner:** $10-$16   **Phone:** 315/685-6600
Location: Center. 11 W Genesee St 13152. **Hours:** 11:30 am-10 pm, Fri & Sat-11 pm, Sun 10:30 am-2 pm. Closed: 1/1, 11/25, 12/25. **Reservations:** suggested. **Features:** Sitting on a fishing pier is never as much
American   fun as it is at this casual grill next to the pier on Lake Skaneateles. Guests can dine outside in fine
weather or inside at the bustling eatery. Baked fresh scrod is a favorite, and Maryland crab cakes and grilled-to-order filet mignon are also tempting. Bumbleberry pie is a good "catch" for dessert. Casual dress; cocktails. **Parking:** street. **Cards:** AX, DC, DS, MC, VI.

DOUG'S FISH FRY
Lunch: $5-$7   **Dinner:** $7-$15   **Phone:** 315/685-3288
Location: Center. 8 Jordan St 13152. **Hours:** Open 5/1-12/31 & 1/15-4/30; 11 am-10 pm; to 8 pm 9/3-5/26. Closed major holidays. **Features:** People flock to the hole-in-the-wall restaurant for a good reason—the
Seafood   food is great. Fried just right, the fish fry is lightly browned, with the fish turning out light and flaky. Crispy, golden fries and tangy slaw are delicious accompaniments. Casual dress; beer & wine only. **Parking:**
on-site. **Cards:** MC, VI.

KABUKI
Dinner: $10-$17   **Phone:** 315/685-7234
Location: Center. 12 W Genesee St 13152. **Hours:** 5 pm-9 pm, Fri & Sat-10 pm; to 10 pm, Fri & Sat-11 pm 5/31-9/6. Closed: 1/1, 11/25, 12/25. **Reservations:** suggested. **Features:** The electic sushi bar sustains a
Asian   cheery, bistro-style atmosphere in which to enjoy Asian-themed foods made from the freshest ingredients. Casual dress; beer & wine only. **Parking:** street. **Cards:** AX, DS, MC, VI.

THE KREBS Country Inn
Dinner: $10-$35   **Phone:** 315/685-5714
Location: On US 20. 53 W Genesee St 13152. **Hours:** Open 5/1-10/30; 6 pm-9 pm, Fri & Sat-10 pm, Sun 10:30 am-2 & 4-9 pm. Closed: 9/6. **Reservations:** suggested. **Features:** The long-established restaurant
American   delivers a seven-course prix fixe meal that includes country-style entrees of lobster Newburg, prime rib and fried chicken. Early American decor pulls together the dining room in a tidy, cohesive theme. Service is prompt. Casual dress; cocktails. **Parking:** on-site. **Cards:** AX, CB, DC, DS, MC, VI.

MANDANA INN
Dinner: $14-$28   **Phone:** 315/685-7798
Location: 6 mi s on SR 41A. 1937 W Lake Rd 13152. **Hours:** Open 5/1-1/1 & 4/2-4/30; 5 pm-10 pm, Sun 4 pm-9 pm. Closed: 12/24, 12/25; also Mon & Tues 4/1-5/31 & 9/3-10/31, Mon-Wed 11/1-1/1. **Reservations:** suggested. **Features:** Near Skaneateles Lake, the former stagecoach tavern is decorated
Seafood   with antique grandfather clocks and local artwork. The menu centers on well-prepared entrees of flavorful seafood and steak. The homemade dessert here has been popular for many years. Casual dress; cocktails. **Parking:** street. **Cards:** AX, DC, DS, MC, VI.

ROSALIE'S CUCINA
Dinner: $10-$28   **Phone:** 315/685-2200
Location: 0.6 mi w. 841 W Genesee St 13152. **Hours:** 5 pm-9 pm, Fri & Sat-10 pm. Closed major holidays; also Super Bowl Sun. **Features:** Scampi Rosalie—a delicious choice with shrimp, garlic butter, angel hair
Italian   pasta, artichokes and oven-cured tomatoes—is just one of the creative dishes on the tempting menu. Tuscan furnishings and warm, wood ceilings decorate the dining room. Lucious, generous desserts are made fresh on premises. Casual dress; cocktails. **Parking:** on-site. **Cards:** AX, MC, VI.

SHERWOOD INN DINING ROOM Country Inn
Lunch: $7-$12   **Dinner:** $12-$27   **Phone:** 315/685-3405
Location: US 20; in Sherwood Inn. 26 W Genesee St 13152. **Hours:** 11:30 am-9 pm, Fri & Sat-10 pm, Sun 4 pm-9 pm. Closed: 12/25; also for dinner 12/24. **Reservations:** suggested. **Features:** Enjoy beautiful views
American   of the water from most seats in the comfortable dining room. The menu centers on generous portions of standard tavern fare—fish, chicken, red meat, salad, sandwiches and pizza. The historic inn was established in 1807. Casual dress; cocktails. **Parking:** on-site. **Cards:** AX, DS, MC, VI.

SMITHTOWN pop. 26,901

————— WHERE TO STAY —————

ECONO LODGE SMITHTOWN   *Book at aaa.com*   **Phone:** (631)724-9000
All Year   1P: $89-$169   2P: $89-$169   XP: $8   F18
Location: On SR 347 (Hauppauge-Nesconset Rd), 2.3 mi e of SR 111. Located in a commercial area. 755 Smithtown
Bypass 11787. Fax: 631/724-9017. **Facility:** 39 one-bedroom standard units. 1-2 stories, exterior corridors.
Motel   **Parking:** on-site. **Amenities:** hair dryers. **Cards:** AX, CB, DC, DS, JC, MC, VI. **Special Amenities:** free continental breakfast and free newspaper.
SOME UNITS

————— WHERE TO DINE —————

CASA RUSTICA
Lunch: $11-$16   **Dinner:** $15-$25   **Phone:** 631/265-9265
Location: Jct SR 111/25A/25, 0.7 mi w. 175 W Main St 11787. **Hours:** noon-3 & 5-10 pm, Fri-11 pm, Sat 5 pm-11 pm, Sun 2 pm-9 pm. Closed major holidays. **Reservations:** suggested, for dinner.
Northern   **Features:** Representative of mouth-watering fare are two specialties: vitello Casa Rustica, which is a
Italian   breaded rack of veal covered with mozzarella in herb and garlic sauce, and pesce in crosta di sale, a flavorful preparation of the fresh catch of the day. Dressy casual; cocktails. **Parking:** on-site. **Cards:** AX, DC, DS, MC, VI.

H2O SEAFOOD GRILL   Lunch: $10-$20   Dinner: $16-$30   Phone: 631/361-6464

▼▼▼▼   **Location:** Jct SR 111/25A/25, 0.8 mi w. 215 W Main St 11787. **Hours:** noon-3 & 5-10 pm, Fri-11 pm, Sat 5
pm-11 pm, Sun 2 pm-10 pm. Closed: 11/25, 12/25. **Reservations:** suggested. **Features:** The stylish hot
Seafood   spot features fresh tastes from the ocean. Guests should come hungry and order often because the
portions allow for the sampling of multiple courses, including artfully presented desserts. Dressy casual;
cocktails. **Parking:** on-site. **Cards:** AX, CB, DC, DS, MC, VI.

IL VIOLINO RISTORANTE   Dinner: $14-$30   Phone: 631/382-9744

▼▼▼▼   **Location:** Jct SR 111/25A/25, 0.5 mi w; center. 53 W Main St 11787. **Hours:** 5 pm-9:30 pm, Fri & Sat-10:30 pm,
Sun 4 pm-9 pm. Closed: 1/1, 7/4, 12/25; also Mon. **Reservations:** suggested. **Features:** Il Violino offers
Northern   fine dining in an intimate atmosphere. Dressy casual; cocktails. **Parking:** street. **Cards:** AX, CB, DC,
Italian   MC, VI.

SOUTHAMPTON pop. 3,965

———— WHERE TO STAY ————

EVERGREEN ON PINE BED & BREAKFAST   Phone: (631)283-0564

▼▼▼▼   5/1-10/31 [ECP]   1P: $150-$450   2P: $150-$450   XP: $25
     11/1-4/30 [ECP]   1P: $100-$195   2P: $100-$195   XP: $25
Bed & Breakfast   **Location:** Jct Main St, just s on Meeting House Ln. Located in a residential area. 89 Pine St 11968. Fax: 631/283-0564.
Facility: Hardwood floors and some antiques add charm to guest rooms at this B&B, which has an inviting
outdoor patio. Smoke free premises. 5 one-bedroom standard units. 2 stories (no elevator), interior corridors. *Bath:* combo or
shower only. **Parking:** on-site. **Terms:** check-in 4 pm, 2 night minimum stay - weekends 4/1-10/31, age restrictions may apply,
14 day cancellation notice-fee imposed, package plans. **Amenities:** high-speed Internet, voice mail. *Some:* irons, hair dryers.
Cards: AX, DS, MC, VI.

SOME UNITS

   FEE

SOUTHAMPTON INN   *Book at aaa.com*   Phone: (631)283-6500

▼▼▼   7/1-9/5   1P: $249-$489   2P: $249-$489   XP: $29   F18
     5/1-6/30   1P: $169-$459   2P: $169-$459   XP: $29   F18
     9/6-10/31   1P: $159-$329   2P: $159-$329   XP: $29   F18
Small-scale Hotel   11/1-4/30   1P: $119-$199   2P: $119-$199   XP: $29   F18
Location: 0.3 mi n from corner of Main St and Jobs Ln. 91 Hill St 11968. Fax: 631/283-6559. **Facility:** 90 units. 89 one-bedroom standard units. 1 one-bedroom suite ($319-$999). 2 stories (no elevator), exterior corridors. *Bath:* combo or shower only. **Parking:**
on-site. **Terms:** 2 night minimum stay - weekends 5/1-10/31, 30 day cancellation notice-fee imposed, package plans - seasonal,
small pets only ($29 extra charge). **Amenities:** video games (fee), voice mail, hair dryers. *Some:* CD players. **Pool(s):** heated
outdoor. **Leisure Activities:** tennis court, exercise room. *Fee:* game room. **Guest Services:** valet laundry, area transportation.
Business Services: meeting rooms. **Cards:** AX, CB, DC, DS, MC, VI.

SOME UNITS

   FEE

———— WHERE TO DINE ————

BARRISTER'S   Lunch: $7-$9   Dinner: $13-$20   Phone: 631/283-6206

▼▼▼   **Location:** Center. 36 Main St 11968. **Hours:** 11:30 am-5 & 5:30-11 pm, Fri & Sat-midnight, Sun 11:30
am-10:30 pm. Closed: 11/25, 12/25. **Features:** The casual tavern is a favorite haunt in which neighbors
American   dine and chat over simply prepared, flavorful dishes. Penne pasta, peppercorn-rubbed tuna steak and
grilled pork loin medallions are representative of menu fare. The covered terrace is relaxing. Casual dress;
cocktails. **Parking:** on-site. **Cards:** AX, DC, DS, MC, VI.

BASILICO   Lunch: $6-$15   Dinner: $14-$25   Phone: 631/283-7987

▼▼▼▼   **Location:** Just w of Main St via Jobs Ln. 10 Windmill Ln 11960. **Hours:** 11:30 am-3:30 & 5:30-10 pm, Fri &
Sat-11 pm. Closed: 1/1, 11/25, 12/24, 12/25. **Reservations:** suggested, for dinner. **Features:** A country
Italian   trattoria ambience punctuates the chic cafe, which presents a menu of dishes prepared with subtle
Mediterranean influences. Fresh ingredients flavor such dishes as spaghetti with broccoli, grilled vegetable
pizza and marinated grilled fish. Dressy casual; cocktails. **Parking:** street. **Cards:** AX, CB, DC, DS, MC, VI.

DRIVERS SEAT RESTAURANT   Lunch: $9-$15   Dinner: $14-$19   Phone: 631/283-6606

▼▼   **Location:** Center. 62 Jobs Ln 11968. **Hours:** 11:30 am-10 pm, Fri & Sat-11 pm. Closed: 11/25, 12/25.
Features: Known for steak and seafood specials, the casual family restaurant serves traditional American
American   fare with a twist. An inviting patio—dotted with nicely spaced tables covered by umbrellas—sits out back.
Service is basic, prompt and friendly. Casual dress; cocktails. **Parking:** on-site. **Cards:** AX, MC, VI.

THE PLAZA CAFE   Dinner: $22-$32   Phone: 631/283-9323

▼▼▼   **Location:** 0.3 mi n from corner of Main St and Jobs Ln/Hill St; downtown. 61 Hill St 11968. **Hours:** 5:30 pm-11 pm.
Closed: 12/25; also Tues & Wed. **Reservations:** suggested, in season. **Features:** Some say this airy East
American   End cottage is a hidden treasure. Yellow textured walls, an iron chandelier, flowers and fireplace make for
subdued sophisticated dining. Seafood is the chef's star with choices of brightly flavored and seasoned fish
and shellfish. Steamed mussels with lemon grass curry broth anyone? Plaza's generous and soul-satisfying shepherd's pie is
the signature dish, filled with chunks of lobster, shrimp, shiitakes and topped with light chive flecked potatoes. Dressy casual;
cocktails. **Parking:** on-site. **Cards:** AX, DC, MC, VI.

The following restaurant has not been evaluated by AAA but is listed for your information only.

SOUTHAMPTON PUBLICK HOUSE   Phone: 631/283-2800
[fyi]   Not evaluated. **Location:** Just e, corner of North Sea Rd. 40 Bowden Sq 11968. **Features:** Homemade, award-winning lagers and ales are always on tap to accompany traditional pub favorites.

SOUTH BRISTOL

─────── **WHERE TO STAY** ───────

BRISTOL HARBOUR RESORT   Phone: (585)396-2200

	6/25-9/7	1P: $149-$169	2P: $149-$169
	5/1-6/24 & 9/8-10/30	1P: $119-$139	2P: $119-$139
Resort	10/31-4/30	1P: $89-$139	2P: $89-$139

Small-scale Hotel **Location:** From Canandaigua, 7.7 mi s on SR 21, 0.5 mi e on CR 16, then 1.1 mi s. Overlooking Canandaigua Lake. 5410 Seneca Point Rd 14424 (5410 Seneca Point Rd, CANANDAIGUA). Fax: 585/394-9254. **Facility:** In a sophisticated Adirondack style, these roomy lodgings, each with a fireplace, offer heated bath floors and balconies overlooking a lake. 31 units. 30 one-bedroom standard units. 1 one-bedroom suite ($139-$229) with whirlpool. 1-3 stories (no elevator), exterior corridors. **Parking:** on-site. **Terms:** 7 day cancellation notice. **Amenities:** voice mail, irons, hair dryers. **Pool(s):** lap. **Leisure Activities:** whirlpool, exercise room. *Fee:* golf-18 holes, massage. **Guest Services:** gift shop. **Business Services:** meeting rooms. **Cards:** AX, DC, DS, MC, VI.

SOME UNITS

SOUTH GLENS FALLS pop. 3,368—*See also GLENS FALLS.*

─────── **WHERE TO STAY** ───────

LANDMARK MOTOR INN   Phone: 518/793-3441

(AAA) [SAVE]	7/26-9/7	1P: $120	2P: $120	XP: $10	F18
	5/1-7/25	1P: $60	2P: $65-$70	XP: $5	F18
	9/8-10/10	1P: $55	2P: $60-$65	XP: $5	F18
Motel	10/11-4/30	1P: $50	2P: $52-$55	XP: $5	F18

Location: I-87, exit 17 N, 1 mi n. US 9 12803 (PO Box 376, GLENS FALLS, 12801). Fax: 518/761-6909. **Facility:** 74 one-bedroom standard units. 1 story, exterior corridors. **Parking:** on-site, winter plug-ins. **Terms:** cancellation fee imposed. **Pool(s):** outdoor, indoor. **Leisure Activities:** whirlpool, putting green, playground, exercise room. **Business Services:** meeting rooms, fax. **Cards:** AX, CB, DC, DS, JC, MC, VI. **Special Amenities:** free local telephone calls and free newspaper. *(See ad p 563)*

SOME UNITS

FEE

SOUTH KORTRIGHT

─────── **WHERE TO DINE** ───────

THE HIDDEN INN Historic   Dinner: $6-$20   Phone: 607/538-9259
American   **Location:** CR 18, just s of SR 10, follow signs. Main St 13842. **Hours:** 5 pm-9 pm, Sun noon-7 pm. Closed: 12/25; also Mon. **Reservations:** suggested, weekends. **Features:** The 1890s restored Colonial home is decorated in a French country motif, with fresh flowers, chandeliers and tableside lighting. The bottomless bowl of shrimp is a favorite offering on a menu of lamb, veal, duck, beef and seafood choices. Casual dress; cocktails. **Parking:** on-site. **Cards:** AX, DS, MC, VI.

SOUTHOLD pop. 5,465

─────── **WHERE TO DINE** ───────

COEUR DES VIGNES   Dinner: $17-$33   Phone: 631/765-2656
(AAA)   **Location:** Just e; downtown. 57225 Main Rd 11971-4704. **Hours:** 5 pm-9 pm, Fri-10 pm, Sat noon-11 pm, Sun 11 am-9 pm. Closed: 12/25; also Mon off season & Tues. **Reservations:** suggested. **Features:** The sophisticated menu changes seasonally depending on what the family catches in the morning or finds in the field. They are expert at providing fresh fish and game and the chef/son prepares the predominately French dishes beautifully. Long stem roses and candles adorn each table but the mood is friendly and relaxed. Dressy casual; cocktails. **Parking:** on-site. **Cards:** AX, CB, DC, DS, MC, VI.

SOUTH WORCESTER

─────── **WHERE TO STAY** ───────

CHARLOTTE VALLEY INN B & B AND ANTIQUES   Phone: 607/397-8164

	All Year [BP]	1P: $80-$100	2P: $90-$150	XP: $20	D12

Historic Bed & Breakfast   **Location:** SR 23, 5.0 mi n on Delaware CR 9/40. 480 County Hwy 40 12197. **Facility:** Handmade quilts cover the four-poster beds at this stagecoach inn overlooking a quiet valley. Designated smoking area. 5 one-bedroom standard units. 2 stories (no elevator), interior corridors. *Bath:* some shared or private, combo or shower only. **Parking:** on-site. **Terms:** 14 day cancellation notice, no pets allowed (owner's pets on premises). **Guest Services:** TV in common area.

SPECULATOR pop. 348

──────── WHERE TO STAY ────────

LAKE PLEASANT INN   **Phone: (518)548-5746**

▽▽▽ ▽▽▽	12/30-4/30	1P: $90-$150	2P: $90-$150
Motel	6/15-9/7	1P: $95-$145	2P: $95-$145
	5/1-6/14	1P: $85-$145	2P: $85-$145
	9/8-12/29	1P: $75-$125	2P: $75-$125

Location: Jct SR 30 and 8, just s. Located by Lake Pleasant. Rt 30 12164. Fax: 518/548-5192. **Facility:** Smoke free premises. 11 one-bedroom standard units, some with whirlpools. 1 story, exterior corridors. *Bath:* combo or shower only. **Parking:** on-site. **Terms:** office hours 7 am-midnight, 45 day cancellation notice, in summer. **Amenities:** irons. **Dining:** Fjord Restaurant, see separate listing. **Cards:** AX, DS, MC, VI.

(ASK) (S◯) (†1) (✕) (DATA PORT)

──────── WHERE TO DINE ────────

FJORD RESTAURANT   **Lunch:** $3-$9   **Dinner:** $15-$20   **Phone:** 518/548-5746

▽▽ ▽▽

American

Location: Jct SR 30 and 8, just s; in Lake Pleasant. Rt 30 12164. **Hours:** 8 am-10 pm; hours vary off season. **Closed:** 1/1, 11/25, 12/25. **Reservations:** suggested. **Features:** Next to Lake Pleasant, the restaurant affords views of the lovely Adirondack scenery. Delicious fare reflects a Norwegian accent. The sinfully rich rice cream pudding is a must. Casual dress; cocktails. **Parking:** on-site. **Cards:** AX, CB, DS, MC, VI. (✕)

SPENCERTOWN

──────── WHERE TO STAY ────────

SPENCERTOWN COUNTRY HOUSE-A BED & BREAKFAST   **Phone: (518)392-5292**

| ▽▽▽ ▽▽▽ | 5/1-10/31 [BP] | 1P: $65-$220 | 2P: $85-$220 | XP: $25 |
| Historic Bed & Breakfast | 11/1-4/30 [BP] | 1P: $65-$175 | 2P: $70-$175 | XP: $25 |

Location: Jct Taconic State Pkwy, 0.4 mi e on SR 203, then 0.9 mi n. 1909 CR 9 12165 (PO Box 279). Fax: 518/392-7453. **Facility:** A brook crosses the grounds of this Federalist-style 1803 mansion in the Berkshires; it also offers a carriage house converted into meeting space. Smoke free premises. 9 one-bedroom standard units. 2 stories (no elevator), interior corridors. *Bath:* combo or shower only. **Parking:** on-site. **Terms:** 2 night minimum stay - seasonal, age restrictions may apply, 14 day cancellation notice-fee imposed. **Amenities:** video library. **Business Services:** meeting rooms. **Cards:** AX, DS, MC, VI.

(占) (✕) (DATA PORT) / (₽Ⅳ) (VCR) (🖥)

SPRINGFIELD CENTER —*See also COOPERSTOWN.*

──────── WHERE TO STAY ────────

BAYSIDE INN & MARINA   **Phone: 607/547-2371**

| (AAA) (SAVE) | 6/18-9/6 | 1P: $149-$189 | 2P: $149-$189 | XP: $10 |
| ▽▽ ▽▽ | 5/1-6/17 & 9/7-10/31 | 1P: $59-$89 | 2P: $59-$89 | XP: $10 |

Motel

Location: 3 mi s. 7090 State Hwy 80 13468. Fax: 607/547-5856. **Facility:** 29 one-bedroom standard units. 1-2 stories (no elevator), interior/exterior corridors. **Parking:** on-site. **Terms:** open 5/1-10/31, 3 day cancellation notice-fee imposed. **Amenities:** voice mail, irons, hair dryers. **Leisure Activities:** canoeing, paddleboats, fishing, children's swimming area, rowboats, picnic tables, barbecue, gazebos, playground. *Fee:* marina, game room. **Cards:** DS, MC, VI. **Special Amenities:** early check-in/late check-out. *(See ad p 269)*

SOME UNITS

(✕) (🎥) (DATA PORT) (🖥) / (✕) (🖥)

COOPERSTOWN LAKE 'N PINES MOTEL   **Phone: (607)547-2790**

| (AAA) (SAVE) | 6/18-9/6 [CP] | 1P: $130-$135 | 2P: $145-$160 | XP: $10 |
| ▽▽ ▽▽ | 5/1-6/17, 9/7-12/1 & 3/18-4/30 [CP] | 1P: $55-$65 | 2P: $65-$85 | XP: $10 |

Motel

Location: Jct US 20, 3 mi s. 7102 State Hwy 80 13326. Fax: 607/547-5671. **Facility:** 35 one-bedroom standard units. 1 story, exterior corridors. **Parking:** on-site. **Terms:** open 5/1-12/1 & 3/18-4/30, 5 day cancellation notice. **Amenities:** hair dryers. **Pool(s):** heated outdoor, heated indoor. **Leisure Activities:** sauna, whirlpool, paddleboats, boat dock, fishing, rowboats, picnic area with grills. *Fee:* game room. **Cards:** AX, DC, MC, VI. **Special Amenities:** free continental breakfast and free local telephone calls. *(See color ad p 269)*

SOME UNITS

(⇴) (✕) (🎥) (🖥) / (✕) /

COOPERSTOWN'S HICKORY GROVE MOTOR INN   **Phone: (607)547-9874**

(AAA) (SAVE)	6/11-9/5	1P: $110-$130	2P: $110-$140	XP: $5
▽▽ ▽▽	9/6-10/23 & 4/16-4/30	1P: $55-$90	2P: $58-$100	XP: $5
Motel	5/1-6/10	1P: $50-$88	2P: $55-$90	XP: $5

Location: Jct US 20, 4.7 mi sw. 6854 State Hwy 80 13326. Fax: 607/547-8567. **Facility:** 12 one-bedroom standard units. 1 story, exterior corridors. *Bath:* shower only. **Parking:** on-site. **Terms:** open 5/1-10/23 & 4/16-4/30, 2-3 night minimum stay - weekends, 5 day cancellation notice-fee imposed, [CP] meal plan available. **Amenities:** hair dryers. **Leisure Activities:** paddleboats, fishing, small stone beach area. **Cards:** AX, DS, MC, VI. **Special Amenities:** free local telephone calls and preferred room (subject to availability with advanced reservations).

SOME UNITS

(✕) (🎥) / (✕) /

LAKE VIEW MOTEL & MARINA   **Phone: (607)547-9740**

(AAA) (SAVE)	6/13-9/1	1P: $109-$197	2P: $109-$197
▽▽ ▽▽	9/2-12/1	1P: $56-$99	2P: $59-$99
Motel	5/1-6/12 [CP]	1P: $56-$99	2P: $56-$99
	4/1-4/30	1P: $56-$99	2P: $56-$99

Location: Jct US 20, 4 mi s. 6805 State Hwy 80 13326 (PO Box 293, SOMERVILLE, NJ, 08876). Fax: 607/547-5080. **Facility:** 35 units. 27 one-bedroom standard units. 3 one-bedroom suites ($89-$162), some with kitchens. 5 cottages ($99-$197). 1 story, exterior corridors. *Bath:* combo or shower only. **Parking:** on-site. **Terms:** open 5/1-12/1 & 4/1-4/30, 2 night minimum stay - weekends, 7 day cancellation notice, 30 day for a stay of 5 days or more, package plans - seasonal. **Amenities:** video library (fee), CD players, high-speed Internet, voice mail, hair dryers. **Leisure Activities:** paddleboats, fishing, rowboats. *Fee:* boat dock. **Cards:** AX, DS, MC, VI.

SOME UNITS

(S◯) (✕) (🎥) (🖥) (🖥) / (✕) (VCR) (🖥) /

SPRING GLEN

──── WHERE TO DINE ────

COUNTY LINE RESTAURANT   **Dinner:** $8-$19   **Phone:** 845/647-3310

◆◆◆   **Location:** US Rt 209 12483. **Hours:** 4:30 pm-9 pm. **Closed:** 12/24, 12/25; also Mon 1/1-2/28 & Tues.
Reservations: accepted. **Features:** The walls are adorned with pictures of spirits from around the world.
American   After sampling from the soups, salad bar and plentiful entrees, guests might find it difficult to save room for
a homemade dessert, such as Black Forest cake. Casual dress; cocktails. **Parking:** on-site. **Cards:** AX,
DS, MC, VI.

SPRING VALLEY —See New York p. 457.

SPRINGVILLE —See Buffalo p. 255.

STAATSBURG pop. 911

──── WHERE TO DINE ────

PORTOFINO RISTORANTE   **Dinner:** $10-$19   **Phone:** 845/889-4711

ⒶⒶⒶ   **Location:** Center. 57 Old Post Rd 12580. **Hours:** 4 pm-9:30 pm, Fri & Sat-10:30 pm, Sun-9 pm. **Closed:**
11/25, 12/25; also Mon & 1/1-1/20. **Features:** Regional Italian dishes mingle with daily-changing specials
◆◆◆   that show piquant influences from the Pacific Rim. Art deco prints decorate the walls of the dining room;
Italian   soft music, ranging from jazz to easy listening pop, plays in the background. Casual dress; cocktails.
Parking: on-site. **Cards:** AX, DC, DS, MC, VI.

STAFFORD pop. 2,409

──── WHERE TO DINE ────

RED OSIER LANDMARK RESTAURANT   **Dinner:** $11-$30   **Phone:** 585/343-6972

ⒶⒶⒶ   **Location:** Center. 6492 Main Rd (SR 5) 14143. **Hours:** 4 pm-8:30 pm, Fri & Sat-10 pm, Sun 1 pm-8:30 pm;
hours may vary in winter. Closed major holidays; also 12/24 & Mon. **Reservations:** accepted.
◆◆◆   **Features:** Casual country dining offers early birds and famous specials as well as their signature prime rib
American   and lobster tail dinner value. Generous portions of aged black angus New York strip steaks and filet
mignon are available or create your own seafood combos with lobster, scallops or Alaskan King crab.
Casual dress; cocktails. **Parking:** on-site. **Cards:** AX, MC, VI.

STATEN ISLAND —See New York p. 448.

STEPHENTOWN pop. 2,873

──── WHERE TO STAY ────

MILL HOUSE INN   **Phone:** (518)733-5606

◆◆◆◆   5/15-10/30 & 12/15-3/15 [ECP]   1P: $105-$115   2P: $115-$130   XP: $15
Location: Jct SR 22, 1.1 mi e. 86 Rt 43 12168 (PO Box 477). Fax: 518/733-6025. **Facility:** Two fireplace rooms
Bed & Breakfast   are among the varied accommodations at this Alpine chalet-style inn, which is characterized by an informal
charm. Smoke free premises. 12 units. 7 one-bedroom standard units. 5 one-bedroom suites ($135-$175). 2
stories (no elevator), interior/exterior corridors. **Bath:** combo or shower only. **Parking:** on-site. **Terms:** open 5/15-10/30 & 12/15-
3/15, office hours 8 am-11 pm, 14 day cancellation notice. **Amenities:** video library. **Pool(s):** small outdoor. **Cards:** AX,
MC, VI.

SOME UNITS

STONY BROOK pop. 13,727

──── WHERE TO STAY ────

HOLIDAY INN EXPRESS STONY BROOK   *Book at aaa.com*   **Phone:** (631)471-8000

◆◆◆   All Year   1P: $134-$215   2P: $134-$215   XP: $10   F
Location: I-495, exit 62, 8 mi n on Nicolls Rd (CR 97), then 0.6 mi e on SR 347. Located in a commercial area. 3131
Small-scale Hotel   Nesconset Hwy 11720. Fax: 631/471-8623. **Facility:** 143 units. 136 one-bedroom standard units, some with
whirlpools. 7 one-bedroom suites, some with whirlpools. 6 stories, interior corridors. **Parking:** on-site.
Amenities: video games (fee), voice mail, irons, hair dryers. **Pool(s):** heated indoor. **Leisure Activities:** playground, exercise
room. **Guest Services:** valet laundry. **Business Services:** meeting rooms. **Cards:** AX, CB, DC, DS, JC, MC, VI.

SOME UNITS

THREE VILLAGE INN   **Phone:** 631/751-0555

ⒶⒶⒶ SAVE   All Year   2P: $179-$225   XP: $20   F10
Location: Jct SR 25A and Main St, just n. Located opposite Village Green. 150 Main St 11790. Fax: 631/751-0593.
◆◆◆   **Facility:** Built as an inn in 1751, this hotel offers a main building and small cottages, all in Colonial style in-
Historic   side and out. Smoke free premises. 26 one-bedroom standard units. 2 stories (no elevator), interior/exterior
Country Inn   corridors. **Bath:** combo or shower only. **Parking:** on-site. **Terms:** [BP] meal plan available, package plans.
Amenities: voice mail, irons, hair dryers. **Dining:** restaurant, see separate listing. **Business Services:**
meeting rooms. **Cards:** AX, MC, VI. **Special Amenities:** free full breakfast and preferred room (subject
to availability with advanced reservations).

——— WHERE TO DINE ———

THREE VILLAGE INN   Country Inn   **Lunch:** $10-$18   **Dinner:** $27-$36   **Phone:** 631/751-0555
▽▼▽▼▽▼   **Location:** Jct SR 25A and Main St, just n; in Three Village Inn. 150 Main St 11790. **Hours:** 7 am-11, noon-4 & 5-9 pm, Fri & Sat 8 am-11 pm, Sun 8 am-11, noon-3 & 4-9 pm. Closed: 12/25. **Reservations:** suggested.
Regional American   **Features:** A Colonial theme weaves through the converted 1751 homestead. Enjoy panoramic views of the village and harbor from the charming dining rooms. Yankee pot roast, roast duckling and seafood pie are examples of traditional New England dishes. Dressy casual; cocktails. **Parking:** on-site. **Cards:** AX, DC, MC, VI.   🍸 ☒

STORMVILLE

——— WHERE TO DINE ———

HARRALDS   **Dinner:** $68   **Phone:** 845/878-6595
▽▼▽▼ ▽▼▽▼   **Location:** I-84, exit 17, 2.5 mi w. 3760 SR 52 12582. **Hours:** 6 pm-9 pm; Sat seatings 5:30 pm & 9 pm. Closed: 1/1, 3/27, 12/24, 12/25; also Sun-Tues. **Reservations:** required. **Features:** You would take a drive up the Taconic Parkway, into the Hudson Valley area, to dine at Harralds. The chef's exceptional six-course meal, complemented by a comprehensive wine list, is an experience in European Continental cuisine. The service is attentive, yet unobtrusive with Old World elegance. Semi-formal attire; cocktails. **Parking:** on-site.   🍸 ☒

Continental

SUFFERN —*See New York p. 457.*

SYLVAN BEACH pop. 1,071

——— WHERE TO STAY ———

CINDERELLA'S COMFORT SLEEP SUITES   **Phone:** 315/762-4280

▽▼▽	5/27-9/6	1P: $79-$179	2P: $79-$179
	9/7-10/31	1P: $69-$129	2P: $69-$129
Motel	5/1-5/26	1P: $59-$129	2P: $59-$129
	11/1-4/30	1P: $59-$119	2P: $59-$119

Location: On SR 13; center. 1208 N Main St 13157. Fax: 315/762-5675. **Facility:** 9 one-bedroom standard units, some with whirlpools. 1 story, exterior corridors. *Bath:* combo or shower only. **Parking:** on-site. **Terms:** 16 day cancellation notice, weekly rates available, package plans, pets ($50 deposit). **Amenities:** irons, hair dryers. **Dining:** Cinderella's Cafe, see separate listing. **Guest Services:** coin laundry. **Cards:** AX, DC, DS, MC, VI.

(ASK) 🛍 🛒 🍽 ☒ 🛏 🖼 🖥
FEE

——— WHERE TO DINE ———

CANAL VIEW CAFE   **Lunch:** $4-$8   **Dinner:** $7-$14   **Phone:** 315/762-5623
▽▼▽   **Location:** On north side of Erie Canal; w of SR 13 S. 9 Canal St 13157. **Hours:** Open 5/1-11/20 & 3/20-4/30; 11:30 am-9 pm, Fri & Sat-10 pm; to 8 pm, Fri & Sat-9 pm off season. Closed: Tues 3/20-5/29 & 9/7-11/20.
American   **Reservations:** accepted. **Features:** Overlooking Oneida Lake and Erie Canal, the casual restaurant has a fresh nautical theme. Patrons can enjoy a meal in the bright dining room or on the deck. Menu favorites include seafood, pasta and steaks. A children's menu is available. Casual dress; beer & wine only. **Parking:** on-site. **Cards:** AX, DS, MC, VI.   🍸 ☒

CAPTAIN JOHN'S PRIME RIB-PASTA & SEAFOOD HOUSE   **Dinner:** $9-$24   **Phone:** 315/762-9949
(AAA)   **Location:** Center. 1424 N Beach (Rt 13) Blvd 13157. **Hours:** Open 5/1-10/31 & 2/14-4/30; 3 pm-10 pm, Sun from noon. Closed: Tues; Wed 3/1-5/30 & 9/8-11/1. **Features:** This is the place for diners with big appetites. Among specialties are two-pound prime-rib cuts, two-pound crab legs and one-pound lobster
▽▼ ▽▼   tails. Nautical appointments set a seafaring tone in the casual dining room. Scrumptious desserts, such as
Steak & Seafood   hot apple dumpling served with ice cream, are homemade. Casual dress; cocktails. **Parking:** on-site. **Cards:** AX, CB, DC, DS, MC, VI.   🍸 ☒

CINDERELLA'S CAFE   **Lunch:** $5-$8   **Dinner:** $8-$16   **Phone:** 315/762-4280
(AAA)   **Location:** On SR 13; center; in Cinderella's Comfort Sleep Suites. 1208 N Main St 13157. **Hours:** Open 5/1-11/30 & 1/15-4/30; 8 am-9 pm; to 10 pm 6/1-8/31. Closed: 11/25. **Reservations:** accepted. **Features:** Pictures of
▽▼   Cinderella decorate the walls of the whimsical family cafe. Breakfast is served until 2 pm. Menu choices
American   range from charbroiled steaks to grilled lemon pepper haddock. On Saturday, guests can sample all-you-can-eat crab legs with free shrimp cocktail. For dessert, enjoy a piece of freshly baked pie or choose from an array of more than 40 flavors of ice cream and yogurt. Casual dress; beer & wine only. **Parking:** on-site. **Cards:** AX, DC, DS, MC, VI.   🍸 ☒

EDDIE'S RESTAURANT   **Lunch:** $5-$12   **Dinner:** $8-$13   **Phone:** 315/762-5430
▽▼   **Location:** Center. 901 Main St 13157. **Hours:** Open 5/1-10/30 & 3/15-4/30; 11 am-11 pm. **Features:** Operated by the Stewarts since 1934, the family-oriented restaurant is a local favorite for seafood, steaks and pasta.
American   Homemade fruit and "mile-high" cream pies are specialties. Surrounded by windows, the bright, friendly dining room is decorated with works by local artists. Servers are pleasant and attentive. Casual dress. **Parking:** on-site. **Cards:** MC, VI.   ☒

YESTERDAY'S ROYAL-ABBY'S RESTAURANT   **Lunch:** $5-$7   **Dinner:** $8-$15   **Phone:** 315/762-4677
▽▼   **Location:** On the canal; next to amusement park. 13 Canal St 13157. **Hours:** Open 5/1-9/30 & 4/14-4/30; 11:30 am-10 pm. Closed: Mon-Wed 9/8-9/30. **Features:** Portions are generous at the old-fashioned family
American   restaurant, which has some old-time memorabilia and a tin-type ceiling. The menu centers on familiar preparations of fish, beef, chicken and pasta. Children of all ages enjoy the ice cream bar and in-house desserts. Casual dress; cocktails. **Parking:** on-site. **Cards:** AX, DC, DS, MC, VI.   🍸 ☒

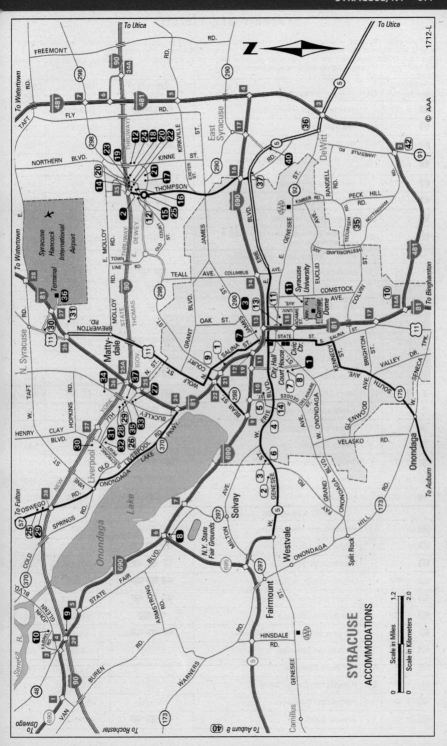

SYRACUSE
ACCOMMODATIONS

Syracuse and Vicinity

This index helps you "spot" where approved accommodations and restaurants are located on the corresponding detailed maps. Lodging rate ranges are for comparison only and show the property's high season; rates are per night, unless only weekly (W) rates are available. Restaurant rate range is for dinner, unless only lunch (L) is served. Turn to the listing page for more detailed rate information and consult display ads for special promotions.

Spotter/Map Page Number	OA	SYRACUSE - Lodgings	Diamond Rating	Rate Range High Season	Listing Page
❶ / p. 577		Hawthorn Suites Armory Square	◈◈◈	$139-$399	580
❷ / p. 577	AAA	Red Roof Inn	◈◈	$52-$73 SAVE	582
❸ / p. 577		The Dickenson House on James	◈◈◈	$115-$150	580
❼ / p. 577	AAA	Econo Lodge University/Downtown - see color ad p 580	◈◈	$55-$80 SAVE	580
❽ / p. 577		Best Western Fairgrounds	◈◈◈	$99	580
❾ / p. 577		Comfort Inn Fairgrounds	◈◈	$79-$179	580
❿ / p. 577	AAA	Holiday Inn/Farrell Road	◈◈◈	$69-$139 SAVE	581
⓫ / p. 577	AAA	Sheraton Syracuse University Hotel & Conference Center	◈◈◈	$300-$370 SAVE	582
		SYRACUSE - Restaurants			
① / p. 577		Antonio's Restaurant	◈◈	$13-$28	582
② / p. 577		China Pavilion	◈	$6-$13	582
③ / p. 577		Mimi's Bakery & Cafe	◈	$2-$7(L)	583
④ / p. 577	AAA	Coleman's Authentic Irish Pub & Restaurant	◈◈	$11-$18	582
⑤ / p. 577		Pascale Wine Bar and Restaurant	◈◈◈	$14-$24	583
⑥ / p. 577		Dinosaur Bar-B-Que	◈	$10-$15	582
⑦ / p. 577		Bistro 238	◈◈◈	$12-$20	582
⑧ / p. 577		Lemon Grass	◈◈◈	$14-$20	583
⑨ / p. 577		Juanita's Mexican Kitchen	◈	$5-$12	583
⑩ / p. 577	AAA	Danzer's Restaurant	◈	$10-$14	582
⑪ / p. 577		Phoebe's Garden Cafe	◈◈	$12-$18	583
⑫ / p. 577		Joey's Restaurant	◈◈◈	$12-$18	582
⑬ / p. 577		L'Adour	◈◈◈	$19-$24	583
⑭ / p. 577		Pastabilities	◈	$8-$20	583
		EAST SYRACUSE - Lodgings			
⓬ / p. 577	AAA	Hilton Garden Inn-Syracuse	◈◈◈	$62-$161 SAVE	282
⓮ / p. 577		Courtyard by Marriott	◈◈◈	$79-$159	282
⓯ / p. 577		Residence Inn By Marriott	◈◈◈	Failed to provide	283
⓰ / p. 577		Candlewood Suites Syracuse	◈◈◈	$89	281
⓱ / p. 577		Holiday Inn East-Carrier Circle	◈◈◈	$89-$109	283
⓲ / p. 577		East Syracuse Super 8	◈◈	$45-$80	282
⓳ / p. 577		Embassy Suites Hotel - see ad p 581	◈◈◈	$129-$229	282
⓴ / p. 577	AAA	Microtel Inn Syracuse	◈◈	$40-$83 SAVE	283
㉑ / p. 577	AAA	Wyndham Syracuse	◈◈◈	$145-$165 SAVE	283
㉒ / p. 577	AAA	Hampton Inn-Carrier Circle	◈◈◈	$89-$135 SAVE	282
㉓ / p. 577	AAA	Fairfield Inn Syracuse	◈◈	$65-$85 SAVE	282
㉔ / p. 577		CrestHill Suites	◈◈◈	$129-$259	282

Spotter/Map Page Number	OA	EAST SYRACUSE - Lodgings (continued)	Diamond Rating	Rate Range High Season	Listing Page
25 / p. 577	🔺	Comfort Inn-Carrier Circle	▽▽▽	$85-$109 SAVE	282
		EAST SYRACUSE - Restaurant			
20 / p. 577	.	Justin's Grill	▽▽	$16-$29	283
		LIVERPOOL - Lodgings			
27 / p. 577		Hampton Inn	▽▽▽	$89-$99	341
28 / p. 577		Homewood Suites	▽▽▽	$109-$219	341
29 / p. 577	🔺	Super 8 Motel Route 57	▽▽	$59-$109 SAVE	341
30 / p. 577	🔺	Best Western Inn & Suites	▽▽▽	$99-$169 SAVE	341
31 / p. 577		Holiday Inn Syracuse Airport	▽▽▽	$114-$139	341
32 / p. 577	🔺	Knights Inn - see color ad p 581	▽▽	$44-$129 SAVE	341
33 / p. 577		Super 8 Motel Syracuse/Liverpool	▽▽	$59-$99	341
		LIVERPOOL - Restaurants			
25 / p. 577		Pier 57	▽▽	$10-$15	342
26 / p. 577	🔺	Ichiban Japanese Steak House	▽▽	$14-$27	341
		NORTH SYRACUSE - Lodgings			
34 / p. 577		Doubletree Club Hotel/Syracuse Airport	▽▽▽	$75-$139	529
35 / p. 577	🔺	Ramada Inn - see color ad p 581	▽▽▽	$99 SAVE	530
36 / p. 577	🔺	Best Western Syracuse Airport Inn	▽▽	$74-$115 SAVE	529
37 / p. 577	🔺	Quality Inn North	▽▽	$79-$139 SAVE	530
		NORTH SYRACUSE - Restaurants			
29 / p. 577		Colorado Mine Company Steakhouse	▽▽	$10-$19	530
30 / p. 577		The Clam Bar	▽	$10-$12	530
31 / p. 577		Hunan Empire	▽▽	$6-$14	530
		DE WITT - Lodgings			
40 / p. 577	🔺	Econo Lodge	▽▽	$62-$120 SAVE	276
		DE WITT - Restaurants			
35 / p. 577		Saratoga Steaks and Seafood	▽▽	$13-$30	277
36 / p. 577		Scotch N' Sirloin	▽▽	$13-$40	277
37 / p. 577		Delmonico's Italian Steakhouse	▽▽	$9-$15	276
		CAMILLUS - Restaurant			
40 / p. 577	.	Inn Between Restaurant	▽▽▽	$18-$23	258
		JAMESVILLE - Restaurant			
42 / p. 577	🔺	Glen Loch Restaurant	▽▽	$11-$32	315

SYRACUSE pop. 147,306 (See map and index starting on p. 577)—See also EAST SYRACUSE & NORTH SYRACUSE.

——— WHERE TO STAY ———

BEST WESTERN FAIRGROUNDS *Book at aaa.com*   Phone: (315)484-0044   8

5/1-10/31 & 4/1-4/30	1P: $99	2P: $99	XP: $10 F12
11/1-3/31	1P: $85	2P: $85	XP: $10 F12

Small-scale Hotel **Location:** I-690, exit 7, 1.3 mi nw, just past fairgrounds. 670 State Fair Blvd 13209. Fax: 315/484-0045. **Facility:** 47 one-bedroom standard units, some with whirlpools. 2 stories, interior corridors. *Bath:* combo or shower only. **Parking:** on-site. **Terms:** 14 day cancellation notice-fee imposed, [ECP] meal plan available, pets ($25 fee). **Amenities:** voice mail, irons, hair dryers. *Some:* high-speed Internet. **Leisure Activities:** exercise room. *Fee:* game room. **Guest Services:** valet laundry. **Cards:** AX, DC, DS, MC, VI.

ASK SD FEE ⛌ 🍴 🍷 &M ⚿ DATA PORT ▣ / ✕ 🖥 🖨 /   SOME UNITS

COMFORT INN FAIRGROUNDS *Book at aaa.com*   Phone: (315)453-0045 9

All Year [ECP]	1P: $79-$169	2P: $79-$179	XP: $10

Small-scale Hotel **Location:** I-90, exit 39 to I-690 E, exit 2 (Jones Rd), just sw. 7010 Interstate Island Rd 13209. Fax: 315/453-3689. **Facility:** 109 one-bedroom standard units, some with whirlpools. 4 stories, interior corridors. **Parking:** on-site. **Terms:** pets ($10 fee). **Amenities:** video library (fee), irons, hair dryers. **Leisure Activities:** exercise room. *Fee:* game room. **Guest Services:** valet laundry. **Business Services:** meeting rooms, fax (fee). **Cards:** AX, CB, DC, DS, MC, VI.

ASK SD FEE ⛌ 🍴 🎦 DATA PORT ▣ / ✕ VCR FEE 🖥 🖨 /   SOME UNITS

THE DICKENSON HOUSE ON JAMES   Phone: (315)423-4777 3

All Year [BP]	1P: $115-$125	2P: $125-$150	XP: $25 D18

Historic Bed & Breakfast **Location:** I-90, exit 35 (Carrier Cir), 1 mi s on Thompson Rd S, then 2 mi w. 1504 James St 13203. Fax: 315/425-1965. **Facility:** Built in 1920 and once a private residence, this restored inn is in an area of historic homes; modern conveniences enhance the cozy guest rooms. Smoke free premises. 4 one-bedroom standard units. 2 stories (no elevator), interior corridors. *Bath:* combo or shower only. **Parking:** on-site. **Terms:** age restrictions may apply. **Amenities:** dual phone lines, hair dryers. **Business Services:** fax. **Cards:** AX, DS, MC, VI.

✕ DATA PORT

ECONO LODGE UNIVERSITY/DOWNTOWN *Book at aaa.com*   Phone: (315)425-0015 7

AAA SAVE

All Year [CP]	1P: $55-$80	2P: $55-$80	XP: $8 F18

Motel **Location:** Downtown. 454 James St 13203. Fax: 315/474-7009. **Facility:** 47 one-bedroom standard units. 3 stories, exterior corridors. *Bath:* combo or shower only. **Parking:** on-site. **Terms:** weekly rates available, small pets only ($8 extra charge). **Amenities:** *Some:* DVD players, irons, hair dryers. **Guest Services:** area transportation-bus & train station. **Business Services:** fax (fee). **Cards:** AX, DC, DS, MC, VI. **Special Amenities:** free continental breakfast. *(See color ad below)*

SD FEE ⛌ 🍴 🎦 🖥 🖨 / ✕ VCR   SOME UNITS

HAWTHORN SUITES ARMORY SQUARE *Book at aaa.com*   Phone: (315)425-0500 1

All Year [BP]	1P: $139-$399	2P: $139-$399	

Small-scale Hotel **Location:** Jct Jefferson St; downtown. 416 S Clinton St 13202. Fax: 315/472-4976. **Facility:** 60 units. 20 one-bedroom standard units with efficiencies. 40 one-bedroom suites with efficiencies, some with whirlpools. 11 stories, interior corridors. **Amenities:** video library, DVD players, high-speed Internet, dual phone lines, voice mail, irons, hair dryers. *Some:* CD players. **Leisure Activities:** exercise room. **Guest Services:** complimentary evening beverages: Wed, valet and coin laundry. **Business Services:** meeting rooms, fax. **Cards:** AX, CB, DC, DS, JC, MC, VI.

ASK SD 🍴 🍷 🎦 DATA PORT 🖥 🖨 ▣ / ✕ /   SOME UNITS

(See map and index starting on p. 577)

HOLIDAY INN/FARRELL ROAD *Book at aaa.com* Phone: (315)457-8700 10
AAA SAVE All Year 1P: $69-$139 2P: $69-$139 XP: $10 F
Location: I-90, exit 39 to I-690 E, exit John Glenn Blvd. 100 Farrell Rd 13209. Fax: 315/457-2379. **Facility:** 152 units. 151 one-bedroom standard units. 1 one-bedroom suite. 2 stories (no elevator), interior corridors. *Bath:* combo or shower only. **Parking:** on-site. **Terms:** cancellation fee imposed, pets ($20 deposit).
Small-scale Hotel **Amenities:** video games, voice mail, irons, hair dryers. **Dining:** 6:30 am-10:30 & 4-10 pm, cocktails. **Pool(s):** outdoor. **Guest Services:** valet and coin laundry. **Business Services:** meeting rooms. **Cards:** AX, DC, DS, MC, VI.

SOME UNITS

(See map and index starting on p. 577)

RED ROOF INN   *Book at aaa.com*   Phone: (315)437-3309   [2]

(AAA) (SAVE)	6/13-10/16	1P: $52-$73	2P: $58-$73	XP: $6	F18
◆◆◆	3/27-4/30	1P: $43-$60	2P: $49-$60	XP: $6	F18
	5/1-6/12	1P: $42-$60	2P: $48-$60	XP: $6	F18
Motel	10/17-3/26	1P: $39-$55	2P: $45-$55	XP: $6	F18

Location: I-90, exit 35 (Carrier Cir), just n. 6614 N Thompson Rd 13206. **Fax:** 315/437-7865. **Facility:** 114 one-bedroom standard units. 3 stories, exterior corridors. *Bath:* combo or shower only. **Parking:** on-site, winter plug-ins. **Amenities:** video games, voice mail. **Cards:** AX, CB, DC, DS, MC, VI. **Special Amenities:** free local telephone calls and free newspaper.

SOME UNITS

🐕 🍴 ♿ 📷 📹 DATA PORT / ✖ 📶 📁 / FEE FEE

SHERATON SYRACUSE UNIVERSITY HOTEL & CONFERENCE
CENTER   *Book at aaa.com*   Phone: (315)475-3000   [11]

(AAA) (SAVE)	1/1-4/30	1P: $300-$370	2P: $300-$370	XP: $10	F12
◆◆◆◆	5/1-12/31	1P: $289-$350	2P: $289-$350	XP: $10	F12

Large-scale Hotel

Location: I-81, exit 18. Located at Syracuse University. 801 University Ave 13210. **Fax:** 315/475-2266. **Facility:** 235 units. 234 one-bedroom standard units. 1 one-bedroom suite ($319-$400) with whirlpool. 9 stories, interior corridors. *Bath:* combo or shower only. **Parking:** on-site (fee). **Terms:** 2 night minimum stay - seasonal, cancellation fee imposed, pets ($100 extra charge). **Amenities:** high-speed Internet, dual phone lines, voice mail, irons, hair dryers. *Some:* fax, safes. **Dining:** 6:30 am-3 & 5-10 pm, cocktails. **Pool(s):** heated indoor. **Leisure Activities:** sauna, whirlpool, exercise room. **Guest Services:** gift shop, valet and coin laundry, airport transportation-Syracuse International Airport, area transportation-downtown. **Business Services:** conference facilities, business center. **Cards:** AX, CB, DC, DS, JC, MC, VI. **Special Amenities:** free newspaper.

SOME UNITS

✈ 🐕 🍴 ♿ 🏊 ✖ 📷 DATA PORT 📶 / ✖ 📶 📁 / FEE FEE

──────── **WHERE TO DINE** ────────

ANTONIO'S RESTAURANT   Lunch: $7-$13   Dinner: $13-$28   Phone: 315-425-1946   [1]

◆◆◆
Italian

Location: Jct E Division and N Salina sts. 700 N Salina St 13208. **Hours:** noon-10 pm, Sat from 5 pm. Closed major holidays; also Sun, except Mother's Day. **Features:** This restaurant is a locally popular spot to enjoy traditional Italian dishes. The portions are large, the service is friendly and the atmosphere is comfortable. Casual dress; cocktails. **Parking:** on-site. **Cards:** AX, MC, VI.

🍴 ✖

BISTRO 238   Dinner: $12-$20   Phone: 315/475-9463   [7]

◆◆◆
Continental

Location: Center; across from the Armory. 238 W Jefferson St 13202. **Hours:** 5 pm-9:30 pm, Fri & Sat-11 pm. Closed major holidays; also Sun. **Reservations:** suggested. **Features:** The bistro is accommodating in its diverse menu selections. The warm and intimate atmosphere perfectly sets off the Continental choices. The menu is changed seasonally to incorporate fresh ingredients. Desserts are fabulous. Casual dress; cocktails. **Parking:** street. **Cards:** AX, DC, DS, MC, VI.

🍴 ✖

CHINA PAVILION   Lunch: $4-$5   Dinner: $6-$13   Phone: 315/488-2828   [2]

◆
Chinese

Location: I-81, exit I-690 W to exit 10, s on Geddes St, then w; in Westvale Plaza. 2318 W Genesee St 13219. **Hours:** 11:30 am-9 pm, Fri & Sat-10 pm. Closed major holidays. **Features:** Among cuisines sampled on the extensive menu are Hunan, Cantonese, Peking and Szechuan. Tangerine beef and the treasure-of-the-sea casserole are particularly flavorful. A luncheon buffet is served daily, and dim sum lunch is a Sunday tradition. Casual dress; beer & wine only. **Parking:** on-site. **Cards:** AX, DS, MC, VI.

✖

COLEMAN'S AUTHENTIC IRISH
PUB & RESTAURANT   Lunch: $5-$9   Dinner: $11-$18   Phone: 315/476-1933   [4]

(AAA)
◆◆
Irish

Location: On Tipperary Hill. 100 S Lowell Ave 13204. **Hours:** 11:30 am-10 pm, Fri & Sat-11 pm, Sun noon-9 pm. Closed: 12/25. **Reservations:** suggested. **Features:** Adding to the cozy, traditional Irish pub decor is a special leprechaun's door. Celtic and regional Irish dishes are served in a bustling atmosphere. Locals often order daily "pub pie" specials, and "green" beer in March makes for a lucky year. Casual dress; cocktails. **Parking:** on-site. **Cards:** AX, DC, DS, MC, VI.

🍴 ✖

DANZER'S RESTAURANT   Lunch: $3-$7   Dinner: $10-$14   Phone: 315/422-0089   [10]

(AAA)
◆
German

Location: I-81, exit 17, 0.7 mi s on E Brighton Ave, then just e. 153 Ainsley Dr 13210. **Hours:** 11 am-11 pm, Fri & Sat-midnight, Sun noon-11 pm. Closed: 1/1, 11/25, 12/25. **Reservations:** suggested, weekends. **Features:** German and American specialties, ranging from steak and seafood to bratwurst and Wiener schnitzel, make up the family-oriented restaurant's menu. In business since 1946, this place resembles a Bavarian chalet. Service is casual but capable. Casual dress; cocktails. **Parking:** on-site. **Cards:** AX, DC, DS, MC, VI.

🍴 ✖

DINOSAUR BAR-B-QUE   Lunch: $7-$11   Dinner: $10-$15   Phone: 315/476-4937   [6]

◆◆
American

Location: Jct Franklin St; downtown. 246 W Willow St 13202. **Hours:** 11 am-midnight, Fri & Sat-1 am, Sun 2 pm-9 pm. Closed major holidays. **Features:** The restaurant is just what you expect: great tasting pork, beef and chicken barbeque, all smokey and delicious. Featuring rough and rustic decor with music and blues offered six nights a week. Casual dress; cocktails. **Parking:** street. **Cards:** AX, DC, DS, MC, VI.

🍴 ✖

JOEY'S RESTAURANT   Lunch: $6-$8   Dinner: $12-$18   Phone: 315/432-0315   [12]

◆◆◆
Italian

Location: I-90, exit 35 (Carrier Cir), just n. 6594 Thompson Rd 13206. **Hours:** 11:30 am-11 pm, Sat from 5 pm, Sun 4 pm-10 pm. Closed: 11/25, 12/25. **Reservations:** suggested. **Features:** Hearty traditional and regional Italian dishes combined with deft service in a warm, intimate dining room will satisfy the most discriminating diner. An extensive wine list enhances the many choices of creative dishes—from veal and seafood to pasta, chicken and beef. Great entree accompaniments include the spinach bread appetizer, greens and beans soup, Caesar salad made tableside and varied dessert temptations that include tiramisu and white chocolate creme brulee. Dressy casual; cocktails. **Parking:** on-site. **Cards:** AX, DC, DS, MC, VI.

🍴 ✖

(See map and index starting on p. 577)

JUANITA'S MEXICAN KITCHEN   Lunch: $5-$10   Dinner: $5-$12   Phone: 315/478-2185   ⑨
▽▽
Mexican
Location: Jct Spring St. 600 Court St 13208. **Hours:** 11:30 am-2 & 5-9 pm, Thurs-Sat to 9:30 pm. Closed major holidays; also Sun. **Features:** Modest, casual dining is the mode in the award-winning Mexican/Southwestern restaurant. Traditional dishes are made promptly from fresh ingredients. Casual dress; cocktails. **Parking:** on-site. **Cards:** DS, MC, VI.

L'ADOUR   Lunch: $7-$12   Dinner: $19-$24   Phone: 315/475-7653   ⑬
▽▽▽
French
Location: Jct Washington St; downtown. 110 Montgomery St 13202. **Hours:** 7 am-2 & 5:30-10 pm, Sat from 5:30 pm. Closed major holidays. **Reservations:** suggested. **Features:** Classic French cuisine is created from fresh, quality ingredients and presented in artistic harmony for an impressive, tantalizing experience. An extensive French wine list complements the a la carte choices offered in the bistro or the prix fixe menus presented in the formal upstairs restaurant. Dressy casual; cocktails. **Parking:** on-site (fee) and street. **Cards:** AX, DC, DS, MC, VI.

LEMON GRASS   Lunch: $6-$8   Dinner: $14-$20   Phone: 315/475-1111   ⑧
▽▽▽
Thai
Location: Center; across from the Armory. 238 W Jefferson St 13202. **Hours:** 11:30 am-2:30 & 5-9:30 pm, Fri-11 pm, Sat 11:30 am-3 & 5-11 pm, Sun 4:30 pm-9:30 pm. Closed major holidays. **Reservations:** suggested. **Features:** Adventuresome diners are treated to a casual atmosphere, intriguing foods with unusual flavor combinations and an extensive wine list. Modern decor, traditional and innovative Thai cuisine choices and Pook Chutinthramond's fabulous dessert all combine to bring guests the quintessential dining event, be it for lunch or dinner. Casual dress; cocktails. **Parking:** street. **Cards:** AX, DC, DS, MC, VI.

MIMI'S BAKERY & CAFE   Lunch: $2-$7   Phone: 315/422-6630   ③
▽
American
Location: I-81, exit Adam St to State northbound, just w on Erie Blvd; exit West and Franklin sts southbound, follow to downtown; across from Clinton Exchange. 260 W Genesee St 13202. **Hours:** 6:30 am-5 pm, Sat 6 am-3 pm. Closed major holidays; also Sun. **Features:** Baked goods are outstanding at the cozy cafe, a favorite for light delicatessen fare. Sandwiches, soups, salads and daily specials have brought this place its devoted clientele. Sidewalk seating lets diners engage in people-watching. Casual dress. **Parking:** on-site. **Cards:** AX, MC, VI.

PASCALE WINE BAR AND RESTAURANT   Lunch: $6-$15   Dinner: $14-$24   Phone: 315/471-3040   ⑤
▽▽▽
American
Location: Corner of Clinton and W Fayette St; downtown. 204 W Fayette St 13202. **Hours:** 5:30 pm-9:30 pm, Wed 11:30 am-2:30 pm, Fri & Sat 5:30 pm-10:30 pm. Closed major holidays; also Sun. **Reservations:** suggested. **Features:** An extensive wine list with rare vintages complements such savory choices as duck breast, venison and king salmon. Stucco walls with original artwork, an open kitchen and marble finishes lend to the contemporary atmosphere. Dressy casual; cocktails. **Parking:** on-site (fee) and valet. **Cards:** AX, DC, MC, VI.

PASTABILITIES   Lunch: $4-$7   Dinner: $8-$20   Phone: 315/474-1153   ⑭
▽
Italian
Location: Jct Fayette St; downtown. 311 S Franklin St 13202. **Hours:** 11:30 am-2:30 & 5-10 pm, Fri-11 pm, Sat 5 pm-11 pm, Sun 5 pm-10 pm. Closed major holidays. **Features:** The centrally located downtown restaurant lets patrons grab fast and fresh cafeteria-style lunches or relax as the friendly staff serves dinner. The casual dining room is walled with bricks and displays interesting decor. Casual dress; cocktails. **Parking:** on-site (fee) and street. **Cards:** AX, DC, DS, MC, VI.

PHOEBE'S GARDEN CAFE   Lunch: $7-$10   Dinner: $12-$18   Phone: 315/475-5154   ⑪
▽▽
American
Location: I-81, exit 18, 0.5 mi e on SR 92. 900 E Genesee St 13210. **Hours:** 11 am-9 pm, Fri-11 pm, Sat 4 pm-9 pm. Closed major holidays; also Sun. **Reservations:** accepted. **Features:** A sunny skylight sheds light on the bright atrium, which is filled with plants, satisfied diners and casual, friendly ambience. Fresh seafood and steak are at the heart of the bistro-like menu. For dessert, savor the specialty creme brulee. Casual dress; cocktails. **Parking:** on-site (fee). **Cards:** AX, MC, VI.

────── *The following restaurant has not been evaluated by AAA* ──────
but is listed for your information only.

AMBROSIA   Phone: 315/426-8800
[fyi]
Not evaluated. **Location:** Jct S Franklin and Walton sts; in Armory Square. 201 Walton St 13202. **Features:** The sushi bar and restaurant uses the freshest quality ingredients available; the contemporary style has an uncomplicated, modern tone.

TANNERSVILLE pop. 448

────── **WHERE TO STAY** ──────

THE EGGERY INN   Phone: (518)589-5363
AAA [SAVE]   All Year [BP]   1P: $110-$125   2P: $130-$155   XP: $40   D12
▽▽   **Location:** Jct SR 23A and CR 16, 1.3 mi s. 288 Platte Clove Rd (CR 16) 12485 (Box 4, CR 16). Fax: 518/589-5774.
Bed & Breakfast   **Facility:** Smoke free premises. 15 one-bedroom standard units. 3 stories (no elevator), interior corridors. *Bath:* combo or shower only. **Parking:** on-site. **Terms:** 2 night minimum stay - seasonal, 14 day cancellation notice-fee imposed, weekly rates available, no pets allowed (owner's pets on premises). **Amenities:** voice mail. **Cards:** AX, MC, VI. **Special Amenities:** free full breakfast.

—————— WHERE TO DINE ——————

LAST CHANCE ANTIQUES & CHEESE CAFE   **Lunch:** $6-$11   **Dinner:** $8-$16   **Phone:** 518/589-6424
◊◊◊◊   **Location:** Town center. 602 Main St 12485. **Hours:** 11 am-9 pm; Fri & Sat-9:30 pm 6/16-9/14 & 12/13-3/31.
American   **Closed:** Mon-Thurs 4/1-6/15 & 9/15-12/12. **Features:** The eclectic eatery has it all—great food, more than
300 beers and 50 cheese selections. The upbeat dining room is hung with old brass instruments.
Porch-sidewalk seating is available. Casual dress; cocktails. **Parking:** street. **Cards:** AX, DS, MC, VI. ⊠

TARRYTOWN —See New York p. 457.

THENDARA

—————— WHERE TO DINE ——————

VAN AUKEN'S INNE   **Lunch:** $4-$8   **Dinner:** $14-$22   **Phone:** 315/369-3033
◊◊◊◊   **Location:** Just behind Thendara Train Station on SR 28. 108 Forge St 13472. **Hours:** Open 5/7-10/10 &
American   12/3-3/13; 11:30 am-2:30 & 5-9 pm. **Closed:** 9/6, 12/25; also Mon-Thurs 5/7-6/19 & 12/3-12/24 and Tues &
Wed 9/5-10/10 & 12/26-3/13. **Reservations:** suggested. **Features:** The tastefully restored,
turn-of-the-20th-century inn has hardwood floors, decorative wood moldings and pressed tin ceilings in an
understated decor. Pan seared Asian sea bass or veal Milanese are two of the flavorful, well-prepared dinners. The wine list
offers a broad selection. The friendly service is attentive and helpful. Casual dress; cocktails. **Parking:** on-site. **Cards:** MC, VI.
⊤ ⊠

TICONDEROGA pop. 5,167—See also ADIRONDACK MOUNTAINS.

—————— WHERE TO STAY ——————

CIRCLE COURT MOTEL   **Phone:** (518)585-7660
◊◊◊◊ SAVE | 6/6-10/30 | 1P: $64-$69 | 2P: $69-$75 | XP: $10 | F12
| 5/1-6/5 | 1P: $58-$64 | 2P: $64-$70 | XP: $10 | F12
◊◊◊◊ | 10/31-4/30 | 1P: $52-$57 | 2P: $57-$62 | XP: $10 | F12
Motel   **Location:** SR 9N; at Liberty Monument traffic circle. 6 Montcalm St 12883. **Facility:** 14 one-bedroom standard units.
1-2 stories (no elevator), exterior corridors. *Bath:* combo or shower only. **Parking:** on-site, winter plug-ins.
Cards: AX, MC, VI.

SOME UNITS
[icons] / ⊠ ▣ /

TONAWANDA —See Buffalo p. 255.

TROY pop. 49,170   (See map and index starting on p. 215)

—————— WHERE TO STAY ——————

BEST WESTERN-RENSSELAER INN   *Book at aaa.com*   **Phone:** (518)274-3210   **43**
◊◊◊◊ SAVE | 7/23-9/1 [BP] | 1P: $89-$99 | 2P: $109-$119 | XP: $5 | F12
| 5/1-7/22 & 9/2-11/15 [BP] | 1P: $84-$89 | 2P: $89-$99 | XP: $5 | F12
◊◊◊◊ | 11/16-4/30 [BP] | 1P: $79-$84 | 2P: $84-$89 | XP: $5 | F12
Small-scale Hotel   **Location:** I-787, exit 9 E, 0.5 mi e, exit downtown, 0.5 mi s. 1800 6th Ave 12180. **Fax:** 518/274-3294. **Facility:** 152
one-bedroom standard units. 4 stories, interior corridors. **Parking:** on-site. **Amenities:** irons, hair dryers.
Dining: 6:30 am-10 & 5-9 pm, Sat & Sun 7 am-11 & 5-9 pm, cocktails. **Pool(s):** outdoor. **Leisure Activi-**
ties: exercise room. **Fee:** game room. **Guest Services:** coin laundry, area transportation-train & bus station. **Business Serv-**
ices: conference facilities. **Cards:** AX, CB, DC, DS, JC, MC, VI. **Special Amenities:** free full breakfast and free local
telephone calls.

SOME UNITS
[icons] / ⊠ ▣ /
FEE

———— *The following lodging was either not evaluated or did not* ————
meet AAA rating requirements but is listed for your information only.

FRANKLIN SQUARE INN & SUITES   **Phone:** 518/274-8800   **42**
[fyi] | 7/20-9/7 | 1P: $106-$269 | 2P: $106-$269 | XP: $5 | F17
| 9/8-4/30 | 1P: $96-$249 | 2P: $96-$249 | XP: $5 | F17
Small-scale Hotel | 5/1-7/19 | 1P: $86-$249 | 2P: $86-$249 | XP: $5 | F17
Under major renovation, scheduled to be completed June 2004. **Last rated:** ◊◊ **Location:** I-787, exit 8, just
e on 23rd to Federal, just e to 4th St, then just s; downtown. One 4th St 12180. **Fax:** 518/274-0427. **Facility:** 62 one-bedroom standard
units, some with whirlpools. 3 stories, interior corridors. *Bath:* combo or shower only. **Parking:** on-site. **Terms:** 5 day cancellation notice-fee imposed, [ECP] meal plan available. **Amenities:** voice mail, irons. *Some:* dual phone lines. **Guest Services:** coin
laundry. **Business Services:** meeting rooms. **Cards:** AX, CB, DC, DS, JC, MC, VI.

SOME UNITS

FEE   FEE

—————— WHERE TO DINE ——————

HOLMES & WATSON, LTD   Historic   **Lunch:** $5-$8   **Dinner:** $11-$15   **Phone:** 518/273-8526   **32**
◊   **Location:** Downtown. 450 Broadway 12180. **Hours:** 11 am-10 pm, Fri & Sat-11 pm. **Closed:** 12/25; also Sun.
American   **Reservations:** accepted. **Features:** The historic pub atmosphere is themed around Sherlock Holmes.
Widely varied menu items are named after book characters or places. Patrons can choose from 70 malt
scotches and a world tour beer list with more than 200 selections. Casual style and service surrounded by
period decor makes for an interesting meal. Casual dress; cocktails. **Parking:** street. **Cards:** AX, DC, DS, MC, VI. ⊤ ⊠

TRUMANSBURG pop. 1,581—See also FINGER LAKES.

―――――― WHERE TO STAY ――――――

TAUGHANNOCK FARMS INN   Phone: 607/387-7711

	6/1-10/31 [ECP]	1P: $75-$400	2P: $100-$400	XP: $25	F10
	4/1-4/30 [ECP]	1P: $75-$395	2P: $100-$395	XP: $25	F10
	5/1-5/31 & 11/1-1/1 [ECP]	1P: $75-$385	2P: $100-$385	XP: $25	F10

Historic Country Inn   **Location:** From Ithaca, 10 mi n on SR 89. Located next to a state park. 2030 Gorge Rd 14886. Fax: 607/387-7721. **Facility:** The inn offers accommodations in an 1873 Victorian mansion as well overlooking Cayuga Lake, just a short drive from Ithaca. Smoke free premises. 11 one-bedroom standard units. 1-2 stories (no elevator), interior/exterior corridors. *Bath:* combo or shower only. **Parking:** on-site. **Terms:** open 5/1-1/1 & 4/1-4/30, 11 day cancellation notice-fee imposed, weekly rates available. **Amenities:** voice mail. **Dining:** dining room, see separate listing. **Cards:** AX, DS, MC, VI.

SOME UNITS

―――――― WHERE TO DINE ――――――

TAUGHANNOCK FARMS INN Historic   **Dinner:** $19-$27   Phone: 607/387-7711

Regional American   **Location:** From Ithaca, 10 mi n on SR 89; in Taughannock Farms Inn. 2030 Gorge Rd 14886. **Hours:** Open 5/1-1/1 & 4/1-4/30; 5 pm-9 pm, Sun 3 pm-8 pm; hours vary in winter. Closed: 12/12-12/30, also Mon & Tues 4/1-4/30. **Reservations:** suggested. **Features:** Overlooking Cayuga Lake, the 1873 Victorian estate is loaded with quaint charm. In addition to such flavorful entrees as prime rib, roast duck, fresh fish and roast turkey, the restaurant serves an excellent chilled strawberry soup. Dinner is prix fixe. Dressy casual; cocktails. **Parking:** on-site. **Cards:** AX, DS, MC, VI.

TULLY pop. 924

―――――― WHERE TO STAY ――――――

BEST WESTERN MARSHALL MANOR   *Book at aaa.com*   Phone: (315)696-6061

AAA SAVE   All Year [ECP]   1P: $74-$154   2P: $74-$154   F12
Location: I-81, exit 14, just e. 5779 Rt 80 13159 (PO Box 156). Fax: 315/696-6406. **Facility:** 44 one-bedroom standard units, some with whirlpools. 2 stories (no elevator), interior corridors. **Parking:** on-site. **Amenities:** voice mail, irons, hair dryers. **Cards:** AX, CB, DC, DS, JC, MC, VI. **Special Amenities:** free expanded continental breakfast and free local telephone calls.

Small-scale Hotel

SOME UNITS

TUPPER LAKE pop. 3,935—See also ADIRONDACK MOUNTAINS.

―――――― WHERE TO STAY ――――――

RED TOP INN   Phone: 518/359-9209

AAA SAVE   All Year   1P: $45-$65   2P: $55-$75   XP: $5   D12
Motel   **Location:** 3 mi s. 1562 SR 30 12986. **Facility:** 21 units. 13 one-bedroom standard units. 4 two-bedroom suites ($75-$95), some with efficiencies. 4 cabins. 2 stories (no elevator), interior/exterior corridors. *Bath:* combo or shower only. **Parking:** on-site, winter plug-ins. **Terms:** 2 night minimum stay - weekends, 7/1-8/31, pets (in cabins). **Leisure Activities:** boat dock, fishing, rowboats. **Cards:** AX, MC, VI. **Special Amenities:** free local telephone calls and free newspaper.

SOME UNITS

SHAHEEN'S MOTEL   Phone: 518/359-3384

	6/18-10/11 [CP]	1P: $53-$77	2P: $61-$81	XP: $6	F5
	12/21-4/30 [CP]	1P: $49-$70	2P: $56-$79	XP: $6	F5
	5/1-6/17 [CP]	1P: $49-$66	2P: $55-$67	XP: $6	F5
	10/12-12/20 [CP]	1P: $49-$56	2P: $55-$67	XP: $6	F5

Motel   **Location:** 0.8 mi e on SR 3/30. 314 Park St 12986. Fax: 518/359-3384. **Facility:** 31 one-bedroom standard units. 2 stories (no elevator), exterior corridors. *Bath:* combo or shower only. **Parking:** on-site, winter plug-ins. **Terms:** 3 day cancellation notice-fee imposed, package plans - seasonal. **Amenities:** irons, hair dryers. **Pool(s):** outdoor. **Leisure Activities:** picnic area, playground. *Fee:* miniature golf. **Cards:** AX, DS, MC, VI. **Special Amenities:** free continental breakfast and free local telephone calls.

SOME UNITS

TUPPER LAKE MOTEL   Phone: (518)359-3381

AAA SAVE   All Year   1P: $45-$65   2P: $53-$79   XP: $5   F3
Motel   **Location:** 0.5 mi e on SR 3/30. 255 Park St 12986. Fax: 518/359-8549. **Facility:** 18 one-bedroom standard units. 1 story, exterior corridors. *Bath:* shower only. **Parking:** on-site, winter plug-ins. **Terms:** 2 night minimum stay - weekends in summer, 3 day cancellation notice-fee imposed, package plans - seasonal. **Pool(s):** outdoor. **Leisure Activities:** picnic table. **Cards:** AX, DS, MC, VI. **Special Amenities:** free continental breakfast and free local telephone calls.

SOME UNITS

―――――― WHERE TO DINE ――――――

―――― *The following restaurants have not been evaluated by AAA* ――――
but are listed for your information only.

THE RED BARN FAMILY RESTAURANT   Phone: 518/359-7555

fyi   Not evaluated. **Location:** 218 Park St 12986. **Features:** The converted red barn makes for fun family dining on any night. Selections range from sandwiches and salads to steaks and prime rib.

THE WAWBEEK RESTAURANT   Phone: 518/359-2956

fyi   Not evaluated. **Location:** Panther Mountain Rd, Rt 30 12986. **Features:** Guests can let their eyes bathe in the beauty that surrounds the sprawling, 40-acre resort in the heart of the Adirondacks. The setting is the driving force behind the inspired menu. Reservations are required.

UNIONDALE pop. 23,011

—————— WHERE TO STAY ——————

LONG ISLAND MARRIOTT HOTEL & CONFERENCE CENTER   *Book at aaa.com*   **Phone:** (516)794-3800

	1/1-4/30	1P: $179-$229	2P: $179-$229
	8/13-12/31	1P: $169-$209	2P: $169-$209
	6/19-8/12	1P: $169-$199	2P: $169-$199
Large-scale Hotel	5/1-6/18	1P: $149-$195	2P: $149-$195

Location: Meadowbrook Pkwy, exit M4 (follow signs to coliseum), exit Hempstead Tpke W. Located in the financial district, next to Nassau Coliseum. 101 James Doolittle Blvd 11553. Fax: 516/794-5936. **Facility:** 618 units. 610 one-bedroom standard units. 8 one-bedroom suites. 11 stories, interior corridors. **Parking:** on-site and valet. **Terms:** check-in 4 pm. **Amenities:** high-speed Internet (fee), dual phone lines, voice mail, irons, hair dryers. *Some:* CD players. **Pool(s):** heated indoor. **Leisure Activities:** saunas, whirlpool. *Fee:* racquetball courts, massage. **Guest Services:** gift shop, valet and coin laundry. **Business Services:** conference facilities, business center. **Cards:** AX, CB, DC, DS, JC, MC, VI.

SOME UNITS

UTICA pop. 60,651

—————— WHERE TO STAY ——————

A-1 MOTEL   **Phone:** (315)735-6698

	5/1-10/31	1P: $50-$55	2P: $55-$60	XP: $8	F6
	11/1-4/30	1P: $35-$45	2P: $45-$50	XP: $8	F6

Motel

Location: I-90 (New York Thruway), exit 31, just s. 238 N Genesee St 13502. **Facility:** 20 one-bedroom standard units. 2 stories, interior corridors. **Parking:** on-site. **Terms:** 3 day cancellation notice, weekly rates available, pets (no cats). **Cards:** AX, DC, DS, MC, VI. **Special Amenities:** free local telephone calls and early check-in/late check-out. *(See ad below)*

SOME UNITS

BEST WESTERN GATEWAY ADIRONDACK INN   *Book at aaa.com*   **Phone:** (315)732-4121

	All Year	1P: $79-$190	2P: $89-$190	F18

Location: I-90 (New York Thruway), exit 31, 0.5 mi s. 175 N Genesee St 13502. Fax: 315/797-8265. **Facility:** 89 units. 88 one-bedroom standard units. 1 one-bedroom suite ($125-$250) with efficiency. 1-2 stories (no elevator), interior corridors. **Parking:** on-site, winter plug-ins. **Terms:** [ECP] meal plan available. **Amenities:** irons, hair dryers. **Leisure Activities:** limited exercise equipment. *Fee:* game room. **Guest Services:** sundries, valet and coin laundry. **Business Services:** meeting rooms, PC. **Cards:** AX, DC, DS, MC, VI. *(See ad below)*

Small-scale Hotel

SOME UNITS

COUNTRY MOTEL

AAA SAVE

Motel

		1P: $40-$60	2P: $52-$75	XP: $5	F13
5/1-10/31		1P: $35-$40	2P: $46-$55	XP: $5	F13
11/1-4/30					

Location: I-90 (New York Thruway), exit 31, 2 mi e on SR 5. 1477 Herkimer Rd 13502. Fax: 315/733-8801. **Facility:** 25 one-bedroom standard units. 1 story, exterior corridors. *Bath:* combo or shower only. **Parking:** on-site, winter plug-ins. **Terms:** package plans. **Cards:** AX, DC, DS, MC, VI. **Special Amenities:** free room upgrade and preferred room (each subject to availability with advanced reservations).

Phone: 315/732-4628

SOME UNITS

HOTEL UTICA

Book at aaa.com

Large-scale Hotel

5/1-8/31	1P: $109-$129	2P: $109-$129	XP: $10	F16
1/1-4/30	1P: $99-$129	2P: $99-$129	XP: $10	F16
9/1-10/31	1P: $94-$114	2P: $94-$114	XP: $10	F16
11/1-12/31	1P: $99-$109	2P: $99-$109	XP: $10	F16

Location: I-90 (New York Thruway), exit 31, 1.1 mi s on Genesee St. 102 Lafayette St 13502. Fax: 315/733-7621. **Facility:** 112 units. 98 one-bedroom standard units. 14 one-bedroom suites ($139-$179), some with whirlpools. 9 stories, interior corridors. *Bath:* combo or shower only. **Parking:** on-site. **Terms:** check-in 4 pm. **Amenities:** video games, dual phone lines, voice mail, irons, hair dryers. **Guest Services:** gift shop, valet laundry. **Business Services:** conference facilities, business center. **Cards:** AX, DC, DS, MC, VI.

Phone: (315)724-7829

SOME UNITS

RADISSON HOTEL-UTICA CENTRE

Book at aaa.com

Small-scale Hotel

5/1-10/31	1P: $139-$169	2P: $139-$169	XP: $10	F17
4/1-4/30	1P: $109-$139	2P: $109-$139	XP: $10	F17
11/1-3/31	1P: $109-$129	2P: $109-$129	XP: $10	F17

Location: Downtown. 200 Genesee St 13502. Fax: 315/797-1490. **Facility:** 158 one-bedroom standard units. 6 stories, interior corridors. **Parking:** on-site (fee). **Terms:** small pets only ($30 deposit, $10 extra charge). **Amenities:** video games, dual phone lines, voice mail, irons, hair dryers. **Pool(s):** heated indoor. **Leisure Activities:** sauna, whirlpool, exercise room. *Fee:* game room. **Guest Services:** valet and coin laundry. **Business Services:** conference facilities, business center. **Cards:** AX, CB, DC, DS, MC, VI. *(See ad below & color ad p 413)*

Phone: (315)797-8010

SOME UNITS

FEE

FEE FEE FEE

RED ROOF INN

AAA SAVE

Motel

Book at aaa.com

6/27-10/30	1P: $64-$88	2P: $70-$94	XP: $6	F18
5/23-6/26	1P: $55-$72	2P: $61-$78	XP: $6	F18
5/1-5/22	1P: $48-$60	2P: $54-$66	XP: $6	F18
10/31-4/30	1P: $44-$60	2P: $50-$66	XP: $6	F18

Location: I-90 (New York Thruway), exit 31. 20 Weaver St 13502. Fax: 315/724-7158. **Facility:** 112 one-bedroom standard units. 2 stories (no elevator), exterior corridors. **Parking:** on-site. **Terms:** small pets only. **Amenities:** video games, voice mail. **Cards:** AX, CB, DC, DS, MC, VI. **Special Amenities:** free local telephone calls and free newspaper.

Phone: (315)724-7128

SOME UNITS

FEE FEE

ROSEMONT INN BED & BREAKFAST

Historic Bed
& Breakfast

| All Year | 1P: $89-$135 | 2P: $99-$145 | XP: $15 |

Location: I-90 (New York Thruway), exit 31, 2.5 mi s on SR 5. 1423 Genesee St 13501. Fax: 315/792-8852. **Facility:** Claw-foot tubs and quality antique period furnishings distinguish this 1860 Italianate-style Victorian B&B. Smoke free premises. 7 one-bedroom standard units. 2 stories (no elevator), interior corridors. **Parking:** on-site. **Terms:** age restrictions may apply, 14 day cancellation notice-fee imposed, [BP] meal plan available. **Guest Services:** TV in common area. **Cards:** MC, VI.

Phone: 315/792-8852

SOME UNITS

——— WHERE TO DINE ———

BABE'S MACARONI GRILL & BAR
♦♦♦♦ ♦♦♦♦
American

Lunch: $5-$10 **Dinner:** $6-$12 **Phone:** 315/735-0777
Location: I-90 (New York Thruway), exit 31, 0.8 mi s. 80 N Genesee St 13501. **Hours:** 11 am-1 am. **Closed:** 11/25, 12/25. **Reservations:** accepted. **Features:** The atmosphere is often boisterous at the bustling restaurant, which is decorated with a wide array of memorabilia and movie posters. The broad menu includes chicken, beef and fish dishes, as well as Mexican fare. Service is casual and friendly. Casual dress; cocktails. **Parking:** on-site. **Cards:** AX, CB, DC, DS, MC, VI.

&M ⛉ ⊗

BEI JING HOUSE
♦♦♦
Chinese

Lunch: $4-$5 **Dinner:** $4-$10 **Phone:** 315/797-3388
Location: 0.5 mi s; center. 1506 Genesee St 13502. **Hours:** 11 am-11 pm, Fri & Sat-midnight, Sun noon-10 pm. **Closed:** 11/25. **Features:** Menu favorites are cooked in an open kitchen while patrons wait or order takeout. This place is just a short hop from central downtown. Casual dress. **Parking:** on-site. **Cards:** MC, VI.

⊗

DELMONICO'S ITALIAN STEAKHOUSE
♦♦♦♦ ♦♦♦♦
Italian

Dinner: $8-$18 **Phone:** 315/732-2300
Location: I-90 (New York Thruway), exit 32, 0.6 mi s. 147 N Genesee St 13501. **Hours:** 4 pm-10:30 pm, Fri-11:30 pm, Sat 3 pm-11:30 pm, Sun noon-10 pm. **Closed:** 11/25, 12/25. **Reservations:** accepted. **Features:** Guests can "dine with the stars" in a room surrounded by caricatures of famous people. The traditional restaurant has a casually upscale feel. The real crowd-pleaser is the 24-ounce Delmonico steak meal. Casual dress; cocktails. **Parking:** on-site. **Cards:** AX, DC, DS, MC, VI.

⛉ ⊗

DOMINIQUE'S CHESTERFIELD RESTAURANT
♦♦♦♦ ♦♦♦♦
Italian

Lunch: $7-$10 **Dinner:** $11-$19 **Phone:** 315/732-9356
Location: At Niagara St. 1713 Bleecker St 13501. **Hours:** 11:30 am-10 pm. **Closed:** 12/25. **Reservations:** accepted. **Features:** Since 1988, the family-owned restaurant has been known for its traditional homemade pasta and desserts made on site. Dishes compile fresh, high-quality vegetables, seafood, certified Angus steak and dry-aged filet mignon. Daily early-bird specials and the fish fry are worth checking out. Casual dress; cocktails. **Parking:** on-site. **Cards:** AX, MC, VI.

⛉ ⊗

THORNBERRY'S RESTAURANT
♦♦♦♦ ♦♦♦♦
American

Lunch: $4-$8 **Dinner:** $9-$20 **Phone:** 315/735-1702
Location: I-90 (New York Thruway), exit 31, 1.5 mi s to Hopper St, just e, then just s. 1011 King St 13501. **Hours:** 11:30 am-2 & 5-10 pm. **Closed:** 12/25; also Sun & Mon. **Reservations:** suggested, weekends. **Features:** Eating downtown won't be ordinary in the bustling restaurant. Relaxed service and ample portions are most satisfying. Original artwork graces the walls and a warm fire brightens any winter day. Hearty soup, salad and dinner specials such as curry chicken with rice or beef and seafood await hungry diners. The worth-waiting-for Thornberry Pie is big enough to share. Casual dress; cocktails. **Parking:** on-site. **Cards:** AX, CB, DC, DS, MC, VI.

⛉ ⊗

VALATIE pop. 1,712

——— WHERE TO STAY ———

BLUE SPRUCE INN & SUITES
AAA SAVE
♦♦♦♦ ♦♦♦♦
Motel

Phone: 518/758-9711

5/1-11/30	1P: $60-$89	2P: $75-$95	XP: $5	D13
12/1-4/30	1P: $60	2P: $70-$80	XP: $5	D13

Location: I-90 (New York Thruway), exit 12, 4 mi s on US 9 via New York Thruway Extension, exit B1. 3093 Rt 9 12184. **Fax:** 518/758-1638. **Facility:** 28 units. 24 one-bedroom standard units. 4 one-bedroom suites ($115-$125) with kitchens. 2 stories (no elevator), exterior corridors. *Bath:* combo or shower only. **Parking:** on-site. **Terms:** 2 night minimum stay - weekends in summer, 3 day cancellation notice, weekly rates available. **Amenities:** irons, hair dryers. **Dining:** 7:30-10 am; closed 12/1-4/30. **Pool(s):** outdoor, wading. **Guest Services:** coin laundry. **Business Services:** fax. **Cards:** AX, DS, MC, VI. *(See color ad p 219)*

SOME UNITS
S/D 🐾 ⓘ 🍴 🐕 📷 / ⊗ 🖥 ▭ / FEE

VARNA —See also FINGER LAKES.

——— WHERE TO STAY ———

EMBASSY INN MOTEL
♦♦♦
Motel

Phone: 607/272-3721

All Year	1P: $55-$75	2P: $69-$99	XP: $10	D12

Location: 4 mi e; 2 mi e of Cornell University. Located in a quiet area. 1083 Dryden Rd (Rt 366) 14850 (1083 Dryden Rd (Rt 366), ITHACA). **Fax:** 607/272-3722. **Facility:** 25 one-bedroom standard units, some with efficiencies (no utensils). 1-2 stories (no elevator), exterior corridors. *Bath:* combo or shower only. **Parking:** on-site, winter plug-ins. **Terms:** 3 day cancellation notice. **Cards:** AX, DS, MC, VI.

SOME UNITS
ASK S/D / ⊗ 🖥

VERNON pop. 1,155

——— WHERE TO DINE ———

MASON JAR RESTAURANT
♦♦♦
American

Lunch: $4-$6 **Dinner:** $8-$12 **Phone:** 315/829-9999
Location: Jct SR 31 and 5, 0.3 mi e. SR 5 13476. **Hours:** 6 am-8 pm, Fri & Sat-9 pm. **Closed:** 12/25. **Features:** The restaurant is known for tasty, no-nonsense, home-style cooking. Among favorites are barbecue ribs, roast pork, prime rib and chicken and seafood dishes. In-house bakery tempts with selections including doughnuts, cakes, pies and other desserts. Casual dress. **Parking:** on-site. **Cards:** AX, MC, VI.

⊗

TOWN & COUNTRY RESTAURANT

Lunch: $3-$8   **Dinner:** $10-$25   **Phone:** 315/829-2450

American

Location: SR 5, 0.3 mi w of jct SR 31. 5366 E Seneca St 13476. **Hours:** noon-8 pm, Fri & Sat 8 am-10 pm, Sun 8 am-8 pm. Closed: 1/1, 7/4, 12/25; also Mon & Tues. **Reservations:** accepted. **Features:** Hearty portions and friendly, casual service are hallmarks of the central New York eatery, just a short drive from Turning Stone Casino. The "country-home" atmosphere is welcoming to families, and selections range from soup and sandwiches to pork steak with dressing, gravy and all the "fixins". Casual dress; cocktails. **Parking:** on-site. **Cards:** AX, DS, MC, VI.

VERNON'S APPLE BETTY DINER

Lunch: $5-$7   **Dinner:** $9-$14   **Phone:** 315/829-4875

American

Location: Jct SR 31, 0.3 mi e. 5350 SR 5 (Seneca St) 13476. **Hours:** 6 am-8:30 pm, Mon & Tues-2 pm, Sun from 7 am; 6 am-2 pm, Fri & Sat-8:30 pm, Sun 7 am-8:30 pm in winter. Closed major holidays. **Features:** The nifty little diner serves locals and hungry travelers tasty comfort food, such as homemade soups, hot and cold sandwiches and freshly baked desserts. Many breakfast choices are served from 7 to 11:30 a.m. Casual dress. **Parking:** on-site.

VERONA pop. 6,425

——— WHERE TO STAY ———

TURNING STONE CASINO RESORT

Phone: (315)361-7711

(AAA) (SAVE)

Large-scale Hotel

7/1-8/31	1P: $138-$199	2P: $138-$199	XP: $10	F16
5/1-6/30 & 9/1-11/30	1P: $124-$185	2P: $124-$185	XP: $10	F16
12/1-4/30	1P: $110-$175	2P: $110-$175	XP: $10	F16

Location: I-90, exit 33, just w, follow signs. 5218 Patrick Rd 13478 (PO Box 126). Fax: 315/361-7665. **Facility:** 279 units. 267 one-bedroom standard units. 12 one-bedroom suites with whirlpools. 4 stories, interior corridors. *Bath:* combo or shower only. **Parking:** on-site. **Terms:** package plans. **Amenities:** video games, voice mail, irons, hair dryers. **Dining:** 8 restaurants, 24 hours, nightclub, name entertainment. **Pool(s):** heated indoor. **Leisure Activities:** saunas, whirlpools, steamrooms, driving range. *Fee:* golf-63 holes, massage. **Guest Services:** gift shop, valet laundry, area transportation, beauty salon, tanning facility. **Business Services:** conference facilities, business center. **Cards:** AX, DC, DS, MC, VI.

SOME UNITS

VERONA BEACH

——— WHERE TO DINE ———

SPAGHETTI FACTORY

Lunch: $4-$7   **Dinner:** $9-$16   **Phone:** 315/762-9948

Italian

Location: Center. 6800 SR 13 13162. **Hours:** Open 5/1-11/6 & 3/23-4/30; 11 am-10 pm; Sun noon-9 pm 5/31-9/7. **Reservations:** accepted. **Features:** Family-owned since 1978, the Italian-American restaurant prepares made-to-order meals in generous portions. Freshly baked desserts will delight. Skylights and vines hanging from beams give the dining room the atmosphere of a vineyard. Neatly uniformed servers are pleasant. Casual dress; cocktails. **Parking:** on-site. **Cards:** AX, DC, DS, MC, VI.

VESTAL pop. 26,535

——— WHERE TO STAY ———

BINGHAMTON COURTYARD BY MARRIOTT

Book at aaa.com   **Phone:** (607)644-1000

Small-scale Hotel

5/1-10/31	1P: $109-$129
11/1-4/30	1P: $89-$129

Location: SR 17, exit 67S eastbound, just s on SR 26, 3.3 mi e on SR 434; exit 70S westbound, 2 mi s on SR 201, then just w on SR 434. 3801 Vestal Pkwy E 13850. Fax: 607/644-1022. **Facility:** 78 units. 70 one-bedroom standard units. 8 one-bedroom suites ($119-$159). 3 stories, interior corridors. *Bath:* combo or shower only. **Parking:** on-site. **Amenities:** video library (fee), video games, high-speed Internet, dual phone lines, voice mail, irons, hair dryers. **Pool(s):** small heated indoor. **Leisure Activities:** whirlpool, exercise room. **Guest Services:** valet and coin laundry. **Business Services:** meeting rooms, fax (fee). **Cards:** AX, DC, DS, MC, VI.

SOME UNITS

HOLIDAY INN AT THE UNIVERSITY

Book at aaa.com   **Phone:** (607)729-6371

Small-scale Hotel

All Year [ECP]	1P: $99-$109	2P: $109-$129	XP: $10	F

Location: SR 17, exit 70S, 2.5 mi s on US 201 to SR 434 W, then right on Bunn Hill Rd. 4105 Vestal Pkwy 13850. Fax: 607/729-6407. **Facility:** 142 units. 140 one-bedroom standard units. 2 one-bedroom suites, some with whirlpools. 2 stories (no elevator), interior/exterior corridors. **Parking:** on-site. **Terms:** check-in 4 pm, pets ($25 fee). **Amenities:** video library (fee), video games, high-speed Internet, voice mail, irons, hair dryers. **Pool(s):** outdoor. **Leisure Activities:** exercise room. **Guest Services:** valet laundry. **Business Services:** meeting rooms. **Cards:** AX, CB, DC, DS, JC, MC, VI. *(See color ad p 231)*

SOME UNITS

FEE

HOWARD JOHNSON EXPRESS INN (BINGHAMTON UNIVERSITY)

Book at aaa.com   **Phone:** (607)729-6181

Motel

All Year	1P: $49-$89	2P: $64-$109	XP: $20	F16

Location: SR 17, exit 70S, 1 mi s on SR 201 S, then 0.5 mi w on SR 434 W. Located in a light-commercial area. 3601 Vestal Pkwy E 13850. Fax: 607/797-0309. **Facility:** 58 one-bedroom standard units, some with whirlpools. 1-2 stories (no elevator), interior corridors. **Parking:** on-site. **Terms:** 3 day cancellation notice, weekly rates available, [ECP] meal plan available. **Amenities:** voice mail, irons, hair dryers. **Pool(s):** outdoor. **Business Services:** meeting rooms. **Cards:** AX, CB, DC, DS, JC, MC, VI. *(See color ad p 218)*

SOME UNITS

FEE   FEE   FEE

——— WHERE TO DINE ———

KAMPAI

Japanese

Dinner: $12-$28   **Phone:** 607/798-7521
Location: SR 17, exit 70S, 2.5 mi s on SR 201 to SR 434 W, 2.5 mi, then just n. 108 Jensen Rd 13850. **Hours:** 4:30 pm-9:30 pm, Sun 3:30 pm-8:30 pm. Closed major holidays. **Reservations:** suggested. **Features:** A respected area fixture since 1975, the Japanese restaurant offers three dining choices: sushi, hibachi and traditional. Casual dress; cocktails. **Parking:** on-site. **Cards:** AX, DC, MC, VI.

P.S. RESTAURANT

Continental

Dinner: $12-$18   **Phone:** 607/770-0056
Location: SR 17, exit 70S, 2.5 mi s on SR 201, exit Endicott/SR 434W, then 3.6 mi w; in the Giant Shopping Center. 100 Rano Blvd 13850. **Hours:** 5 pm-9 pm, Fri & Sat-9:30 pm. Closed: 1/1, 11/25, 12/24, 12/25; also Sun & Mon. **Reservations:** suggested. **Features:** The versatile chef/owner of this unassuming but cozy restaurant creates innovative, fusion-style cuisine. Classic French and Thai/Asian influences dominate on a menu that includes filet mignon, poached salmon and vegetarian fare. Diners are encouraged to ask the professional, knowledgeable staff for help with choosing a selection from the award-winning wine list. Casual dress; cocktails. **Parking:** on-site. **Cards:** AX, DC, DS, MC, VI.

VICTOR pop. 2,433—See also FINGER LAKES.

——— WHERE TO STAY ———

EXIT 45 MOTEL

Motel

	1P: $38-$62	2P: $48-$68	XP: $8	F12
5/1-10/31				
11/1-4/30	1P: $38-$49	2P: $42-$49	XP: $8	F12

Phone: (585)924-2121
Location: I-90, exit 45, 0.8 mi s. 7463 SR 96 14564. Fax: 585/924-0468. **Facility:** 34 one-bedroom standard units. 1 story, exterior corridors. **Parking:** on-site. **Cards:** AX, DC, DS, MC, VI.

SOME UNITS

HAMPTON INN AND SUITES-ROCHESTER/VICTOR   *Book at aaa.com*

Small-scale Hotel

	1P: $124-$149	2P: $124-$149
5/1-11/1 [ECP]		
11/2-4/30 [ECP]	1P: $113-$139	2P: $113-$139

Phone: (585)924-4400
Location: I-90 (New York Thruway), exit 45, just n. 7637 NY SR 96 14564. Fax: 585/924-4478. **Facility:** 123 units. 68 one-bedroom standard units. 55 one-bedroom suites with efficiencies, some with whirlpools. 3 stories, interior corridors. *Bath:* combo or shower only. **Parking:** on-site. **Amenities:** dual phone lines, voice mail, irons, hair dryers. **Pool(s):** small heated indoor. **Leisure Activities:** whirlpool, exercise room. **Guest Services:** valet and coin laundry, area transportation-local businesses. **Business Services:** meeting rooms, fax (fee). **Cards:** AX, CB, DC, DS, MC, VI. **Special Amenities: free expanded continental breakfast and free local telephone calls.**

SOME UNITS
FEE

MICROTEL   *Book at aaa.com*

Small-scale Hotel

	1P: $54	2P: $69	XP: $8	F18
5/1-10/31 [ECP]				
11/4-4/30 [ECP]	1P: $49	2P: $64	XP: $8	F18

Phone: (585)924-9240
Location: I-90 (New York Thruway), exit 45, just s off SR 96. 7498 Main St Fishers 14564. Fax: 585/924-9241. **Facility:** 99 one-bedroom standard units. 2 stories (no elevator), interior corridors. *Bath:* combo or shower only. **Parking:** on-site. **Terms:** 3 day cancellation notice. **Amenities:** video games, voice mail, safes. **Cards:** AX, CB, DC, DS, MC, VI.

SOME UNITS

——— WHERE TO DINE ———

BRENDA'S FAMILY RESTAURANT

American

Lunch: $3-$7   **Dinner:** $5-$8   **Phone:** 585/924-5025
Location: I-90 (New York Thruway), exit 45, 3.1 mi s on SR 96 S. 34 E Main St 14564. **Hours:** 6 am-7 pm, Thurs & Fri-8 pm, Sun-2 pm. Closed: 12/25. **Reservations:** accepted. **Features:** The downtown family restaurant serves American favorites, including sandwiches and home-style entrees, for breakfast, lunch and dinner. Casual dress. **Parking:** on-site. **Cards:** DS, MC, VI.

INDIA HOUSE

Indian

MC, VI.

Lunch: $6-$10   **Dinner:** $8-$20   **Phone:** 585/742-2030
Location: I-90 (New York Thruway), exit 45, 0.5 mi s. 7343 Rt 96 14564. **Hours:** 11:30 am-2:30 & 5-9:30 pm, Fri & Sat-10 pm. Closed: 7/4, 11/25, 12/25. **Reservations:** accepted. **Features:** A feast for the senses begins with the freshest, quality ingredients, herbs and spices. In addition to vegetarian choices, the menu lists tandoori lamb, chicken, beef and seafood. Casual dress; cocktails. **Parking:** on-site. **Cards:** AX, DC, DS,

WAPPINGERS FALLS pop. 4,929

——— WHERE TO DINE ———

AROMA OSTERIA

Italian

Lunch: $9-$13   **Dinner:** $14-$23   **Phone:** 845/298-6790
Location: Jct US 9 and CR 28, just se off US 9. 114 Old Post Rd 12590. **Hours:** 11:30 am-2:30 & 5-10 pm, Fri & Sat-11 pm, Sun 4 pm-9 pm. Closed: 1/1, 11/25, 12/25; also Mon. **Reservations:** suggested. **Features:** Patrons might be reminded of an Italian hilltop villa at this restaurant in the heart of the Hudson Valley. This place is nestled away from the hustle of the area's commercial strip. Casual dress; cocktails. **Parking:** on-site. **Cards:** AX, CB, DC, DS, MC, VI.

WARRENSBURG pop. 3,208—See also ADIRONDACK MOUNTAINS.

------ WHERE TO STAY ------

ALYNNS BUTTERFLY INN BED & BREAKFAST   Phone: 518/623-9390
All Year [BP]   1P: $89-$169   2P: $99-$179
Location: I-87, exit 23, 3.3 mi n on US 9, then just w. Located in a quiet, rural area. 69 Rt 28 12885.
Bed & Breakfast Fax: 518/623-9396. **Facility:** Smoke free premises. 5 one-bedroom standard units, some with whirlpools. 2 stories (no elevator), interior corridors. Bath: combo or shower only. **Parking:** on-site. **Terms:** 2 night minimum stay - seasonal, 14 day cancellation notice-fee imposed, weekly rates available, no pets allowed (owner's pets on premises). **Amenities:** irons, hair dryers. **Leisure Activities:** cross country skiing, hiking trails. **Cards:** MC, VI.
SOME UNITS

SUPER 8 WARRENSBURG   Phone: (518)623-2811
All Year   1P: $55-$110   2P: $65-$120   XP: $10   F17
Location: I-87, exit 23, just w. 3619 SR 9 12845. Fax: 518/623-2874. **Facility:** 32 one-bedroom standard units. 2
Motel stories (no elevator), interior corridors. **Parking:** on-site, winter plug-ins. **Terms:** pets (in smoking units).
Cards: AX, DC, DS, MC, VI.
SOME UNITS

------ WHERE TO DINE ------

GRIST MILL ON THE SCHROON   Phone: 518/623-8005
Location: I-87, exit 23, 0.9 mi n on US 9, jct CR 418, 0.5 mi w along river. 100 River St 12885. **Hours:** Open
5/1-10/31; 5 pm-9 pm. Closed: Mon-Wed 5/1-7/3 & 9/2-10/31. **Reservations:** suggested.
American **Features:** Whether watching the Schroon River in springtime flood or lazy summer flow, you'll find a
delightful vista from your table. Attentive and expert servers bring creations such as orange- and
basil-marinated chicken, pan-seared prawns and scallops and pepper-crusted venison. Don't hesitate to blow your diet on a
dessert of chocolate mousse with phyllo pastry surrounded with bananas Foster. Casual dress; cocktails. **Parking:** on-site.
Cards: AX, MC, VI.

MERRILL MAGEE HOUSE Country Inn   Dinner: $15-$24   Phone: 518/623-2449
Location: Center; opposite bandstand. 3 Hudson St 12885. **Hours:** 5 pm-9 pm. Closed: Sun.
Reservations: suggested. **Features:** On the grounds of a historic country inn, the restaurant sustains a
Continental romantic and modestly elegant atmosphere, thanks to soft background music and attractive table settings.
The menu choices and presentation should please big-city diners. Casual dress; cocktails. **Parking:**
on-site. **Cards:** AX, CB, DC, DS, MC, VI.

WARWICK pop. 6,412

------ WHERE TO DINE ------

CHATEAU HATHORN Country Inn   Dinner: $18-$24   Phone: 845/986-6099
Location: Jct SR 17A, 0.6 mi sw on SR 94. 33 Hathorn Rd 10990. **Hours:** 5 pm-9 pm, Sun 3 pm-8 pm. Closed:
12/24, 12/25; also Mon & Tues. **Reservations:** suggested. **Features:** On a small hill surrounded by
Continental impressive landscaping and stone walls, the Tudor-style mansion with field stone and red brick face is
charming. Vaulted beam ceilings, large arched windows and an ornately carved fireplace are a few of the
architectural details. A superior list of wines stored in the cellar complements seafood, chicken and steak dishes. A few
German dishes spot the menu, and an exotic dish or two may surprise. Dressy casual; cocktails. **Parking:** on-site. **Cards:** AX,
MC, VI.

WARWICK INN Historic   Dinner: $15-$26   Phone: 845/986-3666
Location: Just s of center on SR 94 and 17A. 36 Oakland Ave 10990. **Hours:** 5 pm-8:30 pm, Sun 1 pm-7 pm.
Closed: 12/24, 12/25; also Mon. **Reservations:** suggested, weekends. **Features:** A
American turn-of-the-20th-century ambience infuses the old Victorian home, which is decorated with antiques, crown
molding and stained glass. The restaurant's signature is fresh seafood and Black Angus sirloin steaks.
Casual dress; cocktails. **Parking:** on-site. **Cards:** AX, MC, VI.

WATERLOO pop. 5,111—See also FINGER LAKES.

------ WHERE TO STAY ------

HOLIDAY INN WATERLOO-SENECA FALLS   Book at aaa.com   Phone: (315)539-5011
7/1-10/31   1P: $89-$130   2P: $89-$130
5/1-6/30   1P: $75-$85   2P: $75-$85
11/1-4/30   1P: $65-$76   2P: $65-$76
Small-scale Hotel **Location:** I-90 (New York Thruway), exit 41, 4 mi s, just n of jct SR 414/5 and US 20. 2468 SR 414 13165 (PO Box 149).
Fax: 315/539-8355. **Facility:** 148 units. 144 one-bedroom standard units. 4 one-bedroom suites with whirlpools. 2 stories (no elevator), interior corridors. **Parking:** on-site. **Terms:** cancellation fee imposed.
Amenities: high-speed Internet, voice mail, irons, hair dryers. **Dining:** Our Heritage Cafe', see separate listing. **Pool(s):** heated
outdoor. **Leisure Activities:** sauna, whirlpool, lighted tennis court, exercise room. **Guest Services:** valet and coin laundry. **Business Services:** conference facilities, PC, fax. **Cards:** AX, CB, DC, DS, JC, MC, VI. **Special Amenities:** free local telephone
calls and free room upgrade (subject to availability with advanced reservations).
SOME UNITS

MICROTEL INN & SUITES   *Book at aaa.com*   Phone: (315)539-8438
AAA SAVE   All Year [CP]   1P: $46-$86   2P: $56-$87   XP: $7   F16
Small-scale Hotel   **Location:** I-90 (New York Thruway), exit 41, 4 mi s on SR 414, then just e. 1966 Rt 5 & 20 13148 (PO Box 807, SENECA FALLS). Fax: 315/539-4780. **Facility:** 69 one-bedroom standard units. 2 stories, interior corridors. *Bath:* combo or shower only. **Parking:** on-site, winter plug-ins. **Terms:** cancellation fee imposed. **Amenities:** video library (fee), video games. **Business Services:** meeting rooms. **Cards:** AX, CB, DC, DS, MC, VI. **Special Amenities:** free continental breakfast.

SOME UNITS

——— **WHERE TO DINE** ———

ABIGAIL'S   **Lunch:** $6-$8   **Dinner:** $16-$18   Phone: 315/539-9300
American   **Location:** I-90 (New York Thruway), exit 41, 4 mi s on SR 414, then just e. 1978 Rt 5 & 20 13165. **Hours:** 11 am-2 & 5-9 pm, Sun 1 pm-9 pm. Closed major holidays; also 12/24. **Reservations:** suggested, weekends. **Features:** Friendly staff members at the popular, all-American-style restaurant serve homemade comfort food. The weekday lunch buffet is a draw. Casual dress; cocktails. **Parking:** on-site. **Cards:** AX, CB, DC, DS, MC, VI.

OUR HERITAGE CAFE'   **Lunch:** $6-$10   **Dinner:** $9-$18   Phone: 315/539-5011
AAA   **Location:** I-90 (New York Thruway), exit 41, 4 mi s, just n of jct SR 414/5 and US 20; in Holiday Inn Waterloo-Seneca Falls. 2468 SR 414 13165. **Hours:** 6:30 am-2 & 5-10 pm, Sun 6:30 am-10 pm. **Reservations:** accepted.
American   **Features:** The restaurant was conceived with a tribute to local history in mind. Genuine artifacts, historical pictures and local facts, trivia and history make this more than a great place to eat. Family favorites are served in ample portions. The salad buffet is plentiful. Casual dress; cocktails. **Parking:** on-site. **Cards:** AX, CB, DC, DS, MC, VI.

WATERTOWN pop. 26,705

——— **WHERE TO STAY** ———

BEST WESTERN CARRIAGE HOUSE INN   *Book at aaa.com*   Phone: 315/782-8000
Property failed to provide current rates
Small-scale Hotel   **Location:** Center. 300 Washington St 13601. Fax: 315/786-2097. **Facility:** 160 units. 150 one-bedroom standard units. 10 one-bedroom suites, some with whirlpools. 3 stories, interior corridors. **Parking:** on-site. **Terms:** pets ($10 fee, in designated units). **Amenities:** irons, hair dryers. **Pool(s):** heated indoor. **Leisure Activities:** saunas, exercise room. **Guest Services:** valet laundry. **Business Services:** conference facilities.

SOME UNITS
FEE

DAVIDSON'S MOTEL   Phone: 315/782-3861
AAA SAVE   5/1-10/31   1P: $46-$49   2P: $49-$55   XP: $5   F12
11/1-4/30   1P: $39-$45   2P: $45-$49   XP: $5   F12
Motel   **Location:** From Town Square, 3.5 mi e on SR 3. 26177 NYS Rt 3 13601. Fax: 315/786-0599. **Facility:** 20 one-bedroom standard units, some with kitchens. 1 story, exterior corridors. *Bath:* combo or shower only. **Parking:** on-site. **Amenities:** voice mail. **Pool(s):** heated outdoor. **Leisure Activities:** grills, picnic tables, barbecue pit, hiking trails. **Cards:** AX, DS, MC, VI.

SOME UNITS
FEE   FEE

DAYS INN   *Book at aaa.com*   Phone: (315)782-2700
7/4-10/1   1P: $92-$112   2P: $97-$112
5/29-7/3   1P: $84-$104   2P: $89-$104
Small-scale Hotel   5/1-5/28 & 10/2-4/30   1P: $79-$99   2P: $84-$99
Location: I-81, exit 45, 0.5 mi e. 110 Commerce Park Dr 13601. Fax: 315/782-7691. **Facility:** 135 units. 115 one-bedroom standard units. 20 one-bedroom suites ($95-$112). 6 stories, interior corridors. **Parking:** on-site. **Amenities:** hair dryers. *Some:* irons. **Pool(s):** small heated indoor. **Leisure Activities:** exercise room. **Guest Services:** valet laundry, area transportation. **Business Services:** meeting rooms, fax. **Cards:** AX, DC, DS, MC, VI.

SOME UNITS

RAMADA INN   *Book at aaa.com*   Phone: (315)788-0700
AAA SAVE   5/1-10/31   1P: $89-$104   2P: $94-$109   XP: $5   F
11/1-12/31 & 3/1-4/30 1P: $79-$94   2P: $84-$99   XP: $5   F
Small-scale Hotel   1/1-2/28   1P: $69-$84   2P: $74-$89   XP: $5   F
Location: I-81, exit 45, just w. Located across from shopping mall. 6300 Arsenal St 13601. Fax: 315/785-9875. **Facility:** 143 one-bedroom standard units, some with whirlpools. 4 stories, interior corridors. **Parking:** on-site. **Terms:** [AP], [BP] & [CP] meal plans available, pets ($200 deposit). **Amenities:** voice mail, irons, hair dryers. **Dining:** 6:30 am-10 pm, Sun 8 am-noon, cocktails. **Pool(s):** outdoor. **Leisure Activities:** limited exercise equipment. *Fee:* game room. **Guest Services:** valet laundry. **Business Services:** meeting rooms. **Cards:** AX, CB, DC, DS, MC, VI. **Special Amenities:** free local telephone calls and free newspaper. *(See color ad p 8)*

SOME UNITS
FEE   FEE   FEE

REDWOOD MOTOR LODGE   Phone: 315/788-2850
All Year   1P: $37   2P: $45   XP: $3   F12
Motel   **Location:** I-81, exit 45, 4 mi se on SR 3/12 S. 24098 Gifford St Rd 13601. **Facility:** 27 units. 26 one-bedroom standard units. 1 two-bedroom suite. 1-2 stories (no elevator), exterior corridors. *Bath:* combo or shower only. **Parking:** on-site, winter plug-ins. **Pool(s):** indoor/outdoor. **Cards:** AX, MC, VI.

SOME UNITS

TRAVELODGE

Book at aaa.com

(AAA) (SAVE)

🔷🔷 🔷

Small-scale Hotel

5/1-9/30	1P: $65-$88	2P: $65-$88	XP: $5	F12
10/1-4/30	1P: $49-$70	2P: $49-$70	XP: $5	F12

Phone: (315)786-8888

Location: I-81, exit 45, 2 mi e. 652 Arsenal St 13601. Fax: 315/788-5676. **Facility:** 48 one-bedroom standard units. 2 stories (no elevator), interior corridors. **Parking:** on-site, winter plug-ins. **Terms:** small pets only ($25 deposit). **Cards:** AX, DC, DS, MC, VI. **Special Amenities:** free continental breakfast and early check-in/late check-out.

SOME UNITS

🆂🅳 🛏️ 🍴 🎥 🖨️ / ✕ 🔒 📠 /
FEE

——— **WHERE TO DINE** ———

BENNY'S STEAK HOUSE

🔷

American

Lunch: $5-$10   **Dinner:** $10-$30   **Phone:** 315/788-4110

Location: I-81, exit 45, 0.6 mi e. 1050 Arsenal St 13601. **Hours:** 11 am-11 pm. Closed: 11/25; also Mon. **Reservations:** accepted. **Features:** An established favorite among locals, the casual restaurant is convenient to many lodgings. The menu lists appetizers, pizza, homemade Italian dishes, steaks and seafood. Delivery is available. Casual dress; cocktails. **Parking:** on-site. **Cards:** AX, MC, VI.

📺 ✕

CAVALLARIO'S CUCINA

🔷🔷 🔷🔷

Italian

Lunch: $7-$10   **Dinner:** $12-$20   **Phone:** 315/788-9744

Location: Jct Prospect St; downtown. 133 N Massey St 13601. **Hours:** 11 am-9 pm, Fri & Sat-9:30 pm. Closed major holidays; also Sun. **Reservations:** accepted. **Features:** Friendly and family-oriented, the new restaurant features gourmet pizza and pasta. Crispy fresh salads, chargrilled Angus beef burgers, stuffed delicatessen sandwiches and such classic dinners as chicken Marsala and veal parmigiana are complemented by Italian wines. Guests can finish off the meal with a rich, homemade dessert. Casual dress; cocktails. **Parking:** on-site. **Cards:** AX, MC, VI.

♿M ✕

WATKINS GLEN pop. 2,149—See also FINGER LAKES.

——— **WHERE TO STAY** ———

ANCHOR INN AND MARINA

(AAA) (SAVE)

🔷🔷 🔷🔷

Motel

5/28-9/12 [CP]	1P: $79-$135	2P: $79-$135	XP: $10	F5
9/13-11/24 [CP]	1P: $69-$99	2P: $69-$99	XP: $10	F5
5/1-5/27 [CP]	1P: $69-$85	2P: $69-$85	XP: $10	F5

Phone: (607)535-4159

Location: 1.2 mi n on SR 14. Located on a hilltop. 3425 Salt Point Rd 14891. Fax: 607/535-4159. **Facility:** 11 one-bedroom standard units. 1 story, exterior corridors. *Bath:* combo or shower only. **Parking:** on-site. **Terms:** open 5/1-11/24, 10 day cancellation notice, weekly rates available, pets ($25 deposit). **Amenities:** voice mail, hair dryers. **Leisure Activities:** rental boats, rental paddleboats, rental sailboats, fishing. *Fee:* charter fishing, jet skis, pontoon boat. **Cards:** AX, DS, MC, VI. **Special Amenities:** free continental breakfast and early check-in/late check-out.

SOME UNITS

🆂🅳 🛏️ 👶 ✕ ✕ 🖧 / 🔒 📠 /
FEE   DATA PORT   FEE FEE

BUDGET INN

(AAA) (SAVE)

🔷

Motel

5/1-10/31	1P: $48-$85	2P: $55-$125	XP: $10	F12
11/1-4/30	1P: $45-$65	2P: $48-$75	XP: $10	F12

Phone: (607)535-4800

Location: On SR 14. 435 S Franklin St 14891. Fax: 607/535-4800. **Facility:** 21 one-bedroom standard units. 1 story, exterior corridors. *Bath:* combo or shower only. **Parking:** on-site. **Terms:** cancellation fee imposed, [CP] meal plan available, pets ($10 deposit, dogs only). **Cards:** AX, DS, MC, VI. **Special Amenities:** free local telephone calls and preferred room (subject to availability with advanced reservations).

SOME UNITS

🆂🅳 🛏️ 🎥 / ✕ 🔒 📠 /
FEE

CHIEFTAIN MOTEL

(AAA) (SAVE)

🔷🔷 🔷🔷

Motel

5/28-9/12 [CP]	1P: $69-$125	2P: $79-$135	XP: $10	F5
9/13-11/24 [CP]	1P: $59-$89	2P: $69-$99	XP: $10	F5
5/1-5/27 [CP]	1P: $49-$79	2P: $59-$89	XP: $10	F5

Phone: (107)535-4759

Location: Jct SR 14A, 3 mi n. 3815 State Rt 14 14891. Fax: 607/535-6091. **Facility:** 14 units. 12 one- and 2 two-bedroom standard units, some with efficiencies. 1 story, exterior corridors. *Bath:* combo or shower only. **Parking:** on-site. **Terms:** open 5/1-11/24, 10 day cancellation notice, weekly rates available, small pets only ($25 deposit). **Amenities:** voice mail, hair dryers. *Some:* irons. **Pool(s):** small outdoor. **Cards:** AX, DS, MC, VI. **Special Amenities:** free continental breakfast and early check-in/late check-out.

SOME UNITS

🆂🅳 🛏️ 👶 🏊 🖧 / ✕ 📼 🔒 📠 🖨️ /
FEE   DATA PORT   FEE FEE FEE

LONGHOUSE LODGE MOTEL

🔷🔷🔷

Motel

5/1-10/31	1P: $69-$139	2P: $69-$139	XP: $5
11/1-4/30	1P: $49-$129	2P: $49-$129	XP: $5

Phone: 607/535-2565

Location: 2 mi n on SR 14 at Abrams Rd. 3625 SR 14 14891. Fax: 607/535-5415. **Facility:** 21 one-bedroom standard units. 1 story, exterior corridors. **Parking:** on-site. **Terms:** office hours 7 am-10 pm, 2-3 night minimum stay - weekends 5/1-10/31, 7 day cancellation notice-fee imposed. **Amenities:** video library, voice mail, irons, hair dryers. **Pool(s):** small heated outdoor. **Cards:** DS, MC, VI.

SOME UNITS

🏊 ✕ 📼 🖧 🔒 🖨️ / 🏊 📠 /
DATA PORT

LONGHOUSE MANOR

🔷🔷🔷

Bed & Breakfast

5/1-10/31	1P: $119-$219	2P: $119-$249	XP: $15
11/1-4/30	1P: $89-$159	2P: $89-$219	XP: $15

Phone: 607/535-2565

Location: 2 mi n on SR 14. 3137 Abrams Rd 14891. Fax: 607/535-5415. **Facility:** Amply sized common areas and finely appointed, spacious rooms enhance this inn, which offers sweeping views of Seneca Lake. Smoke free premises. 4 one-bedroom standard units. 1 story, interior corridors. **Parking:** on-site. **Terms:** 2-3 night minimum stay - weekends 5/1-10/31, age restrictions may apply, 14 day cancellation notice-fee imposed, [BP] meal plan available. **Amenities:** video library, voice mail, irons, hair dryers. **Pool(s):** heated outdoor. **Leisure Activities:** putting green, game room. **Guest Services:** complimentary evening beverages. **Cards:** AX, DS, MC, VI.

🏊 ✕ 📼 🖧 🔒 🖨️ 🖨️
DATA PORT

SENECA CLIPPER INN
Phone: 607/535-2441

(AAA) SAVE

Motel

5/1-10/31   1P: $61-$83
11/1-4/30   1P: $45-$66
Location: Jct SR 14 and 414 W, just s on SR 14. 436 S Franklin St 14891. Fax: 607/535-4340. **Facility:** Smoke free premises. 15 one-bedroom standard units. 1 story, exterior corridors. **Parking:** on-site. **Terms:** 7 day cancellation notice-fee imposed, [CP] meal plan available. **Amenities:** voice mail. **Cards:** AX, DS, MC, VI. **Special Amenities:** free continental breakfast and free local telephone calls.

SOME UNITS

FEE

——— **WHERE TO DINE** ———

GRAPEVINE DELI & CAFE
Lunch: $3-$6   Phone: 607/535-6141

Deli/Subs
Sandwiches

Location: Corner of 5th St; center. 418 N Franklin St 14891. **Hours:** 7 am-3 pm. Closed major holidays; also Sun. **Features:** Only the finest Boar's Head meats, cheeses and deli products are used in the eatery's made-to-order sandwiches. Homemade soups, nine different salads, quiche, grilled sandwiches and breakfast are also served. Casual dress. **Parking:** on-site. **Cards:** MC, VI.

HOUSE OF HONG
Lunch: $5-$11   Dinner: $5-$11   Phone: 607/535-7024

Chinese

Location: Corner of 4th St; center. 400 N Franklin St 14891. **Hours:** 11 am-10 pm, Fri & Sat-11 pm, Sun noon-10 pm. Closed: 11/25, 12/25; also Mon in winter. **Features:** The little corner restaurant is big on taste and choices. Staffers at the friendly, family-owned spot serve all guests' needs. Casual dress; beer & wine only. **Parking:** on-site. **Cards:** AX, MC, VI.

JERLANDO'S RISTORANTE
Lunch: $4-$8   Dinner: $4-$14   Phone: 607/535-4254

Italian

MC, VI.

Location: Center. 400 N Franklin St 14891. **Hours:** 11 am-9 pm, Fri & Sat-10 pm. Closed: Mon in winter; 2 weeks for New Years. **Features:** The smoke-free atmosphere makes this a nice spot for casual family dining. The menu offers Italian fare, as well as seafood, steak and veal choices. Pizza, burgers, subs and chicken wings are available for take-out. Casual dress; beer & wine only. **Parking:** on-site. **Cards:** AX, DS,

SAVARD'S FAMILY RESTAURANT
Lunch: $3-$7   Dinner: $6-$10   Phone: 607/535-4538

American

Location: Center. 601 N Franklin St 14891. **Hours:** 6 am-3 pm, Wed-Sun to 8 pm. Closed major holidays; also 12/24. **Features:** Comfort food is prepared the old-fashioned way. The popular downtown location serves homemade soups, hot and cold sandwiches, fish fry and daily specials. Casual dress; beer & wine only. **Parking:** on-site. **Cards:** AX, DS, MC, VI.

SENECA HARBOR STATION
Lunch: $6-$10   Dinner: $9-$30   Phone: 607/535-6101

American

Location: SR 14; lakefront. 3 N Franklin St 14891. **Hours:** Open 5/1-11/30 & 4/1-4/30; 11:30 am-3:15 & 4:30-9 pm, Fri & Sat-10 pm. Closed: 11/25, 12/24, 12/25. **Features:** Guests can dine in casual style in a restored 1876 train station on the Seneca lakefront at the end of the Seneca Lake Wine Trail. The covered patio provides a more advantageous view of the lake in season. Seafood pasta, Bubba Gump shrimp gumbo, crostini fresca and New England clam chowder top the list of popular dishes, which match well with a good wine list. Casual dress; cocktails. **Parking:** on-site. **Cards:** AX, DS, MC, VI.

SENECA LODGE
Lunch: $4-$9   Dinner: $11-$23   Phone: 607/535-2014

American

Cards: AX, DC, DS, MC, VI.

Location: Just s on SR 329 W; at Watkins Glen State Park, south entrance. Walnut Rd 14891. **Hours:** Open 5/1-10/12; 8 am-10:30 & 6-9 pm; 11:30 am-2 pm Mon-Fri in summer; hours may vary. Closed: for dinner Fri holidays. **Features:** Family operated since 1948, the rustic log cabin-style restaurant offers casual dining with a varied but limited no-nonsense menu of favorites. Casual dress; cocktails. **Parking:** on-site.

WILDFLOWER CAFE
Lunch: $4-$8   Dinner: $4-$20   Phone: 607/535-9797

(AAA)

American

Location: On SR 14; downtown. 301 N Franklin St 14891. **Hours:** 11:30 am-10 pm, Fri & Sat-11 pm; hours may vary off season. Closed major holidays. **Reservations:** accepted. **Features:** Fine art hangs throughout the moderately upscale dining room. The broad menu centers on Northern Italian cuisine as well as Cajun entrees. Homemade desserts such as white chocolate cheesecake and Dublin rice pudding provide much temptation. Casual dress; cocktails. **Parking:** street. **Cards:** AX, MC, VI.

WEBSTER pop. 5,216

——— **WHERE TO STAY** ———

FAIRFIELD INN BY MARRIOTT ROCHESTER EAST/WEBSTER
Book at aaa.com   Phone: (585)671-1500

Small-scale Hotel

All Year [CP]   1P: $104-$119   2P: $104-$119
Location: SR 104, exit Hard Rd, just s. Adjacent to shopping center. 915 Hard Rd 14580. Fax: 585/671-1610. **Facility:** 63 one-bedroom standard units. 3 stories, interior corridors. *Bath:* combo or shower only. **Parking:** on-site. **Amenities:** video library (fee), video games, high-speed Internet, irons, hair dryers. **Pool(s):** small heated indoor. **Leisure Activities:** whirlpool. **Guest Services:** valet laundry. **Cards:** AX, DC, DS, MC, VI.

SOME UNITS

FEE

WEBSTER SUPER 8 MOTEL   Phone: 585/671-6990

AAA SAVE

7/1-8/31 [CP]	1P: $64-$88	2P: $69-$93	XP: $5	F12
5/1-6/30 [CP]	1P: $59-$84	2P: $64-$89	XP: $5	F12
9/1-10/31 [CP]	1P: $54-$71	2P: $59-$76	XP: $5	F12
11/1-4/30 [CP]	1P: $49-$65	2P: $54-$70	XP: $5	F12

Small-scale Hotel **Location:** I-590, exit 8, 3.9 mi e on SR 404. 2450 Empire Blvd 14580. Fax: 585/671-7494. **Facility:** 42 one-bedroom standard units, some with whirlpools. 2 stories (no elevator), interior corridors. **Parking:** on-site. **Guest Services:** valet laundry. **Cards:** AX, DC, DS, MC, VI. **Special Amenities:** free continental breakfast and free local telephone calls.

SOME UNITS

[SD] [CATV] / [X] /

WEEDSPORT pop. 2,017—See also FINGER LAKES.

———— **WHERE TO STAY** ————

BEST WESTERN WEEDSPORT INN   *Book at aaa.com*   Phone: (315)834-6623

AAA SAVE

7/1-8/31 [CP]	1P: $69-$150	2P: $79-$160	XP: $10	F12
5/1-6/30 [CP]	1P: $45-$140	2P: $55-$160	XP: $10	F12
9/1-10/31 [CP]	1P: $45-$140	2P: $50-$150	XP: $10	F12
11/1-4/30 [CP]	1P: $45-$69	2P: $50-$79	XP: $10	F12

Motel **Location:** I-90 (New York Thruway), exit 40, just s to jct SR 34 and 31, then 0.3 mi w on SR 31. 2709 Erie Dr 13166. Fax: 315/834-6626. **Facility:** 34 one-bedroom standard units. 1 story, exterior corridors. **Parking:** on-site. **Amenities:** irons, hair dryers. **Pool(s):** outdoor. **Cards:** AX, CB, DC, DS, MC, VI. **Special Amenities:** free continental breakfast and free room upgrade (subject to availability with advanced reservations).

SOME UNITS

[SD] [T] [~] [cartoon] [data] / [X] [B] [img] /

DAYS INN-WEEDSPORT   *Book at aaa.com*   Phone: 315/834-6198

AAA SAVE

All Year	1P: $59-$110	2P: $64-$125	XP: $5	F12

Motel **Location:** I-90 (New York Thruway), exit 40, just s at jct SR 31 and 34. 9050 SR 34 13166. Fax: 315/834-9849. **Facility:** 40 one-bedroom standard units, some with whirlpools. 2 stories (no elevator), exterior corridors. *Bath:* combo or shower only. **Parking:** on-site. **Terms:** [CP] meal plan available. **Amenities:** irons, hair dryers. **Business Services:** fax (fee). **Cards:** AX, DS, MC, VI. **Special Amenities:** free continental breakfast and free newspaper.

SOME UNITS

[SD] [T] [c] [cartoon] [data] / [X] [B] /

———— **WHERE TO DINE** ————

ARNOLD'S FAMILY RESTAURANT   **Lunch:** $4-$8   **Dinner:** $7-$9   Phone: 315/834-6251

[diamond] **Location:** I-90 (New York Thruway), exit 40, just s to jct SR 34 and 31, then 0.5 mi w on SR 31. 2667 Erie Dr 13166. **Hours:** 7 am-9 pm. Closed: 12/25. **Features:** The popular family restaurant is known for friendly, American hometown service and a menu of comfort food. Casual dress. **Parking:** on-site. **Cards:** AX, DS, MC, VI.

[X]

———— **The following restaurant has not been evaluated by AAA** ————
but is listed for your information only.

OLD ERIE RESTAURANT   Phone: 315/834-6641

[fyi] Not evaluated. **Location:** I-90, exit 40, just s to jct SR 34 and 31, 0.5 mi w on SR 34 S. 8924 N Seneca St 13166. **Features:** Traditional American favorites are deliciously prepared by the seasoned CIA owner-chefs.

WELLSVILLE pop. 5,171

———— **WHERE TO STAY** ————

LONG-VUE MOTEL   Phone: (585)593-2450

AAA SAVE

All Year	1P: $40-$90	2P: $44-$90	XP: $10	F16

Motel **Location:** Jct SR 19, 3 mi w. 5081 Rt 417 W 14895 (PO Box 463). Fax: 585/593-2450. **Facility:** 19 units. 18 one-bedroom standard units. 1 one-bedroom suite ($59-$90). 1 story, exterior corridors. *Bath:* combo or shower only. **Parking:** on-site, winter plug-ins. **Terms:** weekly rates available, small pets only (in designated units). **Amenities:** video library, irons. **Guest Services:** valet laundry. **Business Services:** fax (fee). **Cards:** AX, DS, MC, VI.

SOME UNITS

[pet] [VCR] [data] / [X] [B] [img] [TV] /
FEE   FEE

MICROTEL INN & SUITES   *Book at aaa.com*   Phone: (585)593-3449

AAA SAVE

All Year [CP]	1P: $43-$84	2P: $43-$84	XP: $5	F17

Small-scale Hotel **Location:** Just n off SR 19 and 417. 30 W Dyke St 14895. Fax: 585/593-4288. **Facility:** 60 one-bedroom standard units. 2 stories, interior corridors. *Bath:* combo or shower only. **Parking:** on-site. **Terms:** cancellation fee imposed. **Amenities:** voice mail. *Some:* hair dryers. **Business Services:** meeting rooms. **Cards:** AX, DC, DS, MC, VI. **Special Amenities:** free continental breakfast and free local telephone calls.

SOME UNITS

[SD] [T] [M] [c] [cartoon] [data] / [X] [B] [img] [TV] /

--------- WHERE TO DINE ---------

THE BEEF HAUS

American

MC, VI.

Lunch: $5-$10   **Dinner:** $7-$15   **Phone:** 585/593-6222
Location: Center. 176 N Main St 14895. **Hours:** 11:30 am-9:30 pm. Closed major holidays; also Sun.
Reservations: suggested. **Features:** More than 500 pounds of beef are cooked and served weekly at the busy, popular dining spot. The restaurant's motto is "best beef on the block, and a whole lot more." Only supreme Angus beef is said to be used. Casual dress; cocktails. **Parking:** street. **Cards:** AX, DC, DS, [X]

TEXAS HOT

American

Lunch: $2-$4   **Dinner:** $5-$9   **Phone:** 585/593-1400
Location: Center. 132 N Main St 14895. **Hours:** 6 am-11:45 pm. Closed: 3/27, 11/25, 12/25.
Features: Family-owned since 1921, the busy downtown restaurant serves American fare, good and fast all day. Try the famous Texas hot, with sauce made from a family recipe. Casual dress; beer only. **Parking:** street.

WEST COXSACKIE

--------- WHERE TO STAY ---------

BEST WESTERN NEW BALTIMORE INN   *Book at aaa.com*   **Phone:** (518)731-8100

5/1-10/31	1P: $99-$139	2P: $104-$144	XP: $5	F17
11/1-4/30	1P: $79-$99	2P: $84-$104	XP: $5	F17

Small-scale Hotel

Location: I-87 (New York Thruway), exit 21B, 0.5 mi s. 12600 Rt 9 W 12192. Fax: 518/731-6266. **Facility:** 63 units. 55 one-bedroom standard units, some with efficiencies and/or whirlpools. 8 one-bedroom suites ($125-$179) with whirlpools, some with efficiencies. 2 stories (no elevator), interior corridors. *Bath:* combo or shower only. **Parking:** on-site, winter plug-ins. **Terms:** [CP] meal plan available, pets ($10 extra charge). **Amenities:** irons, hair dryers. **Pool(s):** small heated indoor. **Leisure Activities:** whirlpool, exercise room. *Fee:* game room. **Guest Services:** valet and coin laundry. **Cards:** AX, CB, DC, DS, JC, MC, VI. **Special Amenities:** free continental breakfast and free newspaper.

SOME UNITS

[icons: SÒ / FEE / 🐕 / 🔧 / ⊗ / 🐾 / DATA PORT / 🛏 / 🖥 / 🖨 / ⊗ / VCR FEE]

WEST FALLS

--------- WHERE TO DINE ---------

COUNTRY BREADS & MORE

American

Lunch: $6-$9   **Dinner:** $10-$20   **Phone:** 716/655-0039
Location: I-90 (New York Thruway), exit 55, just e on SR 240 (Orchard Park Rd). 1089 Davis Rd 14170. **Hours:** 9 am-3 pm, Fri-9 pm. Closed: 1/1, 11/25, 12/25; also Mon in winter. **Reservations:** accepted.
Features: Guests can sample a sophisticated country meal in a relaxed setting that blends aspects of a country store, bakery and banquet facility. Fresh-baked goods and cinnamon-glazed French toast fill the dining room with mouthwatering aromas. A lunchtime favorite is the grilled chicken breast with sun-dried tomato basil bread. Casual dress; cocktails. **Parking:** on-site. **Cards:** AX, MC, VI. [Y][X]

WESTFIELD pop. 3,481

--------- WHERE TO STAY ---------

THE WILLIAM SEWARD INN

Historic Country Inn

Phone: 716/326-4151
All Year [BP]   1P: $80-$185   2P: $90-$195   XP: $20   F8
Location: I-90 (New York Thruway), exit 60, 4 mi se on SR 394. 6645 S Portage Rd 14787. Fax: 716/326-4163. **Facility:** High-post beds are among the antiques furnishing individually appointed guest rooms at this historic mansion. Smoke free premises, 12 one-bedroom standard units, some with whirlpools. 2 stories (no elevator), interior corridors. *Bath:* combo or shower only. **Parking:** on-site. **Terms:** 2 night minimum stay - weekends, age restrictions may apply, 7 day cancellation notice. **Amenities:** hair dryers. **Business Services:** meeting rooms. **Cards:** AX, DS, MC, VI. [🍴][X][🌊][🐾][☎]

WEST HENRIETTA   (See map and index starting on p. 550)—*See also HENRIETTA.*

--------- WHERE TO DINE ---------

THE CARTWRIGHT INN

American

Lunch: $6-$8   **Dinner:** $13-$20   **Phone:** 585/334-4444   [22]
Location: I-390, exit 12 northbound; exit 12A southbound, 0.5 mi w on SR 253, then 0.8 mi s on SR 15 (W Henrietta Rd). 5691 W Henrietta Rd 14586. **Hours:** 11:30 am-3 & 4:30-10 pm, Sun 12:30 pm-9 pm. **Reservations:** suggested. **Features:** This 1831 hotel turned roadside restaurant offers a menu consisting of steak and seafood. It is primarily known for its signature clam chowder and fresh lobster. Casual dress; cocktails. **Parking:** on-site. **Cards:** AX, DC, DS, MC, VI. [Y][X]

WEST ISLIP pop. 28,907

--------- WHERE TO DINE ---------

LA GRANGE INN

Continental

Lunch: $9-$14   **Dinner:** $15-$25   **Phone:** 631/669-0765
Location: 1 mi e on SR 27A (Montauk Hwy) at Higbie Ln, 1 mi w of Robert Moses Cswy, exit 2. 499 Montauk Hwy 11795. **Hours:** noon-10 pm, Fri-11 pm, Sat 2 pm-11 pm, Sun 11:30 am-8 pm. Closed: 12/25; also Mon & Tues. **Reservations:** suggested. **Features:** Sauerbraten is among delicious German specialties on the restaurant's traditional menu. The atmosphere is serene and welcoming, with bright, homelike decor. Casual dress; cocktails. **Parking:** on-site. **Cards:** AX, CB, DC, DS, MC, VI. [Y][X]

WESTMORELAND pop. 6,207

——— WHERE TO STAY ———

CARRIAGE MOTOR INN   Phone: (315)853-3561

AAA SAVE

Motel

7/1-8/31	1P: $45-$50	2P: $50-$65	XP: $5	F8
5/1-6/30 & 9/1-10/31	1P: $45-$50	2P: $50-$60	XP: $5	F8
11/1-4/30	1P: $35-$40	2P: $42-$48	XP: $5	F8

Location: I-90, exit 32, just n. Located in a rural area. 5370 SR 233 13490 (PO Box 379). Fax: 315/853-3563. **Facility:** 24 one-bedroom standard units. 1 story, exterior corridors. *Bath:* shower only. **Parking:** on-site, winter plug-ins. **Terms:** 5 day cancellation notice, [ECP] meal plan available, small pets only ($20 deposit, $5 extra charge). **Guest Services:** coin laundry. **Cards:** AX, CB, DC, DS, MC, VI. **Special Amenities:** free continental breakfast and free local telephone calls. *(See ad p 586)*

SOME UNITS

🅂🄳 🐾 [DATA PORT] / ⊠ 🖪 /
FEE

WEST POINT pop. 7,138

——— WHERE TO STAY ———

THE THAYER HOTEL   *Book at aaa.com*   Phone: (845)446-4731

▽▽▽

Historic
Small-scale Hotel

5/1-11/19 & 4/16-4/30 [BP]	1P: $150-$200	2P: $150-$200	XP: $10	F
11/20-4/15 [BP]	1P: $130-$160	2P: $130-$160	XP: $10	F

Location: Jct US 9W and 6, 2.8 mi n on US 9W, then 1.9 mi n on SR 218 to West Point's South Gate. 674 Thayer Rd 10996. Fax: 845/446-0338. **Facility:** Originally a dormitory for cadets, this 1926 property features a Gothic-style stone and red-brick facade. 151 units. 149 one-bedroom standard units. 2 one-bedroom suites. 5 stories, interior corridors. **Parking:** on-site. **Terms:** cancellation fee imposed. **Amenities:** video games (fee), dual phone lines, voice mail, irons, hair dryers. *Some:* high-speed Internet (fee). **Leisure Activities:** exercise room. **Guest Services:** valet and coin laundry, beauty salon. **Business Services:** conference facilities. **Cards:** AX, CB, DC, DS, MC, VI. *(See color ad p 202)*

SOME UNITS

🍽 🍸 ✎ ⊛ [DATA PORT] 💻 / ⊠ 🖪 /

WEST SENECA —*See Buffalo p. 255.*

WHEATFIELD —*See Niagara Falls p. 481.*

WHITE PLAINS —*See New York p. 459.*

WHITNEY POINT pop. 965

——— WHERE TO STAY ———

POINT MOTEL   Phone: (607)692-4451

AAA SAVE

▽

Motel

All Year	1P: $36-$44	2P: $41-$50	XP: $4	D14

Location: I-81, exit 8, just e. 2961 US 11 13862 (PO Box 468). Fax: 607/692-4450. **Facility:** 13 one-bedroom standard units. 1 story, exterior corridors. *Bath:* combo or shower only. **Parking:** on-site. **Guest Services:** coin laundry. **Cards:** AX, DS, MC, VI. **Special Amenities:** free local telephone calls and preferred room (subject to availability with advanced reservations).

SOME UNITS

🅂🄳 🍽 ⊛ / ⊠ /

——— WHERE TO DINE ———

AIELLO'S RESTAURANT/PIZZERIA   **Lunch:** $4-$6   **Dinner:** $7-$15   Phone: 607/692-4114

▽▽

American

Location: I-81, exit 8, corner of US 11 and Main St. SR 11 & Main St 13862. **Hours:** 11 am-10 pm, Fri & Sat-10:30 pm. Closed: 3/27, 11/25, 12/25. **Reservations:** required. **Features:** Locally popular since 1982, the family restaurant features a large selection of fresh seafood, tender veal, prime rib, homemade pasta and sauces. Casual dress; cocktails. **Parking:** on-site. **Cards:** AX, DS, MC, VI.

⊠

WILLIAMSVILLE —*See Buffalo p. 255.*

WILLISTON PARK pop. 7,261

——— WHERE TO DINE ———

RIVERBAY SEAFOOD BAR & GRILL   **Lunch:** $8-$13   **Dinner:** $12-$22   Phone: 516/742-9191

▽▽▽

Seafood

Location: I-495, exit 37; Northern State Pkwy, exit 28 S, 1.5 mi s. 700 Willis Ave 11596. **Hours:** noon-4 & 5-10 pm, Fri-11 pm, Sat 5 pm-11 pm, Sun 11:30 am-9:30 pm. Closed: 11/25, 12/25. **Features:** Rich, mahogany beams, antique light fixtures and beveled glass add to the comfortable charm of the relaxed dining room. Many varieties of oysters are among well-prepared selections of fresh seafood, nicely complemented by a lengthy wine list. Casual dress; cocktails. **Parking:** on-site. **Cards:** AX, DC, MC, VI.

🍸 ⊠

WILMINGTON pop. 1,131—*See also ADIRONDACK MOUNTAINS.*

——— **WHERE TO STAY** ———

GRAND VIEW MOTEL Phone: (518)946-2209

(AAA) (SAVE)

| | 12/26-3/21 | 1P: $69-$99 | 2P: $69-$99 |
| | 6/4-10/12 | 1P: $54-$84 | 2P: $59-$99 |

Motel

Location: On SR 86, 1 mi e. HC 2, Box 121A (SR 86) 12997. **Facility:** 17 one-bedroom standard units. 1 story, exterior corridors. *Bath:* shower only. **Parking:** on-site, winter plug-ins. **Terms:** open 6/4-10/12 & 12/26-3/21, small pets only. **Pool(s):** heated outdoor. **Leisure Activities:** badminton, playground, basketball, horseshoes. **Cards:** MC, VI.

SOME UNITS

HUNGRY TROUT RESORT Phone: (518)946-2217

(AAA) (SAVE)

| | 5/15-10/31 | 1P: $89-$179 | 2P: $89-$179 |
| | 12/26-3/31 | 1P: $69-$179 | 2P: $69-$179 |

Motel

Location: On SR 86, 2 mi w. Rt 86 12997. Fax: 518/946-7418. **Facility:** 20 units. 18 one- and 2 two-bedroom standard units, some with efficiencies. 1 story, exterior corridors. **Parking:** on-site, winter plug-ins. **Terms:** open 5/15-10/31 & 12/26-3/31, 7 day cancellation notice-fee imposed, [MAP] meal plan available, package plans - seasonal, pets ($5 extra charge). **Dining:** 2 restaurants, 5 pm-10 pm, cocktails, also, The Hungry Trout Restaurant, see separate listing. **Pool(s):** outdoor, wading. **Leisure Activities:** fishing, guide services for fishing & hunting, cross country skiing, hiking trails, playground. **Cards:** AX, DS, MC, VI.

SOME UNITS

LEDGE ROCK AT WHITEFACE MOUNTAIN *Book at aaa.com* Phone: (518)946-2379

(AAA) (SAVE)

| | 6/16-10/20 | 1P: $99-$139 | 2P: $99-$139 |
| | 5/1-6/15 & 10/21-4/30 | 1P: $69-$129 | 2P: $69-$129 |

Motel

Location: On SR 86, 3 mi w. Placid Rd (SR 86) 12997 (HCR 2, Box 34). Fax: 518/946-7594. **Facility:** 19 units. 16 one-bedroom standard units. 3 two-bedroom suites, some with kitchens. 2 stories (no elevator), exterior corridors. **Parking:** on-site, winter plug-ins. **Terms:** 2 night minimum stay - weekends, 10 day cancellation notice-fee imposed, pets ($10 fee). **Amenities:** video library, hair dryers. **Pool(s):** outdoor, wading. **Leisure Activities:** paddleboats, cross country skiing, ice skating, tobogganing, ski waxing room, recreation programs, hiking trails. **Business Services:** meeting rooms. **Cards:** AX, DS, MC, VI. **Special Amenities:** free local telephone calls and early check-in/late check-out. *(See color ad p 331)*

MOUNTAIN BROOK LODGE Phone: 518/946-2262

	5/1-10/15	1P: $58-$99	2P: $58-$99
	11/21-3/28	1P: $64-$95	2P: $64-$95
	10/16-11/20	1P: $55-$75	2P: $55-$75
	3/29-4/30	1P: $55-$70	2P: $55-$70

Motel

Location: Center. Rt 86 12997 (PO Box 145). Fax: 518/946-7536. **Facility:** Designated smoking area. 12 one-bedroom standard units. 1 story, exterior corridors. *Bath:* combo or shower only. **Parking:** on-site. **Terms:** cancellation fee imposed. **Pool(s):** outdoor. **Guest Services:** gift shop. **Cards:** AX, MC, VI.

SOME UNITS

NORTH POLE MOTOR INN Phone: 518/946-7733

(AAA) (SAVE)

| | All Year | | 2P: $49-$99 | XP: $5 | F12 |

Motel

Location: On SR 86, just w of jct CR 431. SR 86 12997 (PO Box 68). Fax: 518/946-7705. **Facility:** 23 units. 22 one-bedroom standard units, some with efficiencies. 1 one-bedroom suite ($89-$139) with efficiency. 1 story, exterior corridors. *Bath:* combo or shower only. **Parking:** on-site, winter plug-ins. **Terms:** 7 day cancellation notice-fee imposed, pets ($3 extra charge). **Pool(s):** heated outdoor, wading. **Leisure Activities:** fishing, shared recreational facilities with adjacent campground, hiking trails, playground, basketball, horseshoes, volleyball. *Fee:* miniature golf, game room. **Guest Services:** coin laundry. **Business Services:** meeting rooms. **Cards:** DS, MC, VI. **Special Amenities:** free local telephone calls and early check-in/late check-out.

SOME UNITS

——— **WHERE TO DINE** ———

THE COUNTRY BEAR Lunch: $3-$6 Phone: 518/946-2691

American

Location: Center. Rt 86 12997. **Hours:** 6 am-2 pn. Closed: 3/27, 11/25, 12/25; also Wed. **Features:** The tiny, small-town restaurant serves early breakfast and lunch. The menu is fairly basic, with soups, sandwiches and burgers, but on the plus side, everything is homemade and delicious, right down to the breads and pies. Casual dress. **Parking:** on-site.

THE HUNGRY TROUT RESTAURANT Dinner: $16-$24 Phone: 518/946-2217

Steak & Seafood

Location: On SR 86, 2 mi w; in Hungry Trout Motor Inn. Rt 86 12997. **Hours:** Open 5/1-11/1 & 12/27-4/30; 5 pm-10 pm. Closed: 4/1-4/30. **Reservations:** suggested. **Features:** The setting will enchant you and the atmosphere charm you. The Hungry Trout offers casual dining with stunning views of the mountains which frame it. Trout, prepared as simply or as elaborately as you like, is the house specialty. Also on the menu, steak, seafood and chicken. Reservations are a must for the popular window seats. Casual dress; cocktails. **Parking:** on-site. **Cards:** AX, DS, MC, VI.

———

The following restaurant has not been evaluated by AAA but is listed for your information only.

R. F. MCDOUGALL'S Phone: 518/946-2217

(fyi)

Not evaluated. **Location:** Rt 86 12997. **Features:** The old-fashioned neighborhood pub serves fish and chips, steak sandwiches and hamburgers. Bottled and draft beers on tap are available.

WILTON pop. 12,511

WHERE TO DINE

CHEZ PIERRE RESTAURANT
WWW WWW
French

Dinner: $16-$23 **Phone:** 518/793-3350
Location: I-87, exit 17S, 3 mi w. 979 Rt 9 12831. **Hours:** 5 pm-10 pm, Sun-9 pm. Closed: 12/24, 12/25; also Mon. **Reservations:** suggested. **Features:** Find the red Eiffel Tower in Wilton and you will also find provincial French cuisine, carefully prepared by the same family for over 30 years. Polished service will smooth the way from complimentary pate to crispy salad and on to seafood, veal and beef prepared in tempting sauces. One attractive dessert is ice cream with candied chestnuts. Casual dress; cocktails. **Parking:** on-site. **Cards:** AX, MC, VI.

WINDHAM pop. 359

WHERE TO STAY

ALBERGO ALLEGRIA HISTORIC BED & BREAKFAST
AAA SAVE
WWW WWW
Bed & Breakfast

Phone: (518)734-5560
All Year 1P: $73-$329 2P: $73-$329 XP: $25
Location: SR 23, just s. 43 SR 296 12496 (PO Box 267). Fax: 518/734-5570. **Facility:** Near the ski slopes, this B&B offers individually decorated guest rooms and friendly and accommodating service. Smoke free premises. 21 one-bedroom standard units, some with whirlpools. 1-2 stories (no elevator), interior/exterior corridors. **Parking:** on-site, winter plug-ins. **Terms:** 2 night minimum stay - weekends, 14 day cancellation notice-fee imposed, no pets allowed (owner's pets on premises). **Amenities:** video library, DVD players, dual phone lines, voice mail, hair dryers. *Some:* CD players, irons. **Leisure Activities:** golf driving net, hiking trails, shuffleboard. *Fee:* bicycles. **Guest Services:** gift shop. **Business Services:** fax (fee). **Cards:** MC, VI. **Special Amenities:** free full breakfast and preferred room (subject to availability with advanced reservations).

SOME UNITS

WOODBURY pop. 9,010

WHERE TO STAY

BEST WESTERN WOODBURY INN   *Book at aaa.com*
AAA SAVE
WWW WWW
Small-scale Hotel

Phone: (516)921-6900
5/1-10/31 & 3/1-4/30 [ECP] 1P: $119-$159 2P: $119-$159 XP: $10 F12
11/1-2/28 [ECP] 1P: $109-$159 2P: $109-$159 XP: $10 F12
Location: I-495, exit 44N, 1 mi e of exit 14 E off SR 135. Located in a commercial area. 7940 Jericho Tpke 11797. Fax: 516/921-6908. **Facility:** 98 one-bedroom standard units, some with efficiencies. 2-3 stories, interior/exterior corridors. *Bath:* combo or shower only. **Amenities:** video games (fee), voice mail, irons, hair dryers. *Some:* CD players. **Dining:** 11 am-11 pm, Sat 5 pm-midnight, Sun 5 pm-10 pm, cocktails. **Pool(s):** outdoor. **Leisure Activities:** exercise room. **Guest Services:** valet laundry. **Business Services:** meeting rooms. **Cards:** AX, CB, DC, DS, MC, VI. **Special Amenities:** free expanded continental breakfast and free local telephone calls.

SOME UNITS

EXECUTIVE INN AT WOODBURY   *Book at aaa.com*
AAA SAVE
WWW WWW
Motel

Phone: (516)921-8500
5/1-10/31 [BP] 1P: $119-$159 2P: $119-$159 XP: $10 F12
3/1-4/30 [BP] 1P: $115-$159 2P: $115-$159 XP: $10 F12
11/1-2/28 [BP] 1P: $109-$159 2P: $109-$159 XP: $10 F12
Location: I-495, exit 44N, 1.3 mi e of 14 E exit off SR 135. Located in a commercial area. 8030 Jericho Tpke 11797. Fax: 516/921-1057. **Facility:** 108 one-bedroom standard units. 1-2 stories (no elevator), exterior corridors. *Bath:* combo or shower only. **Parking:** on-site. **Amenities:** video games (fee), voice mail, irons, hair dryers. *Some:* CD players. **Pool(s):** outdoor. **Leisure Activities:** exercise room. **Guest Services:** coin laundry. **Business Services:** meeting rooms. **Cards:** AX, CB, DC, DS, MC, VI. **Special Amenities:** free full breakfast and free local telephone calls.
(See color ad p 344)

SOME UNITS

WYOMING pop. 513

WHERE TO DINE

GASLIGHT VILLAGE CAFE
WWW WWW
American

Lunch: $6-$8 **Dinner:** $8-$19 **Phone:** 585/495-6695
Location: Corner of SR 19 and Main St; center; in the Gaslight Commons. 1 Main St 14591. **Hours:** Open 5/1-12/31 & 4/1-4/30; 11:30 am-3 pm, Fri & Sat to 9 pm, Sun-6 pm. **Features:** Built in 1846, the building is appointed in charming country decor. Hearty American fare with homestyle meatloaf, ribs and pork chops along with some Italian favorites are carefully prepared to order. The adjacent pub features automotive memorabilia collected by the founder of Car & Driver magazine. Casual dress; cocktails. **Parking:** street. **Cards:** AX, DS, MC, VI.

YONKERS —*See New York p. 460.*

YORKVILLE pop. 2,675

WHERE TO DINE

SYMEON'S
WWW WWW
Greek

Lunch: $5-$13 **Dinner:** $10-$20 **Phone:** 315/736-4074
Location: On SR 5A, 0.5 mi e of Sangertown Square Shopping Center. 4941 Commercial Dr 13495. **Hours:** 11 am-10 pm, Fri & Sat-11 pm, Sun noon-9 pm. Closed: 3/27, 11/25, 12/24, 12/25. **Features:** Greek artwork, posters and pottery decorate the newly renovated, intimate dining rooms. Among well-prepared traditional dishes are the specialty souvlaki, spanakopita and crisp, tasty salad. Casually uniformed servers are pleasant and efficient. Casual dress; beer & wine only. **Parking:** on-site. **Cards:** AX, DS, MC, VI.

YOUNGSTOWN —*See Niagara Falls p. 482.*

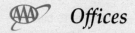

Offices

Cities with main offices are listed in **BOLD TYPE** and toll-free member service numbers in *ITALIC TYPE*.
All are closed Saturdays, Sundays and holidays unless otherwise indicated.

The type of service provided is designated below the name of the city where the office is located:
+ Auto travel services, including books/maps, marked maps and on-demand Triptik maps
● Auto travel services, including books/maps, marked maps, but no on-demand Triptik maps
■ Provides books/maps only. No marked maps or on-demand Triptik maps available
▲ Travel agency services

NATIONAL OFFICE: 1000 AAA DRIVE, HEATHROW, FLORIDA 32746-5063, (407) 444-7000

NEW YORK

ALBANY—AAA HUDSON VALLEY, 618 DELAWARE AVE, 12209. MON-FRI 9-5, THU 9-7, SAT 9-1. (518) 426-1000.+▲

AMSTERDAM—AAA NORTHWAY, 118 SANFORD FARMS, 12010. MON-FRI 9-5, TUE & THU 9-6. (518) 684-0064.+▲

BATAVIA—AAA WESTERN AND CENTRAL NEW YORK, 8351 LEWISTON RD, 14020. MON-FRI 9:30-5:30, SAT 10-1. (585) 344-1910.+▲

BINGHAMTON—AAA SOUTHERN NEW YORK, 21 WASHINGTON ST, 13901. MON-FRI 8:30-5, MON & THU 8:30-6. (607) 722-7255.+▲

BROOKLYN—AUTOMOBILE CLUB OF NEW YORK, 2334 RALPH AVE, 11234. MON-FRI 8:45-5:30, SAT 9-5. (718) 224-2222.+▲

BUFFALO—AAA WESTERN AND CENTRAL NEW YORK, 100 INTERNATIONAL DR, 14221. MON-FRI 9-5:30, MON & THU 9-7, SAT 9-2. (716) 633-9860.+▲

BUFFALO—AAA WESTERN AND CENTRAL NEW YORK, 2658 DELAWARE AVE, 14216. MON-FRI 9-5:30, TUE 9-7, SAT 10-2. (716) 873-0111.+▲

CAMILLUS—AAA WESTERN AND CENTRAL NEW YORK, 5103 W GENESEE ST, 13031. MON-FRI 9-5:30, THU 9-7, SAT 9-1. (315) 487-2700, *(866) 432-9005.*+▲

COOPERSTOWN—AAA TRI COUNTY MOTOR CLUB, 72 ELM ST, 13326. MON-FRI 8-5:30, SAT 9-2. (607) 547-2519.+▲

CORNING—AAA WESTERN AND CENTRAL NEW YORK, 273 W PULTENEY ST, 14830. MON-FRI 8:30-5:30. (607) 936-4166.+▲

DUNKIRK—AAA WESTERN AND CENTRAL NEW YORK, 3968 VINEYARD DR, 14048. MON-FRI 9-5:30, THU 9-7, SAT 9-1. (716) 366-3599.+▲

ELMIRA HEIGHTS—AAA SOUTHERN NEW YORK, 99 W MCCANNS BLVD, 14903. MON-FRI 8:30-5, THU 8:30-6. (607) 734-5246.+

ENDICOTT—AAA SOUTHERN NEW YORK, 124 WASHINGTON AVE, 13760. MON-FRI 9-5, MON & THU 9-6. (607) 754-1060.+▲

GARDEN CITY—AUTOMOBILE CLUB OF NEW YORK, 1415 KELLUM PL, 11530. MON-FRI 8:45-5:30. (516) 746-7141. [Administrative office only]

GARDEN CITY—AUTOMOBILE CLUB OF NEW YORK, 229 SEVENTH STREET, 11530. MON-FRI 8:45-5:30, SAT 9-5. (516) 746-7141.+▲

HERKIMER—AAA UTICA & CENTRAL NEW YORK, 246 N MAIN ST, 13350. MON-FRI 8:30-5:30. (315) 866-1830, *(800) 640-6144.*+▲

HUDSON—AAA HUDSON VALLEY, 179 HEALY BLVD, 12534. MON-FRI 9-5, THU 9-7. (518) 828-4537.+▲

ITHACA—AAA WESTERN AND CENTRAL NEW YORK, 723 S MEADOW ST, 14850. MON-FRI 9-5, THU 9-5:30, SAT 9-1. (607) 273-6727.●▲

JAMAICA—AUTOMOBILE CLUB OF NEW YORK, 186-06 HILLSIDE AVE, 11432. MON-FRI 8:45-5:30, SAT 9-5. (718) 224-2222.+▲

JAMESTOWN—AAA EAST CENTRAL, 111 W 5TH ST, 14701. MON-FRI 8:30-5. (716) 488-1981.+▲

LIVERPOOL—AAA WESTERN AND CENTRAL NEW YORK, 7485 HENRY CLAY BLVD, 13088. MON-FRI 9-5:30, SAT 9-1. (315) 451-1115.+▲

LOCKPORT—AAA NIAGARA-ORLEANS AUTO CLUB, 7135 ROCHESTER RD, 14094. MON-FRI 9-5, THU 9-8. (716) 434-2865.+▲

NEW YORK—AUTOMOBILE CLUB OF NEW YORK, 1881 BROADWAY AT W 62ND ST, 10023. MON-FRI 8:45-5:30, SAT 9-5. (212) 757-2000.+▲

NIAGARA FALLS—AAA WESTERN AND CENTRAL NEW YORK, 1629 MILITARY RD, 14304. MON-FRI 9-5, TUE & THU 9-6:30, SAT 9-12. (716) 298-5651.+▲

NORWICH—AAA TRI COUNTY MOTOR CLUB, 1 S BROAD ST, 13815. MON-FRI 8-5:30, SAT 9-2. (607) 334-9269.+▲

OLEAN—AAA WESTERN AND CENTRAL NEW YORK, ONE BLUE BIRD SQ ST 4, 14760. MON-FRI 9-5. (716) 372-3511.+▲

ONEONTA—AAA TRI COUNTY MOTOR CLUB, 195 ONEIDA ST SUITE A, 13820. MON-FRI 8-5:30, SAT 9-2. (607) 432-4512.+▲

ORCHARD PARK—AAA WESTERN AND CENTRAL NEW YORK, 3364 SOUTHWESTERN BLVD, 14127. MON-FRI 9-5, TUE & THU 9-7, SAT 9-2. (716) 675-4900.+▲

PENFIELD—AAA WESTERN AND CENTRAL NEW YORK, 2156 PENFIELD RD, 14526. MON-FRI 9-5, TUE & THU 9-7, SAT 9-2. (585) 377-8500, *(800) 836-2582.*+▲

PLATTSBURGH—AAA NORTHWAY, 20 BOOTH DR, 12901. MON-FRI 9-5, TUE & THU 9-6. (518) 563-3830.+▲

QUEENSBURY—AAA NORTHWAY, 345 BAY RD, 12804. MON-FRI 9-5, TUE & THU 9-6. (518) 792-0088.+▲

ROCHESTER—AAA WESTERN AND CENTRAL NEW YORK, 1100 LONG POND RD, 14626. MON-FRI 9-5:30, MON & WED 9-7, SAT 9-2. (585) 227-9600, *(800) 836-2582.*+▲

ROME—AAA WESTERN AND CENTRAL NEW YORK, 5783 ROME-TABERG RD SR 69, 13440. MON-FRI 9-5. (315) 337-0240.+▲

SARATOGA SPRINGS—AAA NORTHWAY, 26 WEST AVE, 12866. MON-FRI 9-5, TUE & THU 9-6. (518) 587-8449.+▲

SCARSDALE—AUTOMOBILE CLUB OF NEW YORK, 111 BROOK ST, 10583. MON-FRI 8:45-5:30, SAT 9-5. (914) 948-4600.●▲

SCHENECTADY—AAA NORTHWAY, 112 RAILROAD ST, 12305. MON-FRI 9-5, TUE & THU 9-6. (518) 374-4575.+▲

SMITHTOWN—AUTOMOBILE CLUB OF NEW YORK, 729 SMITHTOWN BY-PASS, 11787. MON-FRI 8:45-5:30, SAT 9-5. (516) 746-7141.+▲

SYRACUSE—AAA WESTERN AND CENTRAL NEW YORK, 3175 E GENESEE ST, 13224. MON-FRI 9-5:30, THU 9-6:30, FRI 9-5, SAT 9-1. (315) 446-3134.+▲

TROY—AAA HUDSON VALLEY, 514 CONGRESS ST, 12180. MON-FRI 9-5, THU 9-7, SAT 9-1. (518) 426-1000.+▲

UTICA—AAA UTICA & CENTRAL NEW YORK, 409 COURT ST, 13502. MON-FRI 8-6. (315) 797-5000, *(800) 640-6144.*+▲

WATERTOWN—AAA WESTERN AND CENTRAL NEW YORK, 19482 US RT 11, 13601. MON-FRI 9-5:30, SAT 10-1. (315) 788-5250.+▲

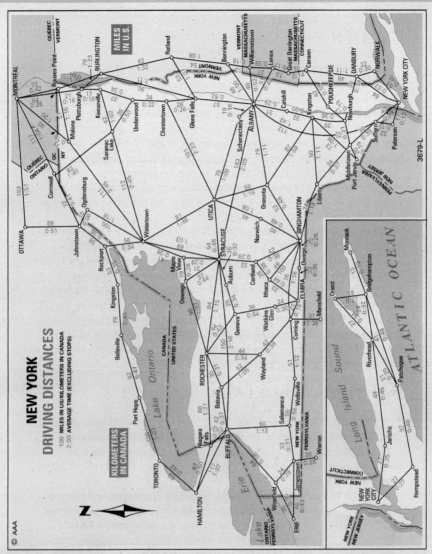

NEW YORK
DRIVING DISTANCES

100 MILES IN US/KILOMETERS IN CANADA
2:00 AVERAGE TIME (EXCLUDING STOPS)

MILES IN U.S.

KILOMETERS IN CANADA

3679-L

© AAA

GOLDEN PASSPORTS

Golden Passports, available in three types, offer benefits and significant savings to individuals who plan to visit federal recreation sites.

The Golden Eagle Passport, available for a **$65** annual fee, is valid for entrance only to all federal recreation areas that have an entrance fee. Sites include those operated by the National Forest Service, National Park Service, Bureau of Land Management and the U.S. Fish and Wildlife Service. The passport admits all occupants of a private vehicle at locations where entrance is on a per vehicle basis. At locations where a per person fee is charged, the pass covers the pass holder, spouse, parents and children.

Citizens or permanent residents of the United States who are 62 and older can obtain Golden Age Passports for a one-time **$10** fee. Proof of age is required.

Golden Access Passports are free to citizens or permanent residents of the United States (regardless of age) who are medically blind or permanently disabled.

Both Golden Age and Golden Access passports cover entrance fees for the holder and accompanying private party to all national parks and sites managed by the U.S. Fish and Wildlife Service, the U.S. Forest Service and the Bureau of Land Management, plus half off camping and other fees. When a per person fee is imposed, the pass covers the pass holder, spouse and children. Apply in person at a federally operated area where an entrance fee is charged.

NATIONAL PARKS PASS

The National Parks Pass, valid for 1 year from its first use in a park, allows unlimited admissions to all U.S. national parks. The **$50** pass covers all occupants of a private vehicle at parks where the entrance fee is per vehicle. At parks with individual entry fees, the pass covers the pass holder, spouse, parents and children.

As a result of a partnership with the National Park Foundation, AAA members may purchase the pass for **$48**, either through AAA's internet site (www.aaa.com) or by visiting a participating AAA office. Members may also phone the National Park Foundation at **(888) 467-2757** or purchase the pass online at www.nationalparks.org. Non-members may purchase the pass through participating AAA offices for the full **$50** price or online at www.nationalparks.org.

For an upgrade fee of **$15**, a Golden Eagle hologram sticker can be added to a National Parks Pass. The hologram covers entrance fees not just at national parks, but at any federal recreation area that has an admission fee. Valid for the duration of the National Parks Pass to which it is affixed, the Golden Eagle hologram is available at National Park Service, Fish and Wildlife Service and Bureau of Land Management fee stations.

Metric Equivalents Chart

TEMPERATURE

To convert Fahrenheit to Celsius, subtract 32 from the Fahrenheit temperature, multiply by 5 and divide by 9.
To convert Celsius to Fahrenheit, multipy by 9, divide by 5 and add 32.

ACRES

1 acre = 0.4 hectare (ha)   1 hectare = 2.47 acres

MILES AND KILOMETRES

Note: A kilometre is approximately 5/8 or 0.6 of a mile.
To convert kilometres to miles multiply by 0.6.

Miles/Kilometres	Kilometres/Miles
15.............................24.1	30.............................18.6
20.............................32.2	35.............................21.7
25.............................40.2	40.............................24.8
30.............................48.3	45.............................27.9
35.............................56.3	50.............................31.0
40.............................64.4	55.............................34.1
45.............................72.4	60.............................37.2
50.............................80.5	65.............................40.3
55.............................88.5	70.............................43.4
60.............................96.6	75.............................46.6
65...........................104.6	80.............................49.7
70...........................112.7	85.............................52.8
75...........................120.7	90.............................55.9
80...........................128.7	95.............................59.0
85...........................136.8	100...........................62.1
90...........................144.8	105...........................65.2
95...........................152.9	110...........................68.3
100..........................160.9	115...........................71.4

Celsius°	Fahrenheit°
100 BOILING	212
37	100
35	95
32	90
29	85
27	80
24	75
21	70
18	65
16	60
13	55
10	50
7	45
4	40
2	35
0 FREEZING	32
-4	25
-7	20
-9	15
-12	10
-15	5
-18	0
-21	-5
-24	-10
-27	-15

LINEAR MEASURE

Customary	Metric
1 inch = 2.54 centimetres	1 centimetre = 0.4 inches
1 foot = 30 centimetres	1 metre = 3.3 feet
1 yard = 0.91 metres	1 metre = 1.09 yards
1 mile = 1.6 kilometres	1 kilometre = .62 miles

LIQUID MEASURE

Customary	Metric
1 fluid ounce = 30 millilitres	1 millilitre = .03 fluid ounces
1 cup = .24 litres	1 litre = 2.1 pints
1 pint = .47 litres	1 litre = 1.06 quarts
1 quart = .95 litres	1 litre = .26 gallons
1 gallon = 3.8 litres	

WEIGHT

If You Know:	Multiply By:	To Find:
Ounces	28.000	Grams
Pounds	0.450	Kilograms
Grams	0.035	Ounces
Kilograms	2.200	Pounds

PRESSURE

Air pressure in automobile tires is expressed
in kilopascals. Multiply pound-force per
square inch (psi) by 6.89 to find kilopascals
(kPa).

24 psi = 165 kPa	28 psi = 193 kPa
26 psi = 179 kPa	30 psi = 207 kPa

GALLON AND LITRES

Gallons/Litres		Litres/Gallons	
5.............................19.0	12...........................45.6	10.............................2.6	40...........................10.4
6.............................22.8	14...........................53.2	15.............................3.9	50...........................13.0
7.............................26.6	16...........................60.8	20.............................5.2	60...........................15.6
8.............................30.4	18...........................68.4	25.............................6.5	70...........................18.2
9.............................34.2	20...........................76.0	30.............................7.8	80...........................20.8
10...........................38.0	25...........................95.0	35.............................9.1	90...........................23.4

Border Information

FOR CANADIAN RESIDENTS ENTERING THE UNITED STATES

PASSPORTS to enter the United States or return to Canada are not required for native-born citizens of either country. However, **a Canadian passport remains the best internationally accepted evidence of Canadian citizenship and its use is strongly suggested.** Proof of citizenship must be carried; a certified birth certificate, accompanied by a photo ID will usually suffice. Proof of residence also may be required. Unmarried parents who share custody of children should carry copies of the legal custody documents.

UNITED STATES CUSTOMS permits you to bring, free of duty, for personal use and not intended for sale: clothing, personal effects and equipment appropriate to the trip. Personal effects may include 200 cigarettes *or* 50 cigars *or* 4.4 pounds (2 kgs) of smoking tobacco *or* proportionate amounts of each, and 1 litre of alcoholic beverage. **Cuban cigars are denied entry.**

If you are planning to be in the United States **at least 72 hours,** you may bring gifts up to a fair retail value of $100 (U.S.), provided you have not claimed this exemption within the preceding 6 months. Family members may not combine their gift exemptions. Perfume containing alcohol and valued at more than $5 retail, tobacco products (except for 100 cigars) and alcoholic beverages are excluded from the gift provision.

RADIO COMMUNICATION EQUIPMENT: You may use your Family Radio Service (FRS) radio and cellular phone in the United States without any restrictions.

RETURNING TO CANADA

CANADIAN CUSTOMS allows you to bring, free of duty and taxes, goods valued up to $200 (Canadian) any number of times per year, provided you have been in the United States **48 hours or more.** All goods must accompany you; a written declaration may be required.

You may claim a $50 (Canadian) exemption on goods, excluding alcoholic beverages and tobacco products, if you are returning after an absence of **24 hours or more** and are not using any other exemption. If more than $50 worth of goods are brought back, the regular rate of duty and taxes will be levied on the entire value. This exemption may apply any number of times in a year.

If you are returning after **7 days or more** in the United States (not counting the day of departure from Canada), you may claim an exemption on goods valued up to $750 (Canadian). Goods, other than alcohol and tobacco products, are not required to accompany you; a written declaration may be required.

Permitted within the $200 and $750 exemptions are up to 50 cigars, 200 cigarettes, 200 tobacco sticks and 7 ounces (200 gm) of tobacco and up to 40 ounces (1.14 L) of liquor *or* 1.6 quarts (1.5 L) of wine *or* 9 quarts (8.5 L) of beer and/or ale (or its equivalent of 24 twelve-ounce bottles or cans). You must meet the minimum age requirement of the province entered to claim alcohol or tobacco products. Northwest Territories and Nunavut do not allow you to bring in more than the duty-free allowance of alcohol.

There is nothing to prevent you from importing any quantity of goods, even if you do not qualify for any kind of personal exemption, provided the goods you are importing are not restricted and you pay the full rate of duty and taxes

Special Tariff: When you exceed your $200 or $750 exemptions, a special rate of 7 percent combined duty and taxes is levied on the next $300 value in goods (except tobacco and alcohol) in excess of maximum exemptible amounts, provided the goods are of U.S. origin. Regular duties apply on any amount over that. For detailed information concerning specific duty rates, consult Canadian Customs before leaving on your trip.

All exemptions are individual and may not be combined with those of another person. You may be asked to verify the length of your visit; dated receipts normally constitute proof.

GIFTS to the value of $60 (Canadian) may be sent from abroad, free of duty or taxes. These may not include alcoholic beverages, tobacco products or advertising matter. Gifts valued at over $60 (Canadian) are subject to duty and taxes on the amount in excess of $60. Gifts sent from abroad do not count against your personal exemption, but gifts brought back must be included as part of your exemption.

Bed & Breakfast Lodgings Index

Some bed and breakfasts listed below might have historical significance. Those properties are also referenced in the Historical index. The indication that continental [CP] or full breakfast [BP] is included in the room rate reflects whether a property is a Bed-and-Breakfast facility.

Country Inns Index

Some of the following country inns can also be considered as bed-and-breakfast operations. The indication that continental [CP] or full breakfast [BP] is included in the room rate reflects whether a property is a Bed-and-Breakfast facility.

Historical Lodgings & Restaurants Index

Some of the following historical lodgings can also be considered as bed-and-breakfast operations. The indication that continental [CP] or full breakfast [BP] is included in the room rate reflects whether a property is a Bed-and-Breakfast facility.

Resorts Index

Many establishments are located in resort areas; however, the following places have extensive on-premises recreational facilities:

Points of Interest Index

Index Legend

☙ GEM: Points of Interest Offering a *Great Experience for Members*®

EXHIBITS & COLLECTIONS-INDIAN

EXHIBITS & COLLECTIONS-MUSIC

EXHIBITS & COLLECTIONS-REVOLUTIONARY
WAR HISTORY

EXHIBITS & COLLECTIONS-SCIENCE

EXHIBITS & COLLECTIONS-SPORTS

EXHIBITS & COLLECTIONS-VEHICLES

MUSIC HALLS & OPERA HOUSES

MYTHICAL PERSONS & ANIMALS

SIGHTSEEING-AIRCRAFT RIDES & TOURS

SIGHTSEEING TOURS

SAVE *Attraction Admission Discount Index*

The One That Does It All

*F*or years, people have turned to AAA for their emergency road service needs. But AAA is more than just towing. Access to AAA's travel services can give you the world. Its financial services can help you pay for it. And AAA insurance can give you the peace of mind to enjoy the ride. Plus, AAA gives you exclusive Show Your Card & Save® offers, bail bond benefits, and much more.

Discover the ways AAA can simplify your life. Call or stop by your nearest AAA office today to find out about the specific products and services they offer.

Comprehensive City Index

Here is an alphabetical list of all cities appearing in this TourBook® guide. Cities are presented by state/province. Page numbers under the POI column indicate where points of interest text begins. Page numbers under the L&R column indicate where lodging and restaurant listings begin.

COMPREHENSIVE CITY INDEX (CONT'D)

COMPREHENSIVE CITY INDEX (CONT'D)

Everyone Has A Dead Battery Story

*J*t happens to each of us sooner or later. Sure, anybody can offer you a battery boost, but your problem isn't really solved, is it? Why get stuck waiting in a repair shop to replace your battery when AAA can offer you a total solution. Be sure to ask if the mobile AAA Battery Service is available in your area.* This new service provides the convenience of on-the-spot battery testing, diagnostics and replacement. Another first from the first name in trusted emergency road services – AAA!

*available in select areas – consult your local AAA club

When You Really Need To Speak Their Language...

Travel

Let the IDP Speak for You

When traveling overseas, carry an **International Driving Permit...** even if you're not planning to drive. Should you need to communicate with foreign authorities, this recognizable form of identification can help you get on your way more quickly. Valid in over 150 countries, the permit contains information translated into ten languages.

Before you travel the world, travel to any AAA office for your International Driving Permit. Bring your valid U.S. driver's license, $10, and two passport-size photos (also available at AAA offices).

Travel With Someone You Trust®

Get more for your money.

Exclusively for AAA members!

- **Best available rate for dates of stay.**
- **Over 1 million rooms to fit your budget.**
- **100% satisfaction guarantee.**

AAA Preferred Lodging Partners

Best Western	Hampton Inn	Quality Inn
Clarion	Hampton Inn & Suites	Renaissance Hotels
Comfort Inn	Hilton Garden Inn	Residence Inn
Comfort Suites	Hilton Hotels	Rodeway Inn
Courtyard by Marriott	Homewood Suites	Sheraton Hotels & Resorts
Days Inn	Hyatt Hotels	Sleep Inn
DoubleTree Hotels	La Quinta Inn	SpringHill Suites
Econo Lodge	La Quinta Inn & Suites	St. Regis
Embassy Suites	Luxury Collection	TownePlace Suites
Fairfield Inn	Mainstay Suites	W Hotels
Four Points by Sheraton	Marriott Hotels, Resorts, Suites	Westin Hotels & Resorts

Visit Over 1,100 AAA Offices **Click** aaa.com **Call** 866-AAA-SAVE

Valid AAA Membership required. Not valid with other discounts or promotions. Good at participating locations only. Other restrictions may apply. Offers subject to change without notice.

Fill 'er Up!

5%* Rebate When You Pay at the Pump!

Put money in your wallet when you put gas in your tank — with the AAA Credit Card.

AAA members — you can now save 5 percent every time you buy gas with your AAA Credit Card. At any automated gas pump. It's fast, easy, and automatic — just pay at the pump and you earn 5 percent!

The AAA Credit Card comes with a wide range of cardholder benefits you won't get with other credit cards. Apply today, and start saving 5 percent on your next tankful.

*For rate, fee, other cost information, or details about the 5% gas rebate program, please contact your local AAA branch or log on to **www.aaa.com**, or call toll-free **(800) 545-7899**.

5%

GAS REBATE

AMERICA ON THE MOVE

A NEW EXHIBITION ON TRANSPORTATION IN AMERICAN HISTORY

Smithsonian
National Museum of American History
Behring Center

National Museum of American History

14th and Constitution Ave. NW
Washington, D.C.

Open Daily: 10 a.m. - 5:30 p.m.
(Except December 25)

americanhistory.si.edu/onthemove
Free Admission

Made possible by generous
support from:

General Motors Corporation

AAA

State Farm Companies Foundation
The History Channel
United States Congress
U.S. Department of Transportation

ExxonMobil

American Public Transportation
Association
American Road & Transportation
Builders Association
Association of American Railroads
National Asphalt Pavement
Association
The UPS Foundation

AMERICA
ON THE MOVE

We'll help you get your beauty sleep.

(Not that you don't look great just the way you are.)

Ahhh, the rejuvenating powers of a good night's sleep. Quiet rooms. Comfortable beds. Unstuffy atmosphere. Not to mention room service, a swimming pool, fitness center, restaurant, lounge, and in-room amenities that include everything from a dataport to a hair dryer.* And with us, Kids Eat & Stay Free.** So both you and your wallet can rest easy.

RELAX, it's
Holiday Inn

For reservations call 1-800-734-4275, your AAA professional or visit holiday-inn.com/aaa.